BLOOMSBURY ENCYCLOPEDIA OF
POPULAR MUSIC OF THE WORLD
VOLUMES VIII–XIV: GENRES

VOLUME XII
GENRES: SUB-SAHARAN AFRICA

Principal Editors

David Horn, Institute of Popular Music, University of Liverpool

John Shepherd, FRSC, Carleton University, Ottawa

Founding Editor

Paul Oliver, Oxford Brookes University, Oxford

International Advisors

Sean Albiez, Anglia Ruskin University, UK

Christopher Ballantine, University of KwaZulu-Natal, South Africa

Nimrod Baranovitch, Haifa University and Hebrew University of Jerusalem, Israel

Rafael José de Menezes Bastos, Universidade Federal de Santa Catarina, Brazil

Theo Cateforis, Syracuse University, USA

Banning Eyre, Afropop Worldwide, Middletown, CT, USA

Juan Pablo Gonzalez, Universidad Alberto Hurtado SJ, Santiago Chile

Werner Graebner, Jahazi Media, Moerlenbach, Germany

Dai Griffiths, Oxford Brookes University, UK

Jocelyne Guilbault, University of California, Berkeley, USA

Bruce Johnson, University of Turku, Finland; Macquarie University, Sydney; University of Glasgow, UK

Steve Jones, University of Illinois, USA

Dave Laing, University of Liverpool, UK

Peter Manuel, City University of New York, USA

Portia Maultsby, Indiana University, USA

Richard Middleton, University of Newcastle, UK

Toru Mitsui, Kanazawa University, Japan

Svanibor Pettan, University of Ljubljana, Slovenia

Paolo Prato, Luiss Creative Business Centre, Rome, Italy

Motti Regev, Open University of Israel, Israel

Raquel Z. Rivera, affiliated scholar, Center for Puerto Rican Studies, Hunter College, City University of New York, USA

T.M. Scruggs, University of Iowa, USA

Martin Stokes, King's College, London, UK

Jim Strain, Northern Michigan University, USA

Will Straw, McGill University, Canada

Paul Wells, Middle Tennessee State University, USA

Peter Wicke, Humboldt-Universität, Berlin, Germany

BLOOMSBURY ENCYCLOPEDIA OF
POPULAR MUSIC OF THE WORLD

VOLUMES VIII–XIV: GENRES
EDITED BY DAVID HORN AND JOHN SHEPHERD

VOLUME XII
GENRES: SUB-SAHARAN AFRICA

EDITED BY
HEIDI CAROLYN FELDMAN,
DAVID HORN, JOHN SHEPHERD
AND GABRIELLE KIELICH

BLOOMSBURY ACADEMIC
NEW YORK • LONDON • OXFORD • NEW DELHI • SYDNEY

BLOOMSBURY ACADEMIC
Bloomsbury Publishing Inc
1385 Broadway, New York, NY 10018, USA
50 Bedford Square, London, WC1B 3DP, UK

BLOOMSBURY, BLOOMSBURY ACADEMIC and the Diana logo are trademarks of
Bloomsbury Publishing Plc

First published in the United States of America 2019

Copyright © Heidi Carolyn Feldman, David Horn, John Shepherd, Gabrielle Kielich,
and Contributors, 2019

For legal purposes the Acknowledgments on pp. xviii–xix constitute an extension
of this copyright page.

Cover photograph: Alpha Blondy © Angel Manzano/Getty

All rights reserved. No part of this publication may be reproduced or transmitted in any form or
by any means, electronic or mechanical, including photocopying, recording, or any information
storage or retrieval system, without prior permission in writing from the publishers.

Bloomsbury Publishing Inc does not have any control over, or responsibility for, any third-party
websites referred to or in this book. All internet addresses given in this book were correct at the
time of going to press. The author and publisher regret any inconvenience caused if addresses have
changed or sites have ceased to exist, but can accept no responsibility for any such changes.

A catalog record for this book is available from the Library of Congress.

ISBN: HB: 978-1-5013-4202-8
ePDF: 978-1-5013-4204-2
eBook: 978-1-5013-4203-5

Series: Encyclopedia of Popular Music of the World, volume 12

Typeset by Deanta Global Publishing Services, Chennai, India
Printed and bound in the United States of America

To find out more about our authors and books visit www.bloomsbury.com and
sign up for our newsletters.

This book is dedicated to the memory
of our colleague and friend Paul Oliver (1927–2017)

Contents

Introduction — xiii
Acknowledgements — xviii
List of Contributors — xx

Maps — 1

Genres: Sub-Saharan Africa

Note regarding treatment of headings for genres found in more than one country:
- *Individual genre or form with regional variants: Genre (in Country), for example, Maringa (in Sierra Leone)*
- *Individual genre in a single country with a name that could be thought to be international: Genre (Country), for example, Jazz Band (Malawi)*
- *International genres: Genre in Country, for example, Reggae in Ghana*

Adaha	E. John Collins	9
Afrobeat	Jesse D. Ruskin	11
Afrobeats	Banning Eyre	19
Afro-Cuban Music in Senegal	Richard Shain	22
Afroma	John Lwanda	24
Afropop	Banning Eyre	27
Afro-Rock	E. John Collins	30
Akan Recreational Music	E. John Collins	34
Amakwaya	Markus Detterbeck	37
Apala	Isaac Yekini-Ajenifuja	43
Aṣíkò	Banning Eyre and Christian 'Dowu Jayeola Horton	46
Azmari Music	Shawn Mollenhauer	48
Azonto	Eric Sunu Doe	50
Ba Gasy	August Schmidhofer	52
Baikoko	Werner Graebner	54
Bajourou	Samuel Dickey	56
Band (Uganda)	Joel Isabirye	57
Bango	Mellitus Nyongesa Wanyama	60
Batuque	JoAnne Hoffman	62

Contents

Bend Skin	Joseph Fumtim	63
Benga	Donald Otoyo Ondieki and Caleb Chrispo Okumo	68
Beni	Donald Otoyo Ondieki and Caleb Chrispo Okumu, with Werner Graebner	73
Bikutsi	Anja Brunner	76
Boeremusiek	Willemien Froneman	78
Bongo Flava	Uta Reuster-Jahn	84
Borborbor	E. John Collins	89
Brass Band Music in Benin	Sarah Politz	90
Brass Band Music in Ethiopia	Shawn Mollenhauer	93
Bubblegum	Lizabé Lambrechts	94
Cabo-Zouk	JoAnne Hoffman	96
Chakacha	Donald Otoyo Ondieki and Caleb Chrispo Okumu	98
Chimurenga	Tony Perman	100
Coladeira	JoAnne Hoffman	105
Concert Party	David A. Donkor	106
Coupé Décalé	Ty-Juana Taylor	120
Cultural Animation Groups (in Gabon)	Alice Aterianus-Owanga	124
Cumbé	Isabela De Aranzadi	131
Discolypso	E. John Collins	137
Ethiopian Modern Music (Zemenawi Muzika)	Michele Banal	139
Fújì	Debra L. Klein	145
Funaná	JoAnne Hoffman	151
Gahu	E. John Collins	153
Ghoema Musical Complex	Sylvia R. Bruinders	153
Ghoemaliedjie	Sylvia R. Bruinders	157
Gule Wa Mkulu	John Lwanda	158
Gumbe/Goombay	E. John Collins with Christian 'Dowu Jayeola Horton	159
Gumbe/Goombay (in Sierra Leone)	Christian 'Dowu Jayeola Horton	162
Guux	Kenedid A. Hassan	164
Hausa Popular Music (Northern Nigeria)	Abdalla Uba Adamu	168
Hawl	Violeta Ruano	178
Heavy Metal in Africa	Edward Banchs	180
Heavy Metal in Botswana	Magnus Nilsson	185
Heavy Metal in Kenya	Ekkehard Knopke	188
Heavy Metal in Madagascar (Metaly Gasy)	Markus Verne	190
Heavy Metal in South Africa	Catherine Hoad	194
Hees	Christina J. Woolner	197
Highlife	E. John Collins	204
Highlife, Igbo	Austin Emielu	216
Highlife, Yorùbá	Olupemi Oludare	221
Hip-Hop in Sub-Saharan Africa	Catherine Appert	225
Hip-Hop in Botswana	Abimbola Kai-Lewis	228
Hip-Hop in Cameroon	Daniel Künzler	234
Hip-Hop in Gabon	Alice Aterianus-Owanga	235
Hip-Hop in Kenya	Mwenda Ntarangwi	243
Hip-Hop in Mozambique	Karen Boswall	248
Hip-Hop in Nigeria	Stephanie Shonekan	254

Contents

Hip-Hop in Nigeria (Hausa Rap)	Abdalla Uba Adamu	258
Hip-Hop in Senegal	Catherine M. Appert	260
Hip-Hop in South Africa	Lee Watkins	265
Hip-Hop in the Democratic Republic of the Congo	Chérie Rivers Ndaliko	267
Hip-Hop in Uganda	Joel Isabirye with John Shepherd	271
Hiplife	Halifu Osumare	273
Hira Gasy	Didier Mauro	278
House Music in Southern Africa	Lindelwa Dalamba, Adimbola Kai-Lewis and Cara L. Stacey	283
Imbyino	Jason McCoy and Tharcisse Biraguma	294
Isicathamiya	Sazi Dlamini	296
Isukuti	Mellitus Nyongesa Wanyama	304
Jazz Band (Malawi)	John Lwanda	308
Jeliya	Eric Charry	310
Jembe Music	Rainer Polak	315
Jit (Jiti)	Banning Eyre	319
Jùjú	Jesse D. Ruskin	321
Kadongo-Kamu	James Makubuya	326
Kaka	Sarah Politz	330
Kalindula	Rick Sanders	331
Kazukuta	Garth Sheridan	333
Kidandali	David Pier	334
Kidumbak	Werner Graebner	336
Kizomba	Rui Cidra	337
Konkoma	E. John Collins	341
Koriana le Moropa	David B. Coplan	343
Kpanlogo	E. John Collins	345
Kuduro	Michael B. Silvers	347
Kwaito	Christopher Ballantine	348
Kwasa Kwasa	David Horn and John Lwanda	355
Kwasa Kwasa (in Botswana)	Pinkie Gomolemo Mojaki	355
Kwasa Kwasa (in Malawi)	John Lwanda	357
Kwela	Lara Allen	358
Litungu Music	Mellitus Nyongesa Wanyama	362
Ma/Gaisa	Shishani Vranckx	366
Makossa	Anja Brunner and Joachim Oelsner	369
Makwayela	João Soeiro De Carvahallo and Karen Boswall	374
Malipenga	John Lwanda	376
Maloya	Guillaume Samson	379
Mamaya	Eric Charry	381
Mande Music	Graeme Counsel	383
Marabi	Christopher Ballantine	387
Maringa	Isabela De Aranzadi	391
Maringa (in Equatorial Guinea)	Isabela De Aranzadi	392
Maringa (in Sierra Leone)	Christian 'Dowu Jayeola Horton	398
Marrabenta	Karen Boswall and João Soeiro De Carvahallo	402
Maskanda	Kathryn Olsen	408
Masse Gohoun	Sarah Politz	412
Mbalax	Patricia Tang	414
Mbaqanga	Lindelwa Dalamba	418
Mbumba	John Lwanda	425

Contents

Mchiriku	Werner Graebner	428
Mdundiko	Werner Graebner	430
Medeh	Violeta Ruano	430
Merengue in Angola	Garth Sheridan	431
Milo Jazz	Christian 'Dowu Jayeola Horton	432
Moppie	Sylvia R. Bruinders	435
Morna	JoAnne Hoffman	436
Mutia	Guillaume Samson	438
Muziki Wa Dansi	Werner Graebner	439
Muziki Wa Injili	Imani Sanga	442
Mwomboko	Mellitus Nyongesa Wanyama	444
Naija Pop	Banning Eyre	448
Ndebele Pop	Banning Eyre	449
Ndombolo	Banning Eyre	451
Nederlandslied	Sylvia R. Bruinders	453
Ngoma	Werner Graebner	454
Ngoma/Ingoma (in Malawi)	John Lwanda	455
Nidal	Violeta Ruano	456
Odonson	E. John Collins	457
Omutibo	Mellitus Nyongesa Wanyama	460
Oromo Popular Music	Shawn Mollenhauer	463
Oviritje	Shishani Vranckx	464
Palmwine Music	E. John Collins	466
Pandza	Karen Boswall	470
Rebita	Rui Cidra	475
Reggae in Sub-Saharan Africa	Jérémie Kroubo Dagnini	477
Reggae in Côte d'Ivoire	Daniel B. Reed	479
Reggae in Ghana	E. John Collins	482
Reggae in Malawi	John Lwanda	484
Reggae in South Africa	David Durbach	486
Rumba	Banning Eyre, Johnny Frias, John Nimis and Mellitus Nyongesa Wanyama	490
Sákárà	Stephen Olusoji	500
Salegy	Banning Eyre	501
Séga	Guillaume Samson	503
Semba	Rui Cidra	507
Shambo	Shishani Vranckx	512
Simpa	E. John Collins	516
Sokwe	Guillaume Samson	517
Soukouss	Bob W. White	518
Sungura	Tony Perman	520
Taarab	Werner Graebner	523
Tabanka	JoAnne Hoffman	527
Takamba	Banning Eyre	529
Takiboronsé	Christophe Hien with John Shepherd	531
Tchinkoume	Sarah Politz	535
Tigrinya Music	Michele Banal	536
Tsaba Tsaba	Sazi Dlamini	540
Tsapiky	Banning Eyre	543
Tuareg Guitar Music	Eric J. Schmidt	545
Tufo	Karen Boswall	548

Umbholoho	Cara L. Stacey	551
Uukorasa	Minette Mans	552
Wákà	Stephen Olusoji	555
Wassoulou	Heather Maxwell	557
Yéla	Ibrahima Wane and Hauke Dorsch	558
Yenyengo	Hauke Dorsch	561
Zamrock	Henning Göransson Sandberg	565
Zenji Flava	Irene Brunotti	568
Zenli	Sarah Politz	572
Zikiri	Emmanuelle Olivier	574
Zilizopendwa	Caleb Chrispo Okumu and Donald Otoyo Ondieki	580
Zoblazo	Ty-Juana Taylor	583
Zouglou	Ty-Juana Taylor	585

Index 589

Introduction

The *Bloomsbury Encyclopedia of Popular Music of the World* had its genesis in the International Association for the Study of Popular Music (IASPM) in the mid-1980s.

IASPM was established in the early 1980s as a response to the increasing number of scholars publishing in the field of popular music. These scholars needed an organization through which to share and comment on their work, advocate the legitimacy and desirability of work on popular music and argue for the inclusion of popular music studies in the academy.

Early in the life of IASPM there was a recognition of the need for a comprehensive and reliable reference work on popular music that would serve the needs of scholars, researchers, students and information and media professionals, as well as the general public. The *Bloomsbury Encyclopedia of Popular Music of the World* (the first eight volumes of which were published as the *Continuum Encyclopedia of Popular Music of the World*) was planned as a response to that need. The first evidence of the progress of the project was *Popular Music Studies: A Select Preliminary Bibliography*, published in 1997.

Part 1 of the *Encyclopedia* was published in 2003 and comprises two volumes: Volume I, *Media, Industry and Society*; and Volume II, *Performance and Production*. Part 2 of the *Encyclopedia*, devoted to *Locations*, was published in 2005. It comprises five volumes: Volume III, *Caribbean and Latin America*; Volume IV, *North America*; Volume V, *Asia and Oceania*; Volume VI, *Africa and the Middle East*; and Volume VII, *Europe*.

The present volume is the fifth in Part 3: *Genres*. Volume VIII, *Genres: North America* was published in 2012, followed by Volume IX, *Genres: Caribbean and Latin America* (2014), Volume X, *Genres: Middle East and North Africa* (2015), and Volume XI, *Genres: Europe* (2017). The remainder of Part 3 will consist of Volume XIII, *Genres: International*; and Volume XIV, *Genres: Asia and Oceania*. (Please note that some regional combinations have been changed and some volumes have been renumbered since the publication of previous volumes in the set.)

When work on the *Encyclopedia* began, no model existed for this kind of comprehensive, scholarly reference work on popular music, and extensive research was undertaken to develop a systematic, subject-based taxonomy for such a new field of study. Throughout the *Encyclopedia*, subjects that would have been scattered arbitrarily by employing one single alphabetical sequence across a set of volumes are brought together and organized coherently to constitute an unprecedented body of knowledge. Because the volumes are organized in this way it is important for the reader to be aware of the overall organization of the volumes (as outlined above) and to consult the table of contents at the beginning of each volume. Each volume also has its own index, making it easy to locate discussions of specific subjects across a range of entries.

The subject-based approach makes the *Encyclopedia*'s volumes distinctive among popular music reference works. They are also distinctive in covering the whole world rather than only specific regions, a motivation responsible for the genesis and character of the volumes in both Part 2 and Part 3. The volumes manifest their scholarly nature by drawing on the expertise of a great many of the world's

Introduction

leading popular music scholars. It is also evident in the detailed end matter that is provided for the great majority of entries: bibliographies, discographies, sheet music listings, filmographies and listings of other visual media.

The present volume has called on the services of an international team of almost 100 contributors from Africa, Europe, North America and Australia. With scholars coming from a wide range of regions, disciplines and traditions it is perhaps inevitable that alert readers may note some disparate accounts or interpretations. The editors have not attempted to reconcile these, or indeed smooth them over, believing that, with the study of such a huge subject still in its relative infancy, such variations of approaches may be used in a constructive way.

Genres

In forming part of the overall taxonomy for the *Encyclopedia*, the volumes in Part 3, like those in Part 2, are organized geographically by volume, rather than being presented in a single alphabetical sequence. Popular music genres have, however, presented a number of additional challenges to the editors, taxonomical and otherwise. Several principles of arrangement were discussed, such as organization by function or character, but were deemed unworkable. It was decided that the only workable principle of arrangement was one in broad geographical divisions – and even that raised a number of issues. In the case of a majority of genres it is possible to determine a country or region where a given genre not only originated but where much of its 'life' was spent. We have judged it to be inadvisable, however, to attempt to make more narrowly focused geopolitical or geocultural sub-arrangements within broad areas, not only because identifiable points of origin are frequently region-wide rather than confined to one country, but also because the meaningful life of a given genre often takes place on a region-wide basis, leaving point of origin with limited significance.

At the same time, it is apparent that many genres have proved to have little respect for even broad geographical or geopolitical boundaries. The importance of international and transnational dimensions in the history of many genres is reflected both in the overall taxonomy for genres across the *Encyclopedia* and in the entries themselves. In addition to the five regional volumes there is a sixth volume for 'international' entries. The majority of entries in that volume will be for genres and forms which have demonstrated an international character from their inception. Two outstanding examples are film music and pop, which therefore have no entry in the present volume, but will be extensively covered in the *International* volume. In the case of genres which have clear regional origins and history and have also experienced significant development in other parts of the world, these are covered either in the original entry for the genre (as, for example, in that for *zarzuela* in Volume XI), or, where this approach would allow insufficient scope, in additional entries for that genre in other volumes; so, for example, in this volume entries are provided for the history of reggae in Sub-Saharan Africa. In the instance of one or two genres whose progress from regional and national to international and transnational history is widely understood not only to be both complex and of major global significance, but also to have had profound local impact, additional entries are also found both in the *International* volume and in regional volumes. A particular example of this approach in the present volume is hip-hop, which is represented by a major entry in the *North America* volume, complemented by another in the *International* volume and by a representative set of geographically focused entries in the majority of regional volumes, including the present one. Rock is unique within the *Encyclopedia* in being a genre that is regarded as originating and occurring simultaneously in more than one country; hence it has been designated as 'international' and the principal entry will be found in the *International* volume. References to rock in Sub-Saharan Africa may be found in the index to the present volume.

The case of jazz has been treated slightly differently. While it would be perfectly possible to argue that jazz should be treated in much the same way as hip-hop – as having identifiable points of origin, a complex global history and local impact – the editors have adopted an alternative approach, seeing a difference in the way in which jazz as a substantially instrumental music does not become regionally and locally owned in quite the same way as does hip-hop, but retains more obvious links with – and often allegiance to – its points of origin and development. As a result of this conclusion, with which some readers may disagree

Introduction

with respect to some of the places where it has been applied, the majority of jazz entries will be found in the *North America* and *International* volumes. The present volume does, however, include entries on genres with distinctive names that are strongly connected with jazz – for example, *marabi* and *mbaqanga*.

The concept of 'genre' itself also poses editorial challenges and the decision to use it as the defining term for the volumes in Part 3 was not taken without due consideration of the debates that have taken place on the use of the term in music and of the limitations that are characteristic of labeling systems. For the most part, the term is used in these volumes in a way that complies with the description given by Franco Fabbri and John Shepherd in the 'Genre' entry in Volume 1 of the *Encyclopedia*: 'In music, genres emerge as labels for defining similarities and recurrences that members of a community understand as pertinent to identifying and classifying musical events.' We have preferred to use 'genre' rather than 'style,' as despite the common use of the latter in English to invoke a wide range of meaning, it tends to prioritize attention to recurring musical features, while 'genre' invokes, as Fabbri and Shepherd say, 'the many activities above and beyond the purely musical that are involved in a musical event.' The use of 'genre' in these volumes also allows authors of entries to reflect where appropriate on issues of power and agency that are often fundamental to the ways in which popular music is categorized.

When identifying genres for inclusion – and in recognition of the importance of naming conventions – the editors have generally abided by the useful principle of 'no name, no genre.' In some instances, however, when a tight adherence to that principle would have meant overlooking a body of music with strong evidence of shared characteristics, we have bent our rule and supplied a generic term to enable the genre-type features of that body of music to be discussed. Examples in the present volume include 'Afro-Cuban Music in Senegal' and 'Tuareg Guitar Music.'

In addition to these two types of label – genres with specific individual names and supplied generic names – one further type has been used in the Genres volumes. These are the collective terms that are commonly used to refer to music with an identifiable function. Examples of this type are 'occupational song' and 'protest song.' Sometimes, as for example in the case of marches, pieces of music that share a function also have musical features in common, but this is by no means always the case. Comic songs, for example, do not necessarily share musical features with each other. Because this type of labeling is a transnational phenomenon with no identifiable starting point or dominant region, the majority of entries of this type are treated as transnational forms and will be found in the *International* volume.

A word is also necessary on dance music. A great deal of the music referred to by genre names is in part at least music for dancing, and this is particularly the case in Sub-Saharan Africa. Whenever dancing is an important element in the makeup and use of a particular genre the entry has endeavored to cover that aspect as, for example, in the entries for *makossa* and *mbalax*. There are also many names which refer to a specific form of dance as, for example, in the entry on *kpanlogo*.

A further word of explanation is in order concerning the spelling of genre names. In many parts of the world, genre names were originally an aural-oral phenomenon. The manner in which such names were then rendered in written form frequently varied both within and between locations. Variation can also be found when names are transliterated into English. The editors have not seen it as their task to impose standardization and their policy therefore has been not to strive unduly for consistency, which could be misleading, but in most cases to accept the spelling supplied by the contributor. Where genres have widely used alternative spellings, for example *gumbe/goombay* and *kwasa kwasa/kwassa kwassa*, these are given in the main entries for the genres concerned, but are not automatically given in other entries where the terms appear. The presence of diacritical marks and linguistic inflections in the rendering of African names and terms is another area where practice among contributors has differed. The editors have attempted to standardize practice as much as possible for terms such as Yorùbá and for genre names that appear regularly throughout the book (for example, *jùjú*), without endeavoring to attain complete consistency.

Popular music genres by their nature are connected in their character and histories to a wide

Introduction

range of performative, sociocultural, technological, economic and other activity. Previous volumes of the *Encyclopedia* contain their own entries for such activity (Volume I contains entries, for example, on sound recording, publishing, marketing and copyright, while Volume II contains entries, for example, on instruments and aspects of musical performance, and Volumes III–VII contain entries on popular musical activity in specific places). Readers are strongly advised to consult these to complement the information given in the volumes in Part 3. *Genres* entries often provide basic contextual information, for example, in terms of location, but do not as a rule duplicate information that has already been presented in a previous volume.

Translation

Several entries in the present volume were originally written in languages other than English and have been translated into English by a number of translators, named and anonymous, to whom the editors are deeply grateful. It has also been an editorial policy to provide English translations of all song and record titles that appear in the texts of the entries, and of the titles of all non-English items in the bibliographies, though some discretion has been used when titles appear self-explanatory.

End Matter

The *Bibliography* for any one entry contains information on virtually all publications referred to in the body of the entry. They are not only lists of references, however, but also contain wherever possible other published items of relevance to the subject of the entry that, in the author's judgment, readers may wish to consult. The increasing number of articles and book chapters available on Internet websites is reflected in the bibliographies. Because such websites vary in their longevity, the dates when sites were accessed are normally given. If no date is present, the item in question may have been removed at the time of publication, but the editors have judged that information concerning the item is useful in its own right.

Some listings of *Sheet Music* are also provided. These are normally limited to items referred to in the text, where it is clear that the reference is to a piece of printed music. Because the availability of reference sources for sheet music and their presence in library catalogs vary considerably around the world, it has not always been possible to give all the necessary information, especially when the author of an entry does not have personal access to an item in question.

A similar situation pertains with *discographical* information, which has in any case never been given the kind of attention commonly given to information for printed sources.

Because the role of sound recording in the history of popular music has been so considerable, it has been the editors' policy to include discographical details that are only partially complete rather than leave items out.

Discographical information is provided in two ways. If a particular recording is referred to in the body of the entry, details of this recording are provided in a section for *Discographical References*. Every effort is made to provide information about the original recording, in the form of record label and release number, date of issue and country of issue. The existence of historical discographical information varies hugely from country to country, however, and complete details have not always been available (though the growth of the remarkable online database discogs.com has been an extremely helpful development in this area). Most entries also have a *Discography*, which offers a list of representative recordings of relevance to the subject of the entry. In this section the details given for any item listed may be those of the original recording or of a reissue that was available at the point at which the entry was signed off. An effect of the transient nature of the record market is that the release details of any one recording are more likely than the remainder of the information to become out of date; nevertheless, the editors believe the policy of listing recommended titles remains a useful one, as there is often a likelihood that a recording will be issued again or will be available as a download.

Details of all films and visual recordings referred to in an entry are also given in a *Filmography* and/or *Audio-visual Media* section. Listings in the filmographies contain information on the director and the length of the film, plus notes on the type of film and, where appropriate, the music.

The present volume also reflects a growing use by scholars of the visual resources provided by YouTube, and despite the sometimes ephemeral nature of these sites it was decided to include some listings that offer both visual and audio recordings of performances that are otherwise very elusive. Useful websites, while often equally ephemeral, have sometimes also been included also, especially when information in printed form is limited.

Popular Music

Editing a comprehensive reference work of the world's popular music inevitably involves a consideration of what counts as popular music: in other words, of the criteria according to which topics should be included in the *Encyclopedia*. The definition of popular music is an issue which continues to be debated. As with previous volumes, the editors have resisted the temptation to attempt a precise definition, both when identifying terms for inclusion on entry lists and when offering guidance to contributors, recognizing that as terms that are discursive in character, 'popular,' 'classical' and 'folk' are used to refer to changing products of historical, social, political and cultural forces, rather than as designations of easily distinguishable musics. The question of where 'the popular' ends and 'the folk' begins has proved particularly difficult. The advice given to contributors has been that music created and disseminated in rural situations in an exclusively oral-aural fashion with little or no currency outside its location of origin does not constitute a prime focus for these volumes. It does not follow from this, however, that such music should not be discussed if it is commonly accepted as 'popular,' if it forms a significant source for later styles or genres commonly accepted as 'popular,' or (as in the case of the entry in the present volume for *hawl*) if modern, electronic instruments have been introduced and the music still has great currency among 'the people.' While the principal emphasis of the *Encyclopedia* is on the urban, the commodified and the mass disseminated rather than on the rural, the oral-aural and the restrictedly local, therefore, this emphasis is far from exclusive. The principal test for including music as 'popular' has been whether it has been so regarded by communities of practitioners or users. The tendency has therefore been to be inclusive rather than exclusive.

The Editors
June 2018

Acknowledgments

The Editors' first debt of gratitude is to Philip Tagg, Professor Emeritus of Music at Université de Montréal who, over a two-year period at the Institute of Popular Music at the University of Liverpool in the early 1990s, developed a detailed taxonomy of popular music, its practice and its study. This taxonomy served as a basic model for developing the structure of the *Encyclopedia*, as well as its major sections and headword lists.

A special word of thanks is due to a number of individuals whose vital role in the development of the *Encyclopedia* over the years has been crucial to the Editors' ability to develop and continue the project:

- Alyn Shipton, whose vision and dedication in the formative period of the *Encyclopedia* were vital to the development and long-term viability of an ambitious publishing project;
- Janet Joyce and Veronica Higgs, both formerly of the Continuum International Publishing Group, whose unwavering support and guidance were crucial to the realization of Parts 1 and 2 of the *Encyclopedia*;
- Jo Allcock, also formerly of the Continuum International Publishing Group, who took over as the Encyclopedia's Managing Editor in September 2002, and who played a major and critical role in bringing Part 2 of the *Encyclopedia* to publication;
- Jennifer Wilson, who was the Encyclopedia's Chief Editor at Carleton University from 1996 until 2005;
- Jennie Strickland, who at Carleton University was central to the commissioning of the entries for Part 2 of the *Encyclopedia*;
- David Barker, formerly at the New York office of Continuum, to whom a huge debt of gratitude is owed for his patient and understanding support as work on Part 3 progressed;
- Ally-Jane Grossan and Leah Babb-Rosenfeld, music editors in Bloomsbury's New York office, for maintaining David's patient and understanding approach and for their own commitment to the project; and Katherine DeChant, who took over temporarily from Leah during the last stages of the editing of Vol. XII.

Thanks are also due to the University of Liverpool, the University of Exeter, the University of Göteborg (Sweden), and especially Carleton University (Ottawa), all of which have made significant financial contributions, as well as contributions in kind, in support of this project.

In the context of Part 3, special thanks go to

- Dr. John Osborne, Dean of the Faculty of Arts and Social Sciences at Carleton University from 2005 until 2015; Dr. Catherine Khordoc, Interim Dean from 2015 to 2016; and Dr. Wallace Clement, the Interim Dean from 2016 to 2018, all of whom have provided financial assistance in support of the guest editors and editorial assistants working on the volumes of Part 3;
- Merilyn Holme, who has acted as Commissioning Editor and Style Editor for the entries in Part 3, and in so doing has provided the Editors with an invaluable level of support and assistance;
- Mandi Crespo, Jessica DeVries, Crystal French, Allison Whalen, Alicia Ott and Alicia Kerr, all of whom have been involved in the project via Car-

Acknowledgments

leton University, and who have rendered important service in various capacities.
- The production team at Deanta Global Publishing Services for their hard work and patience.

All those involved in editing Volume XII would like to extend thanks to those who have contributed entries, and in doing so have often been called on to complement their scholarship by showing great patience with the editorial process. Special words of thanks are due to all those who translated entries, especially André Loiselle, and to the many individual scholars who gave their help in response to the numerous specific questions that arose over the time this volume was being prepared, in particular Christopher Ballantine, Edward Banchs, Eric Charry, John Collins, Banning Eyre, Werner Graebner, Pamela Narbona Jerez, Janet Topp-Fargion and Markus Verne. A special word of thanks is due to Nishlyn Ramanna, who began the long editing process for this volume. It is with sadness that we also wish to mark the passing of Caleb Chrispo Okumo while the book was in process.

List of Contributors

Abdalla Uba Adamu is a professor of Media and Cultural Communication at Bayero University, Kano, Nigeria. His ethnomusicological focus is on Muslim Hausa performing arts and its transcultural influences.

Lara Allen is Executive Director of the Centre for Global Equality and Affiliated Lecturer of the Centre of Development Studies at the University of Cambridge, UK. She was previously Associate Professor in Ethnomusicology at the University of the Witwatersrand in South Africa.

Catherine M. Appert is Assistant Professor in the Department of Music at Cornell University, New York, USA.

Isabela de Aranzadi is Associate Professor of Ethnomusicology in the Department of Music at the Autónoma University of Madrid. She specializes in the music of ethnic groups in Equatorial Guinea and is the author of *Instrumentos musicales de las etnias de Guinea Ecuatorial* (Apadena, 2009).

Alice Aterianus-Owanga is an anthropologist and a documentary maker, currently a postdoctoral researcher at the University of Lausanne, supported by the Ambizione excellence program of the Swiss National Science Foundation.

Christopher Ballantine is Professor of Music Emeritus, and University Fellow, at the University of KwaZulu-Natal, Durban, South Africa.

Michele Banal studied ethnomusicology at SOAS-University of London and is currently an audio cataloguer at the British Library Sound Archive working on the project Unlocking Our Sounds Heritage.

Edward Banchs is a freelance writer, independent scholar and the author of *Heavy Metal Africa*. He lives in Pittsburgh, PA, USA.

Tharcisse Biraguma is a Rwandan citizen and master of traditional Rwandan music. He has held teaching positions at the University of Rwanda's Centre for Arts and Drama in Butare and at Green Hills Academy in Kigali and has also toured extensively throughout Africa and Europe with Ikobe Music Group. He currently lives in Kampala, Uganda, where he works as an architect.

Karen Boswall is an Anglo-Mozambican filmmaker, anthropologist, ethnomusicologist and musician based at the University of Sussex in the UK.

Sylvia R. Bruinders is Associate Professor and Head of Ethnomusicology and African Music at the South African College of Music, University of Cape Town, South Africa.

Anja Brunner is a postdoctoral researcher/lecturer in ethnomusicology at the Department of Musicology at the University of Bern (Switzerland).

Irene Brunotti is currently a lecturer of the Swahili Language and Swahili Studies at the Institute for African Studies, University of Leipzig, Germany.

Eric Charry is Professor in the Music Department at Wesleyan University in Middletown, CT, USA.

Rui Cidra is a researcher at the Instituto de Etnomusicologia (INET-md; Lisbon) and professor

List of Contributors

at the Music Department of the New University of Lisbon, Lisbon, Portugal.

E. John Collins has been involved in the Ghanaian/West African music scenes since the late 1960s as a musician, bandleader, music-union activist, record engineer, writer, archivist and university lecturer. (Editors' note: The author appears in his publications as both John Collins and E. John Collins. In the bibliographies in this volume the form of name has been left as contributors have provided it.)

Graeme Counsel is a lecturer in Music and Cultural Studies at the University of Melbourne, Australia.

Lindelwa Dalamba teaches music history at the University of the Witwatersrand's School of Arts, Music Division.

Marcus Detterbeck holds a Ph.D. from the University of Natal, Durban, South Africa. Since returning to Germany, he has worked as a music teacher, conductor, composer and author.

Sam Dickey is a freelance guitarist, composer, and bandleader living in New Orleans, USA.

Sazi Dlamini is a musician and lecturer in music at the University of KwaZulu-Natal in Durban, South Africa.

Eric Sunu Doe is a Ph.D. student in applied ethnomusicology at the University of KwaZulu-Natal, Durban, South Africa.

David Afriyie Donkor is Associate Professor and Director of Graduate Studies in the Department of Performance Studies (joint appointment in Africana Studies) at Texas A&M University, College Station, TX, USA.

Hauke Dorsch is Director of the African Music Archives and teaches at the Department of Anthropology and African Studies at the Johannes Gutenberg University, Mainz, Germany.

David Durbach is a freelance writer and DJ living in Johannesburg, South Africa. He runs the record store and label Afrosynth Records.

Austin Emielu is Professor and Visiting Scholar at the Department of Music, University of Ghana, Legon, Ghana.

Banning Eyre is an author, guitarist and Senior Producer for public radio's Afropop Worldwide. He lives in Connecticut, USA.

Heidi Carolyn Feldman is an author, editor, educator and independent scholar. In 2018–19, she is an AAUW American Fellow and a Visiting Scholar at the Center for Iberian and Latin American Studies of the University of California, San Diego, USA. Her award-winning book, *Black Rhythms of Peru*, was published by Wesleyan University Press in 2006.

Johnny Frías is a performer of Afro-Cuban music and a Ph.D. candidate in ethnomusicology at the CUNY Graduate Center, New York, USA.

Willemien Froneman is a research associate at the Africa Open Institute at Stellenbosch University, South Africa.

Joseph Fumtim is a writer and film director living in Yaoundé, Cameroon.

Werner Graebner is a freelance writer, journalist and music producer living in Dar es Salaam, Tanzania and Mörlenbach, Germany.

Kenedid A. Hassan is Director of the Centre for Frankincense, Environmental and Social Studies (CFEES), Hargeysa, Somaliland.

Christophe Hien is Researcher in ICT and Lifelong Learning at the Institute of Society Sciences in Burkina Faso, and a consultant in ICT and development.

Catherine Hoad is a lecturer in the School of Music and Creative Media Production at Massey University, Wellington, New Zealand.

JoAnne Hoffman is an independent scholar living and working in New York City, USA.

David Horn is Senior Fellow at the Institute of Popular Music (IPM), University of Liverpool. He was Director of the IPM from 1988 until his retirement in 2002. He lives in Devon, UK.

Christian 'Dowu Jayeola Horton was Adjunct Professor of Music at Macon State College and at Mercer University, Macon, GA, USA. He is now retired.

Joel Isabirye is Assistant Professor of Mass Communication at Kampala International University, Uganda. As a media consultant he has helped set up several radio and television stations in East Africa.

List of Contributors

Abimbola Kai-Lewis is a special education teacher in the New York City Department of Education. She has a Ph.D. in Ethnomusicology from the University of California Los Angeles.

Gabrielle Kielich is a Ph.D. candidate in the Department of Art History and Communication Studies at McGill University in Montreal, Canada.

Debra Klein is Professor and Director of the Anthropology Program in the Department of Social Science at Gavilan College, Gilroy, CA, USA.

Ekkehard Knopke is a research assistant to the Chair of Media Sociology at the Bauhaus-Universität, Weimar, Germany.

Daniel Künzler is Lecturer in Sociology, Social Policy and Social Work at the University of Fribourg, Switzerland.

Lizabé Lambrechts is a research fellow at Africa Open Institute for Music, Research and Innovation at Stellenbosch University, South Africa.

John Lloyd Chipembere Lwanda, an honorary Senior Research Fellow in Sociology at Glasgow University, Scotland, UK, is a social historian, music publisher and writer specializing in Malawi music, medicine and culture.

James Makubuya is Professor of Music at Wabash College in Crawfordsville, IN, USA. Born and brought up in the culture of the Baganda in Uganda, he is an ethnomusicologist with a disciplinary focus in organology, a choreographer and a proficient performer on several East African traditional instruments.

Minette Mans is a retired Associate Professor of Music and Dance and Chair of Performing Arts at the University of Namibia.

Didier Mauro is a social anthropologist, film producer and professor of cinema. Since 1988 he has dedicated himself to research in Madagascar and has been elected a member of the Académie des Sciences d'Outre-Mer de la République Française.

Heather Maxwell is Host and Producer of the worldwide music radio program *Music Time in Africa* on the Voice of America.

Jason McCoy received his Ph.D. from Florida State University. He currently lives in Fort Worth, TX, USA, and teaches courses in musicology at Dallas Baptist University.

Pinkie Gomolemo Mojaki is an ethnomusicologist and lecturer in the Department of Music at the Teacher Training College in Molepolole, Botswana.

Shawn Mollenhauer holds a Ph.D. and an MA in Ethnomusicology from the University of California, Riverside, USA.

Chérie Rivers Ndaliko is an assistant professor of music at the University of North Carolina at Chapel Hill and Executive Director of the Yolé!Africa Institute in Goma, Democratic Republic of the Congo.

Magnus Nilsson is Professor of Comparative Literature at Malmö University, Sweden.

John Nimis received his Ph.D. in French from New York University, and taught African Cultural Studies at the University of Wisconsin-Madison.

Mwenda Ntarangwi is a cultural anthropologist, researcher and administrator with an interest in the popular music of East Africa.

Joachim Oelsner founded the musical archive Arc Musica in Yaoundé, Cameroon, where he has lived since 1991.

Caleb Chrispo Okumu was the Executive Dean, Faculty of Liberal and Professional Studies, and Associate Professor of Music in the School of Creative and Performing Arts at Kenya Polytechnic University College. He died in 2012.

Emmanuelle Olivier, an ethnomusicologist, is Research Fellow at Centre National de la Recherche Scientifique and Lecturer at the École des Hautes Études en Sciences Sociales, Paris, France.

Kathryn Olsen is a lecturer in the School of Arts, University of KwaZulu-Natal, South Africa.

Olupemi Oludare, Ph.D., is a lecturer in the Department of Creative Arts (Music), University of Lagos, Nigeria.

Stephen Olusoji is Associate Professor in Music in the Department of Creative Arts (Music), University of Lagos, Nigeria.

Halifu Osumare is Professor Emerita of African American & African Studies at the University of California, Davis, USA. She is the author of *The Hiplife in Ghana: West African Indigenization of Hip-Hop* (2012).

List of Contributors

Donald Otoyo Ondieki is Director of the Permanent Presidential Music Commission, Vice-Chairman of the Kenya Music Festivals and Director at the Kenya Copyright Board, Nairobi, Kenya.

Tony Perman is Assistant Professor in the Department of Music at Grinnell College in Grinnell, IA, USA.

David Pier is Associate Professor in the Department of African, African American, and Diaspora Studies at the University of North Carolina, Chapel Hill, USA.

Rainer Polak is a postdoctoral researcher at the Max Planck Institute for Empirical Aesthetics, Frankfurt, Germany. He specializes in West African dance-drumming and rhythm perception.

Sarah Politz is Visiting Assistant Professor of Ethnomusicology at Williams College, Williamstown, MA, USA.

Daniel B. Reed is Laura Boulton Professor of Ethnomusicology and Associate Professor in the Department of Folklore and Ethnomusicology at Indiana University, Bloomington, IN, USA.

Uta Reuster-Jahn, Ph.D., is Lecturer in Swahili at the Asien-Afrika-Institut, University of Hamburg, Germany. She has carried out extensive research on Swahili popular literature and *bongo flava* music in Tanzania.

Violeta Ruano is an independent researcher and project manager working and living between London, UK, Algeria and Spain.

Jesse D. Ruskin is Evaluation & Development Associate at the Ford Theatre Foundation in Los Angeles. He holds a Ph.D. in ethnomusicology from the University of California Los Angeles, where he lectured on global popular music from 2013 to 2016.

Henning Gorenson Sandberg is Project Manager and Senior Consultant at FCG Swedish Development AB. He was previously Research Manager at the BBC's international development NGO BBC Media Action, based in Juba, South Sudan.

Rick Sanders is a freelance writer and musician living in Ely, UK.

Imani Sanga is Associate Professor of Music, Composer and Choral Director in the Department of Creative Arts at the University of Dar es Salaam, Tanzania.

August Schmidhofer is Assistant Professor at the Department of Musicology, University of Vienna, Austria.

Eric J. Schmidt is Assistant Director of the Boston University African Studies Center. He holds a Ph.D. in ethnomusicology from the University of California, Los Angeles, USA.

Richard M. Shain teaches African and Caribbean history at Thomas Jefferson University, Philadelphia, USA.

John Shepherd is Chancellor's Professor of Music and Sociology at Carleton University, Ottawa, Canada.

Stephanie Shonekan is Associate Professor of Ethnomusicology and Chair of the Department of Black Studies at the University of Missouri, Columbia, USA.

Michael B. Silvers is Assistant Professor of Musicology at the University of Illinois at Urbana-Champaign, USA.

João Soeiro de Carvahallo is Associate Professor of Music at the New University of Lisbon, Portugal. He has a Ph.D. from Columbia University, New York, USA (1997).

Cara L. Stacey is a postdoctoral fellow at the South African College of Music at the University of Cape Town, South Africa.

Patricia Tang is Associate Professor of Music at the Massachusetts Institute of Technology, Cambridge, MA, USA.

Ty-Juana Taylor is a music scholar and advocate for children's rights and the amplification of their voices through speech and the arts. She holds a Ph.D. in ethnomusicology from the University of California Los Angeles, USA.

Markus Verne is Professor of Anthropology at the Department of Anthropology and African Studies, Johannes Gutenberg University, Mainz, Germany.

Shishani Vranckx is a singer, songwriter, drummer, guitarist, creative cultural entrepreneur and researcher (anthropology and musicology), based in Amsterdam, the Netherlands.

Ibrahima Wane is Professor of African Oral Literature at the Cheikh Anta Diop University of Dakar, Senegal.

List of Contributors

Mellitus Nyongesa Wanyama is Professor and Founding Dean, School of Music and Performing Arts, at Kabarak University in Nakuru, Kenya.

Lee Watkins is the Director of the International Library of African Music and is based at Rhodes University in Grahamstown, South Africa.

Bob W. White is a professor of anthropology at the University of Montreal, Canada.

Christina J. Woolner is a Ph.D. candidate in the Department of Social Anthropology at the University of Cambridge, UK.

Isaac Yekini-Ajenifuja, Ph.D., is Senior Lecturer at the Department of Theatre Arts and Music, Lagos State University, Ojo, Nigeria.

Maps

Maps

Maps

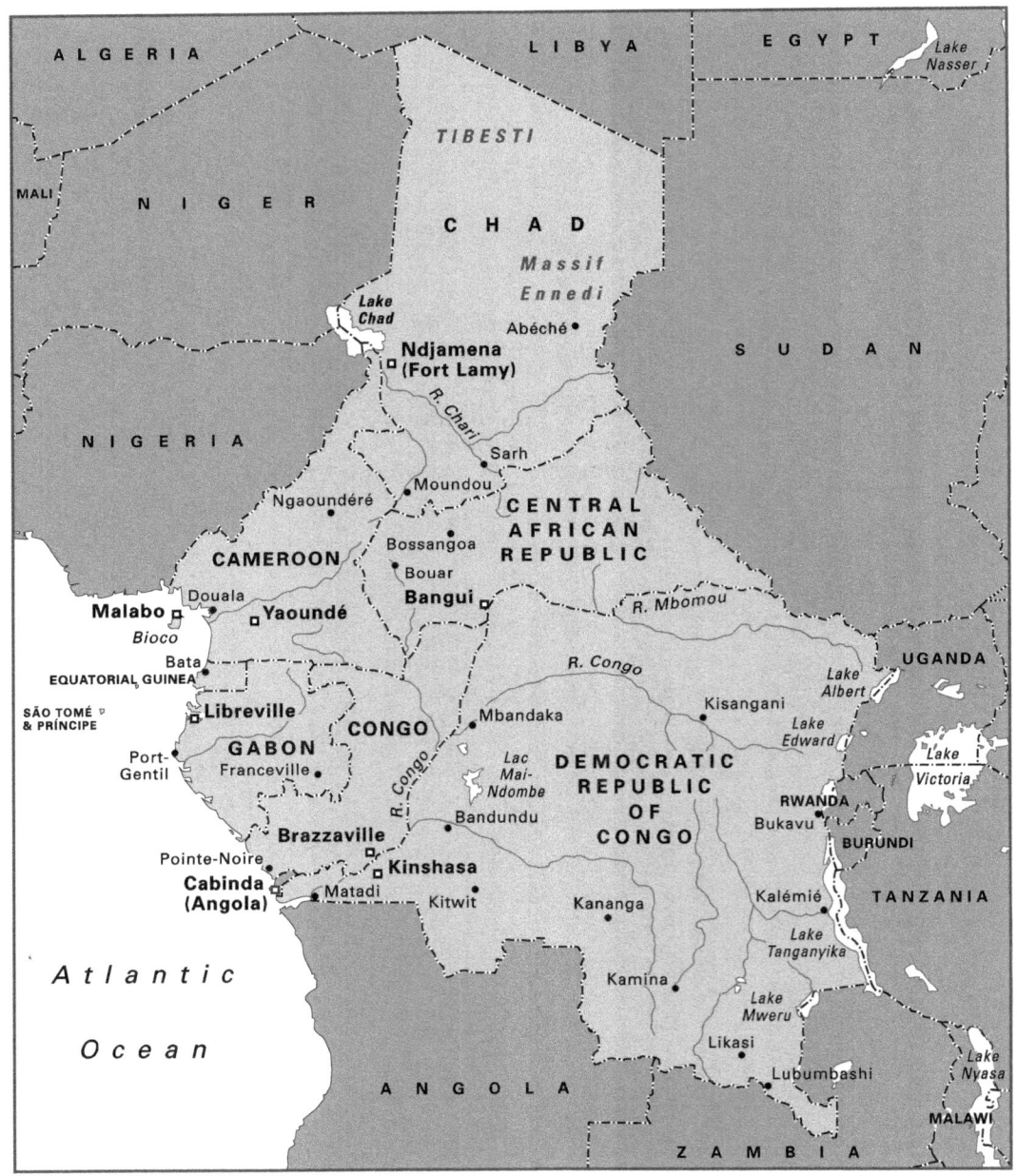

Maps

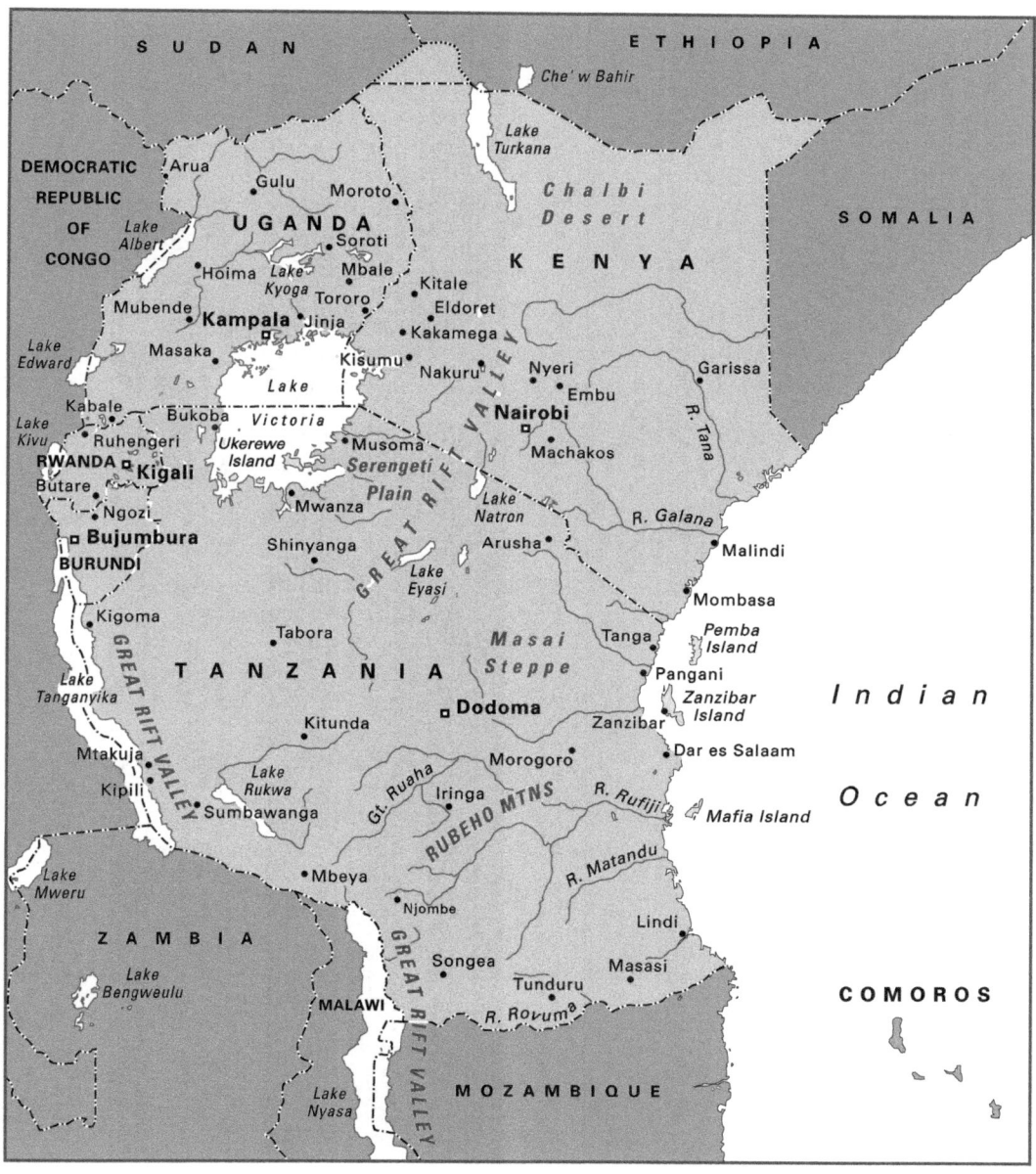

5

Maps

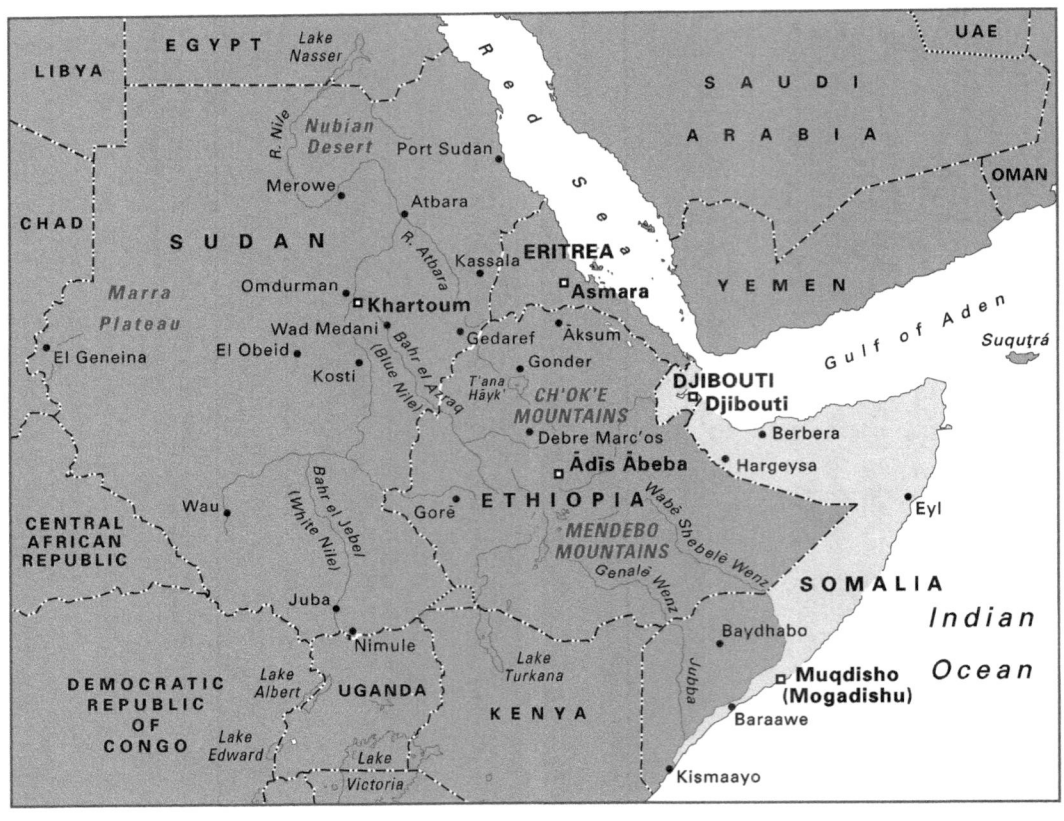

Maps

Maps

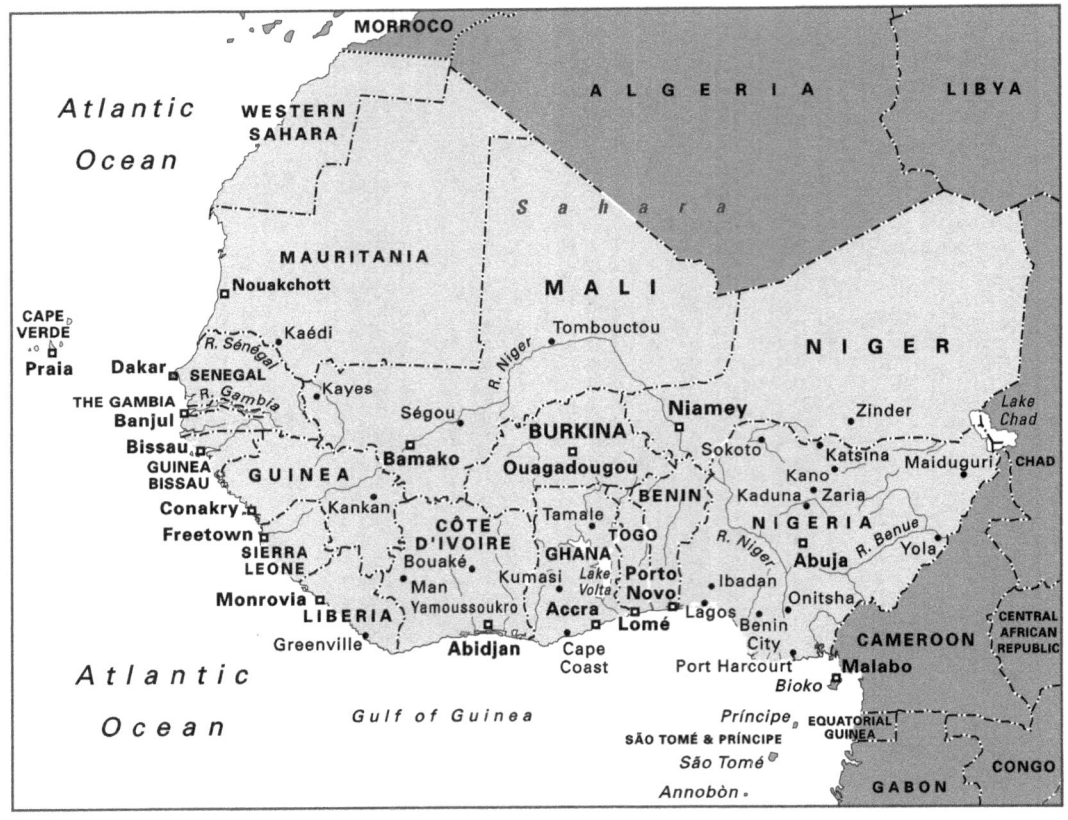

Genres: Sub-Saharan Africa

Adaha

Adaha is an Africanized form of brass band music that emerged on the Ghanaian coast in the 1880s, created by local musicians who had been associated with the fife-and-drum and later brass bands of the European military forts. It is both marched and danced to and utilizes syncopated 4/4 rhythms and 6/8 polyrhythms. *Adaha* is a recreational music, played during street parades and at local festive ceremonies. *Adaha* bands also accompany the local street masqueraders that are featured during Fanti Easter and Christmas holidays.

Because some of the marching groups' instruments (such as side drum and bugles) were used for battlefield communication, Europeans during colonial times were at first reluctant to allow local Africans to play these sonic symbols of British power. The very first recorded case in Ghana (De Graft-Johnson 1932) was the use of British uniforms, drums and fifes by the Cape Coast Akrampa Number Six Asafo (Warrior) Company, formed in 1665, which consisted of the mixed-marriage children of Europeans living at Cape Coast Castle. The Fantis (an Akan subgroup of the southern coast of Ghana) became the allies of the British in their early nineteenth-century struggle against the inland Ashanti kingdom and Wolfson (1958, 122) comments on the use of regimental music of the Royal African Corps before the 1824 Battle of Bonsaso, with the opposing Ashantis also bringing out their 'talking' war drums. Beecham (1841, 1) refers to a 'native' military band at Cape Coast Castle in the 1840s playing English martial and popular tunes.

There is, however, no evidence that any of these African military bands played local music until the latter half of the nineteenth century, when West Indian troops were stationed in English-speaking West Africa. The British stationed West Indian Regiments in Sierra Leone as early as 1819 (Harrev 1987, 6; Fyfe 1962) and, during the late nineteenth century, in Nigeria (Waterman 1990) and Ghana. According to A.A. Mensah (1969/70), this stationing of black Caribbean soldiers catalyzed the Africanization of brass band music in Ghana, where, in the coastal Fanti area, there is the earliest noted evidence of a distinct West African variety of brass band music. In Mensah's opinion, the clue to the seminal West Indian influence is that one of the earliest *adaha* tunes, 'Everybody Likes Saturday Night,' is based on a calypso melody. Furthermore, although *adaha* bands were recreational and not linked directly to the army, their members wore the colorful 'zouave' uniforms (red-rimmed black uniforms and matching red hat with tassels) that were also worn by the West Indian Regiment (Boonzajer-Flaes 1999).

According to Aboagye (1999), from 1873 to 1901 between five and seven thousand West Indian soldiers (mainly from English-speaking Jamaica, Trinidad and Barbados) spent three-year periods of duty stationed at Cape Coast and the neighboring El Mina Castle to help the British in their Sangreti War against the inland Ashanti kingdom. From Mensah (1969/70), we learn that these English-speaking Caribbean soldiers played calypsos in their spare time, which stimulated local military-trained Ghanaian musicians to create their own syncopated *adaha* brass band music, the earliest form of which later became known as 'highlife' music. *Adaha* groups began by playing syncopated African-Caribbean tunes and utilizing West Indian offbeat *clave* rhythms, but by the 1880s were adopting features of Akan recreational styles (including *adenkum, sikyi* and *adzewa*) such as offbeats, hemiolas and 6/8 polyrhythms.

By 1900 *adaha* brass bands in the Fanti traditional area were supplying march rhythms for street parades and festivities and dance rhythms for local picnics and events at open spaces. In Cape Coast, for instance, these *adaha* bands included the Lion's Hearts, Edu Magicians, Diamond Players and Coker's and Biney's brass bands, while a little later the town of Winneba had its Yamoah's and Acquah's brass bands set up by Fanti merchant trading houses. *Adaha* bands had not only hijacked and Africanized European martial music; they also played at competitive street parades, resulting in objections from the Europeans. The British missionary Rev. Denis Kemp (1898) described the sound of local Cape Coast drum-and-fife bands as 'hideous' and 'tormenting' and warned of the danger of allowing Sunday school processions to be led by them, as they would 'ultimately lead to the ballroom, the heathen dance and other worldly amusements' (cited in Boonzajer-Flaes 1999, 14 f/n 23). In 1908 A. Foulkes, the district commissioner of Cape Coast, prevented the town's five local brass bands from playing their 'objectionable native tunes' as these allegedly led to competitive quarrelling, obstruction of roads, dancing and drinking (Ghana National Archives). Incidentally, there were also reports in the 1882 *Gold Coast Times* of drunkenness among West Indian troops (see Akyeampong 1996).

Despite these colonial objections and bans, during the early twentieth-century local proto-highlife music played by *adaha* brass bands spread like wildfire into provincial and cocoa-rich towns in southern Ghana. The towns and villages that could not afford expensive brass instruments made do instead with *konkoma* (or *konkomba*) highlife groups that used uniforms and conductors but did away with expensive imported brass instruments by employing only voices and local drums (Sackey 1989). It should be noted that when the term 'highlife' was invented in the 1920s it was used generically to describe any form of Ghanaian popular music, whether played by guitar bands, brass bands, dance bands or *konkoma* groups. These *konkoma* bands marched through towns and villages to open spaces where they performed recreational dance music for the youth. Interestingly, Ranger (1975) and Kerr (1995) refer to a similar East African 'tribalization' of European regimental brass band music in the early twentieth century by local *mbeni* bands.

Beginning in the 1890s the European missions (Wesleyan, Basel and Bremen) also set up marching brass bands. However, when missionaries turned their backs or were out of earshot, the church-trained Ghanaian musicians played local dances instead of sedate hymns. As a result, this musical church initiative was discontinued. It was only after World War II and Independence that the churches (especially in the Volta Region) again began to utilize brass bands, eventually incorporating local drums and dance steps. Although secular *adaha* brass bands largely died out in the late 1940s and 1950s due to the rise of highlife dance bands and guitar bands, there were still pockets of this celebratory street music in the Fanti Cape Coast, El Mina, Winneba and Agona Swedru areas in the early twenty-first century.

Bibliography

Aboagye, Lt-Colonel Festus B. 1999. *The Ghanaian Army*. Accra: Sedco Publications.

Akyeampong, Emmanuel. 1996. *Drink Power and Social Change: A Social History of Alcohol in Ghana c. 1800 to Recent Times*. Portsmouth, NH: James Currey/Oxford.

Beecham, John. 1841. *Ashanti and the Gold Coast*. London: John Mason.

Boonzajer-Flaes, Robert. 1999. *Brass Unbound: Secret Children of the Colonial Brass Band*. Amsterdam: Royal Tropical Institute (Book and accompanying CD).

Collins, E. John. 1987. 'Jazz Feedback to Africa.' *American Music* 5(2): 176–93.

Collins, E. John. 1992. *West African Pop Roots*. Philadelphia: Temple University Press.

Collins, E. John. 1994. 'The Ghanaian Concert Party: African Popular Entertainment at the Crossroads.' Unpublished Ph.D. Dissertation, State University of New York, Buffalo.

Collins, E. John. 1996. *Highlife Time*. Accra: Anansesem Press.

De Graft-Johnson, J. C. 1932. 'The Fanti Asafu.' *The Journal of the Institute of African Languages and Culture* V: 307–22.

Fyfe, Christopher. 1962. *A History of Sierra Leone.* New York: Oxford University Press.

Ghana National Archives. Letter from District Commissioner's Office, 1909. Document number 134e, 16 March.

Harrev, Flemming. 1987. 'Goumbe and the Development of Krio Popular Music in Freetown Sierra Leone.' Paper read at the 4th International Conference of IASPM, Accra, Ghana, 12 to 19 August.

Kemp, Dennis. 1898. *Nine Years at the Gold Coast.* London: Macmillan.

Kerr, David. 1995. *African Popular Theatre: From Pre-Colonial Times to the Present Day.* Oxford: James Currey.

Mensah, Atta Annan. 1969/70. *Highlife.* Unpublished manuscript, J.COLLINS/BAPMAF Archives.

Mensah, Atta Annan. 1971/2. 'Jazz – the Round Trip.' *Jazz Forschung/Research* 3/4: 124–37.

Ranger, Terence. 1975. *Dance and Society in Eastern Africa 1890–1970.* London: Heinemann.

Sackey, Chris K. 1989. *Konkoma: A Musical Form of Fanti Young Fishermen in the 1940's and 50's in Ghana West Africa.* Berlin: Dietrich Reimer Verlag.

Waterman, Christopher. 1990. *Jùjú: A Social History and Ethnography of an African Popular Music.* Chicago: University of Chicago Press.

Wolfson, Freda. 1958. *Pageant of Ghana.* London: Oxford University Press.

Filmography

Brass Unbound, dir. Robert Boonajer-Flaes et al. 1993. Holland. 105 mins. TV documentary.

E. JOHN COLLINS

Afrobeat

Afrobeat is a blend of highlife, jazz, funk and Yorùbá social dance music that emerged in the late 1960s through the musical experiments of Nigerian multi-instrumentalist bandleader Fela Anikulapo-Kuti (born Ransome-Kuti) and drum set player Tony Allen. Although Afrobeat's origins are inseparable from these two artists, the roots of its hybridity lie in the long history of Afro-diasporic cultural exchange that is the legacy of transatlantic slavery, mercantile capitalism and colonialism, on the one hand, and of pan-Africanism and African nationalism on the other. From the return of emancipated black Brazilians to Lagos in the late nineteenth century to the American soul revues that toured the continent in the 1970s, the cultures of the African diaspora – especially those of the Americas and the Caribbean – had a significant impact on the development of twentieth-century African popular music. Afrobeat is an extension of this legacy, refracted through the creative minds of Kuti and Allen, whose backgrounds as highlife musicians and shared love of jazz brought them together.

Origins

Highlife music was born in the coastal towns of West Africa at the turn of the twentieth century. Drawing on African, American, Caribbean and European sources, it became the dominant form of popular music in Ghana and Nigeria by the 1950s. Fela Kuti is a product of this musical world and Afrobeat bears its stylistic stamps, namely, a blend of Afro-diasporic and local music orchestrated for jazz big band. Among his first musical mentors was trumpeter Victor Olaiya, an alumnus of Bobby Benson's pioneering Nigerian highlife band. But it was not until after his sojourn in the UK that Fela made the genre his own, introducing novel ideas based on his experiences in London's jazz and Caribbean music scenes.

When Fela went to study in London in the late 1950s, he was immediately drawn to its vibrant jazz scene. Bebop and Afro-Cuban jazz, although they had emerged a decade earlier in the United States, were in ascendance in the UK. Big band arrangements of calypso and mento were also wildly popular, promoted by artists including the Trinidadian Lord Kitchener. Fela also benefited from his exposure to a new form of highlife – actually a revival of early Lagosian highlife with a West Indian sensibility – brought to the UK by Ambrose Campbell and Brewster Hughes, both veterans of the Jolly Orchestra, one of Nigeria's most popular dance bands in the 1930s. The London scene whetted Fela's appetite for the harmonic complexity and virtuosic improvisations of bebop, the instrumentation and *ostinato*-based arrangements of Afro-Cuban jazz and Campbell's hybridization of West African and Caribbean popular music. With these inspirations, Fela returned to Nigeria and set out to forge a new highlife-jazz hybrid with his band

Koola Lobitos. It was in the United States, however, that Fela's critical and political sensibility emerged and Afrobeat as a genre crystalized.

The 1960s was an era in which the intimacies of musical pleasure were tied to the growth of international black consciousness – a pan-African and black diasporic sensibility shaped by African independence abroad and civil rights struggles at home. Black American music of the era – modern and avant-garde jazz as well as rhythm 'n' blues and soul – both reflected and regenerated this consciousness. By the late 1960s the James Brown sound had swept through Ghana and Nigeria and spawned imitators including Sierra Leonean Geraldo Pino, whose band Fela admired and who was one of his prime competitors in the Nigerian market. In search of new opportunities, Fela brought his band Koola Lobitos to Los Angeles in 1969, where he met Sandra Iszadore (née Smith), an activist who introduced him to black revolutionary culture. Alongside the many books Iszadore gave him to read, notably the *Autobiography of Malcolm X*, Fela drank in the sounds and sensibilities of soul and the jazz avant-garde.

Ornette Coleman, Cecil Taylor, John Coltrane, the Art Ensemble of Chicago, Sun Ra and others of the avant-garde sought not only a break with jazz tradition, but also models for music-making that resisted Western frameworks altogether (Veal 1995, 11). While the avant-garde sensibility became obvious in Fela's later experiments with polytonality, it was the politics of liberation inherent in this new aesthetic that initially moved him. This was a movement of black artists urgently aware of their own potential and seeking the musical foundations from which to realize it. Fela had finally found what he had been looking for, a sentiment captured in his famous statement that it was not in Nigeria, but in America, that he discovered 'Africa.'

Yorùbá Performance Practice

Fela returned to Nigeria with his band in the early 1970s determined to make his music more 'African.' Yet, he had distaste for much of what made music African at the time. Yorùbá music is dominated by panegyrics – forms of chanting, singing and drumming that valorize wealth, power and authority. Fela felt that such music only served to reinforce entrenched structures of social inequality by legitimizing a Nigerian elite who had benefited from colonialism. He also rejected *dundun* and *bata* drums for their roles in the panegyric tradition. Fela did, nonetheless, adopt a number of Yorùbá performance practices. On a general level, these include the use of layered *ostinato* and cyclical variation-in-repetition in the manner of Yorùbá drum polyphony, pentatonic melodies, homophonic parallelism and call-and-response arrangements.

But there is a deeper level of Yorùbá cultural reference in Fela's music. First is the use of folk material, as in the songs 'Alu Jon Jonki Jon' (1972) and 'Gbagada Gbogodo' (1972), both of which derive from the Yorùbá tradition of moonlight tales, and 'Who're You' (1970, *Fela's London Scene*), which features an electric piano solo built on the melody of a children's song. Although these are the only published songs in which Fela directly borrows folk material, he does occasionally quote folk melodies and use parables to convey moral and political sentiments. Second, in eschewing panegyrics, Fela turned instead to the sanctified language of abuse and satire found in many Yorùbá performance practices. While praise is widely accepted as public discourse, derision tends to be reserved for ritual contexts, where the potentially destabilizing awareness of individual faults and societal fault lines can be better contained. However, for Fela, who viewed the Nigerian postcolony as fundamentally unstable and untenable, ritualized derision *was* his primary mode of public discourse. Third, many of Fela's songs are ritualistic in more than metaphoric ways; they also incorporate deep ritual language and follow the structural logics and energetic trajectories of Yorùbá ritual practice (Olorunyomi 2003, 99). The songs 'Original Sufferhead' (1981), 'Confusion Break Bone' (1990) and 'Overtake Don Overtake Overtake' (1989), for example, make use of lamentations drawn from Oro and Ogboni ritual language, while 'I.T.T. (International Thief Thief)' (1979) and the unreleased 'Big Blind Country' unfold in the manner of masquerade and Ifa divination rituals, respectively. Many of Fela's songs, especially in his late period, also offer ritual homage to the Yorùbá *orisa* (deities) (see Olorunyomi 2003, chap. 3, on the Yorùbá ritual dimensions of Afrobeat).

Antecedents: Koola Lobitos and Highlife-Jazz

Fela's first steps toward Afrobeat began with his band Koola Lobitos, which he formed in the early 1960s as an effort to bring jazz to Nigeria but which soon transformed into a vehicle for the re-hybridization of jazz and highlife. Many of the features that would eventually coalesce into Afrobeat were evident in Koola Lobitos in varying proportions. The group's early work, in songs including 'Awo,' 'Egbin' and 'Lagos Baby' (*Lagos Baby 1963–1969*), for example, is in many ways consistent with the highlife music of the time, with its tonic-dominant-chord progressions, Caribbean melodic lilt and Latin rhythms, but it also showcases a genre-stretching tendency toward the complex harmonies, arrangements and horn improvisations of jazz. The band's unreleased 1965 *Voice of America Sessions* highlights Fela's taste for calypso-jazz and the work of Sonny Rollins, whose version of 'St. Thomas' is quoted in the opening of 'Igba l'Aiye.' By the late 1960s the band was experimenting with the layered *ostinato* of Latin jazz, the bluesy tinges of hard bop (Horace Silver and Art Blakey were favorites) and the backbeat drive of soul. 'Wayo (1st version),' for example, is a fast-paced *mambo*-like number with horns phrased around the *clave*, while the second version features a horn melody reminiscent of hard bop (for comparison of the two, see *Koola Lobitos 64–68/The '69 Los Angeles Sessions*). 'Funky Horn,' from the same 1969 sessions, highlights the band's turn toward soul, with its hints of blues harmony, up-tempo backbeat and punchy horn lines. Fela's inclination toward slow, syncopated grooves is evident in the songs 'My Lady Frustration' and 'This Is Sad,' which demonstrate his approach to vamp-based forms and minor-key modalism, respectively (Veal 2000, 72–3).

Early Afrobeat

After their transformative sojourn in the United States, Fela and the members of Koola Lobitos (renamed Nigeria '70 by that time) returned to Nigeria in 1970 with a clearer sense of how to integrate their many influences into a coherent style. Sensing that 'highlife-jazz' was no longer viable in a market overtaken by soul and funk, Fela renamed his music 'Afrobeat' and, in the pan-African spirit of the times, rebranded his outfit the Africa '70. After further refinements of style and changes in personnel between 1971 and 1972, Africa '70 stabilized as a unit with Fela on lead vocals and electric piano (also tenor saxophone after Igo Chico's departure in 1973); Tony Allen on drum set; a horn section that included future bandleader Lekan Animasaun on baritone sax, Coltrane-inspired tenor saxophonist Igo Chico (until 1973) and hard bop stylist Tunde Williams on trumpet; Okalue Ojeah, Leke Benson and Oghene Kologbo on rhythm, tenor and bass guitars, respectively; Shina Abiodunn and Nicholas Addo on *congas*; percussionists James Abayomi and Isaac Olaleye on clips and *sèkèrè* (rattle), respectively; and a rotating chorus of female singers (see Veal 2000, 261–2 for complete list of personnel).

The Afrobeat sound further solidified in the early 1970s. In the period between his breakthrough hit 'Jeun K'o Ku' (1971) and the release of *Shakara* in 1972, Fela increasingly turned from the dominant-chord vamps of James Brown toward the cooler sounds of minor modes (Dorian and Aeolian in particular) overlaid with pentatonic melodies. In terms of texture, Afrobeat is characterized by layered *ostinato*, with multiple strata of short interlocking rhythms and melodies – a technique probably owing as much to funk music as to West African polyphony. Like James Brown's funk, Afrobeat is composed of a melorhythmic gestalt over which horn and vocal themes and variations are introduced. Brown's influence is especially evident in Fela's juxtaposition of rhythm and tenor guitars – the first scratching out a syncopated chord pattern and the second playing a single-line *ostinato*. This was an unusual innovation in the context of West African popular music, where even in brass bands the guitar plays a leading melodic role. In Afrobeat, by contrast, the rhythm, tenor and bass guitar unit functions as a bridge between the rhythmic strata of *conga* drums, rattle and *claves*/clips, on the one hand, and the harmony-melody strata of horns, electric piano and vocals, on the other. Fela uses layered *ostinato* to maximum effect by staggering the entrances of different parts and by varying textural density to create tension and release. And the parts lock together melodically as well. Motives are typically extracted from the song's larger themes and then arranged in responsorial formats in order to build a sense of melodic unity across the ensemble's many moving parts (see Omojola 2012, 175–88, for an analysis of these features in the 1976 song 'Zombie').

Afrobeat would be unimaginable without the innovations of drummer Tony Allen. Well versed in jazz independence, he uses the drum set to musically link the ensemble's different layers. He locks his bass drum in with the bass guitar *ostinato*, weaves snare drum and hi-hat cymbal rhythms into the guitar and percussion layers and brings the whole kit into play to accentuate horn section hits and breaks. Respected in equal measure for their feel and originality, Allen's grooves bring together Nigerian social dance rhythms, the *clave* or 'timeline'-oriented phrasing of highlife, a nimble jazz vocabulary and the tight syncopation of James Brown's funk. In early Afrobeat songs such as 'Egbe Mi O' and 'J'Ehin J'Ehin' (1970, *Fela's London Scene*), for example, Allen reconfigures the standard highlife drum set rhythm by slowing the tempo, placing hi-hats on beat '2' and '4,' re-orchestrating the *clave* pattern around the drum set and syncopating the ride and snare parts. But Allen's palette was rich with ideas and he created a variety of patterns that hinted at his influences. Similarities with James Brown's funk drummers can be heard in a number of Allen's grooves, which satisfyingly balance syncopated rhythms with an emphasis on the downbeat of '1.' Allen's grooves, however, with their orientation toward jazz, highlife and traditional rhythms, are looser and more 'conversational' in style, favoring 'off-beat' phrasing over backbeat emphasis. (For a more detailed analysis of Allen's drumming, see Stewart 2013.)

The typical Afrobeat song of the 1970s begins with a solo prelude or introductory overture, sometimes including melodic gestures on the piano or horns that anticipate the main theme. The ensemble then proceeds to the 'head' or main horn theme. Improvised horn solos follow, with the horn section providing responsorial riffs. After the solos, Fela sings the lyric and performs call-and-response passages with the horn section and chorus. He also adds extemporaneous declamations, didactics and dialogues, all addressed to an imagined audience and intended to convey not just the moral or political message but also the emotional truth behind the song. This part of his songs became increasingly longer with Fela's growing political radicalization. The compositions typically conclude with a return to the choral refrain and a recapitulation of the main horn theme(s). Since the tonality and rhythmic character remain constant throughout, formal contrast is built through the progressive elaboration and juxtaposition of melodic motives and through the strategic addition or subtraction of musical layers – variations in textural density that build and release tension.

Leaving behind the frivolous lyrics of his highlife days, Fela's early 1970s work addresses the complexity of postcolonial life through the lens of individual morality, that is, through matters of personal character and social conduct that he sees as having racial or cultural significance (Olaniyan 2004 divides Fela's stylistic innovations and ideological stances into three overlapping stages: 'apolitical avant-pop hustler,' 'afrobeat social reformer' and 'afrobeat political activist'). The song 'Gentleman' (1973), for example, is on one level a satire of African men who dress like Westerners and on another level a critique of the African elite as a class for their perceived 'colonial mentality' and dislocation from indigenous culture. The song may also be read as a reference to the older generation of highlife musicians, like 'Gentleman Bobby' (Bobby Benson), from whom Fela was determined to differentiate himself. Other examples of this era include 'Lady' (1972), a popular piece that addresses the perceived Westernization of African women, and 'Buy Africa' (1970, *Fela's London Scene*), a nationalist song that criticizes Nigerians' taste for foreign goods. The songs of this era also demonstrate Fela's emerging populism – more specifically, his identification with the working-class masses of Lagos – signaled by his turn from Yorùbá lyricism toward the rough-hewn idioms of Pidgin English. The cityscape of Lagos itself, both as a lived space and as a determining structure, was the subject of the album *Roforofo Fight* (1972), among many others throughout Fela's career (Olaniyan 2004, 37, refers to these as Fela's 'metro songs'). 'Ikoyi Mentality versus Mushin Mentality' (1971) illustrates this duality by connecting the intimacies of language use and home life to the class stratification of modern Lagos and the differing notions of 'civilization' it implies.

Political Afrobeat

By the mid-1970s Fela's political radicalization increasingly found its outlet in his Afrobeat lyrics. He became more direct in his attacks on what he saw as the authoritarianism, militarism, corruption and general incompetence at the heart of the Nigerian state. He also adopted a more structuralist perspective, identifying the ideological and social conditions that perpetuate inequality and the illegitimate exercise of power (Olaniyan 2004, 57). Fela's transition from the language of moralism to that of social systems mirrors his transformation from brash African nationalist to political dissident and working-class hero, his public and private life increasingly intertwined. In a libertine interpretation of 'tradition,' Fela adopted polygamy and formed a 'village' compound in the heart of Lagos, where he, his wives and hangers-on lived. Fela's Afrika Shrine, a nightclub located across the street from his compound, became the central context not only for Afrobeat music, but also for Fela's public musings on politics, his experiments with reconstructed Yorùbá ritual and an outlet for the Lagos counterculture that sustained him. He was first arrested and temporarily imprisoned on fabricated charges of marijuana possession in 1974. Fela reports that this experience, in which he saw 'society' imprisoned and 'criminals' in positions of authority, forever changed his orientation toward the system (see Moore [1982] 2009, 122–7, for the complete anecdote). 'Alagbon Close' (1974), his first direct attack on the legitimacy of the Nigerian state, is a response to this experience expressed through the metaphor of the soldier's uniform, which Fela rhetorically downgrades from a sign of authority to a mere piece of cloth. Fela also signaled his move toward political dissidence and direct opposition to the Nigerian state by naming his urban commune the Kalakuta Republic ('Rascals' Republic') and declaring it an independent state. Fela's confrontations with the authorities only intensified after this, as did the sharpness of his discourse. Significant work of that era includes his best-selling 1976 albums *Zombie* and *Kalakuta Show*, the title songs of which are anti-state compositions that respectively lampoon the mindless militarism of Nigeria's dictatorships and describe the destruction they leave in their wake. Fela also viewed Christianity and Islam in Nigeria as vestiges of imperialism and denounced them in the most uncompromising manner. His album *Shuffering and Shmiling* (1978) best captures this sentiment, juxtaposing images of poverty-stricken and suffering worshippers with the exhortations of wealthy imams and bishops who urge their congregants to 'suffer for world, enjoy for heaven' (suffer in this world, enjoy/rejoice in heaven) – a discourse that Fela saw as just another screen for neo-colonial exploitation.

Late-Period Afrobeat

In 1981 Fela renamed his group Egypt '80 to signal the band's reorganization, his growing interest in Egyptological Afrocentrism and his reclamation of precolonial 'African' culture, broadly conceived. The period from 1978 to 1979 had seen the death of Fela's mother, Funmilayo Ransome-Kuti, from wounds inflicted during a police raid on the Kalakuta Republic; the dismantling of the original commune; and the departure of drummer Tony Allen. Fela and the genre of Afrobeat were irrevocably changed. He became increasingly political – in the sense of getting more directly involved in the discourses and contests through which power and resources are distributed. In his attempt to run for the Nigerian presidency in the national elections of 1979, he formed a political party, Movement of the People (MOP), and became known informally as the Black President. Although his political aspirations were never realized, Fela's testimony to the suffering of the poor and his condemnations of the state continued unabated and took on a more personal dimension. The album-length works 'Unknown Soldier' (1979) and 'Coffin for Head of State' (1981), for example, detail the army's attacks on Kalakuta and the subsequent death of his mother. These two pieces, along with 'Army Arrangement' (1985), 'I.T.T. (International Thief Thief)' (1979) and 'Beasts of No Nation' (1989) call out politicians, judges and chief executives by name, deriding them for what Fela saw as their wrongheaded or outright criminal activities. And Fela no longer limited himself to politics of a local order. The cover of the album *Beasts of No Nation*, for example, caricatures Ronald Reagan, Margaret Thatcher and P.W. Botha as animals with sharp, blood-stained teeth. The lyrics decry their accommodations to apartheid and note the irony of a UN governing body that professes human rights yet is made up of 'beasts' that feed on the suffering masses.

Fela's Egypt '80 grew to nearly twice the size of Africa '70, with nine horn players, two guitarists, two bassists, a second keyboardist, five percussionists and a large group of singers and dancers. Aspiring to create a form of 'classical African music,' Fela extended his multi-movement compositions to the length of an LP. The music of this period is richer in texture with more complex arrangements. Still largely modal in quality, the pieces occasionally include sections in contrasting tonalities or polytonal ensemble passages. Textural and timbral variation continue to be a central source of formal contrast, from the lush overlap of guitars and second piano to the brash wall of sound created by the interlocking choral and horn parts. Other differences from 1970s Afrobeat include more varied thematic material; greater interplay between the vocal and horn parts; longer and more abstract horn solos, with hints of modal and avant-garde jazz; and more extended vocal sections that include solo lyrics, choral themes, responsorial chants and schoolyard game songs.

As the vocal sections became more elaborate and the Yorùbá cultural references deeper, the density of ideas and layers of meaning in Fela's lyrics only increased. He came to see words themselves as having spiritual efficacy and began to incorporate and imitate the incantations, lamentations and divinations of Yorùbá ritual. The metaphor of magic also began to surface in Fela's lyrics. 'Just Like That' (1990), for example, draws a parallel between acts of magic and the occult economies of the Nigerian postcolony in which the powerful can make the people's money, electricity, food and water disappear or appear as if by force of the supernatural. Other notable works of this era include 'Army Arrangement' (1985), 'Teacher Don't Teach Me Nonsense' (1986) and 'Confusion Break Bone' (1990).

Afrobeat's success during the 1970s was largely a Nigerian phenomenon and the genre was so closely identified with Fela and his political activities that its musical ideas were explored only by an intrepid few. Jùjú star King Sunny Ade was one of the first. While Afrobeat influences can be detected in Ade's work as early as 1976's *Syncro System Movement*, it was not until the early 1980s that Ade most effectively mobilized the genre's sound to propel his African Beats band to international acclaim (Veal 2000, 188–90). This Afrobeat-inflected *jùjú* music, with its simultaneously African and African-American references, enhanced as it was by Ade's charismatic performances, would cut a wide path for African popular music of all kinds in the global marketplace. Largely resistant to the imperatives of the nascent 'world music' industry, Fela nonetheless saw in Nigeria's post-oil boom implosion and his own declining fortunes the necessity of pursuing international audiences.

Fela's early European appearances drew polarized reception – German jazz fans lambasted his musicianship and autocratic style, while French students idolized him as a countercultural hero – but the move served to revive his career. Despite Fela's isolationist stance, Afrobeat had, in fact, already grown well beyond the purview of its creator by the early 1980s. Its influence extended from Nigerian artists like Dele Abiodun, Segun Adewale, Sonny Okosun and Ephraim Nzeka to those beyond, including Roy Ayers, Ginger Baker, Lester Bowie, David Byrne, William 'Bootsy' Collins, Brian Eno, Branford Marsalis, Hugh Masekela, Paul McCartney, Randy Weston and Stevie Wonder, among many others.

Afrobeat after Fela: The Second Wave

Fela Kuti died in 1997 from AIDS-related complications. More than a million people came out to the streets of Lagos to bid him farewell along the route to his resting place in the Kalakuta compound. By the time Fela died, Afrobeat was well on its way to becoming a global genre. His music has been sampled by numerous hip-hop artists and is credited with sparking the Afrohouse and broken beat movements of 1990s New York and London (Patel 2003, 33–4). Fela's music saw a full-scale resurgence at the millennium, with a series of reissues by MCA/Universal and their affiliates. A number of tribute albums have also appeared featuring original music by second-wave Afrobeat artists, creative remixes and reinterpretations of classic Fela tunes and Afrobeat-inspired contributions by a variety of contemporary musicians. These include *Afrobeat No Go Die* (2000), *Red Hot & Riot* (2002), *Underground Spiritual Game* (2004) and *Black Man's Cry: The Inspiration of Fela Kuti* (2010). Other tributes include the New York exhibition *Black President: The Art and Legacy of Fela Anikulapo-Kuti* and its companion publication *Fela: From West Africa to West Broadway* (2003). The musical *Fela!*, under the direction of Bill T. Jones, opened in New York in 2009 and morphed into a touring show with musical direction from members of Antibalas, one of the torchbearers of Afrobeat's second generation.

The first to pursue Afrobeat in a sustained way outside the context of Fela's band was the drummer who helped create the genre, Tony Allen. Allen began working as a bandleader on Afrobeat projects while he was still a member of Africa '70.

With Fela as producer, the band backed Allen on his first three albums, *Jealousy* (1975), *Progress* (1977) and *No Accommodation for Lagos* (1979). In 1979, however, he left Africa '70 and formed his own band, the Afro Messengers, with whom he released *No Discrimination*. Allen's title track, with its wah-wah synth lines, bluesy guitar licks and backbeat groove, signaled his departure from genre conventions and his entrance into a period of musical experimentation. Allen's 1985 release *NEPA (Never Expect Power Always)* showcases his ability to flex the framework of Afrobeat enough to incorporate different instruments and styles, in this case the synth-driven sounds of 1980s boogie funk, without losing the essence of the genre. He would in turn explore Afrobeat fusions with dub, rap and other forms of electronic music. It was not until 2006 with *Lagos No Shaking* that Allen returned to a more conventional Afrobeat sound.

The next to pursue Afrobeat independently was Fela's eldest son Femi, who cut his teeth with his father's Egypt '80 band. Femi Kuti left Egypt '80 in 1986 to form his own band, Positive Force. At first ridiculed by his father for this move, Femi and his group persisted and achieved moderate success in the global market. Fela would eventually reverse his position and recast Femi as the only true heir apparent. Femi's music, however, is different from his father's. The compositions tend to be shorter, more closely adhering to the jazz-inspired form of early Afrobeat than to the more complex multi-movement forms to which his father aspired. At the same time, Femi's music is unabashedly oriented toward global tastes in popular music, with its brisk dance tempos, liberal use of backbeat grooves and synthesized timbers. In short, Femi is far less concerned with the status of Afrobeat as authentically 'African' music (Olaniyan 2004, 179). His popular 1998 album *Shoki Shoki*, for example, was rereleased in 1999 with remixes by a number of electronic music producers and his Grammy-nominated album *Fight to Win* (2001) features American artists Common, Mos Def and Jaguar Wright. Femi's songs are generally written along themes of cultural or national concern and generally avoid the derisive lyrics and confrontational style of his father.

Fela's youngest son Seun Kuti, who took over leadership of Egypt '80, blends his father's aggressive verbal style with his brother's more direct approach to songwriting. Generally faithful to the Egypt '80 sound, with its rich overlapping choral and horn textures, he pushes genre boundaries with *A Long Way to the Beginning* (2014), which is co-produced by American pianist Robert Glasper and features Nneka, M-1 of Dead Prez and Blitz the Ambassador.

If Femi and Seun have reformulated Afrobeat for the international market, Lagbaja (Bisade Ologunde) has brought it back into conversation with the forms of Yorùbá traditional and popular music that Fela so long rejected. Instruments shunned by Fela for their roles in the Yorùbá panegyric tradition, the *dundun* and *bata* in particular, are given center stage in Lagbaja's music. Although expressly influenced by Fela, Lagbaja has sought to distinguish his music from Afrobeat, renaming the neo-traditional drum-centered sound 'africano.'

Brooklyn-based Antibalas, formed in 1998 by Martín Perna, is widely recognized as the pioneer of second-wave Afrobeat. Translated from Spanish as 'anti-bullet,' the band's name is intended to connote both a durable musical sound and an anti-militaristic stance. In their own words, Antibalas plays 'unadulterated' Afrobeat, meaning that they stick closely to the genre conventions established by Fela in the 1970s. In fact, their interpretation of the 1970s sound was so convincing that band members Aaron Johnson and Jordan MacLean were tapped to be musical director and assistant musical director, respectively, of the musical *Fela!*. But there are important differences. While giving their front man Amayo ample space, Antibalas feels more like a collective than does Africa '70 – a band designed only to do the bidding of its master. In Fela's spirit, Antibalas writes songs that comment on social issues, like the popular 'Dirty Money' (2012), but they generally avoid directly confrontational content.

The tension between Afrobeat as 'political' music and as music for aesthetic enjoyment runs through the genre's history. It has only become more pronounced with the emergence of the international second wave, in which artists share with Fela an aesthetic and political progressivism, but have experienced little of the abject conditions that fueled his fiery ideology and activism. Fela knew, however, that politics and pleasure could never be separate and that the spiritual charge necessary to spark political change could only be found in music. It is with this knowledge that primarily instrumental bands such as the Chicago Afrobeat Project and Australia's Shaolin Afronauts are pursuing the spirit of avant-garde jazz in Afrobeat – the commitment to music-making as an expression of protest and prayer, an act of revelation and a call to action. Afrobeat has thus become not so much a platform for one man's radical ideology and confrontational politics, but rather a musical language for conveying the many truths of global progressivism.

Bibliography

Allen, Tony, with Michael E. Veal. 2013. *Tony Allen: An Autobiography of the Master Drummer of Afrobeat*. Durham, NC and London: Duke University Press.

Collins, John. 1985. *Musicmakers of West Africa*. Washington, DC: Three Continents Press.

Collins, John. 2009. *Fela: Kalakuta Notes*. Amsterdam: KIT Publishers.

Dosunmu, Oyebade Ajibola. 2010. 'Afrobeat, Fela and Beyond: Scenes, Style and Ideology.' Unpublished Ph.D. thesis, University of Pittsburgh.

Moore, Carlos. 2009. *Fela: This Bitch of a Life. The Authorized Biography of Africa's Musical Genius*. Chicago: Lawrence Hill Books. (First published London: Allison & Busby, 1982.)

Olaniyan, Tejumola. 2004. *Arrest the Music! Fela and His Rebel Art and Politics*. Bloomington, IN: Indiana University Press.

Olorunyomi, Sola. 2003. *Afrobeat! Fela and the Imagined Continent*. Trenton, NJ: Africa World Press.

Omojola, Bode. 2012. *Yorùbá Music in the Twentieth Century: Identity, Agency and Performance Practice*. New York: University of Rochester Press.

Patel, Joseph. 2003. 'Power Music, Electric Revival: Fela Kuti and the Influence of His Afrobeat on Hip-Hop and Dance Music.' In *Fela: From West Africa to West Broadway*, ed. Trevor Schoonmaker. New York: Palgrave Macmillan, 25–35.

Sanneh, Kelefa, and Kuti, Femi. 2000. 'Here Comes the Son.' *Transition* 85: 114–39.

Schoonmaker, Trevor, ed. 2003. *Fela: From West Africa to West Broadway*. New York: Palgrave Macmillan.

Stewart, Alexander. 2013. 'Make It Funky: Fela Kuti, James Brown and the Invention of Afrobeat.' *American Studies* 52(4): 19–118.

Veal, Michael E. 1995. 'Jazz Music Influences on the Work of Fela Anikulapo-Kuti.' *Glendora Review* 1(1): 8–13.

Veal, Michael E. 2000. *Fela: The Life and Times of an African Musical Icon*. Philadelphia: Temple University Press.

Waterman, Christopher A. 1998. 'Chop and Quench.' *African Arts* 31(1): 1, 4, 6, 8–9.

Discographical References

Ade, King Sunny. *Syncro System Movement*. African Songs Limited AS26-L. *1976*: Nigeria.

Afrobeat No Go Die: Trans-Global African Funk Grooves. Shanachie 66030. *2000*: USA.

Allen, Tony. *Jealousy* (with Africa '70). Sound Workshop SWS1004. *1975*: Nigeria.

Allen, Tony. *Lagos No Shaking*. Astralwerks ASK51322. *2006*: USA.

Allen, Tony. *NEPA (Never Expect Power Always)*. Celluloid-Moving Target MT002. *1985*: USA.

Allen, Tony. *No Accommodation for Lagos* (with Africa '70). Phonogram POLP035. *1979*: Nigeria.

Allen, Tony. *Progress* (with Africa '70). Coconut PMLP1004. *1977*: Nigeria.

Allen, Tony, and The Afro Messengers. *No Discrimination*. Shanu-Olu GSLP1012. *1979*: Nigeria.

Anikulapo-Kuti, Femi. *Fight to Win*. Barclay 589 264. *2001*: France.

Anikulapo-Kuti, Femi. *Shoki Remixed*. Barclay 543 190. *1999*: UK.

Anikulapo-Kuti, Femi. *Shoki Shoki*. Barclay 559 035. *1998*: UK.

Anikulapo-Kuti, Seun, and The Egypt '80. *A Long Way to the Beginning*. Knitting Factory Records KFR1132. *2014*: USA.

Antibalas. 'Dirty Money.' *Antibalas*. Daptone DAP028. *2012*: USA.

Black Man's Cry: The Inspiration of Fela Kuti. Stones Throw-Now-Again NA 5056. *2010*: USA.

Fela Ransome-Kuti and His Koola Lobitos:

Koola Lobitos 64–68/The '69 Los Angeles Sessions. Wrass 054. *2001*: UK.

Lagos Baby (1963–9). Vampisoul 097. *2008*: Spain.

Voice of America Sessions. United States Information Agency. *1965*: Nigeria.

Fela Ransome-Kuti and the Africa '70:
'Alagbon Close.' *Alagbon Close.* Jofabro Nigeria JILP1002. *1974*: Nigeria.
'Alu Jon Jonki Jon.' *Afrodisiac.* Regal Zonophone-EMI 1E 062-81290. *1972*: UK.
'Coffin for Head of State.' *Coffin for Head of State.* Kalakuta KALP003. *1981*: Nigeria.
'Gbagada Gbogodo.' *Open and Close.* EMI HNLX 5090. *1972*: Nigeria.
'Gentleman.' *Gentleman.* EMI NEMI 0009. *1973*: Nigeria.
'Ikoyi Mentality versus Mushin Mentality.' *Why Black Man Dey Suffer* (with Ginger Baker). African Songs AS0001. *1971*: Nigeria.
'I.T.T. (International Thief Thief).' *I.T.T. (International Thief Thief).* Kalakuta K002. *1979*: Nigeria.
'Jeun K'o Ku.' EMI-HMV HNS 1075. *1971*: Nigeria.
Kalakuta Show. EMI (catalogue number unknown). *1976*: Nigeria.
'Lady.' *Shakara.* EMI 008N. *1972*: Nigeria.
Music of Fela – Roforofo Fight. Jofabro JILP001. *1972*: Nigeria.
Shuffering and Shmiling. Phonogram-Coconut PMLP1005. *1978*: Nigeria.
'Unknown Soldier.' *Unknown Soldier.* Phonodisk Skylark SKLP003A. *1979*: Nigeria.
Zombie. Coconut PMLP1003. *1976*: Nigeria.

Fela Anikulapo-Kuti and the Egypt '80:
'Army Arrangement.' *Army Arrangement.* Celluloid CELL6115. *1985*: USA.
'Beasts of No Nation.' *Beasts of No Nation.* Kalakuta K008. *1989*: Nigeria.
'Confusion Break Bone.' *Confusion Break Bone.* Kalakuta K010. *1990*: Nigeria.
'Just Like That.' *Just Like That.* Kalakuta K011. *1990*: Nigeria.
'Original Sufferhead.' Original Sufferhead. Lagos International LIR 2. *1981*: Nigeria.
'Overtake Don Overtake Overtake.' *Overtake Don Overtake Overtake.* Kalakuta K009. *1989*: Nigeria.
'Teacher Don't Teach Me Nonsense.' *Teacher Don't Teach Me Nonsense.* Polygram-Phillips PH2004. *1986*: Nigeria.

Fela Ransome-Kuti and the Nigeria '70:
Fela's London Scene. EMI HNLX 5200. *1970*: Nigeria.
'Who're You.' Fela's London Scene. EMI HNLX 5200. *1970*: Nigeria.
Red Hot & Riot. MCA 088 113 075. *2002*: USA.
Rollins, Sonny. 'St. Thomas.' *Saxophone Colossus.* Prestige LP7079. *1956*: USA.
Underground Spiritual Game (produced and mixed by Chief Xcel). Wrasse 133. *2004*: UK.

JESSE D. RUSKIN

Afrobeats

'Afrobeats' (sometimes written Afro Beats) is an umbrella term that emerged in the 2000s to describe the modern, urban music of Africa and its diaspora communities around the world. The music features both singing and rapping, a variety of danceable rhythms that are most often played electronically, and frequent use of Auto-tuned vocals. The term was first employed by DJs in London around 2009 as a way to describe the new music emerging from West African cities and from young African artists in European cities. This was a time when a Ghanaian popular dance and music style called *azonto* was gaining ground rapidly in West African diaspora communities. *Azonto* was one of a number of new pop dance genres springing up in Anglophone African cities in particular. All these genres became increasingly lumped together under the Afrobeats banner. Afrobeats as a descriptor was not immediately embraced in Africa, but by 2012 a CNN reporter in Lagos, Nigeria, described it as a 'movement' particular to the 'Anglophone West African music scene' (Duthiers and Kermeliotis 2012). Afrobeats has remained a rapidly evolving phenomenon, ever-morphing through the channels and filters of digital media – the Internet, social media and satellite television.

African popular music has been in an ongoing condition of change ever since the early twentieth century when the first urban bands began to make recordings and receive radio play. By the dawn of the twenty-first century the arrival of affordable recording and mixing equipment and digital media had coincided with the rise of hip-hop around the world. Starting in the mid-1990s there were burgeoning African rap scenes in cities including Dakar, Dar es Salaam and Johannesburg. Congolese music, which had previously dominated the dance floors of Africa, was becoming more electronic and driving, incorporating the spirit, if not the sound, of hip-hop.

It was increasingly rivaled by slickly produced *coupé-décalé* dance music from the Ivory Coast. Meanwhile, pop singers emulating African-American R&B music began to dominate the airwaves of independent radio stations in countries including Tanzania, Zambia, South Africa and Kenya. By the early 2000s syndicated satellite television networks were beginning to broadcast music and music video contests, crossing national borders and especially putting Anglophone countries in touch with each other's popular culture in an unprecedented way. Facebook and YouTube also played a role in empowering entrepreneurial young artists, connecting them across national borders, and even oceans.

All of these factors presaged the crystallization of Afrobeats. There is a dispute between two London-based DJs as to who coined the term: Kenyan DJ Edu of BBC 1Xtra's program 'Destination Africa' and Ghanaian DJ Abrantee of Capital XTRA's 'Afrobeats' show. Writing in *The Guardian* in 2012, Dan Hancox credits Abrantee, who describes Afrobeats as 'a 21st-century melting pot of western rap influences, and contemporary Ghanaian and Nigerian pop music.' While the original impetus may have come from West Africans, Afrobeats went on to encompass music from Angola, Tanzania, Kenya and South Africa.

Rab Bakari, a Ghanaian-American DJ, producer and agent, was an architect of the Ghanaian genre known as hiplife – a merger of hip-hop and highlife that coalesced in the mid-1990s. Bakari has traveled frequently to Lagos, Accra, Nairobi, Pretoria and Johannesburg, keeping up with changes in popular music. He notes that, starting around 2005, many African producers came to an emerging consensus regarding the ideal bpm (beats per minute) for dance music: somewhere around 125 bpm (Bakari 2016). Once that happened, it became possible to segue easily between current songs from Nigeria, Kenya, Angola, South Africa and Ghana. *Coupé-décalé* from the Ivory Coast also works within this flow. Since then, other tempos have been commonly used, particularly slower ones and rhythms using a 12/8 time signature. So while this moment of stylistic consensus opened the door to a pan-African dance floor flow, it has not created orthodoxy. Congolese music, for example, which is organized around a *clave* rhythm and relies on speed variations, fits less easily and continues to stand on its own; no one would refer to Congolese music as part of the Afrobeats genre.

Bakari notes that Afrobeats producers are skilled at working local African rhythms into this shared rhythmic flow, for example from different regions of Ghana or Nigeria (Bakari 2016). There is room for individual cultural expression without fundamentally changing the dance momentum of the music, which is created for the nightclub and for mixes of songs regularly posted by DJs on YouTube and elsewhere. While some critics view Afrobeats as a generic version or Americanization of African pop, others see it as opening a space for more local cultural expression within a shared context. DJ Abrantee told *The Guardian* that Afrobeats should be seen as 'an amalgamation of beats' (Hancox 2012).

Accompanying this emphasis on rhythm is a noteworthy decrease in the importance of language. In earlier times, language was a barrier to marketing music within Africa. Listeners tended not to embrace music when they could not understand the lyrics, the clear exception being Congolese music, whose Lingala melodies were widely embraced because the music was so universally danceable. In the era of Afrobeats, Bakari says that the groove is more important than the language (2016). In fact, listeners enjoy hearing the urban patois of other African cities. For example, the Ghanaian rapper Sarkodie raps almost exclusively in Twi, an Akan language. His distinguishing mark is the fast speed of his raps, and he has found an audience all over the continent and has collaborated with artists from countries including Angola, South Africa and Morocco, always rapping in Twi.

Afrobeats has arisen at a time when hip-hop artists in the United States and Europe frequently combine rapping and singing. Since the late 1990s hip-hop vocalists have used pitch correction software generally described as Auto-tune. Auto-tune began as a way of disguising imperfections in the performances of rappers who were not trained singers. When the correction required was sufficiently large, it resulted in a trilling sound, which soon became a desired effect. Auto-tune is no longer seen primarily as a tool for repairing vocal recordings; it has become an instrument in itself, an effect employed artistically by many vocalists and producers, including artists within the Afrobeats movement.

Artists interviewed for the syndicated public radio program *Afropop Worldwide* at the 2016 One Africa Music Festival concert at the Barclay's Center in Brooklyn, USA, which featured stars from Nigeria, Ghana, Tanzania and Kenya, offered a variety of definitions of Afrobeats. The artists generally agreed that the Afrobeats genre's place of origin encompasses not only West Africa but also the entire continent as well as diaspora locations, particularly urban ones. DJ Tunez, who works with one of Nigeria's most popular singers, Wizkid, cited Fela Kuti as 'a big, big founder of Afrobeats,' even 'the King of Afrobeats.' Wizkid himself, famously, has Fela's name tattooed on his forearm. Efya, one of the most popular young women singers in Ghana said, 'When you say Afrobeats, it goes all the way back to Fela' (Efya 2016). She specifically cites Fela's use of foreign and local influences in his sound which is known as Afrobeat (with no 's') (see entry on Afrobeat).

The similarity of these two genre terms has created inevitable confusion. In a recent interview, Fela's youngest son Seun Kuti noted that he was 'okay' with the adaptation of his father's term – 'Afrobeat' – though he would have preferred that the new music be called something else (Kuti 2016). He sees the appropriation of his father's genre name as a kind of crutch relied upon by promoters of the new music to popularize an upcoming roster of artists and songs. Kuti predicted that the term would not last long. Rab Bakari (2016) does not consider the term Afrobeats to be a homage to Fela, primarily because the music reflects none of Fela's outspokenness on social and political issues. In the early twenty-first century, when musicians could not profit from recordings but had to fill large venues with live audiences and look for corporate sponsors or powerful patrons, it did not pay to sing or rap about politics as Fela did.

Afrobeats is thus decidedly recreational music, for dancing, partying and forgetting one's cares. Nigerian music promoter Cecil Hammond made the point clearly to CNN in 2012, noting that 'Nigerian artists don't really want to get into politics.' Hammond cited the risk to an artist of becoming associated with a political party, and stressed that, given the stresses of life in a city such as Lagos, young people want music to 'make you loosen up, make you happy.'

In Lagos, a key city for the production of Afrobeats music, industry professionals have continued to resist the term, preferring to project a more local stamp by using the term Naija pop. However, Afrobeats has remained a far more widely used term, encompassing Naija pop, *azonto*, South African house and many other locally identified genres. Rab Bakari sees the true significance of Afrobeats in the way it connects Africans of different cultural backgrounds, and also the many Africans living or born abroad, with their ancestral homes. Afrobeats provides a shared space that no previous popular genre really did, and, as such, it is easily compatible with the social media lifestyle, where the breadth of connections and communications tends to outweigh their depth. Given how quickly artists and songs come and go in the Afrobeats milieu, the music is sure to continue changing. Afrobeats appears to have established itself as a durable descriptor. Its imprecise definition may well prove the key to its survival.

Bibliography

'African Music at the Crossroads.' *Afropop Worldwide*. Online at: http://www.afropop.org/32206/african-music-at-the-crossroads/ (accessed 19 October 2017).

'Afrobeats Comes to America.' *Afropop Worldwide*. Online at: http://www.afropop.org/32879/afrobeats-comes-to-america/ (accessed 19 October 2017).

Bakari, Rab. 2016. Interview with the author. Brooklyn, New York.

DJ Tunez. 2016. Interview with the author. Brooklyn, New York.

Duthiers, Vladimir, and Kermeliotis, Teo. 2012. 'Afrobeats: The New Sound of West Africa That's Going Global.' *CNN* (19 December). Online at: http://edition.cnn.com/2012/12/19/world/africa/afrobeats-music (accessed 9 November 2017).

Efya. 2016. Interview with the author. Brooklyn, New York.

Hancox, Dan. 2012. 'The Rise of Afrobeats.' *The Guardian* (19 January). Online at: https://www.theguardian.com/music/2012/jan/19/the-rise-of-afrobeats (accessed 19 October 2017).

Kuti, Seun. 2016. Telephone interview with the author: the author in Brooklyn, New York and Seun Kuti in Lagos, Nigeria.

Discography

Afrobeats Hot Hits: New Urban Dance Grooves from Africa. Shanachie SHANCD 66044. *2017*: USA.

Afrobeats with Love: Volume 2. Freeme Digital. *2015*: Nigeria.
Essential Afrobeats with Love, Volume 1. Freeme Digital. *2014*: Nigeria.
Fresh Afrobeats, Volume 1. iROKING. *2013*: Nigeria.

Websites
'Afrobeats Nation.' http://afrobeatsnation.com/ (accessed 9 November 2017).
'Afrobeats with Abrantee.' http://www.capitalxtra.com/radio/afrobeats (accessed 9 November 2017).

BANNING EYRE

Afro-Cuban Music in Senegal

Afro-Cuban music has served as one of the foundations of numerous African popular musics. However, its impact has proved most pervasive and enduring in the West African nation of Senegal. In the 1990s some Senegalese began to call Senegalese Afro-Cuban music 'salsa,' but the preferred term in Senegal for these genres remains 'Afro-Cuban music.' The dominant model for most Senegalese Cuban music has been Cuban *son* from the 1920s and *danzón* from the 1950s, with electric guitars replacing pianos and violins. Senegalese musicians who play Latin music adhere to the Cuban *clave* rhythm but from the 1960s on Senegambian rhythms have increased in importance. In place of Cuban *bongó* drums, which don't exist in Africa, Senegalese *sabar* and *tama* drums have been incorporated into percussion sections. Lyrics are sung both in Spanish and, increasingly, Wolof, the most widely spoken Senegalese language. Singers retain the typically nasal quality of much of Afro-Cuban vocal music but often sing in a higher register than would be the norm in Cuba.

Early History

Senegal was one of the first West African countries to participate in the southern Atlantic economy. From the sixteenth century on European ships sailed to the Senegambian region. When the Caribbean sugar cane plantation complex emerged in the seventeenth century, the Senegambian region was an important source of enslaved laborers for Cuba and other islands. There is some speculation that among the many cultural practices and concepts enslaved Africans brought to the Caribbean was the *clave*, the rhythmic core of Afro-Cuban music. Between the sixteenth and nineteenth centuries there was extensive maritime contact between Senegambia and the Caribbean, with some Senegambians crewing European ships. It is likely that these sailors exposed the coastal population of Senegal to early forms of Cuban music. In the nineteenth century the guitar and banjo began to reach Senegal. There already was a tradition of playing string instruments (e.g., the three-stringed *hoddu/xalam*) and the Senegalese adapted these new instruments to local traditions and, later, to Afro-Cuban music.

In the twentieth century records and radio played an important role in introducing Senegalese listeners to Afro-Cuban music. In 1930 the bandleader Don Azpiazú recorded the Cuban *pregón*, 'El Manisero' (known in English as 'The Peanut Vendor'). The song became a worldwide hit. It reputedly sold a million copies in West Africa alone and instilled in African publics a taste for Afro-Cuban music. Initially, Senegalese students studying in Paris brought 78-rpm discs of Afro-Cuban music with them when they returned home. They also carried with them knowledge of Latin music dance steps, which they taught friends and family. Throughout the colonial period Senegal had a large French population, many of whom loved Afro-Cuban music, and Senegalese musicians who played in hotels and clubs that catered to this population began playing Cuban music. In the late 1930s the French established a radio station in Dakar. The programming on this station was oriented to French musical taste, which, in that period, gravitated toward Afro-Cuban music. Many Senegalese heard this music, even though it wasn't meant for their ears. During World War II, many Allied soldiers were based in Dakar and they brought with them Afro-Cuban music and a desire to dance to this music when they were not on duty. The circulation of Afro-Cuban discs among the Senegalese increased as a result, as did work for Senegalese musicians specializing in Cuban styles.

The Belle Époque

By the end of World War II an increasing number of Senegalese associated Afro-Cuban music with modernity. Dancing to the music with mixed-gender couples created new spaces for leisure in Senegal and represented a radical break with 'local' practice of the era. For many Senegalese, the music allowed them to embrace the African diaspora and be modern in a way that commanded international respect but eluded French cultural hegemony. Young Senegalese formed record clubs that staged private parties. A network of record shops in Dakar, mostly owned by Lebanese businessmen, supplied these clubs with the latest recordings of groups and orchestras from Cuba. Clubs competed fiercely with one another to have the best collection of Afro-Cuban music. During this period the Senegalese were especially attracted to three genres/types of Cuban music – *son*, *charanga* ensembles, and *guajira* music. They regarded these musics as productive examples of *métissage* – a blending of European and African culture that struck them as quintessentially elegant and modern.

The increased tempo of economic life in 1950s Dakar resulted in the further professionalization of Senegalese Afro-Cuban musical groups, who often sang in a phonetic Spanish and who previously had played a variety of styles ranging from French music hall to calypso. By the late 1950s the most famous of these groups was the Star Band, the house ensemble at a nightclub in one of Dakar's African neighborhoods. By the early 1960s the Star Band included two of the most famous figures in the history of Afro-Cuban music in Senegal: the instrumentalist Dexter Johnson, originally from Nigeria, and the singer, Laba Sosseh, originally from the Gambia. Together, this duo established a higher standard of fidelity to the Cuban tradition with a more faithful adherence to the *clave* and a greater degree of musical proficiency. Over the years the Star Band was the incubator for many of the most famous Senegalese Afro-Cuban musicians who went on to form such notable groups as Number 1, Orchestre Baobab and Étoile de Dakar. These groups were primarily guitar bands with some brass sections and both Cuban and African percussion. Throughout the 1970s these groups worked to indigenize Afro-Cuban music, singing in Senegalese languages such as Wolof, and employing Senegalese rhythms and vocal styles, especially the percussive *mbalax* rhythms and a high, keening vocal timbre. However, the Cuban influence, represented by *son* and *danzón* music, usually remained dominant in their cultural mix, in part because it embodied a tradition of cosmopolitanism that the musicians were hesitant to abandon or undermine. The success of these groups ensured that Afro-Cuban music became a symbol of national unity and inclusiveness in Senegal as well as one of elegance and modernity. Afro-Cuban music became so popular in Senegal that Cuban, Dominican and Puerto Rican musicians, including the members of Orquesta Aragon and Orquesta Broadway and Johnny Pacheco, began to perform in Senegal on a regular basis.

Decline and Revival

In the 1980s younger Senegalese embraced 'local' musical styles such as *mbalax* instead of Afro-Cuban music. They regarded the latter as a relic of a colonial past, out of step with the trend toward *authenticité*, a movement that entailed the revitalization of 'traditional' African forms. It seemed certain that Senegalese Afro-Cuban music was destined for the dustbin of history. However, starting in the late 1980s and early 1990s the music was revitalized. The generation in power had never wavered in its love for Afro-Cuban music and ensured that the music remained in the public eye – and ear. Senegalese Afro-Cuban musicians including Pape Fall and James Gadiaga developed a genre called *salsa mbalax* that largely stayed true to Cuban musical practice but replaced the Cuban *montuno* with the popular Senegalese indigenous music form in 12/8 time. This mélange found favor with a segment of the listening public. As world music carved a niche for itself in music shops and performance venues, some Senegalese groups, such as Orchestre Baobab, had successful second careers as world music icons. The group Africando, a combination of New York studio musicians and Senegalese *soneros*, enjoyed both local and international success. The popularity of these groups abroad created a new legitimacy for them and the music they championed at home. In 2001 a Senegalese all-star group finally toured Cuba as a result of Senegal establishing diplomatic relations with Cuba. The tour, for a variety of reasons, was not the triumph they had hoped for. Still, it attested to the continuing vitality of the transatlantic conversation between Senegal and Cuba that has continued for almost 400 years. In 2014 at least six major Senegalese Afro-Cuban ensembles were active in Dakar, Senegal's capital. While recording opportunities for these ensembles had diminished and audiences had shrunk, they were able to maintain an active performing schedule at nightclubs and private parties.

Senegalese radio and television continue to devote considerable broadcast time to both Senegalese and Cuban performers of Afro-Cuban music.

Bibliography

Benga, Ndiouga Adrien. 2002. '"The Air of the City Makes Free': Urban Music from the 1950s to the 1990s in Senegal – Variété, Jazz, Mbalax, Rap.' In *Playing with Identities in Contemporary Music in Africa*, eds. Mai Palmberg and Annemette Kirkegaard, 75–86. Uppsala: Nordiska Afrikainstitutet.

Jaji, Tsitsi Ella. 2014. *Africa in Stereo: Modernism, Music and Pan-African Solidarity*. Oxford: Oxford University Press.

Morgan, Andy. 'Afrocubism: An Old Transatlantic Love Story.' Online at: www.andymorganwrites.com (accessed 24 May 2017).

Roberts, John Storm. 1985. *The Latin Tinge: The Impact of Latin American Music on the United States*. Tivoli, NY: Original Music.

Shain, Richard M. 2002. 'Roots in Reverse: *Cubanismo* in Twentieth Century Sénégalese Popular Music.' *International Journal of African Historical Studies* 35(1): 83–103.

Shain, Richard M. 2009. 'The Re(Public) of Salsa: Afro-Cuban Music in Fin-de-Siècle Dakar.' *Africa* 79(2): 186–205.

Discographical References

Azpiazú, Don. 'El Manisero.' His Masters Voice – G.V. 1. *1930*: USA.

Discography

African Salsa. Sterns/Earthworks STEW41CD. *1998*: UK.

Africando. *Trovador*. Sterns Africa STCD 1045. *1993*: UK.

Azpiazu, Don. *Don Azpiazu* (reissue of 78 rpm recordings). Harlequin HQCD 10. *1991*: UK.

Los Afro-Salseros de Senegal. *Los afro-salseros de Senegal en La Habana*. Popular African Music 407. *2001*: Germany.

Orchestre Baobab. *Pirates Choice: The Legendary 1982 Session*. (Recorded 1982.) World Circuit WCD014. *1989*: UK.

Sosseh, Laba. *El Maestro: 40 Años De Salsa*. Mélodie 00022. *2002*: France.

RICHARD SHAIN

Afroma

The popular music of Malawi at the time of the country's change from colonial rule to self-government in 1963 was largely acoustic, a carry-over from the guitar and banjo-based acoustic music of the 1950s and 1960s. *Rumba, kwela*, soul and rock 'n' roll were dominant on Lusaka Radio, Radio Laurenco Marques and later, Radio Malawi (Lwanda and Kanjo 2013). Self-government and independence brought with it a cultural imperative (Phiri 1983) to create a Malawi sound acceptable to a growing urban population using the electric instruments that were then becoming available. The resulting music, afroma (the name of which combines the first two letters of the words 'Africa,' 'rock' and Malawi), is usually (but not exclusively) electrified music that fuses Malawi melodies and rhythms with Western and other African styles.

History

The musical superstars of 1950s and 1960s Nyasaland (pre-independence Malawi), such as Luka Maganga, Thailo and Kapiye and the Paseli Brothers, all used acoustic backing. This guitar and banjo music usually featured vamping guitar backing a lead banjo played in finger-picking style, as on Thailo and Kapiye's 'Dziko,' which was easy to imitate on electric guitar. The bridge between 1950s acoustic sounds and the electric phase was provided by musicians such as Ndiche Mwalale who, in the 1960s, played acoustic slide guitar ('Andiche alombele') but who also lived and played through the early stages of afroma.

The roots of afroma can be traced back to army and police bands that trained musicians in both world wars. Both marching and dance bands, led by Europeans, mixed African and European melodies and rhythms in songs, including 'Tilikuyenda' (King's African Rifles, n.d.).

Pioneer Malawi electric musicians played mostly covers of soul and jazz classics such as the Platters' 'The Great Pretender' and Chubby Checker's 'The Twist.' One seminal band was Naison Seke's Jazz Giants. Later led by Morson Phuka and renamed New Scene, Jazz Giants at one point included many of the pioneers of afroma, including Botswana's John Selolwane Longwe who later played with US musician Paul Simon (Chechamba 1997, 33). Although Seke's Jazz Giants played mostly soul they also tackled Western jazz arrangements of local songs such as 'Chitukutuku' and 'Kumanda Kwa Bambo Wanga.'

Morson Phuka's trajectory offers a case study of how his group Jazz Giants combined the elements of African (afro), rock (ro) and Malawian (ma) to form afroma. In 'Gule wina' he started by playing the original 'Peanut Butter' (The Marathons 1961), then he indigenized the lyrics and finally increased the syncopation, without changing the chords. In another composition, 'Mtsinje' (1969), he took a tune from the female dance genre *chiwoda* and rearranged it using a rock tempo, chords and sensibility. New Scene offshoots included the True Tones and Muzipasi, which featured Maria Chidzanja Nkhoma, Malawi's veteran lady singer who emulated Miriam Makeba's mix of Western and African beats with Muzipasi's version of 'Music Man.'

Five bands were crucial training and experimental grounds for afroma: the Malawi Police Orchestra; the Army Strings Band, the Malawi Broadcasting Band (MBC Band), the Jazz Giants/New Scene and Kalimba. Under Mjura Mkandawire and Kapote Mwakasungura and with musicians including guitarist William Malikula and arranger and saxophonist Wyndham Chechamba on board, the MBC Band was led by trained musicians interested in composition and arranging. The results of these experiments are recorded on the band's only LP to date, *Kokoliko ku Malawi* (1974). The LP and several singles on Nzeru Records featured different afroma experiments: jazzy arrangements ('Echipini,' 'Kumanda kwa bambo wanga'), and reggae ('Zivute zitani tili pa mbuyo pa Kamuzu') from the LP *Kokoliko ku Malawi*; and *mbumba* ('Angwazi kawiri kawiri'), *rumba* and *simanjemanje* ('Wayaka moto'). The Police Orchestra experimented with swinging reggae-style afroma arrangements such as 'Mwana wanga Koli' and 'Sapota' (Supporter), while the Army Strings Band ('Ndavutika') produced a more *rumba*-influenced sound.

At the same time as the MBC and Police Orchestra, the Katenga Humming Bees, a folk group, was also updating Tonga songs for a new generation; they used both the Jazz Giants and the MBC Band as backing groups, respectively, on their afroma arrangements of 'Kankhali wilawila' and 'Ilala' (Chechamba 1997, 28–35). The Katenga Humming Bees were active at the same time as Daniel Kachamba and his brother Donald were creating one of the main exceptions to the afroma sound. The Kachamba Brothers Band largely remained acoustic, although Daniel liked to play blues guitar live on stage. The Kachamba Brothers Band played two broad types of music: the *kwela* music for which they are well known, due to the work of Gerhard Kubik (1987); and the acoustic afro-jazz soul of 'Unoroti phwanya,' 'Mlendo ndi mame,' 'Kodi atani mbale' and 'Kwa inu matsoka.' Daniel's sound in this case used Western chords but traditional Malawi beats and syncopation; his lyrics dealt with socially relevant issues including debt, drink and disease.

A younger generation led by Nassau Mkukupha and Griffen Mhango took the mantle from Phuka and formed Kalimba in 1976, where they continued fusing Malawi music with rock, soul, ska and reggae. Kalimba achieved a BBC chart-topping hit in 1982 with their soul reggae song 'Sometimes I Wonder.' Makasu (a splinter group from Kalimba that included Brite Nkhata and Stain Phiri) and Love Aquarius (which included Overton Chimombo) continued this trajectory. The brothers Isaac and Nassau Mkukupha also broke away to form Super Kaso Band. Super Kaso, as their hit 'Jessie ndimakukonda' showed, was a move toward a less rock-oriented and more afro (Zambian/Zairean) influence, as shown by their use of the mi-solo rhythm and lead guitars. A decade later, a Police Band offshoot, Mulangeni Sounds, created one of the first local *kwasa kwasa* hits with 'Tinadya Chambo.' In a separate development Elias Kaliati and Kenneth Ning'anga from the Army Strings, started arranging traditional wedding songs on electronic keyboards.

Another cohort of musicians, at their creative peak in the 1980s and 1990s, developed a harder riff-based and more syncopated afroma sound aimed at the rural and peri-urban audience with more socially conscious but apolitical lyrics. These bands included Deaf Ears, Masaka Band of the song 'A Molotoni' fame, Chitipi Capital Sounds, The Roots, Maurice Maulidi and Songani Swing Stars of *Ulendo wanga* fame, Robert Fumulani and Likhubula River Dance Band, Africa Express and Saleta Phiri and AB Sounds, who recorded 'Zinthu zasintha, malamulo sanasinthe' (Things Have Changed but the Laws Remain the Same, 1994). This group cultivated more influences from Zimbabwe, Zambia and Zaire.

Afro jazz is one area where afroma has achieved international exposure with a number of subgenres: Wambali Mkandawire, recording in South Africa, achieved a Kora Award nomination; Masauko Chipembere of Blk Sonshine, Chris Kele and Eric Paliani are also playing versions of Malawi afro jazz internationally. Others, such as Tiwonge Hango and Peter Mawanga are continuing the experiments locally in Malawi.

In a separate but related development, younger musicians (both trained and some self-taught, such as Agorosso) have returned to the original afroma experiments and created an urban afroma, in some cases by fusing Malawi rhythms, raps and melodies with rhythm and blues music. Prominent among these are the Real Elements (Lewis Chikuni, Qabaniso Malewezi and Kimba Anderson) and, on the international scene, Esau Mwamwaya. As of 2015 many consider the Malawi acoustic afro-jazz musician Francis Phiri (Lawi) to be the leading exponent of afroma within Malawi.

Conclusion

Afroma was created by the convergence of history, economics, politics and culture at a time of possibility for Malawi musicians and consumers. Hotels, previously restricted to Europeans, were opening their doors to African clients and, with expansion in education, a youth market was developing. However, the onset of a one-party dictatorship in 1964 affected the trajectory of the economic possibilities for the musicians, if not the form of the music. As afroma required more studio time and was more expensive to promote, it did not prosper as well as reggae or gospel.

Bibliography

Chechamba, Wyndham R. 1997. 'Chechamba's Music Story.' *WASI* 9(1): 28–35.

Kubik, Gerard, et al. 1987. *Malawian Music: A Framework for Analysis*. Zomba: Centre for Social Research.

Lwanda, John. 2006. 'Sounds Afroma.' In *The Rough Guide to World Music: Africa & Middle East*, eds. Simon Broughton et al. London: Penguin, 210–18.

Lwanda, John, and Kanjo, Chipo. 2013. 'Computers, Culture and Music: The History of the Recording Industry in Malawi.' *Society of Malawi Journal* 66(1): 23–42.

Phiri, Kings M. 1983. 'The Concept of Culture in Malawi: A Brief Report and Working Bibliography.' *The Society of Malawi Journal* 36(2): 19–26.

Discographical References

Checker, Chubby. 'The Twist.' *The Twist*. Parkway 811. *1960*: USA.

Jazz Giants. 'Chitukutuku.' MBC Archives. *Circa 1968*: Malawi.

Jazz Giants. 'Gule wina.' MBC Archives. *Circa 1967*: Malawi.

Jazz Giants. 'Kumanda kwa bambo wanga.' MBC Archives. *Circa 1968*: Malawi.

Kachamba, Daniel. 'Kodi atani mbale' and 'Kwa inu matsoka.' MBC Archives. *1982*: Malawi. (Reissue: Daniel Kachamba. 'Kodi atani mbale' and 'Kwa inu matsoka.' *Acoustic and Electric Dance Hits from Malawi*. MC Pamtondo PAM 030. *1991*: UK.)

Kachamba Brothers. 'Unoroti phwanya' and 'Mlendo ndi mame.' MBC Archives. *Circa 1985*: Malawi.

Kalimba. 'Sometimes I Wonder.' Dephon Promotions SCL 5302. *1982*: South Africa.

Katenga Humming Bees. 'Kankhali wilawila.' MBC Archives. *1969*: Malawi.

Katenga Humming Bees. 'Ilala.' MBC Archives. *1969*: Malawi.

Kings African Rifles and East African Land Forces Officers Dinner Club. 'Tilikuyenda.' *Regimental Marches of the King's African Rifles Collection*. George Shepperson Collection (Cassette.) *N.d.*: UK.

Malawi Army Strings Band. 'Ndabvutika.' MBC Archives. *Circa 1982*: Malawi.

Malawi Police Orchestra. 'Mwana wanga Koli.' MBC Archives. *1983*: Malawi.

Malawi Police Orchestra. 'Supporta.' MBC Archives. *1988*: Malawi.

Marathons. 'Peanut Butter.' Arvee Records A50271. *1961*: USA.

Masaka Band. 'A Molotoni.' MBC Archives. *Circa 1985*: Malawi. (Reissued on *Various Electric and Acoustic Hits from Malawi*. Pamtondo PAM 001. *1991*: UK.)

Maulidi, Maurice, and Songani Swing Stars. 'Ulendo wanga.' MBC Archives. *1988*: Malawi.

MBC Band. 'Angwazi kawiri kawiri.' Ngoma Records 002. *1973*: Malawi.

MBC Band. *Kokoliko ku Malawi*. Ngoma Records MW LP001. *1974*: Malawi.

MBC Band. 'Wayaka moto.' MBC Archives. *Circa 1971*: Malawi.

Mulangeni Sounds. 'Tinadya Chambo.' *Mulangeni Sounds*. MBC Archives. *1994*: Malawi.

Muzipasi. 'Music Man.' MBC Archives. *Circa 1983*: Malawi.

Ndiche Mwalale. 'Andiche alombele.' MBC Archives. *Circa 1960s*: Malawi. (Reissue: Ndiche Mwalale. 'Andiche alombele.' *Banjoes, Guitars and Fifties: Malawi Music of the 1950s*. Pamtondo PAM050. *2006*: UK.)

Phiri, Saleta. 'Zinthu zasintha/Ndirande Blues.' (Self-published cassette.) *1994*: Malawi. (Reissued on *Ndirande Blues*). Pamtondo. *2001*: Malawi.

Phuka, Morson, and Jazz Giants. 'Gule wina.' Nzeru Records. *1969*: Malawi.

Phuka, Morson, and Jazz Giants. 'Mtsinje.' Nzeru Records SOM. *1969*: Malawi.

Platters, The. 'The Great Pretender.' *The Great Pretender*. Mercury 70753. *1955*: USA.

Super Kaso. 'Jessie ndimakukonda.' MBC Archives. *1983*: Malawi.

Thailo and Kapiye. 'Dziko lino ndi lathu.' Label unknown. 1958?: Malawi. (Reissued on *Banjos, Guitars and Fifties: Malawi Music of the 1950s*. Pamtondo PAM050. *2006*: UK).

Discography

Banjos, Guitars and Fifties: Malawi Music of the 1950s. Pamtondo. *2006*: UK.

Fumulani, Robert, and Likhubula River Dance Band. 'Mwana wanga.' *Let's Go and Dance*. Likhubula Productions MOM/C001. *1990*: Malawi.

Hango, Tiwonge. *Chinyengo*. T Hango. *2008*: Malawi.

Kaliati, E., and Ning'ang'a, K. *Wamkulu ndani mbanja?* Studio K. *N.d.* : Malawi.

Lawi. *Lawi*. Lawi Multimedia Garage 661256254652683244. *2014*: Malawi.

Mkandawire, Wambali. *Zani muwone*. Instinct Africaine. *2002*: South Africa.

Various Electric and Acoustic Hits from Malawi. Pamtondo PAM 001 - 003. *1991*: UK.

JOHN LWANDA

Afropop

'Afropop' is a general term used by journalists, recording industry professionals and authors of books about African music to designate the modern, mostly urban, popular music of Africa. The term applies to music from all regions of Africa, though generally not to music designated with another loosely defined designator: 'traditional.' Such styles as highlife, soukous, mbalax, mbaqanga, makossa, rai, Naija pop and many others have all been described as Afropop. Though less problematic than the much-maligned descriptor 'world music,' for reasons discussed below, Afropop (sometimes Afro Pop or Afro-pop as the *New York Times* would have it) is nevertheless difficult to define with precision. It has been used in a variety of ways since the 1970s: as an aggregator of a broad array of popular music unfolding out of the African continent and the Afro-Atlantic slave trade: as a way to differentiate contemporary musical expressions from more traditional or rural varieties; and sometimes, as a mild pejorative suggesting a watering down through fusion with foreign influences of something perceived as 'pure.' Of course, no form of contemporary music may accurately be described as pure.

As an aggregator, the term Afropop has been used since the 1970s to make a vast universe of music comprehensible to a steadily growing general audience around the world. Listeners who might relate to reggae or *salsa*, but not to the inexhaustible compendium of genre names used to describe the many varieties of African music, find entry here. The entire breadth of musical styles from the African continent and even its various diasporas is subsumed and perceived using one convenient collective.

Like 'world music,' the term Afropop oversimplifies a vast musical landscape, and a number of writers and artists avoid the word in favor of more precise genre names. That said, there is logic to the umbrella classification, however broad. The dissemination of Africans in past centuries, principally through the forced movement of enslaved peoples, has led to the creation of a large family of loosely connected musical styles. If one hears resonances between North African vocal techniques and Mississippi Delta blues, between Brazilian *samba* rhythms and Angolan traditional music, between Afro-Cuban music and the modern dance sounds of the Democratic Republic of Congo, or between rhythmic accordion music from Madagascar to Louisiana, history offers explanations. The network of African musical influences through the decades and around the world imposes a broad, if imprecise, interpermeability that sets all of these genres apart from, say, Celtic, Balkan or Chinese music.

In the early twenty-first century, leaving aside diaspora settings that increasingly assert their own individual identities expressed in terms such as *cumbia* (Colombia), *soca* (Trinidad) and *khaliji* (Persian Gulf), Afropop may be defined broadly as music created in African towns and cities, combining elements of village tradition with influences from outside, including rock, funk, jazz, reggae, rap, electronic dance music or other forms of Afropop. This process gathered momentum throughout the twentieth century and continues in the twenty-first century, driven by the ongoing arrival of new technologies: radios, phonographs, cassettes, televisions, CDs, the Internet, MP3 technology and cell phones.

Origins and Applications of the Term 'Afropop'

In the 1950s, as independence movements swept the African continent, and in the 1960s, when most African countries gained autonomy from colonial powers, the creation of new urban music styles surged. Some aficionados view the 1950s to 1970s as a kind of golden age of African popular music, an era in which the collision of local and imported influences yielded the freshest and most memorable results. Music became a metaphor for the entire process of honoring and reclaiming African identity after the trials of slavery and colonialism, while at the same time embracing and incorporating the best influences emanating from North and South America, Europe, the Caribbean and the Arabic-speaking world during a particularly creative and productive period.

The first known usage of the term Afropop may have been in an article in *Billboard* Magazine as far back as the 1970s, but it did not become a common term in print until the 1980s. The phenomenon of contemporary music styles connected through the forces of history is the driving idea behind the late John Storm Roberts's seminal 1972 book *Black Music of Two Worlds*. While the term Afropop does not appear in the book, Roberts makes the case that such a term is needed. He urges his readers to view music as encoded history, and to think of twentieth-century popular music genres in global terms.

A May 1983 article in San Francisco's *City Arts Monthly* ran the headline 'AfroPop Around the Bay.' At the time, a number of important Nigerian musicians, notably O.J. Ekemode (later known as Orlando Julius) from Nigeria and Hedzoleh Soundz from Ghana, had settled in the Bay Area. They were building followings in a milieu open to new sounds, and finding talented local musicians to collaborate with them in new bands. As far back as the late 1960s South African legends Miriam Makeba and Hugh Masekela had penetrated American popular music consciousness, but they were perceived at that time as individual artists, not part of a larger movement or scene. But in the early 1980s the San Francisco Bay Area was becoming known as a scene – a haven for 'worldbeat,' a term that enjoyed more currency at the time than Afropop. Despite that *City Arts Monthly* headline – 'AfroPop Around the Bay' – the accompanying piece refers only to 'African pop' in its text – not Afropop.

Musicologist, archivist and author John Collins notes that in the early 1980s in London, popular awareness of African music was growing rapidly. New hybrids were proliferating, and writers, artists and commercial entrepreneurs alike were scurrying to find new terminology to describe them. Labels were releasing recordings of African acts, and these acts were turning up in European venues. There was a pressing need for terminology. 'And the word that was coalescing was Afropop,' Collins stated in a 1993 interview. He went on to say that young people, especially in England, turned to African music in the early 1980s because they viewed it as fresh, organic and highly danceable. For Collins, this seemed to be the logical conclusion of an ongoing historical process that began with the slave trade. The 'African element' infiltrated mainstream culture through 'cultural time bombs' such as ragtime, minstrelsy, swing music and Elvis Presley. Even white performers channeled African cultural elements.

For Collins, the ascendancy of explicitly African popular music was far more than the next popular trend. It was part of a tectonic redefinition of popular music and culture. In his view, 'Practically every major style of European dance music has come indirectly from Africa, or through the diaspora' (personal interview, 1993). When Europeans dance to music in 3/4 time, he noted, the dance descends not from the once-popular waltz, which has vanished, but from an African or African-derived 12/8 rhythm.

Veterans of the UK popular music scene recall a legendary meeting at a London pub in 1986, at which a set of influential writers, record company executives and arts presenters agreed that a new phenomenon in transnational popular music should be marketed as 'world music,' not Afropop. For Collins, this was a fateful error, as it sidelined a sensible, coherent and profoundly provocative idea with what he viewed as an incoherent mish-mash. 'Everything is world music,' he noted. 'It doesn't really mean anything.' The consequences of this decision, Collins recalled, were immediate. For example, a formerly successful Afropop DJ in London, who had done well playing a mix of African, black American and Caribbean dance music, gradually found it harder to get work because he knew nothing about Bulgarian wedding songs. And so began the rise of a generation of world music journalists who knew, as Collins put it, 'a little about a lot,' but not very much about anything (ibid.). The incisive logic of the burgeoning Afropop movement became subsumed in the murkiness of world music marketing.

Radio provided the real breakthrough for the currency of a new terminology in the United States. In 1986 a pilot for the eventual 'Afropop' radio series, produced by the show's creator Sean Barlow and hosted by Bob Yassi of Howard University, aired on American public radio. This was the first time the word Afropop had enjoyed broad exposure on the American airwaves, and the effect was amplified two years later with the arrival of the syndicated weekly *Afropop* program series, hosted by veteran Cameroonian broadcaster Georges Collinet. The program enjoyed rapid success, picked up by nearly 200 stations around the country in its first year. Coming at a time when few Americans knew anything about contemporary music from Africa, this was the first nationally syndicated media showcase for African music in the United States (the program was later renamed 'Afropop Worldwide' in order to specifically include global relatives from Brazil to Louisiana and the Middle East). Georges Collinet, the host of 'Afropop Worldwide,' became for many American listeners a friendly, auditory embodiment of an otherwise intimidating world of rhythms, languages, names and cultural specifics. Beginning in the 1990s the Rough Guide series of CDs later provided listening material for this audience, including many volumes focused on individual countries, artists and styles falling under the Afropop umbrella.

Several books on African popular music were published in the United States and the United Kingdom in the 1980s. These books catered to new Afropop audiences, although in many cases they did not explicitly use the term (or used it while acknowledging its shortcomings). In 1987 Chris Stapleton and Chris May published a groundbreaking book on contemporary African music, *African All-Stars: The Pop Music of a Continent*. The text refers to 'Afro-pop' just three times. Afrobeat, by then an established Nigerian genre, is referenced frequently, and the text also uses terms including Afro-rock, Afro-reggae, Afro-carnival, none of these clearly defined. Afro-pop is contrasted with Afrobeat. On one occasion, Afro-pop is used to describe a London-based group combining Kenyan and British musicians (Shokolokobangoshay) (235). For Stapleton and May, the term 'pop' seems to suggest a high degree of fusion, as in a description of the Gambian Super Eagles who 'covered just about everything in sight' (269).

Soon afterwards, in 1991, Graeme Ewens published *Africa O-Ye!: A Celebration of African Music*. Here we find the terms *Afro-Music* (the name of a magazine) (211), also 'African pop' and 'Afro-fusion' (206). The text refers to Guinea's Mory Kante and Zimbabwe's Thomas Mapfumo as 'pop stars' (23). The only time the term Afropop appears is in a nod to the American public radio program (206, 213). The term 'worldbeat,' still in circulation, turns up briefly (213). But all these references come in the book's final chapter, 'Music in the Marketplace.' The bulk of the text, as in the case of Stapleton and May's book, is concerned with introducing individual artists and styles, not with trying to describe them collectively. More precise genre names, such as highlife, *mbalax*, *makossa* and Afrobeat, proliferate. Umbrella terms are mostly avoided. The same is true for Ronnie Graham's exhaustive compendium of African genre blurbs and discographies, first published in 1988 as *The Da Capo Guide to Contemporary African Music*, and in 1991 as *The World of African Music*.

In 1995 Sean Barlow and Banning Eyre coauthored the first US-published book on the subject of African music. Prominently featuring photographs by Jack Vartoogian, *Afropop! An Illustrated Guide to Contemporary African Music* specifically notes that Afropop is not a genre signifier per se, but rather a reference to 'the immense and richly varied landscape of contemporary African music' (vii). The book lays out the philosophy that has guided the *Afropop Worldwide* radio series and website (afropop.org, launched in 1997) ever since. Both the radio program and the website have consistently emphasized the interconnections between African-derived popular music styles, wherever they are found, and the historical circumstances that engender them. Nevertheless, newspapers, magazines and websites that cover popular music increasingly began using Afropop as a genre signifier. Many still do, no doubt viewing the term as a necessary oversimplification of a subject with great relevance, but little familiarity, to most Americans.

All the aforementioned books were consumed by small, specialized audiences. None were bestsellers, and none are still in print. They were also quickly outpaced by rapid developments in African cities and diaspora hotspots, which have continued to churn out new stars and styles year by year. However, these texts do describe the underpinnings of the continent's musicality and global influence in an enduring way. Viewed from the perspective of Roberts's and Collins's theories of cultural tectonic shift, they remain relevant sources.

Conclusion

The proliferation and diversification of Afropop music absolutely continues in the age of hip-hop, the Internet and digital music. The conversation among artists around the world unfolds at unprecedented speed, with social media and visual tools such as YouTube creating the possibility for instantaneous influence and innovation in music, dance and fashion. As such, the term Afropop is likely to endure, its imprecision more an advantage than a weakness in the ever more hybridized milieu of global popular culture.

Bibliography

Barlow, Sean, and Eyre, Banning. 1995. *Afropop! An Illustrated Guide to Contemporary African Music*. Edison, NJ: Chartwell Books.

Collins, John. 1993. Interview with the author in Accra, Ghana.

Ewans, Graeme. 1991. *Africa O-Ye! A Celebration of African Music*. London: Guinness Publishing.

Field, David. 1983. 'AfroPop Around the Bay.' *City Arts Monthly* (May).

Graham, Ronnie. 1992. *The World of African Music: Stern's Guide to Contemporary African Music, Volume Two*. London: Pluto Press.

Roberts, John Storm. 1972. *Black Music of Two Worlds*. Tivoli, NY: Original Music.

Stapleton, Chris, and May, Chris. 1987. *African All-Stars: The Pop Music of a Continent*. London and New York: Quartet Books.

Discography

Africa: Never Stand Still. (3 CDs.) Ellipsis Arts CD 3300. *1994*: USA.

Africa: 50 Years of Music/50 And D'Indépendance. (18 CDs.) Discograph 3218462. *1960/2010*: EU.

The Rough Guide to the Music of Mali. World Music Network RGNET1311. *2014*: UK.

The Rough Guide to Acoustic Africa. World Music Network RGNET1297. *2013*: UK.

The Rough Guide to South African Jazz. World Music Network RGNET1341. *2016*: UK.

Website

'Afropop Worldwide': http://www.afropop.org/

BANNING EYRE

Afro-Rock

Afro-rock is a West African popular dance music that arose from the impact of imported rock music of the 1960s on African popular music. It therefore uses typical Western pop band instrumentation but with the addition of some African instruments and is sometimes sung, or partly sung, in an African language. It is played in the standard 4/4 time of most Western popular music, but also in the 12/8 time of traditional polyrhythmic African music. For instance, the pioneering London-based Ghanaian Afro-rock group Osibisa was fond of using the polyrhythms of the traditional Akan *adowa* dance and utilizing traditional hand-drums, xylophones (the *gyil*) and *atenteben* flutes. Osibisa's members were predominantly Ghanaian (the band also included some West Indians and Nigerians), but, after the band's huge 1970s success with African youth, other brands of Afro-rock appeared around Africa that were flavored with particular regional instruments, rhythms and languages.

Emergence and Early History

Afro-rock was created in 1969 and 1970 by Osibisa. The group, originally called the Cats Paw, played rock music for British dance fans in the late 1960s, but noticed that these youths enjoyed the Africanized rock songs the group occasionally played and called 'Afro-rock' – and so the band decided to focus on this music. They renamed the group 'Osibisa,' led by the Ghanaians Teddy Osei, Mac Tontoh and Sol Amartio, who had previously all been dance band highlife musicians. Indeed, the band's name is derived from the old Akan name for highlife, *osibisaaba* – and some of Osibisa's songs such as 'Music for Gong Gong,' were based on highlife rhythms. Over a 20-year period from 1970 on this band toured all over the world and released dozens of top-selling records.

The influence of rock music itself on African popular music goes back to the 1950s and 1960s rock 'n' roll and the twist (Chubby Checker made an African tour in 1967). This was followed by US soul music introduced through records and films – with James Brown actually playing in Nigeria in 1970 and Wilson Pickett and Tina Turner featured at Ghana's Soul to Soul concert in 1971. As a result, many imitative Western-type pop bands were formed by African youth, especially in English-speaking Africa. The earliest of these bands that included rock 'n' roll in its repertoire was the Heartbeats, formed in Sierra Leone in 1961 by Geraldo Pino. By the mid-1960s other student rock groups in Freetown included the Echoes, Red Stars and Golden Strings, while the Heartbeats began to specialize in soul music.

Ghana's first rock band was Gabby Nick Valdo's Avengers, formed in 1962 by members of the Red Devils army group that had spent time training in England, home of Cliff Richard and the Shadows. The Avengers subsequently inspired 'pop chains' (the name for local pop competitions) for schoolboy and student pop bands. These included Ricky Telfer's Bachelors, the Road Runners, Blues Syndicate, Circuit Five, Mathew Chapter Five and the Saints that all played the music of the Beatles, Rolling Stones and Spencer Davis. In the late 1960s the 'progressive' or 'psychedelic' rock music of Jimi Hendrix, Sly and the Family Stone and Cream also started to become popular in Ghana and was played, for instance, by Ricky Telfer's Magic Aliens (formed 1967), sometimes known as the Psychedelic Aliens. Some other youthful groups that played rock music (as well as soul music) were Blue Magic, the Barristers and Stanley Todd's El Pollos.

Student and schoolboy rock bands likewise appeared in Nigeria in the early 1960s, including the Blue Knights and Cyclops of Lagos, followed later by the soul-influenced Hykkers, Segun Bucknor's Assembly and Bobby Benson's Strangers. Early Liberian pop bands were the Dynamics, the Psychedelic Six and Shades. From Gambia came Badou Jobe's Super Eagles that played both local African popular music and rock and toured West Africa in 1968, introducing the Western rock guitar wah-wah pedal (the group later became known as Ifang Bondi). In southern Africa there was the Chicken Run Band of Zimbabwe (which included the young Thomas Mapfumo) and the Beaters of South Africa, while the West African Francophone country of Togo boasted its singing diva, Bella Bellow, who sang pop songs in Ewe.

The 1970s–1990s

During the 1970s, due to various factors, an intensely experimental phase began that led to several forms of music that fused Western pop music and African music. Afro-rock first established itself in the English-speaking West African countries of Ghana and then Nigeria. Afrobeat arose at roughly the same time as Afro-rock, but was more closely related to the soul and funk influence on African popular artists, particularly those in Nigeria.

The factors that enhanced the creative musical explosion of Afro-rock (and indeed Afrobeat) in Ghana and Nigeria included the continuing Africanist and Africanization policies of the early independence period, as well as imported Afrocentric messages and 'Afro' fashions associated with US soul music that started to become popular in Africa from the mid-1960s. This was followed by the experimental psychedelic rock of Jimi Hendrix, the Latin-rock fusion music of Santana, who played at Ghana's 1971 'Soul to Soul' concert, and early 1970s trips to West Africa by two British rock stars: Paul McCartney (formerly of the Beatles), whose band Wings recorded 'Band on the Run' in 1973 in Lagos, and the rock drummer Ginger Baker (of Eric Clapton's Cream and Blind Faith), who made a filmed trans-Saharan trip to West Africa in 1971, when he briefly visited Ghana and helped establish the ARC recording studio in Lagos.

After the Ghanaian Osibisa band's international success (and African tours), its Afro-rock, together with Afrobeat, began to influence many African bands and artists. From Sierra Leone came Francis

Fuster (of the Baranta and later Ninkribi bands) and the London-based Super Combo. Liberian bands included Kapingdbi, the Afrodelics and Oxygen. From the Cameroons came Manu Dibango of 'Soul Makossa' fame, while Kenya's top Afro-rock bands of the 1970s were Matata and Makonde. From South Africa there was Harare, Johnny Clegg's and Sipho Mchunu's multiracial Jaluka band (renamed Savuka in the mid-1980s) and the London-based Assagai, set up by the South African exiles Louis Moholo, Mongezi Feza and Dudu Pukwana.

Later, in the 1990s, Angelique Kidjo of the Benin Republic became internationally famous for fusing rock music with her native Fon rhythms. This was in the period when 'world music' was becoming globally popular and famous Western rock stars such as Paul Simon, Sting, Peter Gabriel, Stewart Copland, Bono and Damon Albarn were beginning to play and record with African musicians.

In Ghana and Nigeria, Afro-rock bands proliferated from the early 1970s. By then there were several Ghanaian bands that played Afro-rock and soul-influenced Afrobeat: the Magic Aliens, Q-Masters, Big Beats (formerly Triffis), Sawaaba Soundz, Barons, the Zonglo Biiz and Boombaya (the latter moved to London). Then, from 1973, Faisal Helwani formed a series of resident Afro-rock bands at his Napoleon Club in Accra that included Basa Basa, the Bunzus and also Hedzoleh Soundz, which had toured the United States with the South African trumpeter Hugh Masekela. These three bands fused rock music with local folksongs, highlifes and traditional Ewe and Akan rhythms and drums, with Basa Basa featuring Amoah Azangeo playing the northern Ghanaian *frafra* rattle.

By the mid-1970s more of these youthful pop bands had surfaced in Ghana, playing highlifes, imported pop and their own renditions of rock and soul music. Some of these included Alpha-Omega, Ionic Revolt, Bisa Goma, Blay Ambolley's Steneboofs, Kukurudu, Tommy Darling's Wantu Wazuri, Szaabu Sounds, Asase-Ase, Pagadeja, the Apagya Show Band, Marijata, the Bediako Band and the London-based Bukutu and Oja groups. Some others were Uppers International that featured the singers Christie Azuma and Bob Pinodo's Sound Casters that created a fusion of rock and local Efutu rhythms he called the 'sonobete.'

In the late 1970s Faisal Helwani set up the Edinkanfo Afro-rock band that in 1980 worked in Accra with the British new wave rock musician Brian Eno. The same year the British rock drummer Mick Fleetwood came to Ghana to make a musical film and album called *Mick Fleetwood: The Visitor*. Later, the Hedzoleh percussionist Okyeremma Asante worked in America with Mick Fleetwood and also joined American rock singer Paul Simon's late-1980s Graceland's tour.

A large number of youthful Afropop bands also surfaced in Nigeria during the 1970s and were influenced by both Osibisa and the soul-influenced Afrobeat style being developed in Nigeria by Segun Bucknor, Orlando Julius and Fela Anikulapo-Kuti. Some of these utilized the traditional Yorùbá 12/8 *kon-kon* polyrhythmic bell rhythm, such as Black Ghosts, run by the musician and painter Twin Seven Seven. The Ofege band, on the other hand, was composed of Igbo students in Lagos and therefore used the 12/8 Eastern Nigerian Igbo *ogene* bell pattern for their rock numbers. The Funkees, formed by Harry Mosco and Jake Sollo in 1969, later relocated to the UK – and Berkley Jones's BLO, formed in 1972, released albums including *Chapter One* and *Phase II* on the EMI and Decca Afrodisia label. It was also in 1972 that the highlife musician Sonny Okosun of Benin City formed his Ozzidi group (named after the Ijaw god of music) that played what he called 'Jungle Rock.' Also important were Joni Haastrup's Mono-Mono, which ended up in the United States, and Larry Ifediorama's Ofo and the Black Company that played what they called 'Afrodelic Funk' and relocated to London where they played at Ginger Johnson's Iroku Club.

Other pop fusion groups in Nigeria during the 1970s were the Shango Babies, Easy Kabaka, the Gondoliers, Cicada, Bongos Ikwue, the Granadians who experimented with Cameroonian *makossa* music and Tee Mac's Afro-Collection that at one point worked with Ginger Baker. Indeed, Baker included Nigerians such as Joni Haastrup, the Lijadu Sisters, Berkely Jones, Laolu Akins and Tunde Kuboye in his Salt band that toured throughout Western Europe and North America in 1971 and 1972.

Due to the rise of Fela Kuti and his Afrobeat in the 1980s and 1990s, later artists in Nigeria (including Lagbaja, Dede Mabiaku, Seun Kuti, Femi Kuti and others) are more influenced by Afrobeat than by

Afro-rock. In Ghana, however, there has been somewhat of an Afro-rock revival since the 1990s and some of the Afro-rock bands that have appeared since that time include Saka-Saka, Blekete, Bawasaba, Dabatram and Dzidudu. More recent ones are Sanekoye (set up by Asabre Quaye who as a youngster had played in Mick Fleetwood's *The Visitor* film), and Amartey Hedzoleh who released some of his Afro-rock songs in 2014 on a European world music label. The Dzidudu band also sometimes backs youthful Ghanaian hiplife (local hip-hop) acts. Also important is Mac Tontoh, the trumpeter and cofounder of Osibisa, who returned to Ghana in the 1990s and set up his Osibisa Kete Warriors that continued Afro-rock experimentations until his death in 2010.

Conclusion

Invented by Osibisa in 1969 to 1970, Afro-rock quickly became popular with both musicians and audiences throughout Africa, particularly in the English-speaking countries. Many of the Ghanaian musicians who passed through the long-lasting Osibisa group became important musicians in their own right, such as percussionist Kofi Ayivor, keyboard players Emmanuel Rentoz and Kiki Gyan, the guitarist Kari Bannerman, as well as the Nigerian bass players Fred Coker and Mike Odumosu. Afro-rock's appearance in Britain around 1969–1970 came at the very time when many Western rock fans had become weary of passively watching superstars on the concert stage and wanted to return to the dance focus of earlier rock 'n' roll. Afro-rock helped fill this popular dance music void in Britain and Europe, before the emergence of new popular dance idioms including disco music, reggae and punk. In doing so, the music of Osibisa and the other pioneers who followed in their wake introduced 12/8 polyrhythmic music to young white dance fans.

Osibisa's Afro-rock was the very first form of West African popular music to cross over to the West, and as such predates the emergence of the 'world music' of the mid- to late 1980s, when African popular music went global. Part of this 'world music' phenomenon was that increasing numbers of Western rock musicians experimented with African music and collaborated with African musicians, in the process inventing various new blends of what could be called 'Afro-rock.' As described above, however, Afro-rock had been created almost 20 years earlier by West Africans who blended rock music into African music.

Bibliography

Andersson, Muff. 1991. *Music in the Mix: The Story of South African Popular Music*. Johannesburg: Ravan Press.

Barber, Karin. 1987. 'Popular Art in Africa.' *African Studies Review* 10(3): 1–78.

Collins, E. John. 1985. *Music Makers of West Africa*. Washington DC: Three Continents Press.

Collins, E. John. 1992. *West African Pop Roots*, Philadelphia: Temple University Press.

Collins, E. John. 1994/6. *Highlife Time*. Accra: Anansesem Press.

Coplan, David. 1985. *In Township Tonight: South Africa's Black City Music and Theatre*. Johannesburg: Ravan Press.

Ewens, Graeme. 1991. *Africa Oh Ye: A Celebration of African Music*. London: Guinness Books.

Graham, Ronnie. 1988. *Stern's Guide to Contemporary African Music*. London: Zwan.

Horton, Christian Dowu. 1984. 'Popular Bands in Sierra Leone, 1920 to the Present.' *Black Perspectives in Music* 12(2): 183–92.

Stapleton, Chris, and May, Chris. 1987. *African All Stars*. London: Quartet Books.

Ware, Naomi. 1978. 'Popular Music and African Identity in Freetown, Sierra Leone.' In *Eight Urban Cultures: Tradition and Change*, ed. Bruno Nettl. Urbana: University of Illinois Press, 196–319.

Zindi, Fred. 1980. *Roots Rocking in Zimbabwe*. Harare, Zimbabwe: Mambo Press.

Discographical References

BLO. *Chapter One*. EMI. *1973*: UK/Nigeria.

BLO. *Phase II*. Decca West Africa Afrodisia Label. *1975*: Nigeria.

Osibisa. 'Music for Gong Gong.' 'Osibisa MCA MDKS8001. *1971*: UK.

Discography

Afro-Rock Vol. 1. Duncan Brooker/Kona Records. *2001*: UK. (Reissued as *Afro-Rock Vol. 1*. Strut Records STRUT059LP. *2010*: UK.)

Assagai. *Assagai*. Vertigo Records VEL 1004. *1971*: UK. (Reissued as Assagai. *Assagai*. Repertoire Records. *1994*: Germany.)

Ayivor. Kofi. *Rhythmology*. Otrabanda Records. *2004*: Holland.

BLO, *Blo Phases 1972–1982*. Strut Records STRUTCD 004. *2000*: UK.

Bucknor, Segun. *Poor Man Get No Brother 1969–75*. Strut Records STRUTACD 005. *2002*: UK.

Clegg, Johnny, and Sipho Mchunu's Juluka Band. *Universal Men*. EMI. *1979*: UK. (Reissued as Johnny Clegg and Sipho Mchunu's Juluka Band, *Universal Men*. Rhythm Safari, P2 57144. *1992*: USA.)

Fleetwood, Mick. *Mick Fleetwood: The Visitor*. RCA Records RCALP 5044. *1981*: UK.

Ghana Special: Modern Highlife, Afro-Sounds and Ghanaian Blues 1968–81. Soundways Records SNDWCD 016. *2009*: UK.

Hedzoleh, Amartey. *Kukurantumi*. Chop Time Music CTM02. *2014*: Holland.

Kidjo, Angelique. *Logozo*. Island/Mango Records 3991828. *1991*: UK.

Masekela Introducing Hedzoleh Soundz. Blue Thumb Records BTS 62. *1973*: USA.

Mono-Mono. *Give the Beggar a Chance*. EMI HLNX5104. *1973*: Nigeria. (Reissue as Mono-Mono). *Give the Beggar a Chance*. Tummy Touch/Soundway Records. *2011*: UK.

Nigeria Special: Modern Highlife Afro-Sounds and Nigerian Blues: 1970–76. Soundway Records SNDWCD 009. *2007*: UK.

Ofege. *Try and Love*. Reissue Academy LP's ACD00. *2009*: USA.

Osibisa. *Osibisa*. MCA MDKS8001. *1971*: UK.

Osibisa. *Woyaya*. MCA *Records* MAPS 5617. *1971*: Germany. (Reissued as Osibisa. *Woyaya*. BGO Records 175. *2012*: UK.)

Osibisa. *Welcome Home*. Bronze label UK, ILPS 9355. *1975*: UK.

Osibisa. *Ojah Awake*. Bronze label UK, ILPS 9412. *1976*: UK.

Osibisa. *The Very Best of Osibisa*. Golden Stool label GSTOCD001 *2009*: UK.

Pino, Geraldo. *Heavy Heavy Heavy*. Retrafric RETRO20CD. *2005*: UK.

Super Eagles Band. *Senegambian Sensation*. Retroafric RETRO17CD. *2001*: UK.

Filmography

Across the Sahara: Ginger Baker in Africa, dir. Tony Palmer. 1971. UK. 53 mins. Documentary.

Soul to Soul, dir. Dennis Sanders. 1971. USA. 90 mins. Concert documentary. Reissue (DVD): *Soul to Soul*, dir. Dennis Sanders, 2004. 90 mins. Concert documentary.

Mick Fleetwood: The Visitor, dir. Mick Fleetwood and Micky Shapiro. 1981. USA. 90 mins. Documentary.

E. JOHN COLLINS

Akan Recreational Music

The term 'Akan recreational music' is used by Ghanaian musicians and musicologists to describe a variety of informal drumming, dancing and singing styles of the various Akan groups of southern Ghana. Since these styles are not linked to the formal ritual, ceremonial and court institutions that take a conservative approach to musical change, traditional recreational music and dance styles are more open to innovation, particularly by young people. As a result, when Western popular music influences were introduced to Ghana and cultural blending took place in the coastal areas beginning in the late nineteenth century, it was local recreational performance that strongly influenced the early development of the acculturated proto-highlife forms (*adaha* and *osibisaaba*) of the Fanti people, a coastal Akan subgroup. So while it was difficult for ceremonial music to be detached from its religious or social function, recreational music could easily be adapted to new circumstances, including the changing tastes of young people.

Recreational performance was, and still is, often associated with the young people, who employ it to entertain themselves on moonlit nights and festive occasions and who playfully experiment with novel stylistic changes in both the music and the dance. As a result there has been in the twentieth century a constant sequence of rapidly evolving recreational styles linked to generation changes. For instance Nketia (1973, 66) provides a list of such a sequence of short-lived Akan 'new musical types for popular use … then abandoned by creative individuals for a new one' including *ompe, dwae, sobom, adakim/adakam, osoode, asaadua* and *Akosua Tuntum*.

According to A.A. Mensah (1969/70), two nineteenth-century Fanti recreational styles that were important for the emergence of highlife music were the *kununku* (or *kurunku*) played by men and the *akrodo* by women. The cantor (lead vocalist) and chorus voices in these styles are accompanied by rattles, bells or wooden *claves* (called 'castanets' and later 'clips' in Ghana) and handclapping. Another, says Mensah, was the Fanti *adenkum* orchestras in which women play a prominent role and whose instruments consist of long-necked *adenkum* gourds, bamboo stamping tubes, rattles, the '*firikyiwa*' finger-bell and drums (see Aning 1969). Kwaa Mensah (personal communication) claims that another formative influence on highlife was Fanti *adzewa* or *densim*, a recreational version of the 6/8 polyrhythmic Ashanti royal *adowa* drum-dance, itself created at the Mampong court in the 1870s from *mpre* funeral music and religious *akom* drumming (Holmes 1984), as well as elements from *kete, akapoma* and *densewu* music (Opoku 1966, 55).

A Fanti recreational style is the *osibi* drum-dance of the fishermen of the Cape Coast area. This is played in 4/4 and 6/8 time on calabashes, drums and bamboo stamping tubes and associated with youthful entertainment and musical wrestling matches. *Osibi* is probably the origin of the word 'osibisaaba,' a form of early highlife that evolved around 1900 in the Cape Coast area, combining combined local recreational music with the guitars and accordions of visiting seamen.

Another Fanti recreational music style that influenced early highlife was *adakam* (or *adakim*) whose principle instrument was a large rectangular wooden box or chest (sometimes with a round hole on the side) that was held between the player's feet and beaten with the palm of the hands and fist. It was accompanied by other male musicians playing gong, iron castanets and hand held frame drums and by the clapping hands of a women's chorus (Bame 1991, 10–11). The *adakam* box-drum was also used by early Fanti *osibisaaba* guitar groups, the best known being that of Jacob Sam (Kwame Asare) whose Kumasi Trio (made up of three Fantis based in the Ashanti capital) recorded for Zonophone in 1928, with Kwah Kantah tapping out rhythms on the *adakam* or playing the wooden 'clips.'

Following the success of *adakam* came *osode* or *osoode* ('you find it sweet'), another Fanti recreational box-drum music that became popular during the 1930s. *Osode* bands employed frame drums, bells and an *adakam* type of box with a crescent-shaped slit cut out of one side and beaten with the right hand and tapped with the fingers of the left hand (Beattie Casely-Hayford and Y.B. Bampoe, personal communication). The 4/4 rhythms of *osode* were used in the late 1960s and early 1970s by the Fanti guitarist C.K. Mann for his very popular '*osode* highlife' compositions.

Sikyi music, which according to J.H.K. Nketia (personal communication) became popular in the Ashanti areas in the 1920s, also had a relationship to highlife. *Sikyi* employs a 4/4 'triple offbeat' *clave* rhythm (played on cowbells, wooden clappers or simply clapped), identical to one of those used in highlife. Although *sikyi* is a contemporary of highlife, the triple offbeat pattern most certainly goes back to earlier traditional Akan rhythms. According to the Ghanaian guitarist Koo Nimo (personal communication) one of the *kwadum* drum patterns used in the *apente* variation of Ashanti royal *kente* music goes back centuries. A later link between *sikyi* and highlife was created in the 1970s when *sikyi* gave its name to the 1974 hit record 'Sikyi Highlife' by Doctor Gyasi's Noble Kings guitar band from Kumasi.

Because Ghanaian popular music and traditional music coexisted during the twentieth century, a circular relationship was forged between them. Not only did highlife draw on traditional music (as discussed above), but conversely highlife also influenced traditional music, particularly informal recreational drum-dance styles. This resulted in what can be called 'neo-traditional' music and dance styles that were pioneered by successive generations of twentieth-century Ghanaian youth. These modern forms of traditional music and dance were influenced by highlife and other forms of popular music but drew on traditional resources, utilizing primarily local instruments and evolving within the social context of traditional music and music-making. In addition to the previously mentioned Akan 'new musical types' (Nketia 1973, 66), there were the Ga *kolomashie* and *kpanlogo* of the 1930s and 1960s respectively, the Ewe *tuidzi* (see Agordoh 1994) and *borborbor* of the 1940s and 1950s, and the northern Ghanaian Dagbon *simpa* and *atika-tika* of the 1930s and 1970s, respectively (see Chernoff 1979 and Collins 1996, chapter 20).

In the case of the Akan there have been three important forms of highlife-influenced neo-traditional recreational music since the 1940s. The earliest was the *ahweya* or *ahwiya*, also known as *aways* (i.e., waist) due to this dance's stress on pelvic movements (Mensah 1971/2,132). *Ahweya* groups utilized cantor and chorus, bells, wooden 'castanets' or 'clips,' rattles, *odonno* pressure drums and three frame drums. These groups also included the double-headed, metal *pati* drum, a copy of the military side drum of 1930s *konkoma* highlife marching groups, themselves influenced by the local *adaha* (proto-highlife) brass band genre (Opoku 1966, 25). *Ahweya* was followed by *assadua* ('sweet berry') for male and female performers, which utilized the same drums as did *ahweya*. It was played in 6/8 time and the singers addressed frivolous, sensual and satirical topics (Nketia 1973, 68). Nketia (ibid.) goes on to mention that around 1960 *assadua* was replaced by a newer Akan recreational dance music called *Akosua Tuntum* (a woman's name) that also featured the large Akan *premprensua* lamellophone (Bame 1991). One of the dance moves associated with these Akan recreational styles of the 1950s and 1960s was *bosoe*, which, according to Nketia (personal communication) means 'hit it' and was shouted out during a dance move that involved young boys and girls flirtatiously slapping their thighs. This expression subsequently inspired the title of Joe Mensah's famous mid-1960s highlife dance band hit record 'Uhuru Special/Bosoe' (first recorded with the Uhuru Dance Band under the name 'Big Beats').

The relatively fast-moving recreational form of traditional Akan music resulted in two important developments in Ghana. First, traditional music was constantly recycled during the twentieth century by successive generations who infused elements of highlife music and dance into traditional drum dances. Second, when early forms of highlife emerged from the blending of foreign and indigenous musical ingredients, they drew their elements largely from the recreational side of traditional music. This process persists in the twenty-first century. For instance, 'azonto,' a new dance craze linked to modern Ghanaian electronic music that surfaced with urban youth around 2010, draws from the dance rhythms and moves of older forms of traditional recreational performance.

Bibliography

Agordoh, Alex A. 1994. *Studies in African Music*. Accra: New Age Publications, Ho Printhony Press.

Aning, Ben. 1968. 'Melodic Analysis of Adenkum.' *Papers in African Studies* (Journal of the University of Ghana) 3: 64–80.

Bame, Kwabena N. 1991. *Profiles in African Traditional Popular Culture: Consensus and Conflict*. New York: Clear Type Press.

Chernoff, John Miller. 1979. *African Rhythms and African Sensibilities*. Chicago: University of Chicago Press.

Collins, E. John. 1994. *The Ghanaian Concert Party: African Popular Entertainment at the Crossroads*. Unpublished Ph.D. dissertation, SUNY Buffalo.

Collins, E. John. 1996. *Highlife Time*. Accra: Anansesem Press.

Holmes, Michael D. 1984. 'The Pulse of the Adowa.' MA Thesis, Wesleyan University.

Mensah, Atta Annan. 1969/70. *Highlife*. Unpublished manuscript. Accra: Collins/BAPMAF Archives.

Mensah, Atta Annan. 1971/2. 'Jazz – the Round Trip.' *Jazz Research* 3(4): 124–37.

Nketia, J. H. Kwabena. [1963] 1973. *Folk Songs of Ghana*. Accra: Ghana Universities Press.

Opoku, Albert M. 1966. 'Choreography and the African Dance.' *African Research Review, University of Ghana African Studies Journal* 3(1): 53–9.

Discographical References

Gyasi, Dr. K, and His Noble Kings. 'Sikyi Highlife.' Essiebons. *1974*: Ghana.

Mensah, Joe, with the Uhuru Dance Band. 'Big Beats.' *1963*: Nigeria.

Discography

Addy, Mustapha Tettey. *Kpanlogo Party*. Tangent Record. *1972*: UK.

Addy, Obo. *Okropong: Traditional Music of Ghana*. Santrofi Records. *1989*: USA.

Music in Ghana: A Selection of Popular African Music from the Archives of the Institute of African Studies, University of Ghana, Legon. PAMAP 601. *1997*: Germany.

Rhythm of Life, Songs of Wisdom: Akan Music from Ghana, West Africa. Smithsonian/Folkways SF CD 40463. *1996*: USA.

The Roots of Highlife: Bamaya to Bosoe. Ghana Arts Council/Community Centre and Faisal Helwani, ACFH 100. *1987*: Ghana.

Filmography

African Cross Rhythms, dir. Peter Bischoff. 1994. Denmark. 52 mins. Documentary. Rereleased in edited form as *Listen to the Silence*, dir. Peter Bischoff. 1996. USA. 30 mins. Documentary.

Repercussions, dir. Dennis Marks. 1983. UK. 50 mins. 7-part television documentary.

When the Moment Sings, dirs. Asiak Aarhus and Ole Brent Froshaug. 1995. Norway. 32 mins. Television Documentary.

E. JOHN COLLINS

Amakwaya

Amakwaya (pronounced 'ah-mah-kwah-yah') refers to the tradition and performance practice of choirs in South Africa that emerged from the mission schools in the nineteenth century. As a syncretic art form, *amakwaya* has roots in hymnody (based on Western four-part functional harmony with a prescriptive dominant melodic line) and indigenous music and folk songs (with a typical call-and-response format, simple harmonic structure, parallel fourths, fifths and octaves and rather complex interwoven rhythmic patterning). Modern concerts and competitions are based on a three-part repertoire, including Western classical compositions, mainly taken from oratorios and operas, African-composed pieces that show a strong Western influence, and neo-traditional songs, often referred to as 'wedding songs.' This choral practice, combining Western music styles with African tradition, bears the marks – both social and aesthetic – of colonial and missionary influences and is closely linked to the emerging black middle class, their process of negotiating identity, and their later quest for a national culture. With political, social and economic mobility restricted in white South Africa, the black middle class turned toward artistic expressions such as choral singing in order to define and express a distinctively African concept of civilization. In this process, *amakwaya* performance developed into a powerful social as well as political means whereby class identity and consciousness could be constructed and communicated.

Missionaries and the Emergence of a Black South African Middle Class

Mission stations and mission schools became localities of a social change that led finally to the formation of a black South African middle class. The declared aim of missionaries was twofold – to produce Christians and to 'civilize' people. Those who chose to follow the missionaries began to construct a new identity. They were eager to render proof that there was a substantial body of educated, progressive, religious and hard-working Africans who had already achieved much in the way of civilized standards.

The endeavors of this new social group were, however, welcomed neither by the *amabhinca* (the traditionalists) nor by the white communities. One of the most important reasons for the resistance of traditional communities to Christianity was the issue of *lobola* (bride price or dowry). Moreover, the king and his chiefs were afraid of losing control over their people. Missionaries ought not to 'become the captains' of those who went to the mission stations. *Amakholwa* ('school-people'), however, recognized their missionaries as leaders: a few missionaries were even accorded the title *nkosi* (chief) in addition to the more common *mfundisi* (teacher). On the other side, white farmers and businessmen felt threatened by Africans who worked independently in agriculture or trade, and it was therefore their main aim to eliminate competition. Education, they argued, would lead to a decrease in the abundant supply of cheap black labor and finally to competition from independent African farmers and merchants. This double rejection, and the resulting isolation, led members of *amakholwa* communities to form an exclusive group.

Music at the mission schools (and in particular singing of hymns) was crucial for the emergence of *amakwaya*. The groups that were formed by the missionaries to lead the singing during the service gradually extended their repertoire and developed a distinctive choral practice. At the schools, singing in a choir soon became an important part of leisure activities. For the mission societies, exhibiting choralism served to showcase the validity of their 'civilizing mission.' By means of choral singing, they argued, as reported in *Ilanga Lase Natal*, a South African newspaper, 'the native people have a chance given them to prove to the world that they are progressive' (23 June 1911).

However, to attribute the advance of *amakwaya* solely to mission education would miss an important precondition that was conducive to the fast and efficient development of the genre. There is a strong indigenous precedent for choral singing that missionaries put to use in their teaching and ministerial strategies. Unlike the instrumental and percussion-based music of more northerly Africans, traditionally South African music has always been predominantly vocal. Drums and other instruments have played a role, mainly in solo performances, but have never been the main means of musical expression. In group dances, still performed in the early twenty-first century, for example, at rural weddings, the singers provide their own dance music without instrumental accompaniment. Communal singing (e.g., of *amahubo* – old clan songs) has always been an important part of celebrations, ceremonies and recreation. In South African Nguni communities, song and dance created and reaffirmed the social values, practices and ideas of the community, and positioned members of the community in relation to their kin, to the 'great-great one' (*nkulunkulu*) and to the ancestral spirits.

Given the political, social and economic restrictions of the world in which they lived, the black middle class turned more and more toward cultural attainment, and especially the development of a syncretic African choral tradition, in order to define and express a distinctively African concept of modern civilization. Despite their re-evaluation of African traditions, the black elite often disapproved of the musical practices of other black South African social groups, both traditional and urban. At the time when ragtime and jazz became the rage in both black and white communities, they tried to counteract the 'jazz disease' by endorsing a mission school performance culture: the Transvaal National Eisteddfod was established in 1931 in order to realize and promote their concept of a national culture. Important agents in the promotion of this 'national culture' were touring choral groups such as Caluza's Ohlange choir. This led to the emergence of a growing number of community choirs with a characteristic repertoire and performance practice.

Repertoire: Negotiation – Tradition and the Modern

Amakwaya repertoire characteristically consists of (1) neo-traditional songs (modernized versions of songs from African folk repertoire), (2) African choral works (by composers of the *amakwaya* community) and (3) Western art music (mainly of European origin). Visual aesthetics reinforce this segmentation. For choirs participating in competitions and festivals it became common practice to wear elaborate robes when presenting Western set pieces and to change into traditional attire for the rendition of traditional songs.

1. Neo-Traditional Songs

The process of modernizing traditional songs happened in two stages. In the first stage, starting in the last quarter of the nineteenth century, traditional African wedding songs (*izingoma zomtshado*), with their distinctive antiphonal and polyphonic call–response structure, were performed in four-part harmony with African movements and Western vocal aesthetics.

The second stage followed in the first quarter of the twentieth century: traditional dance-songs arranged for choir (*amagama 'sizulu*) were blended with American popular song styles and local ragtime styles (*amagama eRagtime*) that had become popular among *amakwaya* groups.

2. African Eclectic Compositions

The styles of African eclectic compositions allow a rough categorization, which is determined mainly by the degree to which Western or African musical aspects and traditions are used. This categorization is marked not by rigid periods but by fluid transitions.

Ntiskana Gaba can be described as the influential precursor of this choral tradition. In his compositions, which were notated decades later by John Knox Bokwe, Ntsikana attempted to make Christian doctrine more accessible to the people. At the center of Ntsikana's worship stood a set of hymns. Four of these have survived to the present day: 'Intsimbi ka Ntsikana' (Ntsikana's Bell), 'Dalibom ka Ntsikana' (Life Creator), 'Elinqukuva lika Ntsikana' (The Round Hymn) and 'Ulo Tixo 'Mkulu' (Thou Great God/The Great Hymn). All four compositions reflect the structure of traditional songs, in which the call (*hlabela*) and response (*landela*) of a leader and chorus determine the cyclical form of the music. His fourth composition, 'Ulo Tixo 'Mkulu,' for instance, is based on a Xhosa *umdudo* (wedding song) and uses the form of a praise-poem (*isibongo*).

The first group of mission-educated composers deviated from Ntsikana's approach. Their works merely imitate the melodic and harmonic structures of hymns taught by the missionaries. In most cases, vernacular words constitute the only African aspect of these compositions. In addition to his achievements as a practicing musician and editor, John Knox Bokwe became the first African composer of national stature. His song collection *Amaculo ase Lovedale* (Lovedale Music, first published in 1885 and named after the mission institution where he taught), is arguably one of the most important early sources of *amakwaya* compositions. In 1897 school choirmaster Enoch Mankayi Sontonga (1873–1905), another important composer of this period, who had trained at Lovedale, wrote the hymn-like tune 'Nkosi siklel' iAfrika' (God Bless Africa). The African National Congress (ANC) adopted it officially as the closing anthem for all its meetings in 1925. For decades, it was regarded as the unofficial national anthem of South Africa by the oppressed, who sang it as an act of defiance against the apartheid regime. Since the fall of the apartheid regime 'Nkosi sikelel' iAfrika' has formed the first part of the official national anthem of South Africa. Other important composers of this period are Tiyo Soga and John L. Dube (1871–1946).

Toward the beginning of the twentieth century, however, composers started to recollect their roots and began to include elements of African traditional music in their compositions, thus contributing to emerging nationalism. The African elements initially involved only rhythm. Gradually composers such as Alfred Assegaai Kumalo (1879–1966), Reuben Tholakele Caluza (1895–1969), Benjamin Tyamzashe (1890–1990) and Polumo Joshua Mohapeloa (1908–81) started to replace Western hymnic square rhythms, introducing polyrhythm, multiple downbeats, syncopated rhythms and interwoven rhythmic patterning into their compositions. At that stage, the harmonic and melodic structures were still largely Western. By raising sociopolitical issues, Caluza's songs became an important part of the emerging national culture, for they 'metaphorically united local (Zulu) traditionalism and a national, "civilized" outlook in an attempt to sketch the outline of a modern, black South Africa' (Erlmann 1991).

It was only toward the middle of the twentieth century that composers started to search for a peculiarly 'African style' of choral composition. Composers found inspiration in the hymns of Ntsikana and in the recordings of traditional song material such as the Zulu bow songs of Mntwana (Princess) Magogo (1900–84), daughter of the Zulu king Dinuzulu KaCetshwayo (1868–1913), who can be regarded not only as a respected performer of the *ugubhu* bow but also an influential authority on Zulu music. Mzilikazi Khumalo, who was at the forefront of this development, started to experiment with traditional linguistic elements such as the tonal glides in the form of grace-notes.

In the late 1980s *amakwaya* composers started to compose large-scale works. At the beginning of the development stood one of Mzilikazi Khumalo's compositions, *Izibongo ZikaShaka*. This was followed by the composition of Khumalo's song cycle, *Haya, Mntwan' Omkhulu!*, which coincided with Durban-based Opera Africa's commissioning of an opera on the subject of Princess Magogo's life. Before taking the step of presenting the country's first opera by a black composer, Opera Africa had experimented with 'Africanizing' opera for five years, setting *The Magic Flute*, *Carmen*, *Fidelio* and *Faust* in local contexts and performing them in local languages. The result of the commission, *Princess Magogo kaDinizulu*, which is commonly regarded as 'the first African opera,' was performed with great success at Durban's Playhouse Opera on 4 May 2002.

3. Western Repertoire

Compositions by Western composers have always had a special importance for members of the choral community, and performing such works is partly viewed as an expression of their sophistication and desire to be progressive.

In the 1970s the choral community began to shift its attention from unaccompanied choral pieces (short *a cappella* compositions such as madrigals and part-songs, mainly from European Renaissance composers) toward compositions with instrumental accompaniment and extensive solo passages taken mainly from oratorios, masses or cantatas. A central figure in this development was the music educator and choral conductor Khabi Mngoma. His influence triggered a process of restructuring *amakwaya* repertoire, with the result that, from the 1980s onwards, most choral competitions prescribed repertoire taken exclusively from oratorios, masses or cantatas.

The major role played by Mngoma in influencing this development should not obscure the fact that choruses taken from oratorios had already been performed in the nineteenth century at the mission stations. Works by Mendelssohn and Brahms, and above all Handel's *Messiah*, had long been significant presences. The performance of oratorios may be understood originally as an endeavor simply to emulate Britishness, whereas the translations of the texts (e.g., Handel's *Messiah* sung in Zulu), undertaken much later, represent a more thoroughgoing process of appropriation, involving the adaptation of Western culture to African needs.

In the first decade of the twenty-first century the trend of concentrating mainly on choruses taken from oratorios, to the exclusion of other forms of Western choral music, gradually developed toward an enthusiasm for opera.

Competition: Meaning and Motivation

It was also at the schools that one of the most important features of *amakwaya* performance practice was initiated: competitive contexts. Interhouse competitions and the annual school competitions organized by the Teachers' Associations grew into the multitude of competitions that today form the backbone of *amakwaya* performance practice.

The urge to compete has strong indigenous precedents. However, when transferred into the urban sphere, the spirit of competitiveness assumed new forms and contexts. In the traditional Zulu wedding ceremony the proceedings culminate in group singing and an elaborate program of choral dances. On such occasions, choral groups representing the bride's party (*umthimba*) and the groom's party (*ikhetho*) strive to outdo one another in artistic excellence.

The development of choral contests in the public sector started in the early 1930s with the Transvaal Eisteddfod. Motivated by the concept of an African national culture, the conductor and teacher Mark Radebe sought to preserve and develop the individuality of native music and at the same time encouraged the 'finer refinements of European music' (*Ilanga*, 19 May 1951).

Whereas initially these competitions were organized only at a provincial level, the various teachers' organizations soon began to coordinate local efforts. The result was the National Music Eisteddfod, which was inaugurated in 1962. The conductor Pansy Tlakula reported in 1965 that competitions soon grew into an obsession. According to his reports in TUATA, the official organ of the Transvaal United African Teachers' Association, the work of school was in many aspects linked with singing with choral competitions being an important event of the school year.

The National Choir Festival (NCF) that developed out of the Ford Choirs in Contest started in 1978. For the first time in the history of *amakwaya* a corporate sponsor provided a material incentive for the champion. Other significant innovations included prescribing pieces with accompaniment, at first with piano and in later years with orchestra, and creating separate categories for large and standard-sized choirs.

In addition to providing a platform to display talent, choir competitions proved to be an ideal framework for the shaping and communication of the choirs' middle-class identity. *Amakwaya* contests were ideal vehicles to promote the conception of an African national culture. First, they put a well-defined distance between the black working class and the educated black middle class as they became an important means of countering the *marabi* culture of the urban centers. In addition to offering a means of keeping a distance from the black working class, they became a medium of competing, on a symbolic level, with the white communities: competitions represented a safe space in their struggle for recognition and emancipation. Here they could render proof that they were capable of achieving 'world-class standards' and attaining the same level as white people.

Conclusion

Whereas early mission converts were required to reject their own musical culture (e.g., by exclusive singing of hymns), the black middle class later began to redefine its attitude toward traditional music when African nationalism took hold in the early twentieth century. In the process of negotiation between tradition and modernity, the endeavor to integrate African and Western elements was to become characteristic of *amakwaya* groups throughout the twentieth century; it shaped individual identity and touched every aspect of the choral tradition, from performance practice to repertoire and aesthetics.

The sectionalized repertoire is, since the emergence of mission school choirs in the nineteenth century, an essential characteristic of *amakwaya* groups, and with the distinct function and meaning of its various parts, this distinguishes it from other choral practices. The choice of repertoire, ranging from simple borrowing in the case of neo-traditional wedding songs to the wholesale imitation of Western aesthetic and performance practice, reveals to what extent *amakwaya* groups mediate foreign influences. The process of negotiation has remained a central concern of *amakwaya* compositions. This is illustrated not least in the project of creating an African opera, in which a Western art form is used to express African content.

Moreover, an important aspect of performance practice of *amakwaya* is manifested in the form of competitions, which have become the major driving force that keeps this choral tradition alive.

Bibliography

Ballantine, Chris. 2002. 'Opera for Africa.' *Opera* 53(8/August).

Bokwe, John Knox. 1904. *Ntsikana: The Story of an African Hymn*. Lovedale: Lovedale Mission Press.

Bruce, Jacob. 195?. *Zulu Hymnology and Hymnody. Natal Missionary Conference 1877-1950*. Manuscript Collection at Killie Campbell Africana Library, Durban, South Africa.

Cockburn, Christopher. 1999. 'Music in Twentieth Century South Africa: The Example of Handel's Messiah.' *26th Annual Congress of the Musicological Society of Southern Africa*. Bloemfontein, 26-7 August.

Cockrell, Dale. 1987. 'Of Gospel Hymns, Minstrel Shows, and Jubilee Singers: Towards Some Black South African Musics.' *American Music* 5(4): 417-32.

Couzens, Tim. 1985. *The New African: A Study of the Life and Work of H.I.E. Dhlomo*. Johannesburg: Ravan Press.

Dargie, Dave. 1982. 'The Music of Ntsikana.' *South African Journal of Musicology* (SAMUS) 2: 9-27.

Dargie, Dave. 1997. *Christian Music Among Africans*. In *Christianity in South Africa: A Political, Social and Cultural History*, eds. R. Elphick and R. Davenport. Cape Town: David Philip.

Detterbeck, Markus. 2010. *South African Choral Music (Amakwaya): Song, Contest and the Formation of Identity*. Helbling, Rum, Austria: Helbling Academic Books.

Detterbeck, Markus, and Giddy, Patrick. 2005. 'Questions Regarding Tradition and Modernity in Contemporary Amakwaya Practice.' *Transformation: Critical Perspectives on Southern Africa* 59: 26-44.

Erlmann, Veit. 1983. 'Apartheid, African Nationalism and Culture: The Case of Traditional African Music in Black Education in South Africa.' *Perspectives on Education* 7(3): 131-54.

Erlmann, Veit. 1991. *African Stars: Studies in Black South African Performance*. Chicago: University of Chicago Press.

Erlmann, Veit. 1999. *Spectatorial Lust: The African Choir in England, 1891-1893*. In *Africans on Stage: Studies in Ethnological Show Business*, ed. B. Lindfors. Bloomington: Indiana University Press.

Etherington, Norman. 1978. *Preachers, Peasants and Politics in Southeast Africa, 1835-1880: African Christian Communities in Natal, Pondoland and Zululand*. London: Royal Historical Society.

Hodgson, Jane. 1980. *Ntsikana's 'Great Hymn': A Xhosa Expression of Christianity in the Early Nineteenth Century Eastern Cape*. Cape Town: University of Cape Town, Centre for African Studies.

Hodgson, Jane. 1981. 'The Genius of Ntsikana.' In *Papers Presented at the Conference on Literature and Society in Southern Africa, held at the University of York, September*. York: University of York, Centre for Southern African Studies, 8-11.

Houle, Robert. 2001. 'Becoming Amakholwa: Revival and the Formation of Group Identity on the Stations of the American Zulu Mission, 1890-1910.' Paper presented at History and African Studies Seminar, African Studies Association Annual Meeting, University of Durban/Natal. Collection of the University of Durban/Natal Library.

Huskisson, Yvonne. [1969] 1983. *The Bantu Composers of South Africa*, 2nd ed., ed. Jacques P. Malan. Pretoria: Human Sciences Research Council.

Johnston, Anne. 2002. 'Memorable Opening for Africa's First Opera.' *The Sunday Tribune* (May), 12.

Kirby, Percival. 1979. 'The Bantu Composers of South Africa.' In *South African Music Encyclopaedia*, Vol. 1, ed. Jacques Malan. Cape Town: Oxford University Press, 85-94.

Matthews, Zachariah Keodirelang. 1986. *Freedom for My People: The Autobiography of Z. K. Matthews. Southern Africa 1901 to 1968*. Cape Town: Africasouth Paperbacks.

Meintjes, Sheila. 1983. 'Aspects of Ideological Formation among the Kholwa of Edendale in Nineteenth Century Natal.' *Centre for African Studies Seminar Papers*. Cape Town: University of Cape Town.

Mthethwa, Bongani. 1988. 'The Songs of Alfred A. Kumalo: A Study in Nguni and Western Musical Syncretism.' *6th Symposium on Ethnomusicology. Rhodes University*. Grahamstown: International Library of African Music.

Rycroft, David. 1971. 'Stylistic Evidence in Nguni Song.' In *Music and History in Africa*, ed. K. P. Wachsmann. Evanston: Northwestern University Press, 213–41.

Rycroft, David. 1975/1976. 'The Zulu Bow Songs of Princess Magogo.' *African Music Society Journal* 5(4): 41–97.

Rycroft, David. 1991. 'Black South African Urban Music Since the 1890s; Some Reminiscences of Alfred Assegai Kumalo (1879–1966).' *African Music* 7(1): 5–31.

Skota, Mweli, ed. 193?. *The African Yearly Register*. Johannesburg: R. L. Esson and Co.

Tlakula, Pansy. 1965. 'Twenty-One Years of Singing.' *TUATA, Official Organ of the Transvaal Untied African Teachers' Association* (December): 18.

Xulu, Musa. 1995. 'Socio-Political Change and the National Anthem in South Africa: A Critical Appraisal of Nkosi Sikelel' iAfrika.' *10th Symposium on Ethnomusicology. Rhodes University, 1991*. Grahamstown: International Library of African Music.

Sheet Music

Bokwe, John Knox. 1922. *Amaculo ase Lovedale*. 5th ed. Lovedale: Lovedale Mission Press.

Bokwe, John Knox. *Solfa Leaflets*. Lovedale: Lovedale Mission Press.

Detterbeck, Markus. 1996. 'Mbube – Chormusik aus Südafrika' (Book and CD.) Oldershausen: Institut für Didaktik populärer Musik.

Detterbeck, Markus. 2006. 'Sing Africa, Sing: 9 Afrikanische Lieder für gemischten Chor.' Rum, Austria: Helbling Verlag.

Gibbins, Clarence. 1946. 'An African Song-Book.' Pietermaritzburg: Tarboton and Mitchell.

Hitchcock, Giley, ed. 1941 'The School Choir.' Lovedale: The American Board Mission.

Khumalo, Mzilikazi. 1998. 'South Africa Sings: African Choral Repertoire in "Dual Notation",' Vol. 1. Johannesburg: SAMRO.

Khumalo, Mzilikazi. 1999. 'Ushaka, Kasenzangakhona – Shaka, Son of Senzangakhona: An Epic in Music and Praise Poetry.' Piano-vocal score in dual notation. Bryanston: Maxym Music.

Kumalo, Alfred. 1967. 'Izingoma zikaKumalo.' South Africa: Shuter & Shooter.

Mohapeloa, Joshua Pulumo. 1935. 'Meloli le Lithallere tsa Afrika.' Lesotho: Morija Sesotho Book Depot.

Rycroft, David, ed. 1996. 'Amagama Abantu.' In *A Zulu Songbook*. Pietermaritzburg: University of Natal Press. (Facsimile reprint of J.L. Dube and N. Dube, 1911. *Amagama Abantu, awe mishado, imiququmbelo, utando, nawe mikekelo no kudhlala*. Phoenix, Natal: Ohlange Institute.)

Shabalala, Sam. 1993. 'I~Mesaya – Umculo kaHandel ngesiZulu' [Handel's Messiah in Zulu translation]. Pietermaritzburg: Reach Out Publishers.

Discography

Cock, Richard. *Songs of Praise 1998 & 1999*. Sarepta Music, Kloof SARCD 060. *1999*: South Africa.

Diop, Mapathé. *Sabar Wolof: Dance Drumming of Senegal*. Village Pulse VPU-1003. *1992*: Senegal.

Imilonji kaNtu Choral Society. *Ukushona Kwelanga – the Sunset*. Gallo Records CDGSP 3078. *2006*: South Africa.

Manhattan Brothers. *The Very Best of The Manhattan Brothers – Their Greatest Hits (1948–1959)*. Gallo Records CDZAC 77. *1999*: South Africa.

Mhumalo, Mzilikazi. *Nation Building – Celebrating 10 Years in Music. Sowetan, Caltex, SABC 1, Massed Choir Festival 10th Anniversary*. Janus Media JANP 33. South Africa.

SABC Choristers. *Education*. Gallo Records CDGMP 40817. *2000*: South Africa.

Filmography

Amandla – A Revolution in Four-Part Harmony, dir. Lee Hirsch. 2002. South Africa. 99 mins. Documentary.

MARKUS DETTERBECK

Apala

Apala is an Islamic-influenced Yorùbá style of popular music from southwestern Nigeria. The genre evolved from an Islamic socio-religious form of music, *were*, which was performed during the Ramadan period of fasting to awaken Muslims to consume a pre-dawn meal, *sari*, before daytime fasting commenced. To mark the celebration at the end of the Ramada period of fasting, *were* musicians competed to determine who were the most skilled, a competition which served to improve their musicianship. These competitions can be traced back to the 1940s. As the music became increasingly popular, more musicians participated and *were* flourished as a genre. In 1943 the *gangan* drum (talking drum) was for the first time introduced to *were* by one of the competing groups from Isale Eko (Ajirire and Alabi 1992). The audience was thrilled by the tunes played by the drummer, Lasisi Layemi. These tunes became known as 'apala.'

It is also believed in certain quarters that 'Apala is an offshoot of the well-known *dundun* (hourglass drum) music of the Yorùbá' (Euba 1989, quoted in Olusoji 2005, 100), and that the term 'apala' was created in order to distinguish this new genre from *dundun* music. Yet what is certain is that the instrumentation, style and creative dynamics of *apala* were all derived from Yorùbá culture, with the exception of an Islamic melismatic vocal style which, however, is not as pronounced as in *fújì* and *sákárà* music.

The principal characteristics of *apala* have therefore been an Islamic vocal style, Yorùbá musical instruments and a percussive style. The themes of *apala* songs are based on indigenous philosophy and proverbs, street jibes and praise songs. *Apala* is performed by all-male bands in Yorùbá and English and has strong roots in Yorùbá tonal inflections. The membership of these bands ranges from nine to 13 members.

Musical Characteristics

Apala is both a vocal and instrumental music. Vocalization is based on a lead singer and backup singers employing mostly Yorùbá call-and-response, call-and-refrain and solo and chorus patterns. With a solo and chorus pattern, the chorus exactly replicates the preceding solo. The leader of the band is the lead vocalist, and it is he who takes the solo or 'call' part while the backup singers perform the chorus or refrain. The singing style is thus antiphonal. The voice of the lead vocalist determines the overall framework of songs. For instance, Haruna Ishola, a leading exponent of *apala*, sang at a low pitch because of his baritone voice. The backup vocalists consequently sang at a higher pitch to achieve balance since all the singers were men. Conversely, the backup vocalists for Ayinla Omowura, another leading exponent of *apala*, had to sing at a low pitch to achieve balance because he had a high tenor voice. Yorùbá tonal inflections and syllabic expressions were more prominent in *apala* than the Islamic melismatic vocal style found in other Islamic-influenced genres such as *fújì*.

The percussion instruments that generally accompany *apala* singing include the *gangan*, *akuba/tomtom*, *sekere*, *agogo* and *agidigbo*. *Apala* bands also use amplification equipment in their performances.

Performance Practices

Apala has been one of the most popular dance genres among the Yorùbá. From the 1960s to the 1980s it enjoyed quite extensive patronage and transcended religious barriers. The genre was performed at virtually all social occasions including weddings, funerals, christenings, birthday parties, coronation parties, club anniversaries, house warmings and entertainment provided in club houses. *Apala* was in general performed for anyone in the community irrespective of gender and religious affiliation. Bands were paid by means of the Yorùbá tradition of 'spraying': with hosts and guests placing money on the foreheads of the musicians.

Apala is performed at designated centers. Unlike *fújì*, *jùjú* and some other genres in which musicians stand to perform, *apala* musicians always perform sitting down in two slightly curved rows. This seating arrangement is a mark of their identity. The first row contains the leader in the center surrounded by the backup singers; the second row contains the drummers and other instrumentalists. At any social event in Yorùbá culture, those to be eulogized alongside their well-wishers expect to be the recipients of a special dance that takes place in front of the band.

Principal Exponents

Following the *were* competition of 1943, a number of musicians began performing *apala*. These musicians included Adisa Alayameta, Rabiu Ishola

Cole, Haruna Ishola, Ayinla Omowura, Kasumu Adio, Raji Owonikoko, Y.K. Ajadi, Saka Olayigbade, Rotimi Atologbe, Ayinla Adegetor, Folorunsho Aribido and Ayinla Omo-Rali, Aminu Olaribigbe, Ligali Mukaiba and Lasisi Onieede. However, the two most important of these musicians were Haruna Ishola and Ayinla Omowura. Haruna Ishola in particular came to be regarded as the icon of *apala*.

Haruna Ishola Bello

Haruna Ishola was among the audience inspired by Lasisi Lauemi's 1943 *gangan* performance. He was born in Ijebu Igbo, Ogun State, in 1919. He received no formal education but had some knowledge of the Quran. He started work as a bicycle repairer but was fond of singing, something he got from his father, who was an indigenous doctor. Haruna Ishola also fell in love with and played the *agidigbo*, a kind of thumb piano. Because of his interest in music he understudied a *sákárà* musician, 'Ejalonibu.' His interest in playing music reached a peak when he relocated to Lagos to live with his uncle and became attracted to *were* music. The inspiration he experienced at the 1943 *were* competition eventually led him to establish his own band back in Ijebu Igbo in 1947. The initial members of his band included Aderan Kareem, Aderan Gabriel, Shittu Bello, Abass Tiyamiu, Bisiriyu Karimu, Ajao Oru and Adisa Aniyameta. Adisa Aniyameta had earlier formed an *apala* band but, after a while, it floundered.

Haruna Ishola, fondly known as 'Baba Ngani Agba,' named his group 'Haruna Ishola and his Apala Group.' The band made its first recording in 1948, 'Orimolusi Adebayo,' in honor of the ruler of Ijebu Igbo, but it was not as successful as expected. In 1955 Haruna Ishola made another recording for Decca West Africa in honor of the same ruler, 'Late Orimolusi Adeboye.' This time the recording was successful and it placed him in the limelight, a position which he successfully maintained. In 1971 he recorded another major breakthrough album, *Oroki Social Club*, which sold about five million copies. Ishola's other major hit records include 'Ina Ran' (1983), which was later released as a remix by his son, Musiliu Ishola, and 'Apala Disco.'

Ishola became the leading figure of *apala*, influential in determining its conventions. As a poet and singer he widened the genre's horizons by making his music more entertaining, educative and challenging, and also by making it more suitable as a vehicle for praise. He became a model for younger musicians, his fans and society at large, and he was always consulting the elders who were custodians of Yorùbá culture to obtain information and ideas which he believed should be passed on to following generations. He traveled the world in order to propagate *apala*. The countries in which he made the most impact included Ghana, Benin, Liberia, Guinea, the United Kingdom, the United States, Italy, Sweden, France, Czechoslovakia, Yugoslavia, Hungary and Saudi Arabia.

The dynamic character of Ishola's music can be traced to the various influences and novel trends he adopted in his music. For example, he inserted some elements of disco into his music when disco was popular in the 1970s, recording a track entitled 'Apala Disco.' However, his innovations did not include the introduction of Western musical instruments as *fújì* did because of his belief in African instruments and the value of their percussive character. Again, as with other *apala* music, Ishola's music was characterized by the inclusion of indigenous philosophy and proverbs.

Before he died in 1983 Ishola had to his credit about 300 albums. Most of these sold in the millions. As a producer, Ishola managed and invested in organizations such as Phonodisc Records. He also had a string of honors and awards including 'Member of the Niger,' an honor conferred on him by the Federal Government of Nigeria. After his death, one of his children, Musiliu Ishola, continued to perform *apala*, introducing elements of hip-hop into the music. As a consequence, Musiliu Ishola was able to breathe new life into the genre.

Ayinla Omowura

Ayinla Omowura was born in the late 1930s at Itoko in Abeokuta, Ogun State. He received no formal education. He was a butcher before he started his musical career in the 1960s with a genre of music, *olalomi*, that was popular in the 1950s but faded after time. In 1970 Omowura decided to take up *apala* and recorded a single, 'Aja t'o foju d' Ejo,' in June of that year. Surprisingly, the single was a tremendous success and he immediately made three other recordings, *Ema Fowo S'oya Si Wamo* (1970), *Danfo O Si'Ere/ Ema Tori Owo Pa'nia* (1971) and *Anjonu Elere* (1971).

This single and the three extended-play records sold 50,000 copies and placed him in the limelight. His music, which was very popular with young people in the 1970s, was a street-bred form of *apala* known as 'ragamuffin apala,' and was targeted mostly at artisans. As was the case with Haruna Ishola, Ayinla Omowura's music was instrumental in establishing the conventions of *apala*. As well as being spiced with indigenous philosophy and proverbs, his lyrics were colored with street jibes and jargon, which is what made the music attractive to his fans. His music threw jibes at lazy men and women, troublesome children, unpopular government programs and government mismanagement. In his music he was blunt and fearless.

Ayinla Omowura was known fondly as 'Alhaji costly' because of his taste for expensive clothes and jewelry. He was second in popularity only to Haruna Ishola. The two musicians were, however, rivals. Omowura died in 1980 as a consequence of a fracas between himself and his band members. After his demise, his younger brother Dauda took over the leadership of his band but could not sustain its popularity. After that his son Akeem also tried to revive the band but was unsuccessful.

Conclusion

Through the contributions of musicians such as Haruna Ishola and Ayinla Omowura *apala* enjoyed overwhelming recognition from the 1950s through to the 1990s, after which its popularity declined significantly. Although there were various attempts to revive the genre, these have been unsuccessful, not so much because there were no creative *apala* musicians, but because of competition from many other genres, such as *fújì* and hip-hop. *Apala* music is not appealing to young people who have fully embraced hip-hop. The attempt by Musiliu Ishola to revive *apala* by introducing elements of hip-hop did not go far, though he did achieve considerable success with a remix of one his father's songs, 'Ina Ran,' entitled 'My Dear (Apala Remix)' on his 2004 album *Soyoyo*, 'My Dear' being the English for 'Ina Ran.' So, while *apala* has persisted, it has not remained as popular as it used to be. Live performances have been largely restricted to outlying locations. However, the recorded works of the major artists have continued to be listened to in the cities.

Bibliography

Agu, Dan C. C. 1999. *Form and Analysis of African Music*. Enugu: New Generation Books.

Ajerire, Tosin, and Alabi, Wale. 1992. *Three Decades of Nigerian Music 1960–1990*. Lagos: Macboja Press.

Euba, Akin. 1989. 'Jùjú, Fújì and Intercultural Aspects of Modern Yorùbá Popular Music.' In *An Essay on Music in Africa 2: Intercultural Perspectives*, ed. Akin Euba. Bayreuth African Studies Series. Iwalewa Haus, Bayreuth: University of Bayreuth.

Olusoji, Stephen. 2005. 'Apala, Sakara and Waka as Entertainment Music.' *African Notes: Journal of the Institute of African Studies, University of Ibadan* 29(1/2): 98–112.

Yekini-Ajenifuja, Isaac. 2012. 'The Influence of Yorùbá Culture in Southwest Nigeria on Islamic Music.' *OBOBDO: Uyo Journal of Aesthetics in Music* 1(2): 129–33.

Discographical References

Ayinla Omowura and His Apala Group. 'Aja t'o foju d' Ejo.' (7-inch single.) EMI Nigeria 01. *1970*: Nigeria.

Ayinla Omowura and His Apala Group. *Anjonu Elere*. (EP.) EMI Nigeria HNEP 534. *1971*: Nigeria.

Ayinla Omowura and His Apala Group. *Danfo O Si'Ere/Ema Tori Owo Pa'nia*. (EP.) EMI Nigeria HNEP 533. *1971*: Nigeria.

Ayinla Omowura and His Apala Group. 'Elekotode Orin Owe 25x40.' EMI Nigeria 20. *1981*: Nigeria.

Ayinla Omowura and His Apala Group. *Ema Fowo S'oya Si Wam*. (EP.) EMI Nigeria HNEP 506. *1970*: Nigeria.

Haruna Ishola and His Apala Group. 'Apala Disco.' *Apala Disco*. (CD.) Star SRPS 34. *N.d.*: Nigeria.

Haruna Ishola and His Apala Group. 'Ina Ran,' *Sule Maito*. Star SRPS 40. *1983*: Nigeria.

Haruna Ishola and His Apala Group. 'Late Orimolusi Adeboye.' (7-inch rpm single). Decca West Africa. *1955*: Nigeria.

Haruna Ishola and His Apala Group. 'Orimolusi Adebay.' (10-inch 78 rpm single). Label unknown. *1948*: Nigeria.

Haruna Ishola and His Apala Group. *Oroki Social Club*. (LP.) Star SRPS 2. *1971*: Nigeria.

Musiliu Haruna Ishola and His Apala Remix. 'My Dear (Apala Remix)' ('Ina Ran'). *Soyoyo*. (Album.) Jat Productions JOCO 04. *2004*: Nigeria.

YouTube

Haruna Ishola. 2011. 'Apala Disco.' https://www.youtube.com/watch?v=-AAqnpAkkaM (accessed 5 April 2018).

Websites

Discography of the recordings of Haruna Ishola and His Apala Group: http://biochem.chem.nagoya-u.ac.jp/~endo/EAIshola.html (accessed 5 April 2018).

Discography of the recordings of Ayinla Omowura and His Apala Group: http://endolab.jp/endo/EAOmowura.html (accessed 5 April 2018).

ISAAC YEKINI-AJENIFUJA

Aṣíkò

The term 'aṣíkò' describes a set of styles that emerged in West Africa in the twentieth century and were popular in several countries in the period from the 1930s to the 1960s. All varieties, whether Sierra Leonean, Nigerian or Cameroonian, may be considered descendants of gumbe (goombay) music, the product of what Collins (1985) describes as a feedback loop between West Africa, the Caribbean and Brazil, as Africans traversed the Atlantic first as captives, later returning as freed slaves or soldiers, particularly during the late eighteenth and early nineteenth centuries. The intermingling of Africans from different backgrounds in places such as Jamaica, Cuba and northeast Brazil resulted in hybrid percussion and vocal traditions, which were later readapted in West African coastal communities.

Aṣíkò in Sierra Leone

Aṣíkò (var. ashiko, assiko) is Sierra Leone's earliest form of popular music, with origins around 1900. In Sierra Leone, the aṣíkò ensemble is associated with the Alikali society, an animistic semi-secret society found among the predominantly Muslim Hausa and Fulani ethnic groups in Nigeria and in other parts of West Africa, whose celebrations feature a set of masquerades. Aṣíkò was one of the African tools used by the Aladura Mission (Church of the Lord), led by Apostle Adejobi from Nigeria, in the 1960s as part of a post-independence movement to Africanize church and secular music. That movement resulted in such popular Sierra Leonean bands as Afro-National and Masokoloko singing songs in ethnic languages, like those of the Mende and Limba, and using instruments such as the segure, the Mende name for a rattle and 'nkali,' the Limba name for a log drum (Horton 1984).

'Alikali' is a word of Islamic origin meaning 'town elder,' 'native speaker' or 'interpreter.' The word 'aṣíkò' is both the name of a genre and a medium of performance (music and dance). In the Yorùbá language, 'aṣíkò' means 'time' or an appointed moment with fate; hence the implication of making the best use of time and of life while we have it. It is therefore not surprising that one aṣíkò song is called 'Feso jaiye,' meaning 'take care to enjoy life.'

In the feedback process as described by Collins (ibid.), the earliest 'homecoming' was a Jamaican frame drum-dance music known as goombay (gumbia) introduced by freed Maroon slaves on 1 October 1800 to Freetown, Sierra Leone, where it is still played and called 'gumbe,' and where it laid the basis for aṣíkò (Horton 1999, 231). The smallest of the aṣíkò drums, known as baba, was similar to Afro-Brazilian samba drums, especially the caixa, whose bright, loud sound enables it to provide driving rhythms. Structurally, however, the baba was octagonal in shape, while the caixa was cylindrical like the Western snare drum.

Music and Lyrics

The instrumental ensemble provides accompaniment for the different masqueraders and is comprised of four drums (see Horton 1979, 166): the bel and marine, which alternate beats to provide the timeline; the rollin, which embellishes the timeline; and the baba, which functions as the master drum. All drums in the ensemble are octagonal in shape. The bel and marine are the largest; the baba is roughly two-thirds of the size of the bel and marine and the rollin is the smallest. Each drum is made of cowhide (ibid., 162). The traditional drums used in Sierra Leone usually have skins made either from sheep, goat, cow, deer, buffalo or leopard. Hence the tabule, used by the Muslims in the call to prayer, the sangbai talking drum of the Mende and the aṣíkò and gumbe drums are all made of cowhide (ibid., 162).

Some aṣíkò songs use Yorùbá lyrics and others have Krio lyrics. Examples of Yorùbá lyrics include 'Feso jaiye' (mentioned earlier) and 'Mo'n lo, mo'n lo' (roughly, 'I am going'). Krio lyrics include 'Mi ko yu ti sie' (roughly, 'whatever happens I'll still survive') and 'Rain kam san kam raray man go beht' (roughly, 'whatever happens, a vagabond will still find something to eat') (Horton 1979, 61).

The Dance and Masquerade Performance in Alikali

Participants celebrate their worship of ancestral spirits with masquerades (masked devils of different sizes and ranks). The smallest masqueraders are known as 'kekere.' They wear jump suits with frills and perform opening dances to the rhythm of the drummers, combining gymnastics with some elements of street dance, dancing on their heads and turning somersaults as a climax of their dance. Dancers in the next category (the Dance of the Fairy [Mama Queen]) wear headpieces and masks of female figures, and in the dance depict the elder women, who must be respected. These dancers are more graceful and portray the 'queen' who, together with the chief (king) of the society, has the exclusive right to use horse tails (*iwukere*). The dancers hold and move their *iwukere* in rhythm gracefully to the left and to the right, and, from time to time, they 'kpejor' by making gentle stooping steps and waving their horse tails to right and left. The third group of masqueraders is the senior elders of society, called 'old Papa.' They wear masks depicting themselves as old men who don't have the energy for lively dances, and who move around the crowd making jokes to entertain and dance in the manner of young men wearing masks of old men. Carrying a supporting cane in imitation of the way old people dance, these dancers also sing humorous songs that cause the young children to clap their hands in rhythm to the music, shouting 'Oli papa, oli papa' (meaning roughly 'Old man, old man dance for us'), to which the old man masqueraders respond with comical gestures.

For the dance, the *bel* and *marine* begin by alternating single beats in 4/4 meter. Next, they are joined by the *rollin*, which fills in the alternating beats of the *bel* and *marine* with rolls, beaten with a pair of drumsticks. Then the song leader introduces a song (usually short in length) and a chorus of non-masqueraders joins in. The song is repeated several times to get the performance moving. When the rhythm is well established, the *baba* master drum comes in, played with bare hands in a variety of complementary patterns to enliven the flow of the music. At this point the masqueraders are excited and ready to perform, from the junior dancer to the most senior. The 'Agba' (roughly meaning the leader of the society) usually functions as the song leader.

Diffusion

Both *gumbe* and its spin-offs, *maringa* and *asikó*, were later partially absorbed into highlife from Ghana and Eastern Nigeria. The *asikó* drum was also incorporated into Yorùbá *jùjú* music and used at peak moments in the *jùjú* music of I.K. Dairo, as well as pan-West African palmwine music styles (Waterman 1990). In fact, *gumbe* and *asikó* subsequently spread from Sierra Leone to many West and Central African countries (Mali, Côte d'Ivoire, Ghana, Nigeria, Gabon, Congo, Cameroon and Fernando Po), creating an important musical building block for various twentieth-century African popular and neo-traditional music styles such as *maringa, Milo jazz*, highlife, *jùjú, gube, gome, le gombe, simpa* and *gahu* (Horton 1999, 231).

Asíkò in Nigeria

In Nigeria, *asíkò* is the Christian counterpart of the Islamic recreational praise music known as *sákárà*. How exactly the process described above – in which African traditions that intermingled in the Caribbean and Brazil and were readapted in coastal West Africa – resulted in Nigerian *asíkò* is difficult to pin down with precision. Whereas, as noted earlier, in Sierra Leone it existed as Muslim recreational practice, in Nigeria, as Waterman notes (1990, 41), *asíkò* took shape in the early twentieth century as a Yorùbá Christian practice, with a dance imported from Sierra Leone. In keeping with the word's association in Yorùbá with making the most of one's time on earth, in Nigerian Yorùbá cultural centers such as Ibadan and Abeokuta, *asíkò* was commonly performed during the 1920s at weddings, wakes, church socials and mission schools. The music incorporated influences from older local Yorùbá forms, but it was essentially a new cultural expression, reflecting the hybridizing realities of the colonial era, when Africanized Christian churches were taking hold in much of Nigeria. Waterman stresses that *asíkò* was 'modernized African music' (1990, 43), as opposed to 'Africanized Western music,' such as the brass band traditions that grew up around the same time. *Asíkò* persisted in Christian and secular settings into the Independence era of the 1960s, though it is not widely performed in Nigeria today.

Initially, *asíkò* was linked to the emergence of syncretic religion in Yorùbáland, such as Cherubim and Seraphim (1925) and Christ Apostolic Church (1931). These were independent entities overseen by charismatic, visionary prophets who relied also on pre-Christian practices such as spells and curses. Meanwhile, mainstream African churches used *asíkò* songs to promote messages of racial equality and Christian faith couched in Yorùbá melody, rhythm and language (Waterman 1990, 42). Here it is significant that *asíkò* groups used frame drums rather than *bàtá* or other drums associated with 'pagan' religious practice.

Generally faster than sákárà, *asíkò* was played with only frame drums and metal or bottle percussion, sometimes a carpenter's saw. A 1937 description speaks of five drummers, and two pairs of dancers – two men, two women, with the drummers singing as a chorus in call-and-response format. The *asíkò* dance was mostly practiced by Christian immigrant families, many from Sierra Leone, but some also, notably, from Brazil. There is a resemblance between the *asíkò* frame drums and those used in Brazilian *samba* of the era. Some elders even referred to *asíkò* as 'samba.' An account of male-female couples dancing, with partners chosen by the wave of a handkerchief, also suggests a practice imported from Brazil (Waterman 1990, 39). The fact that the audience did not join in the singing was taken as a sign of European influence, where the separation between performer and audience – an un-African concept – had been introduced.

The lyrics in *asíkò* songs, sung in Yorùbá and Pidgin English, draw upon Christian hymns, urban slang and Yorùbá proverbs, apparently with the goal of easing listeners into emerging Christian churches. The song 'Sáwá Sáwá' condemned prostitution with playful humor. Some songs implicitly urged listeners to reject the *orishas* (deities) central to Yorùbá religion. Others simply commemorated social events, large and small, from the landing of the first airplane in Lagos in 1928 to a tenant brandishing a machete at his demanding landlord.

Bibliography

Collins, E. John. 1985. *Music Makers of West Africa*. Washington, DC: Three Continents Press.

Horton, Christian Dowu. 1979. *Indigenous Music of Sierra Leone: An Analysis of Resources and Educational Implications*. Unpublished Ph.D. dissertation, University of California, Los Angeles.

Horton, Christian Dowu, 1984. 'Popular Bands of Sierra Leone, 1920 to the Present.' *The Black Perspective of Music* 12(2): 183–92.

Horton, Christian Dowu. 1992. 'Fela Anikulapo Kuti Protest Songs: Zombi and Beast of No Nation.' Case study presented at Society for Ethnomusicology Regional Conference, California State University, Dominguez Hills.

Horton, Christian Dowu Jayeola, 1999. 'The Role of the Gumbe in Popular Music and Dance Styles in Sierra Leone.' In *Turn up the Volume! A Celebration of African Music*, ed. Jacqueline Cogdell DjeDje. Los Angeles: UCLA Fowler Museum of Cultural History, 230–5.

Jackson, Rachel. 2012. 'The Trans-Atlantic Journey of Gumbé: Where and How Has It Survived?' *Journal of International Library of African Music* 9(2): 128–53

Stapleton, Chris, and May, Chris. 1987. *African All-Stars: The Pop Music of a Continent*. London and New York: Quartet Books.

Waterman, Christopher. 1990. *Jùjú: A Social History and Ethnography of an African Popular Music*. Chicago: University of Chicago Press.

Discography

Calender, Ebenezer. 'Fire, Fire, Fire'/'Mi ko yu ti si.' Decca WA 2502. *Late 1940s/ early 1950s*: Sierra Leone. Online at: http://sounds.bl.uk/World-and-traditional-music/Decca-West-African-recordings/025M-1CS0043709XX-0100V0 (accessed 19 October 2017).

Donkor, Eddie. *Asíkò Darling*. Melody Sound. *2012*: Ghana.

BANNING EYRE (INTRODUCTION AND NIGERIA) AND
CHRISTIAN 'DOWU JAYEOLA HORTON (SIERRA LEONE)

Azmari Music

The term *azmari* has long identified the wandering minstrel–musicians of the area that became present-day Ethiopia. The *azmari* play and sing almost entirely pentatonic music, using instruments that lend themselves to the performers' traditionally itinerate existence, such as fiddles (e.g., the *masenko*) and lyres (e.g., the *krar*). Historically occupying a low social position in the hierarchy of Ethiopian culture, they were nonetheless respected for fulfilling vital social roles, acting as oral historians, critiquing power structures and so on. Although the social context has been altered since the overthrow of the socialist dictatorship in 1991, with greater political democratization and the dissemination of technologies from radio to MP3, contemporary *azmari* continue to fulfill similar social functions.

Azmari are in many ways similar to the *griots* or *jeli* of western sub-Saharan Africa. Musical performance, intimate knowledge of a specific set of instruments and mastery of improvisation are all a constituent part of their existence. Both function as oral historians and both, although occupying lower rungs on the social ladder, have paradoxically been freer to criticize political and religious authority when compared to their fellow citizens. *Jeli* and *azmari* musics are easily distinguished from each other, as the former uses chordophones such as the *kora*, which has 21 strings rather than the *krar*'s five, thus offering more notes and spanning a wider range of pitches. Also, the singing style of the *azmari* typically includes more prominent vibrato than that of the *jeli*. Unlike the *jeli*, the *azmari* are not identified as such by being part of a caste system. Additionally, the *azmari* have traditionally been itinerate, making a living by wandering around and playing at *tej bets* (honey wine drinking houses), parties and festivals, and even accompanying noblemen during a journey to liven up their travels.

With increasing modernization and infrastructure tying populations more permanently to one location, and emerging technologies carrying music faster and farther than any *azmari* travel, a new route was taken by *azmari* to find a place where their services could be utilized. *Azmaribets* (literally *azmari* houses, performance venues with a nightclub atmosphere in which *azmari* are the focal point of entertainment) began forming in Addis Ababa in the early twentieth century. As the *azmari* changed from being itinerate musicians to being settled, the money now came from setting up their own cabaret-style businesses. These *azmaribets* have proliferated since the fall of the Derg, the socialist regime that ruled Ethiopia from 1974 to 1991. During the Derg period, nightlife such as the *azmaribets* was brought to a halt by curfews. In a culture where the preeminent musical role in a song is given to melody because it is the carrier of the poetry and lyrics that are the most important element overall, government censorship essentially stamped out all possibilities of free and unfettered musical performance.

Since the lifting of the curfew after the overthrow of the Derg in 1991, the *azmari* have created a new musical genre called *bolel*, literally meaning 'car exhaust fumes,' a reference to one of the most ubiquitous aspects of urban life in the capital city. Musically, this style often uses much that is traditional (i.e., instrumentation, song structures, poetry). However, in terms of itineracy *bolel* has broken with tradition, as *azmari* have found it worth their while financially to perform in various entertainment establishments on a regular basis, becoming in many places something akin to the 'house-band.' *Azmari* music includes *krar*, *masenko* and *kebero* (Ethiopian harp, fiddle and drums). Pentatonic scales are used. Voice is more important than instruments, because, of all the ways to judge the skill of an *azmari*, it is their facility with poetry that is of greatest importance. Throughout the Horn of Africa, especially in Oromo and Somali cultures, poetry is one of the most important art forms. This is perhaps unsurprising in areas with historically nomadic people, who avoid production of cultural artifacts that are difficult to transport. Vocal music is easily transportable, and skill is judged by various abilities such as memorization, improvisation and the ability to compose texts with many layers of possible meaning and interpretation. Improvisation, sarcasm, codes and double meaning are what make it possible for an *azmari* to say almost anything. This double meaning is called *sem-ena-wreg*, literally 'wax and gold.' What is presented as an outer layer, the wax, contains a gold core that one can only see if one knows how to look for it.

As with many traditional performance practices, those of the *azmari* are an important cultural symbol for many Ethiopians, despite the fact that the conditions in which they have historically operated have changed or disappeared. Since many are no longer itinerate, it has become difficult to distinguish them from any group of trained musicians. However, the *azmari*'s facility with extemporized poetry and verse seems to set them apart in the minds of many Ethiopians, and is often their defining performance practice. That ability is so highly valued throughout Ethiopia that it seems unlikely to diminish in importance, even if urban encroachment and the adoption of new instrumentation changes the social and musical contexts in which it operates.

Bibliography

Falceto, Francis. 1998. Liner notes for 'Tetchawet!' from *Tetchawet! Urban Azmaris of the 90's*. Buda Musique/Distribution Melodie 82952-2 DK016. Vincennes, France.

Kebede, Ashenafi. 1976. 'Zemenawi Muzika: Modern Trends in Traditional Secular Music of Ethiopia.' *The Black Perspective in Music* 4(3): 289–301.

Kebede, Ashenafi. 1977. *Secular Verse and Poetry in Ethiopia*. International Institute for African Music.

Discography

Ethiopiques 2: Tetchawet! Urban Azmaris of the 90's. Buda Musique/Distribution Melodie 82952-2 DK016. *1998*: France.

Ethiopiques 27: Azmari Tessema Eshete. Buda Musique/Distribution France Socadisc 860192-SC868. *2010*: France.

The Music of Ethiopia: Azmari Music of the Amharas (recordings and notes by Ashenafi Kebede). Anthology AST-6000. *1967*: USA.

SHAWN MOLLENHAUER

Azonto

Azonto is a popular dance-oriented genre that originated at the turn of first decade of the twenty-first century among the young people of Ghana. The genre is characterized by a digitally layered electronic sound fused with rhythmic inflections from indigenous Ga *kpanlogo*, a neo-traditional dance style first performed by the Ga, most of whom live in and around Ghana's capital city, Accra, but subsequently performed throughout the country. Jesse Weaver Shipley has expanded this description in noting that *azonto* 'is a subgenre which is characterized by digital beats, lyrical references, styles of dress and dance moves that are shared across a variety of locales' (2013, 371). *Azonto* employs many synthesizers and is arranged in a verse–chorus format within a major or minor tonal framework but with its most popular chordal progressions occurring in minor keys. The sound of *azonto* has been created largely to facilitate dancing. As a result, musicians have focused more on layering percussive idioms than on the harmonic nuances of these idioms. The themes of *azonto* songs are drawn largely from the daily struggles of young people in Accra and are sung mainly in Akan, although there are instances in which other local languages such as Ga are employed. While these songs are sung in Ghanaian languages, English nonetheless features predominantly in most of the songs. The use of English could be attributed to the fact that principal progenitors of *azonto* were young men and women who had experienced a high school or university education.

Origins and Terminology

Azonto therefore owes its development to the dance craze that emerged in the streets of some of the coastal towns neighboring Accra in Ga communities such as Jamestown, Bukom, Chorkor and Tema. There has been relatively high unemployment within these communities among young people, who as a consequence have spent most of their time learning to dance and practicing other forms of culture (Ofosu and Dei 2013). For these young people, this activity has represented a cathartic release, a veiled expression of freedom in the face of economic hardships (Brefo 2013). It is within this sociocultural context that *azonto* emerged. The unique character of the dance could be said to hinge on the amalgamation of different idioms from other indigenous dances performed largely by the Ga people.

Ever since *azonto* began to develop there has been controversy as to who was its first exponent. Whereas one school of thought attributes its creation to musicians such as Sarkodie, other musicians such as Gasmilla have claimed to be the originator. Continuing discussion has, however, demonstrated that *azonto* arose as a communal creation resulting in a music whose significance has propelled it to international prominence. Brefo acknowledges and situates *azonto* and *kpanlogo* alongside each other within the Ga communities and proposes that although its precursor 'strictly remained in the cultural ownership of the Ga people,' *azonto* moved on to assume a national character (2013). Akrong, on the other hand, notes that *azonto* embraces the nuances and essence of traditional music and dance expressed within a contemporary context (2012, 70). These references to indigenous creative resources solidify the communal ethos of *azonto*. Although there is debate on the specific origins of the dance, scholars and cultural critics in Ghana do on the whole agree that many of the elements that comprise the dance are in the main subtle details derived from such indigenous dance forms as *kpanlogo, apaa* and *gome* as well as more contemporary forms such as *gbeohe, korgon, kpe* and *awukye* (Ofosu and Dei 2013). For instance, examining the nuances of *azonto* performances in church, Thompson identifies some salient features of *kpanlogo*, which goes to support the general theses on borrowings in *azonto* as espoused by Ofosu and Dei (Thompson 2016, 414).

The term 'azonto' is ambiguous in meaning. Tracing its meanings requires understanding some of the jargon commonly used by senior high school students. 'Azonto' usually refers to a 'loose lifestyle,' and is often uttered in reference to promiscuous women. However, there are instances in which young men have been addressed as 'azonto boys.' The term gained popularity when it became associated with the music of some hiplife musicians. These musicians capitalized on the developing dance form to write songs that suited its performance, songs such as 'African Girls' by Castro, featuring Asamoah Gyan, 'U Go Kill Me' by Sarkodie, featuring E.L., 'Aboodatoi' by Gasmilla, 'Azonto' by Fuse ODG, featuring Itz Tiffany and 'Lapaz Toyota' by Guru.

Performance Practices and Characteristics

Since *azonto* is an electronic style of music, a typical performance will involve a disc jockey playing either a sound track or the original recording of the song with the artist miming or, in certain cases, engaging in a voice over on stage. As part of their performance these musicians will also include choreographed versions of the dance forms that they have taken the time to learn. Like many of its antecedents, *azonto* engages in a set of synchronized hand and foot movements that involve bending the knees slightly as well as moving the hips in a stylized manner to mimic such everyday activities as bathing, washing, boxing and driving. The improvisatory nature of the dance allows the context of performance to determine which set of movements a dancer will rely on.

Azonto melodies are couched mostly in minor scales with some occasionally occurring in major scales. The melodies are nonetheless usually bright and cheerful with simple catchphrases known as 'punch lines.' Because the music also focuses on encouraging people to dance, it tends to have very simple lyrics that blend rapping and singing. Keyboards and sometimes guitars provide the principal harmonies, resulting in a 'chunking' feeling. *Azonto* essentially employs primary chords that revolve around two progressions: vi – V (or *vice versa*) as, for example, in Nii Funny's 'Broken Heart'; or I – V (or *vice versa*) as, for instance, in Sarkodie's 'Down on One,' featuring Fuse ODG. There are some rare occasions in which a I – IV – V progression occurs, as, for example, in the harmonic progression for Fuse ODG's 'Azonto.' This song is constructed around a looping I – IV – V progression similar to that found in Ghanaian highlife music.

International Presence

Two main reasons can be identified for *azonto* gaining international prominence, a development which resulted in the genre becoming attractive to other age demographics. First, during the 2010 FIFA World Cup soccer tournament in South Africa, Ghana's Black Stars, the national soccer team, engaged in an *azonto* dance led by Asamoah Gyan every time a goal was scored. Gyan had featured on Castro's 'African Girls' and is seen performing the dance in the song's video. The second reason is related to the YouTube video of Fuse ODG's song 'Azonto.' In this video, Fuse is seen learning and teaching the dance in the streets of London, as suggested in the lyrics. This video went viral, being viewed about 27 million times and resulted in prominent figures attempting the dance. Ameyaw Debrah (2012) reports that at a charity event in memory of his mother, Princess Diana, Prince William was seen engaging in some *azonto* dance routines with Ghanaian-born Vanessa Boateng. In addition, US comedian Kevin Hart is seen moving to the steps of the dance while singing Fuse ODG's song, 'Azonto,' on a YouTube video made from the radio program Choice Breakfast.

Conclusion

Azonto first emerged as a form of dance created on the part of young Ghanaians as a means of survival in communities with high rates of unemployment. Its evolution from a dance form to a style of music speaks to the way in which young Ghanaians continually find creative avenues of expression. As with hiplife or highlife, these young people have continued to push the boundaries of popular culture in Ghana. The soundscape in the late 2010s demanded something new as hiplife, a progenitor of *azonto*, was experiencing a decline. The advent of *azonto* represented a new development in popular culture, the spread of this distinctive form of music being aided considerably by the advent of the Internet. Ghanaian diasporas, which had yearned for a vehicle of identity or a symbol of home, could now easily access a music and dance they could celebrate. As Shipley (2013, 378) points out, 'azonto celebrates self-actualization, continuous upward and outward mobility. It is a style of cosmopolitan self-making that allows practitioners to align a range of specifically Ghanaian attachments while ultimately eluding attachment itself.'

Bibliography

Akrong, Isaac R. N. K. 2012. *Hip Life Music: Re-defining Ghanaian Culture (1990–2012)*. Unpublished Ph.D. dissertation, York University, Toronto.

Anangfio, Ebenezer. 2013. 'Sarkodie Did Not Create Azonto.' *GhanaWeb*, 9 September. Online at: https://www.ghanaweb.com/GhanaHomePage/entertainment/Sarkodie-did-not-create-Azonto-285203 (accessed 12 January 2018).

Brefo, Henry. 2013. 'Azonto – A Dance of Defiance.' *What's On Africa*, 21 November. Online at: http://whatsonafrica.org/azonto-a-dance-of-defiance/ (accessed 10 January 2018).

Collins, John. 1992. *West African Pop Roots*. Philadelphia, PA: Temple University Press.

Debrah, Ameyaw. 2012. 'Prince William Dances Azonto with Kate at Diana's Homeless Charity.' *AmeyawDebrah.com*, 10 January. Online at: https://ameyawdebrah.com/prince-williams-azonto-with-kate-at-dianas-homeless-charity/ (accessed 15 May 2018).

Ofosu, Terry Bright K., and Dei, Tabitha. 2013. 'The Azonto Dance – A Ghanaian New Creation: Exploring New Boundaries of Popular Dance Forms.' *African Performance Review* 7(1): 45–64.

Owusu, Atta Stephen. 2012. 'Azonto – The New Music and Dance Craze in Ghana.' *ModernGhana*, 4 February. Online at: https://www.modernghana.com/news/376302/azonto-the-new-music-and-dance-craze-in-ghana.html (accessed 17 May 2018)

Owusu-Bediako, Victor. 2016. 'Ghana: Azonto Is Dead – Music Producer.' *allAfrica*, 28 September. Online at: http://allafrica.com/stories/201609290147.html (accessed 10 January 2018).

Shipley, Jesse Weaver. 2013. 'Transnational Circulation and Digital Fatigue in Ghana's Azonto Dance Craze.' *American Ethnologist* 40(2): 362–81.

Thompson, Joan. 2016. 'Azonto and the Church: The Place of Dance in Worship.' In *The Bible, Cultural Identity, and Missions*, eds. Daniel Berchie, Daniel Kwame Bediako and Dziedzorm Reuben Asafo. Newcastle-upon-Tyne: Cambridge Scholars Publishing, 409–34.

Yankah, Kwesi. 1995. *Speaking for the Chief: Okyeame and the Politics of Akan Royal Oratory*. Bloomington: Indiana University Press.

Discographical References

Castro, featuring Asamoah Gyan. 'African Girls.' Online at: http://www.youtube.com/watch?v=87MSNRfDKEQ (accessed 13 April 2018).

Fuse ODG. 'Azonto.' 3beat (2). *N.d.*: UK. Online at: https://www.youtube.com/watch?v=VetNdbu-ZNc (accessed 8 May 2018).

Gasmilla. 'Aboodatoi.' Online at: https://www.youtube.com/watch?v=wQ6npJdH24Q (accessed 12 January 2018).

Guru. 'Lapaz Toyota.' Online at: https://www.youtube.com/watch?v=vIp8ipJ3sYI (accessed 10 January 2018).

Nii Funny. 'Broken Heart.' Online at: https://www.youtube.com/watch?v=9qvNW1w00OM (accessed 13 April 2018).

Sarkodie, featuring Fuse ODG. 'Down on One.' Online at: https://www.youtube.com/watch?v=uBH5W6nSUCo (accessed 13 April 2018).

Sarkodie, featuring E.L. 'U Go Kill Me.' Online at: https://www.youtube.com/watch?v=QTJ3bwDIyWc (accessed 10 January 2018).

YouTube

Kevin Hart does the Azonto on Choice Breakfast. https://www.youtube.com/watch?v=2Yu21YQRYoA (accessed 17 May 2018).

ERIC SUNU DOE

Ba Gasy

'Ba gasy' is a term primarily, but not exclusively, associated with the repertoire of Malagasy musical plays, frequently referred to as 'Malagasy operetta.' These plays emerged in Antananarivo, the capital of Madagascar, in the first half of the twentieth century. 'Ba' derives from the French verb 'battre' (la mesure) (to beat [time]), 'gasy' being an abbreviation of 'Malagasy' (an adjective relating to Madagascar or its inhabitants). *Ba gasy* therefore denotes a specific Malagasy rhythm as opposed to the rhythms of music introduced by Europeans.

In *ba gasy*, influences from French musical theater, which had been present in Madagascar since the end of the nineteenth century, were assimilated and blended with elements of the performances of *mpilalao* troupes which perform at *famadihana* (reburials), circumcisions and other traditional celebrations. These troupes combined in their plays music, dance, dialogue and declamatory speech. After the establishment of a French protectorate in 1895, theatrical companies from France regularly appeared in Madagascar. Their programs included comedies, operettas and operas. The interest of the Malagasy public was great, and this encouraged the formation of local theatrical troupes. As early as the first years of the twentieth-century Malagasy adaptations of French plays were staged, subsequently followed by original Malagasy plays written by Malagasy writers and composers and performed by Malagasy actors. A 'malgachization' of the genre with regard to its form and content took place from the 1920s onwards.

The best-known companies were Antananarivo Teatra, Kintana Telonohorefy, Ny Tropy Analamanga and Troupe Jeannette, with the latter being named after the outstanding singer Marie Jeanne Jeannette (1903–81). Also included in this number was Troupe Théâtrale Malgache, which participated in the *Exposition coloniale internationale* (International Colonial Exposition) in Paris in 1931. Some of these troupes undertook tours throughout Madagascar in addition to their regular appearances in Antananarivo. The most important composers were Andrianary Ratianarivo (1895–1949), who wrote some 500 songs for the theater, Justin Rajoro (1889–1949), Naka Rabemanantsoa (1892–1943), Therack (1899–1976) and Rasamy Gitara (1899–1970).

As far as form is concerned, these operettas had one to three acts and consisted of a sequence of dialogues and songs. Very often, the contents were amusing or tragic stories about thwarted love between two young people from different castes. These stories were ironic and humorous, were loaded with proverbs and generally displayed a tendency to moralize.

Many of the Malagasy songs composed for the theater enjoyed great popularity, not least thanks to the record industry and the radio. Beginning in 1929 numerous solos, duets, trios and choral pieces were released on shellac records by leading companies such as Odeon, Columbia, Decca and Polydor.

Apart from these *hira teatraly* (songs of the theater), the record industry released many more songs by female and male stars. These songs were attributable to the *ba gasy* repertoire because of their musical structure. Among the most famous composers of such songs of the late shellac period (the 1950s) were Fredy Raolifahanana, Naly Rakotofiringa, Noelson Lalao, Tseheno, Ranaivo Ranarivelo, Dadapaoly, Nest, Ramarokoto, Paul Ratianarivo and Barijaona. Favorite interpreters were Ossy, Ludger Andrianjaka, Jeanne Naly, Salomon, Romule, Gabhy and others.

Musical Characteristics

The term 'ba gasy' refers to music evidencing several musical features of which rhythm is the most significant. 12/8 meter is prevalent, but without regular binary or ternary subdivisions. Instead, the rhythm follows closely the meter of the verses. This results in irregular and asymmetric pulse groupings. A bipartite structure of phrases consisting of 7+5 beats is, however, frequent. The close alliance of language and music becomes particularly apparent in the accentuations of both. Since the difference between stressed and unstressed syllables is rather significant in the Malagasy language, accents are distinguished musically, notably with different note values (for example: unstressed syllables: sixteenth notes; stressed syllables: eight notes; and so on).

Songs are performed by a four-part mixed chorus, a duet, a trio or a solo singer; the chorus can alternate with solo passages. Short passages by the bass singers which interconnect with the phrases of the choir are typical. Tonality and harmony based on tonic, dominant and subdominant chords exhibit a strong European influence; nearly the whole *ba gasy* repertoire uses the major scale. A complex tripartite form including strophic elements is most common. The middle part of a song is frequently in the dominant key, the first and third parts in the tonic.

Ba gasy is a declamatory art in which it is most important that messages are well heard and understood. Singing is therefore performed in a didactic and declamatory manner accompanied by expressive gestures. Loud volume throughout a piece is a characteristic element. A very special vocal technique is *angola*, the undulating singing style of women in a high register embellished with a great deal of ornamentation. The percussive staccato-like singing of bass singers contrasts with the fluid melodic lines performed by sopranos.

The instruments used to accompany *ba gasy* songs are primarily the piano, which is played in a markedly percussive way and, more rarely, the guitar and the accordion. The instrumental accompaniment consists mainly of the doubling of the sung melodic lines, an introduction and short motifs that connect the sung parts.

Contemporary *Ba Gasy*

Many *ba gasy* songs, referred to as *kalon'ny fahiny* (songs of old times), *hira tranainy* (old songs) or *hira taloha* (songs of the past), have continued to be popular in Madagascar, especially with the older generation. This is in part due to the ambitious efforts of a number of aficionados who have successfully devoted their artistic activities to preserving and reviving this musical heritage. In 1965 the *Association Théâtrale et Artistique des Universitaires de Madagascar* (the Theatrical and Artistic Association of Malagasy University Scholars: ATAUM) was founded by students. An outcome of their activities was the foundation of Solika, one of the most acclaimed groups in this musical style. Other well-known *ba gasy* ensembles have been R'Imbosa, Angola Itokiana, Aro Kanton'ny Fahiny, Diarin'ny Kintana, Ny Sakelidalana and – still going strong in the late 2010s – Troupe Jeannette. Sehatra ba gasy, an association promoting the *ba gasy* heritage, is made up of about 20 groups that perform in concerts and organize workshops. The special way of playing *ba gasy* on the piano (*piano ba gasy*) and on the guitar (*gitara ba gasy*) is taught in several places, for example, the *Cercle Germano-Malagasy* (German-Malagasy Circle), the *Alliance française* (French Alliance), and the *Centre national d'études musicales* (National Center of Musical Studies).

Bibliography

Dez, Jacques. 1964. 'Lexique des mots européens malgachisés' [Lexicon of Malagasy Words of European Origin]. *Annales de l'Université de Madagascar, Série Lettres et Sciences Humaines* 3: 63–86.

Gérard, Albert. 1973. 'The Birth of Theatre in Madagascar.' *Educational Theatre Journal* 25(3) (October): 362–5.

Rabenasolo, Imboasalamaniaina, et al. 2015. *Tiona Ba Gasy. Sol-fa sy sorapeo, Boky voalohany* [Ba Gasy Tunes, Solfa (Notation) and Staff (Notation): the First Volume]. Antananarivo: Self-published.

Rakotomalala, Mireille Mialy. 2003. *Madagascar – La musique dans l'histoire* [Madagascar – Music in History]. Fontenay-sous-Bois: Anako Editions.

Rambeloson-Rapiera, Jeannine, et al. 2001. 'Madagascar.' In *The World Encyclopedia of Contemporary Theatre, Volume 3, Africa*, eds. Don Rubin et al. 2nd ed. London: Routledge, 176–81.

Discography

Madagascar: Musiques de la côte et des hauts plateaux [Music of the Coast and the Tablelands], 1929–1931. (2 CDs.) Frémeaux & Associés FA 058. *1997*: France.

The Music of Madagascar. Classic Traditional Recordings of the 1930s. (CD.) Yazoo 7003. *1995*: USA.

AUGUST SCHMIDHOFER

Baikoko

Baikoko is a dance and music genre that took Tanzania by storm in the 2010s. Its origins lie with the Digo ethnic group and an exclusive, women-only dance called *ngoma ya ndani* that was part of girls' coming-of-age ceremonies. *Baikoko* developed into one of the most favored night entertainment forms around Dar es Salaam, Tanzania's principal city, performed either in small bars, at weddings or as an added attraction for modern *taarab* club nights.

Baikoko originated as youth music in the Digo villages around the town of Tanga, a seaport near Tanzania's northern border with Kenya, in the early 1990s. There, it evolved out of a number of older Digo *ngoma* genres including *gita*, *chera* and *mdindiko*. *Baikoko* grew directly out of the latter, from which it inherited the long *msondo* drum, the shakers and the *mabuyu*, a type of trumpet originally made from gourds. To the original drum lineup *baikoko* added an array of *dogole* – three bass-range drums – that guide the dancers. The sensual, erotic dance style is directly linked to *ngoma ya ndani*, formerly only practiced 'inside' (as the name suggests), so as not to be visible to men. *Ngoma ya ndani* is known among all the Mijikenda people (along the Kenya coast) from the Bajuni to the Digo. Elsewhere on the coast and in Zanzibar it can be likened to *msondo* or *unyago*, formerly a rite of passage of girls into adulthood.

Baikoko was first seen in the Kisosora area of Tanga in the late 1990s, performed by a group called Bazoka. In town, the instrumentation changed and was adapted to materials available in the city. Thus the drums are made from plastic drainage pipes of varying sizes, the *maboya* from buoys otherwise used to guide ships in their approach to the harbor, the pipes used to blow into the *maboya* also of plastic, and the rattles from empty tins. It has been suggested that the name *baikoko* derives from the fact that it was first seen in the Kisosora area – in the dark, close to the sea and the *mikoko* (mangrove forests). However, the name actually derives from the final song of *mdindiko* performances: *koko* is Digo for 'the kernel of a fruit,' the last thing to be eaten, and *bai* translates as 'the end' or 'the final thing.'

The repertoire of *baikoko* groups is a mixture of songs in the Digo and Swahili languages. The songs in Digo are described as being 'traditional,' which is borne out by the fact that all groups sing and play them without claiming them as their own compositions. The Swahili songs in the repertoire are more recent and sections are often improvised on the spot to suit the occasion or audience. Musically, *baikoko* is characterized by an intricate interplay of the percussionists and the *maboya* horns (of two different sizes/pitches), the latter enhancing the rhythm through notes played in hocketing fashion. The singer floats freely on top, either giving cues for particular songs, improvising or urging on the dancers. The hour-long sets typically start *a cappella* and develop from a slow groove that accelerates as the different rhythmic parts work into each other. The dancers' moves build relationships with individual rhythmic parts, all culminating in patterns used by the lead drummer to guide a dancer's hips, and where they precisely 'cut' it in perfect synchronization.

The group that introduced *baikoko* into Dar es Salaam nightlife in 2009 was Dogo Dogo Stars Baikoko, led by singer Maya (Juma Hussein). *Baikoko* rapidly achieved huge popular success and the band soon had more gigs than available days of the week. The success created its own problems and before long the group started to split up into many branches as individual members were lured away to launch their own groups. Thus, by the mid-2010s *baikoko* was performed by many groups in Dar es Salaam and had gained a following in Zanzibar and the Kenyan city of Mombasa as well.

Possibly related to its origins in *ngoma ya ndani*, the public image of *baikoko* is one of dubious quality, often based on hearsay. Performance contexts have positioned *baikoko* in circumstances beyond the artists' control; in addition to bars, one of the major contexts for *baikoko* is as part of coastal wedding celebrations, either as an added live music attraction to *rusha roho* – a disco featuring modern *taarab* recordings – or in an event called 'kitchen party.' The latter takes part inside and may be likened to a hen party, with dancing and the drinking of a great deal of alcohol. The strict women-only image facilitates a comparison to *ngoma ya ndani*. Kitchen party events in Dar es Salaam have become notorious for the hiring as *agents provocateurs* of groups of women prepared to dance half-naked and in explicit poses of sexual intercourse, inciting other guests at the celebration to join in. Videos secretly filmed with mobile phones made the round in the city, popularizing the events and the associated dancing and leading to a spread to lower-class areas where, for lack of space, performances take place outside. A new name was also coined for the dance: *kigodoro*, or 'the mattress thing.'

For the general public, *baikoko* has increasingly become associated with the contexts just described. Thus, the majority of video clips tagged with *baikoko* on East African music websites or YouTube actually show dances including *kigodoro* and *ndombolo*, accompanied by various musical forms from modern *taarab* to *soukous* to unrelated local *ngoma*. With new groups pushing into a ready market, *baikoko* practitioners themselves have become confused, and many feel that more and more of the original aesthetic values of the style and its subtleties are in danger of being lost.

Bibliography

Graebner, Werner. 2016. 'Other Flavas from Bongo: Mchiriku-Segere-Baikoko.' In *Mambo Moto Moto: Music in Tanzania Today*, eds. Tiago de Oliveira Pinto and Bernhard Hanneken. Berlin: VWB – Verlag für Wissenschaft und Bildung, 73–94.

YouTube

Kaya Baikoko – Ngoma ya Tanga. https://www.youtube.com/watch?v=I8nggTQhaGw

WERNER GRAEBNER

Bajourou

Bajourou is a genre of music found in the West African nation of Mali. Translated alternately as big string/big tune or mother string/mother tune, it occupies a unique space in Malian culture between tradition and modernity, and this is reflected in the genre's instrumentation, which often combines traditional instruments like the *kora* (21-stringed harp), *bala* (wooden marimba) and *djelingoni* (traditional lute) with Western instruments like the guitar and drum machine. *Bajourou* has its roots in the centuries-old traditions of the Mandé *jelis* (hereditary musicians/historians). However, it is a modern and less formal rendering of the tradition, with hints of Western harmony and lyrics that deal with personal topics like love rather than focusing exclusively on commemorating historical figures and events. As Lucy Duràn describes it, *bajourou* is an expression of 'the dual identity of many young Malians – caught between urban and rural ways of life, and old and new social values.' (Duràn 1993, 2) With its unique position at the intersection of tradition and modernity and its ubiquity at weddings, baptisms and other social gatherings, *bajourou* is a reflection of Malian society's ongoing reconciliation of a profound traditional culture with the complexities of modernization.

The album generally recognized as the first recorded example of *bajourou* is *Musique de Mali*, Vol. 1 (1972), the debut album of vocalist Fanta Sacko, on which she is accompanied by guitarists Foussenou Diabaté and Mamadou Tounkara. In addition to older traditional pieces, Sacko performs her own piece, 'Jarabi,' which is about the importance of love in marriage. This was and still is a controversial topic in a society where arranged marriages are common. The guitars are played in what has become the typical *bajourou* style, drawing on the heavily ornamented melodies of the *kora* and *djelingoni*. In describing this style, Eric Charry notes the use of 'quick grace notes and trills that explode out of the more leisurely unfolding of the piece' (Charry 2000, 298). Through audacious, personal lyrics and innovative guitar work, Sacko's debut sets the defining characteristics of *bajourou* in place.

In the wake of Fanta Sacko and other female *jeli* vocalists such as Fanta Damba and Sira Mory Diabaté, a new generation of female vocalists came to prominence in the 1980s and 1990s, with Ami Koita, Tata Bambo Kouyaté, and Kandia Kouyaté at the forefront (Charry 2000, 276). This era of *bajourou* was also defined by brilliant guitarists, most notably Bouba Sacko and Modibo Kouyaté (husband of Tata Bambo). Bouba Sacko is held in particularly high esteem by other guitarists, with some saying that during his heyday in the 1980s and 1990s virtually every *jeli* vocalist hired Bouba to play on their albums. More recent guitarists like Aboubacar 'Badian' Diabaté have taken *bajourou* guitar in new, virtuosic directions, but reverence for Bouba Sacko is still ubiquitous among both musicians and listeners.

Djelimady Tounkara, the famous guitarist and leader of the Rail Band, must also be mentioned for his contribution to *bajourou* guitar playing. Although he is known primarily for his work in the context of larger dance orchestras built around bass, drums and horns rather than the smaller *bajourou* ensembles featuring guitar alongside traditional instruments, Tounkara has assimilated a great deal of the melodic language of *bajourou* guitar into his playing. Furthermore, his landmark collaboration with Bouba Sacko and vocalist Lanfia Diabaté entitled *Bajarou: Big String Theory* (1993) shows the ease with which Tounkara moves into a *bajourou* setting. The album stands as a prime example of *bajourou* in its most subtle, stripped-down form.

Bibliography

Charry, Eric. 2000. *Mande Music: Traditional and Modern Music of the Maninka and Mandinka of Western Africa*. Chicago: University of Chicago Press.

Duràn, Lucy. 1993. Liner notes to *Bajarou: Big String Theory*. Ace Records CDORBD 078; Green Linnet, GLCD 4008.

Eyre, Banning. 1993. Unpublished interview with Bouba Sacko.

Eyre, Banning. 2000. *In Griot Time: An American Guitarist in Mali*. Philadelphia: Temple University Press.

Nourrit, Chantal, and Pruitt, Bill. 1978. *Musique traditionelle de l'Afrique noire: Discographie. 1. Mali*. Paris: Centre de documentation Africaine, Radio-France international.

Discographcal References
Bajourou: Big String Theory. Ace Records CDORBD 078. *1993*: UK. (Also issued on Green Linnet, GLCD 4008. 1993: USA.)
Musique du Mali. Vol. 1. Fanta Sacko. Bärenreiter Musicaphon BM 30L 2551. 1972: Germany.

Discography
Coumaré, Koni, with Fotiqui Diabaté. *Folklore Bambara* … Fiesta, 360.059. 197?–?: France.
Diabaté Family of Kela. *An bè kelen/We Are One: Griot Music from Mali*. PAN 2015CD. *1994*: Netherlands.
In Griot Time – String Music from Mali. Compiled by Banning Eyre. Sterns Africa, STCD 1089. *2000*: UK.
Kouyaté, Kandia. *Amary Daou présente Kandia Kouyaté*. Amary Daou AD 001. *1983*: Mali. (Reissued on Oriki Music. ORK 003. *2006*: France.)

Filmography
Bajourou: Music of Mali, dir. Jeremy Marre. 1995. UK. Documentary made by BBC Open University Productions.
Bamako Beat: Music from Mali, dir. and prod. Mark Kidel. 1991. UK. Television documentary made for BBC.
Da Kali: The Pledge to the Art of the Griot, dir. and prod. Lucy Duran. 2015. UK. 80 mins. Documentary produced at the School of Oriental and African Studies, London. (Online at http://www.growingintomusic.co.uk/the-growing-into-music-film.html.)

SAMUEL DICKEY

Band (Uganda)

The use of the term 'band' in the context of Ugandan popular music is a convenience that accommodates a fusion of indigenous and foreign forms of popular music. Although the term refers to an identifiable sound, band is nonetheless an ambiguous and polyrhythmic form of music encompassing elements of *soukouss, zouk, rumba*, dancehall reggae, *bakisimba* and vocal rhythm and blues (R&B). Its development has also been influenced by various North American, Latin American, Caribbean and global genres such as soul, *chachachá*, calypso, jazz and rap. The fusions that followed these encounters were a result of influences drawn from various cover versions of these musics performed by band musicians for audiences in bars, nightclubs and hotels. Musicians, audiences and the media gradually came to recognize and identify this form of music through the way these fusions were performed. Band has been recognized as one of the two broad streams in Ugandan popular music, the other being *kadongo-kamu* music (see separate entry).

The music has its origins in the big band era of the 1950s and 1960s. 1950s band music was characterized more by Latin American influences, while in 1960s band music the influence of Caribbean and other African genres became more prominent. Some of the earliest recordings of band music are from the 1960s and include Bill Mbowa's 'Jane Wange,' Fred Kigozi's 'Mega Jukira,' Charles Sonko's 'Wano Tulimuba' and Fred Masagazi's 'Ekommera.' All these recordings are to be found on the compilation album, *The Kampala Sound – 1960s Ugandan Dance Music*.

The term 'band' itself in reference to this genre arose at the height of its revival in the early 2000s. Previously, band music was referred to by the name of the artist performing the music rather than a particular term that could be applied across the board. Some band musicians were, indeed, solo artists, but they nonetheless used bands in live performance. By contrast, the recording of band music has occurred rather differently, and has not necessarily entailed having a complete band in the studio. Musicians have worked with producers who digitally produce the music. As part of this process, musicians have hired some backup vocalists or have sung the choral sections themselves.

The Vintage Period of Band Music

There are numerous accounts of the origins of band music in Uganda. One of these accounts traces its foundation to the big band period shortly before and immediately after Uganda's independence from the United Kingdom in 1962. During this period bands such as the Top Ten Band, Crazy Gang, the Uganda Kezaala Band, Peterson Mutebi and the Tames, Elly Wamala and the Mascots, Kampala City 6, the Crane Band and the Rwenzori Band were already in existence or were being formed. Some Ugandan musicians such as Charles Sonko were associated with the Equator Sound Band in Nairobi, Kenya, the city from which most band musicians recorded (Isabirye 2004).

In 1975 the Crane Band, which had become the most prominent band, split up. From its ranks sprouted the Afrigo Band. Afrigo has remained the most enduring band in the history of Ugandan popular music. Founding leader and saxophonist Moses Matovu noted (2015) that 'after the split Tony Ssenkebejje, Jeff Sewava, Ssekyanzi, Jessy Gitta and I decided to form Africa Go (Black Power), which later became the Afrigo Band, on August 31, 1975.'

The 1970s and the 1980s were difficult times for band music. On 25 January 1971, Idi Amin Dada, an army officer, staged a military coup and wrested power from President Milton Oboto. Amin presided over a regime during whose tenure the country experienced widespread insecurity. It was therefore risky for musicians to pursue a performing career in the country. Not only were the musicians a potential target for undisciplined soldiers, but also the robberies and murders that took place in broad daylight as well as at night made it difficult to stage concerts. With Amin's expulsion of the merchant Asian class in 1972, the economy declined sharply. Resulting economic hardship made it almost impossible for band musicians to hold concerts or to sell records to people who were struggling to make ends meet.

In due course, many band musicians fled the country for their own safety and to seek out better opportunities. Some of those who went into exile were Philly Lutaaya, Frank Mbalire, Tony Senkebejje and Hope Mukasa. Lutaaya, Mbalire and Mukasa went to Sweden and formed the Savannah Band, while Senkebejje settled in Mombasa, Kenya. Some band musicians nonetheless stayed, and were strategic enough to record songs in praise of Idi Amin. According to Moses Matovu, Idi Amin – surprisingly – treated them quite well until the liberation war to depose him began in 1979. Then, 'all our instruments were looted and we were back to zero!' (Matovu 2011). The period that followed was equally difficult, as Matovu's bandmate Herman Sewanyana (2011) has confirmed.

In the early 1990s Tony Sengo, a member of the Afrigo Band, left and formed the Big Five Band. Along with singer Juliet Ssesanga, they became an alternative to Afrigo. Newfound political stability under President Museveni, who came to power in 1986, provided an environment within which several other bands could develop and thrive. At the same time, exiled musicians began to return home. Bands that came to the fore at this time included the Central Volcano Band, the Waka Waka Band, the Hot Springs Band and the Simbangoma Band (founded by the late legendary guitarist Dede Majoro).

The history of band music in Uganda has been characterized over the years by acrimony between band members over financial matters and personal relationships. Following internal disagreements with his bandmates, Sengo also left the Big Five Band and started the Badindaz Band. A few years later, with Tony Sengo ailing, most of the members of the Badindaz Band joined the newly formed KADS Band. The KADS Band folded in the mid-2000s. Joe Tabula, another member of the Badindaz Band, moved to BK Studios and established himself as one of the leading producers of contemporary band music. Iconic contributors to the growth of band music during this vintage period were Sam Kauma, Fred Kigozi, Moses Matovu, Joanita Kawalya, Rachel Magoola and Jimmy Katumba.

The Contemporary Period of Band Music

The period from 1995 to 2005 witnessed the contemporary revival of band music. During this period, band musicians began to be heavily influenced by Congolese musicians in song structure, costume and dance. These musicians were popular in Uganda at the beginning of the contemporary period.

In 1995 a parallel movement in band music inspired by Jimmy Katumba and the Ebonies began to appear in theaters. Jimmy Katumba was a 1980s theatrical icon. Directors of theatrical plays such as Omugave Ndugwa, Abbey Mukiibi, Kato Lubwama, Charles James Senkubuge, Andrew Benon Kibuuka and Aloysius Matovu Joy Sr began composing songs to enhance scenes in plays. Gradually, such songs took on a life of their own. Some were released as records while musicians such as Fred Maiso, Mariam Ndagire, Sarah Birungi and Kato Lubwama began careers singing this kind of music. Some of the hit records of this era were Fred Maiso's 'Ekimuli Kya Rosa' (1997), Mariam Ndagire's 'Bamugamba' (1998), Sarah Birungi's 'Obulamu Bwa Kisera' (1997) and Ronald Mayinja's 'Clare' and 'Necklace' (1998). In 1997 actor and director Kato Lubwama formed the band Diamond Production. He recruited musicians Ronald Mayinja, Mesach Semakula, Geoffrey Lutaaya, Grace Sekamatte, Haruna Mubiru, Angela Kalule and Immaculate Nabiryo. Following disagreements, some members left to start Eagles Production. Eagles Production included Fred Maiso, Geoffrey Lutaaya, Mesach Semakula, Ronald Mayinja and Grace Sekamatte, and signed other artists such as Sofia Nantongo, Haruna Mubiru, Catherine Kusasira, Irene Namatovu, Stacia Mayanja and Maureen Nantume. The band became the most successful of the contemporary era.

In 1998 Kasiwukira studio, a new production house which focused on band music, was launched. It was owned by the late Eria Sebunya. Sebunya had started out with a cassette distribution store that retained a network all over East Africa. Tim Kizito, a prominent producer among band musicians, became the resident producer at Kasiwukira. In due course he attracted many band musicians to record at Kasiwukira.

Key contributors to the development of contemporary band music have been Mariam Ndagire, Fred Maiso, Travis Kazibwe, Mesach Semakula, Geoffrey Lutaaya, Ronald Mayinja, Kato Lubwama, Catherine Kusasira, Stacia Mayanja, Maureen Nantume and Haruna Mubiru. All these performers have been recognized for their role in successfully promoting the genre.

Beyond the Contemporary Era

In 2013 Haruna Mubiru left Eagles Production to form Kream Production. A year later, Eagles Production was dissolved and the former members created two new bands, Golden Production and Da Nu Eagles. Competition from emerging genres such as Afrobeat, *Luga flow*, *Luga ragga* and *bax ragga* has occasioned changes in the aesthetics and performance of band music. Some of these changes have been in the general sound and structure of the music, while others have been in the costumes worn by band musicians and the videos they produced. Musicians such as Chris Evans, Lytto Boss, Bettina Namukasa, Karitas Kario, Izon T and Carol Natongo have more recently cemented their presence within band music.

Performance, Themes and Language in Band Music

The performance of band music involves a big band format with various instrumentalists and backup vocalists supporting a lead singer. The particular way in which these lineups are used varies from artist to artist. There is also a marked emphasis on stage presentation. And as with many genres of African music, dancing is integral to the performance of band music, with women fulfilling the role of 'dancing queens' and men providing the music.

Since their inception, vintage band music and contemporary band music have mainly explored themes to do with love. For example, most of the songs that emerged from the theaters and the band musicians of the contemporary era have been about romantic relationships and marriage. Occasionally band musicians may sing about politics, tragedy, economic issues and domestic violence. For example, one of the few exceptions to the prevailing trend has been songs from Ronald Mayinja such as 'Tuli ku bunkenke' (Situation Is Tense) and 'Tuwalana nguzi' (We Are Against Corruption). However, the theme of love has dominated the lyrics of band music. Band music's focus on romantic relationships and marriage has generated a large market for its musicians through weddings and other kinds of engagements. Weddings are held literally every week of the year. As the demand for band musicians at wedding ceremonies has grown, so has their urge to compose more songs tailored to these functions.

It is because of this dominant theme that band music appeals mainly to a middle-aged female audience. A core preoccupation of this group is, indeed, with love, relationships and marriage. A large segment of this audience is engaged in business in the downtown areas of urban centers in the central region of Uganda, a fact which renders them a lucrative market for band music.

The language used in band music is Luganda, the language of the Baganda, the largest and most economically active ethnic group in Uganda. Luganda is also spoken in other major urban centers of the country and has become the dominant language of the music industry.

Bibliography

Isabirye, Joel. 2004. 'Ugandan Popular Music as Expression: A Marked Historiography.' Keynote Address: Uganda Music Forum. Kampala, Uganda.

Kafumbe, Damascus. 2014. 'Could Afrigo's Semadongo be Uganda's Zilizopendwa?' *The World of Music (New Series)* 3(1): 113–32.

Matovu, Moses. 2011. '36 Years of Mellow Music' (interview with Robert Kaluma). *Saturday Monitor*

(10 December). Online at: http://www.monitor.co.ug/artsculture/Reviews/691232-1286616-12ijrdlz/index.html (accessed 28 May 2018).
Matovu, Moses. 2015. 'Uganda's Afrigo Band Marks 40 Years of Music' (interview with Bamuturaki Musinguzi.) *The East African Newspaper*, 27 November. Online at: http://www.theeastafrican.co.ke/magazine/Uganda-s-Afrigo-Band-marks-40-years-of-music/434746-2973600-tnh5y9z/index.html (accessed 28 May 2018).
Sewanyana, Herman. 2011. '36 Years of Mellow Music' (interview with Robert Kaluma). *Saturday Monitor*, 10 December. Online at: http://www.monitor.co.ug/artsculture/Reviews/691232-1286616-12ijrdlz/index.html (accessed 28 May 2018).

Discographical References
Birungi, Sarah. 'Obulamu Bwa Kisera.' *1997.* Online at: https://www.howwe.biz/song/3530/obulamu-bwa-kisera/844/sarah-birungi (accessed 28 May 2018).
Kigozi, Fred. 'Mega Jukira.' Reissue: *The Kampala Sound – 1960s Ugandan Dance Music.* Original Music African Classics OMCD 013. *1988*: USA.
Maiso, Fred. 'Ekimuli Kya Rosa.' *1997.* Reissue: *Ekimuli Kya Rosa.* Uganda Performing Right (AFROBEATS) Soci 9705925. *2015*: Uganda.
Masagazi, Fred. 'Ekommera.' Reissue: *The Kampala Sound – 1960s Ugandan Dance Music.* Original Music African Classics OMCD 013. *1988*: USA.
Mayinja, Ronald. 'Clare.' *1998.* Online at: http://www.djerycom.com/player?id=1946&a=ronald-mayinja (accessed 28 May 2018).
Mayinja, Ronald. 'Necklace.' *1998*: Online at: https://www.howwe.biz/song/1926/necklace/166/ronald-mayinja accessed 28 May 2018).
Mayinja, Ronald. 'Tuli ku bunkenke.' Online at: https://www.youtube.com/watch?v=mhumaRiWGnI (accessed 28 May 2018).
Mayinja, Ronald. 'Tuwalana nguzi.' Online at: http://www.djerycom.com/player?id=1961 (accessed 28 May 2018).
Mbowa, Bill. 'Jane Wange.' Reissue: *The Kampala Sound – 1960s Ugandan Dance Music.* Original Music African Classics OMCD 013. *1988*: USA.
Ndagire, Mariam. 'Bamugamba.' *1998.* Online at: https://www.howwe.biz/song/6081/bamugamba/1287/mariam-ndagire (accessed 28 May 2018).

Sonko, Charles. 'Wano Tulimuba.' Reissue: *The Kampala Sound – 1960s Ugandan Dance Music.* Original Music African Classics OMCD 013. *1988*: USA.

Discography
Afrigo Band, The. *Music Parade Vol. 8.* The Afrigo Band TAB 008. *1990*: Uganda.
Afrigo Band, The. *Julie.* Michele International Ltd. MICH 9701. *1997*: USA.

JOEL ISABIRYE

See also Uganda (Vol. VI. Locations: Africa and the Middle East)

Bango
Bango music was created by Joseph Ngala (also known by his stage name as *Mzee Bango*, or Mzee Ngala) in the late 1980s on the east coast of Kenya. A mixture of Portuguese, Arabic, African and Swahili musical arts and cultures, the genre is largely performed at weddings and also as evening entertainment at restaurants in urban settings along Kenya's coastal region. In wedding contexts, the music's lyrics advise the bride and bridegroom about how to live harmoniously as a couple, and highlight for them the challenges of married life that they will work to overcome.

Kioko and Wanjohi (2010) argue that *bango* draws much from Swahili *rumba*, a form that developed in the 1960s, after Jean Bosco Mwenda, a prominent Congolese finger-style *rumba* guitarist, came to live in Nairobi. His music spread to the Coast Province, was adopted by upcoming tourist bands singing in the Swahili language and developed into Swahili *rumba*. Ngala built on Swahili *rumba* and integrated the brass band drum rhythm and, later, influences from Stan Getz's *bossa nova*-inflected cool school of jazz. Among other musical influences that were incorporated were *tango*, waltz and rock 'n' roll, the latter associated with urban life in the 1960s. As a prolific composer and arranger, Ngala was then able to craft his ideas into what became *bango* music, which draws also from the rhythms, proverbs and setting of the Mijikenda community of the Kenyan coast.

Ngala was born on 14 October 1935 to John Anderson Katana and Mary Mbeyi in the coastal town of Mombasa, Kenya. As a young saxophonist he joined a group led by Edmund Silvera at the

Nyali Beach Hotel in the early 1960s, and here his music developed in character and style, especially through his performance of solo sections. He began to carefully embellish his music with saxophone riffs that were lyrical in style and incorporated longer solo sections into the music through improvisations around various melodic themes. Both Ngala and Silvera were passionate about jazz, which influenced how they performed together and, in due course, how Ngala's compositions evolved.

Between 1981 and 1986 Ngala taught his children, who were still in school, how to play various instruments: his eldest son, Sidney Kilonga, played the bass guitar and his other son, Jimmy Mjimba, played drums. One day, after a successful performance at a wedding in Kilifi, Ngala's younger brother Jimmy Dzimba, a guitarist, asked if he could join the band. Ngala consulted with his children and his vocalist, Joseph Kondo, and they agreed to form a band that they called Teusi Five.

In 1987 Ngala's sister-in-law asked him to perform at her daughter's pre-wedding event, an all-night function where women would gather to prepare food. Although his new band had no experience performing at such an event, he agreed and the performance began at 9 pm. By 2 am they had performed all the songs in their repertoire, except a simple song entitled 'Naitaka Bango' (I Want My Shilling Coin), which Ngala had composed after leaving a group called the Bahari Boys. Despite his reservations that the song was rather childish and unfit for such an occasion, he yielded to Kondo's insistence. To his surprise, the audience loved the song and kept asking the band to repeat it. It was performed until daybreak, with the audience repeatedly joining in the refrain.

Ngala had composed this song with the idea of entertaining young people, incorporating the style of soul music that was popular with them in the 1980s. The song is structured in stanza and refrain form, and wherever it is performed the audiences join in singing the chorus (Kioko and Wanjohi 2010). The song's lyrics, which concern a person who loans money and finds it difficult to be repaid, illustrate how a minor issue (a shilling) can strain a relationship. The use of the word *bango*, which was slang for shilling at the time, helped ensure the song's popularity. In the following months Ngala was kept busy performing at weddings, where audiences repeatedly requested the song and started referring to him as Mzee Bango, a name that stuck (*mzee* is a Swahili word meaning 'old man,' and in this case it is used to mean 'respected old man').

Ngala's Teusi Five Band became so popular in Mombasa that Ngala thought it was important to create a unique style with which he would be identified. Every other band in Mombasa was performing different *rumba* varieties that were popular at the time. Eventually, Ngala decided to incorporate the rhythms from the bass drum of the brass bands of the 1940s and 1950s, which shared elements with Kenyan music genres. As a result, his music became very popular with people from the Kenyan Coast. Some fans commented that the music had the feel of local styles characterized by dance movements of the Mijikenda people in moderate tempo, such as *chela* from Rabai and *mabumbumbu* from Giriama. This new style of music became widely known as 'bango' (Kioko and Wanjohi 2010).

Ngala's elder brother, Patrick Moemba, challenged him to record his music and introduced him to an Italian recording studio owner in Malindi who, realizing the band's potential, loaned them a full set of musical instruments and negotiated contracts on their behalf with hotels in Malindi until they were able to pay for the equipment. Ngala recorded one cassette with Idlios Studio under the title *Bango Teusi Five*, and the cassette sold well (Kioko and Wanjohi 2010).

In 1991 Ngala retired from the East African Railway and concentrated fully on his music. In 1994 he and his brother, Dzimba, parted ways due to differences over the identity of the band. Dzimba wanted to retain the name Teusi Five while Ngala wanted to secure his musical identity within *bango*. Ngala continued to perform with his children and vocalist Kondo under the name Bango Sounds Band.

Bango Style

Bango music is characterized by the Congolese *rumba* style, which was adopted in Mombasa from the 1950s as part of urban town life and later developed in the tourist industry (Kioko and Wanjohi 2010). Silvera (in Kioko and Wanjohi 2010) describes Ngala's vocal music as based on the parallel harmonies of fourths and fifths that are characteristic of polyphonic singing in much African music. The *bango* style is rich in poetic content and is also characterized by the unique way in which Ngala addresses issues of social concern in daily life, as a respected musician and prolific composer who earned the status of a figure of authority (elder) in the community.

Ngala explores three themes in his music (Kioko and Wanjohi 2010): love, weddings, and topics to do with education or instruction. His poetry is as important as his musical arrangements in his compositions, and he carefully crafts his text to communicate to his audience at both the individual and the communal level. The demand for Ngala to perform at weddings is such that his schedule is fully booked a year in advance. Each of his wedding songs is individually crafted and bears the name of the bride and groom in the text and the title. However, the applicability of these songs to people's daily lives ensures that they are also popular among the general public, especially when they are played in places of social gathering such as hotels (Kioko and Wanjohi 2010).

Ngala has suffered immensely from copyright infringement, a practice which became ingrained in the Kenyan music industry from the 1970s. In 1986 he recorded his first CD with Bango Sounds Band at Mushrooms recording studio in Nairobi under the name *Bango Volume II*. This was followed by *Bango Volume III* in 1988. In December 2002 he recorded *Bango Volume IV* with Kelele Studios in Nyali Beach, Mombasa. However, before the launch of the CD, Ngala was surprised to find it had been pirated and was being sold in the streets by vendors. He has, therefore, decided not to record his music anymore, and writing in 2010 Kioko and Wanjohi observed that many hundreds of songs exist that have never been recorded. As radio presenter Donde Samora has also noted (ibid.), Ngala's music is popular on radio talk shows, especially the songs with themes covering issues of social concern to Kenyan coastal audiences.

Conclusion

Bango is truly a single-artist phenomenon, and Ngala's style is quite distinct in terms of choice of lyrics, saxophone-dominated instrumentation and performance context. That is not to deny, however, that the music style may be replicated by other musicians in the future, albeit with variations in the lyrics. The genre is very relevant to local Kenyan coastal identity and culture, resonating directly with daily happenings in society while offering advice to Kenyan society as a whole and specifically to young people in the Kenyan coastal region.

Bibliography

Kioko, Mumbua, and Wanjohi, Peter. 2010. 'Joseph Ngala.' In *A Biography of Kenyan Musicians*. Nairobi: Permanent Presidential Music Commission. (Includes personal interviews with Joseph Ngala, Donde Samora and Edmund Silvera.)

Discographical References

Bango Sounds Band. *Bango Vol. II*. Mushrooms. *1986*: Kenya.

Bango Sounds Band. *Bango Vol. III*. Mushrooms. *1988*: Kenya.

Bango Sounds Band. *Bango Vol. IV*. Kelele Studios. *2002*: Kenya.

Teusi Five Band. *Bango Teusi Five*. Idios Studios. N.d.: Kenya.

MELLITUS NYONGESA WANYAMA

Batuque

Batuque (or *batuko*) is a music and dance genre traditionally performed by Badiu women from the island of Santiago in Cabo Verde. The Badiu were the descendants of slaves who escaped to the center of the island and maintained their own traditions in defiance of the Catholic Church and the Portuguese, who considered *batuque* to be rebellious and immoral. It is the oldest genre of music in Cabo Verde, and, more than any other local genre, its rhythms, dance and call-and-response structure are clearly derived from the African continent. The word 'batuque' is derived from the Portuguese *batucar* – to beat or drum.

In *batuque* a group of women, sitting in a semicircle, beat contrasting rhythms with their palms on folded cloths – known as *panos* – held between their thighs, creating a polyrhythm through the juxtaposition of two against three, building to rhythmic patterns called *bam-bam*, *rapica* and *galeom*. Lyric topics are wide-ranging but are limited to a few phrases in a narrow melodic range initiated by the leader and repeated by the seated women. Though less common, men such as the well-known Antoni Denti d'Oro, have been known to lead the *batuque*.

At the beginning of the piece, a solo dancer, with a *pano* wrapped low around her hips, travels to the center where she slowly begins the *torno* dance, moving her hips and feet in sync with the two-against-three rhythm. The music gradually picks up speed and energy, leading up to the *tchabéta* section, when the women sing and pound the rhythm exuberantly and the dancer's hip movements become rapid and staccato. At the end of the song the *pano* is handed over to the next dancer and the process begins again, often lasting for many hours.

In the past, *batuque* (also known as *sambuna*) was performed at weddings, baptisms and saint's day festivals in combination with sung extemporized poetry known as *finaçon*. In contrast to *batuque*, the focus in *finaçon* is on the clever use of language to tell topical stories and relay the memory of past events. There is no dancing or chorus, but there may be quiet rhythmic accompaniment. Because of the skill level required, only a few have been considered masters of this genre, among them Nácia Gomi, Gida Mendes and Bibina Kabral.

At the time of Cabo Verde's independence in 1975, the new socialist government purposefully supported *batuque* as a manifestation of national culture. The genre, often *sans* the more challenging *finaçon*, was reborn, first as a staged performance in government-sponsored events, and then later as a tourist attraction.

In the 1990s the composer Orlando Pantera referenced the rhythms and sensibilities of *batuque* in his popular music. After his untimely death in 2001, what some call the 'Post-Pantera' generation, including performers such as Lura, Vadú and Tcheka, has continued this trend in their compositions and performances.

Since independence in 1975, *batuque* has become an accepted part of the repertoire of Cabo Verdean music, but cannot be considered pan-Cabo Verdean because it has maintained such strong ties to the Badiu. On Santiago there are many performing groups of varying quality, and despite its transformations it still serves as a social outlet to mitigate the hard lives of women with little economic means.

Bibliography

Hurley-Glowa, Susan. 1997. 'Batuko and Funáná: Musical Traditions of Santiago, Republic of Cape Verde.' Unpublished Ph.D. dissertation, Brown University, Providence, RI.

Lobban, Richard A., Jr. 1995. *Cape Verde: Crioulo Colony to Independent Nation*. Boulder, CO: Westview.

Monteiro, Vladimir. 1998. *Les musiques du Cap-Vert* [The Musics of Cabo Verde]. Paris: Éditions Chandeigne.

Silva, T. V. da. 1985. *Finasons di Na Nasia Gomi: Tradisons oral de Kauberdi* [Finaçons of Nasia Gomes: Oral Traditions of Cabo Verde]. Praia, Cabo Verde: Institutu Kauberdianu di Libru.

Silva, T. V. da. 1988. *Nha Bibina Kabral: Bida y óbra* [Senhora Bibinha Cabral: Life and Work]. Praia, Cabo Verde: Institutu Kauberdianu di Libru.

Silva, T. V. da. 1990. *Na Gida Mendi: Simenti di onti na txon di manan* [Senhora Gida Mendi: Seeds of Yesterday in the Earth of Tomorrow]. Praia: Instituto Caboverdiano do Disco e do Livro.

Spinola, Daniel. 1986. 'Para cada letra um som; para cada som uma letra' [For Each Lyric a Sound, for Each Sound a Lyric]. *Voz di Povo* XII (572): 9.

Discography

Cap Vert: Anthologie 1959–1992. Buda Musique 92614-2. *1994*: France.

Dez granzin di tera, Cabo Verde. A viagem dos Sons, 11. Tradisom VS11. *1998*: Portugal.

Gomi, Nácia. *Cu sê mocinhos*. Sons D'Africa CD 285. *1999*: Cabo Verde.

Lura. *Di korpu ku alma* (w/DVD). Escondida 6511-2. (Lusafrica *362912.*) *2005*: France.

Tcheka. *Nu monda*. Harmonia 023352 (CD) and 023348 (DVD). *2007*: Portugal.

Filmography

Songs of the Badius, dir. Gei Zantzinger. 1986. USA. 36 minutes. Original music by Bibinha Cabral and Antoni Denti d'oro. Documentary.

JOANNE HOFFMAN

Bend Skin

A style of music and dance involving complex percussive rhythms, *bend skin* (*ben skin*) is a genre of urban popular music that emerged in the late twentieth century from the oral traditions of the people of the Bamiléké plateau in the Highlands of Western Cameroon. The first musicians to popularize *bend skin* actually came from the Ndé division, which forms part of the Bamiléké plateau. Initially sung in the Medumba language, the main language spoken in Ndé, contemporary *bend skin* is characterized in terms of both lyrics and music by a diversity of languages as well as a blending of melodies, rhythms and instrumentation that accounts for its vitality.

The Development of *Bend Skin*

The term 'bend skin' is a Pidgin English expression that means 'bending the back,' 'bending down,' 'working' or 'producing before consuming' (Fandio 2004). The term refers to the motorcycle-taxis that made an unusually brutish appearance in Cameroon's cities in the late 1980s. This onset of the motorcycle-taxis occurred at a time when groups such as Kouchouam Mbada were trying to reach audiences with their performances in the popular neighborhoods of Douala: Bepanda, Brazzaville, Bonébéri, New Bell and so on. Referred to as 'zémijan' in West Africa (Benin and Togo), 'jakarta' in Senegal and 'okada' in Nigeria (Keutcheu 2015), bend skin motorcycle-taxis are driven by unemployed young people (some of whom are highly educated) willing to take any job in order to survive. Bend skin drivers must bend down while riding their motorcycle to keep their balance as they navigate the substandard city streets. The similarity between the position of the driver and the choreography of *bend skin* explains the use of the term.

Initially, the singers in *bend skin* groups were mostly women from various professions who gathered according to ethnicity around organizations promoting tontines (tontines, which are common throughout Africa, are a form of savings organization that allow for different forms of group savings and microcredit schemes) (Nkakleu 2009). These women generally did not have any formal musical training. They were accompanied instrumentally by men mostly from the trades: casual salesmen, taxi and motorcycle-taxi drivers or unemployed people. Some of these men would have had a musical background from participating in church choirs.

The popularization of this musical genre throughout Cameroon and its inclusion in urban musical culture resulted from the simultaneous work of André-Marie Tala (b. 1950) and the Kouchouam Mbada group at the end of the 1980s. At the time, André-Marie Tala was already an internationally renowned musician, winner of the Charles Humel Prize awarded by La Société des Auteurs, Compositeurs et Éditeurs de Musique de France (SACEM; the Society of Authors, Composers and Music Publishers of France) in 1981. As a composer and performer attentive to the musical trends of his country and the world, Tala's trademark sound soon came to represent a national integration of diverse influences. Although his music has remained strongly anchored in the traditional rhythms of the Bamiléké plateau of West Cameroon, Tala has never hesitated to introduce elements from other traditions, such as *makossa*, blues, reggae, rock and jazz. These external elements can be found in the melodies and rhythms of his music, as well as in the lyrics, which are sung in many languages: French, English, Bamoun, Fufuldé, Ghomala and so on. His first experiments with what would later become *bend skin* can be heard in several songs recorded in the 1970s and 1980s, including 'Che Mutok' (1981), 'Mwouop' (1974), 'Mete nè msè' (1981) and, in particular, 'Odoya' (1975). 'Odoya,' sung in Bamoun, is melodically based on the musical styles of the Noun division of Cameroon, which include *mendu* and *mekoumbou*.

As a shrewd connoisseur of music, Tala refined and honed his own style through astute observation and reflection. In Douala, he noticed the excitement occasioned by the performances of women's groups such as Kouchouam Mbada, who originated from Ndé. Tala recognized that *mangambeu*, the genre preceding *bend skin*, as well as the musical lineages which fed into it (*meuto, kwa and ngeugnia*), possessed the rhythmic, melodic and harmonic elements necessary to create a modern urban music in the vein of the popular successes of Nami Jean-de-Boulon, Pierre Didy Tchakounté, Antoine Bamou, Daniel Njiké and Nya Director. Most importantly, Tala realized that this music could support a new social and political discourse, especially in this period at the end of the 1980s when alternative political voices sought free expression. This was also the time when an economic crisis started to seriously affect Cameroon, presaging the decline of the welfare state and disrupting established patterns of social life. Following these beginnings, Tala was able to capitalize on his insights and, in 1993, he released 'Bend skin,' the eponymous song of an album that signaled the modern production, promotion and consumption of the genre. The album was arranged by Justin Bowen Tchounou, who skillfully interspersed the songs with breaks borrowed from jazz and rock, counteracting the characteristic monotony of most traditional rhythms from the Bamiléké plateau of Western Cameroon.

Simultaneously, in the Bangangté district of New Bell, a historic quarter of Douala, a unique experiment was being carried out by groups of women from the Western Highlands of Cameroon, including Bangangté and the surrounding areas of Bangoulap, Balengou, Bazou and Bamena. During the funerals of community members, women would organize themselves around a small group featuring one or two drummers, two or three xylophone players and three or four musicians playing rattles. Initially these musicians were men. However, as time went on, women became increasingly active in these groups. Dancers would wear bells on their anklets and sing, while the lead singer would accompany the performance with a military or referee's whistle repurposed for the occasion. In the fertile cultural mix centered around the Bangangté district, one group began to stand out. A certain Njike Ibrahim got into the habit of bringing together young people from the neighborhood to breathe life into funeral vigils. From one performance to the next, the group enjoyed growing success through their dancing, singing and theatrical presence. Several people joined the group, but only a few distinguished themselves through their abilities in dancing and singing: Jean-Berlin Kamtchoum, Toncha, Toubet Sidonie, Tchokui, Noumi Stephanie and Irene Feuyang. It is around this core that the Kouchouam Mbada group was created, the name itself serving as an expression of friendliness and cheerfulness.

At first, the group was only an amateur organization performing at funeral vigils without any ambition of becoming famous even if, by the early 1990s, they already had a vast repertoire of songs. But when André-Marie Tala released 'Bend skin,' the group became aware of its own potential. These musicians with no professional experience in the studio decided to approach one of the biggest stars of the Cameroonian music scene of the 1980s, Sam Fan Thomas (Samuel Ndonfeng, born in 1952 in Bafoussam). Thomas, who began his career as a member of André-Marie Tala's band, The Black Tigers, had a studio (the Makassi Plus Studio) in Douala which employed highly skilled artists such as Tala Jeannot (keyboards), Keng Godefroy (bass) and Kotto Bass (a renowned *makossa* singer and bass player who died unexpectedly in 1996). Shortly after, in 2001, Kouchouam Mbada's first album, *Ancien Koutchoua Mbada*, was released with the flagship single 'Essola' under the artistic direction of Sam Fan Thomas with production being handled by Jean Pierre Sar of JPS Production. Several other songs, such as 'Swèga menzu,' 'Adonis' and 'Yaya belong,' were also hits with Cameroonian music lovers. Thanks to the broadcasting of several music videos on the national television station, Cameroon Radio and Television (CRTV), audiences quickly became enamored of *bend skin* in the cities and countryside of Cameroon.

Performance Characteristics

Bend skin in its classical form is based on a battery of percussion instruments structured around membrane drums (*Faʾ*) and castanets or rattles (*ShŨʹ ShŨʹ*). Three types of membrane drums are necessary to perform *bend skin*: a call drum, a response drum and a drum for accompaniment. A slit drum (*nduʾ*) can also be used for accompaniment. This instrument is hit with hard mallets (De Mégahshi 2014, 55). Rattles can be made of any material that can encase small solid objects such as pebbles, seeds, glass or metal marbles. The material traditionally used is the outer fibers of woven palm raffia; however, some performers have more recently used recycled pop cans. Rattles provide the tempo throughout a performance of *bend skin*, serving as a metronome and background pulse to create the acoustic dynamic of the music. Instruments also used include the xylophone (*Djaʾ*), the double-gong (*krəəhʹ*) and various other rattles (*kwaʹ*). The meter of *bend skin* is the same as that of most of the music of the Bamiléké plateau of Western Cameroon, namely, 6/8. Given its percussive nature, a *bend skin* performance usually starts with a very strong beat with a percussion instrument at the forefront, this beat being interrupted by a break, a drum roll or a song.

The musical genealogy of *bend skin* reflects the diversity of rhythms from the Bamiléké plateau of West Cameroon. This diversity is skillfully synthesized in 'kwa,' a generic rhythm which originates with women singers and dancers who wear ankle rattles (*kwaʹ*) that produce a wall of sound. The *kwa* rhythm derives from women's music such as *meuteu*, *ngueuguia* and *koʹdjaʹ*. (As well as referring to a rhythm and ankle rattles, 'Kwa' also refers to a language spoken between the Ndé division and the Littoral region in Western Cameroon.) The women performers are generally dressed in a cloth uniform called 'kaba ngondo,' a kind of women's boubou, a long, loose-fitting, flowing and brightly colored garment first utilized by the Douala women of the Cameroonian coast. In colonial times, this dress was imposed by the clergy to hide the nakedness of African women (*Masoso ma Nyambe*, 2011). Wearing scarves of the same fabric as the boubou, as well as necklaces and pendants with various patterns, the women form a circle surrounding the singer, the lead vocal, who can use a whistle either to animate or to accelerate the pace of the performance. A second circle is formed by the spectators who applaud and encourage the dancers.

Apart from the mastery evidenced in the singing and other aspects of the musical performance, crowds have above all been delighted by the *bend skin* dance (De Mégahshi 2014, 60). As explained earlier, *bend skin* owes its name to its choreography. The dance is executed by highlighting the posterior of the women performers (Nzessé 2015, 40). The convention is to dance while being stooped over, tightening the legs and producing patterns with the feet, generally made up of small steps forward and backward, but also from side to side. Highlighting the posterior of the women performers does not happen in any erotic sense, but serves more as a process of maintaining an identity, a means of being oneself in the face of a society sometimes characterized by misogyny. Moreover, in a context where stability in family and collective life has been undermined by poverty and unemployment, this emphasis on the posterior can also be understood as a kind of 'nihilism of emptiness' intended to alleviate the weight of stress and anguish arising from daily life (Monga 2009, 128).

Other developments were noteworthy as *kwa* morphed into *bend skin*. The most notable of these, referred to earlier, is *mangambeu*, a genre performed by men. This precursor of *bend skin* changed from being a purely oral tradition to being recorded in studios, thereby effecting an important transition for the development of *bend skin*. *Mangambeu* was broadcast on the radio, and distributed through discs and cassettes. In terms of instrumentation, pioneers from the 1970s such as Nami Jean-de-Boulon and Bamou Antoine maintained the battery of percussion instruments common to the rhythms of West Cameroon, but also introduced wind instruments such as the trumpet or saxophone as well as the *sanza*. The *sanza* is an idiophone, a type of *mbira* made up of a platform in the form of a soundboard on which are fixed hardwood slats or recycled flexible metal rods from umbrella frames. It is played by being plucked. Pierre Didy Tchakounté, Justin Tchatchoua and Jack Djeyim made a lot of money by making the *sanza* a main instrument of accompaniment. They 'rediscovered' the instrument, Tchakounté from the elders in his village and Djeyim during a visit to Zimbabwe. The use of the instrument represented a real break in their respective careers. Djeyim can be heard performing on the instrument in 'Magni,' a track on his album, *Sanza Trio Family*.

Musical arrangers such as Justin Bowen, Brice Wassy, Fan Sam Thomas, Tala Jeannot, Prince Tchetche and Emmanuel Kuaté have significantly diversified the instrumentation of *bend skin*. In the late 2010s, thanks to the advent of the synthesizer and programming software such as GSelector, Musik Maker and Ableton Live, arrangers have increased the sonic spectrum of the genre. Brass, drums and the rhythms of the Charleston have become part of the *bend skin* world. This trend can be heard in contemporary songs by Marole Tchamba, Guy Watson, Wank's Nya, Dj Gérard Ben, Charly Yonkeu, Prince Patrice and Passy La Noblesse. This stylistic diversity is also apparent in various linguistic and musical influences derived from other traditions. For example, DJ Gérard Ben sprinkles his song 'Il y a pas de match' (2016) with rhythms from *coupé décalé*, a genre from the Côte d'Ivoire. And in his 'African Dances' (1995), the main instrument is the trombone. Marole Tchamba's 'Un homme qui m'aime' (2015) replicates *bikutsi*, a genre from the forests of Central and Southern Cameroon. Tchamba also sings in Ewondo, French and Medumba. In 'Waka' (2014), the newcomer JJ Créas sings 70 percent in French. However, it should also be noted that, in a landscape that is mainly focused on popular urban music, some people still hold fast to traditional *bend skin*, performed in a self-controlled manner, using conventional instruments and only rarely borrowing from modern influences. This is the case for Justin Tchatchoua ('Nve Numga,' 2009; 'Lali,' 2009), Jack Djeyim ('Bangoulap,' 1995), Brice Wassy ('Ku Ngabeu,' 1996) and Guy M'biro ('Poulno,' 1996).

Conclusion

Although *bend skin* has gained an audience in Cameroon, the fact remains that its national and international expansion remains a challenge. It has continued to struggle to establish itself as a legitimate genre within modern Cameroonian music. Unlike other genres such as *bikutsi*, which has had its own locations for creativity and production, *bend skin* is heard mainly by chance. An introduction to the genre often results from improvised street shows, for example. The lack of specialized producers is another major constraint, as most of the songs currently available on the market are self-produced. Initially, the involvement of Jean Pierre Sar of JPS Production put the Kouchouam Mbada group in the spotlight. Similarly, the rise of Guy Watson's song 'Mignoncité' in 2010 resulted from the groundbreaking work undertaken by Raymond Tchengang of the RT Production House and Star 2000 (which provides media support as well as negotiation services with professional promoters). But all these initiatives have remained fragmented and represent serious shortcomings in terms of marketing and career development.

Bibliography

De Mégahshi, Stéphane. 2014. *Bana: Essai d'histoire*. Yaoundé: Editions Grassfields.

Fandio, Pierre. 2004. 'Nouvelles voix et voies nouvelles de la littérature orale camerounaise' [New Voices and New Ways in Cameroon Oral Literature]. *Semen*. Online at: http://journals.openedition.org/semen/2298 (accessed 5 January 2018).

Keutcheu, Joseph. 2015. 'Le "fléau de motos-taxis": Comment se fabrique un problème public au Cameroun' [The 'Scourge of the Moto-Taxis': How to Manufacture a Public Problem in Cameroon]. *Cahiers d'études africaines* [African Studies Notebook] 219: 509–34.

Masoso ma Nyambe. 2011. 'L'Histoire du "Kaba Ngondo"'. Online at: http://masoso.unblog.fr/lhistoire-du-kaba-ngondo/ (accessed 11 March 2018).

Monga, Célestin. 2009. *Nihilisme et négritude* [Nihilism and Negritude]. Paris: Presses Universitaires de France.

Nkakleu, Raphaël. 2009. 'Quand la tontine d'entreprise crée le capital social intra-organisationnel en Afrique: Une étude de cas' [When the Tontine Enterprise Creates Intra-organizational Social Capital in Africa: A Case Study]. *Management & Avenir* 27(7): 119–34.

Nzéssé, Ladislas. 2015. *Inventaire des particularités lexicales du français au Cameroun (1990–2015)* [An Inventory of French Lexical Peculiarities in Cameroon (1990–2015)]. Nice: Institut de linguistique française. Online at: http://www.unice.fr/bcl/ofcaf/29/le%20Francais%20en%20Afrique%2029.pdf (accessed 5 January 2018).

Discographical References

Créas, J. J. 'Waka.' Label unknown. *2014*: Cameroon. Online at: https://www.youtube.com/watch?v=ML7aCg0ykcA (accessed 11 March 2018).

Dj Gérard Ben. 'African Dances.' Label unknown. *1995*: Cameroon. Online at: https://www.youtube.com/watch?v=9BB1yn4qA-Q (accessed 11 March 2018).

Dj Gérard Ben. 'Il y a pas de match.' Label unknown. *2016*: Cameroon. Online at: https://www.youtube.com/watch?v=Co4q8pzGTkI (accessed 11 March 2018).

Djeyim, Jack. 'Bangoulap.' *Dance Around the Fire*. Label unknown. *1995*: Cameroon. Online at: https://www.youtube.com/watch?v=5dGSq3vvUCo (accessed 11 March 2018).

Djeyim, Jack. 'Magni.' *Sanza Trio Family*. *2012*: Cameroon. Online at: https://www.youtube.com/watch?v=ye62AVDvawo (accessed 10 March 2018).

Kouchouam Mbada. 'Adonis.' *Swèga Menzu*. JPS Production. *N.d.*: France.

Kouchouam Mbada. 'Essola.' *Ancien Koutchoua Mbada*. JPS CDJPS. *2001*: France.

Kouchouam Mbada. 'Swèga menzu.' *Swèga Menzu*. JPS Production. *N.d.*: France.

Kouchouam Mbada. 'Yaya belong.' *Ancien Koutchoua Mbada*. JPS CDJPS. *2001*: France.

M'biro, Guy. 'Poulno.' *Mendu*. Bolibana. *1996*: France.

Tala, André-Marie. 'Bend skin.' *Bend Skin*. *1993*: France.

Tala, André-Marie. 'Che mutok.' *Bend Skin Beats*. RetroAfrique RETRO23CD. *2009*: UK.

Tala, André-Marie. 'Mete nè msè.' *Tala 81*. Andy's Productions AND 33802. *1981*: France.

Tala, André-Marie. 'Mwouop'/'NaMala ebolo.' (7-inch single.) Fiesta 51.213. *1974*: France.

Tala, André-Marie. 'Odoya.' *Hot Koki*. Fiesta (7) 360.057. *1975*: France.

Tchamba, Marole. 'Un home qui m'aime.' Label unknown. *2015*: Cameroon. Online at https://www.dailymotion.com/video/x2nokd3 (accessed 22 September 2018).

Tchatchoua, Justin. 'Lali.' *Lali el sueño africano*. 2009: Spain.

Tchatchoua, Justin. 'Nve numga.' *Lali el sueño africano*. 2009: Spain.

Wassy, Brice. 'Ku ngabeu.' *N'ga Funk*. B&W Music BW036. *1996*:UK.

Watson, Guy. 'Mignoncité.' Société Rt et Star l'an 2000 Sarl. *2010*: Cameroon.

Discography

Djeyim, Jack. *Dance around the Fire*. Cross-over. *2014*: Belgium.

Jean-de-Boulon, Nami, *Le Cameroun et son folklore/ Cameroun partout vol 7*. Disques Cousin DC 8032 y. *N.d.*: France.

Jean-de-Boulon, Nami. *Roi de mangabeu*. Secret De La Musique – SM5001. *N.d.*: Cameroon.

Jean-de-Boulon, Nami, and Moise Ngandja, *Choc*. DM 008. *1980*: Cameroon.

Tala, André-Marie. 'Mwouop.' *Best of André-Marie Tala Volume 2*. Touré Jim's Records – CDAT 167. *1997*: France.

Tchakounté, Pierre Didy. *Meguela*. BBZ Productions – BZL 7013, RCA – BZL 7013. *1977*: France.

Tchatchoua, Justin. *Oh ! Kokoriko*. EMI. *1994*: Spain.

Tchatchoua, Justin. *Vuela*. Antar Productionnes. *2000*: Spain.

Watson, Guy. *Calculé*. Kboy. *2017*: Cameroon.

YouTube

Tala, André-Marie. 'Che Mutok.' https://www.youtube.com/watch?v=dkKymUMVEa8 (accessed 11 March 2018).

Tala, André-Marie. 'Mwouop.' https://www.youtube.com/watch?v=okHbeFpjBBc (accessed 11 March 2018).

JOSEPH FUMTIM (TRANSLATED BY ANDRÉ LOISELLE WITH JOHN SHEPHERD)

Benga

In the early decades of the twenty-first century *benga* is considered one of the definitive and most renowned Kenyan popular music genres; it is also one of the most-recorded and most-performed genres in the Kenyan popular music scene. The style utilizes fundamental modern African popular song-and-dance components: vocals, guitar accompaniment and contemporary story lines. The key to the popularity of *benga*, however, lies in its development of local and international variants. Evolving predominantly as a popular music genre of the Luo people, *benga* became a national phenomenon with representative variants in different parts of the country. A major contributory factor in its nationalization was *benga*'s appropriation of indigenous musical idioms combined with modern sounds; the result, with its characteristic danceable grooves, resonated well with audiences. A second important reason for the widespread dissemination of the genre was the savvy and extensive way in which it was promoted and distributed. Credit for being the leading producer, promoting Luo *benga* to both local and international markets, is usually given to Phares Oluoch Kanindo, while David Amunga, the first producer of Kikuyu and Kamba *benga*, abetted the spread of *benga* into other communities. Kanindo and Amunga, alongside other producers, helped to shape the genre by providing competitive recording opportunities that popularized it not only in Kenya but also in other parts of Africa from the 1960s to 1980s.

The Luo people, to whom *benga*'s beginnings are attributed, are predominantly found in the Nyanza region of southwestern Kenya on the eastern edge of Lake Victoria. From their indigenous music *benga* borrowed its lyrical melodies and syncopated rhythms. The vocal melodies, mostly sung solo or in two-part harmony, sometimes doubled by the bass guitar, engage in musical conversation with the lead guitar while the rhythm guitar provides the groove alongside the bass guitar and drum set. The genre, however, also acquired variants associated with different ethnic groups such as the neighboring Abagusii in Nyanza region, southwestern Kenya, the Abaluyia of western Kenya, the Akamba of eastern Kenya, the Kikuyu of central Kenya and the Kalenjin of the Rift Valley region. In the 1970s and 1980s *benga* music was the dominant local popular product. It was also exported to the neighboring countries of Uganda and Tanzania and consumed as far as Congo, Malawi and Zimbabwe.

Origins and Development

Graham (1988) dates the beginnings of *benga* to the late 1940s and early 1950s, Ewens (1991) to the late 1960s and Stapleton and May (1987) to the 1970s.

However, Osusa (2008), in documentary interviews with pioneer recording artists, credits the origins of the genre to three Luo musicians: John Ogara Odondi (a.k.a. Ogara Taifa), Samuel Aketch Jabuya (a.k.a. Aketch Oyosi) and Nelson Ochieng' Orwa (a.k.a. Ocheing' Nelly). In the early 1960s these three musicians formed the Ogara Boys Band. Prior to starting the band, Aketch had worked in Mombasa and Nairobi alongside the renowned Congolese musician Jean Bosco Mwenda, from whom he learned to play the guitar. He is featured in Bosco's recording 'Tajiri na mali yake' (1959; [Rycroft 1962, 102]). 'Ocheing' Nelly acquired his guitar skills from another pioneering Congolese musician, Adolf Banyore. By the early 1960s Ogara had established himself as a one-man guitarist. The trio recorded 'Selestina Juma' at African Gramophone Stores (AGS) in Nairobi in 1963 (Osusa 2008).

Upon relocating to their rural homeland, and in an effort to make music that appealed to the local community, the trio developed a unique guitar sound that was heavily influenced by indigenous Luo styles such as *nyatiti*, *orutu*, *ohangla*, *ramogi* and *dodo*. The sound appropriated the idiom of the *nyatiti*, an eight-stringed lyre, while the singing style and interaction of the guitar and vocals reflected that of the *orutu*, a one-stringed fiddle. Later the rhythms and tempo of the *ramogi*, *ohangla* and *dodo* styles were incorporated. The resulting style was named *benga* around 1963. Other founding recording artists of *benga*, who recorded in the 1960s, were Owiti Origo and Olima Anditi.

The source of the term *benga* has elicited numerous debates. Musician Daniel Owino Misiani (popularly known as D. O. Misiani) claims he named the style after his mother (Mwaura 2006, 30). However, the seminal recording artists Nelson Ochieng' and Samuel Aketch attribute the genesis of the term to a cloth that women tied around their waists while dancing (Osusa 2008; Amateshe and Ondieki 2013). The women danced until the cloth fell and the band would exclaim in Luo 'lawo bengore,' meaning 'the cloth has fallen,' leading to the chanting of the term 'benga.' The two musicians, Samuel Aketch and Nelson Ochieng' first encountered 'the cloth has fallen' syndrome during their tour in Uganda in the early 1960s. There, *benga* was played at a slightly faster dance tempo than later versions. In 1965 the Ogara Boys trio recorded the song 'Samuel Aketch' in praise of band member Samuel Aketch. It is in this recording that the term 'benga' was used for the first time, thus dating the commercial use of the term to 1965.

Benga grew rapidly in Luo Nyanza with the rise of these and other artists, such as George Ramogi, D. O. Misiani, Ochieng' Kabaselleh (real name Hajullas Nyapanji) and Collela Mazee (real name Richard Owino) in the 1960s and 1970s. Many of these musicians released singles under their own names alongside albums with bands such as the Ogara Boys Band, Victoria Jazz Band, Luo Sweet Band, Continental Kilo Jazz Band (C.K. Jazz), C.K. Dumbe Dumbe Jazz Band, Tausi Band and D.O. 7 Shirati Jazz Band, among others. Recording labels for these early *benga* artists included the Kenyan label AIT, originally set up by the South African Gallo label, and the international company EMI. Phares Oluoch Kanindo, who was to become the leading local and international promoter of the genre (as well as a member of the Kenyan parliament), worked as CEO in Kenya, before setting up his own labels, including Sungura, Lolwe, POK (his own initials), Duol and Oyundi. Kanindo's business acumen and work experience with recording companies facilitated the spread of *benga* to South Africa, Zimbabwe, Congo and other African countries. In 1972 renowned guitarist Gabriel Omolo raised *benga* to the next level when he recorded the song 'Lunchtime' in the national language Kiswahili. The recording sold over 250,000 copies, earning a Gold Disc Award.

Musical Characteristics of *Luo Benga*

Most *benga* pieces are structured in two large sections, a characteristic common in popular urban styles in the 1950s to 1980s and still practiced in *rhumba* and *benga* in the twenty-first century. In the first section, the story is recounted in several stanzas, punctuated by instrumental interludes. The second section, mostly instrumental with the solo guitar taking the lead, acts as a climax and is characterized as the dancing section, similar to the *montuno* section of Cuban *rumba*. In this section musicians praise themselves or other prominent members of their society (the Luo term for these praises is *pakruok*).

Luo *benga* melodies often imitate the quick and syncopated melodies of the *nyatiti* (eight-stringed lyre) and the *orutu* (one-string fiddle). The bass line typically doubles the main melody as well as outlining the chord progressions and their variants through arpeggios and broken chords. *Benga* chord progressions, since the genre's inception in the 1960s to 1970s, have remained constant and are usually I–IV–V–I and/or I–IV–I–V–I. It is characteristic for the solo and rhythm guitars to interplay in a lively manner. The drumming and rhythm borrow heavily from the *ohangla* drums but the hi-hat percussive quality is based on *pekee* (shakers made from flattened bottle tops). The singing is often high-pitched and in two-part harmony, mainly in parallel thirds (Okumu 2005).

Benga musicians initially appropriated ideas from the indigenous music of the Luo, and the songs borrow compositional techniques and approaches from indigenous tunes. The melodic and rhythmic articulations of the *nyatiti* idiom provided the backbone groove for the rhythm guitar. The vocal harmonies and interaction with the solo guitar lines were similar to *orutu* stylings. In the *orutu* style, the instrument always derived its melody from the voice and interacted with the singer. Similarly, in *benga*, the guitar not only engaged in a solo-responsorial conversation but also doubled the voice. The bass and lead guitar derived their melody lines from the voice, although the bass guitar had a lot more flexibility in delivery. This meant that the vocal lines were always shadowed by the lead guitar and at times by both the lead and bass guitars.

Lyrics usually narrate an elaborate storyline, often in strophic form, and mainly in the Dholuo (Luo language), with occasional Kiswahili or English words inserted to emphasize certain ideas. *Benga* lyrics always focus on themes that reflect current issues of the day. These can be chronicles of important social events or political drama. Many song lyrics dwell on love, extol beauty, praise virtues, lament bad behavior and so on. Some songs recount real-life personal experiences, money, hardships, struggles and challenges. Some praise senior citizens, high-profile leaders, politicians and musicians. A few songs castigate the same leaders for their errors toward the community (Amuka 2000; Ogude 2007).

The original *benga*, as played by the seminal *benga* ensemble the Ogara Boys Band, was very fast in tempo. In the 1970s the tempo was slowed down and borrowed from the gentle and graceful *dodo* dance in response to competition from Congolese *rhumba*. Also, in the 1970s the rhythm guitar began to borrow from the *ramogi* beat and developed an *ostinato* groove that heralded the climax sections of the piece. This rhythm became a signature of *benga* music and was borrowed by other communities that adopted the genre. The rhythm, represented in Example 1 below, is prominent in the climax section of *benga* recordings from other parts of Kenya.

Example 1: *Benga ostinato* rhythm, transcribed by Donald Otoyo Ondieki

The Ogara Boys Band was made up of vocals and guitars that were at first accompanied by the 'conductor,' a small metallic box with lamella. The instrument was initially used by the East African Railways train conductors to announce meal times in train cabins. It was subsequently adapted and adopted by the early *benga* musicians as a percussion instrument. Later it was replaced by the Fanta bottle to play percussive grooves similar to those of the Latin American *guiro*. In time the acoustic guitars were replaced with electric guitars and the 'conductor,' along with the Fanta bottle, was superseded by the drum set and other instruments such as the *congas* and cowbell.

Because of its roots in the indigenous music of the Luo, *benga* was initially considered music of the 'rural and uncultured' while *rhumba* was considered music for the upper class. However, benga's appropriation of indigenous idioms gave it a unique flavor, not only locally and nationally, but also in the international sphere.

Benga Variants

Most of the *benga* musicians in the 1960s to 1980s recorded with the local and/or international record labels that were based in Kenya, whose capital Nairobi was the recording hub for East and Central Africa during this period. Both the international and local record companies had networks within the region and beyond, thus contributing immensely to the spread of the style. In Zimbabwe, for example, the genre was commonly referred to as 'Kanindo,' the name of the most prominent record label distributing *benga* in the country. This in turn influenced variants of *benga* in Zimbabwe such as the genre known as *sungura* (Pfukwa 2010). Consequently, the spread of *benga* was largely attributed to the great promotion and distribution by the record labels both nationally and internationally.

Locally in Kenya, the spread of *benga*'s first variants – that is Kikuyu *benga* and Kamba *benga*, and much later the Luhyia *benga* – is largely attributed to prominent Kenyan musician and producer David Amunga, who recorded the pioneer artists in the 1970s. Amunga's ingenious idea of fusing Kikuyu, Kamba and Luhyia popular music with *benga* not only repackaged the artists he was producing but spread their music's appeal to a wider Kenyan audience. This idea inspired more artists and communities to adopt the same approach, leading to other *benga* fusion variants.

The Akamba people of central Kenya successfully adapted and adopted the *benga* style in the 1970s and 1980s, and it became their most prominent popular music genre. Early Kamba *benga* recording artists include the Kilimambogo Brothers led by Kakai Kilonzo. Kamba *benga* gained traction when the Kilimambogo Brothers began to sing in the national Kiswahili language, including a series of national patriotic songs. These songs gave the band airplay on the national radio, whence the group gained government support and special invitations to perform for Daniel Toroitich arap Moi, the second president of the Kenyan Republic. Other prominent Kamba *benga* artists include Peter Muambi, Bosco Mulwa, Sammy Wambua, Francis Danger and Ken wa Maria (known as the king of Kamba *benga* in the twenty-first century).

Kikuyu *benga* may be traced to Daniel Kamau Mwai, popularly known as 'DK.' Though DK recorded his first song in 1967, it was 'Murata/I Love You,' produced by David Amunga in 1970, that garnered national attention as the first Kikuyu *benga* hit. The recording used two rhythm guitars and one solo guitar, which was not common in Kikuyu popular music at the time. Following this hit other Kikuyu artists recorded in the new style. Some of them include Kamande wa Kioi, Simon Kichera Musa, John Ndichu, John De Mathew, Musaimo, Mike Murimi, Kefa Maina, Queen Jane and Lady Wanja.

In the 1990s the *benga* craze hit the Rift Valley, evidenced by the popularity of the Kalenjin Sisters, made up of Angelica Chepkoech and Elizabeth Chepkorir. In a community that did not recognize female musicians, this was a great breakthrough both in cultural tradition and on the national music scene. In 1989 the Kalenjin Sisters rose to fame with their *benga* hits such as 'Paulo my Lover' and 'Kwaheri Yohana.' By the 1990s they were a household name, receiving prominent airplay by the Kenya Broadcasting Corporation (KBC), formerly named Voice of Kenya (VoK), national radio station. After Elizabeth Chepkorir passed away, Angelica Chepkoech continued performing as one of the most popular Kalenjin *benga* artists in the Rift Valley. Angelica was later based in Eldoret, a major town in the North Rift Valley region of Kenya, where she performed with the Jamnazi Band from 2006 until her death in 2014. Other prominent *benga* artists in the region include Kipchambai arap Tapotuk and his Koilonget Band, Chebaibai and Kipchambai arap Butuk.

The Abagusii adopted *benga* due to their proximity to the Luo as neighbors. As a vibrant market and economy in the region, Kisii town attracted and hosted several Luo guitarists. These guitarists were contracted by Kisii musicians to accompany recordings of their own version of Kisii *benga*. One of the pioneer Kisii *benga* artists was Christopher Monyoncho. However, prominent Luo *benga* artists such as Okatch Biggy began their career in Kisii in the early 1990s and later moved to the Luo regional headquarters Kisumu after gaining national popularity.

Despite their proximity to the Luo, the Luhya were slow to adopt *benga*, due to the prominence of their own *omutibo* genre. One of the earliest Luhya *benga* artists still going strong in the early twenty-first century is Wilson Omutere Ongaro (a.k.a. Sukuma bin Ongaro). Sukuma bin Ongaro was initially produced by David Amunga. His early 1990 hits include 'Leonida Anyango,' 'Nereah Wekomola' and 'Kazi ya Musumeno ime Nishinda.' Another prominent Luhya *benga* artist is Fanuel Amimo.

While the structure of the first section of *benga* has remained unchanged in recordings and performances since the 1990s, the second section (guitar section) evolved to a more *sebene*-influenced approach (*sebene* is the Congolese beat used similarly on the second-half guitar section of the Congolese *rumba*), with vocal choruses inserted in the previously guitar-dominated improvised section that was also used to showcase the technical skills of the lead guitarist (Mboya 2009, 4). This characteristic has been adopted by the various local *benga* variants and is a perceived Congolese influence on the genre. The *benga* variants continue to develop in their own right, attracting recording opportunities and widespread audiences nationally and internationally.

Conclusion

Benga has developed from the 1960s ensembles of two to three musicians to a huge band sound incorporating more musicians and giving birth to several variants, both nationally and internationally. The genre, initially rooted in the indigenous Luo idioms, has metamorphosed with infusions from other indigenous idioms, engendering deep cultural significance for its diverse audiences across Kenya. New and young *benga* musicians also record in the national 'Kiswahili' language, targeting a wider national audience and generating an international outlook. Some of these artists, including Suzanna Owiyo, Eric Wainaina and Dan Chizi among others, have achieved global exposure through international festivals. Thus, the genre continues to stand out as one of the most celebrated Kenyan popular music styles.

Bibliography

Amuka, Peter S.O. 2000. 'The Play of Deconstruction in the Speech of Africa: The Role of Pakruok and Ngero in Telling Culture in Dholuo.' In *African Philosophy as Cultural Inquiry*, eds. Ivan Karp and D. A. Masolo. Bloomington, IN: Indiana University Press, 89-104.

Barz, F. Gregory. 2001. 'Meaning in *Benga* Music of Western Kenya.' *British Journal of Ethnomusicology* 10(1): 107-15.

Ewens, Graeme. 1991. *Africa O-ye: A Celebration of African Music*. London: Sage Publications.

Graham, Ronnie. 1988. *Stern's Guide to Contemporary African Music*. London: Zwan ('Reissued as The World of African Music.' London: Pluto Press, 1992.).

Mboya, Tom Michael. 2009. '"My Voice Is Nowadays Known," Okatch Biggy, *Benga* and Luo Identity in the 1990s.' *Muziki: Journal of Music Research in Africa* 6(1): 14-25.

Mwaura, Bantu. 2006. '"*Benga* ni Damu Yake D.O. Misiani" [*Benga* Is His Blood].' *Jahazi* 1(1): 28-32.

Ogude, James. 2007. '"The Cat that Ended up Eating the Homestead Chicken": Murder, Memory and Fabulization in D. O. Misiani's Dissident Music.' In *Urban Legends, Colonial Myths: Popular Culture and Literature in East Africa*, eds. James Ogude and Joyce Nyairo. Trenton, NJ and Asmara: Africa World Press, 173-200.

Okumu, Caleb Chrispo. 2001. 'Conceptualising African Popular Music: A Kenyan Experiment.' *Bulletin of the Council for Research in Music Education* 147: 145-8.

Okumu, Caleb Chrispo. 2005. 'A World View of *Benga*: Truths and Lies about the Region's Popular Music.' Paper presented at the Lake Victoria Festival of Arts, 26 May-1 June, Kisumu, Kenya.

Ondieki, Donald Otoyo. 2010. 'An Analysis of Zilizopendwa for the Development of Instructional Materials for Music Education.' Unpublished Ph.D. thesis. Kenyatta University, Nairobi.

Ondieki, Donald Otoyo, and Amateshe, Maurice. 2013. 'The *Benga* Phenomenon: Unmasking a "Relentless" Musical Genre in Kenya.' In *Readings in Ethnomusicology: A Collection of Papers Presented at Ethnomusicology Symposium 2013*, ed. Mitchel Strumpf. Dar es Salaam: University of Dar es Salaam Press. (Also published in *East African Journal of Music* 3(1) [2015]: 26ff.)

Osusa, Tabu. 2008. Liner notes to *Retracing the Benga Rhythm* CD and DVD. Nairobi: Ketabul Music.

Osusa, Tabu. 2010. Liner notes to *Retracing Kikuyu Popular Music* CD and DVD. Nairobi: Ketabul Music.

Pfukwa, Charles. 2010. 'When Cultures Speak Back to Each Other: The Legacy of *Benga* in Zimbabwe.' *Muziki: Journal of Music Research in Africa* 7(1): 169-78.

Roberts, John Storm. 1968. 'Popular Music in Kenya.' *African Music Society Journal* 4(2): 53-5.

Rycroft, David. 1962. 'The Guitar Improvisation of Mwenda Jean Bosco (Part II).' *African Music Society Journal* 3(1): 86-102.

Stapleton, Chris, and May, Chris. 1987. *African All-Stars: The Pop Music of a Continent*. London: Quartet Books Limited.

Stapleton, Chris, and May, Chris. 1990. *African Rock: The Music of a Continent*. New York: Penguin Books.

Discographical References

Kalenjin Sisters. 'Kwaheri Yohana.' Label unknown. N.d.: Kenya. (Reissued as Kalenjin Sisters. 'Kwaheri Yohana.' *Retracing the Benga Rhythm*. Ketebul Music. 2008: Kenya.)

Kalenjin Sisters. 'Paulo my Lover.' Label unknown. 1997: Kenya.

Mwai, Daniel Kamau. 'Murata/I Love You.' 1970: Kenya. (Reissued as Daniel Kamau Mwai. 'Murata/I Love You.' Various Artists. *Retracing the Benga Rhythm*. Ketebul Music. 2008: Kenya.)

Mwenda, Jean Bosco. 'Tajiri Na Mali Yake.' Gallo C.O. 199. 1959: Kenya.

Ogara Boys Band. 'Selestina Juma.' AGS Records. 1963: Kenya.

Ogara John, and Ochieng', Nelly. 'Samuel Aketch.' 1965: Kenya. (Reissued as John Ogara and Nelly Ocheing'. 'Samuel Aketch.' Various Artists. *Retracing the Benga Rhythm*. Ketebul Music. 2008: Kenya.)

Omolo, Gabriel, and the Apollo Komesha Band '71. 'Lunchtime' and 'Tutakula Vya Ajabu.' Apollo. APL 618. 1971: Kenya.

Ongaro, Sukuma Bin. 'Kazi ya Musumeno imenishinda.' Label unknown. N.d. : Kenya.

Ongaro, Sukuma Bin. 'Leonida Anyango.' Label unknown. N.d. : Kenya.

Ongaro, Sukuma Bin. 'Nereah Wekomola.' Label unknown. N.d. : Kenya.

Discography

Kilimambogo Brothers Band. 'Katulu na Bell-Bottom' and 'Eka Kuia Beatrice.' Kilimambogo Brothers. KLB 7-001. 1976: Kenya.

Kilimambogo Brothers Band. 'Kelitu Ka Kanyole Pt. 1' and 'Kelitu Ka Kanyole Pt. 2.' Kilimambogo Brothers. KLB 7-002. 1976: Kenya.

Kilimambogo Brothers Band. 'Muindi Wa Mang'ala' and 'Dr. Kalau.' Kilimambogo Brothers KLB 7-003. 1976: Kenya.

Kings, Victoria B. *The Mighty Kings of Benga*. Globe Style CDORB 079. 1993: UK.

Misiani, Daniel Owino. 'Kiseru Pek Chalo Kidi.' POK records. N.d.: Kenya

Misiani, D.O., and the Shirati Jazz Band. *Benga Beat*. World Circuit WCB 003. 1987: UK.

Misiani, D.O., and the Shirati Jazz Band. *Benga Blast*. Earthworks STEW EWW13. 1989: UK.

Misiani, D.O., and the Shirati Jazz Band. *Piny Ose Mer: The World Upside Down*. Globe Style ORB 046. 1989: Germany.

Misiani, D.O., and the Shirati Luo Voice Jazz. Shirati Luo Voice Jazz. Sungura. SGA-LP-103. 1972: Kenya.

Ramogi, George, and C. K. Dumbe Dumbe Jazz Band. *1994 USA Tour: Safari ya Ligingo*. Dumbe Dumbe Records, Dumbe 01. 1994: USA.

Retracing the Benga Rhythm. Ketebul Music. 2008: Kenya. (CD. DVD and accompanying booklet).

DONALD OTOYO ONDIEKI AND CALEB CHRISPO OKUMO

Beni

Beni is among the very first popular music genres that originated as a result of the slave trade, colonialism, Westernization, industrialization and urbanization in East Africa. It was popular along the coastal towns of East Africa and in the capitals of the regions from the 1890s to the 1960s. Historically, the genre represented a localized version of the military brass bands that were ubiquitous from the 1890s through World Wars I and II and that disappeared soon after the end of colonial rule in the early 1960s.

Beni was originally performed by the Swahili people of the eastern African coastline. It was a hybrid of the old Arab pageant, the indigenous 'ngoma' (song and dance) and semi-military evolutions, welded together with European brass band instruments, costumes and culture (Ranger 1975, 93). *Beni* is a Swahili adaptation of the English word 'band' referring to groups of musicians. The genre takes its name from its essential musical feature – the reproduction of a military brass-band effect (Ranger 1975, 5). However, unlike military brass band music, *beni* was accompanied by dancing that varied considerably from one region to another. The dancing took the forms of parade, procession, march, or dance in platoon form. Singing was also an important part of *beni* performances, thus the alternate title *beni ngoma*.

Beni songs normally took the form of rhyming commentaries on current affairs of the day in the Kiswahili language. The songs comprised both instrumental and vocal sections. The instrumental sections at times repeated the vocal melodic motifs and/or provided interludes, bridges and development sections. The bands belonged to societies that were organized through a hierarchy of men and women officers, elaborate ranks, uniforms and titles of honor as was found within the British military formation. The leaders participated in the dance and were in charge of the administration and welfare functions of the societies. The *beni* societies founded subordinate branches (Ranger 1975, 5).

Ranger (1975) gives a unique and detailed chronicle of how the *beni* tradition was an integrating phenomenon from the northern coast of Lamu, which almost borders Somalia, to the lakeside villages of the Zambian shore of Lake Tanganyika. In Lamu and Mombasa, the *beni* associations first emerged in the 1890s, coexisting with colonial rule, and were phased out in the early 1960s. *Beni* was initially a consequence of the traumatic experiences of eastern Africans taken out of their own communities into slavery. The slaves were taken to the coast and loaded onto slave ships. If the ships were intercepted by the Royal Navy, the freed slaves were placed in the care of missionaries 'whose absolute power was made all the more absolute by their benevolence' (ibid., 10). The rescued slaves were instructed that their original customs were wrong and were offered selected European customs as a new way of life. The freed slaves then learned how to read, write and speak English, among other accomplishments that included playing military band instruments.

The earliest-known formations of *beni* are described by Ranger (1975, 15), who traces it to the Swahili quarters of the coastal towns of Kenya and Tanzania as early as the 1890s. While Ranger (ibid., 21) attributes the emergence of the genre to the 1890s, Salim (1973, 158) asserts that *beni* emerged in Mombasa just prior to World War I, and that it gained popularity during and after the war. According to Ranger (1975), *beni* was characterized by performance groups marching with brass instruments and portable percussion instruments in the style of the military marching bands they emulated. *Beni* from the Kenyan coast emulated the British military bands while on the Tanzanian coast it imitated the German military bands. The groups consisting of the band, singers and dancers were popularly known as *chama* (an association of a group of people). The dancers usually paraded their skill at drills while costumed in ceremonial military uniforms that displayed loyalty to the British Crown (Ranger 1975, 9). Some features of *beni* were alien to the local Swahili communities, such as the instrumentation and some of the British repertoire they learned. There were also inherited features from the coastal traditions such as the competitions of dance, poetry and song. Competitions among the groups were common, organized by the group leaders. Elements that were adjudicated by the audience included the cleanliness and 'smartness' of the marching troupes.

According to Ranger (1975, 21) Khamis Mustafa is normally credited with being the founder of *beni*. Mustafa established the Kingi Beni (King's Band), the first of the coastal *beni* societies, in the late 1890s (ibid., 22). It is said to have started as a flute band before adding bugles. This concept was soon imitated in a competitive manner and another group, this time emulating the Scottish, was formed and named Scotchi Beni. The Scotchi Beni also used kilts in their attire and added bagpipes. In Malindi, the two early *beni* associations were Sultani, which flew the Zanzibar flag, and the Kingi, which flew the Union Jack. Lamu was divided into two halves, namely the Zena and the Suudi, which were later named Mtambweni and Mkomani. The people of Lamu selected their *beni* tradition from Mombasa with the Mtambweni association adopting the Kingi Beni and, as a reaction, the Mkomani adopting the Scotchi Beni. The two competed in public displays as well as weddings and other ceremonies. From these beginnings, *beni* culture spread along the coast from Kismayu in the north to Lindi in the south and then to the interior regions of Tanganyika, Nyasaland and Mozambique.

Beni grew out of the preexisting dance association tradition and was an indication of the adaptability of Swahili culture. The Swahili people were passive and reluctant to serve in World War II, and the British mainly recruited in up-country communities. But the presence of the King's African Rifles (KAR) in Lamu created a reaction among the Lamu youth. Thus the Kingi Beni split, giving rise to two extra splinter groups, namely Keya (KAR) and Chura (Frog) associations. These two splinter groups stressed more military aspects of *beni* than Kingi (Ranger 1975, 45). Later the Sadla group broke away with a more liberal style of dress that included a more casual bush hat and khaki clothes representing the European settlers' informal lifestyle (ibid. 46).

The busy nature of the port of Mombasa and the docking of many naval ships during World War I encouraged *beni* activities to place even greater emphasis on naval and military symbols and ranking. Toward the end of World War I, the Mombasa form of *beni* disappeared as the town became more cosmopolitan, moving to the interior of Nairobi and rural Kamba areas, which joined the coastal region with central Kenya. One of the African quarters of Nairobi that hosted the Swahili people from the coast, called 'Mombasa Village,' started a branch of Scotchi Beni around 1919. The 'Pangani Village,' another African quarter in Nairobi that also settled Tanzanian prisoners of war, developed a Tanzanian version of Arinoti Beni. Tanzania had two main *beni* societies – Marini and Arinoti – that were influenced by German military band music. Soon the Nairobi competitions featured the Arinoti versus the Scotchi *beni*. The Scotchi reported to the main office in Mombasa and the Arinoti reported to the main office in Tanga, Tanzania.

Beni prospered during World War II but slowly lost popularity after independence, due in part to the economic challenge of managing the *beni* societies' competitions, especially after the economic depression that followed the end of the war. In Mombasa, the influence of *rumba* and jazz was slowly taking hold. With the need to support the bands, most of them took up the market for hiring and rebranded themselves as Kingi Jazz Band, Skotchi Jazz Band and Sadla Jazz Band. They were later known as 'Brass Bands Jazz' or 'Brasso.' These 'brasso' bands have continued to exist in the periphery of the music industry; the most popular of the twenty-first century in Kenya is the Mazeras Brasso Band, based on the outskirts of Mombasa in the town of Mazeras. The Mazeras Brasso Band has continued to feature in all 'coast-nite' concerts organized to celebrate the musical culture of the Kenyan coastal region.

The Mazeras brasso bands are made up mainly of Digo people from the Mijikenda community, as opposed to Swahili people. This led to other genres developing from small bands hired to provide entertainment at private weddings, Eid ul-Fitr celebrations and special observances. The small bands began to take over after World War II due to the influx of war veterans who came back with additional musical skills on other instruments such as the guitar and banjo, and other musical influences such as *rumba*. These war veterans also introduced new European-style dancing that was similar to ballroom dancing. Hence, a new dance form emerged, known as *muziki wa dansi*, deriving its name from the adoption of the English word, dance (see separate entry). The use of the term *dansi* also highlighted the difference between the *ngoma* dancing and games practiced with *beni* music, thus the term *beni ngoma* and the *dansi* that was associated with the annexation of the guitar, accordion and banjo instruments by smaller groups of young musicians mostly after World War II (Ranger 1975; Kavyu 1978). While *beni* was founded basically on the principles of brass band, *dansi* was played on accordion and guitar.

The Survival of *Beni*

The popularity of *dansi* marked the end of *beni* in the 1960s and the start of other eastern Africa popular music styles that were based on the guitar. Among the coastal Islamic Swahili people, however, *beni* has stayed an integral part of festive life, surviving the onslaught of the fashionable *dansi* that has elsewhere made the form obsolete.

In 1980s Mombasa some of the old *beni* clubs would still come out for the Eid-ul-Fitr celebrations at the end of Ramadhan, one even sporting two bagpipes. In Zanzibar *beni* continued as a night entertainment in the suburban areas through its association with the illicit liquor trade, which earned it the alternative name of *mbwa kachoka* ('the dog is tired') after one of the drunkards' dances that had turned into a fashion. *Beni* was also performed as a march band music for the *fensi* carnivalesque parade on the eve of the Ramadhan fasting month.

Still current in the 2010s, wedding *beni* takes on two different modes: one is a street procession that accompanies the sending of the bride's belongings to the place where the newlyweds are going to live; the other one is a women's dance where the wedding guests perform in a circle around the band with solo dancers or pairs of dancers entering the circle for special hip-gyrating routines. The lead trumpet gives the cues for new songs and all participants join for the chorus. A typical lineup may feature one to four trumpets (cornets), occasional trombone or baritone horn/tuba. Rhythm is provided by bass drum, snare drum and small local percussion instruments. Clash cymbals form an integral part of the *beni* sound. If imported ones are not available a local piece or pieces of sheet metal may be substituted for this important part of the sound, which is also borne out by the alternative Swahili name for the genre, *beni bati* (bati = 'sheet metal').

Wedding *beni* usually shapes melodies and catchphrases of songs of different origins – mainly *taarab* – into suite-like medleys. In turn, *beni* rhythms and the sound of the trumpet are continuing into the 2010s to be an inspiration for modern *taarab*, where many keyboard solos in the faster chorus/dance sections are modeled on the sound and style of *beni* brass.

In Zanzibar and Dar es Salaam any kind of street procession – like the celebration after winning a soccer match – may feature a small accompanying *beni* ensemble. In Dar es Salaam the boundaries between *beni* and *mdundiko* are fleeting.

Bibliography

Anyumba, Henry Owunor. 1970. 'Historical Influences on African Music: A Survey.' In *Hadith* 3, ed. Bethwell Allan Ogot. Nairobi: East African Publishing House, 192–204.

Kavyu, Paul Ndilya. 1978. 'The Development of Guitar Music in Kenya.' *Jazz Research* 10: 111–19.

Lambert, Harold Ernest. 1962-3. 'The Beni Dance Songs.' *Swahili* 33(1): 18–21.

Lonsdale, John M. 1968. 'Some Origins of Nationalism in East Africa.' *Journal of African History* 9(1): 119–46.

Macintyre, Kate. 1986. *The Nairobi Guide*. London: MacMillan Publishers.

Martin, Stephen. 1991. 'Brass Bands and the Beni Phenomenon in Urban Africa.' *African Music* 7(1): 72–81.

Ranger, Terence Osborn. 1975. *Dance and Society in East Africa 1890–1970: The Beni Ngoma*. London: Heinemann Educational Books.

Salim, Ahmed Idha. 1973. *The Swahili Speaking Peoples of Kenya's Coast 1895–1965*. Nairobi: East African Publishing House.

Discography

Beni ya Kingi. 'Beni Medley.' *Zanzibar: Soul & Rhythm – De l'âme à la danse*. Virgin JAHM CD 511-12. *2004*: France.

DONALD OTOYO ONDIEKI AND CALEB CHRISPO OKUMU, WITH WERNER GRAEBNER

Bikutsi

Bikutsi (also written *bikudsi*) is a distinctive dance music genre that is connected to the ethnic groups of the Beti living in the southern parts of Cameroon. The genre is named after a dance movement involving stamping on the ground: 'kut' means to beat or to hit, 'si' is the earth or the floor, and the particle 'bi' means repeatedly or continuously. The term *bikutsi* also refers to a women-only song-and-dance genre that is renowned for its socio-critical lyrics and frequently described as 'original' *bikutsi*. The popular music genre *bikutsi*, however, is played by modern music ensembles consisting of electric guitars, drum set, vocals and various additional percussion instruments. It arose from the imitation of xylophone music on electric guitars in the 1960s and 1970s and was successfully introduced in the Cameroonian music market in the 1980s. Since then, *bikutsi* has evolved to become one of the most popular music genres of the country.

Bikutsi music is first and foremost music for dancing. It is regularly performed live in nightclubs, especially in the areas inhabited mainly by Beti, including the capital Yaoundé. Songs are commonly in a fast tempo and based on a pattern in 12/8 pulse structure with the accented beat, played by the bass drum, on every third pulse. The drum set provides the rhythmic foundation, with repetitive chords and interlocking guitar lines on top. The lyrics are in Ewondo (and dialects thereof), the language spoken by the Beti, and, rarely, in French. The songs are in call-and-response form or structured along the verse-refrain model. The lyrics cover topics including love and relationships, daily life, social pressures and moral issues; they frequently include direct or indirect references to sexual and erotic matters, more or less hidden through metaphorical language use.

In the 1960s musicians in Cameroon were dedicated to transferring traditional music styles to 'modern' instruments, including Beti dance music played by *mendzan* xylophones. Guitarist Messi Martin, nicknamed 'Father of Bikutsi,' is credited with having invented the so-called *balafon* guitar ('xylophone guitar') in the late 1960s by threading a sponge or folded paper between the strings, at the side of the body, right at the bridge, to make his guitar sound like a *mendzan*. In addition, the fast and interlocking lines of the xylophone ensembles and the rhythmical structures were taken from traditional dance music and transferred to modern musical instruments. The lead guitar, the accompanying guitar and the bass guitar in a modern music group all have a corresponding *mendzan* xylophone.

During the 1970s important music groups were the band Los Camaroes (with guitarist Messi Martin), the band Les Titans, the singer Mama Ohandja and the band Elanga Maurice et Les Grands Esprits.

In the 1980s this 'modern' Beti music was labeled *bikutsi*. By means of the media and music industry, it was established as a distinctive popular music genre on the Cameroonian music market. This development was facilitated by political changes including a Beti president in 1982 and the introduction of television in 1985. Important groups that promoted *bikutsi* music in the 1980s were Les Vétérans and Les Têtes Brulées and the singer Ange Ebogo Emerent.

Musically, in the 1990s, the bass guitar became more important within the instrumental setting. Also, women entered the field of modern *bikutsi*, first and foremost the singer Katino (later K-Tino) who became famous for her erotic dance style and her use of sophisticatedly metaphorical language in her lyrics. Since the 1990s *bikutsi* has been accompanied by a public discourse over morality due to outspoken sexual references in lyrics and presentation of many *bikutsi* songs. Popular male musicians of the 1990s include Mbarga Soukouss, Fam Ndzengue and Zélé le Bombardier. An annual *bikutsi* festival has been held in Yaoundé since the late 1990s.

Since the 2000s video clips have been established as essential for the initial dissemination of *bikutsi* songs, which are then adapted for live performance. Stars of *bikutsi* since the 2000s include Lady Ponce, Majoie Ayi, Richard Amougou and Tonton Ebogo.

Bikutsi songs appeal to all ages and socioeconomic groups, especially to members of the Beti ethnic groups. The respective generations have 'their' *bikutsi* musicians; younger stars within the field rather appeal to the younger generation and vice versa. *Bikutsi* is disseminated in the country by way of radio, televised video clips, audio cassettes and compact discs, and the Internet. In the international world music market, *bikutsi* is rarely seen. In the late 1980s the group *Les Têtes Brulées* brought *bikutsi* to some fame in Europe, and the Paris-based Cameroonian singer Sally Nyolo has featured *bikutsi* songs since the 2000s.

Bibliography

Brunner, Anja. 2012. 'Local Cosmopolitan Bikutsi.' *Norient Academic Online Journal*. Online at: http://norient.com/academic/local-cosmopolitan-bikutsi (accessed 24 May 2017).

Brunner, Anja. 2014. *Bikutsi – Popular Music in Postcolonial Cameroon in the 1970s and 1980s. The Rise of a Beti Dance Music Genre*. Unpublished Ph.D. thesis, Vienna University (Austria).

Mbala, Agnès Marie épouse Nkili. 1985. *Bikutsi: Chants des femmes chez les Mvele* [Bikutsi: Women's Songs of the Mvele]. Unpublished Ph.D. thesis, Université de Lille.

Noah, Jean Maurice. 2004. *Le Bikutsi du Cameroun. Ethnomusicologie des Seigneurs de la forêt* [The Bikutsi of Cameroon. Ethnomusicology of the Lords of the Forest]. Yaoundé: Carrefour/Erika.

Onguene Essono, Louis-Martin. 1996. 'La Démocratie en chanson: Les Bikut-si du Cameroun' [Democracy in Song: the Bikut-si of Cameroon]. *Politique Africaine* 64: 52–61.

Owona Nguini, Mathias Eric. 1995. 'La Controverse bikutsi-makossa: Musique, politique et affinités régionales au Cameroun (1990–1994)' [The Controversy Bikutsi-Makossa: Music, Politics and Regional Affinities in Cameroon (1990–1994)]. *L'Afrique politique:* 267–76.

Owono-Kouma, Auguste. 2004. 'Langage de la sexualité et tendances de la pratique sexuelle chez les Beti aujourd'hui. Essai d'analyse lexico-sémantique des textes de quelques chanteurs de bìkùd sí des années 1990' [Language of Sexuality and Trends of Sexual Practices of the Beti Today. Analytical Essay of Lexical Semantics of Lyrics of Some Bikutsi Singers of the 1990s]. *Cahier de l'UCAC* 7: 37–67.

Rathnaw, Dennis Michael. 2010. 'The Eroticization of Bikutsi: Reclaiming Female Space Through Popular Music and Media.' *African Music* 8(4): 48–67.

Discography

Aï-Jo Mamadou. *Action Réaction*. Les Editions Achille Production 016. *N.d.*: Cameroon.

K-Tino. *7è Ciel*. Les Editions Achille Production. *2006*: Cameroon.

Les Têtes Brulées. '*Best Of*.' *Bikutsi Fever*. Africa Fête Diffusion 004/Night & Day 215. *2000*: Senegal/France.

Les Vétérans. *Au Village.* Vol. 3. Ebobolo Fia Production TC 0007/Safari Ambiance 103. *1985:* Cameroon.

Majoe Ayi. *Horizon.* Originespro. *2010?:* Cameroon.

Mama Ohandja dit Rossignol et l'orchestre Confiance Jazz. *Consequences de la prison.* La Vox Africa 228. *1980:* Nigeria.

Mbarga Soukous. *Essamba.* Ebobolo Fia KTC 043. *1990:* Cameroon.

Nkodo, Sitony: *Bikutsi Super Vision.* JPS Production 0011. *1998:* France.

Olinga, Gaston, and l'Echo Jazz de la Capitale. 'Sogolo befam.' Sonafric 1762. *1975:* Cameroon.

Orchestre Los Camaroes. 'Bekono Nga N'konda/Mengala Maurice.' Sonafric 1501. *1969?:* Cameroon.

ANJA BRUNNER

Boeremusiek

Boeremusiek is a widely ridiculed form of mostly instrumental folk music, predominantly (but not exclusively) practiced by white Afrikaans-speaking South Africans. Primarily intended to accompany informal social dancing, the genre developed out of collisions between nineteenth-century European dance forms, South African indigenous music, blackface minstrelsy and American and British dance hall music of the early twentieth century.

In twenty-first-century South African popular culture, *boeremusiek* is often employed as musical typecast for a conservative brand of working-class, white-Afrikaans social clumsiness. However, *boeremusiek*'s boorish cast often masks the fact that the music arouses – among a much broader cross-section of South African society – powerful affective associations with a bygone era of South African pioneer life. These affective associations are often expressed in barely perceptible linguistic inflections: an edge of apologetic nostalgia here, a touch of embarrassment there.

The 'boer' in *boeremusiek* – which translates directly from Afrikaans as 'farmer' – belongs at least in part to a deep rural South African dreamtime. The whimsical materialism of *boeremusiek* titles such as 'Dirt Road Setees' (*Stofpad seties*); 'Dust Storms in the Free-State' (*Stofstorms in die Vrystaat*); 'Under the Baobab Tree' (*Onder die kremetartboom*); 'The Sad Waltz' (*Die hartseerwals*); and 'Aunt Anne Smells Like Glue' (*Tant Antjie ruik na gom*) help conjure up this time outside time. Mostly, however, the genre's nostalgic resonances are tied up with the sound of the concertina, the lead instrument in a typical dance band. Pointing to its braying sound, its mechanisms of respiration and, perhaps, its stubbornness in yielding to the commands of its owner, the instrument is also known as a *donkielong* – a 'donkey's lung.' In the language of enthusiasts the instrument is a living, breathing extension of themselves. Its 'voice' is said to 'quiver' with emotion when players shake the instrument on held notes to effect a vibrato of sorts, or to 'sigh' in slow exhalations of breath. The concertina is repeatedly described as 'screeching' and 'wailing' in a mesmerizingly unpleasant way.

Supported by a combination of rhythm guitar, banjo, piano, bass (and electronic and percussive instruments for the nontraditionalists), the concertina cranks out familiar and mostly formulaic ditties. Although earlier forms of *boeremusiek* sometimes included a vocal chorus, the sung element began to wane in the 1950s and most of the music produced beginning in the second half of the twentieth century is purely instrumental. A typical *boeremusiek* 'number' is in a major key and consists of two 16-bar themes (8+8), also called 'draaie' (turns). An important musical feature is a contrasting section, colloquially called 'minors,' which usually occurs after the statement of both themes. Nothing to do with the minor mode, 'minors' often features a modulation to the fifth-scale degree and is mostly characterized by fast concertina tremolos over lingering harmonies. Here the focus shifts from the musicians to the dancers who are encouraged to whirl around enthusiastically. 'Minors' is followed by an often inelegant modulation back to the tonic key, which either marks the end of the piece or an abrupt return to the first theme. Some bands embellish the basic formula with frequent secondary dominants and diminished, augmented, seventh and ninth chords, but others regard deviations from the norm as show-offish and corrosive.

Origin Myths

Through the appellation 'Boer' as an interchangeable term for 'Afrikaner,' *boeremusiek* is inevitably set against the context of apartheid South Africa. In tune with the political ideology of separate racial development, the genre's Creole origins were largely suppressed during the latter half of the twentieth century. Most *boeremusiek* enthusiasts of the era preferred to draw a direct and uncomplicated (if historically inaccurate) link between *boeremusiek* dance forms – notably the waltz, *mazurka, polka* and *settees/schottische* – and their European and Anglophone counterparts. 'Boeremusiek is what it says,' argued the president of the largest *boeremusiek* organization in South Africa, the Boeremusiek Guild, in 1995 (Ferreira 1995, 5): 'It is the interpretation of the music that was brought by the European to Africa and which the South African, in his isolation in remote districts and farms, kept up as part of his own culture.' Ferreira claims that the development of *boeremusiek* was 'in reality nothing but an extension of European civilization.'

Before the 1940s, however, there was little sense of *boeremusiek* as a defined genre, or of concertina music as an exclusively white European musical tradition. Many nineteenth- and early twentieth-century accounts of *boer* domestic life describe music making as an activity that involved the entire household – servants included (see Froneman 2012, 49–76 and Worrall 2009, 1–65). Following the Cape colonial tradition of outsourcing musical entertainment to locals and slaves, the influence of so-called colored musicians on the development of the genre was significant. In fact, the type of music that was by the mid-twentieth century touted as 'boeremusiek' – the national folk music of the *Boere* – was earlier commonly referred to as 'hotnotsmusiek' – a derogatory term for the music of South Africa's indigenous Khoi people (see Hartman 1955).

In terms of musical characteristics, traces of *boeremusieks*'s hybrid beginnings are most noticeable in the guitar-driven *vastrap* beat that undergirds many *boeremusiek* numbers. A common feature of *langarm*, and closely related to the *ghoema* beat associated with *klopse* and Cape Town jazz, *vastrap* has begun to function as a salient marker of hybridity and creolization in South African popular music (see Martin 2009 and Kombuis and Kramer 2004). There are also significant similarities between the repertoire and playing techniques of *boeremusiek*, *klopse* and *langarm*. As Denis-Constant Martin (2013, 143) has noted, *boeremusiek* banjo playing of the 1930s 'evoked the Klopse approach to the instrument' and Cape Town-born concertinist Japie Laubscher 'used a singular kind of tremolo, akin to the characteristic vibrato of *langarm* saxophonists.'

Although it remains somewhat sketchy and elusive, there is further indication of convergence between 'boeremusiek' and 'hotnotsmusiek' in nineteenth- and early twentieth-century blackface minstrelsy. The connection is most apparent in the correspondence of popular minstrel songs and the Afrikaans folk music repertoire and in the history of concertina playing in South Africa. The concertina was, by many accounts, an important feature of local minstrel performance. Jan Bouws (1982, 81–2), for example, refers to an 1874 concertina competition in Cape Town with the prize of a gold watch where a 'duet was performed in the manner of the minstrels to the accompaniment of a banjo and "bones."' Dale Cockrell (1987, 419) includes the concertina in a list of instruments featured in a 'typical minstrel show' in the South African context. The concertina also featured regularly in English and American minstrel groups in the nineteenth century, leading Dan Worrall (2009, 47) to deduce that the concertina 'found a ready place in Cape Town "Christy Minstrel" knockoff bands.'

Politics and Pleasure

It is not only its Creole origins that are underplayed in Eurocentric accounts of the genre's development, but the fact that *boeremusiek* has generally not found acceptance in the upper echelons of Afrikaner society. The overlaps between the cultural agendas of Afrikaner nationalism and *boeremusiek* as a popular form are uneven and irregular. Although the music functioned as a powerful emblem of white-Afrikaner identity for the better part of the twentieth century – and although *boeremusiek* discourse has been influenced by Afrikaner cultural politics in pronounced ways – the music has promulgated working-class values that have often been at odds with the ideal-type civilized European culture to which Afrikaans cultural leaders wanted the *volk* to aspire.

The incongruous relationship between popular sentiment and ideological positioning is evident from one of the very first documented debates about the genre, where the issue at hand was the aptness of the term 'boeremusiek' for the type of concertina-driven dance music it would come to describe.

The name 'boeremusiek' emerged as part of the Great Trek centenary celebrations in 1938. The movement of the Boers from the Cape colony to the southern African interior during the 1830s has been constructed by Afrikaner historiographers as a key myth of Afrikaner nationalism, and the commemoration and reenactment of the event in 1938 formed an important moment in the emergence of Afrikaner nationalist consciousness (Giliomee 2003, 432–3; Hofmeyr 1988).

As well as symbolizing a political watershed, the 1938 celebrations had a profound influence on Afrikaner popular culture. Conjunctions with the word *boer* – including *boerewors* (boer sausage) and *boeretroos* (coffee) – were all the rage, and a range of everyday activities, such as the *braai* (barbecue), was resurrected as typical of Afrikaner culture in South Africa. The conjunction 'boeremusiek' was not assimilated without contestation into this newly popular vocabulary, as the letter columns of Afrikaans newspapers of the time suggest.

At the center of the 1938 debate about *boeremusiek* was David de Lange's hit song 'Suikerbossie' ('Sugarbush,' 1937), which sold over 200,000 copies in an era when the South African recording infrastructure was so sparse that master recordings had to be shipped to Britain for production. In contrast to claims that the song represented 'the soul of the Afrikaner,' the so-called colored origins of the song were repeatedly raised in objection to its being considered an example of 'authentic boeremusiek.' The song met resistance not only on racial grounds, however; debates around its relative merits also hinged on Calvinist notions of bodily restraint (see Froneman 2014a). Most important, the debates exposed class-based tensions within Afrikaner society that are often glossed over in historiographical accounts of the event.

From the early 1930s Afrikaans dance music as recorded by, among others, Die Vyf Vastrappers, Die Vier Transvalers and Die Vyf Takhare, gave voice to a particular working-class urban Afrikaner identity. These groups usually featured the concertina as lead instrument, accompanied by a combination of guitar, banjo, accordion, piano, clarinet or double bass. It was not uncommon for *boeremusiek* recordings from this era to include a sung component, and the lyrics of some of these tunes referenced a world far removed from the idealized white-Afrikaner home of the 1930s. Often directly adapted and translated from American vaudeville hits, David de Lange's lyrics – in particular – regularly featured alcohol abuse, sex, parties, poverty or domestic violence as themes. For the ideologically minded sector of 1930s Afrikaner society, *boeremusiek* represented an alien influence on Afrikaner cultural life and the moral degeneration of the Afrikaner people.

'Light' Afrikaans Music

The problem of generalizing about *boeremusiek* during the period from 1930 to 1950 is that the term was applied to divergent musical styles that employed different instrumental settings and performance practices. When one reads, for example, that *boeremusiek* formed part of the official events at the culmination of the 1938 celebrations on 16 December, it is not the working-class style that is referenced, but Hendrik Susan's more sophisticated reinterpretation that is sometimes called 'light Afrikaans music.'

The events leading up to the formation of Susan's sleek outfit in 1938, and the role of his business associate Pieter de Waal, are well documented (see Froneman 2012, 121–35). De Waal, an extremely popular radio announcer at the South African Broadcasting Corporation (SABC) at the time, saw a commercial opportunity for the formation of a band playing 'boeremusiek' appropriate for radio broadcasts. An important factor in their entrepreneurial endeavor was establishing explicit – albeit highly tenuous – links between the band and Afrikaner nationalist concerns. Although the band members were portrayed in the media as 'sons of the *volk*,' for example, only three of the original band members actually spoke Afrikaans and the other members changed their names to avoid criticism (Trewhela 1980, 50).

Whereas working-class musicians drew on vernacular styles and vaudeville, the Susan band initially took the official songbook of a prominent Afrikaner cultural organization as springboard, and once this repertoire was depleted, supplemented it with newly composed patriotic songs. Although the repertoire of the original Susan 'boere-orkes' (*boer* orchestra) was Afrikaans, their performance style was at first quite indistinguishable from other popular jazz forms of the time. Relatively quickly, however, the band began to absorb vernacular *boeremusiek* formulas into their jazz idiom, especially after prominent Afrikaans concertinists including Fanie Bosch, Neels Steyn and Manie Bodenstein were recruited.

Nico Carstens, the name many South Africans associate most closely with *boeremusiek*, propelled the 'light Afrikaans music' strand of *boeremusiek* to new heights. Once the highest-paid musician in South Africa, Carstens began his career with Susan, but broke away to form his own band in the early 1950s. As bandleader, accordionist and songwriter, Carstens had a diverse musical output that transgressed stylistic boundaries. Much of his commercially successful music of the 1950s and 1960s, however, relies heavily on *boeremusiek* conventions.

Not only did he record multiple successful albums with well-known concertinists such as Rassie Erasmus, Neels Steyn and Nic Potgieter, but his unique accordion style features clear adaptations of techniques prevalent in *boeremusiek* concertina playing: his pervasive use of octave unison tremolos and downward-sliding major sixths, for example. Carstens's best-known hits in the *boeremusiek* style include 'Jampotpolka' (Jam Pot Polka), 'Warmpatat' (Hot Sweet Potato) and the less locally infused 'Klokkiewals' (Little Bell Waltz).

'Traditional' versus 'Modern' *Boeremusiek*

Perhaps because of the intensified focus on locating and defining an Afrikaner folk tradition that could form the basis for a national art music (Bouws 1957), *boeremusiek* bands of the 1950s – including that of Hendrik Susan and Nico Carstens – were increasingly criticized for playing 'unafrikaans,' 'alien' and 'hybridized' music, too strongly influenced by jazz (Hartman 1955). By the mid-1950s it was clear that a new category had emerged: that of 'old-fashioned' or 'traditional' *boeremusiek*. The SABC played a tangible role in the construction of this idea.

In 1951 the SABC launched an extensive campaign to source old *boeremusiek* tunes from its listeners. The biggest response came from Jo Fourie, an avid *boeremusiek* collector, who sent in about 250 tunes (for more on her remarkable story, see Froneman 2012b). Some of these tunes were recorded for the SABC's transcription service and included in a program series *Uit die jaar vroeg* (From Years Yonder), aired in 1952. *Uit die jaar vroeg* represented a conscious intervention on the part of the SABC to endorse 'traditional boeremusiek' as opposed to an 'Afrikaans Tin Pan Alley'. In the opening program of the series, coordinator Bosman de Kock established the parameters of 'real' *boeremusiek* in what can only be described as an invention of tradition: 'Real' *boeremusiek* never makes use of syncopation, rhythm is derived from the melody and not arbitrarily provided by a rhythm section, only primary chords are used and ornamentation always occurs within these set boundaries.

Throughout the 1960s and 1970s *boeremusiek* – in both its 'modern' and 'traditional' guises – continued to be heard on SABC radio, mostly in niche time slots.

Boeremusiek Organizations

The distinction between 'modern' and 'traditional' *boeremusiek* was formalized in the 1980s with the founding of two *boeremusiek* organizations in South Africa that became involved in fierce rivalry and an ongoing feud over matters of musical aesthetics.

The Traditional Boer Music Club of South Africa (TBK), originally called The Concertina Club of South Africa, was founded in 1981 when a group of enthusiasts embarked on a project of finding and renovating the grave of Faan Harris, a legendary concertinist from the 1930s. The aims of the club have been described as 'the collection and fostering of traditional *boeremusiek*' and 'the inviolate preservation of the inalienable and unique character of traditional *boeremusiek*.' To this end the club has, since the earliest years of its existence, primarily engaged itself with the collection and reissuing of rare historical recordings. Although the TBK organizes dances and other live *boeremusiek* gatherings, the club is distinctly discourse-oriented. Under its banner have appeared numerous newsletters, three volumes on *boeremusiek* legends (Bester 1987; 1993; 2003), a history of the origins and development of *boeremusiek* (Schultz 2001) and an important digital archive (Die tradisionele boeremusiekklub van Suid-Afrika, n.d.).

In 1989 the Boeremusiekgilde (Boeremusiek Guild or BMG), looking further to explore the possibilities of 'modern' *boeremusiek*, branched off from the original organization, due to the former's rigidity around upholding 'traditional' musical aesthetics. The TBK demands unplugged instruments, the omission of a rhythm section and the use of primary chords, while the BMG embraces the use of electric guitars, drum kits and keyboards, sound engineering and musical experimentation. The activities of the BMG are also focused on attracting new audiences for *boeremusiek* and supporting new players.

Boeremusiek in Postapartheid South Africa

It has mostly been business as usual for the BMG and TBK in the postapartheid years. On the fringes of South African society, the stale air of school halls has persistently filled up with concertina music on Saturday nights. Members from different branches have carried on convening at tired holiday resorts and camping sites over weekends. Swathed by their respective organizational paraphernalia – uniforms, insignia, banners and pamphlets – the two organizations have continued to rehearse the arguments that keep the rivalry between them alive.

The position of women in the BMG has shifted quite markedly during the 2000s. From mostly being tasked with flower arranging and food preparation, female musicians – and female-only bands – became increasingly common at BMG events. The most prominent of these bands is Die Kaapse Affodille, whose first album *Jy sal dit nie glo nie* (You Won't Believe It) was released in 2011.

Outside the subcultural world of the organized *boeremusiek* scene there have been some attempts since 1994 at fusing *boeremusiek* with other styles. Notable in this regard was Nico Carstens's so-called boereqanga project *Made in South Africa* (1996), which attempted a musical alignment of *boeremusiek* and *mbaqanga*. The group Beeskraal (2004) has explored a fusion between *boeremusiek* and rock.

Following international roots revivalist trends, *boeremusiek* featured prominently in Afrikaans public discourse between 2007 and 2012. This was mainly due to the efforts of Rian Malan and his band Radio Kalahari Orkes (2007), who rerecorded David de Lange's hits from the 1930s, and repositioned De Lange as South Africa's original rock star (see Malan 2006). A much-publicized collaboration between Afrikaans rocker Valiant Swart and *boeremusiek* accordionist Ollie Viljoen, *Vuur en Vlam*, was also released in 2007.

In post-millennial mainstream Afrikaans pop traces of *boeremusiek* – the sound of the concertina, in particular – have resurfaced as a powerful affective marker in a growing nostalgia industry focused on white audiences. The symbolism that gives the concertina its power centers on the sentimental Afrikaner every day of the bygone *boereplaas* (boer farm). Steve Hofmeyr's enormously popular 'DKW' (2010), for example, recalls finding love in the 'old Transvaal' – a reference to Boer republic geography and the Afrikaans folk song 'Sarie Marais.' The concertina threads through the nostalgic imagery of the song, replete with classic cars, outdoor picnics and inopportune mentions of oxwagons to guarantee mass appeal. More ironic is the idyllic farm imagery in Radio Kalahari Orkes's 'Heuningland' (Land of Honey) (2009), where Manie Bodenstein's concertina enters on the refrain.

Conclusion

Perhaps more so than any other genre of South African popular music, *boeremusiek* is steeped in associations with the oppressive history of white power in South Africa. The impact of political ideology lurks everywhere in the house of *boeremusiek*. At the same time, the genre opens up a view on an Afrikaner popular culture often in opposition to the segregationist white politics of twentieth-century South Africa. *Boeremusiek* is a genre that refuses unproblematic classifications of identity, race and class and one that exists across conflicting planes of political and aesthetic experience.

Bibliography

Bester, Piet. 1987. *Tradisionele boeremusiek: 'n gedenkalbum* [Traditional *Boeremusiek*: A Commemorative Volume]. Pretoria: Afrikanervolkswag.

Bester, Piet. 1993. *Boeremusiek: tweede gedenkalbum* [Traditional *Boeremusiek*: A Second Commemorative Volume]. Pretoria: Afrikanervolkswag.

Bester, Piet. 2003. *Boeremusiek: derde gedenkalbum* [Traditional *Boeremusiek*: A Third Commemorative Volume]. Pretoria: Afrikanervolkswag.

Bouws, Jan. 1957. *Suid-Afrikaanse komponiste van vandag en gister* [South African Composers of Today and Yesterday]. Cape Town: A.A. Balkema.

Bouws, Jan. 1982. 'Die minstrels skyn die ewige lewe te hê' [Minstrels Seem to Go on Forever] In *Solank daar musiek is ..: musiek en musiekmakers in Suid-Afrika (1652–1982)* [As Long as There Is Music … Music and Musicians in South Africa (1652–1982)]. Cape Town: Tafelberg, 80–2.

Cockrell, Dale. 1987. 'Of Gospel Hymns, Minstrel Shows, and Jubilee Singers: Toward Some Black South African Musics.' *American Music* 5(4): 417–32.

Die Boeremusiekgilde [The Boeremusiek Guild]. N.d. Online at: http://www.boeremusiekgilde.co.za (accessed 19 May 2017).

Die tradisionele boeremusiekklub van Suid-Afrika [The Traditional Boeremusiek Club of South Africa]. N.d. Onnline at: http://www.boeremusiek.org and http://www.boeremusiek.org.za (accessed 19 May 2017).

Ferreira, I.L. 1995. *Die Boeremusiekgilde se vyf goue jare 1989-1994* [The Boeremusiek Guild's Five Golden Years 1989-1994]. Valhalla: Boeremusiekgilde.

Froneman, Willemien. 2012a. *Pleasure Beyond the Call of Duty: Perspectives, Retrospectives and Speculations about Boeremusiek.* Unpublished Ph.D. thesis, Stellenbosch University.

Froneman, Willemien. 2012b. 'She Danced Alone: Jo Fourie, Songcatcher of the Groot Marico.' *Ethnomusicology Forum* 21(1): 53-76.

Froneman, Willemien. 2014a. *Seks, ras en boeremusiek: agter die retoriek van gebrekkige sanglus by die 1938 Voortrekkereeufees* [Sex, Race and Boeremusiek: Behind the Rhetoric of Lacklustre Singing at the 1938 Great Trek Centenary]. *Litnet-Akademies* 11(2).

Froneman, Willemien. 2014b. 'Subjunctive Pleasure: The Odd Hour in the Boeremusiek Museum.' *Popular Music* 33(1): 1-17.

Giliomee, Hermann. 2003. *The Afrikaners: Biography of a People.* Cape Town: Tafelberg.

Hartman, Anton. 1955. 'Waarheen boeremusiek?' [Whither Boeremusiek?]. *Dagbreek en Sondagnuus*, 13 February.

Hofmeyr, Isabel. 1988. 'Popularizing History: The Case of Gustav Preller.' *Journal of African History* 29(3): 521-35.

Kombuis, Koos, and Kramer, David. 2004. *Is Afrikaanse rock 'n leë gebaar?* [Is Afrikaans Rock an Empty Gesture?]. Online at: http://www.oulitnet.co.za/mond/kkramer.asp (accessed 19 May 2017).

Malan, Rian. 2006. *Consider your verdict ... in die saak Puris v. Rian Malan* [Consider Your Verdict ... in the Case of Puris vs. Rian Malan]. Online at: http://www.oulitnet.co.za/senet/senet.asp?id=48859 (accessed 19 May 2017).

Martin, Denis-Constant. 2009. '"My Culture Is a Creole Culture": Alex van Heerden Talks About Cape Music and His Relationship to It.' *Journal of Musical Arts in Africa* 6(1): 77-82.

Martin, Denis-Constant. 2013. *Sounding the Cape: Music, Identity and Politics in South Africa.* Somerset West: African Minds.

Muller, Stephanus. 2008. 'Boeremusiek.' In *Van volksmoeder to Fokofpolisiekar: Kritiese opstelle oor Afrikaanse herinneringsplekke* [From Volksmoeder to Fokofpolisiekar: Critical Essays on Afrikaans Sites of Memory], eds. Albert M. Grundling and Siegfried Huigen. Stellenbosch: Sun Press, 189-96.

Schultz, Wilhelm. 2001. *Die ontstaan en ontwikkeling van boeremusiek* [The Genesis and Development of Boeremusiek]. Pretoria: AVA Systems.

Trewhela, Ralph. 1980. *Song Safari.* Johannesburg: Limelight Press.

Worrall, Dan Michael. 2009. *The Anglo-German Concertina: A Social History.* Vol. 2. Fulshear, TX: Concertina Press.

Discographical References

Beeskraal. *Plaasdorp.* Leo Musiek LEOCD128. *2004*: South Africa.

Carstens, Nico, and Boereqanga. *Made in South Africa.* Lion's Head Records LHR 001/96. *1996*: Cape Town.

Carstens, Nico. 'Jampotpolka,' 'Warmpatat' and 'Klokkiewals.' *Die lewenslied van Nico Carstens.* Gallo CDREDD 67. *2001*: South Africa.

De Lange, David. *Suikerbossie/Roosterkoek Settees.* Singer GE 264. *1937*: South Africa.

Die Kaapse Affodille Dames Boereorkes. *Jy sal dit nie glo nie.* Select Music SELBCD 866 *2011*: South Africa.

Hofmeyr, Steve. 'DKW.' *Duisend en een.* EMI CDEMIM 361. *2010*: South Africa.

Radio Kalahari Orkes. *Die Nagloper: Musiek van David de Lange.* Sony BMG TERRACD01 *2007*: South Africa.

Radio Kalahari Orkes. 'Heuningland.' *Heuningland.* Rhythm Records RR110. *2009*: South Africa.

Swart, Valiant, and Viljoen, Ollie. *Vuur en Vlam.* Rhythm Records RR 077. *2007*: South Africa.

Discography

Bodenstein, Manie. *Deur die jare 1947-1996.* Gallo CDTGE 170 *2008*: South Africa.

Boeremusiektreffers - So het hulle gespeel 3. Gallo CDTGE 2. *1997*: South Africa.

Konsertina Klub Volume I. EMI CDEMIMD 340. *2009*: South Africa.

Konsertina Klub Volume II. EMI CDEMIMD 380. *2010*: South Africa.

Susan, Hendrik. *Hendrik Susan: So het hulle gespeel 1.* Gallo CDTGE 6. *1996*: South Africa.

Vier Transvalers. *Vier Transvalers: So het hulle gespeel.* Gallo CDTGE 23. *1999*: South Africa.

WILLEMIEN FRONEMAN

Bongo Flava

Bongo flava is a heterogeneous music that developed in Tanzania after the end of the country's socialist era in 1985. This development was facilitated by political change toward multiparty democracy, along with economic liberalization, globalization and affordable digital audio technology. After the opening toward music from the West, young people particularly embraced hip-hop, reggae, rhythm and blues (R&B), *zouk* and dancehall, and *bongo flava* emerged through the appropriation and localization of these music genres. Apart from the US styles, *bongo flava* uses elements from Nigerian Afrobeats, the Tanzanian urban music genres *muziki wa dansi* (itself influenced by Congolese *rumba*) and *taarab* (Swahili coastal music of Arabic origin and with Indian influence), and musical elements from the various ethnic groups in Tanzania. Because of *bongo flava's* connection to the immediate post-socialist era, it is also called the music of the new generation. The name *bongo flava* (often also phonetically spelled bongo fleva) was coined by Tanzanian radio DJs in around 2000, just as the new music was gaining momentum. Bongo is a nickname for Tanzania's metropolis Dar es Salaam, while flava, meaning flavor, is an English loanword. While *bongo flava* began as a localized version of hip-hop, it gradually encompassed other localized foreign styles, so that hip-hop has become a subset of *bongo flava*.

Bongo flava has attracted scholarly interest since the mid-1990s. Studies have mostly evaluated it positively in terms of its role in Tanzanian urban youth identity, its character as a youth movement and socially critical medium, its function as a mouthpiece for youth, and its capacity for employment opportunities. What they sometimes overlooked were negative factors such as piracy, corruption and the exploitation of artists by distributors, managers and media personnel that weakened *bongo flava* as a movement. Moreover, entertainment and media conglomerates that formed since the mid-2000s favor commercially oriented *bongo flava* songs while marginalizing hip-hop (Clark 2013; Reuster-Jahn 2014a).

The Beginning: Reception and Imitation of US Hip-Hop in the 1980s

Hip-hop reached Tanzania through music and video cassettes when the ban on Western music was lifted at the end of the socialist period in 1985. Because these cassettes were at first only accessible through relatives or friends in Western countries, the first people to obtain them were young people from middle- and upper-class families, usually secondary school students. They copied the cassettes, shared them with each other, and watched US hip-hop films together (Remes 1999, 2, 8). Secondary schools were thus the cradle of the Tanzanian hip-hop movement. Soon, sampled beats from US rap stars including Tupac Shakur, Public Enemy and Naughty by Nature were copied and circulated, and rapping in English became the favored pastime of many predominantly male secondary school students. Initially, they imitated both the music and the language of their US idols when they performed at school events and discotheques, striving for closeness to the original. Local rappers attained a certain fame through competitions, and the first Tanzanian rap crews were formed.

The 1990s: The Emergence of *Bongo Flava* Through Localization

Rap music could only be fully appreciated in Tanzania if the songs were performed in Swahili, as most of the Tanzanian youth at that time had a very limited knowledge of English. Consequently, the Swahilization of rap music became a powerful trend, starting in 1991 with Saleh J's Swahili version of 'Ice Ice Baby' by the white US rapper Vanilla Ice from 1989 (Remes 1999, 6–7). Saleh J did not merely translate the English text into Swahili; he also altered the content from drive-by shootings to warnings about HIV/AIDS and promiscuity, thereby setting the path for using the music as a vehicle for social commentary. His album *Swahili rap*, released in 1994 (Perullo 2007, 271), was one of the first hip-hop music cassettes to be produced for sale. While some purist and elitist hip-hop pioneers initially resisted the trend toward Swahilization, they eventually accepted it in order to remain part of the Tanzanian hip-hop scene. Swahilization meant that topical or controversial issues could now be communicated to a broad swath of young people, who were thirsting after facts, feelings and attitudes to which they could relate. It facilitated the spread of hip-hop to poorer neighborhoods and to economically deprived youth, who used rap music to speak out about their lives.

During the early 1990s hip-hop became a broader movement, and groups formed to represent certain areas in Dar es Salaam in competition with each other. The first such group was Kwanza Unit (First

Unit), which was launched in Dar es Salaam in 1991 and represented the affluent neighborhood Oysterbay and Masaki. Other groups followed, for example, Hard Blasterz (representing Upanga), Gangsters with Matatizo or GWM (representing Temeke) and Kino Clan (representing Kinondoni). These groups identified with certain US groups, which they tried to resemble in such aspects as clothing and attitudes (e.g., Kwanza Unit with Mobb Deep, GWM with Naughty by Nature, Hard Blasterz with Fu-Schnickens). This pattern was reproduced in other cities, such as Dodoma, where Chamber Squad and Monsters of the East rivaled with G'z Mobb (Mwanjoka 2011, 15).

From 1990 onwards the new hip-hop culture became increasingly popular through live competitions organized in hotels and clubs; recording and selling albums came later. The only recording studio was owned by the government, which did not allow Western music to be recorded. Private recording studios were set up in Dar es Salaam starting in 1990, beginning with Don Bosco, Soundcrafters and Mawingu studios. In addition, distributors were at first reluctant to invest in the new music. It was only in 1995 that the Dar es Salaam-based distribution company Mamu Stores distributed the first album, Mac Mooger's *The Mac Mooger* (Perullo 2007, 260, 263). It proved successful on the market, and from then on albums were produced in substantial numbers. New studios were formed to meet the growing demand for songs and albums, and by the end of the decade there were about 15 in operation in Dar es Salaam (Mangesho 2003, 39). These studios shaped the new music to a great extent. Bongo Records, in particular, was very influential in developing the sound of what later became known as *bongo flava*.

After private broadcasting was allowed in 1993, FM radio stations became pivotal for the further spread of the new music. In 1994 Radio One was established as the first private radio station in Tanzania dedicated to entertainment. Its DJ, Taji Liundi, was a driving force in the popularization of Swahili hip-hop. Not only did he initiate the broadcasting of such music, he also encouraged young people to bring demo tapes to be played. In 1998 Radio Clouds FM was established, which became the dominating entertainment station in Tanzania, and further FM radio stations followed. They organized talent shows in clubs, where young rappers were invited to rap over instrumentals played by the DJs. Studio producers went to the shows to find new talent. A number of famous artists started there, such as T.I.D., Solo Thang, Mwanafalsafa, Sister P, Wagosi wa Kaya and Juma Nature (Mangesho 2003, 52).

By the end of the 1990s the new music had become a mouthpiece for urban youth. It also offered them business opportunities and thus a way out of difficult living conditions. The music attained enormous popularity and could be heard everywhere. Many songs conveyed a message that rang true for older people as well, and the artists lost their negative image as hooligans. Often related in the first person, the songs centered on the life experience and worldview of the artists. Topics included life in shared rented rooms, HIV/AIDS, problems of health service and the educational system, corruption, unemployment and difficult love relationships. By 1997 many rap lyrics were socially conscious and in Swahili. The artist II Proud was a leading proponent of conscious rap. In his album *Ndani ya Bongo* (Inside Dar es Salaam), he exposed inequality and injustice and challenged state authority. Thus, rap was used as a medium of social empowerment, enabling urban Tanzanian youth to create a sense of community with other urban youth elsewhere in the world (Perullo 2005, 75).

The new music was a source of income both through the sale of albums and through live performances. Moreover, the artists' mobilizing power was harnessed by NGOs and advertisers. As early as 1993 II Proud's crew, Niggaz 2 Public from Mbeya, performed rap shows for the German Technical Cooperation agency's AIDS prevention campaign in the region (Sugu n.d., 32). Musicians also performed at rallies during election campaigns. At the end of the millennium Tanzania had the second largest hip-hop scene in Africa, after Senegalese *rap galsen*.

From 2000 to 2010: Diversification and Commercialization of *Bongo Flava*

In 2000 the Hard Blasterz Crew released their immensely popular song 'Chemsha bongo' (Think Hard), which kicked off the subsequent 'bongo explosion.' Rap was in the air – in streets, shops and minibuses. Hip-hop clothing and hairstyles were widespread, and breakdance was popular. The trend for socially conscious and critical lyrics continued. Songs with meaningful lyrics, especially by artists such as Mr. II, Professor Jay (a former member of the Hard Blasterz crew), and the crew Wagosi wa Kaya contributed substantially to *bongo flava*'s standing as a legitimate form of Tanzanian culture, and in 2001 rap was officially acknowledged by the National Arts Council (BASATA) (Saavedra Casco 2006, 233). Some artists even became rich from their songs. According to Perullo (2007, 268), between 1999 and 2001 the albums of some rappers reached sales of up to 100,000 copies, a high number in Tanzania. Some toured East Africa, while Mr. II and the crew X-Plastaz from Arusha performed at festivals in Europe and produced albums there. In 2004 a compilation of *bongo flava* hits was released by the German label Out Here Records. In the early 2000s *bongo flava* dominated the East African music market, and songs were sold even among the Swahili-speaking expatriate communities in Europe and North America (Saavedra 2006, 230).

With growing popularity and commercialization, *bongo flava* artists became the first centers of attention in Tanzania in a star cult initiated and groomed by the entertainment media. Their private lives and scandals filled the gossip papers, which multiplied during those years. The stars became role models for young Tanzanians looking for ways to escape poverty. This quest was enacted in the film *Girlfriend – filamu ya muziki na maisha* (Girlfriend: A Film of Music and Life [2003]), which relates the story of a poor and struggling young rapper who becomes a star overnight. The film became immensely popular, partly because the actors were real stars from the East Coast Team and partly because of its *bongo flava* soundtrack. In an atmosphere resembling a gold rush, many young people wanted to become rich through *bongo flava*. However, few succeeded. One of them was Juma Nature, who was discovered at a talent show in Dar es Salaam. This artist from a poor family later became the central figure of the Wanaume TMK crew, who represent the Temeke area of Dar es Salaam with its lower-income residents. He invented the *mugambo* ('guard') dance style with its military movements. Juma Nature worked with Bongo Records studio, owned by the sound engineer Paul Matthysse ('P. Funk'), who shaped the stylistic development of *bongo flava* in the 2000s. There, Juma Nature produced one of his most popular tracks, 'Umoja wa Tanzania' (The Union of Tanzania), in which he urged Tanzanians of opposing party affiliations not to fight against each other. In the general elections of 2005, Juma Nature and many other artists campaigned for Jakaya Kikwete, the candidate of the dominant party CCM, through numerous songs and performances (Reuster-Jahn 2008). It is thus apparent that the popularity of *bongo flava* was used by the party to influence people politically. A few independent artists, however, commented critically in their songs on corrupt practices during the elections.

Throughout the country, even in remote towns, young people raised the money to pay for recordings, and the number of studios multiplied. By 2010 there were several hundred studios in Dar es Salaam, many of which, however, were rudimentarily equipped. Most used digital production software such as Fruity Loops and Cubase, which they downloaded themselves or shared with one another. Many of the tracks they produced were never widely heard because the artists did not have the money to promote them. Artists still struggling to make it are called 'undergrounds' (*maandagraundi*) in Tanzania. They try to compensate for their lack of financial resources through networking and musical collaboration (Reuster-Jahn and Hacke 2014; Kerr 2014). They also adopt a mixing strategy with regard to language, topic and musical style in order to reach the widest audience possible (Englert 2008). This mixing strategy is, however, not restricted to the *maandagraundi*. Most artists mix musical styles such as rap, *zouk*, reggae, Congolese *rumba*, Indian music and traditional tunes and instrumentals, either within their songs or in their repertoire.

During the 2000s problems in the *bongo flava* scene emerged; they concerned fraudulent practices vis-à-vis individual artists or crews as the weakest members of the chain. In the production and distribution of cassettes and later CDs, contracts were often not fair and artists could not monitor actual sales. This led to the rise of middlemen, who dealt with distributors on behalf of the artists. However, they usually did not make transactions more transparent for artists but rather established a patron–client relationship with them. Another major problem was promotion fees, which even today in Tanzania include getting airtime for songs, in addition to interviews and feature articles. After the radio stations had used *bongo flava* to win over young audiences, they no longer courted the *bongo flava* artists. On the contrary, artists now usually had to pay radio DJs and program managers for airtime. Piracy by youth using the mp3 format, enabled by the spread of computers, was yet another problem; it also caused a decline in CD production.

In addition to declining sales, live performances gradually became less frequent during the 2000s.

One reason for this was the rapid spread of television in Tanzania, which launched music programs and broadcast music videos. The first music videos had been produced around 1996 by TV stations. From 2000 the increasing demand for these videos led to the emergence of video production companies. With almost all Tanzanian TV stations offering music TV channels and music programs, they soon contributed significantly to music promotion, which increased investment cost. The studio generally considered to have the best reputation in Tanzania in 2015 was Adam Juma's Visual Lab.

Female artists have always played a minor role in *bongo flava*. Hip-hop artists Zay B and Sister P were famous for some time because of their audacious lyrics and their personal rivalry, which they expressed in songs and performance. Most female *bongo flava* artists chose R&B, *zouk* or *kwaito* as their style. The best-known singer is Lady Jaydee, who was once a member of the East Coast Team and rose to fame in 2000 with her hit 'Machozi' (Tears).

2010 to 2015: From Internal Conflicts to Going International

Concentration processes in the entertainment and media sector transformed *bongo flava* from a youth movement into commercial mainstream music, with a niche for rappers. In 2010 a bitter conflict broke out between a group of veteran rappers on the one side and the Clouds Media Group, along with the closely connected Tanzania House of Talent (THT), on the other. Under the name 'Antivirus,' the rappers accused the Clouds Media Group and THT of mainstreaming *bongo flava* and favoring consenting artists while denying independent and critical artists airtime and other forms of promotion (Reuster-Jahn 2014a). THT, a center for the training of musicians, songwriters and dancers, was accused of exploiting its trainees in its commercial production of songs, music videos and live events. THT promotes singers, not rappers, and has produced stars such as Barnaba and Amini, and the female singers Mwasiti, Linah and Rachel. The rebels, who felt increasingly excluded from business opportunities, produced two *Antivirus* mixtapes with caustic songs (2010 and 2011), some in abusive language, which were particularly directed against THT's director and the staff at Clouds FM. The conflict was covered by the media and for a while reinforced the artists involved in their struggle. Joseph Mbilinyi, one of the most long-standing Tanzanian rappers, with the stage name of Sugu (a.k.a. Mr. II), became the leader of the rebels. He also campaigned for the opposition party CHADEMA and was elected Member of Parliament of Mbeya urban constituency in the 2010 elections. In 2011, however, he settled his personal dispute with THT, and the Antivirus movement lost its force.

Another change in *bongo flava* was caused by the growing popularity of Nigerian music (Afrobeats) in Tanzania and on the international music market, particularly in the United Kingdom. Consisting of mostly party songs, this up-tempo and danceable music is called Naijabeats in Tanzania. From roughly 2011 *bongo flava* artists began imitating Naijabeats, which has also led to an increased use of English in the songs (Reuster-Jahn 2014b). Simultaneously, the international success of Naijabeats has raised hopes that *bongo flava*, which is supported by growing international TV networks such as DSTV and MTV, could enjoy similar fame in Africa and beyond. The mega-star of *bongo flava* in the 2010s was Diamond Platnumz, who made his breakthrough in Tanzania in 2010 with 'Mbagala,' a song about a young man so poor he cannot keep his girlfriend. In 2013 his song 'Number One' became a hit all over Africa, and Diamond even released a remix version in collaboration with the Nigerian star Davido. Thanks to this song, Diamond was nominated for several highly prestigious prizes in 2014, such as the MTV Africa Music Award and the MTV Europe Music Award, and he won the Channel O Music Video Award. In 2014 he produced the song 'Bum Bum,' in collaboration with the Nigerian artist Iyanya. In fact, this song could be called the first Tanzanian Naijabeats song (Reuster-Jahn 2014b). However, Diamond and other *bongo flava* stars constantly make sure that they also produce songs for the domestic audience, which demands a slower tempo and lyrics in Swahili. Thus, the well-tried mixing strategy is being used as much as ever. Three decades after its beginnings, in 2015 *bongo flava* is mainly commercial mainstream pop music driven by the entertainment and media industry. Hip-hop and rap music, however, continue to exist as subsets of *bongo flava*, albeit in a niche. They are considered part of *bongo flava* in the historical sense of being 'music of the new generation' but do not influence the mainstream music characteristic of *bongo flava*.

Bibliography

Bancet, Alice. 2007. 'Formation of a Popular Music: Hip-hop in Tanzania.' In *Songs and Politics in Eastern Africa*, eds. Kimani Njogu and Hervé Maupeu. Dar es Salaam: Mkuki na Nyota, and Nairobi: IFRA, 315–54.

Clark, Msia Kibona. 2013. 'The Struggle for Hip Hop Authenticity and Against Commercialisation in Tanzania.' *Journal of Pan African Studies* 6(3): 5–21.

Englert, Birgit. 2003. 'Bongo Flava (Still) Hidden "Underground": Rap from Morogoro, Tanzania.' *Stichproben. Wiener Zeitschrift für kritische Afrikastudien* 5: 73–93.

Englert, Birgit. 2008. 'Kuchanganyachanganya: Topic and Language Choices in Tanzanian Youth Culture.' *Journal of African Cultural Studies* 20(1): 45–55.

Gesthuizen, Thomas. 2002. *Tanzanian Hip Hop: The Old School*. Online at: http://www.africanhiphop.com/archive/index.php?module=subjects&func=printpage&pageid=100&scope=all (accessed 1 November 2010).

Hacke, Gabriel. 2014. 'Tanzanian Music Videos in the Black Atlantic: The Production, Distribution and Visual References of Bongo Flava Video Clips.' In *Bongo Media Worlds: Producing and Consuming Popular Culture in Dar es Salaam*, eds. Matthias Krings and Uta Reuster-Jahn. Cologne: Köppe, 79–107.

Kerr, David. 2014. *Performing the Self: Rappers, Urban Space and Identity in Dar es Salaam*. Unpublished Ph.D. thesis, University of Birmingham.

Mangesho, Peter. 2003. 'Global Cultural Trends: The Case of Hip-Hop Music in Dar es Salaam.' Unpublished MA thesis, University of Dar es Salaam, Tanzania.

Mwanjoka, Gerrard (G-Solo). 2011. *Harakati za Bongo Fleva na Mapinduzi* [The Bongo Fleva Movement and Revolution]. Dodoma: self-published.

Omari, Shani. 2009. *Tanzanian Hip Hop Poetry as Popular Literature*. Unpublished Ph.D. thesis, University of Dar es Salaam.

Perullo, Alex. 2005. 'Hooligans and Heroes: Youth Identity and Hip Hop in Dar es Salaam, Tanzania.' *Africa Today* 51(4): 74–101.

Perullo, Alex. 2007. '"Here's a Little Something Local": An Early History of Hip Hop in Dar es Salaam, Tanzania, 1984–1997.' In *Dar es Salaam: The History of an Emerging East African Metropolis*, eds. Andrew Burton et al. London: British Institute and Mkuki na Nyota, 250–72.

Perullo, Alex. 2011. *Live from Dar es Salaam: Popular Music and Tanzania's Music Economy*. Bloomington and Indianapolis: Indiana University Press.

Perullo, Alex, and Fenn, John. 2003. 'Language Ideologies, Choices, and Practices in Eastern African Hip Hop.' In *Global Pop, Local Language*, eds. Harris Berger and Michael Carroll. Jackson: University Press of Mississippi, 19–51.

Raab, Klaus. 2006. *Rapping the nation. Die Aneignung von HipHop in Tansania* [The Appropriation of Hip-Hop in Tanzania]. Berlin: LIT.

Remes, Pieter. 1999. 'Global Popular Musics and Changing Awareness of Urban Tanzanian Youth.' *Yearbook for Traditional Music* 31: 1–26.

Reuster-Jahn, Uta. 2007. 'Let's Go Party! Discourse and Self-Portrayal in the Bongo Fleva Song Mikasi ("Sex", Ngwair 2004).' *Swahili Forum* 14: 225–54.

Reuster-Jahn, Uta. 2008. 'Bongo Flava and the Electoral Campaign 2005 in Tanzania.' *Stichproben. Wiener Zeitschrift für kritische Afrikastudien* 14: 41–69.

Reuster-Jahn, Uta. 2012. '"Am Walking on the Way Kuiseti Future Yangu." The Use of English in Bongo Flava Music in Tanzania.' In *Listening to Africa: Anglophone African Literatures and Cultures (Anglistik & Englischunterricht 80)*, eds. Jana Gohrisch and Ellen Grünkemeier. Heidelberg: Winter, 145–73.

Reuster-Jahn, Uta. 2014a. 'Antivirus: The Revolt of Independent Bongo Flava Artists Against a Media- and-Entertainment Empire in Tanzania.' In *Bongo Media Worlds. Producing and Consuming Popular Culture in Dar es Salaam*, eds. Matthias Krings and Uta Reuster-Jahn Cologne: Köppe, 43–78.

Reuster-Jahn, Uta. 2014b. 'English versus Swahili: Language Choice in Bongo Flava as Expression of Cultural and Economic Changes in Tanzania.' *Swahili Forum* 21: 1–25.

Reuster-Jahn, Uta, and Hacke, Gabriel. 2014. 'The Bongo Flava Industry in Tanzania and Artists' Strategies for Success.' In *Bongo Media Worlds. Producing and Consuming Popular Culture in Dar es Salaam*, ed. Matthias Krings and Uta Reuster-Jahn. Cologne: Köppe, 24–42. (First published as No. 127 of Arbeitspapiere des Instituts für Ethnologie und Afrikastudien der Johannes Gutenberg-Universität Mainz. 2011. Online at: http://www.ifeas.uni-mainz.de/Dateien/AP127.pdf [accessed 26 October 2017]).

Roch, Anna, and Hacke, Gabriel. 2006. *HipHop in Tansania zwischen Message und Flava* [Hip-Hop in Tanzania Between Message and Flava]. (Sozialanthropologische Arbeitspapiere 101). Berlin: Schiler.

Saavedra Casco, José Arturo. 2006. 'The Language of the Young People: Rap, Urban Culture and Protest in Tanzania.' *Journal of Asian and African Studies* 41(3): 229–48.

Sugu [Joseph Mbilinyi], n.d. [2011]. *The Autobiography. Muziki na maisha [Music and Life]. From the Streets to Parliament.* Dar es Salaam: Deiwaka.

Suriano, Maria. 2007. '"Mimi ni msanii, kioo cha jamii [I'm an Artist, a Mirror of Society]." Urban Youth Culture as Seen Through Bongo Fleva and Hip-Hop.' *Swahili Forum* 14: 207–23.

Thompson, Katrina D. 2008. 'Keeping It Real: Reality and Representation in Maasai Hip-Hop.' *Journal of African Cultural Studies* 20(1): 33–44.

Discographical References

Bongo Flava: Swahili Rap from Tanzania. Out Here Records OH003. *2004*: Germany.

Diamond Platnumz. 'Bum Bum.' Wasafi Classics. *2014*: Tanzania.

Diamond Platnumz. 'Mbagala.' Sharobaro Records. *2010*: Tanzania.

Diamond Platnumz. 'Number One.' Wasafi Classics. *2013*: Tanzania.

Hard Blasterz. 'Chemsha bongo.' Label unknown. *1999*: Tanzania.

II Proud. *Ndani ya bongo*. FM Music Bank. *1996*: Tanzania.

Juma Nature featuring Prof. Jay. 'Umoja wa Tanzania.' Bongo Records. *2003*: Tanzania.

Mac Mooger. *The Mac Mooger – Maisha magumu*. Mamu Stores. *1995*: Tanzania.

Saleh J. 'Ice Ice Baby.' Label unknown. *1991*: Tanzania

Saleh J. *Swahili Rap*. *1994*: Tanzania.

Vinega (various rap artists). *Antivirus mixtape 1*. *2010*: Tanzania.

Vinega (various rap artists). *Antivirus mixtape 2*. *2011*: Tanzania.

Discography

Juma Nature. *Ugali*. GMC. *2003*: Tanzania.

Lady Jaydee. *Machozi*. Smooth Vibes Music Project/GMC. *2001*: Tanzania.

X-Plastaz. *Masai Hip Hop*. Out Here Records OH002. *2004*: Germany.

Filmography

Girlfriend: Filamu ya Maisha na Muziki [A Film of Music and Life], dir. George Tyson. 2003. Tanzania. 110 mins. Feature film.

UTA REUSTER-JAHN

Borborbor

Borborbor of the northern or 'Ewedome' Ewe people of the southeastern Volta Region of Ghana is a drum-dance music that became popular in the 1950s. The recreational music is performed in duple meter and utilizes the 2/4 and 4/4 bell rhythms found in highlife music.

Borborbor mainly employs traditional Ewe hand drums and percussion, as well as some percussion and brass instruments from brass band *adaha* highlife and its *konkoma* offshoot. However, unlike the marching and freestyle competitive dances of *adaha* and *konkoma* highlife music that influenced it, *borborbor* is accompanied by a traditional-type ring dance performed by men and women who shuffle in a counterclockwise direction waving handkerchiefs and bending down from time to time, thus the name 'borborbor' which means bend down (from the Ewe 'borbor'). *Borborbor* drum-dance music is played in syncopated 4/4 time and, unlike Akan *adaha* and *konkoma*, the cantor and chorus sing in the Ewe language and there is no marching associated with the genre.

The instruments of *borborbor* include the double *gankogui* cowbell, the *axatse* rattle and small *asivui* peg drums that are all found throughout the Ewe region, where they are used for traditional religious, ceremonial and social purposes. In addition there are the tenor and bass barrel-shaped peg drums, unique to *borborbor*, that are open-ended and so provide a deep bass for solo passages, especially when these hand drums are lifted off the ground with the knees. Three *odonno/dondo* hourglass-shaped pressure drums are also employed (originally a Hausa instrument that became popular throughout northern and southern Ghana), along with one or two *pati* side drums played with sticks. *Pati* drums are a Ghanaian copy of a Western brass band side drum that was used in the local *adaha* brass band music developed by coastal Fanti people during the late nineteenth century. Since they are influenced by the local brass band music, it is not surprising that *borborbor* groups also include a bugle or b-flat trumpet. These are used to signal rhythmic changes and also play short melodic bursts over syncopated and polyrhythmic drumming.

There were several formative influences on *borborbor*, including the already mentioned Fanti *adaha* brass band music. Another was *konkoma* highlife, a local 'poor man's' version of Fanti *adaha* marching music that utilized voices and local drums and spread through southern Ghana during the 1930s and 1940s, when it influenced various neo-traditional music styles. In the case of *borborbor*, indigenous Ewe drums replaced the frame drums of *konkoma*. It should be noted that two Ewe recreational drum styles preceded the emergence of *borborbor*. One was *tuidzi*, which employs the *pati* drum (Agordoh 1994). The other was *akpese* recreational music that included frame drums and became popular in the town of Kpalime in Togo during the 1940s (Lareau 2002). Like *borborbor*, these two preexisting forms of neo-traditional music were sung in Ewe and used a combination of local drums with modern ones (i.e., *konkoma* frame drums and the *pati* side-drum). Indeed, local *tuidzi* and *akpese*, as well as imported Fanti *konkoma*, are the formative influences on *borborbor*.

The first *borborbor* group was formed in the town of Kpandu by the policeman Francis Cudjoe Nuatro and other young people who had been playing in the town's *konkoma* band. The name *borborbor* was invented by Nuatro (see Badasu 1988; Agordoh 1994, 112; Agawu 1995 and Younge 1992).

Borborbor music is associated with formal clubs that have a hierarchy of officers (chairman, secretary, treasurer, women's leader, etc.) and act for their members as mutual benefit societies and funeral clubs. *Borborbor* music is therefore played at funerals and also at weddings, 'outdoorings' (local christenings) and festivals. Early *borborbor* also became identified with Kwame Nkrumah's Convention Peoples Party (CPP) that led Ghana to independence beginning in the late 1940s. Indeed, since Nuatro's original group was composed of young men and women sympathetic to the CPP, his group became known as 'Osagyefo's [i.e., Nkrumah's] Own Borborbor' (Badasu 1988). One of the Osagyefo's Own Borborbor Group's most popular 1950s patriotic songs was 'Ghana le a azoli dzi' (Ghana Is Moving Forward). This connection between *borborbor*, politics and political rallies continued. Badasu (1988) mentions the genre's use for Colonel Acheampong's People's National Party (PNP) military government political rallies in the 1970s, while Lareau (2002) refers to this music being played at presidential rallies during the 2000 elections.

Borborbor music became a favorite neo-traditional recreational music of the 'Ewedome' Ewe in the northern Volta Region, as well as those who have migrated to the urban areas such as Accra. However, according to Lareau (2002), local Christian churches in the Volta Region also began to use *borborbor* with choirs who sang local hymns in the Ewe language. By the early twenty-first century *borborbor* performances were also an established part of the repertoires of both professional dance companies (such as the National Dance Company and Ghana Dance Ensemble) and semi-professional and amateur 'cultural groups' that play a cross-section of Ghana's ethnic music in nightclubs, at hotels and at folkloric events.

Bibliography

Agordoh, Alexander A. 1994. *Studies in African Music*. Accra: New Age Publications, Ho Printhony Press.

Agawu, Kofi. 1995. *African Rhythm: A Northern Ewe Perspective*. Cambridge: Cambridge University Press.

Badasu, Ambrose. 1988. 'Tribute to FC: Originator of Borborbor.' *Ghana Times*, 3 June, 4.

Collins, E. John. 1994. *The Ghanaian Concert Party: African Popular Entertainment at the Crossroads*. Unpublished Ph.D. dissertation, SUNY Buffalo, NY.

Collins, E. John. 2005. 'The Decolonisation of Ghanaian Popular Entertainment.' In *Urbanization and African Cultures*, eds. Toyin Falola and Steven Salm. Durham, NC: Carolina Academic Press, 119–37.

Lareau, Joseph. 2002. 'The Borborbor of the Northern Ewe: Functional and Technical Aspects.' M. Phil thesis, University of Ghana, Legon.

Younge, Yao Paschal. 1992. 'Musical Tradition of Ghana Volume 2.' Unpublished manuscript.

Discographical References

Nuatro's Osagyefo's Own Borborbor Group. 'Ghana Le A Azoli Dzi.' Label unknown. *1950s*: Ghana.

Discography

Abebe and the Bantus. 'Original Borborbor: Mehiawo.' Cassette album recorded at Bokoor Studio Accra and produced by Jonathon Kakraba Abebe. Self-produced. *Late 1980s*: Ghana.

Tsito Agbeyeye Group. 'Borborbor Music Vol. 1.' Cassette album recorded at Bokoor Studio. Self-produced. *Late 1980s*: Ghana.

E. JOHN COLLINS

Brass Band Music in Benin

Brass band music in Benin is a diverse genre. It includes local ensembles called *fanfares* that accompany ceremonies such as funerals, weddings and baptisms, as well as brass bands that record albums and tour abroad. The repertoire of these groups is influenced by a wide variety of local and Afro-diasporic musics, from Afrobeat, *soukous, salsa* and all forms of jazz to Protestant hymnody, Vodun drumming and Brazilian and Nigerian street band styles.

In general, the French term *'fanfares'* refers to amateur affinity music groups that center around churches, the police and the military. They developed around the 1940s before the English term 'brass band' was in use in Benin (then Dahomey). Their repertoire draws from Protestant hymns and well-known local songs, and they perform mostly in processional form. So-called brass bands, which developed in the 1990s, have a more expanded repertoire and tend to draw upon more influences from jazz, Afrobeat and New Orleans second line styles. They typically employ more elaborate arrangements and play for programmed stage concerts, although the groups may also have a processional (*ambulatoire*) component. Brass bands are more likely to be professional ensembles with members who play music full-time.

Beninois brass bands and *fanfares* have developed the status of a postcolonial tradition, one that takes the instruments of the colonizer and turns them into vehicles for traditional songs and rhythms that praise the ancestors. While musical mixtures were not explicitly censored in French Dahomey, the colonists brought their own musicians to staff marching bands and dance bands and did not allow African musicians to join. Dahomeans could form their own groups, but they needed the sponsorship of a church, a school or local political leaders to obtain instruments. In other words, early groups were dependent on the patronage of religious or political institutions. The few brass and wind musicians in the 1950s learned to play their instruments in church-sponsored *fanfares*, such as those in the independent Cherubim and Seraphim and Celestial Christian churches, where they learned basic solfège and choral harmony and had access to instruments. The instrumentation originally included trumpets and trombones, with the occasional baritone horn, along with snare, bass and cymbals for percussion. The percussionists interpreted rhythms from local genres, especially genres that were popular in Christian communities in Nigeria, such as aṣíkò (*ashiko, assiko*), the street drumming style developed by Brazilian returnees to Lagos, and Ouidah and Porto Novo in Benin. *Fanfares* played for Christian funerals, Sunday worship and other religious ceremonies. After independence in 1960, recordings of international genres, such as early Congolese *soukouss*, Cuban *salsa* and US jazz and R&B, became more available in stores in Cotonou, and musicians began to incorporate these sounds as well.

New opportunities were also available through the military police station in the capital of Porto Novo, which formed a band, Orchestre National du Jazz, in 1962. Political instability in Dahomey sidelined the Orchestre National in 1963, but, with the support of the military general Mathieu Kerekou's administration, it returned in the early 1970s as the Orchestre National de la Gendarmerie (known as Les Volcans de la Capitale), the *gendarmerie*'s premiere dance band, famous for its legendary horn section. The band's modern guitar and horn-based dance music was considered to be the sound of the revolutionary People's Republic of Benin. Les Volcans released four albums between 1974 and 1976, and they were very influential for the generations of musicians that followed.

The *gendarmerie* also became a center for musicians to network, practice and share their skills. This inspired the creation of large *fanfares* in the major churches in Porto Novo, first in the Protestant Church Atinkame, then in the Celeste Church at their Porto Novian *paroisse mere* (mother parish), and finally in the Cherubim and Seraphim Church, with the *fanfare* Imole Christi. The *gens d'armes* who participated musically in these religious communities shared their skills with other members. These bands divided the responsibilities of playing for the wide variety of weddings, funerals and baptisms that took place, performing a combination of hymns and popular songs. In the early twenty-first century the sound of *fanfares* is ubiquitous throughout southern Benin on any given weekend, and it is difficult to spend time in any city or village without hearing them processing along the major routes, calling listeners out of their homes to join in.

While musicians in Benin draw a distinction between the local *fanfares* and international brass bands, the members of major international ensembles such as the Gangbé Brass Band and Eyo'nlé Brass Band come out of the *fanfare* tradition, particularly in independent African churches including the Celestial Church of Christ and Cherubim and Seraphim, and the *gendarmerie*. Many of these musicians also studied music theory, performance and jazz improvisation, either at institutions in other parts of West Africa or overseas in France or Canada. This kind of travel and study became possible after 1990 when Benin embraced democracy and opened its borders and its economy to the world. A pluri-religious and creative renaissance followed in Beninois music and art worlds. This new context gave brass band musicians an opportunity to reinterpret their country's musical history and culture and curate it for the interest of the international audience.

The generation of brass band musicians that came up in the 1990s and 2000s has had to make difficult, strategic musical and professional choices in order to promote their music. As the first and most visible ensemble to break into the Western world music market, Gangbé faced the challenging task of representing Benin's wide cultural diversity through its music. So the band sought out members from different ethnic regions of the country, from the Mahi in Savalou, the Toffin in Cotonou, the Gun in Porto Novo and the Fon in Abomey and Ouidah. Gangbé also recruited members with special training in jazz and in composition, arranging and orchestration. Soon after the group formed in 1994, its members participated in a master class with the Rebirth Brass Band of New Orleans. The musicians from Rebirth encouraged Gangbé's drummers to replace their military bass and snare drums with local forms of percussion to give the group a distinctive, African sound. In their efforts to represent Vodun ritual repertoires, the Gangbé musicians visited the chief Vodun priest in Ouidah to ask for his blessing on the project and to obtain permission to record and distribute the sacred rhythms.

The members of Gangbé grapple with significant musical challenges in their work, including how to represent traditional styles such as *masse gohoun* or *zenli*, which normally require at least six or seven musicians to execute all of the call-and-response parts, with only three percussionists on tour. They created several innovative solutions to this problem, including condensing multiple drum parts and creating alternatives for instruments they could not access while traveling. For example, they cover the fragile clay *kpezin* drums in iron, and make them into a set of three played by one person, who also sings. Another percussionist plays the *assan* (shaker) pattern on the hi-hat, the *gan* (bell) as itself, and a calabash as an all-purpose bass drum to represent the *gota* (gourd) or other low parts. A third drummer plays the lead parts on the *kpawle* drum or one of the talking drums such as *gbon* or *gangan*, depending on the style. It can be difficult to fit these lead drum parts, which depend on text-based phrases and proverbs, into a jazz arrangement that assumes squared-off, four-bar phrases. The rhythmic heterophony of many traditional genres poses particular challenges for studio recording, especially with the use of a click track for postproduction editing. But Gangbé's lead drummers have learned how to adapt the phrases so that they fit into the arrangement, sometimes altering their meaning. The Gangbé Brass Band has also adapted many sacred styles, including *agbotchebou*, *agbehun* and *kaka*, for new instrumentation, and sometimes in original compositions.

In contrast to Gangbé's project of national representation, the Eyo'nlé Brass Band, which formed later in the 1990s, was launched by musicians mostly from Porto Novo and the surrounding villages. The band's emphasis is on local Gun, Torri and Nago styles from the Porto Novo area. The group also tends to use more diatonic, 'trad-jazz' harmonic cycles in its arrangements, while Gangbé's orientation is more texture-oriented, centering around the percussion, blues tonality and the development of vamps and grooves. Unlike Gangbé, Eyo'nlé uses standard *fanfare* instrumentation with snare and bass drums, with the addition of a lead drum depending on the style. This requires special virtuosity from the snare drummer, who must use this instrument to represent as many different drum parts with as many different sounds as possible. Eyo'nlé has also benefited from long-standing collaborations with French folk musicians, especially the groups Jaune Toujours and Les Ogres de Barback. Eyo'nlé's strategy has been to spend as much of the year as possible in France to maintain residency, returning to Benin for only a few weeks each year. Gangbé, on the other hand, tours in Europe and the United States during the summers, and spends the rest of the year in Benin. The members of Eyo'nlé describe their project as 'tradi-modern,' 'feet in the tradition, head in the modern,' placing their practice squarely and productively in the center of historical debates over the politicization of culture in Benin.

Fanfares and brass bands have become key sites for the production of postcolonial identities in contemporary Benin. Through their use of multiple styles from other parts of Africa and the diaspora, these ensembles communicate a rich spectrum of information about local history and the international circulation of music practices. They continue to confront obstacles of travel and economics with creative solutions, and are among the primary representatives of Benin's culture in the wider world.

Bibliography

Boonzajer Flaes, Robert. 2000. *Brass Unbound: Secret Children of the Colonial Brass Band*. Amsterdam: Royal Tropical Institute.

Harrev, Flemming. 1992. 'Francophone West Africa and the Jali Experience.' In *West African Pop Roots*, ed. John Collins. Philadelphia: Temple University Press, 209–43.

Waterman, Christopher. 1990. *Jùjú: A Social History and Ethnography of an African Popular Music*. Chicago: University of Chicago Press.

Discographical References

Les Volcans de la Capitale. *Les Volcans de la Gendarmerie, République Populaire du Bénin*. SATEL VG 0001. *1974*: Benin.

Les Volcans de la Capitale. *Les Volcans de la Gendarmerie, République Populaire du Bénin*. SATEL VG 0002. *1975*: Benin.

Les Volcans de la Capitale. *Les Volcans de la Gendarmerie, République Populaire du Bénin*. SATEL VG 0003. *1975*: Benin.

Les Volcans de la Capitale. *Les Volcans de la Gendarmerie, République Populaire du Bénin*. SATEL VG 0004. *1976*: Benin.

Discography

Eyo'nlé Brass Band. *Empreinte du père*. Irfan EY0002. *2015*: France.

Gangbé Brass Band. *Togbé*. Contre-jour CJ009. *2001*: Belgium.

Gangbé Brass Band. *Whendo*. Contre-jour CJ015. *2004*. Belgium.

Gangbé Brass Band. *Assiko!* Contre-jour CJ021. *2008*: Belgium.

Gangbé Brass Band. *Go Slow to Lagos*. Buda Musique 4734804. *2015*: France.

SARAH POLITZ

Brass Band Music in Ethiopia

Brass band music has been one of the driving forces of modern music in Ethiopia since 1924, when it was enthusiastically embraced by the Prince Regent of Ethiopia Tefari Makonen (later known as Emperor Haile Selassie), and has occupied a place at the core of Ethiopia's musical link with the rest of the world. Through brass band music, jazz and other Western musical styles have been part of musical language and practice in Ethiopia for nearly a century.

In April 1924, while in Jerusalem, Tefari Makonen was welcomed by a brass band of 40 Armenian orphans displaced by the genocide carried out by the Turks in 1915. Makonen was so impressed that he approached the Armenian bishop of Jerusalem, the orphans' legal guardian, and signed the musicians to a four-year contract to be the official musicians of the empire. Known as the Arba Lijotch (Amharic for the '40 children'), this group of mostly teenage musicians was led by their instructor Kevork Nalbandian, whose knowledge of Western music theory and pedagogy came to shape musical practices beyond those of the Arba Lijotch. Musical elements including tertiary harmony and group performance became part of a musical culture in Ethiopia where traditional music was almost entirely without harmony and largely consisted of solo performance repertoire. 'European' music was now firmly established in Ethiopia. For the next several decades, such music was often associated with government institutions.

Groups including the 'Imperial Body Guard Band,' 'Police Band,' 'Army Band' and various municipality bands began to emerge. These bands often featured a dozen performers, entirely male, who performed for large nightclub audiences. The brass section of these bands developed a 'jazz section' in which swing-jazz arrangements of tunes ranging from US jazz to Ethiopian traditional melodies were created. More traditional Ethiopian melodies were played on instruments constructed to conform to the Western harmonic system. As a result, certain sets of Western scales whose intervallic interrelationships approximated Ethiopian ones came to constitute the distinct sound of what would become Ethiopian jazz. For example, two of the most common traditional scales used in Ethiopian jazz are *tezeta* and *ambasel*. Both are pentatonic, with *tezeta* having a more major key sound (C D E G A C), and *ambasel* having a harmonic minor sound (C Db F G Ab C). The intervallic relationships of these scales are approximate, as the division of the octave in traditional Ethiopian music does not quite match the Western European one.

Much traditional Ethiopian instrumental music is solo music, in which the performer needs only to tune the instrument to his or her own voice. With brass band music, a standard was adapted so groups of four to fifteen musicians could play together. This meant that players not only had to adopt a fixed-pitch tuning system, but also had to change the entire social dynamic in which they would normally play.

Out of the many municipality bands in existence, individual band leaders and singers emerged in the late 1950s who continued to use large brass sections in their groups, as this had become accepted as the standard sound of Ethiopian jazz. Saxophonist Getatchew Mekuria became famous for the almost avant-garde playing of his saxophone in the style of a *shellela*, an ancient Ethiopian war horn. Artists including Mahmoud Ahmed and Mulatu Astatke took the jazzy brass sections in new directions in the 1960s and 1970s and through the early twenty-first century with groups such as Either/Orchestra. The music of such groups is relatively new in historical terms, and conspicuously a hybrid of two very different musical systems/practices. They will, no doubt, continue to provide a performative space in which dialogues between tradition and modernity will take place.

Bibliography

Falceto, Francis. 2001. *Abyssinie Swing: A Pictorial History of Modern Ethiopian Music*. Addis Ababa: Shama Books.

Discography

Ethiopiques 1: Golden Years of Modern Ethiopian Music 1969–1975. Buda Musique/Distribution Melodie 82951-2 DK016. *1998*: France.

Ethiopiques 3: Golden Years of Modern Ethiopian Music 1969–1975. Buda Musique/Distribution Melodie 82963-2 DK016. *1998*: France.

Ethiopiques 13: The Golden Seventies: Ethiopian Groove. Buda Musique/Distribution Melodie 82255-2 DK016. *2003*: France.

Ethiopiques 20: Either/Orchestra & Guests Live in Addis. Buda Musique/Distribution Socadisc 860121 SC881. *2005*: France.

SHAWN MOLLENHAUER

See also **Adaha, Beni**

Bubblegum

Bubblegum, or township pop as it is also called, is a musical style that developed in South Africa during the 1980s. Largely popular among urban black youth, bubblegum shares certain similarities with disco pop or bubblegum elsewhere in the world, most notably the United States and Europe. However, the content of songs moved beyond that of its light, bouncy counterparts in the rest of the world to reflect also on social and political issues during the final years of apartheid. The term 'bubblegum' is therefore not an unproblematic taxonomy in South Africa and some leading scholars point out that it has been used in a derogatory fashion to refer to the music's supposed superficial characteristics.

The genre is a vocal style characterized by its use of keyboard and drums, with short overlapping call-and-response vocal patterns. Artists and producers exploited the newest technology of the time and the music is dominated by synthesizers, signal-processing effects such as reverb, chorus and echo, and a disco beat, usually supplied by a drum machine. Songs are mostly sung in English with the addition of vernacular languages including Zulu, Xhosa and Sotho. The lyrics tend to be repetitive, covering topics from love and betrayal to violence, township culture and political sentiments. Proponents of the genre include early albums by Sipho 'Hotstix' Mabuse (1984, 1991), and music by Brenda Fassie, Yvonne Chaka Chaka, Sello 'Chicco' Twala and Dan Tshanda.

Brenda Fassie established herself in 1983 as the queen of township pop with her first single 'Weekend Special.' This song, recorded with her band the Big Dudes, speaks out against the status of being a weekends-only girlfriend, while her man is off with others during the week. Although Fassie's lyrics are typically more in line with the carefree attitudes of bubblegum, she did engage more serious political content in some of her songs. For example, her 1990 album, *Black President*, produced by Sello 'Chicco' Twala, contained two songs written by Twala including 'Black President,' a praise poem predicting the rise of Nelson Mandela as the first black president of South Africa, and 'Shoot Them Before They Grow,' depicting a debate between a white liberal and a racist on the future of young black kids, their powerlessness and police brutality during peaceful protests.

In addition to his work with Brenda Fassie, Sello 'Chicco' Twala is also known for his work with Yvonne Chaka Chaka, Sipho Mabuse and his top-selling backing group Chimora. Some of his biggest hits include 'We Miss You Manelo' (1989), a hidden tribute to the political activist Nelson Mandela, and 'Papa Stop the War' (1990), featuring the voice and poetry of Mzwake Mbuli. The song, spoken by Mbuli over Chicco's synthesizers and vocals, describes the dream of a new society free from racism and war. Another producer, composer and artist who produced successful township pop artists is Dan Tshanda, best known for his success with the group Splash. Splash's first hit single entitled 'Peacock' was released in 1986. Tshanda is also known for his work with the Dalom Kids, Patricia Majalisa and Matshikos.

In 1985, shortly after Brenda Fassie's first big hit, Yvonne Chaka Chaka released her first single 'I'm in Love with a DJ,' launching her on the path to stardom. With her song 'Umqombothi' (1987), celebrating the indigenous grain beer prepared in South Africa, Chaka Chaka became known across the African continent, giving rise to her nickname as the 'Princess of Africa.' With a string of gold and platinum disks behind her, she has performed to great acclaim across the African continent including Nigeria, Malawi, Congo, Uganda and Tanzania.

Bubblegum remained popular until the mid-1990s when township youth turned to new musical styles including house, techno, hip-hop and ragga which merged into a style known as *kwaito*. Fassie had a lasting influence on *kwaito* and local pop music, and, in spite of her ever-increasingly self-destructive lifestyle, she continued to release hit albums during the 1990s and early 2000s, including *Now Is the Time* (1996), *Memeza* (1999) and *Myekeleni* (2002). Many view her rise to stardom in 1983 and her death in 2004 due to a drug overdose as the beginning and end of the bubblegum pop era.

Bibliography

Allen, Lara. 1997. 'South African Women of Song, Their Lives and Times.' In *A Common Hunger to Sing: A Tribute to South Africa's Black Women of Song, 1950–1990*, ed. Z. B. Molefe and Mike Mzileni. Cape Town: Kwela Books, 3–12.

Allen, Lara. 2001. 'Bubblegum.' In *Grove Music Online*. Online at: http://www.oxfordmusiconline.com/public (accessed 6 September 2017).

Allingham, Rob. 1994. 'Township Jive: From Pennywhistle to Bubblegum. The Music of South Africa.' In *World Music: The Rough Guide*, eds, Simon Broughton et al. London: Rough Guides, 373–90.

Coplan, David. 2007. *In Township Tonight! South Africa's Black City Music and Theatre*, 2nd ed. Chicago: University of Chicago Press.

Meintjes, Louise. 2003. *Sound of Africa! Making Music Zulu in a South African Studio*. London: Duke University Press.

Discographical References

Chaka Chaka, Yvonne. 'I'm in Love with a DJ.' *I'm in Love with a DJ*. World Record Co., RBS-029. *1985*: Kenya.

Chaka Chaka, Yvonne. 'Umqombothi.' *Thank You Mr. D.J.* Roy B. Records, RBL 123. *1987*: South Africa.

Fassie, Brenda. 'Black President.' *Black President*. Mercury, 4064851. *1990*: Nigeria.

Fassie, Brenda. *Memeza*. CCP Record Company, CDBREN 98. *1999*: South Africa.

Fassie, Brenda. *Myekeleni*. EMI Music (South Africa), CDBREN (WL) 2002. *2002*: South Africa.

Fassie, Brenda. *Now Is the Time*. CCP Record Company, CDBREN (WL) 96. *1996*: South Africa.

Fassie, Brenda. 'Shoot Them Before They Grow.' *Black President*. Mercury, 4064851. *1990*: Nigeria.

Fassie, Brenda, and the Big Dudes. 'Weekend Special.' *Weekend Special*. Family Records (13), FLY(V) 4. *1983*: South Africa.

Splash. 'Peacock.' *Peacock*. Gallo GRC, MCGMP 40353. *1986*: South Africa.

Twala, Sello. 'Papa Stop the War.' *Papa Stop the War*. Dephon, MCRBL 175. *1990*: South Africa.

Twala, Sello. 'We Miss You Manelo.' *We Miss You Manelo*. Philips, 874 870-7. *1989*: France.

Discography

Chaka Chaka, Yvonne. *Princess of Africa: The Best of Yvonne Chaka Chaka*. Teal Records, CDRBL 190. *1999*: South Africa.

Fassie, Brenda. *The Best of Brenda and the Big Dudes*. CCP Record Company, CDBREN (WR) 001. *1993*: South Africa.

Mabuse, Sipho 'Hotstix.' *Burnout*. Gallo Record Company, HUL 509. *1984*: South Africa.

Mabuse, Sipho 'Hotstix.' *The Best of Sipho 'Hotstix' Mabuse*. Gallo Record Company, 3020. *2001*: South Africa.

Twala, Sello. *The Best of Chicco*. Teal Records, CDRBL 189. *1999*: South Africa.

LIZABÉ LAMBRECHTS

Cabo-Zouk

Cabo-zouk (also known as Cabo Verdean *zouk*, or *cola-zouk* when combined with *coladeira*) is a product of the Cabo Verdean diaspora in Europe. A modern, highly technical urban dance music generally produced on synthesizers and drum machines, it began in the mid-1980s among Cabo Verdeans living in Rotterdam. The music is studio-produced, and the recording engineer's expertise plays a seminal role in creating the *zouk* sound. Its identifiable, ubiquitous rhythm (see Example 1) and much of its technical, instrumental and vocal style were unabashedly appropriated from Antillean *zouk*, which developed in the French West Indies in the mid-1980s and quickly swept the international music scene. The main difference between *cabo-zouk* and Antillean *zouk* is the former's characteristic romantic lyrics in the Kriolu language.

In the late 1980s Cabo Verdeans first came into contact with *zouk* in the discotheques of Paris and Holland. Young Cabo Verdeans were deeply affected by this music, and in relatively short order the appropriation process began in the Cabo Verdean communities in Rotterdam and Paris when musicians began composing *zouk* with lyrics in Kriolou. *Cabo-zouk* musicians and fans initially were citizens who came of age in an independent Cabo Verde, but the *cabo-zouk* community came to include those born after independence in 1975. This new generation was characterized by a greater sense of freedom, since they did not see music in terms of resistance to colonial oppression, nor did they feel limited by traditional forms.

Musical Characteristics

In *cabo-zouk*, synthesizers and a drum machine accompany romantic lyrics sung in the Kriolu language by a solo vocalist and a small, primarily female chorus, in either a call-and-response pattern or strophe and refrain. The solo singer's voice often has a hushed, sensual quality, including a boy band-style 'throb' at the end of lines. In some songs the chorus takes over the refrain altogether. Choruses are small, but in some ways numbers don't matter, since much of the effect is created by the sound engineer. The form is generally AABAAB, often with exact repetition of verses or of the last line of a verse, as in other Cabo Verdean musical forms such as *morna* and *coladeira*.

Example 1: *Cabo-zouk* rhythm

The most distinguishing feature is the ubiquitous syncopated rhythm (see Example 1). Tempos vary, but the slow and sensual variation known as *zouk-love* is by far the most popular. *Zouk*-love is also harmonically more complex than faster versions of *cabo-zouk*, which often employ only a three-chord progression (I-IV-V) in comparison to *zouk-love*'s use of more passing and seventh chords. The close physical proximity promoted by the accompanying couples' dance is an important part of the social life between Cabo Verdean men and women, who see little point in dance styles where men and women do not touch. Generally, in the *cabo-zouk* dance, the woman's arms are around the man's neck and his arms are around her waist or buttocks. The buttocks move to one side on the long part of the rhythm and then execute a sort of double-time move to the other side. The dance is smoother than Antillean *zouk*, which is more overtly sexual, with even more movement of the woman's buttocks. No doubt due to the melding of musical styles, languages and Lusophone connections, today *zouk*-love and *kizomba*, a music and dance genre from Angola derived from *semba* and *zouk* and sung in Portuguese, are identified virtually synonymously.

Origins and History

The pop group Cabo Verde Show, formed in Dakar, Senegal in 1977 by Cabo Verdean immigrants Manu Lima and Luís da Silva, laid the groundwork for this new phenomenon. Cabo Verde Show moved its base to Paris to take advantage of the world music phenomenon and better recording studios in the early 1980s, but they often performed in Holland as well. Their influence on the new generation is clear in that they changed and increased the role of the synthesizer and, while singing in Kriolu, consciously incorporated foreign rhythms, including *zouk*.

Starting in the late 1980s Rotterdam became the epicenter of a flood of new musical activity in the Cabo Verdean international community. Due to recurring droughts and lack of opportunity, Cabo Verde has a high rate of emigration, which has created many diaspora communities worldwide. The oldest of these are in the northeastern United States and Lisbon, Portugal. After World War II, Cabo Verdeans went to Rotterdam and various cities in France to find work in the shipping industry.

There are several possible reasons why Rotterdam occupied the central role for *cabo-zouk* in the Cabo Verde diaspora. The long-standing and conservative Portuguese diaspora community primarily recorded traditional *mornas* and *coladeiras*. Paris, where the diaspora community was more segregated from the native population, was a center for Antillean *zouk*. French law limited the amount of foreign language music that could be played (Antillean *zouk* was considered 'foreign' due to its use of a Creole language), so radio time was limited, but Antillean *zouk* dominated clubs. In Holland, however, Cabo Verdeans received equal time on radio and television programs when compared to other ethnic groups. Moreover, *cabo-zouk* musicians characterize Rotterdam's Cabo Verdean community as comparatively open to innovation, integrated into Dutch society and international in their views – in other words, Cabo Verdean but not afraid to include other music and languages.

Livity, formed in 1987, was the first successful group of the new Rotterdam-based style, but many others would follow. Gil and the Perfects, formed by Gil Semedo in 1991, was the first 'superstar' of the Dutch groups. In 1990 Splash! was formed, initially serving as a studio band for individual singers who wanted to record *cabo-zouk* and other modern dance styles. Due to the prohibitive cost of touring with a band, only the best-funded and best-known groups brought musicians, and the same musicians played for both the group and their warm-up band, generally in outdoor parks or soccer stadia. Less famous groups typically performed live vocals in small dance clubs to prerecorded music. Although this made it financially possible to reach the disparate and relatively small transnational Cabo Verdean communities, the intrinsic reason for this performance practice lies in the fact that the sophisticated equipment used to create the music means neither Antillean nor Cabo Verdean *zouk* lends itself to completely live performance (Benoit 1993). The recorded backup created initially by an essentially small group of musicians living in Holland provided a homogenous, identifiable sound, the aesthetic of which remained when *cabo-zouk* began to be produced elsewhere.

Until the late 1990s Cabo Verde had no recording studios, so all recordings were produced off the islands. Several groundbreaking recordings were made in Rotterdam in the 1960s (e.g., by the group Voz de Cabo Verde which was the first group to record *coladeiras* using electric instruments), and in the late 1970s, after independence (when Bulimundo recorded *funaná* with electric instruments). Initially, most *cabo-zouk* recordings were made in Holland, but due to the complexities of the music and the important role sound engineers played in the production of the *cabo-zouk* sound, mixing was often done in Paris by engineers who had extensive experience with the Antillean *zouk* sound. Early in its development, a small group of financiers and producers expanded musical distribution networks simultaneously with touring schedules, as the groups tour not only the islands themselves, but Cabo Verdean communities in Europe, the United States and the other Lusophone African countries. Because of logistics and a lack of copyright laws, distribution rights are sold locally within separate countries. The small record companies lack the necessary international structure to coordinate sales and copyright violations on a broad scale. Performers make their profits only in concert tickets, which makes frequent touring imperative for survival (Romer 2004).

In the 1990s groups and individual performers began to appear, with varying degrees of success and quality, in the other diaspora communities in the USA and Portugal. One of the most striking changes was in the number of female *cabo-zouk* performers, who had previously been relegated to the lesser choral parts. Notably, Suzanna Lubrano, from Rotterdam, released *Tudo pa bo* (All for You) in 2002, and won the Kora All African Music Award for Best Female Artist in 2003.

In the early 1990s Cabo Verde moved from a socialist government that heavily sponsored music, PAICV (Partido Africano da Independencia de Cabo Verde), to a free market-inclined government, MpD (Movimento para a Democracia). *Cabo-zouk*'s rise coincided with this change because the new government refused state sponsorship to any group that had had ties with the previous regime, a development which essentially stopped musical production for many established groups in the islands.

Cabo-zouk filled this lacuna in Cabo Verde because it had no connection with the previous regime and, more importantly, was popular music that could support itself.

Outside of Cabo Verde and its diaspora communities, *cabo-zouk* has a small but consistent presence in the increasingly international *zouk* charts. *Cabo-zouk* has expanded its audience by incorporating English and French lyrics and other dance styles, such as Angolan *kizomba* and *kuduro*, or American rap.

Despite strong criticisms regarding the authenticity of *cabo-zouk*, primarily by those of the older generation who had experienced Portuguese colonial oppression and felt that this 'lower-quality' music was essentially not Cabo Verdean and represented a disintegration of Cabo Verdean culture and identity, it has continually gained such popularity that in the early twenty-first century it dominates the airwaves, nightclubs and stages of Cabo Verdean communities throughout the world.

Bibliography

Benoit, Édouard. 1993. 'Biguine: Popular Music of Guadeloupe, 1940–1960.' In *Zouk: World Music in the West Indies*, ed. Jocelyne Guilbault. Chicago: University of Chicago Press, 53–67.

Guilbault, Jocelyn. 1993. *Zouk: World Music in the West Indies*. Chicago: University of Chicago Press.

Hoffman, JoAnne. 2008. 'Diasporic Networks, Political Change, and the Growth of Cabo-Zouk Music.' In *Transnational Archipelago: Perspectives on Cape Verdean Migration and Diaspora*, eds. Luís Batalha and Jørgen Carling. Amsterdam: Amsterdam University Press, 205–20.

Romer, René. 2004. Personal Communication, Rotterdam, 27 December.

Discographical References

Lubrano, Suzanna. *Tudu pa bo*. Kings Records 9792. *2002*: Netherlands.

Discography

Cabo Verde Show, The. *Les 10 meilleures chansons*. Lusafrica/Melodie 08722-2. *N.d.*: France.

Elizio. *Confirmação*. Sushiraw/Section Zouk 634479754913. *2008*: France.

Gil. *Best of Gil: 1991–2001*. Giva 9928. *2001*: Netherlands.

Livity. *Rapaz Novo*. Sons D'África CD 292. *1994*: Portugal.

Mendes, Mika. *Mike Mendes*. Sushiraw/Section Zouk SR 7014-2 SP70. *2008*: France.

Mendes, Mika. *Sem Limite*. Real Touch/Mika Mendes (Mp3 format). *2013*: France.

Monteiro, Philip. *Philip Monteiro – Greatest Hits*. Globe Music C-058. *2006*: USA.

Splash! *Africana: The Best of Splash!* Islands Music, Inc. RB0299. *1998*: USA.

JOANNE HOFFMAN

Chakacha

Chakacha is indigenous dance music of the Mijikenda people of Kenya that has been popularized by the Swahili people. Originating as a female wedding dance of the Mijikenda community, it was later integrated into Swahili all-night wedding celebrations (Senoga-Zake 1986, 55), and from the 1980s developed into a popular genre using modern instruments.

Both peoples live in the Kenyan coastal region. In general, the Mijikenda are found on the Kenyan coastline while the Swahili are found on the larger East African coastline. In Kenya, the Swahili people live on the coast both to the north of the Tana River through the islands of the Lamu archipelago and to the south through the towns of Malindi and Mombasa. They are mainly Islamic and share a set of values, beliefs, traditions and customs, in addition to speaking dialects of the Swahili language (Campbell and Eastman 1984, 467). The Swahili perform various indigenous dances commonly referred to as *'ngoma'* – a Swahili term that means 'drum' but has an extended meaning that encompasses music and dance. In addition to *chakacha*, *ngoma* types performed by the Swahili include *vugo*, *mdurenge* and *msondo* (see Campbell and Eastman 1984). However, some of these dances (e.g., *msondo*) are adopted from neighboring non-Swahili cultures (Senoga-Zake 1986).

The term *chakacha* is a Swahili verb that refers to the crackling or rustling noise made by the grinding of dry leaves. In its indigenous setting, *chakacha* was performed during weddings by young women, generally virgins. Older women often joined the dance, ostensibly to guide the young girls to dance correctly, but also for the fun of it. *Chakacha* as dance formed part of the process of young women's sex education in readiness for marriage, including the proper form of hip rotation (Campbell and Eastman 1984, 472).

All young adult girls were expected to perform *chakacha* correctly during their wedding ceremony and to exhibit their ability to please their husbands. Normally, the young ladies started to perform this dance after puberty. The socially significant lyrics stressed social values of honesty, fidelity, faith in God, respect for elders and proper sexual behavior within the female domain. The lyrics were composed using poetry, sayings, rhyme and scansion.

Despite *chakacha* being a dance for women, the instrumentalists were mostly male. In addition to the *nzumari* (later replaced by the trumpet), other accompanying instruments included the *msondo* drum (a tall, approximately three- to four-foot drum); two to three *kunda* drums (a smaller stool-shaped drum); metal shakers and other idiophones from the coastal communities.

In the twenty-first century *chakacha* is still performed in a circle that moves counterclockwise. The female dancers fold and tightly tie decorated wraparound garments, with local sayings encrypted on them, around their waists. These garments are known as 'leso' or 'kanga' and assist in accentuating the rotating hip movement characteristic of the dance. The dance normally continues around the circle with periodic stops when sets of the women go into the center of the circle and compete to demonstrate their prowess in hip rotation. As they dance, they continue singing short responses to the cues of the soloist and/or *nzumari* (a double-reeded aerophone). In the popular version of *chakacha*, most bands have replaced the *nzumari* with the trumpet (locally referred to as *tarumbeta*).

Chakacha as Popular Music

Since the mid-1980s *chakacha* has developed into a modern popular genre. The indigenous instrumental ensembles have been replaced by modern band instruments, but the dancing and singing have remained heavily influenced by the indigenous idiom. The development of *chakacha* from its traditional setting and role in sex education to a popular genre and a more entertainment-based theme also moved it from private performance spaces to more exposed settings. Traditionally, performances of *chakacha* were conducted by elderly women to teach young girls the etiquette of being a woman, marriage and motherhood, and were held in secret chambers where men were not allowed. From the mid-1980s *chakacha* was taken into the public sphere and appropriated by coastal bands such as Mombasa Roots Band, Safari Sound Band and Them Mushrooms, retaining its characteristic slow and sensuous hip and waist movements. These coastal bands first began to perform *chakacha* songs as fillers in their shows because the lyrics contained sexual overtones. As these became popular with the local people from the coast, the genre soon spread to the wider audience of tourists visiting the coastal towns. The bands went on to record *chakacha* songs that most had arranged from the indigenous *chakacha* melodies. The genre was further promoted through *chakacha* dancing competitions sponsored by companies advertising their brands, with generous prizes awarded to the winners.

In the popular version of the genre, the traditional music structure has remained, though with modern instrumentation. The role played by the *nzumari* has been taken over by the trumpet, and the calls are also normally undertaken by the trumpet as in the indigenous idiom and style. The traditional drums have been replaced by modern drum sets and *congas*, and the rhythms initially played on the *upatsu* are replicated on the high hat. The short melodic calls by the soloists and their answers in exact repetition by the dancers are still considered synonymous with the genre. Lyrics remain in the indigenous idiom and the meaning is hidden and not overtly ribald in nature.

Dancing in the popular version of *chakacha* is performed in a circle that moves counterclockwise, as in the indigenous form. The fact that it may be performed by both sexes or in the presence of both sexes is an interesting syncretism. However, the majority of dancers remain female. It is customary in *chakacha* to reward the best dancers with money. This money may be slotted in the hip belt or in the bust of the best dancer. Traditionally, jewelry was also used.

The artist who perfected the *chakacha* dance in the public limelight was Princess Farida (real name Farida Mafoudh), who became famous after winning a *chakacha* dancing competition where she was crowned 'Queen of Chakacha.' She was later engaged as a dancer for several bands in Nairobi before starting her own band, African Rhythms Band, with her younger brother, Kanda Kid. Princess Farida eventually left the Islamic faith to become a Christian, was married in church and began raising a family while singing Christian gospel music and working as a television presenter for a Christian organization.

Chakacha has remained popular in the coastal regions and capitals of East Africa. This popularity has been enhanced by the relocation of some bands, such as Them Mushrooms, from the coastal region to the national capital of Nairobi, and by an increase in the number of road shows and performing tours. The style also enjoyed radio airplay in the 1980s and 1990s. The sensual dancing associated with the genre is one particular reason why it has remained a less-practiced form of popular music. The *indigenous* version of *chakacha* is among the very few dances not allowed at the Kenya Music Festivals, due to its intended context and age group.

Bibliography

Anyumba, Henry Owunor. 1970. 'Historical Influences on African Music: A Survey.' In *Hadith*, Vol. 3, ed. Bethwell Allan Ogot. Nairobi: East African Publishing House, 192–204.

Askew, Kelly. 2002. *Performing the Nation: Swahili Music and Cultural Politics in Tanzania*. Chicago and London: University of Chicago Press.

Campbell, Carol A., and Eastman, Carol M. 1984. 'Ngoma: Swahili Adult Song Performance in Context.' *Ethnomusicology* 28(3): 467–93.

Graham, Ronnie. 1989. *Stern's Guide to Contemporary African Music*. London: Pluto Press.

Harrev, Flemming. 1989. 'Jambo Records and the Promotion of Popular Music in East Africa.' In *Perspectives on African Music*, ed. Wolfgang Bender. Bayreuth: Bayreuth University Press, 103–38.

Kavyu, Paul Ndilya. 1978. 'The Development of Guitar Music in Kenya.' *Jazz Research* 10: 111–19.

Manuel, Peter. 1988. *Popular Music of the Non-Western World*. Oxford and London: Oxford University Press.

Musau, Paul. 2004. '*Taarab* Songs as a Reflection of the Changing Socio-Political Reality of the Swahili.' In *Swahili Modernities: Culture Politics and Identity on the East Coast of Africa*, eds. Pat Caplan and Farouk Topan. Asmara: African World Press, 175–91.

Ntarangwi, Mwenda. 2003. *Gender, Identity and Performance*. Asmara: African World Press.

Ranger, Terence Osborn. 1975. *Dance and Society in East Africa 1890–1970: The Beni Ngoma*. Oxford: Heinemann Educational Publishers.

Roberts, John Storm. 1968. 'Popular Music in Kenya.' *African Music Society Journal* 4(2): 53–5.

Salim, Ahmed Idha. 1973. *Swahili Speaking Peoples of Kenya's Coast 1895–1965*. Nairobi: East African Publishing House.

Senoga-Zake, George. 1986. *Folk Music in Kenya*. Nairobi: Uzima Press.

Stapleton, Chris, and May, Chris. 1987. *African All Stars: The Pop Music of a Continent*. London: Quartet Books.

Topp Fargion, Janet. 2000. 'Hot Kabisa! The Mpasho Phenomenon and Taarab in Zanzibar.' In *Mashindano: Comparative Music Performance in East Africa*, eds. Frank Gunderson and Gregory Barz. Dar es Salaam: Mkuki na Nyota, 39–53.

Discography

Mombasa Roots Band. 'Disco Cha-ka-cha Part 1 & 2.' Polydor. POL 561. *1985*: Kenya.

Mombasa Roots Band. 'Karibishe/Reggae Sound of Africa.' Polydor. POL 560. *1985*: Kenya.

Mombasa Roots Band. 'Mezea tu (Lele Mama)/Kasha Langu.' Polydor. POL 592. *1985*: Kenya.

Mombasa Roots Band. *Msa-Mombasa*. Polydor. POLP 319. *1987*: Kenya.

Safari Sound Band. *Mambo Jambo*. Arc Music. *2001*: Kenya.

Them Mushrooms. *At the Carnivore*. Polydor. POLP 562. *1987*: Kenya.

Them Mushrooms. *Unakula Huu/Kazi ni Kazi* (Tribute to Bob Marley). Kelele Records. 20.3508-KE. *1999*: Germany.

DONALD OTOYO ONDIEKI AND CALEB CHRISPO OKUMU

Chimurenga

From the revered ancestral warrior Murenga Sororenzou (Vambe 2004, 167), *chimurenga* means 'struggle' in Shona, the dominant language of Zimbabwe. It first came into common use when Zimbabwe's Shona and Ndebele communities openly resisted colonial oppression by the British during the First Chimurenga in 1895–6. Although ultimately unsuccessful, the First Chimurenga had a lasting influence on nationalist politics and the direction of popular music. In a musical context, *chimurenga* typically refers to a genre of popular music from Zimbabwe that combines lyrics of resistance and struggle drawn from Zimbabwe's war of liberation in the 1970s with musical material drawn from the indigenous music of Zimbabwe's Shona majority, especially the *mbira*, a handheld lamellaphone with metal keys typically played in spirit possession ceremonies that are unique to the Shona. The best-known performer of *chimurenga* music is Thomas Mapfumo. He so dominates the style that *chimurenga* is often used to refer solely to his music. But *chimurenga* is much more complicated than this. It has been used inconsistently to refer to a wide array of musical practices ranging from songs sung specifically by soldiers during the war, to contemporary music celebrating Zimbabwe's ruling party ZANU-PF, and to any and all Zimbabwean popular music. After President Mugabe's removal from office in 2017, the future of *chimurenga* music is unclear.

The Second Chimurenga

As nationalism emerged in the 1950s and coalesced in the 1960s, two highly organized and effective political parties emerged, each with an armed wing that successfully fought the armies of what was then white-ruled Southern Rhodesia and won independence in 1980. Over time, the Zimbabwe African National Union (ZANU) acquired predominantly Shona membership whereas the Zimbabwe African People's Union (ZAPU) relied on primarily Ndebele membership. From 1966 to 1979 the affiliated armies of ZANU and ZAPU jointly fought for and won independence. This successful armed struggle is known as the Second Chimurenga.

Based on the military training of their communist backers in China and the Soviet Union, the historical role of music in rural communities, and the didactic role of collective singing in Christian churches, soldiers increasingly used music as a way to educate the masses and lift people's spirits during the war. Musically inclined ZANU soldiers such as Dick 'Comrade Chinx' Chingaira drew from a wide range of musical sources including Shona dance-drumming genres, the *mbira* and Christian hymnody to appeal to a broad spectrum of Zimbabwe's Shona majority. This continued a long legacy linking song and resistance that predates formal nationalism (Chikowero 2011). Lyrics were often changed to inspire support for the nationalist armies, educate people in colonial history, advocate for war or engender a future Zimbabwe. These Chimurenga songs were staples on popular ZANU radio broadcasts and at all-night rallies called *pungwes* that recalled the all-night ancestral ceremonies central to Shona spirituality. Although participation in *pungwes* was often coerced, they became key moments of education, recruitment and solidarity. Alec Pongweni famously called these the 'Songs That Won the Liberation War' (Pongweni 1982). In one example, 'Tora Gidi Uzvitonge (Take up Arms and Liberate Yourselves)' (ZANU n.d.), the singing soldiers managed to educate their recruits, connect the ancestral heroes of the First Chimurenga (Mbuya Nehanda) to the heroes of the Second Chimurenga (Herbert Chitepo), advocate for war as the only means to freedom, and reiterate their own modernity all at once:

> Take up Arms and Liberate Yourselves
> Mbuya Nehanda died with these words on her lips
> 'I'm dying for this country'
> She left one word of advice
> 'Take up arms and liberate yourselves'
> Aren't you coming with us to fight
> We are running about carrying sub-machine guns
> We carry anti-air missiles
> 'Take up arms and liberate yourselves' Chitepo
>   died with these words on his lips
> 'I'm dying for the fatherland.'
> He left one word of advice.
> 'Take up arms and liberate yourselves' (translation
>   by Alec Pongweni).

The Chimurenga songs inspired a generation of young Zimbabweans, including musicians, and helped shape a growing sense of Zimbabwean nationalism. These musicians brought the sounds and ideas of Chimurenga beyond the military rally and radio propaganda into the recording studio and onto the concert stage.

Popular Music in Zimbabwe before Independence

Musical life in Zimbabwe changed dramatically during the colonial period (1880s–1980). The guitar became popular, foreign recordings and bands arrived, and music became a viable professional activity leading to concert performances and commercial recordings. Cosmopolitan bands catering to the growing black middle class played what Thomas Turino calls 'concert' music that reflected hymn-like harmonies and foreign musical models (Turino 2000).

As war grew closer, nationalism spread and the call for independence grew stronger. In the late 1960s musicians relied more and more on indigenous music as a model for an ever-evolving Zimbabwean popular music. Bands like Thomas Mapfumo and the Springfields, with 'Chemutengure' in 1966 and the Harare Mambos with 'Manhanga Kutapira' in 1967, added Shona songs to their repertoire of rock and roll and foreign covers, as did Saint Paul's Band, the Zebrons and the Beatsters (Turino 2000). In the early 1970s three bands recorded songs that drew on *mbira* classics and employed musical techniques that became signatures of the style. M.D. Rhythm Success recorded 'Kumutongo' (1974), based on the classic *mbira* song 'Kuzanga'; Lipopo Jazz, a popular band known for playing Congolese rumba, recorded 'Ndozvireva' (1974), based on the *mbira* classic 'Taireva'; and the Hallelujah Chicken Run Band recorded 'Ngoma Yarira' (1974), based on 'Kariga Mombe.' Co-credit for 'Ngoma Yarira' was given to the singer Thomas Mapfumo and the lead guitarist Joseph Hlomayi Dube. Their collective efforts helped shape the distinctive musical characteristics of *mbira* guitar music that became the most recognizable feature of Mapfumo's version of *chimurenga* music: dampened guitar strings mimicking the percussive attack of *mbira* keys; *mbira* parts split into lead, rhythm and bass guitars; the driving triple rhythms of the *hosho* shakers played by the kick drum and the high hat; and the unique vocal techniques of *mbira* music, including yodeling.

The *mbira* these guitarists emulated is unique to Zimbabwe. It is a handheld instrument with 22–8 metal keys often derisively called a 'thumb piano' in English. It is usually played in pairs with lead and follow parts to accompany dancing, singing and spirit possession during all-night ceremonies. Because the spirits and local spirit mediums became so closely associated with the nationalist movement leading up to independence, the *mbira* itself became a strong index of Shona nationalism. Its cyclical melodies, call-and-response vocals, and dense harmonies became signature musical elements of Mapfumo's *chimurenga* music (for further information on the *mbira* and classic *mbira* songs see Berliner 1993). *Mbira* music and the popular music inspired by it relies heavily on the polyrhythmic framework of duple versus triple rhythms, interlocking instrumental parts (either in the two *mbira* parts or complementary lead, rhythm and bass guitar parts), and cyclical, easily learned call-and-response vocals.

Thomas Mapfumo

Although Pongweni (1982) includes other important bands from the 1970s such as the Green Arrows, Oliver Mtukudzi, Lipopo Jazz and the Inter Jazz Band in his analysis of *chimurenga* music, it is Thomas Mapfumo who typically defines the style. Mapfumo started his career singing 'concert' music with the Cosmic Four Dots and first made his name as a lead singer with the Springfields in the late 1960s before joining the Hallelujah Chicken Run Band. His innovative combination of indigenous musical material, signature dreadlocks and early utilization of explicitly spiritual stage elements (such as the cloth and walking stick used by spirit mediums) brought him notoriety in the popular press of the time. He explicitly blended ideas of 'tradition' and 'modernity' in a successful attempt to appeal to all Shona Zimbabweans, across age, class and gender barriers. In his subsequent bands, the Acid Band followed by the Blacks Unlimited, Thomas Mapfumo developed a strong local following and an international reputation for his renditions of well-known *mbira* standards. Joshua Dube and Jonah Sithole were the two guitarists most widely credited for innovating the unique *mbira* guitar style, although Mapfumo's other guitarists Leonard 'Pickett' Chiyangwa, Ashton 'Sugar' Chiwsehe and Ephraim Karimaura all played a role. Thomas Mapfumo's music quickly became synonymous with *chimurenga*, despite the fact that *mbira* music was always only one element of his repertoire. He still played rock and roll, some reggae and other more idiosyncratic pieces that had little to do with Zimbabwe's Shona heritage. But it was his combination of resistance lyrics, suggested spirituality and indigenous musical material that made him an international world music star (Turino 2000).

In response to Mapfumo's success and as a result of Zimbabwe's post-independence euphoria and embrace of indigenous expressive practices, several bands in Zimbabwe performed popular music based on the *mbira* and other indigenous Shona genres. The freedom to travel and perform throughout the country as well as the growing recording industry in Harare allowed young musicians in Zimbabwe to make a living through music. Mapfumo's style and stage show were frequently emulated. Joshua Dube and Jonah Sithole each left Mapfumo to form their own bands. Dube and Shangara Jive incorporated *mbira* and the Shona dance style *shangara*. Sithole, first with the Storm and later with Deep Horizone, used his innovative *mbira* guitar technique to perform his own, similar, music. Sithole and Dube were the primary innovators behind the performance of *mbira* music on the guitar. Their playing was characterized by long, single-note melodies, a constant 2 versus 3 polyrhythmic feel, and even dampened strings to imitate the quick decay of the *mbira*'s metal keys. But neither could replicate the success they had with Mapfumo. Other bands of the 1980s, including Pio Macheka and the Black-Ites, Robson Banda and the New Black Eagles, Taurai Pekiwe and the Legal Lions, Ilanga, Comrade Chinx, Vadzimba and Flavian Nyathi, emulated Mapfumo's style but were always overshadowed, often criticized for being derivative and marginal to Zimbabwe's popular tastes. These musicians were never as adept at translating the *mbira* and other indigenous musical styles to the guitar and Mapfumo was always able to frame *chimurenga* music (especially *mbira* guitar music) as his own.

Since the 1970s, when Mapfumo first began playing guitar versions of *mbira* songs, he has looked more and more to the tastes of his international audience and placed greater emphasis on the *mbira* itself, even adding an *mbira* player, Chartwell Dutiro, in the mid-1980s. Similarly, *mbira* players like Ephat Mujuru and Stella Chiweshe incorporated guitars and lyrics related to *chimurenga*, but are not typically defined as *chimurenga* musicians. In the early 2000s Mapfumo moved to the United States. Living abroad has undermined his popularity at home where his recordings are typically outsold by *sungura*, *jit* and gospel performers. Popular music based on indigenous antecedents, regardless of lyrical content, are less popular with Zimbabwean audiences than they were when Mapfumo began.

The 2010s: Increasing Politicization

The term 'chimurenga' itself has also been co-opted by the government of Robert Mugabe in an effort to draw parallels between the Second Chimurenga and recent land reacquisition programs that the government calls the Third Chimurenga. The minister of information in the first decade of the twenty-first century, Jonathan Moyo, even produced a series of recordings called '3rd Chimurenga Music,' 'Hondo YeMinda' (War of the Agricultural Lands) and 'Back2Black' by PaxAfro, an ensemble he created to sing urban grooves music in support of the government and land reform. Expensive state-sponsored promotional jingles called 'Chave Chimurenga' by Tambaoga and others used indigenous musical influences and pro-land reform lyrics to link ancestral authority, the liberation struggle and land reform (Sibanda 2004). At the turn of the twenty-first century artists including Simon Chimbetu, Andy Brown and Comrade Chinx sang songs about war, land reform and Chimurenga, tying current political struggles to the 1970s fight for independence. Although Chimbetu, for instance, has little in common with Mapfumo musically, his explicitly pro-ZANU texts often elicit *chimurenga* music as a description. As the term becomes more politicized, its use as a genre term becomes less common. For example, the Zimbabwe Music Awards replaced the category 'Chimurenga' with that of 'socially conscious lyrics.' In the 2010s Mugabe's ZANU-PF government explicitly employed *chimurenga* music as a form of propaganda and marketing. Zimbabwean airwaves were inundated by the music of the Mbare Chimurenga Choir who performed songs based on Shona dance/drumming styles and the original Chimurenga sound from the liberation war to celebrate Robert Mugabe, ZANU-PF and land reform. Their appeal to older, rural audiences was balanced by government-friendly hip-hop groups who used the rhetoric of Chimurenga to appeal to urban youth, such as the Born Free Crew and VaMugabe Chete Crew. These groups' continued relevance is in doubt after Mugabe's removal from power, but the Mbare Chimurenga Choir immediately released songs in praise of his successor, President Emmerson Mnangagwa. As Zimbabwe moves forward, it remains to be seen whether Chimurenga will continue to apply to all Zimbabwean popular music, political songs, the music of Thomas Mapfumo or the soldiers' songs that comprised the original *chimurenga* music.

Bibliography

Berliner, Paul. 1993. *The Soul of Mbira*. Chicago: University of Chicago Press.

Chikonzo, Kelvin, Nyimai, Joel, and Sambo, Kudakwashe Shane. 2016. '"Violations" of the

Chimurenga Genre in the Music of *Mbare Chimurenga Choir*.' In *Sounds of Life: Music, Identity and Politics in Zimbabwe*, eds. Fainos Mangena, Ezra Chitando and Itai Muwati. Newcastle upon Tyne: Cambridge Scholars Publishing, 182–95.

Chikowero, Moses. 2011. 'The Third Chimurenga: Land and Song in Zimbabwe's Ultra-Nationalist State Ideology, 2000–2007.' In *Redemptive or Grotesque Nationalism: Rethinking Contemporary Politics in Zimbabwe*, eds. Sabelo J. Ndlovu-Gatsheni and James Muzondidya. New York: Peter Lang, 291–314.

Eyre, Banning. 2015. *Lion Songs: Thomas Mapfumo and the Music that Made Zimbabwe*. Durham, NC: Duke University Press.

Frederikse, Julie. 1982. *None But Ourselves: Masses vs. Media in the Making of Zimbabwe*. Harare: Zimbabwe Publishing House.

Gonye, Jairos. 2013. 'Mobilizing Dance/Traumatizing Dance: Kongonya and the Politics of Zimbabwe.' *Dance Research Journal* 45(1): 64–79.

Guchu, Wonder. 2008. 'Zima's Decision Ill-Advised.' *The Herald* (8 October).

Kwaramba, Alice Dadirai. 1997. *Popular Music and Society: The Language of Chimurenga Music: The Case of Thomas Mapfumo in Zimbabwe*. Oslo: University of Oslo.

Marongwe, Ngonidzashe. 2013. 'Political Aesthetics, the Third Chimurenga, and the ZANU-PF Mobilization in Shurugwi District of Zimbabwe.' *Journal of Developing Societies* 29(4): 457–85.

Pongweni, Alec J. C. 1982. *Songs That Won the Liberation War*. Harare: The College Press.

Sibanda, Maxwell. 2004. 'Complete Control: Music and Propaganda in Zimbabwe.' *Freedom of Music Expression*, 20 September. Online at: https://freemuse.org/news/zimbabwe-complete-control-music-and-propaganda-in-zimbabwe/ (accessed 21 August 2018).

Thram, Diane. 2006. 'Patriotic History and the Politicisation of Memory: Manipulation of Popular Music to Re-invent the Liberation Struggle in Zimbabwe.' *Critical Arts* 20(2): 75–88.

Turino, Thomas. 2000. *Nationalists, Cosmopolitans, and Popular Music in Zimbabwe*. Chicago: University of Chicago Press.

Vambe, Maurice T. 2004. 'Versions and Sub-Versions: Trends in Chimurenga Musical Discourses of Post Independence Zimbabwe.' *African Study Monographs* 25(4): 167–93.

Zindi, Fred. 1985. *Roots Rocking in Zimbabwe*. Gweru: Mambo Press.

Discographical References

3rd Chimurenga Series. More Fire. Sebwe Music ROS 5. *2002*: Zimbabwe.

Chiangwa, Last. *Chave Chimurenga*. National Events Trust. *2003*: Zimbabwe.

Comrade Chinx and the Police Band. *3rd Chimurenga Series. Hondo Yeminda Vols. 1 & 2*. Shed Studios. *2001*: Zimbabwe.

Hallelujah Chicken Run Band. 'Ngoma Yarira.' Afro Soul AS 105. *1974*: Southern Rhodesia. (Reissued in *Take One (1974-1979)*. Analog Africa AACD062. *2006*: Germany).

Harare Mambos. 'Manhanga Kutapira.' RBC #9948B. *1967*: Zimbabwe.

Lipopo Jazz. 'Ndozvireva.' Gallo GB.3868. *1974*: Zimbabwe.

Mapfumo, Thomas, and the Springfields. 'Chemutengure.' RBC #9196B. *1966*: Zimbabwe.

M. D. Rhythm Success. 'Kumutongo.' Gallo GB.3815. *1974*: Zimbabwe.

Pax Afro. *Back2Black Tapes 1 & 2*. Talunosiza Music. *2004*: Zimbabwe.

Discography

Banda, Robson, and the New Black Eagles. *Greatest Hits, Vol. 1*. Zimbob ZIM5. *1996*: USA.

Black-I-Tes. *Mabweadziva*. RTP L4RTLP33. *1991*: Zimbabwe.

Harare Mambos. *Ngatigarei Tese*. ZML 1025. N.d.: Zimbabwe.

Mapfumo, Thomas, and the Acid Band. *Hokoyo!*. Gramma ZASLP 5000. *1978*: Zimbabwe.

Mapfumo, Thomas, and the Blacks Unlimited. *Gwindingwi Rine Shumba*. Afro Soul ASLP 5002. *1980*: Zimbabwe.

Mapfumo, Thomas, and the Blacks Unlimited. *Ndangariro*. Gramma ASLP 5003. *1983*: Zimbabwe.

Mapfumo, Thomas, and the Blacks Unlimited. *The Chimurenga Singles, 1976–1980*. Earthworks ELP 2004. *1984*: UK.

Mapfumo, Thomas, and the Blacks Unlimited. *Zimbabwe-Mozambique*. Gramma TML 100. *1988*: Zimbabwe.

Mapfumo, Thomas, and the Blacks Unlimited. *Chamunorwa*. Gramma TML 102. *1989*: Zimbabwe.
Mapfumo, Thomas, and the Blacks Unlimited. *Corruption*. Island CCD 9848. *1989*: UK.
Mapfumo, Thomas, and the Blacks Unlimited. *Vanhu Vatema*. Zimbob ZIM2. *1994*: USA.
Mbare Chimurenga Choir. *Nyatsoteerera*. Gramma. *2010*: Zimbabwe.
Nyathi, Flavian, and Blues Revolution. *Ropa ReZimbabwe*. Gallo Records KK13. *1980*: Zimbabwe.
Pekiwe, Taurai, and the Legal Lions. *Samero*. *1991*: Zimbabwe.
Shangara Jive. *Shangara Jive*. CC Shangara 001. *1993*: Zimbabwe.
Sithole, Jonah, and Deep Horizon. *Zimbabwe Beat*. L4 RTLP 115. *1995*: Zimbabwe.
ZANU (Zimbabwe African National Union). *Chimurenga Songs: Music of the Revolutionary Peoples War in Zimbabwe*. Gramma L4VZ5. *N.d.*: Zimbabwe.

TONY PERMAN

Coladeira

The modern Cabo Verdean *coladeira*, considered the first urban music and dance style of the archipelago, developed after World War II in the lively musical environment of Mindelo, a port city with vacillating fortunes on the northern island of São Vicente. With the proliferation of recordings played on radio programs and in dance halls, *coladeira* had a meteoric rise in the turbulent 1960s, as Cabo Verde headed into the war for liberation. As dance music with no obvious political agenda, it avoided some of the increasingly oppressive censorship enforced by the Portuguese colonial authorities. It became a symbol of modernity and the future in a country on the cusp of independence.

The name 'coladeira' is derived from the *Cola SanJon*, a lively circle dance which is part of the Festival SanJon (Saint John) popular in the northern islands. Women who sang and clapped in the festival's processions were known as *coladeiras*. As early as the 1920s partygoers who wanted the slow dance tempos of the *morna* to speed up would use a reference understood by all, and yell out to the band, 'Hey old man, turn it into a *coladeira*!' (Monteiro 74).

Musical Features

Coladeiras are always played fairly up-tempo in 2/4 or 4/4 and in a major key. Traditionally they are accompanied by guitars, *cavaquiño* (a small, ukelele-like stringed instrument), and a wind instrument, often a clarinet. Later bass, drums and additional wind instruments were added. The *cavaquiño* player sets the pace and keeps time with an underlying rhythm:

The music is accompanied by an exuberant and, depending on the social situation, potentially close couple's dance in which the upper body is still while the hips and feet move back and forth with the duple meter. Lyrics are in a verse and refrain format, with each verse sung twice before moving to the refrain, which is also repeated. Themes are full of social and domestic satire, sharp criticisms, off-color jokes and sarcasm, all based in the reality of the hardship of day-to-day life on islands that were often plagued by drought and famine. They contrast sharply with the serious, idealized romantic lyrics of the slower-paced and elegiac *morna*, also in 4/4 with a strophe and refrain format. Early *coladeiras* were written exclusively in the Kriolu (*sampadjudo*) language of Mindelo, but starting in the 1960s composers throughout the islands began to write them using the expressions, locations and situations specific to their own island or diaspora community. Nonetheless, the form retains a cultural connection to the city of its birth.

Composers

The form coalesced around the compositions of Ti Goy (born Gregório Gonçalves), who was a leader in the Mindelo music scene beginning in the 1920s. Although he never left the islands, there can be no doubt that the myriad of cultures that passed through Mindelo influenced his work. His lyrics are quite biting and humorous, especially when it comes to women in songs such as 'Terezinha' and 'Vaquinha Mansa' (Sweet Little Cow), both of which appear on Cesaria Évora's recording *Café Atlantico*.

Later composers such as Manel D'Novas, Frank Cavaquim and Luis Morais were well traveled and incorporated the Latin American rhythms of *mambo*, *cumbia* and *merengue* into the *coladeira*. Manel D'Novas, who died in 2009, left a large body of work which added harmonic complexity and lyrics that were often political or patriotic in nature.

In 1967 Luis Morais formed the group Voz de Cabo Verde (Voice of Cabo Verde) in Rotterdam, which played an important role in modernizing the genre with new arrangements and electric instruments. On tour following the release of their first album, *Dançando com Voz de Cabo Verde* (Dancing with Voz do Cabo Verde), their newly electrified *coladeiras* were a cultural turning point in a country firmly under the grip of Portuguese censorship. The popular Os Tubarões (The Sharks), formed in Praia in 1969 and, headed by the vocalist Ildo Lobo with arrangements by Zeca Couto, continued to expand and develop the form as well. For the first time, Cabo Verdeans heard a live, modernized version of their *own* music.

As dance music, *coladeira*'s popularity waned in the 1980s in favor of *funaná*, an accordion-based music from Santiago. Starting in the late 1980s Cesaria Évora's international success created a renaissance of neo-traditional *coladeiras* paving the way for new opportunities for many composers. But the *coladeira* is not fixed; it is a flexible and evolving form, with the ability to absorb and reconfigure many influences while maintaining its Cape Verdean identity. Paulino Vieira's arrangements incorporate Latin rhythms and African instruments; Gerard Mendes and Téofilo Chantre integrate jazz improvisation and African rhythms; and even *cabo-zouk* composers acknowledge the influence of *coladeira* in their music.

True to its origins in the cosmopolitan melting pot of Mindelo, the *coladeira* continues to play an important role in Cabo Verde's musical connection to the world. Although no longer considered popular music by the younger generation, it holds an important place in the Cabo Verdean psyche, expressing the quintessentially Cabo Verdean quality to laugh at the ridiculousness of life even in the direst conditions. (For more on *coladeira* in the Cabo Verdean diaspora, see Coladeira [in Europe], Vol. XI, *Genres: Europe*.)

Bibliography

Ferreira, Manuel. 1973. *Aventura crioula ou Cabo Verde: Uma síntese cultural étnica* [The Creole Experience or Cabo Verde: An Ethnic Cultural Synthesis]. 2nd ed. Lisbon: Plátano Editora.

Gonçalves, Carlos. 1998. 'Kab verd band.' In *Descoberta das Ilhas de Cabo Verde* [Discovery of the Cabo Verde Islands], ed. José Maria Almeida. Praia, Cabo Verde: Archivo Histórico Nacional (Cabo Verde), 178–207.

Monteiro, César Augusto. 2003. *Manel d'Novas: Música, vida, caboverdianidade* [Manel d'Novas: Music, Life, Caboverdianidade]. Mindelo, Cabo Verde: Self-Published.

Monteiro, Vladimir. 1998. *Les musiques du Cap-Vert* [The Musics of Cabo Verde]. Paris: Éditions Chandeigne.

Discographical References

Évora, Cesaria. 'Terezinha' and 'Vaquinha Mansa.' *Café Atlantico*. Lusafrica 74321 65401-2. *1999*: France.

Voz de Cabo Verde. *Dançando com Voz de Cabo Verde*. Morabeza Records. *1967*: Netherlands.

Discography

Évora, Cesaria. *Miss Perfumado*. Melodie 79540-2. *1992*: France.

Évora, Cesaria. *Cesaria*. Nonesuch 79379-2. *1995*: France.

Évora, Cesaria. *Cabo Verde*. Nonesuch 79450-2. *1997*: France.

Évora, Cesaria. *Voz d'amor*. Bluebird 54380. *2003*: France.

Évora, Cesária. *Radio Mindelo: The Early Recordings*. Lusafrica 562202. *2008*: Mindelo, Cabo Verde.

Paris, Tito. *Dança ma mi Criola*. MB Records. *1994*: USA.

Tubarões, Os. *Best of Os Tubarões*. Sons d'Africa 605277 080021. *2006*: Portugal.

JOANNE HOFFMAN

Concert Party

In Ghana, *concert party* refers to a variety show consisting of live dance band music, stand-up and sketch comedy punctuated with songs (often parodies), and a melodramatic musical play peppered with farcical situations and slapstick antics. During the early decades of the twentieth century the same term was used in Great Britain to refer to small troupes of multitalented variety artists – called 'Pierrot troupes,' after a naïve, buffoonish stock character of the European stage – that toured the seaside towns with 'Pierrot shows' made up of songs, dances, juggling and jokes.

The British and Ghana concert parties have a mutual historical connection to British music hall. However, there is no solid, traceable link between them. Scholars and practitioners of Ghanaian popular music and theater link the Ghana *concert party* with the African-European cultural encounter in Ghana and place the local origin of the term in the distinctions that Africans made between performances that they saw the Europeans present and the ones in their own African cultural life. Colonial-era Africans observed that, in contrast with the looser temporal stage structures, multiple centers of visual focus and fluid spatial audience–performer relationships within their own performances, Europeans presented performances in an 'ordered,' pre-established program on a raised platform and with a marked proscenium style separation between the performers and audience. Therefore 'concert,' a term that was loaned from the English language, developed in the African popular parlance for any performances that followed these presumed European conventions. *Concert party* is, nevertheless, a multi-rooted genre forged, not only from the social/political/economic conditions and the creative-artistic consequences of the African-European contact, but also from long-standing homegrown cultural performance practices.

The Precursors of the Genre

One precursor of *concert party* – musicals and theatricals in colonial schools – was part of the colonial project to produce English-literate Africans in Gold Coast. British-style education in Gold Coast began in the mid-eighteenth century on a small scale, with a school in the trading fort at Cape Coast (a seaboard city) for mulatto children of European administrators, missionaries and traders, and children of African chiefs and wealthy merchants. Britain declared the area a colony in 1821 but could afford only a small presence because Europeans frequently died of malaria and yellow fever there. To fill the gap, the British set up more schools to train Africans as clerks in the mercantile houses and civil service, and as teachers and catechists in the schools and churches. From the 1900s onwards these schools regularly staged musical and theatrical concerts on special occasions such as Empire Day, an annual ritual to celebrate Queen Victoria's birthday. Empire Day began in the schools with a morning parade by fife-playing African pupils before their teachers and colonial administrators. On such special days, pupils expressed loyalty to Britain in songs such as 'Armada,' 'Our Home is the Ocean Blue,' 'You Gentlemen of England,' 'Hurrah for England' and 'Britannia and Her People.' They danced the Scottish reel and the sailors' hornpipe, staged Shakespeare's *Macbeth* and *Twelfth Night*, adapted the 'Trial of Bardel v. Pickwick' (from Dickens's *Pickwick* Papers) for the stage, enacted operas such as *The King of Sherwood*, and – in consort with the British turn-of-the-century orientalist imaginary – acted out folk tales such as *Aladdin and the Magic Lamp* and fables such as Aesop's *The Wolf and Lamb*.

British colonization in Gold Coast had a missionary front as well as those more directly concerned with political-imperial and mercantile affairs. Many schools in the Gold Coast were government-controlled/funded but a good many more were controlled by church entities. Perhaps even more than government schools, church entities actively promoted musical/theatrical concerts in their programs. One favorite musical-theatrical tradition among these church entities was the cantata, a dramatized vocal composition (this, in its Gold Coast manifestation, was a musical morality play) done to the accompaniment of musical instruments and/or a choir. In the 1930s the head teacher of the Bishop's School in Accra was a producer-cum-musician well known for producing dramatic cantatas. Church-related groups such as Swedru Twelve Apostles, the Wesley (Methodist) Church Choir and the Mass (Anglican) Sunday School Choir of the Holy Trinity and St Mary's Churches, staged cantatas entitled *The Rolling Seasons, Nativity, Bethlehem, Joseph and His Brethren* and *Esther the Beautiful*. That these church entities shared an interest with the colonial government in promoting musical/theatrical concerts is evident, for instance, in the fact that the chairperson on the occasion of the Wesley Church Choir's performance of *The Rolling Seasons* was none other than the British Colonial Secretary himself.

Around the start of the twentieth century concerts were to be found also in the activities of social/literary clubs in Gold Coast. Among these, European clubs aimed to provide private variety amusements to stave off tropical boredom and offer a semblance of European culture for nostalgic colonial administrators and the staff of British trading companies. One such amusement was a costumed Ball and Concert. Rogers Club called its Ball and Concert in 1932 'the first of its kind in the colony' (*The Times of Africa* cited in Agovi 1993, 8). This was a slight exaggeration, as in 1903 there had been one in Cape Coast fort with prominent Europeans and Africans in the city dressed as Ben Hur (from Lew Wallace's 1880 novel *Ben-Hur: A Tale of the Christ*), as the Queen of the Night (from Mozart's opera *The Magic Flute*), and as the Pierrot character of the European stage, along with magic shows, brass band music and 'Two Macs' (a comic routine from the late-Victorian London variety theaters). In any case, European clubs like the Rogers Club served as models for African ones like the Ladies Club of Cape Coast and the Optimism Club of Sekondi. African clubs hosted concerts with performances such as *Belshazzar's Feast* (a cantata by William Walton) and *Accomplished Lover* (a comic drama); choral renditions of 'God Save the King' and 'God Bless the Prince of Wales'; recitations of 'Colonial Loyalty' and 'Loss of the Royal George'; readings of Shakespeare; dramatic sketches of a 'Mock Trial,' 'Playing at Parliament' and the 'Battle of the Books'; and comic scenes of 'Camp Life.'

Beside the concerts in/by colonial schools, church entities and social and literary clubs, another *concert party* precursor was the type of popular amusement found in Gold Coast seaboard cities such as Sekondi (west of Cape Coast) and Accra (the easterly replacement of Cape Coast as colonial capital in 1877). By the early twentieth century these cities had grown and their populations had become more cosmopolitan, developing a taste as they did so for new-fangled entertainments. Silent films, which were imported into the Gold Coast by the firm of G.B Olivant, served this appetite. Several cinema houses went up in Accra and other locations that showed the films from abroad. Accra had the Palladium Theatre, which sat over 1,000 people and took after the famous London Palladium, a music hall building. Albert Ocansey, owner of the copy, was inspired to build his after seeing the original during a visit to the UK. At Sekondi the Arkhurst Hall showed films distributed by Ocansey. By the end of the 1920s favorite film stars of the urban audiences included Charlie Chaplin, himself a former British music hall actor, and Al Jolson, the vaudevillian star of the first sound-synchronized 'talking' film, *The Jazz Singer* (1927), among others.

In addition to film shows, Gold Coast's urban cinema houses held variety entertainments that drew liberally on foreign, often Western, theatrical and musical practices copied from movies and other sources. At Ocansey's Palladium a regular feature of the entertainments were Augustus Williams, 'actor, tap dancer, guitarist and singer of comic songs,' and his partner Joseph Marbel (*The Gold Coast Spectator*, cited in Agovi 1993, 11). Wearing bowler hats, tailcoats and tattered pants (as in Chaplin's tramp character) and accompanied by a small brass dance orchestra (acoustic bass, drums, piano) and a chorus of singers, they combined dances, popular songs and short, simply plotted, physically comedic dramatic sketches in their variety entertainments. They imitated the dance routines and the blackface makeup of minstrel characters – especially that played by Al Jolson – from the films. Like many of the Gold Coast's urban-dwelling Africans, the duo studied dances such as the foxtrot, waltz, blues, quickstep, tango and Charleston from local formal and informal dance schools, newspaper columns, books, sheet music and the vaudevillian silent films. From foreign variety artists such as Hoyte and Fineran and Glass and Grant (whom Ocansey brought to the Palladium Theatre from abroad), Williams and Marbel also studied tap dancing, ragtime music, makeup and the quick costume-change artistry of the vaudevillian musical-theatrical performance tradition.

The vaudevillian musical-theatrical fares – with their 'Negro jokes and songs' – were already a part of the concerts in the social and literary clubs and colonial schools by the 1930s. For instance, in a variety show hosted by the Ladies Musical League in Accra in 1932, a certain Aurora Cato performed a vaudeville act in which she impersonated the African-American singer-actress Ethel Waters's performance of 'Am I Blue' from the movie *On with the Show*. Also, at a 1930 Empire Day concert put on by the Bishop School of Accra, schoolmaster Ayitey followed his pupils' 'humorous plantation songs' and 'Negro spirituals' with a comic routine in which he wore blackface makeup and nearly set himself and his master on fire. Yet another schoolmaster, Yalley, dubbed 'Laughter Maker of Tarquah' (he hailed from the mining town of Tarkwa), wore 'fancy clothes, wigs, a false moustache,' oversized shoes and blackface makeup for his one-person variety act at his school's Empire Day concert in 1918. Yalley's one-person acts included comedy sketches as well as ragtime, foxtrot and waltz numbers: 'He sang, he danced and talked a lively patter' to the accompaniment of a pedal organ and trap drums (Sutherland 1970, 7). By 1926 Yalley's three-hour-long show was a regular feature at Sekondi's Optimism Club. Essentially, Williams and Marbel, Ayitey, and Yalley were early members of a cadre of semi- and fully professional twentieth-century Gold Coast variety entertainers in the precursors of *concert party* form and content.

The Progenitor of the Genre

The artistic evolution from concerts and amusements to *concert party* took a significant turn in the 1930s when a distinct type of variety performance emerged among Africans in Gold Coast. Ishmael Johnson, the 'most influential artist' in this crucial development is the immediate progenitor of *concert parties* (Bame 1985, 9). Johnson grew up in Cape Coast and, later, Sekondi under assorted theatrical and musical influences, from silent and later 'talkie' films and African-American seamen's jokes, songs and dances (with harmonica, banjo and accordion accompaniment), to sea shanties that Liberian stevedores sang alongside guitars and musical saws. As a schoolboy Johnson had tried often to get into schoolmaster Yalley's shows at Sekondi Optimism Club, but social restrictions to the elite space barred him until 1927, when he found his way in as Yalley's helping hand. Johnson loved the cantatas that were performed by his Methodist School across the street from the Club. He also loved the excitement of the Empire Day parades and concerts for which colonial pupils spent long hours of preparation. In the concerts, he thrilled teachers and schoolmates so much with his singing and dancing skills that they usually made him the opening and closing act. After Empire Day concerts, he and his friends would gather in the school compound to stage their own 'mock' versions for their schoolmates' amusement. Johnson recalled saying to himself as a schoolboy that 'if song and dance is what makes concerts,' he too 'can become a performer' (Sutherland 1970, 7).

Inspired by the positive reception of his Empire Day acts and afterschool mock versions, Johnson teamed up with his friends in 1922 to form the Versatile Eight, touring the local villages and towns with an improvised variety act of songs, dances (many copied from the films), speeches and short dramatic scenes for a small group. The group retained the infusion of originally English songs and dialogues with mock, funny, Fante versions. In fact, their supreme purpose on stage was laughter and, to that end, they filled their acts with horseplay, slapstick and general buffoonery. After elementary school in 1930 Johnson and two schoolmates Charles Hutton and Bob Ansah formed a new group, Two Bobs and Their Carolina Girl. They toured Gold Coast cities and towns on the seaboard and inland to rural areas. Their shows were roughly two hours long, beginning around 8:00pm with a quickstep to drums and music from a hired school orchestra till a sizeable audience assembled. They continued with 'ragtime' (then a catch-all term for tunes from abroad), a 'Duet' with dance and comic dialogue, and a 'Scene' or play punctuated with song and dance. These were in English with occasional translations into – and parodies in – Fante. Popular songs such as English music hall actor Dick Henderson's recording of J.P Long's 'Crowning of the Cotton Queen,' and 'Minnie the Moocher' by American jazz singer Cab Calloway, turned into a Fante hymn and a Fante account of Liberian stevedores' love for rice, respectively. Johnson created – for his group – a stock character 'Bob,' whose name he took from the way that African-American sailors in Sekondi hailed school children for errands: 'Hey Bob!' Johnson's Bob wore large mismatched shoes and baggy trousers based on Chaplin's tramp character and blackface makeup similar to that of Al Jolson's minstrel in *The Jazz Singer*.

The artistic influences on Johnson were not purely foreign/Western-derived. His Bob figure, for example, was a hybrid of Chaplin's tramp, Jolson's minstrel, comic stereotypes of the seafaring Liberian Kru laborer and a homegrown figure, trickster Ananse of the Akan storytelling tradition called *Anansesem*. Like Ananse, Bob was an ambiguous character who lived to indulge his ravenous appetite, transgressed the social norms, survived by his wit and was loved and hated by audiences. *Anansesem* influenced more elements of Johnson's art than the Bob character. The mix of dialogue and song (Johnson's Akan term, *kasa-ndwom*, means speech-song) and use of female impersonators (Charles Hortons was so convincing in one impersonation that an Englishman in the audience called him 'Oh My Carolina Girl,' from which the Two Bobs and Their Carolina Girl derived their name) in Johnson's art, were as much features of Akan storytelling as they were of American vaudeville and British music hall. Plays by the group typically (although not exclusively) revolved around three stock characters: a wife, a cuckolded husband and a servant. The infidelity arose from the couple's mismatch and led to quarrels between them, but the plays emphasized comedy and fun. With the Two Bobs and Their Carolina Girl Johnson began not just an itinerant performance tradition in Gold Coast, but a dramaturgical model as well, for which he is usually credited as the 'father' of *concert parties*.

The Emerging Genre in Context

Notwithstanding its comedy or light-heartedness and fun, the musical-theatrical variety performance that Johnson and company pioneered reflected serious socioeconomic and political aspects of Gold Coast colonialism. Indeed, by the 1930s it was quite common in Gold Coast for entertainers to imitate blackface minstrels, particularly as performed by Al Jolson (Augustus Williams and a comedian called Smart Abbey performed imitations from another Jolson talkie, *The Singing Fool* [1928], in 1932 and 1934, respectively). Johnson's group, therefore, got in on the act of something that was already popular. For one, his copying of blackface minstrelsy was part of a nascent anti-imperialist diaspora consciousness in Gold Coast in the 1930s and 1940s. Literature circulating in Gold Coast then, like the Paris-based *Negro Worker* and Marcus Garvey's *Negro World*, invoked 'Negro' as a transnational/transcultural identity to expose racist foundations of imperialism and promote broader-based affiliation and struggle against racial and class/capitalist exploitation. The British colonial government deemed such publications seditious and censored them but permitted the circulation of films with racist stereotypes of black people. The result was a complex doubleness about local imitations of minstrelsy. What forged blackface minstrelsy in North America was the ideology of white supremacy and the related history of exploitation, segregation and derisive stereotyping of black people. Gold Coast Africans consumed minstrelsy without these racist connotations: they (mis)construed the films as actual or at worst comic representations of black culture. Thus, their imitations were the embodied way by which they imagined themselves a part of the transnational/transcultural black community. In other words what motivated the imitation was, among other things, a sense of racial affinity with the diaspora at a time black people were mobilizing blackness across national/cultural borders with anti-imperialist verve.

Johnson and other Gold Coast Africans' blackface was part of a broader tendency of emulation in the colony. School concerts had played a key role in inculcating this tendency by asking African pupils to show off English-singing, -speaking and -dancing abilities to demonstrate their mastery of the behaviors of Western culture. Recall that Western education began in Gold Coast for mulatto children of Europeans and children of African chiefs and wealthy merchants. Chiefs' and merchants' interest in such education arose from the socioeconomic transformations and cash economy that trade with Europeans created: aside from traditional modes of authority one could suddenly obtain rank, status and mobility also by acquiring wealth and developing a Western frame of reference (including speech, manners, dress). Privileged children of this 'new wealth' – a small, highly 'educated' African elite – saw itself ordained to prove the capabilities of a maligned black race by helping to 'uplift' it to 'equality of achievement … with the white man.' With that sense of ordination, this elite founded African literary/social clubs as 'centers of continuing adult education' – adjuncts to the formal schools – to offer opportunities for self-improvement to elementarily educated Africans. The African clubs' activities – lectures, fine dining and assorted performances, from concerts of Mozart's piano music and readings of Shakespeare to ballroom dances, masked/costumed galas and variety entertainments (all modeled after European clubs' activities) – extended the culture of emulating Western behaviors and lifestyles that the colonial school concerts were already inculcating through performance.

The elementarily educated Africans whom the elite wished to uplift with literary and social clubs were those who had taken advantage of the expansion of colonial education in the African population. They were an incipient class for which the literary/social clubs provided a space to socialize as Africans who were literate in English, uninhibited by prevailing ethnic considerations. This class was drawn to the literary/social clubs partly because behind the concerts and other educational experiences in which the colonial school immersed it – experiences that held up Western ways as models for this class to imitate – was a colonial ideology that placed British rituals and behaviors atop African ones (in fact at the apex) in a hierarchy of civilization. This incipient class, lacking the social and economic means to access advanced education, was drawn to social/literary clubs also from a pragmatic recognition of the rewards of personal advancement or mobility that the successful performance of Western culture promised. Therefore, as the supply of elementary education in the colony outstripped available salary-earning jobs for this class in the private and public sectors of the economy, it became more and more the case that this class's aspirations for personal advancement failed to match the reality of its everyday experiences. Ishmael Johnson and the other members of his group belonged to this incipient class of elementarily educated Africans in Gold Coast. The musical-theatrical variety show they pioneered reflected the emulation by, but also the aspirations and frustrations of, their incipient class in colonial society and economy. One aspect of this was the way they highlighted the desirability but also artifice of the life of the Westernized/educated Gold Coast Africans

One manifestation of the wife, husband and servant (the group's stock characters) was the Lady, Gentleman and Houseboy. The Lady was a stereotype of educated Gold Coast African women from the colonists' point of view: with white femininity as her model, she adopted the English language, dress (frock, pearl necklace, earrings, spectacles, lipstick, gloves, shoes, purse etc.) and manners, in contrast with the 'uneducated,' illiterate, drudge, cloth-wearing woman. Her disdain for menial occupation, her inability and unwillingness to do household chores and her fickleness in love were reasons for her infidelity and the sources of conflict and moral focus in the plays. The Gentleman was a penniless man with pretensions to affluence and English fluency (he was particularly bad at the latter). The Houseboy was a familiar stereotype – a night-soil-carrying, joke-cracking Kru man but also an intrigue-full Ananse figure. He instigates and stokes the conflict yet manages to be on the good side of it and is always the audience's comic delight. The Lady and Gentleman, in the former's enactment of Englishness and latter's pretensions to it, embodied the aspirations of the incipient class in the colonial society and economy. Yet they also indicated a disjuncture between representation and reality, between the attachment of personal advancement to the performance of European-ness – that is, European-ness as the means, mode and mark of success – and the frustrating reality of the lives of those in this incipient class. Interaction between these stock characters, including the antics and commentary of the Houseboy (ironically the most adjusted of the trio), captured the social/economic tumult that colonialism unleashed in the lives of Gold Coast's incipient class in the early twentieth century.

In 1935 the Two Bobs and Their Carolina Girl broke up. The group had persuaded Sugar Babies, a Cape Coast dance band, to allow it to perform alongside the band on the latter's tour of Nigeria but group members Ansah and Hutton later declined to honor the deal out of fear that remuneration would not be fair. Johnson therefore joined E.K. Dadson and Charles Turpin as the Axim Trio for the trip. The Two Bobs and Their Carolina Girl finally disbanded in 1937 and Johnson toured permanently as one of the Axim Trio. The Axim Trio continued the touring tradition, mixing the Fanti language with English not just for parody or to make a thematic point but also as a pragmatic move to reach the growing non-English-speaking audiences for that kind of performance that Johnson had pioneered. Axim Trio shows opened with the same introductory elements as the Two Bobs and Their Carolina Girl but had longer and relatively more serious plays with a wider range of historical and social/political themes.

Plays by the Axim Trio continued to reflect the social-political sentiments Gold Coast Africans held about British colonialism. At one level Axim Trio's *The Coronation of King George VI* (a re-enactment of the 1936 event) had something colonial school concerts – indeed colonial education – inculcated: the attachment of value to British rituals, practices, manners and the development of a sense of loyalty to Empire. However, the play's success was possibly more theatrical than ideological: countrywide ferment of excitement over it seemed to derive more from the thrilling achievement of executing the entire coronation with the quick-change artistry of three actors. *Bond of 1844* (about a historic bond of allegiance to British power/jurisdiction by local chiefs) was clearly less differential but still ambivalent. The play presents the Bond, a legal foundation for Britain's colonial hold in Gold Coast, as the result of a British man's deception of an unsuspecting local fisherman. The fisherman's educated/literate son, on returning from a sojourn in Britain, sees the fraudulence of the Bond and gets his people out of it. They congratulate him for his learning, praise education and decide to send their children to school. In turn, he advises them to be proud and jealous of their land and see it as a legacy for their children. In the show's participatory atmosphere, audiences cheered wildly at his words, and condemned and booed the British man offstage. The Axim Trio celebrated Western education but whipped up nationalist and anti-colonial sentiment in a manner unprecedented in Johnson's work. The Axim Trio grew in popularity and was a major attraction at assorted indigenous festivals across Gold Coast, also touring the neighboring countries of Nigeria, Ivory Coast, Liberia and Sierra Leone.

By World War II other itinerant groups modeled after the Axim Trio had formed. Some of them, like the Dix-Covian Jokers, had names that emphasized the comic underpinning of their art. However, the names of many more, like Happy Trio, Saltpond Trio, and Keta Trio, acknowledged their inspiration in the archetypal three-person group that Johnson had established. As 'trios' crisscrossed the colony with shows, they helped forge public consciousness of a national identity. By the end of the War nationalist activism in Gold Coast had shifted from a politico-legal struggle for fair representation, which relied on a lawyer-dominated educated elite, to mass calls for immediate independence. The socioeconomically disgruntled incipient class drove this shift, but under the leadership of the Lincoln College (Pennsylvania)-educated and proletarian sensitive Kwame Nkrumah. The trios were at the forefront of these disaffected class sensibilities and made their support for Nkrumah known. Although by the time of independence itself in 1957 the Axim Trio had disbanded, it led the troupes in giving Nkrumah support, staging plays such as *Nkrumah Will Never Die*, *Nkrumah Is a Mighty Man*, and *Nkrumah Is Greater than Before*. Thereafter, World War II veteran Bob Vans showed support for transforming Gold Coast into the independent Ghana by changing the name of his Burma Jokers to the Ghana Trio. In the mid-1950s the Ghana Trio's shows included *The Disappointed Lady* and its latest, entitled *Why Self Government by Ultimatum*, which echoed the mass demand for immediate independence.

Establishing the Genre

The period after the end of World War II, from the late 1940s to roughly the first decade after Ghanaian independence, is when much of the format of *concert party* that exists today was established. During this period the name *concert party* was in wider use for the genre although many troupes still identified themselves with the trio designation. Also, during this period, most troupes were abandoning the Western ballads and vaudevillian songs their forbears appropriated from colonial school concerts and entertainments, and integrating a popular syncretic homegrown music genre, called highlife, into the shows. Highlife was the resulting assortment of acculturated styles from the 1920s onwards, when traditional music in Gold Coast's seaboard cities assimilated Western musical instruments such as piano, fife, guitar, banjo, brass horns, harmonica and concertina, together with styles such as sea shanties, marching music, ballroom dance music and hymns. Brass bands, dance orchestras (a more Westernized variant aimed at the African elite, hence 'highlife'), and guitar bands were three types of ensembles that played highlife. The confluence of *concert party* and highlife music was gradual. In the 1920s the Optimism Club Dance Orchestra of Sekondi had comedians perform during the intermission at its shows. In 1940 the Axim Trio teamed up with Sam (Kwame Asare) Jonah, the first Ghanaian guitarist of importance to have recordings made of his music, by granting him a spot appearance on stage alongside Bob Johnson, a move that encouraged Jonah to develop a one-man show in the manner of Schoolmaster Yalley. Also, the Axim Trio, on its tour with the Sugar Babies Band, performed 'floor shows' during the intermission at the band's concerts as an appetizer for the troupe's full-scale performance the following day.

Concert party truly integrated highlife when, in 1950, guitar-band musician E.K. Nyame forayed into theater performance by forming the Akan Trio. E.K. Nyame's integration of highlife into *concert party* was part of a broader redirection from what had begun as a predominantly English-language urban music-theater tradition to an appeal to the interests of a local language-speaking, rural-inclusive audience between World War II and the Independence years. Of the three variations of highlife ensembles that of the guitar band was seen as the least respectable. In the relative prosperity of the postwar period, young people from rural areas were attracted to urban centers – beehives of trade and commercial activity – to seek employment and opportunity, while also being viewed as people who often drank away their wages to the music of guitar bands in the many drinking bars that had discovered that music was a good way to attract customers. So the music was tagged 'palmwine' music (after the drink most regularly consumed in the bars) and associated with 'wayward' youth. However, palmwine music was also the most popular music of the day, attracting listeners everywhere in rural and urban areas. The availability of gramophones and records helped fuel this popularity. Major trading companies like the United Africa Company, G.B. Olivant, SCOA, CFAO and the Union Trading Company acted as agents between guitar-band artists and British recording companies (HMV, Decca, Parlophone, etc.) to record 78 rpm records in Ghana. Gramophone artists such as Jacob Sam and E.K. Nyame thus gave palmwine music cultural capital and helped make it more accessible to its expanding audience.

E.K.'s Akan Trio revolutionized *concert party* by linking it closely with popular highlife music, bucking the trend of using imported (mostly English-language) songs and, instead, composing Akan guitar-band song lyrics for its shows. Desirous of the Akan Trio's commercial success and popularity, other guitar bands set up as *concert parties* and existing troupes incorporated guitar-band music, expanding their musical sections of trap drums and organ to include guitar, standing bass and additional percussion. Some musicians linked the preference for palmwine music over Western songs to the nationalist Pan-African ethos of the time: as a signifier that highlife is our black people's 'greatest music.' The integration of highlife into *concert party* also meant a more intricate weaving of music into the fabric of plays. Highlife songs such as E.K.'s compositions often contained densely signifying proverbs. Troupes wove plays around the maxims and aphorisms of proverbs. For example, the Akan Trio play *Wosum Brodie A, Sum Kwadu* (if you plant plantain also plant banana, lest you need one if the other fails you) has a song, 'Wosum Brodie A.' In the plot built around this song, a man with two wives favors one over the other but when he falls destitute it is the less favored wife's son who rescues him. In highly melodramatic plots, with their mercurial, miraculous reversals of fortune (rags, health, respect, popularity to and from riches, sickness, contempt and abandonment), songs such as Akwaboa Band's 'Awisia Ye Mobo' (Orphan Is Pitiable) in their play *Treat Somebody's Child as Your Own* worked as character exposition and a signal of high stakes for tense or climatic scenes. Ranging from sentimental (e.g., Akan Trio's 'Woamma a Mewu' [Come to Me Lest I Die]) to philosophical (e.g., Kakaiku Band's 'Ohia Ma Adwendwen' [Necessity Makes for Invention]), it was music, more than realism in plot development, that signified and intensified moments of anguish, despair and jubilation to create and reflect the mood of plays. All in all, there developed in the plays of this period a level of unity between the popular music and dramatic action unprecedented in *concert party*.

Concert parties in the 1950s and 1960s remained attuned to the interests and experiences of their expanding audiences and so dramatized the conflicts, problems and dilemmas familiar to these audiences. Firmly planted in the quotidian domestic life in contemporary Ghana (and going beyond the Euro-aspirational class pretensions seen in the plays of the 1930s–40s) they kept the previous themes of marital conflicts and master-servant relationships but added fresh ones with current appeal: the fate of orphans/stepchildren, housemaids and widows; inheritance disputes; infertility; witchcraft; competition between (or designs against and exploitation of) colleagues, friends and relatives; and problems of labor migration, all of which were concomitant of the monumental social transformations at that period of the nation's life. Sometimes themes were evident in the titles of plays, such as *Treat Somebody's Child as Your Own, Orphan Avert Your Eyes, Orphan Child, The Ungrateful Husband, The Jealous Wife, Man is Ungrateful, Fix Your Will Before You Die, The Taxi Driver and The Wicked Friend*, and *Don't Covet Your Neighbors Possessions*. Even when troupes challenged traditional social practices, as in Ahanta Trio's critique of the exploitation of bereaved families in *Abusua*

Do Funu (*The Matriclan Loves A Corpse*), they kept a didactic moral tone against vices like alcoholism, bad company, prostitution, laziness, disobedience, etc., contrasting them with corresponding virtues and showing their consequences. Nevertheless, unpredictability and ambivalence marked this moralism/didacticism and provided entertainment value. One moment chastising a character enamored with city life, the next moment glorifying that very life, plays maintained a clownish, makeshift and very nearly chaotic aesthetic of slapstick and farce and thus easily detoured into complicated, amoral, comic scenes and asides. The result: a dizzying but delightful 'rattletrap ride … from sentimental pathos to ridiculous buffoonery' that often obscured the very moral lessons they were teaching (Cole 2001, 150).

The 1960s marked the heyday of *concert party*. The greater economic wealth and social status of Ghanaians after independence allowed more of the population to afford radio and gramophones, making interest in highlife music *concert parties* more and more popular. The state broadcasting service put *concert party* plays on radio and the state-sponsored Workers Brigade Concert Party included women such as Adelaide Buabeng, Esi Kom, Margaret Quainoo and Confort Dompo on stage although female impersonation continued well into the 1980s among many troupes. As the *concert parties* expanded their themes, their comic sketches became complex extended narratives. Plays had a wider range of characters – children, aunts, uncles, grandparents, chiefs, 'traditional' priests, farmers, government agents – swelling troupe sizes from the archetypal three to, at times, 25 members. Plays also featured traditional belief-, folklore- and Christian-influenced supernatural characters – dwarfs, forest monsters, witches, demons, ancestor spirits and hymn-singing choruses. *Concert party* shows had an established format by this time: about an hour-long of danceable highlife opening music; 'comedies' (from short stand-up routines and magic shows to juggling, body contortions and other acrobatics) and, finally, plays themselves – unscripted, song-interspersed, humor-filled melodramas that allowed performers to show their skills as actors, singers, dancers and masters of improvisation. Historically removed from earlier concerts in Gold Coast, *concert parties* abandoned the hard audience–performer separation of proscenium stages for highly participatory experiences like those in *Anansesem*. Also, the troupes used microphones, often no more than one in which actors spoke between stage movements, making for an anarchic aesthetic that appealed – over theatrical realism – to the audiences.

The Momentum of the Genre

If the 1950s and 1960s were the decades of *concert party*'s establishment as a genre, the 1970s and 1980s are best described as a 'momentum era.' This does not mean there were no innovations in *concert party* during this decade, but whereas the earlier decades saw the development of features that remained defining qualities of the genre into the 2000s (such as: its integration of popular music; its incorporation of microphones [and other new technology], fresh themes and new characters; its opening to female performers; its use of lesser 'Western' staging conventions; its redirection to appeal to a broader base of Ghanaians; and its consolidation of a performance format), in the 1970s and 1980s more troupes (between 50 and 60) were operating than ever before. Not since Ishmael Johnson toured with Two Bobs and Their Carolina Girl, however, had performers had to struggle so hard to keep the profession alive. *Concert parties* survived Nkrumah's overthrow in 1966, perhaps because the majority successfully pursued their commercial interests outside the purview of the state. Between 1966 and 1973 Ghana saw two military coups with an aborted period of elected civilian rule in between. Economic dissatisfaction fueled these successive military interventions but by 1974 Ghana was once again in economic shambles worsened by an international oil crisis and inflation worldwide. Amidst the political economic tumult, some performers hit the big screen in the Ghana Film Industry Corporation's *I Told You So*, a 1970 film in the *concert party* style. Also, about 24 troupes participated in the 'National Festival of Concert Parties,' organized by the state-run Arts Council in 1973.

As the decade proceeded, *concert party* troupes remained attuned to the cultural pulse of both rural and urban population, even as state recognition became something of a prize among the troupe members for the prestige and cultural capital it bestowed on them. Television sets were, by this time, more common items in the households of (at least) the Ghanaian middle class. The state-owned Ghana Broadcasting Corporation brought *concert party* plays onto its single-channel television lineup and in 1972 awarded Y.B Banpoe of Jaguar Jokers the accolade of 'outstanding comedian of the year'. The Corporation's television series *Showcase* featured non-Akan language troupes such as Adabraka Drama Troupe, Ewa Brothers and Tsui Shito, but even more famous was a multi-episode series featuring a troupe of Akan-language actors and titled *Osofo Dadzie* after a lead character and moral voice (he was a reverend) in the episodes. For the purpose of these television series, which were recorded inside closed television studios (no live audiences) and served audiences (including those of 'upscale' classes) who were for the most part invisible, the *concert party* troupes tweaked the genre's format and style for a shorter length and more 'realistic' experience. They eliminated female impersonation and blackface makeup almost altogether, except for comic effect in certain instances. The presence of *concert party* women on television reflected on the composition of the troupes, as more and more women were admitted into them. Televised shows also abandoned the opening dance music and 'comedies' of their live counterparts, made more use of stage sets and props, and aimed at less melodrama in their resolutions to dramatic conflicts (even if occasionally they let in a supernatural entity). Performers, particularly the by-then-celebrity *Osofo Dadzie* actors, also appeared in printed photo-comics (comic magazines with photographs rather than illustrated images for sequential storytelling).

Even as *concert party* performers branched into film, television and print arenas in the 1970s, itinerant live-audience performances remained the primary variety of this popular musical theater practice. Far from passive, the audiences at these performances remained exuberantly participatory, much like audiences at an *Anansesem* storytelling event: they would cheer or applaud one moment, then hiss, hoot, jeer and shout expletives the next. They would answer questions directly posed by actors, or finish off actors' dialogue. Audience members would walk on stage to join a dance, shout advice to or reward a character with money and/or food. There were nevertheless a few developments in the *concert party* tradition. Troupes went to great lengths to represent supernatural figures on stage, with improvised but spectacular visual effects. Also, in the earlier times, troupes hired a brass band or used a *Yefun Pee*, a masked, bell-ringing, stomach-stuffed child dressed in Charlie Chaplinesque outfit and sandwiched between two poster-plastered boards, to promote the coming attraction in a town or village. By the 1970s they were sending minivans with a mounted megaphone and putting up billboards with near-life-size oil paintings of cartoons (supernatural beings, usually) to promote a coming show. Troupes equipped with electric guitars, keyboards and amplifiers played not just palmwine music but included – especially during the opening dance session – covers of records from abroad: from American rock 'n' roll and Cuban *pachanga* to the funk and soul of James Brown and Wilson Pickett and the reggae of Jimmy Cliff and Bob Marley. Dance music from other parts of Africa by Fela and Prince Niko Mbarga of Nigeria, Manu Dibango of Cameroun, Miriam Makeba of South Africa and Papa Wemba of Congo also found its way into shows.

Troupe organization also went through changes in the 1970s. In the early years troupes were cooperative undertakings in which members divided the income from shows more or less equally among themselves. By the 1970s we find, in the Jaguar Jokers troupe for example, a tiered system – a revolving periphery of performers (usually bandsmen) who earned fixed wages, and a core executive of performers who shared profits. *Concert party* tours had long been precarious work that resulted in everything from extravagant windfalls and pittances of profits to big losses. Sustained good earnings were possible only by developing a good sense of the vagaries of road life to properly adjust to them. As Ghana's economy worsened in the 1970s and touring got more unpredictable and precarious, some troupes started to rely on external tour promoters for fixed seasonal payments, less financial risk and a chance to focus more on their art. However, many troupes soon chafed at what they considered to be exploitative contracts with promoters. Paid work on television and radio or at state-sponsored events – few and far between for the majority of troupes, if there were any at all – were opportunities for troupes to diversify work and in that way cushion themselves from financial downturns. Some troupes also toured

Nigeria and Côte d'Ivoire, where stronger, less inflated economies promised higher earnings. Rivalry and competitiveness between different *concert party* troupes intensified, leading them to make renewed efforts at unionization – the members of a union formed in 1960 to 'control the theatrical profession' and manage the affairs of the *concert party* artists among other goals, had felt cheated by its leaders – but the fatal blow came in 1966 when the union was dissolved by the military regime that overthrew President Nkrumah (Barber, Collins and Richard 1997, 17). In 1977 over 40 concert parties and highlife bands teamed up to launch another union for their mutual benefit.

The period between 1978 and 1982 was another politically tumultuous period, with three military coups, in the third of which an elected civilian government was overthrown. In 1980 the union that formed in the previous decade folded and the highlife bands that were part of it joined the then re-formed Musicians Union of Ghana, which had also been proscribed in 1966, but was now government recognized. This development reflected and portended the state of affairs of both guitar bands and concert parties during the 1980s. Political instability (the early 1980s saw several more attempted but unsuccessful coups) and economic depression worsened by drought and famine all took a toll on audiences, who were less able to spend on shows, and performers alike. Military curfews and general instability curtailed the country's active nightlife: with the advent of home videos and more television sets in even modest households, people preferred to stay at home rather than risk going out. Imported musical instruments like guitars, keyboards, trap drums and brass horns, considered de rigueur at highlife band and *concert party* shows by then, were harder to obtain in the badly depressed, inflated economy. The highlife bands that managed to stay afloat in all this were usually those whose music was better known than their plays, and so managed to sell their records and cassettes against stiff competition from popular mobile discos which provided young people with the original records of the soul, funk (and by this time disco) music that they preferred, rather than a live cover version. The situation was even bleaker for *concert parties*. Increasingly, the scarcity of imported fuel and a debilitated road infrastructure turned the business model of itinerancy into something too costly, cumbersome and dangerous to be worthwhile. By the early 1990s nearly all *concert party* troupes were on the verge of disbanding, if they had not already done so.

A Revival of the Genre

Although women were not admitted into *concert party* troupes to a significant degree until the 1970s and 1980s, it was from the persistent efforts of a pioneering *concert party* actress, Adelaide Buabeng, that the revival stemmed. Concerned about the destitution of many of her peers, Buabeng convened a meeting of veteran and budding *concert party* artists to found the Ghana Concert Party Union (GCPU), with the goal of reviving the genre and attending to performers' welfare. She successfully petitioned the Ghana National Theatre to collaborate in hosting fortnightly revival *concert party* shows. In the 'gentleman's agreement' between the Union and the Theatre both parties understood that, given limited slots (performers would have to audition and for even the most successful there were only so many available slots) and low-income working-class/underclass audiences, gate proceeds from the proposed shows could not sustain performers as the full-time professionals they once were. Neither could the Theatre itself offer that sustenance with its own limitations as a cash-strapped, state-owned, non-profit enterprise. So, the collaborators agreed that the Theatre would contribute logistic (performance space, stage equipment, transportation, publicity) and managerial support as part of its public service mandate. For their part, the Union members would create and perform the shows for a token remuneration from the gate proceeds. In essence, in this collaboration with the Theatre, members of the Concert Party Union postponed their long-standing commercial interests as profit-seeking entrepreneur artists.

On 11 November 1994 the Theatre and the Union jointly launched the Concert Party Show, a fortnightly variety event comprising live band (mostly highlife) music, stand-up comedy and/or sketches and comic melodramatic plays at the Folks Place, a small open-air stage in the Theatre complex. Thus, concert party activity, previously itinerant across the country, settled at the Theatre complex in Ghana's capital city,

Accra. In the early days of the Concert Party Show public patronage was poor because the collaborators could not afford the necessary publicity blitz. Things changed when the Theatre secured commitment from a sister state institution, Ghana Television, to record the show and broadcast it in weekly installments. The immediate dramatic increase in patronage prompted the collaborators to move the Show from the Folks' Place to the larger Main Hall of the Theatre complex. However, the production costs, as the revival soared in popularity, pushed the Concert Party Show to the forefront of the Theatre's budget concerns. By this time Ghana's government had targeted the Theatre for partial divestiture, which meant decreased state funding and increased political pressure on the Theatre to find non-state revenue sources for its programs. The resulting new mission of the Theatre, which emphasized 'customer-oriented programming' and 'profitability,' caused consternation among critics who feared that the view of its audiences as paying customers instead of as cultural wards would undermine the artistic integrity of its programs and thus the Theatre's ability to execute its mandate of promoting national culture.

Critics' fears seemed to materialize when the Theatre obtained sponsorship for the Show from the local subsidiary of an Anglo-Dutch multinational conglomerate Unilever Ghana, especially after Unilever demanded – in return for the sponsorship – that the Show be renamed after its Key Soap brand and that performers mention Key Soap on the stage. Locked by the divestiture policy into dependency on private funding, the Theatre insisted that its shows would remain culturally authentic under that funding. Authenticity is a fine horse to ride, but has to be ridden somewhere, so the Theatre forged its own ideal of cultural authenticity in the form of an orientation to social development that emphasized responsible behavior by ordinary citizens, and presented the privately sponsored Concert Party Show as a showcase of this ideal. The Theatre's narrative in this was that whereas itinerant concert parties of the past had followed their audiences' whims instead of leading them to socially responsible choices through morally clear didactic messages, the Unilever-sponsored Show would not be rudderless – *concert party* performers would lead audiences to responsible social behavior under strict dramaturgical terms determined by the Theatre. Unilever itself had long identified itself with that ideal, presenting itself as an 'enlightened firm with social responsibility and concern for public affairs' – a 'force for progress in the world' (Jones 1995, 323–9). In July 1995 the Theatre, the Union and Unilever came together for a 'mega-launch' of the Key Soap Concert Party Show.

Keeping with the effort to showcase their capability for cultural authenticity under the aegis of private corporate sponsorship, Unilever and the Theatre required performers to address themes such as HIV/AIDs awareness, family planning, civic responsibility, environmental protection, etc. to qualify for a slot in the Show. What could have been progressive about this showcasing was dented by the Theatre and Unilever's reduction of the moral ambiguity and anarchic tomfoolery of itinerant concert parties to triviality, and by the paternalism with which they tried to drag concert party art away from its typically ambivalent and light-hearted satiric dramaturgy toward unequivocally framed social messages. The Union did not push against this, perhaps because it had a multigenerational membership – from veterans of the 1940s trios to fledglings whose only sense of *concert party* was versions on television since the 1970s – and thus represented such mixed ideas about the art that it was unable to offer either united support for, or resistance to, the corporate-driven changes in the genre. Perhaps the Union's restraint was strategic long-sightedness. Throughout *concert party* history an intractable social prejudice had cast performers as the vagrant purveyors of frivolous, irresponsible, low-class entertainment. This was part of the reluctance to admit women on the *concert party* stage; women who embraced the profession were seen as prostitutes, or at least as sexually 'loose.' The Theatre and the Union's 'gentleman's agreement' included their mutual expectation that by associating itself with the state enterprise the genre would accrue enough social dignity – a boon to performers' intended return to the independent commercial-entrepreneurial interests they had always had. It seems therefore, that whatever its opposition to the institutional paternalism, the Union was prepared not to bite the hands that fed it but to play a long waiting game till it could rid itself of – that is, feed itself without – those overbearing hands.

In 1997 the Union decided to defer to the Theatre no longer. It was unhappy that whereas the Theatre had shifted its mission to profit making (the Union believed the Theatre was reaping windfalls from the arrangement with Unilever), performers were expected to postpone their own commercial interests until some future return to *concert party* glory. It was miffed, for instance, that the Theatre's remuneration of performers did not properly reflect the increased patronage of, and Unilever's infusion of sponsorship funds into, the shows. It demanded increases in members' remuneration, and a set amount for itself on the basis that as collaborator in the revival from the start – even if by a 'gentleman's agreement' – it deserved, by itself, a share of any gains from Unilever's sponsorship package. The Theatre demurred, refusing to meet those demands on the basis that the production costs of the Show had increased commensurately with the gate proceeds and that the Union deserved no additional payment because it was not party to the arrangement with Unilever. The Union asked members to strike till negotiations for better terms were completed. The Theatre refused to negotiate, so the Union severed its then two-and-a-half-year partnership with the Theatre. It teamed up with Brismen, an advertising company, to attempt a rival revival effort, but that folded within a year, effectively diminishing the Union's influence and compelling many members to return to the Theatre outside the Union's purview. Between 1998 and 2001 the Theatre and Unilever asserted more control over performances in the Key Soap Concert Party Show. As part of their stipulation that acts in the show unequivocally voice social responsibility, they censored the old *concert party* style of using supernatural beings for plot conflict resolution, on the basis that this detracted from an *explicit* message of *human* social responsibility.

Unilever and the Theatre could not *completely* censor the artful, delightful, socially subversive ethos of trickster-like duplicitousness at the heart of the *concert party*'s historically anarchic aesthetic and moral messaging. Even under the Theatre and Unilever's intensified surveillance of the Key Soap Concert Party Show a comedian like Bob Okalla managed to take swipes at Unilever and Key Soap in such a double voice (innocuous at one level but critical and/or defiant at another). With the copious comic parodies of highlife music to intersperse his stand-up comedy Okalla would, at one semiotic level, praise the efficacy of Key Soap, fulfilling Unilever's expectations of a positive product mention, and on another level question the value of the soap or critique Unilever's monopoly on the soap market. The King Karo troupe's 2001 play *Afutuo Nsakra Nnipa* (People Do Not Heed Counsel) displayed similar doubleness. The play's protagonist Ma Red learns painfully that the cost of her peevish attitude toward participating in her community's development is her own ill health. Thus, at one level the play incorporated the progressive themes required by the Theatre and Unilever, with an over-the-top didacticism; on the other hand it portrays Ma Red as a Key Soap distributor, thus indirectly attaching social irresponsibility to the sponsors. Also, while on one hand, *Afutuo Nsakra Nnipa* pictures Ma Red as the object lesson of social irresponsibility, on the other hand it imbues her with an attractively independent freewheeling spirit that could as well be the yearnings of Key Soap Concert Party performers, against the institutional stipulations and constraints on their art.

The experiences of performers in the Key Soap Concert Party Show during the millennial decade (i.e., 1995–2005), described above, reflected the fact that the *concert party* had been revived in an age of the market in Ghana, that is, an age in which – in a manner unlike ever before – citizens were envisioned as consumers and more and more aspects of social, cultural and political life were sucked into relationships of economic exchange. For *concert party* artists, creators and creatures of a musical theater market long before the market became a dominant organizing force of social and cultural relationships in Ghana, it was deeply frustrating that their hope of getting out of the constraining grip of the Theatre and Unilever and returning the art to its former itinerant, institutionally independent, commercial status seemed more futile than ever. However, it could also well be that in the new millennium the genre itself had outlived its currency. In the mid-2000s the Theatre and Unilever sponsored the last Key Soap Concert Party Show, and in the subsequent decade or so there was no similarly significant *concert party* activity in the country. A legacy of the Show was an atomization of the genre. Before, troupes had their own bandsmen for music and jokers for comedy. However, troupes in the revival had mainly actors and almost exclusively performed plays. Troupes, comedians and highlife bands, in any edition of the Show, for the most part existed and operated separately from each other, auditioning for and signing on to shows distinctively. Consequently, highlife music, which revolutionized the *concert party* in the 1950s when E.K. Nyame incorporated it into the genre, became peripheral to the drama. In the fewer instances of song in a play, playmakers were more likely to find and use a suitable cover version of an existing popular tune, than to have one specially composed for it.

Bibliography

Agovi, Kofi. 1993. 'The Origins of Literary Theatre in Colonial Ghana.' *Research Review* 6(1): 1–23.

Amegatcher, Adelaide. 1968. 'The Concert Party: A Manifestation of Popular Drama in Ghana.' MA thesis, University of North Carolina Chapel Hill.

Austen, Dennis. 1964. *Politics in Ghana*. New York: Oxford University Press.

Bame, Kwabena N. 1985. *Come to Laugh: African Traditional Theatre in Ghana*. New York: Lilian Barber Press.

Barber, Karin, Collins, John, and Richard, Alain. 1997. *West African Popular Theatre*. Bloomington, IN: Indiana University Press.

Cole, Catherine M. 2001. *Ghana's Concert Party Theatre*. Bloomington, IN: Indiana University Press.

Collins, John. 1996. *Highlife Time*. Accra: Anansesem Publications.

Damptey, Nathan B. 1981. 'Popular Music in Contemporary Ghana: A Study of Guitar Band Music.' Diploma thesis, University of Ghana.

Donkor, David A. 2016. *Spiders of the Market: Ghanaian Trickster Performance in a Web of Neoliberalism*. Bloomington, IN: Indiana University Press.

Donkor, David A. 2017. 'Trickster's Doubleness: The Cultural Performance of Akan Storytelling.' In *Cultural Performance: Ethnographic Approaches to Performance Studies*, eds. Kevin Landis and Suzanne MacAulay. London: Palgrave, 19–29.

Fieldhouse, David Kenneth 1978. *Unilever Overseas: The Anatomy of a Multinational*. Stanford, CA: The Hoover Institution Press, 1978.

Foster, Phillip. 1965. *Education and Social Change in Ghana*. Chicago: University of Chicago Press.

Hagan, Kwa O. 1968. 'The Literary and Social Clubs of the Past: Their Role in National Awakening in Ghana.' *Okyeame* 4(2): 81–6.

Ince, Bernard. 2018. 'The Neglected Art: Trends and Transformations in British Concert Party Entertainment, 1850–1950.' *New Theatre Quarterly* 31(1): 3–16.

Jones, Geoffrey. 1995. *Unilever: Transformation and Tradition*. New York: Oxford University Press.

Kedjanyi, John. 1966. 'Observations on Spectator-Performer Arrangements of Some Traditional Ghanaian Performances.' *Research Review* 2(3): 61–6.

Kerr, David. 1995. *African Popular Theatre: From Pre-Colonial Times to the Present Day*. London: James Currey.

Kimble, David. 1963. *A Political History of Ghana: The Rise of Gold Coast Nationalism, 1850–1928*. Oxford: Clarendon Press.

Plageman, Nate. 2013. *Highlife Saturday Night: Popular Music and Social Change in Urban Ghana*. Bloomington, IN: Indiana University Press.

Shipley, Jesse W. 2012: *Living the Hiplife: Celebrity and Entrepreneurship in Ghanaian Popular Music*. Durham, NC: Duke University Press.

Sutherland, Efua T. 1970. *The Story of Bob Johnson: Ghana's Ace Comedian*. Accra: Anowua Educational Publications.

Toll, Robert C. 1974. *Blacking Up: The Minstrel Show in Nineteenth-Century America*. New York: Oxford University Press.

Ziorklui, Emmanuel. 1993. *Ghana: Nkrumah to Rawlings*. Osu-Accra: Emzed Books.

Discographical References

Calloway, Cab, and His Orchestra. 'Minnie the Moocher.' Brunswick Records 6074. *1931*: USA.

Henderson, Dick. 'The Crowning of the Cotton Queen.' Edison Bell Radio 1349. *1930*: UK.

Kakaiku's Band. Ohia Ma Adwendwen. *Adadam Paa Nie Vol.1*. Ambassador Records LPEX 005. *1975?*: Ghana.

Nyame, E. K. 'Wosum Brodie A.' *Madi Amia*, Aduana PN 07-93992. *195?*: Ghana.

Discography

A.B. Crentsil's Ahenfo Band. *Highlife in Canada*. Highlife King RAP 002. *1987*: Canada.

African Brothers International Band of Ghana. *Highlife Time*. Afribros PAB 003. *1973*: UK.

Black Beats Band. *Black Beat Rhythms*. Decca WAL 1006. *1959*: Ghana.

E.K.s Band. *This is E.K.'s No. 1*. Phillips 6354 003. *1973*: Ghana.

Ghana Popular Music 1931–1957. Arion Music ARN 64564. *2001*: France.

Hansen, Jerry, and the Ramblers Band. *Dance with the Ramblers*. Decca WAP 24. *1967*: Ghana.

Kumasi Trio, The. 'Amponsah Part I & 2.' Zonophone. EZ 100. *1928*: UK.

Stars of Ghana. Decca WAP 21. *1962*: Ghana.

Filmography

I Told You So, dir. Egbert Adjeso. 1970. Ghana. 97 mins. Comedy-drama.

On With the Show, dirs Alan Crosland and Larry Ceballos. 1929. USA. 103 mins. Musical.

The Jazz Singer, dir. Alan Crosland. 1927. USA. 96 mins. Musical.

The Singing Fool, dir. Lloyd Bacon. 1928. USA. 105 mins. Musical.

The Tramp. dir. Charlie Chaplin. 1915. USA. 32 mins. Comedy.

DAVID A. DONKOR

Coupé Décalé

Coupé décalé is a music and dance genre that was created by immigrants from Côte d'Ivoire in the cosmopolitan city of Paris, France, in the early twenty-first century but that gained its popularity in the immigrants' home country. The inventors of the genre are believed to be Douk Saga (Stephane Hamidou Doukouré), Molare, Solo Beton, Lino Versace and Bobo Sango, all of whom were middle-class immigrants from Côte d'Ivoire who amassed a substantial amount of wealth while living in Paris. 'Coupé décalé,' literally meaning in French 'cut and shift,' has an alternate meaning among the genre's young urban Ivoirian Nouchi-speaking audience (Nouchi is an argot composed of Ivoirian French and several different indigenous languages), for whom the phrase connotes 'cheating someone and running away,' a reference to the playful, frequently fraudulent way in which its inventors acquired funds and wealth. The genre's primary purpose is to accompany dance. Lyrically, it is noted for its flaunting of wealth, materialism and sexual desires and/or for introducing a new dance.

Before the genre itself emerged, a subculture of *coupé décalé* centering on extravagance began in the late 1990s and early 2000s, when those who would become the founding figures of the genre became imitators of the sharp-dressing men who called themselves *les sapeurs*. With origins among the Congolese in Brazzaville, *les sapeurs* forged a society, S.A.P.E. (Société des Ambianceurs et des Personnes Elégantes [Society of Tastemakers and Elegant People]), which over time has become a subcultural movement as much as a fashion statement. *Les sapeurs* were and are men from the working and middle classes who dress in fine designer suits. The culture has significant roots in colonialism, as the extravagant dress style was initially an attempt to imitate the colonizers. Nearly half a century after independence, such trends continue. For some they signify Western acculturation, while other practitioners view the style as a sophisticated art, where men cleverly use themselves as the canvas and their clothing as the paint. Aside from aesthetics, *les sapeurs* also have a political inclination. They are known for being pacifists, which is significant given the environment of hostility in much of Central Africa where this culture started.

Douk Saga, though Ivoirian, was part of a group of immigrant Africans who embraced the culture of *les sapeurs*, adorning himself in luxurious clothing from France and Italy and matching his attire with a hedonistic lifestyle that fully embraced dancing, drinking and partying, while flaunting his wealth (the source of which was never publicly known or determined) to others in the clubs, in particular Club Atlantis. In the process, he acquired a following. His dance moves resembled the Congolese dance *ndombolo*, which is the foundation of the *coupé décalé* dance.

It was at Club Atlantis that the song that would become Douk Saga's first release, 'Sagacité,' was first performed in 2002. From there it spread quickly to Abidjan in Côte d'Ivoire through Saga, his fellow 'jet set' (as they became known) and various DJs. It was only after David Monsoh (producer at OBOUO Music) produced 'Sagacité' as Saga's first release in 2004 and financed the video that the performer became a musical star and *coupé décalé* was introduced as a musical genre to the world. Along with Douk Saga, artists such as Boro Sandji, Molare, Versace and Solo Beton, were a part of the first generation of *coupé décalé* artists. Between 2004 and 2008 a second generation emerged in the form of the disc jockeys such as DJ Jacob, DJ Caloudje and DJ Jonathan who were providing the music for the men to dance to (singing their praises all the while). Later, in the third generation and most contemporary style of *coupé décalé* (beginning in 2008), emphasis was placed primarily on dance. With artists such as DJ Arafat, Serge Beynaud and Kiva Kedjevara break dancing, crumping, street dancing and acrobatics became crucial components of the genre.

When *coupé décalé* became popular in Abidjan, Côte d'Ivoire, shortly after gaining recognition in the Francophone African community in Paris, the nation was facing a civil crisis and many were looking for distractions from the violence and war. In this context the flamboyant dress and flaunting of material items associated with *coupé décalé* became a source of amusement and distraction for many listeners and established a mood of happiness. At the same time many music television shows were produced offering artists such as Douk Saga the opportunity to promote and disseminate their new music.

After the nation recovered from the 2010–11 crisis (caused by the refusal of former President Laurent Gbagbo to step down from his position after elections), peace concerts toured Côte d'Ivoire, typically presenting a lineup of artists from several different genres. Included, for example, were reggae star Alpha Blondy, *zouglou* artists Les Patrons, several *coupé décalé* performers, as well as popular figures from Nigeria, Ghana and other surrounding countries. Thus, the genre came to be used as one tool in the process of cultural exchange and the expression of national peace.

In addition to original founders Douk Saga (who died in 2006) and Molare, other performers who have gained celebrity through the performance of *coupé décalé* include DJ Arafat, DJ Lewis and Serge Beynaud. In the late 2010s DJ Arafat (a.k.a. Yoro Gang), most commonly known for his *blockage* (mnemonic phrases), accompanying dance movements and raspy vocal quality, is the most distinctive figure among contemporary exponents of the genre, and by far the most popular. Other *coupé décalé* performers often mimic his performance style and quality. At the young age of 17, DJ Arafat released his first major hit, 'Hômmage à Jonathan' (a song in memory of a deceased DJ) in 2000. Though rumored to have been a street child, DJ Arafat (Ange Didier Houon) was the son of a famous pop singer, Tina Glamour, known for her sultry and seductive lyrics, and began his own career as a DJ at a grand *maquis* (open-air restaurant) called La Shangaï in Rue Princess, a major party district in Youpougon, Abidjan.

Musical Antecedents

Coupé décalé is in many ways aurally similar to its historical musical predecessor *zouglou*, which was bred in the streets of Abidjan in the late 1980s and early 1990s. It also draws significantly from the Congolese genre *soukouss* in rhythm and instrumentation. Although both *zouglou* and *coupé décale* are popular among urban youth, *zouglou* was geared toward the generation of youth and young adults at the end of the twentieth century and was created as a platform for disenchanted youth. Due to the use of the same distinctive popular dance rhythm heard in *soukouss* and *ndombolo* (see below), the genres have an audibly similar musical foundation not only to each other but also to other Congolese popular music genres. Unlike *zouglou*, however, which has indigenous roots and initially utilized traditional membranophones (*djembe*) and idiophones (shakers, bottles), *coupé décalé* was bred in the electronic world music scene, dependent upon the mixing, variation and layering of synthesized sounds and beats by DJs, and it is primarily the influx of layered electronic beats, together with the lack of vocal harmony, in *coupé décalé* that differentiates it musically from its predecessor.

Musical Characteristics

Alongside its similarities with both *zouglou* and *soukous*, *coupé décalé* has a unique sound and structure of its own. The music is constructed of several different percussive instrumental riffs repeated and layered continuously in a 4/4 meter. The overall musical form, varying in order with each song, has four possible components: intro, A (chorus/call and response), B (verses) and C (dance break). The introduction (not a mandatory section) is usually at a slow tempo and in a completely free form. The A-section usually has repetitive lyrics and resembles a chorus or extended refrain in performance. The B-section consists of actual verses, sometimes providing a brief narrative or scenario. The C-section is generally at a quicker tempo and the lyrics consist of onomatopoeias and serve as accompaniment to dance movements. During the dance break in the C-section, the dancers exclaim mnemonic phrases, also known as *blockage*, to replicate the punctuation of the dance movements.

These components are basic to most *coupé décalé* songs, making the general form: Intro/A/B/A/C. Within this overall structure there is frequent formal variety. For example, some songs only have a chorus and dance break with no actual verses, while others have no introduction and the chorus and dance break form the basis of the song. The lyrical structure and melodic structure complement one another.

Douk Saga's 'Sagacité' commences with the familiar popular dance rhythm (see Example 1) and with an introduction by the singer.

Example 1: *Coupé décalé*'s popular dance rhythm

Following this introduction, a *soukouss*-style riff on picked guitar accompanies the call-and-response chorus. The lyrics have no particular form and are primarily comprised of repetitive short phrases and words, such as 'coupé décalé,' 'sagacité' and a variety of vocables. Throughout the song vocables are injected and lyrics praising individuals (Douk Saga, Versace) and places (New York, Abidjan, Bouake, London) can be heard. The vocal style is a mixture of speaking and singing that is slightly more melodic than rap, and the accompanying music evolves from the original motif (after a few bars a guitar motif enters, and more digital instruments and digitally modified motifs are added to the mix). The song lacks any distinct lyrical or structural form, appearing to be an exchange of ideas from one singer to another.

Many contemporary artists, such as Serge Beynaud and DJ Arafat, write songs that have become more formulaic in form and structure, reflecting the intro/A/B/A/C form described earlier. Because the genre lacks much in the way of musical complexity, being dependent upon short electronically created motifs, and because it evolved minimally in musical terms over its short period of existence, many scholars deem *coupé décalé* to be a genre composed by non-musicians.

Dance and Content

Since the genre's original inception in 2002 numerous substyles have developed under its umbrella (e.g., *guantanomo*, *sauté-mouton*, *prudenica*, *fouka-fouka* and *decalé chinois*). With only subtle musical differences between these, if any, it is predominantly the dance movements that distinguish most of these substyles from one another. The basic bodily movement performed to all *coupé décalé* songs is a pelvic rotation in a slightly squatted position. The bent arms and legs then move in ways specified in the song or by the singer. For example, *prudencia* requires small cautious movements, while *décalé chinois* mimics the movements of martial arts. Both men and women perform the very sexualized dance movements, although male *coupé décalé* singers and dancers far outnumber females.

After the genre was introduced in Côte d'Ivoire, many Ivoirians thought of *coupé décalé* (music and dance) as a method to cope with and escape the daunting realities at home (including war, lack of jobs, national instability, economic decline and so on). This function differentiates the genre from its popular music predecessor, *zouglou*. As noted above, *zouglou* was a tool to express the sentiment of dissatisfaction of a younger generation with injustice and mistreatment; by contrast, *coupé décalé* aggrandizes a culture of materialism and the appropriation of wealth. In present-day Côte d'Ivoire, the genre is predominantly known as party and dance music. However, some artists have used the popularity of the genre as a platform to express their discontent with the government and to discuss the civil war between 2002 and 2007, and the general political and economic condition of the nation. Songs such as Gadji Celi's 'Ne touchez pas à mon pays' (Don't Touch My Country, 2005) and A Nous Les Petits' 'Pays de joie' (Country of Joy, 2005), which are quite contrary to the typical fantastical images of wealth and prosperity shown and discussed in most *coupé décalé* songs, projected messages of peace and fraternity to counter the war.

Conclusion

Although rap, *azonto* and other African popular genres have gained popularity in Côte d'Ivoire, *coupé décalé* continues to create iconic figures in the eyes and minds of children and young people within the country. On the popular Ivoirian summer children's television program *Wozo Vacances* children between the ages of 3 and 15 are given the opportunity to view and/or imitate their favorite popular artists. Often, the artists chosen are *coupé décalé* artists, demonstrating that children throughout the country are familiar with this music and its lyrical content.

While *coupé décalé* is far from being the sole or even dominant popular music genre in Côte d'Ivoire, it appears to be the most readily mediated through television, radio and amplified external speakers at clubs on the weekends. Music television channels such as Trace Africa allot a time slot specifically to it, and in overall terms *coupé décalé* is a thriving genre that draws an audience at the simple invocation of its name. However, as Ghanaian and Nigerian Afrobeats/Afropop artists (such as Yemi Alade, Davido, Timaya, P-Square, Wizkid, K-Cee) and Southern and East African hip-hop artists (e.g., AKA, Cassper Nyovest) have climbed the charts in the 2010s, a slow descent of *coupé décalé* musicians from the top slots has become apparent.

Bibliography

Boka, Anciet. 2013. *Coupé-décalé: Le sens d'un genre musical en Afrique* [*Coupé-Décalé*: The Direction of an African Musical Genre]. Paris: L'Harmattan.

Evancie, Angela. 2013. 'The Surprising Sartorial Culture of Congolese "Sapeurs": The Picture Show.' *NPR*. Online at: https://www.npr.org/sections/pictureshow/2013/05/07/181704510/the-surprising-sartorial-culture-of-congolese-sapeurs (accessed 29 November 2017).

McGovern, Mike. 2011. *Making War in Côte d'Ivoire*. Chicago: University of Chicago Press.

Mediaville, Hector. 2014. 'Meet the *Sapeurs* – The Men Behind the Story of Style, Honour and Integrity.' *The Journal.ie*. Online at: http://www.thejournal.ie/guinnes-le-sapeurs-1258133-Jan2014/ (accessed 29 November 2017).

Mitter, Siddhartha. 2011. 'The Hip Hop Generations: Ghana's Hip Life and Ivory Coast's Coupé Decalé.' Online at: www.afropop.org (accessed 29 November 2017).

Monsoh, David. N.d. 'David Monsoh: President Fondateur de Black!Africa: @biadj@n.net. Qui est qui?' Online at: https://abidjan.net/qui/profil.asp?id=785 (accessed 29 November 2017).

Tanon-Lora, Michelle. 2008. 'La codification de la grivoiserie dans la chanson moderne ivoirienne' [The Codification of Sensuality in Modern Ivoirian Music]. In *Actes du Colloque International: Francophonie Conflit ou Complémetarité Identitaire* [International Colloquium: French-Speaking Conflict or Complimentary Identity], ed. Georges Dorlian. El-Koura, Lebanon: Université de Balamand, 953–72.

Discographical References

A Nous Les Petits. 'Pays de Joie.' *Coupé Décalé Explosion*. Créon/Aztec. *2005*: France.

Celi, Gadji. 'Ne touchez pas a mon pays.' *Coupé Décalé Explosion*. Créon/Aztec. *2005*: France.

DJ Arafat. 'Hômmage à Jonathan.' *Femmes*. Obouo Music. *2000*: France.

Mike, Don. 'Prudencia.' *Coupé Décalé Explosion, Vol. 2 (Retour de la compilation officielle du Coupé Décalé)*. *2006*: Créon/Aztec. N.d.: France.

Papa Ministre. 'Décalé chinois.' *Drogbacité*. Momo de Paris. *2011*: France.

Saga, Douk. 'Sagacité.' *Coupé Décalé Explosion*. Créon/Aztec Music MK8798. *2004*: France.

Discography

Beynaud, Serge. *Seul Dieu*. Obouo Productions. *2012*: France.

Côte d'Ivoire 1960–2010, Vol. 3 (Histoire de la Musique Contemporaine Moderne). Obouo Music. *2010*: France.

Coupé Décalé Explosion. Créon/Aztec Music. MK8798. *2004*: France.

DJ Arafat. 'Hômmage à Jonathan.' *Femmes*. Obouo Music. *2000*: France.

DJ Arafat. *Gladiator*. Tori Publishing, Nouvelle Donne. *2010*: France.

DJ Lewis. *Stop Grippe Aviaire*. Musiki. *2012*: Côte d'Ivoire.

Molare. *Autre dimension*. Couleurs Music Publishing. *2012*: France.

Saga, Douk. *Heros National Bouche-Bee*. Obouo Music. *2011*: France.

TY-JUANA TAYLOR

Cultural Animation Groups (in Gabon)

In Gabon, as in other African countries, cultural animation groups (*groupes d'animation culturelle*) represented an important branch of musical creativity during the era of one-party rule from 1968 to 1990, and they continued their activities after that date to a lesser extent. The Gabonese groups were made up of women assembled according to ethnic and territorial origins, and constituted a section of the Union des femmes du Parti démocratique gabonais (UFPDG) (Union of Women of the Gabonese Democratic Party), on which they depended for their funding and schedule of activities. They performed songs in French and in local languages, dedicated to the core political figures of the country and above all to the glory of the president, Omar Bongo. Praising the success of his regime, their dancing and singing, accompanied by male musicians and with choreographies known for their sexual symbolism, formed a distinctive element of national and official events. As symbols of a past period of political hegemony and authoritarianism, these groups of women represented an ever-present part of the music and dance life in urban Gabon from the 1960s to the 1990s. They also exerted a strong influence on the popular music that developed after their decline following the abrogation of one-party rule in 1990, which occurred during the national conference organized in Libreville in March of that year. The conference was arranged in response to the current social crisis and to significant protests on the part of syndicates, opposition parties and students, which in turn led to the emergence of new rights and freedoms, and to a critique of the use of music as propaganda. As a result, groups of cultural animation declined, and the accompanying decrease in the control and censorship of musical productions by the state enabled the emergence of new musical content and lyrics.

History and Origins

The emergence of cultural animation groups in Gabon coincided with the installation in November 1967 of the second president, Albert Bernard Bongo, who changed his name in 1973 to become Omar Bongo. The newly elected president abrogated multipartism and created the Parti démocratique gabonais (PDG, Gabonese Democratic Party) on 12 March 1968. With this instrument and with his concept of 'Renovation,' he asserted an ideology that broke profoundly with the previous era, one marked by ethnic and territorial divisions, in order to promote national unity. Bongo defined 'Renovation' as 'the projection on the political stage of the deep tendency among the people towards unity, harmony and peace' (quoted in Minko 2010; author's translation). The development of the country depended on the union of all 'tribes,' 'clans' and 'ethnic groups' through the central figure of the president and the state (Ndombet 2009; Minko 2010; Mbah 2015). President Bongo insisted upon amplifying the strong feeling of national belonging that had existed since the colonial period and the era when Gabon was part of French Equatorial Africa (Pourtier 1989), and upon the cohesion of the country's values of peace and unity. He maintained his hegemony with the help of several communication institutions, including media (radio, television, press) and music, and these became core ways to spectacularize and embody the power of the state.

Two main kinds of musical groups were at the center of state politics and of urban popular life from 1967 until the 1980s. First, from 1950, the new citizens of Libreville – which was in the midst of a demographic explosion resulting from the rural exodus – embraced 'modern' instruments (such as piano, guitar, bass, drums, trumpets and saxophone) in brass bands and orchestras. These orchestras went through a period of great turmoil around the time of independence, between the end of the 1950s and the 1960s, and they enlivened Libreville's nightlife. Their emergence was enabled by the development of festive venues, bars and dance halls, and inspired by African-Caribbean and Congolese orchestras who were invited to perform in Libreville during their African tours. Composed almost exclusively of men, these musical formations, ever-present in Libreville's nightlife during the 1960s, were requisitioned by national armed forces and turned into national military orchestras in 1971. Musicians who performed in informal musical groups such as the Sorciers Noirs (Black Wizards), Négro Tropical or Afro-Succès (Afro-success) were forced to join the ranks of the orchestras created in the armed forces: they entered in the group Gena (for 'Gendarmerie nationale'), the Orchestra of the National Police Forces, Akweza, les Diablotins (the Little Devils), or the Forces armées gabonaises (FAG, Gabonese armed forces), where they were obligated to uphold the messages and serve the preferences of the law enforcement and police chiefs.

The second type of musical group to occupy the musical foreground after the creation of the single party in 1968, was the cultural animation group. In Gabon and other African countries such as the Democratic Republic of Congo, the notion of *animation culturelle* (also called *animation politique et culturelle* in the Democratic Republic of Congo) referred to a kind of 'state-sponsored singing and dancing that came to be synonymous with the image of the state and the system of the one-party rule' (White 2008, 73). The term *animation* was synonymous with the idea of enlivening (*ambience*) the official events and the public sphere. In Gabon, cultural animation groups were created as a ramification of UFPDG, a partisan organization created for the promotion of women and their autonomy and equal rights in the new modern society. Consisting exclusively of women, these ensembles danced and sang to praise the glory of the single party and the president. An organization for the promotion of women had already existed under the previous government (the Organisation nationale des femmes gabonaises, ONFG). In 1971 it was renamed Union des femmes du Parti démocratique gabonais and integrated into the PDG by Omar Bongo in order to involve women in state politics and militancy (Mouélé 2009, 58). Cultural animation groups mainly took charge of *animation* and popular propaganda (Nzengue 1989).

Josephine Bongo, honorary president of UFPDG, wife of President Bongo and a passionate music lover, created the first cultural animation group on 23 November 1968. Initially called Akébé II, in reference to the borough in Libreville where several members of the group lived, it was later renamed Kounabeli and then Mbil'asuku (in languages from the eastern province of the High Ogooué) to give it a more 'authentic' and traditional appeal. The group gathered women mainly from the eastern province of the High Ogooué, the birthplace of President Bongo, Josephine Bongo and the presidential family. Accompanied by their orchestras of musicians (the Superstars, also known as Banowita), and often by the First Lady herself, their mission was to create ambience at the events and political activities of the president and his single party. As the first, most popular and closest to the party, Kounabéli remained the most important cultural animation group during the golden era for these groups in the 1970s and 1980s. Its 1985 album *One* was arranged by US jazz and funk trombonist Fred Wesley, through Josephine Bongo's connections within the American music markets. After her separation from Omar Bongo in 1986, Josephine Bongo left for the United States where she worked under the stage name of Patience Dabany and recorded several albums before returning to Gabon in the late 1990s. She subsequently toured with James Brown, contributed to the tours of Gabon of pop stars such as Michael Jackson and promoted the spread and adoption of new modern and pop music in Gabon. In his biography Fred Wesley recounts his work with Patience Dabany for Kounabeli's album, and their ambition to 'Americanize this African music' (Wesley 2002, 255).

Following the model of Kounabeli, several other groups arose after 1968 to represent first each province of the country, then each department within each province, where they added to the ambience at parties, official ceremonies, invitations of political personalities, cultural festivals, celebrations and inaugurations. During the 1970s and 1980s the country counted 13 main groups, among them Centre-ville, Nkol Engong, Dimossi, Nyenzi, Missema and Mikouagna, each of which could sometimes gather thousands of members. In 2008, 17 cultural animation groups were still active and recognized by the PDG (Mouélé 2009, 62).

Each of the country's major groups was ruled by a hierarchically organized committee containing 15 different levels of status (ibid.). The committees were in charge of the supervision of smaller groups inside the country, connecting the capital with its hinterland peripheries and with the new citizens who had been arriving in Libreville as part of the rural exodus from the beginning of the twentieth century, under the control of political institutions and figures.

Groups of Animation in Africa and African Studies

Far from being a national anomaly in Gabon, political animation by musical groups has been common in many African countries, serving the messages of the party in power. Some cultural animation groups have become famous, for example, in Togo, during the presidency of Gnassingbé Eyadema, where they were named 'groupes de choc' (shock groups) (Toulabor 1986). In Malawi, the one-party period (from 1964 to 1993) was also synonymous with the creation of female musical groups (*mbumba* groups), linked to the Malawi Congress Party, that sang the praise of leadership and of the president, Kamuzu Banda. Female groups appropriated *mbumba* culture and traditional melodies that they mixed with popular rhythms and political lyrics (Lwanda 2008). In the genre's manifestation in Democratic Republic of Congo (previously Republic of Zaïre), Gazungil Sang'Amin Kapalanga considers – in the only monograph concerning this genre in the Democratic Republic of Congo – that 'animation is a resurgence of traditional artistic forms in a new form of representation' (Kapalanga 1989, 118; author's translation), because these spectacles honor the chief, just as in traditional cultures. He notes how consent was made through these groups, comparing this mass choreography to a 'rape of the crowds' whose aim was to conceal incoherence and to arouse a collective delirium (ibid., 118). Also writing about the Democratic Republic of Congo, Bob W. White has analyzed the connections between these groups and the construction of cultural authenticity under Mobutu's regime (White 2006) and their importance for the diffusion of a certain vision of 'culture' as a political tool in Congo. White returns to the discussions concerning the origins of cultural animation, which is often considered to be a product of Mobutu's inspiration in Northern Korea and in China, defending the point of view that they were probably also inspired by previous folkloric animations from the colonial era.

In Gabon, it is also commonly supposed that Omar Bongo was inspired to create these propaganda spectacles by socialist regimes and by his travels in the Democratic Republic of Congo (Mouélé 2009). Therefore, before the emergence of the name 'groupes d'animation culturelle' and of the PDG, the early creation of dance and music groups before independence and their participation in colonial animations (Bernault 1996) corroborate the idea that orchestras and practices of folkloric music and dances were predecessors of the genre during the colonial era.

While some articles and books address the existence of these groups (Matsahanga 2002; Rossatanga-Rignault et al. 2005; Tonda 2009; Minko 2010), only a few studies and monographs are devoted specifically to this genre, in particular, two masters theses (Nzengue 1989; Mouélé 2009). In the existing studies, these organizations have been analyzed from the perspective of their political meanings and functions rather than their musical dimensions.

Furthermore, while many documents from the archives of the national press in Gabon describe the musical scene with its orchestras, dance troupes and solo singers, and identify their role in the representation of the nation, it is very hard to find journalistic articles devoted to cultural animation groups. These groups were only cited in articles about the official ceremonies and travels of the president, or later, in portraits of singers who came from these musical formations. In summary, these musical formations have, above all, been considered in public and scholarly discourses as political instruments, and not so much for their aesthetic and musical contents. Nevertheless, they created a genuine aesthetic, endowed with musical and choreographic characteristics, that remains, for a part of the population, as an emblem of this historical era and of Gabonese identity, and that has deeply influenced the subsequent generation of musicians.

Cultural Animation Groups: Social Contexts and Musical Contents

Cultural animation groups that developed during the second part of the twentieth century in Africa can generally be defined, using White's words, as 'a particular kind of spectacle that allied the sensibility of folklore with popular music, but that sang at the same time the praises of the single party and its chief' (2006; author's translation). Even if the attempts to create fusions of modern Western instruments with traditional songs and instruments were numerous in this period, the spectacle presented in cultural animation groups came from a special dialogue with politics and ideologies of each nation-state, highlighting local singularities, in musical contents, political impacts and gender norms associated with these groups.

In Gabon, groups of animation were constituted on the basis of common provincial or ethnic origins, and mostly led by important women from the country, such as wives of state ministers or rich political personalities. Of the dozens of groups supported since 1968, many also depended on the main political figures of their provinces; described as 'sponsors,' they provided general funds for the group, costumes, the small amount of material remuneration that the members received for their travels, drinks and food, and sometimes meager financial support; they also intervened to provide jobs for some members and partisans of the PDG (Mouélé 2009, 61).

Cultural animation groups aimed to represent local features of an 'authentic' African culture, which was called for by several nation-state ideologies after independence (White 2006). As a consequence, ethnicity and provincial singularities were strongly highlighted in music, languages and textual contents. The common linguistic element that linked members of each group was predominant in their songs. Their mother tongue was mixed with French, which remains Gabon's national language and which is used to avoid the ethnic claims to which the ideology of national unity in the PDG is strongly opposed. Henceforth, the group Dimossi, for example, produced texts in *ipunu* and in French, northern cultural animation groups while Kounabeli used *bateke* and *obamba* languages in its songs.

Lyrics were mainly dedicated to a description of Bongo's successes, presented as 'Camarade Bongo Ondimba,' 'Papa Omar,' 'Yaya Bongo,' 'father of the nation,' 'strong man of the country' or 'great guide.' Depending on concerned groups and provinces, some dedications were made to other ministers, deputies or senators. Songs were then punctuated by shouts of the solo singer such as 'Bongo Oyé!,' 'Josephine Bongo, Oyé!' or 'PDG, Oyé!,' repeated by the whole choir of women. In these praise songs, themes of peace, development, national wealth, national unity and solidarity were also very present, and they progressively included other social issues, such as the prevention of AIDS. These songs were used to spread the idea of nation, political values and social norms among popular classes; through singing, the repetition of political slogans by women from diverse generations and social classes permitted the incorporation of the single party's messages by large audiences and the recruitment of new militants.

Most of the songs were musically structured around short verses of two to four sentences, repeated several times by the lead singers with a few variations, and insisting on the grandeur of the political figure and the success of his program, concepts and politics. The lead singer could also shout and deliver slogans. The rest of the group (numbering from dozens to thousands of women) answered in unison to the leader's verse repeating the main sentence or vocalizing around phrases such as 'oyo oh,' 'eh eh eh,' etc. As such, the structure of singing partly reproduced the responsorial scheme ('call-and-response') of many traditional and ritual songs that inspired them. Melodies were often repetitive, allowing easy memorization, but lead singers could also perform virtuoso vocals around the core sentences and verses of the song, punctuated by dedications to sponsors. The sound included several diverse melodic phrases and breaks with changes of rhythms and melodies.

From the end of the 1960s to the mid-1980s cultural animation groups mainly performed live, as they were solicited to perform during official and political events. Some, however, also made records after 1985, first in France and later – thanks to the support of their benefactor – in the first local studios that were created during the 1980s.

During their performances, cultural animation groups were systematically organized in the same way: the women, sometimes in huge numbers, from teenagers to the elderly, occupied the background of the stage, placed in lines and led by one or several solo singers who occupied the foreground. They were dressed mainly in traditional textiles ('pagne'), either with a loincloth wrapped around the waist or in modern costumes and dresses, sometimes with a T-shirt with the emblem of the party and an effigy of the president or the name of the cultural animation group. A few were also dressed in traditional costumes and raffias.

The groups were accompanied by an orchestra consisting of modern and traditional musicians (mainly men), playing guitar, drums, bass or brass instruments, and also very often traditional percussion instruments, such as *nkul* or *ngom* for northern cultural animation groups (Nkol Engong), *mosomba* drums or *obaka* (a rack made of hardwood and hit with two sticks) for southern groups. Musical instrumentation at the time was very much inspired by African *rumba* sounds, but they also included traditional rhythms and 'folklores' of each province, such as *ikoku* rhythm for the group Dimossi – mostly composed of *Punu* – or the *elombo* ritual music for groups of the province of Estuary and Maritime Ogooué. A song usually lasted around 15 minutes, and could continue until the president of the ceremony decided to stop the performance. Songs often contained a special part called 'chauffé,' with an acceleration of the rhythm usually in the middle of the song and a solo performance of the guitarist, as in *rumba* music (White 2002), which was appropriate for solo improvisations of the best dancers.

Although often considered a women's musical genre, cultural animation groups therefore involved male musicians in their performances whether it was as members of entire orchestras that had their own activities apart from those accompanying cultural animation groups, or as single musicians hired especially for a particular show. This presence of male orchestras was due to the fact that a huge majority of instrumentalists and musicians were men. Placed in the foreground of the stage, they did not participate in dance performances or in singing, and they were absent from record covers and music videos, with just a few exceptions.

Dance represented a core aspect of each performance. In musical terms, dance and choreographies were a mix of *ndombolo* (or other popular urban moves from Congo) and traditional dances coming from ritual ceremonies or festivities. Most of these dances particularly emphasized the swaying hips and the eroticism of waist movements, a feature present both in popular dances and in traditional moves such as *ikoku*, a symbolic celebration of fertility (Plancke 2010). The consequent sexual suggestiveness and extreme eroticization of the cultural animation groups have been subjected to strong criticism (particularly since the end of the one-party rule in 1990), while also being seen as representing the location of the groups' power.

Debate: Domination or Agency

Whereas cultural animation groups in Congo and Togo involved the coming together of both male and female participants, with women in the majority, in Gabon actual membership in these groups was exclusively reserved for women, and they represented a strong sense of gender identity. Under the one-party government, a gendered division structured the emerging musical scene; while the category of musician was designated principally for men, women occupied the duties of spectacularization and embodiment of the power through dance. The abstract dimension of state power and its virile value in Africa (Mbembe 2001) were both present and became reality through the women's bodies and through their singing and dancing for the leadership. Demonstrating the infinite devotion of women to Omar Bongo and the objectification of their bodies by the state, the cultural animation groups have been considered by some scholars as a spectacularization of the body presented as a sexual object to be consumed by high government officials, for the benefit of the political hegemony of the PDG and of Omar Bongo (Mouélé 2009). Several authors have insisted on the political alienation resulting from participation in these musical groups (Kapalanga 1989; Mouélé 2009; Tonda 2009), where women were led to put their body at the disposal of the leaders and to sing in their honor.

However, it may be argued that these groups allowed their members to develop their agency in a society defined by the control of the nation-state, and to reconstitute social links in a context of urbanization and transformation of solidarity relations; they also helped members to improve their chances for a professional promotion or to meet male partners with high influence and power in the political organization of the one-party rule. During the mid-1980s, when Gabon entered an economic crisis and strong inequalities divided urban society, the spectacularization of their bodies, their seductive power and beauty gave women the opportunity to escape precarious life situations. For some poor women who could not be hired in the public sector or in private companies since they lacked the necessary diplomas and/or contacts to family patronage, these groups provided a way to meet important political personalities who helped them to find a job, or with whom they had intimate relationships in exchange for material support, leading potentially, in a few cases, to official relationships. As Bob White affirms (2006), the representation of these artists as alienated and passive individuals is therefore insufficient to take into account all the subtle forms of criticism expressed by these singers and dancers behind the scenes, and to understand all the interdependence that was progressively established between these groups and the single party. If, on the one hand, the single party imposed the frame for musical creation and the life of the musicians, on the other, its authority also became dependent on these organs of communication, whose presence was an unavoidable condition for holding political and official ceremonies.

Decline and Continuity

In 1990, with the establishment of multi-partism and the end of the hegemony of PDG, cultural animation groups went through an important shift. As icons of Omar Bongo's domination of the masses and symbols of his objectification of women they were strongly denounced during the national conference by opposition parties and leaders, and its members were criticized as 'buttocks shakers.' The title 'cultural animation groups' disappeared and these groups were renamed 'sociocultural groups' during the fifth congress of the PDG, organized in August 1991 with the intention of transforming their political duties into a more cultural and folkloric value.

During the 2000s and the 2010s some sociocultural groups have continued to be active and to record albums and popular music videos (one title 'La botte' [The Barrel], released by Omengo in 2008, rapidly became a hit), and their discs have continued to represent a major part of the sales in street markets of original and pirated CDs (Mouélé 2009). They are sometimes invited to perform in official ceremonies, where they praise the grandeur of President Ali Bongo (Omar Bongo's son, who succeeded his father in 2009). However, their power and their omnipresence on musical stages have suffered from the initiation of freedom of expression, the development of new music markets and the emergence of new themes in songs, since artists have been freed from obligatory involvement in the PDG's activities and from the official censorship from the single party.

At the same time, many artists who were trained in these cultural groups controlled by UFPDG progressively turned themselves toward solo careers during the same period (e.g., Maman Dede, who became one of the most famous Fang singers after her career in the Nkol Engong cultural animation group). Some former military musicians who accompanied these groups have also seen brilliant subsequent careers, such as, for example, Kacki Disco, a guitarist in the group Missema, who was inspired by his many experiences in sociocultural groups to create his own orchestra. He became famous for promoting a dance entitled 'oriengo' that consists of holding the waist of a partner and shaking the hips back and forth. Other groups that appeared at the turn of the 1990s, such as Empire and its singer Amandine, have clearly reproduced some aspects of cultural groups of animation in their texts or in the line formation of their choreographies. In other words, a considerable number of musicians from the generation who have pursued their careers since the decline of cultural animation groups have established themselves in these new formations, which have then had a strong influence on the form and content of contemporary choreographic and spectacle creations.

Conclusion

In the twenty-first century popular discourses concerning cultural animation groups (or sociocultural groups) are colored with ambivalent feelings between nostalgia and condemnation. On the one hand, many critics have appeared, for example, in YouTube comments or in popular discussions about music videos of cultural animation groups, condemning the lewdness of their choreographies and the vulgar image of women promoted as sex objects. Since the emergence of new musical genres and freedom of expression, cultural animation groups represent, from the engaged singers' points of view, a negative emblem of subjection, passivity and alienation toward the authoritarian state. Engaged rappers, for example, have used the term as an insult to discredit other rappers who released a song and performed in meetings in favor of the candidate of PDG (Ali Bongo) during the 2009 election.

On the other hand, the mention of these groups also often leads to nostalgia for a lost past, and is associated with the image of the seductiveness and eroticism of 'authentic' African women. For some people, images and songs from cultural animation groups are also linked to family memories, as many housewives were part of these groups.

Cultural animation groups have progressively been transferred into a symbol of a common national history and heritage, particularly for militants from the PDG. Some TV programs devoted to the past music of Gabon accord special tributes to this part of Gabonese musical heritage; channels on YouTube provide links to their music and to video archives as well as new music videos. Since the turn of the new millennium, cultural animation groups have continued to be invited to participate in official events as emblems of the country or of their province, and they are instituted as part of the local market of music. They tend to become expressions of traditional folklore and cultural authenticity (White 2006). This authenticity mostly relies on the image of the African woman that they promoted: in this ideology, women's bodies and creativity were at one and the same time devoted to the demonstration of men's power and endowed with a sexual power that men depended on and tried to monopolize. This representation of relations between genders underlying cultural animation groups later led to other kinds of representations of women's bodies in musical scenes, such as the ones observed in a subsection of hip-hop and rap creation in Gabon (Aterianus-Owanga 2013). At the same time, the culture of *animation culturelle* has pervaded many sectors of musical production, and even apart from the one-party rule and the cultural animation groups, musical production in Gabon remains partly an instrument for the spectacle of power and the '*ambiancement*' (enlivenment) of public life.

Bibliography

Aterianus-Owanga, Alice. 2013. 'A Rap Music "Based on Strength".' *Cahiers d'études africaines* [Journal of African Studies] 209–10(1): 143–72.

Bernault, Florence. 1996. *Démocraties ambiguës en Afrique centrale* [Ambiguous Democracies in Central Africa]. Paris: Karthala.

Kapalanga, Gazungil Sang'Amin. 1989. *Les spectacles d'animation politique en République du Zaïre: Analyse des mécanismes de reprise, d'actualisation et de politisation des formes culturelles africaines dans les créations spectaculaires modernes* [Spectacles of Political Animation in the Republic of Zaïre: Analysis of Mechanisms of Appropriation, Actualization and Politicization of African Cultural Forms in Modern Performance Creations]. Louvain-la-Neuve: Cahiers théâtre Louvain.

Lwanda, John. 2008. 'Music Advocacy, the Media and the Malawi Political Public Sphere, 1958–2007.' *JAMS* (Journal of African Media Studies) 1(2): 135–54.

Matsahanga, Hugues Gatien. 2002. *La chanson gabonaise d'hier et d'aujourd'hui: Cinquante ans de musique moderne gabonaise* [The Gabonese Song of Yesterday and Today: Fifty Years of Modern Gabonaise Music]. Libreville: Editions Raponda-Walker.

Mbah, Jean-Ferdinand. 2015. *La construction de l'état au Gabon (1957–2009)* [The Making of the State in Gabon (1957–2009)]. Paris: L'Harmattan.

Mbembe, Achille. 2001. *On the Postcolony*. Berkeley and Los Angeles: University of California Press.

Minko, Emmanuelle Nguema. 2010. *Gabon: l'unité nationale ou la rancune comme mode de gouvernance* [Gabon: National Unity or Resentment as a Mode of Governance]. Paris: L'Harmattan.

Mouélé, Patricia Noëlle. 2009. 'Spectacularisation du corps féminin et construction de l'hégémonie politique au Gabon postcolonial' [Spectacularization of the Female Body and Construction of Political Hegemony in Postcolonial Gabon]. Unpublished MA thesis in Sociology, University Omar Bongo, Libreville.

Ndombet, Wilson-André. 2009. *Partis politiques et unité nationale au Gabon* [Political Parties and National Unity in Gabon]. Paris: Karthala.

Nzengue, Dieudonné. 1989. 'Les groupes d'animation du Parti démocratique gabonais' [Animation Groups of the Gabonese Democratic Party]. Unpublished MA thesis, University of Bordeaux.

Obiang, Jean-François. 2007. *France-Gabon: Pratiques clientélaires et logiques d'État dans les relations franco-africaines* [France-Gabon: Clientelism Practices and State Logics in Relations Between France and Africa]. Paris: Karthala.

Plancke, Carine. 2010. 'On Dancing and Fishing: Joy and the Celebration of Fertility among the Punu of Congo-Brazzaville.' *Africa* 80(04): 620–41.

Pourtier, Roland. 1989. *Le Gabon: Espace, histoire, société* [Gabon: Space, History and Society]. Paris: l'Harmattan.

Rossatanga-Rignault, Guy, Metegue N'Nah, Nicolas, Tonda, Joseph, et al. 2005. *Rupture-Solidarité 6: Le Gabon malgré lui* [Gabon Despite Itself]. Paris: Karthala.

Tonda, Joseph. 2009. 'Omar Bongo Ondimba, Paradigme du pouvoir postcolonial' [Omar Bongo Ondimba, Paradigm of Postcolonial Power]. *Politique Africaine* [African Politics] 114(2): 126–37.

Toulabor, Comi M. 1986. *Le Togo sous Eyadéma* [Togo Under Eyadema]. Paris: Karthala Editions.
Wesley, Fred. 2002. *Hit Me, Fred: Recollections of a Sideman*. Durham, NC: Duke University Press.
White, Bob W. 2002. 'Congolese Rumba and Other Cosmopolitanisms.' *Cahiers d'études africaines* [Journal of African Studies] 168(4): 663–86.
White, Bob W. 2006. 'L'incroyable machine d'authenticité: L'animation politique et l'usage public de la culture dans le Zaïre de Mobutu' [The Amazing Authenticity Machine: *Animation Politique* and the Public Use of Culture in Mobutu's Zaire]. *Anthropologie et Sociétés* [Anthropology and Societies] 30(2). Online at: http://id.erudit.org/iderudit/014113ar (accessed 3 April 2018)
White, Bob W. 2008. *Rumba Rules: The Politics of Dance Music in Mobutu's Zaire*. Durham, NC: Duke University Press.

Discographical Reference
Kounabeli et Orchestre Banowita. *One*. (producers: Patience Dabany and Fred Wesley). Nkoussou Productions. *1985*: Gabon.

Discography
Dabany, Patience. *Associé*. Believe, Le Monde des artistes. *1985*: Gabon.
Disco, Kacky. *Best of Oriengo*. Kage Pro. *2013*: Gabon.
Maman Dédé avec les Anges. *Omar bongo notre chef bien aimé / Attention au sida*. 33T. Nkol'Engong, Anzal 1344. *1986*: Gabon.
Mikouagna de Mounana. *Rabi kounga*. MKA: MK102A. *1990*: Gabon.
Missema. *Centenaire*. Missema Production / Sonodisc: MI 2003. *1986*: Gabon.
Missema, *Missema 10 ans chante Omar Bongo 20 ans*, Missema Production / Sonodisc: MI 2005. *1986*: Gabon.
Missema. *Missema 11 ans, PDG 20 ans*. Missema Production: MI 2006. *1988*: Gabon.
Omengo. 'La botte.' *Ya Omar*. Omengo productions. *2008*: Gabon.

ALICE ATERIANUS-OWANGA

Cumbé

Cumbé is a neo-traditional music and dance genre among the Annobonese people in Equatorial Guinea. It originated in the multiethnic environment of Malabo (the capital city, located on the island of Bioko, formerly known as Fernando Po), from where it was exported to the island of Annobon in the early twentieth century. In Equatorial Guinea, *cumbé* music is played and danced in Palé, the only city on Annobon Island (with approximately 2,000 inhabitants) and also in Malabo. The dance is accompanied by several instruments: a square drum with a double frame and four legs that is also called *cumbé*; the *tambali*, a tambourine constructed in the same way and in different sizes; the *chin*, an iron sheet that is struck; *katá* (two sticks); a bottle; and a carpenter's saw, which is played with a nail, a knife or any other available implement. The music's rhythmic *clave* (timeline) is in quadruple meter with a Caribbean feel and is played by the bottle and *katá* sticks and sometimes by the saw (see Example 1).

Example 1: *Cumbé* timeline pattern

The Annobonese live on the small island of Annobon, located about 350 miles south-west of mainland Equatorial Guinea (see Maps), and have established themselves as a group since the Portuguese colonization of the island in the sixteenth century, with slaves brought from Angola and Sao Tomé. The island was a Spanish colony from 1778 until it became a province of Equatorial Guinea after independence in 1968. The island of Bioko, some four hundred miles to the north, off the coast of Cameroon, is also home to many Annobonese who moved there in search of work and who also dance *cumbé*.

In Annobon, there is an official *cumbé* association, with a president and bylaws. Children up to the age of 12 learn by watching and listening and ask to participate as instrumentalists. They also ask to be 'blessed' and, in exchange for patronage, receive instruction and the 'blessing' of the connoisseurs. From that moment, the initiated may be called upon to play for celebrations and commemorations on the island. For example, 'Papa Pavil' was the master teacher of Ruperto Cachina, who plays *cumbé* in Annobon and Malabo.

Historical Overview of *Cumbé* and Related Caribbean and African Genres

In Annobon, *cumbé* is the result of complex trajectories from the Atlantic and from movements along the African coasts. Since 1800 these trajectories have influenced the development of African popular music. The Jamaican genre *goombay* evolved in the late nineteenth century and, at the beginning of the twentieth century, extended its influence from Sierra Leone throughout West Africa, at the crossroads of genres and styles that influenced the popular music of Ghana, Nigeria and Equatorial Guinea. Related versions of this drum-dance have various names on both sides of the Atlantic: *gumbe*, *goombay*, *goomba* (Bahamas, Trinidad, Jamaica), *goombay*, *gome* (Ghana), *gumbay*, *gumbe* (Sierra Leone), *gube* (Mali), *goumbé* (Ivory Coast), *kumbeh* (Nigeria), *maringa* or *malinga* (Gabon) and *patenge* (Congo). The isolation of Annobon Island, where these elements were borrowed from Bioko, resulted in a greater level of preservation of original styles, maintaining Caribbean-style rhythms but with reinterpretations in the language and the melody.

The Sierra Leoneans who founded the city of Malabo on the island of Fernando Po in 1827 were descendants of liberated slaves, Jamaican Maroons and Black Loyalists. These groups established Krio culture throughout the nineteenth century in Freetown, Sierra Leone (Aranzadi 2013, 2016). The *gumbe/goombay* genre, which employs the square drum and which was brought by Jamaican Maroons who arrived in Freetown in 1800 (Rankin 1836, Vol. 1, 108), is documented by authors such as Wyse (1979, 412) and is still played in the early twenty-first century (see also separate entry). Around 1830 use of the *gumbe* drum started to spread among other ethnic groups in Freetown (Sibthorpe 1970 [1868], 52). Hutchinson, consul in Fernando Po between 1855 and 1858, describes *goombee* as one of the 'immoral' dances of the inhabitants of Freetown (1858, 112). Later, and throughout the nineteenth century, the common use of this drum-dance resulted in its propagation to other African countries.

The link with Sierra Leone in terms of the dissemination of the square drum by workers off the coast of Africa went as far as Gabon and the Congo. In Gabon, the *maringa*, or *malinga*, a square drum with accordion accompaniment, was recorded and photographed by Herbert Pepper (1958, 49).

The *cumbé* drum from Annobon is virtually the same as the *gumbe* or *gome* from Accra and the *goombay* or *gumbe* from Freetown, and shares the same type of construction as the *gumbe* from Jamaica with double frame and legs. The timeline (see Example 1) is the same in Annobon and Sierra Leone, but faster in Freetown (to compare the *cumbé* sung by Desmali and his group in Annobon with the *goombay* in Freetown, see the websites BBC Radio 3 World Routes and 'Sierra Leone Heritage'). In Sierra Leone, Ghana and Equatorial Guinea, the drum has the same shape and is played in the same way: with the musician sitting astride the drum, beating it with their hands and the heel of the foot (Aranzadi 2009). In Freetown, it is played in this way and also by placing it between the knees, which corresponds to the way it is played in Jamaica. *Maringa*, associated particularly with the late famous Freetown guitarist Ebenezer Calender, also utilizes the giant *goombay* frame-drum upon which a player sits (Collins 2007, 180). In 2016 Congolese musicians stated that the square drum *patenge*, linked to the *maringa* style in Congo, was also played with the musician sitting astride (personal communication).

In several Bubi villages in Bioko the Bubi people have used the square drum *kunké*. The villages are located near the two cities, Malabo and Luba, which are the main nucleus of the Creoles (originally from Sierra Leone) who had contact with the Bubi throughout the nineteenth century and exerted an influence upon them. In the 1950s the drum's use spread along the island (see Manfredi 1950, 150; Crespo 1949, 104–8), with the dance being performed by men and women. In Basakato (a Bubi village), a group called 'Elegancia' danced the *kunke*. Villages on the island that were further away from the influence of the Creoles did not adopt the drums, and in the village of Moka they were forbidden as the elders said that their sound frightened the female spirits (Aranzadi 2009, 75).

A related dance and drum were found among a group of Bioko Island Creoles that had been formed by African-American former slaves, who had settled in Sierra Leone, and their descendants, together with the passengers from boats carrying slaves that had been recaptured by the British Navy on the African coast. The Bioko Island Creoles called the square drum and the dance *kunki*, a term for which there was no written record in Africa. However, freed former slaves in Freetown, Sierra Leone danced the *koonken* or *koonking* in 1830, as recorded by the traveler Rankin (1836, 268). Fernandino Creoles on the island of Bioko stopped using this drum in 1976 during the era of upheaval under the dictatorial president Macias Nguema, when many Creoles fled the island for Nigeria (Aranzadi 2012, 194).

There were some differences between *kunki* and the Annobonese *cumbé*. *Kunki* was a female-only dance (as was *koonken* in Freetown in 1830) while, for the Annobonese, *cumbé* was and is a mixed-gender dance. The guitar was added to *kunki* later during the twentieth century, brought by the Spaniards. The *kunki* songs were in the Creole Pidgin language, a language that spans the island of Bioko as a lingua franca among the different ethnic groups. The dance was performed using the same rhythmic timeline found in Freetown (although at a slower tempo) and with the same instruments, in addition to the accordion.

Kunki has not been danced since 1976, but *cumbé* is still danced among the Annobonese. In Freetown, the saw is used to mark the same timeline, which is performed at a much faster tempo, and *gumbe* is accompanied by an iron called *angul* (Horton 1999) and other instruments. Creoles also used these instruments along with the drum (Aranzadi 2009).

In the evolution of Jamaican *goombay*, a separate variant emerged – *aṣíkò* (*ashiko, assiko*) – which became popular in Ghana and Nigeria (Collins 1994, 346) and later traveled to Bioko. In Ghana, other local styles merged *gombe* and highlife in a second cultural integration among certain ethnic groups and, even up to the 1970s, square tambourines were played in three sizes – bass, medium and soloist (Collins 1992, 33, 35), as in Annobon and Bioko.

In the 1940s and 1950s a large flow of workers went back and forth from Ghana to the island of Fernando Po, as it then was. The Ga workers from Ghana learned to use the drum and the songs from Sierra Leonean artisans who were in the city of Santa Isabel (later called Malabo), working on cocoa farms or fishing. The songs that accompanied the drum were in Pidgin English. In Bioko, the songs were performed by workers from multiethnic origins and were meant as entertainment on the day of rest – usually Sunday (Hampton 1979, 5). A musical group using the drum who called themselves Kpehe Gome Group was formed in Ghana in 1954 by the Ga fishermen who returned from Fernando Po (Collins 2007, 5).

The *Cumbé* Dance in Annobon

The *cumbé* on Annobon is known for the elegance displayed in the dance and its slow and cadenced rhythm. The songs are in Fa d'Ambô, a Portuguese-related Creole language spoken originally on the small island. They are composed by a member of the community and integrated into the traditional repertoire of popular songs. The lyrics speak of events, of the suffering of the Annobonese caused by their isolation and their repression under the Macias dictatorship (1968–79), and other themes. Recitative singing is employed, half-spoken, half-sung, with ascending and descending vocalizations on the syllables 'a-yéé in a manner similar to the lamentations used in flamenco. A soloist sings and the ensemble makes occasional responses, sung in thirds. The elderly may act as soloists, expressing the hardships of their history or any recent event. Both pathos and humor are present. An Annobonese musician affirmed (in a personal communication with the author), 'although we are [descendants of] slaves, we are people.'

The slow couples' dance begins with all participants forming a circle, standing on flat ground, alternating men and women. One dancer leads the dance and may be positioned with a partner either at the center or in the circle. The *cumbé* drum is played with the hands alone until the moment known as the *punt*, marked by the rhythm of all the drums (the leader of the dance is called *pe punt*). From that moment onwards, it is also played with the heel of the foot and the music acquires a greater dynamism and energy. Also at that moment, when the leader of the dance gives the signal, the women turn around and stand facing the men. This dance is performed on holidays (especially on Saint Anthony's Day) and for commemorations including Epiphany. The dance often takes place in the town square of Palé, the main city on the island (Aranzadi 2009, 145).

During the dance, the performers elicit humor. The men wear suit jackets and a tie and usually have

Genres: Sub-Saharan Africa

Example 2: *Cumbé* music (reprinted from Aranzadi 2009)

a walking stick and sunglasses. The performance style is similar to *gome* from Ghana (see Example 2), in which the songs are often accompanied by humorous dance-dramas. However, whereas *gome* music is played in duple meter and the timeline is played by the bell, in *cumbé* the timeline is played by the bottle and *katá* (two sticks) and the accompanying instruments are two drums – the main bass drum and the *cumbé* – and the *tambali* (see Example 3).

Instruments

The *cumbé* drum is a square, double frame drum, 40 to 50 centimeters wide, with four legs, built with modern joinery methods. The inner frame pushes the skin taut using a system of wedges. Four fixed legs attach to the outer frame and four movable legs are attached to the inner framework, moving with the inner framework to tighten the skin. Between two of the four legs, there is a table on which the musician sits to play. The drum is played with the hands and with the heel of the foot. Usually it is made of goatskin or the skin of the *fritambo* antelope. It has the same type of construction as its counterpart in Jamaica in 1920, described and illustrated by Helen Roberts (1924).

Tambali is a square tambourine with the same type of construction as the *cumbé*. It measures from 20 to 25 centimeters in diameter. The skin is stretched over a wooden frame, under which there is another frame with two strips of cross-shaped wood, which tightens the skin underneath and which in turn is held by wedges (*cuin*). The skin may be goat or antelope, and it is also made with wild cat or dog skin. There is a special *tambali* for more agile and complicated rhythms: the *doblá*, whose sound is higher-pitched. Another *tambali* is the *tan tuk* (Aranzadi 2009, 204). The *tan tuk* plays the bass part. Among the Fernandino Creoles, two sizes of tambourines were used to accompany the big square drum. The *tambali* is played with the hands and one or two thin sticks called *opa tombol*. With the left hand holding the tambourine, the

Example 3: *Gome* music of Ghana (score by Sonja Rentik, reprinted with permission from Aranzadi 2009)

tambali remains parallel to the body on the chest while the right hand plays with great dexterity using the stick on the drum. In Ghana, there is a drum exactly like the Annobonese *tambali* called *tamalin* (a possible corruption of the word 'tambourine' according to John Collins [personal communication]). In Sierra Leone, the same drum is called *sikko* or *assiko* (Aranzadi 2009, 74).

These tambourines that accompany the music of the *cumbé* dance are also used in *dadj'i* (an Annobonese dance for age groups in which the *tambali* is the only instrument played) and in Annobonese popular songs. Two replicas of the square tambourines are on display at the Music Museum of Barcelona.

Katá are two sticks, ten centimeters wide and one meter long, which are used in *cumbé* to mark the timeline. The Annobonese living in Malabo on Bioko Island also mark the timeline with the bottle and sometimes use the iron. In Jamaica, the word *katá* is used to refer to the sticks accompanying the drum in Kumina ceremonies. In Cuba, *katá* are two bamboo sticks. Thus, Caribbean heritage may also be seen in the words used for musical instruments on Annobon.

The Annobonese do not play the accordion, but the Creoles on Bioko Island did play it. The accordion was introduced in Africa in the nineteenth century and in the 1860s was played in Freetown (Harrev 1987, 6). Later, it was associated with *maringa* and the *aṣíkò* style (with square tambourines) in Senegambia, after having been set up by the Aku community (Yorùbá) of the Krio group in Freetown. In the twentieth century it was also used with square tambourines in Ghana, the Ivory Coast and other West African countries (Harrev 1993, 3) and Gabon (Pepper 1958, 49). In Santa Isabel (now Malabo), it was used in the *kunki* dance of the Sierra Leonean Creoles, with the square drum and tambourines accompanied by the saw and the bottle during the twentieth century until 1976.

The saw was used in Africa in the *gumbe* style, along with other tools of the carpentry trade. On Bioko Island, Creoles used the saw in *kunki*, as in Sierra Leone. This was one of the tools exported to Annobon. In the early twenty-first century Juan Murcia plays the saw on Annobon Island and other Annobonese people play it to accompany the *cumbé* in Malabo.

Chin is a sheet of iron hanging from a rope and struck by an iron cylinder. Its name is onomatopoeic. It is played to accompany the *cumbé* dance and provide polyrhythms. In Jamaica in 1924, Helen Roberts mentioned an iron sheet on a rope as a tool used by musicians in the markets (1924, 242). In Sierra Leone, *angul* is a U-shaped piece of metal beaten with a metal stick, used in the Milo jazz ensemble (Van Oven 1982, 8), a variation of *goombay* music in Sierra Leone. This instrument was present in the three areas of the Atlantic (Jamaica, Sierra Leone and Equatorial Guinea), and is now kept on Annobon and adapted to the Annobonese language and rhythms.

The bottle is played with a nail, a spoon or other metal object or sometimes even with a fingernail. Sometimes two bottles are used.

Flemming Harrev (1993, 6) and John Collins (2007, 184) point out that carpentry influenced the musical style and instrumentation of *gumbe* and its related genres, since tools were used as instruments (the saw, nails for percussion, and so on) in several countries where the use of the drum spread. It was the workers at the beginning of colonization who shared these pre-popular styles of music in Africa. In 2016, in Malabo, Annobonese carpenter and musician Hipólito Teruel, who accompanies the celebrated musician Desmali, makes the drum (Aranzadi 2010).

Identity

Cumbé is considered a symbol of tradition and an important part of identity in Annobon (Aranzadi 2012). The *cumbé* style also has influenced popular Annobonese music and other dances. Desmali, for example, who is considered one of the best contemporary musicians in Equatorial Guinea, uses the *tambalí*, a small tambourine symbol of the Annobonese, in his concerts. The key rhythms of *cumbé* can also be heard in many popular songs, for example on Desmali's album with his group Dambo de la Costa, *Luga da ambo* (2008).

The Annobonese have been isolated for centuries, having little contact with other people, except those from the island of Bioko. Among their cultural expressions, the adoption of 'imported' musical instruments or performances has assumed a reinterpretative character; by adapting certain aspects such as the rhythm the Annobonese make them their own. In local culture, these 'imported' elements, such as Pidgin terms, songs, rituals and instruments, are nevertheless associated with a higher status because Bioko was the 'metropolis' of the Spanish colony. Once adopted, these musical elements form part of Annobonese idiosyncrasy.

Thus, *cumbé* songs express Annobonese identity, including that of the slaves who were brought to the island centuries ago. Even the short steps and the walking in line formation at the beginning of the dance reflect this expression of cultural heritage, according to Desmali. This dance and its music are considered truly Annobonese both by the people themselves and by other ethnic groups in Equatorial Guinea.

Bibliography

Aranzadi, Isabela de. 2009. *Instrumentos musicales de las etnias de Guinea Ecuatorial* [Musical Instruments of Ethnic Groups in Equatorial Guinea]. Madrid: Apadena.

Aranzadi, Isabela de. 2010. 'A Drum's Trans-Atlantic Journey from Africa to the Americas and Back after the End of Slavery: Annobonese and Fernandino Musical Cultures.' *African Sociological Review* 14(1): 20–47.

Aranzadi, Isabela de. 2012. 'Musical Objects and Identities in Transit within Groups in Equatorial Guinea: Musical Connections with Sierra Leone and Cuba following the Abolition of Slavery.' In *In and Out of Africa, Exploring Afro-Hispanic, Luso-Brazilian, and Latin-American Connections*, ed. Joanna Boampong. Newcastle upon Tyne: Cambridge Scholars Publishing, 190–215.

Aranzadi, Isabela de. 2013. *Memoria africana en el Atlántico. Cultura musical en un espacio de criollización: La isla de Bioko* [African Memory in the Atlantic and (in) Material Musical Culture in a Space of Creolization: The Island of Bioko]. Unpublished Ph.D. thesis, Universidad Autónoma de Madrid.

Aranzadi, Isabela de. 2016. 'El legado cultural de Sierra Leona en Bioko. Comparativa de dos espacios de Criollización africana' [The Cultural Legacy of Sierra Leone in Bioko. Comparison of Two Spaces of African Creolization]. *ÉNDOXA: Series Filosóficas* 37. Madrid: UNED, 237–78.

Beni Salem. 1954. 'Estampas coloniales. Chrismas en Santa Isabel' [Colonial Scenes. Christmas in Santa Isabel]. *La Guinea Española* 1401 (10 January): 7–12.

Bilby, Kenneth. 2005 (2008). *True-Born Maroons*. Gainesville: University Press of Florida.

Cervera Liso, Desiderio (Desmali). 2007–15. Personal communications with the author.

Collins, John. 1992. *West African Pop Roots*. Philadelphia: Temple University Press.

Collins, John. 1994. *The Ghanaian Concert Party: African Popular Entertainment at the Cross Roads*. Unpublished Ph.D. dissertation, State University of New York at Buffalo.

Collins, John. 2007. 'Pan African Goombay Drum-Dance Music: Its Ramifications and Development in Ghana.' In *Legon Journal of the Humanities*, Vol. 18, eds. Gordon Adika and Kofi Ackah. Accra: Faculty of Arts, University of Ghana, 179–200.

Crespo Gil-Delgado, Carlos. 1949. *Notas para un estudio antropológico y etnológico del bubi de Fernando Poo* [Notes for an Anthropological and Ethnographic Study of Bubi from Fernando Po]. Madrid: Instituto de Estudios Africanos y Bernardino de Sahagún de Antropología y Etnología. C.S.I.C.

Hampton, Barbara. 1979–80. 'A Revised Analytical Approach to Musical Processes in Urban Africa.' In *African Urban Music*, ed. Kazadi wa-Mukuna. Special issue of African Urban Studies (winter), East Lansing: Michigan State University Press, 1–16.

Harrev, Flemming. 1987. 'Gumbe and the Development of Krio Popular Music in Freetown, Sierra Leone.' Paper presented at IASPM's 4th International Conference, Accra, Ghana, 12–19 August.

Harrev, Flemming. 1993. 'The Origin of Urban Music in West and Central Africa.' Paper presented at 23rd World Conference of the ICTM, Berlin, 16–22 June.

Harrev, Flemming. 2001. 'The Diffusion of Gumbe Assiko and *Maringa* in West and Central Africa.' Paper presented at 12th Triennial Symposium on African Art by the Arts Council of the US African Studies Association, St Thomas, Virgin Islands, 25–9 April.

Horton, Christian Dowu Jayeola. 1999. 'The Role of the Gumbe in Popular Music and Dance Styles in

Sierra Leone.' In *Turn Up the Volume. A Celebration of African Music*, eds. J. DjeDje and Ernest Brown. Los Angeles: UCLA Fowler Museum of Cultural History, 230–5, 349.

Hutchinson, Thomas J. 1858. *Impressions of Western Africa, with Remarks on the Diseases of the Climate and a Report on the Peculiarities of Trade Up the River in the Bight of Biafra*. London: Longman, Brown, Green, Longmans, & Roberts.

Lewin, Olive. 2000. *Rock It Come Over, The Folk Music of Jamaica*. Jamaica, Trinidad and Tobago: University of the West Indies Press, Barbados.

Manfredi, Domingo. 1950. *Ischulla (La Isla)* [The Island]. Madrid: C.S.I.C. Instituto de Estudios Africanos.

Pepper, Herbert. 1958. *Anthologie de la vie africaine. Congo-Gabon* [Anthology of African Life. Congo-Gabon]. Paris: Ducretet Thomson.

Rankin, F. Harrison. 1836. *The White Man's Grave; A Visit to Sierra Leone in 1834*, 2 vols. London: R. Bentley.

Ricketts, Major. 1831. *Narrative of the Ashantee War; With a View of the Present State of the Colony of Sierra Leone*. London: Simpkin and Marshall.

Roberts, Helen. 1924. 'Some Drums and Drum Rhythms of Jamaica.' *Natural History* 24(2): 241–51.

Sibthorpe, A. B. C. 1970 [1868]. *The History of Sierra Leone*. London: Routledge.

Van Oven, Cootje. 1982. *An Introduction to the Music of Sierra Leone*. (Supplement.) Culemborg: Cootje van Oven.

Wyse, Akintola. 1979. 'On Misunderstandings Arising from the Use of the Term 'Creole' in the Literature on Sierra Leone: A Rejoinder.' *Africa: Journal of the International African Institute* 49(4): 408–17.

Discographical Reference

Desmali e Dambo de la Costa. *Luga da ambo: Musique de l'île d'annobon-Guinée Équatoriale*. ICEF. 2008: Equatorial Guinea.

Discography

Música tradicional de Guinea Ecuatorial, Vol. I (compiled by Isabela de Aranzadi). CD accompanying *Instrumentos musicales de las etnias de Guinea Ecuatorial* [Musical Instruments of Ethnic Groups in Equatorial Guinea]. Apadena. 2009: Spain.

Web References

BBC Radio 3 World Routes: http://www.bbc.co.uk/programmes/p019j2zl (*Cumbé*) (accessed 8 November 2017).

'Sierra Leone Heritage': http://sierraleoneheritage.org/video/gallery/ (*Gumbe*) (accessed 8 November 2017).

ISABELA DE ARANZADI

Discolypso

Discolypso was a blend of West African and Caribbean popular music that was aimed at young people who were attracted to the new dance-oriented disco music being played at discotheques during the 1970s. Like Western disco music, this West African offshoot was not usually presented in live performances, but rather primarily produced by studio bands for records (including 12-inch disco singles). Again, like Western disco music, the lyrics of discolypso were mainly concerned with romantic and erotic love.

'Discolypso' was the creation of London-based Sierra Leonean producer Akie Deen, who moved into the African-Caribbean disco market that emerged in the 1970s by combining disco music with West African music. One of the effects of the international 'disco fever' of the time was the updating of calypsos, *meringues*, *sambas* and *rumbas* by West Indian artists into the *salsa* of Cuba and Puerto Rico, the *zouk* music of the French Antilles and soca (soul calypso) of Trinidadian artists such as Ed Watson, Lord Shorty and also the old-time calypsonian Lord Kitchener, who had a massive international recording hit in the late 1970s with his revamped disco version of 'Sugar Bum Bum.' Disco music itself was a combination of US soul-funk and drum-machine music (popularized by Boney M, Donna Summers, Abba, Kraftwerk, Michael Jackson and others) that was played on records at discotheques and became immensely popular with youthful American, European and Caribbean dance fans of the 1970s. Akie Deen simply moved into this Afro-Caribbean soca side of disco music with his hi-tech studio versions of Sierra Leonean *maringas* and Ghanaian/Nigerian highlifes which, incidentally, during the 1950s had themselves been influenced by the post–World War II calypso music of Lord Invador, Lord Kitchener and Mighty Sparrow. Akie Deen called his sound 'disco calypso' or simply 'discolypso,' as it combined elements of West African popular music with disco versions of Trinidadian calypso and soca.

Akie was born in Freetown, Sierra Leone, in 1947 and first became interested in music production when he served as social secretary of the Sierra Leonean Students' Union in England in 1972 and 1973. In that capacity he helped organize tours of the top guitar bands of Sierra Leone and Ghana, the Afro Nationals and the African Brothers. In 1974 Akie produced the London-based Sierra Leone group Super Combo, with whom he made the highlife 'Merigueoko.' The following year members of the Afro Nationals, under the name Sabanoh 75, came to London again and, assisted by Akie, released three singles, 'Susanna,' 'Konko' and 'Carry On,' all of which became hits in Sierra Leone. Sabanoh 75 returned yet again in 1977 and released a 12-inch single (under the name the 'Wagadugu' band) of the Nigerian Prince Nico Mbarga's best-known highlife hit 'Sweet Mother,' produced by Akie. Akie continued to release recordings of his new discolypso sound on his Afro-Disco label, with Teddy Davies's version of Lord Kitchener's calypso 'Just a Little Bit,' the two singles 'Tumba' and 'Carolina' by Addy Foster Jones of Sierra Leone television and 'Amo Sakee Sa' by the Liberian singer Miatta Fahnbulleh. These productions drew on West African and West Indian popular dance music influences, combined electric guitars, percussion and keyboards with the drum machines of disco, and were sung in English, Pidgin English or Krio.

However, the major breakthrough into the African-Caribbean disco market for Akie Deen came in 1979 with the release of 'Easy Dancing' by Wagadugu, followed by 'Discolypso' and 'Funny Lady' by the Freetown musician Cecil Bunting McCormack (or Bunny Mack). In 1980 Bunny Mack (backed by the Ghanaian and Nigerian musicians Alfred 'Kari' Bannerman, George Lee, Paapa Mensah and Jake Solo) had his first Afro-Disco label entry on the British pop charts, 'Love Me Love You Forever,' which reached number five on the disco charts and number 76 on the UK singles charts. This song was also a hit song in the West Indies and Africa, earning a gold disc in Nigeria in 1981 for the Tabansi label.

Akie Deen followed this success with more disco singles, including 'Weakness for Your Sweetness' by Jimmy Senyah from Barbados, which reached number 25 on the British disco charts and was subsequently released by Scorpion Records in France, where it was included in the hit parade. When Akie Deen released Bunny Mack's second album *Supa Frico* in 1981, he also organized tours of Nigeria for Bunny Mack. Other discolypso artists that Akie began producing on his Afro-Disco label in the 1980s included the Ghanaian keyboard player Emmanuel Rentoz, the West Indian singers Nina da Costa and Leon Charles, South Africa's Yvonne Mobambo and the Nigerian singer Martha Ulaeto.

Akie Deen's disco version of Sierra Leonean and other African popular music was part of a larger move by young West African artists from the late 1970s toward new forms of 'technopop' that utilized drum machines and synthesizers and depended on records, cassette and music video sales rather than live performance. For instance, local forms of disco music were popularized in Nigeria by Chris Okotie, Patti Boulaye and Sonny Okosun, while Ghana's George Darko and Daddy Lumba produced a disco form of highlife they called 'burger' highlife. Discolypso, burger highlife and Nigerian disco music tended to dwell on the topic of romantic love and were immensely popular with the West African youth of the 1980s. These local disco forms of West African technopop music were, however, gradually superseded during the 1990s by local versions of US rap and hip-hop music, such as the 'hiplife' of Ghana and the '*naija* rap' of Nigeria. In Sierra Leone, Krio rap and hip-hop artists including Kao Denero, Daddy Saj and the Wan Pop Sojas also surfaced in the 1990s, particularly after the country's 11-year civil war ended in 2002.

Like disco music itself, Akie Deen's discolypso music declined in the 1990s with the rise of hip-hop and rap. Nevertheless, it had been a success with both African and Caribbean fans and, as such, helped pave the way for the later international cross-over of African popular music and world music to the West from the mid- to late 1980s.

Bibliography

Collins, E. John. 1994–6. *Highlife Time*. Accra: Anansesem Press.

Collins, E. John. 1985. *Music Makers of West Africa*. Washington DC: Three Continents Press.

Collins, E. John. 1992. *West African Pop Roots*. Philadelphia: Temple University Press.

Horton, Christian Dowu. 1984. 'Popular Bands in Sierra Leone, 1920 to the Present.' *Black Perspectives in Music* 12(2): 183–92.

Ware, Naomi. 1978. 'Popular Music and African Identity in Freetown, Sierra Leone.' In *Eight Urban Cultures: Tradition and Change*, ed. Bruno Nettl. Urbana: University of Illinois Press, 196–319.

Discographical References

Davies, Teddy. 'Just a Little Bit' (song by Lord Kitchener). Afro-Disco. *1978*: UK.
Fahnbulleh, Miatta. 'Amo Sakee Sa.' Afro-Disco. *1978*: UK.
Jones, Addy Foster. 'Carolina.' Afro-Disco. *1978*: UK.
Jones, Addy Foster. 'Tumba.' Afro-Disco. *1978*: UK.
Lord Kitchener. 'Sugar Bum Bum.' Ice Records GUY 7-12. *1978*: UK.
Lord Kitchener and Ed Watson. 'Just a Little Bit.' Charlie's Records CR 338. *1978*: USA.
Mack, Bunny (Cecil Bunting McCormack). 'Discolypso.' Afro-Disco. *1979*: UK.
Mack, Bunny (Cecil Bunting McCormack). 'Funny Lady.' Afro-Disco. *1979*: UK.
Mack, Bunny (Cecil Bunting McCormack). 'Love Me Love You Forever.' Afro-Disco. *1980*: UK.
Mack, Bunny (Cecil Bunting McCormack). *Supa Frico*. Afro-Disco. *1981*: UK.
Mbarga, Prince Nico, and Rocafil Jazz. 'Sweet Mother.' Roger All Stars label ASALPS 6, 1. *1976*: Nigeria.
Sabanoh 75. 'Carry On.' Afro-Disco. *1975*: UK.
Sabanoh 75. 'Konko.' Afro-Disco. *1975*: UK.
Sabanoh 75. 'Susanna.' Afro-Disco. *1975*: UK.
Sabanoh 75. 'Wagadugu.' Afro-Disco. *1977*: UK.
Senyah, Jimmy. 'Weakness for Your Sweetness.' Afro-Disco. *1981*: UK.
Wagadugu. 'Easy Dancing.' Afro-Disco. *1979*: UK.

E. JOHN COLLINS

Ethiopian Modern Music (Zemenawi Muzika)

Ethiopian modern music (*zemenawi muzika*) emerged in the years after World War II from the encounter between Ethiopian musical traditions and Western popular music. As an umbrella term, it encompasses several subgenres and stylistic shifts that have punctuated the history of popular music in Ethiopia since the 1950s. Ethiopian modern music may be described, albeit with some simplification, as the fusion of Ethiopian lyrics, vocal style, melodies and often also rhythms, with instrumentation, arrangements, performance style and imagery drawn from Western popular music.

Although unsatisfactory for its lack of specificity, the term 'Ethiopian modern music' is able to encompass the whole complex of Ethiopian popular music. In its early stages, it was called *zemenawi zefen* or *zemenawi muzika* – *zemenawi* meaning 'modern' in Amharic, *zefen* being the Amharic word for secular folk music, and '*muzika*' a borrowed term which further separated modern music from its traditional counterpart. In the 2010s, however, modern music is mostly defined by its regional subgenres, and the word *zemenawi* is used only in contrast to *bahlawi* ('cultural'), which indicates music employing traditional instruments. Some authors have used the terms 'Ethio-jazz' or 'Ethio-groove' to define Ethiopian modern music in general, but this can be misleading, since Ethio-jazz is a subgenre of Ethiopian modern music mostly associated with the work of Mulatu Astatke, and 'Ethio-groove' is a journalistic term used in the West to describe either the 'vintage' music of the Éthiopiques series, or new international music inspired by it.

Musical Description

Ethiopia is a vast country inhabited by several different language groups, each with distinct musical traditions and practices. However, its modern music derives mostly from the secular highland music of the Amhara, Tigrinya, Oromo and Gurage people. Historically, the Amhara have constituted the cultural and political elite in the country, and as such their influence on Ethiopian modern music has been particularly significant, especially in the first period of the genre's history.

Like the traditional music from which it descends, Ethiopian modern music is mostly pentatonic. The melodic material of a song is normally based on one of four pentatonic modes called *kignit* (also transliterated as *qenet*), each characterized by a specific sequence of intervals, regardless of the starting pitch. Taking C as an arbitrary starting point, the four principal *kignit* are

Tezeta: C-D-E-G-A
Bati: C-E-F-G-B
Ambassel: C-Db-F-G-Ab
Anchihoye: C-Db-F-Gb-A

Variations on the main *kignit* are also found, notably:

Tezeta minor: C-D-Eb-G-Ab
Bati minor: C-Eb-F-G-Bb

This system of tempered pentatonic modes derives from the secular music tradition of the Ethiopian highlands, where sets of intervals close to the tempered *kignit* are frequently found. However, these are not conceived as a musical system, but rather as a pool of distinct tunings and melodic contours upon which different types of song are based. Moreover, Ethiopian traditional music is not tempered, and intervallic variations and discrepancies abound. Thus, the tempered *kignit* of modern music appear to be the result of a process of Westernization and standardization of the most common sets of intervals found in the traditional repertoire, a compositional and pedagogical method developed within music schools and other institutions in order to adapt Ethiopian music to Western instruments, staff notation and functional harmony. Not all Ethiopian modern music is rigidly based on the *kignit* system, and exceptions and experimentations with 'imported' scales abound, especially in more recent music. Still, and despite them being a somewhat recent construction, it is nonetheless the distinctive sound of the four *kignit* that many musicians and listeners identify as the 'truly Ethiopian' element of Ethiopian modern music.

Modal harmony is prevalent, that is, chords and chord progressions are built using the notes of a single mode (or *kignit*) and tend not to modulate. This results in different chord sequences being associated with different modes. For example, because the *tezeta* and *bati* minor *kignit* are, respectively, equivalent to the Western major pentatonic and minor pentatonic scales, the chord sequences built on them will be quite similar to progressions found in Western popular music. Conversely, because of their peculiar set of intervals, songs in the *ambassel* and *anchihoye kignit* will have a more 'dissonant' sequence of chords or, even more commonly, be based on a single chord or vamp throughout.

Triple meters are particularly common, and so are compound meters such as 6/8 and 12/8. Cross-rhythms that play on a two-over-three feel are also frequent, the most popular example being the drum kit accompaniment called *tchik-tchik-ka* beat. Borrowed rhythms are also used, changing through the decades depending on what foreign music is popular at a given moment (e.g., rock 'n' roll rhythms were common in the 1960s, replaced by more funk-oriented rhythms in the 1970s). Finally, rhythms belonging to the different Ethiopian nationalities play an important part in the country's popular music, despite the fact that its early history was largely Amhara-dominated. Some of these distinctive rhythms – such as the Guraginya with its driving 4/4 beat, or the Tigrinya with its asymmetrical accents – have over time become fully fledged subgenres of Ethiopian dance music.

The vocal style is highly melismatic, and an important part of a singer's skills is his/her ability to embellish a melody with glissandos, microtonal variations and rhythmic *rubato*. Vocal harmony is rare, and call-and-response sections may be found. Since the late 2000s the use of the Auto-tune digital effect on vocals has become widespread, giving a digital texture to the voice, which is sought for aesthetic reasons.

If the vocal style of Ethiopian modern music may be traced back to traditional music, the main element signifying the 'modernity' of Ethiopian modern music is its instrumentation. Although traditional instruments such as the *krar* (a five- or six-stringed lyre) or the *masinqo* (a one-stringed spike fiddle) were used in the postwar years for Westernized arrangements of Ethiopian traditional music, modern (*zemenawi*) bands were so called because they employed almost exclusively imported instruments. The dance bands of the 1950s, modeled after USA jazz orchestras, featured large brass and woodwind sections, piano, drum kit, double bass and often an accordion (the latter most probably an inheritance from the Italians). During the 1960s, smaller combos, modeled on foreign rock and soul bands, gained popularity over the larger dance bands. Brass sections became smaller, the acoustic bass was replaced by the electric bass guitar, and electric guitars and organs increasingly took the place of pianos and accordions. This type of ensemble remained common until the 1980s, when electronic keyboards and drum machines started appearing. Because they made it possible to accompany a singer without having to hire a full band, these new instruments became increasingly popular among music producers, and only live bands that already enjoyed a considerable level of success were able to stay in business. Even though exceptions abound, this trend continued in the early 2010s, with keyboards, digital samplers and computers being the favorite tools of the trade of most music producers.

Ethiopian Modern Music (Zemenawi Muzika)

The main language of Ethiopian modern music is Amharic. However, and especially since the 1990s, other Ethiopian languages are also used. In the early twenty-first century the landscape of Ethiopian popular music is comprised of several regional subgenres, and the language of the lyrics varies accordingly. Ethiopia has a rich tradition of lyrical improvisation with virtuosic use of *doubles entendres* and metaphors (a technique known as 'wax and gold,' still very much alive among the *azmari*, the traditional poet-musicians of the Ethiopian highlands). However, it has been noted that performers of popular music use much simpler lyrical techniques, with no improvisation, limited vocabulary, and direct and obvious meaning (Kebede 1976). The subject matter of songs is varied and includes the usual topics of popular music, foremost of all romantic love. A very popular song style is *Tezeta*, which in Amharic means 'memory' and by extension also 'nostalgia' (it is also the name of one of the four Ethiopian modes). *Tezeta* is a ballad, usually slow, that centers on feelings of longing, nostalgia and loss, and most singers include their own version of *Tezeta* as part of their repertoire.

Iskista is the name of Ethiopia's most popular dance style, which can be performed to both modern and traditional music. It involves shaking the shoulders and chest, along with rhythmic movements of the head and neck, while the lower part of the body remains relatively still.

History

With the exception of a short-lived military occupation by Mussolini's Italian forces (1936–41), Ethiopia was never colonized by European powers. Boasting an almost uninterrupted lineage of Amhara kings and queens dating back at least to the thirteenth century, and an even older Christian Orthodox Church, Ethiopia's encounters with the West – with its missionaries, armies, diplomats and merchants – have mostly taken place on a level of parity. These circumstances, unique among African countries, played an important part in shaping another encounter, that between Ethiopian and Western music, which eventually led to the birth of Ethiopian modern music.

According to record producer and Ethiopian music historian Francis Falceto (2002), the first significant event in the history of modern Ethiopian music was the gift of 40 brass instruments by the Russian Tsar Nicholas II to the Ethiopian emperor Menelik II in 1897, shortly after an Italian attempt to occupy the country was trounced at Adwa by the Ethiopians. A Polish musician was appointed as musical director of what became the first official brass band of the Ethiopian court, and, because being a musician was deemed an undignified profession by the Amhara, the band members were recruited from among Ethiopia's southern peoples. The function of the new court band was to play military marches in European style and national anthems for visiting foreign dignitaries, and it is worth noting that the military brass band, usually considered a legacy of colonial domination, was in this case deliberately adopted as a symbol of modernity and cosmopolitanism by the only African nation that resisted colonization (see separate entry, Brass Band Music in Ethiopia). During a 1924 visit to Jerusalem, Ras Tafari (the Ethiopian regent who would become Emperor Haile Selassie I) hired a group of young refugees from the Armenian genocide as the new official band of the Ethiopian court. Leading the orchestra was Kevork Nalbandian, an Armenian musician who during the following years set in motion a system of musical education that would be crucial in training Ethiopians in Western music performance.

After World War II Ethiopia underwent a period of state-led reconstruction and modernization which saw the foundation of a national school of music and a national theater (the latter including both a folkloric and a modern music orchestra), and the establishment of several institutional bands, such as the Addis Ababa Municipality Orchestra, the Imperial Bodyguard Band, the Police Orchestra and the Army Band. As a consequence, a new cohort of full-time salaried musicians started to consolidate in Addis Ababa and other urban centers. A number of European conductors, composers and educators were hired by Haile Selassie's government to oversee the modernization of Ethiopian music (Haile Selassie himself had spent the years of the Italian occupation in England). Throughout the 1950s and 1960s their contribution was vast and varied: among other things, they established Western art music curricula, devised compositions and arrangements for orchestras and smaller ensembles, and introduced the new sounds of Western dance music and orchestral jazz into the country. Most important, they included Ethiopian music in their work as teachers and composers, for instance by incorporating traditional Ethiopian melodies in Western art music compositions and jazz arrangements for dance bands. Thus, the practice of taking melodic (and often rhythmic) material from the secular music tradition of one of Ethiopia's many nationalities, and then giving it a modern twist by means of Western instruments, arrangements and style of performance – a formula which constitutes the very core of Ethiopian modern music – was established within institutions under the direct control of the state, and was the result of a deliberate attempt by the cultural elites of the time to train a new generation of bi-musical composers, performers and teachers proficient in both Western and Ethiopian music and able to combine the two in their work.

A perhaps less positive aspect of this institutionalization of music was that no musical activity, be it public performance, recordings or school teaching, could happen without the sanction of the state. In December 1960 a failed coup against Haile Selassie led the government to cautiously relinquish control over certain aspects of public life, and during the following decade the state's monopoly over music was also progressively loosened. In the same years, also due to the fact that in 1963 Addis Ababa had been chosen as the seat of the new Organisation for African Unity (OAU), Ethiopia's capital city underwent a further period of modernization, becoming a truly cosmopolitan metropolis. Several music clubs opened in different parts of the city, thus catering to a larger part of the population – most crucially, the urban young people – and nightlife in Addis blossomed. *Addis zemen* ('modern Addis') was how people referred to this new social and cultural era, and the music played by the modern, cosmopolitan dance bands was accordingly called *zemenawi muzika* ('modern music').

Whether accompanied by the Police Orchestra, the Army Band or another of the institutional bands, singers were the real stars of the period. Among the most popular were Tilahun Gessesse, Mahmoud Ahmed and Alemayehu Eshete, but their popularity was constantly challenged by the scores of young newcomers hoping to make it as the next big star. Being a professional musician was frowned upon by traditional Ethiopian society, but performers of modern music seemed to make an exception. Unlike the *azmari*, who played in semi-private drinking houses for small audiences, the modern performers – if successful in their career – had a real chance to climb the social ladder, gaining fame and money in the process. This changed attitude toward music performance also affected women. Prior to this period, a female performer was mostly considered a disgraceful thing, but the comparative respectability of a career in *zemenawi muzika* attracted several women to the stage, some of whom – for example, singers Bizunesh Bekele and Hirut Bekele – became leading stars of Ethiopian music.

Meanwhile, the younger generations were discovering the new, rebellious sounds of rock 'n' roll and rhythm and blues, brought to Ethiopia via imported records, the American Peace Corps volunteers stationed in the country, and the radio station of the American military base of Kagnew in the then province of Eritrea. A sizeable group of young musicians, trained within the institutional orchestras, started experimenting with those foreign genres, as well as with the imagery and performance style associated with them. As the 1960s progressed, smaller groups with electrified instruments gained popularity over the bigger dance bands, with many performers replicating the moves and stage antics of Elvis Presley, Chuck Berry and other US music icons of the time. Faster and rowdier rhythms were introduced to accompany the latest dance steps imported from the United States, as young Ethiopians were boogying, shaking and twisting their nights away on Addis's dance floors. Yet, the music wasn't just an uninventive copy of foreign genres, because in spite of its Western coating it remained unmistakably Ethiopian at its core. Melodies, vocal style, lyrics and often also rhythms were drawn from local repertoires and styles, and merely adapted to fit in with the modern arrangements required by the times. Also, not everybody embraced the new music with equal enthusiasm, and while some singers went as far as sporting an Elvis-like haircut and using English lyrics in order to better resemble their foreign models, others remained closer to the Ethiopian melodic tradition. As in so many other societies, the 1960s were a period of intense intergenerational conflict, and music clearly reflected this rift, with younger generations using the foreign, modern sounds and attitudes to distance themselves from the more traditional values and tastes of their parents.

An exception in the musical landscape of the time was Mulatu Astatke. A pianist, vibraphonist and composer trained in the United States, he returned to Ethiopia at the end of the 1960s, quickly becoming one of the most prolific composers and arrangers of the local scene. In addition to working with several singers and bands, Astatke developed a modern style of Ethiopian instrumental music – he called it Ethio-jazz – which mixed Ethiopian modes and traditional melodies with jazz and Latin arrangements. Although Ethio-jazz was not very popular at home, Astatke's influence on Ethiopia's music scene lasted for decades, and in recent years he has become an important ambassador for Ethiopian music abroad.

In 1969 the state monopoly over music production was challenged when the first truly independent Ethiopian record label, Amha Records, opened for business. Independent bands also started to appear, competing with the still-popular institutional dance bands. And when it became clear that the state would not stop these new independent ventures, the already thriving modern music scene gained even more momentum, as witnessed by the large quantity of records published and the numerous new bands formed in the five years between 1969 and 1974.

Emperor Haile Selassie was deposed through a coup in 1974, and soon after a military junta headed by Colonel Mengistu took control of the state and adopted a Marxist-Leninist ideology. Under the Derg, as Mengistu's junta was popularly called, civil life in Ethiopia became once again heavily controlled by the state. All music groups were again nationalized, permanent curfews starting as early as 6:00 p.m. virtually killed off Addis's nightlife, and the heavy censorship of the state made life very difficult for composers and performers. A further, if unrelated, challenge was presented by the introduction of cassettes, which replaced vinyl records in the mid-1970s and engendered widespread music piracy in the country, greatly reducing the income of singers, musicians and producers.

Despite these obstacles, music in Ethiopia did continue to progress. New influences such as funk and psychedelic rock were integrated into the sound of successful bands such as the Ibex Band and Walias Band, and the late 1970s and 1980s also saw a renewed interest in incorporating Ethiopia's traditional instruments into modern music, for example, in the work of Mulatu Astatke and the Tukul Band. Arguably the most popular Ethiopian band of all time, the Roha Band was formed at the end of the 1970s from the ashes of the Ibex Band and it performed extensively both in Ethiopia and abroad throughout the 1980s. Another key development of the Derg period was the introduction of electronic keyboards and drum machines, which cut the costs of music production but also reduced employment opportunities for musicians.

The new circumstances and the deep economic crisis that hit Ethiopia in the 1980s pushed several musicians to leave the country and settle abroad. One of them was singer Aster Aweke, who moved to Washington DC – home of one of the largest Ethiopian expatriate communities – after starting her career in Addis Ababa. She would become one of the most loved Ethiopian singers of the 1990s and 2000s and, having attracted the attention of the world music industry, one of the first Ethiopian musicians to gain international recognition. Another expatriate singer who has experimented with world fusion sounds is Gigi, whose albums depart from the sounds and conventions of Ethiopian modern music, yet still clearly nod to the singer's musical roots.

After the end of the dictatorship in 1991, the Ethiopian music scene started to pick up again. Finally free of the curfews, live music returned to Addis Ababa and other urban centers, to the benefit of a new generation of performers who had grown up under the Derg and could now reach a wider public by playing in nightclubs and other music venues. Most of the old veterans, such as Mahmoud Ahmed and Alemayehu Eshete, were still active after almost 20 years of dictatorship, but Ethiopian young people were mostly looking elsewhere, for example, at singer Netsanet Mellesse, one of the most popular young voices of the 1990s.

In 1998 French music producer Francis Falceto started releasing a series of CDs called *Éthiopiques*, which mostly focused on out-of-print Ethiopian 'oldies' from the late 1960s and early 1970s. The *Éthiopiques* series sparked a wave of interest among international journalists, musicians and world music fans for what was hailed as 'the golden age of Ethiopian music'. The instrumental Ethio-jazz of

Mulatu Astatke has proved particularly successful with Western listeners, and he has since toured extensively abroad and collaborated with many international musicians. Although not a mainstream phenomenon, the *Éthiopiques* series has also inspired several international bands to experiment with Ethiopian rhythms and modes, and to launch collaborative projects with Ethiopian musicians.

At the turn of the millennium Ethiopian modern music was still heavy on keyboards and drum machines, and seemingly oblivious to the international success of the *Éthiopiques* series' vintage sounds. Teddy Afro, a singer and musician who fuses Ethiopian modern music with reggae and politically engaged lyrics, emerged as the biggest Ethiopian star of the post-2000 era, but younger singers and their laptop-carrying producers soon started challenging his dominance. Since the late 2000s online videos have become the main distribution channel for new music, and while some musicians bring forward the ideas of Ethio-jazz and others experiment with reggae or hip-hop, the popular music landscape is mostly divided in regional subgenres, with Ethiopian music websites categorizing songs and videos according to their linguistic affiliation (Amharic, Tigrinya, Afaan Oromo, Guraginya, etc.). Each style comes with its language, rhythm and specific imagery, but it would be wrong to think of contemporary Ethiopian music as ethnically divided. The musicians of the new generation, while proud of their people's heritage, are also the product of a shared history shaped by modern Ethiopia's unique conditions in Africa, and as such they are a paradigm of what it means to be Ethiopian in the modern era, constantly negotiating their own positions between regional roots, Ethiopian citizenship and cosmopolitan aspirations.

Historiography

Little ethnographic research has been published on the history and practice of Ethiopian modern music, either at home or in the diaspora (see Kebede 1976; Kimberlin 1994; Shelemay 2010; Teffera 2013), and no comprehensive study has appeared to date. The writings of music producer and historian Francis Falceto remain the most extensive source of information on the first decades of Ethiopian modern music, while more recent music has so far only been addressed in popular music magazines and Internet websites.

Conclusion

Ethiopian modern music was born in the postwar years as the product of a modernizing African society that had managed to resist colonization, but still embraced cosmopolitanism. It is a form of musical expression in which cultural nationalism and modernism go hand in hand, and also one through which complex networks of affiliation can be successfully articulated. Besides having become the most popular music at home, since the early 2000s Ethiopian modern music – with its distinctive modes and rhythms – has also influenced musicians and audiences abroad, thus becoming truly international in scope.

Bibliography

Bekele, Zenebe. 1987. *Music in the Horn: A Preliminary Analytical Approach to the Study of Ethiopian Music*. Stockholm: Författares Bokmaskin.

Falceto, Francis. 2002. 'Un siècle de musique moderne en Éthiopie (precedé d'une hypothèse baroque)' [A Century of Modern Music in Ethiopia (Preceded by a Baroque Hypothesis)]. *Cahiers d'études africaines* 42(168): 711–38.

Falceto, Francis. 2005. *Abyssinie Swing: A Pictorial History of Modern Ethiopian Music*. Addis Ababa: Shama Books.

Falceto, Francis. 2006. 'Ethiopia: Land of Wax and Gold.' In *The Rough Guide to World Music: Africa & Middle East*, eds. Simon Broughton et al. London: Rough Guides, 108–16.

Kebede, Ashenafi. 1976. 'Zemenawi Muzika: Modern Trends in Traditional Secular Music of Ethiopia.' *The Black Perspective in Music* 4(3): 289–301.

Kimberlin, Cynthia Tse. 1980. 'The Music of Ethiopia.' In *Musics of Many Cultures: An Introduction*, ed. Elizabeth May. Berkeley and Los Angeles: University of California Press, 232–52.

Kimberlin, Cynthia Tse. 1994. 'Traditions and Transitions in Ethiopian Music: Events as a Catalyst for Change.' In *Proceedings of the Eleventh International Conference of Ethiopian Studies, Vol. II*, eds. Bahru Zewde et al. Addis Ababa: Addis Ababa University, Institute of Ethiopian Studies, 643–52.

Shelemay, Kay Kaufman. 2009. 'Musical Scholarship and Ethiopian Studies: Past, Present, Future.' *Journal of Ethiopian Studies* 42(1–2): 175–91.

Shelemay, Kay Kaufman. 2010. 'Music in the Ethiopian American Diaspora: A Preliminary Overview.' In

Research in Ethiopian Studies: Selected Papers of the 16th International Conference of Ethiopian Studies, Trondheim July 2007, eds. Harald Aspenet et al. Wiesbaden: Harrassowitz Verlag, 321–33.

Teffera, Timkehet. 2013. 'Canvassing Past Memories Through Təzəta.' *Journal of Ethiopian Studies* 46: 31–66.

Weisser, Stéphanie, and Falceto, Francis. 2013. 'Investigating Qənət in Amhara Secular Music: An Acoustic and Historical Study.' *Annales d'Éthiopie* 28: 299–322.

Discography

Afro, Teddy. *Yasteseryal*. Nahom Records. *2005*: Ethiopia.

Ahmed, Mahmoud. *Éthiopiques 7: Mahmoud Ahmed – Ère mèla mèla 1975*. Buda Musique 82980-2. *1999*: France.

Astatke, Mulatu. *Éthiopiques 4: Ethio Jazz & Musique Instrumentale 1969–1974*. Buda Musique 82964-2. *1998*: France.

Aweke, Aster. *Aster*. CBS Records CT 46848. *1990*: USA.

Eshete, Alemayehu. *Éthiopiques 9: Alèmayèhu Eshèté*. Buda Musique 82983-2. *2000*: France.

Éthiopiques 1: Golden Years of Modern Ethiopian Music 1969–1975 (ed. Francis Falceto). Buda Musique 82951-2. *1997*: France.

Éthiopiques 3: Golden Years of Modern Ethiopian Music 1969–1975 (ed. Francis Falceto). Buda Musique 82963-2. *1998*: France.

Éthiopiques 10: Tezeta – Ethiopian Blues & Ballads (ed. Francis Falceto). Buda Musique 82222-2. *2002*: France.

Éthiopiques 13: Ethiopian Groove – The Golden Seventies (ed. Francis Falceto). Buda Musique 82255-2. *2002*: France.

Gessesse, Tilahoun. *Éthiopiques 17: Tlahoun Gèssèssè*. Buda Musique 82266-2. *2004*: France.

Mellesse, Netsanet. *Dodge*. Dona Wana 198682. *1992*: France.

Roha Band. *Roha Band Tour 1990*. AIT Records AIT001. *1990*: Ethiopia.

Walias Band. *The Best of Walias*. Walias Records WRS 100. *1981*: USA.

Filmography

Under African Skies: Ethiopia, prod. Richard Taylor for BBC. 59 mins. Documentary.

MICHELE BANAL

Fújì

During the 1960s in post-independence Nigeria, Síkírù Àyìndé Barrister (1948–2010) pioneered and coined the term *fújì*, a Yorùbá genre of popular dance music. While Barrister was a soldier in the Nigerian army in the late 1960s, he transformed *wéré/ajísari* music, songs performed by and for Muslims during the Ramadan fast, into this new style of dance music. *Fújì* is characterized by its Islamic-influenced vocal style, Yorùbá praise poetry (*oríkì*) and driving percussion. *Fújì*'s popularity hit a peak in Nigeria and on the global stage in the late 1980s and early 1990s, and *fújì* bands continue to record their music and perform throughout Nigeria and across the globe into the twenty-first century.

After Barrister, *fújì*'s most renowned and prolific bandleader is K1, King Wasiu Àyìndé Marshal (b. 1957), credited with expanding the original *fújì* ensemble of Yorùbá drums, percussion and vocals. In the early 1980s Àyìndé introduced synthesizer, saxophone, electric and pedal steel guitar, and drum set into his band. *Fújì*'s rise to popularity in the 1980s coincided with the proliferation, marketing and pirating of audio and video recordings. From the 1980s through the early 2000s *fújì* recordings provided the soundscape for public markets, bus depots, restaurants and parties. In Nigeria, *fújì*'s performers and fan base are predominantly Yorùbá Muslims, due to the cultural specificity of *fújì*'s Yorùbá-language lyrics, praise song interludes and associations with Islam. Overseas *fújì* audiences are dominated by Yorùbá expatriates. However, the addition of synthesizer, saxophone and electric and pedal steel guitar to the *fújì* sound has made *fújì* more accessible to fans of highlife, *jùjú* and Afrobeat, the most popular genres of Nigerian dance music prior to *fújì*'s emergence on the competitive Nigerian music scene.

Origins

During the yearly Ramadan fast, aspiring male vocalists created *wéré* music – vocals accompanied by harmonica, bells or drums – to wake up Muslims in their towns to prepare the morning meal, called *sari* in Arabic, before sunrise. *Wéré* means 'quick,' referring to the music's wake-up call function. *Ajísari*, an interchangeable name for *wéré*, means 'waking up for *sari*.' Toward the end of the colonial period, in the 1950s, Yorùbá kings began to invite town performers to their palaces for *wéré* competitions to celebrate the end of the annual month-long fast. Whole towns attended to enjoy the show, judges were appointed and kings awarded the best groups with trophies. These annual competitions gave talented performers status and recognition, inspiring them to rehearse throughout the year. *Wéré* competitions became much-anticipated and competitive events, ultimately producing the first generation of *fújì* vocalists.

The origin of *fújì* is traced to what is believed to have been Barrister's divine inspiration to transform *wéré* into a popular dance music that would exist alongside other forms of Yorùbá popular music. When Barrister was making the decision to leave the army for a career in music, his friends, mentors in the music industry (notably Ebenezer Obey and King Sunny Ade) and royal advisers (including the kings of Ìbàdàn and Ìlọrin) gave him their blessings and encouragement. They believed that Barrister's talent was God-given and that he was destined to succeed as a professional musician and founder of *fújì*. Barrister was particularly inspired by the *sákárà* (round, single-skinned frame-drum) music of Yusuf Ọlátúnji and the highlife-*jùjú* fusion music of Ebenezer Obey. Barrister created the *fújì* sound by combining the *sákárà* drum, drums from the Yorùbá *dùndún* ensemble and *wéré*-style vocals.

After seeing a poster of Mount Fuji in an airport, Barrister is reputed to have named his new music after Japan's mountain of love and peace. Nigerian newspapers often described *fújì*, upon its arrival on the music scene, as 'high-energy trance dance music.' In 1973 Kollington Àyìnlá, one of Barrister's best friends in the Nigerian army, started his own *fújì* band and became a prolific performer and Barrister's musical rival. The competition between Barrister and Kollington became *fújì*'s original 'big man' rivalry and helped to propel it into national popularity.

The *Fújì* Sound

Fújì's signature sound is dominated by vocals and percussion. In order to produce a full-bodied sound, bands include many members: several vocalists, often 15 to 20 percussionists and since the 1980s a keyboardist, saxophonist/s and/or electric and pedal steel guitarist/s. Barrister's first band, Alhaji Sikiru Ayinde Barrister and His Fuji Group, was a 25-piece band. Many *fújì* bands employ percussionists who have trained within Àyàn (the spirit of the drum) lineages, extended families whose boys and young men apprentice to the profession of drumming and perform in local ensembles. While most popular music in southwestern Nigeria incorporates drumming, *fújì* relies on its extensive and diverse drum section for its sound and 'vibe.'

Àyàn lineages train professionals in two distinct drumming, singing and dancing traditions: *bàtá* and *dùndún*, each ensemble comprising at least three different drums in the same drum family. Each of these ensembles performs a repertoire whose rhythms interlock and create a rich sound for dancing and/or summoning the spirits. The supporting drums of each ensemble are responsible for the underlying rhythms that sustain and drive each song, while the master (lead) drums improvise within rigorous rhythmic structures and text frameworks. Both ensembles employ surrogate speech technologies to intone praise poetry and proverbs to communicate with the spirits and entertain. Rhythms and songs use binary (2/4 and 4/4) or ternary (12/8 and 6/8) meters, foundational patterns in West African musical styles.

Dùndún drums are the most numerous in any *fújì* ensemble, particularly the *gángan*, the smallest of the double-headed, hourglass-shaped drums. Players hold the drum, often with a strap over the left shoulder, under the left arm while striking the forward-facing goatskin head with a curved wooden stick called *ò.pá*. *Dùndún* drums are commonly known as 'talking' drums; drummers mimic the tones of the Yorùbá language by squeezing and releasing the tension straps to change the pitch of the skin to imitate speech. In the context of a *fújì* band, however, *dùndún* drums do not normally intone speech; their role is to provide a fast-paced and constant groove.

Bàtá drums are double-headed and conical, said to have been commissioned by King Ṣàngó during his fifteenth-century reign of the town of Ò.yó. Since Ṣàngó's death, *bàtá* drums have been played to invoke the Yorùbá spirits as well as for entertainment. Kollington introduced the *bàtá* rhythmic accompanying drum into the *fújì* ensemble during the 1980s. Since then several *fújì* bands include the *bàtá omele akọ* (two small drums joined together), played with two cowhide beaters called *bílálà* striking the upward-facing goatskin heads called ṣàṣá. In the 1970s bàtá drummers added another drum to the omele cluster, called omele mé.ta (three), so they could mimic the tones of the Yorùbá language. Fújì drummers have added even more drums to the cluster, increasing the melodic range. Like the dùndún drums, however, the role of the omele akọ (double) bàtá drum is not to talk but to fulfill a rhythmic function. The inclusion of bàtá in fújì bands can be controversial, particularly for devout Muslims who reject anything associated with the Yorùbá spirits. When Kollington added bàtá drums to his band, he was celebrating his cultural heritage while experimenting with a new sound, for which he coined the term 'Bàtá Fújì.'

The sákárà drummer, typically male, plays a key role in fújì bands; he constantly communicates with the lead singer/band leader, percussion section and dancers. He sits on a chair very close to the lead singer as they collaboratively determine the breaks and transitions throughout the performance. The sákárà is made of goatskin tightly stretched over a round frame. The sákárà drummer can produce different pitches by pressing his left thumb into the back of the membrane while striking the other side with a stick in his right hand. By varying the pitch in this way, skilled sákárà drummers 'talk' by mimicking the melodic contour of Yorùbá, a true-tone language with three relative pitches (Villepastour 2010, 51). Like the lead drummer in a bàtá or dùndún ensemble, the sákárà player often improvises and/or talks against the steady rhythmic accompaniment provided by the percussion section. The sákárà drummer also frequently decides when to break into a faster dance rhythm and when to pull back again into a slower-paced section that features vocals.

Fújì percussion often includes a drum set in addition to bells and rattles used in various styles of Yorùbá music. Most fújì bands include ṣè.kè.rè (gourd rattles), and many bands include agogo (metal gongs) and aro (a pair of circular iron idiophones clapped together). Syncopated chords played on the synthesizer often provide hooks, which help to make fújì songs and albums recognizable and memorable. Synthesized sound effects, such as strategically placed, high-pitched glides, were perceived as modern and edgy additions in the 1980s. Fújì saxophone and guitar styles borrow from jùjú pedal steel guitar (appropriated from country and western) and horn arrangements recalling highlife, creating a more laid-back vibe.

Fújì's vocal style is typically melismatic (whereas most Yorùbá song is syllabic) and has a nasal timbre, characteristic of Arabic singing and Quranic recitation. Vocalists frequently employ glissandi, which are often imitated by synthesizers. While most fújì vocalists have informal or no vocal training, they have learned to sing in wéré competitions, Quranic schools, prayer groups and/or social events. Teachers or group leaders often encourage talented vocalists to join competitions, after which aspiring singers may find sponsors to help launch their careers.

Many successful fújì vocalists are also skilled praise singers who have learned to sing oríkì, a Yorùbá performance genre that most Yorùbá speakers know and appreciate as part of the fabric of Yorùbá culture (Barber and Waterman 1995, 249). Since the spread of Islam into Yorùbá cities and towns from the late sixteenth century onward, Islamic singing and chanting have influenced and shaped preexisting vocal styles in the region. Thus fújì vocal styles are a synthesis of indigenous Yorùbá praise singing, Arabic singing and Quranic recitation. While many fújì songs, recordings and performances open with a prayer-like song in Arabic, often recited from the Quran, fújì's popularity transcends boundaries of religion and culture.

Fújì lyrics include a wide range of themes concerning social and political issues, morality and audience members' histories. Such themes emerge from artists' everyday lives and are stylistically rooted in ewì, a neo-traditional style of moral and topical Yorùbá poetry. Ewì songs often begin with invocations of Allah, the ancestors and/or the òrìṣà (Yorùbá gods and goddesses) and include praise songs, prayers, proverbs and stories. Some common ewì and fújì themes are wealth and poverty, success and failure, politicians and their legacies, good versus evil, people's sources of power, infidelity, secrecy, magic, greed, pregnancy, money, loyalty, war and love. True to its wéré and ewì roots, fújì artfully weaves its moral and spiritual foundation into its popular dance music themes about having fun on and off the dance floor.

Fújì as Performance and Profession

In Nigeria, in Yorùbá diasporic communities and in venues across the globe, fújì bands play for weddings, funerals, baby-naming celebrations, birthday parties and other social events, and the more famous bands play concerts for ticket holders. In Nigeria, typical *fújì* performances start in the evening and end early in the morning, lasting from six to eight hours. In addition to charging their hosts a flat rate, *fújì* bands count on the cash they earn throughout their performances as audience members 'spray' (place bills on the band members' foreheads or on the stage) the performers in exchange for being praised and entertained.

Throughout Nigeria, *fújì* performers are unionized by the state under the umbrella of The Fújì Musicians Association of Nigeria (FUMAN). FUMAN is one branch of the larger union, The Performing Musicians Association of Nigeria (PMAN). FUMAN chapters are responsible for helping performers organize, negotiate fair pay and working conditions, launch new CDs and DVDs and discuss all aspects of their profession. *Fújì* bands revolve around their bandleaders who are responsible for hiring, managing and firing band members. Successful bandleaders work with managers and promoters to secure recording contracts, performance venues and marketing deals. Some managers collaborate creatively with bandleaders, helping them with album concepts and song content.

As in other Yorùbá musical genres, *fújì* 'songs' typically last for periods of 45 minutes to an hour; thus most *fújì* CDs contain only one, two or three tracks. Typical of Muslim forms, *fújì* vocal choruses are predominantly sung in unison and employ minimal harmony. Thus, *fújì* differs from other popular Yorùbá music styles, such as *jùjú*, where vocal choruses are performed in three- to four-part harmony, derived from Christian hymnal forms. Songs generally consist of an opening prayer, lyrics sung by the lead vocalist, sections of improvised text sung by the lead vocalist and a chorus sung by lead and backup vocalists in unison. The leader (usually male) and chorus sing in call-and-response style, typical of Yorùbá vocal music. Live performances and albums consist of expansive sections, which are almost always improvised praise songs for audience members. An exemplary *fújì* front man, Barrister released over 150 recordings (1966–2010) and is revered for the tone of his voice and his gift for poetic text improvisation.

Male musicians dominate *fújì*, reflecting *fújì*'s origins in *wéré* and drumming styles. However, female Muslim artists have developed *fújì*-related styles called Islamic, *azikir and wákà*. Islamic and *azikir* are interchangeable names for this genre of women's *fújì*-related music (particularly in and around the city of Ìlọrin), while *wákà* is a more general pan-Yorùbá term for this Muslim women's genre. While numerous labels reflect slight regional variations, these styles emerged in the late 1950s and were originally performed by women vocalists for Islamic events such as weddings and celebrations for pilgrims returning from Mecca. Since the 1980s professional Muslim women vocalists have fronted their own bands and these are identical to *fújì* bands in their instrumentation. This genre differs from *fújì* in text content, aesthetics and in the gender of its performers. While its themes and aesthetics are more closely tied to Muslim morality than *fújì*, there is a significant overlap between this women's genre and *fújì*. The majority of *azikir* and *wákà* bandleaders and backup vocalists are women, while the rest of their bands are typically men. Unlike *fújì*, women performers of *azikir* and *wákà* have a dominant presence on stage and in videos.

Fújì appeals to young and old dancers alike. Signature dance steps and moves are rooted in Yorùbá dance styles that feature small and precise movements of the buttocks, hips and shoulders, while the torso is pitched slightly forward. Skilled dancers who recognize the drum breaks might choose to accentuate the drum parts with sharp movements of their buttocks, shoulders or feet. Guests often spray the hosts of the event on the dance floor with individual bills, thanking them for throwing a great party. Guests also spray other guests to compliment one another's dancing. *Fújì* videos are either mini-films, interpreting the theme of a song, or a series of dance scenes. Women dancers are often featured for their skillful and provocative dance moves. Videos are popular for their portrayals of luxury and excess through a proliferation of imagery featuring expensive clothing, cars, jewelry, clubs, nightlife and Nigerian and overseas cityscapes.

Conclusion

Fújì continues to be a favorite dance music genre for many Nigerians. Distinct from highlife, *jùjú* and Afrobeat, *fújì* grew out of Yorùbá Muslim communities. Diverse audiences appreciate *fújì*'s philosophical and moral themes as well as its infectious and danceable rhythms. New generations of *fújì* artists draw from hip-hop, rap and other popular genres to produce fusions for Nigerian and global markets, inspiring debate about the future of *fújì*'s status, style and aesthetics. While its sound has changed since its birth in the 1960s – with the inclusion of synthesizer, electric and steel pedal guitar, horn sections and drum set in the 1980s – *fújì* is still rooted in Yorùbá percussion and vocal styles that emerged from nineteenth-century drumming and centuries-old vocal genres.

Bibliography

Abiodun, Olowoseunre. 2011. *Applause for a Lyric Reformer: Late Chief (Dr.) Mohammed Sikiru Ayinde Balogun MFR Baala of Lagos, Agbaakin Babagunwa of Ibadan Land*. Lagos: Great Nation Publication.

Barber, Karen, and Waterman, Christopher. 1995. 'Traversing the Global and the Local: Fújì Music and Praise Poetry in the Production of Contemporary Yorùbá Popular Culture.' In *Worlds Apart: Modernity Through the Prism of the Local*, ed. Daniel Miller. London: Routledge, 240–62.

Euba, Akin. 1971. 'Islamic Musical Culture Among the Yoruba: A Preliminary Survey.' In *Music and History in Africa*, ed. Klaus Wachsmann. Evanston, IL: Northwestern University Press, 171–81.

Euba, Akin. 1989. 'Jùjú, Fújì and the Intercultural Aspects of Modern Yoruba Popular Music.' In *Essays on Music in Africa, vol. 2: Intercultural Perspectives*. Bayreuth, Germany: Bayreuth African Studies and Elekoto Music Center, 1–30.

Euba, Akin. 1990. *Yoruba Drumming: The Dùndún Tradition*. Bayreuth, Germany: Bayreuth African Studies Series.

Klein, Debra L. 2007. *Yorùbá Bàtá Goes Global: Artists, Culture Brokers, and Fans*. Chicago, IL: University of Chicago Press.

Klein, Debra L. 2012. 'A Political Economy of Lifestyle and Aesthetics: Yorùbá Artists Produce and Transform Popular Culture.' *Research in African Literatures* 43(4): 128–46.

Ọlátúnji, Michael O. 2012. 'Modern Trends in the Islamized Music of the Traditional Yorùbá: Concept, Origin, and Development.' *Matatu* 40: 447–55.

Omojola, Bode. 1995. *Nigerian Art Music*. Ibadan: Institut Français de Recherche en Afrique (IFRA), University of Ibadan.

Omojola, Bode. 2012. *Yorùbá Music in the Twentieth Century: Identity, Agency, and Performance Practice*. Rochester, NY: University of Rochester Press.

Peel, John D. Y. 2000. *Religious Encounter and the Making of the Yoruba*. Bloomington, IN: Indiana University Press.

Villepastour, Amanda. 2010. *Ancient Text Messages of the Yorùbá Bàtá Drum: Cracking the Code*. Farnham, UK: Ashgate Publishing Limited.

Discography

Wasiu Àyìndé

Àyìndé, Alhaji Wasiu Barrister, and His Fuji Commanders. *Mecca Special*. Omo Aje OLPS 0268. *1981*: Nigeria.

Àyìndé, Alhaji Wasiu Barrister, and His Tarazo Fuji Commanders. *Ise Logun Ise*. Omo Aje OLPS 1315. *1984*: Nigeria.

Àyìndé, Alhaji Wasiu Barrister, and His Tarazo Fuji Commanders. *Talazo System*. Omo Aje OLPS 0311. *1984*: Nigeria.

Àyìndé, Alhaji Wasiu Barrister, and The Royal Inter-Fuji Messiah. *Adieu Awolowo*. Talazo TRLP 001. *1987*: Nigeria.

Àyìndé, Alhaji Wasiu Barrister, and The Royal Inter-Fuji Messiah. *Talazo in London*. Omo Aje OLPS 1351. *1987*: Nigeria.

Àyìndé, Dr. Wasiu Barrister, and The Tarazo International Fuji Messiahs. *Consolidation*. The Ultimate Music TUMMC 001. *1994*: Nigeria.

Àyìndé, King Wasiu Marshal 1, and The Ultimate Band with Blakky & Bunmi Sanya Legacy. *Legacy*. The Ultimate Music TUMLP 003. *1996*: Nigeria.

Àyìndé, King Wasiu Marshal 1. *Talazo Fuji Music Party*. Womad WSCD 101. *1997*: Nigeria.

K1 De Ultimate. *K1 at 50*. Sarola J. Music & Films. *2006*: Nigeria.

K1 De Ultimate. *Tribute to My Mentor Barry Wonder*. Omega Music. *2011*: Nigeria.

Kollington Àyìnlá

Àyìnlá, President Kollington, and His New Fuji System. *Omo Mariwo*. Emi Nemi 075. *1975*: Nigeria.

Àyìnlá, Kollington. *Africa Apartheid*. Emi Nemi 298. *1978*: Nigeria.

Àyìnlá, Alhaji Kollington, and His African Fuji 78 Organization. *American Yankee*. Kollington KRLPS 021. *1987*: Nigeria.

Àyìnlá, Alhaji Kollington, and His African Fuji 78 Organization. *Late Chief Obafemi Awolowo*. Kollington KRLPS 020. *1987*: Nigeria.

Àyìnlá, Alhaji Kollington, and His African Fuji Eaglets. *Ijo Yoyo*. Kollington KRLPS 035. *1990*: Nigeria.

Àyìnlá, Alhaji Kollington, and His African Fuji Eaglets. *Ijo Mbe*. Kollington KRLPS 039. *1993*: Nigeria.

Àyìnlá, Alhaji Kollington, and His African Fuji Eaglets. *Democracy*. Kollington KRLC 048. *1998*: Nigeria.

Àyìnlá, Alhaji Kollington, and His African Fuji Eaglets. *Fuji Raggae*. Babs Video & Music Co. KRLC 051. *2001*: Nigeria.

Àyìnlá, Alhaji Kollington, and His African Fuji Megastar. *Kebe Lomo*. Babs Video & Music Co. KRLC 055. *2003*: Nigeria.

Àyìnlá, General Kollington. *Back to Sender*. Corporate Pictures. *2007*: Nigeria.

Adewale Àyùbá

Àyùbá, Adewale. *Bubble*. Flame Tree FLTRCD 518. *1994*: London.

Àyùbá, Adewale, and His Bonsue Fuji Organization. *Fuji Time*. Agogo/Qbadisc AG 9501. *1996*: New York.

Àyùbá. *Gunshot*. Cooperate Pictures and Records CPRLC 08. *2001*: Nigeria.

Àyùbá. *Ijo Fuji*. Jooat Records Company. *2004*: Nigeria.

Àyùbá. *Mellow*. BFB Nigeria Ltd. *2004*: Nigeria.

Síkírù Àyìndé Barrister

Barrister, Síkírù Àyìndé, and His Ajisari Group. *Ejeka Gbo T'Olorun*. Niger Songs. *1966*: Nigeria.

Barrister, Síkírù Àyìndé, and His Supreme Fuji Commanders. *E Sinmi Rascality*. Siky Oluyole SKOLP 017. *1982*: Nigeria.

Barrister, Síkírù Àyìndé, and His Supreme Fuji Commanders. *Nigeria*. Siky Oluyole SKOLP 022. *1983*: Nigeria.

Barrister, Síkírù Àyìndé, and His Supreme Fuji Commanders. *Military*. Siky Oluyole SKOLP 025. *1984*: Nigeria.

Barrister, Síkírù Àyìndé, and The African International Music Ambassadors. *America Special*. Siky Oluyole SKOLP 034. *1986*: Nigeria.

Barrister, Síkírù Àyìndé, and The African International Music Ambassadors. *Barry Wonder at 40*. Siky Oluyole SKOLP 040. *1987*: Nigeria.

Barrister, Síkírù Àyìndé, and The African International Music Ambassadors. *Fuji Garbage*. Siky Oluyole SKOLP 041. *1988*: Nigeria.

Barrister, Síkírù Àyìndé, and The Musical Legend of Common-Wealth. *Precaution*. Siky Oluyole SKOLP 054. *1995*: Nigeria.

Barrister, Síkírù Àyìndé. *Millennium Stanza*. Ivory Music BBML 05. *2000*: Nigeria.

Barrister, Síkírù Àyìndé, Àyìnlá, General Kollington, and K1 D Ultimate. *Great Day/Ojo Nla*. Lati Alagbada & Sons Co. *2007*: Nigeria.

Alao Adekunle Malaika

Malaika, King Sule Alao Adekunle. *Masterpiece*. 1995. Babalaje Music. *2013*: Nigeria.

Malaika, King Sule Alao Adekunle. *Proper Music*. Babalaje Music. *2013*: Nigeria.

Malaika. *Malaika*. Sony Music Entertainment South Africa. *2003*: South Africa.

Malaika. *Sekunjalo*. SBME Africa (Pty) Ltd. *2007*: South Africa.

Malaika. *Mmatswale*. SBME Africa (Pty) Ltd. *2009*: South Africa.

Abass Àkàndé Obesere

Obesere, Abass Akande. *Asakasa*. Master Sound Ltd. *2012*: Nigeria.

Obesere, Abass Akande. *OBTK*. Master Sound Ltd. *2012*: Nigeria.

Obesere, Pk1st. *American Faaji Series*. *2010*: Stingomania Records: Nigeria.

Saheed Oṣupa

Oṣupa, Saheed. *Fuji Fadisco*. Alasco Films and Records. *1992*: Nigeria.

Oṣupa, Dr. Saheed Saridon P. *London Delight*. Bayowa Films & Records International. *N.d.*: Nigeria.

Oṣupa, King Dr. Saheed. *Saraki of Ilorin*. High Kay (Q) Dancent Ltd. *2013*: Nigeria.

Wasiu Àlàbí Pasuma
Pasuma, Wasiu Àlàbí. *Recognition*. 1993. Sarolaj Music & Films Int'l. *2013*: Nigeria.
Pasuma, Wasiu Àlàbí. *Orobokibo*. 1995. Sarolaj Music & Films Int'l. *2013*: Nigeria.
Pasuma, Wasiu Àlàbí. *Judgement*. 2004. Sarolaj Music & Films Int'l. *2013*: Nigeria.
Pasuma, Alhaji Wasiu Àlàbí. *Entertainer*. 2001. Sarolaj Music & Films Int'l. *2013*: Nigeria.
Pasuma, Otunba Fuji Wasiu Àlàbí. *Fuji Motion*. Sarolaj Music & Films Int'l. *2013*: Nigeria.

DEBRA L. KLEIN

Funaná

Funaná is an accordion-based dance music from the island of Santiago in Cabo Verde that is associated with the Badiu, residents of the interior who have stubbornly maintained their own traditions despite Portuguese repression. During the colonial era *funaná* was denounced by the Portuguese authorities for its 'revolutionary' content and by the Catholic Church for the perceived erotic nature of the accompanying dance.

Musical Features

Traditional *funaná* is played on the *gaita*, a two-button melodeon, and the *ferro*, a meter-long iron rasp that is scraped with a kitchen knife. When there are lyrics, the *gaiteiro* (*gaita* player) alternates between four bars of singing and four bars of playing. The performers are generally male, but occasionally the wife or daughter of the *gaiteiro* may sing or play the *ferro*.

The harmony is built on the alternation of the *gaita*'s two chords: one chord on the push, one on the pull. The rate of harmonic change is one chord per bar. Depending on the key of the *gaita*, the relationship between the two chords can be a whole step (I-VII or i-VII) or a perfect fourth (I-V or i-vm7). The melodic range is fairly narrow and disjunct, typically arpeggiations of the alternating chords.

The *ferro* player subdivides the pulse into a pattern that repeats every two beats and interlocks with the push-pull movement of the *gaita* (see Example 1).

Tempos are relatively quick and specifically chosen to match the accompanying couples' dance, which

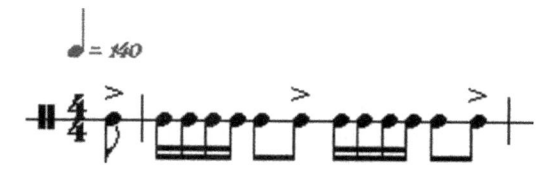

Example 1: *Ferro* rhythm

can be very close or more chaste, depending on the occasion.

Traditionally *funaná* is sung in the Kriolu of Santiago, which is sometimes unintelligible to other Cabo Verdeans and certainly to the Portuguese. Prior to independence, lyrics dealing with the realities of Badiu life (such as hunger, starvation, lack of rain, difficulty of travel, romantic problems and sexual innuendo), based on concrete geographical references to Santiago's countryside, were forbidden because they reflected negatively on the Portuguese administration and were believed to foment revolution.

History

Funaná is associated with the Badiu, descendants of slaves who escaped to the interior of Santiago from the fifteenth century onwards and who, owing to geography and distance, were able to retain a degree of cultural autonomy from the Portuguese government. The term itself is derived from the Portuguese verb '*vadiar*,' meaning 'to idle or loaf,' and was applied derogatorily to a population considered backward and more African than other Cabo Verdeans. After independence the term came to be used with pride by those from the entire island of Santiago, not just the interior.

The *gaita*, initially called *gaita de fole* (literally 'bagpipe'), may have arrived in the interior of the island as early as 1902. No doubt due to its portability and strident volume, it was quickly adopted to accompany dances at parties and life cycle festivities, often appearing in conjunction with the *batuque* dance. Initially the *gaita* was used to play waltzes, *mornas*, *viras* and marches, and by the middle of the 1920s a genre built around *badjo di gaita* (accordion dances) began to take form. Around the 1930s a rhythm known as *camino de ferro* (railroad), perhaps based on the march, developed from the *badjo di gaita* repertoire. This rhythm, along with adaptations of existing couples' dances, the sound of the *gaita* and lyrics reflecting the realities of Badiu life, came together to create what is now known as *funaná*. Most sources agree that the term itself is a recent development, probably dating from the 1970s. The derivation of the term is unknown, but the popular version involves a humorous story about two well-known players, Senhores Funa and Naná.

By the late 1960s the popularity of traditional *funaná* faded in favor of recordings at private parties and *boites* (discotheques). However, after independence in 1975 the new socialist regime supported music and arts in order to forge a postcolonial identity for Cabo Verde. In 1980 a group known as Bulimundo (Shake up the World), led by the charismatic figure known simply as Katchás and with the distinctive vocals of Zeca di Nha Reinalda, made musical history by performing a modernized version of *funaná*. This new electrified form replaced the *gaita* with guitar or keyboards and the *ferro* with a drum set, and it added an electric bass. The music of Bulimundo, and, later, Finaçon, became the sound of Cabo Verdean independence and the music of an entire generation, in both the islands and the diaspora communities. There were, however, many Cabo Verdeans who were highly critical of *funaná*'s post-independence popularity because they felt that the music of the Badiu, whom they considered backward and uneducated, was not representative of Cabo Verde.

In the 1990s the popularity of *funaná* waned in favor of *cabo-zouk*; however, in 1997, the group Ferro Gaita produced a powerful new hybrid combining electric bass and percussion with the *gaita* and *ferro*. This re-popularized *funaná* gave traditional *gaita* players such as Semi Lopi and Kode di Dona opportunities to join the ensembles.

Conclusion

Repressed by the Portuguese during the colonial period and criticized as unsophisticated after independence, *funaná* has lost much of its political divisiveness. Although its roots clearly lie on the island of Santiago, it is not uncommon for those from other islands and the diaspora to perform *funaná* as it has taken its place in the pan-Cabo Verdean musical repertoire. (For more on *funaná* in the Cabo Verdean diaspora, see Funaná [in Portugal], Vol. XI, Genres: Europe.)

Bibliography

Gonçalves, Carlos. 1998. 'Kab verd band' [Cabo Verde Band]. In *Descoberta das Ilhas de Cabo Verde* [Discovery of the Cabo Verde Islands], ed. José Maria Almeida. Praia, Cabo Verde: Archivo Histórico Nacional (Cabo Verde), 178–207.

Hurley-Glowa, Susan. 1991. 'Cape Verdean Funaná: Voice of the Badius.' Unpublished master's thesis, Department of Music, Brown University.

Hurley-Glowa, Susan. 1997. *Batuko and Funáná: Musical Traditions of Santiago, Republic of Cape Verde*. Unpublished Ph.D. dissertation, Brown University.

Monteiro, Vladimir. 1998. *Les musiques du Cap-Vert* [The Musics of Cabo Verde]. Paris: Éditions Chandeigne.

Veiga, Emanual Antero Garcia da. 1982. '"Badjo di gaita" na Ilha de Santiago (1 & 2)' [Accordion Music on the Island of Santiago]. *Voz di Povo*, VII(312): 6–7; VII(313): 5.

Discography

Bulimundo. *Djâm Branku Dja*. Black Power Records 17013, LP 1942. *1981*. Netherlands.

Bulimundo. *Bulimundo*. Black Power Records 17014, LP 1943. *1982*: Netherlands.

Cap Vert: Anthologie 1959–1992. Buda Musique 92614-2. *1994*: France.

Ferro Gaita. *Fundu Baxu*. CDS Productions FG970108. *1997*: Cabo Verde.

Ferro Gaita. *Rei di Tabanka*. Ferro Gaita Productions (no number). *1999*: Cabo Verde.

Finaçon. *Funaná*. Mélodie CD 79539 2. *1990*: France.

Finaçon. *Kel Ki Ta Da … Ta Da*. Sonovox 11.316-4. *1995*: Portugal.

Tavares, Noberto. *Volta pa Fonti*. Do-La-Si (no number). *1979*. Portugal.

Filmography

Journey of a Badiu: The Story of Cape-Verdian Musican Norberto Tavares, dir. Susan Hurley-Glowa. 2010. USA. 54 minutes. Documentary.

Songs of the Badius, dir. Gei Zantzinger. 1986. USA. 36 minutes. Original music by Bibinha Cabral and Antoni Denti d'oro. Documentary.

JOANNE HOFFMAN

See also **Funaná (Vol. XI, Europe)**

Gahu

Gahu or (*agahu*) is a West African neo-traditional drum-dance that became popular during the mid-twentieth century in Ghana, Togo and Benin. It is an up-tempo, polyrhythmic music played in syncopated 4/4 and 2/2 time, and its ensembles consist of male drummers and male and female singers and dancers. The singers use call-and-response between cantor and chorus, while the dancers perform in a counter-clockwise circle. *Gahu* music is not a ceremonial or ritual music, but rather a recreational musical type played at festive social occasions. *Gahu* groups are organized as social clubs with treasurers, chairman and other specialized leaders and these clubs not only play music but also serve a social welfare function.

According to Kobla Ladzekpo and Alan Eder, *gahu* was created shortly before World War II by Egun-speaking people from the Republic of Benin (formerly Dahomey) who were living in the coastal town of Badagry, Lagos State, Nigeria. Egun is a Yorùbá dialect spoken in Lagos State and also in parts of the neighboring republic of Benin. Badagry itself was a slave port and area of early missionary activity situated halfway between Lagos and Cotonu, the Capital of the Benin Republic. These Egun speakers had played *gumbe/goombay*, a frame drum dance music itself originally imported by Jamaican Maroons in 1800 to the West African city of Freetown in Sierra Leone, from where it spread into about 20 West and Central African countries, including the Republic of Benin and Nigeria.

When the Egun speakers modified the preexisting recreational music style around the 1930s and began using local hand-carved peg drums rather than frame drums, they changed the name to *agahu*, which means 'metal vehicle' or 'airplane' from the names for iron (*ga*) and vehicle (*hu*). According to Ladzekpo and Eder, the name was created around the time the Egun-speaking people saw their first airplane, although it has also been said that *gahu* means 'money,' specifically metal coins (Locke 1987).

Ewe migrant fishermen visiting the Badagry area of Nigeria adopted the music and, according to Ladzekpo and Eder, it was the Ewe fisherman Kofi Dey who brought *gahu* to the Volta Region in southeastern Ghana in 1950. *Gahu* subsequently became a popular recreational music of the southern Ewe of southeast Ghana and continues to be played there using local rattles (*axatse*), double-headed bell (*gonkogui*) and peg drums constructed with wooden slats and metal hoops in the manner of wooden barrels. The four types of drum are the lead *boba* and the accompanying *sogo*, *kidi* and small *kagan* drums.

After Ghana's independence in 1957, the government encouraged the performance of traditional and neo-traditional music and dance as part of Ghana's national cultural policy to use indigenous artistic resources to help develop a national identity. As a result, *gahu* began to be played at national festivals and arts councils. Moreover, *gahu* and other forms of ethnic music were taught at schools and universities. As a result, beginning in the 1960s *gahu* music and dance were choreographed and taught by Professor A.M. Opoku and others of the School of Performing Arts of the University of Ghana. In the early twenty-first century this music is still featured in university students' drumming and dancing classes. At the same time, *gahu* continues to be played in the Ewe-speaking Volta Region of Ghana – and indeed Ewe communities in the big cities – as a communal activity for local social events such as marriages, the festive side of local funerals and children's naming ceremonies.

Bibliography

Eder, Alan and Ladzekpo, Kobla. 1989. Personal communication with the author (18 February).

Gorlin, Dan. 2000. *Songs of West Africa*. Forest Knolls, CA: Alokli West African Dance. (includes CD.)

Hartigan, Royal. 1995. *West African Rhythms for Drumset*. Miami: Manhattan Music Inc.

Jones, A.M. 1959. *Studies in African Music*. London: Oxford University Press.

Locke, David. 1987. *Drum Gahu: An Introduction to African Rhythm*. Incline Village, NY: White Cliffs Media Company. (Includes CD.)

Nketia, J. H. Kwabena. 1963. *African Music in Ghana*. Evanston, IL: Northwestern University Press.

E. JOHN COLLINS

Ghoema Musical Complex

In Cape Town, South Africa, the summer season, which coincides with Christmas and New Year, is a particularly festive time. These two dates are celebrated with centuries-old cultural practices to which lower-middle- and working-class Capetonians look forward with much anticipation. Three practices, referred to as 'disciplines' by the participating members, are particularly prevalent in the city and its neighborhoods. These disciplines are located within the Creole community, referred to as colored people since the beginning of the twentieth century. 'Colored' is a racialized designation for people of mixed descent, often perceived as of mixed race by the segregationist colonial and apartheid ideologues. They are constituted from the autochthonous Khoekhoe, slaves whom the Dutch imported, once they had colonized the Cape in 1652, from places such as Indonesia, India, Mozambique and Madagascar, as well as the Europeans who intermingled with the slaves. In the complexity of race relations in South Africa, colored communities have emerged largely within the black/white interstices and have remained marginal to the sociocultural and political landscape. Their ancestral area is the Western Cape, where most still live and where several of their expressive practices can be witnessed over the festive season in the summer months from December through March. The three disciplines may be designated as the ghoema musical complex (Bruinders 2017), as all three are characterized by a particular syncopated rhythm, which has become emblematic of Cape Town and is referred to as the *ghoema* rhythm (see entry on Ghoemaliedjie).

The three disciplines are the Minstrel troupes (referred to as *klopse*), the Malay choirs and the Christmas bands. All three share much in terms of their organizational operations, although they are distinct cultural practices, associated with distinct performance genres and repertoires (except that the *klopse* and the Malay choirs have some repertoire in common) and the members perceive them as separate cultural practices. Other shared commonalities are the annual street parades; house visitations with the consumption of food; the wearing of uniforms; performing music; and competitions held at stadia. The main street parades take place in close temporal proximity to each other: the Christmas bands ring in Christmas morning and the Malay choirs and *klopse* announce the New Year on 31 December and 2 January, respectively. While the members of the Christmas bands are predominantly Christians, the Malay choirs are predominantly Muslims who, like most of the South African Creole community, trace part of their ancestry to the Southeast Asian slaves brought to the Cape by the Dutch.

Three Parading Disciplines
Minstrel/Klopse Carnival

Of the three disciplines, the *klopse* are by far the largest grouping and the best known, not only due to their long history but also because of the excitement they arouse at each annual parade. Thousands of colorful participants join the parade, which can last well into the night. People line the city streets, some booking their places a day or two beforehand so that they obtain the best spot to see and cheer for their favorite troupe. Their costumes are made of satin, a loose-fitting, colorful jacket and trousers, somewhat like pyjamas, with sandshoes, topped off with a hat and a little umbrella. Along the parade they perform *passies* (inimitable dance steps) accompanied by a large brass band, *ghoema* drums (single-headed barrel drum) and the *tamboor* (a little frame drum) as well as tambourines and bass drums. The younger generation often perform a special dance or movement routine at prime spots along the route. A *voorloper* (drum major) leads the entire carnival group – which can number anything from a couple of hundred to a couple of thousand – performing his individual *passies* and other specially rehearsed movements.

The *klopse* have historically paraded in the city center on the second day of New Year, which was the annual slave holiday in the Cape under Dutch rule, a day when slaves paraded in the city center wearing outlandish costumes and playing on musical instruments (Martin 1997). The *klopse*, associated with carnivalesque celebrations, were influenced by US blackface minstrelsy (see Cockrell 1987 and Erlmann 1991, 1996) and were referred to by the English as 'coons.' They consist of members of both religious groups and have for years been regarded in a derogatory manner, particularly by those colored people aspiring to middle-class respectability. Their annual competitions, which occur in stadia from 2 January, have been formalized since 1907, although the annual occurrence was not always regular at first. The *klopse* participate in these competitions every Saturday in January and February, until each troupe has taken part in the various knockout and final rounds. Various trophies are competed for and are adjudicated in several categories, including musical items, marching, costumes and dance routines.

Malay Choirs

On New Year's Eve the Malay choirs, now referred to as *Nagtroepe* (night troupes), parade in the city center in dull-colored tracksuits, performing *passies* in a similar manner to the *klopse*, singing *moppies* (comic songs) along designated streets, brandishing long sticks covered in two-tone striped wrapping paper and used as percussive instruments, beating rhythms on the streets as they dance along. The parade ends in front of a community hall in Rose Street, *Bo-Kaap* (literally above the Cape) – a historical Muslim neighborhood on the slopes of Signal Hill above the city of Cape Town. At this venue, they sing the 200- to 300-year-old *Nederlandsliedjies* (Dutch songs) with suitable reverence. Their competitions occur in large city or community halls from the early evening on Saturdays and Sundays in February and March. They perform a repertoire of songs for chorus and soloists such as the *moppie* and *Nederlandslied* (see separate entries). Their final competition occurs at a stadium, where they perform marching routines and present carnival floats on which they are also adjudicated. For the competitions their uniform consists of a suit or blazer with contrasting colored trousers and a red fez, which symbolize their religious affiliations. Malay choirs proffer a sung repertoire accompanied by string instruments such as violins, cellos, double bass, mandolins, ukuleles, guitars and banjos, giving the music an Iberian texture. The *ghoema* drum is used only to accompany the *moppie*.

Christmas Bands

The Christmas bands are far less visible than the celebrated Minstrel Carnival or the Malay choirs, even though their reach is much wider across the Western Cape Province. There are about 80 bands in the Western Cape, ranging in membership from 20 to over 200 members, which makes them, in comparative terms, much smaller bands than the *klopse*. They are nominally Christians; they have close relationships with churches but are not affiliated to them. They subscribe to Christian ethics and perform Christian hymns and marches and are busiest on Sundays, the Christian Sabbath. Their competitions consist of several categories, the most important being: the 'solo,' the prescribed piece; 'best-dressed band,' the uniform review; and the 'grand march past,' in which bands march in strict platoon formation. Their uniform consists of dull-colored trousers with matching shoes, a brighter-colored blazer with matching shirt and tie, and a hat with a feather placed dashingly on the right-hand side. The band consists of various wind instruments, accompanied by a small string section; guitars, banjos and cellos plucking a bass line; and an accordion filling in the harmonies.

Christmas bands belong to Christmas Bands Unions, which in turn belong to two Christmas bands boards (large affiliations). The unions and boards organize the competitions at different levels: bands compete against each other in the union competitions, and unions compete against each other in the board competitions. It is particularly when they are out in the streets, parading in the city or neighborhoods, that their ethical principles of discipline, order and respectability are revealed. They march in strict tempo, executing platoon-like marches while respectfully playing Christian songs (mostly) on wind and string instruments, thus announcing their Christian affiliations.

Commentary

All three disciplines have been influenced by Western cultural and military practices on display in the early years of the Cape Colony. Practices such as carolling, Dutch traditions around Twelfth Night, military uniform reviews, Salvation Army and Church Lads Brigade marches as well as church brass bands have all been absorbed into these disciplines. Their annual house visitations mark their renewal of friendships with feasting and goodwill messages. They are almost defiant in their maintenance of erstwhile neighborhood connections, which have been destroyed through apartheid policies of forced removals, resulting in the dislocation of colored communities and, for a short while, their cultural practices. Since the late twentieth century they have hired buses to take them to greet their former neighbors on the day of their annual city parade and over weekends throughout the festive season. The buses stop a distance from the former neighbors' homes; the members disembark and then parade to these homes. In this way they map out and enact a sense of community and place through the memory of and nostalgia for those places once regarded as home. Their house visitations are especially poignant, as the community members' responses are often very emotional – either jubilant or, in the case of older people in particular, quite tearful as they remember days gone by.

The notions of discipline and order underline all these practices. Even though the *klopse* parade through Cape Town on 2 January may appear disorderly and chaotic, with members doing different steps – some dancing, others walking rather tiredly toward the end of the parade – they have usually spent many hours rehearsing what they are going to present. With such large numbers involved, in order for them to pull off anything at all they need to adhere to very strict discipline. Martin (2001) suggests that there is a play on dis/order in many carnival practices around the world, and it is useful to think about carnival as a temporary social disorder (a spectacular disruption) before a return to the necessary and much-appreciated social order of the everyday.

These notions of discipline and order relate to the politics of respectability that emerges strongly within the Malay choirs and Christmas bands. Often this idea of respectability is expressed in relation to the *klopse*, who, like all carnival revelers, are seemingly about wild abandonment and the lack of decency. Malay choir and Christmas band leaders often distance themselves from the *klopse* and this express lack of decency and disorder. Nevertheless, the members of these cultural practices are very supportive of each other and their organizations and the musicians often double up in the different disciplines where they are needed. Although it may seem contradictory, being a minstrel almost calls for a different person(ality) than that of a Christmas band or Malay choir member. In these cases, the subjective and ontological condition of participating in these different practices requires a conscious shift in one's relation to the world and way of being in the world. The behavior expected from a minstrel can never be condoned in the more 'respectable' disciplines, while the various uniforms, which act as masks, condone or disdain the different behaviors within the disciplines.

Bibliography

Bruinders, Sylvia. 2017. *Parading Respectability: The Cultural and Moral Aesthetics of the Christmas Bands Movement in the Western Cape, South Africa*. Grahamstown: NISC Publishers, African Humanities Edited Series.

Cockrell, Dale. 1987. 'Of Gospel Hymns, Minstrel Shows, and Jubilee Singers: Towards Some Black South African Musics.' *American Music*. 5(4): 415–32.

Erlmann, Veit. 1991. 'A Feeling of Prejudice: Orpheus McAdoo and the Virginia Singers in South Africa.' In *African Stars: Studies in Black South African Performance*. Chicago and London: University of Chicago Press, 21–53.

Erlmann, Veit. 1996. *Nightsong: Performance, Power, and Practice in South Africa*. Chicago and London: University of Chicago Press.

Martin, Denis-Constant. 1997. '"The Famous Invincible Darkies," Cape Town's Coon Carnival: Aesthetic Transformations, Collective Representations, and Social Meanings in the Twentieth Century.' In *Confluences: Cross-Cultural Fusions in Music and Dance. Proceedings of the First South African Dance Conference Incorporating the 15th Symposium on Ethnomusicology*, ed. Andrew Tracy. Cape Town: University of Cape Town School of Dance, 297–333.

Martin, Denis-Constant. 2001. 'Politics Behind the Mask: Studying Contemporary Carnivals in Political Perspective; Theoretical and Methodological Suggestions.' Unpublished paper, Centre for International Research and Studies, Paris.

YouTube

(all accessed 23 April 2018)

Klopse

Minstrel Carnival Rocks Cape Town: https://www.youtube.com/watch?v=nvOyK4w-N0c

Malay Choirs

Marines Malay Choir 1st Prize Nederlandslied: https://www.youtube.com/watch?v=mC9kKEg4BOk

Ottomans Sporting Club Malay Choir Afrikaans Moppie Gertie Top 8: https://www.youtube.com/watch?v=Qi9oyCP-4YY

Waseef Piekaan Afrikaans Music / The Cape Argus Bo Kaap DISTRICT 6 RAW @ Cape Town Stadium 2018: https://www.youtube.com/watch?v=h_nA_yDLd1A

Christmas Bands

Boland Xmas Choir Bands (2015): https://www.youtube.com/watch?v=m_i6Kn9ptLs

SYLVIA R. BRUINDERS

Ghoemaliedjie

The *ghoemaliedjie* (older spelling is *ghommaliedjie*, literally meaning 'little drum song') is a medley of ditties, composed spontaneously and accompanied by the *ghoema* (pronounced goomah) drum, which is performed at life-cycle celebrations and community events of the Creole peoples in the Western Cape, South Africa. It is a lively song, with what may often seem like nonsensical words and unrelated texts, and it has historically accompanied couple dancing. Kirby (1939, 480) suggests that the name *ghomma* (or *ghoema*) is related to the Bantu word *ngoma*, which is a common term for drum in many sub-Saharan African cultures. *Ngoma* also refers to various drum dances in East Africa and it is used by the Arab people of Zanzibar as well.

Ghoemaliedjies emerged from the pastimes of enslaved Africans and ex-slaves who were brought by the Dutch to the Cape Colony beginning in the mid-1600s from Dutch territories in the East Indies and other places situated in the Indian Ocean. The majority of slaves came from present-day Indonesia, India, Madagascar and Mozambique. On 2 January the slaves were given the day off and they spent it making music and dancing at picnics. Historically, the *ghoemaliedjie* or *afkloplied* (rhythm song) was sung between the verses of a Dutch song which accompanied a circle dance, while the *ghoemaliedjie* facilitated couple dancing at the picnics.

Ghoemaliedjies have simple repetitive melodies and chord structures. The *ghoema* drum, a single-headed barrel drum originally made from a wine cask, is held under the left arm and played with both hands alternating; the left hand marks the beat and the right hand plays the syncopated *ghoema* rhythm (Example 1).

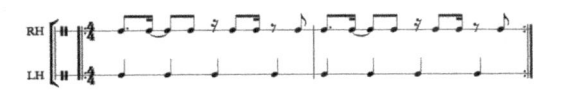

Example 1: The *ghoema* rhythm

The *ghoema* rhythm, an underlying rhythm also found in Western Cape musical practices such as the minstrels, Malay choirs, Christmas bands and Cape jazz, has become emblematic of the music of Creole peoples.

'Daar kom die Alibama' ('Here comes the *Alabama*') is the most well-known and quintessential *ghoemaliedjie*. Textually, the subject matter of the first melody and verse concerns the arrival of the Confederate steamer, *Alabama*, in Table Bay in 1863 and its capture of the Federal ship *Sea Bride*. The second melody and verse refer to a bed made of reeds offered to the first freed female slave and also imply a sexual promise, while the third melody and verse name the months of the year, referring to the practice of renaming slaves with surnames derived from the months in which they arrived at the Cape.

Closely resembling the *ghoemaliedjie* rhythmically is the *moppie*, a comic song used to poke fun at serious matters, which is a competitive genre sung at the Minstrel Carnival and Malay Choir competitions held during the summer months (January to March). According to Ballantine (1991), aspects of the *ghoemaliedjie* were incorporated into the early black South African urban musical genre called *marabi*. Nonetheless, the music of the Cape played an influential role in other urban genres in South Africa as Cape Town was the first city established in the country and often took the lead in terms of city life and culture.

Bibliography

Ballantine, Christopher. 1991. 'Concert and Dance: The Foundations of Black Jazz in South Africa between the Twenties and the Early Forties.' *Popular Music* 10 (2): 121–45.

Bradlow, Edna, and Bradlow, Frank. 2007. *Here Comes the Alabama: 'Daar kom die Alabama.'* Cape Town: Westby Numm Publishers.

Du Plessis, David Izak. 1935. *Die Bydrae van die Kaapse Maleier tot die Afrikaanse Volkslied* [The Contributions of the Cape Malays to the Afrikaans Folksong]. Monograph of Doctoral Degree, University of Cape Town. Cape Town: Nationale Pers Beperk.

Kirby, Percival R. 1939. 'Musical Instruments of the Cape Malays.' *South African Journal of Science* 36: 477–88.

Discography
Tulips The. *South Africa: The Cape Town Minstrels*. Musique du Monde. *1999*: France.

YouTube
Aquarius All Stars. 'Daar kom die Alibama': https://www.youtube.com/watch?v=KW_jillvuVg.

SYLVIA R. BRUINDERS

Gospel Music in Africa, see Gospel Music (Volume XIII, International)

Gule Wa Mkulu

The term *Gule wa mkulu* refers to a traditional dance and its related music that have survived the imposition of colonialism, Christianity and Islam in Malawi to continue to provide the performative aspect of Chewa traditional culture and religious belief. The Chewa (or aChewa) is a major Bantu ethnic group found in Malawi, Mozambique and Zambia. *Gule wa mkulu*, or *nyau*, as it is also called, is the ritual dance of the Nyau, a secret association with cultural and religious aspects at the heart of Chewa traditional society. Membership in Nyau is by initiation of 'all true Chewa' males into the association. The society has secret codes and a language, and those who betray secrets are punished. In its traditional context, *gule wa mkulu* is performed at funerals, commemorations of funerals or whenever a Nyau spirit expresses in a dream his or her desire that *gule wa mkulu* be danced. *Gule wamkulu* is connected to strict rituals pertaining to male and female initiation into adulthood, performances, places of occurrence (which may be *bwalo* [arena] or *dambwe* [place of initiation]) and times when it may be performed. Although they cannot be initiated into the Nyau, women are an important part of both the private and public performance, in which they sing the chorus and participate as hand clappers. Also, masked *nyau* dancers make an entry at a crucial part of the *chinamwali* girls' initiation ritual, perhaps to remind the initiates of the perils of breaking taboos and customs.

Since self-government in 1964 some *gule wa mkulu* has been increasingly performed as entertainment at public occasions. With the spread of *gule wa mkulu* into the secular environment two types of performance have emerged: for the initiated and for the general public. These performance types are similar except for the context and the audience. The performances that take place in secret involve initiated chiefs and dancers, the *zirombo* (wild animals). In line with the history of secrecy, performers, the *zirombo*, are always masked.

The *zirombo* represent the complicated connection between the living and the dead, the good and the bad, and they are intended to celebrate everyday life and to demonstrate various formative and normative aspects of morality and respect for ancestors. The masked dancers symbolize spirits or represent contacts with spirits. Their masks, because *gule wa mkulu* is intended to educate initiates, also demonstrate various aspects of human behavior from the point of view of Chewa Nyau cosmology, such as kindness, charity, immorality, use and abuse of power or money. The genre also satirizes aspects of colonialization as part of its resistance to colonialization. A full arrangement will also include animal structures and figures. As figures were made from maize husks in the past, the best period for traditional *gule wa mkulu* is after harvest, from August to November. Costumes can also be made from grass and wood. In its representations of the spirit world, *gule wa mkulu* includes a growing number of representations of specific animals, some more important than others, such as elephant, hare, snake and lion. Similarly masked dancers also take on different human figures including *maliya* (Maria, a demure girl), *chabwera kumanda* (the returnee from the grave), *chadzunda* (old man), *kachipapa* (the mourner), *kamkhwindi* (the wicked one) and *gutende* (the cruel one). The animal and human figures represent various elements from the world of spirits and the dead, and their role is to teach morality through the dramatic dance and music. This is why the figures in *gule wa mkulu* have evolved over time, in order to keep up with contemporary evils and misdeeds.

Musical Characteristics

In traditional cultural settings, the ceremonies are performed at the *dambwe* (places of initiation usually on river banks). In public *gule wa mkulu is* usually performed in the village *bwalo* (square) or in stadia at political or cultural events. Typically a battery of drummers, in a full ensemble about five to seven or more, is positioned at one end of the *bwalo*. A shaker may be used, in which case the shaker player accompanies and directs the dancers. The basic drum setup involves the long *mpanje* drum, the big *mbalule* drum, two *mbandambanda* and two *kamkumbe* smaller drums. The first drum establishes the beat and the other drums follow, creating a complex polyrhythmic pattern. One of the lead drums provides accompaniment to the dancers' movements. A characteristic of the drumming is the rhythmic thrill or tremble achieved by playing fast notes on the large *mbalule* drums as a particular dance reaches a crescendo. The women sing, in Chewa, songs about the various aspects of life alluded to above as accompaniment to the *zirombo*, who, emulating wild animals, sing in muffled falsetto or nasal tones. The melodies are structured in a call-and-response pattern with polyphonic texture. The dancing is vigorous, requiring physical stamina and fitness. The choreography emulates animal movements and appearances.

Bibliography

Birch de Aguilar, Laurel. 1994. 'Nyau Masks of the Chewa.' *Society of Malawi Journal* 47(2): 3–14.
Breugel, J. W. M. Van. 2001. *Chewa Traditional Religion*. Blantyre: Kachere/CLAIM.
Kamlongera, Christopher, Nambote, Mike, Soko, Boston, et al. 1992. *Kubvina: An Introduction to Malawian Dance and Theatre*. Zomba: CSR.

Discography

Kwandege Cultural Troupe. *Chileka Traditional Village Ensemble*. PAM 033. *2004*: UK.

JOHN LWANDA

Gumbe/Goombay

Gumbe or *goombay* (other variations: *gumbay, gumbe, gumbeh, gombay, goombah*) is a syncopated 4/4-time recreational drum-dance accompanied by songs sung in Patois and found in West and Central Africa. Originating in Jamaica, it was introduced to Sierra Leone in 1800 when rebel Jamaican Maroons (Africans who had escaped slavery, fought the British and been deceived on surrendering) were transported by the British to their new colony of Sierra Leone. Consequently, *gumbe* became part of the culture of the Krio (Creoles), freed slaves who came to Sierra Leone in the period from the late 1780s to 1800 as part of three main groups: Black Loyalists (freed slaves who had fought in the American Revolutionary War and were brought to the new colony to settle what became the city of Freetown); Maroons; and liberated slaves from slave ships captured by the British Navy on the high seas. The Black Loyalists and the Maroons came to Africa from Nova Scotia, to which they had both been initially evacuated. After arriving in Sierra Leone, these peoples developed a homogenous ethnic entity with their own unique lifestyle and cultural practices (see Horton 1979, 15, fig. 5). (For the twentieth-century Bahamian genre called goombay or rake-n-scrape, see 'Goombay,' Vol. IX, *Genres: Caribbean and Latin America*.)

Origins

The Jamaican drum (often spelled 'goombay' when referring to the Caribbean) that is fundamental to the music is a rectangular frame drum that comes in various sizes and is found in several parts of West Africa and the Caribbean (see Horton 1999, 230–1, figs. 18.1 and 18.2). In most instances, it consists of a single membrane made of goatskin that is stretched and nailed over a square wooden form or stool and raised off the ground on four legs. It is held in the hands or between the knees. Documentation of the drum in the Caribbean dates back to the nineteenth century, which suggests that the instrument was probably in use there from the eighteenth century or earlier.

In Jamaica, runaway Maroon slaves created the *goombay* drum during the late eighteenth century as a response to the suppression of traditional African hand-carved peg drums by the British authorities in the island. The British feared these drums for two reasons: first, their typical complex 6/8 cross-rhythms (polyrhythms) made slaves brave by triggering spirit possession by their ancestors in ceremonies that the slave masters called 'pagan' rituals and second, by mimicking the pitches of tonal West African languages, peg drums could literally 'talk.' Indeed, the polyrhythmic music and 'talking drums' of Vodún in neighboring Haiti helped inspire, organize and communicate during the successful Haitian black slave revolt in the late eighteenth century.

In comparison, *goombay* drums and drumming were considered 'safe' by the white authorities, so *goombay* music was able to find its way to various other Caribbean countries. Unlike the peg drums, the *goombay* drum was made by modern methods of carpentry and was typically played in quadruple time rather than the polyrhythmic 6/8 time of ritual. Despite its use of African musical resources such as syncopation, offbeating, call-and-response and a close relationship between the music and dance, *goombay* was not clearly connected to neo-African religious cults and the carved talking drums of rebellion; rather, it was a recreational music associated with Caribbean John Canoe/Jonkonnu masquerades, carnival and other slave celebrations.

Gumbe/Goombay in Africa

As has been discussed by Harrev (1987, 1993), *gumbe/goombay* (hereafter *gumbe*) was introduced to Freetown, Sierra Leone in October 1800 by some 600 Jamaican Maroons. The British were never able to conclusively defeat these runaway slaves and so negotiated a peace treaty with them, which involved some of them being settled in West Africa. Again according to Harrev, the first references to *gumbe* in Freetown were in the 1820s and 1830s, where it was initially received with hostility by Christianized members of the Krio elites, for whom this Maroon music was 'a cause of many vices' (Harrev ibid.). Nevertheless, *gumbe* had become firmly established in Freetown by the mid-nineteenth century and during the twentieth century became associated with 'Jolly Masquerades' street carnivals.

Gumbe went on to influence some of Sierra Leone's twentieth-century popular dance-music styles that combined frame drums with guitars, concertinas and accordions. The first was *aṣíkò* (*ashiko, assiko*), which by 1900 had become a pan-West African popular music style. Later came *maringa* music that was sung in the Krio language of Freetown and popularized by local musicians such as Ebenezer Calender. (For further information on *gumbe* in Sierra Leone see separate entry on Gumbe/Goombay (in Sierra Leone).)

Not only did the *gumbe* drum-dance become a craze in Freetown from the mid-nineteenth century, but it was later spread inland and along the coast to around 20 West and Central African countries by migrant workers, carpenters and fishermen. In Nigeria it was called *goumbe* or *kumbeh*, in Mali *gube*, in Equatorial Guinea *cumbe*, in Côte d'Ivoire *le goumbey* and among the Ghanaian Ga people of Accra *gome*.

One particular route along which *gumbe* spread was through Sierra Leonean artisans who worked alongside other English-speaking West African contract laborers in the 'Free Congo' owned by Belgium's cruel King Leopold between 1885 and 1908. As Leopold did not want to train local people in these skills, Sierra Leonian, Ghanaian, Nigerian and Liberian 'West African Coastmen' were employed as carpenters, blacksmiths and clerks to work in the port of Matadi at the mouth of the Congo, or as paddleboat sailors on the Congo River.

In the case of Ghana, for instance, the Congo route was the earliest way in which *gumbe* music was introduced to the country by Ga carpenters and blacksmiths returning to Accra after working in the Congo for some years. According to the elderly Ga musicians Squire Addo and Frank Torto (personal communication, early 1970s), it was the Ga artisans working on contract labor for firms in the Congo who brought back with them this Sierra Leonean music sung in Pidgin English. According to the musicologist Barbara Hampton (1983), a later wave of *gumbe* was introduced to Accra between 1947 and 1954 by Ga fishermen returning from extended stays on the island of Fernando Po, off the Nigerian/Cameroonian coast. But again there is a Sierra Leone connection since, although Fernando Po was a Spanish colony from 1778, the Spanish allowed a British antislavery squadron to be stationed there from 1827 to 1872, during which time the British settled some Sierra Leoneans in the town of Malabo (see also entry on cumbe).

Over the years *gumbe* became integrated into Ga society, where it became known as 'gome' and was increasingly sung in the Ga language. As such, *gome* became a component of local Ga celebrations, and elements were worked into new forms of Ga traditional (i.e., neo-traditional) recreational music, such as the *kolamashie* of the 1930s and *kpanlogo* of the 1960s. *Gome* dances often involve a man wearing a suit and tie and holding a carpenter's box flirting with a lady wearing an enormous bustle. In the mid-late 2010s *gome* was still performed by Ga communities.

In addition to influencing Sierra Leonean *aṣíkò* and *maringa* music, *gumbe* frame drum music also helped lay the foundations for some other early forms of Anglophone West African popular music.

One is Ghanaian *konkoma* music that sprang up in the 1930s and used various sized frame drums. Very early Ghanaian and Nigerian highlife and *jùjú* guitar bands also employed frame drums, an example being the 1940s Accra-based highlife guitar band of Appiah Adjekum. Moreover, *gumbe* frame drums and rhythms were also incorporated into various forms of West African neo-traditional drum-dance music during the 1930s, one being the *simpa* music of the Dagbon people of northern Ghana, and the other the *gahu* of the Egun and Fon people of the Benin Republic and the Ewe of Togo and Ghana in which frame drums were replaced by cylindrical peg drums.

Gumbe is therefore West Africa's first modern transcultural urban music in that it emerged in West Africa in the early nineteenth century and includes three of the key components of so many seminal forms of African popular music: namely the African-American, the Western and the African. The first component is obviously the Jamaican origin of *gumbe*. The Western component is the construction of the drum by modern methods of carpentry and joinery rather than the African-type, hand-carved drum. The third component is the African development of *gumbe* that first took root in Freetown and subsequently spread throughout West and Central Africa, where regional variants appeared, sung in different local languages.

Taking into account that *gumbe* drum-dance was created by Jamaican slaves who partly drew on African musical resources, *gumbe* is also the first documented case of an African-American dance music being brought to Africa, thus completing a transatlantic musical cycle that began in the days of slavery and then made a return journey or 'homecoming' to Africa (Mensah 1971/2, 124). This pattern began with *gumbe* in 1800 and was followed in the late 1800s by the Brazilian *samba* and Trinidadian calypso, and later by a succession of twentieth-century dance-music styles that range from American jazz and blues to Latin *rumba* and *mambo* through to soul, R&B, reggae and hip-hop.

Bibliography

Aranzadi, Isabela de. 2009. *Instrumentos musicales de las etnias de Guinea Ecuatorial* [Musical Instruments of Ethnic Groups in Equatorial Guinea]. Madrid: Apadena.

Bilby, Kenneth. 1985. *The Caribbean as a Musical Region*. Washington DC: The Woodrow Wilson International Center for Scholars.

Campbell, Mavis. 1988. *The Maroons of Jamaica 1655–1796: A History of Resistance, Collaboration & Betrayal*. South Hadley, MA: Bergin & Garvey,

Clifford, Mary Louise. 1999. *From Slavery to Freetown: Black Loyalists After the American Revolution*. Jefferson, NC: McFarland.

Collins, E. John. 1987. 'Jazz Feedback to Africa.' *American Music* 5(2): 176–93.

Collins, E. John. 1996. *Highlife Time*. Accra: Anansesem Press.

Collins, E. John. 2007. 'The Pan-African Goombay Drum-Dance: Its Ramifications and Development in Ghana.' In *Legon Journal of the Humanities* 63, eds. Gordon Adika and Kofi Ackah. Legon: Faculty of Arts, University of Ghana Legon, 179–200.

Hampton, Barbara. 1983. 'Towards a Theory of Transformation in African Music.' In *Transformations and Resilience in Africa*, eds. Pearl T. Robinson and Elliott P Skinner. Washington DC: Howard University Press, 211–29.

Harrev, Flemming. 1987. 'Goumbe and the Development of Krio Popular Music in Freetown Sierra Leone.' Paper read at 4th International Conference of IASPM (International Association for the Study of Popular Music), Accra, Ghana, 12–19 August.

Harrev, Flemming. 1993. 'The Origin of Urban Music in West and Central Africa.' Paper read at 23rd World Conference of the International Council for Traditional Music, Berlin, 16–22 June.

Meillasoux, Claude. 1968. *Urbanisation of an African Community*. Seattle: University of Washington Press.

Mensah, Atta Annan. 1971/1972. 'Jazz the Round Trip.' *Jazz Forschung/Jazz Research* 3/4: 124–37.

Van Oven, Cootje. 1981/1982. *An Introduction to the Music of Sierra Leone (and Supplement)*. Culemborg: Technipress.

Personal Communication

Squire Addo and Frank Torto. Early 1970s.

Discography

Kpanlogo Party, with Oboade. Tangent Records TGS 115. *1973*: UK.

E. JOHN COLLINS WITH CHRISTIAN 'DOWU JAYEOLA HORTON

Gumbe/Goombay (in Sierra Leone)

In Sierra Leone, *gumbe*, *maringa* and *Milo jazz* are important genres of popular music in the Krio (Creole) culture. All three genres are used for social occasions in Krio life circle ceremonies. *Gumbe* music is primarily used to celebrate wedding periods. Therefore, the lyrics of the songs praise and extol the wedding party, namely the bride (*iyawo*), bridegroom (*okor*), bride's mother (*iyawomami*), bride's father (*iyawodadi*), bridegroom's mother (*okormami*) bridegroom's father (*okordadi*) and other relatives. In Sierra Leone, *maringa* music surpassed *gumbe* in popularity in the 1940s, and since the 1970s and 1980s *Milo jazz* has become more popular than *maringa*. In the twenty-first century Krio elders still request that *gumbe* and *maringa* music recordings be played as wedding entertainment.

The arrival of the *goombay* drum in Sierra Leone around 1800 had far-reaching implications. Significantly, it is the first instance of the reconnection of the African expressive culture that was transported by the slave trade with its place of birth (Collins 1985). The 200th anniversary of this event was celebrated in the year 2000 in both Sierra Leone and the Caribbean. The earliest 'homecoming,' when *goombay* was introduced by the freed Maroon slaves in Freetown (where it is still played), laid the basis for the country's first popular music (c. 1900), known as *aṣíkò*. *Goombay/gumbe* and *aṣíkò* subsequently spread from Sierra Leone to many West and Central African countries (Mali, Côte d'Ivoire, Ghana, Nigeria, Gabon, Congo Cameroons, and Fernando Po in Equatorial Guinea), creating an important musical building block for various twentieth-century African popular and neo-traditional music styles (see separate entry on Gumbe/Goombay).

Instrumentation

The *gumbe* ensemble took its name from its master drum, the *gumbe*, which was used to perform elaborate improvisations (the early Jamaican *gumbe* drums are pictured in Horton 1999, 230, 231, figs. 18.1 and 18.2). Also included in the ensemble was the bass-box (ibid., fig. 18.3). In colonial times, this instrument was made from the wooden container used to transport kerosene tins. This container was selected because of the sonority produced by the light wood used to construct it. As containers of this type are no longer used – fuel now being more safely delivered by tanker trucks – a similar lightweight wood is procured to make bass-boxes for *Milo jazz*. The *gumbe* bass-box was rectangular in shape with square ends, and it was open at the bottom. It was used to keep the timeline, which is the underlying rhythmic pulse in polyrhythmic arrangements of many types of African instrumental music. The bass-box player sat astride the instrument and alternated beats between two of its surfaces using the hands. Additional beats could be made using the heels of both feet (see Horton 1999, 232, fig. 18.3).

The saw *en nef* (or simply 'saw') was also a component of the *gumbe* ensemble. Its serrated edges were scraped in rhythm with a knife to create a rasping, rhythmic effect. Over the years the *gumbe* ensemble typically incorporated a player or two using some form of friction idiophone – for example, rubbing empty milk tins together. This made the tone color of such an ensemble, as one would expect, rather mellow. It was brightened from time to time with the loud improvisatory rhythmic pattern played on the *gumbe* in its role as master drum. The *gumbe* player was also the lead singer of folk tunes, for example, 'Lili pepeh lili sal drai bonga go match am' (roughly, 'All that it takes to make a quick, cold sauce for eating fufu [a staple made from tapioca starch] is to mix pieces of smoked bonga fish, hot powdered pepper, salt and lime'); ballads; and hint songs, for example, 'De up nay u garret, lef mi na mi two by foe' (roughly, 'Stay up in your storied house, leave me in my small and humble dwelling'). The rest of the ensemble provided appropriate vocal responses to the lead singer. An ensemble of this nature was best suited to a small outdoor area where all could hear its interacting parts distinctly. If used in a procession, the group would have to be of a moderate size so everyone could hear and enjoy the interacting roles.

With the advent of *Milo jazz* in the 1970s, the *gumbe* ensemble augmented its instrumentation to include the *bátá* drum (see Horton 1999, 232, fig. 18.6) and *koto* (a type of triangle with loud sonority) in order to reach a larger, more youthful dance crowd. In so doing, its earlier characteristic sonority was lost, even though its name did not change. Hence it has been said that *Milo jazz* supplanted the *gumbe* ensemble by virtue of its inclusion of bright-sounding instruments, such as the bugle, *koto* and the two-in-one drum (i.e., two single drums differently pitched and connected by a wooden frame to make it easier for the player to produce the alternate tones). These drums appealed to the crowd of dancers at *Milo jazz* events.

Dance Style

Gumbe and *maringa*, the oldest of Krio traditional dance styles in Sierra Leone, were individualized and competitive as dances. The dancer who outlasted the others was hailed as the best and might have paper money stuck in his or her mouth as an indication of audience approval. The *gumbe* dance style consisted of four movements: (1) *olewase*, in which the dancer moved rather slowly, swaying the torso to the rhythm, and rested the palms of the hands on the hips; (2) *cut beleh*, where the dancer became more involved in the dance, contracting and expanding the stomach muscles rhythmically and alternating that movement with the first for variety; (3) *shake wase*, the third movement, which involved moving the hips and was alternated with the first two movements and (4) alternation of *cut beleh* and *shake wase*, which occurred at the climax of the dance when the instrumentalists increased the pace of the music to excite the dancers. At this point the onlookers typically became excited and began to comment and to applaud those dancers who were displaying their skills to the fullest (see Horton 1979, 313–14, plates 26 and 27, 'Four Styles of Gumbe Dancing').

Gumbe dancing also involved solo and group dances. The solo dances were the highlight of the dance. The master drummer concentrated on each solo dancer, improvising to suit the style of the dancer as he or she brought the dance to a climax. One *gumbe* master drummer, the late Peter Johnson, was also known as 'Peter na Lepet,' roughly meaning 'Peter the Leopard.' He earned this nickname because one of his feet had an ulcer and sometimes skilled dancers, while concentrating on the beating of the master drummer, would dance too close and step on his ulcerous foot, causing him to jump up like a leopard and scream aloud. This, in turn, caused the dancer to flee for fear of being hit by the drummer (see Horton 1979, 189, plate 13 'Peter na lepet'). Another late master drummer was called 'Pa Araico.' He was healthier than Peter Johnson, and drummed so vigorously to attract the dancers to the rhythm of his instruments that they would dance close to him and cover his head with their headscarves as a climax of the dance. At that point, someone from the wedding party would shout the vocables 'Ibi ibi!' and others would answer, 'urah urah urah!' Yet others would shout, 'marade nordey yah!' and the response would be 'marade dey!' (loosely, 'this is a wedding ["marade"] ceremony, let us all be merry and happy!') Both Peter Johnson and Pa Araico died in the 1970s.

Gumbe Lyrics

Since *gumbe* music was performed at weddings, song lyrics (by Ebenezer Calender, who learned *gumbe* songs in the 1940s from traditional *gumbe* drummers and then composed his own *gumbe* songs, which became more popular than those of the original *gumbe* drummers) usually dealt with praise for and adoration of the bride and bridegroom and their parents. For example, 'Yawo mami ebi so' translates roughly as 'mother of the bride is well dressed and looking sharp.' Some of the songs are petitions to the bridegroom, to take good care of the bride ('Baio baio o mi beh' roughly means 'please take good care of my child who has become your wife'). Others are salacious commentary on the body movement of the dancers, such as the sexy movement of the buttocks (for example, 'Kainde, Kainde shake am foh mi yah' translates roughly, as 'Kainde, please dance well and roll the hips for our pleasure'). A few of the songs are adorations of the bride and bridegroom's parents who are expected to display their wealth in their dress and the quality of the food served (e.g., 'yawo mami wi donh kam' may be understood as 'mother of the bride, we have honored your invitation by attending your child's wedding now treat us as befits your status'). Other songs lament public criticisms (e.g., 'na mi yone dehn see' translates roughly as 'people criticize my faults even though they are also guilty of similar crimes. People gossip about my faults instead of working to correct theirs'). A few songs are 'hint' songs (e.g., 'us soup sara cuk so nar wata wata' translates roughly as 'the food served is tasteless,' which could be a hint about the food prepared by a woman who doesn't know how to cook).

As people danced to the rhythm of songs such as these, Calender was in the habit of making exclamations such as 'O Congo man' or 'O San tomi people' in admiration for *gumbe* dancers and their skillful style of dancing in the Congo (Congo Brazzaville) and on the island of São Tomé in the Gulf of Guinea, testifying to the popularity of *gumbe* and its dance styles in those West African cities.

Bibliography

Collins, E. John. 1985. *Music Makers of West Africa*. Washington DC: Three Continents Press.

Dixon-Fyle, Mac, and Cole, Gibril, eds. 2006. *New Perspectives on the Sierra Leone Krio*. New York: Lang.

DjeDje, Jacqueline Cogdell. 1998. 'West Africa: An Introduction.' In *The Garland Encyclopedia of World Music, Vol. 1: Africa*, ed. Ruth Stone. New York and London: Garland Publishing, 442–70.

Hall-Alleyne, Beverly, White, Garth, and Cooke, Michael. 1982. *Towards a Bibliography of African-Caribbean Studies, 1970-1980*. Kingston: African-Caribbean institute of Jamaica.

Harrev, Fleming. 1987. 'Goumbe and the Development of Krio Popular Music in Freetown, Sierra Leone.' Paper read at the 4th International Conference of IASPM, Accra, Ghana, 12–19 August.

Horton, Christian Dowu. 1979. *Indigenous Music of Sierra Leone: An Analysis of Resources and Educational Implications*. Unpublished Ph.D. dissertation, University of California, Los Angeles.

Horton, Christian Dowu Jayeola. 1999. 'The Role of the Gumbe in Popular Music and Dance Styles in Sierra Leone.' In *Turn Up The Volume! A Celebration of African Music*, ed. Jacqueline Cogdell DjeDje. Los Angeles: UCLA Fowler Museum of Cultural History, 230–5.

Ortiz, Fernando. 1952. *Los instrumentos de la musica afrocubana* [The Instruments of Afrocuban Music], 5 vols. Havana: Direccion de Cultura del Ministerio de Educacion.

Wyse, Akintola J. G. 1989. *The Krio of Sierra Leone: An Interpretative History*. London: Hurst.

Personal Communication

DjeDje, Jacqueline Cogdell. Personal communication with the author, 28 December 1998.

Discography

Calender, Ebenezer. 'Ariya Bebi'; 'Why yu nor go buy ogboro.' Decca WA 2501. *Late 1940s*: Sierra Leone.

Calender, Ebenezer. 'Du yu yone lef mi yone'; 'Si mi no mohr.' HMV JZ 5240. *Late 1940s*: Sierra Leone.

Calender, Ebenezer. 'Gbe nyama [Leave Me Alone]; Konni Rabbit En Kondo.' HMV JZ 5241. *Late 1940s*: Sierra Leone.

Calender, Ebenezer. 'If na boy gi sm ehn dadi name, if na girl gi am ehn mami name.' HMV JZ 523. *Late 1940s*: Sierra Leone.

Calender, Ebenezer. 'Na marade ring yu want'; 'Yuba noh geht Papa.' HMV JZ 5256. *Late 1940s*: Sierra Leone.

Gumbe Music of Sierra Leone. (Cassette tape, recorded by Christian Horton, personal collection to be deposited at the UCLA Music Library.) *1970s*: Sierra Leone.

Plates Depicting *Gumbe* Music

'Gumbe Player,' 'Bass box Player' and 'Gumbe Ensemble Including 'Saw en Nef.' Horton personal collection, to be deposited at the UCLA music library.

CHRISTIAN 'DOWU JAYEOLA HORTON

Guux

Guux is a popular Somali musical style that emerged in Djibouti in the latter part of the 1960s and flourished during the independence movement period of the 1970s. Previously known as French Somalis' Coast – French Somaliland (1896–1967) and the French Territory of the Afars and Issas (1967–77), Djibouti gained independence on 27 June 1977. While Djibouti's population is made up of Afars, Arabs and Somalis, *guux* is a Somali genre that is linked to the development of a number of new art forms that emerged across the Somali-inhabited Horn of Africa in the 1950s. The genre has particularly close links to developments in neighboring British Somaliland (today the self-declared Republic of Somaliland), which gained independence in 1960 and joined with what had been Italian Somaliland to form the Somali Republic. Djiboutian Afar and Arab musicians developed their own specific musical style drawing mainly on Sudanese and African-American traditions (for a discussion of Afar music see the entry on Djibouti in *Volume VI: Locations – Africa and the Middle East*).

The term 'guux' literally means 'to moan' or 'a loud roar,' and may be used to describe the sound made by camels in search of water. In relation to the Somali expressive arts the term 'guux' was first used to refer to a 'miniature' genre of poetry (*heello yar-yar*) that was popular among young, disenfranchised men in the early twentieth century, sometimes known also as 'Somali blues.' Using poems composed in this style, Djiboutian musicians later transformed *guux* into a popular musical genre that incorporated elements of traditional poetry, other emerging genres of Somali popular song as well as African-American musical influences. In Djibouti's transition to independence, *guux* became a genre through which issues about inequality, colonial rule, gender, marriage, the place and role of the musician and urban/rural dynamics were explored.

Origins and Early Development of Somali Popular Song

Like other genres of Somali popular song the origins of *guux* can be traced to a confluence of influences in the 1950s during the British and French colonial administrations. In both British Somaliland and French Somaliland the birth of popular music is linked to the pre-independence period of the 1940s and 1950s, a crucial era in Somali life across the Somali-inhabited Horn of Africa that witnessed rapid migration and urbanization accentuated by colonial oppression. Although Somali artists were under relatively oppressive colonial rule, they at times paradoxically experienced the unwitting approval of the colonial powers, thereby making possible a way to translate poetry into new musical styles. In time these new styles supplanted more established expressive arts. Historically and culturally the origin of Somali musical sounds in Djibouti is closely related to that of the Somalis in the then British Somaliland Protectorate. While important differences did develop between mainstream Somali *hees* and Djiboutian styles, they share a common ancestor, *belwo*, a genre created by Abdi Sinimo in the 1940s in Borama, a town in the western part of the self-proclaimed Republic of Somaliland (Qarshe 1997; Aidarus 2017). Similar to other miniature genres (*heello yar-yar*) – *wiglo, hirwo, dhaanto* and *guux* (in its early poetic form) – *belwo* were short lyrical poems performed with *jiibka iyo jaanta* (Somali dance). *Belwo* were composed predominantly by young people who mostly focused on individual themes such as love. The genre quickly spread to neighboring towns, including Djibouti City. Many observers (Aidarus 2017; Ali 2017) have argued that Sinimo's new popular art form played an important role in changing artistic and cultural tastes, eventually leading to the birth of popular song (see also the entry on *Hees*).

The *belwo* movement and the emergence of popular song that it precipitated brought about a number of important changes. Catering to a young urban group affected the way in which people gathered to perform the nascent genre. New artists abandoned Somali traditional open-air dance in favor of sitting in private houses for sessions using newly adopted musical instruments (Aidarus 2017). Some poems explored gender issues, although somewhat timidly. A handful of women participated in the artistic community's musical innovations, though women artists made only minor advances and the genre did little to question issues of gender inequality and access to the arts for women. The new art form that was emerging from *belwo* did, however, serve as a vehicle to challenge the prominence of long poetic forms such as *gabay*, a poetic genre regarded as the highest art form by many Somalis and non-Somalis, as well as the predominance of two other traditional poetic genres, *jiifto* and *geerar*.

Sensing new developments in artistic and cultural tastes, colonial offices in both territories (British Somaliland and French Somaliland) sponsored the emerging popular music as a means of galvanizing support for their policies and undertook 'modernization' programs for the expressive arts. The mission of modern music for the European powers was to help change Somali culture, which was viewed as archaic. This 'modernization' initiative was intended to dismantle the subversive drive of independence movements in the post–World War II era. However, musicians and cultural practitioners rejected the initiative, in part because it limited their creativity and in part because it restricted their political aspirations (Qarshe 1997). Musicians performing this emerging popular music thus started to give life to a new anti-colonial discourse without the sexual undertones often associated with their artistic productions. The 1950s marked the emergence of the figure of the musician as a patriot and nationalist.

Djibouti Musical Innovations and the Development of *Guux*

While Djibouti musical innovations share their history with other Somali music, the differing colonial histories as well as the influence of the large Arab communities in Djibouti (which do not exist in other Somali-inhabited regions of the Horn of Africa) were to have an impact on the development of Djibouti-specific genres such as *guux*. In an immediate sense it was a change in French policy that led to the establishment of the first Djibouti 'band.' Before the advent of radio the French colonial administration relied on Dar Akhbar (News Tower), one of the tallest buildings in the main public square of Djibouti City, to broadcast traditional Somali dance and poetry through loudspeakers; this square served also as a site where traditional folklorists and others regularly performed *jiib iyo jaanto* (Somali dance), including during festivities (Aidarus 2017; Kamal 2017). With the creation of Radio Djibouti in 1956 the French colonial office, in line with the policy of the *Loi Cadre* of 1956 (designed to grant internal autonomy to each of its overseas territories), decided to change the way in which it exercised power over the colony and abandoned its practice of organizing cultural and artistic events in the main public square. As a consequence, the French administration created a small studio group of Arab musicians who performed as a backup band on all Djiboutian recordings. The group was led by the versatile Taha Nahari and mainly played the drums, oud and tambourine (Aidarus 2017; Kamal 2017).

By the end of the 1950s *guux* as a *heello yar-yar* poetic genre was a relatively well-established artistic practice with lyrics that emphasized individual misfortunes. Typical *guux* poems would construct individual existential narratives, as the following poem illustrates:

Adduunyo hal baan lahaa	In this world, I owned only one she-camel
Hashina oroob ba iga dilay	And my she-camel died after a long journey

This poetic genre quickly spread across the Somali-inhabited Horn of Africa, especially when, in 1960, the British and Italian Somalilands gained independence and formed the Republic of Somaliland. As in other *heello yar-yar*, poets used *guux* to express their disenchantment with the union of these two colonies (Adam 2008; Ducaale 2006; Samatar 1997). Simultaneously, Djibouti artists were using this genre to give expression to a new anti-colonial discourse.

In the mid-1960s Somali-Djiboutian musicians began experimenting with new instruments and sounds, in turn transforming *guux* into a distinct Djiboutian musical genre. At this time, a group of Somali-Djiboutian musicians formed the first band not under colonial sway in order to gain independence from the radio station's studio group. The Somali-Djiboutian group was led by Somali-Yemeni oud player Said Abdi and received financial backing from Jama Nur Da'ar, a Somali-Djiboutian businessman who had sponsored members of Walaalaha Hargeysa (Hargeysa Brothers), the first band in British Somaliland. Other members of the group included Said Ismail Buh 'Hamargod,' Hawa Geelqaad (the first woman) and Abdi Matan. Said Abdi taught Said Harmagod and others how to incorporate harmony, melody and rhythm into their music, as well as how to absorb non-Somali sounds (Aidarus 2017). Whereas Somali musicians in British Somaliland drew mainly on Indian, Arab and Sudanese sources, Somali-Djiboutian musicians were exposed to more Euro-American sounds and were particularly influenced by African-American genres. Inspired by the new sounds arriving on the airwaves, Said Hamargod, who was early on fusing Somali sounds with non-Somali genres, recorded a Somali version of Ray Charles's 'Hit the Road Jack,' entitled 'Mooyi' ('Who Knows?'). The recording incorporated the melody of Ray Charles's song with lyrics that explored the vicissitudes of Djibouti's political climate under colonial rule. After much experimenting with various non-Somali musical genres Hamargod uncovered a close similarity between *guux*'s pattern repetition and the African-American shuffle (Aidarus 2017). With the help of new instruments – accordion, drums, flute and oud – he recorded the first *guux* song, 'Hiddiiyooy Hiddi' ('Hope'). The song expressed Djiboutians' discontentment with colonial oppression using the long-practiced technique of veiling sensitive messages.

Harmagod's 'Hiddiiyooy Hiddi' became one of the most famous Djibouti songs and served as a model for the new musical style in a period during which dramatic changes were occurring in pre-independence Djibouti. At the time, however, musical success barely translated into financial gain. Yet artists' financial situation and their ability to innovate continued to increase as more and more supporters contributed to their work. Of particular importance in this regard was Ibrahim Barre, a famous Somali-Djiboutian music manager. In 1964 he brought a number of instruments from abroad, including electric guitars, bass guitars, pianos and drums kits, and established Mont Arrey, a band regrouping some of Djibouti's rising musicians such as Abdi Bobo and the Hamargod brothers (Abdo and Said). Using Said Hamargod's shuffle/*guux* fusion with a more pronounced role for the electric guitar that suited the upcoming urban elite, Abdi Bobo perfected the genre with his 'Arrey,' a song that addressed increasing colonial state violence and the importance of unifying Djiboutians against the foreign power.

Guux performers were perceptive in understanding that music was continually open to all kind of influences and responsive to changing musical styles. Stimulated and moved by the endless music experimentations of Mont Arrey's band members, a younger generation of musicians embraced the *guux* tradition and explored new influences after Djibouti's independence in 1977. During and after the 1980s the genre was further developed by guitarist Abdi Houssein 'Aidarus,' a professor of music at the Institut Djiboutiens des Arts (IDA). Trained in Russia, Aidarus recorded some of the most memorable *guux* songs. His cover of Said Hamargod's 'Hiddiiyooy Iyo Hiddi' represents the durability and popularity of Djiboutian *guux*. In 2017 two famous young bands, Abdillahi dj and The Guux Brothers Band, paid tribute to the ingenuity of Said Hamargod's *guux*, a musical style that has continued to appeal to a mass audience.

While Djibouti popular music has continued to evolve, *guux*'s undiminished popularity suggests that it will continue to influence future musical innovations. The genre's fusion with African-American shuffle has continued to captivate contemporary audiences who associate *guux* with a distinctive Djiboutian identity.

Bibliography

Adam, Hussein. 2008. *From Tyranny to Anarchy: The Somali Experience.* Trenton, NJ: Africa World Press & Red Sea Press.

Aidarus, Hussein. 2017. Interview with author, 1 December.

Ali, Kamal. 2017. Interview with author, 2 December.

Andrzejewski, Bogumil Witalis, and Lewis, Ioan Myrddin ·1964. *Somali Poetry: An Introduction.* Oxford: Oxford University Press.

Ducaale, Yusuf. 2006. *Diiwaanka Maansada: Cabdillahi Suldan Maxamed (Timacadde)* [Poetry Anthology: Cabdillahi Suldan Maxamed (Timacadde)]. Addis Ababa: Flamingo Printing Press (2nd ed.).

Qarshe, Abdillahi. 1997. Interview with author, 23 August.

Samatar, Meygag. 1997. 'Light at the End of the Tunnel: Some Reflections on the Struggle of The Somali National Movement.' In *Mending Rips in the Sky: Options for Somali Communities in the 21st Century*, eds. Hussein M. Adam and Richard Ford. Lawrenceville: Red Sea Press, 21–48.

Touval, Saadia. 1963. *Somali Nationalism.* Cambridge, MA: Harvard University Press.

Discographical References

Aidarus, Houssein. 'Hiddiiyooy Hiddi.' Self-produced. N.d. (2000s): Djibouti.

Bobo, Abdi. 'Arrey.' Self-produced. N.d. (1960s): Djibouti.

Hamargod, Said. 'Hiddiiyooy Hiddi.' Self-produced. N.d. (1960s): Djibouti.

Hamargod, Said. 'Mooyi.' Self-produced. N.d. (1960s): Djibouti.

KENEDID A. HASSAN

See also **Djibouti (Volume VI – Locations: Africa and the Middle East)**

Hausa Popular Music (Northern Nigeria)

The Hausa people of northern Nigeria are predominantly an African Muslim group. Islam has made inroads in the region since the thirteenth century through trading networks headed by Malian Muslim clerics from West Africa. The Hausa are predominantly peasant farmers, traders and itinerant merchants following long caravan routes that saw a Hausa mercantile and social presence in cities in the North African countries of Tunisia, Morocco, Algeria and Libya. They were the original source of the *gnawa* music genre of North Africa. The spread of the Hausa over the Sahelian regions of West Africa gave them distinct diversity, and yet they retain a culturally homogeneous identity. Beside northern Nigeria, they are also spread across the countries of Niger, Cameroon, Côte d'Ivoire, Chad, Togo, Ghana and the Sudan. This entry is concerned with the urban popular music of the Hausa of northern Nigeria, although diasporic Hausa share more or less the same musical traditions.

This entry begins with an account of Hausa traditional music, which forms a backdrop to the development of urban Hausa popular music. This account is followed by a section on *nanaye filmi* music. Although not the only impetus for the development of urban Hausa popular music, the music of Hindi films was undoubtedly the major one. It gave rise to a form of music known as *nanaye* for Hausa video films. The music known as *nanaye* gradually came to have a life of its own as a genre somewhat distinct and independent from Hausa films. *Nanaye filmi* music played a significant role in the development of two other forms of Hausa popular music, *madhee* or *madhu* (Islamic gospel music of northern Nigeria) and technopop, genres that are the subject of the entry's final two sections.

Hausa Traditional Music

Despite its long history and variety of styles, Hausa traditional music has retained a consistent structure that has defined it over the centuries. A distinct characteristic of the genre is that its creative focus is not on instrumental accompaniment but on the lyrics the bandleader sings, delivered in a verse-chorus (*amshi*) structure. This structure came to later pervade nontraditional performances that rely on electronic instruments. Hausa songs relying exclusively on acoustic (as opposed to electronic) instrumentation define Hausa music and are referred to as *wakokin gargajiya* (traditional songs). It is very common for Hausa musical groups to play only one type of instrument, typically a percussion instrument such as the *kalangu* or 'African' drum, maintaining more or less the same beat throughout the song. The skills of the bandleader, who is always male, are essentially measured by the philosophy and poetry of his lyrics rather than the musical accompaniment.

This focus on singing rather than instrumental Hausa music creates a social world where Hausa musicians are given a low social status because of the client-focused nature of Hausa lyrical performance (Smith 1959). With its main function of appeasing specific clients, the music thus is viewed as a nonart form – in the sense of 'art for art's sake' – because the *maroka* (praise singers) praise their clients in return for money or other material goods. A client who is not generous receives the short end of the singer's stick, often with sarcastic barbs thrown in for good measure. Naturally, a very generous patron enjoys the full-blown poetic powers of the singer.

Hausa traditional music does not, however, include poet–musicians, who often recite their poetry without any accompanying instrumentation. Older *madhu* singers are cast in the same mold of not using musical accompaniment. These older *madhu* poets, such as Sheikh Nasiru Kabara, Sheikh Bala Maiyafe, Mallam Magaji 'Yantandu and Sani Hasasan Kafinga, often focused their repertoire on classical Arabic poetry and restricted themselves to the a capella tradition of such performance. They provided inspiration for the younger *madhu* singers who initially used the frame drum (*bandiri*) and then, later, Yamaha synthesizers for musical accompaniment. Secular Hausa singers in other traditions have not been influenced by these poet–singers.

Non-*madhu a cappella* poets do not perform publicly for payment and, subsequently, have been seen as representing the Hausa oral art form and the cultural characteristics of quintessentially elite Hausa forms of entertainment. Mainly highly educated (both in Western and Islamic traditions, in contrast with traditional 'lowbrow' musicians who often have had only an Islamic education), these poets tend to employ either political or religious thematic elements. Aliyu Namangi's nine-volume *Imfiraji*, for instance, is a Dante-esque exposition of life and death, and what comes after death – all admonishing the Muslim to lead a pious life. Ahmadu Danmatawalle's *Waƙar Tsuntsaye* is a blistering critique of the ruling house of one of the emirates of northern Nigeria, structured in the form of an Orwellian *Animal Farm* landscape in which the characteristics of the various courtiers are juxtaposed with characteristics of specific birds and animals in a jungle in their quest for a new ruler.

The Three Elements of Hausa Traditional Music

Hausa traditional musicians perform in a single cluster of three elements. The first is the singer (*mawaƙi*). Considered the bandleader, the singer provides the central focus of any Hausa traditional music performance, whether on stage or in the studio. The pure 'classic' traditionalist singers rarely play an instrument themselves, preferring to provide the lead vocals only. The few exceptions include musical groupings of stringed instruments, where the singer often plays one-stringed instrument or another. Examples of such bandleaders include Hassan Wayam and Garba Supa, as well as solo performers such as Danmaraya Jos.

The second element is the backing musicians (*makaɗa*), who provide the music to accompany lyrics sung by the bandleader. The musicians are often made up of about three to five individuals, usually playing percussion instruments (*kalangu*, *jauje*) of various pitches. Wind instruments are unusual. The drummers rarely sing, but may form part of the chorus.

The third element is the backup choristers ('*yan amshi*), who provide a call-and-response soundscape for the singer's lyrics. These '*yan amshi* are often made up of between three and ten individuals of the same gender; mixed-gender musical formations do not exist in Muslim Hausa traditional music because of Islamic prohibitions.

The Four Categories of Hausa Traditional Music and Musicians

Historically, Hausa traditional music and musicians were often divided into four categories. These categories did not merge into each other, but rather developed concurrently, with the last category, *makaɗan jama'a*, gaining predominance from the 1980s.

The first category was *makaɗan yaƙi* (war musicians), who flourished from the mid-nineteenth century up to 1920. Singing for palace armies of Sokoto territories such as Gobir, Kebbi and Argungu, these included Wari Mai Zarin Gobir (d. 1800), Ata Mai Kurya (d. 1899), Kara Buzu Mai Kan Kuwa (d. 1920) and so on. Their instruments included *zari* (any piece of equipment used to create a musical tone, such as a ring beaten with a metal rod), *kurya* (a variety of drum) and *molo* (a three-stringed 'guitar' like a lute) each accompanied by a backing choir.

The second category, *makaɗan sarakuna* (emir's palace musicians), centered their musical performance around drum orchestras. Again found predominantly around the Sokoto basin, these musicians included Buda Dantanoma Argungu (1858–1933), Ibrahim Gurso Mafara (1867–1954), Salihu Jankidi Sakkwato (1852–1973), Aliyu Dandawo Argungu (1925–66), Ibrahim Narambaɗa Isa (1875–1960), Muhammadu Sarkin Taushin Sarkin Katsina (1911–90), Musa Danƙwairo (1909–91), Sa'idu Faru (b. 1932), Sani Aliyu Dandawo Yauri (b. 1949) and Abu Dankurma Maru (b. 1926). Their main music styles were based on a variety of drum rhythms accompanied by slow, mournful and elegant vocals, as befitting one in the presence of royalty. The main drums were *kotso* (a drum with only one diaphragm), *taushi* (a conical drum with only one diaphragm, beaten softly), *kuru* (a drum about one meter long) and *turu* (a large drum). Although predominantly palace musicians, they nevertheless used their skills to sing about issues such as politics and the importance of traditional culture.

The third category was *makaɗan sana'a/maza* (those who sang for members of specific occupational guilds and professions, predominantly male). Perhaps the most famous of these was Muhammadu Bawa Dan Anace (1916–86), whose main – although not exclusive – specialty was singing for traditional boxers, the most famous of whom was Muhammadu Shago. Dan Anace also sang for farmers and members of the aristocracy.

The most eclectic category was the fourth, *makaɗan jama'a* (popular singers). Although often singing for emirs and other gentry, their predominant focus was on ordinary people and their extraordinary lives. And while other musicians tended to favor the drum in its various forms, popular singers employed a variety of musical instruments and incorporated a variety of styles and subject matter – marking a departure from a closeted traditional society to a more cosmopolitan product reflecting the transnational flow of media influences.

Departing from the dominance of Sokoto musicians and the staid emir's courts, Hausa popular folk musicians also adopted new instruments to replace the predominantly percussion-based music of the emir's courts and occupational guild singers. Thus percussion instruments, such as *duman girke, ganga, tauje, banga, taushi, kotso, turu, kalangu* and *kwaira,* wind instruments such as *algaita, kakaki* and *kubumburuwa,* and stringed instruments including *garaya, kuntigi, molo, kwamsa, goge* and *kukuma* all became the vogue among Hausa street and popular folk musicians up until the 1990s before the introduction of the Yamaha PSR series of synthesizers created new forms of urban musics that eclipsed the folk music genre among the Hausa. For instance, Mamman Shata, the most famous of all Hausa traditional and popular entertainers, used the *kalangu* in his band and Danmaraya Jos used the *kuntigi* (a small, one-stringed fiddle-type instrument). Equally diverse was their subject matter. Shata was predominantly a praise singer (*maroki*) for emirs, gentry, women, the infamous, high society, civil servants and so on, having composed thousands of songs for all categories of people, while Danmaraya Jos devoted his repertoire to social philosophy.

Women Singers in Hausa Traditional Music

Very few popular singers in Hausa traditional music have been women – perhaps due to the low-class status often afforded to musicians in Islamicate Hausa society. Generally, music and popular entertainment are not seen as credible or acceptable career options for women in a traditionally closeted society. This results from the mixed-gender nature of public performances of many forms of music. Islamicate societies – societies with Islamic social institutions that do not operate with strict Islamic constitutions because of the secular nature of the larger nation-state – nonetheless do not encourage mixed-gender social spaces. The few women performers in traditional music often include what is considered bawdy subject matter in their performances. These are seen as being too loud, and contrary to the expectations that women keep out of sight in the public sphere.

The most notable of female traditional performers were the late Uwaliya Mai Amada (active between the 1960s and the early 1980s) and the late Sa'adatu Barmani Choge (active from the 1970s to the 1990s), both of whose accompanying bands used calabashes as percussion. Restricting their performances exclusively to all-female audiences, these two elderly female performers were accepted by the larger Hausa society, which gave them opportunities to 'tour' the various naming and marriage ceremony circuits providing entertainment to exclusively female audiences. Between the two of them, Uwaliya and Barmani provided entertainment for well-heeled Hausa women during ceremonies.

The Diminishing Fortunes of Hausa Traditional Music

In the early twenty-first century the patronage system of Hausa traditional music relegated the genre to the status of a quaint archival performance, valued essentially because of its preservation of Hausa cultural performing heritage. Modernization reduced the desire to sustain the patronage of the musicians, whose creativity is driven by clients, with compositions made in honor of their generosity. With performing as a musician viewed increasingly as a lowbrow and unrewarding occupation, many Hausa traditional musicians were unwilling to see their offspring follow in their footsteps. As a consequence, an entertainment vacuum developed for Hausa young people, filled initially in the 1970s and 1980s by African-American disco. At the same time, however, modern Hausa music began to make inroads into northern Nigeria with music principally from Ghana and Niger. Wide acceptance of such musics, particularly among young people, accelerated the diminishing fortunes of traditional Hausa performing artists. In this environment, the main impetus for the development of modern urban music among young Hausa people came from Hindi film music rather than African-American music, although Western musical structures more generally did exercise an influence on Hausa *nanaye filmi* music once synthesizers became available, and African-American disco, R&B and rap became one impetus for the development of Hausa technopop. Rap, in particular, became an important impetus for Hausa rap.

One challenge in adopting African-American music was that it required skills on the instruments used to perform it, skills not easily accessible to young Hausa people. In addition, the largely hostile attitude toward US entertainment maintained by the Muslim Hausa cultural establishment also militated to a degree against the adoption of African-American music. By contrast, Hindi films had themes more consistent with those of Hausa culture. These themes included those of arranged marriages, gender hierarchies and colorful but modest dress. As a consequence, Hindi films enjoyed significant exposure and patronage among Hausa young people from the 1960s onward. In addition, Hindi film music could be easily reproduced using the cheap synthesizers that came onto the market in the 1980s (Adamu 2006, 19–21).

Hausa *Nanaye Filmi* Music

The expression '*filmi* music' evolved in relation to Indian cinema, where 'music is often used as a transformative medium accompanying moments when the protagonists achieve illumination and enlightenment, particularly during traumatic events or turning points in their lives' (Sarrazin 2016, 91). This is precisely the same style of soundtrack music that has been adopted by Hausa video filmmakers in northern Nigeria. This Hausa music genre became known locally as *nanaye*, and is made up of music and songs composed for, and performed during, the choreographed song-and-dance sequences that have become central motifs in Hausa video film dramas of northern Nigeria. These are films that from 1990 onward were initially recorded on videocassettes (as opposed to the usual celluloid film stock of the professional film industries) due to the low-cost availability of video cameras and tapes. However, with the increasing availability of digital recording media, especially from 2013 onward, these films began to be recorded with digital cameras containing internal hard drives or digital memory storage devices.

Hausa *nanaye filmi* music evolved from the Muslim Hausa cinema of northern Nigeria. It was created as a consequence of immersion in the Indian films which were screened by resident Lebanese cinema theater owners throughout northern Nigeria beginning in 1960, when Nigeria became independent from British colonial rule. Young, urban and male Muslim cinema audiences saw reflections of their cultural milieu in the depictions of life in India. Women were excluded from going to cinemas because of the strict Islamic culture of gender separation. However, women became audiences for the films after the state-run television stations established in the 1970s began broadcasting them and making tapes available for home consumption. Radio stations had also began broadcasting the soundtracks of popular Hindi films in the 1960s.

The appeal to young, urban and male Muslim cinema audiences occurred especially through films in the 1960s to early 1970s, in particular where dress codes, behavior toward parents and communal cohesion were concerned. Films from the United States, the United Kingdom and Chinese-language 'chopsocky' films were favored by the older educated elite. However, the vast majority of young people preferred Indian films with their spectacular and attractive song-and-dance routines. Eventually, the songs in these films, played intensively over the radio, provided onomatopoeic meters for young audiences in playgrounds to create equivalent Hausa lyrics. This development was crucial in the changing gender relations of Hausa popular music, as these audiences, made up mainly of boys, also included girls. Women's voices eventually emerged as a central characteristic of *nanaye* music. These lyrics were subsequently adapted by Islamic school clerics to create *madhu qasida* (panegyric poetry) in praise of the Prophet Muhammad. This adaptation constituted an attempt to 'Islamize' the Hindu-based lyrics while retaining the same musical structure. Girls were also prominent as students in the Islamiyya schools whose teachers were instrumental in 'Islamicizing' the Hindu-based lyrics.

When urban young men in the city of Kano in northern Nigeria decided to enter into the film industry, their immediate creative reference point was Indian film. These young men created a video film industry principally because of an inability to purchase the right equipment and film stock to shoot on celluloid. Videotape technology in the 1980s was leading-edge, cheap and easily available. Storylines were not aimed at creating artistic, social, political or intellectual statements. Using Indian film templates and, in many cases, completely appropriating popular Indian films, the storylines focused on the romantic theme of love triangles – a social phenomenon quite familiar to the young filmmakers. By 1999 the young filmmakers had labeled the video film industry

'Kanywood' after Bollywood and Hollywood and long before Nigeria's 'Nollywood,' a term coined in 2002 by *The New York Times*. Kanywood films subsequently became popular in other Hausa-speaking parts of Africa, such as Niger, Ghana and Cameroon, and provided templates for the local production of diasporic Hausa films in these African countries.

Hausa video films do not use music scores in the same way as conventional cinema, as a musical accompaniment to or emphasis of the film's moods. Instead, the films use specially composed soundtracks that do not interact with the film's storyline; indeed, in most cases, the musical interludes are unrelated to the film's narrative. They do, however, serve as sub-narratives superimposed on the main plot. These sub-narratives often occur when the contents of a song narrate a story or event that differs radically from the main plot. They are achieved through flash-forward scenes shot in futuristic vignettes that recount the fantasies of the protagonists (the main narrative is often frozen until the sub-narrative song is concluded).

So powerful were the *nanaye filmi* soundtracks in Hausa video films that they often determined the name of the film. This was because the songs were often composed first, before the script was written. In some cases, lyricists would promote an independent song and, if it were considered catchy enough, it could be purchased by a film producer. A film would then be created around the song.

Hausa *nanaye filmi* music was composed using standard commercial piano synthesizers, mainly from the Yamaha and Casio companies. Like other forms of Hausa music, including traditional acoustic performances, this music follows the verse-chorus form in its lyrical composition, the verse-chorus form (referred to as '*amshi*') being a fundamental characteristic of Hausa singing. However, unlike Indian filmi music, *nanaye filmi* is not based on traditional Hausa musical harmonies; if anything, *nanaye filmi* musicians go out of their way to create a sound more in tune with Western musical structures, made possible by the numerous stored samples of various genres of Western music stored in the databanks of the synthesizers they used.

The verses are arranged so that each one ends with a specific rhyming word (referred to as '*ƙafiya*'). The verse structures themselves may be couplets (*ƙwal biyu*), tercets (*ƙwal uku*), quatrains (*ƙwal huɗu*) or quintets (*ƙwal biyar*). *Nanaye* singers usually adopt one of these structures, interspacing them with a chorus, which then acts as the hook of the song.

The lyrics are in Hausa and often recorded separately from the accompanying music, with alternating male and female voices singing each verse. There is no fixed number of verses in a song. The lyrics are then mixed with the music later by session musicians in the studio. The mixed-gender structure of the songs, which is quite different from that of Hausa traditional music with its strict gender segregation, was as a result of the Indian film duets after which the musical structure is patterned. The choruses, with their memorable hooks, are always sung by female voices, perhaps providing an outlet for women's social power. The female voices are often enhanced with Auto-tune software after the recording when editing the song, creating a higher-pitched vocal delivery that approximates famous and popular Hindi female playback singers – singers such as Asha Bhosle and Lata Mangeshkar whose prerecorded performances were used as soundtracks with actors then miming the songs during shooting sequences.

The word '*nanaye*' refers to the chorus of traditional Hausa girls' playground songs in a style referred to as *gada* (handclapping). Oil wealth in Nigeria resulted in rapid infrastructural development in cities during the 1970s, which in turn resulted in increasing urbanization. As a consequence, the quintessential 'village playground' of most Hausa towns and villages started giving way to housing expansion and the clustered playgrounds where children played and sang *nanaye* songs disappeared. This style of music was, however, revived with the development of Hausa video films because it was a style that seemed suited to the domestic themes and plots of the films. Both the music and storylines of the films target women and explore domestic issues such as romantic relationships as they affect women.

The first Hausa video films, made from 1990 to 1994, relied on Hausa traditional acoustic music ensembles for their soundtracks. These soundtracks were just that: incidental background music to accompany the film that was not integral to the storyline. The Hausa video film that pioneered a changeover to electronic music was *In Da So Da Ƙauna* (dir. Ado Ahmad, 1994), whose score was composed with a Casiotone MT-140 keyboard. With 20 instrumental sound samples and rhythms, this keyboard was seen as providing a 'modern' sound for Hausa music as opposed to the limited acoustic instruments used by the more classical, traditional Hausa musicians.

Clearly seeing the future in keyboard music, Hamisu Lamiɗo Iyan-Tama, a Kano-based Hausa entrepreneur who was also an actor, decided to invest in a pioneer music studio, establishing the Iyan-Tama Multimedia studio in Kano in 1996. The studio's first purchase was the Yamaha PSR-220, which provided an instant appeal for modern Hausa musicians seeking to explore a combination of sounds without being hampered by the inability to play traditional acoustic instruments. Traditional Hausa music performances are usually based on a single musical instrument of various types, one example being provided by Aliyu Dandawo's ensemble, which plays about six different types of drums. Performers such as Hassan Wayam and Nasiru Garba Supa, who use different musical instruments in the same event, are rare. The availability of the Yamaha PSR series of synthesizers thus enabled modern Hausa musicians to combine different musical sounds in the same performance – creating truly innovative outcomes in Hausa music that broke the monopoly of the single instrument characteristic of traditional Hausa music. In so doing, synthesizers enabled Hausa video film *nanaye* artists to creatively approximate Hindi film music, a music which they copied avidly.

The first *nanaye* hit that set the pace was 'Sangaya,' composed on a Yamaha PRS-730. Written in 1999 by Alee Baba Yakasai at the Iyan-Tama Multimedia Studios in Kano, it was the leading *nanaye* song in the film *Sangaya* (dir. Muhammad Sabo, 1999). The success of *Sangaya* sent a strong message that *nanaye* music could achieve massive sales, especially if executed with what practitioners called a '*fiyano*' (the Hausa word for 'piano'). The flexibility afforded by the Yamaha PSR series of keyboard synthesizers enabled improvisations that would not have been possible with Hausa traditional orchestras and propelled *nanaye* as a pioneer Hausa urban music style.

Hausa *nanaye* songs are derived from many sources including, importantly, Hindi film songs. The main sources, however, are independent lyricists such as Sani Yusuf Ayagi, Musbahu Ahmed, Sadi Sidi Sharifai, Yakubu Muhammad and Rabi Mustapha. Their lyrics have been set to music by a burgeoning group of Yamaha synthesizer instrumentalists in the numerous studios that emerged in Kano in the aftermath of the *nanaye* music revolution, especially after 2000.

As *nanaye* songs do not have to relate to the storyline of any particular film, they are inserted at any point in a film where the director needs a song-and-dance sequence. The CD of the song is then taken to the location where the actors – who have learned the lines of the song by heart – mime the song while the finished recording plays in the background. The first Hausa video film to incorporate this process of *nanaye* mixed-gender miming was *Badaƙala* (dir. Ɗan Azumi Baba, 1997). The lyricists rarely contribute to the musical structure of the songs, leaving decisions about the beat and the rhythm to the studio musician. An exception was *nanaye* lyricist Adam A. Zango, who composed his own music and became a famous actor and lyricist, having started his career as a studio technician.

A lull in Hausa video film production in 2007 forced *nanaye* singers to start releasing songs not intended for any film. However, the songs did retain the format used in Hausa film song-and-dance routines. These singers, including Aminudeen Ladan Abubakar, Binta 'Fati Nijar' Labaran, Maryam Fantimoti and Mahmud Nagudu, created a new substyle which came to be referred to by Hausa social media fans as *sabon alƙawari* (new testament, new future), because the songs were composed for general popular consumption rather than for a particular film. In addition, they have been considered 'modern' because of the role of Yamaha synthesizers in their composition. This substyle also included burgeoning Islamic gospel music, centered around praise of the Prophet Muhammad, that used the same *nanaye* performance format. This development echoes Indian filmi music for, as Sarrazin (2014, 178) has noted, 'filmi music has become so powerful that quite often its aesthetics in turn influenced the original co-opted genre outside of the cinemas.' The development of *madhu* religious poetry and political songs all based on the *nanaye* format attests to the enduring power of *nanaye* and its technologies of production among Hausa young people (see below). Indeed, audiences often want to know which particular film featured a particular political or religious song, indicating a complete crossover in musical styles across the genres.

In 2008 the emergence of *nanaye* songs totally disconnected to the Hausa film industry heralded the emergence of what can only be called 'post-*nanaye*' – a musical style with a massive output rooted in Hausa urban cultures. Without any film outlet, the lyricists simply keep recording song after song – sometimes in the hundreds – and uploaded what they could into MP3 sharing websites. Social media features heavily in the dissemination of *nanaye*. This is because young urban Hausa people have ready access to the Internet through commonly available smartphones that make it easy to upload songs to social media sites such as Instagram, YouTube and MySpace, as well as social network sites such as Facebook. Bureaucratic processes associated with record labels and the professional pressing of CDs have made social media the most effective way for both performers and their audiences to participate in wide-scale music dissemination, often for free.

Hausa *nanaye* has come to reflect the dynamism of the contemporary music scene in urban Africa. By focusing on women's voices as its central characteristic, it has redefined social spaces for women, particularly in northern Nigerian Muslim cultures. The duet, its central feature, gives greater prominence to women and has brought them out of the social 'cold.'

Madhee (Madhu) – Islamic Gospel Music in Northern Nigeria

Madhee is a style of music performed by Muslim peoples based on panegyrics in praise of Allah, the Prophet Muhammad, as well as of venerated sheikhs of Islam. It has been significantly influenced in its development by *nanaye filmi* music.

Among the Muslim Hausa of northern Nigeria, this style of *madhee* music is referred to as '*madhu*' and originated in religious schools referred to as Islamiyya schools. It is, to all intents and purposes, Islamic gospel music. Established in the 1960s, and based on similar schools in the Sudan, Islamiyya schools provided a modernized, expanded and inclusive curriculum, as opposed to the older traditional and more established religious schools that teach only the Qur'an. These schools' more inclusive religious curriculum is based on Hadith (sayings of the Prophet Muhammad), Fiqh (Islamic jurisprudence), Tauhid (oneness of God), Seerah (Prophetic biography), Tahfeez (memorizing and fluently reciting the Qur'an) and Nasheeda (*a cappella* poetry, although, in some schools, especially those of the Sufi brotherhoods – mystics of Islam – the *bandiri*, a frame drum, is used as accompaniment).

While *madeeh* poetry is original to the Islamiyya schools, the schools nevertheless always incorporate three classical poems into the Nasheeda curriculum as a template for the subsequent development of not only the style but also the content of popular Islamic poetry. Hausa *madeeh* poets differ from traditional poet–musicians in the sense that they focus on purely religious narratives, whether modern or classical, while traditional poet–musicians tended to philosophize about life.

The first Islamic poem incorporated by Hausa *madeeh* poets was Al-Fazazi's *Ishriniyyat*, originally composed in 1208 by Abu Zayd Abd al-Rahman ibn Yakhlaftan ibn Ahmad al-Fazazi from Córdoba. Its full title was *Al-Wasail al-Mutaqabbala* (The Accepted Paths), or more commonly, *Qasid al-Ishriniyyat fi Madh Saiyidna Muhammad* (Poem in the Praise of Muhammad). The second was Al-Busiri's *Al-Burda*. This was composed in the thirteenth century by Abu Abdallah Muhammad ibn Sa'id ul-Busiri Ash Shadhili from Morocco, commonly referred to as Al-Busiri. *Al-Burda* is commonly referred to by its longer title of *al-Kawakib ad-Durriya fi Madḥ Khayr al-Bariya* (The Celestial Lights in Praise of the Best of Creation). The third is the *Hamziyya*, also composed by Al-Busiri. The *Hamziyya* is a poem, all of whose verses rhyme with the letter '*hamza*.' Imam al-Busiri wrote a *Hamziyya* with more than 400 verses, which contains the biography and history of the Prophet Muhammad. Between them, these three classic poems provide the Islamiyya school students with an effective summary of the Seerah of the Prophet Muhammad, and became templates to be used as a basis for the development of similar poems.

When Hindi films became very popular in northern Nigeria from the 1960s onward, their Hausa audiences became enamored with the catchy music of the films. It was mainly young boys who, having heard the songs played on the radio, started mimicking them, in playgrounds. Noticing this, Islamiyya school teachers took the step of 'Islamizing' the Hindi film songs by composing songs in praise of the Prophet using the Hindi songs' vocal harmony.

This 'Islamizing' was a deliberate step motivated by an understanding that a lot of the Hindi film songs were either odes to various gods of the Hindu religion or romantic songs. These adaptations, which were purely vocal, emerged principally in the 1980s during an Islamic religious resurgence in northern Nigeria after the 1979 Iranian Islamic revolution, a revolution which had a significant impact in the region. The basic idea was to wean Hausa children away from repeating Hindi film lyrics which they did not know, and which, in marked contrast to the monotheism of Islam, could contain references to the multiplicity of deities characteristic of Hinduism.

With the establishment of a system that got children to sing something considered more meaningful than a substitution of Hindi words from Hindi film soundtracks, more structured performance groups started to appear from 1986 onward, principally in Kano, but soon spreading to other parts of northern Nigeria. Devoted to singing the praises of the Prophet Muhammad in local languages with performances based on the templates of the three classical poems, the groups were referred to collectively as *Kungiyoyin Yabon Annabi* (Panegyric Singers of the Prophet). The more notable of these included Usshaqul Nabiyyi (established in 1986), Fitiyanul Ahbabu (1988), Ahawul Nabiyyi (1989), Ahababu Rasulillah (1989), Mahabbatu Rasul (1989), Ashiratu Nabiyyi (1990) and Zumratul Madahun Nabiyyi (1990). These groups used the *bandiri* instead of the *a cappella* performance of the Islamiyya schools. The *bandiri* itself has a special place in Hausa Muslim Sufi religious performances, a practice that has often led to controversies about the use of music in Islam, as well as the use of music in mosques during Sufi religious activities. The *bandiri* was used by the groups to attract audiences to their performances.

Emerging in an era of Nigerian political turbulence (1979 to 1983) that saw an increased number of gangs made up of young people come into existence as well as an increase in political thuggery, Yabon Annabi poets formed themselves into groups of young people aimed at curbing the miscreant excesses of their peers. These groups felt the best way to achieve their ends was to emphasize love for the Prophet Muhammad in the belief that intense love for the Prophet alone was a significant enough deterrent to offset bad behavior by young people. In effect, the Yabon Annabi poets were preachers, adopting the motif of popular culture to preach rather than the usual fire and brimstone approach of elder clerics.

In the 1990s a new style of Islamic gospel music emerged, riding on the coat tails of the Hausa film industry's use of Yamaha PSR keyboards to compose the predominantly romantic songs embedded in the narrative of Hausa films. Noting an overwhelming tendency on the part of young people to recite the songs of the Hausa video films, a new group of Islamic gospel singers emerged who also relied on a Yamaha synthesizer to accompany their poems – thus lending them a 'modern' sound that was in competition with Hausa film songs. This approach worked. The *majalisi* (concert) organized by these performers usually drew mammoth crowds. This music was instrumental in attracting people, and young people in particular, to the religious messages embedded in the poems. Led by Rabi'u Usman Baba – a Sufi poet in Kano who became the first individual to use a Yamaha piano synthesizer in his performances – other poets followed, and the electronic sound became a signature of both secular and Islamic singers. Some of the most successful of the singers to emerge as 'modern' Islamic gospel performers include Umar Abdul'aziz Wudil, with the stage name of 'Fadar Bege' (The Palace of Yearning'), Auwalu Habib Bichi, Kabiru Dandogarai, Kabiru Maulana and Ibrahim Autan Sidi. With increased access to recording technology, these modern Islamic singers quickly moved from compact cassette recordings of their performances to CDs that were sold in markets across northern Nigeria. These CDs were neither produced nor marketed by major recording companies since these did not exist for this genre of music. They were produced and marketed through amateur recording studios with limited pressings that sold for less than 50 cents each.

Islamic gospel music in northern Nigeria has therefore evolved as a rallying point for the revival of the Islamic mysticism of Sufism through panegyric performances which focus on the Prophet Muhammad. However, with increasing emphasis on the Seerah (biography) of the Prophet, performers of this music became increasingly devoted to veneration of the two main classical Sufi sheikhs, Sheikh Abdul Qadir Jilani (1077–1166), Iran, founder of the Qadiriyya, and Sidi Ahmad al-Tijani (1737–1815), Morocco, founder of the Tijaniyya Sufi order. In Kano, most of the Islamic popular singers were Tijaniyya, embracing technology and using the Internet to spread their gospel.

While Islamic gospel songs were targeted initially at moving young people away from secular songs containing undesirable subject matter (mainly romantic in character), their proliferation has served only to add color to the musical landscape in northern Nigeria rather than diminishing the existing and increasingly burgeoning secular music scene.

Hausa Technopop

Hausa technopop is an urban music style created in Kano. Although it made appearances on northern Nigerian radio as early as the mid-1990s, it only emerged as a fully formed style from 2008 onward, when it ran counter to the dominance of Hausa *nanaye*, the romantic urban music style created initially for the song-and-dance routines of Hausa video films. Hausa technopop performers consider *nanaye* less macho and more 'girlish' due to the latter's dependence on women's voices. While Hausa technopop artists often use women's voices in their chorus to attract larger audiences, the main focus of their performance is on men's voices. The subject matter of Hausa technopop is as diverse as the music. However, unlike *nanaye* singers, Hausa technopop singers focus less on romantic themes and more on social and educational issues. Most often the words are simply assembled to form a rhyme, since the main essence of Hausa technopop is to provide a dance-oriented entertainment within a matrix of 'modern' beats.

The style emerged as a result of the desire on the part of young Hausa people in urban areas to create modern musical forms that respected musicians in Hausa society, since music and musicians were considered to be of a low status among mainstream conservative Hausa – a legacy stemming from Hausa traditional music. This modernity was triggered by the increasing popularity of transnational urban music styles of dance music, R&B and, significantly, rap. This popularity created a desire among young urban Hausa to domesticate these music styles.

The opportunity to create Hausa technopop first presented itself in 1996 when 18-year-old Nasir Gwale, based in Kano, received the gift of an old Casiotone MT-140 keyboard. With over 20 sound samples and rhythms, the keyboard provided him with an opportunity to sequence the various samples into a soundscape that approximated 'modern' music, although reflecting no particular distinctive style. This keyboard was eventually replaced by the Yamaha PSR series of synthesizers, which provided the main creative template for the composition of *nanaye* music for Hausa video films (see Hausa *nanaye filmi* music above). Technopop thus came to be based exclusively on sounds generated by the Yamaha PRS series of synthesizers. Hausa instrumentalists have used the term 'dance-hall' to refer to the samples stored in the Yamaha synthesizers they used and it is not to be confused with the Jamaican music genre of the same name.

Due to the variety of ways technopop musicians use synthesizers to create their music, there is no single, recognizable style preferred by session and studio musicians. Lyricists usually either come to the studios with lyrics that are written down or simply pay to enter the recording studio and sing to a beat that in general is created by a studio musician. Consequently, dance rhythms are the only connecting tissue in all Hausa technopop music in Kano and other parts of northern Nigeria.

Vocals are sung mainly in the Hausa language, although lyrics in English are occasionally used in order to create a sound that is 'authentically modern.' In adopting this latter style of delivery, Hausa technopop musicians copy southern Nigerian Afropop counterparts such as D'Banj, Davido, Wizkid, P-Square and 2Face Idibia – although most of these southern Nigerian musicians prefer to see themselves as rap artists in that they combine Afropop (a contemporary, urban, electric popular music style targeted at dance clubs) with elements of rap (with lyrics targeting audiences that can easily compare them with those of mainstream US rap artists such as Ice Cube or Snoop Dogg).

Due to the diversity of approaches adopted by the various musicians who compose the instrumental parts for Hausa technopop songs, the style has no specific musical pedigree. It is generally recognized as technopop because of its disco beat. Like most Hausa modern music, the technopop rhythm and beat follow the oral contours of the song, in that the rhyming words correspond to the beat, while the musician creates a sound equivalent to the rhyme (*kafiya*). This lyrical structure is borrowed from the Arabic poetic structures to which most Hausa musicians are exposed through the compulsory Islamic education they undergo at various stages of their lives. Technopop thus becomes poetry set to music that conforms to the structure of the rhymed lyrics.

In the Muslim states of northern Nigeria that from 1999 onward have implemented Shari'ah Islamic law, strict Islamic rules governing entertainment for young people in public spaces has severely limited performances of technopop (or any other form of music) in clubs. There was as a consequence an absence of a structured culture of nightclubs and concert venues in Kano. Young people, especially unmarried women, could be arrested for vagrancy by the morality police after 10 pm. This initially restricted the reception of technopop to iPods and smartphones and its distribution to Bluetooth. The form of technopop known as 'dance-hall' was thus paradoxically prohibited from use for dancing in public due to restrictions on public gatherings for the purposes of nonreligious entertainment. As a consequence, audiences for this form of technopop came to appreciate its dance beats at small gatherings in the privacy of their homes. In the absence of CDs until 2005, radio stations gradually became the main platform in northern Nigeria for Hausa technopop musicians.

In December 2003 a new FM radio station, Radio Freedom, was opened in Kano. Within two years the station had become a catalyst in showcasing the increasing pool of emerging Hausa technopop stars. These were led by Bello Ibrahim (Billy-O). His demo (a studio recording distributed exclusively to other users through Bluetooth technology) 'Rainy Season' received massive airplay on Freedom Radio in 2005. Its appeal to young urban audiences was due to its use of Enghausa – starting a verse in Hausa and ending almost every line of the verse with an English word that captures a particular emotion.

By 2006 Hausa technopop musicians were still in what may be called the 'demo mode' because of a lack of record deals and a total absence of record companies willing to market Hausa music. The 'demo' method of production consisted of a lyricist going to a studio with a song and asking the resident musician to listen to the song and create a tune based on its rhyme. Eventually the song was set to music, recorded on a CD and disseminated as an MP3 in club circuits and on FM stations, and shared by fans through Bluetooth technology.

The first Hausa technopop CD was Abdullahi Mighty's *Taka*, released in 2005 in Kano. Its lead track, 'Sanya Zobe,' was a pure dance-hall composition. Aimed squarely at the commercial side of the music industry, it attained its success through its adoption of a technopop dance matrix over-layered with a thin veneer of Hausa *nanaye*-style singing. This form of Hausa technopop music was followed by others, despite the contempt technopop singers felt toward *nanaye* singers. Indeed, the competition and scorn with which the rising Hausa technopop musicians treat *nanaye* lyricists and musicians were brought to the fore in one of the top-selling independent CDs of 2007 – *Jeeta*, by Kabiru 'Shaba' Shariff. Shariff was a resident session musician-turned lyricist in Kano who put down some of the *nanaye* stars.

A crisis in the Hausa video film industry in 2007 led to the banning of the film industry by the Kano State Censorship Board, the government agency responsible for regulating all creative activities in Kano. This ban affected the music industry because the musicians and lyricists relied on the film industry for their trade. Some of the *nanaye* singers such as Adam A. Zango reinvented themselves as technopop artists, at least until the film industry revived in the middle of 2008. Zango thus combines the two styles in his performances. The lull in film production also led to the emergence in 2008 of a new crop of singers that included X-Dough, Double D, Cast, AY Fashion and Funkiest Mallam. Funkiest Mallam differs from the other singers in using comedy in his lyrics. This has given him a sizeable following on YouTube. Using a variety of subject matter mainly drawn from social issues, all these performers have catapulted technopop to a new height of Hausa urban cool. With a regime change in 2011, when a new, less puritanical governor was elected in Kano, technopop came to be performed more publicly at 'shows' or concerts at the end of major religious festivals.

Bibliography

Adamu, Abdalla Uba. 2006. 'Transglobal Media Flows and African Popular Culture: Revolution and Reaction in Muslim Hausa Popular Culture.' Mary

Kingsley Zochonis Lecture presented at the African Studies Association UK Biennial Conference, School of Oriental and African Studies, University of London, London, 12 September.

Adamu, Abdalla Uba. 2008. 'The Influence of Hindi Film Music on Hausa Videofilm Soundtrack Music.' In *Global Soundtracks: Worlds of Film Music*, ed. Mark Slobin. Middletown, CT: Wesleyan University Press, 152–76.

Adamu, Abdalla Uba. 2009. 'Hausa Video Films – Yesterday, Today and Tomorrow: Intellectualizing Hausa Video Films in Retrospect.' Paper presented at the International Workshop on Hausa Home Video Films, Ahmadu Bello University, Zaria, Nigeria, 13–15 August.

Adamu, Abdalla Uba. 2010. 'The Muse's Journey: Transcultural Translators and the Domestication of Hindi Music in Hausa Popular Culture.' *Journal of African Cultural Studies* 22(1): 41–56.

Ames, David W., and King, Anthony V. 1971. *Glossary of Hausa Music and Its Social Contexts*. Evanston, IL: Northwestern University Press.

Furniss, Graham. 1996. *Poetry, Prose, and Popular Culture in Hausa*. Washington, DC: Smithsonian Institution Press.

Gusau, Saidu Muhammad. 1996. *Makaɗa da Mawaƙan Hausa* [Hausa Musicians and Singers]. Kaduna, Nigeria: Fisbas Media Services.

Kofoworola, Ziky, and Lateef, Yusef. 1987. *Hausa Performing Arts and Music*. Lagos: Department of Culture, Federal Ministry of Information and Culture.

Kvetko, Peter. 2009. 'Individualism, Authenticity and Genre Boundaries in the Bombay Music Industry.' In *Popular Culture in a Globalised India*, eds. K. Moti Gokulsing and Wimal Dissanayake. London: Routledge, 111–24.

Larkin, Brian. 2003. 'Itineraries of Indian Cinema: African Videos, Bollywood and Global Media.' In *Multiculturalism, Postcoloniality and Transnational Media*, eds. Ella Shohat and Robert Stam. New Brunswick, NJ: Rutgers University Press, 170–92.

Larkin, Brian. 2004. 'Bandiri Music, Globalization and Urban Experience in Nigeria.' *Social Text* 22(4): 91–112.

Larkin, Brian. 2008. *Signal and Noise: Media, Infrastructure and Urban Culture in Nigeria*. Durham, NC: Duke University Press.

McCain, Carmen. 2013. 'Nollywood, Kannywood and a Decade of Hausa Film Censorship in Nigeria.' In *Silencing Cinema: Film Censorship Around the World*, eds. Daniel Biltereyst and Roel Vande Winkel. London: Palgrave MacMillan, 223–40.

Sarrazin, Natalie. 2014. 'Devotion or Pleasure? Music and Meaning in the Celluloid Performances of Qawwali in South Asia and the Diaspora.' In *Music, Culture and Identity in the Muslim World: Performance, Politics and Piety*, ed. Kamal Salhi. New York: Routledge, 178–99.

Sarrazin, Natalie. 2016. 'Magic, Destruction and Redemption in the Soundtracks of *Aashiqui 2*, *RockStar*, and *Rock On!!*' In *Music in Contemporary Indian Film: Memory, Voice, Identity*, eds. Jayson Beaster-Jones and Natalie Sarrazin. London: Routledge, 91–104.

Sheme, Ibrahim, et al. 2006. *Shata: Mahadi Mai Dogon Zamani* [Shata: The Evergreen Singer]. Kaduna: Informart Publishers.

Smith, Michael G. 1959. 'The Hausa System of Social Status.' *Africa* 29(3): 239–52.

Discographical References

Abdullahi Mighty. *Taka*. De-Hood Records. *2005*: Nigeria.

Baba, Yakasai Alee. 'Sangaya.' Iyan-Tama Multimedia Studios. *1999*: Nigeria.

Ibrahim, Bello (Billy-O). 'Rainy Season.' *Ba A Rawa*. Global Records. *2005*: Nigeria.

Shaba. *Jeeta*. Shaba Musical Studio. *2009*: Nigeria.

Filmography

Badakala, dir. Dan Azumi Baba. 1997. Nigeria. 132 mins. Crime drama. Original music by Nasir Ishaq Gwale.

In Da So Da Kauna, dir. Ado Ahmad. 1994. Nigeria, 222 mins. Romantic drama. Original music by Nasir Ishaq Gwale.

Sangaya, dir. Muhammad Sabo. 1999. Nigeria. 175 mins. Romantic drama. Original music by Alee Baba Yakasai.

ABDALLA UBA ADAMU

Hawl

El-hawl is the most representative classical music style of the northwest-African region of Trab el-Bidhân, which mainly encompasses present-day

Mauritania and Western Sahara. The *Bidhân* people, a traditionally crossroads culture of Arab, Berber and sub-Saharan descent, were nomadic shepherds who were constantly on the move searching for green pastures for their camel herds; however, nowadays most people are settled in urban centers across the territory. *El-hawl*, deeply rooted in the *Bidhân* oral traditions in *Hassâniya* (the region's dialect of Arabic), is the perfect example of the blends of northern and southern musical practices in northwest Africa.

El-hawl is usually performed by the *iggâwen*, the traditional hereditary musicians and storytellers closely related to the 'griot' culture in other West African countries such as Mali, Guinea and Senegal (Hale 1998). The *iggâwen* are more common in the southern areas of the Bidhân region (Mauritania) than in the north. These musicians normally perform sitting down, accompanying their singing with two traditional string instruments distinguished by the gender of their players: the men play the *tidinit* – a small four-stringed plucked lute related to the Bambara *ngoni* (Mali) and the Wolof *xalam* (Senegal) (Charry 1996); while the women play the *ardin* – an 11-stringed harp that is linked to the West African *kora* and whose body is made from a calabash gourd cut in half and partially covered with animal skin. In the early twenty-first century, male musicians also play the electric guitar and the keyboard (here, as elsewhere, symbols of musical modernity), transferring to them the traditional playing techniques of the *tidinit*. On some occasions, both male and female musicians play the traditional *tbal* drum.

Compositions of *el-hawl* are expected to be a perfect combination of poetry and music (Norris 1968). The themes of Hassâniya poetry are varied and include the full range of human experience. Common poetry genres among the *Bidhân* are *thaydin* (epic tales), *adlal* (landscape poems), *as-sababa* (ardent love; fervent longing), *ghazâl* (about the beloved and torments caused by love), *nasib* (about nostalgia), *hikma* (didactic and moral wisdom), religious praise, history and genealogy, elegy, satire, insult and a range of social commentary (Deubel 2012).

The music of *el-hawl* is the *azawaan*, a complex musical system divided into four modes (*kar*, *fâghu*, *senima* and *lebteit*) called *bhor* ('seas'). Between *senima* and *lebteit*, musicians usually perform a transitory bridge named *liyen*, with its own musical characteristics. In turn, each *bhâr* can be performed in what is conceived as a 'black' (*lakhal*) or 'white' (*labiad*) way. Each of these modes relates to a different mood and age. For example, *fâghu* evokes scenes of war and feats of courage, strength and pride. Traditionally, musicians used it to inspire warriors on the battlefield, and it is today one of the most commonly used modes in the contemporary resistance music of Western Sahara (see *nidal*). *Kar*, on the contrary, is associated with praises and religious chants (see *medeh*), and is used to recognize the achievements of certain saints. In traditional *hawl* performances, the *bhor* were arranged in a very specific order, and performances were not complete until the whole suite was finished. However, modern musicians may choose one mode for each individual song (Guignard 2005).

El-hawl is commonly performed at weddings and other social gatherings, requiring a relaxed environment in which the audience can enjoy the performance, normally being accompanied with conversation or with their tea-making ceremony. This music expresses feelings that normal speech cannot convey, such as deep love, connection with the land, the joy of a victory or the sorrow of a defeat, and it is the responsibility of the lead vocalist to convey them effectively. These musical expressions of feeling are especially emphasized at the beginning of the songs with a poetic recitation, or with a melodic improvisation called *mawwâl*, typical of the Arabic singing tradition. In *el-hawl* there is also a characteristic expressive device of Berber origin called *barmât* that consists of very quick vibrations of the voice (Guignard 2007). The mixture of all these influences into a single style is an example of the hybridity of *Bidhân* identity.

Bibliography

Charry, Eric. 1996. 'Plucked Lutes in West Africa: An Historical Overview.' *The Galpin Society Journal* 49: 3–37.

Deubel, Tara. 2012. 'Poetics of Diaspora: Sahrawi Poets and Postcolonial Transformations of a Trans-Saharan Genre in Northwest Africa.' *The Journal of North African Studies* 17(2): 295–314.

Guignard, Michel. 2005. *Musique, honneur et plaisir au Sahara: Étude psycho-sociologique et musicologique de la société maure* [Music, Honor and Pleasure in the Sahara: Psychosociological and Musicological Study of Moorish Society]. Paris: Librairie Orientaliste Paul Geuthner.

Guignard, Michel. 2007. 'Les griots maures et leur musique: Origine et évolutions contemporaines' [The Moorish *Griots* and Their Music: Origin and Contemporary Changes]. Presentation at *Conference on Music in the World of Islam*, Assilah (Morocco), 8–13 August.

Hale, Thomas A. 1998. *Griots and Griottes*. Bloomington and Indianapolis: Indiana University Press.

Norris, Harry Thirlwall. 1968. *Shinqiti Folk Literature and Song*. Oxford: Oxford University Press.

VIOLETA RUANO

Heavy Metal in Africa

While not often discussed outside North America and Europe, heavy metal has solidified itself into a global genre. The spread of the genre has come about organically as fans outside these two heavy metal epicenters have gravitated toward this music for years not only in Latin America, but also in Asia and Africa. The latter, not typically associated with a proclivity for Western ways, has embraced hard rock and later heavy metal for decades with little notice being taken outside the continent.

Early Years

Since the 1970s aspects of rock 'n' roll and psychedlic rock have existed in Africa, notably in Zambia during an era known as 'Zamrock,' with artists such as Musi-O-Tunya, WITCH (or W.I.T.C.H.), Paul Ngozi and the Ngozi Family, The Peace and Amanaz performing original songs characterized by the 'fuzzy' guitar sounds, repetitive riffing and thunderous rhythms of international acts Black Sabbath, Deep Purple and Jimi Hendrix. While there were other fuzzy-guitar scenes in Nigeria, Zimbabwe (then known as Southern Rhodesia) and South Africa, it was the Zamrock scene that produced the most salient records of this time. With the music of these acts purchased and reissued by the US label Now-Again during the 2010s, much of what was recorded has since been discovered for the first time by Western audiences. The songs of Zamrock artists were significant reflections of Zambian life, marked lyrically by their nation's 'economic despair … and also the controversy of wider politics in Africa and the world' (Sandburg 2013). However, most of what Zamrock-era artists created did not translate well for successive generations, and thus was not able to foster a viable fan base. Musicians in Africa would later be influenced by this same British music, but in a markedly different way.

The next wave of rockers in sub-Saharan Africa built on previous developments but were influenced additionally by groups such as AC/DC, Van Halen and Judas Priest, thus ushering in acts that were notably heavier and more intense. Heavy metal's development in Africa occurred in parallel with Western developments, as Africans were able to connect to global scenes through heavy metal's tape-trading culture of the 1980s and early 1990s, which allowed them to access the wider world of extreme music. As Kahn-Harris explains, this cultural exchange largely took place through local bands in different countries trading 'demo tapes, live tapes and rehearsal tapes' (2007, 7) that were often accompanied by letters and leaflets. These letters and leaflets would advertise other bands as well as metal magazines and fanzines that were also being exchanged between fans on a global basis.

Metal's largest impact in Africa came about as a result of the burgeoning of two types of infrastructure: digital and musical. The former has witnessed strong growth in the continent since the 1990s, especially in cosmopolitan settings. The Internet has dramatically assisted the spread of metal outside traditional markets as it is 'low cost and allows for incredible specialization' (Weinstein 2011, 51). Furthermore, as Frith has noted (2000, 315), 'this technology (made) for a new music culture, organized around neither local traditions nor global corporate trends.' With the advent of chat rooms, message boards, video streams, various forms of social media, Skype and YouTube, Africans have been able to connect with their Western metal peers, not only to access music, but also to discuss the experience of performing heavy metal. Knowledge needed to perform heavy metal could in this way be acquired in various forms of peer-to-peer communication, mostly by amateurs, or downloaded in situations where printed material 'would otherwise be limited' (Ebert 2017, 179): the availability of music lessons through the Internet has steadily increased.

Musical infrastructure relates to music as a viable and commercial form of art: the marketing and live performance of bands, the establishment of spaces for consumption and promotion as well as a culture of transferring knowledge to other musicians that can involve musical instruction and business acumen. This infrastructure has developed significantly in Africa's various metal scenes as musicians and fans have gained experience, even embedding themselves in Western metal scenes as expatriate participants and observers. This involvement has allowed those participating to accrue a wealth of knowledge that would otherwise have been difficult to obtain. Furthermore, an increase in performances by international artists has resulted in interactions with local musicians and fans, allowing for a better understanding of professional rules and guidelines.

The Spread of Heavy Metal in Africa

With the growth of these types of infrastructure, the number of nations in Africa identified as having heavy metal bands has increased substantially since 1990, with the largest increase having occurred since the early 2000s. According to the *Encyclopedia Metallum* (2014), only seven African nations had been identified as having heavy metal bands in 1990. As of 2018 the number of African nations boasting metal bands was 20. This growth has been notable in countries with substantial colonial vestiges, a tendency to adopt Western ways, trade relationships with former colonial governments and both emigrant and immigrant expatriate communities. Established metal bands exist in most of the nations of North Africa; the West African states of Ghana, Nigeria and Togo; Cameroon in Central Africa; the Southern African countries of Angola, Botswana, Mozambique, Namibia, South Africa and Zimbabwe; Kenya and Uganda in East Africa; and the African Islands of Madagascar, Mauritius and Reunion.

In Central Africa, the prospect of heavy metal evolving has been considerably limited, despite its presence in Cameroon. Physical infrastructure in nations including the Congo (Brazzaville), the Democratic Republic of Congo (especially outside the capital, Kinshasa), Chad and the Central African Republic remains undeveloped. Economic progress has frustrated everyday life as resource issues have hindered economic progress, fueled conflicts and impaired development. Literacy rates and life expectancies have been among the lowest in the world (The Africa Report 2017–18, 161–9).

The Sounds of African Metal: the Global and the Local

Heavy metal, even among its most active and loyal consumers, is a term that evokes ambiguity. The term encompasses a multitude of sounds, having been applied to acts from the pop-soaked sounds of British rockers Def Leppard to the extreme guttural growls of Florida's Cannibal Corpse. Despite the wide swath of acts that have made up this huge category of music, from Blue Cheer to Black Sabbath in the early days through Iron Maiden and Metallica, the sound of heavy metal is unmistakable to fans globally. In Africa, this is no different. Fans across the continent have been able to connect to this music and convey their emotions and life experiences through the formation of their own bands.

Musically, metal in Africa is structured on the sounds of Western bands. While heavy metal's musical palette allows for the incorporation of many sounds outside the instrumentation customarily used in its performance, traditional African influences have remained minimal: musicians have incorporated local instrumentation to only a modest extent. In most nations, musicians have eschewed such influences as a means of seeking validation from their Western counterparts while solidifying the genre in their home nations, and doing this based on the unwritten code to which heavy metal's sound and instrumentation adheres: drums, electric guitars, electric bass, vocals and – with some subgenres – keyboards (Weinstein 2000, 6).

However, there are a few instances where local influences are apparent. One notable example would be the exclusive use of the Malagasy language as well as the influence of a local oral tradition known as *hainteny* in the lyrics of heavy metal in Madagascar. These lyrics include many allusions to precolonial existence as well as a close affinity to the land (Bookman 2007, 9). While the country has a history somewhat distinct from other African nations because of a unique culture stemming from the Austronesians who initially settled the island, Madagascar's deep-seated musical traditions are otherwise absent as musicians lean on their Western heroes as exemplars.

Kenya's metal scene boasts an ethnically diverse group with musicians coming from any one of Kenya's 42 ethnic groups. This disparity has musicians divided regarding the inclusion of traditional elements in their music. Musically, Kenya's metal scene has been involved in a dialogue contrasting global and local traditions (Knopke 2015, 117–18), tension arising as some bands choose to perform portions of their lyrics or even entire songs in Swahili as a way of bringing in more local listeners. Swahili is seen as a unifier because, unlike English, it is not a colonial language and could be used to bring fans from rural Kenya into the heavy metal scene. However, its use is still sparse – primarily occurring among rock bands, as some rockers see the use of Swahili as a move away from rock and metal's *lingua franca*: English.

Other bands, such as Botswana-based Skinflint, whose sound is marked by strong influences from the New Wave of British Heavy Metal (NWOBHM), have ensured that their music is 'distinctly African' by incorporating 'African mythologies and spirituality' (Allegrezza 2015) as their main lyrical themes. Countrymen Wrust have included Setswana traditional music on their 2013 album, *Intellectual Metamorphosis*. In Ethiopia, Jano Band have experimented with different musical elements to create a mixed sound called 'Ethio-rock' (Ilado 2018), one seemingly distant from the familiar sounds of hard rock and metal. In the West African nation of Togo, Arka'n have used the term 'African metal' to describe a sound that encapsulates a dynamic range of rhythms; heavy, distorted, detuned, chugging guitars, double-bass drumming and aggressive vocals have become a familiar feature to metal fans, yet dynamic enough to raise the curiosities of the Togolese as their sound is laced with the band's regional influences of Agbajda, Gazo and Blekete music.

In Mauritius, heavy metal bands have benefited from life in one of Africa's political and economic success stories. The local metal scene grew steadily throughout the 1980s and into the 1990s, with early bands such as Strength and Paranoid leading the charge with hard rock. Influences were thin as many musicians relied on expatriate family members to send them music. They relied equally on television signals carrying rock and metal from nearby Reunion Island. Metal received its greatest impetus with the formation of the progressively influenced groups Feedback and the extreme metal act Scar in the 1990s. With little exposure outside the island, metal fans engaged with a national identity that has celebrated the various cultures of the island in addition to its Creole music, *séga*. Creole identity, as Thomas Hylland Erikson has explained, belongs to those 'of African/Malagasy or mixed descent' (2007, 161). The music identified as Creole is often linked to the era of slavery on the island and is commonly referred to as the 'slave beat.'

Acts from nearby Reunion Island have also incorporated traditional music. *Maloya*, also referred to locally as 'the slave beat,' has allowed heavy metal to reach a larger audience as it embraces an art form associated with the island's history of slavery, an art form unique to the island's cultural identity. Heavy metal on Reunion Island has grown significantly since the turn of the millennium, as bands have benefited from French citizenship and European Union membership, both of which have provided significant arts endowments and funding for recordings and performances as well as allowing metal bands to travel easily to perform on the European mainland.

This trend for African metal bands – of not being influenced too much by traditional music – may change as many other bands in the West have begun to experiment with local elements. Though gradual, there has been an increase in Northern European bands releasing records with more local instrumentation and musical elements. Acts such as Finland's Korpiklaani, Latvia's Skyforger, Israel's Orphaned Land and Taiwan's Cthonic have contributed to the dialogue of what is possible in heavy metal. This development stems from having within their cultures something that can be referred to as 'fatigue generation' in terms of which a band may be more inclined to challenge norms or rules as a result of the multigenerational history of metal in their part of the world. In Africa, metal was in the 2010s still in its first or second generation; as a consequence, the incorporation of local elements was to take a while. Musicians are likely to be hesitant in compromising the sounds of heavy metal for a risky experiment challenging the norms of a genre to which they are still becoming acclimatized.

The incorporation of local languages in some African metal has facilitated the inclusion of local subject matter. While heavy metal has never distanced itself from social issues that are predominately Western, African heavy metal acts have used their music to reflect on their environment. Daily life for musicians in Africa can be arduous given circumstances of political knavery, economic struggles and social norms that portray metal culture as jejune and, in some cases, odious. However, metal fans and artists in sub-Saharan Africa have persisted with this genre as both a positive form of expression and a transgressive experience. The music has established itself globally outside the mainstream and has continued to grow as the Internet has reached into corners of the earth that might otherwise be forgotten – such as the African continent.

Metal's Viability in Africa

Heavy metal bands in Southern Africa have benefited from being located in one of the continent's largest regions of economic success, a region with a well-developed musical infrastructure. The result has been established metal cultures in which different subgenres have been able to flourish, even though with precarious beginnings. The most influential metal scene in sub-Saharan Africa has been in South Africa, where metal survived the troubled era of apartheid, during which an authoritarian government established agencies to monitor cultural activities under the strong censorship laws of the Publications Act of 1974 (Drewitt 2003). Rock and metal attempted to sidestep authority during this period, but did so with caution, providing just one example of heavy metal's clash with political and social forces in the continent.

Zimbabwe, a nation that enforced racial policies during the pre-independence regime of Ian Smith, also boasted a stable rock scene during this era of white rule with bands such as Eye of Liberty, Dr. Footswitch and Wells Fargo. While these bands enjoyed success locally with mixed audiences (WNYC 2016), performing songs of liberation and protest, the post-independence period witnessed a vacuum in talent as many musicians fled or were killed in the war of independence. Because musicians experienced performance as challenging because of an unreliable technical infrastructure left derelict throughout the late 1990s and 2000s, and because performing could at times be life-threatening under the authoritarian grip of Robert Mugabe's government, which enacted strong censorship laws that often resulted in imprisonment, bands established an underground metal scene that only began to reveal itself during the 2010s.

The metal scenes of Mozambique and Angola originated after both countries' horrendous post-independence civil wars in the early part of the 2000s. While both countries share a Lusophone colonial history and common language, neither of them have a history of rock giving birth to metal. While Mozambique has stumbled in postwar rebuilding, Angola's rapid development has correlated with the growth of metal as the Internet has connected local fans to metal scenes both in and outside the continent. Angola is home to one of the larger rock/metal festivals in Africa, the annual Rock No Rio Festival, as well as the Huambo Metal Festival (*Death Metal Angola* [2012], directed by Jeremy Xido). However, against many odds, Mozambique has been slowly building a solid metal scene with bands and fans traveling to neighboring South Africa for instruments, recording studios and merchandise, as well as to attend performances of South African and international bands.

Elsewhere, Namibia – whose government has been ranked third in the annual Africa's Ibrahim Index assessment of democratic transparency (2017) – has enjoyed a small rock and heavy metal scene since independence in 1994, even playing host to the short-lived Windhoek Metal Festival. Metal scenes have also begun to blossom in Uganda, Ghana, Cameroon and Nigeria.

Conclusion

Heavy metal is the longest surviving genre of rock as a result of a solid foundation of faithful, dedicated fans whose passion has been the soul of this music. It has become not just a fringe genre with a niche appeal in specific, wealthy societies, but a global phenomenon that permeates all aspects of local culture.

While colonial governments may have left political and social quagmires in the nations they ruled, there remained vestiges that benefited the spread of metal in the years following. These vestiges resulted in the transfer of knowledge, the advent of radio and facilitated travel between African and European nations. After the colonial era waned, these connections remained, allowing those that had heard and liked the heavier music of the time to pursue this music without a scene of their own. African young people started reaching out for more metal, eventually creating it on their own, albeit in varying degrees of isolation.

Heavy metal's reach expanded throughout the late 1990s as more countries witnessed increasing advancements in infrastructure. With ever-increasing developments on the African continent, musicians have found themselves within a greater global metal collective. With the ability to learn from others in the West through chatboards, social media and video streams, and being able to engage with their favorite acts, African metal musicians have become capable of furthering the musical infrastructure of their countries, building a shared knowledge beneficial to later generations.

However, musicians have remained keen on performing according to global norms. Yet this could change as metal is very much an open genre capable of accepting various cultural infusions, including those of language and instrumentations. Once metal scenes have rooted themselves and local bands have been able to influence a generation locally, a process of 'genre fragmentation' will likely occur, much as in various scenes in Europe and even Asia, where metal bands in the Middle East and Southeast Asia have incorporated local influences into their metal without compromising heavy metal's true spirit. As journalist Ian Christe states in his seminal work on the matter, 'Heavy metal is durable and unmistakable, even when channeled in new forms' (2004, 373–4). The concept of 'African metal' has a prosperous future ahead of it. Heavy metal has proven to be a genre that embraces an ever-changing world, the individual, the community and the 'tribe' (O'Boyle and Scott 2016, 341), continually engaging fans and musicians with local responses to global conditions (Green 2011, 121). Heavy metal has a viable home in Africa because fans and musicians alike have embraced a form of expression that best exemplifies their emotions and ambitions, while challenging the perceptions of what is possible in the modern continent.

Bibliography

Allegrezza, Kim. 2015. 'Is Africa the Future of Heavy Metal?' Online at: https://www.axs.com/is-africa-the-future-of-heavy-metal-64133 (accessed 19 January 2018).

Bookman, Elly. 2007. 'Songs from Imerina: A Creative Study of the Evolving Craft of Merina *Hainteny* in Madagascar.' Independent Study Project (ISP) Collection 122. Online at: http://digitalcollections.sit.edu/isp_collection/122/ (accessed 8 May 2018).

Christe, Ian. 2004. *Sound of the Beast: The Complete Headbanging History of Heavy Metal*. New York: Harper Collin.

Drewitt, Michael. 2003. 'Music in the Struggle to End Apartheid.' In *Policing Pop*, eds. Martin Cloonan and Reebee Garafolo. Philadelphia: Temple University Press, 143–65.

Ebert, Kevin. 2017. 'But That Doesn't Help Me on Guitar! Unraveling the Myth of the Self-Taught Metal Guitarist.' In *Connecting Metal to Culture: Unity in Disparity*, eds. Mika Elovaara and Bryan Bardine. Chicago: Intellect Books, 115–89.

Encyclopedia Metallum: The Metal Archives. 2014. Online at: https://www.metal-archives.com/ (accessed 11 January 2018).

Erikson, Thomas Hylland. 2007. 'Creolization in Anthropological Theory and in Mauritius.' In *Creolization: History, Ethnography, Theory*, ed. Charles Steward. Walnut Creek, CA: Left Coast Press, 153–77.

Frith, Simon. 2000. 'The Discourse of World Music.' In *Western Music and Its Others: Difference, Representation, and Appropriation in Music*, eds. Georgina Born and David Hesmondhalgh. Berkeley, CA: University of California Press, 305–22.

Greene, Paul D. 2011. 'Electronic and Effective Overdrive: Tropes of Trangressions in Nepal's Heavy Metal Scene.' In *Metal Rules the Globe: Heavy Metal Music Around the Globe*, eds. Jeremy Wallach, Harris M. Berger and Paul D. Greene. Durham, NC: Duke University Press, 109–34.

Ibrahim Index of African Governance (2017). Online at: http://mo.ibrahim.foundation/iiag/ (accessed 24 June 2018).

Ilado, Lucy. 2018. 'Ethiopia's Jano Band Talks New Album.' *Music in Africa* (7 February). Online at: www.musicinafrica.net https://www.musicinafrica.net/magazine/ethiopias-jano-band-talks-new-album (accessed 14 March 2018).

Kahn-Harris, Keith. 2007. *Extreme Metal: Music and Culture on the Edge*. New York: Berg Publishers.

Knopke, Ekkehard. 2015. 'Headbanging in Nairobi: The Emergence of the Kenyan Metal Scene and Its Transformation of Metal Code.' *Metal Music Studies* 1(1): 105–25.

Monnakgotla, Motlabana. 2017. 'Money, Witchcraft and Beer: This Is Metal from Soweto.' *Forbes Africa* (25 September). Online at: https://www.forbesafrica.com/life/2017/09/25/money-witchcraft-beer-metal-soweto/ (accessed 15 January 2018).

O'Boyle, Tom, and Scott, Niall W. R. 2016. 'The Future of Metal Is Bright and Hell Bent for Genre Destruction: A Response to Keith Kahn-Harris.' In *Global Metal Music and Culture: Current Directions in Metal Studies*, eds. Andy R. Brown et al. New York: Routledge, 333–42.

Sandburg, Henning Goranson. 2013. 'Why Zamrock Is Back in Play.' *The Guardian*, 22 July. Online at: https://www.theguardian.com/world/2013/jul/22/zamrock-zambia-music-rerelease (accessed 9 January 2018).

The Africa Report. 2017–18. No. 96 (December–January). Online at: http://www.theafricareport.com/ (accessed 24 June 2018).

Weinstein, Deena. 2000. *Heavy Metal: The Music and Its Culture*. Boston, MA: Da Capo Press.

Weinstein, Deena. 2011. 'The Globalization of Metal.' In *Metal Rules the Globe: Heavy Metal Music around the World*, eds. Jeremy Wallach, Harris M. Berger and Paul D. Greene. Durham, NC: Duke University Press, 34–59.

WNYC. 2016. 'Zim Heavy: Rock and Revolution in Zimbabwe, Snap #717-Shake, Rattle and Roll.' June 24. Online at: https://www.wnyc.org/story/zim-heavy-rock-and-revolution-zimbabwe-snap-717-shake-rattle-and-roll/ (accessed 7 March 2018).

Discographical Reference

Wrust. *Intellectual Metamorphosis*. Self-Produced. *2013*: Botswana.

Discography

Amanaz. *Africa*. Zambia Music Parlour. *1975*: Zambia. (Reissue: Amanaz. *Africa*. Now-Again NA5123. *2014*: USA.)

Apost. *Didy X*. Self-Produced. *2000*: Madagascar.

Feedback. *A Moment of Transition*. Self-Produced. *2009*: Mauritius.

Groinchurn. *Sixtimesnine*. Happy Hamster HHR5972-97. *1997*: South Africa.

Jano Band. *Ertale*. M.O.D. Technologies MOD0009. *2012*: USA.

Kazar. *Apokalipsa*. Self-Produced. *2002*: Madagascar.

Musi-O-Tunya. *Wings of Africa*. M.O.T Records LMOT 1017. *1975*: Zambia.

Nazca. *The White Wheel*. Brennus Music BR8106. *2003*: France.

Ngozi Family. *Day of Judgement*. Now Again NA5115. *2014*: USA.

Overthrust. *Desecrated Deeds to Decease*. Self-Produced. *2013*: Botswana.

Parking Lot Gras. *Tusk at Hand*. Self-Produced. *2015*: Kenya.

Scar. *Neutralizers*. Self-Produced. *2001*: Mauritius.

Skinflint. *Nyemba*. Self-Produced. *2014*: Botswana.

subMission. *Blind Sighted*. Deaf Metal Publications. *2009*: Namibia.

Vale of Amonition. *Those of Tartarean Ancestry*. Self-Produced. *2017*: Uganda.

Voice of Destruction. *Bloedrivier*. Morbid Records MR 026. *1996*: Germany.

Welcome to Zamrock! Volume 1. Now-Again NA 5147. *2016*: USA.

Welcome to Zamrock! Volume 2. Now-Again NA5148. *2016*: USA.

Wells Fargo. *Watch Out!* *1976*: Southern Rhodesia (Zimbabwe). (Reissue: Wells Fargo. *Watch Out!* Now Again NA5130. *2016*: USA.)

Witch. *We Intend to Cause Havok* (Box Set: 6 LPs.) Now-Again NA5091. *2012*: USA.

Zombies Ate My Girlfriend. *Retrocide*. Burning Tone Records BTRCD003. *2015*: South Africa.

Filmography

Death Metal Angola, dir. Jeremy Xido. 2012. USA. 83 mins. Documentary.

EDWARD BANCHS

Heavy Metal in Botswana

In Botswana, as in many other countries in Africa and elsewhere, heavy metal does not constitute a single genre from a strictly musical perspective, but rather functions as an umbrella term embracing several specific subgenres of global heavy metal, such as classic heavy metal, death metal and black metal. At the same time, however, a number of heavy metal bands in Botswana incorporate elements from traditional African music and culture in their music, thereby contributing to the genre sometimes called 'Afro Metal' or 'Tribal Metal.'

One such band is Skinflint, which is probably the contemporary metal act from Botswana that is best known internationally. A typical African feature in their music is the use of the syncopated handclapping characteristic of Borankana music (a traditional music usually practiced or performed by the Bakwena tribe in the Kweneng District of Botswana). A good example of this can be found in the song 'Borankana Metal,' which is the opening track on the album *Chief of the Ghosts*, originally self-released in 2016 and rereleased in Germany in 2017. However, Afro Metal is not defined only by musical features, but also by its connections to African culture in a broader sense. Here, too, Skinflint serves as a good illustration, since the band's works incorporate several African cultural elements. Among other things, Skinflint's lyrics are inspired by African folklore, occultism and storytelling. In addition, members of the band sometimes sing in their native language of Setswana. Another metal act from Botswana that uses African elements in their work – mainly rhythms from African music and references to African mythology and folklore – is the heavy metal band Metal Orizon, who self-identify as playing 'Afro tribal heavy metal' (Audio Inferno 2017a).

While heavy metal in Botswana is musically diverse, the country's heavy metal scene itself is singularly coherent and characterized by a distinct style of fashion that has attracted worldwide attention. Some of the most important features of this style are black leather clothes that are often decorated with metal studs and spikes, cowboy hats and boots, animal horns and skulls, and T-shirts with band logos (foreign as well as domestic). This style is often associated with biker culture, the dystopian postapocalyptic Mad Max films, cowboy culture or some aspects of the fashion of the New Wave of British Heavy Metal. In addition, members of the heavy metal scene in Botswana are known for their camaraderie and for various bonding rituals that include complex handshakes, embraces, dances and so on. One rather intricate greeting ritual among the country's metal fans has been described as 'a kind of showdown cowboy jig' in which the fans 'circle each other and perform martial arts moves' (Marshall 2012, 65).

It is often said that the roots of heavy metal in Botswana go back to the classic rock band Nosey Road, which was founded in 1972 by two Italian brothers (McGroarty 2016). However, the contemporary scene – which features mainly Botswanan musicians and almost exclusively Botswanan fans – emerged as late as in the early 1990s. Sometimes, the founding of Metal Orizon in 1990 (*Soundcloud*, n.d.) is described as the birth of modern heavy metal in Botswana.

Compared, for example, to European countries or neighboring South Africa, the total number of heavy metal bands and fans in Botswana is modest. Nevertheless, the metal scene extends to all parts of the country with important centers in two locations: the county's capital, Gaborone, and the city of Maun, which is a center for the nation's tourism industry (and referred to by metal fans as 'Maun Rock City'). Important heavy metal bands in Botswana include – in addition to the ones already mentioned – the death metal bands Wrust, Overthrust and Crackdust, and the black metal band Raven In Flesh.

Since about 2010 Botswana's metal scene has received quite a lot of international attention. However, the music itself has not stirred as much interest as the fashion style developed by its fans. One example of this attention is that several photographers have documented the people involved in the scene. One of these is the South African Frank Marshall whose exhibition, 'Renegades' (2010), received international attention. Another is the Spanish photographer Pep Bonet who, in 2016, put together the series 'Hellbangers: Botswana's Underground Metal Culture,' which was published in, among other publications, the German magazine *Der Spiegel*. The heavy metal scene in Botswana has also been presented in an episode of CNN's television program, *Inside Africa*, in June 2012.

The attention given to heavy metal in Botswana by international media has had some positive effects. One of these is that it has created a curiosity among metal fans worldwide that has made it possible for some bands from Botswana to play concerts in other parts of the world. For example, in 2017 Skinflint supported Tarja Turunen (the former singer of the Finnish band Nightwish) on her European tour and in 2016 Overthrust played several concerts in

Germany and Switzerland, including one at the prestigious Wacken festival. It cannot be ignored, however, that northern hemisphere media outlets, as one commentator puts it, tend to regard heavy metal in Botswana as 'a freakish novelty' (Madondo 2017). This is the result of an ethnocentric understanding of European and North American heavy metal music as the core of global heavy metal culture, and of heavy metal music in other parts of the world as being peripheral, exotic or backward (Nilsson 2016, 260). One important feature of this view is that heavy metal is considered to be a 'white' cultural phenomenon (Weinstein 2000, 101–2; Walser 1993, 17). Thus, the fact that almost all heavy metal musicians and fans in Botswana are black attracts attention even if, within the country's heavy metal scene, skin color is not necessarily important (Nilsson 2016, 266). This ethnocentrism runs the risk of producing too strong a focus on what sets heavy metal in Botswana – as well as in other African countries – apart from heavy metal in the global North and, thus, in its misrepresentation. For example, it overlooks the fact that the use of elements from African music and culture in Afro Metal is very similar to the use of Nordic musical and cultural elements in so-called Viking Metal. This can be illustrated by a comparison between Skinflint and the band Tyr from the Faroe Islands. Both draw on local mythology in their lyrics, incorporate elements from traditional music in their works and sometimes sing in their native languages. However, Viking Metal bands such as Tyr are seldom cast as the Other in heavy metal discourses.

Bibliography

Audio Inferno. 2017a. '[Interview] Metal Orizon to Play at Botswana Metal Festival "Rock the Nation".' Online at: https://audioinferno.com/2017/09/19/interview-metal-orizon-play-botswana-metal-festival-rock-nation/ (accessed 24 February 2018).

Audio Inferno. 2017b. '[Interview] Raven In Flesh to Play at Botswana Metal Festival "Rock the Nation".' Online at: https://audioinferno.com/2017/09/13/interview-raven-flesh-play-botswana-metal-festival-rock-nation/ (accessed 24 February 2018).

Der Spiegel. 2016. 'Fotoserie – "Hellbangers" in Botswana: Heavy Metal ist ihre Religion' [Photoseries – 'Hellbangers' in Botswana: Heavy Metal Is Their Religion] (8 November). Online at: http://www.spiegel.de/stil/heavy-metal-fotoprojekt-hellbangers-aus-botswana-a-1119030.html (accessed 24 February 2018).

Madondo, Bogoni. 2017. 'The Hell Bangers of Botswana's Underground Metal Scene: Far Beyond Driven.' *Huck*. Online at: http://www.huckmagazine.com/art-and-culture/hellbangers-botswana-underground-heavy-metal-culture/ (accessed 24 February 2018).

Marshall, Frank. 2012. 'Visions of Renegades: *Transition* Speaks with Photographer Frank Marshall about Heavy Metal in Botswana.' *Transition* 109: 62–71.

McGroarty, Patrick. 2016. 'Heavy Metal's Leather and Chains Find a Home in the Kalahari: The Genre's Raucous Vibe and Apocalyptic Fashion Serve as a Counterpart to Botswana's Conservative Culture.' *The Wall Street Journal* (7 June). Online at: https://www.wsj.com/articles/heavy-metals-leather-and-chains-find-a-home-in-the-kalahari-1465317612 (accessed 24 February 2018).

Nilsson, Magnus. 2016. 'Race and Gender in Globalized and Postmodern Metal.' In *Heavy Metal, Gender and Sexuality: Interdisciplinary Approaches*, eds. Florian Heesch and Niall Scott. London and New York: Routledge, 258–71.

Soundcloud. N.d. 'Metal Orizon.' Online at: https://soundcloud.com/metal-10 (accessed 5 March 2018).

Walser, Robert, 1992. *Running with the Devil: Power, Gender, and Madness in Heavy Metal Music*. Middleton, CT: Wesleyan University Press.

Weinstein, Deena, 2000. *Heavy Metal: The Music and Its Culture*. Rev. ed. New York: Da Capo Press. (First published 1991.)

Discographical Reference

Skinflint. 'Borankana Metal.' *Chief of the Ghosts*. Pure Steel Records PSRCD 148. *2017*: Germany.

Discography

Crackdust. *Dented Reality*. Core Riodic Records CR 67860-1. *2007*: Botswana.

Metal Orizon. *Metal Örizon*. *2009*: Botswana.

Nosey Road. *Freeway(28)*. Gallo ACP 653. *1983*: South Africa.

Overthrust. *Descrated Deeds to Decease*. *2015*: Botswana.

Wrust. *Soulless Machine*. Witchdoctor Records. *2007*: South Africa.

Wrust. *Intellectual Metamorphosis. 2013*: Botswana.

Website

https://www.cnn.com/2014/02/13/world/africa/africa-botswana-metal-heads/index.html (accessed 4 March 2018).

MAGNUS NILSSON

Heavy Metal in Kenya

Heavy metal found its way into Kenya's capital, Nairobi, in the mid-1990s. On the one hand, travelers to the region brought with them recording devices containing Western heavy metal tracks. On the other hand, the spread of heavy metal among Nairobi's young people was fostered through the advent of the Internet. College students in particular listened online to grunge, punk, hardcore and heavy metal songs. Heavy metal tracks were initially consumed only by individuals or small groups. However, during the early 2000s collective consumption increased and heavy metal tracks were played in local discotheques. In addition, the first heavy metal bands such as Class Suicide and Last Year's Tragedy were established, and the local scene switched from being passive to active: heavy metal was no longer just consumed but also came, initially, to be reproduced. Shortly afterward, original songs were produced. A marked variation in style resulted. Certain bands, such as Last Year's Tragedy, Mortal Soul, In Oath and Lust of a Dying Breed, can be thought of as 'fundamentalist' heavy metal bands because they were involved with the more transgressive metal subgenres such as death metal, metalcore and deathcore. In contrast, bands such as Seismic and Rash performed music that sounded more like classic metal while Parking Lot Grass performed music closer to the mainstream. This group could therefore be described as a 'light metal' band.

The Kenyan heavy metal scene has mainly been restricted to and concentrated in Nairobi. Rural regions are excluded from this scene, most likely because of a lack of infrastructure. Popular meeting places, such as the Choices and Carnivore clubs, are only to be found in Nairobi. Along with regularly occurring concerts in these venues, there have also been festivals such as the Nairobi Rock Fest in 2009 and the Nairobi Metal Festival in 2017 at which heavy metal bands have been featured. At the same time, the Kenyan metal scene has opened up internationally. For example, Parking Lot Grass was invited to perform in Bayreuth, Germany, in 2013, and in the late 2010s bands from other African countries such as Skinflint from Botswana and Boargazm from South Africa came to Nairobi to perform on stage.

The Contemporary Scene

A young and aspiring heavy metal music scene has thus been under development in Nairobi. Despite precarious production conditions, several bands have been established which range widely along the continuum of heavy metal music. Sound, language, performance practices and iconography in the Kenyan music scene have been strongly oriented toward Western heavy metal; there are mosh pits during concerts, as well as CD covers and websites that use the metaphorical language typical of heavy metal. Clothing styles have also been adapted from the global heavy metal scene. Lyrics have been predominantly in English, and influences from traditional Kenyan music have only been marginal. In addition, the content of Kenyan songs has been quite similar to that of heavy metal songs in general and includes themes of protest, hate, violence, injustice and so on. However, the absence of satanic themes in Kenyan heavy metal might be ascribed to the Christian values typical of Kenyan society. There is as well an awareness of political dissension as evidenced in the songs of the band, Last Year's Tragedy. The Kenyan heavy metal scene is also not without its social structures and hierarchies. It emulates heavy metal as the music of heterosexual men with a middle-class background. The scene's elite – musicians, promoters and owners of recording studios – are usually black men with a higher education. Some have attended universities overseas. The borders of the scene are negotiated very carefully as a hard distinction exists between 'rockers' and 'metalheads.' However, strong influences from rock music can also be found, as in the case of one of the most popular bands, Parking Lot Grass.

Heavy Metal in Kenya or Kenyan Heavy Metal?

The sounds of Kenyan heavy metal bands thus reveal strong Western influences. However, on closer examination, a distinction does need to be drawn between heavy metal in Kenya and Kenyan heavy metal. The former is played by a large number of bands – the sounds are predominantly oriented toward US and European audiences, and the language used is English. The latter, by contrast, contains local influences including traditional rhythms or Swahili lyrics, such as those found in the song 'Shimo Mfukoni' by Parking Lot Grass. However, as of the late 2010s traditional Kenyan or African instruments had not made an appearance in Kenyan heavy metal.

Language is treated to a degree ambivalently. Some members of the Kenyan scene see recourse to Swahili as an opportunity to promote Kenyan heavy metal bands, to enable them to receive a special status within the global scene and to spread heavy metal music among the Kenyan population. Other metalheads are skeptical of any use of Swahili. For them, this language appears to be tied to traditional values and does not stand for progress and modernization. In addition, some heavy metal fans might see the use of Swahili as providing an opening for the playing out of ethnic tensions prevalent in Kenya. For them, heavy metal in Kenya should not as a consequence sound too African. In general, the metal scene is quite apprehensive about reproducing political dissension in Kenya. Metalheads perceive themselves as Kenyans and not as an amalgamation of different ethnic groups. As such, language choice functions as a filter that confers equanimity. African dialects such as Luo are not used in heavy metal songs in order to prevent discord in auditoriums and the sparking of conflicts. Due to its seeming ethnic neutrality and connotations of prestige and progress, English has remained the *lingua franca* of the Kenyan heavy metal scene.

Conclusion

The Kenyan heavy metal scene is comparatively young and has undergone a big change since the beginning of the twenty-first century. It has transformed from a scene that was highly dependent on Western music production and recording devices to a scene that has its own infrastructure of recording studios and venues. The future development of this scene is an important topic of discussion for Kenyan metalheads. These discussions need to focus on the tension between local sounds and global trends as well as on the need to position heavy metal in relation to the political history of Kenya and the lives of its citizens. Ultimately, these negotiations will decide the extent to which there will be heavy metal in Kenya and Kenyan heavy metal.

Bibliography

Banchs, Edward. 2016. *Heavy Metal Africa: Life, Passion, and Heavy Metal in the Forgotten Continent*. Tarentum, PA: Word Association Publishers.

Banchs, Edward. 2016. 'Swahili-tongued Devils: Kenya's Heavy Metal at the Crossroads of Identity.' *Metal Music Studies* 2(3): 311–24.

Knopke, Ekkehard. 2013. 'Kenya. Feedbacks. Metal.' *eject. Zeitschrift für Medienkultur* 3: 39–46.

Knopke, Ekkehard. 2014. 'Headbanging in Nairobi: The Emergence of the Kenyan Metal Scene and Its Transformation of the Metal Code.' *Metal Music Studies* 1(1): 105–25.

Knopke, Ekkehard. 2015. '"Redykyulass Generation Light": Metal und Politik in Kenia' ['Redykyulass Generation Light': Metal and Politics in Kenya]. In *(Un)Politischer Metal? Musikalische Artikulationen des Politischen zwischen Ideologie und Utopie*, eds. David Stoop and Roman Bartosch. Trier: Wissenschaftlicher Verlag Trier, 135–50.

Discographical Reference

Parking Lot Grass. 'Shimo Mfukoni.' *Shimo Mfukoni*. Andromeda Music. *2012*: Kenya.

Discography

Absence of Light. *Vyom Chakra*. Depressive Illusions Records. *2012*: Ukraine.

In Oath. *Eulogy*. Andromeda Music. *2012*: Kenya.

In Oath. *The Bread of Disposition*. Andromeda Music. *2017*: Kenya.

Last Year's Tragedy. *Challenge Accepted*. Andromeda Music. *2013*: Kenya.

Last Year's Tragedy. *Bury Your Fallen Dreams*. Andromeda Music. *2015*: Kenya.

Lust of a Dying Breed. *Cat of Nine Tails*. Independent. *2012*: Kenya.

Mortal Soul. *Ashes in the Wind*. Shinigami Studios. *2013*: Kenya.

Parking Lot Grass. *Shimo Mfukoni*. Andromeda Music. *2012*: Kenya.

Parking Lot Grass. *Tusk at Hand*. Andromeda Music. *2015*: Kenya.

Reva. 'Luanda Magere.' Heavyweight Records. *2017*: Kenya.
Rish. 'The Hate Song.' Andromeda Music. *2015*: Kenya.
Underscore the Architect. Andromeda Music. *2016*: Kenya.
Void of Belonging. 'Dream Again.' Yagami Mastering. *2015*: Kenya.

Filmography

Un Monde de Metal [A World of Metal], dir. Olivier Richard. 2015. France. 52 mins. Documentary.

Television

Du metal au Kenya – ou l'internationale des riffs rugueux [From Metal to Kenya – or International Rough Riffs], Tracks ARTE. 2017. France. 10 mins. Documentary. Online at: https://www.youtube.com/watch?v=kl3CwTaQVEw (accessed 4 June 2018).

Headbanging Bands Put Kenyan Metal on the Map: RASH, Parking Lot Grass, and Kanyeki Are Rousing the Nairobi Rock Scene, CNN. 2017. USA. 7 mins. Documentary. Online at: https://edition.cnn.com/videos/world/2017/07/28/inside-africa-headbanging-bands-put-kenyan-metal-on-the-map-c.cnn (accessed 8 June 2018).

EKKEHARD KNOPKE

Heavy Metal in Madagascar (Metaly Gasy)

Madagascar's heavy metal subculture was established around the mid-1980s in the island's capital city, Antananarivo. At this time, Madagascar's socialist Second Republic, which lasted from 1975 to 1993 and was the second of four major constitutional periods in the history of the country after it achieved independence from France in 1960, became bankrupt. In order to obtain credit from the World Bank and the International Monetary Fund, the Republic had to end a ten-year policy of national seclusion toward the West. Living conditions soon improved and Western culture, which had significantly influenced Madagascar's urban highlands for the previous 200 years, became part of everyday life again. At the time, heavy metal was already enjoyed by a small number of young people who had come in touch with bands such as Van Halen, Iron Maiden, Scorpions, Rainbow and Metallica through records brought in by migrants or foreign workers. For these young people, this political and economic change not only meant that they could now appreciate their music publicly; they were also able to buy instruments and technologies without which heavy metal music, for which the sound of distorted guitars is a defining feature, is impossible to perform. Soon, bands like Green, Apost, Kiaka, Tselatra, Lokomotiva and Kazar were being established. According to the conventions of international heavy metal all these bands composed their own songs. As a result, an increasingly diverse heavy metal subculture emerged that explored the different heavy metal subgenres current at the time: glam metal, the New Wave of British Heavy Metal and thrash metal. Malagasy metal musicians (Madagascar was previously known as the Malagasy Republic) also composed, performed and recorded highly successful power ballads, and thereby rendered heavy metal a part of the island's pop music mainstream.

After ten successful years, the importance of Malagasy heavy metal began to decline (Mauro 2003) in line with international trends and the sudden rise of grunge and alternative rock. However, from the mid-2000s onward, and again corresponding to global developments, Malagasy heavy metal experienced an enormous comeback. Previously established bands and genres reappeared. In addition, many new bands emerged and explored more recently developed heavy metal subgenres such as death metal, nu metal, black metal and symphonic metal. Facebook and Internet pages such as Mozika Mavesatra Malagasy (heavy music from Madagascar) and hardrockmg.com have provided information about more than 80 bands, the music of which ranges from classic hard rock and heavy metal to extreme death and black metal variants as those performed, for example, by Children of Bodom (Finland), Arch Enemy (Sweden), Cannibal Corpse (United States), Cradle of Filth (United Kingdom) or Immortal (Norway). An increasing number of younger bands have also engaged in the fast but highly melodic power metal or symphonic metal genres, drawing inspiration from internationally acclaimed bands such as Nightwish, Stratovarius (both from Finland) or Angra (Brazil).

The Sound of *Metaly Gasy* (I): Authenticity and Technology

From its beginnings Malagasy metal musicians took great pains to perform their music in an authentic metal style. Different from many genres of popular music which circulate on a global scale but which are contextualized both sonically and culturally in the various locations they reach, Malagasy metalheads have enjoyed metal music in its original form. For the musicians, this enjoyment has resulted in an attempt to reproduce the aesthetic forms of the respective metal subgenres as reliably as possible; for the fans, the desire to experience the performance of 'actual' metal music becomes clear during concerts: audiences loudly criticize musicians who do not meet accepted standards. A key element with respect to the assessment of the music is the production of a proper metal sound. Even though this sound is quite different within different metal genres, it demands a certain degree of 'power,' which is basically achieved through distorted guitar signals. In order for a distorted sound to be powerful, however, a certain technological standard has to be met. For financial reasons, Malagasy musicians often fail to meet this standard. Many cannot afford to buy an original instrument; neither do they have the means to purchase adequate effects or amplification units. They therefore have to make do with highly limited technological infrastructure and cheap Asian equipment. As a result, Malagasy metal often does not attain its own standards of 'authenticity' when it comes to the sound of the music. In live performances, where distortion needs to be coupled with a fair degree of loudness, the sound of the music is often distorted beyond recognition; where recordings are concerned, the music often does not evoke the 'heaviness' required and therefore fails to produce a proper metal ambience (Verne 2012).

Malagasy heavy metal has been struggling with this problem since its beginnings in the mid-1980s. During the late 2010s, however, Malagasy metal musicians enjoyed considerable improvements with respect to sound because of developments in computer-based sound and recording technologies. While high-quality instruments, audio effects and amplification units have remained out of reach for most Malagasy musicians, most have had access to computers and (pirated) high-end software products. Thus, somewhat paradoxically, the increasing digitization of heavy metal music has helped Malagasy musicians meet the demand for sonic authenticity.

The Sound of *Metaly Gasy* (II): Heaviness and Sentimentality

Malagasy metal musicians espouse two fundamentally different ideologies. On the one hand, they try to keep up with international developments and satisfy the needs of Madagascar's underground metal community. Here, bands and fans together engage with metal's championing of increasingly extreme sounds and images in an attempt to push already established boundaries. In Madagascar, this attempt has involved notions of speed and virtuosity, as in power metal (as exemplified by the music of bands such as Resurrection, Allkiniah and L'Imby), as well as of heaviness and darkness, as in thrash metal (as exemplified by the music of bands such as Kazar, Sharks and Sasamaso), death metal (as exemplified by the music of bands such as Samar and Behind the Mask) or black metal (as exemplified by the music of bands such as Golgotha and Lamasy). On the other hand, Malagasy metal has been seriously engaged with sentimentality, an engagement best evidenced through the power ballad. This second orientation has had as its clear purpose the attainment of fame and commercial success within the island's pop music mainstream. Power ballads, most of which deal with the topic of unrequited love, are thought to speak to a general Malagasy fondness for sentimentality. Several metal ballads have managed to become classics in Malagasy pop music. Once they have become hits, these ballads not only constitute the climax of the respective band's concerts since everyone knows them by heart. They also are covered during the live performances of other bands. In addition, they are played on a regular basis by radio and television stations, which can result in royalties being paid by l'Office Malagasy du Droit d'Auteur (OMDA), Madagascar's society for musical performing and mechanical reproduction rights, even if the sums paid are usually rather modest. Besides engaging in 'actual' metal music, it has therefore become common for many Malagasy metal bands to compose epic ballads, trying to reproduce the enormous success other metal bands have had before them (for example, Apost with 'Dila,' Green with 'Hafatra' or Mage4 with 'Maratra hampom-po').

The Economics of *Metaly Gasy*

Besides offering the chance to become famous and be recognized as outstanding musicians, success with ballads has also been a means for Malagasy metal musicians to earn money. Usually, heavy metal is performed publicly in rather small locations such as bars, restaurants or minor concert halls, with three to five bands performing. In these cases, bands will be paid only small amounts by organizers, as entrance fees are usually needed to cover costs (rental of the venue and PA system). The only exceptions to this are open-air concerts such as the 'Tana in Rock' event, a big rock and metal festival that is held once a year at one of the city's larger concert locations. These concerts are usually well attended, often by thousands of fans; still, with several rock and metal bands performing, financial rewards are rather modest. However, if a metal band manages to score a hit with a ballad, it can rent a large venue and perform its music in front of thousands of fans. This results in considerable financial gains for band members, even though entrance fees need to be kept very low, at about 3,000 to 6,000 ariary (the currency of Madagascar: 3,000 to 6,000 ariary are roughly one to two US dollars), for large crowds to take part.

This possibility of earning money from metal music in the context of the stressful financial situation in which many Malagasy people find themselves has had consequences for Malagasy metal music, as many metal bands expend a disproportionate amount of time, energy and money in the production of ballads. To become hits, songs need as much airplay as they can get, and they will receive this only if the sound quality is of an exceptional standard. In addition, because much music is consumed through television or increasingly through Internet channels such as YouTube, successful songs need to be accompanied by videos. Since the production of high-quality sound and videos is expensive, such steps are taken mainly in the case of ballads, which are thought of as investments resulting in possible future financial gains. As a result, while *metaly gasy* is often quite heavy in live performances, it tends to be rather light in mediated formats; in fact, with respect to their sonic qualities, the music of many Malagasy metal ballads only differs from mainstream pop music in its occasional use of distorted guitar sounds. It is for this reason that even bands such as Ambondrona, Madagascar's hugely successful pop rock band, are often considered by a wider public to be part of the island's heavy metal scene (Verne 2017).

Contemporary Developments

As of the late 2010s Malagasy heavy metal was still developing, with new bands being established and older groups continuing to perform. Once established, Malagasy metal bands seldom cease to exist. However, band members do often change, whether because of disagreements, other attractive engagements or because musicians leave town to work or live elsewhere. Bands may also go 'on standby' for quite extended periods of time, spending years without producing new songs, performing in public or even rehearsing. But not unlike dead ancestors, who in Madagascar are believed to still be around and to get in touch with the living every now and then, bands that have become part of Madagascar's metal scene never dissolve completely. This is even more the case for a band that has become well known for a particular song, whether within or beyond the metal community. As a result, Madagascar's active metal community has not only continued to grow in size, but also transformed itself into a highly diversified scene in which many metal subgenres are represented (Banchs 2016, 183–246). *Metaly gasy* has developed its history, with founding luminaries such as Tselatra, Green, Apost, Kiaka and Kazar; anthems, such as, preeminently, Apost's 'Apocalipsy'; stars such as Nini of Kiaka, Mage4's frontman Ken, female rocker Iary and Poun, Green's virtuoso guitarist; and a musical evolution that resembles that of metal worldwide yet places special emphasis on the melodic dimensions of heavy metal. These melodic dimensions come to the fore in metal ballads, but also strikingly in genres such as classic heavy metal, power metal, symphonic metal and, in a somewhat new strand within *metaly gasy*, melodic death metal (as exemplified in Lamasy's eponymous single, 'Lamasy').

With respect to the sound of *metaly gasy*, digitization has continued to fundamentally change its overall ambience. During its analog period, Malagasy metal always suffered from a lack of technological means and thus consistently struggled with the production of a proper metal sound. Since about the 2010s, however, digitization has provided Malagasy musicians with easy access to standard metal sounds and high-quality recording processes. Malagasy metal musicians have no longer needed to pay significant amounts of money to rent studios, pay sound engineers and buy audio tape. Instead, many of them record their music themselves, at home and in as many takes as necessary. Besides having access to a huge number of digital sounds and sound effects, they can record scores of tracks, take their time in mixing the sounds, and add tracks programmed on their computers to those they actually recorded. This latter possibility is of utmost importance for drum tracks, as modern metal formats require enormous speed, complexity and precision on the part of the drummer. This means that drum tracks are almost impossible to record in a satisfying way without a considerable technological infrastructure. Digitization thus helps musicians increase the quality of *metaly gasy* and cope with the requirements of metal's international standards. Because it rendered the production of both sounds and images relatively cheap, however, digitization has also continued to change the general sound of Malagasy heavy metal: fewer and fewer recordings, as uploaded on YouTube and other similar sites, represent ballads designed for the market, but are rather representative of 'actual' metal music. Combined with increasing access to the world wide web that urban Malagasy enjoy, the digitization of music may finally enable the biggest dream of Malagasy metal musicians to come true: to be recognized beyond Madagascar's borders and become part of the 'global metal ecumene' (Wallach et al. 2011, 20).

Bibliography

Banchs, Edward. 2016. *Heavy Metal Africa: Life, Passion, and Heavy Metal in the Forgotten Continent*. Tarentum, PA: Word Association Publishers.

Mauro, Didier. 2003. 'Rocking in Madagascar: Aspects sociologiques du rock'n roll malgache' [Rocking in Madagascar: Sociological Aspects of Malgache Rock 'n' Roll]. *Madagascar Magazine* 31: 54–7.

Verne, Markus. 2012. 'Heavy Conditions: Power Metal in Madagascar.' In *Heavy Metal Generations*, eds. Andy Brown and Kevin Fellesz. Oxford: Inter-Disciplinary Press, 37–47.

Verne, Markus. 2017. '"A Highland Thing": Heavy Metal and the Construction of Cultural Difference in Madagascar.' *Journal of World Popular Music* 4(1): 58–77.

Wallach, Jeremy, et al., eds. 2011. *Metal Rules the Globe: Heavy Metal Music around the World*. Durham, NC: Duke University Press.

Discographical References

Apost. 'Apocalipsy.' *Mipoitra avy Hafitra*. (Reissue). *2012*. Madagascar. Online at: https://www.youtube.com/watch?v=augYdBQaPMk (accessed 3 June 2018).

Apost. 'Dila.' Online at: https://www.youtube.com/watch?v=Mj9tsgkPkzU (accessed 2 June 2018).

Green. 'Hafatra.' Online at: https://www.youtube.com/watch?v=tTDoqqGmTWo (accessed 2 June 2018).

Lamasy. 'Lamasy.' Online at: https://www.youtube.com/watch?v=EoXYmxsu8cQ (accessed 3 June 2018).

Mage4. 'Maratra Hambom-Po.' *Fo Vaovao*. N.d.: Madagascar. Online at: https://www.youtube.com/watch?v=BUcnp1VgGVU (accessed 2 June 2018).

Discography and YouTube

Allkiniah. 'Andro farany.' 2014. Online at: https://www.youtube.com/watch?v=Kn0-y3a1KBY (accessed 4 June 2018).

Allkiniah. 'Setrin'ny fahotana.' 2016. Online at: https://www.youtube.com/watch?v=W_R4Pp1wlkk (accessed 4 June 2018).

Ambondrona. 'Antso.' *Eto @ tanána (Live Colliseum)*. Lay tanana & saryfeo.malagasygraphic. *2014*. Madagascar. Online at: https://www.youtube.com/watch?v=L4OuZqKfYLA (accessed 21 June 2018).

Ambondrona. 'Maraina vao.' 2018. Online at: https://www.youtube.com/watch?v=H8D-nRmh-xs (accessed 4 June 2018).

Ambondrona. 'Tiako hitoetra.' *2016*. Online at: https://www.youtube.com/watch?v=g4UWQ1ifRmY (accessed 4 June 2018).

Behind the Mask. 'The Message.' *2016*. Online at: https://www.youtube.com/watch?v=8JsJCGVKTKM (accessed 4 June 2018).

Golgotha. 'Fikotrohanify.' Online at: https://www.youtube.com/watch?v=30l4lrqAWaI (accessed 4 June 2018).

Golgotha. 'Vangy.' *2013*. Online at: https://www.youtube.com/watch?v=UcsD42uJcjg (accessed 4 June 2018).

Green. 'Atsimo sy Avaratra.' Online at: https://www.youtube.com/watch?v=yHEWm2oxPYc (accessed 21 June 2018).

Iary. 'Modia am'zay'. *Di'ary*. *2007*: Madagascar. Online at: https://www.youtube.com/watch?v=uh3kbsxd6G0 (accessed at 21 June 2018).

Iary. 'Aoka ihany.' *2016*. Online at: https://www.youtube.com/watch?v=9NHDDL1celA (accessed 4 June 2018).
Iary. 'Isaorako ianao' [Iary's band]. *2017*. Online at: https://www.youtube.com/watch?v=fVFawOCz3SM (accessed 4 June 2018).
Kazar. 'Mpanota.' *1988*: Madagascar. Online at: https://www.youtube.com/watch?v=VSaEkhuVfBg (accessed 21 June 2018).
Kazar. 'Hades.' *Kazar*. *2007*: Madagascar. Online at: https://www.youtube.com/watch?v=IPJsqga0tkY (accessed 21 June 2018).
Kiaka. 'Ilay mahantra.' *1985*: Madagascar. Online at: https://www.youtube.com/watch?v=q4-pVAphV3I (accessed 21 June 2018).
Kiaka. 'Izy roa kely.' *Collection*. N.d.: Madagascar. Online at: https://www.youtube.com/watch?v=nEobw775X-Y (accessed 21 June 2018).
L'Imby. 'Ilay sangany.' Online at: https://www.youtube.com/watch?v=wl_F2F32lvk (accessed 21 June *2018*).
L'Imby. 'Mpihaza Mahery.' Online at: https://www.youtube.com/watch?v=jzh66UZzp3U (accessed 21 June 2018).
Lokömotiva. 'Jiholahy-Jambo.' Online at: https://www.youtube.com/watch?v=iJdIPIO3wgU (accessed 21 June 2018).
Lokömotiva. 'Lokomotiva.' *Nomad*. *2014*: Madagascar. Online at: https://www.youtube.com/watch?v=9tPOt1C69eE (accessed 21 June 2018).
Mage4. 'Fefy tsilo.' Online at: https://www.youtube.com/watch?v=dNH8wej6U3M (accessed 21 June 2018).
Resurrection. 'Eyes of Soul.' Online at: https://www.youtube.com/watch?v=5rvxF-XR_MQ (accessed 21 June 2018).
Resurrection. 'Rangotry ny omaly.' Online at: https://www.youtube.com/watch?v=qGWhEupr6u8 (accessed 21 June 2018).
Samar. 'No Salvation.' *2015*. Online at: https://www.youtube.com/watch?v=9H506L7dQIQ (accessed 4 June 2018).
Sasamaso. 'Fariseo.' Online at: https://www.youtube.com/watch?v=FIZUvlq-1ic (accessed 21 June 2018).
Sasamaso. 'Fotamandry.' *2017*. Online at: https://www.youtube.com/watch?v=ypawp6HrCdY (accessed 4 June 2018).
Sharks. *Mahery Fo*. *2012*: Madagascar. Online at: https://www.youtube.com/watch?v=NcWCJmnfxf8 (accessed 21 June *2018*).
Tselatra. 'Manantena an'iza.' *Best of Tselatra: Rock*. SM Pro. N.d.: Madagascar. Online at: https://www.youtube.com/watch?v=8kQKzDBobts (accessed 21 June 2018).
Tselara. 'Matoky.' *2011*. Online at: https://www.youtube.com/watch?v=t6HkQrfU1Ho (accessed 4 June 2018).
Tselatra. 'Misy andro.' *Best of Tselatra: Ballad*. SM Pro. Madagascar. Online at https://www.youtube.com/watch?v=MGKwLSi1kW8 (accessed at 21 June 2018).

MARKUS VERNE

Heavy Metal in South Africa

Heavy metal in South Africa has experienced a distinctly political development historically. South Africa's global marginalization during apartheid meant that many international bands boycotted the country, or simply did not regard South Africa as a viable market for touring: Metallica, for example, did not tour South Africa until 2006. Such marginalization also meant that the domestic metal scene in South Africa went largely unrecognized. As Banchs observes, 'Away from the eyes of the world' (Banchs 2013), heavy metal scenes had been steadily developing in South Africa prior to the official end of apartheid in 1994. The South African metal scene developed from existing punk and alternative rock subcultures in the 1980s and continued to diversify throughout the 1990s, supported by live scenes in urban areas. The 1990s saw the growth of varied regional scenes encompassing thrash, death, grindcore, doom and Christian Metal and, crucially, the development of an Afrikaans-language metal scene.

Cape Town was the major center for South African metal in the 1990s, driven by bands such as death metal act Sacraphyx and thrash act Pothole. During the late 2010s heavy metal scenes continued to center largely around the major metropolitan areas of Johannesburg, Cape Town, Durban, Pretoria and Bloemfontein. Kahn-Harris further notes that 'even in the Rainbow Nation [South Africa] the scene is mostly white' (Kahn-Harris 2010). While women are present in South African metal, coverage of the scene is overwhelmingly centered on men. The infrastructure of scenes further lends itself to the genre's largely urban demographics. The South African scene has been supported through institutions such as radio stations Voice of Rock and MK Ondergrond, dedicated rock and metal clubs in metropolitan areas, and festivals such as RAMfest and Witchfest. Since the mid-2000s the scene has gained wider reach through online spaces such as the comprehensive Metal 4 Africa, which also supports a metal festival of the same name. The relative strength of South Africa's recording industry is also reflected in the metal scene, with labels Witchdoctor and Burning Tone serving as notable players in a small but comparatively well-represented sector.

The identity of South African metal is in many ways born from the entanglement of the genre with the politics of apartheid. Heavy metal and rock scenes served as important sites of anti-government protest both during the years of apartheid (Banchs 2016; van der Waal and Robins 2011, 764) and in its immediate aftermath. As Clifford Crab, the lead singer of the thrash metal band Agro, has observed, '[Our] role as metalheads during Apartheid was to speak out against Apartheid, and we did so blatantly' (quoted in Banchs 2013). The injustice and violence of apartheid is manifest in the music of several bands from this period: Retribution Denied's blackened-death album *The Meek Shall Inherit the Earth* (1992) serves as a significant example of criticism of the ruling National Party's policies and, moreover, the perceived failure of the United Nations to adequately disassemble the architecture of apartheid.

Foreign influences including those of heavy metal had been heavily censored and often banned outright by the ultra-conservative National Party during apartheid. Heavy metal communities were closely monitored by police during this period. Clifford Crab has recalled that 'if you stepped out of line, you got messed up' (quoted in Banchs 2013). As Paul Blom, the former drummer of Voice of Destruction has observed, 'the government was more concerned with keeping the black population under their thumb, and with that mind-set comes the fascist attitude that anyone different is an enemy, so fans and supporters were often harassed by cops' (quoted in Banchs 2013). Heavy metal and hard rock scenes thus acted as small but important sites of resistance in the latter decades of the twentieth century. Nonetheless, political divides, particularly those articulated along ethno-national lines, have continued to permeate the national scene.

The varied histories, subgenres and regional influences of South Africa's metal communities make it difficult to identify a distinctly South African metal sound. However, the development of Afrikaans-language metal is in many ways a marker of a distinctively South African contribution to heavy metal, albeit one which represents regional tensions. Heavy metal in the latter years of apartheid and its immediate aftermath became one of the many voices speaking to young people who had to find their place in a transitional phase of a country with a problematic history (Klopper 2011, 187). Afrikaans metal, which utilizes the Afrikaans language and voices the concerns of the Afrikaner community, is bound up in an intricate network of postapartheid identities within the 'new' South Africa. Stylistically, Afrikaans metal, represented by bands such as Kobus! and Mind Assault, traverses a range of genres from the guttural vocals and down-tuned guitars of death metal to mid-tempo groove, though the unifying convention of the scene remains the use of the Afrikaans language.

These characteristics have stylistic purposes: Jacques Fourie, the lead singer of death metal band Mind Assault, points out that the harsh sonority of Afrikaans makes it 'great language for metal just because of how it sounds. [It is] more true to the nature of metal' (quoted in Ramon van H. 2009). Nonetheless, there are also explicit political reasons for singing in Afrikaans. Afrikaans metal is bound up with what van der Waal and Robins have called the 'post-apartheid Afrikaner culture industry,' a market which allows for a celebration of a revamped but less party-political Afrikaans identity while reasserting the imagined boundaries of white Afrikaanerdom and a feeling of disenfranchisement (van der Waal and Robins 2011, 763). The Afrikaans metal scene, Senekal has suggested, may be seen as propagating self-imposed marginalization, rather than being marginalized by an external force (Senekal 2011, 96). The political tensions which accompany Afrikaans metal thus indicate that South African metal has remained very much entangled with complex architectures of power and identity as realized through the spaces of popular music.

Despite these ongoing complexities, South Africa's heavy metal scenes have grown and diversified considerably since their earliest incarnations, becoming part of the increasingly crowded 'cultural festival tent' (Klopper 2011, 185) of modern South African music. In the postapartheid era, however, heavy metal in South Africa has remained a relatively marginal genre. As Mind Assault's Jacques Fourie, has observed, 'very few South Africans are even aware that SA metal bands exist. We get zero radio, TV or media coverage' (quoted in Ramon van H. 2009). Nonetheless, South Africa's metal scenes have gained increased international attention. In 2013 Infanteria won the first-ever South African 'Metal Battle' competition and were awarded a spot on the lineup of Wacken Open Air, the biggest metal festival in the world. Wacken has also served as a platform for South African stalwarts Agro in 2012, Zombies Ate My Girlfriend, who featured on the 2016 bill and Megalodon in 2017. The success of Demogoroth Satanum, stars of the entertainment and popular culture news website Uproxx's documentary on 'South Africa's first all-black black metal band' (Bramucci 2017), has also been vital in breaking down the racial and regional divides which have continued to beleaguer South African metal. Such growth will see the South African heavy metal scene further develop and diversify into the future.

Bibliography

Banchs, Edward. 2013. 'The Quiet Rise of Heavy Metal in South Africa.' *This is Africa*. Online at: https://thisisafrica.me/lifestyle/quiet-rise-heavy-metal-south-africa/ (accessed 19 March 2018).

Banchs, Edward. 2016. *Heavy Metal Africa: Life, Passion, and Heavy Metal in the Forgotten Continent*. Tarentum, PA: World Association Publishers.

Bramucci, Steve. 2017. 'Meet South Africa's First All-Black, Black Metal Band.' *Uproxx*. Online at: https://uproxx.com/life/soweto-death-metal/ (accessed 20 March 2018).

Hoad, Catherine. 2014. 'Ons is saam – Afrikaans Metal and Rebuilding Whiteness in the Rainbow Nation.' *International Journal of Community Music* 7(2): 189–204.

Hoad, Catherine. 2015. 'Whiteness With(out) Borders: Translocal Narratives of Whiteness in Heavy Metal Scenes in Norway, South Africa and Australia.' *Medianz* 15(1): 17–34.

Kahn-Harris, Keith. 2010. 'Metal in Africa.' *Norient*. Online at: http://norient.com/stories/metalafrica/ (accessed 19 March 2018).

Klopper, Annie. 2011. 'Reshaping Remembrance – "In Ferocious Anger I Bit The Hand That Controls": The Rise of Afrikaans Punk Rock Music.' In *Reshaping Remembrance: Critical Essays on Afrikaans Places of Memory*, eds. Albert Grundlingh and Siegfried Huigen. Amsterdam: Rozenberg Publishers, 179–89.

Ramon, van H. 2009. 'Mind Assault.' *Lords of Metal ezine*. Online at: http://www.lordsofmetal.nl/nl/interviews/view/id/3022 (accessed 29 October 2018).

Senekal, Burgert A. 2011. 'Vervreemding in die ekstreem: 'n Oorsig oor normloosheid en sosiale isolasie in Afrikaanse ekstreme metal' [Alienation in the Extreme: An Overview of Normlessness and Social Isolation in Afrikaans Extreme Metal]. *LitNet Akademies* 8(1): 76–109.

van der Waal, Kees C. S., and Robinse, Steven. 2011. '"De la Rey" and the Revival of "Boer Heritage": Nostalgia in the Post-apartheid Afrikaner Culture Industry.' *Journal of Southern African Studies* 37(4): 763–79.

Discographical Reference

Retribution Denied. *The Meek Shall Inherit the Earth*. Inhouse Records MINHC 153. *1992*: South Africa.

Discography

Agro. *Rewriting History*. Tritone (8) TTCD/D007. *2010*: South Africa.

Demogoroth Satanum. 'Kingdom ov Hell.' *Mixtape 2017*. We Did This Records. *2017*: South Africa.

Infanteria. *Where Serpents Conquer*. Burning Tone Records BTRCD 004. *2015*: South Africa.

Kobus! *100% Skuldgevoelvry*. Ent Entertainment CDENT 002. *2004*: South Africa.

Kobus! *Kobus!* Ent Entertainment CDENT 001. *2002*: South Africa.

Kobus! *Swaar Metaal*. Rhythm Records (3) RR 075. *2007*: South Africa.

Megalodon. *Darkness in Sonance*. Burning Tone Records BTRC 002. *2013*: South Africa.

Mind Assault. *Stigma*. Self-produced. *2008*: South Africa.

Pothole. *Force-fed Hatred*. Way Cool WCR/005. *1997*: South Africa.

Pothole. *Showdown.* Way Cool. WCR 014. *1999*: South Africa.

Sacraphyx. *The Shades of Hate.* Witchdoctor Records. *2003*: South Africa.

Voice of Destruction. *Bloedrivier.* Morbid Records (2) MR 026 CD. *1996*: Germany.

Zombies Ate My Girlfriend. 'Appropriate Hate Crimes.' *Live at Wacken 2016.* Silver Lining Music SLM077P17. *2017*: Europe.

Websites

http://metal4africa.com/ (accessed 19 March 2018)

CATHERINE HOAD

Hees

Hees (pl. *heeso*), or 'song,' refers broadly to a genre of Somali oral poetry that is sung by both men and women to unique melodies with instrumental accompaniment. The term 'hees' may also be applied to songs that accompany dances (*heeso ciyaareed*) and songs sung to accompany specific work activities (*heeso hawleed*, or 'work songs'). However, since the 1960s the term 'hees' has usually been deployed to describe a distinct form of urban popular song that emerged in the 1940s and has remained popular since then. *Hees* are differentiated from other forms of oral poetry in their use of instruments, the unique melodies (*laxan*) to which they are sung and their performance by and for both men and women. Most *hees* are composed on the theme of love (*hees jacayl*), though songs that address political themes (*hees siyaasadeed*) have long been an important part of the genre's development and popularity. *Hees* may also be classified by their period of origin, with 'classic' used to describe songs from the period before the Somali civil war, and 'modern' used to describe songs produced since the 1990s that rely on electronic instrumentation. Since their emergence in the late colonial period *hees* have been a site of both pride and contestation, variously used to push the boundaries of expectations regarding gender, love and marriage, to advance the cause of Somali nationalism, to veil critique of the powers that be, and to stake a claim in the shaping of postwar and diasporic public spaces.

Origins and Development

The origins of *hees* can be traced to a convergence of social, political and technological forces in the late colonial era. This was a period of significant sociopolitical change, when increasing urbanization, transformations in the economic sphere, developments in education and the rise of bureaucratic governance prompted the emergence of a new urban elite. The opening of Radio Hargeysa (first Radio Goodir) in 1943, followed by Radio Muqdisho in 1951 exposed new city dwellers to Sudanese, Arab and Indian sounds, and facilitated the dissemination of new genres that expressed the changing personal (romantic) and political (anti-colonial, nationalist) aspirations of the new elite. This confluence of forces, combined with the pioneering influence of key individuals such as Cabdi Deeqsi 'Sinimo' and Cabdullahi Qarshe, created an environment ripe for artistic innovation.

The birth of *hees* is most immediately traced to the *belwo* movement. The first *belwo* was reportedly composed in 1943 after a mechanical failure forced Cabdi Deeqsi 'Sinimo,' a truck driver, to the side of the road somewhere between Boorame (Borama) (a town in the west of the then British Protectorate of Somaliland) and Djibouti City. To air his frustrations Cabdi Sinimo, known to be a skilled joke- and story-teller (hence the nickname 'Sinimo' from 'Cinema'), composed a short, lyrical poem that improvised on the vocative form of the word 'belwo' from the Arabic *balwā* or *balā*, meaning 'trial,' 'tribulation' or 'calamity.' Once back in Boorame, the poem was repeated to instant success. Encouraged by this warm reception, Cabdi Sinimo and others began meeting regularly in homes to compose similar short poems. Accompanied by empty petrol cans and using the standard opening formula 'belwooy, (belwooy), hoy belwooy!' (which means something like 'woe is me!' [Johnson 1996a, 59]), they produced a body of two- to three-line poems on themes ranging from everyday events (or calamities) to the pains of love and descriptions of the women they liked. While other genres of Somali poetry are composed by and for single-sex audiences, the *belwo* movement was mixed-gendered and women such as Khadiija Ciye Dharaar (later known as Khadiija 'Belwo') became some of the genre's earliest torchbearers. These poetic innovations were not without their detractors: considered 'frivolous' by established poets, the mixed-gendered nature of *belwo* gatherings and the intimate content of their verse also drew the ire of religious authorities, and the fathers of Khadiija 'Belwo' and Cabdi Sinimo were barred from entering their mosques. Nevertheless, by the mid-1940s *belwo* had a strong (young) urban following and had reached neighboring towns such as Hargeysa (Hargeisa), Djibouti City and Muqdisho (Mogadishu).

As *belwo* spread to other urban centers it began to undergo transformations in both its poetic and musical form. More and more instruments began to join the tin drum, including the tambourine, *cuud* (oud, ʿūd), flute, violin and guitar. The opening of radio stations in Hargeysa and Muqdisho provided a timely platform for artists to air their new musical creations. Along with musical innovations came changes to the *belwo* form. Multiple *belwo* were strung together to make longer songs and in time were eventually replaced with longer unified poetic texts and standardized alliteration. The introductory formula changed from 'belwooy, (belwooy), hoy belwooy!' to 'heelloy heellelloy': whereas the term 'belwo' carried with it connotations of promiscuity, drinking and womanizing, 'heello' came from traditional poetry and thus served to make the genre more acceptable (Johnson 1996a, xii). Furthermore, whereas *belwo* were recited to a standard melody, *heello* came to have their own distinctive tunes. For the first time, individual poems were identifiable by their melody alone. By the late 1940s *belwo* had metamorphosed into *heello*, and popular song was born.

While Cabdi Sinimo's poetic complaint precipitated the *belwo* movement, the musical innovations that transformed *belwo* into *heello* are usually credited to Cabdullahi Qarshe. Raised in Aden, Qarshe grew up surrounded by the sounds of Sufi praise songs, Arabic music and Indian films, yet was perplexed as to why Somalis did not have a similar musical tradition. 'Want[ing] music to be for Somali as for the other languages' (Qarshe, quoted in Johnson 1996a, 82), Qarshe eventually bought a *cuud*, even though to his religious family (who believed music to be prohibited by Islam) it was considered blasphemous. When he moved to the British Protectorate of Somaliland in 1945, he took his instrument with him and found a teacher. Qarshe soon began setting Somali texts to distinct melodies with musical accompaniment, starting with the widely circulating love poetry of Cilmi Boodhari, the 1930s baker-turned-poet who by then was infamous as the poet who 'died for love.' These early love songs, known as *qaraami* (from the Arabic *gharāmī*, meaning 'amorous' or 'passionate'), have remained widely loved and enjoyed, and represent some of the earliest instantiations of *heello*. For bringing differentiated melodies and musical accompaniment to Somali poems, Qarshe is fondly referred to as 'the father of Somali music.'

In addition to his musical innovations, Qarshe also helped to raise the prestige of the new genre and the artists that produced it from something considered frivolous and immoral to a more serious and acceptable art form. Under Qarshe's leadership, the first Somali artistic collective was formed in 1955. Named Walaalaha Hargeysa (The Hargeysa Brothers), the group included a number of poets, playwrights, actors and musicians such as Saxardiid Maxamed 'Jebiyay,' Cumar Dhuule and Xuseen Aw Faarax, who would shape the artistic sphere for decades to come. In addition to *hees*, a new literary genre of dramas had also by this point become popular across the Somali territories, an innovation pioneered by Somali teachers in the north and political organizers in the south (Kapteijns 1999, 106). Walaalaha Hargeysa soon began producing songs and plays for performance on the radio and at open-air venues. In addition to themes of love and marriage, their work began to critically engage political issues. Songs such as Qarshe's 'Ka Kacaay' (Wake Up! Arise) and the patriotic 'Dhulkayaga' (Our Country) reflected on the evils of colonialism and the sacrifices to be made in the pursuit of independence (Johnson 1996a, 84–90). *Heello* thus played a critical role as 'the mouthpiece for the drive towards independence' (Johnson 1996a, 83), fueling anti-colonial sentiment and promoting *Soomaalinnimo* (a pan-Somalist nationalist identity*)*.

The independence of British and Italian Somalilands and the formation of the Somali Republic in 1960 brought with it further changes to the form and content of *heello*, which came to be more generally known as *hees*. In terms of form, songs became longer and began incorporating a refrain and the introductory 'heelloy heellelloy' was eventually dropped. Love remained a prominent theme. Kapteijns (1999) suggests that the genre helped the new urban elite to 'mainstream' the ideal of companionate marriage and put the issue of women's equality on the national agenda, even if appealing to tradition in ways that limited debates about women's rights. Many songs also continued to address political issues. However, as the ruling powers were now Somalis themselves, increasingly complicated imagery and metaphor were deployed to disguise sensitive messages (Johnson 1996a, 117–18). Given the existing preponderance of love as a theme in songs, love and marriage were frequently used as a cover for political critique, allowing the poet the escape of claiming his work was 'just about love' if he came under attack. Determining whether any given song is a *hees jacayl* or *hees siyaasadeed* is thus not always a straightforward affair. As a key means through which the new country's political elite articulated both their personal and political aspirations, the genre continued to gain in respectability and popularity. In the span of just over two decades the poetic experimentations of urban young people had metamorphosed into a genre of popular song increasingly central to social and political life in postcolonial Somalia.

Music-Making under Socialism

While *hees* gained in acceptance and popularity throughout the 1960s, it was after the 1969 socialist coup led by Maxamed Siyaad Barre and the Supreme Revolutionary Council that Somali music really flourished, with massive state investment leading to an unprecedented outpouring of new music. As with other socialist regimes, Barre saw the arts as a potential means of both educating the population and promoting support for his government. He thus effectively nationalized the entire artistic sphere. This nationalization led to the building of national theaters in both Hargeysa and Muqdisho and the organization or artists into collectives associated with (and usually employed by) different government ministries and organizations. New talent was regularly recruited through school singing competitions (*heesaha hirgalay* [new singing talent]), and cultivated in a number of groups aimed at young people (for instance, Ubaxa Kaccanka ['flowers of the revolution'] or the young pioneers). The most prolific and well-known government-sponsored collectives include Waaberi (the largest national collective), Iftiin (the band of the Ministry of Education), and the military bands Jeneraal Daa'uud and Horseed. These various government-affiliated bands were responsible for playing at government functions while the larger groups, such as Waaberi and Iftiin, regularly toured across the country to perform (educational) dramas, produced content for the radio and performed at popular entertainment venues in the evening (alongside the few private bands that survived into this period such as Shareero and Durdur). Members of Waaberi also represented Somalia at music competitions abroad and performed across Africa and the Middle East. Many 'giants' of Somali music who have remained popular – such as Hibo Nuura, Magool, Khadra Daahir, Xasan Aadan Samatar, Axmed Cali Cigaal – rose to fame as performers with these groups.

While the socialist regime provided an unprecedented amount of support to artists, the increasingly repressive nature of Barre's regime had mixed effects on musical production. On the one hand, increased support meant increased access to instruments and an ever-expanding number of professional musicians with time to develop their craft. Virtuosos on the *cuud*, such as 'Jiim' Sheekh Muumin (so-nicknamed for abilities comparable with those of Jimi Hendrix), Xudeydi and Cumar Dhuule took *cuud* playing to new heights. Growing orchestras began integrating more and more instruments, including the saxophone, bass guitar, drum kit and organ. However, increasingly strict censorship policies meant that the themes that songs and plays could address were progressively curtailed and the quantity of musical production was not always matched by quality. This situation did at times lead to creative attempts to bypass government censors and subversive songs banned from the radio circulated on cassette tapes (sometimes leading to the artists' imprisonment or exile). By the mid-1980s the artistic energy that had characterized the 1970s had waned as popular support for the regime also turned to opposition. The 1988 aerial bombardments of Hargeysa by government forces that razed the National Theatre (and much of the rest of the city) index the complete collapse of the artistic sphere that was to come and the beginning of a devastating war that soon engulfed the entire country. Yet, despite this eventual destruction, or perhaps because of it, the 1970s and early 1980s continue to be fondly recalled as the 'golden era' or 'heyday' of Somali music, a time when artists were celebrated as national icons and when *hees* were an integral feature of the soundscape of the city.

Hees in the Aftermath of War

The massive displacement and destruction brought on by war has left an indelible scar on Somali musical production. In the immediate term, artists' homes and radio archives were looted, instruments were lost or destroyed, and artists were displaced to refugee camps in neighboring Ethiopia and Kenya or sought asylum in Europe or North America. In the north (subsequently the self-declared state of Somaliland), musicians affiliated with the Somali National Movement (SNM) did use their craft to support armed resistance against the government and even continued to play in refugee camps. However, the destruction precipitated by the war led to a serious decline in artistic morale. Combined with a lack of instruments, weakened financial and institutional support and growing anti-music sentiment from conservative religious quarters, new musical production in the Somali territories was nearly nonexistent in the 1990s and 2000s.

Despite massive setbacks, *hees* have survived, even if in a continually evolving form. A number of national artists displaced to Europe and North America began performing again, with some even recording commercial albums for the first time (for example, Maryan [Maryam] Mursal's album *The Journey*) and incorporating the sounds of diverse musical collaborators (for example, The Sahra Halgan Trio's *Faransiskiyo Somaliland* ['France and Somaliland']). New diaspora-based groups also began to emerge, such as Walaalaha Sweden ('The Brothers Sweden,' a name no doubt inspired by Walaalaha Hargeysa). Informal studios opened in London, Minneapolis and Toronto to record emerging young talent, including some children of popular prewar performers such as Hodan Cabdiraxmaan. Although it took more than two decades, and despite continued hostility toward musicians from some religious authorities, by the early 2010s new groups had started to operate in the Somali territories themselves. Hargeysa-based Xidigaha Geeska ('The Stars of the Horn') have had the most success, and their principal singers – such as Maxamed BK and Yurub Geenyo – have had a strong following at home and in the diaspora.

While *hees* produced in the postwar period share much with earlier *hees*, particularly in terms of the themes they address and the poetic meters and pentatonic melodies they employ, they are differentiated by their instrumentation. In a period marked by displacement and lack of access to instruments (or learning support), the synthesizer has effectively come to stand in for all other instruments. Whereas prewar *hees* were frequently performed live by multiple musicians, postwar *hees* have almost always been prerecorded, and the work of instrumentation is now usually completed by a single individual with a keyboard and digital recording/editing software. In the 2010s songs were being shared primarily through YouTube and Facebook and, when young artists have performed, they rely heavily on 'playback.' Such practices have led some fans of prewar music to decry new music as 'fake' and of inferior quality. However, such technological innovations have served to make the production of *hees* accessible to a younger and geographically dispersed generation that has lacked the support, resources and training provided by the socialist regime.

In addition to new musical production, the postwar period has been marked by a nostalgic resurgence and celebration of prewar *hees*, often described subsequently as 'classic' songs. While there were no commercial recording studios under Barre, the cassette collections of individuals uploaded onto YouTube or copied and distributed by diaspora-based studios have made these songs accessible to Somalis across the globe. Hargeysa-based Horn Cable TV has had a 24-hour music channel devoted to playing a mix of prewar and postwar songs, broadcast globally via satellite. Some of the archives of Radio Hargeysa and Radio Muqdisho survived the war, and in the late 2010s there was increased interest in preserving and digitizing these collections for future generations. An archive established at the Hargeysa Cultural Centre in 2015 containing cassettes acquired from a Djibouti studio and private donations was the source of tracks (which include *hees*, as well as Benaadiri and Djiboutian songs – for an account of Benaadiri songs, see the entry on Muqdisho in Volume VI) for the Grammy-nominated compilation, *Sweet as Broken Dates: Lost Somali Tapes from the Horn of Africa* (2017). Motivated by a desire to expose a younger generation to Somalis' musical heritage and carve out a space for musicians in postwar Hargeysa, SNM-singer Sahra Halgan and others opened Somaliland's first postwar music venue in 2014. Hiddo Dhawr ('Take Care of Heritage') has hosted live-music evenings two to three nights a week, playing exclusively prewar 'classics' accompanied by the *cuud* and drums, and has provided a platform for both established and emerging artists to share their craft (Woolner 2016; 2018). If the enthusiasm of the venue's audiences or the number of songs regularly uploaded to YouTube has been any sign, *hees* will continue to play an important role for Somalis across the globe into the foreseeable future.

Form, Content and Composition

Both prewar and postwar *hees* are nearly always the result of a collaboration between a poet (*abwaan*), melody writer (*laxamiste*), vocalist (*fannaan/fannaaniin* or *cod* [voice]) and one or more musicians. Both men and women help to produce *hees,* though women's participation is usually limited to singing. *Hees* nearly always begin as poems inspired by real-world events. The composition process is guided both by the individual creativity of the artists as well as the poetic, rhythmic and melodic motifs and expectations of the genre.

As a genre of oral poetry, the texts of *hees* follow the same basic principles of other Somali poetic genres, including the use of alliteration and conformity to strict scansion/metrical rules which determine the pattern of long and short vowels and syllable-final consonants in any given line. From *belwo* through to the early phases of *heello* (including all *qaraami),* songs adhered to the scansion pattern of *dhaanto,* a genre of traditional dance song. As the melodies of songs became increasingly differentiated, so too did the scansion patterns in which songs were composed. From the 1960s *jiifto,* a poetic genre traditionally used by men of religion, became a particularly popular form. By some estimates, up to 90 percent of Somali songs written since the 1960s employ this poetic genre (Weedhsame, pers. corr. 2017). Song texts may employ a range of scansion patterns, yet invariably must adhere to some generic scansion form. Additionally, the texts of individual songs employ universal alliteration. Every line of a song must therefore include at least one word beginning with the same vowel or consonant.

The texts of *hees* are overwhelmingly reflections on intensely personal and often painful experiences of love. Poets often compose based on their own experiences, although they also frequently write about the love experiences of those around them or those who seek their counsel. Common themes include the pains of unrequited love, love thwarted by social or familial expectations, longing for lovers separated by distance, love that cannot be expressed due to expectations of (women's) modesty, love that has turned sour and descriptions of ideal partners/partnerships. *Hees jacayl* are sometimes classified by the particular love emotion that a song depicts: for example, *calaacal* depict mournful experiences of longing while *foorjo* contain rebukes of scorned lovers. The imagery employed in songs has changed over time, with prewar love songs frequently employing pastoral images and metaphors to describe the beauty of a woman (for example, by comparing her eyes to that of an antelope, her stature to that of a tree or her virginity to untouched pastures) or the pains of love (for example, by comparing one's longing to that of a she-camel crying for her calf). Postwar lyrics employ such pastoral imagery less frequently and lyrics composed in particular by diaspora poets often speak more frankly. However, the experiences of love on which songs reflect remain very similar. The texts of *hees jacayl* are almost always written in the first person even when the poet is giving voice to another's experience. This means that poets must be adept at empathizing with others' experiences of love and are expected to convey the emotion of the original experience in their words.

While the overwhelming majority of *hees* are about love, politics and other social issues have remained common themes. Patriotic or nationalistic songs (*hees waddani*) as well as songs that address issues of common social concern (such as a spate of contemporary songs about illegal migration [*tahriib*]) tend to use straightforward text. However, *hees* that contain potentially sensitive political commentary or critique (often called *anti* songs) have long employed more complicated imagery, sometimes appearing on the surface to be love songs. While the practice of disguising political critique as love songs was more common in times of strict censorship, it has continued to be practiced in the late 2010s, though with less frequency, by young artists. Because of the expectation that love songs begin in real-world experiences, as well as in the practice of veiling political critique as reflections on love, group listening is often punctured by lively debate about the real-world origins of songs, and poets are frequently asked to expound on their motivations and inspiration.

When the text of a *hees* is complete, the *laxamiste* is responsible for setting it to a melody. The *laxamiste* is often a musician, though he may be a poet or other inspired party. Melodies employ one of a set of pentatonic scales. Words are generally sung syllabically with melismatic phrasing at the end of lines and verses (melismatic phrasing is especially pronounced in *qaraami*). The influences of Indian, Arab, Ethiopian and particularly Sudanese music, as well as traditional poetic genres and Sufi praise songs, can be heard in these melodies (though Somali scales lack the microtones or even semitones of Arabic *maqām*). Melodies must also be capable of being sung to a set number of rhythmic motifs which for the most part comprise offbeat 4/4 patterns. Some of these are drawn directly from earlier dance genres such as *dhaanto*. Afrobeat rhythms were also popular in the 1970s and 1980s. The *laxamiste* may sometimes make alterations to the text to make it more amenable to a particular melodic or rhythmic mode, though will usually consult the poet before doing so. Like the poet, the *laxamiste* should take the original emotional experience on which a song is based into consideration when creating the melody so that listeners may 'taste' the experience in the melodic movement of the words. A *calaacal*, for instance, should sound mournful, while the melody of an openly patriotic song should contain the conviction and celebration of its lyrics.

Once words have been provided with a melody, the song is given to a vocalist to sing. Love songs are most often performed as solos by either a man or a woman, depending on the gendered perspective of the song. Some songs are also written as duets (*talantalli*) in which a man and woman alternate singing different verses and refrains but never singing in harmony. Patriotic songs may be sung by individuals or by a group singing in unison. Vocalists are often selected by the poet who takes into consideration an individual's vocal range, timbre and ability to effectively convey the emotion of a given song. In some cases the selected vocalist is the individual who inspired the lyrics. As is the case for much Western popular music, particularly that influenced by African-American genres, an 'aesthetic of sincerity' (Middleton 2000, 32) defines expectations for 'good' vocal performances, especially for love songs: that is, singers should sing with emotional conviction 'from the heart.'

After the text and melody are set and the vocalist has prepared the vocal line, it is the work of one or more musicians to set the song to music. *Hees* begin with an instrumental introduction, in which the instrument(s) elaborate on the pentatonic motif of the song, sometimes using elements of the vocal *laxan*; instrument(s) then double or embellish the vocal line when the singer is singing and expand on the vocal line in between sung stanzas. During live performance there is a degree of improvisation in how instrumentalists play and the best performers are those adept at adding *xawaash* ('spice') to their sound. Songs that use the synthesizer are created by layering lines that mimic what different instruments (the drum, *cuud* and others) would have previously played individually.

Conclusion

As a genre birthed by the tumultuous sociopolitical changes of the late colonial period, refined in the early years of Somalia's independence and then indelibly shaped by Somalia's socialist regime and subsequent decades of war, *hees* represent a fascinating window into the personal and political aspirations of nearly seven decades of mainly young and mainly urban Somalis. While the massive upheavals that have occurred since the late 1980s have indelibly disrupted Somali artistic production, the genre's deep roots in Somalis' rich tradition of oral poetry and its ability to integrate the sounds and sentiments of a community in flux suggest that *hees* will continue to play an important role in the sociopolitical fabric of Somali communities for years to come.

Bibliography

Abokor, Axmed Cali. 1993. *Somali Pastoral Work Songs: The Poetic Voice of the Politically Powerless*. Uppsala: EPOS, Research Programme on Environmental Policy and Society, Department of Social and Economic Geography, Uppsala University.

Banti, Giorgio, and Giannattasio, Francesco. 1996. 'Music and Metre in Somali Poetry.' In *Voice and Power: The Culture of Language in North-East Africa: Essays in Honour of B.W. Andrzejewski. African Languages and Cultures, Supplement No. 3*, eds. Richard J. Hayward and Ioan M. Lewis. London and New York: Taylor and Francis, 83–127.

Hassan, Mohamed-Rashid Sheikh. 2008. 'Interview with the Late Abdullahi Qarshe (1994) at the Residence of Obliqe Carton in Djibouti.' *Bildhaan* 2: 65–83.

Johnson, John William. 1996a [1974]. *'Heelloy': Modern Poetry and Songs of the Somali*. London: Haan Publishing.

Johnson, John William. 1996b. 'Musico-Moro-Syllabic Relationships in the Scansion of Somali Oral Poetry.' In *Voice and Power: The Culture of Language in North-East Africa: Essays in Honour of B.W. Andrzejewski. African Languages and Cultures, Supplement No. 3*, eds. Richard J. Hayward and Ioan M. Lewis. London and New York: Taylor and Francis, 73–82.

Johnson, John William. 2010. 'The Politics of Poetry in the Horn of Africa: A Case Study in Macro-level and Micro-level Tradition.' In *Milk and Peace, Drought and War: Somali Culture, Society and Politics*, eds. Markus Hoehne and Virginia Luling. London: Hurst Publishing, 221–44.

Kapteijns, Lidwien (with Ali, Maryan Omar). 1999. *Women's Voices in a Man's World: Women and the Pastoral Tradition in Northern Somali Orature, c. 1899–1980*. Portsmouth, NH: Heinemann.

Kapteijns, Lidwien. 2009. 'Discourse on Moral Womanhood in Somali Popular Songs, 1960–1990.' *Journal of African History* 50: 101–22.

Kapteijns, Lidwien, and Ali, Maryan Omar. 2001. '"Come Back Safely": Laments about Labor Migration in Somali Love Songs.' *Northeast African Studies* 8(3): 33–46.

Laurence, Margaret. 1970 [1954]. *A Tree for Poverty: Somali Poetry and Prose*. Hamilton, ON: McMaster University Library Press.

Middleton, Richard. 2000. 'Rock Singing.' In *The Cambridge Companion to Singing*, ed. John Potter. Cambridge: Cambridge University Press, 28–41.

Woolner, Christina. 2016. 'Hiddo Dhawr: Singing Love in(to) Somaliland.' *Camthropod: The Cambridge Anthropology Podcast*, Episode 5. Online at: https://www.socanth. cam.ac.uk/media/listen-and-view/camthropod#episode-5--hiddo-dhawr--singing-love-in-to--somaliland---by-christina-woolner (accessed 18 March 2018).

Woolner, Christina J. 2018. 'Singing Love in(to) Somaliland: Love Songs, "Heritage Preservation," and the Shaping of Post-War Publics.' In *Music and Dance Research in Eastern Africa: Current Research in Humanities and Social Sciences*, eds. Kahithe Kiiru and Maina Mutonya. Nairobi: IFRA and Twaweza Communications, 76–90.

Personal Communication

Xasan Daahir Weedhsame, 29 December 2017.

Discographical References

Note: The texts of Cabdullahi Qarshe's songs 'Ka Kacaay' and 'Dhulkayaga' are available in Johnson (1996a, 84–90). 'Ka Kacaay' was composed in 1948, before the advent of compact cassettes; 'Dhulkayaga' dates to the 1950s. A recording of unknown origin is available online (though the accompanying images are not of Somali origin): https://www.youtube.com/watch?v=zEeUGisxNyo (accessed 22 March 2018).

Maryam Mursal. *The Journey*. Real World Records CAR 2370-2. *1998*: USA.

Sahra Halgan Trio. *Faransiskiyo Somaliland*. Universal Music 4758652. *2016*: France.

Sweet as Broken Dates: Lost Tapes from the Somali Horn of Africa. Ostinato Records OSTLP003. *2017*: USA.

YouTube

Examples of 'Classic' Songs (1950s–1980s)

Cabdullahi Qarshe, 'Waryaadhaay,' https://www.youtube.com/watch?v=WrY24XSweFY (accessed 22 March 2018).

Cumar Dhuule, 'Xafuun,' https://www.youtube.com/watch?v=1y39Ye238OA (accessed 22 March 2018).

Hibo Nuura, 'Sabab Kale' https://www.youtube.com/watch?v=6S-kosdWyCY (accessed 22 March 2018).

Khadra Daahir, 'Caashaqu Ogeysiis Ma Leeyahay?' (from the play *Xishood iyo Jacayl*, performed by members of Waaberi), https://www.youtube.com/watch?v=SBkXXqKDny8 (accessed 22 March 2018).

Xaliimo Khaliif Magool, 'Daydayaa Ma Daalee,' https://www.youtube.com/watch?v=C-OsCfTLqX0 (accessed 22 March 2018).

Xasan Aadan Samatar, 'Beledweyn,' https://www.youtube.com/watch?v=ALPMztHdHDA (accessed 22 March 2018).

Examples of 'New' Songs (2010s)

Hodan Cabdiraxman, 'Saddex Saddex' https://www.youtube.com/watch?v=7ZDOdoxt5D4 (accessed 22 March 2018).

Maxamed BK, 'Nolosha Cusub,' https://www.youtube.com/watch?v=ZQjd7SIkprY (accessed 22 March 2018).

Nimcaan Hilaac, 'Jamasho,' https://www.youtube.com/watch?v=-L5pxdEmuNg (accessed 22 March 2018).

Xidigaha Geeska 2018 New Year's Concert, https://www.youtube.com/watch?v=NqL9xMbtraw (accessed 22 March 2018).

Yurub Geenyo, 'Qaamuus,' https://www.youtube.com/watch?v=DWBdIhnZWhI (accessed 22 March 2018).

CHRISTINA J. WOOLNER

See also **Muqdisho (Mogadishu) (Vol. VI. Locations: Africa and the Middle East)**

Highlife

Highlife is a West African urban popular dance music that utilizes African rhythms, melodies and languages and is played by brass bands, guitar bands and dance bands. It first developed in southern Ghana during the nineteenth and early twentieth centuries from a fusion of three cultural influences: the African, the European and the New World Black Diaspora. As the imported music of missionaries, brass bands and Western popular music came to West Africa via European and American ships during the nineteenth century, highlife developed initially in the coastal areas before moving inland. (This entry is concerned mainly with highlife in Ghana. For highlife in areas of Nigeria see separate entries on Highlife, Igbo and Highlife, Yorùbá. See also separate entries on Adaha, Concert Party, Hiplife, Konkoma, Odonson and Palmwine Music.)

Origins

Although the term 'highlife' was not coined until the 1920s, progenitors of this music existed before then under various names. Its creation occurred in three contexts: the coastal military-fort brass bands that played 'adaha' music; the ports where seamen and fishermen played guitar and accordion 'palmwine' music; and the local dance orchestras of the Christian elites of towns such as Accra, Cape Coast and Winneba that went on to play ballroom versions of local tunes called 'highlife.' By the 1940s all these various early Ghanaian popular music styles – brass-band highlife, guitar-band highlife and dance orchestra and dance-band highlife – became known collectively as 'highlife.'

The very earliest form of proto-highlife, *adaha*, arose due to the Africanization of Western regimental brass-band music in the late nineteenth century. Earlier in that century, fife-and-drum and brass bands were set up at the European military forts. For instance, in the 1830s a 'native band' (a brass band) was set up at Cape Coast Castle in the southern Fanti (an Akan subgroup) area of Ghana to play Western military marches and dance music, but not local songs. This changed with the emergence of local *adaha* brass-band music in the 1880s, catalyzed by the arrival of five to six thousand West Indian troops at Cape Coast and El Mina Castle who, between 1873 and 1901, helped the British fight the inland Ashantis. In their spare time, these soldiers from the English-speaking Caribbean played their own syncopated African-Caribbean music such as calypsos. Ghanaians who had been trained in military brass bands followed suit, and beginning in the 1880s they set up competing brass bands playing their own blend of syncopated marching music that fused imported Caribbean and local rhythms. Ghanaian brass-band musicians borrowed calypso melodies to create *adaha* songs such as 'Everybody Loves Saturday Night.' At first, syncopated five-pulse 4/4 Caribbean *clave* rhythms were utilized, but local bell patterns in both 2/4 and 6/8 time were quickly added. *Adaha* thus became the earliest recognized form of the coastal Ghanaian transcultural music that later became known as highlife.

Attempts were made by the colonial authorities to ban *adaha* music street parades for being noisy and encouraging drunkenness. Nevertheless, *adaha* bands spread like wildfire throughout southern Ghana, supported by money from the cocoa boom. Less well-off towns and villages that could not afford expensive imported brass-band instruments made do with a poor man's version of *adaha* called *konkoma* (or *konkomba*), which employed voices and local percussion and spread as far eastwards as Nigeria. By the early twenty-first century *adaha* brass bands had largely died out, except in the Agona Swedru areas (near Cape Coast) where they were associated with masquerade parades.

The term 'palmwine music' retrospectively describes the various early twentieth-century music styles that combined small local percussion instruments with the portable instruments played by visiting seamen, such as the concertina, accordion, penny whistle, mandolin, banjo, harmonica and, particularly, the guitar. By around 1900 this music was being played at low-class dockside bars and local bars that sold a local alcoholic drink called 'palmwine' made from the fermented sap of the palm tree. It included subgenres such as the *osibisaaba* of the local Fanti fishermen, Sierra Leonian *aṣíkò* music popular all along the West African coast, and the *dagomba*, *fireman* (i.e., ships' stoker) and *mainline* guitar styles of visiting Liberian Kru sailors and stevedores. The maritime Krus worked aboard European and American sailing ships throughout the nineteenth century. Consequently it was on the high seas that they developed a distinctive West African two-finger guitar plucking technique which they spread up and down the West African coast via the Kru-town settlements they established from the mid-nineteenth century onward. A Kru taught Ghana's most famous pioneer highlife guitarist, Kwame Asare (also known as Jacob Sam). Later, Asare and his Fanti group, the Kumasi Trio (working in Kumasi at the time) made some of the first highlife recordings (including the famous song 'Yaa Amponsah') for Zonophone in London in 1928. These recordings were part of a lucrative African or 'Native Record' music market that developed in Anglophone West Africa at the time when companies such as Zonophone, HMV and EMI brought African artists to London to record.

When the coastal Fanti *osibisaaba* style of palmwine music moved inland during the 1930s, it incorporated the lyrics, rhythms and modulations of the traditional Akan *seprewa* (or *seprerewa*) harp lute, creating the more 'rootsy' Akan guitar style known as *odonson* or 'Akan blues.' During the 1930s and 1940s guitar and concertina records of the various palmwine styles featuring artists such as Kwesi Pepera, Appianing, Mireku, Osei Bonsu, Kwesi Menu and Appiah Adjekum were distributed by HMV and Parlophone in cocoa-rich southern Ghana. These groups all consisted of a guitarist or two plus a percussionist who played 'clips' (the local name for *clave*-type percussion sticks), a bell or a drum. Based on the music of the *seprewa*, the *odonson* style did not follow Western chord progressions but rather the Akan modal melodic style of moving between two tonal centers. Like *seprewa* music, the lyrics were highly proverbial and many *odonson* songs utilized the traditional Akan polyrhythmic 6/8 bell pattern.

A third and separate development, beginning with the Accra Excelsior Orchestra in 1914, was the establishment by educated Ghanaians of a number of large dance orchestras that played European and Latin American ballroom music and ragtime for the local black elite audience. These orchestras included a brass and woodwind section, kit drums, a piano or harmonium and a large string section of violins, cellos, guitars and banjos. Many such prestigious groups, composed of Western-educated Akan and Ga musicians, were formed in the 1920s and 1930s, such as the Jazz Kings, Rag-a-Jazzbo, the Cape Coast Sugar Babies, the Accra Orchestra, the Accra Rhythmic Orchestra, the Winneba Orchestra, the Ashanti Nkramo Band and the Sekondi Nanshamak. During the 1920s orchestrated renditions of local melodies and street songs were added to their repertoires. Listeners who stood outside the elite venues but were too poor to enter called this orchestrated local music 'highlife' (i.e., high-class life). Despite the high-status context of this term, the name 'highlife' subsequently became an umbrella for all the early varieties of Ghanaian popular music, whether played by posh dance orchestras and bands, low-class *konkoma* bands or rustic palmwine guitar groups. Indeed 'highlife' became the generic name for all forms of local Ghanaian popular dance music right up to recent forms, such as the 'burger' disco-style highlife of the 1980s and the rap-influenced 'hiplife' (i.e., hip-hop highlife) of the 1990s.

At the same classy venues where the top-hatted elites danced to ballroom music they were also entertained by silent movies and a 'concert party,' which combined ragtime, tap-dancing and vaudeville sketches performed in English. Ragtime music was introduced through records, sheet music and African-American 'black-jack' seamen. American vaudeville (in the UK called 'music-hall') was introduced during the 1920s through visiting artists from the United States, Liberia and Britain and early film. Ghanaians copied these imported forms of popular entertainment and created what they called 'concert parties' in which they performed ragtime, quicksteps, tap dances foxtrots and vaudeville sketches wearing the blackface makeup of the US minstrel show. In

Ghana, blackface was not perceived as racist, as it was in the United States, but simply as the uniform of ragtime and its associated dances.

Although the Ghanaian *concert party* initially started as a Ghanaian elite art form, in the 1930s the blackface comedian Bob Johnson hijacked the *concert party* from the elites and took it and its associated ragtime music to the rural hinterland. Consequently, the first steps in the indigenization of this local form of comic theater took place when Johnson's Versatile Eight (and later the Axim Trio) incorporated motifs from traditional Akan legends about Ananse the spider that were popular with rural audiences. Johnson pioneered the stage character 'Bob,' still found in the early twenty-first century, who looks like an American blackface comic but behaves like the mischievous West African trickster Ananse.

For the rural and provincial tours the concert parties continued to employ ragtime, foxtrots and quicksteps for their performances. However, since village people did not speak English, these pioneering itinerant popular theatrical groups also performed partially in the vernacular (i.e., Fanti) and used *konkoma* highlife music for their preshow publicity. By the 1940s about ten concert parties were operating in Ghana, taking their musical plays to rural audiences and the urban poor, who mainly consisted of new rural migrants. Some concert parties also began to use an occasional highlife song in their performances. However, as will be mentioned later, highlife music only became central to the concert parties in the early 1950s.

Highlife from World War II to the 1980s

Ghana was deeply involved in World War II, with over 60,000 Ghanaians being recruited into the British army, with many fighting the Japanese in Burma. Conversely, thousands of US and British servicemen were stationed in Ghana. Not surprisingly, World War II had a great impact on Ghanaian popular music. For instance, the British used *konkoma* highlife marching songs for recruiting Ghanaian youth into the British army, and the West African Theatre was set up to entertain the African troops in Burma by seven Ghanaian servicemen who were also *concert party* actors and *konkoma* highlife musicians. At the same time British and American Allied soldiers stationed in Ghana loved swing and jazz, and together with Ghanaian dance orchestra musicians who could read music they established the swing bands Black and White Spots and the Tempos to entertain the Allied troops.

The Tempos survived the war and the departure of the foreign servicemen and became an all-Ghanaian group which, beginning in 1948 and, under the leadership of E.T. Mensah, began to concentrate more on local highlife with a strong swing, jazz and calypso touch. In fact, the band's lineup was basically that of a small swing combo with a drummer, double bassist, guitarist and small horn section. The Tempos' drummer, Kofi Ghanaba (then called Guy Warren), added Afro-Cuban percussion (*congas* and *bongó*) after briefly working in London with Kenny Graham's Afro-Cubists, a Cu-bop band that combined bebop with Afro-Cuban percussion. The jazz influence increased when Louis Armstrong and His All Stars visited Ghana in 1956 and again in 1960.

The ten-piece Tempos, with its blend of the imported and indigenous, became so successful that during the 1950s and 1960s many West African dance bands modeled themselves on it: the Black Beats, Rhythm Aces, Red Spot, Ramblers, Stargazers, Messengers, Broadway (later called Uhuru), Comets and Rakers of Ghana, the Black Santiagos of Benin, as well as bands from Nigeria (where the Tempos often toured) run by Bobby Benson, Victor Olaiya, Zeal Onyia, Victor Uwaifo and Rex Lawson. Indeed, the postwar highlife dance bands, with their then-sophisticated jazz-type lineup, reflected the spirit (*zeitgeist*) of the early independence era, for just as these bands successfully combined Western instrumentation with African content (i.e., highlife), so independence was ushering in a modern Western-type nation-state, but one run by Africans. In short, highlife became the sound symbol and indeed the soundtrack of the early independence era in Ghana and elsewhere in Africa where institutional Africanization was taking place.

World War II intensified the Ghanaian nationalist struggle, particularly after the 1948 anti-British demonstrations by Ghanaian war veterans demanding back pay. When some of the soldiers who marched on the colonial headquarters at Christiansborg Castle in Accra were shot, widespread riots and lootings of European shops resulted. The British began to lose their colonial nerve and so elections were held in 1952. They were won by Kwame Nkrumah and his Convention People's Party (CPP), resulting in

Ghana's full independence in 1957. This nationalist upsurge affected the country's popular music during the period leading to independence. E.T. Mensah's Tempos and other similar highlife dance bands wrote independence songs and played at Nkrumah's CPP rallies. When the members of the wartime West African Theatre returned home they formed the Burma Jokers *concert party*, renamed the Ghana Trio in 1948 in line with the rising nationalist sentiments of the times. The Axim Trio and Bob Ansah's concert parties staged pro-Nkrumah comic party plays and in fact Ansah was arrested by the colonial authorities on several occasions for his *concert party*'s anti-British plots.

Palmwine music was influenced by the postwar dance bands. By the 1950s the earlier palmwine ensembles had expanded to include double bass, *bongó* and other imported percussion. These became known as 'guitar bands' and many of them, like those of Kwaa Mensah and E.K. Nyame, also wrote pro-independence highlife songs. Indeed E.K. Nyame sometimes accompanied Nkrumah on state visits.

When E.K. Nyame expanded his guitar band to include local popular theater by forming the Akan Trio *concert party* in 1952, he completed the indigenization process begun during the 1930s by Bob Johnson and the Axim Trio. The musical plays of E.K. Nyame's Akan Trio were performed totally in the vernacular and were accompanied by guitar band highlife music rather than the ragtime of earlier concert groups. Nyame's 'comic highlife opera' format subsequently became the template of practically all succeeding guitar bands: Kakaiku's and Yamoah's bands, the Jaguar Jokers, Dr. Gyasi's Noble Kings, Bob Cole's Ghana Trio, Onyina's Royal Trio and many others. Beginning in the 1950s scores of *concert party* bands operating in southern Ghana constantly toured or 'trekked' up and down Ghana bringing their plays, music, urban fashions and sociopolitical commentaries to even the tiniest villages, using acoustic instruments and kerosene pressure lamps for illumination. The *concert party* plays and highlife songs presented themes that dealt with the dangers of modern times, such as prostitution, alcoholism and juvenile delinquency. The favorite topic of the time was a story of broken homes and orphan children, reflecting the collapse of traditional African extended and polygamous families under pressure from Western economic and social norms (class stratification, migrant work, patrilineal inheritance and the ideal of the nuclear family). Like the highlife dance bands, many of these guitar bands wrote and recorded songs in support of the independence struggle and Nkrumah's policies of Pan-Africanism, Africanization and national identity (which Nkrumah called 'African Personality'). For instance, E.K. Nyame released 40 highlife songs in support of Nkrumah and his CPP, while Onyina wrote the 'Destiny of Africa' about the foundation in Ghana of what is now the African Union. Similarly, Bob Cole released both highlife records and staged *concert party* plays that supported Nkrumah and the CPP.

During the 1960s the guitar bands-cum-concert parties went electric and batteries and portable generators were used to run their musical and lighting equipment. In the early 1960s there were around 30 concert parties, and by the 1970s these highlife-cum-theatrical groups had become so popular that there were almost 100 of these groups operating. Some of the most famous were the African Brothers, Kofi Sammy's Okukuseku, F. Kenya's Riches Big Sound, the City Boys and Kumapim Royals.

Due to the support popular performers gave to the independence struggle the Nkrumah CPP government began establishing state highlife bands and concert parties as part of its Africanization and 'African Personality' policy. Moreover, Nkrumah's ideal of political gender equality led to the employment of female actresses in the state concert parties, instead of the earlier practice of using female impersonators which had emerged due to the difficult life-on-the road of these touring bands. In 1960 the CPP government also facilitated the establishment of two separate trade unions, one for the urban-based highlife dance bands and the second for the more provincial-oriented guitar bands-cum-concert parties. Since both of these were affiliated with Nkrumah's CPP, they were dissolved after the anti-Nkrumah coup of 1966 that followed the destabilization of Ghana by Western powers who considered Nkrumah to be too close to the Communist bloc. Eight years would elapse before another music union (MUSIGA) was formed.

State radio and television had begun occasionally broadcasting concert plays and their highlife songs during the Nkrumah period. However, by the 1970s this led to long-running *concert party* TV series such as the *Osofo Dadzie* and *Obrah* programs that featured the concert parties of these names. *Obrah* was led by one of the new generation of female *concert party* artists, Grace Omaboe, who appeared as the stage character 'Mami Dokonu.'

By the early 1970s there were almost 100 *concert party* bands traversing the villages and provincial towns of Ghana, with some of the most loved being the African Brothers, Okukuseku, F. Kenya's Riches Big Sounds, F. Micah's band, the Jaguar Jokers, Happy Stars, City Boys and Kumapim Royals. At the same time there were scores of dance bands modeled on the Tempos format that focused exclusively on urban audiences.

During the 1960s and 1970s a sequence of popular music styles from the United States and Europe influenced Ghanaian music. It began with the rock 'n' roll of Elvis Presley, Fats Domino, the twist of Chubby Checker, the beat music of the Beatles – and was followed by the progressive rock of Jimi Hendrix and Cream and the wide-ranging fusion of Sly and the Family Stone. Then came the soul and funk of James Brown and Otis Redding, followed by the reggae of Jimmy Cliff and Bob Marley, whose 'Afro' fashions and 'black and proud,' 'do your own thing' and 'African roots' messages helped spark a period of intense musical experimentation by Ghanaian pop and highlife musicians during the 1970s. This musical emphasis on 'doing your own thing' was augmented by the 1971 Soul to Soul concert in Accra, which featured the African-American soul artists Tina Turner, Wilson Pickett and Roberta Flack as well as the Latin rock band Santana.

This creative phase of adapting and localizing imported popular music began around 1970 when the London-based Ghanaian supergroup Osibisa (led by highlife dance-band musicians) created its internationally acclaimed Afro-rock style, followed by bands in Ghana such as Hedzoleh, the Psychedelic Aliens, Boombaya and Zonglo Biiz. At the same time in Nigeria, Fela Anikulapo Kuti (initially a highlife musician) created his militant and soul-influenced Afrobeat, which was taken up in Ghana by youthful pop bands such as the Big Beats and Sawaaba Sounds. As a result Afro-rock and Afrobeat music were also incorporated into the repertoires of highlife bands.

For instance, Nana Ampadu's African Brothers guitar band developed their 'Afrohili' and 'Locomotive' styles, while highlife artists including C.K. Mann, Smart Nkansah, Blay Ambolley and Ebo Taylor played funky highlife. After reggae started to become popular in Ghana in the early 1970s various forms of 'reggae-highlife' were developed by the African Brothers, Teacher and His Afrikana and the City Boys, followed later by Amakye Dede, K. K. Kabobo and Kojo Antwi.

During the mid-1970s to mid-1980s the Ghanaian music industry declined as a result of the economic mismanagement and corruption of the regimes of Colonel Acheampong and Colonel Akuffo. Ghanaians call this the 'kalabule' (i.e., corruption) period. In 1979 and again in 1981 came the military coups of Flight Lieutenant J.J. Rawlings, which resulted during the early 1980s in his PNDC government instituting a cultural revolution. This was a difficult time for the Ghanaian entertainment sector as it involved almost three years of night curfews from 1982 to 1984 and the consequent closure of many nightclubs, ultra-high 160 percent import duties on musical equipment (classed as luxuries), followed by the demotion of music in the school curriculum as it was not considered relevant to a technical syllabus. The difficulties of this period were made worse by the 1983 drought and the sudden expulsion of a million or so Ghanaians from Nigeria.

During the *kalabule*/corruption and the revolutions of the various military governments of the 1970s and early 1980s, record companies, including Ambassador and Polygram, folded and there was a 'brain drain' of musicians who went overseas to find better economic prospects. Highlife bands and concert parties could not obtain equipment and at one point there was only one recording studio operating in the country. On the positive side, in 1982 the Rawlings PNDC government recognized the new musicians' union MUSIGA (formed back in 1974), promulgated the 1985 Copyright Law and set up organizations to combat cassette piracy. However, beginning in the mid-1980s under pressure from the IMF and World Bank's 'structural adjustment program' the economy began to be liberalized. In 1992 the Rawlings government moved the country back to democracy in 1992 and the airwaves and mass media were deregulated.

Highlife since the 1980s: Burger Highlife, Gospel Highlife, Hiplife and the Highlife Revival

Although the older forms of guitar-band and dance-band highlife declined during the military era, new forms of highlife have appeared since the 1980s. Four specific developments within highlife music can be identified: disco-influenced burger highlife; the gospel highlife of the independent African churches; a local form of rap called hiplife (i.e., hiphop-highlife); and various forms of contemporary highlife enhanced by the boom in foreign tourists and the world music industry.

Burger Highlife

Burger highlife was created by Ghanaians who from the late 1970s on, due to the economic downturn of their country, migrated abroad in a 'brain drain.' Those who settled in Germany were influenced by the disco music of Kraftwerk, Boney M and Donna Summers that was all the rage with German youth. As a result, the Ghanaian musicians there created a form of technopop highlife that used guitars, disco drum machines and synthesizers. Many of these musicians settled in the port town of Hamburg as it already had a small established Ghanaian community, and this new style of music became known as 'burger highlife,' named for both the city of Hamburg and the German word for 'citizen.' When the economy began to pick up in Ghana beginning in the late 1980s, some Ghanaian musicians who had gone abroad began returning home, bringing with them this 'made in Germany' style of highlife as well as new recording equipment, technopop techniques and musical know-how.

The first burger highlife band, Bus Stop, was formed in Hamburg by guitarist George Darko, singer Lee Duodu, keyboard player Bob Fischian and bassist B.B. Dowuona. Darko and the Bus Stop band released the first burger highlife hit in 1983, the song 'Akoo Te Brofo' that appears on the album *Friends*. Some of the other Ghanaian 'burger' musicians who settled in (or frequently visited) Germany included Pat Thomas, Bob Pinodo, Allan Cosmos Adu, Charles Amoah, Andy Vans, Seth Dako, Nii Edmund Aryittey, McGod, Rex Gyamfi, the Lumba Brothers (Nana Acheampong, Charles Kojo Fusu and Sarkodie) and Ekow Savage Alabi. Ghanaian musicians abroad who followed the disco-type burger highlife trend included Sloopy Mike Gyamfi, Charles Tetteh, Chikinchi and Captain Moro in Holland, Ben Brako and the late John Kay in Britain and the late Khodjo Aquai in the USA. This 'burger' music subsequently became popular in the mid-1980s with the youth of Ghana, who began to treat the older brands of highlife that used live percussion and horns as 'colo' or old-fashioned. The burger highlife use of drum machines and synthesizers reduced the number of musicians needed in a band (particularly percussionists and horn players) and so they were smaller than the highlife big bands. Consequently they were more economical to operate, an important consideration when taking into account the decline of live-music venues and revenues and the 160 percent import duty on musical instruments. Burger highlife bands generated most of their income from recordings rather than live shows, as this style of highlife is mainly played at indoor discotheques, open-air 'spinner' (mobile disco) events and also on FM radio and music video clips.

The most popular of the burger highlife artists of the late 1990s was Daddy Lumba (Charles Kojo Fusu) who broke away from the Lumba Brothers and released an enormous hit in 1998 with his contentious song 'Aben Wo Ha' (It Is Cooked), which was banned by some radio stations due to its lyrics thinly disguising the portrayal of a sexually aroused woman. Other burger highlife artists promoted the ideals of romantic love, with examples including songs by 'Lover Boy' Nana Acheampong, Charles Amoah's song 'Eye Odo Asem' and also Nana Aboagye Da Costa who, with Nana Acheampong, released a major hit in 2000 called 'Odo Menkoaa.' Indeed, most of the lyrics of burger highlife are about 'odo' (i.e., love). In this way they are quite different from the lyrics of old-time highlife in which romance was a minor theme, with the majority of lyrics covering topical and social issues, family problems, moral advice, poverty and philosophical and proverbial comments on life and death.

Gospel Highlife

The economic decline of the 1970s led in southern Ghana to a massive increase in Christian churches, mostly of the African separatist kind (apostolic, spiritual charismatic, and pentecostal), which, unlike orthodox Western churches, use local percussion and allow worship through dancing. In the 1950s there were just 17 such African denominations in southern

Ghana (Acquah 1958) rising to 800 by 1991 according to statistics gathered by the National Commission on Culture. From these churches came the practice of using local percussion instruments (beginning in the 1920s with the early separatist churches). Then, in the 1930s, came *a cappella* singing bands that often used light percussion and sang in highlife style, followed from the 1950s on by some local churches using brass band instruments and playing in a dance club style (Baeta 1962, 15–16, 36, 92). The very earliest Ghanaian gospel highlife was created in the early 1970s by Reverend Andersson and the Joyful Way Singers, a church-based band in Cape Coast. At the same time gospel highlife records were also released by the well-known guitar band highlife composers Love Nortey (Happy Stars guitar band) and Kofi Abraham (Sekyedumasi Gospel Singers and later Nyame Bekyere Band).

By the end of the 1970s/early 1980s the economic slump in Ghana under the military regime and the resulting collapse of the music industry led to gospel highlife acquiring an increasing importance. Many unemployed or underemployed secular highlife dance musicians moved under church patronage, while churches themselves began to use popular dance as part of their outreach programs. High taxes on the commercial music industry during the 1980s (import duties on musical instruments, entertainment tax and so on) and the fact that the churches, as charitable organizations, were not taxed, also promoted this drift of highlife from secular to sacred spheres. Some of the pioneering 1980s bands and recording artists who reflected this trend include Mary Ghansah, the Tagoe Sisters, Cindy Thompson, Ola Williams, Javes Johnathon Addo, Stella Dugan, Reverend Yaw Agyeman Baidoo, and the Genesis Gospel Singers. During the 1980s some of the top commercial highlife artists also turned in varying degrees to lucrative gospel highlife, including A.B. Crentsil, C.K. Mann, Paapa Yankson, Kofi Sammy, F. Kenya, Nana Ampadu, Jewel Ackah, T.O. Jazz, A.K. Yebuah, Ani Johnson, Daddy Lumba and Akosua Agyempong.

By 1990 local gospel represented about 60 percent of local music airplay. In fact, the Rawlings military government of the time, which was just emerging from a quasi-Marxist-socialist cultural revolution and wanted the media to propagate its views, instructed state radio to reduce the amount of gospel music airplay time by half (*Christian Messenger* 1990). Despite these government sanctions, gospel music continued to expand. Beginning in the 1990s a host of new local gospel artists and stars emerged, including Diana Akiwumi, the Daughters of Glorious Jesus, Reverend Michael Osei Bonsu, Suzzy and Matt, Reverend Owusu Ansah, Cindy Thompson, Joe Beecham, Amy Newman and many others.

Women singers featured prominently in gospel highlife. Whereas previously it was almost impossible for a woman to appear onstage and maintain her respectability, the local gospel that emerged in the 1970s introduced large numbers of female artists (particularly as singers) to the Ghanaian popular music industry. According to the Ghanaian newspaper the *Graphic Showbizz* (Doku 2004), by 2002 over half of the emerging gospel singers were women. In 2013 gospel highlife comprised well over half (some sources estimate as high as 70 percent) of the commercial cassette and CD output and airplay of local popular dance music in Ghana. There were also numerous church recording studios, music production and promotion companies, gospel music unions and competitive organizations that gave gospel awards.

Hip-Hop Highlife (Hiplife)

A third type of highlife emerged in the 1990s and became the rage with Ghanaian youth. Called hiplife (i.e., hip-hop highlife), a name coined by Reggie Rockstone in 1995, it was based on US hip-hop and rap and Jamaican ragga but was sung in local languages, including Twi, Ga, Hausa and Ewe. After Rockstone released the first rap in a local language this trend was quickly taken up by artists including Lord Kenya, Nana King, Daasebre Gyamena, Ex Doe, Chicago, Lifeline Family, Buk Bak, VIP, TicTac, Obrafour and the Native Funk Lords. The older generation condemned hiplife artists for their profane lyrics, 'kasa harri' (fast talk) presentation and for lip-synching over a preprogrammed backing-track at public performances rather than singing live. On the positive side, hiplife provided many young people with a voice to express their ideas, as it is easy to chant and rap over preprogrammed beats, even if one does not know how to play a musical instrument. This is an important consideration when taking into account the lack of live performance role models for young people resulting from the collapse of the local live-music highlife scene in the 1970s and 1980s, as well as the demotion of music in the school curriculum in the late 1980s.

Beginning in the early 2000s, however, some hiplife artists began to change the format and presentation of their music. Sydney, VIP and Batman Samini started to perform live rather than lip-synch, while others used more indigenous musical resources than the imported beat-box rhythms of earlier hiplife. Traditional rhythms and instruments were increasingly used by hiplifers such as Omanhene Pozo, Akatakye, Okonfo Kwade Castro, Buk Bak and Bones Nkasei, while others turned toward highlife. Lord Kenya, Kontihene, Akyeame, Tic Tac and Adane Best rap over highlife samples whereas others collaborate with highlife singers. For example, Obour worked with the highlife singer A.B Crentsil, Ex Doe collaborated with Paa Bobo and Omanhene Pozo with the lady highlife singer Ewurama Badu. Indeed two new hiplife subgenres emerged around 2005. One was the 'jama' or 'djama' (an 'animated dance' in the Ga language) sound of artists such as Wuta, Batman/Samini and K.K. Fusu (produced in Jeff Quaye's Hush Hush Studio) that included some live percussion and local rhythms in their electronic mixes to back vocalists in rap, ragga and highlife style.

The other hiplife subgenre is 'contemporary highlife.' This began with hiplifers such as Daasebre Gyamena, the late Terry Bonchaka and Slim Busterr, who focused on singing rather than rapping, and it was continued by the 'contemporary highlife' artists Ofori Amponsah, Nana Quame, Papa Shee, Nana Fynn, Praye, Wunluv, Okyeame Kwame and Kwabena Kwabena. These artists hardly rap at all, but rather sing in a highlife vein. Even though early hiplife, despite its name, had little connection with highlife music, these newer *jama*- and highlife-oriented hiplifers have become part of the early twenty-first-century highlife music scene.

Highlife Revival

As noted earlier, live performance highlife bands suffered a setback during the military regimes of the late 1970s and 1980s, due to corruption, curfews, high import duties and a musical brain drain abroad. It was also during the 1980s that the Ghanaian commercial highlife scene was dominated by the 'spinners' and disco-type burger highlife studio bands who largely did away with the need for large bands and live performance and instead mimed to recorded works, both on television and at public performances. However, during the early 1990s there were complaints from members of the viewing public about the mimed ('lip-synched') music videos on prime-time television, and as a result live-music programs such as *For Your Dancing Feet* were established.

This revival of live highlife was also affected by the liberalization of the economy and move toward democracy that began in the late 1980s and which resulted in the deregulation of the airwaves (250 private broadcasting stations by 2013) and large numbers of tourists coming to Ghana (1.2 million in 2012 according to Ministry of Tourism statistics). Moreover, during the 1990s the government established tourist-oriented international festivals such as PANAFEST and Emancipation Day and many beach resorts, private cultural centers and live-music venues were established for foreign visitors. The tourists were not very interested in the hi-tech lip-synched music of burger highlife and early hiplife; they preferred traditional musical performances, live highlife and Afro-fusion (Afrobeat/rock) music. This revival of live and old-time highlife music was also reflected by the fact that some of the FM radio stations that proliferated from the mid-1990s on began broadcasting programs that specialized in 'classic' old-time highlife; the first being Paa K. Holbrook-Smith's program on Groove FM. Furthermore, a number of Ghanaian music archives were established during the 1990s that included a highlife and popular music component, including the Gramophone Museum at Cape Coast, the Bokoor African Popular Music Archives Foundation (BAPMAF) in Accra, Professor Nketia's International Centre for African Music and Dance (ICAMD) at the University of Ghana, Legon and Kofi Ghanaba's African Heritage Library at Medie.

All of these factors helped rekindle an interest in old-time highlife as did the forming of a new generation of highlife bands from the early 1990s onward. These include the Golden Nuggets, Western Diamonds, Ankobra, the Ghana Broadcasting Band (under Stan Plange), Marriots, Ozimzim and more recently the Megastar Band, Desmond Ababio's Alpha Waves, the late Komla Amoaku's Visions, Wellington's

Band, Avalon's Gold Coasters and the reconstituted Ramblers dance band. Moreover, beginning in 2002 university music department highlife bands were set up, directed by highlife veterans including Ebo Taylor and Bob Pinodo. Beginning in the 1990s a number of live performance Afro-fusion bands were also established, such as Dzidudu, Bawasaba, Dabatram and later the Kete Warriors of the late Mac Tontoh, a founder of Osibisa. Some of the older generation of 'classic' highlife artists who survived the 1970s and 1980s downturn in live music also made a comeback in the 1990s, some of them having managed to survive by residing abroad or making frequent overseas trips. These include Jewel Ackah, Paapa Yankson, Amekye Dede, Pat Thomas, C.K. Mann, Eric Agyeman, Prince Osei Kofi, J.A. 'Black Chinese' Ampofo, Nana Tuffour, Koo Nimo and Gyedu-Blay Ambulley.

Another factor in the highlife revival was interest from international fans of the African and world music that attained global commercial success beginning in the mid-1980s. This was when African stars such as Sunny Ade, Fela Kuti, Franco, Papa Wemba, Youssou N'Dour, Salif Keita, Thomas Mapfumo and Angelique Kidjo became globally recognized, while Western rock superstars Peter Gabriel, Stewart Copeland and Paul Simon began to incorporate African elements into their music. As part of these developments, Ghanaian drummer Okyerema Asante performed on the South African 1987 'Graceland' tour with Paul Simon, who went on to release the *Rhythm of the Saints* album which included the old highlife melody 'Yaa Amponsah' in the track 'Spirit Voices.' Okyeremma himself moved on to highlife when he was involved with the 1998 release of a highlife big band album called *Crabs in a Bucket*.

During the 1990s many young Ghanaian musicians turned to live highlife performance, including NAKOREX, an acronym for Nat 'Amanzeba' Brew, Akosua Adjepong and Rex Omar. This highlife band was formed under Smart Binete's SECAPS management in 1990 and went on to have several hits of world music-oriented highlife hits such as 'Amu Money' and 'Kpanlogo Yede.' Other world music-influenced Ghanaian highlife musicians include Felix Owusu, Afro Moses and the Ngogo Highlife Orchestra (based in Denmark and later Australia), Nana Tsiboe and Smilin' Osei. Two NAKOREX members became solo artists and have toured and released highlife hits popular throughout West Africa, including Amanzeba's 'Kpanlogo' and 'Demara' and Rex Omar's 'Abiba Wadonkoto Ye Me Fe' (Abiba's Beautiful Movements Sweet Me). As mentioned earlier, the highlife revival was also boosted by a new generation of hiplifers who collaborated with old-time highlife artists or created *jama* hiplife and 'contemporary highlife.'

This rekindling of Ghanaian interest in live bands and old-time highlife, as well as the impact of foreign tourists and world music fans also created an interest in acoustic Akan palmwine highlife and highlife bands. T.O Jazz, Koo Nimo and Kwabena Nyama released palmwine records in the early 2000s for the world music market. Both Koo Nimo and the late Kwabena Nyama also made international tours, with Koo Nimoo often playing for the foreign visitors coming to Ghana. Bands that are very popular with visitors and world music fans that include highlife songs in their repertoires and use various combinations of Western and traditional instruments include Kojo Essah's Takashi, the Sensational Wulomei, Hewale Sounds, Local Dimension and Salaam's Cultural Imani Group. Furthermore, because world music fans have become sensitized to the Sahelian style of Malian and Senegalese musicians (such as Ali Faka Toure, Oumou Sangare, Salif Keita and Baaba Maal), artists from Ghana's northern Sahelian or savanna region, such as Atongo Zimba, Aaron Bebe Sukura, the African Show Boys and King Ayisoba, have become popular with foreigners and Ghanaians alike. Indeed, the northern lute player King Ayisoba won the Ghana Music awards in 2007 and collaborated with the new generation of *jama*-style hiplifers who were turning to highlife and other local rhythmic resources.

In the late 2010s the Ghanaian highlife scene appears to have a bright future. Hundreds of recording studios and FM radio stations operate in Ghana, the booming musical tourist industry enhances both folkloric music and live highlife performance, the church utilizes popular dance music, there is international interest in African and world music and highlife is now studied at Ghana's universities. So, despite 20 years of military rule, the local music industry has experienced a boom, and as a result successive Ghanaian governments have taken an interest in it. Between 2004 and 2005

President Kuffour reduced the import duty on musical instruments and integrated the music sector into its Poverty Reduction Strategy, and since then governments have continued to integrate the popular music industry into various medium-term strategic plans. At the same time, highlife is being enriched by many creative streams of music. A wealth of trained 'gospel highlife' bandsmen and female singers have emerged from the churches. Hiplifers continue to experiment with highlife while some highlifers turn to traditional instruments. A new crop of contemporary highlife artists has appeared and there is a revival of old-time 'classic' highlife and 'unplugged' acoustic palmwine highlife. Furthermore, musicians from Ghana's Northern and Upper Regions have, for the first time, made a significant contribution to highlife. This reworking of the old and new imported and local, northern and southern, male and female bodes well for the continued creative development of highlife music.

Bibliography

Acquah, Ione. 1958. *Accra Survey*. London: University of London Press.

Agordoh, Alexander Akorlie. 2000. 'Contemporary African Music in the Ghanaian Church.' Unpublished paper presented at 'Playing with Identities in Contemporary Music in Africa' Conference, Nordic African Institute, Turku/Abo Finland.

Agovi, Kofi E. 1989. 'The Political Relevance of Ghanaian Highlife Songs Since 1957.' *Research in African Literatures* 20(3): 194–201

Baeta, C. G. 1962. *Prophetism in Ghana*. London: SCM Press.

Bame, Kwabena N. 1985. *Come to Laugh: African Traditional Theatre in Ghana*. New York: Lillian Barber Press.

Barber, Karin, Collins, E. John, and Ricard, Alain. 1997. *West African Popular Theatre*. Bloomington: Indiana University Press.

Bender, Wolfgang. 1986. *Sweet Mother: Africanische Musik*. Munich: Trickster Verlag.

Brempong, Owusu. 1984. 'Akan Highlife in Ghana: Songs of Cultural Transition.' Unpublished Ph.D. dissertation, Indiana University.

Charry, Eric, ed. 2012. *Hip Hop Africa: New African Music in a Contemporary World*. Bloomington, IN: Indiana University Press.

Christian Messenger [Ghana], July–August 1990, Vols. 1, 4. Ghana.

Collins, E. John. 1976a. 'Comic Opera in Ghana.' *African Arts* 9(2): 50–7.

Collins, E. John. 1976b. 'Ghanaian Highlife.' *African Arts* 19(1): 62–8, 100.

Collins, E. John. 1977. 'Postwar Popular Band Music in West Africa.' *African Arts* 10(3): 53–60.

Collins, E. John. 1985. *Music Makers of West Africa*. Washington DC: Three Continents Press.

Collins, E. John. 1987. 'Jazz Feedback to Africa.' *American Music* 5(2): 176–93.

Collins, E. John. 1992a. 'Some Anti-Hegemonic Aspects of African Popular Music.' In *Rockin' The Boat: Mass Music and Mass Movements*, ed. Reebee Garofalo. Boston: Southend Press, 185–94.

Collins, E. John. 1992b. *West African Pop Roots*. Philadelphia: Temple University Press.

Collins, E. John. 1996. *E.T. Mensah, the King of Highlife*. Accra: Anansesem Press.

Collins, E. John. 1996. *Highlife Time*. Accra: Anansesem Press (First published 1994.).

Collins, E. John. 1999. 'The Evolution of West African Popular Entertainment.' In *The Encyclopedia of Africa South of the Sahara*, ed. John Middleton. New York: Charles Scribner and Sons.

Collins, E. John. 2004a. 'Ghanaian Christianity and Popular Entertainment: Full Circle.' *History in Africa* 31: 407–23.

Collins, E. John. 2004b. 'Urban Anxiety and Its Sonic Response.' *Glendora Review* 3(2 and 4): 23–8.

Collins, E. John. 2007. 'The Entrance of Women into Ghanaian Popular Entertainment.' In *The Legacy of Efua Sutherland and Pan-African Cultural Activism*, eds. Anne V. Adams and Esi Sutherland-Addy. Banbury: Ayebia Clark Publishing, 47–54.

Collins, E. John. 2009. *Fela: Kalakuta Notes*. Amsterdam: Dutch Royal Tropical Institute.

Collins, E. John. 2009/2010. 'Highlife and Nkrumah's Independence Ethos.' *Journal of Performing Arts* 4(1): 93–104.

Collins, E. John. 2012. 'Contemporary Ghanaian Popular Music since the 1980s.' In *Hip Hop Africa: New African Music in a Globalising World*, ed. Eric Charry. Bloomington: Indiana University Press, 211–33.

Collins, E. John. 2016. *Highlife Giants: West African Dance Band Pioneers*. Abuja and London: Cassava Republic Press.

Collins, E. John, with Ronnie Graham. 1999. 'Ghana.' In *The Rough Guide to World Music, Volume One: Africa, Europe and the Middle East*, eds. Simon Broughton, Mark Ellingham and Richard Trillo. London: Rough Guide/Penguin, 488–98.

Collins, E. John, and Richards, Paul. 1989. 'Popular Music in West Africa: An Interpretive Framework.' In *World Music, Politics and Social Change*, ed. Simon Frith. Manchester: Manchester University Press, 12–46.

Darkwa, Asante. 1974. *New Musical Traditions from Ghana*. Unpublished Ph.D. dissertation, Wesleyan University.

Doku, Francis. 2004. (Gospel Music). *Graphic Showbizz*, 4–10 March.

Emielu, Austin 'Maro. 2013. *Nigerian Highlife Music*. Lagos: Centre for Black African Arts and Civilisation.

'Ghana Broadcasting Corporation News.' 29 December 1991. Accra: National Commission on Culture's Religious Affairs Department.

Graham, Ronnie. 1988. *Stern's Guide to Contemporary African Music, Volume I*. London: Pluto Press.

Graham, Ronnie. 1992. *The World of African Music: Stern's Guide to Contemporary African Music, Volume 2*. London: Pluto Press.

Haydon, Geoffrey, and Marks, Dennis, eds. 1985. *Repercussions: A Celebration of African-American Music*. London: Century Publishing.

King, Bruce. 1966. 'Introducing the Highlife.' *Jazz Monthly* (July): 3–8.

Mensah, Atta Annan. 1971 and 1972. 'Jazz the Round Trip.' *Jazz Research* 3(4): 124–37.

Nketia, J. H. Kwabena. 1956. 'The Gramophone and Contemporary African Music in the Gold Coast.' In *Proceedings of the Fourth Annual Conference of the West African Institute of Social and Economic Research*. Ibadan, Nigeria: University College, 191–201.

Osumare, Halifu. 2012. *Hiplife in Ghana*. New York: Palgrave Macmillan.

Plageman, Nate. 2013. *Saturday Night: Popular Music and Social Change in Urban Ghana*. Bloomington: Indiana University Press.

Ricard, Alain. 1977. 'The Concert Party as a Genre: The Happy Stars of Lome.' In *Forms of Folklore in Africa*, ed. Bernth Lindfors. Austin: University of Texas Press, 222–36.

Roberts, John Storm. 1974. *Black Music of Two Worlds*. New York: William and Morrow.

Sackey, Chris K. 1989. *Konkoma: A Musical Form of Fanti Young Fishermen in the 1940's and 50's in Ghana West Africa*. Berlin: Dietrich Reimer Verlag.

Schmidt, Cynthia. 1994. 'An Interview with John Collins on Cultural Policy, Folklore and the Recording Industry of Ghana.' *The World of Music* 36(2): 138–47.

Shipley, Jesse. 2013. *Living the Hiplife*. Durham, NC: Duke University Press.

Smith, Edna M. 1962. 'Popular Music in West Africa.' *African Music* 3(1): 11–14.

Sprigge, Robert. 1961. 'The Ghanaian Highlife: Notation and Sources.' *Ghana Music Society's Music in Ghana Journal* 2: 7–94.

Stapleton, Chris, and May, Chris. 1987. *African All Stars*. London: Quartet Books.

Sutherland, Efua. 1970. *The Original Bob: The Story of Bob Johnson Ghana's Ace Comedian*. Accra: Anowuo Educational Publications.

Van der Geest, Sjaak, and Asante-Darko, Nimrod K. 1982. 'The Political Meaning of Highlife Songs in Ghana.' *American Studies Review* 25(1): 27–35.

Yankah, Kwesi. 1984. 'The Akan Highlife Song: A Medium for Cultural Reflection or Deflection?' *Research in African Literatures* 15(4): 568–82.

Discographical References

Acheampong, Nana, and Aboagye Da Costa, Nana. 'Odo Menkoaa.' Megastar. *2000*: Ghana.

Amandzeba. 'Demara.' *Demara*. Native Breww Musik. *2006*: Ghana.

Asante, Okyerema. *Crabs in a Bucket*. Asante/Oyigbo IAO1. *1998*: USA.

Daddy Lumba. 'Aben Wo Ha.' Lumba Records. *1998*: Ghana.

Darko, George. 'Akoo Te Brofo.' *Friends*. Racket Records RRK 15011. *1983*: Germany.

Kumasi Trio. 'Yaa Amponsah.' Zonophone EZ 1001. *1928*: UK. (Reissued on *Kumasi Trio, 1928*. Heritage Records HTCD 22. *1993*: UK.)

NAKOREX. 'Kpanlogo Yede.' *Kpanlogo*. Asona. *1966*: Ghana.

Omar, Rex. 'Abiba Wadonkoto Ye Me Fe.' *Collection*. New Ashanty. *2006*: Ghana.

Simon, Paul. 'Spirit Voices.' *Rhythm of the Saints*. Warner Brothers W1-26098. *1990*: USA.

Discography

General Highlife Compilations and Old Recordings

Aingo, George. *Roots of Highlife 1927*. Heritage HTCD17. *1992*: UK.

Early Guitar Music from West Africa 1927–9. Heritage Records HTCD33. *2003*: UK.

Electric Highlife: Sessions from the Bokoor Studios. Naxos World 760302. *2002*: UK.

Ghana Muntie: Recordings from the GBC Ghana Radio Gramophone Library 1947–62. Centre for World Music. *2012*: Germany.

The Guitar and Gun: Highlife Music from Ghana. Stern's Music Centre, STEW50CD. *2003*: UK

Mensah, E. T., and His Tempos. *All For You: Classic Highlife Recordings from the 1950's*. Retroafric RETRO 1. *1986*: UK.

Mensah, E. T., and His Tempos. *Day by Day: Classic Highlife Recordings of the 1950's and 1960's*. Retroafric RETRO3CD. *1991*: UK.

Popular Music Ghana 1931–57. Disques Arion ARN64564. *2002*: France.

Rough Guide to Highlife. (2 CDs.) Rough Guide Music/World Music Network. RGNET1280CD. *2003*: UK.

Vintage Palmwine. Otrabanda Records OTB02. *2003*: Netherlands.

Highlife: Folk and Palmwine

King Ayisoba. *Modern Ghanaians*. Pidgen Music PMR 001. *2005*: Ghana; Makkum Records MR8. *2013*: Netherlands.

Local Dimension. *N'yong*. Disques Arion. *2003*: France.

Nimo, Koo. *Highlife Roots Revival*. Riverboat Records/World Music Network TUG1064. *2012*: USA.

Nimo, Koo. *Tete Wobi kA*. HumanSongs Records. *2000*: USA.

Nyama, Kwabena. *Sunday Monday*. Disques Arion. *2000*: France.

Zimba, Atongo. *Savannah Breeze*. Hippo Records HIP003. *2005*: Netherlands.

Highlife Bands (Dance, Funk and World Music)

Afro Moses. *Makola*. Riddimtrax Records /GMF. *1998*: Denmark.

Agyeman, Eric. *Highlife Safari*. Sterns. *1994*: UK.

Ambolley, Gyedu-Blay. *Son of Ghana*. Simigwa Records. *2005*: USA.

Ambolley, Gyedu-Blay. *Mumunde*. Hippo Records. *2012*: Netherlands.

Bannerman, Kari. *Ghana Gone Jazz*. Seprewa Records. *2001*: UK.

Bentsil, Kofi, and the Western Diamonds Band. *Diamonds Are Forever*. Westline. *1994*: Ghana.

Bokoor Beats. Otrabanda Records. *2007*: Netherlands.

Brew, Nat (Amanzeba). *Wogbe*. Amanzeba Productions. *2006*: Ghana.

Ghana Funk from the 70s. Hippo Records. *2009*: Netherlands.

Gyamfi, Sloopy Mike. 'Telephone Nkomo.' *Mid-1990s*: Netherlands/Ghana.

Mann, C. K. *Party Time with Ceekay*. Eassiebons. *1970s*: Ghana.

Mann, C. K. *Womma Yengar*. Essiebons. *1979*: Ghana.

Smilin' Osei. *Alarm Blo*. Dakar Sounds. *2001*: Netherlands.

Sweet Talks & A. B. Crentsil. *Popular African Music Compilation*. Gunter Gretzt Production. *1998*: Germany.

Thomas, Pat. 'Sika Ye Mogya.' Tropic Vibe. *2005*: USA.

Tsiboe, Nana, and the Supa Hilife Band. *Ahom*. Tuntumi. *2003*: UK.

Tuffour, Nana. *Genesis*. Shuffle Music. *1996*: Germany.

Tuffour, Nana. *Sankofa*. G Money Productions. *1997*: USA.

Highlife Guitar Bands

African Brothers Band (leader Nana Ampadu). *Afrohili Sounds*. Happy Bird LPJN 05. *1973*: Ghana.

African Brothers Band International of Ghana. *Locomotive Train (Keteke)*. Happy Bird LPJN 08. *197-?*: Ghana.

Donkor, Eddie. 'Na Me Cause Am. Gapophone. *1970s*: Ghana.

Frimpong, K., and the Super Complex Band. *Ahyewa*. Ofori Brothers. *1970s*: Ghana.

Gyasi, K. *Sikyi Highlife*. Essiebons. *1972*: Ghana.

K.K.'s No. 2. *K.K.'s No. 2*. Ambassador Records. *Mid-1970s*: Ghana.

Kenya, F. *Power House*, Essiebons. *1975*: Ghana.

Mensah, Kwaa. *Wayo Christ*. Ambassador Records. *1975*: Ghana.

Parrots (Nkoo) Band. *The Parrots (Nkoo) Band, Led by Kofi Ani Johnson*. Obuoba LPJN 06. *197-?*: Ghana.

Burger Highlife

Acheampong, Nana, and Aboagye Da Costa, Nana. *Odo Menkoaa*. Megastar. *2000*: Ghana.

Best of Lee Duodu and Cantata. Nakasi Record Productions. *2006*: Ghana.

Daddy Lumba. 'Aben Wo Ha.' Lumba Records. *1998*: Ghana.

Hiplife

Black Stars: Ghana's Hiplife Generation. Out Here Records. *2008*: Belgium.

Lord Kenya. 'Sika Mpo Nfa Neho.' Mount Kenya Productions. *N.d.*: Ghana.

Obour and Crentsil, A.B. *The Best of the Life: Hiplife Meets Highlife*. Family Tree Entertainment. *2006*: Ghana.

Obrafour. 'Paa Mu Ka.' OM Studio. *1999*: Ghana.

Okyeame Kwame. 'M'anwensem.' One Mic Entertainment. *2008*: Ghana.

Rockstone, Reggie. 'Makaa Makaa.' *1997*: Ghana.

Rockstone, Reggie. 'Me Na Me Kae.' Kassa Records. *1999*: Ghana.

Tic Tac. 'Accra Connection.' TN Records. *2006*: Ghana.

VIP. 'Ahomka Womu.' Goodies Music. *2006*: Ghana.

Local Gospel Highlife

Abraham, Kofi. 'Kyere Wotumi.' CSM Productions. *N.d.*: Ghana.

Addo, Javes. 'Jesus Power.' Edikwabo Productions. *1995*: Ghana.

Akiwumi, Diana. 'Ebesi Me Yie.' Despite. *1990*: Ghana.

Bonsu, Reverend Michael Osei. 'Yebedi Mkurim.' Big Ben. *2005*: Ghana.

Daughter of Glorious Jesus. 'Aseda.' His Majesty's Production. *2003*: Ghana.

Genesis Gospel Singers. 'Onyame Baba.' Produced by Joyce Offori Atta. *1985*: Ghana.

Ghansah, Mary. 'Jesus.' Label unknown. *2005*: Ghana.

Onyame Bekyere Singers led by Kofi Abraham. 'Psalm 23 – Yehowa Nema Hwefo.' Mid-*1980s*: Ghana.

Tagoe Sisters. 'Nyame Ye Kese.' Produced by Nana Mensah Bonsu. *1988*: UK.

Filmography

African Cross Rhythms, dir. Peter Bischoff. Denmark. 52 mins. Documentary. (Rereleased as *Listen to the Silence*, dir. Peter Bischoff. USA. 1996). 30 mins. Documentary.

Brass Unbound, dir. Rob Boonjafer-Flaes. 1993. Netherlands. 105 mins. Documentary.

Highlife: From Yaa Amponsah to Telephone Lobi, dir. Theo Uittenbogaard. 1999. Netherlands. 30 mins. Documentary.

Living the Hiplife, dir. Jessie Shipley. 2007. USA. 62 mins. Documentary.

Repercussions, dir. Dennis Marks. 1983. UK. 50 mins. BBC Channel 4/Third Eye Production. 7-part television documentary.

Rhythms of the World: Highlife in Ghana, dir. Wolfgang Huschert. 1993. Germany. 28 mins. Documentary.

Soul to Soul, dir. Denis Sanders. 1971. Ghana. 96 mins. Documentary.

Stage Shakers: Ghana's Concert Party Theatre, dir. Kwame Braun. 2001. USA. 100 mins. Documentary.

When the Moment Sings: The Muse Within, dir. Aslak Aarhus and Ole Bernt Frøshaug. 1995. Norway. 32 mins. Documentary.

Who Is Highlife, dir. Wilma Kiener and Dieter Matzka. 2009. Germany. 105 mins. Documentary.

E. JOHN COLLINS

Highlife, Igbo

Igbo highlife is a popular music style with lyrics in the Igbo language (including its various dialects) as well as in Pidgin English. Themes of songs are drawn from a rich reservoir of Igbo folklore, native philosophies and social commentaries. Igbo highlife is a product of several socio-musical influences which include Igbo traditional dance music, the brass-band tradition of the colonial period in West Africa, *samba, tango, calypso* and jazz from the Americas, guitar styles from East and Central Africa as well as Ghanaian highlife. Igbo highlife has two main musical streams: the brass-band highlife of artists such as Stephen Amechi, E.C. Arinze, Osita Osadebe, Paulson Kalu and Celestine Ukwu; and guitar highlife of the period following the Nigerian civil war (from 1970), epitomized by the music of Ikenga Super Stars of Africa, Oriental Brothers, Sir Warrior, Emeka Morocco, Muddy Ibe, Nico Mbarga and Oliver de Coque (real name Oliver Sunday Akanite). These two musical streams also represent the first and second generations of Igbo highlife.

The Igbo people live in South-East Nigeria, spread along the banks of the River Niger and its tributaries. The roots of Igbo highlife are derived from a number of traditional dance music genres such as *egwu ekpiri* (*ekpiri* music/dance), *egwu ogene* (*ogene* music/dance), *ekwe* and *nkwa*. The introduction in the early to mid-twentieth century of Western musical instruments such as the acoustic guitar, accordion and harmonica into these otherwise traditional music ensembles, created many syncretic forms. These forms were subsumed under an amorphous label of 'palmwine music' because of their predominance in palmwine bars (referred to as *tombo* bars in local parlance). These various 'palmwine styles' formed the scaffold of what later became known as Igbo highlife.

Again, the fluid state of the West African subregion in the colonial period provided room for social interactions and mobility across borders such that socio-musical developments in one area were easily replicated or adapted to existing forms in other areas. In about 1915, for example, *aṣíkò* music was introduced to the Rivers Province in then Eastern Nigeria by crew workers aboard merchant vessels from the Gold Coast (now Ghana). Around the 1930s–1940s, also, *konkoma* (*kokoma, kokomba*) music spread from the Gold Coast to Igbo land. Musicians such as Israel Nwaba, G.T. Onwuka and Okonkwo Adigwe played in the current of *konkoma*, combining traditional drums with the Igbo lamellophone known as *ubo aka* and the acoustic guitar (Omojola 1995, 15). The frequent tours to eastern Nigeria of Emmanuel Tettey Mensah (who is believed to have brought the highlife structure from Ghana to Nigeria), as well as the availability and popularity of the records of Ghanaian *concert party* practitioner/highlife musician E.K. Nyame in the 1950s, were important exogenous influences in the development of Igbo highlife. In the 1950s, also, Igbo musicians such as Zeal Onyia, E.C. Arinze, Osita Osadebe and Stephen Amechi were resident in Ghana while in the 1970s Ghanaian musicians and bands such as Opambo, Amachie Dede, Konadus International Band (led by Robert Danso) and T.O. Jazz were based in Igbo land. Igbo highlife therefore reflects, significantly, the cross-fertilization of musical ideas between Ghanaian and Nigerian highlife.

A typical Igbo highlife ensemble consists of two to three electric guitars, a drum kit, other percussion (especially the *conga* drum which plays both *ostinato* rhythms and improvised solos), a brass section (except in guitar bands), a lead vocalist and two or three male backup vocalists who could also double as instrumentalists. The keyboard is rarely used except in a few recordings by Celestine Ukwu, Oliver de Coque and since the 1990s, in the music of Bright Chimezie and other new entrants. Usually the rhythm/lead guitarist and the lead vocalist (most times the leader/proprietor of the band) are the two most important figures in the ensemble. The guitarist provides the 'palmwine guitar' chords, which are broken harmonies of basic chords with passing notes and short fills between chord changes (similar to East African and Spanish guitar styles). This style is intended to hold the band's sound together harmonically and at the same time allow for long solos to stimulate dancing. The lead vocalist projects the entire image of the band. Generally speaking, the lead vocalist is the 'show man' (vocalists are usually male) and he is also supposed to be a good singer and composer of the songs. The overall appeal of the band is therefore tied around him. Apart from a few 'bands of equals' such as Oriental Brothers and Ikenga Superstars of Africa where everyone has an equal say in business matters, Igbo highlife ensembles exhibit a hegemonic relationship between the leader/boss/proprietor who acts as the music director and chief accounting officer and band members/employees/musicians who are on the payroll of the 'master.'

Melodies of Igbo highlife are derived from diatonic major scales, with no strong evidence of the use of chromatic notes. Melodies are usually bright and cheerful, and they also reflect the tonal inflections of the Igbo language. There is a very thin line between speech and song in Igbo, and most songs begin with or include a section of declamation and/or recitative. Vocal harmony is provided by a chorus of about two or three males singing parallel melodies in thirds and sixths, sometimes using the head voice to provide a feminine feel. The rhythm guitar provides the main harmony using essentially primary chords with occasional use of secondary chords of the major scale. Usually, the harmony is cyclic, with just a few chords no matter the length of the song. The I-V-V-I and straight I-IV-V progressions are common musical properties of Igbo highlife. For example, the harmonic progression of Osita Osadebe's 'Peoples' Club' (a 32-minute-long commercial recording) is built on a cyclic I-V-V-I chord progression. In a similar vein his 'Kedu America' track, which is 16 minutes in duration, uses a cyclic I-IV-V-IV-I chord progression.

Most early recordings of Igbo highlife from the 1950s to the outbreak of the Nigerian civil war in 1966 were made by Polygram (then Philips Records) and Decca (West Africa), both of which were based in Lagos. These recordings were in short track format, a consequence of the technical limitations of the 45rpm disc, rather than compositional design. When the LP record was introduced into the Nigerian recording industry in the early 1970s, Igbo musicians also adopted this format, leaving greater room for instrumental solos and praise singing. From the 1970s Rodgers All Stars Recording Studio based in Awka came to epitomize Igbo highlife industry in then Eastern (now South-East) Nigeria. Most Igbo highlife songs have distinctive, loud and deep bass guitar lines with little or no variation at all, no matter the length of the song. Songs such as 'Sweet Mother' and 'Akie' by Prince Nico Mbarga, 'Osondi Owendi' by Osita Osadebe and 'Ana Enwe Obodo Enwe' by Oliver de Coque are memorable more for their alluring bass guitar lines than for their vocal melodies.

Three main gong rhythms are common to Igbo highlife (see Example 1).

Example 1: Igbo highlife gong rhythms

There are also variations of these basic patterns based on artistic creativity and regional peculiarity, but by and large these patterns are close approximations of the rhythmic characteristics of the genre. There is a very close relationship between music and dance in Igbo land, hence the word *egwu* carries a double meaning: music or dance. Dance movements are therefore usually derived from their associated musical styles. Igbo highlife includes an impressive array of dance movements which have traditional roots and range from slow elegant movements, characteristic of royalty and old age, to the more vigorous youthful dances. The late Igbo highlife legend Chief Osita Osadebe describes Igbo highlife music/dance as *ọyọlima* (enjoyment). According to Osadebe, when one dances to highlife one does not perspire (Nwachukwu 2007, 26–7).

Patronage of Igbo highlife cuts across age groups and gender. However, apart from a few women such as Uche Ibeto and Onyeka Onwenu who have recorded songs in the current of Igbo highlife, and the inclusion of female dancers in current music videos, the practice of Igbo highlife is male-dominated. Igbo highlife in a very broad sense represents a form of neo-traditional music, due to its popularity and acceptance in traditional and social ceremonies. Musicians therefore costume themselves in traditional Igbo attire. The use of the red cap, coral beads, bull/elephant/cow tusk/horn, handheld cow tail (all of which symbolize chieftaincy and royalty) and the walking stick have grown to become important parts of the iconography of Igbo highlife. Although Igbo highlife has been popularized mostly by musicians from the South-East, there are many musicians of ethnic groups such as Ika, Aniocha/Anioma, Oshimili, Ukwuani, Asaba (referred to collectively as Delta Igbo), Kalabari, Ijaw (the home of Cardinal Jim Rex Lawson), Efik and Ibibio in the South-South geopolitical zone who share linguistic similarities with Igbo. Many musicians from these ethnic groups play similar styles which for theoretical considerations may not be subsumed under the generic name 'Igbo highlife.'

Igbo Highlife in the Twenty-First Century

Igbo highlife exists within a broader stylistic and sociological framework of what is generally known and referred to as 'Nigerian highlife.' This in turn is subsumed under a wider context of West African highlife. Although highlife music developed as a West African musical phenomenon in the 1950s and 1960s, its articulation in various societies reflects the social and cultural dynamics of the environment.

The growth and development of Igbo highlife represents, therefore, the indigenization of West African highlife to reflect the musical aesthetics and cultural sensibilities of the Igbo-speaking people who inhabit South-East Nigeria. However, with increasing exposure to foreign socio-musical and technological influences of the twenty-first century and the increasing craze for 'crossovers' from secular to gospel music in Nigeria since the late 1990s, coupled with generational modifications and new market demands, the definitive framework of Igbo highlife has become increasingly fluid and amorphous.

Igbo artists of the 2000s such as Flavour, Bracket, Phyno, Desperate Chicks, Timaya, MC Loph, Wizboy, Nigga Raw, Harrysong and Stormex, who play what is known as Nigerian hip-hop (Naija Jams) continue to explore Igbo highlife rhythms and harmonic vocabulary. They also borrow themes, terms and concepts from the works of the older generations of Igbo highlife musicians. For example, in 'Financial Woman' Phyno uses the term 'Iworiwo,' borrowed from the chorus line of Jim Rex Lawson's hit song 'Love Adure,' while Timaya's song 'Money' features the term 'Oyolima,' which Chief Osita Osadebe used to describe highlife music. Also, themes and terms such as 'Onye m' echi' (who knows tomorrow), 'Ada' (first daughter of the family), 'Fada Fada' used by highlife musicians such as Chief Osita Osadebe, Oliver de Coque and Sir Warrior have been explored by Phyno and Flavour, Flavour even made a remix of Chief Osadebe's classic 'Osondi Onwendi,' as well as Jim Rex Lawson's ' Sawale,' which he titled 'Nwa baby (Ashawo remix)' in his *Uplifted* album in 2010.

While we may for academic purposes classify these innovations as new developments in Igbo highlife music reflective of generational change, some of the older generations of Igbo highlife musicians would beg to differ. For example, the swift reaction of the late Chief Osita Osadebe in 2005 to innovations that Sunny Neji was introducing to highlife music in songs such as 'Tolotolo' was to say (in *The Vanguard* newspaper in 2005) that Sunny Neji's desire to fuse pop music with highlife would not work because 'highlife is highlife.' Many older-generation Igbo highlife musicians have continually stressed the idea of 'original highlife' to distinguish it from highlife music instigated by generational innovations. Quite unlike the Ghanaian situation, where new developments and generational innovations still acknowledge the highlife root, reflected in labels such as 'gospel highlife,' 'burger highlife' and 'hiplife,' the generational bias in Igbo highlife complicates the attempt to rethink its definitive framework. It also makes it harder to consider the music of contemporary Igbo hip-hop artists, such as those mentioned above, as belonging to the Igbo highlife genre. However, given that the pioneers and defining icons of Igbo highlife music such as Jim Rex Lawson, E.C. Arinze, Celestine Ukwu, Osita Osadebe, Oliver de Coque, Charles Iwegbue, St. Augustine, Prince Nico Mbarga and many others are no longer alive, and that highlife has been described as the most popular dance music among the Igbo, generational reinterpretation of Igbo highlife music becomes inevitable, and will indeed serve to ensure continuity and generational relevance.

Of great importance also in the twenty-first century is the crossover from secular to gospel highlife. Much of this crossover is the product not only of the increasing religious fervor in Nigeria since the late 1990s, but also of the new and booming music market created around ever-expanding church congregations and ministries. The young Igbo highlife musician Anyo, for example, who in 2006–7 was building a style based on the highlife of Chief Osita Osadebe, Oliver de Coque and Sir Warrior, was advised by marketers and promoters to change from secular to gospel themes in his highlife music if he wanted to break into the music market in Igbo land. This he did in later years with some success.

In practical terms, there is no such genre label as Igbo gospel highlife, or simply gospel highlife, in Nigeria. Gospel highlife in Nigeria did not follow the typical path of a developing genre; rather, the first bold use of the term was on the cover of Voice of the Cross's album of the same name in the early 1990s. Voice of the Cross, a very successful Igbo singing duo of Brother Lazarus and Brother Emmanuel, were and are renowned for their hymnal-style singing with organ accompaniment, reminiscent of the music of the late Ikoli Harcourt-White, referred to as the 'father' of Igbo church music. In their songs and recordings in the 1970s and 1980s, Voice of the Cross had deliberately avoided the use of percussion and dance rhythms. With *Gospel Highlife* the duo signaled a major shift from hymnal style to one incorporating dance rhythms in their music. Such an innovation provided both encouragement and a model for many other prominent Igbo gospel musicians in the 2000s, such as Evangelist Amaka Okwoha (Chioma Jesus) and Prince Gozie Okeke, who have continued to develop the idea of incorporating dance rhythms in Igbo gospel music.

That the crossover from secular to gospel highlife is principally a shift in terms of explicit issues and concerns, from social to Christian, and is not matched by changes in instrumentation, form and performance practices, is seen in the example of Paulson Kalu (also known as Paulson Kanu Afrikhanah), a prominent Igbo highlife musician and a mentee of Chief Osita Osadebe, Kalu changed from secular to gospel in the early 2000s, and in an interview included on his CD *Africana*, declared that he would continue playing highlife music but would henceforth use only gospel themes. A second change is that of performance context, from the nightclub/hotel environment where highlife began to a more 'Christianized' environment.

Bibliography

Collins, John. 1992. *West African Pop Roots*. Philadelphia: Temple University Press.

Collins, John. 1996. *E.T Mensah: King of Highlife*. Accra: Anansesem Publications.

Emielu, Austin. 2013. *Nigerian Highlife Music*. Lagos: Centre for Black and African Arts and Civilization.

Idonije, Benson. 2007. 'Highlife Veteran, Osadebe, Exits.' *The Guardian* (Nigeria), 16 May, 66. Online at: https://groups.google.com/forum/#!topic/wief/O_7dv0jwzDA (accessed 12 April 2018).

Nwachukwu, Cletus. 2007. 'Osadebe OON: Dignified Exit of a Maestro.' *The Guardian* (Nigeria), 8 May, 25-7.

Ọmọjọla, Bode. 1995. *Nigerian Art Music*. Ibadan: IFRA.

Oti, Sonny. 2009. *Highlife Music in West Africa: Down Memory Lane*. Lagos: Malthouse Press.

Vanguard [Nigeria]. 2005. January 8. Online at: https://www.vanguardngr.com/.

Discographical References

De Coque, Oliver. 'Ana Enwe Obodo Enwe.' Panovo Entertainment. *2000*: Nigeria.

Flavour. 'N'abiana.' Obiano Music. *2005*: Nigeria.

Flavour. 'Nwa baby (Ashawo remix).' *Uplifted*. Obiano Music and 2nite Entertainment. *2010*: Nigeria.

Kalu, Paulson. *Africana*. *N.d.*: Nigeria.

Mbarga, Nico. 'Akie.' *Sweet Mother*. Rodgers All Stars ASALPS 6. *1976*: Nigeria.

Mbarga, Nico. 'Sweet Mother.' *Sweet Mother*. Rodgers All Stars ASALPS 6. *1976*: Nigeria.

Neji, Sunny. 'Tolotolo.' *Unchained*. Blue Pie. *2007*: Nigeria.

Osadebe, Osita. 'Kedu America.' Panovo Entertainment. *N.d.*: Nigeria.

Osadebe, Osita. 'Osondi Onwendi.' Panovo Entertainment. *N.d.*: Nigeria (Also released on *OsondiOnwendi*. Polydor POLP120. *1984*: Nigeria.)

Osadebe, Osita. 'Peoples' Club.' Premier Music KMCD 017. *N.d.*: Nigeria.

Phyno, featuring P-Square. 'Financial Woman.' Penthauze Music. *2016*: Nigeria.

Phyno, featuring Olamide. 'Augment.' Penthauze Music. *2017*: Nigeria.

Timaya, featuring Flavour. 'Money.' DM Records. *N.d.*: Nigeria.

Voice of the Cross. *Gospel Highlife*. *N.d.*: Nigeria.

Discography

Chimezie, Bright. *Oyinbo Mentality*. Premier Music KMCD 083. *2007*: Nigeria.

De Coque, Oliver. *Destiny (Akalaka)*. Ogene Records ORLP 07. *1993*: Nigeria.

De Coque, Oliver. *Classic Hits*. Panovo Entertainment. *2000*: Nigeria.

De Coque, Oliver. *Vintage Hits Vol. 3* Olumo Records ORCD 003. *2001*: Nigeria.

Flavour. *Blessed*. 2nite Entertainment MGSFB. *2012*: Nigeria.

Highlife Kings Vol. 2. Premier Music KMCD 02. *N.d.*: Nigeria.

Highlife Kings Vol. 4. Premier Music KMCD 051. *N.d.*: Nigeria.

Ibe, Muddy. *The Best of Capt. Muddy Ibe and His Nkwa Brothers*. Rodgers All Stars RASCO 144. *N.d.*: Nigeria.

Kalu, Paulson. *Uche Chukwu Mee*. Philips 6361 057. *1973*: Nigeria.

Lawson, Rex Jim. *The Classics Vol. 1*. Premier Music KMCD 010. *N.d.*: Nigeria.

Onwenu, Onyeka. *Onyeka!* Benson and Hedges Music. *1991*: UK.

Oriental Brothers. *Vintage Hits Vol. 1*. Afrodisia DWACD 001. *2001*: Nigeria.

Osadebe, Osita. *10th Anniversary Peoples' Club Special*. Premier Music KMCD 017/Polydor POLP 070. *1982*: Nigeria.

Osadebe, Osita. *Ife Onye Metalu*. Polygram Records POLP 165. *1987*: Nigeria.

Osadebe, Osita. *Kedu America*. Panovo Entertainment. N.d.: Nigeria.

Ukwu, Celestine. *Igede*. Premier Music KMCD 012. N.d.: Nigeria.

Sir Warrior. *Agwo Loro Ibe Ya*. Afrodisia DWACD 012. *2006*: Nigeria.

AUSTIN EMIELU

Highlife, Yorùbá

While Islamic-influenced genres such as *fújì, àpàlà, sákárà and wákà* and Christian-influenced *jùjú* are genuinely indigenous popular music genres of the Yorùbá of Nigeria, the same cannot be said of highlife. As one of Africa's most popular and predominant forms of music, highlife spread to the coastal regions of Sierra Leone and Nigeria from Ghana in the first half of the twentieth century. However, with music ingrained in a culture as distinctive as it is syncretic, Yorùbá highlife became a medium for the preservation and dissemination of a musical and cultural identity. In the period from the 1940s to the 1960s highlife was the foremost urban popular dance music among the Yorùbá, quintessentially encapsulating their indigenous and syncretic musical and cultural sensibilities. Despite being engendered through a richness of foreign musical influences, highlife attained an iconic social status and became a symbol of identity for the Yorùbá and a national idiom for Nigeria.

Highlife's emergence in Yorùbáland was not simply a story of twentieth-century musical movement between African countries, but was predicated on earlier historical changes, in which Nigeria and its people experienced almost simultaneously two different foreign religious and cultural transformations. The first resulted from the incursion of Islamic–Arabic cultural influences which swept through the northern parts of Nigeria from west to east up until the fourteenth and fifteenth centuries, reaching southern Yorùbá regions by the first four decades of the nineteenth century. The second was the arrival of a Euro–Christian influence which occurred in the southern coastal regions of the country with arguably much greater musical impact and creative force than the Islamic–Arabic influence. While the former resulted in the creation of *wéré, àpàlà, sákárà, wákà* and later *fújì*, the latter resulted in the creation of highlife, *jùjú* and gospel. These neo-traditional genres all developed as a result of a need for nonliturgical genres to satisfy the social needs of the people.

In Nigeria, the evolution of Yorùbá highlife music can be traced from two perspectives. The first is that of the intercontinental musical influences on the traditional musical forms and practices already existing in the country, particularly in the coastal city of Lagos. The second is the musical influence of the neighboring nation of Ghana, beginning in the early 1950s.

The Evolution of Yorùbá Highlife to the Mid-Twentieth Century

In tracing the first of these directions of influence, it is important to establish the importance to the Yorùbá of their indigenous musical tradition. Long before the incursion of colonial masters, the Islamic jihadists and the Christian missionaries into the Yorùbá societies of southwestern Nigeria, the Yorùbá people had been practicing their indigenous music, which is an inseparable component of their culture. The history of Yorùbá music, particularly in the city of Lagos, can be traced as far back as the sixteenth century. The period from around 1500 to 1700 saw the indigenization and creation of traditional forms established by custom. The major musical forms were those used for religious and ritual processes. These simple vocal (songs and chants) and instrumental (drums, bells and winds) forms were also employed for the cycle of life celebrations. The period from around 1700 to 1840 saw the introduction of new traditional forms from migrants such as those from Benin, Badagry and so on. These include music celebrating deities and masquerade music as well as dance-dramas for liturgical and entertainment functions.

It was in the period from around 1840 to 1914 that foreign musical influences began to increase significantly. In this transitional period foreign forms were explored alongside the existing practices. For example, by 1841, Christian missionaries had reached Badagry, bringing their church hymns with them. Although they discouraged songs praising individual deities, missionaries in due course allowed Yorùbá melodic and rhythmic elements into the hymn form. Similarly, as Yorùbá musical practice appeared to them to be without form and structure, missionaries introduced their own, but later accommodated Yorùbá patterns, while making them conform to Western structure and notation. In this way, foreign and indigenous practices came together, helping to prepare the ground for the creation in due course of neo-traditional Yorùbá genres, of which highlife would be one.

By 1855 two groups of repatriated Yorùbá slaves had migrated to Lagos and had started putting their musical skills acquired in the 'new worlds' to practice on the Lagos streets. The first group consisted of the emancipated Yorùbá slaves from Brazil and Cuba, also known as the 'Aguda,' together with other African-American migrants from the United States and British West Indies. They introduced a range of syncretic genres which further aided the creation of new forms by the local Yorùbá musicians, as prototypes for highlife. The second group comprised the freed Yorùbá slaves who were taken to Sierra Leone (see entry on Gumbe/Goombay) and later migrated to West African coastal cities, including Lagos Island, together with visiting Liberian Kru sailors. The latter introduced their native 'blues' and a two-fingered guitar-style music known as the 'Krusbass,' which were adapted by the local palmwine music performers. All these external elements, adopted into the traditional musical practices of the Yorùbá people, paved the way for the emergence of highlife music among them.

The period dating from 1914 witnessed the emergence of Islamic and Christian nonliturgical Yorùbá music performed solely for social events. This period also saw the rise of nightclub, dance-party and ballroom music. Traditional music was 'Europeanized' through the appropriation of Western musical elements and the arrival of foreign instruments such as the piano, organ, guitar, woodwinds and brass. Local palmwine musicians and other dance bands adopted the foreign instruments, and on the one hand metamorphosed into the brass bands that started performing ballroom, concert hall and European music and, on the other, into the guitar bands which played dance rhythms for entertainment. All these innovations underwrote new forms of music, including highlife.

In the emergence of Yorùbá highlife, two main branches of the genre's development in West Africa at the turn of the twentieth century were thus especially significant: dance-band music and guitar band music. Dance-band music emerged from the music of British and European dance orchestras and military bands as performed in Nigeria. This elite musical style, which developed as a result of the Westernization of indigenous Yorùbá music, was a reflection of the exclusive high-class life and economic status of colonial masters and European missionaries as adopted by educated Nigerians. Guitar band music developed as a result of the music of Kru sailors and fishermen visiting from neighboring countries. These two types of music represented the musical styles of the post–World War I bands of the 1930s, with the guitar band style coming to influence the more elite style. These bands, which flourished in cities such as Lagos, Calabar and Onitsha, included the Chocolate Dandies of Nigeria, the Triumph Club Dance Orchestra and the Sugar Babies Band. They were known in Lagos as the *kokoma* bands and laid the foundations for the evolution of Yorùbá highlife.

The Ghanaian Influence

The introduction of Ghanaian highlife into the Yorùbá musical scene occurred in 1950 when E.T Mensah brought his music to Nigeria. It was the beginning of the golden years of unification between Ghana and Nigeria. In those days, highlife was to rank second only to football (soccer) as a unifying factor between the two countries.

Highlife's reputation as a sophisticated form of musical expression accompanied it to Nigeria. Its very name, however, embodied a cultural division between the affluent who, when highlife emerged in Ghana in the 1920s, could afford the price of imported drink in dance clubs, bars and hotels where the music was played, and those who could only gaze in from the outside, listening to the mesmerizing music, watching couples enjoying themselves late into the night, and coming to the exasperated but resigned conclusion that such music was indeed for a life of 'high' enjoyment.

When Mensah performed in major cities across Nigeria, including Lagos, the Yorùbá were also already experimenting with the development of a form of brass band and jazz-influenced dance music. His visit left an indelible mark on Yorùbá musicians, bringing alive a hotbed of highlife music within Nigeria. Shortly after Mensah's visit most of the Yorùbá neo-traditional brass band and jazz musicians transitioned from their original musical repertoires into highlife. These musicians included Adeolu Akinsanya, who first performed indigenous Yorùbá Agidigbo music, Bobby Benson, who first had a disdain for highlife while playing brass-band music and jazz, and even Victor Olaiya, who was a trumpeter in several brass bands before forming his highlife band, the Morning Star Orchestra, in 1957.

If Mensah's visit is taken to be a catalyst that enabled Yorùbá musicians to build something new on existing practices, the period from 1940 to 1960 can be seen as representing the golden age of Yorùbá highlife as a deliberate move away from conventional Western ballroom and brass-band music. As a hybrid form, it reflected on the cultural impact of European colonization and how local Yorùbá musicians reacted to this. The musical content and style of Yorùbá highlife symbolized an elitist identity associated with European social and cultural values. As a consequence, it was strongly associated with elite members of Nigerian society during the colonial era, with the music performed mainly at dinner parties, nightclubs and banquets of rich, political and highly placed Yorùbá leaders.

In the 1960s highlife experienced a decline in Nigeria, due mainly to the gruesome 30-month-long civil war which started in 1967. Most of the Igbo highlife artists who were key highlife players in Lagos left for eastern Nigeria. On their return from the east at the end of the war in the 1970s, highlife musicians found that the highlife scene had been taken over by jùjú. Among the musicians who kept the genre alive were Fela Ransome Kuti and Victor Uwaifo, both based at the Kakadu Night Club in Lagos. Musicians such as Victor Olaiya and Roy Chicago were conscripted during the civil war.

The Characteristics of Yorùbá Highlife

Yorùbá highlife is a dance-band style which over the years has adopted the guitar band style. The bands started initially by playing foxtrots, waltzes and Latin dances, later incorporating arrangements of popular Yorùbá folksongs. The highlife band is a type of big band, with trumpets, horns, baritone saxophones, trombones, guitars and percussion instruments including traditional drums (*dundun, akuba*), gong (*agogo*), rattles (*sekere*) and woodblocks. There are two types of rhythm employed in Yorùbá highlife: simple and compound quadruple meters. The former is a simple divisive rhythmic structure, the characteristic rhythm of Yorùbá highlife, which employs a straightforward 'walk-along' bass line. The latter employs a compound additive rhythmic structure. The music is usually in ternary form, with an improvisatory rhythmic and instrumental middle section, and employs melodic figures and *ostinato* rhythms which are characteristic features of West African highlife. Yorùbá highlife customarily uses simple diatonic melodies, the primary chords of the Western tonal system and chord progressions with chromatic embellishments. Due to the tonal inflections of the Yorùbá language, its melodic patterns often employ harmonies in thirds and sixth mixed with traditional harmonic features, and are usually played in a moderate tempo. Yorùbá highlife is frequently measured in character, with lyrics derived from Yorùbá folklore in local dialects, English or pidgin languages. The lyrics are usually topical, based on cultural events and current affairs, and deal with familiar themes and political and social issues of the day, all of which makes Yorùbá highlife widely acceptable. The subjects of these songs are similar to those of traditional songs: they eulogize, commemorate and insult; they are about love and death and extol cultural and moral values.

Major Figures in Yorùbá Highlife

One of the pioneering legends of Yorùbá highlife has been Victor Olaiya (b. 1930), dubbed the 'evil genius of highlife' by the media because of his skills and contribution to the genre in Nigeria. Recognized equally as the 'Don of Highlife,' and with a career dating back to the late 1940s, Olaiya was a distinguished trumpeter and group leader. He formed his own band, the Morning Star Orchestra, in 1957 and renamed the group 'The Blue Spots' band in 1961. The band trained and boasts some of the most popular musical icons, including the drummer Tony Allen and vocalist Fela Kuti. Olaiya collaborated with E.T. Mensah, a collaboration facilitated in 1983 by Polydor Records which resulted in the 1984 release of an album featuring these two giants of highlife in

Nigeria and Ghana. The album was a compilation of their individual hits. Olaiya's popular recordings include 'Odale Ore' and 'Mofe Muyon' (1958), *Olaiya's Victories* (1961), *Highlife Reincarnation* (1982), *Baby Jowo (Baby Mi Da)* with 2Face Ibidia (2013).

Another, earlier pioneer of highlife in Nigeria was Bobby Benson (1922–83), also recognized for his role in Nigerian show business. Benson provided successful apprenticeships for the first generation of highlife musicians including Victor Olaiya, creating the highlife scene and setting the pace of its development. Benson was the first musician to own a nightclub (Caban Bamboo) as well as the first to own a hotel (Hotel Bobby). Bobby Benson & His Combo was the first Nigerian highlife band to be recognized by audiences across the country. Other prominent highlife musicians to pass through Benson's tutelage included Victor Uwaifo, Roy Chicago, Billy Friday, Eddy Okonta, Zeal Onyia and Joe Mensah.

Other notable Nigerian highlife musicians of both western and eastern origin include E.C. Arinze, Baller Miller, Rew Williams, Adeolu Akisanya, Stephen Osadebe, Rex Lawson, Crosdale Juba, Chris Ajilo, Wura Fadaka, Chief Billy Friday, the Harbours Band, Bola Johnson, Sunny Oti, King Kenny Tone, Nico Mbarga, Nelly Uchendu, Inyang Henshaw, the Peacocks, the Oriental Brothers and the Professional Seagulls. One of the prominent musicians who helped spread the gospel of highlife music overseas was Ambrose Campbell (1919–2006). He performed for some years at London's Club Afrique to a cross-section of highlife devotees.

Contemporary Trends in Yorùbá Highlife in Nigeria

Although the popularity of highlife has declined significantly, it has continued to be performed in Nigeria as well as in other African countries. It has remained highly commercialized. Due to advanced technology, modern audio and visual media and the Internet, the music has become readily available anywhere in the world. Contemporary artists such as Lagbaja, Kola Ogunkoya and the duo Bracket have contributed immensely to the life of the genre, increasing its popularity to near its previous level.

Other contemporary artists who incorporate older forms of highlife into their music include Paul Play Dairo, 2Face Idibia, Korede Bello and King Oge Nwanne. At the end of the 2010s highlife appeared to be on the increase, particularly with songs and videos such as 'Ada Ada,' which won Flavour N'abania a Nigerian Music Video Award for Best High Life Video in 2013. Just as contemporary forms of highlife have developed in Ghana, referred to variously as burger highlife, gospel highlife and hiplife, so too have contemporary forms in Nigeria: hip-hop highlife, Afro-highlife, gospel highlife and so on. These developments have helped in the reshaping, rebranding, and reinvigoration of highlife in Nigeria as well as in Ghana and other West African countries, where this enigmatic and iconic musical form has continued to be practiced.

Bibliography

Agawu, Kofi. 2016. *The African Imagination in Music*. New York: Oxford University Press.

Ajirire, Tosin, and Alabi, Wale. 1992. *3 Decades of Nigerian Music 1960–1990*. Lagos: Limelight Showbiz Publication.

Collins, John. 1976. 'Ghanaian Highlife.' *African Arts* 19(1): 62–8, 100.

Emielu, Austin 'Maro. 2010. 'The Concept of Change and Genre Development: A Case Study of Highlife Music.' Paper presented at the First International Conference on Analytical Approaches to World Music, University of Massachusetts, Amherst, USA. 19–21 February. Online at: http://www.aawmconference.com/aawm2010/images/1aawmemielupaper.pdf (accessed 21 June 2018).

Emielu, Austin 'Maro. 2013. *Nigerian Highlife Music*. Lagos: Centre for Black African Arts and Civilisation.

Esho, Femi. 2010. 'Africa: A Repository of Indigenous Sound.' Unpublished speech delivered at the 14th International Conference on African Music, University of Lagos.

Esho, Femi. 2016. 'Highlife Must Not Die.' Unpublished speech given at the Tribute to Benson Idonije, Lagos, 13–16 June.

Euba, Akin. 1988. 'Juju, Highlife and Afro-Beat: An Introduction to Popular Music in Nigeria.' In *Essays on Music in Africa*, ed. Akin Euba. Bayreuth: Iwalewa Haus, 119–39.

Ọmọjọla, Bode. 2012. 'Yorùbá Popular Music: Hybridity, Identity and Power.' In *Yorùbá Music in the Twentieth Century: Identity, Agency and*

Performance Practices. New York: University of Rochester Press, 162–203.

Ọmọjọla, Bode. 2014. *Popular Music in Western Nigeria: Theme, Style and Patronage*. Nairobi: Institut Français de Recherché en Afrique.

Ọmọjọla, Bode. 2017. 'Music and Dance in Culture and Performance.' In *Culture and Customs of the Yorùbá*, eds. Toyin Falola and Akintunde Akinyemi. Austin, TX: Pan-African University Press, 407–20.

Stone, Ruth, ed. 2000. *The Garland Handbook of African Music*. New York: Garland Publishing Inc.

Vidal, Tunji. 2012. *Selected Topics on Nigerian Music*, ed. Femi Adedeji. Ile-Ife: Obafemi Awolowo University Press.

Waterman, Christopher. 1990. 'Sakara, Asiko, Highlife and Palmwine: Lagosian Popular Music between the World Wars.' In *Jùjú: A Social History and Ethnography of an African Popular Music*. Chicago: University of Chicago Press, 27–54.

Discographical References

Flavour. 'Ada Ada.' *Blessed*. 2nite Entertainment. *2012*: Nigeria.

Mensah, E. T., with Victor Olaiya and His International All Stars Band. *Highlife Giants of Africa – Highlife Souvenir Volume 1*. Polydor POLP 102. *1984*: Nigeria.

Olaiya, Victor, with 2Face Ibidia. *Baby Jowo (Baby Mi Da)*. 2013. Nigeria.

Olaiya, Victor, and His All Stars. 'Odale Ore'/'Mofe Muyon.' (7" single). Philips-West African-Records ß03 012 P.F. *1958*: Nigeria.

Olaiya, Victor, and His All Stars. *Olaiya's Victories*. Philips P 13403 R. *1961*: Nigeria.

Olaiya, Victor, and His International Stars Band. *Highlife Reincarnation*. POLP 073. *1982*: Nigeria.

Discography

Akinsanya, Adeolu. *Baba Eto*. Afrodisia DWAPS 2185. *1983*: Nigeria.

Fatai Rolling Dollar. *Won kere si numba wa*. Jazzhole Records. *2012*: Nigeria.

Highlife Kings vol. 1. KMCD 01 Lagos: Premier Music. *2000*: Nigeria.

Highlife Kings vol. 2 (2000). KMCD 02. Lagos: Premier Music. *2000*: Nigeria.

Olaiya, Victor. *Olaiya in the 60s*. Polydor POLP 066. *1982*: Nigeria.

Olaiya, Victor. *3 Decades of Highlife Music*. Premier Music. *2002*: Nigeria.

Olaiya, Victor, and His International Stars Band. *Ilu le o*. Polydor POLP 096. *1983*: Nigeria.

YouTube

Flavour, 'Ada Ada.' Online at: https://www.youtube.com/watch?v=2lUFM8yTtUc (accessed 25 April 2018).

OLUPEMI OLUDARE

Hip-Hop in Sub-Saharan Africa

While hip-hop's arrival and initial adoption in various sub-Saharan African countries was, for the most part, strikingly similar, subsequent adaptations reflect locally specific realities of language, social norms, colonial histories, and contemporary economic and political structures. The fact that Africans have been making hip-hop for nearly as long as Americans means that discussions of African hip-hop must take into account not only multiple and shifting national contexts but also multiple generations of hip-hoppers effecting continuous change and development. The articles included here – representing case studies from Anglophone and Francophone West Africa, East Africa, Central Africa and Southern Africa – are only the tip of the iceberg; hip-hop has taken root in countless other countries, including North African ones.

Hip-hop is generally represented as a complex of performance practices – rapping, DJing, graffiti writing and breakdancing – that developed in the South Bronx in the late 1970s and early 1980s as an aesthetically mediated youth response to the racially fraught struggles of daily life in the postindustrial US inner city. This somewhat simplified narrative, while obscuring the role of West Indian and Latino contributors and rendering hip-hop an almost mythical musical creature, has carried weight throughout hip-hop's global spread. Despite hip-hop's roots in social dancing, the music's role as a conduit for social commentary, particularly in the 1980s and early 1990s, has often led scholars and practitioners to define the music as a tool for consciousness raising, as exemplified in the 'Godfather of Hip-Hop' Afrika Bambaataa's addition of 'knowledge' to the four elements of hip-hop culture noted above. This perspective often leads to a devaluing of hip-hop music that demonstrates explicitly commercial goals or whose lyrics emphasize sex, gangsterism or conspicuous consumption rather than overt political or social messages.

Hip-hop arrived in Africa very early on in its history, carried there largely through cassettes and videos brought or sent home by African immigrant workers in North America and Europe. This meant that in most cases young people from socioeconomically privileged backgrounds became hip-hop's point of entry into various African countries. Almost without exception, the earliest African engagements with hip-hop performance – inspired by globally circulating hip-hop films such as *Beat Street* – took the form of breakdancing; perhaps due to linguistic barriers, rapping came slightly later, particularly in non-Anglophone countries.

Nevertheless, African youth soon began to rap, first mimicking US lyrics in English, and eventually (usually in the 1990s) transitioning to original lyrics in local languages: Wolof in Senegal, Swahili in Kenya and Tanzania, Lingala, Kiswahili and Luba in the Democratic Republic of the Congo, and so on. An exception is *Luga flow* in Uganda, which was performed primarily in English until the late 1990s and therefore had little impact in a country where the majority of the population did not speak this official national language. In Gabon, the lack of an indigenous lingua franca posed a problem for rappers seeking to localize the music without drawing on colonial languages; they eventually chose to use widespread urban slang over French. In other countries, we find a greater variety of ethnically specific subsets of hip-hop; Nigeria, for example, has produced Yorùbá, Igbo and Hausa scenes in addition to English-language rap. In all contexts, locally produced musical tracks followed closely behind these linguistically localized lyrics.

Hip-hop has intersected in multiple ways with indigenous African musical practices as well as with local African popular music genres. Sometimes this entails drawing on local traditional musics or instruments, while in other cases, new hip-hop-pop hybrids form; these processes vary not only from one country to the next but between regions of the same country. Often, generational differences are tied up in changing norms of hip-hop musical production. For example, the earliest Senegalese hip-hoppers favored heavily indigenized musical tracks, while hardcore rappers in the mid-1990s rejected traditional music; rappers in the 2000s, however, have begun to re-embrace traditional music while insisting on the centrality of hip-hop rhythms. In Ghana, after initial forays into hip-hop that reproduced US styles, some hip-hoppers in the 1990s combined hip-hop with highlife, a West African popular music with roots in the palmwine guitar and Cuban *son* popular in the early twentieth century; the resultant hiplife genre has continued to evolve into the 2010s. Zanzabari artists have incorporated elements of indigenous *ngoma* performance into their *zenji flava*. Popular genres including Angolan *kuduro*, Congolese *busipa* and South African *kwaito* have roots in hip-hop as well as other local musics; hip-hoppers in Botswana in turn have drawn heavily on *kwaito* to create the hip-hop subgenre *motswako*. In many cases, hip-hop beats without these local elements are understood as more 'hardcore' and the artists who make them sometimes draw criticism for copying US hip-hop too closely.

Hip-hop's expansion from elite urban pockets to larger audiences coincided with the development of local recording and increasingly accessible channels of dissemination, as African media spread to encompass private, non-state-regulated channels. Although early on in hip-hop's trajectory we see artists rising to prominence through national competitions, and despite the increasingly democratic musical production of the mid-1990s and onward, in most cases the localized popular genres that preceded hip-hop continued to dominate local music industries and media outlets. Hip-hop takes a back seat to genres including *mbalax* in Senegal, *kwaito* in South Africa, *rumba* and *ndombolo* in the Democratic Republic of the Congo, and more pop-oriented incarnations of *bongo flava* in mainland Tanzania and *zenji flava* in Zanzibar. This unequal access to media play has, in some instances, exacerbated existing tensions between what are understood as 'underground' versus 'commercial' varieties of hip-hop and/or popular music. Although referring largely to lyrical content and concepts of social consciousness, debates over the 'underground' or 'commercial' properties of a particular artist's music are often tied to musical choices; for example, *bongo flava* artists in Tanzania describe commercialism in terms of how much a song draws on pop genres other than hip-hop, and hip-hop in Senegal is sometimes viewed as too commercial if singing and traditional music obscure a hip-hop beat.

In fact, despite widespread claims to hip-hop as a form of resistance, the music's connection to political figures and processes varies widely within and between national scenes. In 2005 Tanzanian political parties used music to influence the elections, and hip-hop artists explicitly endorsed candidates. Hip-hop in Gabon has held strong ties to the political elite since its inception, largely due to its roots in the privileged sectors of society that produced those same political leaders. Hausa hip-hop in Nigeria has faced religious censorship; its messages therefore tend to focus more on general social change than on explicit political critique. Hip-hop played a shifting role in the 2000, 2007 and 2012 Senegalese presidential elections, in the first instance endorsing a new candidate through music and speeches, in the second, failing to push that same president out of power, and in the third, mobilizing extramusical political demonstrations to enact a shift in leadership without, in this instance, endorsing any particular candidate. In South Africa, early hip-hop took a stance against apartheid, but its political proclivities have waned in the 2000s. In the Democratic Republic of the Congo, rappers have generally focused on raising awareness of social issues rather than engaging in overt political action.

Language use, musical localization and engagement with local social and political issues are not only byproducts of local music industry and state involvement in hip-hop, but are also directly related to hip-hop's widespread use in identity building. As African countries are increasingly urbanized, music – and hip-hop in particular – provides a means for young people to place themselves in a modern, globally interconnected world while also (re)connecting to indigenous modes of performance and ethnically specific identities that are sometimes blurred in cosmopolitan contexts. Hip-hop imagery of the ghetto often comes into play here, as African youth connect their own urban contexts to US hip-hop representations of the inner city. Hip-hop provides a forum for challenging established norms of intergenerational communication in many African cultures, where youth are expected to respect their elders to a point that limits their own voices. It also mediates between ethnic and racial identities, from joint projects between Igbo and Yorùbá Nigerian rappers to Senegalese group Bideew Bou Bess's use of Fulani music in a Wolof-dominated urban context to the use of hip-hop to mediate between black, white and 'colored' identities in South Africa. The white South African group Die Antwoord, which has a large following in the United States, has built its distinctive style around the figurative and literal uses of blackface in its videos and personas.

In general, however, hip-hop's potential for youth identity construction and a break with traditional norms has been largely limited along the lines of gender, with female artists representing a minority in each hip-hop scene. Although a few female artists have risen to prominence in different countries, social constraints related to marriage and the role of women in the home often render their careers more fleeting than those of their male counterparts. The success of women in other popular genres suggests that their scarcity within hip-hop may reflect the easy reconciliation of hip-hop misogyny imported from abroad and local patriarchies that place women at a disadvantage in public forums.

Despite hip-hop's wide reach throughout Africa, African hip-hop has not yet made a significant impact on audiences outside of the continent, with a few exceptions such as Senegal's Positive Black Soul and Daara J Family, and South Africa's Die Antwoord. Musics that sound more immediately 'African,' such as Zimbabwean *chimurenga*, South African *isicathimiya*, Congolese *soukouss* and West African Afrobeat, generally have proven more attractive to Western (world music) audiences. In contrast, as the entries in this volume indicate, scholarly interest in African hip-hop continues to grow. The continent's immense diversity provides a challenge for any scholarly treatment of Africa as a whole. However, shared histories of colonization, urbanization and migration allow one to draw connections between diverse African hip-hop scenes while acknowledging the music's local specificity.

Bibliography

Charry, Eric, ed. 2012. *Hip Hop Africa: New African Music in a Globalizing World.* Indianapolis: Indiana University Press.

Clark, Msia Kibona, and Koster, Mickie Msasia, eds. 2014. *Hip Hop and Social Change in Africa: Ni Wakati.* Lanham, MD: Lexington Books.

Ntarangwi, Mwenda. 2010. 'African Hip Hop and the Politics of Change in an Era of Rapid Globalization.' *History Compass* 8(12): 1316–27.

Saucier, Paul Khalil, ed. 2011. *Native Tongues: The African Hip Hop Reader*. Trenton: Africa World Press.

Saucier, Paul Khalil. 2014. 'Continental Drift: The Politics and Poetics of African Hip Hop.' In *Sounds and the City: Popular Music, Place, and Globalization*, eds. Brett Lashua et al. New York: Palgrave Macmillan, 196–208.

Filmography

Beat Street, dir. Stan Lathan. 1984. USA. 105 mins. Drama.

CATHERINE APPERT

See also Bongo Flava, Hiplife

Hip-Hop in Botswana

Hip-hop music began developing in Botswana during the late 1990s, following the emergence of breakdance crews in the preceding decade. Like its international counterparts, early hip-hop music in Botswana consisted of MCs reciting lyrics over an electronically generated beat which typically had a 4/4 rhythm. Other features of the music included the use of keyboards, synthesizers, drum kits and samples (snippets of songs that were recorded by other artists). Such instrumentation embodied 'technologizing the band,' a characteristic which involved substituting electronically generated sounds for live instruments such as pianos, pipes and drums (Keyes 1999). One key distinguishing characteristic of hip-hop music in Botswana was the insertion of local languages such as Setswana and Kalanga as well as English, especially in the local *motswako* style that became popular in the country beginning in the 1990s and eventually spread to South Africa.

As in the United States, hip-hop in Botswana was part of an arts movement encompassing four core elements: aerosol or graffiti art, breakdancing, DJing and MCing or rapping (Keyes 2002, 1). Young Batswana (citizens of Botswana, plural) who became acquainted with hip-hop culture in the USA set to work on cultivating local manifestations. Before the rise of MCing in the 1990s local interpretations of hip-hop culture in Botswana were extensions of the early US hip-hop youth movement that began in the 1970s.

The socioeconomic climate of Botswana was vastly different from that of the United States during the period when hip-hop came into existence. For example, Botswana did not suffer from the urban 'decay' that was associated with the beginnings of hip-hop in the United States (George 2005, 10). Indeed, it gained international accolades for being a peaceful country that had smoothly transitioned from a British protectorate (Bechuanaland) to an effective democracy. It maintained stable governance and booming industries, and was commended for being one of the world's 'fastest growing economies' between 1965 and 1995 (Beaulier 2003, 231). The nation was rich in diamonds and remained a leading producer of the gem. Botswana forged a partnership with the diamond conglomerate DeBeers, resulting in the formation of Debswana, a mining enterprise that was a leading national employer and source of revenue (De Beers 2014). The second Debswana mining location opened in 1982, 15 years after the first mine was established in Orapa, launching further chances for employment across different economic strata. Additional job opportunities were also available to Batswana who migrated to South Africa, the country that lies along Botswana's southern border, as did many other southern African workers, for employment (Bond, Miller and Ruiters 2001).

In neighboring South Africa, young people started embracing hip-hop music and culture as an artistic expression to resist the apartheid regime. Politically charged lyrics openly opposed the government and were controversial due to their 'subversive' content (Coplan 2007, 334). Breakdance was one of the primary means through which hip-hop culture was first adopted in South Africa. Similarly, and at much the same time, among young people in Botswana the dance form was at the forefront of how hip-hop culture materialized.

During the 1980s breakdance crews (fans who explored different breakdance moves) flourished in South Africa. Their link to the foundations of South African hip-hop has been studied widely by artists, journalists and scholars, namely in cities such as Cape Town, where the music thrived and spread regionally throughout southern Africa at the time (Perkins 1996; Neate 2004; Warner 2007; Warner 2011; Watkins 1999; Watkins 2004; Watkins 2012; Williams and Shroud

2010). This newfound attraction to hip-hop music in South Africa was attributable to an emergent 'cassette culture' where people used networks of friends living in the United States to acquire the latest hip-hop recordings of artists of the (see Abrahams and Ariefdien 2006; Manuel 1993). These cassettes, which were mainly traded through person-to-person interactions and across borders, became the primary means through which hip-hop music was disseminated at the beginning of the movement in Botswana.

In the late 1980s when hip-hop music was infiltrating Botswana's capital city of Gaborone through breakdance and the exchange of recorded music on cassettes, other genres of music such as *kwaito* (a fusion of house, R&B and ragga music) and *kwasa kwasa* (a combination of electric guitar, drums and vocals) were extremely popular. Thus it took almost another 10 years before Batswana audiences fully embraced local hip-hop music and it became a commercialized entity in the country with the release of the first hip-hop album in 1996. According to Batswana DJs, MCs and producers, the process underwent several phases.

The Beginnings: Breakdance Battles and Early MCing

According to MC/producer David 'Draztik' Balsher (personal communication, 2013), breakdancing competitions were an integral part of the hip-hop movement in Botswana. He notes that Batswana students attending high schools and universities in the United States in cities such as New York brought back the latest breakdance moves and music. Many of these students were in the United States while their parents attained international educational or employment opportunities. Upon returning to Botswana, some of the youth joined crews that started battling one another over the sounds of American hip-hop recordings to demonstrate their dance skills and physical dexterity. Dancers deftly displayed techniques associated with breakdancing, such as popping, locking and spinning. The moves mirrored those seen in hip-hop films released in the United States, such as *Breakin'* and *Wild Style*. Breakdancers also emulated the style of dress popularized by US breakdancers: loose-fitting sweat suits and comfortable T-shirts. Their breakdance battles took place at school talent shows, namely at Maru-a-Pula School (MAP) and Gaborone Secondary School (GSS), as well as at Gaborone's Main Mall. The battles were also part of variety shows held around the country (J. Kai-Lewis 2009).

MCing evolved in Botswana during the 1990s. Sidney 'DJ Sid' Basitsile remembers two artists approaching him in 1992 with a request to record a jingle for his show while he was working at Radio Botswana 2 (RB2) (personal communication 2013). At the same time, an assortment of other DJs, including Bass, Dolphus, Eddie Ed and Kicking Clectic, began playing hip-hop records. Consequently, there were additional hip-hop radio broadcasts, such as *Rap Blast*, aired on RB2 by Thabo 'Shakes the Mix' Matthews. Each of these DJs became renowned for playing records straight through without including the scratching techniques that DJs implemented in other parts of the world. Scratching was promoted in Botswana with the appearance of the Beat Premiers after 2000. This DJing duo, comprised of DJ Khenzo and DJ Dext, perfected their craft while living in the United States. They were locally celebrated in Botswana for the techniques of cutting and scratching records while spinning them on turntables.

The hip-hop crews 12 Gauge and P-Side formed during the era of early DJing and MCing in Botswana. DJ Bass was at the forefront of 12 Gauge and DJ Sid pioneered P-Side. The first hip-hop group release came from Third Mind (Kagiso Presley, Azizz Metshe, Modise 'Dee' Moletsane and Mokhabi 'Bumpy' Moeletsi) with their album *Player for Life* (1996). According to DJ Sid, the collective was greatly influenced by Bone Thugs-n-Harmony, a US hip-hop group that gained notoriety in the late 1990s for their slowed-down, lyrical flow blended with portions of sung lines. Third Mind adopted a similar style of MCing, relying on a combination of MCing and sung lyrics. With songs such as 'Dilokile' and 'Ngoma,' their music merged English and Setswana lyrics and is considered one of the first *motswako* recordings. They went on to release a second album, *The Second Coming*, in 2005.

DJ Sid recalls that, despite the appearance of Third Mind, it was difficult for MCs to gain a following in the 1990s. Local hip-hop music was still in its early stages and artists had to actively find ways to market themselves. MCing competitions such as the Sprite Rap Activity Jam, subsequently known as I Got Skills, gave new MCs exposure. Thato 'Scar' Matlabaphiri, for example, gained visibility as an artist this way and was noticed by DJ Sid, who placed him on the P-Side double compact disc release *DJ Sid Presents P-Side* (2000). The album also served as a platform for other hip-hop artists such as Mr. Doe, Kast, Mr. T (who adopted the name Nomadic), and Orakle.

Microphone Masters: The Rise of Solo MCs and Groups

MCing continued growing in Botswana following the release of *DJ Side Presents P-Side*. Scar and a host of other hip-hop artists emerged as leading figures. Scar went on to release his debut solo album, the first record by a hip-hop artist in Botswana, titled *Illegal Act* (2002). The album represented his efforts to secure financial support from the company Vivid Vision in order to become a successful solo act. His accomplishments represented new ventures for Batswana hip-hop artists. It demonstrated artists' ability to build a fan base with a genre of music that was still relatively new. Batswana still preferred the aforementioned *kwaito* and *kwasa kwasa*, but this did not deter Scar from pursuing his album, which earned two Botswana Hip-hop Music Awards (BHIPMA) for Lyricist of the Year and Track of the Year for the song 'My People.' Scar's early achievements spurred other talented Batswana to embark on careers as solo hip-hop artists.

Ralph 'Stagga' Williams, III provided another perspective on local hip-hop music from a solo artist. His songs differed from Scar's in that they depicted his experiences residing in both Botswana and Britain, thereby capturing his Motswana (citizen of Botswana, singular) and Jamaican heritage. Stagga's lyrics were delivered in English, his signature Jamaican patois and Setswana. He spotlighted his solo MC skills with the release of his EP *Staggalicious* (2003). On his second album, *Music for Your Movement* (2007), Stagga relied more heavily on local producers and artists. He turned to the production skills of Henry 'AK' Segopa and Tumelo 'Qbio' Segopa of Sinewave Productions as well as Thabo 'Grandpa' Letsale. Guest hip-hop artists were Orakle (on the track 'Things Done Changed' featuring vocalist Fasia) and Jerry 'Black Intellect' Kai-Lewis of the hip-hop collective Cashless Society (on the track 'Soldier' alongside singer Mmaphala Letsatle).

Monametsi 'Apollo Diablo' Nkhuhku (also known as Billy Blunts) is also among the ranks of celebrated Batswana solo MCs. He released the first hip-hop song in Botswana recorded in Kalanaga in 2004 ('Ikalanga Chedu'). Apollo Diablo broke into the local hip-hop scene through involvement in a crew called 5th Generation made up of himself, Orakle, Feeno Shallah, Nytro and EQ. 5th Generation merged with artists Azziz, Illustrate and King Ming to form another collective, Uncanny Sessman. They collaborated to release a collection of mixtapes, 'Cipher Divine,' which were produced by Zambian producer 'Don The Icon.' Apollo Diablo worked with Draztik and a range of other producers, releasing EPs and participating in MC battles including the Sprite Rap Activity Jam. He went on to put out his first single, 'The City Owes Me,' in 2004 and his album *The Meaning of Life* a year later.

A substantial number of solo MCs of this period were male, but female MCs also strived to make an imprint on the hip-hop movement in Botswana. Noteworthy female MCs are Ice Queen, Jezzabelle and Michelle. They have been embraced by their male counterparts, appearing collaboratively in both stage performances and on recordings. Jezzabelle and Ice Queen were featured on the compilation *Lyrical Mix Xpressions: Life and Times of GC* (2005). Fellow artists Nomadic, Mister Doe, Konkrete, Black Caesar, H.T., Qbio and Nytro, Kelimann, Orakle, Scar, Man-E, Pongo Rista, Short Dog and K.T. also made musical contributions to the project. Ice Queen offered a freestyle, while Jezzabelle recorded the song 'Verse in the Making.' Michelle appeared on recordings for Ramco Records, performing with other artists such as K-Bos. She was one of the featured artists on K-Bos's 2009 album *BosMan*. Michelle appeared on the songs 'In Tha Spot' alongside Magosi, Scar, Third Mind, Goof, Mosako, Kast and Fosta Juliano as well as on 'Ke Yone' and 'On Paper.' Ice Queen, Jezabelle and Michelle have all continued recording independent projects.

In addition to the surge of solo MCs, the group Cashless Society was also gaining momentum and spotlighting Batswana artists. Cashless Society was a group of MCs from Botswana and South Africa. David 'Draztik' Balsher (Cashless Society MC and producer) and Salim 'Fat Free' Mosidinyane (Cashless

Society MC) were Batswana, but they had spent portions of their adolescence in the United States (Balsher lived in California and Mosidinyane in New York City). Upon returning to Botswana, Draztik hosted a radio show broadcast on RB2 called *Strictly Hip-hop Live*. He moved to South Africa, honing his skills as both a producer and an MC and starting the record label Unreleased Records, which has continued to serve as home to some of the country's leading hip-hop talent. Cashless Society attracted a considerable fan base in both Botswana and South Africa. Their single 'Blaze Tha Breaks' garnered the attention of New York DJ Robert 'Bobbito' Garcia, who worked out a distribution deal and circulated the single on his now defunct Definitive Jux record label. It also appeared on the album *Farewell Fondle 'Em*. This made Cashless Society the first African hip-hop group to receive international distribution on a US record label. They went on to release their debut album, *African Raw Material, Volume One*, in 2003 before finally disbanding.

Motswako Flow: The Popularity of *Motswako* MCs

The expansion of hip-hop in Botswana in the 1990s led to the popularity of the *motswako* style, which is described by DJ Sid as 'hip-hop in indigenous languages often infused with *kwaito* beats' (personal communication, 5 August 2013). Thus the music consists of a mixture of English, Kalanga and Setswana. Despite the musical contributions of Third Mind, it is another hip-hop artist who is considered the pioneer of *motswako*. In Botswana, MC Tebogo 'Nomadic' Mapine is credited with starting *motswako* with the release of his demo tape. Nomadic appeared on albums including *Imbizo Street Mixtapes, Vol. 1* (2005) and DJ Rade's *The Motswako Tender Mixtape* (2009). *Motswako* is also widespread in South African hip-hop and is a staple in the music of artists such as Hip-hop Pantsula (HHP). As H. Samy Alim indicates, the use of local languages in hip-hop music contributes to 'complex local remixing' that gives the music distinctive linguistic features. These features are, consequently, imbued with specific cultural associations (Alim 2008, 7). The originality of many *motswako* artists has been celebrated through awards such as BHIPMA, a one-time awards ceremony that took place in 2004, and the Channel O Awards in South Africa. Two of the most recognized artists are Scar and Game 'Zeus' Bantsi. Scar characterizes *motswako* as a way for local audiences to identify with hip-hop music. He has used it on his songs in both the choruses and the verses. This was the case with some of his hit songs such as 'Metlholo,' 'Psycho' and 'Khenya' as well as others appearing on his albums. Consequently, he has demonstrated his commitment to localizing his music through *motswako*, which appeals to youth and builds a degree of cultural pride through the music.

Zeus popularized *motswako* on the albums *Freshly Baked* (2008) and *Flip Side* (2010). He has built his success through his *motswako* flow, and he has proven that he can adopt different approaches to his MCing. Zeus earned a Channel O Award for Best Hip-hop Video for 'Gijima,' a track where he details his range of lyrical skills and encourages others to run from him when they see him coming, appearing on *Freshly Baked* in 2008. He received a second Channel O Award for the song 'Dats Wassup,' featuring AKA and Tumi, a song he classified as an old-school boom bap hip-hop track, meaning that it was bass heavy and did not contain many additional electronic elements (Molabi 2013). He has shown the range of his versatility on the house-inspired song 'Dancing Shoes' (2011), in which he experiments with singing rather than MCing. On another single that he released, 'You Knows Me' (2013), Zeus borrows the slowed-down MCing style and synthesized sounds associated with the music of American MCs such as Clifford 'T.I.' Harris. On the track 'MaAfrika' (2013), Zeus describes the beauty and diversity of the African continent over a looped guitar riff, hi-hats and synthesized drums.

Aerosol Art: Visualizing Hip-Hop Culture

MCing and DJing have undergone tremendous changes since the 1990s. Nevertheless, aerosol art remains an area that has not been heavily practiced by visual artists. However, some Batswana are carving out a niche for themselves in this area, particularly from 2010 to the present. One example is aerosol artist/MC Khwezi Mphatlalatsane. Although Mphatlalatsane began recording songs through P-Side Studios in 2003, he has been dubbed 'the originator of modern graffiti' (Makgekgenene 2010). He created an aerosol art installation for the National Museum in 2010 and has been commissioned to create works for institutions such as FNB Botswana and Boitekanelo College.

Mphatlalatsane, who prefers referring to his artistry as 'street art' rather than graffiti, believes that his pieces are largely inspired by aerosol artwork, namely in his use of spray paint. Mphatlalatsane is broadening the scope of his work by traveling to South Africa and partnering with other aerosol artists there to design pieces and murals. He is also an accomplished photographer whose work has appeared in the pages of the magazine *Elle South Africa* ('Eye on the Khoi-Fro'). Other areas of interest include Mphatlalatsane's recent fashion line Cotton Mouth Wear, which is widely available to Batswana customers.

The Future of Hip-Hop in Botswana: International Dissemination

In the early twenty-first century other young artists such as ATI, Ozi F. Teddy, Noello and Klasick also have become acclaimed hip-hop figures in Botswana. Artists are releasing mixtapes, recorded collections of newly released or remixed songs, and have the opportunity to reach audiences through Internet websites such as Reverbnation and Soundcloud. One example is Zeus's *Honey I'm Home* mixtape, which was released in 2012 and featured artists such as Don Juan, KEB, Ozi F. Teddy, ThatodaPoet and Vusi. This has created greater exposure and a larger following for hip-hop music in Botswana on an international level. Radio stations such as Yarona FM remain integral in broadcasting hip-hop music throughout the nation as well as internationally through live online streaming. Access to hip-hop by Batswana artists is increasing through Internet-based stores such as iTunes as well as through video footage on YouTube. Thus, more global hip-hop fans are listening to Botswana hip-hop music and learning about its origins and development.

Bibliography

Abrahams, Nazli, and Ariefdien, Shaheen. 2006. 'Cape Flats Alchemy: Hip-Hop Arts in South Africa.' In *Total Chaos: The Art and Aesthetics of Hip-Hop*, ed. Jeff Chang. New York: Basic Citvas, 262–70.

Alim, H. Samy. 2008. 'Straight Outta Compton, Straight aus München: Global Linguistic Flows, Identities, and the Politics of Language in a Global Hip-Hop Nation.' In *Global Linguistic Flows: Hip-hop Cultures, Youth Identities and the Politics of Language*, eds. H. Samy Alim, Awad Ibrahim and Alastair Pennycook. New York: Routledge, 1–23.

Beaulier, Scott A. 2003. 'Explaining Botswana's Success: The Critical Role of Post-Colonial Policy.' *Cato Journal* 23(2): 227–40.

Bond, Patrick, Miller, Darlene, and Ruiters, Greg. 2011 'The Southern African Working Class: Production, Reproduction and Politics.' *Socialist Register* 37: 119–42.

Coplan, David. 2007. In *Township Tonight! Three Centuries of South African Black City Music and Theatre*. Auckland Park: Jacana.

De Beers. 2014. 'Debswana.' Online at: https://www.debeersgroup.com/Operations/Mining/Mining-Operations/Debswana/ (accessed 16 March 2014).

Gaotlhobogwe, Monkagedi. 2010. 'Rapper Apollo Diablo Now on eBotswana.' Online at: http://www.mmegi.bw/index.php?sid=7&aid=2301&dir=2010/May/Tuesday11 (accessed 23 March 2018).

George, Nelson. 2005. *Hip-Hop America*. New York: Penguin Books.

Kai-Lewis, Jerry. 2009. 'History of Hip-Hop in Botswana.' *Mmegi*. Online at: http://www.mmegi.bw/index.php?sid=7&aid=19&dir=2009/November/Thursday12 (accessed 23 March 2018).

Kai-Lewis, Jerry. 2009. 'Zeus Wins Channel O Award.' *Mmegi*. Online at: http://www.mmegi.bw/index.php?sid=7&aid=225&dir=2009/November/Wednesday4 (accessed 23 March 2018).

Keyes, Cheryl L. 1999. 'Musical Collages of Sound: Technologizing the Band in the Rap Music Tradition.' In *Turn Up the Volume! A Celebration of African Music*, eds. Jacqueline Cogdell DjeDjeand Ernest Brown. Los Angeles: UCLA Fowler Museum of Cultural History, 210–19; 348.

Keyes, Cheryl L. 2002. *Rap Music and Street Consciousness*. Urbana: University of Illinois Press.

Makgekgenene, Ale-Esi. 2010. 'Khwezi Mphatlalatsane: The Articulate Graffiti Artist.' *Sunday Standard*. Online at: http://www.sundaystandard.info/article.php?NewsID=7314&GroupID=2Accessed (accessed 15 August 2013).

Manuel, Peter. 1993. *Cassette Culture: Popular Music and Technology in Northern India*. Chicago: University of Chicago Press.

Molabi, Galaletsang. 2013. 'Zeus Scoops Channel O Award for Most Gifted Male Video.' Online at: http://www.gazettebw.com (accessed 5 January 2014).

Mphatlalatsane, Khwezi. 2013. 'Eye on the Khoi-Fro.' *Elle South Africa*, October 2013. Online at: http://www.elle.co.za/eye-on-the-khoi-fro/ (accessed 31 August 2014).

Mphatlalatsane, Khwezi. 2013. Personal communication with the author. 18 October 2013.

Neate, Patrick. 2004. *Where You're At: Notes from the Frontline of a Hip-Hop Planet*. London: Riverhead.

Perkins, William Eric. 1996. 'Youth's Global Village: An Epilogue. In *Droppin' Science: Critical Essays on Rap Music and Hip-Hop Culture*, ed. William Eric Perkins. Philadelphia: Temple University Press, 258–73.

Rose, Tricia. 1994. *Black Noise: Rap Music and Black Culture in Contemporary America*. Middletown, CT: Wesleyan University Press.

Warner, Remi. 2011. 'Colouring the Cape Problem Space: A Hip-Hop Identity of Passions.' In *Native Tongue: An African Hip-Hop Reader*, ed. Paul Khalil Saucier. Cape Town: Africa World Press, 105–44.

Warner, Remi. 2007. *Battles Over Borders: Hip-Hop and the Politics and Poetics of Race and Place in the New South Africa*. Unpublished Ph.D. dissertation, York University.

Watkins, Lee. 1999. 'Tracking the Narrative: The Poetics of Identity in Rap Music and Hip-Hop Culture in Cape Town.' Unpublished Master's thesis, University of Natal, Durban.

Watkins, Lee. 2004. 'Rappin' the Cape: Style and Memory, Power in Community.' In *Music, Space, and Place: Popular Music and Cultural Identity*, eds. Sheila Whiteley, Andy Bennett and Stan Hawkins. Burlington, VT: Ashgate, 124–46.

Watkins, Lee. 2012. 'A Genre Coming of Age: Transformation, Difference, and Authenticity in the Rap Music and Hip-Hop Culture of South Africa.' In *Hip-Hop Africa: New African Music in a Globalizing World*, ed. Eric Charry. Bloomington: Indiana University Press, 57–78.

Williams, Quentin E., and Shroud, Christopher. 2010. 'Performing Rap Ciphas in Late-Modern Cape Town: Extreme Locality and Multilingual Citizenship.' *Afrika Focus* 23(2): 39–59.

Personal Communications

Balsher, David 'Draztik.' 2013. Personal communication with the author, 2 August 2013.

Basitsile, Sidney 'DJ Sid.' 2013. Personal communication with the author, 5 August 2013.

Discographical References

Apollo Diablo. 'Ikalanga Chedu.' Independent release. *2004*: Botswana.

Apollo Diablo. 'The City Owes Me.' Independent release. *2004*: Botswana.

Apollo Diablo. *The Meaning of Life*. Independent release. *2005*: Botswana.

Cashless Society. *African Raw Materials, Volume One*. Unreleased Records CDUR 1000. *2003*: South Africa.

Cashless Society. 'Blaze Tha Breaks.' *Farewell Fondle 'Em*. Definitive Jux DJX 19. *2001*: USA.

Cipher Divine. Label unknown. *N.d.*: Botswana.

DJ Sid Presents P-Side. Small House Records. *2000*: Botswana.

Jezzabelle. 'Verse in the Making.' *Lyrical Mix Xpressions: Life and Times of GC*. Label unknown. *2005*: Botswana.

K-Bos. *BosMan*. Eric Ramco Records. *2009*: Botswana.

K-Bos, Fosta Juliano, Goof, Kast, Magosi, Michelle, Mosako, Scar, and Third Mind. 'In Da Spot.' *Bos Man*. Eric Ramco Records. *2009*: Botswana.

K-Bos and Michelle. 'On Paper.' *Bos Man*. Eric Ramco Records. *2009*: Botswana.

K-Bos, Azziz, and Michelle. 'Ke Yone.' *Bos Man*. Eric Ramco Records. *2009*: Botswana.

Lyrical Mix Xpressions: Life and Times of GC. Label unknown. *2005*: Botswana.

Nomadic. 'Artistry n I.' *The Motswako Tender Mixtape*. Direct Drive Entertainment. *2009*: Botswana.

Nomadic and Young Nations. 'Fight Night.' *Imbizo Street Mixtapes, Vol. 1*. Unreleased Records. *2005*: South Africa.

Scar. *Happy Hour*. Breakthrough Records. *2007*: Botswana.

Scar. *Illegal Act*. Vivid Vision. *2002*: Botswana.

Scar. 'Metlholo,' 'Psycho,' and 'Khenya.' *Happy Hour*. Breakthrough Records. *2007*: Botswana.

Scar. 'My People.' *Illegal Act*. Vivid Vision. *2002*: Botswana.

Scar. *Open Bar*. Breakthrough Records. *2009*: Botswana.

Stagga. *Music for Your Movement*. XLT Records. *2007*: Botswana.

Stagga. *Staggalicious*. Creative Kingdom CKCD 007. *2003*: South Africa.

Third Mind. 'Dilokile' and 'Ngoma.' *Player for Life*. Ramco Records. *N.d.* : Botswana.

Third Mind. *The Second Coming*. Ramco Records. *2005*: Botswana.
Uncanny Cessman. 'Cipher Divine.' *N.d.*: Botswana.
Zeus. 'Dancing Shoes.' Label unknown. *2011*: Botswana.
Zeus. 'Dats Wassup.' *African Time*. Universal. *2013*: South Africa.
Zeus. *Freshly Baked*. D.I.Y Entertainment. *2008*: Botswana.
Zeus. *Honey I'm Home Mixtape*. Label unknown. *2012*: Botswana.
Zeus. 'MaAfrika.' *African Time*. Universal. *2013*: South Africa.
Zeus. *The Flipside*. D.I.Y Entertainment OCCD001. *2010*: Botswana.
Zeus. 'You Knows Me.' *Honey I'm Home Mixtape*. Label unknown. *2012*: Botswana.

Filmography

Breakin', dir. Joel Silberg. 1984. United States. 90 mins. Feature film.
Wild Style, dir. Charlie Ahearn. 1982. United States. 82 mins. Feature film.

ABIMBOLA KAI-LEWIS

Hip-Hop in Cameroon

In the late 1980s and, especially, the early 1990s rapping and to a lesser extent DJing were adapted to the Cameroonian context. The main characteristic that defines the emerging genre of Cameroonian rap music is rhymed lyrics that are rhythmically spoken or chanted. The languages, rhythms and instruments used are heterogeneous.

History

In the mid-1980s young Cameroonians, mainly in urban secondary schools in Yaoundé, were exposed to hip-hop from the USA through video, tapes, LPs and the newly established public television. They started to imitate dance steps seen on videos and form break dance and rap groups, mimicking US models and increasingly also models from France and elsewhere. While breakdancing was also established, it was particularly hip-hop music that was adapted to local conditions. Rappers in the early 1990s increasingly translated texts into languages spoken in Cameroon, freestyled and wrote their own lyrics. Starting in the late 1980s rap festivals, shows and competitions, mainly in the capital Yaoundé, increasingly offered opportunities for performances. This was the main exposure to audiences, as it took some time before the first rappers were able to record an album. In this period groups such as Bantou Pô-si and Negrissim and mainly male rappers such as Teek, Valsero and Tony Nobody started to rap. Rappers were initially considered deviant good-for-nothings, especially by adults, but toward the end of the 1990s Cameroonian rap music became increasingly popular among urban youth and was also beginning to be practiced in Douala and smaller regional cities. Exposure on radio and television, as well as in bars and public transport, helped rappers gain a popular audience, which, however, has remained limited to Cameroon and its diaspora with a few exceptions.

In the 1990s the first Cameroonian rap albums were produced and the first specialized studios were founded. However, Cameroonian rappers faced strong competition from other Cameroonian and foreign music genres, nearly absent royalties, different forms of piracy and the lack of organized distribution. The latter two issues made it very difficult to sell legal copies, even for the most successful artists. Among the main sources of income were concerts with corporate sponsorship, but most Cameroonian rappers were not able to make a living from their music.

Musical Characteristics

Cameroonian rap music is sometimes also called 'rap kamer' (alluding to the French term 'amer,' meaning bitter, and the old German colonial name of the country, *Kamerun*) or 'rap mboa' ('mboa' means homeland in the Douala language). The word is also used in Camfranglais (occasionally also called Franglais or Frananglais), a slang based on French, (Pidgin) English, Cameroonian and other languages. Besides Camfranglais, the languages used by Cameroonian rappers, with frequent code-switching, include English, French, Pidgin, Bassa, Douala, Ewondo, Bulu and, less frequently, Féfé and Bafia.

Cameroonian rap is a highly heterogeneous genre. While this is not a genre-defining characteristic, rappers are partly influenced by a cultural field of Cameroonian musical genres rooted in different ethnic groups. The most important is *makossa*, and others include *bikutsi, assiko, tchamassi, bend skin, mangabeu* and *essewe*. Rappers sometimes refer in their lyrics to these genres, produce remakes, use samples, rhythms and melodies inspired by these genres or make use of instruments such as talking drums, slit drums, *mvet* (a string instrument), flutes or the xylophone-like *balafons* and *mendzans*. However, there are also clearly cosmopolitan influences that include African popular music such as Congolese *rumba* and Nigerian highlife, in addition to different forms of European and American popular music such as rap, reggae and ragga.

Neither music labels nor the Cameroonian audience significantly distinguish sub-variants of Cameroonian rap music. As a rough etic distinction, however, there are two broad variants. In the first variant, instruments are recorded. The bass guitar is rather melodic and less central to the beat. The rapping is sometimes close to spoken words or accompanied by melodic singing and acoustic or electric guitars. Many songs by Bantou Pô-si, Koppo, Teek, S-Team and Lady B and earlier songs of Negrissim are examples of this variant, which was more common in the 2000s than after 2010. A second and more common variant of Cameroonian rap music is less based on instruments and is instead computer-produced. Both bass and percussion are used as beats over which rappers rhyme, accompanied by rather sparsely used melodic elements. Some recent productions of this variant are increasingly inspired by contemporary developments in US and European rap music and electronic music styles such as dubstep. Artists such as Krotal, in his newer productions, Jovi and Stanley Enow deliver more complex raps including Auto-tune effects over sophisticated rhythm and bass patterns. Thus, Cameroonian hip-hop continues to evolve.

Bibliography

Künzler, Daniel. 2012. 'Intergenerational Relations and Cameroonian Rap Music: "This Country Kills the Young People". In *L'Afrique des générations: Entre tensions et négociations* [The Africa of Generations. Between Tensions and Negotiations], ed. Muriel Gomez-Perez and Marie Nathalie LeBlanc. Paris: Karthala, 765–99.

Nitcheu, Gervais. 1999. 'Cameroun: Rap cherche messie' [Cameroon: Rap Is Looking for a Messiah]. *Africultures* 21: 32–5.

V.Thf, and Barlet, Olivier, 1999. 'Le rap au Cameroun. Entretien avec UMAR CVM' [Rap in Cameroon. Interview with UMAR CVM]. *Africultures* 15: 104–9.

Discography

Ak Sang Grave. *Du fonds de l'Afrique*. Mapane Records. *2006*: Cameroon.

Bantou Pô-si. *Bantou Pô-si 1 Album*. RTM Productions CD 001 RTM. *2001*: Cameroon.

Big B-Zy. *Le gringo au mic*. K-Mer Sound. *2005*: Cameroon.

Enow, Stanley. *Tumbuboss*. Sawaz Music/PEP/Motherland Empire. *2014*: Cameroon.

Jovi. *H.I.V*. New Bell Music. *2013*: Cameroon.

Kamèr Konnexion Abiali. Mapane Records SDRM N° 14 883. *2004*: Cameroon.

Koppo. *Si tu vois ma go*. BB Prod. *2004*: Cameroon.

Krotal. *La B.O. des nos life*. Ndabott'Prod. *2012*: Cameroon.

Lady B. *Ma colère*. K'entertainment/papisrecords. *2007*: Cameroon.

Manhitoo. *Indépendence now*. Living in Africa. *2011*: Cameroon.

Negrissim. *La Vallée des Rois*. Negsound Productions. *2009*: Cameroon.

Parol. *La zik pour la vie*. Mapane Records. *2007*: Cameroon.

Raid Tape Vol. 1. Red Zone. *2010*: Cameroon.

Sumanja. *Le Chiffre 3*. Zomloa Recordz. *2011*: Cameroon.

Teek. *Nangaboko*. Nangarecords CD NNG0801. *2008*: Cameroon.

Tony Nobody. *Love Peace Respect*. Blaxity. *2010*: Cameroon.

Valsero. *Répond et Réédition Collector Politikement Instable*. Betaa Scorpio Production. *2010*: Cameroon.

VBH. *Jeunes*. So Sounds Productions. *2010*: Cameroon.

Zomloa Familia. *Au Pays de Kush – La voix de la sagesse*. Zomloa Recordz. *2002*: Cameroon.

DANIEL KÜNZLER

Hip-Hop in Gabon

Since the end of the 1980s Gabon has emerged as one of the main areas of hip-hop creation in Francophone Africa. The country has hosted major media programs, festivals and shows including the annual festival Gabao Hip-Hop. Although Gabon is not known internationally for having created a specific local genre inspired by hip-hop – along the lines of *bongo flava* in Tanzania (Perullo 2005, 2007; Englert 2008) or hiplife in Ghana (Shipley 2013) – a significant number of rappers have adopted Gabonese rap as a nationally identified form. Contemporary Gabonese rap (called *gaboma* rap) is eclectic, drawing from several subgenres of rap and from other musical genres, but it is nevertheless composed of some traceable linguistic, musical and textual features such as the use of the local slang Toli Bangando and the description of ordinary life in the slums of Libreville, the country's capital and largest city, called *mapanes*.

1980s: The Arrival of Hip-Hop in Libreville and Democratic Transition

Rap music in Libreville represents the most famous and popular Gabonese expression of the diverse disciplines that constitute the hip-hop cultural movement. In this coastal city, the adoption of hip-hop culture and rap music has built on a long history, going back to the colonial era, of the appropriation of African-American and African-Caribbean musical genres, from the playing of *beguine* and *salsa* in the first dance clubs up to the huge success of soul, funk and disco in Libreville orchestras and nightclubs in the decades after independence (1960).

The end of the 1980s saw the arrival of new sounds and oral practices in the streets of Libreville, where young citizens were gathering in dance troupes and organizing dance competitions around the rhythms of Michael Jackson's hits and the diverse urban dances coming from the Republic of Congo. Part of young people's fondness for urban dances and aesthetics was inspired by the discovery of US and French rap music, which Gabonese youth first tried to copy and recite, before writing their own poetry.

The first rap groups that appeared during this period were deeply influenced by the sociopolitical upheavals that disrupted the country. On the one hand, the content of the first rappers' songs was clearly an expression of the rebellion taking place in Libreville's boroughs. For this generation, rap music was the first media of expression to criticize directly the malfunctions of the Gabonese government. On the other hand, the explosion of rap in Libreville's scenes and media would not have been possible without the development of new rights and freedom of expression that came about following the upheaval and the rebellion in 1990 against increasing poverty.

The mid-1980s had brought an unprecedented economic crisis that jeopardized the life conditions of Gabonese people and increased criticism of a political elite that had monopolized control and resources since independence. With the oil crash and the growth of unemployment, the urban zones saw the rise of deprived neighborhoods and slums called *mapanes* and *matitis*. Gabon had implemented austerity measures and suffered the social consequences of structural adjustment plans – specifically, loans from the IMF and the World Bank designed to reduce the economic crisis and which were contingent upon those economic adjustments. The regime of the Bongo family, which had held power since 1967, was considered responsible for this crisis and was condemned by opposition parties, syndicates and students. The latter criticized corruption, authoritarianism and the unequal ethnically based system of wealth distribution that the single party, the Parti Democratique Gabonais (PDG), and Omar Bongo imposed. A wave of opposition parties arose, and a movement of strikes was set up among workers and students. As this intensified among all the sectors of activity, it led to a general strike and to popular protests, pillaging and violent repression. The extent of the social crisis forced Omar Bongo and the PDG to recognize the fundamental rights of the citizens – such as freedom of movement and expression – and to organize a national conference in March 1990. This conference gathered together the single political party and the opposition groups and led to the re-establishment of multiparty rule in May 1991 and to a new constitution.

During this troubled period of social instability, the transformation of political life and the opening up of Gabonese society a new freedom of expression facilitated the appearance of the first rap groups in Libreville's boroughs. Motivated by a desire to express their quest for change and inspired by identification with expressions of revolt shared by young people around the world, several rap groups emerged, led by two progenitor groups in particular. The first, Si'ya Po'ossi XI, a quartet from the working-class city of Owendo, located south of Libreville, discovered hip-hop culture through a friend who brought cassettes and CDs back from a visit to France. The group's name refers to an English-language hip-hop concept (also used in other countries, such as Italy) the posse, that is, the hip-hop 'crew,' but in the Fang language it means 'the land to knock down.' Through their sound systems and performances on street corners they popularized rap music in Libreville's boroughs. After their victory at a competition organized by the French Cultural Center (CCF) they also released the first cassette of Gabonese rap in Libreville. With this cassette, *Seyougame,* and with their subsequent CDs, Si'ya Po'ossi X exerted a strong influence on the production of an underground rap scene, using their lyrics to describe the precarious daily life of ordinary citizens.

The second pioneer group of Gabonese rap originated in a very different social class. V2A4 (short for the French 'Vis tout et fort' or 'live everything and strongly'), comprised two students who went to study in France, where, in 1990, they recorded the first-ever CD of Gabonese rap music to be successfully broadcast in Libreville. The lyrics offer a crude depiction of the corruption to be found in Libreville and the necessity of political transformation, calling for an 'African revolution'. The group embodied a paradox, however, as one of its members was the son of the defense minister and the other belonged to a business family. The fact that these young people were directly descended from the country's elite led to discussions regarding authenticity and the class identity of rap music, and about what some rappers viewed as the 'intrinsic' distance that rap music should have between itself and the 'system'. Since the emergence of these two contrasting groups, hip-hop music in Gabon has continued to be marked by such class issues and by ambiguous relationships with authorities. The rap network has in effect reproduced the broader connection between politics and music in Libreville, demonstrated since the 1960s by the use of musicians and bands during campaigns (for the promotion of political personalities or parties), and by the ubiquitous presence of members of the presidential family and ministers of government in local music labels.

After these first two groups emerged, a local scene rapidly grew in Libreville, thanks to concert halls and media outlets that hosted rappers, such as the radio program *Les rappeurs de la côte ouest africaine* (Rappers from the West African coast). Broadcast in many French-speaking African countries from 1991 to 1993 by the international radio channel Africa n°1, this program offered rappers one of the first broadcasting vehicles for self-expression.

Meanwhile, competitions in rap music and hip-hop were organized in a concert hall named Cabaret des Artistes, contributing to the attraction of new devotees to this music. Nevertheless, the older generation considered the adoption of rap music and hip-hop aesthetics to be an imitation of Western culture and an expression of young 'outlaws' with no respect for social order, and state institutions did not support rap events and other hip-hop activities – that is, breakdancing, DJing, graffiti.

1990s: The Second Generation and the Growth of Rap Music Production

From the mid-1990s a second generation of rappers witnessed the real explosion of hip-hop in Gabon, thanks to support from some journalists, promoters, producers and studio owners who between them set up concert venues, home studios and radio programs devoted to rap music. This emerging rap scene progressively gained autonomy from other musical markets in Gabon, created its own audience and found a place in official media. The main rap groups from this period, including New School, Hay'oe, Movaizhaleine and Raaboon, were composed of young urbanite males from the middle and lower classes. Many rappers from these groups are still active in the rap scene in the late 2010s, and are famous both locally and abroad. Some have become state-employed workers or have entered politics.

Since the beginning of Gabonese rap in 1990, female rappers have been a rarity. Obliged to confront masculine control throughout the diverse steps of the production, along with a gendered logic of patronage that often contributes to the exclusion or the belittling of women, women in the rap scene are often reduced to the role of groupie, dancer and/or object of male consumption (Aterianus-Owanga 2013). Hip-hop lyrics often assert homophobic and conservative visions of gender identities. However, a few women, such as Naneth and Tina, have succeeded in making a name for themselves in hip-hop networks. Between the reproduction of accepted standards of womanliness and the transgression of social orders, they adapt diverse local and global models of womanliness in order to call some gender inequalities into question.

In the second generation of rap, lyrics are influenced by several contexts. One subset condemns corrupt

African governments and neo-colonial relationships that link Gabon and Africa with France – and more broadly with the former colonizing countries. This tendency, sometimes presented as a 'pro-black' message, corresponds with the denunciation of the French military presence and French directors in major companies. These rappers blame the racial inequalities and implicit social hierarchies that are still observed in ordinary life in Libreville, French education and public educational institutions in Gabon, or in the broad range of intimate relations involving material or money exchange. This criticism resonates more broadly with the description of the poverty of Libreville *mapanes* inhabitants and with the expression of anger against social inequality and government corruption. The depiction of Libreville's bars, parties and nightlife also plays an important part in rap texts.

Two songs remain core emblems of the 2000s golden era of rap music in Gabon for its fans. 'Aux choses du pays' (The Things of the Country), released by the duo Movaizhaleine in 2000, quotes a chorus from the Gabonese singer Pierre Claver Akendengué and samples traditional harp sounds. The lyrics describe in poetic terms all the popular ways of being, beliefs, social practices, and relationships that constitute these Gabonese 'things of the country'. This track is usually correlated with another hit from that same period, released by Raaboon, the other main group from the second generation, 'Vie de haine' (Life of Hate), that describes the dirty conditions of ordinary life, economic inequality and young people's desire for upward mobility and wealth. These two groups of the second generation, Raaboon and Movaizhaleine, are emblematic of the anchoring of rap music in the popular street life in Libreville, and they confronted each other during the most important event of this era: the 'Clash Raaboon / Movaizhaleine'. In hip-hop culture, the notion of clash refers to a duel between two performers and to a performance competition including dance, rap, DJing or verbal sparring. In this case, the clash was between the two main groups of the Libreville rap scene at the end of the 1990s, each of which performed its song in turn in front of the crowd. After three songs each, Raaboon emerged victorious by measurement of the length and volume of the applause. In 2000 this event, sponsored by large companies, gathered thousands of young people for the first time in rap history in Gabon, demonstrating the huge presence of rap as a phenomenon in urban life.

At the same time, rappers from the first and second generations have also rapidly asserted their desire to perpetuate the inheritance from previous musicians and from traditional practices of the elders, who considered the appropriation of rap music to be an illegitimate copy of Western culture, and 'gangster' music. On the contrary, many rappers considered hip-hop to be the product of a common black culture descended from oral African traditions. For them, the mission has thus rapidly become to 'Gabonize' and localize rap music, and also to be recognized by the rest of the hip-hop community and by international markets. This attempt to construct a typical Gabonese rap style was expressed in a desire to rap in local languages, sample traditional instruments, and express claims focused on the rights of African and black people, involving what some call *a posteriori* a 'pro-black movement.' With the advice of their elders from the group Si'ya Po'ossi X, who were the first to produce original beats, several artists learned the techniques of beatmaking and created their own instrumentals, sometimes with samples from previous recordings of Gabonese tradi-modern musicians or traditional instruments.

The multifaceted rap style that has arisen from this attempt to 'Gabonize' rap music is characterized by a deep heterogeneity and by all the tensions that surround the issue of national identity in Gabon (Enongoué 2001; Rossatanga-Rignault and Enongoué 2006; Tonda and Bernault 2009). Still, it is possible to identify several main subgenres with some common features. The first one, which can be called 'popular *gaboma* rap music,' is anchored in the way of talking and daily life in Libreville's slums; while the second one comprises proponents of a tradi-rap genre who use symbols and instruments of religious and oral traditions and call for a return to roots.

Gaboma's Toli Bangando and Body Language

One important element of localization for Gabonese rappers lies in the use of Toli Bangando, a slang born in Libreville's slums and *mapanes* and still deeply connected to this territory. Used mainly by young men, it mixes English, French, vernacular Gabonese words and other African languages present in Libreville, similar to the use of Camfranglais in Cameroon (Kiessling 2005) and Nouchi in Ivory Coast (Schumann 2009). In this generational urban slang, *toli* means talking, and *bangando* refers to the young boys who hang out on the streets. The word *gaboma* belongs to this urban slang and is used by the young people to express their 'alternative nationalism' (Kiwan 2014).

This linguistic creation attests to the sociolinguistic situation in urban Gabon, where no common language is shared by the different ethnic groups of the population. Contrary to Senegal or Congo, where African national languages are shared across the population, French is the only vehicular language commonly used by all the population in Libreville and in many Gabonese cities (Auzanneau 2001; Moussounda Ibouanga 2008). In comparison with Senegalese rappers, who have built a part of their style on their ability to rap both in Wolof and in French, Gabonese rappers often express frustration and a feeling of acculturation because they do not have their own language and feel doomed to use the linguistic legacy of the former colonizer. In reaction to this situation, Toli Bangando allows them to distinguish themselves from the French, and to create a generational marker; at the same time, contrary to vernacular languages, it protects them from ethnic or 'tribalist' presumptions (Bernault 2003) that can sometimes appear when rappers intend to rap in their mother tongue (Aterianus-Owanga 2013). This idea is often connected to the trope of the 'rapper-as-*griot*' asserted by different African and African-American rappers (Tang 2012; Sajnani 2013; Aterianus-Owanga 2015).

Since 2000 Toli Bangando has had a strong presence in rap songs, and rap songs themselves have influenced the creation of new words and expressions in Toli Bangando. The main representatives of Toli Bangando are the rappers of the third generation that has appeared since 2000, such as F.A.N.G., the duo 241 or more recently the duo Tris and NG Bling. The slammer Le Wise (in Toli Bangando, 'wise' means clever or clear-sighted), who won the Slam Cup in Libreville in 2010, became so famous with his Bangando description of Gabonese daily life that he was hired by President Ali Bongo to record videos and slam tracks recounting the success of the president's politics of 'emergence' (see, for example, Le Wise's video 'Pog official,' promoting the economic success of the city Port-Gentil). Slam is a kind of urban poetry competition invented in the United States in the 1980s; in Gabon, it has been spread by rappers and rap producers and is deeply connected to hip-hop culture and rap music. Famous rappers of the second generation are also known for their use of Toli Bangando. For example, the group Movaizhaleine released a track presented as a dictionary of Toli Bangando ('Le bilangom,' 2008).

In addition to this linguistic aspect, *gaboma* rap music also marks its anchoring in Libreville's popular life through particular dance moves. Invented in bars and nightclubs in Libreville or in hip-hop dance troupes, these dance moves associated with hip-hop music in Gabon play an important part in the animation of hip-hop shows and in audience appreciation of rap music videos. Since 2009 Gabonese towns have seen the appearance of several ephemeral urban dances linked to hip-hop rhythms that have nearly become national urban dances, similar to what *coupé décalé* has been for Ivory Coast, *ndombolo* for contemporary Congo or *azonto* for Ghana. *Ntcham*, *ndem* and *jazzé* are the main urban dances that have recently created enthusiasm among young Gabonese dancers and, consequently, rappers; most of them are a mix of pop dance and *bôlo*, a preexisting urban Gabonese solo dance performed both on the floor and standing up, characterized by little steps, movements of the bust and swaying hips. A distinctive feature of these dances is the movement of the arms around the body, which often symbolizes the demonstration of elegance, dress code and the boasting of the dancer. For rappers, the dance dimension of their music and their ability to 'divert' people in bars and nightclubs have become main criteria, transforming partly local rap music into an 'entertaining music,' corresponding to marketing and political factors.

Inventing Religious and Oral Traditions in Tradi-Rap Music

Another part of the creation of rap in Gabon has oriented music around a 'back to roots' identity project that affirms Gabonese traditions, leading to the incorporation of local instruments, and sometimes to the showcasing of ritual practices on stage. Some artists belonging to the Fang ethnic group, the demographic majority in Gabon, have, for example, employed *Mvet*, which is the name of a musical instrument and also of a mythic epic (often also written *mvett*) that relates the origins of the world and the Fang people. *Mvet* poetry is traditionally sung in a guardhouse by initiated men (called *mbome mvet*) accompanied by the four-stringed harp-zither called *mvet* (Zame Avezo'o 2013). The epic *Mvet* has been appropriated by many artists in order to transform it from the oral to a written form, as in *The Mvett* written by Tsira Ndong Ndoutoume (1970, 1983, 1993). Since the beginning of rap practice in Gabon, *Mvet* poetry performance has constituted a core domain of inspiration for rappers from the Fang ethnic group, sampled to create typical instrumentals and beats. In 2010 Okoss, the grandson of the famous writer and *mbome mvet* Tsira Ndong Ndoutoume, recorded a rap album with his group 241 that reproduces oral recordings of his grandfather's *Mvet* and samples extracts of his texts.

Several artists produce rap songs and music videos in which they stage these traditional instruments or dress codes, and others have strived to create rap adaptations especially anchored in local provinces or ethnic groups, such as 'rap ikoku.' *Ikoku* is a traditional festivity dance celebrating fertility from the Punu ethnic group in South Gabon. A southern rap group of the early 2000s named Communauté Black popularized a rap genre based on the *ikoku* rhythm with great success in their province and among national audiences.

However, one group is especially known as the progenitor and most successful example of this kind of 'tradi-rap': Movaizhaleine. This duo unites a rapper and beatmaker from the north of Gabon with a rapper and singer from the south of Gabon who emerged in the 1990s. It has rapidly become very famous for the political engagement of its texts, its inspired depiction of symbolic, political and social life in Gabon, and its musical style, mixing electronic hip-hop beats and reggae rhythms and employing traditional instruments such as the *mvet* or the harp used in traditional religious rituals, the most famous of which is the *bwiti*. The *bwiti* is a male initiation society that developed from rituals of ancestor worship and originated in the south of Gabon but spread to a large western area of the country with many variations and syncretism with Christianity. Despite the fact that missionaries fought and demonized the *bwiti* and other traditional initiation societies during colonization, since independence the *bwiti* has become one of the main elements of the construction of a national heritage and an authentic precolonial culture (Mary 2005; Bonhomme 2007).

The two performers who make up Movaizhaleine are both initiated members of this secret society and their singular rap style is known for the core place they dedicate to the *bwiti* and its symbols. They employ *bwiti* initiation as a metaphor for their quest for knowledge, inviting their audience and their fans to 'know themselves' and to return to traditional ways of talking, behaving, thinking and playing music. For example, the harp *ngombi* plays an important part in their staging and in the ideology that they intend to promote; this instrument is placed at the center of the stage during several moments of their scenes, and it is presented as a feminine character transmitting her message through the vehicle of the rapper's voice. This staging is then inspired by the traditional harp symbolism that is considered to be the voice of a female mythical ancestor (Bonhomme 2014) in the *bwiti* ritual and central in the rituals of several other initiation societies (Sallée 1978, 1985). In several songs, members of Movaizhaleine present themselves as members of the 'harp community,' and they are frequently presented locally as authors of a so-called 'rap *bwiti*.' Thanks to this style, they were the most famous Gabonese rap group in African festivals and rap music networks in the first decade of the twenty-first century, touring in several other African countries and working with peers including Didier Awadi and Daara J., who are also involved in the promotion of a 'conscious' hip-hop with a pan-African message. Several contemporary rappers are continuing with this staging of *bwiti* on the rap scene.

Twenty-First-Century Transformations of Rap Music in Gabon

Around the turn of the millennium, the tremendous growth of enthusiasm for hip-hop drove some wealthy individuals, promoters and sponsors to invest in new means of production in this burgeoning musical market. Some big labels were created at the beginning of the 2000s, under the oversight of individuals close to the presidential family (such as AFJ, EBEN, Promedia and, later, Mayena Production). The new structures that have supported the coming of the third generation of rappers have thus promoted a close relationship with authorities. The arrival of private producers and funding sources, linked to the broader emergence of big markets for hip-hop music in African countries (mainly in Nigeria, Ghana and South Africa), has allowed the construction of a stronger system of production of rap and R&B, the upgrading of sound and video productions, and the growth of entrepreneurship among rappers and hip-hop artists (beatmakers, dancers, DJs).

Furthermore, since the election of Ali Bongo in 2009, rap networks and systems of production have gone through many transformations. During the political shift that followed after the death of Omar Bongo in June 2009 and his 42 years in power, rappers played an important part and were the main artists involved in the campaign for the presidential elections. Several rappers from the group Hay'oe, Tina and other famous rappers produced a song that became very popular among young people and that expressed their claims to the future president. Initially apolitical and directed toward a hypothetical candidate in the presidential elections, this song entitled 'La parole aux jeunes' [Young People May Now Speak] was used in favor of the candidate Ali Bongo as soon as the official campaign started, and these rappers officially asserted their support of him. They participated in Bongo's campaign meetings all over the country, and they even invited him on stage to do a rap performance during a huge rap show in Libreville in August 2013. This collaboration and this performance by Ali Bongo helped him gain a new image, positioning him close to young people's interests and musical tastes (Aterianus 2011). Consequently, Bongo's relationship with the hip-hop community has allowed him to modernize the image of the state and to assert that his election could be synonymous with a change, although his candidacy was criticized by opponents and by some citizens as a perpetuation of a dynastic system.

After Bongo's election, one rapper (Massassi) and a rap producer (Joe Da Crazy Boy), both of whom were engaged in the campaign, were promoted to the position of project executives (*chargés de mission*) in the government. Also, new radio stations and recording studios were created and have provided new funding for hip-hop activities. International hip-hop celebrities are often invited to Libreville for big shows, whose costs lead to some criticism among underground artists. Still in deep connection with the political elites, some rappers have also been increasingly involved in helping to promote the president's program or to perform as music entertainers. While underground rap activities tend to decrease and informal censorship leads to the erasure of some of the direct criticism expressed against the source of the country's social and political crises, the huge success of popular R&B from the United States and Nigeria has driven a growth in 'mainstream' and commercial music dealing with gender issues, fun, quests for material wealth and symbols of success or fame. Nevertheless, in the diaspora, through social networks or informal labels and systems of production, some rappers and slammers maintain a critical stance concerning Gabonese society and governance. In 2016, on the edge of the presidential elections, several rappers (such as Keurtyce E., Movaizhaleine, Buung Pinz, or Saïk1ri with his track 'Mister Zero') actively denounced in rap songs and public marches the authoritarianism of Ali Bongo's regime and his candidacy for a second presidential mandate.

Whether in one or the other part of this multifaceted and sometimes conflicted movement, different groups and individuals use rap music as a vehicle to debate their diverging conceptions of national identity, political commitment and society. Considered renegade music in the 1990s, in the late 2010s rap and hip-hop music are presently recognized as the musical expression of a generation that appeared with the democratic transition and have grown up with the sociopolitical transformations consecutive with the privatization of the state and the structural adjustment plans. Hip-hop has become, for members of this generation, a medium to connect themselves to the elders and to local traditions, to invent new national identifications, to create new musical careers or to access local celebrity, and to enter into a dialog with broader black cosmopolitanism and pan-African claims in the Black Atlantic.

Bibliography

Aterianus, Alice. 2011. 'Rap et démocratie dans le Gabon contemporain' [Rap and Democracy in Contemporary Gabon]. *Émulations. Revue des jeunes chercheurs en sciences sociales* [Emulation. Journal of Young Scholars in Social Sciences] 9.

Online at: http://www.revue-emulations.net/archives/n9/aterianus (accessed 11 January 2017).

Aterianus-Owanga, Alice. 2013. *Pratiques musicales, pouvoir et catégories identitaires: Anthropologie du rap gaboma* [Musical Practices, Power and Identity Categories: Anthropology of *Gaboma* Rap Music]. Unpublished Ph.D. dissertation, Université Lyon 2, France.

Aterianus-Owanga, Alice. 2015. '"Orality Is My Reality": The Identity Stakes of the 'Oral' Creation in Libreville Hip-Hop Practices.' *Journal of African Cultural Studies* 27(2): 146–58.

Aterianus-Owanga, Alice. 2017. '"Le rap, ça vient d'ici!" Musiques, pouvoir et identités dans le Gabon contemporain.' (Rap Comes From Here! Music, Power and Identity in Contemporary Gabon). Paris: Editions de la MSH.

Auzanneau, Michelle. 2001. 'Le rap, expression de dynamiques urbaines plurilingues. Le cas de Libreville' [Rap, An Expression of Dynamic Urban Multilingualism. The Case of Libreville]. *Plurilinguismes* 18: 11–47.

Auzanneau, Michelle. 2005. 'Rap in Libreville, Gabon: An Urban Sociolinguistic Space.' In *Black, Blanc, Beur: Rap Music and Hip-Hop Culture in the Francophone World*, ed. Alain-Philippe Durand. Lanham, MD: Scarecrow Press, 106–23.

Bernault, Florence. 2003. 'Dévoreurs de la nation: Les migrations fang au Gabon' [Devourers of the Nation: Fang Migrations in Gabon]. In *Être étranger et migrant en Afrique au XXe siècle* [Being a Foreigner and Migrant in Africa During the Twentieth Century], eds. Catherine Coquery-Vidrovitch and Issiaka Mandé. Paris: L'Harmattan, 169–87.

Bernault Florence, Tonda Joseph. 2009. 'Le Gabon: Une dystopie tropicale' [Gabon: A Tropical Dystopia]. *Politique africaine* 115(3): 7–26.

Bonhomme, Julien. 2007. 'Anthropologue et/ou initié' [Anthropologist and/or Initiate]. *Journal des anthropologues* 110–11: 207–26.

Bonhomme, Julien. 2014. 'La voix du mongongo ou comment faire parler un arc musical' [The Voice of the Mongongo or How to Make a Musical Arch Speak], in *L'Image rituelle* [Ritual Image]. *Cahiers d'anthropologie sociale* 10, eds. Carlos Fausto and Carlo Severi. Paris: L'Herne, 93–111.

Englert, Birgit. 2008. 'Ambiguous Relationships: Youth, Popular Music and Politics in Contemporary Tanzania.' *Wiener Zeitschrift Fur Kritische Afrikastudien* 14(8): 71–96. Online at: https://uscholar.univie.ac.at/get/o:245519.pdf (accessed 11 January 2017).

Enongoué, Flavien. 2001. 'La Gabonité: Un noeud vide?' [Gabonity: An Empty Nub?]. Groupes ICES, *Le Gabon. Enjeux et perspectives* [Gabon. Stakes and Perspectives]. Corbeil Essonne: Editions ICES, 39–61.

Kiessling, Roland. 2005. '"Bak Mwa Me Do" – Camfranglais in Cameroon.' *Lingua Posnaniensis, The Journal of Poznan Society for the Advancement of the Arts and Sciences and Adam Mickiewicz University, Institute of Linguistics* 47: 87–107.

Kiwan, Nadia. 2014. 'Moroccan Multiplicities. Performing Transnationalism and Alternative Nationalism in the Contemporary Urban Music Scene.' *Cahiers d'études africaines* 216(4): 975–97.

Mary, André. 2005. 'Le Bwiti à l'heure du village global' [The *Bwiti* in the Time of the Global Village]. *Rupture-solidarité 6: Le Gabon malgré lui* [Rupture-solidarity 6: Gabon Despite Itself]: 83–103.

Moussounda Ibouanga, Firmin. 2008. 'Le *toli bangando*: La variabilité de réalisation à libreville et ses conséquences sur le français (du Gabon)' [Toli Bangando. Variability of Realisation in Libreville and Its Consequences for the French (in Gabon)]. *Revue gabonaise des sciences du langage* 4: 135–52.

Ndong Ndoutoume, Tsira. 1970. *Le Mvett I*. Paris: Présence africaine.

Ndong Ndoutoume, Tsira. 1983. *Le Mvett: Epopée Fang* [The *Mvett*: A Fang Epic]. Paris: Présence africaine.

Ndong Ndoutoume, Tsira. 1993. *Le Mvett: L'homme, la mort et l'immortalité* [The *Mvett*: Man, Death and Immortality]. Paris: L'Harmattan.

Perullo, Alex. 2005. 'Hooligans and Heroes: Youth Identity and Hip-Hop in Dar Es Salaam, Tanzania.' *Africa Today*, 75–101.

Perullo, Alex. 2007. '"Here's a Little Something Local": An Early History of Hip Hop in Dar Es Salaam, Tanzania, 1984–1997.' In *Dar Es Salaam: The History of an Emerging East African Metropolis*, eds. Andrew Burton, James Brennan and Yusuf Lawi. London: British Institute and Dar es Salaam: Mkuki wa Nyota, 250–72.

Rossatanga-Rignault, Guy, and Enongoué, Flavien. 2006. *L'Afrique existe-t-elle? A propos d'un malentendu persistant sur l'identité* [Does Africa Exist? Concerning a Persistent Misunderstanding about Identity]. Paris: Dianoïa.

Sajnani, Damon. 2013. 'Troubling the Trope of "Rapper as Modern Griot."' *The Journal of Pan African Studies* 6(3): 156–80.

Sallée, Pierre. 1978. *Deux études sur la musique du Gabon* [Two Studies on Music in Gabon]. Travaux et documents de l'ORSTOM 85. Paris: O.R.S.T.O.M.

Sallée, Pierre. 1985. *L'arc et la harpe: Contribution à l'histoire de la musique du Gabon* [The Bow and the Harp: Contribution to the History of Music in Gabon]. Unpublished Ph.D. dissertation, Université Paris X, France.

Schumann, Anne. 2009. 'Popular Music and Political Change in Côte d'Ivoire: The Divergent Dynamics of Zouglou and Reggae.' *Journal of African Media Studies* 1(1): 117–33.

Shipley, Jesse Weaver. 2013. *Living the Hiplife: Celebrity and Entrepreneurship in Ghanaian Popular Music*. Durham, NC: Duke University Press.

Tang, Patricia. 2012. 'The Rapper as Modern Griot: Reclaiming Ancient Traditions.' In *Hip Hop Africa: New African Music in a Globalizing World*, ed. Eric Charry, Bloomington: Indiana University Press, 79–91.

Zame Avezo'o, Léa. 2013. 'Le mvet: Origine, contextes et acteurs de la résistance au Gabon' [The *Mvett*: Origins, Contexts and Actors of Resistance in Gabon]. Communication presented for the congress *De la résistance dans les Arts de la parole* [Resistance in Oral Arts]. March 2013, Beni Mellal (Morocco).

Discographical References

'La parole aux jeunes.' AJF Productions. *2009*: Gabon.

Movaizhaleine. 'Aux choses du pays.' Zorbam Produxions. *2000*: Gabon.

Movaizhaleine. 'Le Bilangom.' *On détient la harpe sacrée Tome 2*. Zorbam Produxions. *2008*: Gabon.

Raaboon. 'Vie de haine.' Dangher Productions. *1999*: Gabon.

Saïk1ry. 'Mister Zero.' Self-produced. *2016*: Gabon.

Siy'a Po'ossi X. *Seyougame*. Jah observer / CCF St-Ex. *1990*: Gabon.

V2A4. 'African Revolution.' (45 rpm record.) Self-produced. *1990*: France.

Discography

Bantu Mix (compilation). *Esse-pou-are*. Kage Pro. *1998*: Gabon.

Bantu rap. *Underground LBV I*. Kage Pro. *2000*: Gabon.

Bantu rap. *Underground LBV II*, Kage Pro. *2004*: Gabon.

Ba'Ponga. *L'animal*. Eben Entertainment. *2005*: Gabon.

Ba'Ponga. *Karnivor*. Eben Entertainment. *2008*: Gabon.

F.A.N.G. *Mon dernier bling*. Engong Inc. *2008*: Gabon.

Movaizhaleine. *On détient la harpe sacrée Tome 1*. Zorbam Produxions. *2005*: Gabon.

Movaizhaleine. *On détient la harpe sacrée Tome 2*. Zorbam Produxions. *2008*: Gabon.

241, Amour, unité. Nofia Sound. *2008*: Gabon.

YouTube

Le Wise. 'Pog official.' Online at: https://www.youtube.com/watch?v=d2rzQ4GhAP0.

ALICE ATERIANUS-OWANGA

Hip-Hop in Kenya

In Kenya, hip-hop is the one of the most popular musics among urban youth. In many contexts, hip-hop comprises the following elements: MCing (rapping or chanting rhyming lyrics that are accompanied by a strong rhythm), beatboxing (the art of producing drum beats, rhythm and musical sounds using one's mouth, lips, tongue and voice), DJing, breakdancing and graffiti art. In Kenya, however, the most widespread forms of hip-hop involve rapping and DJing, with only a few manifestations of graffiti art and breakdancing that happen in controlled spaces (such as sponsored hip-hop events in Nairobi at which artists are provided with canvases). Since a majority of artists depend on computer-generated beats for their music, there is no culture of beatboxing. Kenyan hip-hop themes focus on the experiences of the artists and their immediate locale/context. The music is composed primarily in Sheng (a mixture of Swahili and English), appeals mostly to younger audiences (under 35 years of age) and seeks to highlight the experiences of the socially, politically and economically marginalized located in specific neighborhoods called *Mtaa* (Swahili for street).

Historical Development

The emergence and expansion of hip-hop in Kenya in the late 1980s and early 1990s coincided with a number of socioeconomic and political factors including neoliberal economic processes, expanded access to computer technology, the retreat of the state from controlling and distributing social services, and increased access to different forms of Western popular cultural products for many youth. Neoliberal economic structures and philosophies that generally promoted ideas about the primacy of markets in shaping social, political and economic policies and practices in Kenya in the 1980s and 1990s had cultural repercussions in the form of encouraging transactional thinking and individual autonomy, greatly affecting music production and consumption. Previously, music-making involved groups of band members who had to own or rent musical instruments, have access to spaces for their practice, and then find a studio to record the music and release it in a form that could then be used at a radio station or other outlet. Much of the time, these music groups performed at clubs to a live audience or at special events such as agricultural shows, weddings and political rallies. There were also limited outlets for music when there was only one state-owned and controlled radio station which restricted music's content. With the availability of electronic devices and global communication channels such as computer-generated sounds, individuals, especially young people in urban areas, were now able to compose, produce and record music with ease, bypassing all the earlier mechanisms of music-making. Along with these changes came multiparty democracy that eased the tight grip the state had on media and political expression. These new opportunities for music performance and production were no longer easily controlled by the state and as a result soon aligned with young people's yearning for the right to self-expression that they had previously been denied under past authoritarian governments and stifled market systems. Young people quickly found themselves situated in the public arena as active participants in political and social discourse that was mediated through hip-hop music.

A wave of multiple commercial radio and television stations replaced the monopoly of state-owned and state-controlled radio and television stations that had been in place since independence in 1963 through the late 1980s. This led to expanded programming that went beyond the prior focus on the state apparatus and leadership. Prior to these changes musicians had only two viable options: sing songs of praise for the government of the day or completely avoid any lyrics with messages that criticized sociopolitical realities. As the new stations needed a new customer base in order to draw lucrative advertisements, they were forced to diversify their products, bringing in local programs as well as international ones that would interest their prospective clientele. Access to recording and studio equipment within this time period, as entrepreneurs were able to purchase the equipment without the prior government restrictions, also led to the local production of high-quality music that was available for airplay in the now-growing number of private radio and television stations. For a fee, a young and upcoming artist could walk into a recording studio and come out with a high-quality compact disc of his or her debut single that could be played on one of the newly instituted FM radio stations. With the availability of numerous musical tunes on computer software such as Fruit Loops and the possibility of selling music through the Internet, a new space emerged for young people to advance themselves through music and produce high-quality local recordings. Another important avenue through which hip-hop developed was rap and dance competitions held in various venues in Nairobi, including the New Florida Nightclub (popularly known as F1), Florida 2000 Discotheque (popularly known as F2), Carnivore Restaurant and Nairobi Cinema. These competitions, termed National Star Search competitions, were open to all Kenyans and provided a number of the now-popular musicians and groups with opportunities to showcase their talent.

Jimmy Gathu was one of the earliest to engage hip-hop as a musical genre when he released his hit song 'Look, Think, Stay Alive' in 1991 as a public service message urging Kenyan drivers to pay keen attention to road safety. The video for the song was the first public broadcast of a hip-hop recording in Kenya. It depicts a scene in a Matatu (public commuter omnibus) nicknamed 'Fair Ride' that operated within the city of Nairobi. Gathu's television shows on Kenya Television Network (KTN) – the first non-state-controlled television station in Kenya – aired every weekday. Gathu popularized rap and hip-hop music in Kenya through his weekly show program known as *Rap 'Em*, which featured different styles of rap and hip-hop music and musicians from around the world. The show, watched by many young people living in Nairobi where the television signal could be received, was very popular. A number of pioneer Kenyan hip-hop artists such as Kama of Kalamashaka cite the program as their source of inspiration and modeling for their own music.

Many Kenyan music groups composing and performing songs in the early 1990s generally tended to copy popular US artists and sang most of their songs in English. In 1995 this trend changed when an artist calling himself MC Mikey rapped in a mix of English and Swahili (commonly known as Sheng) during the National Star Search Competition at the Carnivore Restaurant in Nairobi, in which he emerged the overall winner. His music style, which he termed 'Kiswa-Centric,' ushered in a local flavor of hip-hop in Kenya. Then in 1997 Hardstone (Harrison Ngunjiri) released the first full album comprising R&B, hip-hop and ragga music (*Nuting But De Stone*), and paved the way for a local style of music that combined some traditional songs with sampled melodies of popular American tunes. Hardstone's hit song titled 'Uhiki' (Wedding) exemplified this style, offering a blend of Kikuyu folk music, synthesized voices, and the beat of Marvin Gaye's popular song 'Sexual Healing.' In the same year, the hip-hop trio Kalamashaka (Roba, Kama and John) introduced rap music in Kenya with their hit song 'Tafsiri hii' (Translate This), and with it (re)presented the social realities of youth in low-income neighborhoods in Nairobi. Other hip-hop artists that had a similar influence were K-South (comprising Jerry Manzekele a.k.a. Dobeez and Tim Kimani a.k.a. Bamboo) and Poxi Presha (Prechard Pouka Olang), with the latter's song 'Dhako' displaying a mix of English and Dholuo in the lyrics.

The group Kalamashaka, which broke into the Kenyan hip-hop scene in 1995, comprised three artists who referred to themselves as 3D Crew before changing to Kalamashaka in 1996. Not only did members of the group come from low-income backgrounds, they also sang about social problems such as unemployment, high rates of crime, poor living conditions, neocolonialism and police brutality, with lyrics exclusively in Sheng. This use of a truly localized medium of communication with lyrics that expressed the hard realities of ghetto life created a new sense of identity for Kenyan hip-hop musicians. Previously, these musicians had lived in a context dominated by European and American music with lyrics in English and content that often had no direct relevance to the lives they led under an authoritarian government with restricted media access. Kalamashaka's song 'Tafsiri Hii,' an example of this newly relevant style, captures the lived realities of youth in poor social conditions. The lyrics affirm that, while life is hard in Dandora (a low-income residential area where the group lived), its residents still keep their heads up. They ask to be given a chance to represent themselves in Kiswahili, a language that symbolizes their own means of communication, and they talk about their aspirations to leave the ghetto where they cannot walk freely without being harassed by the police.

Mention of places where artists live represents a popular trend among hip-hop musicians in Kenya, as in other parts of the world, as a mark of identity. Dandora, where the members of Kalamashaka live, symbolically represents other low-income residential areas in Nairobi. Before the rapid expansion of the city of Nairobi, Dandora was the designated dumping site for the city's refuse. Hip-hop artists such as Octopizzo (Henry Ochieng) and K-South spotlight Kibera and Kariobangi South residential areas respectively.

In 2002 hip-hop duo Gidi Gidi Maji Maji elevated hip-hop to a larger national platform with their song 'Who Can Bwogo Me?' (i.e., 'Who Can Defeat Me?') from the album *Unbwogable* (Undefeatable). The song, which itself became known as 'Unbwogable,' was quickly appropriated by the 2002 Kenyan political bloc known as the National Rainbow Coalition (NARC) that ousted Daniel Moi's 24-year rule. Moi's regime completely limited any political freedom or opposition until December 1991, when Section 2A of the Kenyan constitution was repealed to allow for multiparty politics. After two general elections that ended in Moi's reelection, plagued by massive rigging and voter suppression, the main political parties finally joined hands to form the Rainbow Coalition as a strategy to defeat the ruling party. Moi, who had reached his term limit and was no longer eligible for reelection, handpicked Uhuru Kenyatta to run under the Kenya African National Union (KANU) party ticket, but Mwai Kibaki, representing the Rainbow Coalition, won the election. The song by Gidi Gidi Maji Maji became popular during political campaigns that pitted KANU against NARC. It almost became a national anthem for opposition politics in Kenya as it was sung and performed by politicians aligned with NARC while merchandise (T-shirts, hats and posters) bearing the title 'Unbwogable' was sold in many parts of the country in 2002. (The political mobilization of the 'Unbwogable' craze is discussed in a documentary on hip-hop in Kenya titled *Hip-Hop Colony*, in which the members of Gidi Gidi Maji Maji perform the song live at a political rally and ask the NARC team to sing along.)

Over the years local styles of hip-hop have emerged, including *genge* and *kapuka*, as artists sought a specific style that reflected their unique Kenyan urban music, comparable to *bongo flava* in Tanzania and *Luga flow* in Uganda. *Genge* is a style that incorporates hip-hop, dancehall and local musical genres with the artist rapping in a conversational style in Sheng. *Kapuka* is characterized by its repeated beats and lyrics meant to enhance a song's appeal for dancing. The name is derived from the constant 'kapu-kapu-kapu' beat. Artists Nonini (Hubert Nakitare) and Jua Cali (Paul Julius Nunda) are mostly associated with *genge* while Ogopa DJs are associated with *kapuka*. There are also artists whose hip-hop music focuses primarily on the artist's image and style of clothing, and whose lyrics are about dancing and having fun. Hip-hop artist Prezzo (Jackson Ngechu Makini), for instance, represents this group of artists, having built his public image around pomp and flare, and is seen by some as a mere entertainer with no 'real' qualities of a hip-hop artist. For example, in 2005 he rented a helicopter at Wilson Airport to drop him off at the Carnivore grounds (a distance of 100 meters) to attend the local Chaguo la Teenies (choice of teenagers) music awards (CHAT).

These competing styles of Kenyan hip-hop have led to opposing perceptions of 'real' or 'underground' hip-hop versus *genge* and *kapuka,* with the latter forms not seen as serious hip-hop music. When it comes to 'real' or 'underground' hip-hop, such names as Kalamashaka, Poxi Presha, K-South, Juliani, Nazizi, Ukoo Flani, Ukoo Flani Mau Mau, Mwafrika, Muki Garang, Mashifta, Wenyeji and others, are often mentioned. These are artists whose music focuses on social, economic and political issues affecting youth and often emphasizes the message rather than the danceable beat. These categorizations and definitions are mostly articulated by the artists themselves, seeing their counterparts in *genge* and *kapuka* as mere entertainers and not hip-hop artists.

With the advent of commercial radio stations such as Capital FM (98.4) and Easy FM (96.3) broadcasting from the center of Nairobi in the mid-1990s and community FM stations such as Ghetto Radio (89.5 FM) and Koch FM (99.9 FM) that broadcast from Nairobi's low-income residential areas in late 2007, many hip-hop artists have wider airplay for their music. Hip-hop programs on FM radio include a show titled *Wakilisha* (Represent), hosted by Kalamashaka and DJ Mosse the Darkchild, that aired on Nation FM (later called Easy FM) every Friday. Another hip-hop show titled *The Joint*, hosted by hip-hop artist Mwafrika on Y FM (later called Hot96 FM), was well received before it was discontinued and Mwafrika moved to Ghetto Radio. There are also various freestyle competitions where upcoming artists can showcase their talent, including G Pange Hip-hop Challenge, Hip-hop Halisi Freestyle Challenge, Usanii Kona Hip-hop Challenge, and WAPI (hosted by Sarakasi Trust) in Nairobi. Many hip-hop artists and groups have endured over the years while others have dwindled and disappeared amid stiff competition from other genres as well as new entrants in the scene. Hip-hop in Kenya continues to grow in many areas of the country but Nairobi continues to be where the bulk of such growth occurs. Some artists, such as Juliani, Octopizzo, Jua Cali, Mwafrika, Kitu Sewer, Mc Kah, Nazizi, Shikow FemiOne and Wenyeji, among many others, continue to produce and perform hip-hop that represents all styles of the genre in Kenya. They also represent different neighborhoods and subgenres, with Juliani representing Dandora, Octopizzo representing Kibera and Jua Cali representing Genge.

Conclusion

Given the expansion of new media and access to recording equipment and studios, hip-hop in Kenya will almost certainly continue to be an important form of sociocultural expression. In the late 2010s young people who earlier had no major opportunities to enter into public space and express their lived experiences are now using hip-hop as an avenue through which to critique and present youth-related socioeconomic and political issues. Expansion of FM radio broadcasting, and the acceptance of local hip-hop music as part of music offerings for the local and regional audiences reached by these stations, have provided opportunities for established as well as new artists to make music that is consumed by many while taking advantage of new technologies to continually improve the music's quality. Moreover, competition for airplay between hip-hop artists as well as a need to make money from their music means that the artists will be paying attention to the taste and music needs of their audience members. Such attention may lead to positive growth of the genre for years to come. Already scholars studying hip-hop in Kenya have highlighted the role of identity formation and projection among youth (Samper 2004), attempts made by hip-hop artists to craft their social relations to specific spaces in the city (Mose 2013), the use of global processes to enter into public discussions of politics and cultural values (Ntarangwi 2009), and the underlying linguistic techniques applied to music text by various artists (Nyairo and Ogude 2005), among others. Such studies look set to grow over the years as scholars acknowledge not only the expanded cultural space hip-hop occupies in expressive culture in general but also the role it plays in reflecting, shaping and critiquing life in Kenya.

Bibliography

Greven, Katharina. 2014. 'Hip Hop and Sheng in Nairobi: Creating Identity Markers and Expressing a Lifestyle.' In *Hip Hop and Social Change in Africa: Ni Wakati*, eds. Msia Kibona Clark and Mickie Mwanzia Koster. Lanham, MD: Lexington Books, 226–56.

Higgins, Christina. 2009. 'The Polyphony of East African Hip Hop.' In *English as a Local Language: Post-Colonial Identities and Multilingual Practices*. Bristol: Multilingual Matters, chap. 5.

Mose, Caroline. 2011. 'Jua Cali-Justice: Navigating the "Mainstream-Underground" Dichotomy in Kenyan Hip-Hop Culture.' In *Native Tongues: The African Hip-Hop Reader*, ed. P. K. Saucier. New York: African World Press, 69–104.

Mose, Caroline. 2013. '"Swag" and "Cred": Representing Hip-hop in an African City.' *The Journal of Pan African Studies* 6(3): 106–32.

Ntarangwi, Mwenda. 2007. 'Hip-Hop, Westernization and Gender in East Africa.' In *Songs and Politics in Eastern Africa*, eds. Kimani Njogu and Hervé Maupeu. Dar Es Salaam: Mkuki na Nyota Publishers.

Ntarangwi, Mwenda. 2009. *East Africa Hip-hop: Youth Culture and Globalization*. Urbana and Chicago: University of Illinois Press; Nairobi and Dar es Salaam: IFRA and Mkuki na Nyota Publishers, 273–302.

Ntarangwi, Mwenda. 2015. 'Hip hop, Globalisation and the Politics of Youth Identity in Kenya.' In *The Youth and Identity Question in Africa*, eds. Nicodemus Fru Awasom and Shumba Almon. Dakar, Senegal: CODESRIA Books, 91–111.

Nyairo, Joyce, and Ogude, James. 2005. 'Popular Music, Popular Politics: *Unbwogable* and the Idioms of Freedom in Kenyan Popular Music.' *African Affairs* 104(415): 225–49.

Nyawolo, Mich. 2014 'Redefining the Struggle: Remembering the Mau Mau Through Hip Hop Music.' In *Hip Hop and Social Change in Africa: Ni Wakati*, eds. Msia Kibona Clark and Mickie Mwanzia Koster. Lanham, MD: Lexington Books, 72–93.

Samper, David. 2004. '"Africa Is Still Our Mama": Kenyan Rappers, Youth Identity, and the Revitalization of Traditional Values.' *African Identities* 2(1): 37–51.

Discographical References

Gathu, Jimmy. 'Look, Think, Stay Alive.' Self-produced. *1991*: Kenya.

Gaye, Marvin. 'Sexual Healing.' *Midnight Love*. Columbia Records, 1198356. *1982*: USA.

Gidi Gidi Maji Maji. 'Unbwogable.' *Unbwogable*. Label unknown. *2002*: Kenya.

Hardstone. 'Uhiki.' *Nuting But De Stone*. Kelele Records ke 31018. *1997*: Kenya. (Also released on Kelele Records 203513-206. *1999*: Germany.)

Kalamashaka. 'Tafsiri hii.' *Ni Wakati*. Blu Zebra. *2001*: Kenya.

Proxy Presha. 'Dhako.' *Total Balaa*. Blu Zebra. *1997*: Kenya.

Discography
Abbas. *Mista Abbas*. Phoenix Records. *2010*: Kenya.
Black Star Kenya Artists. *Black Star Kenya Hip-Hop Sampler*. Black Star Kenya Records. *2005*: Kenya.
Juliani. *Mtaa Mentality*. Gatwitch Records. *2008*: UK.
Juliani. *Pulpit Kwa Street*. Juliani. *2011*: Kenya.
K-South. *Nairobbery*. Samawati Studios. *2002*: Kenya.
Nairobi *Yetu. Kilio Cha Haki*. Uptoyoutoo/Guava Productions/Ukooflanimaumau. *2004*: Kenya.
Ukoo Flani Mau Mau. *Dandora Burning*. *2006*: Kenya.

Filmography
Hip-hop Colony, dir. Michael Wanguhu. 2006. 90 mins. USA. Documentary.

YouTube
Gahu, Jimmy. 'Look, Think, Stay Alive.' Online at: https://www.kenyatalk.com/index.php?threads/tbt.15362/ (accessed 26 March 2018).

MWENDA NTARANGWI

Hip-Hop in Mozambique
Hip-hop has been popular in Mozambique since the 1980s. Initially imitating US and Portuguese hip-hop closely, it soon evolved into a proudly Mozambican genre in the 1990s, unique not only because of the often controversial lyrics which gave voice to the daily concerns of the Mozambican people, but also because of the inclusion of rhythms, instruments and voices both from local genres such as *marrabenta* from the south of Mozambique as well as from neighboring southern African countries, most notably *kwaito* from South Africa and *kizomba* and *kuduro* from Angola.

The Story of 'MC Moçambique'
In 2013 one of Mozambique's most popular and long-standing hip-hop artists, Yveth (born Ivete Rosária Mafundza Marlene), released a rap history of Mozambican hip-hop entitled 'MC Moçambique.' This song tells the 30-year history of Mozambican hip-hop in rhyme. Opening with the line 'Era uma vez um MC chamado Moçambique' ('Once upon a time there was an MC called Mozambique'), Yveth describes how Mozambican hip-hop has been 'representing' the people of Mozambique since the 1980s:

Desde os anos 80 (heeee)	Since the 1980s (Heeee)
Que ele nos representa (hooo)	He's been representing us (Hooo)
Que ele se aguenta (heee)	May he keep going on (Heee)
E o público movimenta	And the public move on
E nos anos 90 (heeeee)	And in the 1990s (Heeeee)
Sua fama aumenta (heeee)	His fame grows (Heeee)
E o sistema enfrenta	And the system is confronted.

The song traces Mozambican rap music since its infancy in the 1980s when the country was led by a communist government and in the midst of civil war. Young Mozambicans began to identify with the revolutionary audacity and freedom of expression of black US rappers whose sounds and styles snuck through the cracks of the Mozambicans' closed world. 'MC Moçambique' describes Mozambique's adolescence in the 1990s, as the war ended, the country opened up and urban young people began rapping in their own languages, holding 'freestyles in the tower blocks' ('freestyles no prédio') and developing an 'addiction without a cure!' ('vícios sem remédio!'). Yveth goes on to tell of the dark times of the genre's maturation in the 2000s when it was plagued by musical rivalries between the rappers of the city and the suburbs:

Rivalidades, uma guerra que nos assola	A rivalry war plagued us
Se esqueceram que todos vestimos a mesma camisoa	They forgot we all wore the same shirt.

In the last verse, Yveth celebrates the durability of the genre as it enters its fourth decade. Despite still being dominated by male MCs and still surviving in the margins, the genre has continued to grow, criticizing the system, intervening in social and political life and bringing its message to the people to wake them up:

E hoje vejo cds na praça, Mcs na desgraça	And today I see CDs in the shops and MCs struggling
Poucas female mcs mas mesmo assim o rap avança	Few female MCs, but nonetheless, RAP is moving forward
Simba, Mr Arsen, levam-nos além fronteiras	Simba, Mr Arsen, take us beyond borders
Xiticu Ni Mbaula, não há aqui barreiras	Xiticu Ni Mbaula, there are no more barriers here
E este Mc hoje é intellectual	And this MC today is intellectual
Critica o sistema e separa o bem do mal	Criticizing the system and separating good from bad
Traz consigo mensagem, desperta o povo do fatal	Bringing with it a message, waking people from death
Digam o que disserem para nós é crucial	They say what was said is crucial to us
Ele intervém é ouvido, por vezes incompreendido	It intervenes, it is heard, sometimes it makes no sense
Censurado e banido, mas pelo povo é protegido	Censored and banned, but protected by the people.

Had the young fictitious MC of Yveth's track existed, 'MC Moçambique' would be a grown adult by the end of the 2010s, possibly with children of his or her own. Yveth and her contemporaries from the 1980s have become the mothers and fathers of Mozambican hip-hop. They have seen the next generation of rappers create their own new hip-hop styles: some combining the popular dance styles of Mozambican *kizomba* and *pandza* and filling the dance floors in urban nightclubs across the country; others, such as André Cardoso, freestyling about the daily news on social media in his self-styled Facebook identity, 'Rap Face.' Mozambican hip-hop has continued to evolve, dominating Mozambique's music scene and forming part of the identity of young Mozambicans as they negotiate their place in the future of their country.

War and Peace

The importance of hip-hop in Mozambique is best understood within the context of the social transformation that has taken place since Mozambique gained independence from the Portuguese in 1975. As hip-hop was emerging from its underground beginnings in New York City, the Frente de Libertação de Moçambique (FRELIMO – Mozambican Liberation Front) took over the governance of Mozambique. The country experienced a few years of euphoria when education, health, housing and land were made available to all, before the conflict erupted again as the global struggle between socialism and capitalism spread into southern Africa. In the early 1980s Mozambique's fledgling government forged an ever stronger political alliance with the Soviet Union and musicians, intellectuals and artists who voiced their concerns about the lack of freedom of expression began to find themselves 're-educated' in camps in the north of Mozambique along with political dissidents, prostitutes and traditional leaders (Sousa 2013).

Before Mozambican Independence there had been little room for the voice of black Mozambicans to be heard in the media or in music. Following independence, another generation of Mozambicans found their voices muted by the threats of 're-education,' prison and even public execution (Hanlon 1991, 27). The films seen in the cinema and the music broadcast on the radio were controlled by the state, as evidenced in the film, *Marrabentando: The Stories My Guitar Sings* (*Marrabentando: As histórias que a minha guitarra canta*) (see also Convents 2011, 87–105). A civil war took hold of the country in the 1980s with the Mozambican Resistance (RENAMO – Resistência Nacional Moçambicana) attacking villages and mounting ambushes on the roads and rail networks across the country in an effort to destabilize the socialist government. Any criticism of the government was considered to be indirect support for their enemies. At this time the tapes mixed by the young people who were growing up in the cities guarded by government forces and cut off from the rest of the country snuck under the radar of censorship. For them, the sounds of the likes of Public Enemy and the Jungle Brothers provided their private 'Walkman soundtrack' to the war raging around them. A peace accord was eventually agreed in 1992 and campaigning began for democratic elections, which were held in 1994. While the groundbreaking sounds of the US groups Wu-Tang Clan were shaking up global hip-hop, Mozambicans were hearing political opposition on national airwaves for the first time. The ruling party FRELIMO maintained its power in those first and all subsequent elections, and while a small number of individuals began to voice their criticisms of the government on the airwaves and in the press, public criticism of the *status quo* has continued to be rare and risky. The young rappers who until then were 'freestyling in their tower-blocks,' as Yveth put it in the lyrics of 'MC Moçambique,' took to the streets prepared to take this risk as they put the voices of young people into rhyme. Following the assassination of Mozambique's 'father of press freedom,' Carlos Cardoso, in 2000, young urban rappers became even more vocal as they vented their anger at the silencing of this independent voice.

Speaking Out through Hip-Hop

By the mid-2000s Mozambican MCs were some of the most daring critics of the government, often expressing anger at the failings of the revolutionary dream of the older generation: their broken promises, the corruption and the growing gap between the rich and poor. This anger is illustrated in the following excerpt from the lyrics of Gpro Fam's song, 'País da *marrabenta*' (Marrabenta country):

Foram 16 anos de uma guerra civil	There were 16 years of civil war
Só de orelhas decepadas foram mais de mil	When more than a thousand ears were cut off
Ainda querem que o povo lhes de ouvidos	They still want the people to give them an ear
Dam! filhos da mãe desses politicos!	Damn! These politicians are sons of bitches!
Deram liberdade de imprensa ao jornalista	They gave the journalists freedom of the press
O carlos teve azar foi o primeiro da lista	Carlos was unlucky. He was top of their list
Pois é o mano esqueceu-se da lei da floresta meu	It's just that our brother forgot the law of the jungle
Antes que abrisse a boca tiro na testa	A shot in the head before he opened his mouth
Dizem que era boa pessoa mas sabia demais	They say he was a good guy who knew too much
Resultado, levou uma facado por trás	And what happened? He was stabbed in the back
E o assassino com certeza foi ao enterro	And the killer went to the funeral for sure
Abracou a viuva e disse: meu companheiro!	And hugged the widow and called her their friend!

Edson da Luz, aka Azagaia, one of Mozambique's most outspoken rappers of this period, viewed the role of Mozambican rappers as lending courage to their generation to stand up to their elders. He described this opposition as part of a generational war. Azagaia was vocal in his songs and his interviews about the legacy he and his generation inherited from their parents. For them, FRELIMO was more than a political party. It was part of Mozambique's history and could not be criticized. His music ignited previously unvoiced dissent and gave young people license to start speaking out:

> Since independence we've had 2 or 3 generations, and this last generation is not feeling very connected to all that happened in the past ... so when my music came, for the young Mozambican, it was like 'ooof, that's what we're saying, now let's say it loud!' I wasn't saying anything new, but perhaps I was giving it a spark – and was saying 'let's talk. Let's speak.' (Azagaia; interview with author, January 2014)

Azagaia was detained by the police on two occasions, accused by the government of inciting violence through his music (Fauvet 2008). The government arrested him following a performance of the provocative lyrics in his song 'Povo no puder' (People in Power), in which he makes an audacious call for the corrupt thieves to leave and cries out for the public to shout with him for them to go. He also makes what could be seen as a veiled threat – that, unless the cost of public transport was lowered or the minimum wage raised, things could get nasty:

Ladrões (fora)	Thieves (out)
Corruptos (fora)	Corrupt ones (out)
Gritem comigo para essa gente ir embora (fora)	Shout with me for these guys to leave (out)
Gritem comigo pois o povo já não chora (fora)	Shout with me so the people cry no more (out)
Baixa a tarifa do transporte ou sobe o salario minimo	Lower the cost of transport or raise the minimum wage
Xé ... isso é o que deves fazer no mínimo	Ah ... this is the least you must do

'Rapid Intervention Music'

Azagaia was released after two nights in a cell and, undeterred, continued to release new tracks on a regular basis for free download. His music was listened to not only by the young hip-hop audience but also by the older generation. This generation had previously been uninterested in the genre, but now discovered that these lyrics spoke to them as well. In 2013, at a time when street protests were being repressed by the well-equipped Força de Intervenção Rápida, which was becoming infamous for its violent crowd-control involving tear gas and water cannons, Azagaia introduced the concept of 'Rapid Intervention Music' with a track of the same name, 'MIR Música de intervenção rápida.' The concept of 'intervention' has a double meaning for Mozambicans. For them, the term 'música de intervenção' referred previously to songs recorded after independence to promote socialist values along with literacy and health campaigns. The idea that music alone could change minds was identified and embraced through Azagaia's track.

O povo pede comida e vocês mandam gás lacrimogéneo e depois soltam os cães	The people ask for food and you send tear gas and then release the dogs
Disparam jactos de água contra os nossos pais e mães	You fire water jets against our mothers and fathers
Já vos demos o poder, afinal o que querem quem mais?	We gave you power already, what more do you want?
Cavar a nossas sepulturas com as nossas próprias pás?	To dig our graves with our own spades?
Avisem o conselho de ministros que na próxima terça-feira	Tell the cabinet that next Tuesday
Eu levo um par de gira discos e colunas lá para a feira	I will take a pair of turntables and speakers to the square
A não ser que queiras fogo nas bombas de gasoline	Unless you want fire at the petrol pumps
Assaltos a padarias, ministérios, imagina	Attacks on the bakeries, ministries, imagine.
Com milhares de kilowatts para os nossos camaradas	With thousands of kilowatts for our comrades
Vou ligar o microfone e lançar um jacto de palavras	I'll switch on the microphone and release a jet of words

(Lyrics reproduced by permission of the author)

Going Global

As the themes of Mozambican hip-hop reflected the lives of those making and listening to it, so too did the sound, which gained an increasingly national identity. Live instruments took the place of samples and drum machines, and established musicians from other popular genres began to collaborate with the younger MCs and hip-hop producers. In 2000 an intergenerational hip-hop/*marrabenta* fusion band Mabulu was formed. Their two albums, *Karimbo* and *Soul Marrabenta*, which were released globally, took them onto international stages at the Glastonbury Festival, Womad and the Montreux Jazz Festival. Featuring two successful young rappers from Maputo, Mr Arssen and Chiquito, and old *marrabenta* musicians Lisboa Matavel, Alberto Mucheca, Dilon Djinji and António Marcos, this hip-hop crossover band received nominations for Best Newcomer at the BBC Radio 3 Awards and Best African Group at the Kora All African Music Awards. In 2013 their track 'AIDS' was included in the World Music Network compilation album *Rough Guide to Acoustic Africa*. In the same year Azagaia released his first internationally distributed album, *Cubaliwa*. In it he collaborated with Mozambican musicians from other genres such as Stewart Sukuma, a pop legend from the 1980s, while also expanding his audience with international collaborations and universal themes. In the track 'Maçonaria,' for example, Azagaia worked with Brazilian DJ Guto to take on the church. The track opens with a prayer pastiche: 'Em nome da ambição, do poder e do espírito materialista,/A graça da ambição, o amor ao poder em comunhão/Com o espírito materialista, estejam convosco' ('In the name of ambition, the power and the grace of ambition and the love of power, may the spirit of materialism be with you'). In the chorus of this song, Azagaia introduced the tight vocal harmonies of the Mozambican women's

Afro-fusion group, Banda Likute, whose jazzy church sounds offset Azagaia's articulate critique of the partnership between church and state in the colonization of Africa:

Europeus a pensarem no teu poder e glória	Europeans thinking of their power and glory
Ocuparam a África e escreveram a nossa história	Occupied Africa and wrote our story
Com a Bíblia numa mão e noutra uma	With the Bible in one hand and a gun pistol in the other
Ergueram uma Igreja e negaram-nos uma escola	They built a church and refused us a school.

(Lyrics reproduced by permission of the author.)

Well-Considered Provocation

Azagaia's powerful and complex lyrics reflect the sharp mind behind his compositions. Speaking several languages and holding a degree from Maputo's Eduardo Mondlane University, Azagaia chose to use his ability with words to speak for disenfranchised Mozambicans. His high level of education has not been uncommon among Mozambican hip-hop stars. The young rapper Laylizzie (born Edson Abel Jeremias Tchamo), considered (and reported as such by CNN in 2016) to be one of Africa's top ten rappers and fastest-rising artists, studied for a master's degree in business law in the United Kingdom before settling on his career as a professional rapper. Two of the most prolific and successful women rappers, Yveth and Dama Do Bling (born Ivânnea da Silva Mudanisse) are both lawyers. Yveth is said to see no conflict between working as a lawyer during the day and an MC and rapper at weekends, rapping about 'things that affect us, men who don't stick around to look after their kids, human rights abuses and our leaders' (Yveth, quoted in Mutch 2013). Dama do Bling likes to think of her work as 'irreverent.' She answers critics who accuse her of wasting her state-financed education with statements such as 'why is it that a lawyer can't sing but a minister who doesn't even have 6th-grade can decide our laws' (Dama do Bling 2008). Her scanty clothes, sexy moves and provocative live shows have been described in the local press as 'an attack on moral decency and a crime' (Mabunda 2007), while sociologists have described these as constituting 'a silent revolution' (Langa 2007), viewing her provocative videos as statements about sexual freedom and who controls women's bodies. For many years Dama do Bling made no public contribution to the debate, leaving the public to come to their own conclusions regarding her motivations. However, in a 2013 interview to discuss her new release, 'Bad Girl,' she went some way to making her position clear: 'A bad girl is a woman who fights for her ideas, a woman who is not intimidated by the opinion of other people. She does what her heart tells her to do. A bad girl owns her life' (Jentzsch 2013).

Conclusion – The Fifth Element

Mozambican hip-hop is both unique and part of the global hip-hop phenomenon. As elsewhere in the world, it amounts to more than just the MC or rapper and the music. A Mozambican hip-hop dance and hip-hop art have grown in parallel in Mozambique and have both developed an equally Mozambican identity. Urban dance moves such as Mozambican *marrabenta*, Angolan *kuduru* and South African *pantsula* have been fused with US break dance and body popping, creating a distinctly Mozambican hip-hop dance style. African iconography and coloring have become increasingly present in hip-hop graffiti. What enables Mozambican hip-hop to take on an identity all its own, however, is an element that unifies all these forms of expression. This element is often referred to as the fifth element of hip-hop: its 'consciousness.' In Mozambique this consciousness is particularly strong, perhaps because it was the vehicle through which the first generation of Mozambicans born into an Independent Mozambique after over 500 years of colonialism expressed themselves. In Madier Rashid's 2009 hip-hop documentary *Os 5 elementos* (The Five Elements), poet, writer and rapper Consciencia Keleza describes this consciousness as 'the most beautiful part of hip-hop' that 'holds it together.' It is apt that this consciousness is reflected in Mozambique's music, because music is situated at the heart of its daily life.

Bibliography

Convents, Guido. 2011. *Os moçambicanos perante o cinema e o audiovisual: Uma história político-cultural do Moçambique colonial até à República de Moçambique (1896–2010)* [The Mozambicans in the Light of Their Cinema and Audiovisual

Culture: A Politico-Cultural History from Colonial Mozambique to the Mozambican Republic, 1896–2010]. Maputo: Docanema.

Dama do Bling. 2008. *Diário d'uma irreverente* [Diary of an Irreverent]. Maputo: Bang Entertrenimento.

Fauvet, Paul. 'Mozambique: Threat of Censorship in Press Freedom Week.' All Africa.com / Agencia de Informacao de Mocambique – May 2008. Online at: freemuse http://freemuse.org/freemuseArchives/freerip/freemuse.org/sw27642.html (accessed 18 April 2018).

Hanlon, Josef. 1991. *Mozambique: Who Calls the Shots?* London: Currey.

Jentzsch, Corinna. 2013. 'Dama do Bling, Mozambique's Queen of Hip-Hop.' *Africa Is a Country*. Online at: https://africasacountry.com/2013/02/dama-do-bling-mozambiques-queen-of-hip-hop/ (accessed 18 April 2018).

Langa, Patricio. 2007. 'O fenómoeno Dama do Bling' [Dama do Bling the Phenomenon]. *Circulo de sociologia*. Online at: http://circulodesociologia.blogspot.co.uk/2007/07/o-fenmeno-dama-do-bling1.html (accessed 18 April 2018).

Mabunda, Lazaro. 2007. 'Ra, re, ri, ro, rua nudez, Bling!' [Ra, re, ri, ro, nudity road, Bling!]. *O País*. Online at: http://mozambique-music.com/sites/pages/articles/mmm033_pais.htm (accessed 18 April 2018).

Mutch, Thembi. 2013. 'Rapping Mozambique's Praises and Faults.' *Inter Press Service News Agency (IPS)*. Online at: http://www.ipsnews.net/2013/05/rapping-mozambiques-praises-and-faults/ (accessed 18 April 2018).

Serra, Carlos. 2007. 'As veredas da sexualidade perigosa' [The Paths of Dangerous Sexuality]. *Diário de um sociólogo*. Online at: http://oficinadesociologia.blogspot.co.uk/2007/07/as-veredas-da-sexualidade-perigosa-3.html (accessed 18 April 2018).

Sitoe, Tirso. 2013. 'Música RAP e identidades na cidade de Maputo: Buscando pegadas e analisando discursos' [Rap Music and Identities in Maputo City: Following Footsteps and Analysing Discourses]. *Agália: Revista de Estudos na Cultura* 1(7): 51–65.

Sousa, Glória. 2013. 'As feridas abertas pelo processo de reeducação em Moçambique' [The Open Wounds of the Reeducation Process in Mozambique]. *Deutsche Welle*. Online at: http://www.dw.com/pt-002/as-feridas-abertas-pelo-processo-de-reeduca%C3%A7%C3%A3o-em-mo%C3%A7ambique/a-16948901 (accessed 18 April 2018).

Discographical References

Azagaia. 'Maçonaria.' *Cubaliwe*. Kongoloti Records. *2013*: Mozambique. Online at: https://soundcloud.com/azagaiafanpage/sets/azagaia-cubaliwa-2013 (accessed 18 April *2018*).

Azagaia. 'MIR Música de intervenção iápida.' (Online Release.) Kongoloti Records. *2013*: Mozambique. Online at: https://www.youtube.com/watch?v=VtO1uPqnG2Y (accessed 18 April *2018*).

Azagaia. 'Povo no puder.' (Original Studio Recording.) *2008*: Mozambique. Online at: http://videos.sapo.pt/fhbJ89NE6PjK8uipDv2F (accessed 18 April *2018*) [See also https://www.youtube.com/watch?v=RfVSUXhQUgA (2015) (accessed 18 April *2018*).]

Dama do Bling. 'Bad Girl.' *Deusa*. *2013*: Mozambique. Online at: https://store.cdbaby.com/cd/damadobling (accessed 18 April *2018*).

Gpro Fam. 'País da *marrabenta*.' *Um passo em frente*. Gpro Fam. *2003*: Mozambique. Online at: https://www.youtube.com/watch?v=_qaKqSKWlYg (accessed 18 April *2018*).

Mabulu. 'AIDS.' *Soul Marrabenta*. Riverboat Records TUG CD 1024. *2001*: UK.

Mabulu. *Karimbo*. Riverboat Records TUG CD 1021. *2000*: UK.

The Rough Guide to Acoustic Africa. World Music Network RGNET 1297. *2013*: UK.

Yveth (Iveth), featuring Hawaio, Rage and Sgee. 'MC Moçambique' ('Karinganas do Rap Moz Mc Moçambique'). Tchaya Records. *2013*: Mozambique. Online at: https://www.youtube.com/watch?v=12HmJEwHMgU (accessed 18 April *2018*).

Discography

Mabulu. *African Classics: Modern Marrabenta Magic*. Sheer SLCD 171. *2009*: South Africa.

Filmography

Marrabentando: The Stories My Guitar Sings/ Marrabentando: As histórias que a minha guitarra canta, dir. Karen Boswall. 2005. Portugal. 52 mins. Documentary with English subtitles, and stories and songs by Antonio Marcos and Dilon Djinji.

Online at: http://vimeo.com/43718451 (accessed 22 February 2018).

Os 5 elementos. Moçambique, dir Madjer Rachid. 2009. Mozambique. 25min. Documentary. Online at: https://www.youtube.com/watch?v=0WmJ55ohkUo (accessed 18 April 2018).

Television

Why Laylizzie Believes in a Better Mozambique. 2016. CNN. Online at: https://edition.cnn.com/videos/world/2016/10/07/african-voices-music-masters-spc-a.cnn (accessed 18 April 2018).

Website

Andre Cardoso. 'Rap Face' (Facebook): https://www.facebook.com/MaisMocambicano/videos/1050230665119357/?hc_ref=ARSv-CEesy30hxtLl6nHM-eQgqUlVsDrcL6whfxGWPIECLMS50joVGn39LbOOfuF3s8&pnref=story (accessed 18 April 2018).

Interview

Azagaia. January 2014.

KAREN BOSWALL

(all translations by the author)

See also Marrabenta and Pandza

Hip-Hop in Nigeria

When James Brown toured Nigeria in 1970, he attended a performance at Fela Anikulapo Kuti's club and concluded that he had found 'the African James Brown.' For Brown, Afrobeat was a unique combination of traditional Nigerian and African-American soul and funk. It is pertinent to regard much of the hip-hop that is created in Nigeria in a similar light, as a Nigerian version of African-American hip-hop. Such an analysis must be carefully and deliberately approached, however, as Fela's Afrobeat was not a simple imitation of James Brown's music. Instead, Fela had created a viable and pulsating hybrid music that combined influences that were both local and global. In other words, there was a recognition of James Brown's performance ethic in the tightly controlled but loosely orchestrated band, but there the similarities ended.

By the 1960s Fela had created a unique form of music that combined West African rhythms and sensibilities with elements of funk, jazz and soul, and infused it with lyrical messages that were relevant to the unique experience of a postcolonial identity. Fela's musical invention, which was recognizably traditional and Western, formed a basis for succeeding generations of Nigerian artists and serves as a critical point of departure to begin a historical overview of Nigerian hip-hop. Appreciating the extent to which Nigerian hip-hop artists allow their work to negotiate the same balance as Afrobeat is fundamental to understanding the genre.

Beginnings

The earliest iterations of hip-hop in Nigeria can be traced to the early 1990s when young people began to experiment with hip-hop. Between the development of Afrobeat and the development of hip-hop, and thanks to the profuse telecasting of foreign music and programming on radio and television, generation after generation of young people in Nigeria were inundated with waves of African-American music, from R&B to soul to disco. In addition, Jamaican reggae also became popular. Fans and artists alike gravitated toward these cultural imports, absorbing and recreating them with varying degrees of success. Unlike Afrobeat, and other uniquely Nigerian popular music genres such as *jùjú*, *fújì* and the Igbo and Yorùbá versions of highlife, traditional genres experienced a decline while the foreign elements dominated the attention and imagination of these new Nigerian artists.

By the 1990s young Nigerian artists had grown accustomed to reproducing foreign music and creating Nigerian versions. However, because of the very essence of hip-hop as an expressive form that allows space for unique and socially relevant narratives, Nigerian hip-hop artists have experienced an opportunity to manage a balance between local and global influences.

In the early 1990s a duo, Igbo rappers Okechukwu Azike and Pretty Okafor, better known as 'Junior and Pretty,' emerged with a local version of hip-hop using mostly Pidgin English. As both rappers were Igbo, their sampling soundscape was influenced by highlife music, which was a popular genre among the Igbo of Eastern Nigeria. Also, because the duo was based in the Western metropolis of Lagos, they also included Yorùbá words in their lyrics. This innovative approach of using local vernacular, taken directly from the Afrobeat playbook, made their version of hip-hop accessible and identifiable in the local setting. Their 'old school' sound was also fashioned along the lines of the light beat and humorous lyrics of US duo DJ Jazzy Jeff and the Fresh Prince, who were successful in the late 1980s and early 1990s. Junior and Pretty's song, 'Bolanle,' in which they profess unending love for the woman, Bolanle, provides a good example of this influence. The devices they used in this song are comical but also resonate with US references, an approach that speaks to a degree of hybridity. For instance, they rap, 'the love I have for you is like hot dog and burger.' Sonically, the track begins with the high-strung sounds of a highlife guitar and a simple repetitive beat. Their other songs such as 'Monika' continued this trend of highlife/rap infused with humor.

During the mid-1990s, another important early figure in Nigerian hip-hop emerged: Adesola Adesimbo Idowu (b. 1970), also known as Weird MC or Da Rappatainer. The first woman of note to join the hip-hop community, she released the pulsating hit 'Allen Avenue,' a dance anthem that calls on listeners to get up and do just that. While the track, which was released in 2006, does not have the intense socially conscious message of Afrobeat, Weird MC laces her lyrics with local references such as 'Allen Avenue,' a popular street in Lagos, and 'Kalakuta,' an important reference to Fela Kuti as an enduring influence on artists like herself. Weird MC's androgynous presence in Nigerian entertainment history is noteworthy given the conservative society that has continued to exist there.

Toward the end of the 1990s another vital group joined the Nigerian hip-hop scene, bringing a level of sophistication to lyrical flow as well as to the depth and complexity of beats. The trio, Trybesmen, also known as Da Trybe, was a Lagos-based group made up of artists Eldee, Kaboom and Freestyle. Their 1999 dance hit 'Shake Bodi' is a more Americanized version of Nigerian hip-hop that benefits from US influences by, for example, delivering a smoother lyrical flow that is more American than Nigerian. In the balance between local and US influences, 'Shake Bodi' in general leans more heavily toward US influences. Although the group uses Pidgin English sporadically, they infuse the track with distinctly US accents and references: 'I'm the big issue now like Clinton and Lewinsky,' 'Rushin' like Chris Tucker and Jackie,' 'Gene Kelly on the dance floor' and, most interestingly, they call on 'Niggas' to get on the dance floor. However, the group still finds a way to localize their lyrics as they compare their skills to those of the popular Nigerian soccer player Taribo West and they issue a call – or a shout-out – to their boys or homies from different communities such as Apapa, Isolo, Ikeja, Agege, VI and Festac. All these communities are distinct parts of Lagos which represent a cross-section of class and ethnicity in the complex, multiethnic city. This situates their Americanized sound back at home in Nigeria. The group exemplifies the hip-hop device of braggadocio and boasting as they repeat the memorable refrain, 'Whether you like am, whether you no like am, we go still dey shake body.' In other words, whether you like it or not, Trybesmen and their people will continue to do their thing on the mic and on the dance floor.

Nigerian Hip-Hop in the Twenty-First Century
The 2000s

The new millennium saw a change in the direction of Nigerian hip-hop. Gathering together the threads established by Junior and Pretty and Trybesmen, artists continued to advance Nigerian hip-hop in a manner fitting more closely with the US model that was consumed so voraciously in Nigeria. Even at the level of choosing stage names it became apparent that the attraction of US hip-hop was beginning to overshadow the identity of new artists. For instance, in 2004, Nigerian rapper 2Shotz released 'Carry Am Go.' Visually, the rapper and his hypeman appear in doo rags, a cloth used mostly by inner city African-Americans to cover the top of their head. (A hypeman in hip-hop is a backup rapper or singer who supports the lead rappers with exclamations and interjections and who attempts to increase the audience's excitement with call-and-response chants.) The obvious imitation of US rapper Too $hort's name is, however, misleading in one sense. The Nigerian rapper has developed a valuable hybrid in 'Carry Am Go,' by rapping entirely in Pidgin English. Despite the fact that Nigeria has over 250 ethnicities and languages, all Nigerians understand Pidgin English. The beats of 'Carry Am Go' are simple and minimal as 2Shotz discusses thievery in the local community. 'Thief, *Ole*, Carry am go!' he raps, an order that Nigerians can relate to in a society where theft has been rampant and where retribution is often handed out vigilante-style.

The most popular rapper of the early 2000s was Eedris Abdulkareem. Born Eedris Turayo Abdulkareem Ajenifuja, he began his career in the late 1990s as a member of the Nigerian group The Remedies. After he went solo, Abdulkareem released a number of hits that introduced a socially conscious element to Nigerian hip-hop, yet his persona is carefully constructed with both local and US influences. With his track 'Jaga Jaga' (2004), Abdulkareem came closest to Fela Kuti in terms of providing a direct commentary on the ills of a corrupt government and its adverse impact on 'poor men' who 'suffer-suffer.' 'Jaga-jaga,' which is a well-known Pidgin English term for destruction, was one of the first truly provocatively political hip-hop tracks in Nigeria. Other tracks by Abdulkareem such as 'Mr. Lecturer' continued to provide some interesting insights into certain aspects of Nigerian society, such as the educational system.

Like Eedris Abdulkareem, Tony Tetuila (Anthony Olanrewaju Awotoye) left the group The Remedies to go solo. Unlike Abdulkareem, Tetuila did not focus as directly on social issues. In 2002 he released his track 'My Car,' a tepid track in Pidgin English that seemed to reach back to the era of Junior and Pretty. While Abdulkareem was famous for sporting a turban that represented his northern, Hausa and Muslim identity (see the entry on Hip-Hop in Nigeria [Hausa Rap]), Tetuila had bleached hair that was reminiscent of US R&B singer Sisqua, who was popular in the late 1990s.

Notable at this time was the emergence of three potentially international artists, 2Face Idibia (b. 1975), M.I. (b. 1981), and the twins P-Square (Peter and Paul Okoye, b. 1981). Unlike most of the other rappers who had hailed from the south-east and south-west of Nigeria, all three acts came from Jos, a smaller town in the middle belt of Nigeria. While these artists were growing up Jos was considered a neutral zone, a melting pot of different ethnicities, which is probably why they do not exhibit as much Pidgin English or local dialect in their lyrics. In 2004 2Face, having just left the R&B group Plantashun Boyz and clearly influenced in his choice of name by US rapper 2Pac, released 'African Queen,' a popular R&B song that extols pride in African beauty. A much-needed message in a postcolonial world, the song has been played at countless weddings and celebrations. Although he is more of an R&B singer than a rapper, 2Face has come to be synonymous with the Nigerian hip-hop generation and certainly paved the way for other artists to cross national and international borders.

Following that lead, Nigerian rapper M.I. (Jude Abaga, also known as Mr. Incredible) burst onto the scene in 2006 with his hit 'Crowd Mentality.' Born in 1981, M.I. (not to be confused with rapper M1 from US duo Dead Prez) took Nigerian hip-hop to another level lyrically. His ability to flow with smooth, smart lyrics won him several awards from MTV Africa Music in 2009, and he was nominated for a BET International Act award in 2010. The issue with M.I. and artists like him is that it is hard to situate many of their tracks as specifically Nigerian. 'Crowd Mentality' is rapped completely in an American accent, and is ironically a commentary on being a unique individual. As the track ends, he urges 'Be Black, Be Beautiful ... Be creative, Be native.' As M.I. continued to rise as one of the most successful Nigerian and African hip-hop artists, he collaborated with artists such as Flavour, who tempered M.I.'s US sound with a local, edgy sound that harkened back to Igbo highlife.

The third influential act that emerged at this time, P-Square, had, since 1999, released several albums that are mostly smooth R&B against a hip-hop background. 'Chop Money' has the Auto-tuned quality similar to popular US-based artists at the time such as Akon and T-Pain, and is performed in Pidgin English against a relentless steady hip-hop beat. The videos for their 2012 song 'Alingo' and 2014 song 'Personally' are two of the most polished and highly produced dance music videos that have come out of Nigeria. The dance moves of the twins and their dancers are intensely choreographed and can compare with any of the best choreographed videos of Usher, the US singer, songwriter, dancer and actor.

Many artists who emerged after 2Face, M.I. and P-Square seemed to use these artists as models to emulate the polished and Americanized versions of R&B and hip-hop. However, there have been artists who have taken a slightly different route with a more local slant. For instance, in his hit 'Yahooze' (2007), Yorùbá rapper Olumide Edwards Adegbolu, otherwise known as Olu Maintain (b. 1976), makes use of some interesting Nigerian elements such as *fújì*, local slang, Yorùbá words and lyrics that are relatable. This much-played song is about the common experience of fraudsters, a situation that has brought notoriety to Nigeria as a whole. Conversely, his accompanying video draws heavily on Americanisms, featuring everything from Hummers to hundred dollar bills and dancing girls. Predictably, he raps, 'It's all about the Benjamins, baby.' This signals the degree to which artists such as Olu Maintain are influenced by US culture, even though the lyrics are in Pidgin English and Yorùbá.

The 2010s

As the profile of Nigerian artists has grown in this new era of Nigerian popular culture, and as Nigerian young people have become more in tune with technology and social media, more artists have emerged to take advantage of the insatiable attraction to hip-hop. The second decade of the 2000s has been rife with hip-hop artists of varying quality who have followed the trend established by US artists in resorting to sharp dance techno beats. The effect is a house music sound that is merged with hip-hop. This approach has actually allowed Nigerian hip-hop to find its unique voice as the beats are often inspired by *fújì* or afrobeat.

Nigerian artists have become well known across the continent and have also reached international audiences. These artists include Naeto C who brilliantly mixes hip-hop and Afrobeat; Ice Prince who has won several awards including a Black Entertainment Television (BET) award; Iyanya, a musician from the Niger Delta region of Nigeria who is not strictly a rapper but sings and speaks over hip-hop beats; female rapper Eva, who leans heavily on appropriated aspects of international artists such as the American Eve and the Barbadian Rihanna; and northern-born artists D'Banj and JJC whose lyrical references are global.

Following a trend in US popular music, Nigerian artists have often collaborated in highly successful recordings. For instance, in 2013 three artists, Chidinma, Ill bliss and Tha Suspect, collaborated on 'Emi Ni Baller.' The track is a bright pulsating mixture of *juju* and *fuji* with hip-hop by artists who bring a hard-edged sound that feels as if it was made in the gritty space of Ajegunle, Lagos. With this song, Igbo rapper Chidinma Ekile (b. 1991) became the first woman to make it to number one on MTV's Naija Top 10 charts. Another prominent collaboration occurred on the 2013 hit 'Won Da Mo' by Burna Boy and D'Banj. The two rappers use Yorùbá and English against a *fújì* soundscape. Burna Boy (b. 1991), who came originally from Rivers State in the Niger Delta, usually includes reggae and dancehall beats in his music. He brings these elements into 'Won Da Mo,' while his collaborator D'Banj contributes an R&B and hip-hop flavor.

The most important Nigerian rapper up until the late 2010s has been Lagos-born artist Ayodeji Ibrahim Balogun, better known as Wizkid. Along with the imitation of US rapper Wiz Khalifa's name, the US rap influence on Wizkid's music is particularly apparent in his 2010 hit 'Holla At Yo Boy.' As the title suggests, this early hit was a track that imitated US hip-hop without much local intervention. He used words like 'swag,' 'frontin' and 'fly.' All these are words that are rooted in African-American vernacular. However, Wizkid did evolve artistically, including more Nigerian elements in his music that resulted in a fuller, more localized sound. His 2014 hit 'Ojuelegba' reflects this new direction. The Afrobeat soundscape is unmistakable and his nod to Fela is evidenced in the lyrics and the theme focusing on the daily struggle of Nigerian people and on one of the most bustling parts of Lagos, Ojuelegba. This song also signals a turning point for Nigerian rappers as global artists such as US superstar Drake and Nigerian-British Skepta remixed and covered 'Ojuelegba.' Continuing to serve as a model to which other Nigerian artists can aspire, Wizkid's 2017 album *Sounds from the Other Side* features successful American stars Drake, Chris Brown and Trey Songz.

Conclusion

The history of Nigerian hip-hop has been both colorful and eventful. The sound and the lyrics have come far from the beginnings of Junior and Pretty. The Nigerian hip-hop scene has been crowded with hopefuls, all of whom look to the West for their inspiration. The artists who rise to the top, certainly those mentioned in this entry, are those who have found a way to flavor their lyrics or their sound with tropes and features that anchor their music as uniquely Nigerian. However, no Nigerian MC has yet achieved that vital balance of hybridity that Fela was able to maintain in Afrobeat.

Bibliography

Adedeji, Wale. 2014. 'Negotiating Globalization through Hybridization: Hip Hop, Language Use and the Creation of Cross-Over Culture in Nigerian Popular Music.' *Language in India* 14(6): 497–515.

Babalola, Emmanuel Taiwo, and Taiwo, Rotimi. 2009. 'Code Switching in Contemporary Nigerian Hip-Hop Music.' *Itupale Online Journal of African Studies* 1: 1–26.

Liadi, Olusegun Fariudeen. 2012. 'Multilingualism and Hip Hop Consumption in Nigeria: Accounting for the Local Acceptance of a Global Phenomenon.' *Africa Spectrum* 47(1): 3–19.

Shonekan, Stephanie. 2011. 'Sharing Hip-Hop Cultures: The Case of Nigerians and African Americans.' *American Behavioral Scientist* 55(1): 9–23.

Shonekan, Stephanie. 2012. 'Nigerian Hip-Hop: Exploring a Black World Hybrid.' In *Hip Hop Africa: New African Music in a Globalizing World*, ed. Eric Charry. Bloomington, IN: Indiana University Press, 147–68.

Shonekan, Stephanie. 2013. 'The Blueprint: The Gift and The Curse of American Hip Hop and R&B for Nigeria's Millennial Youth.' *Journal of Pan African Studies* 6(3): 181–98.

Veal, Michael. 2000. *Fela: The Life and Times of an African Musical Icon*. Philadelphia, PA: Temple University Press.

Waterman, Christopher Alan. 1990. *Jùjú: A Social History and Ethnography of an African Popular Music*. Chicago, IL: University of Chicago Press.

Discographical References

2Shotz. 'Carry Am Go.' *The Big Picture*. Tribe Records. 2003: Nigeria.

Abdulkareem, Eedris. 'Jaga Jaga.' *Jaga Jaga*. Kennis Music. 2004: Nigeria.

Abdulkareem, Eedris. 'Mr. Lecturer.' *Mr. Lecturer*. Kennis Music. 2002: Nigeria.

Burna Boy and D'Banj. 'Won Da Mo.' Aristokrat Records. 2013: Nigeria.

Chidinma. 'Emi Ni Baller.' 2012: Nigeria.

Face. 'African Queen.' *Face 2 Face*. Kennis Music. 2004: Nigeria.

Junior and Pretty. 'Bolanle.' *Life*. Kokoma KLMP 023. 1994: Nigeria.

Junior and Pretty. 'Monika.' *Fufu Flavour*. Storm Productions. 1991: Nigeria.

M.I. 'Crowd Mentality.' *Talk About It*. Chocolate City Music. 2008: Nigeria.

Maintain, Olu. 'Yahooze.' *Yahooze*. Reloaded Records. 2007: Nigeria.

P-Square. 'Alingo.' *Greatest Hits*. Square Records. 2012: Nigeria

P-Square. 'Chop Money.' *The Invasion*. (CD.) Flytime Music MGSPSDT. 2011: Nigeria.

P-Square. 'Personally.' *Double Trouble*. (CD.) Square Records MGSPSDT. 2014: Nigeria.

Tetuila, Tony. 'My Car.' *My Car*. (CD.) Kennis Music KMMC 024. 2002: Nigeria.

Trybesmen. 'Shake Bodi.' *L.A.G. Style*. Storm Records. 1999: Nigeria.

Weird MC. 'Allen Avenue.' *Simply Weird*. 1997: Nigeria.

Wizkid. 'Holla At Yo Boy.' *Superstar*. Empire Mates Entertainment. 2010: Nigeria.

Wizkid. 'Ojuelegba.' *Ayo*. Starboy Entertainment. 2014: Nigeria.

Wizkid. *Sounds from the Other Side*. Starboy/RCA. 2017: Nigeria.

Discography

D'Banj. 'Oliver Twist.' *Elton* vs. Pnau – Oliver Twist / Good Morning to The Night*. Universal. *2012*: UK and USA.

Eva. 'High.' *GIGO*. 3UD. *2011*: Nigeria.

YouTube

JJC. 'Afro Shank': https://www.youtube.com/watch?v=9xvdVCJvDOc (2012) (accessed 22 April 2018).

Olu Maintain. 'Yahooze': https://www.youtube.com/watch?v=0Jh8tCns-Bg 2007) (accessed 22 April 2018).

P-Square. 'Alingo': https://www.youtube.com/watch?v=IJUUbxZHmiM (2012) (accessed 22 April 2018).

P-Square. 'Personally': https://www.youtube.com/watch?v=ttdU19Kwce8 (2013) (accessed 22 April 2018).

STEPHANIE SHONEKAN

Hip-Hop in Nigeria (Hausa Rap)

The availability of new forms of musical reproduction from the mid-1990s (particularly the Yamaha PSR series of synthesizers with stored dumbreat samples), coupled with the easy access to rap samples on the Internet and the massive popularity of US rap music meant it was only a matter of time before Hausa musicians in northern Nigeria created their own version of rap. Hausa rap emerged as a counterpoint, in both the musical and urban sense of the word, to the increasing spread of southern Nigerian rap. Hausa rappers seek to reorient the musical landscape of at least northern Nigeria toward a more focused messaging in their lyrics, striking a balance between transnational rhythms and the Hausa philosophy in their lyrics. Not only do their songs appeal to their young audiences, but they are also considered acceptable to the more traditionalist Hausa establishment.

In 2004 Kano-born and Lagos-based Yoruba rapper Eedris Abdulkareem released the CD *Jaga-Jaga*. The title track, sung in the popular Nigerian Pidgin English, was a blistering attack on Nigeria's social and political conditions. The main attraction to the Hausa audience was a Hausa-language track, 'Segarin Kano' (in Hausa, 'Sai Garin Kano' [Going to Kano City]). This proved that Hausa language could be used in rap. Right across the border to the north in the Republic of Niger, Nigerien Hausa rap musicians such as Kaidan Gaskia, Lafiya Matassa, Nazari, Dan Kowa, Fa-Baako and Lakal Kaney were combining musical styles by copying the US hip-hop beat and delivery style of artists such as Run DMC, 50 Cent, Snoop Dogg, 2Pac and DMX, while using the Hausa language and thus confirming the credibility of Hausa-language hip-hop. When in 2005 ZM (Zara Moussa) from Zinder released 'Kirari' ('praise epithet' or 'battle-cry,' rereleased in her album *Ma Rage* in 2012) she shot to stardom as the first female Hausa Muslim rapper in Africa. This was remarkable because neither Nigerian nor Nigerien public spaces provide an opportunity for women to participate in mixed-gender public culture. Further, rap music, perhaps the world over, has long been associated with male macho posturing. ZM therefore broke many barriers – misogynistic, patriarchal, cultural and even religious – as a Muslim female rapper in Africa. Her lyrics, especially on 'Rappo' from the album *Kirari*, drew attention to the poverty and ignorance that bedeviled rural women.

By 2006 a definite interest in creating Hausa rap had been established, particularly among urban youth. Repeated airplay of US rap music over local radio stations generated a lot of interest among young people, while evoking derision from adults who viewed US rap lyrics as antisocial. Soon, undeterred, young people started picking up the microphone and imitating the rap rhythms they heard over the radio, using Hausa words to create onomatopoeic meters that approximate the original rap lyrics they were appropriating.

The music industry in Nigeria is informal, without structured labels and catalogs, so most songs recorded in studios are simply passed around via Bluetooth to friends and often uploaded to MySpace, Hausahiphop blogspot or other MP3 portals. Although they did not offer record deals, the abundance of music studios in Kano made it possible for young aspiring lyricists to have their compositions set to music for a fee of as little as NGN2,500 (US$11 in 2015). The result was an avalanche of Hausa rappers including Northern Soldierz, K-Boys, X-Man Sarari, Kano Riders, J-Man, Ontos, Minor Mistake and Buzu 'Dan Pullo. These Hausa rappers came to public attention through the four FM radio stations then existing in Kano.

With no specific professional training in the use of musical instruments, these Hausa rap artists have relied heavily on a coterie of session musicians spread across the recording studios in Kano using music software such as Cubase, Cakewalk Pro, Sound Forge and FruityLoops (all available as pirated full-version copies – with cracks, serials or keygens – for less than US$4 on mega-compilation CDs from Malaysia and Indonesia) accompanied by the increasing use of Yamaha PSR keyboards (or 'fiyano') and Behringer mixing consoles.

Kano Riders acquired high international status when they collaborated on their demo track 'Rayuwa Cikin Kunci' with a member of the most successful Nigerian rap group, Lakal Kaney, in 2005. On 30 July 2011, Radio Freedom, an FM station based in Kano, debuted the pilot of *Kano Music Express*, hosted by half of K-Boys crew, Hassan M. Sheriff. This program provided the only opportunity for Hausa Rappers to be heard and seemed to galvanize students from high school to college age, young civil servants and just about anybody who wanted to rap to do so – and be heard.

By 2015 more Hausa rap 'crews' had emerged in northern Nigeria. These included Mixter Bash, Mic Flammer, IQ, TEAxY, K-Arrowz, G-Fresh, Dr Pure, Daddy Fresh and Nomiis Gee – only about three of whom had released CDs. Nomiis Gee hosted a Satellite TV program, Arewa24, that showcased emerging Hausa Rap artists in both Nigeria and Niger.

Ziriums released a CD, *This Is Me*, on Amazon in 2010. However, due to nonrenewal of the distribution license with the portal, the CD was removed from Amazon. The artist, one of whose songs, 'Girgiza Kai' (Shake Your Head), was banned by the Kano State Government in 2008, relocated in 2011 to Florida in the United States, where there is more creative freedom for rappers and an absence of government-enforced censorship of music and lyrics.

Almost all Hausa rappers sing in the Hausa language, accompanied most often by hardcore rap tunes, much to the bemusement of the general audiences in Kano, who perceive such musical performances as merely an attempt to imitate US rappers. The tunes are either composed by a studio session musician or simply downloaded from sites providing free hardcore beat samples on the Internet over which the lyricists lay their songs. A few rappers, such as IQ and G-Fresh, prefer to rap in English. The Islamicate nature of cities such as Kano make it difficult to create a true hip-hop culture, in the sense of an urban youth lifestyle, including personal appearance and clothing; the Hisbah Islamic police are always on the lookout for 'un-Islamic apparel' and admonish youth who wear such clothing. Rap crews must censor their lyrics, especially in the local Hausa language, to escape the wrath of the local Censorship Board. Thus Hausa rap lyrics tend to emphasize social sermonizing about good behavior and respect for all. There are exceptions, however. TEAxY's 'Allah Ya Isa' (God Is Our Adjudicator) was a blistering attack on the political culture of Nigeria in 2013. The pungency of the lyrics prevented radio play. IQ's 'Founding Fathers,' released in 2012, offers a similar, although muted, attack on the political leadership in Nigeria as having betrayed Nigeria's founding fathers. Sustained by enthusiasm rather than professionalism, Hausa rap provides urban Hausa young people with an opportunity to be part of a transnational music process by domesticating the genre as part of their social culture.

Bibliography

Adamu, Abdalla Uba. 2014. 'PDP Reloaded: Political Mobilization Through Urban Musics in Kano.' *Bayero Journal of Political Science* 1 June: 65–89.

Discographical References

Abdulkareem, Eedris. 'Jaga-Jaga.' *Jaga-Jaga*. Kennis Music. *2004*: Nigeria.

Abdulkareem, Eedris. 'Se Garin Kano.' *Jaga-Jaga*. Kennis Music. *2004*: Nigeria.

IQ. 'Founding Fathers.' Kastiq Media Production. *2012*: Nigeria.

Kano Riders. 'Rayuwa Cikin Ƙunci.' *Sababbin Mawakan Hausa*. Isiyaka Yellow. *2007*: Nigeria.

Moussa, Zara. 'Kirari.' *Kirari*. La source studio. *2005*: Republic of Niger.

Moussa, Zara. 'Kirari.' *Ma Rage*. Label Caravan. *2012*: France.

Moussa, Zara. 'Rappo.' *Kirari*. La source studio. *2005*: Republic of Niger.

TEAxY. 'Allah Ya Isa.' *Taba Ka Lashe*. Teaxy Jamz. *2015*: Nigeria.

Ziriums. 'Girgiza Kai.' *This is Me*. ReverbNation. *2010*: Nigeria.

Ziriums. 'This is Me.' *This is Me*. ReverbNation. *2010*: Nigeria.

Discography

Dr Pure. *Just the Beginning*. Reverbnation. *2014*: Nigeria.

G Fresh & Al-Amin. *Forget Your Enemies*. Kastiq Media Production. *2015*: Nigeria.

K-Arrowz. 'Sakayya.' S&A Records. *2014*: Nigeria.

K-Boys. 'Bonus Tracks on Harigido.' El-Isah Enterprises. *2010*: Nigeria.

Kano Riders. *Sababbin Mawakan Hausa*. Isiyaka Yellow. *2007*: Nigeria.

TEAxY. *Taba Ka Lashe*. Teaxy Jamz. *2015*: Nigeria.

Zara Moussa. *Ma Rage*. Label Caravan. *2012*: France.

Filmography

Recording a Revolution: A Story of Music, Religion, and Identity, dir. Alex Johnson and Saman Piracha. 2010. USA. 108 mins. Documentary. Original music by Ziriums, K-Boys, Kano Riders, Nasiru Garba Supa and Arewa, Adam A. Zango. Billy-O, Desert Caravan, and Osama bn Music.

ABDALLA UBA ADAMU

Hip-Hop in Senegal

Since the early 1980s Senegalese youth have embraced hip-hop as a global cultural import and as a local cultural practice, refashioning it to their own realities through musical production, sartorial practices, entrepreneurship, political movements, and education and health initiatives. Inspired by the *verlan* (inverted slang) of Arab and African rappers in France, Senegalese hip-hop is locally referred to as 'rap galsen,' an inversion of the first and last syllables of the word *Sene-gal*. Musically indistinguishable from US hip-hop, whose numerous substyles all share the same primary elements of rapped texts over cyclical, layered instrumental tracks, *rap galsen* features localized lyrical content in French and Wolof and sometimes incorporates West African instruments and singing.

Early History and Development

Young people in Dakar's affluent neighborhoods first encountered hip-hop through films including *Beat Street* and *Wild Style*, and through hip-hop cassettes acquired from family members who traveled internationally. In the early 1980s these youths formed dance crews using US hip-hop music as the soundtrack for performances and competitions. When they first began rapping in the mid to late 1980s, it was to repeat the English lyrics of US artists without necessarily understanding their meaning.

Artists Mbacke Dioum and MC Lida are both popularly credited with recording the first original Senegalese rap songs. They were quickly followed by musical groups who had grown out of Dakar's hip-hop dance crews, including Positive Black Soul (comprising DJ Awadi and Doug E. Tee), and Pee Froiss (Xuman, Kool Koc VI, Bibson, Sista Joyce and Gee Bayss). *Rap galsen*'s big break came in 1992, when Positive Black Soul, whose music featured primarily French-language lyrics and sung refrains, opened for Senegalese-French rapper MC Solaar's performance at Dakar's French Cultural Center. The performance led the way to an international market for the group, who released their 1995 album *Salaam* on Mango, a division of Island Records. In the meantime, radio and television programming ensured local hip-hop's spread throughout Senegal.

The mid-1990s witnessed a shift in *rap galsen*. In Medina, the overpopulated, colonially designated 'native quarter,' the group Rap'Adio (rappers Keyti, Iba and Bibson – formerly of Pee Froiss) was inspired by the politicized hip-hop of black nationalist US groups including Public Enemy. Although Rap'Adio had been around for quite some time, their 1998 album *Ku weet xam sa bop* (One Knows Oneself in Solitude) ignited an ever-expanding hip-hop movement. Rapping hard-hitting lyrics entirely in Wolof, the dominant indigenous language, and abandoning the melodic refrains of earlier hip-hop records, Rap'Adio, along with Yatfu and Wa BMG 44, who released their first albums the same year, helped create a new, 'hardcore' identity for Senegalese hip-hop. Membership in these early hip-hop groups shifted frequently, as rappers matured and diverged in their musical tastes.

Hip-Hop's Second Wave and Senegalese Politics

Emerging under the wing of Rap'Adio, groups and artists including Bis bi Clan, Sen Kumpë, 5kiem Underground, Tigrim Bi, Nix, 23.3 Wisdom Connection and Zair ak Batine represented some of the next wave of Dakar rappers in the late 1990s and early 2000s. These groups often coalesced around recording studios/labels such as Jolof4Life in Medina (run by Simon, formerly of Bis bi Clan) and Def Dara in Parcelles Assainies (owned and operated by Gaston, formerly of Sen Kumpë). Hip-hop had spread through the impoverished *banlieues* (under-serviced periphery neighborhoods of the city) through groups such as Wa BMG 44, Bat'haillons Blin-D and Tigrim Bi, while at the same time new hip-hop was emerging from various regions of Senegal. As rappers throughout the country spoke out against government corruption, some faced political persecution. For example, the members of the Kaolack-based group Keur Gui were imprisoned several times in the late 1990s. The 2000 presidential elections became the testing ground for this new wave of Senegalese hip-hop. Encouraging young people to vote for change, rappers were instrumental in the first shift in political power in 30 years, overwhelmingly backing the successful candidate, Abdoulaye Wade. But 2007 found the same rappers who had supported Wade's ascent to power disillusioned by the change they had helped enact. Wade's reelection that year fueled hip-hop's political mission, and in 2011 rappers Thiat and Kilifeu of Keur Gui and rapper Foumalade initiated the Y'en a Marre ('We've had enough') movement. Protesting against the president's manipulations of the constitution, Senegalese youth took to the streets in sometimes violent demonstrations that hip-hoppers themselves, as well as local and foreign journalists, carefully publicized and documented. Prior to Wade's defeat in the 2012 elections, Y'en a Marre focused on voter registration and advocating for a NTS (New Type of Senegalese) that took responsibility for urban cleanliness and development. A new generation of rappers from the poorest peripheral neighborhoods of the city took part – including Fuk n Kuk, Niamu Mbaam and other artists too numerous to name.

It is important to note, however, that not all hip-hoppers embraced the primarily extramusical Y'en a Marre movement; some emphasized that their music-making itself was sufficient as a medium for social commentary and change. Whether involved in Y'en a Marre or not, Senegalese rappers overwhelmingly concerned themselves with social issues, including poverty, rampant power outages and flooding, unemployment, dangerous illegal immigration to Europe and HIV and health education.

Hip-Hop Markets and Media

Hip-hoppers often juxtapose *rap galsen*'s social and political leanings with Senegal's preeminent popular music *mbalax*, whose traditions of praise singing for political and religious figures make it unattractive as a tool for social change. Although *mbalax* was omnipresent in Senegal in the early twenty-first century, dominating the best performance venues and prime television and radio programming, hip-hop's popularity and media exposure was constantly growing. In particular, televised hip-hop competitions and awards shows launched several rappers' careers (notably Canabasse, Reskape and Mame Xa). While the perceived violence of the hardcore movement of the late 1990s alienated mainstream audiences and discouraged young women and girls from attending hip-hop concerts, the 2010s saw hip-hop's mainstream appeal grow steadily, particularly with artists such as Canabasse, Nix and Da Brains.

At the same time, the increasing democratization of hip-hop production – the availability of beatmaking software, access to up-to-the-moment hip-hop from the United States and France, and *rap galsen*'s increased visibility in local media – has meant that more and more Senegalese youth actively make hip-hop. The hip-hop cultural center Africulturbain in Pikine, established by rapper Matador (founder of Wa BMG 44) and directed by Amadou Fall Ba, hosts local and international festivals, organizes influential hip-hop competitions to further the careers of young talent and provides hip-hop education – beatmaking labs, film editing instruction, breakdance and DJing workshops – for local youth.

This increased access to hip-hop does not leave space for everyone, however. Because in Senegalese society most women marry at a fairly young age, and married women are often discouraged from pursuing hip-hop careers that would keep them out late at night and away from their families, the vast majority of Senegalese rappers are male. Notable female hip-hoppers have included the group Alif, Sister Fa (known for her activist work against female genital cutting), Fatim (of Wa BMG 44) and the newer collective Gotale, spearheaded by rapper Anta. Gotale's shifting roster has included Toussa, Sista Coumbis, Zeyna, Sista Dia and other young woman rappers. These women negotiate a tricky balance between the masculine-coded aesthetic norms that are associated with hip-hop (globally and in Senegal) and local pressures to perform cultural norms of femininity as a part of their social and artistic personas.

Since Senegal's first wave of hip-hop artists, few other groups (proportionate to the thousands of young people engaging in hip-hop) have found international recognition. Daara J (originally comprising Fada Freddy, Ndongo D and Aladjiman) achieved international acclaim with their third album *Boomerang* in 2003, and Bideew Bou Bess, a group of brothers whose career was launched by *mbalax* star Youssou N'Dour, performs frequently at world music festivals in Europe and the United States. Wa BMG 44 recorded their 2004 album, *44 4 Life*, in Belgium, and since then founding member Matador has toured Europe extensively. The groups Wagëblë and Gokh bi System, while also popular in Senegal, have made their careers largely in Europe and the United States, respectively, and rapper Sister Fa resides and performs in Germany. The founders of Y'en a Marre, Keur Gui and Foumalade, have had several performance and speaking engagements in the United States. The US Department of State has given significant financial support to *rap galsen*, particularly as the genre matures in its political sensibilities, awarding grant money to Africulturbain and funding artists Toussa and PPS the Writah to come to the United States as part of the State Department's OneBeat program.

Outside of international tours, hip-hop success in Senegal is largely measured through fandom (often centered on neighborhood affiliations) and performance opportunities. While hip-hop is fairly well represented on television and radio, the lack of a structured industry, the prevalence of piracy, and the inefficacy and corruption of the BSDA (Bureau Senegalais des Droits des Auteurs – the national copyright office) in procuring royalties, all mean that hip-hop in Senegal is rarely a profitable enterprise. Rappers are generationally divided in their attitudes toward copyright and piracy, with the established first generation expressing greater concern than the more ambivalent younger generations (Melendez-Torres 2014). Although albums play an important role in legitimizing an artist and garnering a fanbase, artists make money from concerts and festivals. In light of hip-hop's unprofitability, rappers increasingly turn to secondary occupations to support themselves. For example, rapper Drygun, of Yatfu, runs a streetwear shop in Dioupel called 'Galsen Shop,' and rapper Reskape launched his now-widespread BancLieuxArts line of T-shirts in 2007. Since then many others have followed suit, and locally produced, locally themed hip-hop clothing is a popular business endeavor.

Hip-Hop Performance and Aesthetics

In live performance, a shortage of high-quality equipment enforces a norm of 'playback,' where artists rap along with the prerecorded vocals of the album versions of their songs rather than over purely instrumental tracks. Performances are communal efforts, with several groups performing at the same concert; often rappers will support other rappers on stage with backup vocals and by egging on the crowd. Performances are typically scripted; 'freestyling' in *rap galsen* refers to the *a cappella* recitation of precomposed lyrics, although some artists – notably Djily Bagdad of 5kiem Underground, are known for their ability to improvise lyrics on the spot.

Musically, *rap galsen* closely follows aesthetic trends in US hip-hop, from early East Coast styles to more contemporary Dirty South beats, but it is localized through the use of indigenous languages and Senegal-specific thematic content. Sometimes, hip-hop musical tracks also include local musical elements, either sampled or directly recorded into the track; these might include the *kora* (harp lute of the Mande ethnic group), 'talking' pressure drums, and traditional and Islamic singing styles among other possibilities. Rappers rely heavily on Wolof, Senegal's lingua franca, and those who are able also incorporate other indigenous languages, as well as French and English. Most hip-hoppers are adamant that these localizing techniques are consistent with US hip-hop culture's history of distinct regional aesthetics (e.g., East Coast, West Coast and Dirty South substyles) rather than representing any kind of musical syncretism.

Senegalese youth have adopted more than hip-hop's musical components. Rappers and hip-hop fans typically sport US hip-hop fashion, including Nike and Adidas sneakers, New Era baseball caps and clothing labels such as Marc Ecco and Rocawear. Hip-hop fashion has sparked local adaptations, such as BancLieuxArts, noted above, and the clothing line Mbeddu Jolof, which incorporates Afrocentric imagery into sportswear-inspired styles.

While generally adhering to US hip-hop production norms in their musical tracks, and despite their enthusiasm for US hip-hop fashion, most Senegalese hip-hoppers describe their music as a socially and/or politically motivated endeavor that they explicitly differentiate from what they portray as mainstream US hip-hop's increasing emphasis, since around the start of the twenty-first century, on consumerism and sex. Other common themes include love for one's mother, praise for Muslim saints, romantic relationships and 'ego trips' or bragging.

Conclusion

While rarely a vehicle for financial success, *rap galsen* has become a social force in Senegal, creating a space for young people to express themselves and to mobilize against political corruption and the lived experiences of underdevelopment. The variety of styles and perspectives that have variously defined *rap galsen* over its 30-year history demonstrate how artists develop and change as the sociocultural context in which they make and consume hip-hop does the same.

Bibliography

Appert, Catherine. 2012. *Modernity, Remixed: Music as Memory in Rap Galsen*. Unpublished Ph.D. thesis, University of California, Los Angeles.

Herson, Benjamin. 2011. 'A Historical Analysis of Hip-Hop's Influence in Dakar from 1984–2000.' *American Behavioral Scientist* 55(1): 24–35.

Lo, Sheba. 2014. 'Building Our Nation: Senegalese Hip Hop Artists as Agents of Social and Political Change.' In *Hip Hop and Social Change in Africa: Ni Wakati*, eds. Msia Kibona Clark and Mickie Mwanzia Koster. Lanham, MD: Lexington Books, 27–48.

Melendez-Torres, Juan Carlos. 2014. 'Claiming Creation: Hip-hop Aesthetics, Authorship, and Copyright Reform in Dakar, Senegal.' Unpublished undergraduate honors thesis, University of Pennsylvania, Philadelphia.

Tang, Patricia. 2013. 'The Rapper as Modern Griot: Reclaiming Ancient Traditions.' In *Hip Hop Africa: New African Music in a Globalizing World*, ed. Eric Charry. Indianapolis: Indiana University Press, 79–91.

Discographical References

Daara J. *Boomerang*. Wrasse Records WRASS105. *2003*: UK.

Da Brains. *Welcome to Senegal*. Rockstar 400. *2011*: Senegal.

Positive Black Soul. *Salaam*. Mango Records CIDM 1114. *1995*: UK.

Rap'Adio. *Ku weet xam sa bop*. Fitna Productions. *1998*: Senegal.

Waa BMG 44. *44 4 Life*. Independent Release. *2004*: Senegal.

Discography

23.3 Wisdom Connection. *Sunu thiono seen noflaye*. Underkamouf Records. *2010*: Senegal.

5kiem Underground. *Yagg bawoul dara*. Jolof4Life/99 Records. *2009*: Senegal.

African Underground: The Depths of Dakar. Nomadic Wax. *2007*: USA.

African Underground Vol. 1 – Hip-hop Senegal. Nomadic Wax. *2004*: USA.

Alien Zik. *Benen Planet*. Alien Zik Records. *2010*: Senegal.

Bat'haillons Blin-D. *2guntaan*. Independent Release. *2003*: Senegal.

Bideew Bou Bes. *Ndoumbelane*. Independent Release. *2010*: Senegal.

Checky Blaze. *Bou kéné tok (Prise de Conscience)*. Independent Release. *2011*: Senegal.

Daara J. *Daara J*. Déclic Communications 842 9482. *1997*: France.

Daara J. *Xalima*. Déclic Communications B10592. *1998*: France.

Daara J. *Exodus*. Studio 2000. *2002*: Senegal.

Daara J Family. *School of Life*. Wrasse Records WRASS262. *2010*: UK.

DJ Awadi. *Sunugaal*. Mr. Bongo MRBCD059. *2008*: UK.

DJ Awadi. *Presidents d'Afrique*. Périphéria PECD – 5467. *2010*: Canada.

Fata aka El Presidente. *R'afrik*. Taflabel. *2005*: Senegal.

Fata aka El Presidente. *Iqra*. Taflabel. *2013*: Senegal.

Foumalade. *Radio Kankan*. Whatawhat Arts. *2005*: Senegal.

Foumalade. *On va tout dire*. Youkoungkoung Production. *2008*: Senegal.

Gaston. *Tutti wakh job lu beuri*. Def Dara Productions. *2011*: Senegal.

Gohk-bi System. *Pour mouy leer*. Siga Production. *2004*: Senegal.

Keur Gui. *Nos connes doléances*. Independent Release. *2008*: Senegal.

Keyti. *Jog ak daanu*. Independent Release. *2003*: Senegal.

Keyti, Gaston, Ass Malick, and Nix. *Dakar All Stars*. Africa Productions. *2006*: Senegal.

Makhtar le Kagoulard. *Sene mafia*. Under Kamouf Records. *2009*: Senegal.

Mame Xa. *Door waar*. Independent Release. *2008*: Senegal.

Matador. *Xippil Xoll*. Optimiste Productions OPTI-052. *2012*: Senegal.

Matador. *Vox Populi*. Amp Music. *2013*: Senegal.

Maxi Krezy. *La Lumière est ma loi lux mea lux*. Shortwave Records. *2008*: Senegal.

Niamu Mbaam. *Guddi leer*. Youkoungkoung Productions. *2011*: Senegal.

Nitdoff. *M'béde bi*. Senprod. *2007*: Senegal.

Nix. *Rimes de vie*. Kénène Productions. *2010*: Senegal.

Pee Froiss. *Wala wala bokk*. Independent Release. *1996*: Senegal.

Pee Froiss. *F.R.O.I.S.S.* Africa Fête Productions. *2001*: Senegal.

Positive Black Soul. *Run Cool*. Palm Tree Enterprises Inc. 8573 86845 2. *2000*: FrancePositive Black Soul. *New York/Paris/Dakar*. Island Records Limited/Africa Fete Diffusions AFD 005. *2002*: France.

Rap'Adio. *Soldaaru mbed*. Independent Release. *2001*: Senegal.

Reskape. *Dafa jot.* Optimiste Productions. *2008*: Senegal.

Sen Kumpë. *Freedom.* Jolof4Life/99 Records. *2008*: Senegal.

Simon Bisbi Clan. *Diggué boorla.* Jolof4Life/99 Records. *2006*: Senegal.

Sister Fa. *Sarabah – Tales from the Flipside of Paradise.* Piranha CD-PIR2334. *2009*: Germany.

Tigrim Bi. *Gëm gëm du faatu.* Jolof4Life/99 Records. *2010*: Senegal.

Undershiffai. *Mafia mbedd. Independent Release. 2004*: Senegal.

Wa BMG 44. *J Hardcore.* Independent Release. *1998*: Senegal.

Wagëblë. *Senegal.* Two Thou TTPCD02. *2005*: Norway.

Xuman. *Gunman.* Independent Release. *2007*: Senegal.

Yatfu. *Fenku Yatfu.* Independent Release. *1998*: Senegal.

Zair ak Batine. *Xel nangouwoul.* Jolof4Life/99 Records. *2008*: Senegal.

Filmography

Beat Street, dir. Stan Lathan. 1984. USA. 105 mins. Drama.

Wild Style, dir. Charlie Ahearn. 1983. USA. 82 mins. Feature film.

CATHERINE M. APPERT

Hip-Hop in South Africa

In South Africa, hip-hop and rap music are visible in all the major cities and in small, rural towns. Arriving in Cape Town in the mid-1980s, when music, dancing and spraypainting were used as a means of articulating resistance to the apartheid regime, the style had traveled a long journey since its appearance in the South Bronx in the 1970s. In 2015 rap music and versions thereof are performed and appreciated by all population groups in South Africa. Rap music is credited as one of the major influences on *kwaito*, a formulaic popular music genre that emerged in South Africa in the early 1990s, as well as South African house music, which attracted worldwide interest among DJs. Rap is associated with both social commentary and freedom of expression. However, although hip-hop has not entirely moved away from the margin, most of its power to resist has been marshaled by the music industry, the print media and the awards ceremonies that present what many critics feel are dubious interpretations of rap music.

Background

The origins of hip-hop in South Africa share elements with counterparts in other areas of the globe. Breakdance, in particular, and also spraypainting were associated with the political struggle against apartheid. Toward the end of the 1980s, following its global spread through films such as *Wild Style*, rap music was added to the repertoire of cultural expressions that could be mobilized against apartheid. Elements of the genre first became visible in Cape Town in the mid-1980s. The main artists at the time were the Prophets of the City (POC) and Black Noise. These artists had a strong presence in Cape Town as well as overseas, especially in the Benelux countries, due to similarities in their respective languages, and in Sweden. These groups played a significant role in introducing the tenets of hip-hop to townships and rural towns (Watkins 2004). Hip-hop and rap music became tools through which marginalized young people learned about developing their capacity to influence change in their social lives. In the beginning, hip-hop and rap music made their presence felt through social activism, but since the early 2000s this has no longer been the case for the most part, as many young people and corporations are more interested in procuring financial gain.

The hip-hop industry is centralized in Johannesburg, the city in South Africa most associated with capitalist enterprise, and consists of music labels, rap artists from across the country, a rap magazine called *Hype*, breakdancing competitions on the state television broadcaster, and numerous awards ceremonies (including the South African Traditional Music Awards, which, strangely, has included rap music within its ambit). What may seem uniform on the surface has become diverse, contested and multilayered. While gloss and crass materialism often appear to dominate the rap music scene and hip-hop, there is another side that is proudly underground. There is a dichotomy, with musicians in one camp maintaining resistance to the dominant interests of the industrial economy, while those in another camp gratuitously consume as much as possible. The latter group is heavily subsidized by the music industry as well as other kinds of corporations such as Adidas and Red Bull.

Rap has manifested as a form shaped by diverse interests, capabilities and racial identifications and it challenges those in power and those who continue to benefit from the spoils of apartheid. In the South African context, one may consequently claim that hip-hop has matured. The music is not only referred to simply as rap. As different artists from different parts of the country, with different everyday life experiences and different backgrounds, take ownership of the music, new permutations emerge such as zef-rap, a term coined by Jack Parow to refer to the rap music from Afrikaner working-class suburbs in Cape Town.

In the first 15 years of the twenty-first century, there has been a remarkable increase of mass-mediated hip-hop acts and performers. Some of them prefer the anonymity of the underground, while others have blasted their way onto the global stage with fanfare and spectacle. The first wave of hip-hoppers and rap musicians in South Africa were strongly committed to the anti-apartheid struggle and indeed, many continue to voice their opposition to perceived acts of oppression. Among these are artists such as Jitsvinger, who has taken up the cudgel against fracking in the Karoo, and Dookom, who sings against the ongoing repression of seasonal farm workers in the Western Cape. Their lyrics are angry, and speak for the voiceless whose plight goes unanswered by those in authority. As in other parts of the country, their lyrics are also heavily influenced by a local patois which tends to make them unintelligible to outsiders. Their lyrics and the tone in which they are articulated represent a frustration which seems irresolute. The music elicits many negative responses from their targets as the lyrics are considered an abuse of the right to freedom of speech and expression. But there are also artists who have been embraced by local and foreign audiences, presenting to audiences performances that are spectacular and carnivalesque. For them, the stage is a site of excess: an excess of noise, spectacle in sight and sound, and inversion. Artists such as Die Antwoord and Jack Parow are leaders of these styles of performances. Both have become international stars. Both are white and through their utterances and performance style they mock the propriety of their legacy and their roots in Afrikanerdom. In their language, which can be pejorative about ethnicity or class, it appears that they identify with working-class people of mixed descent in Cape Town who are intimately connected to them in race if not the space of Cape Town.

There is a tendency in the music scholarship of South Africa to privilege the Cape Town–Johannesburg axis but it is equally important to describe the sites and towns that are not as well-known as these cosmopolitan cities. The coastal towns such as Durban in KwaZulu-Natal and Port Elizabeth in the Eastern Cape on the eastern littoral deserve mention. Durban's demographics enable hip-hoppers to articulate their various identifications in terms of color, where isiZulu speakers and people of Indian descent live in close proximity. Zulu Boy is a prominent rapper from KwaZulu-Natal who has made an impact on the rap music scene in Johannesburg. His lyrics and songs are about identifying as a Zulu person but there are also strong messages about corruption and the Marikana massacre in 2012. There are a number of mixed-race groups who sing about various topics including romantic love and the effects of pollution in an area south of Durban where oil refineries do not respect environmental laws or human settlement. In Port Elizabeth, there are groups representing different populations, and since it is a closely connected city they share a sense of the hip-hop community and strive toward social development in their communities. Since many believe that the main industry or broadcasting stations in Johannesburg do not have an interest in them, these rappers conduct workshops, produce their music independently, and their music is mainly broadcast on community radio stations and distributed using the Bluetooth application on their devices. Many of these performers, however, express a strong desire to be a part of the scene in Johannesburg and occasionally they perform in Johannesburg and other parts of the country (Watkins 2012).

Style

A key feature of rap music globally is the use of local languages or 'spectacular vernaculars' (Potter 1995). Some of these languages, such as Chinese for instance, present a challenge which adds to the different articulations of rap style and, in this sense, South African rap has made a dramatic contribution to global rap style. South Africa has 11 official languages but there is a range of dialects including tsotsi-taal and the Afrikaans patois spoken in Cape Town, in addition to foul language copied from US artists as well as swear words that are unique to South Africa. These vernaculars have specific tones and rhythms, and are delivered with choreographed postures. The tones and rhythms are readily employed in South African rap songs.

South African rappers have observed that, in addition to language, pools of sounds are unique to each particular location. In Cape Town, rap employs the practice of using local humor and the *ghoema* sound; in Durban, music is influenced by *maskanda* and *isicathamiya*; and in Port Elizabeth the rap music is influenced by Christian hymns and songs associated with the anti-apartheid struggle. The sounds reinforce their differences and emphasize the sense of locale, but rappers are also drawn to another source of music, that is, popular music, particularly of black Americans. South African rappers use samples from US R&B, jazz, soul and middle-of-the-road popular music. Combining North American popular music with a South African style such as *maskanda* results in rich textures. Through these practices, rappers reveal their education in music and they also enjoy rendering the sound as unique compositions. Their ongoing experimentation with sounds, and the rise of new generations of rappers in South Africa, reveals that rap music remains a fluid form in which style is negotiable and mutable.

Conclusion

Hip-hop and rap music have become pervasive to the point where it is nearly impossible to separate them from other forms of popular culture in South Africa. In the early twenty-first century it is not easy to tell how the hip-hop scene in South Africa will evolve. What is certain is that it simply won't stop.

Bibliography

Abrahams, Nazli, and Ariefdien, Shaheen. 2006. 'Cape Flats Alchemy: Hip-Hop Arts in South Africa.' In *Total Chaos: The Art and Aesthetics of Hip-Hop*, ed. Jeff Chang. New York: Basic Citvas, 262–70.

Hawkins-Mofokeng, Raymond Hilary. 2016. *Marketing Implications of Hip-Hop Culture in Durban, South Africa*. LAP Lambert Publishing (on-demand publisher).

Potter, Russell A. 1995. *Spectacular Vernaculars: Hip Hop and the Politics of Postmodernism*. Albany, NY: State University of New York Press.

Swartz, Sharlene. 2008. 'Is Kwaito South African Hip-Hop? Why the Answer Matters and Who It Matters to.' *The World of Music* 50(2): 15–33.

Watkins, Lee. 2004. '"Rapp'in" the Cape: Style and Memory, Power in Community.' In *Music, Space and Place*, ed. Sheila Whiteley. Abingdon: Ashgate, 124–46.

Watkins, Lee. 2012. 'A Genre Coming of Age: Transformation, Difference, and Authenticity in the Rap Music and Hip-Hop Culture of South Africa.' In *Hip Hop Africa: New African Music in a Globalizing World*, ed. Eric Charry. Bloomington: Indiana University Press, 57–75.

Williams, Quentin E. 2016. 'Youth Multilingualism in South Africa's Hip-Hop Culture: A Metapragmatic Analysis.' *Sociolinguistic Studies* 10(1–2): 109–32.

Williams, Quentin E., and Stroud, Christopher. 2010. 'Performing Rap Ciphas in Late-Modern Cape Town: Extreme Locality and Multilingual Citizenship.' *Afrika Focus* 23(2): 39–59. Online at https://ojs.ugent.be/AF/article/viewFile/5005/4939 (accessed 23 March 2018).

Discography

Die Antwoord (The Answer). O. Self-released. *2009*: South Africa.

Jack Parow. *Eksie Ou* [I'm the Dude]. Parowphernalia. *2011*: South Africa.

Jitsvinger. *Skeletsleutel* [Skeleton Key]. KMD – VOLT005. *2006*: South Africa.

Zuluboy. *Inqolobane* [Conqueror]. Native Rhythms Records/EMI/CCP. *2008*: South Africa.

Filmography

Wild Style, dir. Charlie Ahearn. 1982. USA. 82 minutes. Feature film.

LEE WATKINS

Hip-Hop in the Democratic Republic of the Congo

Hip-hop culture, and rap music in particular, began to gain popularity among young people in the Democratic Republic of the Congo (DRC) in the early 1990s, though still eclipsed by established genres such as *rumba* and *ndombolo*. While some artists have incorporated indigenous instruments and compositional elements into their songs, the majority of Congolese hip-hop music conforms to the globally ubiquitous norms of rapped lyrics over rhythm-heavy, predominantly electronic beats, making it musically indistinguishable from its US and European counterparts. In terms of content, in the DRC artists, producers and audiences insist that hip-hop is 'political' compared to other popular genres such as R&B, *rumba* or *soukouss*, yet its political nature is measured in terms of raising awareness rather than fomenting overt action. Further, because of the DRC's vast geographic territory and the distinct histories of different parts of the country, claims for hip-hop as a political genre vary notably from region to region, as do associated aesthetic elements.

Early History and Development

Hip-hop became popular in the DRC (then Zaire) in the early 1990s when the nation was still laboring under the dictatorship and strict cultural regulations of Mobutu Sese Seko. During his 32-year rule, Mobutu imposed *authenticité*, a regime that banned Western cultural practices – including music, dance, clothing, names and so on – in an effort to enforce a nationally unifying 'traditional' Congolese (then Zairian) culture. Under *authenticité*, popular music became a source of national pride, indeed the nation was globally recognized as 'the capital of African music,' yet, simultaneously, Mobutu's strategic deployment of music in political negotiations positioned it as a vehicle of strict authoritarian control. When his power began to decline in the early 1990s, young people discovered hip-hop music, dance and fashion and gravitated toward them as an outlet that represented novelty and a burgeoning sense of global belonging.

As hip-hop gained momentum over time, aspiring hip-hop artists sought to distinguish themselves – and the genre – from other popular music forms so as not to be overshadowed by the overwhelming popularity of *rumba*, *soukouss* and *ndombolo*. Highlighting the historic link between hip-hop, African-American protest and the African diaspora more broadly, early rappers in the DRC positioned hip-hop in opposition to the nationalist cultural policies of *authenticité*, thus establishing it as a genre of political dissent and as the unique popular music genre in the DRC to challenge rather than align itself with politicians or political parties. However, while this stance was comparatively radical and remains a formative element in the identity of Congolese hip-hop, at the time artists did not have sufficient audiences to pose any real threat and were uniformly ignored by established power structures.

One important gauge of hip-hop's evolution as a political project in the DRC is language. The first hip-hop available in the DRC was American and, while Congolese youth adopted the dance, fashion and overall aesthetic of the genre, the English lyrics were incomprehensible to them. It was only when Francophone artists including MC Solaar and Benny B were introduced that young people began to rap. Initially they did so exclusively in French, which affirmed the perception of hip-hop as a middle- and upper-class genre in the DRC. Indeed, it was only comparatively wealthy families with immediate connections to Europe who had access to the cassettes and VHS tapes that introduced hip-hop into the DRC; consequently, it was young people from such families – well educated within a system, enforced during colonialism, that equated French-language proficiency with social status and economic class – who were the pioneers of Congolese hip-hop. In the DRC, the use of French clearly distanced hip-hop from other cultural projects under *authenticité* that were in indigenous languages (primarily Lingala), but the increasingly troubling contradiction between the elitist language and the populist aspirations of hip-hop eventually led artists to rap in indigenous languages (most frequently Lingala, Kiswahili and Luba), the use of which notably diversified and popularized hip-hop in the DRC.

Regional Variations in Congolese Hip-Hop

Like the cultural factors surrounding the emergence of hip-hop in the DRC, the political history of the period had a significant influence on the evolution of the genre. Since its independence from Belgium in 1960 the DRC's political climate has been particularly volatile yet, while all regions of the country are affected by political instability, dramatically different immediate political experiences shape cultural trends along regional lines. In the case of hip-hop, the temporary separation of the nation between 1998 and 2002 exacerbated nascent regional distinctions within the genre. During this period the DRC was divided between east and west, with different languages and currencies on respective sides as well as a travel ban preventing citizens from traversing the country. Although popular music was the one commodity officially distributed nationwide, hip-hop was not yet established enough to qualify. Thus, during the formative years of the genre, artists and audiences from different parts of the DRC were unable to hear the works of their peers. Consequently, although technically speaking the first hip-hop song recorded was Fatima CIA's 'Septembre noir' (Black September) recorded in Shabani Records' digital studio in Kinshasa in 1993, there were a number of other 'first' hip-hop songs produced in isolation from one another by artists pioneering the genre through different channels. For example, in Kisangani (north/central DRC), Relate Soul released a whole album, *tu te croix likolo* (You Think You're Above) on tape in 1995, which was extremely popular and received local radio play for years; in Goma (in the east), South Cross recorded *Expression* in 1995, which was never released or distributed for lack of infrastructure; and in Lubumbashi (in the south) MC Kallé recorded *3x mbui* (pronounced *trois fois mbui,* meaning 'three times *mbui*') in 1999.

Regional isolation, coupled with geographic distance, led to distinct musical influences in hip-hop across the DRC. In the capital city, Kinshasa, the second serious rap group, Bawuta-Kin, began the trend of incorporating *soukouss* and *ndombolo* into their music, giving hip-hop a distinct sound in the capital. By contrast, in Kisangani, where a historic abundance of European consulates and Western-funded cultural centers imported the strong influence of US rappers such as Coolio and Tupac, typical Western influences dominated the first wave of hip-hop. Then, in the second wave, Alesh introduced indigenous instruments such as *marimba, kalimba* and *bongos* into his music, which gave rise to another distinct sonic trend in Kisangani. In the east, most notably in Goma, the geographic proximity and ease of travel to the Great Lakes Region resulted in a strong influence of East African, most specifically Tanzanian, hip-hop, which was already well established by the time hip-hop became popular in the east of the DRC. Finally, in Lubumbashi, which has strong commercial trade relationships with South Africa, hip-hop artists frequently incorporate South African dance music in their songs.

Regional distinctions in Congolese hip-hop are further entrenched through political experiences. While the DRC has both commercial and politically engaged rappers, the magnitude and scope of political influences are indisputably formative of the genre. For example, in Kinshasa, where hip-hop was initially exclusive to the children of politicians and high-ranking civil servants, the rampage of looting and mass killings in Kinshasa by Mobutu's soldiers in September 1991 ('Black September') prompted aspiring artists to take an overtly political stance. The ongoing corruption and popular dissatisfaction with government has been reflected in subsequent hip-hop songs including the collective 2003 single, 'Une nouvelle paix' (A New Peace); Marshal Dixon's 2006 single 'On est fatigué' (We Are Tired); Lexxus Legal's 2009 solo album *L'art de la guerre* (The Art of War); and Radek Supreme's 2011 track 'K—' (pronounced *ka tiré* and meaning 'game over'), for which he was imprisoned for incorporating political language from a militant Congolese diaspora organization.

In Kisangani, which experienced an unprecedented collapse of cultural infrastructure when European countries imposed embargos against Mobutu and withdrew their extensive funding for arts, hip-hop emerged to fill the cultural void among young people. Originally a blatant imitation of US rap, hip-hop became increasingly political in Kisangani in the aftermath of the deadly Six-Day War, fought between Ugandan and Rwandan armies in Kisangani in 2000. In 2002 Ally Bhutto Kaponda (founder of Relate Soul) formed a new group, Tersch, which was the first in Kisangani to produce socially conscious hip-hop. Between the immense popularity of the groups Relate Soul, Negra Soul, Tersch and Hot Boys and the successful solo careers of Pasnas (from Tersch), Dr. Deep (from Hot Boys) and Alesh (from Hot Boys), Kisangani became the first and only city in the DRC to attract large audiences to ticketed hip-hop concerts. Kisangani's hip-hop scene was elevated on the international stage when Studios Kabako sponsored the European tour of rapper Pasnas in 2006 and, further, when Alesh was selected for the inaugural session of OneBeat (2012), then as a Mandela Washington Fellow under US President Obama's Young African Leaders Initiative.

Hip-hop in the eastern regions of the country developed in the political aftermath of the Rwandan genocide and the series of wars it triggered in North- and South-Kivu provinces. In the face of ongoing violence, rape and extensive human rights violations, the burgeoning political nature of early hip-hop evolved into potent critiques of the monumental political failures that allowed more than 5 million people to be killed. That the first recording technology was imported into Goma by a Rwandan fleeing the violence in his own country was a constant reminder for rappers in the east of the DRC of the importance of political protest. In the chaos of war, hip-hop took longer to gain traction in the east and, in the aftermath of the 2002 eruption of volcano Nyiragongo, all recordings of early songs were lost. Over time, with support of local organizations including the Yole!Africa cultural center, rappers from Goma have gained international status – for example, both rapper Emma Katya's 2010 single 'How Long?' and rapper S3's 2012 song 'Conscience' won the Fair Play Anti-Corruption Youth Voices award, organized by Jeunesses Musicales International and the World Bank Institute. The recent online series *Art on the FrontLine*, featuring younger artists including Madibo, DJ Couleur, Fal G, Bin G and Placid Muhinder, confirms the continued political nature of hip-hop in the east of the DRC.

In Lubumbashi, capital of Katanga Province, the evolution of hip-hop was influenced by still other factors. Katanga is a historic hub of political activity and business, with many wealthy businessmen campaigning for high-level national office. Lubumbashi is thus comparatively developed in terms of infrastructure yet has a staggering discrepancy between wealthy and poor, with few middle-class citizens. The prevalence of political rhetoric combined with extreme economic inequity influenced the production of hip-hop in the region, which vacillates between commercial and politically engaged. Pioneering artists included MC Kallé, Lubum-Connection and ARM, then in 2004 RJ Kanyera joined the scene and began to mix popular Congolese and South African music into his songs, which resulted in a local style called *busipa* that has been gaining popularity in Lubumbashi since 2006. *Busipa* is a distinct blend of hip-hop and dance music that incorporates criticism of economic inequity in the lyrics with danceable beats. Compared to places such as Kinshasa, Kisangani, and Goma, hip-hop in Lubumbashi struggles with a lack of producers and viable distribution channels, yet there are still notable artists emerging including M Joe, Kamikaze, Genja and Majoos.

Conclusion

While hip-hop initially emerged throughout the DRC in reaction to a dictatorial cultural regime, ongoing political volatility and geographic distance have influenced the evolution of the genre along regional lines. There are, however, nationwide trends including the increasingly active role many international NGOs play in commissioning hip-hop songs for sensitization projects and promoting these works in the West. Ironically, Congolese hip-hop is perhaps best defined globally by the immense fame of diaspora artists living in Europe (such as Youssupha, Baloji, Maître Gims, Pitcho and others), many of whom are the children of popular musicians from the Mobutu era. With digital technologies and connectivity advancing in the DRC, there are promising new channels of production and distribution that suggest increased visibility of Congolese hip-hop in the years to come.

Bibliography

Ndaliko, Chérie Rivers. 2016. *Necessary Noise: Music, Film, and Charitable Imperialism in the East of Congo*. New York: Oxford University Press.

Nzongola-Ntalaja, Georges. 2002. *The Congo: From Leopold to Kabila: A People's History*. London: Zed.

Nzongola-Ntalaja, Georges. 2004. *From Zaire to the Democratic Republic of the Congo*. Uppsala: Nordiska Afrikainstitutet.

White, Bob W. 2006. 'L'incroyable machine d'Authenticité: l'animation politic et l'usage public de la culture dans le Zaïre de Mobutu.' *Anthropologie et Sociétés* 30(2): 43–63.

White, Bob W. 2008. *Rumba Rules: The Politics of Dance Music in Mobutu's Zaire*. Durham: Duke University Press.

Interviews

Baya, Ciamala. 'Narsix.' Interview with the author via Skype. January 2016.

Bin, G., and Fal, G. Live interview with the author. June and July 2015.

Canonne, Alain. Interview with the author via email. December 2015.

Icey, Dyna. Interview with the author via Skype and email. September 2014.

Kanyera, R. J. Interview with the author via Skype. January 2016.

Kaposo, Alesh. Interview with the author via Skype. December 2015 and January 2016.
Katya, Emma. Live interview with the author. December 2015 and January 2016.
Ndaliko Katondolo, Petna. Live interview with the author. December 2015 and January 2016.

Discographical References
Alesh. *La mort dans l'âme*. Studios Kabako. *2011*: DRC.
Congo All Stars. 'Une nouvelle paix.' Independent Release. *2003*: DRC.
Fatima CIA. 'Septembre noir.' Shabani Records. *1993*: DRC.
Katya, Emma. 'How Long?' Yole!Africa Studio. *2010*: DRC.
Lexxus Legal. *L'art de la guerre*. Independent release. *2009*: DRC.
Marshal Dixon. 'On est fatigué.' Independent release. *2006*: DRC.
MC Kallé. '3x mbui.' Independent release. *1999*: DRC.
Radek Supreme. 'K—.' Independent release. *2011*: DRC.
Relate Soul. 'Tu te croix likolo.' Independent release. *1995*: DRC.
S3. 'Conscience.' Mutaani Label. *2012*: DRC.
South Cross. 'Expression.' Independent release. *1995*: DRC.

YouTube and Other Online Video
'Art on the FrontLine.' Produced by Yole!Africa. https://www.youtube.com/channel/UCufvkji7Wvo_4CHE5v47Dfg (accessed 1 January 2016).
Bawuta-Kin. *Dificile à contruire*. https://www.youtube.com/watch?v=oWf-3h1BZvU (accessed 15 January 2016).
'Conscience.' Written and performed by S3. Produced by Mutaani Label. May 2012. http://www.anticorruptionmusic.org/?videos/conscience (accessed 1 January 2016).
'How Long?' Written and performed by Katya Emma and Ndungi Githuku. 6 February 2012. http://www.youtube.com/watch?v=5Rn4edmLchM&feature=player_embedded (accessed 28 March 2018).
Jupiter's Dance. Directed by R. Barret and F. de La Tullaye. Belle Kinois Films (Copyright Idéal Audience International), 2007. https://www.youtube.com/watch?v=TxkaVmpgHcs (accessed 27 March 2018).
L'art de la guerre. Written and performed by Lexxus Legal, with Ekila. Directed by Ronnie Kabuika. 2009. https://www.youtube.com/watch?v=7dJYaFfiIlo (accessed 28 March 2018).
'Le jour d'après / Siku ya Badaaye.' Written and performed by Baloji, 5 May 2010. http://www.youtube.com/watch?v=-h4kPKcAotU&feature=channel (accessed 28 March 2018).
Majoos. *Big Boss*. https://www.youtube.com/watch?v=eMaOTqDzHmA (accessed 15 January 2016).
'Ndoto Yangu.' *Alternative to TV*. Alkebu Productions, 2007. http://metropolistv.nl/en/correspondents/petna-goma/balume-15-years-old-and-already-a-producer (accessed 28 March 2018).
Pasnas. Live Concert. https://www.youtube.com/watch?v=Dc686a6RzCw (accessed 15 January 2016).
Rj Kanyera. *Atuta lala*. https://www.youtube.com/watch?v=pcOQDYu-_jk (accessed 15 January 2016).
Rj Kanyera. *Césarienne*. https://www.youtube.com/watch?v=WLN_AZI8FpU (accessed 15 January 2016).
'Saisir l'avenir.' Performed by Salaam Kivu Allstars. Alkebu Productions, 2010. http://www.youtube.com/watch?v=SgqZPcXyyFw&context=C3f1292fADOEgsToPDskLRIgnDt0jNQQKLTvTlwnz0 (accessed 28 March 2018).

CHÉRIE RIVERS NDALIKO

Hip-Hop in Uganda
Hip-hop in Uganda, known as 'Luga flow,' owes its origins to US hip-hop's influence upon the rest of the globe in the early 1990s. The term 'Luga flow' is a coinage that synthesizes two words: 'Luga,' which represents the local Luganda language and 'flow,' which signifies the performance aspects of the hip-hop genre. Although some analysts limit the term 'Luga flow' to hip-hop in the Luganda language, the term has also been interpreted more widely to embrace rap in other languages of Uganda.

In traditional hip-hop, 'flow' (the interaction between the rapper's rhymes and the underlying beats) is an essential aspect of the oral performance of a song. Like other hip-hop forms, *Luga flow* consists of organized rhythm and rhyme. Recordings and performances of *Luga flow* are characterized by an artist rapping over beats that are pre-produced for a record or a performance. Rarely do *Luga flow* artists employ live instrumentation in studio or on stage.

One of the distinctive characteristics of *Luga flow* is sampling of other works by borrowing aspects of lyrics, rhythms or other references from those works. Sampling plays many roles in *Luga flow*. First, it connects *Luga flow* audiences to multiple genres in Uganda's recording history, giving it a heritage and foundation. As such, *Luga flow* artists have sampled Ugandan music that was recorded as far back as the 1960s. Two of the most representative samples in *Luga flow* have been GNL Zamba's 2009 adaptation of early Ugandan recording artist Elly Wamala's 'Ani Yali Amanyi' and Navio's 2010 sample of Charles and Freda Sonko's 1968 recording 'Nawuliranga.' Sampling also serves a strategic function for *Luga flow* artists, generating appeal for their records by adopting elements of songs that were hugely popular in the past.

The main audience for *Luga flow* in Uganda is people aged under 30. Ironically, although this group constitutes over 78 percent of Uganda's population, *Luga flow* has not always been a mainstream genre. However, its fan base is considered the most passionate in Uganda.

The exact origins of *Luga flow* are debated. The hip-hop movement in Uganda, which provided the context for the emergence of *Luga flow*, began in the early 1990s. After decades of civil war, a semblance of stability returned to the country when the National Resistance Movement (NRM) came to power in 1986. Following the silence of the guns of war, exiled Ugandans began sending video recordings of Western music to relatives back home, among other gifts. Many of these videos were recorded from MTV. In this way, videos of songs by hip-hop artists including Naughty By Nature, Snoop Doggy Dogg, KRS One and Queen Latifah found their way into video libraries in Uganda.

Ugandan young people began forming youth groups in their urban neighborhoods that emulated these US artists. Some of the groups included Muyenga Youth, Bugolobi Youth, Sharing Youth, Bukoto Youth and Makindye Youth. It was from these youth groups that some of the pioneer *Luga flow* artists emerged. During the 1990s a major source of inspiration for young people who became *Luga flow* artists was DJ Berry, a popular DJ of Rwandan origin who began performing short rap compositions over instrumentals of several US hip-hop songs that he played in nightclubs or at trans-day parties for young people at LIDO Beach and the Rwenzori Ballroom at the Sheraton Hotel. DJ Berry inspired several other artists who entered the field, including DAMAC PAC, MC Afrik, Bataka Underground, D 'N' D Slam, Prim and Propa, Roger M, Positive Power and Zulu Squad.

In its nascent years in the 1990s *Luga flow* failed to attain mainstream success. One of the impediments to its growth was the use of English in recordings and performances. Uganda at the time had a literacy rate of six percent, and, although English was the official language, it was not widely spoken. The majority of the population was not literate and sarcastically referred to themselves as 'Abatasoma,' loosely translated as 'those who did not go to school.' *Luga flow* did not appeal to them. At this time there also existed an anti-indigenous language policy spearheaded by the Ministry of Education, based on the supposition that indigenous languages in schools promoted ethnic tensions that had accounted for decades of civil strife in Uganda. Since the majority of *Luga flow* artists were young people in high schools who could understand the records sent to their families by relatives abroad, the early proponents of the genre used English to record and perform to a limited audience.

Compared to other Ugandan music genres that used local languages, such as *kadongo kamu*, Luga dancehall and band, *Luga flow* artists struggled to attain mainstream acceptance because of the language barrier. In the late 1990s the emergence of *bongo flava*, a form of Tanzanian hip-hop recorded and performed in Kiswahili, gave Ugandan hip-hop artists a useful model with which to rework *Luga flow* to make it more relevant. In 1998 Bataka Underground recorded 'Atoba,' a song in Luganda that enjoyed moderate mainstream popularity but garnered huge underground success. In the same year Young Vibrations recorded a full-length album in Luganda, using references to various localities in Uganda, which was seen as an attempt to create more appeal.

As output from Uganda's music scene riding on a wave of preference for local languages grew exponentially, so did the number of artists performing *Luga flow*. In the mid-2000s hip-hop artist Navio, a member of the hip-hop group Klear Kut, decided to venture out on a solo career. Some of his earliest recordings did not register mainstream success, because they were sung in English. In the same period,

Luga flow artist GNL Zamba, after years of failing to break through with hip-hop sung in English, emerged with a radically different approach to the genre. He recorded mainly in Luganda, and he integrated popular folktales into his lyrics. GNL Zamba achieved monumental success in the early 2000s, becoming the first *Luga flow* artist to break through within the mainstream market in Uganda. His success sparked a wave of *Luga flow* artists recording in Luganda and other languages from different parts of the country. *Luga flow* artists who adopted this trend, such as Mun G, Rabadaba, Victor Kamenyo, Gravity Omutujju, Ruyonga, Santana and Babaluku, became household names in Uganda.

Luga flow artists address a range of sociocultural, economic and political issues in their recordings. For this reason, they have been employed by others as vehicles for communicating with a critical mass of young people. For example, Babaluku, a cofounder of the Bataka Squad and the visionary force behind The Bavubuka Foundation, a nonprofit organization that believes that connecting young people with music can transform lives, has been instrumental in empowering young Africans through music, as evidenced in his 2009 album, *Luga Flow Revolution*. Babaluku's career is featured in the 2009 documentary, *Diamonds in the Rough: A Ugandan Hip-Hop Revolution*, a film which illustrates the impact a number of Ugandan hip-hop artists have had on young people, as well as the challenging social and economic conditions faced by these young people. Yet although music has been adopted by political actors to advance a political agenda in Uganda, it has remained the case that *Luga flow* artists are understood to have a limited audience and have not been co-opted, despite the perception that they appeal to a youthful majority. For example, when the National Resistance Movement (NRM) contracted popular artists to endorse and campaign for its candidate President Yoweri Museveni in the 2016 general elections, *Luga flow* artists, except for Mun G, were sidelined. The party worked with artists of other genres who were perceived to appeal to the youthful majority.

Bibliography

Ntarangwi, Mwenda. 2009. *East African Hip Hop: Youth Culture and Globalization*. Urbana: University of Illinois Press.

Discographical References

Babaluku. *Luga Flow Revolution*. Bavubuka All Starz. *2009*: Uganda.
Bataka Underground. 'Atoba.' *1998*: Uganda.
GNL Zamba. 'Ani Yali Amanyi.' *Koyi Koyi (Riddles of Life)*. Platinum Records. *2009*: Uganda.
Navio. 'Nawuliranga.' *African Hustler Music*. Navcorp Records. *2010*: Uganda.
Sonko, Charles, and Freda. 'Nawuliranga.' *1968*: Uganda. (Reissued as *The Kampala Sound: 1960s Ugandan Dance Music*. Original Music. *1988*: USA.)
Wamala, Elly. 'Ani Yali Amanyi.' (Reissued as 'Ani Yali Amanyi.' *Ani Yali Amanyi*. Uganda Performing Right Society. *2015*: Uganda.)

Filmography

Diamonds in the Rough: A Ugandan Hip-hop Revolution, dir, Brett Mazurek. 2009. 72 mins. USA. Documentary featuring Babaluku, Saba-Saba and others. Online at: https://www.imdb.com/videoplayer/vi3978009625 (accessed 1 June 2018).

YouTube

(accessed 26 May 2018)
Sonko, Charles and Freda. 'Nawuliranga.' https://www.youtube.com/watch?v=eRSm_-Ry1nY
Wamala, Elly. 'Ani Yali Amanyi.' 2012. https://www.youtube.com/watch?v=ka53Z5hwoYo.

JOEL ISABIRYE WITH JOHN SHEPHERD

Hiplife

Hiplife is a popular music genre that began in Ghana in the mid-1990s as a mixture of West African highlife music and US hip-hop. Its origination is often credited to Reggie Rockstone (Reginald Yaw Asante Ossei), a London-born Ghanaian who returned to his homeland in 1994, coining the term to represent his hip-hop sound as he began to rap in his native language of Twi. By that time, however, several local Accra rappers had already used indigenous dialects, making Rockstone the first to commercialize indigenized Ghanaian rap. Musically, hiplife utilizes the melodic and rhythmic phrasings of guitar-based highlife music, along with synthesized hip-hop beats. Linguistically, hiplife musicians often mix English, hip-hop slang, Ghanaian Pidgin English, and Ghanaian languages including Twi, Ewe, Ga, and Hausa. Lyric content blends local sociocultural references and indigenous proverbs with international hip-hop 'gangsta' and dance club imagery. Hiplife, therefore, combines US hip-hop and indigenous Ghanaian music and dialects to create a new genre, one that has since become known throughout the African continent, and increasingly the world.

Hiplife as African Hip-Hop

Rap in African countries, as opposed to many other parts of the world, may be viewed as a 'connective marginality of culture' that creates a deeper link with received hip-hop aesthetics (Osumare 2007, 69–73). African hip-hop engages with the aesthetics already present within the cultural matrix that circulates between Africa and its diaspora and that has become an 'arc of mutual inspiration' (Osumare 2012, 1–2; see below). In the case of hiplife music in Ghana, mutual inspiration becomes apparent as local pop music figures centrally in the hip-hop indigenization process.

The development of hiplife in Ghana took place in what has been identified as a series of somewhat fluid phases (see Table 1). Obour (Bice Osei Kuffour), one of Ghana's most visible hiplife MCs, who was elected president of the Musicians Union of Ghana (MUSIGA) in 2011, clarified five overlapping stylistic phases of highlife and hip-hop music in Ghana (2008). These may be correlated with two of the three Ghanaian generations of hip-hop researched by Osumare, emerging after the first generation (mid-1980s–1993). Obour's five phases of hiplife (which are not always linear) correspond to Osumare's second and third generations, beginning in the mid-1990s, when the second generation first adapted hip-hop to various local dynamics, and continuing halfway through the first decade of the new millennium, when hiplife morphed into a third generation, utilizing various musical indigenization processes to create a completely new genre.

Obour's designated first phase is the early hiplife sound that Reggie Rockstone and others originally introduced, and it represents the transition from a 1980s and early 1990s imitation phase of US hip-hop into an adaptation that launched hiplife's first generation. The early Ghanaian imitation phase of US hip-hop does not appear in his five phases of the development of hiplife, because it is pre-hiplife. In Obour's second and third phases, the indigenizing stages that solidified hiplife differentiated the genre from hip-hop originally inherited from the United States.

One example of this musical shift by the second generation was the Kumasi-based group Akyeame, consisting of Okyeame Kwame (Kwame

Table 1 Comparison of Obour's and Osumare's periodization of hiplife development

Obour's Five Phases of Hiplife (no years given)	Osumare's Three Generations of Hiplife
	First Generation (mid-1980s–1993): Imitation of US hip-hop
Phase 1: Strictly hip-hop rhythm with lyrics in a local dialect	**Second Generation (1994–9):** Adaptation
Phase 2: Hip-hop mixed with local beats and a local dialect	(Adaptation moving into indigenization)
Phase 3: Extremely traditional highlife rhythms and instrumentation with traditional highlife lyrics, with Twi or any other local dialect	Indigenization
Phase 4: English lyrics with local dialects set to the local highlife beat	**Third Generation (2000–):** Continuation of indigenization, with emphasis on international market
Phase 5: Gradual return to the hip-hop beat with a fusion of hip-hop English language and some Twi	(Indigenization cyclically returning to more hip-hop)

Nsiah Appau) and Okyeame Quophi (Daniel Kofi Amoateng). As young high school students who had been listening to American rap, they began rapping in Twi in 1995 when they performed at a local beauty pageant. It was such a hit that by the release of their first album, *BreBre Ohaa Hemma*, in 1997, they incorporated the signature Asante *adowa* percussion rhythm, ubiquitous throughout Ghana, in several of their songs' musical structures. Okyeame Kwame said in a news interview, 'Our debut was big; it was the first hiplife song that had both highlife and rap with *adowa* fusion. What Reggie was doing then was hip-pop with Twi lyrics; we sold fourteen thousand copies, which was big then' ('Ghana Base Music Meets Okyeame Kwame,' 2007). The second generation not only utilized rap in local languages but also began to include experimentation with indigenous musical production, introducing West African highlife guitar phrasings, as well as hundreds-of-years-old drum rhythms such as *adowa*, into their hip-hop tracks. These increasing experimentations with indigenity eventually produced the third generation that solidified the new sound of hiplife.

The tendency of popular music to avoid a linear trajectory in its continual evolution is apparent in the third generation of hiplife musicians' recapturing of some of the original hip-hop 'flava' together with new splinter genres including GH rap, Afropop and Twi-pop. The subsequent interplay between US hip-hop and Ghanaian highlife moves between the two musical genres, based on individual and generational emphases. This continual play between inherited global music and the local indigenous adaptations between Africa and its diaspora is what Osumare calls the 'arc of mutual inspiration,' in which 'the circle of musical and dance influences from Africa to its diaspora and back again' (Osumare 2012, 1). Viewed from this historical perspective, the hiplife music phenomenon becomes a kind of cultural pan-Africanism.

Early Blending of Highlife and Hip-Hop

In addition to Reggie Rockstone, many other MCs and producers percolated through the beginnings of Ghanaian adaptive hip-hop, helping to develop the local sound in the first phase of hiplife music, between 1994 and 1997. Producers including Panji Anoff, Abraham Ohene Djan and Michael Cook, all of whom started in London with Rockstone, along with Rab Bakari, Zapp Mallet, Talking Drums, NFL and Adinkra Clan, contributed different aspects to the hardcore hip-hop beats and local highlife rhythms that developed into Ghanaian hiplife. Anoff started Talking Drum with Kwaku-T and Abeeku The Witch Doctor, producing a song called 'Aden?' around 1993-4. Michael Cook wrote the first recorded rap in Twi, 'Tsoo boi' (Heave Ho) for Rockstone, using the term 'hiplife' in the second verse. Ohene Djan, owner of one of the oldest music and video studios in Accra, OM Studios, remembers these two songs as the beginning of recorded hiplife music.

Highlife, as the worldwide-acknowledged Ghanaian pop music, is central to the birthing of the second and third generations of hip-hoppers turned hiplifers. Ghanaians had already mastered the indigenization of Western music through 100 years of highlife music, evolving from the late-nineteenth-century European ballroom orchestra-oriented sound to the smaller mid-twentieth-century highlife rhythmic combos of E.T. Mensah and others. During the World War II-era, musical indigenization was occurring through the incorporation of earlier guitar-inflected palmwine bands popular in the rural areas, coupled with the calypso sounds of the diaspora filtered through London. Highlife's own indigenization process created the musical mix that resonated with early twentieth-century Ghanaians and became *the* popular music circulating throughout West Africa. So, it was only natural that the localization of hip-hop had to include ubiquitous highlife guitar riffs, melodic singing sensibilities, and a propensity for social commentary.

In the 1980s, before the wholesale introduction of hip-hop into urban Ghana, hiplife musicians point to one major transitional highlife artist, Gyedu-Blay Ambolley. Just as US hip-hop historians credit artistic precursors of rap music, such as the Last Poets and Gil-Scott Heron, who used spoken word in melodic form, so too does Ambolley serve a similar role in the development of the hiplife sound in Ghana. Hiplife artists validate Ambolley's highlife 'simi-gwa-do' sound, his name for his particular blend of Fante and English that created his own pidgin slang, along with typical calypso/soca-like rhythms and melodic highlife horn riff. He chanted texts along with his melodic sung phrasings to comment on male–female relationships, as well as community social conditions. Tracks such as 'Abrentsie' that used his *simi-gwa-do* rapping on his 1988 album *Partytime Revisited* became an important influence on the development of localization of hip-hop in Ghana.

The First, Second and Third Phases of Hiplife

When Rockstone's first album *Maaka maka* (If I Said So, I Said It) 'dropped' in 1997, there was little hiplife music being played on the radio and certainly few music videos on television, but it was his fearless bravado that caught youth and media attention. The first generation, for which Rockstone became the visible media indicator, was characterized by a continuing imitation of hardcore hip-hop music production, but with the new twist of rapping in Twi. Along with Rockstone in the first generation was an important trio from the poor Nima district of Accra called VIP (Vision in Progress). VIP consisted of Lazzy (Abdul Hamidu Ibrahim), Promzy (Emmanuel Ababio) and Prodical (Joseph Nana Ofori). Emerging from Accra's Nima ghetto as young saggy-pants hip-hop teens, they produced their first album *Biibiiba* (Something Is Coming) in 1998. In contrast to many hiplife MCs, including Reggie Rockstone, who come from relatively privileged backgrounds and are well educated, the members of VIP have 'branded' their story as replicating the familiar rags-to-riches and fame tales of many MCs in the USA. Interestingly enough, in contemporary times Promzy left the group, and in 2012 Reggie Rockstone joined the remaining two artists to create the group now called VVIP.

Growing up in a strong Christian family, Obrafour (Kwabena Okyere Darko) is another early pioneer of the first generation of hiplife. He developed a gospel sensibility running throughout his thematic approach to hiplife. His gospel rap song, the first ever in Ghana, called 'Enyeɛ nyame a,' was recorded on his second album *Asem sebe* (2001). Musicians such as Obrafour began to introduce more highlife instrumentation into the musical production; in Obrafour's specific case, he developed the use of well-known Akan proverbs as a source of rap lyrics. Thus, he adapted aspects of local culture that introduced Obour's second phase of hiplife. Although his hiplife name Obrafour, meaning 'Executioner,' follows an American gangsta trope, he is also known as the Rap Sofo, or Rap Priest, denoting his social moralizing tendency, admonishing Ghanaians to do 'the right thing' through proverbial passages with which local consumers were familiar.

Just the opposite of Obrafour in public persona, Kwaw Kese (Emmanuel Abrompah Botchwey) calls himself 'Abodam,' or The Menace. He was a part of the development of the second hiplife phase, cultivating a 'bad boy' image in the hiplife scene based on speaking his mind and creating controversy. Kwaw Kese was first heard on Obrafour's breakthrough 2004 *Execution Diary* compilation with his single 'Oye Nonsense' that was an immediate hit with the growing hiplife audience. This album, with Kwaw Kese's hit single, solidified the adaptation that included highlife musical phrasings along with indigenous rap of the second generation of Ghanaian youth using hip-hop.

The Ghana Music Awards (GMA) began in 2000 at the same time that the third phase of hiplife emerged. The Charter House Production and Events Management company, with its GMA, was established at the turn of the twenty-first century, and its executives realized that hiplife music, as Ghana's new popular music form, had the potential for continent-wide popularity. The new organization helped promote hiplife music, which in turn led to the country's first professional music awards. Over the years, the GMA privileged many hiplife musicians with the Artist of the Year award, starting in its initial year with Obrafour.

Okyeame Kwame, introduced above as a part of the duo Akyeame (plural of Okyeame), became a popular solo artist in 2006 with his first album *Bohye ba*. It was his second album, *M'awensem* (My Poetry, 2008), however, that transformed him into an award-winning artist, making him the Artist of the Year at the GMAs in 2009 as a part of the second hiplife generation. His hit single 'Woso,' remixed with the Ghanaian R&B singer Richie, received significant radio airtime and awards in 2008, continuing to establish hiplife as one of the most popular music genres in the country.

Batman Samini (Emmanuel Samini) is considered a hiplife/reggae musician in the equally popular 'raga' style in Ghana. Previous to the hip-hop wave, reggae music enjoyed a significant following from the 1980s throughout Africa. With the arrival of hip-hop in Ghana various artists have merged the two into what Ghanaians call raga, and Samini has become synonymous with the genre. He markets his style as 'African dancehall,' a mixture of highlife, dancehall, reggae and hip-hop. In 2004 he released his first album, *Dankwansere*, which included his hit track 'Linda' that launched his international award-winning career.

Hiplife's third generation emerged in Ghana in the latter part of the first decade of the twenty-first century. Trigmatic (Nana Yaw) is a third-generation Ga hiplife artist who grew up in the Osu district of Accra and represents another approach to the development of Ghanaian pop music. True to the hip-hop tenet of 'flippin' the script,' or changing the social narrative, Trigmatic challenges the very categorization of his music as hiplife. He stated: 'I wouldn't want to call it hiplife. Why? Because I'm still waiting for that solid definition of hiplife to see where it started. Then I could be a part of it, because I would then understand it' (2010). Trigmatic's style of hiplife or hip-hop music may also be categorized by US standards as 'emo-rap,' or emotional rap, where, in a manner uncharacteristic of hardcore rap, this MC is willing to reveal the personal vulnerabilities of his inner life. US rappers Eminem and Kanye West have been positioned in this category of rap, and one of Trigmatic's most famous tracts, 'My Life,' fits this genre in Ghana.

Trigmatic's critique of the lack of discernment in labeling different strains of music categorized under the term 'hiplife' is a valid one. In the second decade of the twenty-first century there is a cacophony of categories of hiplife music among the third generation that can be mind-boggling to the non-Ghanaian. New descriptive appellations include 'Afropop' and 'Gh rap' and even language-specific 'Twi-Pop,' through which contemporary Ghanaian artists are beginning to perceive their music, all under the larger banner of hiplife. *Azonto* dance music, becoming commercial in 2010, has developed into an important inclusion for successful hiplife artists, which also complicates categorization.

An important third generation hiplife artist is Sarkodie, a protégé of Obrafuor. He started rapping after hearing Obrafour's first album when he was a junior at Achimota Secondary School, one of the oldest and most prestigious high schools in Ghana. Sarkodie's penchant for a rapid-fire Twi style of rap brought a new aesthetic to hiplife and caused him to eventually record the single 'In This Life' with his revered mentor. By 2009 Sarkodie, born and raised in the port city of Tema outside of Accra, was making major waves in Ghana, West Africa and even the United States.

In 2010 Senegalese-American pop singer Akon and his Konvict Records initiated 'Konvict Musik Africa' with Sarkodie as one of its first artists. This business venture signifies how hiplife music and a generation of pop musicians across Africa in general are boosted by sons of Africa, including Akon, who have achieved American and European pop music clout. Akon provides African artists such as Sarkodie with an international platform to globally popularize little-known music genres in Africa, including hiplife. One Sarkodie early single was 'I'm So Hood Our Way (Ghana)' with a line from the track succinctly stating the indigenous process that hip-hop in Ghana is undergoing: 'I sacrifice my life for hiplife; we taking it local.' Thus, imported global discursive practices are translated into local relatable imaginaries. Black Atlantic diasporic connections are made relevantly specific for native consumption.

Although, as in US hip-hop, male hiplife musicians outnumber females, creating a 'male dominance' identified by Ghanaian singer Mimi (Wilhemina Abu-Andani), this fact also renders 'our competition not as tough as the guys' according to Mimi. Mimi represents the female wing of the hiplife genre, first started by Abrewa Nana and Mary Agyepong in the 1990s, both of whom have ceased performing. Along with Mimi, Mzbel (Nana Akua Amoah) and Eazzy (Mildred Ashong) are categorized as female hiplife artists. The latter three sing with an Afropop style that includes rapped verses, while often featuring collaborations with male hiplife MCs. The exigencies of a patriarchal pop culture industry force female hiplife artists often to play the objectified body role, while also inserting their anti-patriarchal messages. Artists such as Mimi and Mzbel do their best to negotiate the 'minefields' of a male-dominated industry, while some female university academics strive to use their research on gender in Ghanaian pop culture to impact gender biases in Ghana's music industry.

Conclusion

Hiplife music in Ghana may be viewed in a continuum of West African popular music, including highlife that evolved out of European contact and colonialism, chronicling an indigenization process of Western cultural influences merging with African musical sensibilities. Over a 20-year period from the mid-1990s to contemporary times, hip-hop evolved in Ghana in various phases across three generations, from imitation of US hip-hop to adaptation using local languages, to its eventual indigenization using local highlife musical phrasing. In the process, as hiplife scholar Jesse Shipley, notes, this new music genre of hiplife became central 'to changing ideas of Ghanaian identity' (Shipley 2013, 4). As a form of West African pop music, hiplife continues to respond to new musical trends from the arc of mutual inspiration between Africa and its diaspora.

Bibliography

'Ghana Base Music Meets Okyeame Kwame,' Ghana Base Music, 15 March 2007. Online at:http://music.thinkghana.com/interviews/200703/34121.php (accessed 10 January 2018).

'Konvict Music Africa officially Unveils Sarkodie.' GhanaWeb, 8 February 2010. Online at: http://www.ghanaweb.com/GhanaHomePage/entertainment/Konvict-Music-Africa-officially-unveils-Sarkodie-176348 (accessed 10 January 2018).

Mimi. 2010. Interview with the author. Accra, 22 September.

Obour. 2008. Interview with the author. 12 December.

Osumare, Halifu. 2007. *The Africanist Aesthetic in Global Hip-Hop: Power Moves*. New York: Palgrave Macmillan.

Osumare, Halifu. 2012. *The Hiplife in Ghana: West African Indigenization of Hip-Hop*. New York: Palgrave Macmillan.

Shipley, Jesse Weaver. 2013. *Living the Hiplife: Celebrity and Entrepreneurship in Ghanaian Popular Music*. Durham, NC: Duke University Press.

Trigmatic. 2010. Interview with the author. Accra, 20 September.

Discographical References

Ambolley, Gyedu-Blay. *Partytime Revisited*. Simigwa Records. UPC: 973230400424. *1988*: Ghana.

Akyeame. *BreBre ohaa hemma*. *1997*: Ghana.

Batman Samini. *Dankwansere*. Lexyrfi Productions. *2004*: Ghana.

Kwaw Kese. 'Oye Nonsense.' *Execution Diary*. Execution Entertainment. *2004*: Ghana.

Obrafour. *Asem sebe*. Bonsu Music Production. *2001*: Ghana.

Obrafour. *Execution Diary*. Execution Entertainment. *2004*: Ghana.

Obrafour and Sarkodie. 'In This Life.' Duncwills Entertainment. *2009*: Ghana.

Okyeame Kwame. *Bohye ba*. One Mic Entertainment. *2006*: Ghana.

Okyeame Kwame. *M'anwensem*. One Mic Entertainment. *2008*: Ghana.

Rockstone, Reggie. 'Maaka maka.' Kassa Records B002BR2N2S. *1997*: Ghana.

Rockstone, Reggie. 'Tsoo boi.' Ossei Mix. *1996*: Ghana.

Sarkodie. 'I'm So Hood Our Way (Ghana).' Duncwills Entertainment. *2010*: Ghana.

Talking Drums. 'Aden?' *1995*: Ghana.

Trigmatic. 'My Life.' *Permanent Stains*. Gab Management. *2010*: Ghana.

Vision in Progress (VIP). *Biibiiba*. Precise Records. *1998*: Ghana.

HALIFU OSUMARE

Hira Gasy

Hira gasy (*hira*; 'song'; *gasy*: 'Malagasy') is a long-standing musical tradition in Madagascar, which is the fourth largest island in the world, situated off the east coast of Africa. The population of Madagascar is derived mainly from Southeast Asian, African, Chinese, Indian and, subsequently, European settlers.

Mpihira gasy (malagasy artists), also known as *Mpihiran'ny Andrianana* in the eighteenth century and *mpilalao* in the twentieth century, have preserved this unique tradition since the fifteenth century, a tradition that is related to both theater and opera. This tradition has lasted well into the twenty-first century and has become increasingly pervasive and influential among the population of Madagascar. In a lengthy spectacle of music, dance and oratory that takes up the good part of a day, these artists convey the religious beliefs of the ancestors, who play a central and fundamental role in Malagasy culture. These beliefs are conveyed in the words of songs during the *fomba* rituals dedicated to the ancestors, as well as during the formalized and poetic speeches (*kabary*), which punctuate *hira gasy* performances. These performances represent a popular form of cultural expression: all *mpihira gasy* are peasants as well as artists, self-taught, and collectively supporting their community.

Hira Gasy in Madagascar's History

Hira gasy is an endogenous form whose origins, according to oral histories, predate the fifteenth century when the first great kingdoms were established in Madagascar. At the end of the eighteenth century the enlightened monarch Andrianampoinimerina conceived a plan to unite all the peoples of the island into a single state. He mobilized *hira gasy* troupes to uplift and sustain the spirit of peasants working on a major expansion of rice fields, rice being the main food consumed by Malagasy people. The artists were elevated to the rank of *Mpihiran'ny Andriana* ('royal artists'). Since then, *hira gasy* has become an emblematic national art form, considered to be a fundamental component of the country's heritage.

The *mpihira gasy* were involved in all the important stages of Malagasy history: unification of the island into the Kingdom of Madagascar in the nineteenth century at the time of King Radama I and Queen Ranavalona I; resistance to colonial aggression by the French during the late nineteenth and twentieth centuries (the *Menalamba* rebellion of 1895, the *Vy Vato Sakelika* secret society formed in 1913 and the formation of the Democratic Movement of the Malagasy Renovation in 1947) until independence was obtained in 1960; the socialist revolution of 1972 to 1975 that resulted in the establishment of Madagascar's socialist-Marxist Second Republic (1975–93); and the democratic revolution of 2002.

The ethos of *mpihira gasy* has constantly evoked Madagascar's precolonial past, the *faha-gasy* (the 'Malagasy times'), when the Kingdom of Madagascar was a sovereign state in full development, associated closely with the United Kingdom of Queen Victoria. At that time, it was recognized internationally, having ambassadors in England as early as 1820, and a full-fledged diplomatic mission in Germany, England, France and the United States in 1883, the year that France attacked the island.

Hira Gasy as a Sacred Art Form

Madagascar is regarded by its inhabitants as a holy land, the land of ancestors, *tanindrazana*, surrounded by blessed water, the sea, *ranomasina*. *Hira gasy* opera forms part of this symbolic space. It has a deep relation with traditional Malagasy religion and *fomban'drazana* (homage to the ancestors). The most important performances take place during the *famadihana* ceremonies. In the course of these ceremonies the bodies of the ancestors of extended families are taken out of the tombs as part of elaborate festivals during which a new shroud, the *lambamena*, is offered to each ancestor. A *famadihana* without a competition between *hira gasy* troupes would be deemed inadequate in honoring the memory of both the ancestors and the living (the descendants of the deceased parents and the villagers from the region where the collective tomb was erected). The performances are offered by the family as a gift to honor the ancestors, and all the inhabitants of the surrounding villages come to attend. These gifts become the subject of a counter-gift: each family that is invited is expected to organize festivals, if possible more prestigious than those of their predecessors, at the next *famadihana*. New Year's Day in Imerina (the Central Highlands region of Madagascar) which, according to the ancestral calendar, occurs in March, occasions performances organized near the tombs of queens and kings in the *doany* sanctuaries which honor monarchs during the *tromba* possession ceremonies that musically invite revered ancestral spirits into the present. When performing in the countryside, artists offer ancestral sacrifices (ducks, pigs, alcohol and so on) at the inauguration of a new song performed for the first time in front of the public.

The *Hira Gasy* Opera

Originating near rice fields, *hira gasy* is an opera-theater genre performed in villages by families of peasants and farmers. The basic unit of performance is the troupe or company, *Tarika*. Each troupe, which has an average of six women and eight men, is centered on a family of artists from which a group is formed. The names of the companies most often include the name of the founder and the region of origin. Thus 'Tarika Ramilison Fenoarivo' means 'troupe founded by Ramilison from Fenoarivo.' The process in terms of which a company operates is that of democratic self-management: decision-making is based on internal democracy. Each troupe has rules that regulate the behavior of its members. Gifts, which are modest, are shared equally. The *mpihira gasy* also have an informal healthcare arrangement for members of troupes to deal with diseases and to attend to pregnancies. This is an essential service in Madagascar, where social safety nets are utterly lacking, with the health and education systems completely abandoned by a deliquescent and corrupt state.

The stage for performances of *hira gasy* is customarily the dark red Madagascan soil at the center of rice fields. Performances thus take place mostly in the open air in the adjoining areas of villages. The spatial organization for performances is as follows:

the troupe settles into a circle around which the public forms a second circle. These two concentric circles represent a symbol of harmony blessed by the ancestors. The performers stand next to each other, organized in accordance with the harmonies of their voices. The troupe then circles on itself so that each spectator can see the performance of each artist. This rotation of artists has given rise to the term '*hiratsangana*,' meaning 'art performed standing and moving.' This relationship between spectators and performers means that no barrier separates the audience from the actors who, most often, are standing while the audience is sitting on the ground. In some cities, such as Manjakandriana in the Central Highlands of Madagascar, stone-edged stages have been erected in market squares and are reserved for these performances. In the capital of Antananarivo two established spaces host the performances: the *kianja* (theaters) of the Andavamamba and Anosybe quarters.

A *hira gasy* performance is structured into acts, and is generally arranged as follows: a prelude performed by men with musical instruments is followed by women who pass majestically through the audience. There is then a succession of scenes: (1) an introductory speech (*kabary*) while the troupe sits in a circle and snare and base drummers beat an accompanying militaristic rhythm (*sasitehaka*); (2) songs of benediction; (3) a transitional speech (*kabary*); (4) *reinihira* or 'queen songs': singers form a circle facing outwards and sing in harmony on a selected theme while musicians, seated to the side, accompany them – *reinihira* are traditionally chanted, as in 'Mandora Mitsolany' (meaning, literally, 'spitting while lying on one's back'), a song that comments on global environment devastation and also on corruption; (5) a transitional speech (*kabary*); (6) acrobatic demonstrations, 'supple dances' and *Dihy* dances (dances which are often acrobatic or take their inspiration from martial arts); (7) a second transitional speech (*kabary*); (8) modern rhythmic songs referred to as *zanakira* or 'children's songs,' one example being 'Fonksionera sy Sofera' (meaning, literally, 'civil servant and get warm'), a song criticizing the corruption which governs the whole of Malagasy existence; (9) a concluding speech (*kabary*). Each song is accompanied by a gesturing of the arms by women and men and a kind of mime which relates to the meaning of the words. A *hira gasy* opera frequently lasts one full afternoon (six to eight hours). It often opposes symbolically two troupes playing alternately (about an hour-and-a-half each), purportedly competing against one another in an artistic contest whose jury is the audience.

The costumes are created by women members of the troupes who become stylists for the occasion with the help of seamstresses from the villages or poor urban neighborhoods. The women's costumes consist of long satin dresses colored pink, red, blue and mauve, and adorned with ruffles, ribbons, creases, braids, folds and secured by buttons. The women are inspired by dresses worn by the queens of Madagascar in the nineteenth century, especially those that Queen Victoria offered to the Malagasy Queen Ranavalona I. Each year a new set of dresses is designed. A silk shawl or *lamba* is wrapped at the waist or around the shoulders and moves in synchrony with the hand gestures (*latsi-tanana*) made during the songs and dances. The hairstyles of the women are traditional and complex. The rule is strict: women often wear multiple 'Afro' braids; hairstyles that do not conform to *hira gasy* conventions must be 'dismantled' before the women enter the performance area. Men's costumes consist of a long jacket (red, khaki, blue and green) that goes down to mid-thigh and is decorated with chevrons (varying according to the 'rank' in the troupe) and shoulder pads. The costumes are inspired by the uniforms of officers in the Malagasy army, which was equipped by Great Britain in the nineteenth century. Pants are made of black cotton and are most often decorated with a military-style side band. The men also wear a *lambaoany*: a cotton loincloth printed with traditional patterns worn at the waist or around the shoulders, which sways rhythmically to accompany leg movements known as *diamanga*. The costume is complemented by a black felt hat or a straw hat adorned with a black cotton headband. Neither men nor women wear shoes: *hira gasy* is performed barefoot.

The musicians transmit their knowledge from father to son and mother to daughter in a self-taught manner in the villages. The main musical instruments used during a *hira gasy* performance are *amponga* drums (a European bass drum), violins, trumpets, clarinets and cornets. Ancestral instruments (chordophones and membranophones) were replaced by European instruments, mainly imported from England at the beginning of the nineteenth century.

Every year each troupe must present to the public a new song that will enrich its repertoire. The writing takes place at the end of the peak season of *hira gasy*, which occurs at the beginning of the rainy season (November). The songs fall into two types. The classics are usually made up of a philosophical poem rooted in a reflection on the world and life and death that relies on proverbs and are sung for several hours, as in 'Mandora Mitsolany'. The texts repeat the tradition of *hainteny*, a form of Malagasy oral literature and poetry integral to daily life. Modern songs recount philosophical stories, often built around characters played by *mpihira gasy* actors and accompanied by dances. These songs combine educational content with a playful aspect. They evoke social problems, including those to do with health, work, food, disagreements, dysfunctional relationships and resistance to corruption. One example is provided by the song 'Zakeline Mama,' in which Zakeline's husband leaves his wife and children for another woman but is sure to be back because 'love is stronger than anything'. The songs also provide advice on ethical living. This advice can cover topics such as birth control, warnings against a rural exodus, delinquency, the prevention of AIDS, the dangers of alcoholism, the protection of the environment, praising the value of work, solidarity and honesty. Social protest is a recurring theme. Artists criticize the extreme egotism of the ruling class in a country that is ravaged by constant exploitation and a culture of corruption. They also express the aspirations of people who demand social justice. Harmony within groups is another constant theme: tips are provided for resolving problems experienced by couples, conflicts between parents and children, and neighborhood quarrels. The use of *ohabolana* proverbs is very common and humor is always present. *Ohabolana* proverbs are one of the oral traditions of *hainteny*. The other tradition is *kabary*. Love is also a recurring theme in these songs. All the stages of a relationship are included from the first encounter to separation.

Hira gasy opera is conceived, written and played in Malagasy, the national language spoken by the entire population. It is a Malayo-Polynesian language belonging to the Grand Barito branch spoken south of Kalimantan in Borneo, Indonesia.

Hira Gasy in the Twenty-First Century

Hira gasy has its roots in Imerina. In 1972 Malgachization took place, a policy implemented during the Second Republic in terms of which French instructors were expelled from the island and Malagasy, the 1,000-year-old language spoken by the entire population, was declared the official language of instruction in Madagascar's education system. Since that time, the influence of *hira gasy* has increased in all the regions of the island. Over the decades the approximately 130 troupes that have come into existence have expanded their range of tours and demand for shows has been growing. The influence of *hira gasy* opera was reinforced during the twentieth century by two artists: Sahondrafinina and Ramilison (also known as 'Besigara' or 'Dadamily'), who founded the most popular troupe, Tarika Ramilison Fenoarivo.

This expansion and demand for shows has continued into the twenty-first century and *hira gasy* has become a growing influence. The peasant artists establish a close relationship with audiences, whose experiences they share. This 'mirror effect' is thus a constant in the narratives of performances. Spectators number in the hundreds of thousands each year. The audience is made up mainly of rice growers and farmers from the Malagasy countryside where more than 85 percent of the population lives. In the city, audiences are made up mostly of casual workers and people living in poor neighborhoods. Students and intellectuals also number among the audiences, as well as some members of the upper classes.

At a more formal level, and since the time of King Andrianampoinimerina (1787–1810), all official ceremonies have included *hira gasy* performances. Good taste and tradition have required it. This practice continued after the creation of the Republic in 1960, with *hira gasy* performances being featured during the investiture of presidents, national festivities, celebrations of the insurrection of 1947 and so on. Moreover, during election campaigns, *hira gasy* shows are put on for the public, but only after partisan speeches have been concluded to ensure that the people who have come for the *hira gasy* performance stay throughout the rally. The inauguration of the Francophonie Games in Antananarivo in August 1997 showcased a fresco of *hira gasy* art. Religious ceremonies, fairs, football games and symposia frequently involve *hira gasy* troupes which are certain to attract large audiences. The media, especially radio and television, have had a multiplying effect. Programs devoted to *hira gasy* always enjoy great success. In stores, even in the most remote areas of the country, *hira gasy* music is heard wherever audio cassettes are sold. CD or DVD recordings are played for passengers on the old and dangerous minibuses, 'bush-taxis,' during long journeys along the hazardous country roads. The Internet has become a new medium for the broadcast of shows, which can generate thousands of views. Finally, in a country ravaged by corruption and which has been undergoing a profound moral, political, economic and social crisis, *hira gasy* has proved to be a means of comradeship, cohesion and hope for a people abandoned by its leaders.

In view of its importance to the cultural identity of Madagascar, steps were underway in the late 2010s to include the *hira gasy* opera in UNESCO's World Heritage list.

Bibliography

Bloch, Maurice. 1971. *Placing the Deads: Tombs, Ancestral Villages and Kingship Organization in Madagascar*. London: Seminar Press.

Bloch, Maurice. 1989. *Ritual, History and Power: Selected Papers in Anthropology*. London: The Athlone Press.

Callet, F. 1974. *Tantaran'ny Andriana nanjaka teto Madagasikara* [History of the Kings of Madagascar]. 3 vols. Antananarivo: Imprimerie Nationale.

Domenichini-Ramiaramanana, Bakoly. 1983. *Du ohabolana au Hainteny: Langue, littérature, et politique à Madagascar* [From Ohabolana to Hainteny: Language, Literature and Politics in Madagascar]. Paris: Karthala.

Edkvist, Ingela. 1997. *The Performance of Tradition: An Ethnography of Hira Gasy Popular Theatre in Madagascar*. Uppsala: Uppsala University.

Houlder, John Alden. 1960. *Ohabolana ou proverbes malgaches* [Ohabolana or Malagasy Proverbs]. Antananarivo: Imprimerie luthérienne.

Mallet, R. 1969. 'Eros et la mort: L'art sakalava à Madagascar' [Eros and Death: Sakalava Art in Madagascar]. *L'œil*, 29 June.

Marion, Marie-Andrée. 1975. *L'art funéraire érotique à Madagascar* [Erotic Funeral Art in Madagascar]. Unpublished Ph.D. dissertation, Université René Descartes.

Mauro, Didier. 1999. *Madagascar: l'Encyclopédie du voyage* [Madagascar: The Travel Encyclopedia]. Paris: Gallimard.

Mauro, Didier. 2001. *L'Opéra Hira Gasy: Un patrimoine mondial* [The Hira Gasy Opera: A World Heritage]. Presented at The National Academy of Arts, Letters and Sciences of Madagascar. Antananarivo: Annales de l'Académie Malgache.

Mauro, Didier. 2001. *Madagascar: L'opéra du peuple, anthropologie d'un 'fait social total': L'art Hira Gasy entre tradition et rébellion* [Madagascar: The Opera of the People – Anthropology of a 'Total Social Fact': Hira Gasy Art Between Tradition and Rebellion]. Paris: Karthala.

Mauro, Didier. 2016. *Testament anthropologique rebelle de Madagascar* [A Rebellious Anthropological Testament of Madagascar]. Paris: L'Harmattan.

Mauro, Didier. 2017. *Veloma Madagascar* [Goodbye Madagascar]. Paris: L'Harmattan.

Mauro, Didier, and Raholiarisoa, Emeline. 1999. *Madagascar: L'Ile-mère* [Madagascar: The Mother Island]. Paris: Nouvelles éditions Pages du Monde.

Mauro, Didier, and Raholiarisoa, Emeline. 2000. *Madagascar: L'Ile essentielle, étude d'anthropologie culturelle* [Madagascar: The Essential Island – A Cultural Anthropological Study]. Paris: Nouvelles éditions Pages du Monde.

Mauro, Didier, and Raholiarisoa, Emeline. 2000. *Madagascar, parole d'ancêtre merina, amour et rébellion en Imerina – contribution à l'ethnoscénologie de l'opéra paysan hira gasy* [Madagascar, Oratory of the Merina Ancestors, Love and Rebellion in Imerina – A Contribution to the Ethnoscenology of Rustic Hira Gasy Opera]. Paris: Nouvelles éditions Pages du Monde.

Molet, Louis. 1979. *La conception malgache du monde surnaturel et de l'homme en Imerina* [The Malagasy Conception of the Supernatural and Human World in Imerina]. 2 vols. Paris: L'Harmattan.

Navone, Gabriele. 1987. *Ny atao no miverina ou Ethnologie et proverbes malgaches* [Ethnology and Malagasy Proverbs]. Fianarantsoa: Librairie Ambozontany.

Ottino, Paul. 1998. *Les champs de l'ancestralité à Madagascar* [Ancestral Territory in Madagascar]. Paris: Karthala.

Paulhan, Jean. 1970. *Le repas et l'amour en Imerina* [Food and Love in Imerina]. Paris: Fata Morgana.

Paulhan, Jean. 1991. *Hain teny Merina: poésies populaires malgaches/recueillies et traduites par Jean Paulhan* [Merina Hainteny: Malagasy Folk Poems (Collected and Translated by Jean Paulhan)]. Antananarivo: Société Malgache d'Editions.

Rabearivelo, Jean-Joseph. 1990. *Traduits de la nuit suivi de vieilles chansons des pays d'Imerina* [Translations of the Night Followed by Old Imerina Songs]. Paris: Orphée – La Différence.

Rakotomalala, Mireille Mialy. 2002. *La musique malgache dans l'histoire* [Malagasy Music in History]. Paris: Nouvelles éditions Pages du Monde.

Ranaivo, Flavien. 1975. *Poèmes Hain-Teny* [Hainteny Poems]. Paris: Publications orientalistes de France.

Ruud, Jorgen. 1960. *Taboo: A Study of Malagasy Customs and Beliefs*. Antananarivo: Trano Printy Loterana.

Verin, Pierre. 2000. *Madagascar*. Paris: Karthala.

Vig, Lars. 1977. *Croyances et mœurs des malgaches* [Beliefs and Customs of the Malagasy]. 2 vols. Antananarivo: Editions Luthériennes.

Discographical Reference

Recordings of the songs, 'Fonksionera sy Sofera,' 'Mandora Mitsolany' and 'Zakeline Mama' may be found on the CD accompanying Mauro and Raholiarisoa 2000 (see Bibliography).

Discography

Ramilison. *Hira Gasy: Un fabuleux opera* [Hira Gasy: A Fabulous Opera]. Buda Musique. *2002*: Madagascar.

Randrianary, Victor. *2001. Madagascar, les chants d'une île* [Madagascar: Songs from the Island]. (Book and CD.) Arles: Editions Actes Sud.

Filmography

L'Opéra Hira Gasy de Madagascar [Madagascan Hira Gasy Opera], dir. Emeline Raholiarisoa. 2018. France. 120 mins. Documentary.

Madagascar, la parole poème, chroniques de l'opéra paysan Hira Gasy [Madagascar: The Poem of Voices – Chronicles of Countryside Hira Gasy Opera], dir. Didier Mauro. 1997. Madagascar. 52 mins. Documentary.

Madagascar l'autre voyage. 1. La pensée malgache [Madagascar: The Other Voyage, Part 1: Madagascan Thought], dir. Didier Mauro. 2001. France. 55 mins. Documentary.

Madagascar l'autre voyage. 2. La vie malgache [Madagascar: The Other Voyage, Part 2: Malagasy Life], dir. Didier Mauro. 2001. France. 52 mins. Documentary.

Madagascar l'autre voyage. 3. La fuite malgache [Madagascar: The Other Voyage, Part 3: The Malagasy Flight], dir. Didier Mauro. 2001. France. 52 mins. Documentary.

Madagascar, l'Île des ancêtres [Madagascar, the Island of Ancestors], dir. Didier Mauro. 2000. Madagascar. 55 mins. Documentary.

Websites

Ramilison ('Dadamily' or 'Besigara'), the master of *hira gasy* opera https://en.wikipedia.org/wiki/Ramilison_Besigara

Hira gasy Opera: https://en.wikipedia.org/wiki/Hiragasy

Perline Raafiarisoa, classic singer of *hira gasy* opera: https://fr.wikipedia.org/wiki/Perline_Razafiarisoa

Research Centers

Antananarivo University. Institute of Civilizations. Museum of Art and Archeology. 17 rue du Docteur Villette. Isoraka. Antananarivo 101. Madagascar. BP 564. Tel : 00.281.20.22210.47.

Malagasy Academy, Madagascar's National Academy of Arts, Letters and Sciences (AcNALS): B.P. 6217, Tsimbazaza. Antananarivo 101. Madagascar. Tel: 00.261.20.22.210.84.

DIDIER MAURO (TRANSLATED BY ANDRÉ LOISELLE)

House Music in Southern Africa

House music first developed in the underground club culture of Chicago in the 1980s. Associated initially with black and gay subcultures, it quickly spread to US cities such as New York and Detroit and then abroad to London. Beginning in the early 1990s, house music moved to the mainstream, influencing pop and dance music internationally. Created by DJs and record producers as well as musicians, it is an essentially electronic form of music characterized by mechanical, repetitive rhythms emanating from drum machines, hi-hat cymbals and synthesized basslines. Like hip-hop, house music has become a global musical phenomenon.

House music in southern Africa is thus to some extent a 'borrowed' culture. However, through a rapid if uneven process of indigenization, acquired local inflections have led to the creation of what became identifiable forms of southern African house music. South Africa has been particularly influential in this process. As a consequence, southern Africa – and South Africa in particular – has become an influential disseminator of new electronic music and house music internationally since the late 1990s. Like other manifestations of house music around the world, house music in Africa is characterized by the inclusion of dub records and instrumentals; instrumentation includes electric guitar, keyboard, horns, synthesizers, hi-hats and drum machines.

This entry begins with a substantial account of the development and history of house music in South Africa. It is then followed by briefer sections on parallel developments in two neighboring countries, Botswana and Swaziland.

South Africa

House music is arguably the most popular genre in postapartheid South Africa's youth music culture in the early twenty-first century. International commentators tend to assign this position to *kwaito*, but this assignation ignores *kwaito*'s musical debt to house and also the fact that house music reclaimed its centrality after *kwaito*'s wane from the mid-1990s.

Founding Fathers

The history of house music in South Africa, as elsewhere, consists of the activities of DJs, of venues, audiences and media networks (Gilbert and Pearson 1999; Thornton 2001; Bennett 2001; Brewster and Broughton 2006; Reynolds 2008). Having observed the extraordinary music activism of their predecessors from the United States and the United Kingdom, South African house DJs furthered the new style through performance, dissemination and active, high-profile promotion. Christos Katsaitis or DJ Christos, who is affectionately known as the country's 'Godfather of House' is a Greek-South African born in Pretoria. His musical skills and entrepreneurship set the standard for emulation in the early history of house music in South Africa. Like others of the first generation (the early 1990s), DJ Christos obtained international house records and played them at parties; beyond this, he also released compilations. From the early 1990s until 2001 Christos owned and ran a nightclub, Club Ellesse, in Pretoria. The club's name indicated house music's desired clientele, since Ellesse was already a favored designer label popular with black urban youth at this time. The club's location in Esselen Street, Sunnyside – an edgy part of the country's capital – was close to Pretoria Technikon, the University of Pretoria and the University of South Africa. It was therefore close to what would become its main audience: black youth. Image, location, youth and house music were thus intertwined early in the genre's local history.

The Pretoria-born Vincent Motshegoa came to fame as DJ 'Vinny Da Vinci' (typical township nomenclature for someone called Vincent). His singular contribution to the early growth of house in South Africa was through his ownership of House Afrika, a shop that sold vinyl recordings of international house music in Johannesburg. Motshegoa was joined by Tim White (a former A&R man for CCP Records) and Glenn Van Loggerenburg, and together they formed the House Afrika Records label which has remained key in the country's house music industry. He also paired up with DJ Christos to form 'DJs at Work,' playing off 'Little' Louie Vega's and Kenny 'Dope' Gonzales's 'Masters at Work' act: 'one of the most respected remix/production teams of the nineties' (Brewster and Broughton 2006, 479). DJs at Work organized their own gigs throughout the country and released compilations that consisted of house tracks from abroad. Separately, Vinny Da Vinci's compilations showed preference for deep house which, along with mid-tempo, has remained the preferred house music style in South Africa. Christos mostly preferred to perform live, either at his Club Ellesse or as the featured act at other venues. As DJs at Work, Christos and Vinny Da Vinci worked on original music rather than mixes, featuring guest artists only occasionally. An important DJ who followed the trends set by DJs at Work was DJ Iggy Smallz (1977–2004) from Atteridgeville township outside Pretoria.

In Soweto, Ganyani Tshabalala or DJ Ganyani played deep house mostly in clubs and was the DJ of choice at neighborhood parties and shebeens or 'spots' that were experimenting with this music. The last of the founding fathers, DJ Ganyani has been affectionately acknowledged in the late 2010s as a mentor who taught aspiring DJs how to mix using vinyl records. He is credited as being one of the first DJs to employ the technique of blended mixing in a compilation meant for public consumption. Prior to this, DJs employed blended mixing only for clubs rather than for commercial release on cassette tapes or, later, on CDs. Ganyani therefore influenced the most important form in which house music in South Africa is consumed: the DJ's compilation album.

Superstars

From this underground, Gauteng-specific scene (Gauteng, meaning 'place of gold,' is one of South Africa's nine provinces, located toward the northeastern tip of the country), South Africa's era of the superstar DJ was inaugurated. The first of these superstars was DJ 'Glen Lewis' Mpotseng Tshinaba, popularly known as 'the teddy bear of the airwaves,' an appellation that illustrates audiences' preference for R&B and soul lyrics' romantic content, usually sung by a female vocalist. Indeed, house music's success in South Africa derives partly from tapping into an already existing fan base for African-American R&B and related styles. Glen Lewis's career began with Radio Bop (of the former apartheid homeland, Bophuthatswana). Post apartheid, he became a main feature in the SABC's Metro FM national network. On television, he presented the music program *Technics Heart of the Beat*, and soon joined the house scene as a pioneer of the local mid-tempo and Latin house trends. This Sowetan is also famous for his compilations, which were distinguished from others because of how they were mixed. Throughout the 1990s mixing was predominantly through cassette tapes. By the time of Glen Lewis's popularity, however, mixing desks and vinyl records were emerging as the preferred musical materials. Importing this equipment and recordings became a marker of a DJ's status, and mixes came to be judged according to what was used and the facility with which it was used. Glen Lewis's road to celebrity is typical of a particular kind of South African house music DJ: by the time of the genre's arrival, the personality is already familiar to a radio and, at times, television audience; the DJ's role is to interpret the new music to devotees, either on radio or on compilations.

The second superstar DJ, Thato Sikwane, professionally known as DJ Fresh, hailed from neighboring Botswana. DJ Fresh entered the country's popular culture scenes as a TV presenter on the music request show 'Pick A Tune.' However, his radio career was more important. He rose to fame in Yfm – a Johannesburg-based independent station whose target was black young people and their music. Yfm remained a profoundly powerful institution, though this was especially from the 1990s to the early 2000s. Its programming was rapidly imitated by the South African Broadcasting Corporation's national (e.g., Metro FM) and regional radio stations (e.g., Durban Youth Radio), and also by university and college campus radios (e.g., 'RMR' Rhodes Music Radio of Rhodes University in the Eastern Cape and 'VOW' Voice of Wits at the University of the Witwatersrand in Johannesburg). Yfm's offshoot, the *YMag* magazine, further disseminated the house music scene and created the celebrity culture that has continued to surround the top DJs in the country. Indeed, *YMag*'s national distribution, unlike the station's regional broadcast, did far more to spread the sound and look of the new scene, merging it with thoughtful and informative features on earlier black popular music cultures and their cultural significance: Sophiatown, African jazz, African-American R&B and South African Black Consciousness politics for example.

Yfm's entry into South Africa's postapartheid soundscape was timely, since at this time public broadcasting was preoccupied with dismantling the ethnic separatism that was created by Bantu Radio in 1960 and, after Bantu Radio's demise, was maintained by radio throughout apartheid (Hamm 1991; Coplan 2011). The extent to which this creation of new listening publics and musical communities led to the making of a new culture is clearest in the naming of this scene, 'Y Culture' (Nuttall 2009). By virtue of his entanglement with this scene, DJ Fresh's house music career was buoyed up by it. Between 1998 and 2003 he released the best-selling *Fresh House Flava* compilation volumes with House Afrika Records' CDGUMBA series. Despite the volumes' popularity – they made house music mainstream – DJ Fresh's compilation aesthetics did not lean toward significant remixing of chosen tracks. Each track remained broadly recognizable and mostly melodic and singable. From Volume 3, and perhaps because of DJ Ganyani's influence, Fresh's main focus was on smooth blending between tunes and, in this way, he fulfilled one of house music's most important ritual features: flow. Fresh's success led to the explosion of compilation releases by South African DJs, mostly through House Afrika Records and, later, through Soul Candi Records – a label formed in 2001.

Among superstar DJs, Oscar Bonginkosi Mdlongwa looms largest. Mdlongwa is known by many names (Oscar Warona, Godzilla or The Big O), but most consistently as Oskido. Oskido was born in Letlhabile Township in Brits, in the north-west of the country. He grew up between Brits and Bulawayo (in Zimbabwe). He completed his schooling in Zimbabwe and returned to Letlhabile in 1988 to run his family spaza shop business (in South Africa, spaza shops are home-based convenience stores). Realizing he wanted to be a musician, he moved to Johannesburg. Once there, he worked as a car mechanic at a BMW dealership, quit after six months and ended up selling *boerewors* rolls (South African hot dogs) on the streets outside the Razzmatazz Night Club in Hillbrow. Oskido's legendary career was born by chance when he was asked to fill in for a DJ who had failed to turn up at Razzmatazz.

Oskido credits the influence of early Chicago DJs including Frankie Knuckles, Steve Silk Hurley and 'Little' Louie Vega of Masters at Work fame. In his early career, he would pick up records, slow down their tempo and reproduce his own sound on cassette as his mixes. He soon became popular on campuses across the country. On radio, Oskido secured a gig with Yfm with its resident DJ Rudeboy Paul to present *Rap Activity Jam*, a show that focused on local and international hip-hop and *ragga* music. Soon thereafter he hosted his own show called Oskido's Church Grooves (because it originally aired on Sunday afternoon) every Saturday afternoon and later he came to work for Metro FM. Oskido's Church Grooves at Yfm is central. Oskido emulated the music's early radio career in Chicago (and Detroit), providing evidence of his high regard for house music's innovators. For example, he regularly invited aspiring DJs to exhibit their skills live on radio, where they tried out their mixes on air or presented fresh original tracks. The show became a kind of 'house workshop,' and listeners were asked to call in and render their verdicts on the new music presented. Oskido's 'house workshop' for him and others in the know recalls earlier experiments by the *Hot Mix 5* show (on Chicago's WBMX radio station) and by *Street Beat* (on Detroit's WJLB radio station) in the mid-1980s, where listeners first heard records being mixed on radio (Brewster and Broughton 2006, 324–6; 350–1). Church Grooves often opened with a recitation of the 'Lord's Prayer' in TshiVenda to mark the onset of the house ritual. This recitation also became a feature in the series of compilations Oskido released with House Afrika Records, the first of which is *Oskido's Church Grooves: The First Commandment* (2001). Ten albums were released in total (the final commandment in 2010). Oskido rarely used original material in these recordings; it was his personality and his reputation in *kwaito* that gave the compilations their high profile.

South African House Music Cultures

These developments created South African house music cultures which, despite their emphasis on clubbing, cannot be read as identical to Euro-American 'club cultures' (Redhead, Wynne and O'Connor 1998). One reason for this is that, unlike in Euro-America, house music was not greeted in South Africa with a variety of moral panics (these were reserved for *kwaito*) and therefore had no underground status: it was everywhere audible and commercially successful, part of South Africa's mass culture. After Christos's Club Ellesse, DJs began to invest in their own clubs as sources of income to supplement tours and radio gigs. Club names changed frequently to keep the scene fresh; the location of the building tended to remain the same. South Africa's leisure industry was quick on the uptake: upmarket sedate restaurants and cafes began to morph into house venues in the evening; the change in function is signaled by the slow crescendo of throbbing deep house beats. In such venues, sponsors of house music – tobacco and alcopops (alcoholic cooler beverages) vendors – promote their discounted wares. Indeed, South Africa's house music cultures differ from those that favor E (ecstasy) because in South Africa they thrive on legal substances, in particular alcohol.

In the early twenty-first century new DJs' first port of call has remained campuses supported by student unions. Top billing at a 'Freshers Bash' during orientation week (with subsequent exposure on campus radio) can make a new career. Minibus taxis that transport the laboring masses and students crisscross cities and the countryside blaring house music, so much so that aspiring DJs regularly give taxi drivers their demos to test on a mobile though captive audience (in Durban, KwaZulu-Natal, a popular myth is that a taxi playing house music with a good sound system is likely to attract more customers, or at least good-looking female customers).

The afterlife of apartheid's racial division of the country is evident in these house music cultures. The genre, despite its urbane and sophisticated 'cool' image, needs to cultivate black township audiences to retain its prominence. Reminiscent of rave gatherings in rural England and Scotland – where 'what began as American urban dance musics became entangled within a skein of pastoral imagery' (Gilbert and Pearson 1999, 43) – house music in South Africa became entangled with the anti-pastoral that townships represent or with gentrified shebeens. In Soweto, for example, gatherings or 'bashes' take place in a demarcated space of ambiguous legality called 'Ubuntu Kraal,' which is a spectacle of Afro-kitsch. Along the east coast of the country, bashes are held on sandy beaches. In both kinds of open spaces, local events allow for listening and dancing; listeners either sit in the bar or *braai* (barbecue) areas.

The scene's embrace of open space bashes has helped to spread house beyond the country's major cities (Johannesburg, Durban and Cape Town). For example, high on the gig calendar is the Mafikeng Sixties Festival at Monare farm in the northern small town of Mahikeng. Clubs remain ideal venues, however, especially when hosting international visiting DJs. Louie Vega was one of the early international DJs invited to South Africa, hosted by Yfm between 1997 and 1999. His visit boosted the local scene because of his stature and because he had remixed Fela Kuti's music (featuring Fela's drummer Tony Allen). The international house music scene reciprocated, as South African DJs were in return invited to observe and perform in Ibiza. As a result, a bewildering transnational traffic of sounds and DJs ensued: Vega remixed Mafikizolo's 'Lotto' (referencing the newly launched National Lottery, 'Lotto,' the track is itself a remix of Osunlade's 'Cantos a ochun et oya'), and renamed it 'Loot.' He also remixed DJ Black Coffee's 'We Are One,' which featured Hugh Masekela.

International connections raised house music's status in the local industry. The South African Music Awards (the SAMAs) and the Metro FM Music Awards created a new category for the genre. New radio publics emerged. Ukhozi FM, a postapartheid equivalent of Radio Zulu which broadcasts in that language, cast off its previous ethnocentric association with and preference for genres such as *maskanda* and became strong purveyors of house music. Umhlobo Wenene, formerly Radio Xhosa, did the same to a lesser degree. Indeed, the dominance of youth programming on radio meant that most 'black' radio stations feature house music. Most significant was house music's adoption by 5FM, formerly Radio 5, which used to be a 'white' English-language station. The most important personality in this move has remained DJ Roger Goode, whose love of the music saw it gain a white youth audience as well as instigating an increased popularity for 5fm with black young people. Goode, in other words, introduced house music styles that were popular with black South Africans to white young people whose preference tended to be techno. Goode's success has transformed 5fm's previous white image. For example, while most Yfm DJs move to Metro FM (traditionally 'black') once they are too old to be associated with a youth market, DJ Fresh was poached by 5fm. House music's multiracial appeal in South Africa has also been evident in independent record companies (where ownership tends to be interracial), in interracial groups and in popular DJs such as 'Crazy White Boy.'

South African House

These developments led to changes in house music's repertoire in South Africa, which had predominantly consisted of variations of existing African-American music. Audiences were becoming more discriminating because of exposure: from SABC TV shows such as *Studio Mix* and gig guides including 'Ziwaphi' ('Where's It At'). The cultivation of value judgments regarding house music was encouraged by anchors at Yfm, who tended to be presenters rather than solely touring DJs. These towering personalities included DJ Khabzela (Isaac Fana Khaba) and DJ Rudeboy Paul (Paul Mnisi). They, among others, shaped ways of talking about house music in South Africa: they critiqued it, praised it and wondered where else it could go. Moreover, they did all this using young South Africa's heteroglot discursive world, employing both the country's African languages (in their Johannesburg 'township lingo' guise) and English to forge an 'Afropolitan' discourse on and about house.

Responses to this were many. They included the formation of sound engineering courses in downtown colleges. Most notable among these has been Allenby College in Bramley, Johannesburg. Others have included Central Johannesburg College, Boston City College's partnership with the Soul Candi Institute of Music (SCIM) and Damelin College satellite campuses. These colleges have been so successful that, each year, university music departments are often approached by applicants who want to be DJs or sound engineers. One reason for these colleges' success (and the resulting applications to study music at university) is that most of their teachers are jazz musicians (who received their degrees or diplomas from a university or a university of technology).

A more important reason is the caliber of DJs these colleges produced and their contribution to house music in South Africa. DJ Fresh graduated from Boston City College and has remained its most high-profile alumnus and ambassador. Allenby College produced DJ Cleo (Cleopas Monyeapo), who worked as Yfm's technical engineer and, as DJ Fresh's apprentice, was the first featured local DJ on the *Fresh House Flava* compilations (in Volume 4) before releasing his own compilation entitled *Es'khaleni* (In the Hood). DJ Cleo's *Es'khaleni* series cleverly alludes to apartheid's partition of black living spaces, variously subtitled 'phase,' 'extension' or 'zone.' Both the reference to place and the language used to reference place are close to *kwaito* albums' linguistic aesthetic. Other Allenby graduates include Amukelani Tshawani ('Ammunition') and the local hip-hop superstar Thabiso Thekisho ('ProVerb'). However, its most maverick graduate has remained Jerah Mothusi: DJ One Eyed Monkey.

One Eyed Monkey has never been a celebrity figure like Fresh or Glen Lewis. However, he revolutionized house music in South Africa because he started remixing classic South African popular music. These remixes included songs by jazz musicians such as Caiphus Semenya and Letta Mbulu. He also teamed up with Rudeboy Paul to remix some repertoire by the *maskanda* guitarist Madala Kunene. Other DJs followed suit, influenced in no small measure by the success and popularity of the Africanism house group, so called because of their emphasis on West African sounds indebted to musics such as soul *makossa*. South African house DJs searched for sounds that would simultaneously be African and 'exotic' *within* South Africa. For this, they relied on musical styles and languages that were not at the time prevalent in either *kwaito* or hip-hop such as XiTsonga and TshiVenda. The most popular exponents were the identical twins from Alexandra Township in Johannesburg, George and Joseph Mothiba, who work together as Revolution. Their career began as backing dancers for DJ Christos. By 2002 their albums were top sellers in the house music genre. The titles of their albums show their adoption of the 'Saffro' trend: *The Journey* (2002), *Roots* (2005), *The Journey Continues* (2008), *Tribal Journey* (2010) and *Meropa* (2011). In *The Journey* in particular, Revolution highlighted the Venda-influenced music of the Afro-Jazz Malombo guitarist and composer Philip Tabane. They have also featured the jazz and Afro-fusion music of legendary pianist Themba Mkhize, Hugh Masekela's rendition of Fela Kuti's 'Lady' and their jazz contemporaries: the guitarist Jimmy Dludlu, saxophonist McCoy Mrubata and kora player Pops Mohammed. In this, they compared favorably with other collaborations such as that of Rudeboy Paul with the jazz saxophonist Zim Ngqawana in the song 'Ibofolo,' which was already a jazz reworking of a Xhosa traditional song.

The response from South African house music lovers was explosive: these were songs black young people remembered from their parents, reconstructed to speak to their postapartheid present. These innovations continued well into the twenty-first century. The most notable exponent has been the jazz vocalist turned super-DJ from the Eastern Cape and KwaZulu-Natal, Nkosinathi Maphumulo or DJ Black Coffee. Trained as a jazz musician, Black Coffee has differed markedly from house music's urbane celebrity DJs, since he has tended to be known as 'bookish,' nerdy and not prone to party unless he is working. His early music career was with Shana, an all-male close harmony vocal group reminiscent of the Manhattan Brothers (Ballantine 1999). Black Coffee most notably collaborated with the jazz composer, arranger and double bassist Victor Ntoni, catapulting the latter to no small fame. Another house music outfit, the band Mi Casa, has drawn on the legacy of South African crossover popular music. Mo-T, who is Mi Casa's trumpeter, was taught by his father Kgasoane Banza, who was the trumpeter for Mango Groove, perhaps South Africa's most celebrated crossover group. Mi Casa has retained this older sound in its house music and it has become the band's trademark.

The cultural significance of One Eyed Monkey's innovations cannot be overstated: postapartheid South Africa was and has remained ambivalent in its relationships to its own pasts. These are often presented to the younger generation as the towering story of the anti-apartheid struggle: inviolable and demanding only piety and gratitude. The remixing of the music from the country's past therefore signals not only aesthetic agency for the house music DJ; it also represents a usable tradition that may be reinterpreted, through dance and through the mix, by the listener. Much like the cultural significance of jungle/drum 'n' bass in the United Kingdom (Gilbert and Pearson 1999, 79–80), One Eyed Monkey's innovations mark the moment when house music in South Africa became South African House.

House and Kwaito

The development of South African house may also be traced from bubblegum (a popular music style of the 1980s) through to *kwaito*. When DJ Oskido was forging his house career touring the country's small towns, he met his future collaborator Bruce 'Dope' Sebitlo in Mmabatho. Together and along with other DJs, they began to add vocals to slowed-down beats of international house tracks, which led to the birth of *kwaito*. Oskido embraced *kwaito* and with Dope Sebitlo, formed the enormously popular *kwaito* band, Brothers of Peace (BOP).

While a *kwaito* performer, Oskido joined forces with DJ Christos and the young jazz pianist Don Laka and formed the record company Kalawa Records (the name is a fusion of *Ka*tsaitis, *La*ka and Mdlong*wa*). The company has been central to postapartheid popular music because the first group it produced was Boom Shaka, the inaugural *kwaito* band, whose cassettes were first sold out of the backs of cars. The company was joined by members of another *kwaito* group, Trompies, whose members were Mandla 'Spikiri' Mofokeng, Jairus 'Jakarumba' Nkwe, Zynne 'Mahoota' Sibika, Eugene 'Donald Duck' Mthethwa and Emmanuel 'Mjokes' Matsane, and was renamed Kalawa Jazmee (Christos left to form his own music label). Kalawa Jazzmee was important because established record companies (Gallo, Sony Music, BMG Records) were unconvinced by the new *kwaito* sound. Kalawa Jazmee, however, consisted of musicians who were schooled in how to succeed in the popular music industry. For example, Jairus Nkwe and Mandla Mofokeng were backing dancers to bubblegum acts of the 1980s, including Sello 'Chicco' Twala, and Eugene Mthethwa played with the internationally acclaimed reggae artist Lucky Dube. With this background knowledge, the record label ensured that the musicians in its stable were featured in events connected with social concerns (such as HIV/AIDS awareness campaigns, and others hosted in particular by the ANC Youth League), thereby establishing their popularity.

Oskido reserved his producing skills for *kwaito*, and it is significant that he did not release his house albums under his own label. In so doing, an attempt at keeping *kwaito* separate from house is evident. This separation spawned the phenomenon of house musicians' 'alter egos.' For example, Trompies member Zynne Sibika cultivated a double act: as a *kwaito* star he is known as 'Mahoota' and he performs house music as DJ Vetkoek. These warring musical personalities combine in his 'DJ Vetkoek vs. Mahoota' shows. Yfm's DJ Sbu's *kwaito* alter ego, 'Mzekezeke,' was another example of this trend. *Kwaito* was, in any case, changing by this time – the heavier music of performers such as Mduduzi 'M'du' Masilela was giving way to the more dance-oriented sounds of the later Arthur Mofokate. Arthur's later music was not only changing in orientation; often the music *was* about a dance style and the song became a vehicle for a style's popularization. *Kwaito's* Doc Shebeleza began to use house music's drum patterns in his songs, at times without slowing them down, layering *kwaito* lyrics on top. A more successful innovator is Durban's Mthokozisi Kathi or DJ Tira. The convergence has never been total and the two musical cultures remain distinct, with artists occupying either extreme at will. Nevertheless, the new *kwaito* sound (later called 'new age *kwaito*') required a lighter music bed to support the body rather than the vocal-melodic line required by its older forms. Thus in the waning years of *kwaito,* the lighter four-on-the-floor house beat was heard creeping in. *Kwaito* circled back to house music to form a different chapter in the history of South African house (see separate entry).

Botswana

House music emerged in Botswana in 1988. Batswana (citizens of Botswana, plural) DJs describe local house music as a mix of 'soulful vocals' and spoken lines recited in a combination of English and Setswana, one of the local languages. Another distinguishing feature of the music is remixing local popular songs. From the beginning of the house movement in the late 1980s the audience has largely consisted of young listeners who attend parties where DJs play their most recent mixes. Partygoers come from a variety of socioeconomic backgrounds and are unified by their love of house music. Since the 1990s house music has attracted a larger following in Botswana and the audience has continued to be primarily Batswana youth.

Motswana (citizen of Botswana, singular) DJ Sidney 'DJ Sid' Basitsile affirms that the house movement in Botswana started when David Molosi, also known as DJ Ski or Skizo, returned to Botswana from Washington, DC during a vacation from Howard University, where he was studying. While there, Molosi was drawn to the house music emanating from both Washington, DC and New York City. At that time, house music was part of a phenomenon called underground dance music (UDM) and was associated with club culture (Fikentscher 2000; Thornton 1996). Similarly, Molosi confirms that house music began as an underground trend in Botswana because the music was still gaining momentum on a national level (personal communication, 2013). At the outset, house music aficionados attended parties where they knew that house music would be played. The rise of nightclubs where DJs specialized in playing house music, along with the growing crowd attendance, led to Molosi's immense popularity.

In addition to Molosi, the aforementioned Sidney 'DJ Sid' Basitsile was also a prominent DJ who was a major force in the establishment of house music in Botswana. Like Molosi, Basitsile attended Howard University, and he was introduced to house music through the Washington, DC scene. He spent substantial amounts of his university stipend purchasing records that he could play for audiences when he came back to Botswana during vacations. DJing was not new to him. Basitsile's turntable skills dated back to his childhood when his father gave him a record player that he tinkered with on his family's farm. His passion for DJing eventually led to playing sets at school dances and was later parlayed into the national role that he played in broadcasting house music on the radio.

Alongside acquiring records during time spent overseas, DJs, including DJ Sid and Skizo, accumulated records to sustain local house music largely through international distributors. Subsequently, records were gathered from Antonio 'DJ Tony' Valinotti, a DJ who relocated to Botswana from South Africa. He hosted 'Tony's Crazy Disco,' a recurring party which was held throughout Botswana in locations such as the Gaborone Club during the 1980s, appealing to followers who looked forward to hearing the latest house music. According to Basitsile, additional record suppliers from South Africa were also a resource for local house music DJs (personal communication, 2013).

Radio became a vehicle for house music DJs to broadcast their music on a national platform. Radio Botswana 2 (RB2) was a forerunner in the promotion of local house music. This station featured Skizo's radio show, *Cklub 103*, on Saturdays, as well as Basitsile's show, *The Smirnoff Party Mix*. Listeners gravitated toward *The Smirnoff Party Mix* and it created a growing demand for the music. Some of the other popular DJs of the period who surfaced in this male-dominated field were Cosmo and Peter Tshiamo, and later DJ Fresh, Dolphus and Kinetic P. Each of these DJs possessed an individual style and unique collection of records that they became known for playing at parties.

Musical partnerships developed between Batswana DJs and other international house DJs such as Thato 'DJ Fresh' Sikwane (South Africa), Oscar 'Oskido' Mdlongwa (South Africa), Victor Simonelli (United States) and Lars Behrenroth (Germany/United States). These affiliations were formed as Batswana DJs traveled internationally to play sets, thereby garnering global attention and building professional networks. Attesting to the resulting popularization of local house music DJs and their music, Molosi asserts, 'The fact that there exists a desire to collaborate, that is a success in itself'(personal communication, 2013). When leading house DJs such as Molosi and Basitsile started playing in Botswana, they were not signed to a label, but ensuing international connections led Molosi to record albums for the South African record labels Big Dawg Productions (Afro Blue: The Rebirth), Gallo (The 69er The Sixty Niner) and Kalawa Jazmee (The Skizo Project: House Rules).

From the beginning of the house music movement in Botswana, technological developments have made it easier for more DJs to get involved. Molosi notes (ibid.) that in the early twenty-first century the emergence of new computer technology has allowed more up-and-coming DJs to experiment with creating songs and producing their own music. Further DJs are appearing due to innovative computer software and CDJs (turntables that enable the manipulation of compact discs during DJ sets). The movement has motivated additional Batswana to master DJ software and related digital programming to break into the industry. Some of the DJs at the forefront of the house movement in the early twenty-first century have been Boogie Sid, Chrispin, Fondo Fire, Groove Cartell and Young Mullar. They have been integral in the expansion of house music from Botswana to audiences outside the country. Their music has received a strong local response in the country, and it has also gained international exposure through online websites that allow DJs to share their latest work. One example is Groove Cartell's appearance at the top of charts on the website Traxsource Charts (www.traxsource.com), which has been deemed one of the world's leading online house music shops. House music DJs in Botswana have been moving the music in new directions by reaching larger audiences and broadening the fan base for house music from the nation.

Swaziland

House music in Swaziland is a microcosm of local, South African and global electronic music influences. With top-earning producers and groups such as Black Coffee, DJ Cleo, Mi Casa and Mafikizolo, South Africa's house anthems stretch beyond her borders and are played at clubs and festivals internationally. Swaziland, being a short journey from the two important South African house-producing cities (Johannesburg and Durban), has been greatly influenced by this music and, as a result, has an ever-growing scene of house producers and appreciators.

In the early 2000s the first DJs and producers credited with making house music in Swaziland were DJ Simza and Swazi Pride. Swazi Pride's hit track 'Viva la vida' from their debut album *House Culture* is regarded as the first Swazi house anthem to enjoy widespread popularity and has been influential for many young producers. Since that time, the scene in South Africa has diversified with the growth of and changes in *kwaito*, Durban's *qhum* music, and the genre-defying sounds of Spoek Mathambo and Fantasma. Alongside these developments, house music in Swaziland has grown in popularity. DJs and producers regularly travel to South Africa to perform and some have moved to South Africa permanently to further their commercial careers. Though no research has been published on the Swazi variation of this global music, local record stores in Swaziland are lined with Swazi and South African house and *kwaito* releases.

Swazi house music can be divided into numerous subgenres ('vernac' or 'tribal house,' 'minimal,' 'nu-disco,' 'deep tech,' 'Latin house' and so on) but it is perhaps more useful to regard the music and its varying characteristics as an ever-changing spectrum (Matsenjwa 2014). House, in its North American and European contexts, is an electronic dance music created from synthesized drum patterns. In South Africa and Swaziland, local sounds, genres and rhythmic grooves twist global house language into a music that speaks to and from this region. For example, DJ Ziyawa defines the 'tribal house' subgenre as any house track that incorporates rattles, shakers, wild animal sounds, flutes and synthesized string pads. He defines the 'Swazi tribal' subgenre as any beat that includes references to Swazi *umhlanga* ('reed dance') vocal songs, or traditional instruments such as the *makhoyane* gourd-resonated musical bow (Matsenjwa 2014). Swazi house loosely borrows and samples songs and instrumental timbres from local traditional genres (such as *umbholoho* and *isicathamiya*) but also from South Africa, Central Africa, South America and the Caribbean. Because there is an impetus among house producers to find musical markers that distinguish their work from house elsewhere, Swazi producers since 2010 have increasingly turned to local musicians, such as guitarist Bholoja, and traditional musicians such as Khokhiwe Mphila and Bhemani Magagula, to help create this sound. Increasingly, producers are using the national language of Swaziland, Siswati, for song lyrics on their tracks.

Swazi house releases tend to be singles, or part of mixes created by DJs, and these are all disseminated widely online via sites such as Traxsource, Mixcloud and Soundcloud, as opposed to in stores as material copies. Though Swaziland has more DJs than producers or composers of original house music, all are important in the sustenance of the scene and have loyal networks of fans. Regular DJ sessions in Manzini and Mbabane, such as the 'Groove

Meditation Sessions,' provide opportunities for house fans to enjoy the latest hits from Swaziland and abroad. In some cases, producers have grouped together to further the music and their careers. An example of this is the group +268 founded in 2008, comprising Senzo Simelane (DJ/producer), Mazwi Myeni (producer/songwriter/instrumentalist) and Vusi Dube (DJ/producer). Within the field, producers see a distinction between DJs who create commercial house and those looking for more 'interesting' sounds. Many Swazi producers criticize those who merely remix international house hits for a local audience. There is an emphasis on originality and local relevance within the genre.

Popular hits that have emerged from Swaziland are Simza and Sabside's 'Mine Bengidzakiwe' (2007, nominated for a Metro Award in South Africa), Nomalungelo Dladla's album *Imiyalo: The House Remixes* (2014), and Nomzamo Dlamini's *Lobola* (2010, produced by +268).

Bibliography

Ballantine, Christopher. 1999. 'Looking to the USA: The Politics of Male Close-Harmony Song Style in South Africa During the 1940s and 1950s.' *Popular Music* 18(1): 1–17.

Bennett, Andy. 2001. *Cultures of Popular Music*. Maidenhead: Open University Press.

Bidder, Sean, ed. 1999. *House: The Rough Guide*. New York: Penguin Books.

Brewster, Bill, and Broughton, Frank. 2006. *Last Night a DJ Saved My Life: The History of the Disc Jockey*. 2nd ed. London: Headline Book Publishing. (First published 2000.)

Coplan, David. 2011. 'South African Radio in a Saucepan.' In *Radio in Africa: Publics, Cultures, Communities*, eds. Liz Gunner, Dina Ligaga and Dumisani Moyo. Johannesburg: Wits University Press, 134–48.

Fikentscher, Kai. 2000. *"You Better Work!": Underground Dance Music in New York*. Middletown, CT: Wesleyan University Press.

Gilbert, Jeremy, and Pearson, Ewan. 1999. *Discographies: Dance Music, Culture and the Politics of Sound*. London: Routledge.

Hamm, Charles. 1991. '"The Constant Companion of Man": Separate Development, Radio Bantu and Music.' *Popular Music* 10(2): 147–73.

Kai-Lewis, Jerry. 2008. 'Big Dawg Throws Weight Behind Compatriots.' Online at: http://www.mmegi.bw/index.php?sid=7&aid=11&dir=2008/April/Tuesday8 (accessed 21 March 2018).

Marumo, Mmoloki. 2008. 'DJ Sid: The Rebirth.' Mmegi. Online at: http://www.mmegi.bw/index.php?sid=7&aid=69&dir=2008/August/Monday4 (accessed 21 March 2018).

Nuttall, Sarah. 2009. *Entanglement: Literary and Cultural Reflection on Post-Apartheid*. Johannesburg: Wits University Press.

Redhead, Steve, Wynne, Derek, and O'Connor, Justin, eds. 1998. *The Clubcultures Reader: Readings in Popular Cultural Studies*. Oxford: Blackwell.

Reynolds, Simon. 2008. *Energy Flash: A Journey Through Rave Music and Dance Culture*. 2nd ed. London: Picador.

Steingo, Gavin. 2016. *Kwaito's Promise: Music and the Aesthetics of Freedom in South Africa*. Chicago: University of Chicago Press.

Thornton, Sarah. 2001. *Club Cultures: Music, Media, and Subcultural Capital*. Cambridge: Polity.

Discographical References (South Africa)

Black Coffee featuring Hugh Masekela. *We Are One*. Vega Records, VR107. *2011*: USA.

DJ Cleo. *Es'khaleni*. Will of Steel Production, CDWOS 001. *2004*: South Africa.

Fresh House Flava 1. House Afrika Records, CDGUMBA (WL) 710. *1998*: South Africa.

Fresh House Flava 2. House Afrika Records, CDGUMBA (WA) 711. *1999*: South Africa.

Fresh House Flava 3. House Afrika Records, CDGUMBA (WA) 716. *2000*: South Africa.

Fresh House Flava 4. House Afrika Records, CDGUMBA (WR) 721. *2001*: South Africa.

Fresh House Flava 5. House Africa Records, CDGUMBA (WR) 739. *2002*: South Africa.

Fresh House Flava 6. House Afrika Records, CDGUMBA (WR) 746. *2003*: South Africa.

Fresh House Flava 7. House Afrika Records, CDHAF 1121. *2013*: South Africa.

Mafikizolo. *Loot*. MAW Records, MAW-064. *2002*: USA.

Oskido's Church Grooves: The First Commandment. House Afrika Records, CDGUMBA (WR) 726. *2001*: South Africa.

Oskido's Church Grooves: The Second Commandment. House Afrika Records, CDGUMBA (WR) 735. *2002*: South Africa.

Oskido's Church Grooves: The Third Commandment. House Afrika Records, CDGUMBA (WA) 742. *2003*: South Africa.

Oskido's Church Grooves: The Fourth Commandment. House Afrika Records, CDGUMBA (WA) 746. *2004*: South Africa.

Oskido's Church Grooves: The Fifth Commandment. House Afrika Records, CDRBL 351 (134). *2006*: South Africa.

Oskido's Church Grooves: The Sixth Commandment. House Afrika Records, CDRBL 400 (134). *2007*: South Africa.

Oskido's Church Grooves: The Seventh Commandment. House Afrika Records, CDRBL 456. *2008*: South Africa.

Oskido's Church Grooves: The Eighth and Ninth Commandments. Universal Music (South Africa), CDSRBL 513. *2009*: South Africa.

Oskido's Church Grooves: The Tenth Commandment. Universal Music (South Africa) CDSRBL 576. *2010*: South Africa.

Revolution. *Meropa*. Universal Music (South Africa), CDRBL 605 (133). *2011*: South Africa.

Revolution. *Roots*. Universal Music (South Africa), CDRBL 346 (134). *2005*: South Africa.

Revolution. *The Journey*. Universal Music (South Africa), TELCD 2077. *2002*: South Africa.

Revolution. *The Journey Continues*. Universal Music (South Africa), CDRBL 322. *2008*: South Africa.

Revolution. *Tribal Journey*. Universal Music (South Africa), CDRBL 569 (133). *2010*: South Africa.

Rudeboy Paul. 'Ibofolo.' *Azanian Pulse – a Rudeboy Mix*. Rudeboy Productions, CDRBP 001. *2003*: South Africa.

Discographical References (Botswana)

Basitsile, Sidney 'DJ Sid.' *The Rebirth*. Small House Records. DHRBD 002. *2008*: Botswana.

Molosi, David 'Skizo.' *Afro Blue 2: Native Tongues Vol. II*. Big Dawg Productions. *2002*: South Africa.

Molosi, David 'Skizo.' *The 69er Sixty Niner*. Gallo CDGURB 003. *2000*: South Africa.

Molosi, David 'Skizo.' *The Skizo Project: House Rules*. Kalawa Jazmee CDCC 001. *2005*: South Africa.

Discographical References (Swaziland)

DJ Simza and Sabside. 'Mine Bengidzakiwe.' *2007*: Swaziland. Online at: https://soundcloud.com/16thnote/mine-bengidzakiwe-by-sabside (accessed 21 March 2018).

Dladla, Nomalungelo. *Imiyalo: The House Remixes.* '*2014*: Swaziland. Online at: http://www.traxsource.com/title/329445/imiyalo (accessed 21 March 2018).

Dlamini, Nomzamo. *Lobola: The House Remixes. 2010*: Swaziland. Online at: http://www.traxsource.com/title/71526/lobola-the-house-mixes (accessed 21 March 2018).

Swazi Pride. 'Vive la Vida.' *House Culture, Vol. 2*. Universal Music. *2009*: Swaziland.

Discography (Swaziland)

+268 (featuring Melusi Super). *What's Going on*. Broadcite Productions. *2012*: Swaziland.

+268 (assorted releases). Online at: https://soundcloud.com/268-records.

Bholoja. *Swazi Soul*. Sheer Sound SLCD 191. *2012*: South Africa.

Black Coffee. *Africa Rising*. 2 CDs. Soulistic Music MESH010. *2012*: South Africa.

Mathambo, Spoek. *Mshini Wam*. BBE Records BBE156ACD. 2010: South Africa/UK.

Mi Casa. *Mi Casa Music*. Soul Candi Records. *2011*: South Africa.

Mphila, Gogo, and Mcina, Phayinaphu. *Akuna'nkomo. 2014*: Swaziland. Online at: https://gogomphilaphayinaphumcina.bandcamp.com/releases (accessed 21 March 2018).

Interviews and Personal Communications

Abimbola Kai-Lewis (Botswana):

Basitsile, Sidney 'DJ Sid.' *2013*. Personal communication with the author, 14 August 2013.

Molosi, David 'Skizo.' *2013*. Personal communication with the author, 11 August 2013.

Cara L. Stacey (Swaziland):

Matsenjwa, Mduduzi (DJ Ziyawa). Interview with the author, 18 September 2014.

Reissman, Mandla (DJ Muscles). Interview with the author, 19 September 2014.

Simelane, Senzo (+268). Interview with the author, 15 November 2014.

LINDELWA DALAMBA (SOUTH AFRICA), ADIMBOLA KAI-LEWIS (BOTSWANA), AND CARA L. STACEY (SWAZILAND)

Imbyino

Imbyino ('eem-BYEE-no') is a tradition of music and dance particular to Rwanda (a similar tradition, *intambo*, is performed in Burundi). The term is derived from the verb *kubyina*, which means 'to perform a song accompanied by dance' or, more literally, 'to dance by stamping one's feet on the ground to the rhythm of a song performed by the dancer and/or others' (Nkurikiyinka N.d.). Though its origins are obscure, *imbyino* was intrinsic to the ceremonial life of the royal dynastic court. Since the abolition of the monarchy in 1959 it has remained popular as a source of entertainment, a celebration of cultural heritage, a means of expressing political solidarity, and a competitive practice with dozens of troupes representing schools and local communities vying for prizes and prestige. *Imbyino* is regularly performed during all-night parties (*inkera*), wedding and birth celebrations, funerals, divination rituals, national festivals and parades, political rallies, the openings of new businesses, gorilla-naming ceremonies, and other commemorative events and social gatherings. Most schoolchildren learn basic movements and an established repertoire of *imbyino* songs, and even in informal dance contexts such as disco clubs or Pentecostal worship services, participants draw upon the choreographic idioms of *imbyino* that they learned as children. Rwanda's more commercially successful musicians typically work in genres imported from elsewhere (especially R&B, hip-hop, reggae, gospel and *zouk*), yet they commonly incorporate *imbyino* musical idioms into song productions in a hybridized, neo-traditional fashion. Indeed, a displayed familiarity with the *imbyino* tradition is all but required to sustain long-term commercial success, so prized is it in Rwanda.

Imbyino is actually an umbrella term encompassing numerous sub-types that are distinguished by style of dance, gender of dancers, tempo, musical texture, lyrical themes, social function, and ethnic and regional associations. A few of the many examples of these sub-types include women's dances (*umushagiriro*) that were originally intended to lull the king to sleep, men's 'stomping dances' (*umudiho*), warrior dances (*umuhamirizo*), hoe dances (*imharamba*) and harvest dances (*umuganara*). *Imbyino* performances ordinarily comprise a set of dances alternating among various sub-types.

Imbyino is danced by a group and always includes singing and rhythmic clapping. A variety of melodic instruments and/or a set of five to ten drums (*ingoma*) may also accompany the dance. A performance troupe (*itorero*) usually consists of approximately a half-dozen to a dozen female dancers, a half-dozen to a dozen male dancers, a mixed chorus of similar number and a smaller number of instrumentalists and drummers; however, performers may take on more than one role depending on their skill sets. A few of the major troupes contain over a hundred members, and in large festival contexts *imbyino* may involve still hundreds more as troupes from throughout Rwanda join together in mass performances.

Musical Features

Most *imbyino* songs have a strophic, responsorial structure. A soloist and choir alternate, respectively, between verse and refrain, each of which sometimes overlaps the first and last few notes of the other. Verses and refrains are quite brief, about two to four measures each, and typically begin in an upper range and then descend. The solo verse is often in a higher range than the choral refrain. When a choir consists of both females and males, as is normally the case, melodies are sung in octave unison, with the exception of a repertoire of Twa polyphonic songs. Most melodies are derived from the anhemitonic pentatonic scale roughly corresponding with the pitches, in ascending order, D F G A C (D), with a modal feel dependent on which pitch constitutes the tonal center.

The rhythmic foundation is supplied by handclaps. The meter may be simple, compound or complex, commonly 5/8, 6/8 or 3/4 time. More than merely laying down the timeline, handclaps are intended, in the words of the renowned Rwandan historian Gamaliel Mbonimana, to express 'the inner-most feelings of the soul' (Mbonimana 1971, 41). Choir members clap more loudly or more softly on certain beats in a way that dynamically corresponds with the emotional tenor of the song lyrics. Choir members may also exercise individual discretion, supplying secondary claps between those that comprise the main timeline in order to further enliven the texture.

Melodic instrumental accompaniment, though not necessary, is often featured. Instruments include *inanga*, a long, trough-shaped zither emblematic of

Rwandan traditional music; *iningiri*, a one-stringed, spiked tube fiddle; *ikembe*, a small, handheld lamellophone with iron keys that are plucked by the thumbs; *umuduri*, a musical bow in which sound is produced by tapping the string with a stick; and a set of single-toned, side-blown horns called *ihembe* that are played with a hocketing technique. A few percussion instruments may also supply rhythmic accompaniment. These include different kinds of rattles as well as bells (*inzogera*) that are worn on dancers' ankles. Finally, many dances are accompanied by a set of five to ten narrow drums, collectively called *ingoma*, that supply a complex polyrhythmic texture anchored to the main timeline. The drums are stood on end and lined up horizontally. A lead drummer establishes the tempo, signals which pattern to play and cues changes. The other drummers are then assigned one to each drum, beating them with two long, wooden mallets that are flatly tapered at the far end. Since the mid-1980s popular music instruments such as guitars, synthesizers and drum machines may also supply accompaniment.

Lyrical Content

Rwandan music is traditionally interwoven with the functions of daily social life. Common themes of *imbyino* songs thus include agricultural practices and events, cattle herding and breeding, military conquests, hunting, beekeeping, artisan trades such as pottery making and basket-weaving, and the ritual activities of the Lyangombe and Nyabingi cults that dominated Rwandan spiritual life before the advent of colonial missionization. Songs related to marriage and familial duties are especially prominent. These tend to be didactic in character, employing humorous parables to instruct audiences in the ways of virtue. Some songs praise the natural beauty of Rwanda's landscape. Others extol the glorious deeds of heroes long gone, though these may be used allegorically to honor recent or current political leaders. Female beauty is another common theme.

Choreology

Most dances are uniformly performed, though allowing for some individual embellishment. Occasionally, especially during male warrior dances, single dancers come forward for a few moments to improvise in a flashier manner against a backdrop of standard movements. The movements are vaguely impressionistic of the lyrical content of the songs they accompany. For example, songs praising cattle are very common, and a typical accompanying dance consists of arms outstretched above the head at a diagonal angle, palms faced outward, and fingers extended and pressed tightly together. This position is intended to convey the image of longhorn ankole cattle, which were, before colonization, the primary form of currency and a symbol of wealth and power.

Dancers must always maintain an enthusiastic smile, with eyes wide, chin up and neck elongated. Dances intended exclusively for male performance tend to be fast and quite aggressive, featuring stomping and leaping motions in which dancers land in a kneeling position with arms stretched out toward the sides. Such movements visually embody traditional Rwandan ideals of masculinity: physical strength, bravery and self-discipline. Dances intended exclusively for women performers, in contrast, tend to be slower and more elegant, featuring flowing, gliding movements meant to embody traditional Rwandan ideals of femininity: grace, purity, kindness and beauty. Some women's dances also task dancers with balancing intricately woven reed baskets on their heads that traditionally held luxury items such as tobacco, milk and honey. Keeping in mind *imbyino*'s historical association with the royal dynastic court, such dances exalted the wealth and power of the king in order to legitimize his authority before the community. Because political power was the province of Tutsi elites, they were traditionally danced by young Tutsi women, often members of the king's own harem. After the monarchy was abolished in 1959 and especially after *imbyino* was revived in the mid-1970s, dancers came to represent any of the region's three autochthonous ethnic groups: Tutsi, Hutu or Twa.

The costuming is integral to the choreography. Female dancers wear long but lightweight, vibrantly colorful dresses called *umushanana*. Draping down from one shoulder and around the opposite hip is a broad, pleated panel of loose cloth. At certain moments, dancers may lightly hold the cloth panel, raise it in front of them and sway it side to side and toward and away from them as they gently stamp the ground, slowly sashay and rotate their bodies in time with the music. Male dancers wear long skirts wrapped around the waist (*ikinimba*) and sashes. For warrior dances, they assume the role of *intore* ('chosen ones'), donning pale yellow, waist-length grass headdresses, which they wildly whip about in thrilling fashion, and bearing spears and narrow, marquise-shaped shields which they use to strike fighting poses.

Sociopolitical Significance

Following independence in 1962, and especially during the Second Republic (1973–94) led by President Juvénal Habyarimana, the government made an active effort to promote *imbyino* as a means of developing nationalist unity and pride. Government radio played an important role in spreading *imbyino* songs. Meanwhile, the government organized numerous troupes, among which arguably the most was the national troupe, *Urukerereza*, which embarked on international tours throughout Africa, Europe and North America. *Imbyino* continues to be employed by politicians and their respective parties to garner public support for new policy initiatives and electoral candidacies.

Bibliography

Mbonimana, Gamaliel. *La musique rwandaise traditionnelle* [Traditional Rwandan Music]. Butare, Rwanda: N.P., 1971.

Nkurikiyinka, Jean Baptiste. N.d. 'Music and Dance in Rwanda.' Online at: http://music.africamuseum.be/instruments/english/rwanda/rwanda.html (accessed 31 December 2017)

Discography

Anthology of World Music: Africa – Music from Rwanda. Rounder Select. *1999*: USA.

Kayirebwa, Cecile. *Rwanda/ Globe Style*. *2004*: UK.

Kayirebwa. *Amahoro*. Ceka i Rwanda. *2015*: Rwanda.

Kayirebwa. *Intamwe*. Ceka i Rwanda. *2015*: Rwanda.

Kayirebwa. *Interuro*. Ceka i Rwanda. *2015*: Rwanda.

Muyango, Jean-Marie. *Inzozi narose*. Self-published. *2003*. Online at: muyango.free.fr.

Samputu, Jean Paul. *Testimony from Rwanda*. Multicultural Media. *2004*: USA.

JASON MCCOY AND THARCISSE BIRAGUMA

Isicathamiya

Isicathamiya is a popular *a cappella* music style performed by black male choirs in South Africa. The genre's beginnings are traced to the nineteenth century. The name is derived from *cathama*, an isiZulu term for 'walk[ing] softly like a cat on tiptoe in a stalking manner,' and it describes the synchronized stepping movements, known as *istep*, that *isicathamiya* choirs execute as they sing. Lyrics are predominantly sung in isiZulu dialect of the Nguni (Bantu).

Isicathamiya choirs are organized by learners in schools, the unemployed, prison inmates, members of the community and cultural activists of the organized worker movements. Among hostel-dwelling labor migrants in the industrialized centers of South Africa, *isicathamiya* exerts a significant influence on choral musical performances of diverse ethnic communities from further afield in sub-Saharan Africa. In 1986 the style garnered a global audience when Joseph Shabalala's Ladysmith Black Mambazo and other South African *mbaqanga* style musicians, including Ray Phiri, Barney Rachabane and Bakithi Khumalo, collaborated with Paul Simon to record the Grammy Award-winning *Graceland* album.

Isicathamiya choirs typically consist of anything upwards of ten members, a growth in size associated with the popularization of *mbube*, a precursor style of *isicathamiya* which emerged in the late 1930s. Paralleling the massive wave of African urbanization and an unprecedented increase in the migrant labor population around the time of World War II, a growing fascination with the style is equally attributable to notoriously exploitative practices of commercial recording, and to ideologically controlled programming on the part of a fledgling South African broadcasting institution. The earliest recorded style of *isicathamiya* singing became known as *mbube* following the phenomenal success of the song 'Mbube' by Solomon Linda and His Original Evening Birds, released by the Gallo recording company in 1939. As the popularity of the *mbube* style grew around the time of World War II, not only did the size and numbers of *isicathamiya* choirs increase but so also did the level of competition among them. Other terms, such as *mbombing* (lit. 'bombing'), *isikhwela Joe* ('climb Joe') and *isikambula* (lit. 'gambling') came into use to describe discrete stylistic approaches while also articulating pervasive socioeconomic conditions and other influential processes in the style's social practice. For example, both *mbombing* and *isikhwela Joe* originally referred to orchestrational vocal elements, with the former describing both the bass texture of the male voices and the explosive sounds of World War II bombings, in contrast to the latter's high, piercing treble voices or concerted vocal 'attacks.' The term *isikambula*, however, refers to the socioeconomic context of a style of performing *isicathamiya* associated with some urban-based choirs, particularly around Johannesburg, that sing at several different venues in one night as a strategy to win more prizes. Similarly, the tradition of staging performances at night earned *isicathamiya* practices and their music the label of *ingomabusuku* ('night music').

Competitive Concert Performances

Isicathamiya concerts are characteristically organized as contests and competing choirs are noted for their discipline and orderliness. In preparation for their turns on the performance stage, choirs often stand in a circular formation with their heads bowed together, as members discuss their competitive strategy and resolve vexing issues amicably without ever raising their voices. The impeccable image is further emphasized in the choirs' strict dress code of neatly pressed matching jackets and pants, often worn with ties or bowties, caps or hats and linen gloves during concerts. References to *isicathamiya* choirs as *ojazibantshi* (from *jasbaaitjie*, Afrikaans for 'tailcoat') or *oswenka* ('swankers') are the result of their immaculately groomed appearance in performance.

All-night *isicathamiya* performance contests are a long-standing tradition of weekend social entertainment of African hostel-dwelling migrant workers in the densely populated areas of Johannesburg, Durban and other major towns and farming areas of rural KwaZulu-Natal and Mpumalanga province. In the urban context, such contests have provided a sociocultural and economic framework for *isicathamiya* practice and have functioned to neutralize the culturally traumatic ramifications of South Africa's historically coercive modernity. The sustenance of performance gatherings through peer and regional homeboy networks reiterates the ideological continuities of *isicathamiya* with traditional performance and also emphasizes its cultural relevance for a rapidly adapting African society.

Competitive performances draw enthusiastic followers and many choirs to contests in which, until the 1980s, the winners were decided upon by a single adjudicator. Ideally chosen from among non-Africans, the incumbent adjudicator was approached randomly to select the best choir of the night. Such persons needed no prior training or familiarity with *isicathamiya* and were deemed suitably qualified and impartial solely on the basis of their non-acquaintance with the style's community of practice. In the late 1980s a newly established South African Traditional Music Association (SATMA) introduced – among other recommendations for *isicathamiya* choir contests – a system of three or more adjudicators. Although rarely observed in the contemporary era, during the early decades of the twentieth century, *isicathamiya* performances were characterized by 'bidding' – a form of fund-raising adapted from aspects of auctioneering. 'Bidding' involved individual members of the audience paying a small sum of money to the concert's master of ceremonies to request a performance item by their favorite choir. In practice, bidding was a robust procedure whose entertainment goal was the unceremonious stoppage of a group in mid-performance in preference for another. Starting from as little as one penny, an audience member could 'buy off' a choir from stage and request their replacement by a different choir. A bidding contest ensued when someone else, by paying a slightly higher amount, reversed the request or proposed that an entirely new act go onstage, in a process that could only end when the highest bidder's request prevailed. In the late 1930s and 1940s weekend concerts in Durban's ICU Hall were known for their thriving bidding activities as part of performances by popular *isicathamiya* choirs and vaudeville troupes from far-flung Natal towns such as Port Shepstone, Ladysmith, Estcourt, Empangeni, Harrismith, Newcastle and Dundee, as well as Johannesburg.

In rural practice *isicathamiya* performance gatherings or *timitins* ('tea-meetings') were primarily for the entertainment of audiences and, particularly, women spectators. A choir that consistently drew the most enthusiastic applause from an audience or received a majority of requests to return to the stage was considered a winner. A choir could win a bottle of lemonade, a rooster or occasionally a goat as a prize, with choirs themselves contributing toward prize money by paying a 'joining fee' – anything from two shillings and six pence to fifty pence. Audiences traditionally paid admission at the door if the venue was a public one, such as a church, school or community hall. Such *isicathamiya* concert gatherings were normally promoted through public announcements and by word of mouth. In the urban areas, printed circulars were usually posted in public spaces such as bus stops, train stations, beer-halls and outside concert venues.

Singing and Synchronized Movement

Primarily as a result of colonial musical influences of the Christian Church and missionary school as well as immigrant European popular culture, *isicathamiya* songs are harmonically based on the major tonalities of the European tonic-subdominant-dominant system. The most commonly found song form is characteristically a vocal call-and-response pattern between leader and a chorus of up to ten voices or more for the largest of choirs. Along with other hybrid black South African popular music styles such as *marabi* and its jazz-influenced *mbaqanga* and *kwela* derivatives, *isicathamiya* shares with the historically influential Protestant Church hymns the *makwaya* school choral music and folk musical styles of European settler culture of the early nineteenth century, with a harmonic basis on the roots I, IV, I6/4 and V of the Western diatonic scale. In practice, the distribution of parts in a ten-voice male choir includes the leader's *fes phathi* (first part) voice that is pitched approximately between alto and tenor in range; one *alitha* (alto) voice; two *thena* (tenor); and the rest of the voices singing *bhesi* (bass). Relative to the size of a choir, *isicathamiya* orchestrations invariably conform to this tradition, which lends the style its characteristic low sonic range and an overall booming, masculine vocal texture.

In performance, a choir approaches the stage in single file, singing and stepping uniformly in a stylized walking movement commonly referred to as *imashi* ('the march') or *ukureka* ('ragging,' 'ragtime'). Such characteristic dancing movements are modeled on the 'grand march' of wedding songs that were popularized by mission-based choirs in the early 1900s. The ragtime influence on *isicathamiya* is commonly attributed to Reuben Caluza's Ohlange Choir which toured large parts of Natal and the mining areas of the Reef in the early 1920s, and whose repertoires included those of traveling US minstrel shows of the late nineteenth century.

On reaching the stage, the choir turns and faces the audience, with the leader – sometimes referred to as *ilida* ('leader') or *ukhondakhti* ('conductor') – positioned a step ahead in the middle (or at the end) of the front line of singers. Normally sung in the Nguni dialect of isiZulu, songs are typically organized into two sections that may be distinguished by difference in tempo, beginning with a slower, *rubato* introduction that is followed by a rhythmic section. The rhythmic section is characterized by a prominent vocal improvisation by the leader, repetition of a rhythmic phrase by the chorus and finally, the execution of accompanying expressive body movements. A vocal call-and-response pattern between leader and chorus introduces the first section and normally involves minimal hand and arm gestures, but is often sung without accompanying body movement. Lyrics in this section are usually dramatized with mimetic hand gestures that are enhanced by the choirs' white costume gloves. In the next section the chorus establishes a cyclic rhythmic phrasing that singers accompany with synchronized *istep* ('stepping') patterns and expressive hand gestures.

Dance in *isicathamiya* involves compact, synchronized toe-stepping patterns punctuated by occasional turns and gentle, mid-body high kicks – similar to traditional Zulu *indlamu* dancing except for the soft landing of shoe-clad feet, which contrasts the thunderous, dust-raising thuds of bare feet in indigenous warrior dances. Characteristic dance patterns in *isicathamiya* are an amalgam of both indigenous cultural performance traditions and those that have changed or are changing as a result of Christian missionary influence and modern cultural socialization.

The blending together of several musical and dance influences in *isicathamiya* is symbolic of the cultural syncretism of *ubugxagxa*, an ambivalent social category and ideological position associated with the style's milieu of practice. Part of historical class stratifications of Africans' adaptation to colonial presence and modernity, the term came into use to refer to Africans who were neither fully Christianized nor traditional in their cultural orientation.

Izingoma zomshado (wedding songs) were popular in Christian mission culture of the Natal countryside at the turn of the twentieth century. Considered an ultimate expression of modernity, the performance of wedding songs was already regarded as both socially and ideologically independent of indigenous *ingoma* and *ukusina* (dancing) traditions of isiZulu-speaking Nguni. As noted earlier, in addition to being significantly shaped by *isishameni* or *umqongqo* dance elements of *ingoma* performance traditions, *isicathamiya* dances also blended with the urban 'ragtime' influences of *ukureka*. In some rural areas 'ragging' movements were known as *umgandayana* or *istishi* (stitches) and characterized by shuffling double-steps, and clicking sounds of steel-capped tap-dancing shoes. As an innovation to indigenous *ingoma* dance forms in the early 1930s, *isishameni*- or *umqongqo*-style dance was fashioned by Jubele 'Lumbu' Dubazane, a farm employee and timber worker in Johannesburg who originally came from the Natal midlands district of Mhlumayo near Ladysmith. Born among migratory laboring subjects of white-owned farms, Dubazane and his clansmen strove to assert distinction from Zulu organizational power institutions and traditions. Among cultural processes through which rural *gxagxa* subjects such as Jubele Dubazane defined their ideological positions with regard to modernity and hardcore Zulu traditionalism was a pioneering absorption and domestication of musical influences of white colonial, Christian mission church and school as well as modern and industrial performance culture. It is such hybridized dance forms as *umqongqo* and *isishameni* that have been adopted and blended with equally syncretic tonal characteristics in the development of a typical *isicathamiya* style performance.

Developmental History of *Isicathamiya*

Isicathamiya's evolution under diverse social, political, economic and other cultural influences spans three eras: a formative period that begins in the 1890s; a mid-nineteenth-century consolidation up to the 1970s; and a phase of diversification and experimentation that is characteristic of the style since the 1990s.

The style's beginnings can be traced to the 1890s, when South Africans began to perform their adaptations of the repertoires of visiting US blackface minstrel troupes. From the 1850s South Africans had been exposed to white mediations of American blackface minstrelsy performed by visiting troupes. Between the years 1890 and 1898 black and white audiences countrywide were introduced to US blackface minstrelsy in two extended South African tours of the Orpheus M. McAdoo's Minstrel, Vaudeville and Concert Company. McAdoo was a graduate of the Hampton Institute in Virginia and his performing troupe, which included young African-American men and women performers, is credited with the popularization of minstrel music and 'jubilee' songs (spirituals) among South Africans.

By the beginning of the twentieth century music hall repertoires, dances, costumes and instruments of minstrelsy such as bone clappers and tambourines had become absorbed into the musical practices of black South Africans. Oral historical references of the term 'coon' and its indigenized form *isikhunzi* ('like the coons') connote *isicathamiya*'s ties with diverse and often contestable trajectories of cultural influence (in South Africa, the term 'coon' was not always considered as racist or derogatory as in the USA; see Erlmann 1991, 62). The incorporation of *isikhunzi* traditions links *isicathamiya* to the Coon Carnival, a revitalized contemporary street-music New Year celebration by Cape Town's multiethnic communities. Historically, both traditions were influenced by US blackface minstrelsy, the performance of which reached the Cape around the middle of the nineteenth century. The Cape 'coon' character is evolved from a repertoire of impersonations that were part of American and British minstrel shows that regularly visited Cape Town in the mid-nineteenth century. In the following decades street parades were to become significant as social musical performance of black urbanizing culture of major South African cities and towns. In Durban's Cato Manor shantytown settlement *nikabheni* (lit. 'give a penny') performers wearing ragged headgear, tattered-looking clothes and white-painted faces entertained onlookers by singing, blowing whistles and playing drums around Christmas and New Year's Eve. In Johannesburg during the 1930s *amacoons* ('the coons') paraded the streets in brightly colored, wide-sleeved shirts, playing on military drums while executing high-kicking and stepping dance movements similar to those of *isicathamiya*.

In other narratives *isikhunzi* is considered to have been a popular practice among mission-based African choirs in the Natal province by 1906. King Edward Masinga, the black South African cultural performance historian and pioneer of isiZulu language radio broadcasting, attributed the beginnings of *isikhunzi* to Dr. John Langalibalele Dube, educationist and founding president of the South African National Native Congress. According to Masinga, mission-based choirs adopted the *isikhunzi* style of singing soon after Dube's return from America in the early 1900s, accompanied by a group of African-Americans who had come to assist in the founding of Ohlange, a trade school for Africans that was modeled after the Tuskegee Institute (founded in Alabama in 1881 by Booker T. Washington to offer practical education to former slaves as well as to train teachers). Masinga recounted that 'when those men were feeling homesick they would sing songs of their American homeland. They would sing about the rivers and the mountains, the valleys, the animals and the towns of their birthplace. Some of the songs spoke about a bashful animal called the raccoon, or the "coon" for short' (Buthelezi 1996, 5). It was the song about a raccoon that caught the musical imagination of local singers who then started naming their groups as 'American Coons,' 'Ohlange Coons,' 'Inanda Coons' and 'Ndwedwe Coons.'

Isikhunzi singers were considered middle class, educated and urban, and their songs in four-part harmony required that they change their natural voices and sing in a style that was closely related to that of *makwaya* school choral tradition. In addition to its repertoires, *isikhunzi* also differed from many of the distinctly working-class *isicathamiya* idioms in terms of its low intensity in delivery and its SATB orchestrations of only one voice per part. From the late 1950s onwards the subculture of black, working-class male competitive singing, while not providing significant stylistic changes, saw a remarkable increase in the size of choirs. This development brought about the characteristic male booming vocal textures of mainstream *isicathamiya*, in contrast to other stylistic approaches such as the high piercing treble voices or concerted vocal 'attacks' of *isikhwela Joe* ('climb Joe').

Isicathamiya in Recording and Broadcasting History

The development of a recording industry, initiated through the establishment by Eric Gallo of South Africa's first recording studio in 1932, is inextricably linked to two successive recording events involving Griffiths Motsieloa and Reuben Caluza. The first of these was the 1931 release, under the HMV (His Master's Voice) label, of a selection of songs out of more than 150 recorded by Reuben Caluza's Double Quartet in London in 1930. Eric Gallo's immediate response was to dispatch Griffiths Motsieloa to collaborate with Ignatius Monare – a South African studying medicine in London at the time – on recording musical items for the Gallo Company, as is heard on the track 'Aubuti Nkikho' (Oh Brother Nkikho). Originally hired as 'talent scout' and producer, Griffiths Motsieloa was a prominent cultural commentator with a degree in elocution and he was also an enterprising founder of several leading vaudeville troupes, among them the widely popular Pitch Black Follies. As a result of his leadership of the touring Ohlange Institute Choir, Caluza's performance innovations in stage costumes, vernacular song texts, instrumental accompaniment, synchronized *ukureka* choreography, satire and action songs had significantly influenced early working-class *isicathamiya* choirs and popular vaudeville troupes such as those led by Griffiths Motsieloa and others. Those influences included Caluza's innovative usage of stage costumes and vernacular song texts, the incorporation in live performance of instrumental accompaniment, and synchronized *ukureka* choreography, as well as his program of satire and action songs. The Double Quartet's recordings of 1930 became immensely popular, with HMV selling over 86,000 copies of its African catalogue by 1935, including Reuben Caluza's 'Ingoduso' and 'Ama-Oxford Bags' which sold 3,800 copies, while his recording of the folk song 'Ngisebenzel' u My Love' alone sold 6,656 copies. As a result, several *isicathamiya* precursor choirs such as The Humming Bees Quartet, Wilberforce Institute Singers, St. Peters Hostel Choir, W.P. Zikhali and Radebe's Trio as well as The Wonderful Three recorded cover versions of Caluza's earlier *isikhunzi*-style repertoires including 'Sanibona' and 'Ixhegwana,' 'Umtshado' (The Wedding) and 'Influenza 1918.'

Recordings by similarly influenced choirs issued on the Columbia, Lafayette, Trutone, Singer and Gallotone labels and in Decca's XU catalogs throughout the 1930s and the 1940s invariably had instrumental accompaniment. In combinations of two or three instruments, such accompaniment often included piano, banjo, concertina, guitar, accordion or violin. In some instances, well-known vaudeville and swing-influenced ensembles such as the Jazz Revellers, Rhythm Kings, the Merry Blackbirds, Pitch Black Follies and Synco Fans or their members provided instrumental backing for choirs. Emily Motsieloa, who was Griffiths Motsieloa's wife and pianist for several top South African vaudeville troupes including the Merry Blackbirds, regularly provided piano accompaniment for *isicathamiya* choirs recording under Gallo's Singer and Gallotone labels. During this period many groups, including eminent choirs such as the African Zulu Male Voice Choir, Isaac Mzobe's Crocodile Male Voice Choir (1939–48), the Dundee Wandering Singers (1941–2), Durban Humming Bees (1938), Mkatshwa' Choir (1937) and Solomon Linda's Original Evening Birds (1938–54), recorded under these conditions, which appear to have been prescribed in musical studio production practice rather than as the norm for *isicathamiya* choirs' live performances.

Griffiths Motsieloa is credited with discovering the talents of Solomon Linda – the leader of the Original Evening Birds – while Linda was working as a packer at Gallo studios. Indeed, the instrumentalists listed for the session during which Solomon Linda and His Original Evening Birds' hit song 'Mbube' was recorded were Emily Motsieloa (piano), Peter Rezant (guitar) and Willie Gumede (banjo) – all members of the legendary orchestra. Recorded in 1939, Solomon Linda's 'Mbube' achieved an unprecedented popularity as a result of its regular broadcasts on the state-sponsored 'Re-Diffusion' radio service of the early 1940s. The song remained indelibly etched in the memories of many South Africans as a sonic symbol of the World War II period. Throughout the 1940s and the 1950s, 'Mbube' was not only emulated by other South African choirs locally but also adapted and recorded under the title 'Wimoweh' by a number of folk revivalists and other musicians internationally, including the Weavers, Jimmy Dorsey, Yma Sumac, the Kingston Trio and Chet Atkins. Miriam Makeba also recorded it, under the original title, 'Mbube.' In 1961 a version on RCA entitled 'The Lion Sleeps Tonight,' with new lyrics and performed by the US doo-wop group the Tokens, rose to number 1 in the Billboard Hot 100. Already widely known, the song achieved the status of a global mega-hit when it was used in Disney's musical film *The Lion King* (1994) and the television series of the same name.

Despite his undisputed role in the creation of 'Mbube,' when Solomon Linda died in 1962 leaving a wife and four children, his family was too poor to give him a decent funeral. In 2006 a suit was filed against Disney and a court ruled that Solomon Linda was a co-composer of 'Mbube.' It also determined that 'Mbube' was the basis of the worldwide hit song 'The Lion Sleeps Tonight.' The settlement awarded Linda's family payment for the song's previous uses and instituted a trust to administer the heirs' copyright and receive worldwide royalty payments on their behalf, which eventually garnered a total of more than 15 million US dollars.

Beginning in the early 1950s the demolition by the apartheid government of inner city black settlements and their jazz-influenced performance culture made way for the South African Broadcasting Corporation (SABC) to take control of production and promotion of *isicathamiya*. By the beginning of the 1960s the bulk of *isicathamiya* recording had become a project of Radio Bantu and directed primarily at consumption by its majority Zulu listenership. In 1962 *Cothoza Mfana!*, a weekly national radio program dedicated to the style, was hosted by the SABC's Alexius Buthelezi, then head of Zulu Service in 1961 in Johannesburg, and soon it expanded to include two additional programs broadcast from Durban. Also involved in *isicathamiya* recording production of choirs throughout the 1960s and 1970s, the SABC became very powerful in shaping the ideological uniformity and acquiescence of choirs to the censorship of its apartheid institutional ethos. Such paternalistic production stances discouraged critical debates and lyrics expressing dissatisfaction with the appalling conditions of black dispensation under apartheid. The condescension that was introduced with these developments is illustrated by 'Cothoza Mfana!' ('Tiptoe, Boy!'), a song composed by Gershon Mcanyana and recorded with his Scorpions choir in 1966. The lyrics of the song heaped praise on the SABC and became a signature tune for SABC's Radio Bantu (Zulu) weekly *isicathamiya* program of the same title.

Isicathamiya in the South African Political Landscape

In popular practice across a wide section of the African working-class society up until the late 1940s, *mbube*-style songs with politically motivated lyrics were normally broadcast in the programs of the pre-SABC studios in Durban. Examples of such songs which deplored the creation by government of an indiscriminate community tax include the Dundee Wandering Singers' 'Poll Tax' and 'S'telel Ama Kanda' (We Pay for Our Heads) by Amanzimtoti Male Voice Choir. Compositions such as 'I Colour Ba' (The Colour Bar) by the African Pride Singers for example, and other *isicathamiya* songs explicitly protesting against racial discrimination and the legal enforcement of the 'colour bar' were never released. Solomon Linda's 'Yetul' isigqoko' (Remove Your Hat) was one among many *mbube* songs whose lyrics were condemnatory of the loss of native liberty and dignity as a result of officially sanctioned racial prejudice in public administrative practices of the 1940s.

With increasing ethnicized patronization by the Zulu Radio Bantu programs of the SABC since the 1960s and the growing conservatism of its paternalistic and religious texts, *isicathamiya* became disparaged by politicized African youth for its benignity and acquiescent stance toward apartheid. Growing perceptions of the SABC's function as a government-sponsored propaganda tool further contributed to *isicathamiya*'s unpopularity, particularly since the emergence in the mid-1970s of a popular urban culture of a politically militant black youth. The beginning of the 1980s, however, saw a sociocultural remobilization of the genre toward resisting popular practices as a result of ideological alliances forged between South Africa's unionized labor movement and apartheid-resisting strategies of township youth. The formation of the SATMA in 1988 reflected in part this new role for *isicathamiya*, beyond its domestication by the SABC and towards a vernacular musical idiom of popular anti-apartheid resistance. The major campaigns and rallies of the Congress of South African Trade Unions' (COSATU) from the mid-1980s began to feature SATMA-affiliated *isicathamiya* groups who sang openly about the exploitation of the black working classes by apartheid institutions of capital, or the Xolo Home Boys' 'Buya Afrika' *(Come Back Africa)*. These and other repertoires by similarly politicized *isicathamiya* worker choirs did not find their way into the recording studios of the country's monopoly music production industry, such as Gallo. Their outspokenness, however, achieved political validation and garnered for *isicathamiya* support from the then-exiled ANC political leadership as an engagement by black South African masses in discourses of anti-apartheid resistance and power.

Conclusion

By the late twentieth century and the end of South Africa's apartheid era *isicathamiya* had grown into one of the most widely practiced grassroots musical genres among working-class Africans. The continuing growth in popularity of the genre is recognized in the staging of the National Isicathamiya Festival, an annual event organized by Durban's Playhouse Company since 1997. The one-night marathon *isicathamiya* concert fields no less than 100 groups and features competition winners of elimination rounds held in at least 14 regions from three provinces of the Eastern Cape, KwaZulu-Natal and Gauteng. The festival program includes competition categories of champion of champions, standard and open categories and also includes *oswenka* (well-dressed male) and *onobuhle* (female beauty) pageants. Prize money of approximately 200,000 rand (in 2014) is split between winners, runner-up and consolation awards, while all participating choirs are paid a minimum fee of R500 for their performances.

Bibliography

Buthelezi, Alexius, H. K. 1996. *Cothoza Mfana (Tiptoe, Boy): The History of Isicathamiya Music*. Pietermaritzburg: Reach Out Publishers.

Clegg, Jonathan. 1982. 'Towards an Understanding of African Dance: The Zulu *Isishameni* Style.' In *Papers Presented at the 3rd Symposium on Ethnomusicology*, ed. Andrew Tracey Grahamstown, South Africa: International Library of African Music, 8–14.

Cockerell, Dale. 1987. 'Of Gospel Hymns, Minstrel Shows, and Jubilee Singers: Toward Some Black South African Musics.' *American Music* 5(4): 417–32.

Erlmann, Veit. 1991. *African Stars: Studies in Black South African Performance*. Chicago: University of Chicago Press.

Erlmann, Veit. 1996. *Nightsong: Performance, Power and Practice in South Africa*. Chicago: University of Chicago Press.

Gunner, Liz. 2008. 'City Textualities: Isicathamiya, Reciprocities and Voices from the Streets.' *Social Dynamics: A Journal of African Studies* 34(2): 156–73.

Hamm, Charles. 1991. 'The Constant Companion of Man: Separate Development, Radio Bantu and Music.' *Popular Music* 10(2): 147–73.
Muller, Carol Ann, 2008. *Focus: Music of South Africa*. 2nd edn. New York and Abingdon: Routledge.
Pewa, Elliot S. 1995. 'Zulu Music Competitions: The Continuity of Zulu Traditional Aesthetics.' Unpublished MA thesis, University of Natal, Durban.
Pillay, Rasagee. 1991. 'Isicathamiya: A Sociohistorical Account.' Unpublished BMus honors thesis, University of Natal, Durban.
Thembela, Alex J., and Hadebe, Edmund P. M. 1993. *Impilo Nemisebenzi ka Joseph Shabalala ne Ladysmith Black Mambazo* [The Life and Works of Joseph Shabalala and the Ladysmith Black Mambazo]. Pietermaritzburg: Reach Out Publishers.

Discographical References

African Pride Singers. 'I Colour Ba.' International Library of African Music (ILAM) 3853 and 2413. *1948*: South Africa. Online at: http://146.230.128.113/samap/content/i-colour-ba?quicktabs_1=2.
Amanzimtoti Male Voice Choir. 'S'telela Ama Kanda.' Better, Trutone XU 38. *1941*: South Africa.
Atkins, Chet. 'Wimoweh.' RCA Victor LSC - 3104. *1969*: USA.
Caluza's Double Quartet. 'Ingoduso' and 'Ama-Oxford Bags.' HMV GU 1. *1930*: UK.
Caluza's Double Quartet. 'Isangoma' and 'Kwati Belele.' Columbia AE 2. *1930*: UK.
Caluza's Double Quartet. 'Ixhegwana' and 'Umtakati.' Columbia AE 4. *1930*: UK.
Caluza's Double Quartet. 'Ngisebenzel' u My Love.' HMV GU 8. *1930*: UK.
Caluza's Double Quartet. 'Sanibona' and 'Ixhegwana.' Columbia GR 13. *1930*: UK.
Caluza's Double Quartet. 'Umtshado' (Wedding) and 'Influenza 1918.' Columbia GR 43. *1930*: UK.
Dorsey, Jimmy. 'Wimoweh.' Columbia 39651. *1952*: USA.
Dundee Wandering Singers. 'Poll Tax.' 1750 Unissued. *1941*: South Africa.
Humming Bees Quartette. 'Influenza' and 'Umtshado.' REGAL Columbia Graphophone Co. GR 43. *1930*: UK.
Kingston Trio. 'Wimoweh.' Capitol Records DT 1612. *1961*: UK.
Linda, Solomon, and His Evening Birds. 'Mbube.' Gallo GE 829. *1939*: South Africa.
Linda, Solomon, and His Evening Birds. 'Yetul' isigqoko.' Gallo GE 887. *1939*: South Africa.
Makeba, Miriam. 'Mbube.' London Records HL 9747. *1963*: UK.
Motsieloa, Griffiths, and Monare, Ignatius. 'Aubuti Nkikho' (Brother Nkikho). Singer GE 1. *1930*: UK.
Scorpions. 'Cothoza Mfana.' SABC LT 6765 and Rounder 5025. *1966*: South Africa.
Simon, Paul. *Graceland*. Warner Brothers 1-25447 *1986*: USA.
St. Peter's Hostel Choir. 'Ixegwana (Ricksha Song).' Regal Columbia Graphophone Co. GR 13. *1930*: UK.
Sumac, Yma. 'Wimoweh.' Capitol Records F2079. *1952*: USA.
Tokens, The. 'The Lion Sleeps Tonight.'/'Tina.' RCA 47-7954 *1961*: USA.
Weavers, The, and Jenkins, Gordon. 'Wimoweh'/'Old Paint.' Decca 9-27928. *1952*: USA.
Xolo Home Boys. 'Buya Afrika' *(Come Back Africa!)*. *Isicathamiya: Zulu Worker Choirs in South Africa*. Heritage HT 313. *1986*: USA.

Discography

Isicathamiya: Zulu Worker Choirs in South Africa. Heritage HT 313. *1986*: USA.
Ladysmith Black Mambazo. *Imbongi*. Motella (Gallo) LPBS 18. *1973*: South Africa.
Ladysmith Black Mambazo. *Phansi Emgodini*. Ezomdabu (Gallo) BL 321. *1981*: South Africa.
Ladysmith Black Mambazo. *Ezulwini Siyakhona*. Ezomdabu (Gallo) BL 548. *1986*: South Africa.
Ladysmith Black Mambazo. *In Harmony*. Gallo CD GMP 40808. *1999*: South Africa.
Wilberforce Institute Singers. 'Sanibona' [Greeting]. Regal Columbia Graphophone Co. GR 13. *1930*: UK.

Filmography

Do It a Cappella, dir. Spike Lee. 1990. USA. 75 mins. Television documentary.
The Lion King, dirs. Roger Allers and Rob Minkhoff. 1994. USA. 88 mins. Musical film.
The Moon Is Walking, dirs. Jerry Kramer, Will Vinton, Jim Blashfield and Colin Chilvers. 1988. USA. 93 mins. Film anthology.

SAZI DLAMINI

Isukuti

Isukuti (var. *isikuti, sikuti, sukuti, sugudi* and *esukuti*) is the name of a set of three drums of the Isukha people, a sub-tribe of the larger Luhya community in Kenya. It is also the name given to the dancing and singing that the drums accompany. With roots in the precolonial era among the Isukha and Idakho sub-ethnic communities of the Abaluhya from Kakamega County in Kenya's Western Province, *isukuti* performance developed as part of indigenous ceremonies (weddings, funerals, etc.) among the Isukha people. In the late twentieth century, drum performance and dance movements became more rapid. When *isukuti* was recognized by UNESCO as Intangible Cultural Heritage in Need of Safeguarding in 2014, it was described as a 'fast-paced, energetic and passionate dance accompanied by drumming and singing.' The citation continued: 'An integral tool for cultural transmission and harmonious coexistence between families and communities, it permeates most occasions and stages in life' (UNESCO 2014). In the twentieth century, too, *isukuti* drums and dancing were influential in the development of the popular genre *omutibo*.

Isukuti Drums

Isukuti performance uses a set of three drums (Mindoti 2005). Together, they symbolize the unity of the family – father, mother and child (Miya 2005). Traditionally, the man is represented by the largest drum (known variously as *musatsa, isatsa and isukuti papa*), the woman by the middle drum (known as *mukhasi, ikhasi, isukuti mama*, meaning 'mother') and the child by the smallest drum, called *isukuti mwana, isutkuti ngapa [isukuti] omutiti or [isukuti] mutiti*. (The latter term literally means 'child' or 'small,' while 'ngapa' denotes the drum's mnemonic sounds: 'ngapa ngapa ngapa.') The performer of the *mutiti* (smallest) drum plays a regulative constant 'melorhythm' (a term developed by Nzewi [1997] to describe the melodic and mnemonic nature of drum music), providing the steady basic pulse of the music. The constant *mutiti* rhythm enables the players of the other two drums to generate their own rhythms while keeping the basic pulse. The middle drum plays the role of motivator to the principal drum. For instance, when the largest drum is quiet or soft, the middle drum supplements the principal theme. The middle drum is not always played continuously and is often used during climaxes, when the dancers intensify their movements. Melorhythms of the biggest drum are very important for the dancers as they guide their dance movements and pattern formations. This drum emits the deepest sounds and is played with much more complicated and faster melorhythms than the other two drums (see Examples 1 to 3 below).

The large and medium drums are made in a bottle-like shape while the smallest drum is cylindrical. The different shapes affect the quality of sound produced. If the shape of a drum were altered, the sound would no longer be consistent with *isukuti* because it would lose a special sound effect called '*amang'uleng'ule*' in reference to the pitch, blend and percussive dialogue among the three drums (Butichi 2005 in Mindoti 2005). The following are the rhythmic patterns of the three drums (reprinted with permission from Miya 2005):

Example 1: Rhythmic pattern for *isukuti mutiti*, *isukuti ngapa* or *isukuti mwana*

Each of the drums has its own tone color and contributes different rhythmic materials to the performances. Within the framework of rhythms notated above, each player employs a personal idiom acceptable by the 'owners' of *isukuti* performance (i.e., the community) (Mindoti 2005). Instrumentalists learn to identify *indigenous* rhythmic patterns upon which they improvise their own. The resulting product is *isukuti* 'harmony,' with its own unique rules. If one of the drums is missing, the 'owners' of the music will notice. They are also able to pinpoint an errant drumbeat that is out of synch or off rhythm. This is the concept of 'harmonic' thinking in *isukuti* performance context.

From his observation, Mindoti (2005) notes that contemporary *isukuti* players, especially schoolchildren, may not follow the rules of traditional *isukuti* 'harmonies' if they have learned by watching and listening. According to Ikutwa (in Mindoti 2005), a master performer of *isukuti* from Itumba village in Lugari region of Kakamega County, *isukuti* players

Example 2: Rhythmic patterns for *isukuti mama*

should have *omusambwa* (special spirits) to stimulate their ability to play the *isukuti*. These spirits are passed down from father to son and cannot be learned by other people from outside a particular *isukuti*-playing clan or lineage. Usually, a male child learns from his father with the guidance of *omusambwa* (special spirit). Novice players rehearse thoroughly in order to meet the standards expected by the community. Mnemonic sounds are used in the teaching of melorhythmic patterns, which aid in the process of *identifying*, remembering and reproducing rhythmic patterns. Those who reach expected standards are highly regarded in the society and may be given free traditional beer and accorded high social status.

Ikutwa argues that this is why there are only a handful of traditional *isukuti* players in Lugari region (2005 in Mindoti 2005). However, Mindoti points out that there may be many more factors perpetuating the scarcity of artists, and that several people have learned to play the *isukuti* drum set and advanced to levels of proficiency.

Some research affirms that the drums are made of logs of wood chopped from the *mukumari* (*Cordia abyssinica*) tree (Senoga-Zake 2000; Mulindi 1984 in Miya 2005), while Shem Tupe (in Wekesa Kusienya 2012) asserts, in contrast, that the wood comes from the *murembe* tree (*Erythrina abyssinica*). The drum makers dig a hollow space in the log and shape it as

Example 3: Rhythmic patterns for *isukuti papa*

desired, and then they make the outside smooth. One end is wider than the other. The wider end is usually covered with the hide of a monitor lizard. *Isukuti* makers are renowned craftsmen and they are usually responsible for blessing the drums before they are played.

According to Tupe (ibid.), initially, *isukuti* music employed only one drum; but through creativity and innovation, another larger drum was made using the same materials. The combination of the two *isukuti* drums caused excitement among the performers, who were accustomed to hearing only one drum. This inspired the idea of adding a third drum, made from the same materials.

The instruments are held by the side under the armpit, allowing both hands to play. The sound is produced by the fingertips and/or open palms. The fingers of the left hand may be pressed on the drum skin to tighten it as the right hand hits it to produce different tone colors and pitches. Change in tone color is also achieved by drifting the playing from the center to the edge of the membrane. An accomplished player is capable of producing different tone colors and rhythms from a single drum (Mindoti ibid.).

Mindoti's research also confirms the importance of accompanying instruments in *isukuti* performance. These include *olwika* (cow horn), played by blowing into the air column of the horn through a small hole toward its thin end while creating melodic variations by opening and closing the wide end of the horn. *Fikhuli* (rattles), which are tied on one leg, are sounded by stamping the foot on the ground in rhythm with the main beat of the music. The *ekengele* (metal ring) is hit with a metal gong or a six-inch nail. Sometimes the *ekengele* remains silent for most of the performance, only to come in at climactic sections especially toward the end. Due to socioeconomic changes, substitute instruments have been adopted, such as plastic pipes with a funnel at the end to replace the *olwika* and metallic rings for the *fikhuli* (rattles).

Isukuti Dance and Song

Traditional *isukuti* performance was initially slow, graceful and dignified (Mindoti 2005), a reminder of the fact that the genre is performed during the *shimambo* and *shiremba* ceremonies (Senoga-Zake 2000 in Miya 2005). *Shimambo* is a type of funeral ceremony conducted when a middle-aged man or woman dies. In such ceremonies the *isukuti* instrumentalists and dancers perform music to console the bereaved family and the community of mourners. *Shiremba* is performed in remembrance of someone who died, or in commemoration of prominent members of the Isukha society. However, toward the end of the twentieth century competition at the Kenya Music Festivals between schools performing their own choreographed versions of *isukuti* led to a rapid tempo with variations in dance patterns and formations. The increased tempo and innovations became more prevalent than the previously dominant slow and elegant *isukuti* beat.

In the twenty-first century, a performance of *isukuti* dancing, though less common than before, is characterized by dancers in two separate rows, women and men, who dance with the rhythm of the drumbeats in an energetic but controlled style using arm and elbows as well as legs (see UNESCO film on YouTube). The dance is often led by a singer, who sings texts related to common experience, keeping to the rhythm of the drums, to which the audience responds.

The Social Role of Isukuti

Miya (2005) argues that *isukuti* performing arts play an important part in relaying social behavior expected by the community at large. They provide a forum for socialization where the community gathers, not only to sing and dance, but also to take part in rituals and other practices such as sporting events. The community, in turn, is educated regarding the social norms required for their cultural survival. Cultural values such as honesty, faithfulness in marriage, peaceful co-existence and the value of hard work are presented, not only through the text of the songs, but also through behavior in the context of the performance and the use of relevant gestures, thereby reinforcing individual and group discipline.

Isukuti performance also educates and reminds the community about their cultural beliefs and practices. For example, Miya observes that the use of the three drums illustrates the unity expected in the family and the roles that each family member assumes. These instruments are played during funerals and commemoration ceremonies to signify the importance of funeral rites and the relationship between the family members and their ancestors. She argues that this unity is just as important culturally as the unity of the living family. Gender roles are also displayed by ideas about instruments, in particular, symbolizing social male dominance in accordance with drums found in many other African societies (Agawu 1995 in Miya 2005).

According to Miya, participating in performing arts groups means that one must have and develop musical imagination and creativity skills – qualities that are mandatory in indigenous music practice. Instrumentalists must learn great skills of coordination among themselves and between themselves and the dancers. Likewise, dancers must listen intently to the music and learn when to perform specific dances and coordinate their movements. Consequently, they all learn to work together as a team, and that team spirit is also vital in the responsorial form of singing. The singers are attentive to the soloist's section so that they can respond to the soloist's call, and especially to changes in text or melody. In dance and drama, they must use their eyes and ears to produce the correct styles. In singing and drama, they use their mouth, eyes and ears as well as their dance creativity. In overall terms, they learn group musical performance skills. Besides playing the instruments, musicians are expected to make their own instruments and take care of them, ensuring that the instruments produce the required sounds. Through this engagement they become well acquainted with their cultural sounds and the skills needed in making the instruments.

Since the performance is 'owned' by the community, the master musicians serve the interests of the community and the community controls where and when to perform the *isukuti* dance. Mindoti (2005), however, adds that during the Kenya Music Festival, these drums are made and played by anyone, regardless of sex, age or lineage. Initially, it was a taboo for women to handle the *isukuti*, let alone play it. However, from the early 1990s girls play the *isukuti* drums in the Kenya Music Festival.

Isukuti and *Omutibo*

As noted above, the *isukuti* drum patterns and dancing styles influenced the development of the popular genre *omutibo*. The mnemonic sound pattern – *tibo, tibo, tibo tibo*, and so on – produced by the small drum (*isukuti mwana*) led to the name *omutibo* – in reference to the last two syllables of the name of the genre, *omutibo*. For further information on the relationship between *isukuti* and *omutibo* see the entry on Omutibo.

Bibliography

Abrokowaa, Clemente K. 1999. 'Indigenous Music in Education in Africa.' In *What Is Indigenous Knowledge? Voices from the Academy*, eds. Ladislaus M. Semali and Joe L. Kincheloe. New York: Falmer Press, 191–208.

Agawu, Kofi. 1995. *African Rhythm: A Northern Ewe Perspective*. Cambridge: Cambridge University Press.

Mindoti, Kaskon W. 2005. 'Trends in Isukuti Performance.' In *Refocusing Indigenous Music in Music Education*. Proceedings of The East African Symposium on Music Education. Nairobi: Kenyatta University, 40–3.

Miya, Florence N. 2005. 'Educational Content in Kenyan Performing Arts: A Case of Isukuti Performing Art.' In *Refocusing Indigenous Music in Music Education*. Proceedings of The East African Symposium on Music Education. Nairobi: Kenyatta University, 80–91.

Mulindi, Luzili R. 1984. 'Music of the Logooli: A Study of Logooli Music with Particular Reference to Children's Songs.' Unpublished MA thesis, Queens University of Belfast.

Nzewi, Meki. E. 1997. *African Music: Theoretical Theoretic Content and Creative Continuum*. Oldhausen: Institut Für Populärer Musik.

Nzewi, Meki E. 2003. 'Instrumental Music Ensemble as a General Musicianship Training Strategy.' In *Emerging Solutions for Musical Arts Education in Africa*, ed. Anri Herbst. Cape Town: African Minds, 203–10.

Senoga-Zake, George W. 2000. *Folk Music of Kenya for Teachers and Students of the Music-loving Public*. Nairobi: Uzima Press.

Thorpe, Shirley A. (1992). *African Traditional Religions: An Introduction*. Pretoria. University of South Africa Press.

Tracey, Andrew, and Uzoigwe, Joshua 2003. 'Ensemble.' In *Musical Arts in Africa: Theory, Practice and Education*, eds. Anri Herbst, Meki Nzewi and Victor Kofi Agawu. Pretoria: UNISA.

Unesco 2014. 'Isukuti Dance of Isukha and Idakho Communities of Western Kenya.' Online at https://ich.unesco.org/en/USL/isukuti-dance-of-isukha-and-idakho-communities-of-western-kenya-00981 (accessed 18 April 2018)

Wekesa Kusienya, Fred. 2012. 'The Evolution of Omutibo Guitar Music of the Abaluhya of Kakamega District of Kenya, from 1960 to 2008.' Unpublished MA thesis. Maseno University, Kisumu.

Informants in Mindoti (2005), Miya (2005) and Wekesa Kusienya 2012

Kofi Agawu 1995 in Miya 2005.
Butichi Gideon 2005 in Mindoti 2005.
Ikutwa Shitambasi in Mindoti 2005.
Ruth Luzili Mulindi 1984 in Miya 2005.
George Senoga-Zake 2000 in Miya 2005.
Shem Tupe 2011 in Wekesa Kusienya 2012.

YouTube

Unesco. 'Isukuti Dance of Isukha and Idakho Communities of Western Kenya.' https://www.youtube.com/watch?v=Zw3WSI8j8Bs (accessed 18 April 2018).

MELLITUS NYONGESA WANYAMA

Jazz Band (Malawi)

The term 'jazz' or 'jazz band' has been used to describe bands in Africa from the 1950s, since the days of Congolese bandleader Joseph Kabasele's African Jazz and South African jazz bands. In Malawi, 'jazz band' is highly syncopated, polyrhythmic music played on homemade instruments by rural and peri-urban males. In Malawi, the term 'jazz' designates the degree of syncopation and improvisation in a piece of music in that rural 'homemade instruments' genre (in contrast to the North American meaning of the term 'jazz'). Musicians also use the term to indicate that 'jazz band' music is dance music (in Chichewa colloquially *kujaza* means 'to dance').

History

Between the attainment of self-government in 1963 and the end of the 1960s, the syncretic form of music called jazz band emerged within rural and peri-urban localities. Malawi jazz, in its various subgenres, incorporates South African *kwela*, *sinjonjo* and *smanjemanje* (Kubik 1987), Zimbabwe *jit*, Zambian *kalindula*, East African *benga* (called *kanindo* in Malawi) and Congolese *rumba* into the major component, which is characterized by highly syncopated local Malawi rhythms derived from traditional dances including *chopa, nyau, beni, chiwoda* and others. A number of subgenres of jazz bands and associated artists may be identified, including rap jazz (Namakwa Brothers Band), folk jazz gospel (Chikowa Jazz), pop jazz (Kasambwe Brothers, Kamwendo Brothers, Mitoche Brothers, Tinyade Sounds), jazz blues (Namoko and Chimvu Jazz, Ndingo Brothers) and jazz jazz (Linengwe River Jazz, Kalambe Jazz, Mulanje Mountain Jazz, Sangalukani Jazz, Mikoko Jazz, Chikowa, Ndingo).

Jazz band music was inspired by a number of factors, including the artistic creativity of the young and the marginalization of nonpolitical youth music from radio, while the high cost of Western instruments led to a resurgence in the manufacture of homemade instruments, encouraging many to take up music. Although not recognized at the time, the emergence of jazz band music was part of the post-independence indigenization of popular music, both in localities and on Malawi radio. The Malawi Broadcasting Corporation (MBC) increasingly played jazz band music, often in lieu of Western pop. The relevance, resonance and, often, subtly rebellious nature of the lyrics, and the rising cost of foreign music recordings, contributed to the popularity of jazz bands (Lwanda 2009).

The evolution of jazz music reflects changing attitudes in gender relations as well as the musical and social growth of the musicians and their society. The jazz band tradition was pioneered mostly by unemployed teenagers (Kubik 1987), school leavers with no prospects of further secondary or tertiary education. Many of these young males who played jazz band music had recent experiences of female environments and influences as teenagers. Until the age of male initiation, or around ten years, boys are allowed around mothers and aunts in the fenced compounds (*kumpanda*) (Lwanda 2003). In rural Malawi, as women pound maize at the mortar (both the pounding act and its environment are called *pamtondo*), they often sing blues, 'gossips,' laments, work songs and songs of joy associated with females and their concerns, all of which are easily traceable in early and later jazz band songs. Lyrics of the early jazz band songs often showed clear influences from local genres associated with women; a significant amount of early jazz band music was, to varying degrees, appropriated from women, especially their pounding songs (Lwanda 2003). Good examples in which elements normally associated only with exclusive women's environments were transferred to the jazz band context include 'Makolo' (Parents) in which the young Mitoche Brothers Band retell a common folk tale; Kamwendo Brothers Band's 'Mwatonyanya nsanje' (You Are Excessively Jealous), which is about a female upbraiding her husband; Sangalukani Jazz Band's 'Aphiri tidzalekana,' about Mr. Phiri, a husband who does not provide for his wife; and Kalambe Jazz Band's 'Nasimelo,' pure female *pamtondo* gossip reserved for social contexts involving only women and uninitiated boys, about a work-shy female who spends all day 'painting her nails.' These songs are all sung in female persona.

Jazz band musicians often employ several sets of lyrics for each melody: one for political or personal praise, one for social critique and the original. 'ANezilia' (about a stubborn unmarried person) by Kalambe Jazz changed to 'Angwazi Banda' (Dr. Banda) on political occasions. 'Mitala' (Polygamy) by Mikoko, with its chorus of 'Palibe ndiona ine' (I earn nothing) highlighted rural poverty (Lwanda 2009), and its melody was also used for political songs.

Musical Characteristics

Malawi jazz is improvised and designed for live performance; lyrics can be changed to suit the occasion. Jazz musicians mostly use homemade musical instruments that include drum kits, banjos, guitars, *babatoni* (one-string bass), various percussion instruments, shakers and flutes.

The music is highly syncopated and mixes chord structures, rhythmic and tempo breaks and drum and bass patterns. The vocal arrangements call for the ensemble to sing in unison, or else to sing parallel harmonies in call-and-response form. The lead singer performs the melody while the rest sing chorus or counter-melody. Various vocal 'tricks' include throat baritone singing, falsetto and yodeling. Some jazz bands feature several lead singers who may sing in unison or in parallel harmonies. Interestingly, many jazz bands, including Linengwe, Ndingo and Chikowa use the *babatoni* bass as the lead instrument, while guitars are usually strummed (Kalambe Jazz). Lead guitars play short bursts that run counter to the main melody while the rhythm guitar plays a steady but often varied pattern. The *bangwe* (zither) is one of Malawi's traditional instruments and its strummed nature has influenced guitar styles in Malawi. However, when a banjo is present, it is usually plucked as lead, particularly by bands such as Mulanje Mountain and Sangalukani Jazz in which sharp lead banjo notes are characteristically the lead feature. Underpinning all of the music is the polyrhythmic drumming. This can be a basic steady pulse with counter-beats and syncopation or a complicated melange with percussion, beat changes and additive drumming.

Dancing is often a part of the performance by the singers or *animateurs*. Where there are *animateurs* they usually base their choreographies on traditional dances or, after 1994, modern styles including *kwasa kwasa* and *ndombolo*. The dancers encourage the crowd to dance and to *fupa* (throw in some money). During the HIV/AIDS awareness campaigns, jazz band music was used to sensitize the rural population about HIV/AIDS issues, with dancers acting out various preventative scenarios.

Conclusion

Jazz band music was a reaction to the social, political and economic circumstances of the 1960s and 1970s. Malawi was a one-party state with constrained modes of expression; educational opportunities were limited; and, given its agro-based economy, job opportunities for school leavers and dropouts were limited also. It is interesting for a number of aspects: its appropriation of female music, its syncretic nature, the relative chauvinism of the lyrics of the early jazz band period, and the fact that it was an important method by which nonpolitical rural males entertained and articulated the grievances of their class. Out of the jazz band tradition have arisen many socially and politically engaged musicians, including Joe Gwaladi and Lawrence Mbenjere who, paradoxically, use keyboards to create a 'bastardized' modern electro-pop jazz that does away with 'real musicians.'

Bibliography

Kubik, Gerhard. 1987. *Malawian Music: A Framework for Analysis*. Zomba: Centre for Social Research.

Lwanda, John. 2003. 'Mother's Songs: Male Appropriation of Women's Music in Malawi and

Southern Africa.' *Journal of African Cultural Studies* 16(2): 119–42.

Lwanda, John. 2009. 'Poverty, Prophets and Politics: Marxist Discourses in Malawi Music, 1994–2008.' Online at: http://www.iaspm.net/proceedings/index.php/iaspm2009/iaspm2009/paper/viewFile/782/77 (accessed 27 May 2017).

Discographical References

Kalambe Band. 'Anezilia.' MBC Records. *Circa 1986*: Malawi. (Reissue: Kalambe Band. 'Anezilia.' *The Last Pound.* Pamtondo PAM007 CD. *1999*: UK.)

Kalambe Jazz Band. 'Nasimelo.' MBC Recording. *Circa 1988*: Malawi.

Kamwendo Brothers Band. 'Mwatonyanya nsanje.' MBC Records. *Circa 1984*: Malawi.

Kamwendo Brothers Band. 'Mwatonyanya nsanje.' Pamtondo CD PAM 027. *1998*: UK.

Mikoko Jazz Band. 'Mitala.' MBC Records. *Circa 1979*: Malawi. (Reissue: Mikoko Jazz Band. 'Mitala.' *The Sizzling Seventies.* Pamtondo PAM 070. *2006*: UK.)

Mitoche Brothers Band. 'Makolo.' MBC Records. *Circa 1978*: Malawi.

Pamtondo's Greatest Hits. Pamtondo PAM 009. *1999*: UK.

Sangalukani Jazz Band. 'Aphiri tidzalekana.' MBC Records. *Circa 1979*: Malawi. (Reissue: Sangalukani Jazz Band. 'Aphiri tidzalekana.' *The Sizzling Seventies*, Pamtondo PAM 070. 2006: UK.)

Discography

Gwaladi, Joe. *Zakanika.* Tempest CD. *2006*: Malawi.

Mbenjere, Lawrence. *Biliwita.* Mbenjere. *2006*: Malawi.

Namoko, Alan, and Chimvu Jazz Band. *Ana osiidwa.* Pamtondo PAM 004. *1992*: UK.

JOHN LWANDA

Jeliya

Jeliya is the art of *jelis*, who are hereditary musicians, singers and oral historians from western Africa (Mali, Guinea, Senegambia and neighboring countries). Called *griots* by early French travelers to the region, *jelis* have developed one of the most sophisticated musical systems in Africa (Charry 2000). They sing and narrate oral history accompanied by three musical instruments, which they have traditionally had the exclusive right to play: *kora* (21-stringed bridge harp); *bala* or *balafon* (xylophone); and *ngoni* (four- or five-stringed lute). *Jeliya* bears hallmarks of a classical tradition, such as a centuries-old venerable heritage, noble, royal and state patronage, professional status and vocal and instrumental virtuosity. By the mid-twentieth century some *jelis* had transferred their repertory to the acoustic guitar, integrating the guitar into their tradition and making it a bona fide *jeli* instrument. In the 1960s *jelis* took up the electric guitar, which was a bridge into the electric guitar- and brass-based dance bands (called orchestras in West African terminology) that became the primary vehicles of the popular music of their newly formed nations. This embrace and usage of both the acoustic and electric guitar are key to understanding how *jelis* have redefined Western concepts of traditional and modern (the term they typically use for 'popular') and how the term 'popular' only partially captures their artistic practice. On the heels of the world music boom in the 1980s *jelis* have also found new international markets by playing their traditional instruments and subsequently have forged unusual collaborations, gaining significant record label and touring support.

Jeliya draws its power in large part from its role in maintaining Mande oral traditions via virtuosic praise singing (and hence its ability to make or break reputations), the protection of the profession by endogamy and its patronage by the noble class associated with the Mande (or ancient Mali) empire. Because *jelis* are believed to inherit the unique ability to harness the power of the highly specialized oral and musical traditions that are foundational for Mande culture and social cohesion, they have been granted an exclusive hold over them. Non-*jelis* would not encroach on this terrain for several reasons: they would be betraying their own birthright; they would not have the necessary spiritual protection; and they would not have adequate access to gaining expertise.

The original Mande homeland, located along the Niger River where modern-day Guinea and Mali meet, became the center of an expanding empire after an epic battle won by the legendary hero Sunjata Keita in the thirteenth century. At its height in the fourteenth to sixteenth centuries it was one of the largest and richest empires ever in all of Africa because of its control of local gold mines and trade routes to the north across the Sahara and south to the coast. A tripartite, mutually dependent social system developed, consisting of nobles, artisans (including blacksmiths, leatherworkers and *jelis*) and slaves. Sunjata is believed to have had his own personal *jeli*, named Bala Faseke Kouyate, whose duty it was to preserve Mande social and political history. The Kouyate family name or lineage has ever since held the highest prestige in Mande society, along with the Diabate lineage, which also stems from Sunjata's time, as guardians of Mande oral and musical traditions.

The ethnolinguistic groups who claim origins in the Mande homeland are Maninka (Malinké in French colonial writing), who live in Guinea and Mali, and Mandinka (Mandingo in British colonial writing), who migrated westward to the Senegambia region (in the Senegambian Mandinka dialect the terms are pronounced *jaliya* and *jali*). Because some neighboring ethnic groups have the social equivalent of *jelis*, the more general and less ethnically specific term *griot* can be helpful. In Senegal, the Wolof equivalent is called *gewel*; the Fulbe manifestation is *gawlo*. The mother of the esteemed Senegalese vocalist Youssou N'Dour was a *gawlo*, although his father was not a *griot*. As *griots* have the exclusive right to take up praise singing and play certain musical instruments, members of the noble class violate a social taboo if they attempt the same. Such was the case with the famous noble Malian vocalist Salif Keita, who shamed his father by entering the music profession (Keita 2011).

The repertory of *jeliya* reflects the diverse musical streams within the vast expanse of territory populated by Mande peoples. The three instruments of the *jeli*, for example, represent different regions and historical eras. The *bala*, predominant in the savanna regions such as southern Mali and Guinea, dates back to the Sunjata era and some of its repertory comes from this time. The *ngoni* is predominant in the sahel regions of Senegal and Mali and also has deep historical roots. The *kora* has more recent roots in the nineteenth century in the Senegambia region. Each of these instruments contributes pieces to the collective repertory of *jeliya*, and pieces originating on one instrument can be played on the others. Modern songs, typically love songs and others addressing topical issues, have recent origins, meaning within the past several generations. In performance, *jelis* will typically perform a mixture of old and new pieces.

The tonal system of the three *jeli* instruments is heptatonic, but they each are tuned differently. The *ngoni* and *kora*, both string instruments, primarily use a scale that is similar to the European major scale (sometimes with a raised fourth degree), along with a few other scales. The *bala* is tuned in seven equidistant steps to the octave. One intriguing aspect of *jeliya* is that instruments with different tuning systems can play with each other without causing alarm as it might in a European context.

The three instruments share the same musical forms, which consist of repeating cycles that are typically 12, 16 or, more rarely, 9 beats long. A musical composition in its most minimal form usually takes up a single cycle, and instrumentalists are expected to weave endless variations in the course of a performance. In *bala* music one can distinguish two, three or four harmonic areas within each cycle (similar to a chord pattern), and the harmonies are laid out polyphonically, with each hand often playing rhythmically independent patterns. *Ngoni* music is more monophonic, with the thumb and index finger of the plucking hand combining to create highly ornamented melodies and variations. The *kora* is plucked by both thumbs and both index fingers, enabling very dense textures created from the interlocking of four independent parts.

Vocal styles are very direct and full-throated, which can make for an intense listening experience. The texts are based on a tradition of praise singing, noting the deeds of various leaders and members of their lineages. The local significance of such texts can easily escape the appreciation of a non-African audience, not only because they are sung in local tongues, but also because praise singing, which can draw on esoteric proverbs, does not translate well. Because *jelis* traditionally receive their patronage from the ruling class, they typically shy away from public social criticism, and so their lyrics praising generous politicians or business people can grate against Western sensibilities honed on countercultural traditions of rock music. Therefore, *jeliya* has had difficulty crossing over into Western pop markets, except in the form of instrumental music for listening or dance music.

Although there are some male *jeli* vocal stars, such as Malian Kasse Mady Diabate (1989) and Guinean Sekouba 'Bambino' Diabate, female *jelis* enjoy the most widespread local appreciation (*Divas of Mali* 1996). In the 1980s the three best-known female *jeli* singers were from Mali: Kandia Kouyate (1999), Ami

Koita (1993) and Tata Bambo Kouyate (see Durán 1995, 1999). They were well represented on the local West African cassette market, but have enjoyed only limited interest from international record labels for CD releases. Slightly younger, Oumou Dioubate (1993) from Guinea gained a significant following in the 1990s.

Guitar and Orchestras

With such a deeply rooted music culture, it is extraordinary that *jelis* embraced the guitar and welcomed it into their tradition. But, similar to processes that occurred throughout Africa, *jelis* took up the acoustic guitar and transferred not only their music onto it, but also the playing styles of the *kora*, *ngoni* and *bala*. In the documentary *Bamako Beat* (1991), *jeli* Modibo Kouyate provides a clear demonstration of how *ngoni* and *kora* styles are played on the guitar in Mali. Immediately following that demonstration is an extended performance in which he plays the acoustic guitar accompanying his wife, Tata Bambo Kouyate, further demonstrating that the guitar has become an accepted *jeli* instrument. The acoustic guitar is even used to accompany narration of the Sunjata epic by expert oral historians, one of the most serious traditional musical practices in Mande culture.

Following political independence in Guinea in 1958, President Sékou Touré initiated government patronage of a national orchestra and then a system of regional orchestras (Counsel 2009). Mali soon followed suit. *Jeli* guitarists (and vocalists) predominate in these dance orchestras, where they are the primary soloists and are largely responsible for the signature sounds associated with their respective countries (Radio Africa 2011). The three best-known and influential electric guitarists, who first emerged in the 1970s, all come from *jeli* families: Sekou 'Bembeya' Diabate of Guinea's Bembeya Jazz (2004); Manfila Kante of Mali's Les Ambassadeurs (featuring vocalist Salif Keita) (2010); and Djeli Mady Tounkara of Mali's Rail Band (2007–9).

Guitar playing styles in Mali and Guinea are shaped by the relative importance of the *ngoni* and *bala*, respectively. For example, Malian Djelimady Tounkara's guitar playing (with Bouba Sacko, 1993) bears great similarities to how the *ngoni* is played, with its linear melodic flourishes, quick hammer-ons, pull-offs, trills and elaborate ornamentation (Eyre 2000). The playing of Sekou 'Bembeya' Diabate (1996) and Manfila Kante (1994), both from Guinea, is strongly marked by extended *bala*-like polyphonic passages. Each of these guitarists has a rich recorded history of electric guitar solos in the context of these orchestras in the 1970s, and they have also recorded more intimate small ensemble guitar albums in the 1990s.

The world music market has encouraged interest in acoustic guitar albums led by *jelis*. Coming out of an intimate guitar tradition recorded in Guinea for the national Syliphone label in the 1970s (African Virtuoses 2007) these groups fall between the cracks, playing neither dance music nor traditional *jeliya*. The Guinean lineage has given rise to unusual guitar trios and quartets (Djessou Mory Kante 1997, Papa Diabaté 1999). In Mali, the genre is called *bajourou* (Tounkara and Sacko 1993).

Guinean *jeli kora* player and vocalist Mory Kante, who also plays the electric guitar (and is nicknamed 'the electric griot'), has had great success electrifying his *kora* and fronting an orchestra – initially the Rail Band (2007–9) in the 1970s, and later his own groups in France. He had a hit song in Europe ('Yeke Yeke') aimed at discotheques in the late 1980s (Mory Kante 1987).

World Music

Ensembles used in *jeliya* can combine any of the three *jeli* instruments as well as the guitar. Traditionally, instruments are often played in like pairs (e.g., two *koras*, *ngonis* or *balas*), although varied ensembles, including the electric guitar, are the norm nowadays. Some groups may add non-*jeli* percussion instruments such as the *jembe* drum. Usually, one or more vocalists are present. Since the 1980s an electronic drum machine has been used to accompany both live and recorded performances of female *jelis*.

Guinean *kora* player and singer Djeli Moussa Diawara's (1983) album *Fote Mogoban* recorded in Abidjan in 1982 with an ensemble of *kora*, *bala*, two acoustic guitars and female chorus did much to spur worldwide interest in acoustic music by *jelis*. Hannibal Records, which reissued the album as *Yasimika* in 1990, provided strong support for the growing genre, especially when it issued a series of albums by Toumani Diabate (1987; with Ketama, 1988; with

Ballake Sissoko, 1998). British journalist, scholar, radio presenter and record producer Lucy Durán (2011) has been crucial in introducing *jeli* music to a broader public outside Africa, working with Toumani Diabate, Kasse Mady Diabate, Bassekou Kouyate and Ballake Sissoko among many others.

Increased access to foreign music as well as the opening-up of new world music markets have spawned imaginative new collaborations with *jeli* instrumentalists. *Kora* player Toumani Diabate is at the forefront of such efforts. As perhaps Africa's best-known instrumentalist, Diabate is in demand and has participated in an extraordinary number of collaborations showing the versatility of the *kora* as well as his unique musical talents. He has collaborated on recordings with the Spanish flamenco group Ketama (1988), US bluesman Taj Mahal (1999), Gorillaz cofounder Damon Albarn (2002), Malian non-*jeli* guitarist/vocalist Ali Farka Touré (2005 and 2010, with both albums receiving Grammy awards in the World Music, Traditional category), US banjo virtuoso Bela Fleck (2005), Cuban vocalist Eliades Ochoa (2010, a belated Buena Vista Social Club project), and US pianist Herbie Hancock (2010). He has also recorded and toured solo with his own Symmetric Orchestra (2006); in performance at its home base in Bamako his orchestra is a rare example of an electrified big band from the region that does not use brass instruments, but rather just strings and percussion.

Malian *jeli ngoni* player Basekou Kouyate and his group Ngoni Ba (2010), an unusual ensemble of *ngonis* of different sizes, has toured European and North American festival circuits and has an album distributed by Seattle-based Sub Pop Records that was nominated for a World Music Grammy in 2011. Malian *kora* player Ballake Sissoko (2008) has recorded a novel string trio album with an *ud* player from Morocco and *valiha* player from Madagascar. While these artists have not migrated abroad, some have, such as Guinean *kora* and *bala* player N'faly Kouyate, who moved to Belgium, formed his own group and then eventually joined Afro Celt Sound System (1999).

In Diaspora

Because of its higher standard of life, Abidjan, Côte d'Ivoire became an important center in the late 1970s and 1980s for *jelis* for recording and performing. A significant number of female singers, both *jelis* (e.g., Ami Koita) and non-*jelis* (e.g., Oumou Sangare) recorded cassettes in Abidjan, which became pop hits back in Mali and occasionally were released as CDs in the international market. For some artists, Abidjan was a stopping-off point before migrating to France, which was at first hospitable to world music from its former colonies. A major community of Malians grew around Paris and *jelis* frequently traveled there to cater to them. *Jelis* took advantage of new opportunities in Paris, having access to high-tech recording studios and willing collaborating musicians (Winders 2006). New York became a destination beginning in the 1990s, but there was initially less integration. Collaborations developed and *jelis* play in both traditional contexts within their own communities and in clubs aimed at a broader public (Badenya 2002; Skinner 2008; Racanelli 2010). One especially novel and well-received collaboration comes from Africando (1996), a New York–based *salsa* band directed by Malian arranger Boncana Maiga (not a *griot*) with guest African vocalists, including *jeli* Sekouba 'Bambino' Diabate singing the modern Guinean classic 'Apollo.'

Conclusion

So pervasive is the influence of *jeliya* on the pop music scene in western Africa that non-*jelis* are often defined by their relation to, or distance from the tradition. For example, Malian vocalist Salif Keita, one of Africa's most successful world music stars, absorbed *jeli* singing styles even though he was not born into the tradition. As he moved from a national to a world stage he redefined himself away from *jeliya* toward an identity more in line with his noble birth (Keita 2011). Mali's most internationally visible female vocalist Oumou Sangare is appreciated not only for her own artistry, but also because the genre she represents, called *wassoulou*, has little relation to *jeliya* and therefore can tackle critical social issues from which *jelis* might shy away (Durán 1999). On the other hand, Rokia Traore (2000), who is not a *griot*, but who belongs to a younger generation that may be less constricted by traditional boundaries, borrows freely from *jeliya* with guest *kora* and *ngoni* players.

Jeliya has an intimate relationship to the popular music of the countries that are its homeland (Durán 2006; Lobeck 2066; Stars of Mali 2003; Eyre 2000). In some respects, in the hands and mouths of its great guitarists and vocalists it is the national pop music. Listeners appreciate its deep roots and continued relevance to certain aspects of their lives. In other respects, it can lack a social immediacy and modern sensibility. Artists with *jeli* roots, from Mory Kante to Habib Koite (1998), can draw from *jeliya*, but also from other local and international musics and sensibilities, to form a hybrid that is directed toward a broader public. And finally, as strong symbols of local culture, *jeli* instruments can be enlisted in the process of making a global current such as hip-hop more locally meaningful (Charry 2012), as has been done by the Malian rap group Les Escrocs (Africa Raps 2001, 'Pirates') or Senegalese rap star Didier Awadi (2002, 'Neye Leer').

Bibliography

Charry, Eric. 2000. *Mande Music: Traditional and Modern Music of the Maninka and Mandinka of Western Africa*. Chicago: University of Chicago Press.

Charry, Eric, ed. 2012. *Hip Hop Africa: New African Music in a Globalizing World*. Bloomington: Indiana University Press.

Counsel, Graeme. 2009. *Mande Popular Music and Cultural Policies in West Africa: Griots and Government Policy since Independence*. Saabrucken: VDM Verlag.

Durán, Lucy. 1995. 'Jelimusow: The Superwomen of Malian Music.' In *Power, Marginality and African Oral Literature*, eds. Graham Furniss and Liz Gunner. Cambridge: Cambridge University Press, 197–207.

Durán, Lucy. 1999. *Stars and Songbirds: Mande Female Singers in Urban Music, Mali 1980–99*. Unpublished Ph.D. dissertation, University of London.

Durán, Lucy. 2006. 'Mali.' In *The Rough Guide to World Music: Africa and the Middle East* (Vol. 1), eds. Simon Broughton, Mark Ellingham and Jon Lusk with Duncan Clark. 3rd ed. London: Rough Guides, 219–38.

Durán, Lucy. 2011. 'Music Production as a Tool of Research, and Impact.' *Ethnomusicology Forum* 20(2): 245–53.

Eyre, Banning. 2000. *In Griot Time: An American Guitarist in Mali*. Philadelphia: Temple University Press.

Keita, Cheick M. Chérif. 2011. *Outcast to Ambassador: The Musical Odyssey of Salif Keita*. St. Paul, MN: Mogoya.

Lobeck, Katharina. 2006. 'Guinea.' In *The Rough Guide to World Music: Africa and the Middle East* (vol. 1), eds. Simon Broughton, Mark Ellingham and Jon Lusk with Duncan Clark. 3rd ed. London: Rough Guides, 136–52.

Racanelli, David. 2010. *Diasporic Jeliya in New York: A Study of Mande Griot Repertoire and Performance Practice*. Unpublished Ph.D. dissertation, City University of New York.

Sinnock, Martin. 2011. 'Sekouba "Bambino" Diabate and Guinée Conakry.' Online at: http://www.africasounds.com/sekouba_bambino.htm.

Skinner, Ryan. 2008. 'Celebratory Spaces Between Homeland and Host: Politics, Culture, and Performance in New York's Malian Community.' In *Migrations and Creative Expressions in Africa and the African Diaspora*, eds. Toyin Falola, Niyi Afolabi and Adérónké Adésolá Adésànyà. Durham, NC: Carolina Academic Press, 279–98.

Winders, James A. 2006. *Paris Africain: Rhythms of the African Diaspora*. New York: Palgrave Macmillan.

Discographical References

Africa Raps: Senegal, Mali, and The Gambia. Trikont US-294. *2001*: Germany.

African Virtuoses. The Classic Guinean Guitar Group. Reissue of material from the 1970s. Stern's Africa STCD3024. *2007*: USA.

Africando. *Gombo Salsa*. Stern's Africa STCD 1071. *1996*: USA.

Afro Celt Sound System. *Release, vol. 2*. Real World 7243 8 47324 2 4. *1999*: UK.

Albarn, Damon. *Mali Music*. Astralwerks ASW 41019; EMI 7243-541019-2-2. *2002*: USA.

Awadi, Didier. *Parole d'honneur – Kaddu Gor*. (Cassette.) *2002*: Senegal.

Badenya: Manden Jaliya in New York City. Smithsonian Folkways SFW CD 40494. *2002*: USA.

Bembeya Jazz National. *The Syliphone Years*. Reissue of material from the 1960s to 1970s. Stern's Africa STCD 3021/3022. *2004*: USA.

Diabate, Kasse Mady. *Fode*. Stern's Africa STCD 1025. *1989*: UK.

Diabate, Papa. *Guitar, Extra Dry*. Popular African Music pam adc 304. *1999*: Germany.

Diabate, Sekou 'Bembeya.' *Diamond Fingers*. Dakar Sound DKS 008. *1996*: Netherlands.

Diabate, Toumani. *Kaira*. Hannibal HNCD 1428. *1987*: USA.

Diabate, Toumani, Ochoa, Eliades, and others. *Afrocubism*. World Circuit/Nonesuch 525993-2. *2010*: USA.

Diabate, Toumani, and Ketama. *Songhai*. Hannibal HNCD 1323. *1988*: USA.

Diabate, Toumani, and Sissoko, Ballake. *New Ancient Strings*. Hannibal HNCD 1428. *1998*: USA.

Diabate, Toumani, and Symmetric Orchestra. *Boulevard de l'indépendence*. Nonesuch 79953-2. *2006*: USA.

Diawara, Djeli Moussa (Jali Musa Jawara). *Fote Mogoban*. Tangent, TAN 7002. *1983*: France. (Reissue: Diawara, Djeli Moussa (Jali Musa Jawara). *Yasimika*. Hannibal HNCD 1355. *1990*: UK.)

Dioubate, Oumou. *Lancey*. Stern's Africa STCD 1046. *1993*: USA.

Divas of Mali: Great Vocal Performances from a Fabled Land. Shanachie 64078. *1996*: USA.

Eyre, Banning. *In Griot Time: String Music from Mali*. Stern's Africa STCD 1089. *2000*: USA.

Fleck, Bela. *Tales from the Acoustic Planet: Throw Down Your Heart*, vol. 3. Rounder 11661-0634-2. *2005*: USA.

Hancock, Herbie. *The Imagine Project*. Hancock Records HR 0001. *2010*: USA.

Kante, Djessou Mory. *Guitare sèche*. Popular African Music pam ag 701. *1997*: Germany.

Kante, Manfila. *N'na Niwalé: Kankan Blues Chapter 2*. Popular African Music pam 402. *1994*: Germany.

Kante, Mory. *Akwaba Beach*. Polydor 833 119-2. *1987*: USA.

Koita, Ami. *Songs of Praise*. Sterns Africa. STCD 1039. *1993*: USA.

Koite, Habib, and Bamada. *Ma Ya*. Contrejour CJ003. *1998*: France. (Issued by Putumayo PUTU146-2. *1999*: USA.)

Kouyate, Bassekou, and Ngoni Ba. *I Speak Fula*. Sub Pop/Next Ambience NXA 001. *2010*: USA.

Kouyate, Kandia. *Kita Kan*. Stern's Africa STCD 1088. *1999*: USA.

Les Ambassadeurs Internationaux featuring Salif Keita. *Mandjou, Seydou Bathily; Mana Mani, Tounkan*. Reissue of material from the *1970s* to 1980s. 2 vols. (4 CDs.) Universal 532 529-2; 532 529-5. *2010*: France.

Rail Band. 3 vols. (6 CDs.) Reissue of material from the 1970s. Syllart/Sterns Africa STCD 3033-34; 3039-40; 3043-44. *2007–9*: USA.

Sissoko, Ballake, Driss El Maloumi, and Rajery. *3MA: Madagascar, Mali, Maroc*. Contre-jour cj020. *2008*: Belgium.

Stars of Mali. Mali Lolo! Smithsonian Folkways SFW CD 40508. *2003*: USA.

Taj Mahal, and Diabate, Toumani. *Kulanjan*. Hannibal HNCD 1444. *1999*: USA.

Tounkara, Djelimady (Jalimady), and Sacko, Bouba. *Bajourou: Big String Theory*. Xenophile GLCD 4008. *1993*: USA.

Touré, Ali Farka, and Diabate, Toumani. *In the Heart of the Moon*. Originally issued on World Circuit; Nonesuch 79920-2. *2005*: USA.

Touré, Ali Farka, and Diabate, Toumani. *Ali and Toumani*. Originally issued on World Circuit; Nonesuch 522937-2. *2010*: USA.

Traore, Rokia. *Wanita*. Label Bleu LBC 2574. *2000*: France.

Filmography

Bamako Beat: Music from Mali. dir. Mark Kidel. *1991*. BBC, UK. 55 mins. Documentary.

Website

Radio Africa. http://www.radioafrica.com.au/ (accessed 18 October 2011).

ERIC CHARRY

Jembe Music

The *jembe* (variants: *jenbe, dyembe, djembé*) is a goblet-shaped drum originating from Mande-speaking societies of West Africa such as the Malinké (Maninka) and Ouassoulounké (Wasulunka), in northeastern Guinea and southern Mali. *Jembe*-centered percussion ensemble music animates local dance events in these societies. In the 1960s *jembe* music and dance also entered the programs of state-sponsored folkloric ensembles and became a national symbol in both Guinea and Mali. At the same time, *jembe* music and dance became part of the urban popular culture in these countries as well as, in the following decades, in neighboring Senegal, Ivory Coast and Burkina Faso. Since the 1980s West African *jembe* music and musicians have migrated to Europe, North America and more recently to Japan, Australia, Brazil, South Africa and many other countries. There, in diverse contexts such as music and dance education, social movement protest culture, interactive drum events (for recreative, health care, team building or human resources development purposes), the drum manufacturing industry's sales strategies and Africa-related tourism, globalized *jembe* music emerged as a popular medium of rhythm and community experience, and a symbol of an imagined Africa, at the beginning of the twenty-first century.

Musical Structure and Performance Context

Mounted with goatskin (or, increasingly since the beginning of the twenty-first century, calfskin) and played with both bare hands, the *jembe* creates a wealth of distinct sounds producing precise timbral melodies. The instrument mostly appears in ensembles of one or two *jembes* (accompaniment and lead) and one to three cylindrical drums called *dunun* (variants: *doundoun, djun-djun*). The latter are beaten with a stick and sometimes come with an iron bell, which is typically attached to the drum and struck with a heavy iron nut or nail, but which can also be fixed to the index and middle fingers of the player's weaker hand and beaten with an iron nut or strong ring slipped on the thumb.

Performed in metric four-beat cycles (or multiples of four) of either binary or ternary subdivision, *jembe* and *dunun* phrases are asymmetrically patterned by both their rhythmic figures and their timbral melodies. Phrases relate to the main beat and to the other ensemble parts in complex ways (offbeat phrasing, cross-rhythm); the ensemble parts produce dense and often intricate polyphonic textures. Repetition and variation are core features of musical form. *Jembe* music thus employs structures that are common in West African percussion ensemble music. A high degree of playful embellishment in the *jembe* lead part, the heavy use of diverse swing feel patterns (asymmetric beat subdivision), shifting between binary and ternary (or ternary and quaternary) beat subdivisions, and the marked acceleration of beat tempo in the course of most pieces are musical characteristics specific to *jembe* music. By contrast, features such as ensemble orientation at *ostinato* timeline patterns and an aesthetic of 'the cool' are less important in *jembe* music than in percussion ensemble music from Ghana, for instance.

Jembe music animates social celebrations of agricultural, religious and life cycle events and aims to make people dance. The *jembe* lead part's role, in particular, is to focus and work out individual dancers' movements in sound. Through dancing, the participants – beyond entertaining themselves – display their commitment to the gathering's social occasion and also identify with the performed piece. Each piece is associated with various meanings that its performance can embody. In the city, pieces can connote a particularly broad range of attributes: ethnic identities, regional origins, and social, professional and age groups, among others. Some pieces also relate to the individual's role in the social occasion, for instance, the role of the bride's *denbaw* (honorary mothers), those few elder female relatives of the jubilee who organize and finance the event. The *denbaw* present themselves to the public by wearing a special headband, which usually is monogrammed with the owner's name or initials, and by dancing the *denbafòli* (honorary mother's rhythm). *Denbafòli* is the most frequently and extensively played drumming piece at Bamako celebrations (Polak 2012).

Who Plays the *Jembe*?

Because of the lack of documentation, the *jembe*'s precolonial history is obscure. Perhaps it was confined to exclusive institutional or ritual contexts, such as those controlled by the so-called blacksmiths (*numu*), who form a hereditary professional group within Mande societies and are, if loosely, associated with *jembe* playing (Charry 2000, 51f). At least since the early twentieth century, however, access to *jembe* playing is open to all social status groups. Taking up *jembe* playing is a matter of gender – female players represent rare exceptions even in modern, urban spaces – and, for boys, of personal taste and commitment.

Jembe music does not belong to the *griots* (*jeli*), who – as a socio-professional group more prominent in public than the blacksmiths – have practiced professional singing and laid hereditary claims to the playing of instruments such as the *kora* (quasi-bridge harp), the *bala* (calabash-resonated xylophone) and the *ngoni* (plucked lute) in Mande societies for centuries. Until their profession's commercialization in the twentieth century, the *griots*' musical genres, described as a 'court,' 'art' or 'classical' music of the Mande, were distinct from the field of percussion ensemble music performed at popular dance events.

Representing Ethnicity, Staging the Nation, Urbanizing Tradition

Throughout the twentieth century *jembe* music performance proliferated in contexts of state formation and urbanization. Under French colonial rule, administrative units were obligated to represent themselves in folkloric shows at official celebrations on occasions such as the *Fête nationale*. In the 1950s the colonial administration set up a system of competitive cultural festivals across all of French West Africa. The regions with populations identifying mainly as Malinké often presented themselves by performing *jembe* music and dance. A formerly rural tradition became an ethnic symbol in the colonial urban space.

After independence from France, the African leaders of Guinea and Mali put much emphasis on their nations' needs for building an identity. Toward this end, they continued the colonial system of competitive cultural festivals. Also, successful artists were recruited for newly formed premier troupes (*ballet national*) meant to represent national folklore to the international public. In pioneering Guinean artistic director Fodeba Keita's concept of an authentic African culture, connecting to ideas of precolonial history was crucial. Folkloric *jembe* music and dance, along with the *griots*' musical traditions, featured centrally in that staging of an imagined past. The *jembe* became a national symbol of both Guinea and Mali.

In the institutional context of state-sponsored ballets, *jembe* players learned of formalized rehearsals under an artistic director, and of performance marked by rigid role distinction between audience and performer. They creatively condensed a multitude of musical repertoires of diverse origins into prearranged pieces and suites. Moreover, they refined the musical support of choreography by providing cues and calls (termed *blocage* or 'break' in modern *jembe* players' jargon) and employed virtuosic playing and showmanship.

Until the 1950s *jembe* music was only one among many regionally and ethnically distinctive traditional music genres performed in the cities of the Mande world. Following its selection as a national art form in the 1960s, however, *jembe* music became a core part of the urban popular culture in Guinea and Mali as well as in neighboring Senegal, Ivory Coast and Burkina Faso. In Bamako, for instance, the female population transcended boundaries of ethnic identity and social class by participating in dancing to *jembe* music for days at the frequent wedding celebrations. Prior to that development, most families would hire ensembles according to their specific ethnic or regional backgrounds, which was less participatory since many attendants such as, for instance, the organizers' neighbors and workmates of different backgrounds did not know exactly how to dance to such music. While the repertoire of *jembe* rhythms broadened and diversified to address the needs of a diversified audience, a supra-ethnic core repertoire of standard pieces, such as *maraka-dòn* (also called *denba-fòli*), *dansa* and *suku* [*soli*]), became particularly popular and representative of the local urban culture. Drumming became a profession. The average size of a typical ensemble increased – from duets of one *jembe* and one *dunun* to quintets of two *jembe* and three *dunun*, and beyond – as did the average tempo and the lead *jembe* player's freedom to expressively embellish and depart from the basic dance-centered phrases and themes.

Jembe Dance Music as Urban Popular Culture

Jembe music is often categorized as traditional (see Charry 2000, 24). People in Mali or Guinea, indeed, would rarely think of *jembe* celebrations as modern affairs. Designated as *fòli*, which denotes percussive dance music performed at social celebrations, *jembe* is distinguished from *musique*, which is a word borrowed from French applied mainly to 'modern' pop music. *Jenbefòli*, in contrast to *musique*, is not performed on stage in the concert context (as it is in Western countries), but rather only in the folkloristic context of state-sponsored dance shows meant to represent 'traditional' culture. Radio and TV rarely broadcast *jembe* music, and it is absent from the cassette market, too. In a word, people in West Africa do not listen much to *jembe* music apart from its live performance in the context of social dance events.

Nonetheless, *jembe* dance music is popular music insofar as it belongs to the large and important class of unofficial art forms which are syncretic, concerned with social change and associated with the masses in twentieth-century Africa (see Barber 1987). It forms a vital framework of public interaction and communication, responds to social change, demonstrates frequent musical changes in its structural and stylistic features and is syncretic in that it draws on diverse cultural sources and creatively merges elements of these into a new artistic form. It is prominent in the cities where it appeals to large parts of the population across social, ethnic, religious and other boundaries (Polak 2012). Individualism, self-employment, competition and market relationships entail artisan-like, work-oriented attitudes to performance and stimulate personal and generation-specific stylistic differentiation and innovation. The audience's demand, through the commercialization of the drummers' work, plays an influential role in the production and style of the music (Polak 2005).

Capturing the North Atlantic

Jembe music made first imprints outside West Africa with the enthusiastically received world tours of the Guinean and Malian national ballets in the 1960s. The Ballets Africains de la République de Guinée's first lead *jembe* player, Ladji Camara, soon broke away from the troupe. Settling in New York City in 1962, his teaching established a small *jembe*-playing community among US African-Americans.

In the mid-1980s two other *jembe* soloists of the Guinean national ballets, Famoudou Konaté and Mamady Keita, began teaching in West Germany and Belgium, respectively. It was the rich experience of staging *jembe* music and dance in the ballets which gave them cues for innovative handling of the contexts of concerts and, above all, formal education. In close collaboration with European percussionists, Konaté and Keita standardized the repertoire of drumming pieces and invented methods of formally teaching *jembe* music. For instance, while simple break phrases served as calls in the ballets and marked the ending of individual dance solos in traditional celebration music, in the teaching context, these breaks were reinterpreted as interfaces between cyclic drumming patterns to work around the difficulty of creating musical form through more flexible changes between phrases and variations.

Konaté and Keita were the cultural brokers of *jembe* music in Europe and thus set in motion the genre's globalization. Other key figures of transcontinental *jembe* music came from the urban tradition of dance music for social celebrations, such as, for instance, Adama Dramé and Soungalo Coulibaly from Bouaké, Ivory Coast.

In the North Atlantic context, *jembe* music has proliferated as a popular medium for approaching rhythm and community experience, which often is associated with an imagined Africa of rural traditions. The genre's most important representatives have been accredited the status of keepers of tradition. Yet, popularizing *jembe* music, both in West Africa and beyond, has been preconditioned exactly by the transcending of traditional forms, contexts and meanings: from dialogic drum and dance performance to modern stage show and classroom to postmodern socio-therapeutic environment (such as drum circle and team building); from local community to ethnic, national and, finally, Pan-African symbol.

Globalization

In the late twentieth century *jembe* music in West Africa and the North Atlantic expressed mutual influences and structures of dependence. Central to this relationship were the large communities of professional players in metropolises such as Conakry, Bamako, Abidjan and Dakar. These players fused local musical styles and repertoires from half of West Africa into urban ballet and celebration music, on the one hand, and provided a pool of artistic knowledge and skill to the European and North American-based world percussion music scene, on the other. Conversely, the *jembe*'s immense popularity in the North – unheard of for an African musical instrument and related genre before – fed back much vitality in the form of money, status and career opportunities into the urban traditions of *jembe* playing in West Africa.

However, the globalization of *jembe* music as a popular medium of rhythm experience also involves processes of cultural appropriation that emancipate the instrument from its association with Mande musical traditions. Agents as diverse as team builders, school teachers, social activists, hand percussion aficionados, tourist animators and instrument traders from many parts of the world make the *jembe* drum and *jembe* music their own to an increasing extent.

Bibliography

Barber, Karen. 1987. 'Popular Arts in Africa.' *African Studies Review* 30(3): 1–78.

Billmeier, Uschi, and Keïta, Mamady. 2000. *A Life for the Djembé: Traditional Rhythms of the Malinké*. Engerda: Arun.

Blanc, Serge. 1993. *Le tambour Djembé (The jembe drum)*. Lyon: Editions Maurice Sonjon.

Charry, Eric. 2000. *Mande Music. Traditional and Modern Music of the Maninka and Mandinka of Western Africa*. Chicago and London: University of Chicago Press.

Doumbia, Abdoul, and Wirzbicki, Matthew. 2005. *Anke Djé Anke Bé: Djembe and Dounou Music from Mali, West Africa*. Self-published.

Dramé, Adama, and Senn-Borloz, Arlette. 1992. *Jeliya: Être griot et musicien aujourd'hui* [Jeliya: Being Griot and Musician Today]. Paris: Harmattan.

Flaig, Vera. 2010. *The Politics of Representation and Transmission in the Globalization of Guinea's Djembé*. Unpublished Ph.D. thesis, University of Michigan.

Konaté, Famoudou, and Ott, Thomas. 1997. *Rhythms and Songs from Guinea*. Oldershausen: Institut für Didaktik populärer Musik.

Polak, Rainer. 2000. 'A Musical Instrument Travels Around the World: Jenbe Playing in Bamako, in West Africa, and Beyond.' *The World of Music* 42(3): 7–46.

Polak, Rainer. 2004. *Festmusik als Arbeit, Trommeln als Beruf. Jenbe-Spieler in einer westafrikanischen Großstadt* [Celebration Music as Work, Drumming as Profession. Jembe Players in a West African City]. Berlin: Reimer.

Polak, Rainer. 2005. 'Drumming for Money and Respect: The Commercialization of Traditional Celebration Music in Bamako.' In *Wari Matters: Ethnographic Explorations of Money in the Mande World*, eds. Jan Jansen and Stephen Wooten. Münster: LIT Verlag, 135–61.

Polak, Rainer. 2006. *The Jenbe Realbook*, Vol. 1. Nürnberg: Bibiafrica (Transcription of CD Dunbia et al. 2006-disc.).

Polak, Rainer. 2007. 'Performing Audience: On the Social Constitution of Focused Interaction at Celebrations in Mali.' *Anthropos* 102(1): 3–18.

Polak, Rainer. 2008. *The Jenbe Realbook*, Vol. 2. Nürnberg: Bibiafrica (Transcription of CD Kone et al. 2008-disc.).

Polak, Rainer. 2010. 'Rhythmic Feel as Meter: Non-Isochronous Beat Subdivision in Jembe Music from Mali.' *Music Theory Online* 16(4.4). http://www.mtosmt.org/issues/mto.10.16.4/mto.10.16.4.polak.html (accessed 24 August 2018).

Polak, Rainer. 2012. 'Urban Drumming: Traditional Celebration Music in a West African City (Bamako).' In: *Hip Hop Africa: New African Music in a Globalizing World*, ed. Eric Charry. Bloomington, IN: Indiana University Press, 261–81.

Zanetti, Vincent. 1996. 'De la place du village aux scènes internationales: L'évolution du jembe et de son repertoire' [From the Village Square to International Stages: The Evolution of the Jembe and Its Repertoire]. *Cahier de Musiques Traditionelles* 9: 167–88.

Discography

Africa Djolé. *Live: The Concert in Berlin '78*. Free Music Production 1. *1978*: Germany.

Camara, Ladji. *Africa, New York*. Lyrichord 7345. *1979*: USA.

Coulibaly, Soungalo. *Percussion and Songs from Mali*. Arion 64192. *1992*: France.

Dramé, Adama. *Rhythms of the Manding*. Philips 6586042 (UNESCO Collection *Musical Sources*). *1979*: The Netherlands.

Dunbia, Yamadu, Jakite, Jaraba, and Madi Kuyate, Jeli. *The Art of Jembe Drumming: The Mali Tradition, Vol 1*. Bibiafrica Records. *2006*: Germany.

Guinée. Musique des Malinké. Le chant du monde CNR 2741112. *1999*: France.

Jakite, Jaraba, Dunbia, Yamadu, and Madi Kuyate, Jeli. *Dònkili: Call to Dance. Festival Music From Mali*. Pan CD 2060. *1997*: The Netherlands.

Keïta, Mamady, and Kan, Sewa. *Wassolon*. Fonti Musicali 159. *1989*: Belgium.

Konaté, Famoudou. *Rhythms of the Malinké*. Museum CD 18. *1991*: Germany.

Kone, Drissa, Madi Kuyate, Jeli, and Jakite, Jaraba. *The Art of Jembe Drumming: The Mali Tradition, Vol 2*. Bibiafrica Records. *2008*: Germany.

RAINER POLAK

Jit (Jiti)

Jit, or *jiti*, is a term used to describe varieties of Zimbabwean music since at least the 1950s. The term's meaning has evolved over the years. In general, *jit* refers to topical, lively songs of daily life, accompanied by anything from a shaker or a single hand drum to an acoustic guitar to a full electric pop band. There is no definitive explanation for the exact origin of the term, though it almost certainly came to Zimbabwe (formerly Rhodesia) from South Africa, along with terms including *jive*, *marabi* and *tsaba tsaba*. Similar to the word 'jazz,' *jit* expresses a feeling, an attitude and a sense of style, but it has no literal translation.

Ethnomusicologist Thomas Turino offers a deep analysis of the term's evolution. He writes that *jit* seems to have been 'superimposed on preexisting recreational dance traditions,' (2000, 229) at least by the 1950s if not earlier. People in the culturally rich town of Murehwa told Turino that what is now called 'jit' used to be called 'serenda.' Others identified older names for these informal village songs as 'concert,' 'chinungu,' and 'chemanjemanje.' Still others considered *jit* a faster variant of the South African popular style *tsaba tsaba*. In any case, by the 1950s *jit* had come into common use as a village term for these topical songs, particularly those from the country's north-east. In the following decades, *jit* also became an urban slang term for recreational music with rural connotations.

Even in the early 1970s the term *jit* was not yet used as a genre label by broadcasters and librarians at the Rhodesian Broadcasting Corporation (RBC). If they used the word at all, it was in reference to dance-drumming songs from villages such as Nyandoro, known for its *jit*, typically accompanied by the tall local hand drum known as *ngoma*.

Jit songs have certain common characteristics: a fast beat, generally in 12/8 time, and a reliance on a I-IV-I-V harmonic progression. In the same way that rural popular music becomes modernized in cities everywhere, these songs began to inspire urban musical cousins that were informally described as *jit*. Turino cites an early example in the 1968 song 'Sevena Nhamo Ichanya' by M.D. Rhythm Success. The harmony and rhythm are consistent with the village songs, but now a trap drummer marks four main beats with the bass drum, with an underlying triplet feel, often played on the hi-hat, while electric bass and one or more guitars fill out the familiar I-IV-I-V harmonic progression. This new sound also has ties to popular songs coming out of South Africa, even the Congo, at the time. However, the 12/8 rhythm clearly distinguishes this as a Zimbabwean sound, one that soon became, and remains, commonplace in the country's popular music.

Once guitar bands began identifying their sound as *jit*, *jiti* or *jit-jive*, the expression began to catch on widely. In the context of Zimbabwe's liberation struggle, music that sounded and felt local delivered a subliminal message of resistance to white rule – even though virtually none of this guitar-band *jit* was overtly political. Most *jit* songs deal with domestic situations, the difficulty of marrying, infidelity, jealousy, betrayal within the family. Shona language lyrics can be humorous, even when telling cautionary tales, but rarely do they seriously address political, economic or religious questions. Some artists, including the politically and culturally engaged singer/bandleader Thomas Mapfumo, rejected the *jit* identifier early on as a 'foreign term.' Mapfumo identifies his music as 'chimurenga' or struggle music. This term has more to do with the music's militant attitude than with any specific musical characteristics. Mapfumo's peer Oliver Mtukudzi embraced the term *jit*, but used it to refer to 'a rhythm,' not a genre as such. Mtukudzi later came to star in a 1992 film called *Jit*, directed by Michael Raeburn.

Both as a word and as a vaguely defined genre, *jit* entered into the contentious arena of popular Zimbabwean culture in the 1970s. By the time of Zimbabwe's independence (1980) *jit* was being used as an umbrella term for music as diverse as that of Thomas Mapfumo, Oliver Mtukudzi, James Chimombe, The Four Brothers, and Zexie Manatsa and the Green Arrows, whether the artists liked it or not. Just as the term's usage was becoming so broad as to lose any precise meaning, it received its biggest boost ever when a group of young musicians came together in 1980 as the Bhundu Boys, and began marketing their music internationally as 'jit.' This further confused the issue because the Bhundu Boys played a wide variety of styles, from the old guitar-band *jit* to *rumba* to *mbira* and other traditional adaptations. As this band became globally popular, touring in Europe and the United States, the term *jit* began to be used in the international music press as a general term for any Zimbabwean popular music.

The Bhundu Boys' career crested with the release of their 1987 album *True Jit*. The album's polished production and its inclusion of light English lyrics, such as 'jit jive in the *bhundu* [the bush] tonight,' lacked the appeal of their original music, and so began the band's dramatic decline. The use of the term *jit* as a designation for popular music also began to diminish, even as *rumba* and *sungura*, also problematic terms, remained in common use. However, Turino notes that the rural usage of the term persisted in 2000, affirming that 'Jit remains a common and vital social activity in the villages of Mashonaland East and Central' (2000, 233).

Bibliography

Eyre, Banning. 1993. Interviews with Oliver Mtukudzi and Biggie Tembo of the Bhundu Boys.

Eyre, Banning. 2015. *Lion Songs: Thomas Mapfumo and the Music that Made Zimbabwe*. Durham, NC: Duke University Press.

Turino, Thomas. 2000. *Nationalists, Cosmopolitans, and Popular Music in Zimbabwe*. Chicago: University of Chicago Press.

Discographical References

Bhundu Boys. *True Jit*. WEA 242203-2. *1987*: UK.

M.D. Rhythm Success. 'Sevena Nhamo Ichanya.' Gallo GB 3739. *1968*: South Africa.

Discography

Bhundu Boys. *The Bhundu Boys*. Rugare RUG 1000. *1983*: Zimbabwe.

Bhundu Boys. *The Shed Sessions*. Sadza Records Sadza 1. *2001*: Germany.

Jit: 6 Essential Songs from Jit the Movie, Plus 6 Other Smash Hits. Earthworks 3-1023-2. *1991*: UK.

Jit Jive: Zimbabwean Street Party. Sheer Sound SSPCD 039. *2004*: South Africa.

Filmography

Jit, dir. Michael Raeburn. 1992. Sweden. 92 mins. Feature film. Original music by Oliver Mtukudzi.

BANNING EYRE

Jùjú

Jùjú is a genre of Yorùbá popular music rooted in the cosmopolitan coastal culture of early twentieth-century Lagos, a city then at the center of British colonial rule in Nigeria. Emerging in the 1930s as a hybrid of the pan-West African urban guitar tradition known as 'palmwine' and neo-traditional street drumming forms, *jùjú* bridges the gap between celebratory social dance music and music for contemplative listening (Alaja-Browne 1989a, 61; Roberts 1972, 241–2). Combining hinterland panegyric traditions with Lagosian musical and technical innovation, *jùjú* proved a crucial medium for the formulation of a Yorùbá identity at once modern and traditional (Waterman 1990b). By remapping local sounds and systems of patronage onto a cosmopolitan urban landscape, *jùjú* artists produced a genre that was culturally specific yet appealed to a wide audience. In less academic terms, *jùjú* star King Sunny Ade describes his music simply as 'traditional roots music that uses some Western instruments' (Topouzis 2002, 67).

Roots and Emergence

Musicians in turn-of-the-century Lagos drew on a rich variety of creative resources emanating from the city's unprecedented confluence of culturally and religiously diverse communities. The Yorùbá population was itself diverse, consisting of migrants from the hinterlands who brought with them traditional drumming and poetic forms; Brazilian and Cuban *empancipados* (Àgùdà/Amaro) who brought with them New World instruments, dances and masquerades; and an elite class of repatriates from Sierra Leone (Sàró) who, in addition to their predilection for European music, encouraged the growth of Yorùbá traditional and West African Creole culture. Another key influence was the mobile population of sailors, railway workers and truck drivers who patronized Lagos nightspots, introducing songs and dances from their West Indian and West African homelands, which they often accompanied on portable instruments, including guitars, banjos and concertinas. The Kru mariners from Sierra Leone, in particular, are credited with introducing a guitar style that is foundational to palmwine and early *jùjú* (Collins 1992, 32–5). The nineteenth-century expansion of Islam and Christianity in Nigeria also left its mark on Lagosian music, with the syncretic commingling of European hymnody and Arabic-derived vocal timbers evident in the earliest recorded *jùjú* repertoire.

Born into Lagos's elite Sàró Yorùbá community, guitarist Tunde King is generally recognized as the first to solidify *jùjú* as a distinct genre. King was educated in Lagos's Christian schools and started his musical career playing *aşíkò*, a neo-traditional social dance performed by Christian youth groups at holidays and festivals. Yorùbá philosophical, religious and topical texts were sung in responsorial fashion to the fast-paced accompaniment of a four-cornered frame drum (known interchangeably as *samba* or *aşíkò*) and carpenter's saw. Although its exact origins are unknown, *aşíkò* drumming and dance is thought to bear strong traces of Afro-Brazilian culture. *Aşíkò* is also a product of the nineteenth-century African church movement in which European hymns were reinterpreted with Yorùbá texts and instruments. Frame drums including the *samba* were incorporated into African Christian worship services because, unlike many other Yorùbá instruments, they did not carry direct associations with traditional religion (Waterman 1990a, 39–42).

By fusing the musical resources of Christian hymnody, Yorùbá poetics, *asíkò* drumming and palmwine guitar to create *jùjú*, King forged a sound that would capture the Lagosian bourgeoisie's desire for a modern national identity rooted in Yorùbá tradition. Although he was not the first to play in this style, King was the first to popularize it under the name 'jùjú,' consolidating an elite patronage base and codifying its sound in his 1936 Parlophone recordings. King's first band consisted of guitar, *samba* drum, *maracas* and a supporting vocalist, but – with the support of a notable patron – he soon made changes that would shape the *jùjú* sound for years to come, replacing the *samba* with a Salvation Army tambourine, the guitar with a six-string banjo-guitar, and the *maracas* with *sèkèrè*, a traditional Yorùbá gourd rattle. Subsequent groups emulated this instrumentation (Waterman 1990a, 64; see Thomas 1992, 162–9 for an illustrated chronology of *jùjú* instrumentation).

With tempos slightly slower than the social dance music from which it was derived, *jùjú* music of the 1930s was amenable to both social dancing and philosophical contemplation. Always attuned to the social dynamics of the events he performed, King used traditional Yorùbá poetic formulations to praise patrons, share proverbial wisdom and comment on social issues. One artist who witnessed King's performances described them as sermons in which the preacher used storytelling to deliver moral and philosophical messages. He was also adept at incorporating non-Yorùbá languages, including Kru, Krio and Twi, as well as Islamic vocal qualities, to appeal to different audiences and patrons. His nasal high-tessitura vocal style influenced the sound of many musicians to come. Representative examples of King's early work include 'Alimi Abade/Oba Oyinbo' (1936), 'Association/John Cole' (1936) and 'Doctor Vaughan/Aronke Macaulay' (1936).

King's Parlophone recordings were the first to explicitly list *jùjú* as the genre. The term, in fact, referred to the tambourine as well as to the new musical style in which the instrument was featured. This has led to some speculation about its meaning. One commonly cited etymology traces the term to King's drummer, who would throw his tambourine into the air and catch it, thus inspiring the phonoaesthetic expansion of the word *jù* ('to throw' in Yorùbá) to *jùjú*, pronounced with a low-tone to high-tone pitch glide (Waterman 1990a, 62–3). Another possibility is that Yorùbá musicians employed the term ironically – originally used by Westerners and African elites to disparage traditional religion, it came to evoke the supposed spiritual associations of the Euro-Christian tambourine (Alaja-Browne 1989a, 60).

Modern *Jùjú*

The end of World War II marks the beginning of modern *jùjú*, when a number of socioeconomic and technological shifts enabled the genre's creators to build their elite patronage networks farther out into the global market, while simultaneously reaching deeper into village tradition for inspiration. Postwar growth and stabilization in the agricultural export industries, as well as expanded access to education and civil service work, drove massive waves of rural-urban migration that in turn sparked an explosion of economic opportunities in big cities like Lagos. From this environment emerged an elite class more broadly based than its prewar counterpart. Newly wealthy Yorùbá merchants and businessmen, whose entrepreneurial savvy had led them to the city and who were eager to be counted among the elite, became some of postwar *jùjú*'s most enthusiastic patrons. Anticolonial political sentiment and a concomitant movement toward self-governance bred a new class of politicians and political aspirants who also proved to be eager patrons of *jùjú* music (Waterman 1993b, 62–4).

Increasing urbanization was accompanied by the growth of transportation and communications infrastructure connecting hinterland to city, which led in turn to an intensification of rural-urban cross-pollination in *jùjú* and other popular cultural forms. The introduction of hereditary talking drummers and the expanded use of Yorùbá poetic forms in *jùjú* are examples of this trend. In 1948 bandleader Akanbi Ege was said to be the first to introduce the talking drum to a *jùjú* ensemble. A year later Ayinde Bakare did the same, adding a small talking drum called the *gángán* and an *agídìgbo*, a bass lamellophone borrowed from the Latin-influenced street drumming style known alternately as *mambo* or *agídìgbo* (Waterman 1990a, 82–4).

Postwar advancements in music technology led to wider availability of portable PA systems, amplifiers and small electric pickups. In the late 1940s Bakare was among the first *jùjú* artists to replace banjo with amplified guitar. Amplification enabled the use of more percussion instruments and the expansion of the vocal chorus. In 1939 Bakare's ensemble consisted of one stringed instrument (ukulele-banjo), two percussion instruments (*jùjú* and *ṣẹ̀kẹ̀rẹ̀*) and one supporting vocalist. But by 1959 his orchestra included one stringed instrument (electric guitar), seven percussion instruments (*jùjú*, *ṣẹ̀kẹ̀rẹ̀*, claves, maracas, *àkúbà*, *ògìdo* and *gángán*) and two supporting vocalists. As instrumentation became more diverse and texture more dense, *jùjú* artists started arranging their music in the hierarchical manner of traditional Yorùbá drum ensembles, employing cyclical patterns and layered *ostinato* to create a stratified polyphonic gestalt (Waterman 1990a, 82–4). Bakare's recording 'Ojo Davies/Elekole of Ikole' (1937) is representative of his small ensemble style, while his large ensemble is on full display in *Live the Highlife* (1968).

In the absence of Tunde King, who had left Nigeria in 1939, Bakare's interventions set the standard for *jùjú* in the 1940s and 1950s. This, along with the expansion of the record industry and radio broadcasting, helped stabilize the genre. Although Parlophone and His Majesty's Voice had been recording in Lagos since the 1920s, it was another three decades before Nigerian music became commercially viable at a large scale. In the 1950s European companies Decca, EMI and Philips, interested in growing their international markets, set up recording studios in Lagos. Nigerian entrepreneurs, notably Peter Badejo (Badejo Sounds), Chief Olayegbe (Jofabro Records) and Chief Abioro (African Songs), played a critical role in this expansion by establishing manufacturing partnerships with European labels. In the mid-1960s *jùjú* stars began founding their own labels, which included I.K. Dairo's Star Records, Ebenezer Obey's Obey Records and King Sunny Ade's Sunny Alade Records (Frankel 2006, 291; Waterman 1990a, 90–1).

Stylistic Diversification

The commercial growth and stabilization of *jùjú* as a genre enabled a variety of alternative styles to emerge (Waterman 1993b, 64). *Jùjú*'s widening patronage base drove stylistic innovation, as artists increasingly drew on diverse sounds, instruments and linguistic material to reach their existing audiences and to draw in new listeners. Afro-Latin musical instruments and Caribbean melodies comingled with church hymnody, Islamic texts, Arabic vocal timbers, US country-and-western tunes and Indian film themes. A greater variety of Yorùbá dialects was employed alongside regionally specific musical material.

I.K. Dairo is the artist typically credited with leading this period of diversification. A carpenter from Ijebu-Ijesa who began his musical career in Ojoge Daniel's band, Dairo formed the Morning Star Orchestra in the late 1950s. The band played life cycle events around Ijesa and garnered a base of wealthy patrons in the city of Ibadan. Dairo took advantage of the widening reach of electronic mass media, appearing on the Western Nigeria Broadcasting Service in 1958 and on a televised *jùjú* competition in 1961, which his band (by then renamed the Blue Spots) handily won. He began recording on Decca in the early 1960s and then founded Star Records with *àpàlà* artist Haruna Ishola in the mid-1960s. Dairo's most noted innovation was the substitution of button accordion for guitar, but his band otherwise adhered to the standard instrumentation laid out by Bakare. An arguably greater contribution – and that which made him a star – was his ability to infuse the music with distinctly regional flavors while maintaining a widely appealing pan-Yorùbá sound (Alaja-Browne 1989b, 235). A member of the Cherubim and Seraphim African spirit healing movement, Dairo employed church hymn melodies and texts alongside Ijesa choral arrangements and regionally specific rhythms. He was known for his deep knowledge of Yorùbá poetry and ritual language, which he could sing in various dialects. By tapping into syncretic Christianity, regional culture and village tradition, he widened *jùjú*'s appeal beyond the elite salons of Lagos. See 'Iku Lumumba/Ore Odale' (1961) and *Ashiko Music* (1971) for examples that contrast Dairo's guitar-driven and accordion-driven sounds.

Dairo's work inspired other artists to diversify and regionalize their sounds. C.A. Balogun and Dele Ojo, for example, used Ekiti Yorùbá dance rhythms and close harmonies, while Rafiu Bankole tapped into concurrent Latin and Congolese traditions. Other artists responded by reconnecting *jùjú* to its Lagosian roots. Bandleader and vocalist Tunde Nightingale, for example, sought to rekindle the 1930s sound with a nasal high-tessitura vocal style reminiscent of Tunde King. J.O. Araba and J.O. Oyesiko revived the prewar *jùjú* sound with toy motion, a style that returns to classic palmwine guitar patterns and Caribbean dance rhythms (Waterman 1990a, 96–7). For examples from this era, see *Jùjú Roots: 1930s–1950s* (1993).

Jùjú After Independence

The post-independence era of the 1960s saw great change in the structure of Nigerian society and in the opportunities available to *jùjú* musicians. The declining fortunes of Igbo artists during the Nigerian civil war (1967–70) hastened the decline of highlife music while *jùjú* artists quickly filled the void, finding many willing patrons among the Yorùbá military leadership. The oil boom of the 1970s led to the formation of a new political and economic elite, whose unprecedented wealth and connections would propel a handful of exceptional bandleaders into the global spotlight. Growth in the local recording industry benefited *jùjú* musicians, as did the genre's increasingly prominent place in commercial radio and broadcasting. *Jùjú*, in other words, had become big business (Alaja-Browne 1989b, 237).

Among the most successful *jùjú* artists of this era were Chief Commander Ebenezer Obey and King Sunny Ade (born Sunday Adeniyi), whose apparent rivalry spurred a wave of musical innovation in which each, with financial backing from patrons and record companies, sought to claim dominance with novel constellations of musical material, instrumentation and electronic technology. Obey began his musical career under the tutelage of Fatai Rolling Dollar, a former *agídìgbo* player and prominent highlife musician. The International Brothers, which Obey founded in 1964, built on Fatai's *jùjú*-highlife foundation, bringing its prewar Afro-Caribbean sound into conversation with Congolese pop, soul and country music (Waterman 1990a, 120). Beginning as a *samba* drummer in Moses Olaiya's group, Sunny Ade formed the Green Spots in 1966. He was a skillful guitarist and his vocal style resembled that of Tunde Nightingale and Tunde King. Signed to the Nigerian-owned African Songs label, he quickly earned acclaim for his records, including a hit song praising the label's owner, Chief Abioro. Following Dele Ojo's lead, Ade introduced bass guitar to his band in 1970 and subsequently began experimenting with other electric instruments. After splitting with Abioro in 1972, Ade renamed his group the African Beats. By 1979 Ade's group consisted of 16 or more musicians, including two tenor guitars, one rhythm guitar, Hawaiian lap steel guitar, bass, two talking drums, drum set and synthesizer, as well as supporting drums and vocalists (Ige and Abulude 1996, 27–8; Waterman 1990a, 132–4).

These articulations of personal style became known as 'systems' (Alaja-Browne 1989b, 239). Examples of Obey's 'miliki system' include his Decca recordings 'Ijo Miliki' and 'Alowo M'ajaiye,' which are found on the album *Chief Commander Ebenezer Obey and his Miliki Sound* (1973). Ade's 'syncro system' is best illustrated on the LP *Syncro System Movement* (1976). As they sought to modernize *jùjú*, Obey and Ade reached deeper into the Yorùbá panegyric tradition, using praise formulae and attributive poetry to eulogize their powerful patrons and reinforce the clientelist social order on which their musical careers depended. They also made masterful use of proverbs and folk parables to comment on social events and convey broader philosophical themes such as the certainty of God in an uncertain world, the dangers of human capriciousness and the ubiquity of competition for power and distinction in social affairs. But the two were also entertainers, a role at which Ade excelled – his celebratory exhortations and dance directives cut with humor and sexual innuendo.

Jùjú music finally hit the global market in the early 1980s when Island Records, looking for new international talent after the death of Bob Marley, released Ade's album *Jùjú Music* (1982) to wide acclaim. Despite being dropped from the label several years later, Ade remains the only *jùjú* artist to have achieved that level of international success, and has continued to tour the United States and the United Kingdom while consistently drawing large crowds in Nigeria.

The late 1970s and early 1980s witnessed the breakthrough of *jùjú* artists such as Admiral Dele Abiodun and Segun Adewale who had been gaining traction with hybrid *jùjú* styles that absorbed the Afro-diasporic sounds of jazz, soul, funk and rock, as well as the influences of other Nigerian popular genres. Abiodun was known for his prominent use of lap steel guitar and dubbed his sound the '*adawa* system,' which is well represented on the album *Adawa Super Ten: Elemu Nget On* (1978). Adewale's 'Yo-pop' music, a style of *jùjú* heavily inflected with Afrobeat, features prominently on *Play for Me* (1983). With distaste for the apparent elitism of praise singing, Abiodun and Adewale sought to detach *jùjú* from its traditional system of patronage and bring it more fully into the global marketplace

(Bergman 1985, 90). Another rising star of this era was Sir Shina Peters, who began his career in Prince Adekunle's Western Brothers with Adewale. The two would later collaborate as Sir Shina Adewale and his Super Stars International (see, for example, *Superstar [Verse 1]*, 1977). Peters first garnered acclaim for his percussion-heavy approach to *jùjú* with the album *Ace/Afro-Jùjú Series 1* (1989). A year later he released *Shinamania/Afro-Jùjú Series 2* (1990), featuring a style of *jùjú* enlivened by the fast tempos, dense percussion and declamatory vocal style of *fújì*, an Islamic popular genre that has dominated Nigerian music since the 1980s. Peters also incorporated elements of Nigerian gospel music, which grew to commercial success at the same time as *fuji*.

Gospel and *fuji* remain steady forces in the Nigerian music industry and they have become increasingly intertwined with *jùjú* since the 1990s. Emerging as a star in the late 1990s, Yinka Ayefele introduced '*tungba*' style, which is essentially a blend of *jùjú* and *fuji* in the manner of Shina Peters but with added hints of *makossa* and a stronger emphasis on Christian hymnody sung in the Euro-American manner (Ajayi 2016). In the track 'My Life Time' from the album *Sweet Experience* (2000), for example, Ayefele interpolates the hymn 'Blessed Assurance' into a Yorùbá-language praise text that is sung to the accompaniment of fast-paced *fuji* drumming. Variations on this stylistic mix are also evident in the '*tungba*-gospel' of Queen Ayo Balogun, the 'gospel-*fuji*' of Dekunle Fuji and the 'gospel-folk' of Opeoluwa Orobiyi (a.k.a., Omo Oba Eledua). Orobiyi brings the story of *jùjú* full circle, offering a performance style that explicitly aims to reconnect Yorùbá popular music to its roots in sacred song and social dance.

Bibliography

Ajayi, Dami. 2016. 'Nigeria: Modern Jùjú Music: An Indigenous Genre Awaiting the Next Superstar.' *The Guardian* (Lagos), 17 July.

Alaja-Browne, Afolabi. 1989a. 'The Origin and Development of Jùjú Music.' *The Black Perspective in Music* 17(1/2): 55–72.

Alaja-Browne, Afolabi. 1989b. 'A Diachronic Study of Change in Jùjú Music.' *Popular Music* 8(3): 232–42.

Bergman, Billy. 1985. *Goodtime Kings: Emerging African Pop*. New York: Quarto.

Collins, John. 1992. *West African Pop Roots*. Philadelphia: Temple University Press.

Frankel, Andrew. 2006. 'Nigeria: Africa's Stumbling Giant.' In *The Rough Guide to World Music: Africa & Middle East* (Vol. 1), ed. Simon Broughton et al. London: Rough Guides, 287–303.

Ige, Clement, and Abulude, Femi. 1996. *King Sunny Ade. Hooked to Music: An Autobiography*. Ibadan: Distinct Publications.

Roberts, John S. 1972. *Black Music of Two Worlds*. New York: Praeger.

Thomas, T. Ajayi. 1992. *History of Jùjú Music: A History of an African Popular Music from Nigeria*. Jamaica, NY: Thomas Organization.

Topouzis, Daphne. 2002. 'The Kings of Jùjú and Palm Wine Guitar.' *Africa Report* 33(6): 67–9.

Waterman, Christopher A. 1990a. *Jùjú: A Social History and Ethnography of an African Popular Music*. Chicago: University of Chicago Press.

Waterman, Christopher A. 1990b. '"Our Tradition Is a Very Modern Tradition": Popular Music and the Construction of Pan-Yorùbá Identity.' *Ethnomusicology* 34(3): 367–79.

Waterman, Christopher A. 1993a. Liner notes. *Jùjú Roots: 1930s–1950s*. Rounder CD 5017. USA.

Waterman, Christopher A. 1993b. 'Jùjú History: Toward a Theory of Sociomusical Practice.' In *Ethnomusicology and Modern Music History*, ed. Stephen Blum et al. Champaign: University of Illinois Press, 49–67.

Discographical References

Abiodun, Dele. *Adawa Super Ten: Elemu Nget On*. Olumo ORPS 83. *1978*: Nigeria.

Ade, King Sunny. *Syncro System Movement*. African Songs Limited AS26-L. *1976*: Nigeria.

Adewale, Segun. *Play for Me*. Segun Adewale Records SARPS 6. *1983*: Nigeria.

Adewale, Sir Shina, and His Super Stars International. *Superstar (Verse 1)*. Wel-Kadeb Records WKLPS 1. *1977*: Nigeria.

Ayefele, Yinka. *Sweet Experience*. Ayefele Records. *2000*: Nigeria.

Bakare, Ayinde. 'Ojo Davies/Elekole of Ikole.' His Masters Voice JZ17. *1937*: Nigeria.

Bakare, Ayinde, and His Group. *Live the Highlife*. Melodisc MLP 12-140AS. *1968*: Nigeria.

Dairo, I. K., and His Blue Spots. *Ashiko Music*. Decca WAPS 33. *1971*: Nigeria.

Dairo, I. K., and His Blue Spots. 'Iku Lumumba/Ore Odale.' Decca NWA 5022. *1961*: Nigeria.

Jùjú Roots: 1930s–1950s. Rounder CD 5017. *1993*: USA.

King, Tunde. 'Alimi Abade/Oba Oyinbo.' Parlophone PO 567. *1936*: Nigeria.

King, Tunde. 'Association/John Cole.' Parlophone PO 500. *1936*: Nigeria.

King, Tunde. 'Doctor Vaughan/Aronke Macaulay.' Parlophone PO 508. *1936*: Nigeria.

Obey, Chief Commander Ebenezer, and His International Brothers. *Chief Commander Ebenezer Obey and His Miliki Sound*. Decca WAPS 78. *1973*: Nigeria.

Peters, Sir Shina. *Ace (Afro-Jùjú Series 1)*. CBS CBS-N-1002. *1989*: Nigeria.

Peters, Sir Shina. *Shinamania (Afro-Jùjú Series 2)*. CBS CBS-N-1006. *1990*: Nigeria.

Tunde the Western Nightingale, and His Band. *Original 'Owa Nbe' Sound (Vol. 1)*. Take Your Choice Records TYC 3-L. [*ca.* late 1960s/early 1970s]: Nigeria.

JESSE D. RUSKIN

Kadongo-Kamu

Kadongo-kamu is a music genre that originated in the south central region of Uganda in the early 1950s. It is regarded as the country's oldest genre of contemporary popular music. A product of the hybridization of traditional Buganda music and Western music elements, its socio-contextual functions include ones with historical resonance such as those of bards, but overall tend more toward modern ideas of entertainment (the guitar-'wielding' *kadongo-kamu* street bards entertain customers from bar to bar, while others feature on the media [Pier 2016, 360]) rather than to the traditional African rites, rituals and/or ceremonies which music was often used to enhance. Beginning as a term denoting something that at the time was considered inferior in every way, *kadongo-kamu* eventually became the brand name of a powerful, successful, multifunctional genre. From its beginning, this genre's novelty and artistic content attracted many prominent artists, among them, Elly Wamala, Fred Masagazi and Paulo Kafeero.

Emergence and Principal Characteristics

In its earliest appearances, which date from the early 1950s, *kadongo-kamu* was so called because it featured accompaniment by a single six-string acoustic guitar (*kadongo-kamu* means 'a solitary guitar'). The 'grandfathers' (respected elders) of *kadongo-kamu* developed a simple guitar style expressed as harmonic *ostinato/s* that combined basic chord progressions with the finger-picking accompaniment of a vocal melodic line (see Manuel 1988, 97).

Kadongo-kamu constituted a major stylistic innovation and marked the beginning of a very different music type in Uganda. At the time, the music of the Baganda was based on approximately equidistant pentatonic scales in which the octave was divided into five intervals of approximately 240 cents (2.4 semitones); this music was not harmony-based and no chords were used. Frequent use was made of parallel octaves. But the introduction of *kadongo-kamu* changed all those features by synthesizing traditional and imported musical elements, and it therefore was considered an avant-garde style. The traditional elements included instruments such as the cone-shaped drums, *endingidi* (single-string tube fiddles) and *enseege* (gourd rattles), while the imported musical instruments included six-stringed guitars, keyboard instruments, cymbals and percussion drum sets. This synthesis inspired many other musicians and also marked the creation of a popular music genre with what was perceived as possessing a true Ugandan identity. The national identity associated with the genre is attributed to a number of elements directly related to or found in Uganda, such as languages, metaphoric statements, local place name, types of plants or fruits and so on.

Since the genre's invention, *kadongo-kamu* performers have predominantly used lyrics in Luganda, the vernacular language spoken by the Baganda people of the Buganda kingdom. In the Luganda tonal language, textual progression of tones significantly determines not only the melodic contours of the songs but also the verbal rhythm of the lyrics which in turn directly influences the songs' melodic rhythms. Words in Luganda have natural pitch accents and the pitched tones are essential in distinguishing between words, especially since nearly all Luganda words automatically bear built-in tunes. The absolute pitches of the words are not precisely prescribed; the term 'tonality' is used in this context to imply that the words are pronounced at high-, middle- or low-pitched tones. *Kadongo-kamu* as a genre, therefore, is characterized among other elements by what van der Merwe refers to as a narrow gap between speech and song in the sense that the words are sung exactly as spoken and vice versa (van der Merwe 1989, 38) (for further discussion of language aspects of *kadongo-kamu*, see Pier 2016).

Traditional Elements and External Influences

The birthplace of *kadongo-kamu* is the kingdom of Buganda and the vast majority of the music idioms that characterize the genre are derived from Buganda culture. Elements of *kadongo-kamu* that are characteristic of Ganda music ('Ganda' is an 'adjective-like' term used to describe things related either to the culture of the Baganda people or to their kingdom, referred to as Buganda) include complex rhythmic textures, unvarying rhythmic *ostinato/s*, melodic *ostinatos*, call-and-response form and arrangements suggesting a musical conversation between the lead singer and main instruments, with sweet, non-harmonized melodies. The key melodies are often sung by the lead singer (male or female) with a choral response by either one or often two or three vocalists. *Kadongo-kamu* also uses the *baakisimba* stylistic characteristics of the Baganda. *Baakisimba* refers not only to one of the traditional music dance genres of the Baganda, noted for its drumming, but also to the stylistic vocal characteristics referred to as *eggono* (describing the scooping vocal style used in *baakisimba*), characterized by natural descending glissandos and brisk, downward-gliding vocal inflections.

Kadongo-kamu also employs polyrhythmic percussive complexity. It produces what van der Merwe refers to as the 'African kick' – an expression used loosely to refer to the initial accent – at the beginning of each note or musical phrase (1989, 39). Using improvisation as an essential feature, *kadongo-kamu* arrangements blend together elements from many sources including traditional, foreign and those offered by new technologies such as electric keyboards and, most recently, electric guitars. In a typical *kadongo-kamu* song all the elements noted above culminate in a rich, complex, polyphonic, polyrhythmic texture with a definite identity reflecting the Ugandan nation.

The overwhelming success of *kadongo-kamu*, including both its popularity and its effectiveness in communicating its intended messages to audiences, has been partly due to its unique, innovative and ever-changing stylistic characteristics. Its style is characterized by persistent creative retentions of traditional elements with an idiosyncratic synthesis of outside influences. The most conspicuous foreign element has been its instrumentation, which incorporates a broad array of instruments of Western derivation along with African ones. The African instruments include *endingidi* (one-string tube fiddles), *engoma* (traditional cone-shaped drums including *embuutu, empuunyi, nankasa*), and *enseege* (gourd rattles). The acoustic and electric guitar, the electric keyboard and, occasionally, the flute have formed the core of the foreign instruments used successfully. Most important is the creative way *kadongo-kamu* musicians use these instruments, which emphatically reflects the origin and traditional music base of the genre. In the musical tradition of Buganda, for example, the *baakisimba* rhythm *ostinato* is played on a cone-shaped double-skinned drum called *embuutu*. *Kadongo-kamu* musicians often reproduce that same drum rhythm *ostinato* on either an acoustic or electric bass guitar. The innovative and creative ways in which foreign instruments such as the bass guitars are played to represent the otherwise traditional *baakisimba* beat fascinate *kadongo-kamu* fans. The latter include especially those people who live in the urban areas but who also happen to be familiar with the traditional *baakisimba* styles that are predominantly based in the rural areas or villages.

The development of *kadongo-kamu* in Uganda was nurtured to a great extent by three circumstances: urbanization, the availability of Western instruments and the growth of what Peter Manuel describes as pan-ethnic social culture identity (Manuel 1988, 101). *Kadongo-kamu* is primarily an urban phenomenon. This is because it is in the towns and cities that most of the foreign musical instruments are present, and other music features, including stylistic characteristics and to some extent languages, not only start but are also more noticeably practiced and experienced. As briefly described above, the change from the 'authentic' Ugandan music-cultural behavior was caused by the exposure of Ugandan musicians to European musical instruments. That contact led to the emergence of the *kadongo-kamu* genre as a result of the processes of acculturation and musical syncretism. Its subsequent existence is the result of the relationship between elements from other cultures – including the above-mentioned European ones – and other pan-ethnic Ugandan cultures. The *kadongo-kamu* genre reveals a certain level of stylistic compatibility between the musical systems in contact. *Kadongo-kamu* cultural borrowing, however, has remained limited to elements that are compatible with the host culture's musical system. *Kadongo-kamu* musicians have made careful, selective decisions that have preserved the basic source and original characteristics of the Ganda tradition. In addition, when the host culture (Buganda) adapts foreign element/s such as harmony, it selectively does so in distinctly idiosyncratic ways that substantially alter the original function of the borrowed element/s. In Manuel's observation, 'borrowed and/or inherited musical elements are often simplified in the process of acculturation' (Manuel 1988, 21) (only basic simple diatonic chords are used, rather than the more complex ones, for example). Even in syncretism and enculturation of *kadongo-kamu*, the vocal production method has been the most resistant to change and remains persistently loyal to its cultural Buganda base.

Key Individuals

The first recording of *kadongo-kamu* is often attributed to Christopher Ssebaduka (see, for example, Nannyonga-Tamusuza 2005; Pier 2016), who made several recordings in the late 1950s and early 1960s, including one of his most popular, 'Eddaame lya Chwa.' Elly Wamala also made recordings in the late 1950s and early 1960s, including 'Nabutono.' Both musicians helped to boost the fledgling Ugandan record industry (Ssemutooke 2014). Wamala appeared often on television and became known for supporting young musicians (ibid.) Other significant figures in the development of *kadongo-kamu* include Fred Magasazi, Don Mugula and Bernard Kabanda. 'Prince' Paul Job Kafeero (also known as Paulo Kafeero), described by Pier in 2016 as 'perhaps the most beloved kadango-kamu singer to date' (2016, 365), came to the fore in the late 1980s after learning from the radio appearances of Dan Mugula and others, releasing his first album *Muvubuka Munange* in 1989, Kafeero (who died at the age of 37 in 2007) sang about many of the contemporary issues touching Ugandan lives, including HIV/AIDS; his 1994 recording 'Walumbe Zaaya' was a 'fifteen minute lament on death' and earned him the sobriquet 'Golden Boy of Africa' (Akyeampong and Gates 2012, 259). The importance attached by his audience to Kafeero's lyrics may be judged from the fact that the words of over 80 albums have been transcribed and published, in Luganda and English (Barret Gaines 2012).

Beginning in the 1980s Matiya Luyima sought to forge together the narrative aspects of *kadongo-kamu* with aspects of Ugandan theater, forming the Kadongo Kamu Super Singers (Pier 2016, 365). *Kadongo-kamu* songs are embedded in his 10-part radio drama *Nakakaawa*, becoming what Mugambi (1994) calls 'radio songs.'

***Kadongo-Kamu* in the 2010s**

As creative musicians continue to refine the musical form – with regard to the overall structure and design of the various sections – and other characteristic elements in *kadongo-kamu*, political and cultural activists have been quick to identify its potential as an effective and influential mass mobilizer. People interested in politics or the 'survival' of cultural ethics have used this avant-garde genre to communicate their respective messages to *kadongo-kamu*'s growing audiences with great effect.

The genre has a magnetic appeal for both young and old. This magnetism may be explained by noting two different reasons. One is simply the successful hybridization of traditional idioms and foreign elements. While the elder class of people identify easily with the traditional elements, the younger ones are just as easily captivated by innovative, incoming, foreign elements. Secondly, *kadongo-kamu* is a 'listening-oriented' style of entertainment music. When a *kadongo-kamu* piece is played, the audiences are first and foremost expected to listen to the lyrics and receive the intended messages from the text. This listening-oriented function serves the generally clear-cut purpose characteristic of many traditions in sub-Saharan Africa. In that role and context, *kadongo-kamu* songs continue to be a powerful and formidable agent in transmitting important messages and mobilizing masses in social, cultural, political and religious matters. They are often didactic in nature. Dan Mugula, for example, in his song entitled 'Mudde Eri Mukama' (Go Back to God), employs lyrics that strongly encourage people to make sure that they 'put God in their life all the time because He is the only solution to any problems' they may have. Paul Kafeero, in his song entitled 'Nantabuulirirwa,' recommends that people should not ignore advice given to them by their 'elders': 'Advice is given to help rather than hurt you,' the lyrics state, while Fred Masagazi, in one of his *kadongo-kamu* pieces entitled 'Atannawa Musolo' encourages the listeners to pay their taxes on time: 'By doing so, you will save yourself the embarrassment of being arrested.'

Conclusion

Kadongo-kamu has persistently adhered to the basic characteristics that identified it when it first emerged. Those basics include the use of Luganda language, and a combination of traditional and pan-ethnic elements and styles for the communication of important cultural, religious, ethical, political and socially required messages. In addition, however, the performing icons of this genre have continued to employ ever-changing music-technological developments, including keyboard instruments and other modernized electronic instruments such as guitars. That way, it has continued to be viewed not only as very appealing but also as a progressive part of the national identity that is constantly challenged to adjust to continuing modern developments without any compromise of basic Ugandan cultural values. There is every hope that it will continue to inspire the upcoming talented musicians who will themselves continue to adjust to modern technologies. In that case, this ever-developing genre will carry on performing the two main roles of (a) entertaining its audiences and (b) effectively communicating the important social, religious, ethical, cultural and political messages without being viewed as outdated.

Bibliography

Akyeampong, Emmanuel K., and Gates, Henry Louis, eds. 2012. *Dictionary of African Biography*, Vol. 6. New York: Oxford University Press.

Barrett-Gaines, Kathryn. 2012. *One Little Guitar: The Words of Paul Job Kafeero*. Kampala: Fountain Publishers.

Kasule, Simon. 1998. 'Popular Performance and the Construction of Social Reality in Post-Amin Uganda.' *The Journal of Popular Culture* 32(2): 39–58.

Manuel, Peter. 1988. *Popular Music of the Non-Western World*. New York: Oxford University Press.

Mugambi, Helen Nabasuta. 1994. 'From Radio to Video: Migratory Texts in Contemporary Luganda Song Narratives and Performances.' Program of African Studies, Northwestern University, 8: 8, 12, 14–15, Online at: https://quod.lib.umich.edu/p/passages/4761530.0008.006/--from-radio-to-video-migratory-texts-in-contemporary-luganda?rgn=main;view=fulltext (accessed 15 June 2018).

Nannyonga-Tamusuza, Sylvia. 2002. 'Gender, Ethnicity, and Politics in Kadongo-Kamu Music of Uganda.' In *Playing with Identities in Contemporary Music in Africa*, eds. Mai Palmberg and Annemette Kierkegard. Uppsala: Nordic Africa Institute, 134–48.

Nannyonga-Tamusuza, Sylvia. 2005. *Baakisimba: Gender in the Music and Dance of the Baganda People of Uganda*. New York and London: Routledge.

Pier, David. 2016. 'Language Ideology and Kadongo Kamu Flow.' *Popular Music* 35(3): 360–79.

Ssemutooke, Joseph. 2014. 'Elly Wamala's Mark on the Recording Industry.' *Daily Monitor*, 8 December. Online at: http://www.monitor.co.ug/artsculture/Reviews/Elly-Wamala-s-mark-on-the-recording-industry/691232-2549024-mvjx08/index.html (accessed 15 June 2018).

Ssewakiryanga, Richard, and Isabirye, Joel. 2011. '"From War Cacophonies to Rhythms of Peace": Popular Cultural Music in Post-1986 Uganda.' *Current Writing: Text and Reception in Southern Africa* 18(2): 53–73.

van der Merwe, Peter. 1989. *Origins of Popular Style. The Antecedents of Twentieth-Century Popular Music*. Oxford: Clarendon Press.

Discographical References

Kafeero, Paul. *Muvubuka Munange*. Label unknown. *1989*: Uganda.

Kafeero, Paul. 'Nantabulirirwa.' *Nantabulirirwa*. Label unknown. *2000*: Uganda.

Kafeero, Paul. 'Walumbe Zaaye.' Label unknown. *1994*: Uganda. (Reissued on *Nabukenya*. Uganda Performing Right [Kandogo Kamu] Society. *2017*: Uganda.)

Masagazi, Fred. 'Atannawa Musolo.' *Atannawa Musolo*. Label unknown. *1961*: Uganda.

Mugula, Dan, with Entebbe Guitar Singers. 'Mudde Eri Mukama.' *Mudde Eri Mukama*. Label unknown. *N.d.*: Uganda.

YouTube

Christopher Ssebaduka, 'Eddame lya Chwa': https://www.youtube.com/watch?v=nxRrwaSL30o

Paul Job Kafeero, 'Walumbe Zaaya': https://www.youtube.com/watch?v=wk99Ib2lZ9s

JAMES MAKUBUYA

Kaka

Kaka is a traditional genre of drumming that originated in and around Porto-Novo, Benin, as the ritual music of the Zangbeto secret society, whose members wear full body masks and incarnate the *zangbeto* spirits during ceremonies. It is characterized by an abundance of interlocking bell patterns, up to six or seven at a time, and the distinctive, dry cracking sound of bamboo sticks, known as 'kaka' in the Gun language. The genre has been modernized and popularized since the 1970s by the 'Homme d'Orchestre' Sagbohan Danialou.

Kaka is primarily played by musicians who are members of the Zangbeto secret society and the genre is associated with the ceremonies of the *zangbeto* spirits, who are covered in long raffia masks and known as the 'guardians of the night'. Their role as the king's secret police began in the nineteenth century, when the *zangbeto* patroled the city at night to catch witches and spies. According to Gilbert Rouget (1996), who conducted research during the reign of King Gbefa (1946–76), the ensembles for the *zangbeto*, as well as those for other religious sects, were under the purview of the king's *migan*, or minister–executioner. The royal dynasties of Porto-Novo, known as Xogbonu and Abomey, were rivals, although both the Porto Novians and the Abomeans share ancestors in Allada and Adja-Tado. The Porto Novian kings established important and controversial alliances with the Yorùbá empire of Oyo and with the French at the beginning of the twentieth century.

Like many traditional genres of Benin, *kaka* was at first played without drums, using only the multiple bells (*ganvinon* and *gangbo*) and the bamboo sticks (*kaka*). The sticks are played against one another and against the ground. One of the sticks sounds the basic underlying bell pattern, while the other plays a repeated accompaniment pattern; together they produce a cross-rhythm. As *kaka* developed, drums, including the *kpezin*, the lead drum *kpahwle* and shakers (*assan*) were added, and the genre began to cross-pollinate with other styles, such as *djegbe* and *avivozenli*, in the region around Porto-Novo. There is some debate about whether the original style of playing only with bells and bamboo sticks should be referred to separately as *kakagbo* or whether it falls under the more general category of *kaka*, which applies to both the older style and to the subsequent developments.

The Porto Novian drummer and bandleader Sagbohan Danialou developed a modernized version of *kaka* in the 1970s. In 1973 he released the track 'Zangbeto' with the *salsa* ensemble Black Santiago on an album of the same name, led by the highlife trumpeter Ignace de Souza of Cotonou. Sagbohan kept the core *kaka* sound on this recording, emphasizing the cracking bamboo sticks, while featuring his voice and his poetic, proverb-filled lyrics in the Gun language. He later hybridized this *kaka* sound with jazz, adding horns and joining the interlocking *kaka* bells with Afrobeat rhythms on the drum set on his 1975 album *Danialou Sagbohan & Les Astronautes*, under the musical direction of the Beninois *salsa* leader El Rego.

Since *kaka* retains its sacred associations, it is rare to find ensembles that specialize in the genre outside of Zangbeto societies. Even Sagbohan's band is not exclusively a *kaka* ensemble, and it plays many different styles, most from outside Benin, such as *soukous* and *salsa*. Singing for *kaka* is usually improvised around pentatonic melodies in the Gun language, and lyrics cover traditional topics such as local politics, advice and proverbs. Dancing is reserved for the *zangbeto* themselves. When the *zangbeto* do appear in public, as they began to do increasingly for festivals in the late twentieth century, spectators are forbidden to touch them. Touching a *zangbeto* may bring an accusation of witchcraft upon the offender. While the masked spirits dance vigorously, it is believed that removing their long raffia coverings will reveal nothing underneath. Some observers have mistakenly described *kaka* as a genre for Vodun, assuming that the *zangbeto* are beings of the same type as the ancestral and natural deities such as Tovodun, Sakpata and Hevioso. But the Zangbeto secret society, like the Yorùbá secret society of *Oro*, is in a separate category from the Vodun deities, tied into the Porto Novian monarchy through a specific historical relationship.

The genre of *kaka* has undergone several transformations since its origins as a ritual genre for Zangbeto ceremonies using only bells and bamboo sticks. With the introduction of the lead drum and the shakers, *kaka* became a part of the regional musical language in Porto-Novo, interacting with other genres in the region. In Sagbohan's recordings, in which *kaka* is fused with jazz and *salsa* and his virtuosic vocals, he called attention to the style as an important marker of Porto-Novo's sonic signature, traditional and modern. In twenty-first-century Benin, the sound of *kaka* is a representation of roots in the ritual traditions of the Porto Novian region, although the increasing popularization of the genre means that it may appear in many different contexts.

Bibliography

Rouget, Gilbert. 1996. *Un roi africain et sa musique de cour: Chants et danses du palais à Porto-Novo sous le règne de Gbèfa (1948–1976)* [An African King and His Court Music: Songs and Dances of the Palace at Porto Novo Under the Reign of Gbefa (1948–1976)]. Paris: CNRS Editions.

Discographical References

Danialou, Sagbohan. *Danialou Sagbohan & Les Astronautes*. SATEL 063. *1975*: Benin.
Danialou, Sagbohan. *Zangbeto*. SATEL. *1973*: Benin.

SARAH POLITZ

Kalindula

Zambia's most famous and memorable style of popular urban music is *kalindula*, which flourished for just over a decade in the late 1970s to early 1990s. *Kalindula* was originally a rural music and dance from Luapula Province in the north of the country. It was played by the Aushi people, a subgroup of the Bemba-speaking peoples. It took its name from the *mbabadoni* or *kalindula*, a large bass guitar. The *kalindula* bass led the ensemble, with smaller homemade string instruments called banjos providing counterpoint and embellishment, and with percussion from *ngoma* drums, *chisekele* shakers and metal bells.

As a genuinely local style from Zambia, *kalindula* songs are exhilarating, distinctive and instantly recognizable. Many feature a ferociously fast 12/8 beat and frenzied bass, but lyrical, harmonized vocal melodies and relaxed lead guitar lines give the music a deceptively laid-back veneer. These are dance songs, driving and energized. However, the subject matter is frequently anything but light: AIDS, alcoholism, moral questions.

A distinguishing mark of *kalindula* is its complexity, the bass playing in particular; low notes are juxtaposed with high notes, two distinct registers being played. Counter-rhythms cut across the beat as the player sees fit. Meanwhile, two guitars play interlocking patterns with subtle variations continually taking place. The kit drummer lays down a steady beat, but it is the bassist who opens up the music and lets it breathe. This bass concept, central to the music, is a traditional element taken directly from the rural homemade *mbabadoni* or *babaton* four-string-bass style. In this part of Africa (Zambia, Malawi, southern Tanzania and southern Congo) the lead instrument is always the lowest and biggest drum. Thus, in *kalindula*, the bass leads.

Closely related to Zambian *kalindula* is modern *karindula* from across the border in the Democratic Republic of the Congo, centered on Lubumbashi. The main instrument is the familiar giant *babaton* banjo made from an oil drum, goatskin and four strings, supported by smaller banjos and percussion. The instruments are homemade, unlike the drums and electric guitars of amplified Zambian *kalindula*. The music inspires extravagant feats of dance and body control, as seen on the DVD accompanying the CD *The Karindula Sessions* recorded by Vincent Kenis for Crammed Discs.

History and Background

With over 70 tribes of Bantu origin, the large and landlocked country of Zambia, previously the British colony of Northern Rhodesia, remains sparsely populated. The country's prosperity or otherwise is heavily dependent on the copper mined in the north. Throughout its history, Zambia has been a crossroad, intersected by important trade routes and enriched by waves of migration, resulting in a varied mix of people and culture and consequently different types of music from many different ethnic backgrounds.

Before *kalindula*, the favorite urban music in Zambia came from the north and to a lesser extent the south. Congolese *rumba* from Zaire – full, rich and highly danceable – was much loved, and remained so 30 years later. In the South, Zimbabwean *chimurenga* was popular. Thus, with the additional popularity of music from the United Kingdom and United States, Zambian pop was mostly imported.

After liberation from British colonial rule in 1964, Kenneth Kaunda's one-party presidential regime took and remained in power for the next 27 years. In a measure reminiscent of Mobutu's campaign for *authenticité* in neighboring Zaire, Kaunda – himself a guitar player – decreed in 1976 that Zambian radio would break its dependence on foreign music. Henceforth, it would broadcast a diet of 90 percent Zambian music.

Among the first beneficiaries of this new policy, answering the new need for national dance music, were the groups playing zamrock in the English rock style of Cream and Hendrix, with fuzz guitar and flared trousers. While this music was derivative of English rock, it was a genuinely local outgrowth, and it was played by Zambians. Even earlier, there was already a tradition of rearranging local music in a modern way. The Big Gold Six, a sophisticated group of professionals that was the resident band at a national radio station, adapted traditional songs from many parts of Zambia in the 1960s and 1970s for electric guitar and bass. But *kalindula*, when it came along, was something else: rural music given a full-blooded electric treatment.

The Serenje Kalindula Band, from Serenje, was apparently the first *kalindula* group to appear. A rural skiffle group playing homemade instruments, the group was seized upon by an entrepreneur, taken to the city of Ndola, given electric instruments and a real drum set and told to rehearse for a week, after which the band released its first record, *Amanyamune*, in 1979. The band became popularly known as the Kalindula Kings – Abene Ba Kalindula. In fact its members were not from Luapula Province, they were Lala people, a group closely related to Bemba found in Central Province. Nor did they restrict themselves to *kalindula*; as well as *kalindula* they played a traditional rhythm from Lala culture called *fwanda fwanda-ing'oma yabalala*.

Michael Baird, record producer and chronicler of Zambian music, maintains (2009) that the first real *kalindula* record was John Mwansa's 'Mukamfwila' (The Witch) (1982); Mwansa played a rural, traditional theme with electric instruments. With a breathless rhythm of triplets and overdriven electric guitar sound familiar from zamrock, it was an immediate national hit. Before Mwansa, Zambian pop had been largely modeled on *rumba*, but now there was a new craze. Played fast and with enormous energy and verve by a host of small bands, typically with two electric guitars, bass and drums, *kalindula* burst into sudden flower.

As the *kalindula* craze spread across the country in the mid-1980s, so the music grew wider in scope and the term more generalized; bands from other areas including North Western, Western, Luapula and Eastern provinces began calling their music *kalindula*. The strict meaning of the term was soon muddled; suddenly nearly all electric pop was referred to collectively as *kalindula*, its roots as Aushi music now obscured. Listeners with local knowledge could tell where these bands came from by the rhythms they favored, such as *imfunkutu* (also from Luapula), *siyomboka* from Western Province, *chitelele*, *akalela* and *mantyantya*, the rhythm favored by the outstanding Masasu Band, who visited the UK in 1990, backing blind *kalindula* singer P.K. Chisala. Another band to tour the UK was Shalawambe from Luapula Province. Of the band's five members, three were brothers and one was a cousin. All were farmers. This closeness was reflected in a form of music that adroitly balanced urban and traditional styles of *kalindula*.

According to Baird (ibid.), Marc Boti played an important role promoting the new music. He broadcast the weekly TV show *Time For Music* from 1984 to 1993, coinciding with the *kalindula* era. All the bands performed at Mike's Car Wash (an auto shop with a bar and performance venue) on the Kafue Road in Lusaka. Recording the music was Peter Musungilo at dB Studios also in Lusaka.

Kalindula did not last, seeming to fade at about the time the Kaunda regime came to an end. From the business end a flood of pirated cassettes, usually blamed on Tanzanians, had a disastrous effect on the indigenous Zambian scene. Also, many musicians died from AIDS. By 1991 *kalindula* was all but over. One band that kept the flame alive was the extremely popular Amayenge. Although this group emerged under the name Amayenge in 1985, its members actually began playing together in 1978, when they popularized *kalindula* in another configuration as the Crossbones (later the New Crossbones). Under its various names, the group was led for 25 years by Kris Chali. Chali died in 2003 but the band carried on. Amayenge played music from all over the country –

kalindula and other kinds of local, traditional material, rearranged and electrified.

In the 2000s Brian 'Rebel' Chilala continued to include *kalindula* songs in his performances and on record. He tended to avoid digitally produced sounds, preferring old-fashioned bass, drums and electric guitar. The Hosanna Gospel Band included *kalindula* in their repertoire, along with *imfunkutu*, *siyomboka*, *chitelele*, *akalela*, *mantyantya* and other local genres, as well as international touches of *rumba*, *chimurenga* and *mutuashi*. The Mondo Music Corporation, set up in 2003, made a policy of re-releasing old *kalindula* hit songs on ancient-and-modern Zambian anthologies: *Shoprite Zambia Hit Parade* includes John Mwansa's 'Mukamfwila' and Serenje Kalindula Band's 'Elo Ya Lila,' while *Sounds of Zambia* Vol. 3 contains tracks from Serenje Kalindula Band, the Five Revolutions, Masasu Band and others.

By the 2010s the days of *kalindula* had passed. References to it were few, CDs hard to find, interest minimal. However, since the related zamrock genre made a comeback around 2013, it is possible that kalindula will see a similar revival.

Bibliography

Baird, Michael. 2009. Liner notes to *Zambush Vol. I – Zambian Hits from the 80s*. Netherlands: Sharp Wood Productions SWP027.

Graham, Ronnie. 1989. *Stern's Guide to the World of Contemporary African Music, Vol 1*. London: Pluto Press.

Graham, Ronnie, and Kandela Tunkanya, Simon. 2000. 'Evolution and Expression.' In *Rough Guide to World Music, Vol. 1: Africa, Europe and the Middle East*, eds. Simon Broughton, Mark Ellingham with James McConnachie and Orla Duane. London: Rough Guides Ltd, Penguin Books, 702–5.

Koloko, Leonard. 2012. *Zambian Music Legends*. Lulu Press (self-published).

Tracey, Hugh. 1948. *Ngoma: An Introduction to Music for Southern Africans*. London: Longmans.

Discographical References

Serenje Kalindula. *Amanyamune*. Zambian Music Parlour ZMPL 31. *1979*: Zambia.

Shoprite Zambia Hit Parade. Mondo Music MCP5MCD. *2003*: Zambia.

Sounds of Zambia Vol. 3. Mondo Music MCP6CD. *2004*: Zambia.

The Karindula Sessions. Crammed Discs CRAW 70. *2011*: Belgium. (With accompanying DVD.)

Discography

Amayenge. *Dailesi*. Mondo Music MZB15CD. *2004*: Zambia.

Masasu Band. *Tuwelele*. Digital Networks International MB002. *1999*: Zambia.

Serenje Kalindula Band. *ZNBC Presents Zambia Legends*. Mondo Music MZL3CD. *2006*: Zambia.

Shalawambe. *Samora Machel* Diabolo DIAB 817. *1989*: UK.

Zambiance! Globestyle CDORB037. *1989*: UK.

Zambush Vol 1: Zambian Hits from the 80s. Sharp Wood Productions SWP027. *2004*: Netherlands.

RICK SANDERS

Kazukuta

Kazukuta is a rhythm and dance style from Angola that is typically performed in Luanda's Carnival. The rhythm became the foundation of the popular *kazukuta* genre that emerged in the 1940s as young musicians began to create music inspired by Carnival and international popular music. The dance style is executed as a slow tap followed by twists of the body that mimic leaning on a cane while weight is shifted between heel and toe.

Kazukuta has its roots in the suburbs of Luanda. The capital in the 1940s was largely segregated. Whites lived in the center, while *assimilados*, the mostly mixed-race middle class who worked for the state or owned businesses, lived in the inner suburbs, and black workers lived in the informal neighborhoods in outlying districts known as *musseques*. As Angola urbanized, Luanda's Carnival maintained its cultural significance and groups in the middle-class Bairro Operário and *musseque* Sambizanga performed the *kazukuta* in the competitions.

Youth groups (known as *turmas*) associated with the anti-colonial movement started in the *musseques* in the 1940s. These predominantly male groups met primarily to sing and dance. The *turmas* and groups such as Grupo dos Sambas played mostly popular Brazilian songs on guitar and piano and incorporated the *kazukuta* rhythm into their developing musical vocabulary. As Moorman (2008) has argued, it was through the practice of Brazilian music that musicians of this era returned to Angolan musical forms and began to 'emphasize the Africanness of their cultural heritage' (2008, 63) that had been marginalized under Portuguese colonial rule. The music and lyrics of these groups reflected the emerging Angolan national identity, or *Angolanidade*, and many members became active participants in the nationalist movement.

By the 1950s popular groups including Kimbandas do Ritmo, Duo Ouro Negro and Elias Dia Kimuezu had become established and included the *kazukuta* rhythm in their repertoire. This grouping of genres became known as *semba*, a name derived from the Carnival dance *massemba*. Although in the early 1960s the Portuguese colonial government banned Carnival and jailed activist performers, *kazukuta* music maintained popularity through clubs and parties in the *musseques* and was played on underground short-wave radio stations broadcast throughout the country. Many groups recorded *kazukuta* songs during the wave of recording that occurred in the late 1960s and 1970s, as labels including Companhia de Discos de Angola, Rebita and Valentim de Carvalho released local popular music.

Guitarists Liceu Vieira Dias of Ngola Ritmos and António Manuel Gonçalves of Águias Reais popularized the use of the *kazukuta* rhythm on melodic instruments and voice. Tenaille (2002) has suggested that Vieira Dias's guitar harmonization tamed 'the circular rhythms of the *marimba* (the xylophone dear to the Mbundu) and the *sanza kissanje* [lamellophone]' (2002, 56–7). Tenaille also highlights the use of the guitar to play counterpoint to the vocal melody and reinforce the counter-rhythm scraped and tapped on the *dikanza* (a hollow, ridged percussion instrument similar to the Brazilian *reco-reco*). Further percussion is played on *tumba* and *bongos*. Trumpet and bugle players, such as União Operário Kabocomeu's Man Nito and António Gonçalves, would often perform the lead melody line in place of vocals.

While the recorded music industry was disrupted for much of the period of the Angolan Civil War (which began in 1975 and lasted into the early twenty-first century), *kazukuta* maintained its popularity during Carnival in the 1970s and 1980s. By the 1990s *kizomba* singers Yuri da Cunha and Dog Murras began performing an interpretation of the genre using a mixture of guitars, live percussion and digital instruments and recorded some music internationally. In the 2010s DJ Djeff Afrozilla revisited *kazukuta* and blended the rhythm with elements of Afrohouse and *kuduro*.

Bibliography

Alves, Carlos Alberto. 2014. 'Conversa com Mário Rui Silva' [Conversation with Mário Rui Silva]. *Multiculturas*. Online at: http://www.multiculturas.com/angolanos/quatro_entrevistas.htm

Barate, Filomena. 2011. 'Dança / Músicas do Carnaval de Angola' [Dance/Musics of Angolan Carnival]. *AEPPEA*. Online at: http://aeppea.wordpress.com/2011/03/08/danca-musicas-do-carnaval-de-angola/ (accessed 6 September 2017).

Birmingham, David. 2006. *Empire in Africa: Angola and Its Neighbors*. Athens, OH: Ohio University Press.

Malumba, Jorge. 2012. Interview with author, Luanda, Angola.

Moorman, Marissa. 2008. *Intonations: A Social History of Music and Nation in Luanda, Angola, from 1945 to Recent Times*. Athens, OH: Ohio University Press.

Tenaille, Frank. 2002. *Music Is the Weapon of the Future: Fifty Years of African Popular Music*. Chicago: Lawrence Hill.

Discography

Africa Show. 'Kazucuta Para Jofre.' N'Gola LD 215. *1973*: Angola.

Os Bongos. 'Kazukuta.' Rebita R.1206. *1974*: Angola.

Os Kotumbas. 'Kazucuta Revoltada.' *Folclore de Angola*. Roda SRL 5541. *1976*: Portugal.

GARTH SHERIDAN

Kidandali

Kidandali is a term used, sometimes disparagingly, sometimes with pride, to categorize pop music that is digitally mass-produced for mainstream Ugandan tastes. In Luganda language, a 'kidandali' (pl. 'bidandali') is a lowdown dance hall where men and women go to drink and socialize all night. *Kidandali* music, correspondingly, is music for social relaxation, without rough edges or artistic pretensions that might spoil a convivial mood. The term refers to these somewhat disreputable local dance venues, as well as, perhaps, to the Jamaican 'dancehall' music from which this Ugandan pop style was consciously derived. The most consistent feature of *kidandali* music is its typical Jamaican dancehall 'riddim,' a globalized digital groove popular throughout Africa since the 1990s. Over this groove, artists sing, in warm, vibrato-laden voices, songs about romantic love, the challenges of work and family life, and aspirations to wealth, travel and middle-class social independence. The root progression IV-I-V-I (or I-IV-I-V) is used to mark out a rhythmic period of eight or sixteen beats, which frames each lyrical line. It must be stressed that 'kindandali,' like most genre terms, is open-ended and contentious, and cannot be conclusively fixed to a closed set of stylistic features or lyrical themes. Artists who are said to sing *kidandali* may themselves reject the term.

While the term 'kidandali' has long been used generically to reference music heard in dance halls, the *kidandali* genre as it exists today first emerged in the mid-1990s, with the arrival of affordable digital music production technologies. Digital producers Tim 'Dr. T' Kizito, David Mukalazi and Joe Tabula are cited as early innovators. As digital technologies have become more widely available, dozens of independent studio producers, working on shoestring budgets, have flooded the Ugandan airwaves with *kidandali* songs that adhere to a proven stylistic formula. This trend has provoked a disdainful response from those Ugandan music fans who believe the nation's popular music has become too digitized, homogenized and commoditized. It is worth noting that, while digital production is essential to *kidandali*'s radio sound, touring shows often feature live band accompaniment. These tours, which travel to small towns throughout rural Uganda, have been dominated by Eagles Production (reformed as Golden Production), a musical corporation strongly identified with *kidandali*. Eagles Production's roster has included Irene Namatovu, Angela Kalule, Juliana Kanyomozi, Cathy Kusasira, Geoffrey Lutaaya, Ronald Mayinja and Mesach Semakula. The roughly equal number of female and male stars under the Eagles banner promotes *kidandali*'s appeal to fans of both genders.

The more neutral term 'afrobeat' is often used to refer to what is otherwise called *kidandali*. Indeed, 'afrobeat' may be the more common name, having been used by the annual Pearl of Africa Music Awards (PAM). Some Ugandan music critics have embraced the term 'kidandali' in order to avoid confusion with the more famous Nigerian Afrobeat style pioneered by Fela Kuti, to which Ugandan afrobeat has no direct stylistic or historical connection. The 'afro' in Ugandan 'afrobeat' reflects the geographical concerns that shape discourse about *kidandali*/afrobeat. It is felt to be neither an assertively 'Western' style, nor a 'local' one, but an 'African' medium between these two extremes. Such geographical considerations are prominent in contemporary Ugandan pop music discourse generally, as artists attempt to position their productions in new, multilevel, markets. They cultivate portfolios of musical songs and videos, some in vanguard global styles (e.g., English-language hip-hop), others in styles meant to appeal to more 'local,' ostensibly less sophisticated, tastes (e.g., *kidandali*). Internationally successful artists who perform some songs in *kidandali* style for their fan base at home include Bebe Cool and Jose Chameleone. On the scale of imagined 'local'-ness, *kidandali* is considered more local than hip-hop or reggae, but less local than *kadongo-kamu*, a style that is not only distinctively Ugandan but also distinctively 'Kiganda,' in that it is associated specifically with Baganda musical traditions and identity (the Baganda, who speak Luganda language and associate with the historical Buganda kingdom, are the largest ethnic group in the South of Uganda). Besides being more explicitly 'traditional' in orientation than *kidandali*, *kadongo-kamu* tends to be more intellectual, musically/poetically virtuosic and politically critical. Both genres, however, touch on many of the same working-class populist themes, and appeal to many of the same fans.

To date, none of the artists most associated with *kidandali* has entered the world music circuit, or garnered the support of an international record label. Thanks to the open flows of digital distribution, however, many *kidandali* songs and albums, old and new, are accessible online, both for free on social media sites such as YouTube and for purchase on retail download sites. These are enjoyed and discussed by members of the Ugandan diaspora as well as by Ugandans at home. With its vernacular-language lyrics, focus on 'local' concerns and stylistic homogeneity, *kidandali* seems likely to remain a national, rather than world, pop-culture phenomenon. Indeed, it is crafted to be 'our music' for Ugandans, rather than a globally successful product. It signifies 'local'-ness without being too local, African-ness without sounding too foreign.

Kindandali may be compared to countless other light, danceable, digital genres that have sprung up around sub-Saharan Africa since the 1990s, many of which share a similar sound and attitude. South African 'bubblegum,' born in the 1980s, may be highlighted as an important progenitor. These genres share an emphasis on fun, consumerist aspiration, and celebrity, perhaps in a continent-wide shift away from both the lofty ideals, and heavy disappointments, of the independence era. For some music connoisseurs and cultural pundits, *kidandali*'s cheap-sounding production, which recycles the same groove over and over again, with minor variations, stands as a symbol of Uganda's cultural decay. Most Ugandan listeners, however, do not share this dour opinion about the genre. *Kidandali* is, for them, a cheerful social lubricant that carries both the familiarity of home and just enough novelty, in its regularly updated sounds, celebrity personalities and lyrical topics to hold their interest.

Bibliography

Asaasira, Anita Desire. 2007. 'Pearl of Africa Music (PAM) Awards: Political Construction of Popular Music in Uganda.' BA thesis, Makerere University.

Nannyonga-Tamusuza, Sylvia. 2006. 'Constructing the Popular: Challenges of Archiving Ugandan "Popular" Music.' *Current Writing* 18(2): 33–52.

Ssewakiryanga, Richard. 2004. '"Bringing the Global Home": Locating Agency in the Reconfiguration of Western Music by Ugandan Youth.' In *Sounds of Change: Social and Political Features of Music in Africa*, ed. Stig-Magnus Thorsén, 135–51. Stockholm: Sida.

Ssewakiryanga, Richard, and Isabirye, Joel. 2006. '"From War Cacophonies to Rhythms of Peace": Popular Cultural Music in Post-1986 Uganda.' *Current Writing* 18(2): 53–73.

Discography

Kusasira, Cathy. *Kankusinze*. Uganda Performing Right Society. *2015*: Uganda.

Lutaaya, Geoffrey. *Agye Munsawoyo*. Uganda Performing Right Society. *2015*: Uganda.

Namatovu, Irene. *Wolokoso*. Uganda Performing Right Society. *2015*: Uganda.

DAVID PIER

Kidumbak

Kidumbak is a dance-centered Zanzibari wedding entertainment performed by small, loosely organized groups, usually consisting of a violin as the single melodic instrument, two *vidumbak* (plural; small clay drums) as the major and style-defining percussive instrument, *sanduku* ('box' in Swahili; similar to a washtub or gutbucket bass) and smaller percussion instruments. Several members of the group alternate as lead singers, with family and wedding guests joining in as chorus and dancers. The style is popular mainly in the lower-class areas of Zanzibar town and the islands' rural areas. It is generally performed in an open space in the vicinity of the bride's home.

Kidumbak is the name of the two small clay drums that form the core of every *kidumbak* ensemble. The meaning of *ki-dumbak* is 'small dumbak' and, in fact, these drums are easy-to-make, low-cost variants of the larger instruments found in the Zanzibar *taarab* orchestras. Additionally, however, they lend their name to and characterize the whole musical genre. The two *vidumbak* are identical in size, though they are tuned differently. The one tuned slightly lower is called *ngoma ya kudunda* ('the sounding drum'). Its player marks the major tempo playing straight through. The *ngoma ya kuchanganya* ('the combining, or mixing drum') improvises on top of the basic rhythm provided by the other drum.

Additional percussion instruments are the *cherewa*, a type of *maracas* manufactured from coconut shells filled with seeds, and *vijiti*, short wooden sticks, played in the manner of *claves*. In the faster and more intense section, the *vijiti* player bangs on the table that is placed amid the instrumentalists. The table also holds a brass tray, into which coins and paper money are tossed as *tuzo*, a gift to the musicians.

The *kidumbak* ensemble consists of a single melodic instrument, customarily a violin. Its player introduces new songs and signals the changes and transitions from one song to the other. In the ensemble, however, the violin's function is not so much to play melody but rather to add texture and a thrill to the proceedings.

The most outstanding instrument of the ensemble, though, is the *sanduku*, or box-bass. It holds special importance for the female wedding audience. Solo dancers frequently draw close to the *sanduku* player, almost pushing him off his instrument as they rub their behinds on his shoulder to incite ever more inventive and arousing rhythmic variations. The *sanduku* playing style is more akin to a deep-tuned drum than to the playing of counter-melodic lines, adding further rhythmic accents to the percussion ensemble.

A *kidumbak* performance typically starts out with a number of slower songs, generally covers of the latest *taarab* hit songs. As tempo and intensity rise, some of the players take turns singing, stringing together fragments or catchphrases of older and well-known songs into an ever-evolving medley that usually lasts about an hour. As for the dancing wedding audience, with the intensity of the music rising to ever new heights, in order to be better visible to the whole congregation, some of them will jump, individually or in pairs, onto the musicians' table and perform a highly erotic hip-gyrating dance, punctuated by ululations from a roaring audience that throws in more *tuzo* money for especially provocative acts.

Kidumbak is sometimes called *ki-taarab*, 'a diminutive type of taarab,' not only because contemporary *kidumbak* often makes use of the latest *taarab* hit songs, but also since many youngsters hone their musical skills in *kidumbak* groups before being admitted into a *taarab* musical club. Against this view of *taarab* as the great tradition, older musicians such as Makame Faki – who for decades has led Zanzibar's most popular *kidumbak* group Sina Chuki, and who is also an eminent *taarab* singer and composer – hold that the original Swahili *taarab* ensembles, before the advent of the *firqah*-style orchestral *taarab* of the 1950s and 1960s, were not so different from modern *kidumbak*, with just two small drums, tambourine, violin and *'ud*, and also performing for dances.

According to oral history, the *'ud* was the original melodic instrument used in *kidumbak*. Bakari Abeid, who became Zanzibar's most celebrated *taarab* singer of the 1960s, led a *kidumbak* ensemble in the 1950s. A *kidumbak* group by the name of Shime Kuokoana was also at the root of the foundation of the Culture Musical Club *taarab* orchestra in 1958. In the 1960s *kidumbak* groups started to include rhythms and elements of *muziki wa dansi* from mainland Tanganyika, a lineage still apparent when, in the faster sections of *kidumbak* medleys, catchphrases or parts of songs by Cuban Marimba and Morogoro Jazz (the most popular bands of the late 1950s and 1960s) are quoted. Even the musical terminology of older *kidumbak* musicians refers to dance music; the fast sections after the main song are called *mapachanga* or *machachácha*, after the *pachanga* or *chachachá* dance crazes of the 1960s. Younger musicians call these parts *mgoma* (i.e., the drum/dance part). The *sanduku* is a 1960s invention as well, possibly also an inspiration taken from *muziki wa dansi* (i.e., an aural equivalent of the bass guitar).

The early development and style of *kidumbak* are not documented on any recordings. Occasional audio and video recordings of wedding celebrations are the only sources that may date back to the 1980s. Some audio cassettes are available from local cassette-duplicating shops. The popular Makame Faki and his group Sina Chuki have self-produced some of their songs and made them available locally on CD-R discs in the 2000s. An in-depth study of the style's history and social significance is urgently required, as so far much academic writing has focused primarily on *taarab*.

Bibliography

Fargion, Janet Topp. 2014. *Taarab Music in Zanzibar in the Twentieth Century: A Story of 'Old is Gold' and Flying Spirits*. New York: Routledge.

Discography

Kidumbak Kalcha. *Ng'ambo: The Other Side of Zanzibar*. Dizim Records 4501. *1997*: Germany.

Zanzibar: Music of Celebration. Topic Records TSCD917. *2000*: UK.

Zanzibar: Soul and Rhythm. De l'ame à la danse. Virgin Records 5957370. *2003*: France.

WERNER GRAEBNER

Kizomba

Kizomba, from the Angolan Bantu language Kimbundu, denotes a set of music and dance styles produced in the countries of Lusophone Africa such as Angola, Cabo Verde, Guinea-Bissau, Sao Tome and Principe and Mozambique, and across their diasporas in Europe, especially in Portugal, France and the Netherlands. In the early 1980s the word, meaning 'party,' began to refer to culturally distinctive appropriations of Caribbean *zouk* among young Angolan musicians. Inspired by *zouk*'s sounds after their global circulation through the music recordings of the Antillean group Kassav, Luanda-based groups such as Afra Sound Stars and SOS (which included the singer and composer Eduardo Paim) introduced *zouk* compositions sung in Portuguese in their repertoires including rhythms and genres such as *kilapanda*, Angolan *merengue*, *kazukuta*, *kabetula*, *trova* and reggae (Prata 2011).

During the Angolan Civil War (1975–2002), when revolutionary songs based on voice and acoustic guitar (known as *trova*) were promoted by the Movimento Popular de Libertação de Angola (MPLA)-controlled state as the main national and cultural expressions (Moorman 2008), *kizomba* reflected the interest of urban youth in modern sounds and new forms of pleasure and creativity intimately related with dance. Some of the first experiments with *kizomba* took shape in 1982 at the studios of Angola's national radio (Rádio Nacional de Angola), where young musicians in charge of the station's jingles, such as Eduardo Paim and members of the group SOS, had access to new musical instruments and technologies – rare goods in the country given its isolation from international contexts during the most intensive years of civil war in the 1980s. Along with SOS concerts, most of them taking place in state-organized events, *kizomba* and Caribbean *zouk* became the main musical choices of radio playlists, a few clubs and weekend backyard parties (*festas de quintal*). These socialities, taking place within the networks of family, friendship and urban neighborhoods, became the main contexts for informally learning and transmitting knowledge of music and especially dance. The old term *kizomba*, synonymous with 'party' and 'conviviality,' was first employed to refer to the new music and dance styles by SOS percussionist Bibi (Prata 2011; Paim 2014) in an interview. The term was chosen to convey the forms of pleasure provided by the social experience of *kizomba*'s music and dance forms.

Musicians involved in *kizomba*'s beginnings reject the idea that the genre emerged as an Angolan version of *zouk*. Although the influence of *zouk* in the period is acknowledged, they prefer to stress the creative synthesis of sound and choreographic materials from Angolan, Central African and Caribbean music and dance genres encompassed by *kizomba*'s aesthetics. The rhythmic and melodic sensibilities of Angolan *merengue* and *semba* have been particularly singled out as crucial in shaping *kizomba* as a fully autonomous music and dance expression. In the same direction, Eduardo Paim (2014) argued that dance moves and steps previously characterizing the dance styles of Latin American genres in Luanda (generically known as *passada* or 'sequence of steps') were adapted to the new *kizomba* choreographies. According to Paim, groundbreaking dancers of Luanda's Carnival and *semba* scene such as Mateus Pelé do Zangado, Joana Pernambuco and Jack Rumba were important actors in the configuration of these dance forms (Paim 2014). While the rhythmic foundation and the synthesized sounds which characterize *zouk* stand out in *kizomba*'s production, some of the vocal and instrumental melodies, the focus on daily social experiences in lyrics, the use of Portuguese punctuated with Kimbundu words, and especially the ever-changing creativity of dance forms seem to express *kizomba*'s roots in *semba* and earlier Angolan expressive forms.

At the end of the 1980s Eduardo Paim headed to Lisbon with a project of acquiring a synthesizer and devoting himself to music recording and production. He produced the first record of the young Angolan singer and composer Paulo Flores (1989), whom he had met in Luanda years earlier, and he started producing his own material (Paim 1991, 1992, 1993). Given the absence of local recording industries in the countries of Lusophone Africa, Lisbon became the main center for musicians from Angola, Cabo Verde, Guinea-Bissau, São Tomé and Principe and Mozambique to record and commodify their musics. In the 1980s Lisbon also became the main location for *kizomba* and other music and dance styles inspired by *zouk* to flourish.

In the late 1980s the term *kizomba* emerged in Europe in close relationship with the dance socialities of the *discotecas africanas* ('African discos') of the Greater Lisbon area, where records of Caribbean and Lusophone African *zouk* were played and danced to, alternating with African dance genres such as Angolan *semba* and Cabo Verdean *coladeira* – both strongly influenced by *zouk* since the late 1980s. The *discotecas africanas* became central spaces for the socialities of African labor migrants and students from the different regions of Lusophone Africa (Bernardo and Lopes Rodrigues 1995), and for their forms of pleasure, style and self-presentation, centered on the sounds and choreographies of *zouk*, *soukous*, *coladeira* and *semba*. Following the popularity and consumption of African *zouk* styles in clubs and private socialities throughout the 1980s, the term *kizomba* became a market label for a burgeoning production of recorded *zouk* styles, connecting musicians, dancers and public in the countries of Lusophone Africa and in the diaspora. Throughout the 1990s Portuguese record companies that normally produced commercially successful Portuguese romantic songs, such as Discossete and Vidisco, as well as the Lisbon-based Cabo Verdean music editor Zé Orlando, released cassettes and CDs of *kizomba* artists covering the expanding music market of Lusophone African communities in Portugal, France, the Netherlands and African countries. In the first years of the twenty-first century, with music consumers enjoying open access to sound files downloadable from the Internet, Zé Orlando/Sons d'África and other small record companies operating between Cabo Verde and the Cabo Verdean diaspora in Europe began commodifying *kizomba* through commercial DVDs circulating in Europe and in the Lusophone African countries. Video clips of the main *kizomba* artists depicting romantic plots and presenting extensive dance scenes became as highly consumed as the recorded sound.

The styles encompassed by the term *kizomba* have had complex histories of circulation in Europe. Whereas Cabo Verdean *zouk* styles began to be produced amid a young generation of Cabo Verdean migrants and descendants of diasporas in the Netherlands not entirely identified with the national genres (which they connoted with older generations) (Hoffman 2008), the production of *kizomba* by other Lusophone Africans was mainly based throughout the 1980s and 1990s in the Greater Lisbon area, the main destiny of Lusophone African migrations and a context with its own established networks of African music production and mediation. Although the Angolan word *kizomba* has been employed among Lusophone Africans and Portuguese to denote a set of creative processes and socialities that depart from *zouk*'s sounds and dance movements, each of the African diasporas has its own music and dance categories. Like *kizomba*, the Cabo Verdean terms *cola-zouk*, *cabo-zouk* and *cabo-love* claim the distinctiveness of national appropriations, stylistic differences from Caribbean *zouk* and complex processes of cultural synthesis involving musical and choreographic materials from Caribbean *zouk* and African national or regional genres.

Musically, *kizomba* is a duple meter dance song characterized by a basic *ostinato* rhythmic pattern (see Example 1), the predominant timbre and texture of multiple synthesized sounds and the dynamics between soloist and chorus voices. *Kizomba* shares the main two-beat rhythmic pattern of Caribbean *zouk*, whose dance groove lies in the accentuation of the strong beat and the ambivalence of the syncopated second beat. The songs develop around short melodic phrases, explored by the singers through high-pitched registers and timbre effects, sometimes whispered, conferring a confidential and intimate character to the vocal part. The lyrics express themes of heterosexual romantic love, seduction and sexuality. While Angolan and Mozambican performers mostly sing in Portuguese and, more rarely, in other national languages, singers from Cabo Verde, Guinea-Bissau and São Tomé use different variants of Creole language.

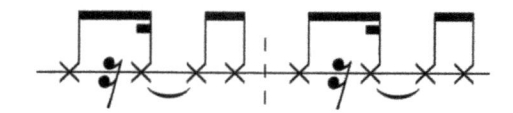

Example 1: *Kizomba* rim shot

The styles encompassed by the term *kizomba* also include other musical elements analyzed by ethnomusicologist Jocelyne Guilbault (1993) in her thoroughgoing study of Caribbean *zouk*: a style of arrangement based on the interaction of rhythmic and melodic patterns; melodic bass lines; the rhythmic and harmonic support of the guitar, also playing melodic riffs and, occasionally, solos; and short melodies of the chorus which, besides adding 'presence to the song and color and expression to the whole arrangement' (Guilbault 1993, 139), reproduce call-and-response patterns with the soloist singer and encourage listeners to interact vocally with the song (ibid., 139–40). Since the late 1990s, vocal styles, digital timbres and rhythmic elements from hip-hop and international mainstream pop styles have also been significant influences on *kizomba*'s music producers and singers.

Kizomba's couple dance is viewed as a romantic and sensual expression embodying deep cultural values and emotions. The dancers stay embraced with their torsos and waists touching each other. The man's left arm curves slightly to hold the woman's right hand. The woman's left arm rests on the top of the man's back. The man's right hand, in turn, is placed on the woman's lower back. While their legs are in tension and their feet remain close to the ground, their hips and torsos must stay relaxed in order to express lightness, grace, creativity and sensuality. *Kizomba*'s dance is based upon different basic sets of short steps (*passadas*) that range from simple moves to highly elaborate ones. The different *passadas* guide the couple's moves and differently accentuate and subdivide the duple meter of the song. This movement vocabulary frames the sensibility and creativity of each dancer.

Although composing fast-tempo *zouk* songs was common throughout the 1980s and 1990s (especially through the pioneering Netherlands-based Cabo Verdean group Livity, and singers Jorge Neto and Gil Semedo), the slow-tempo and romantic *zouk love* songs became predominant within *kizomba* styles. This change was also gradually accompanied by the transition from *zouk* recorded by musical groups (including bass, drums, electric guitar and synthesizers) to digital styles. Among the musicians who stood out in the transnational scene of *kizomba* production were the groups Cabo Verde Show, Livity, Splash!, the producers Kim Alves and Dabs Lopes, and the singers Jorge Neto, Grace Évora, Kino Cabral, Gil Semedo, Beto Dias, Edson Dany and the Kora All African Music Award winner for 'female artist' (2003) Suzanna Lubrano (all Cabo Verdeans or descendants of the Cabo Verdean diaspora, mostly living in Europe, particularly in France and the Netherlands); Afra Sound Stars, SOS, Eduardo Paim, Paulo Flores, Ruca Van-Dunem and Irmãos Verdades (Angola); Justino Delgado (Guinea-Bissau); and Camilo Domingos (São Tomé and Principe).

Since *kizomba* styles became popular among young generations of Lusophone Africans and the descendants of diaspora in the 1980s, they have been considered by musicians, intellectuals and agents of cultural politics as a threat to national genres and musicianship in Lusophone African countries. Despite the controversy, *zouk* has had a considerable impact on the performance of dance genres such as Angolan *semba*, Cabo Verdean *coladeira* and Guinean *ngumbé*, particularly on their rhythmic patterns and grooves and recent adoption of synthesized sounds. These stylistic intersections are patent in *cola-zouk*, a style of *coladeira* whose rhythmic configuration has been compared to *zouk*'s rhythmic foundation, while upholding *coladera*'s melodic style and historical tradition of social critique.

Since about 2010 *kizomba*'s dance has sparked great interest beyond Lusophone African communities. This circulation, which started in the Greater Lisbon area in the 1990s when Portuguese dancers increasingly sought to learn to dance *kizomba*, reached countries such as Spain, France, Germany, Estonia, Brazil, Australia and Israel. *Kizomba*'s dance began to be taught in dance academies and to be part of international ballroom dance competitions and African dance festivals. International recognition of *kizomba*'s music and dance led Angolan audiences, musicians and dancers to claim it as an important national contribution to the world's heritage of dancing cultures, a phenomenon that is stressed in the documentary film *A Minha Banda e Eu* (2011). This public discourse seems to be displacing the previous opposition between national and international cultural expressions, represented, in the case of Angola, by *semba* and *kizomba*. In the twenty-first-century, despite public debates, *kizomba* styles are the main popular musics enjoyed and danced by different generations of Lusophone Africans and their descendants in public and private socialities that involve recorded music.

Bibliography

Bernardo, Viegas de Sousa, and Lopes Rodrigues, Carlos Alberto. 1995. *O fenómeno das discotecas africanas: Espaços, representações e estratégias* [The Phenomenon of African Discos: Spaces, Representations and Strategies]. Seminário de Investigação Sociológica 1994–1995. Lisbon: Universidade Nova de Lisboa, Faculdade de Ciências Sociais e Humanas, Departamento de Sociologia.

Cidra, Rui. 2010a. 'Kizomba.' In *Enciclopédia da música em Portugal no século XX: C–L* [Encyclopedia of Music in Portugal in the Twentieth Century, C–L], ed. Salwa Castelo-Branco. Lisbon: Círculo de Leitores/ Temas e Debates, 674.

Cidra, Rui. 2010b. 'Zouk.' In *Enciclopédia da música em Portugal no século XX: P–Z* [Encyclopedia of Music in Portugal in the Twentieth Century, P–Z], ed. Salwa Castelo-Branco. Lisbon: Círculo de Leitores/ Temas e Debates, 1357–9.

Guilbault, Jocelyne. 1993. *Zouk: World Music in the West Indies*. Chicago: University of Chicago Press.

Hoffman, JoAnne. 2008. 'Diasporic Networks, Political Change, and the Growth of Cabo-Zouk

Music.' In *Transnational Archipelago: Perspectives on Cabo Verdean Migration and Diaspora*, eds. Luís Batalha and Jorgen Carling. Amsterdam: University of Amsterdam Press, 205–20.

Moorman, Marissa. 2008. *Intonations: A Social History of Music and Nation in Luanda, Angola, from 1945 to Recent Times*. Athens, Ohio: Ohio University Press.

Prata, Vladimir. 2011. 'Eduardo Paim "Sou o precursor da kizomba"' [Eduardo Paim 'I am the precursor of *kizomba*'], *O País*, 17 May 2011. Online at: *Angola, Debates & Ideas* http://angodebates.blogspot.pt/2011/05/eduardo-paim-sou-o-precursor-da-kizomba.html (accessed 7 June 2017).

Discography

Dany, Edson. *Merece*. Cabo Verde Productions, MMC CV *0011*. *2003*: Netherlands and Cabo Verde.

Domingos, Camilo. *Nada a ver*. Sonovox Sono 11-302-2. *1994*: Portugal.

Flores, Paulo. *Kapuete Kamundanda*. Carlos Flores. *1989*: Portugal.

Flores, Paulo. *Sassasa*. Disconorte LP 5019. *1990*: Portugal.

Flores, Paulo. *Thunda Mu Njilla*. Discossete ADD CD 815872. *1992*: Portugal.

Flores, Paulo. *Brincadeira tem hora e a hora é essa*. Discossete DDD CD 944972. *1993*: Portugal.

Gil & Perfects. *Separadu*. Sons d'África SPA 94. *1994*: Portugal.

Gil & Perfects. *Verdade*. Giva Productions GIVA 9601. *1998*: Portugal.

Livity. *Harmonia*. Som D'África 029/ 91. *1991*: Portugal.

Lubrano, Suzanna. *Tudo pa Bo*. Kings Records. *2003*: n.p.

Lubrano, Suzanna. *Saida*. Mass Appeal Music. *2008*: USA.

Lubrano, Suzanna. *Festa Mascarado*. Mass Appeal Music MAS CD 7E. *2009*: USA.

Neto, Jorge. *Dia Diferenti*. Sons d'África. *2003*: Portugal.

Neto, Jorge. *Dja Ca Da*. Sons d'África. *2005*: Portugal.

Paim, Eduardo. *Luanda Minha Banda*. Zé Orlando 031/91. *1991*: Portugal.

Paim, Eduardo. *Do Kaiaia*. Zé Orlando LP 002. *1992*: Portugal.

Paim, Eduardo. *Kambuengo*. Vidisco 11.80. 2008. *1993*: Portugal.

Van-Dunem, Ruca, and Abreu, Ricardo. *Sem Kigila*. Zé Orlando LP 0392. *1992*: Portugal.

Filmography

A Minha Banda e Eu, dirs. Inês Gonçalves and Kiluanje Liberdade. *2011*. Portugal. 90 mins. Documentary.

YouTube

Paim, Eduardo. 2014. 'Entrevista com Eduardo Paim sobre a Kizomba' ['Interview with Eduardo Paim on Kizomba.' *RDP África*, 26 November. Online at: https://www.youtube.com/watch?v=j2GRCyIxlfw; https://www.youtube.com/watch?v=TWgYUE1XjG8 (both accessed 6 September 2017).

RUI CIDRA

Konkoma

Konkoma (or *konkomba*) was the earliest and most widespread of a number of early twentieth-century music styles played by southern Ghanaian processional/marching groups that were influenced by late-nineteenth-century local *adaha* highlife brass-band music. Other *adaha*-influenced styles were the Ga *kolomashie* and *kainka*, which were popular with the Akan Ga and Ewe ethnic groups. According to Ghanaian arts and media figure Beattie Casely-Hayford and theater arts academic K.N. Bame, *konkoma* highlife became popular in southern Ghana during the 1930s and 1940s in towns and villages that could not afford expensive brass instruments and made do instead with marching groups that did away with imported instruments (personal communication with the author, 1987 and 1990). Instead, *konkoma* groups employed voices and local instruments such as the double cowbell, the finger bell, the *awaasa* rattles and three handheld rectangular *konkoma* frame drums: the alto, tenor (*tantaba*) and bass (bass-*kese*). *Konkoma* groups also employed the *pati* (modeled on a European military side-drum), occasionally a bugle and, according to Kwaa Mensah (cited in Collins 1985, 16), sometimes a large regimental bass-drum. *Konkoma* emerged around 1930 and Sackey (1989) locates its origin in the Fanti coastal town of Mumford (also known as Dwanba).

According to Kwaa Mensah (cited in Collins 1985, 16 and 1994, 4) *konkoma* groups played the same local proto-highlife and imported music as did their *adaha* brass-band counterparts: namely, local Akan *adesim*,

Ashanti 'blues' and *dagomba* guitar songs, as well as Western *rumbas*, foxtrots, bumps-a-daisy, *sambas* and *la congas*. Like *adaha* bands, *konkoma* parades were led by a baton-throwing conductor and often featured Western-style sychronized marching, using the European military-type 'oom pah' 4/4 tempo that emphasizes the first and third beat of the measure. However, *konkoma* groups also marched in Fanti non-synchronized style and, after parading through town, ended at a location where they performed ring dances in typical African fashion (in syncopated time and with the musicians forming a semicircle inside which the dancers executed solo, ring and team dances).

Also like the *adaha* bands, *konkoma* performers wore uniforms modeled after those of the military, police, fire-brigade and railway workers. These were checked shirts, shorts with multiple pockets for silk handkerchiefs and peaked caps with tassels of varying colors, depending on the particular *konkoma* group, for these groups were highly competitive. This competitiveness was also reflected in the dancing itself; the performers inside the dance circle tried to knock each other down. Indeed, according to A.M. Opoku (personal communication, 1990) the word 'konkoma' is a nonsense word and is part of the Akan expression 'me twa konkoma me bo fum' (I cut *konkoma* and fall down), which was used when the dancers purposely bumped into each other and fell down on the phrase 'ko' of 'konkoma.'

Sackey (1989) and Opoku (personal communication, 1990) affirm that *konkoma* was created by 'school dropouts' and 'ruffian boys' and this connection between *konkoma* and the youthful generation of the times suggests that it was not simply an inexpensive imitation of local brass-band music, but rather that it evolved through Westernizing influences that were absorbed into the Akan recreational music of the 1930s generational age-sets. The association of *konkoma* with youth, together with its military-type marching, is probably the reason why the British colonial government adopted *konkoma* songs for recruiting during World War II. Opoku (1966) recalls a *konkoma* route-march song that translates from Twi as 'we are now in uniform Nana Afuri [i.e., Afuri-Atta], come let's go, Nana we have got soldier work.' Sackey (1989, 98) and Cobbina (1972) refer to anti-German Axis *konkoma* songs. Even in 2013 the Ghanaian army and police used *konkoma* route-marches sung in Akan, along with the earlier tradition of employing Hausa songs (a result of local soldiers being initially recruited into the nineteenth-century British colonial army from northern Ghana).

Whether viewed as an indigenized poor man's version of brass bands, or as a continuation, albeit Westernized, of youthful Akan recreational music, *konkoma* had a profound impact on popular and neo-traditional music. *Konkoma* drums were used by 1940s highlife guitar bands (including Appiah Adjekum's [see Collins 1985, 23 or 1994, 13]) and the genre influenced several forms of postwar recreational music such as Akan *akyewa* or *aways* (Opoku 1966, 25) and Ewe *borborbor* music.

Konkoma spread even further afield and became popular in western Nigeria beginning in the late 1930s. The Nigerian musician Segun Bucknor stated in 1975 that *konkoma* was a low-class informal music that came from Ghana to Lagos in the 1930s and was similar to 'what you would now call highlife, but without the guitar.' It was played, he said, by 'labourers or carpenters who would form a group to play at naming ceremonies for some few drinks' (cited in Collins 1985, 137). He went on to say that this dance step was later called *agidigbo*, a Yorùbá recreational music that features large lamellophones. The Nigerian highlife dance band musician Victor Olaiya stated in 1974 (personal communication with the author) that prior to the dance band variety of highlife introduced to Nigeria in the early 1950s by E.T. Mensah's Tempos there was an earlier craze for the less prestigious *konkoma* highlife. These comments regarding *konkoma* are also confirmed in various writings on Nigerian popular performance. The Nigerian musicologists Alaja-Browne (1985, 64) and Ajayi Thomas (1992) both state that *konkoma* came from Ghana, probably via Togo in the late 1930s and 1940s, brought by Ewe and Fanti migrants. Likewise Chris Waterman (1990, 85) notes that *konkoma* was introduced to Lagos by Ewe and Fanti migrants and also mentions that this music influenced Yorùbá *agidigbo* lamellophone music in the 1940s. For instance, one of the principal pioneers of *agidigbo* music, Adeolu Akinsanya and his Rancho Boys, was influenced by *konkoma*. Waterman (ibid.) also goes on to say that both *konkoma* and *agidigbo* music influenced Yorùbá *jùjú* guitar band music in the 1950s. Further evidence of the importance of *konkoma* in western Nigeria is that the Nigerian dramatist Jeyifo (1984, Preface) refers to *konkoma* as a form of 'low' highlife used at his school concerts in Ibadan in the early 1950s. Finally, regarding the impact of *konkoma* in Nigeria, in 2012, Dr. Charles Onomudo Aluede (of Ambrose Alli University) observed that many decades earlier *konkoma* had influenced the Bini neo-traditional *odide* music of Edo State that was still played in the early twenty-first century (personal communication with the author).

Despite its importance, *konkoma* was held in such low esteem by educated and urbane Ghanaians that it was never commercially recorded, unlike the highlife music of guitar bands, dance orchestras and dance bands of the 1930s to 1950s. Indeed, by the 1960s *konkoma* had largely died out in the country of its birth. However, in the early twenty-first century there were still pockets where *konkoma* was played by elderly people in certain parts of the Volta Region in the southeastern part of the country. For instance, Senyoh Adzei (a graduate student at the University of Ghana Music Department) reported that there was such a group in Tsito Awudome, where *konkoma* was introduced by the local man Dzikum Kwesi in 1947, after he returned from working as a fisherman in Cape Coast for seven years (personal communication with the author).

Bibliography

Alaja-Browne, Afolabi. 1985. *Juju Music: A Study of Its Social History and Style*. Unpublished Ph.D. dissertation, University of Pittsburgh.

Cobbina, F. 1972. *Konkoma Music and Dance*. Diploma thesis, Dance Department, University of Ghana.

Collins, E. John. 1985. *Music Makers of West Africa*. Washington DC: Three Continents Press.

Collins, E. John. 1994. *The Ghanaian Concert Party: African Popular Entertainment at the Crossroads*. Unpublished Ph.D. dissertation, SUNY Buffalo.

Jeyifo, Biofun. 1984. *The Yoruba Popular Travelling Theatre of Nigeria*. Lagos: Nigeria Magazine.

Opoku, A. M. 1966. 'Choreography and the African Dance.' *African Research Review, University of Ghana African Studies Journal* 3(1): 53–9.

Sackey, Chrys Kwesi, 1989. *Konkoma: A Musical Form of Fanti Young Fishermen in the 1940s and 1950s in Ghana, West Africa.'* Mainzer Ethnologische Arbeiten, Bd. 8. Berlin: Dietrich Reimer Verlag.

Thomas, Ajayi. 1992. *History of Juju Music*. New York: Thomas Organisation.

Waterman, Christopher A. 1990. *Jùjú: A Social History and Ethnography of an African Popular Music*. Chicago: University of Chicago Press.

Personal Communications with the Author
Adzei, Senyoh, n.d.
Bame, K. N., 1990.
Casely-Hayford, Beattie, 1987.
Olaiya, Victor, 1974.
Opoku, A. M., 1990.

E. JOHN COLLINS

Koriana le Moropa

The Basotho people from Lesotho have been migrating to work in South Africa since the 1820s. Out of the experience of generations of labor migration came a number of popular Basotho musical styles. Most prominent among these are declamatory songs accompanied by the piano accordion and drum (*koriana* is the Sesotho word for piano accordion; *moropa* means drum) that developed in the small informal taverns and speakeasies found in shack settlements on the outskirts of the mine compounds or in urban black shantytowns and ghettos in South Africa, rather than in Lesotho itself. The accompanying songs, often sung vigorously by chanteuses who doubled as barmaids, embroider the infectious swing of the dance rhythms with lyrical and moving depictions of the hardships of Basotho life. These *koriana le moropa* songs consist of a declamatory extemporized solo, performed antiphonally with a backing choral refrain, accompanied by a concertina or piano accordion and a drum.

Returning home, migrants enjoyed performing new dances and instrumental music learned at the workplace, bringing wider regional influences to bear on village performance styles. Their 'trade-store' instruments achieved such wide distribution that by the early 1900s guitars, concertinas, autoharps and harmonicas came to be considered fully 'traditional' and part of the *Sesotho* (indigenous) as opposed to *Sekhooa* (Western) musical culture. Purists argue that melodic lines and polyrhythms are less clearly articulated and tonal contrasts less subtle on Western instruments than they are on the more delicate gourd resonated bows of precolonial times. The identification of Western instruments with urban life and their flexibility both for creating and performing neo-traditional and syncretic styles and for providing lively music for dances, however, made their adoption inevitable. The old trade-store instruments also gave way in their turn, and Basotho musicians point out that their favorite instrument since the 1960s, the piano accordion, not only provides a larger sound but also allows for greater melodic and tonal variety and solo improvisation than does the concertina, and is far more portable than the once-beloved pedal organ.

During the early 1960s the *koriana* appeared in South African music stores and was adopted by Basotho instrumentalists in the mining compounds and speakeasies. The instrument enabled its most serious exponents to make live performance a full-time profession. The musicians could sling the instrument over their backs and tour by bus and foot from the black townships of urban South Africa to the remotest village bars (*bara*) in Lesotho. Ensembles were completed by the addition of a *moropa* constructed of a 20-liter tar tin topped with a piece of tire inner-tubing, above which was fastened a row of bottlecaps or metal jangles (*manyenenyene*) to provide a jingling beat that alternated with the thump on stretched rubber of drumsticks made from slices of tire. Male *koriana le moropa* instrumentalists played the accompaniment for women who sang improvised lyrics about their troubles in life and danced the sexy *famo*.

By the 1970s *koriana le moropa* and *famo* dancers and singers were everywhere that working-class Basotho gathered for home-brewed drink and entertainment. What was needed to turn this neighborhood barrelhouse revelry into a Basotho national popular music was the emergence of major recording personalities among composer/singers and accordionists. The major recording companies in South Africa, in particular EMI, saw a ready market for this characteristically Basotho migrants' music, and producers such as EMI's Solly Khoza brought them into their studios in Steeldale, Johannesburg.

Among the first and most enduring of these professional recording ensembles was Tau ea Matskeha ('Lion of Matsekha,' a district in northern Lesotho). Both the accordionist Forere Motloheloa and the vocalist/composer Apollo Ntabanyane acquired their performing skills and experience at the mines during the 1970s, where they entertained their fellow workers in their spare time and played in taverns for extra cash. The group's early albums, such as *Ha-Peete Kea Falla* (Peete's Place I'm Quitting, 1981) were phenomenally successful, and their name became synonymous with the form itself, so that this type of music was often called 'Tau ea Matsekha.' Ntabanyane, an athletically comic stage dancer as well as vocalist/composer, left to lead his own group. In 1974 he had himself proclaimed 'King of Famo Music' at a major concert at Maseru's Airport Hotel, an occasion attended by Her Majesty Queen 'MaMohato of Lesotho herself.

Among women, the acknowledged pioneer of the *famo* songs is 'Malitaba, who achieved wide recognition after she was recorded and played on Radio Sesotho in South Africa starting in the early 1960s. For three decades between 1970 and 2000 the long-time champion was indisputably Puseletso Seema. The success of her recordings evoked some jealousy and gentle satire among Lesotho's tavern singers, including Thakane Mahlasi, who sang in her *famo* entitled 'Peka' (a town in northern Lesotho): 'Puseletso, little girl of Seema, Her short stature is hers by nature; Her light complexion is self-made, [with skin lightening creams] Oh girl! …' In the typical women's *koriana le moropa* song 'Peka,' Thakane Mahlasi's vocals conform to the rhythm of the accordion and drum, since *famo* songs are organized both rhythmically and tonally by their instrumental accompaniment. As in traditional southern Bantu song, the soloist follows the principle of 'staggered entry,' overlapping her breath groups with the phrase cycle of the chorus, which in this instance is both played on the accordion and sung by the male accordionist. Similarly, her melody is consistent with the polyphonic 'root progressions' (Rycroft 1967, 96) employed by the accordionist, although the intensity of her declamation leads to only microtonal variation within the body of a given breath group, and her tones are often pushed beyond stabilized pitch to forceful plaints shattered off the upper palate of the mouth; virtual shouts or vibratory cries.

Up until the 1990s *koriana le moropa* ranked low on educated Basotho listeners' scales of musical prestige because of its nonliterate participants, its bar-room origins, and the rather risqué dancing and lyrics that it accompanied. Since the 'African revival' spurred on by democratic elections in Lesotho in 1993 and in South Africa in 1994, however, a more populist and nostalgic indigenism has arisen among all classes of Basotho raised in Lesotho, with *koriana le moropa* serving as an identifying national musical form wherever in this wide world they may have been scattered. The identification of *koriana le moropa* with 'Sesotho' as a national music has arisen out of the need to differentiate Lesotho as a nation from South Africa, and from South African Basotho who are not from Lesotho. There are other forms of 'modern' Basotho music, such as secular and sacred choral compositions, but nothing says 'Lesotho' like the stalwart farmers' and migrants' music of *koriana le moropa*. Even educated Basotho, many of whom may not care much for this music personally and would never perform it, readily agree that *koriana le moropa* takes them back to their 'grass roots.'

Bibliography

Coplan, David B. 1988. 'Musical Understanding: The Ethno-Aaesthetics of Migrant Workers' Poetic Song in Lesotho.' *Ethnomusicology* 32(3): 337–68.

Coplan, David B. 1991. 'Fictions That Save: Migrants' Performance and Basotho National Culture.' *Cultural Anthropology* 6(2): 164–91. (Reprinted in *Rereading Cultural Anthropology*, ed. George Marcus. Durham, NC: Duke University Press, 267–95.)

Coplan, David B. 1992. *The Meaning of Sesotho*. Occasional Paper, *Journal of Research*, National University of Lesotho, No. 3: 1–55.

Coplan, David B. 1993. 'History Is Eaten Whole: Consuming Tropes in Sesotho Auriture.' *History and Theory* (special issue, History Making in Africa, supplement) 32: 80–104.

Coplan, David B. 1994. *In the Time of Cannibals: Word Music of South Africa's Basotho Migrants*. Chicago: University of Chicago Press; Johannesburg: Witwatersrand University Press.

Coplan, David B. 1995. *Lyrics of the Basotho Migrants*. (Translations of African Historical Documents. David Robinson, Series ed.) Madison, WI: University of Wisconsin Press.

Coplan, David B. 2006. '"I've Worked Longer Than I've Lived": Lesotho Migrants' Songs as Maps of Experience."' *Journal of Ethnic and Migration Studies* 32(2): 223–41.

Rycroft, David K. 1967, 'Nguni Vocal Polyphony.' *Journal of the International Folk Music Council* 19: 88–103.

Discographical Reference

Tau Ea Matsekha. *Ha-Peete Kea Falla*. EMI (South African Kwasa Records pressing) KWALP(E) 7006. *1981*: South Africa.

Discography

Africa Today! Best of Contemporary Sotho Folk Music. ARC Music 1577. *2000*: UK.

Best of Lesotho Music Center Compilation. Talk About It Music. *2009*: Lesotho.

Chakela, Mosotho. *Manka le Phallang* 1. Shear Records. *1999*: South Africa.

Ntabanyane, Apollo. *The Best of Apollo Ntabanyane*. Cool Spot Music. *1999*: South Africa.

Ntabanyane, Apollo. *Golden Hits, vol. 2*. Cool Spot Music. *1994*: South Africa.

Puseletso Seema and Tau Ea Linare. *He O Oe Oe!* Globe Style ORB 003. *1985*: UK.

Setumo. *Mantsa Collection*. Tajane music ef7/2008/0225. *2008*: Lesotho.

Sephetho. *The Best of Sephetho, Vol 1*. Makaota Music ef7/2011/1091. *2011*: Lesotho.

DAVID B. COPLAN

Kpanlogo

Kpanlogo (pronounced PAH-loh-goh) is a drum-dance created by Ghanaian youth in the 1960s that combines traditional Ga drum-dance with elements from contemporary Ghanaian and Western popular music. The genre may be viewed as part of a succession of Ga neo-traditional recreational performance styles of the greater Accra region of Ghana. These include *gome*, a Ga version of Sierra Leone's *goombay/gumbe* drum-dance that became popular in the late nineteenth century, followed by the processional Ga *kolomashie* of the 1930s and 1940s that used local drums but was affected by colonial marching bands (thus the possible origin of the word '*kolo*,' which means colonial and *mashie*, which means march). These genres were followed in the 1950s by the guitar/hand-piano/percussion '*something*' music genre of Ga fishermen and by *oge* drumming, introduced to Accra by visiting Liberian Kru seamen.

The *kpanlogo* drum-dance was invented around 1962 by Otoo Lincoln, Okule Foes, Ayitey Sugar, Frankie Lane and other youth of the Bukom fishermen's area of Accra. According to Otoo Lincoln the name *kpanlogo* comes from a traditional Ga *adesa*, or folk-story, told to him by his grandfather in 1956 about three Ga princesses called Kpanlogo, Mma Mma and Alogodzan. Lincoln put this story to music and then went on to write other early *kpanlogo* compositions including 'ABC Kpanlogo' and 'Ayinye Momobiye.' The dances were in local freestyle mode but dance moves from imported rock 'n' roll and the twist were also incorporated, for these Bukom 'area boys' (in the local parlance, young men who are part of local culture and community life) were also members of the Black Eagles rock 'n' roll dance club. Sons of local Ga fishermen and other workers, they were both familiar with traditional drumming and fascinated by the Western pop music being introduced though films and records. Using local hand-drums, bells and rattles they combined the above-mentioned local Ga recreational drumming styles with 4/4 time highlife bell or *clave* patterns. Kpanlogo was performed mainly on the streets, for the 'outdooring' (birth ceremonies) of children, at weddings and in dance clubs that catered to urban youth. This new style of street-music became so popular with the Accra youth that by the mid-1960s there were at least 50 *kpanlogo* groups operating in Accra.

Because of the exaggerated hip movements of the *kpanlogo* dance, borrowed from rock 'n' roll and the 'twist' movements of 'Elvis the Pelvis' and Chubby Checker, the older generation initially opposed this new-fangled version of a traditional genre, claiming it was too sexually suggestive. Due to this opposition, no recordings were made in this early stage. Otoo Lincoln stated that the director of the Ghana Arts Council 'wanted to spoil the name of *kpanlogo*. ... and said my dance was no good as one of the beats in the dance makes the body move in an indecent way' (Collins 1992, 45). The Ga musician Jones Attuquayefio noted in the mid-1970s that some early *kpanlogo* performers were even arrested by the police, their drums seized, with some of the musicians caned and put in cells for a few days (personal communication with the author). Besides containing what the older generation considered as erotic movements, another reason for this harassment, says Attuquayefio, was that early *kpanlogo* (and indeed rock 'n' roll) was popular with the fashionably dressed young 'Tokyo Joes,' with their distinct pompadour haircuts, drainpipe-style trousers and winklepicker shoes. The Tokyo Joes were Ga supporters and 'action troops' of Dr. Busia's United Party which opposed the one-party rule of President Nkrumah's Convention Peoples Party. These rough political activists from the Bukom area used *kpanlogo* rhythms to accompany their anti-Nkrumah songs. Another factor contributing to the initial harassment of *kpanlogo* groups may have been that the content of the short street dance-dramas that accompany *kpanlogo* sessions was sometimes antiestablishment. A specific example of such a dance-drama that took place later in the early 1970s was one presented by the *kpanlogo* group of Frank Lane (the dancer for Otoo Lincoln's original *kpanlogo* group) about a drunken government health inspector trying to summon some street sellers to court for not erecting fly-proof netting over their foodstuffs.

As a result of the friction between Ga youth and some older members of the Accra public, a number of displays of this new traditional music were organized in the mid-1960s to demonstrate its respectability. The most important was one held in 1965 at Black Star (now called Independence) Square in Accra where Mr. G.W. Amarteifio and other members of President Nkrumah's CPP government who were present as arbitrators endorsed this percussion-backed dance music as genuine 'cultural' music. As a result *kpanlogo* moved from the Accra streets onto the stages of national and university dance companies. In fact, by the early 1970s *kpanlogo* was endorsed by Ga elders, the Arts Council and the general Ghanaian public as an acceptable form of traditional or 'cultural' music. Furthermore, *kpanlogo* was internationalized in the early 1970s when Mustapha Tettey Addy and Obo Addy's Obuade group began releasing a string of records, the most famous being *Kpanlogo Party*, released by the British record label Tangent Records in 1973. In 1983 the original *kpanlogo* pioneers appeared in a seven-part Channel Four television series on black music called *Repercussions* (produced by Third Eye).

In the early twenty-first-century *kpanlogo* drum-dance music was an important component of the Ghanaian music scene. It was popular with traditional Ga performance groups that played local ceremonies and also with stage-oriented folkloric groups such as Wulomei (or the Sensational Wulomei), Ebaahi Sounds and Hewale Sounds that performed for the numerous tourists and world music fans who visited Ghana. *Kpanlogo* rhythms in electronic form were also incorporated into local Ghanaian rap known as hiplife (i.e., hip-hop highlife). At first, in the mid-1990s, hiplife drew mainly on American hip-hop beats, but the use of local rhythms, including those of *kpanlogo*, became more prominent beginning in the mid-2000s with the rise of the '*djama*' hiplife style (pronounced *jama* – the Ga word for an animated dance). This led to the craze for the *azonto* dance that began around 2010 and accompanied hiplife and other current forms of Ghanaian technopop. The origin of the *azonto* dance was the young people of Accra, including those of the Bukom area, and some of its moves and gestures were drawn from the *kpanlogo* dance.

Bibliography

Collins, E. John. 1983. 'The Man Who Made Traditional Music.' *West Africa*, 19–26 December: 2946.

Collins, E. John. 1992. *West African Pop Roots*. Philadelphia: Temple University Press.

Collins, E. John. 1996. *Highlife Time*. Accra: Anansesem Press.

Collins, E. John 2002. 'The Generational Factor in Ghanaian Music: Concert Parties, Highlife, Simpa, Kpanlogo and Gospel.' In *Playing With Identities in the Contemporary Music of Africa*, eds. M. Palmberg and A. Kirkegaard. Apo, Finland: Nordic African Institute/Sibelius Museum, 60–74.

Collins, E. John. 2005. 'The Decolonisation of Ghanaian Popular Entertainment.' In *Urbanization and African Cultures*, eds. Toyin Falola and Steven Salm. Durham, NC: Carolina Academic Press, 119–37.

Collins, E. John. 2007. 'The Pan-African Goombay Drum-Dance: Its Ramifications and Development in Ghana.' *Legon Journal of the Humanities* 18: 179–200.

Haydon, Geoffrey, and Marks, Dennis, eds. 1985. *Repercussions: A Celebration of African-American Music*. London: Century Publishing.

Nketia, J. H. Kwabena. 1958. 'Traditional Music of the Ga People.' *African Music* 2(1): 212–17.

Odote, Irene. 1991. 'External Influences on Ga Society and Culture.' *Research Review* 7(1&2): 61–7.

Salm, Steve. 2003. *The Bukom Boys: Subcultures and Identity Transformation in Accra Ghana*. Unpublished Ph.D Dissertation, University of Texas, Austin.

Personal Communication with the Author
Attuquayefio, Jones, mid-1970s.

Discographical Reference
Addy, Mustapha Tettey. *Kpanlogo Party*. Tangent Records TGS 115. *1973*: UK.

Discography
Addy, Mustapha Tettey. *Come and Drum*. Weltwunder Records101-1. *1994*: Germany.

Addy, Mustapha Tettey. *Smart Boys*. Weltwunder Records CD 117-2. *2006*: Germany.

Addy, Mustapha Tettey. *Secret Rhythms*. Weltwunder Records CD 113-2. *2007*: Germany.

Ebaahi Sounds. *Oye Tsei Lo*. Oshuma Sounds. *1995*: Ghana.

Hewale Sounds. *Trema*. Cowry Shell. *2005*: Ghana.

Wulomei. *Sani masye* eko. (Nii Tei Ashitey and the Sensational Wulomei.) Tropic Vibe Records. No number. *2001*: USA.

Wulomei. *Wulomei Returns*. Creative Storm Production. *2006*: Ghana.

Filmography
Repercussions: A Celebration of African-American Music, dirs Dennis Marks and Geoffrey Haydon. 1983. UK. 7-part television documentary (Channel 4/Third Eye Productions).

E. JOHN COLLINS

Kuduro

Kuduro (pronounced ku-'du-ru) is a genre of popular dance music from Luanda, the capital of Angola. It first emerged in the 1990s and has remained popular into the second decade of the twenty-first century. In the 1980s Angolan urban youth danced to house music, techno and Angolan rhythms including *semba* and *kizomba*, as well as a local hybrid of those rhythms called 'batida,' meaning 'beat.' This local electronic dance music came to be known as *kuduro*, initially the name of a dance move, in the mid-1990s. According to the genre's most common origin story, dancer and DJ Tony Amado invented *kuduro* dancing after watching the 1989 film *Kickboxer*, starring Jean-Claude van Damme. In one scene, van Damme's character combined fighting with dancing. Amado's new moves joined those of van Damme with Angolan Carnival dances and breakdancing. The word *kuduro* is a *portmanteau* of the Portuguese words *cu* (ass) and *duro* (hard), literally meaning 'hard ass.' The word can also be understood to mean 'hard surroundings,' 'in hard times,' or 'in a hard place,' as the prefix *ku* is the locative case in the Kimbundu language.

Kuduro music combines *kizomba*, *semba* and Angolan *zouk* with *soca* and electronic dance music, such as house and techno. Its tempo is typically between 130 and 140 bpm. MCs, rapping in either Portuguese or Calão, a Portuguese/Kimbundo pidgin, typically rap in half time over the music's fast tempo. *Kuduro* lyrics tend to be apolitical and often concern dancing and sexuality.

There have been three generations of *kuduro*, each with its own characteristics and locus of production. The first generation, based in both Luanda and Lisbon, was largely the domain of producers with access to recording studios. In the second generation, *kuduro* producers adopted beat-making software such as FL Studio, formerly known as Fruity Loops, democratizing the genre by allowing it to be produced mostly in home studios. The third generation is marked by greater international collaboration and a growing international audience.

Many *kuduro* dance moves imitate movements associated with war, such as crawling on the ground, convulsing, falling backward as if hit by a bullet, dancing on one leg as if the other leg were lost in a land mine, and so on. In addition, many *kuduro* dancers are themselves disabled, victims of land mine injuries, disease and other consequences of Angola's 27-year civil war.

Early *kuduro* recordings were disseminated on cassette to be played on sound systems in buses called *candongeiros* that park on street corners and circulate Luanda's *musekes* (or *musseques*), the city's unpaved neighborhoods. The music can also be heard in Luanda's upscale nightclubs, on television programs including DJ Sebem's *Sempre a Subir*, and online. Since its early days, *kuduro* has been produced by DJs in both Luanda and Lisbon, and Portugal-based *kuduro* groups Batida and Buraka Som Sistema popularized the genre internationally. Between 2010 and 2013 the son of Angola's president José dos Santos promoted *kuduro* culture in the United States and Europe through two consecutive advertising campaigns, 'I Love Kuduro' and 'Os Kuduristas.'

Bibliography

Alisch, Stefanie, and Seigert, Nadine. 2011. *Angolanidade Revisited: Kuduro*. Norient. Online at: http://norient.com/academic/kuduro (accessed 6 September 2017).

Alisch, Stefanie, and Seigert, Nadine. 2013. 'Grooving on Broken: Dancing War Trauma in Angolan Kuduro.' In *Art and Trauma in Africa: Representations of Reconciliation in Music, Visual Arts, Literature and Film*, eds. Lizelle Bisschoff and Stefanie Van de Peer. London: I.B.Tauris, 50–68.

Moorman, Marissa. 2008. "'Estámos Sempre a Subir': Kuduro Music in Angola and Portugal.' Conference paper presented at *Africa in Portuguese, the Portuguese in Africa: An International Research Conference*, University of Notre Dame. Online at: https://www.scribd.com/document/337111358/Moorman-Marissa (accessed 6 September 2017).

Sheridan, Garth. 2014. 'Fruity Batidas: The Technologies and Aesthetics of Kuduro.' *Dancecult* 6(1): 83–96.

Sheridan, Garth. Forthcoming. 'Luanda and Lisbon: Kuduro and Musicking in the Diaspora.' *Hispano-Lusophone Community Media: Identity, Cultural Politics, Difference*, eds. Rosana Martins, Miguel de Barros and Ana Stela Cunha. Canon Pyon: Sean Kingston Publishing.

Discography

Batida. *Batida*. Soundway Records SNDWCD038. *2012*: UK.

Buraka Som Sistema. *Black Diamond*. Fabric/Sony BMG 88697398072. *2008*: Portugal.

Cabo Snoop. *Bluetooth*. Bizness Music / Power House. *2010*: Angola.

Dog Murras. *Bué Angolano*. Vidisco 11.80.8218. *2003*: Portugal.

Helder Rei do Kuduro. *Angola Me Leva Pais Do Futuro*. Sons d'Africa. *1995*: Angola.

Titica. *Chão*. LS Produções 53483. *2012*: Angola.

Filmography

Kickboxer, dir. Mark DiSalle and David Worth, 1989. USA. 103 mins. Feature film.

MICHAEL B. SILVERS

Kwaito

Symptomatic of the time and place of its making, and widely regarded as one of the most important forms of South African cultural innovation in the postapartheid era, *kwaito* is a popular and influential song and dance genre based on a variety of local and international sources. Rap and house music are perhaps the most obvious of these, but *kwaito*'s use of such genres is utterly distinctive and, moreover, the idiom has continued to develop in astonishingly eclectic ways. *Kwaito* first came to prominence in the wake of Nelson Mandela's release from prison in February 1990; it evolved as the music of black, urban, township youth, who danced and reveled in the freedoms and opportunities made possible by the defeat of apartheid and the first democratic elections in 1994.

History

Weary of protest and its symbolic form – the *toyi-toyi* 'marching dance,' which had been used to powerful effect in anti-apartheid street rallies – urban-based young people in the postapartheid era needed new, expressive musical symbols appropriate to the dawn of democracy. Resources were not in short supply. By the late 1980s house music had a significant presence in South Africa. One of the foundations for *kwaito* was laid when DJs began remixing house tracks, slowing the pulse to about 100 bpm and adding percussion, locally derived melodies and new lyrics. Also significant was the identification of young people with aspects of the culture and music of hip-hop, the ready availability of inexpensive, home-based, digital sound-production technology, and the fact that such resources could be put to use without formal, institutionally derived knowledge. Influences from abroad included, from the United States, rapper MC Hammer, DJs and record producers Frankie Knuckles and David Morales, and Michael Jackson remixes; and from Europe, the techno group Technotronix, the dance groups Black Box and Ace of Bass, and British soul singer Gabrielle (Allen 2004, 89). Mimicry was never the intention: for example, the imprint of hip-hop notwithstanding, *kwaito*'s lyrics are typically delivered more slowly than hip-hop's, and are intoned – chanted – rather than rapped.

Though the genre embraces substyles that have gone by such names as *guz*, *d'gong*, *isgubhu* and *swaito*, the term *kwaito*, as the encompassing name, was fixed early. It seems to have been derived from *kwaai*, an Afrikaans word normally denoting anger. On the street, however, *kwaai* has come to signify, as a term of approval, traits such as cool, bad or wicked – very likely as a consequence of the *AmaKwaito* (The Bad Ones), a notorious gang that struck fear into the hearts of Soweto residents in the 1970s and 1980s.

Record companies spurned early *kwaito*, believing that the new music was just a passing fad. So the earliest CDs were sold on the streets, or from trunks of cars. Later a number of black-owned record companies sprang up, with the specific aim of producing and marketing the music. Kalawa Jazmee, Triple 9, M'du Music, Wicked Sounds and Ghetto Ruff were among the most successful, and were led by such pioneering producers as Don Laka, Oscar 'Oskido' Mdlongwa, Christos Katsaitis, Arthur Mafokate, M'du Masilela and Gabi Le Roux. Thus emerged many of kwaito's most popular, creative and resilient performers, including Boom Shaka, Brothers of Peace, Bongo Maffin, Mafikizolo and TKZee.

The genre grew rapidly. By 1993, still operating without a major distributor, Boom Shaka managed to sell more than 40,000 units in a single year. As the decade drew to a close, approximately 1,000 new *kwaito* CDs were being released each year and sales of the most popular albums sometimes exceeded 100,000 units. Unsurprisingly, it was not long before major labels began to take interest and started recording and issuing *kwaito* discs, which they distributed along with albums released by smaller local companies.

Within ten years, *kwaito* had come to rival gospel as the country's best-selling idiom, and had established itself as a pillar of the South African recording industry. Between 1999 – when the genre's penetration of the market was at its height – and 2004, *kwaito* songs accounted for 30 percent of all hits, and 31 percent of adults considered themselves members of a collective they termed the '*kwaito* nation' (Stanley-Niaah 2007). In part, this had been made possible by a significant increase in the number of private and regional radio stations; many of these broadcast in local languages and focused on community issues. Largest and most popular of the new broadcasters was YFM. Established in Johannesburg in 1996 to cater to the musical needs of black youth, its relationship with *kwaito* was deeply symbiotic. Other media played their part, too – notably *Y* magazine (YFM's glossy offspring), and locally made movies and TV series that used *kwaito* soundtracks and performers, with narratives that sometimes involved the lifestyles and subculture of *kwaito* fans. Hailed for its freeing of the black body from the rigors of political agitation (Stephens 2000, 263) and for its embrace of the norms, opportunities and potential identities of the democratic order (Swartz 2008, 19), *kwaito* also became the first locally made music to be 'controlled by black engineers, producers and promoters' (Impey 2001, 46). Although the genre was predominantly male, even masculinist, some female performers achieved fame as *kwaito* artists and *kwaito* groups (such as the singer Lebo Mathosa and the group Ghetto Luv). Thus the genre slowly came to offer significant examples of how, against the odds, young black women could empower themselves and define new modes of postapartheid self-representation (Impey 2001, 47–8).

Yet, *kwaito*'s very success was also problematic, at least ideologically. The genre's affirmation, during its first decade, of an ethic of self-enrichment and entitlement took place within a sea of township poverty. Untroubled by conscience, this ethic chimed comfortably with official policy, particularly after 1996, when the government of the African National Congress (ANC) adopted a neoliberal, macroeconomic outlook that made possible the rapid rise of a self-obsessed and massively acquisitive new elite. 'The two issues young people are facing today,' Bongo Maffin's lead singer, Thandiswa, was reported as saying, 'are making a lot of money and making sure you don't die from all the sex you're having' (Pan 2000).

But *kwaito*'s embrace of this hedonistic and antisocial pleasure principle also unleashed serious criticisms of the genre. It was, for example, blamed for low voting figures, such as the mere 25 percent of the country's eligible youth who voted in the 2000 elections, according to figures issued by the Human Sciences Research Council (Jubasi 2000); even Thabo Mbeki, when he was president, famously referred to 'the distraction of *kwaito*' (ibid.). Conversely, some election campaigns have sought to harness *kwaito*'s popularity: they have signed up musicians both to perform at rallies and to solicit votes from young people.

Under apartheid, particular languages were associated with particular racial and ethnic groups. In the interests of coercing and differentiating group identities, languages were imposed, or at least tightly regimented. The new order changed this. Once language was allowed to be a matter of preference, spaces opened for a freer development of identities. *Kwaito*'s primary language is *iscamtho*, a township argot developed by gangs and then adopted by young men. In the new democracy, the attraction of *iscamtho* was manifold: it resisted the brutalizing 'discourses of ethnicity' (Vokwana 2007, 14) by cutting across 'all linguistic, political and ethnic barriers created in the past by the apartheid state' (Ntshangase 1995, 291), and it displayed a hoped-for superiority by signifying youthfulness, strong metropolitan identity, distance from the ordinary, and qualities of emancipation and creativity (Satyo 2008, 93–101).

Music signifies in important ways here too, of course. In *kwaito* artist Zola's appropriately named 'Ghetto Fabulous,' for example, music and words conjointly – and explicitly – reinforce affirmatory identifications with both the township ghetto (often called the 'location' during apartheid) and the newly emergent 'location' culture (*loxion kulcha*, in *kwaito* parlance). What's more, *kwaito* claims these as *home* and 'imbue[s them] with humanistic qualities of sociality' (Vokwana 2007, 15). For *kwaito* youth, however, this home is far from insular. As was already clear in the genre's founding eclecticism, its followers aspire to international connectedness – an identity both local and global, South African and cosmopolitan. Corroboration of these international aspirations is found in the number of songs written in English, as *kwaito* performers seek, with considerable success, to extend their reach to the United States, Europe, other parts of Africa and elsewhere.

Given its standing as a post-liberation idiom, it is noteworthy that *kwaito* has also tentatively facilitated the growth of postracial, or at least interracial, identities. This appears to have happened more by accident than by design. Though some white producers (particularly DJ Christos and Gabi 'Ibomvu' Le Roux) are regularly acknowledged for their role among those who helped shape *kwaito*, in its early incarnation it was an exclusively black genre. But before long its appeal became significantly multiracial. Its predominance on YFM was crucial in changing the radio station from a black to a multiracial broadcaster, its songs began to be played on stations (such as 5FM) with a largely white listenership, and performers such as Mandoza and Zola appeared at Oppikoppi and other historically white music festivals. Mandoza's songs in particular – 'Nkalakatha'

(2000) most notably – became *kwaito* hits across the 'race' spectrum; and *kwaito* songs were played at major sporting events featuring not just the national football team, but – despite their still predominantly white following – the rugby and cricket teams as well. Stylistic identifications of this kind have enormous potential. Ascriptions of 'race' tend to be fixed; but style identities – 'taste' practices, as Dolby calls them – are 'primary mechanisms through which race is produced and reproduced,' and changes in these practices can 'change the constitution of what race is, how it is expressed, and how it is lived' (Dolby 2000, 12, 17).

Motifs

For members of the '*kwaito* nation,' style does not subsist in songs alone; among its other domains it is, notably, a dress aesthetic. Basing their work on motifs used by *kwaito* musicians, young black designers or owners of fashion labels – the best known being Loxion Kulcha – have flourished. Like the music, these fashions reclaim the ghetto in order to transmute it into a statement of high, urban 'chic,' and so signify a notion of beauty at once local, global and black. Thus, for example, the 'Spotti,' a floppy sun hat, was adopted in preference to the baseball cap, and inexpensive canvas *takkies* (trainers) known as 'All Stars' become the shoes of choice. An important local influence on *kwaito* – particularly on its styles of dance and dress – has been *mapantsula*, originally a gang-based, township youth subculture whose virtuosic, all-male dance troupes became famous in the 1980s for their light-footed, highly synchronized, rapid-step routines. *Kwaito*'s dance patterns are many, are regularly invented and are often highly erotic – such as the circle dances, notorious for their sexual connotations, in which the men and women face each other, or the men dance behind the women.

Since a dedication to the pleasure principle and to capitalist consumerism were among the founding values of the genre, it is no surprise that these found direct expression in the lyrics of many *kwaito* songs, especially during the genre's first decade. Songs celebrating both ostentatious wealth and a rampant, often exploitative male sexuality were common. Typically occupying the performance foreground, male vocalists frequently gave voice to strident masculinities, using misogynist lyrics that objectified women and portrayed them as sexual playthings. But all this began to change somewhat in the new millennium. With soaring unemployment, little progress in the alleviation of poverty, rampant crime and a government in denial about the AIDS pandemic, the partying ethic began to wear thin. A more mature and socially critical voice developed within *kwaito*, and the stronger it became, the more it propelled the genre to new heights of musical and lyrical accomplishment. For example, songs by performers such as Bongo Maffin and M'du took issue with various antisocial attitudes; Boom Shaka sought to empower young women both socially and sexually by dealing with topics of concern to them; songs by Zola promoted responsible parenting and denounced sex with underage girls; and he and Trompies promoted learning and sang in support of abused women. Moreover, several leading performers took up AIDS issues, not just in their songs but also as celebrity campaigners, some singers (Mzekezeke, for instance) criticized government policy, and others (such as M'du) released powerful songs painting a bleak picture of crime and its consequences.

Style and Significance

From the point of view of musical style, *kwaito* developed significantly in, roughly, the first two decades of its existence. Though predominantly a studio product, it has also flourished in live performance and made prominent use of instruments or backing bands; women, too, have come to play a somewhat bigger musical role. In its standard format, however, gender divisions remain firmly in place: the men are in the vocal foreground, chanting alone or in groups; the women are behind them – if they are there at all – singing more melodic phrases.

But the truly signal musical development has been *kwaito*'s ever more confident incorporation and synthesis of a proliferating range of indigenous and exogenous idioms. Frequently this has involved the inclusion, within the performing group, of musicians who are masters of the incorporated idiom. The resulting hybrids are complex and diverse; they involve fusions with, for example, precolonial idioms, 'neo-traditional' styles, local popular music of the 1950s, protest music of the apartheid era, Western popular music, gospel, jazz, classical music and ethnically marked music from other parts of the globe.

Performers who have sometimes looked to so-called 'neo-traditional' idioms include M'du, who incorporated the Sotho migrant-worker idiom known as *famo* (as in his 'Dipabi' of 1999) and also donned traditional Sotho dress, and Boom Shaka, whose collaboration with Ihhashi Elimhlophe, a leading exponent of the Zulu migrant-worker music known as *maskanda*, helped create a version of *kwaito* identified as '*kwaito-maskanda*' or, more rarely, '*amaskwaito*' (as in 'Bambanani' of 2001). In contrast to such atavistically inspired hybrids, many artists have made use of idioms of more recent, and more frankly urban, provenance. Brothers of Peace, for example, incorporated the *mbaqanga* of Mahlathini and the Mahotella Queens (in 'Meropa/Pitseng Tse Kgolo' [2001]), Bongo Maffin used Miriam Makeba's 1957 hit 'Pata-pata' (in 'Makeba' [1997]), and blends by Zola ('Mzioni' [2001]), Senyaka ('Thembalami' [2001]) and others led to what is sometimes referred to as 'gospel-*kwaito*'. Given the historic involvement of jazz in South African popular music, it is no surprise that *kwaito* musicians have drawn local jazz idioms into the mix. Examples include Kabelo's 'Diepkloof' (2002); songs drawing on the music of leading jazz pianist Moses Molelekwa (such as TKZee's 'Moses' in 2001 and 'Phambili siyaya' by Brothers of Peace in 2002); Mafikizolo's manifold references to the *marabi*-jazz style of the 1940s and 1950s ('Ndihamba Nawe' of 2002, for example); Mafikizolo's use of *kwela* (a 1950s penny whistle idiom derived from *marabi*-jazz) to forge what is sometimes called '*kwaito-kwela*' (as in 'Kwela Kwela' [2003]); and jazz pianist Don Laka's '*kwaito*-jazz' or '*kwaai*-jazz' (as in 'Tlang Sekolong' [2007]).

Kwaito's stylistic expansiveness has clearly been crucial to the internationalism it aspired to and hoped to convey. The idiom has stretched to include styles, songs and recordings sourced from, or principally identified with, places elsewhere in Africa or the world. For example, both TKZee ('Fiasco' [1999]) and Bongo Maffin ('Mari ye Phepha' [1999]) have developed Latin-inflected *kwaito*; Boom Shaka has looked to the Caribbean and to recordings by Shabba Ranks (*Greats Collection: 7th Anniversary* [2001]); and Brothers of Peace has drawn *kwaito* closer to house, and thus back to one of its original sources (*Project 4* [2002]). Even Western 'classical' music – along with its performers, sometimes – has made appearances (on, for example, Bongo Maffin's 1998 release, *The Concerto*, and TKZee's album from 2001, *Guz 2001*). Elsewhere, TKZee's international sources have included Madonna, Joni Mitchell, Andrae Crouch, Lionel Ritchie, Quincy Jones, Lisa Stansfield, George Michael (with Wham!), and Dennis Edwards (of the Temptations).

Yet these musical integrations often *mean* more than internationalism alone. Remarkably, where songs give voice to social or political criticism, their critique is often focused, sharpened or deepened through techniques involving musical hybridity. In such instances, 'foreign' musical elements (as we might call them) seem to have been imported into *kwaito* songs for their normative significance; their combinations with *kwaito* thus become symbolic enactments of core aspects of the songs. Because of the associations carried from their home domains, these imported 'vehicles of meaning' (to use Clifford Geertz's term) are able to do particular kinds of work in their new and unfamiliar *kwaito* contexts. So when, for example, *kwaito* artists make explicit allusions to music with 'precolonial' characteristics – as M'du does in his 2001 song 'Ku Hemba' (Telling Lies) – they associate the *gravitas* of local cultural knowledge with the point being made by the lyrics. Boom Shaka's 'Bambanani' (Hold Each Other [2001]) is a particularly vivid example: it is a passionate song whose call for a peaceful and non-sectarian future is both embodied in and enacted by an extraordinary fusion of *kwaito* and *maskanda*. These idioms are as different, even as contradictory, as the social sectors that identify with them and claim them as their own – fashionable, consumer-oriented, outward-looking, modern city dwellers on the one hand, impoverished, tradition-minded, inward-looking, rurally-based migrant workers on the other. In a quite different example, when TKZee (with 'Come Intro' [1998]) begins an album by drawing Western 'classical' music into the *kwaito* mix, the connotation of 'educated seriousness' creates a context for the songs that follow.

Conclusion

Creative innovations of this kind – on a scale unprecedented in South African popular music – have become so prevalent within the practice of *kwaito* that they demand recognition as essential to the genre's identity. They are also an important insight into the identities – hybrid, Creole, in the making – of the so-called '*kwaito* nation.' *Kwaito* might well be the most significant development in South African popular culture since the end of apartheid, but its love of musical miscegenation – an openness to alterity that, in light of the country's past, connotes social hope – might paradoxically also be its undoing. If *kwaito*'s remarkable inclusiveness propels it to continue evolving in unexpected and unpredictable directions and across idiomatic boundaries, then its lifespan as a recognizable genre will have been a short one.

Bibliography

Allen, Lara. 2001. 'Bubblegum.' In *Grove Music Online*. Online at: http://www.oxfordmusiconline.com/public (accessed 6 September 2017).

Allen, Lara. 2004. 'Kwaito Versus Crossed-Over: Music and Identity during South Africa's Rainbow Years, 1994–1996.' *Social Dynamics* 30(2): 82–111.

Ballantine, Christopher. 2009. 'Popular Music and the End of Apartheid: The Case of Kwaito.' *Proceedings of the 12th Biennial IASPM-International Conference Montreal 2003*. Online at: http://info.comm.uic.edu/lyniv/IASPM03.pdf (accessed 6 September 2017).

Bogatsu, Mpolokeng. 2002. '"Loxion Kulcha": Fashioning Black Youth Culture in Post-Apartheid South Africa.' *English Studies in Africa* 45(2): 1–12.

Boloka, Gibson. 2003. 'Cultural Studies and the Transformation of the Music Industry: Some Reflections on Kwaito.' In *Shifting Selves: Post-Apartheid Essays on Mass Media, Culture and Identity*, eds. Herman Wasserman and Sean Jacobs. Cape Town: Kwela Books, 97–107.

Bosch, Tanja. 2008. 'Kwaito on Community Radio: The Case of Bush Radio in Cape Town, South Africa.' *World of Music* 50(2): 75–89.

Coplan, David B. 2005. 'God Rock Africa: Thoughts on Politics in Popular Black Performance in South Africa.' *African Studies* 64(1): 9–27.

Coplan, David B. 2008. *In Township Tonight! South Africa's Black City Music and Theatre*, 2nd ed. Chicago: University of Chicago Press.

Dolby, Nadine. 2000. 'The Shifting Ground of Race: The Role of Taste in Youth's Production of Identities.' *Race Ethnicity and Education* 3(1): 7–23.

Dolby, Nadine. 2001. *Constructing Race*. New York: SUNY University Press.

Impey, Angela. 2001. 'Resurrecting the Flesh? Reflections on Women in Kwaito.' *Agenda* 49: 44–50.

Jubasi, Mawande. 2000. 'Dancing in the Dark.' [Johannesburg] *Sunday Times*, December 10.

Livermon, Xavier. 2006. *Kwaito Bodies in African Diaspora Space: The Politics of Popular Music in Post-Apartheid South Africa*. Unpublished Ph.D. thesis, University of California, Berkeley.

Mbembe, Achille, et al. 2004. 'Soweto Now.' *Public Culture* 16(3): 499–506.

McCloy, Maria. 'Kwaito.' Online at: http://www.rage.co.za/readArticles.php?articleCat=samusic&articleSubCat=kwaito.

Motshegoa, L. 2005. *Township Talk – The Language, The Culture, The People: The A–Z Dictionary of South Africa's Township Lingo*. Cape Town: Double Story Books.

Neate, Patrick. 2004. *Where You're At: Notes from the Frontline of a Hip-Hop Planet*. New York: Riverhead Books.

Ntshangase, Dumisani K. 1995. 'Indaba yami i-straight: Language and Language Practices in Soweto.' In *Language and Social History: Studies in South African Sociolinguistics*, ed. Rajend Mesthrie. Cape Town: David Philip, 291–97.

Nuttall, Sarah. 2003. 'Self and Text in Y Magazine.' *African Identities* 1(2): 235–51.

Nuttall, Sarah. 2004. 'Stylizing the Self. The Y Generation in Rosebank, Johannesburg.' *Public Culture* 16(3): 430–52.

Pan, Esther. 2000. 'Kwaito Blows Up.' *Newsweek*, 5 November.

Peterson, Bhekizizwe. 2004. 'Kwaito, "Dawgs", and the Antimonies of Hustling.' *African Identities* 1(2): 197–213.

Satyo, Sizwe. 2008. 'A Linguistic Study of Kwaito.' *World of Music* 50(2): 91–102.

Stanley Niaah, Sonjah. 2007. 'Mapping Black Atlantic Performance Geographies: Continuities from Slave Ship to Ghetto.' In *Black Geographies and the Politics of Place*, eds. Katherine McKittrick and Clyde Woods. Toronto: Between the Lines Press and Boston: South End Press, 193–217.

Steingo, Gavin. 2005. 'South African Music After Apartheid: *Kwaito*, the "Party Politic," and the Appropriation of Gold as a Sign of Success.' *Popular Music and Society* 28(3): 333–57.

Steingo, Gavin. 2007. 'The Politicization of Kwaito: From the Party Politic, to Party Politics.' *Black Music Research Journal* 27(1): 23–44.

Steingo, Gavin. 2008. 'Producing Kwaito: Nkosi Sikelel'iAfrika After Apartheid.' *World of Music* 50(2): 103–20.

Steingo, Gavin. 2010. *After Apartheid: Kwaito Music and the Aesthetics of Freedom*. Unpublished Ph.D. thesis, University of Pennsylvania.

Stephens, Simon. 2000. 'Kwaito. In *Senses of Culture*, eds. Sarah Nuttall and Cheryl-Ann Michael. Cape Town: Oxford University Press, 256–77.

Swartz, Sharlene. 2008. 'Is Kwaito South African Hip-Hop? Why the Answer Matters and Who It Matters to.' *World of Music* 50(2): 15–33.

Swinke, Simone. *Kwaito: Much More Than Music*. Online at: http://www.southafrica.info/what.happening/arts.entertainment/kwaitomental.htm (accessed 6 September 2017).

Viljoen, Martina. 2008. 'On the Margins of Kwaito.' *World of Music* 50(2): 51–73.

Vokwana, Thembela. 2007. '*Iph'indlela*? Where Is the Way? Resurrecting an African Identity Through Popular Music in Post-Apartheid South Africa.' In *Music and Identity: Transformation and Negotiation*, eds. Eric Akrofi et al. Stellenbosch: Sun Press, 3–20.

Discographical References

Bongo Maffin. 'Makeba.' *Final Entry*. Sony Music CDBOG *001. 1997*: South Africa.

Bongo Maffin. 'Mari ye Phepha.' *IV*. Columbia CDCOL 8131. *1999*: South Africa.

Bongo Maffin. *The Concerto*. Columbia CDCOL 8080. *1998*: South Africa.

Boom Shaka. 'Bambanani.' *Greats Collection: 7th Anniversary*. Bula Music CDBULA (WLM) 092. *2001*: South Africa.

Brothers of Peace. 'Meropa/Pitseng Tse Kgolo.' *Zabalaza: Project B*. Kalawa Jazmee Records CDCOL *8187. 2001*: South Africa.

Brothers of Peace. 'Phambili siyaya.' *Project 4*. Columbia CDCOL 8149. *2002*: South Africa.

Kabelo. 'Diepkloof.' *Rebel With a Cause*. Electromode Music CDRBL 304. *2002*: South Africa.

Laka, Don. 'Tlang Sekolong.' *Destiny*. Sony Music CDBK 21. *2007*: South Africa.

M'du. 'Dipabi.' *24 Seven*. Epic CDEPC 8128. *1999*: South Africa.

M'du. 'Ku Hemba.' *The Godfather*. Epic CDEPC 8185. *2001*: South Africa.

Mafikizolo. 'Kwela Kwela.' *Kwela*. Columbia CDCOL 8243. *2003*: South Africa.

Mafikizolo. 'Ndihamba Nawe.' *Sibongile*. Columbia CDCOL 8212. *2002*: South Africa.

Makeba, Miriam. 'Pata Pata.' *Miriam Makeba – The Best of the Early Years*. Wrasse Records Wrass 088. *2003*: UK.

Mandoza. 'Nkalakatha.' *Nkalakatha*. CCP Record Company CDCCP2 (WB) 012. *2000*: South Africa.

Senyaka. 'Thembalami.' *O Shwa Jwang O Nkolota*. Sony CDEPC 8180. *2001*: South Africa.

TKZee. 'Come Intro.' *Halloween*. BMG Africa CDHOLA(LSP) 3000. *1998*: South Africa.

TKZee. 'Fiasco.' *Guz 2001*. BMG Africa CDHOLA(LSP) 7. *1999*: South Africa.

TKZee. 'Moses.' *Trinity*. BMG Africa CDHOLA(CLM) 8. *2001*: South Africa.

Zola. 'Ghetto Fabulous.' *uMdlwembe*. Ghetto Ruff CDGRUF 019. *2000*: South Africa.

Zola. 'Mzioni.' *uMdlwembe*. Ghetto Ruff CDGRUF 019. *2000*: South Africa.

Discography

Aba Shante. *Ayoyo*. CCP Record Company CDART (WB) 143. *2001*: South Africa.

Arthur. *Mnike*. CCP Record Company CDART (WB) 136. *2000*: South Africa.

Big Nuz. *Undisputed*. Kalawa Jazmee CDRBL487. *2009*: South Africa.

Bongo Maffin. *Bongolution*. Kalawa Jazmee Records CDCOL 8159. *2001*: South Africa.

Boom Shaka. *Words of Wisdom*. Polygram CDRBL 262. *1998*: South Africa.

Brickz. *Stop Nonsense*. TS Records CDTSR *011. 2008*: South Africa.

Brothers of Peace. *The D Project: Life 'Iskorokoro*. Kalama Jazmee CDCOL *8245. 2004*: South Africa.

DJ Bongz. *Spacebongz*. Hola Music CDHOLA2020. *2009*: South Africa.

Kabelo. *And the Beat Goes On*. Universal Music CDRBL 323. *2003*: South Africa.

M'du. *The Godfather Chissa*. 2002. Sony CDEPC 8214. *2002*: South Africa.

Mafikizolo. *Gate Crashers*. Kalawa Jazmee CDCOL 8156. *2000*: South Africa.

Mahlathini and the Mahotella Queens. *The Best of Mahlathini and the Mahotella Queens*.

Gallo Record Company CDGSP 50. *2007*: South Africa.

Mandoza. *Godoba*. CCP Record Company CDCCP2 (WB) 020. *2001*: South Africa.

Music Safari. The Best of South African Dance. Sony CDCOL 8117. *1999*: South Africa.

Mzambiya. *Still I Rise*. Universal CDRBL 498. *2009*: South Africa.

Mzekezeke. *Ama B.E.E*. TS Records CDTSR 002. *2006*: South Africa.

O' Da Meesta. *Wena U Bani…?* Ghetto Ruff ODMCD 001. *N.d.*: South Africa.

Phat Joe 3650 Days Of Kwaito (2 CDs). Universal CDSRBL 279. *2000*: South Africa.

Professor. *University of Kalawa Jazmee*. Kalawa Jazmee CDRBL 566. *2010*: South Africa.

Skeem. *Ozwa*. Ghetto Ruf CDGRUF (WB) *009*. *1999*: South Africa.

Thebe. *The Vibe Continues*. Kalawa Jazmee CDCOL 8095 P. *1999*: South Africa.

TKZee. *Coming Home*. Hola Music CDHOLA *2018*. *2009*: South Africa.

Trompies. *Shosholoza*. Kalama Jazmee CDCOL 8074. *1998*: South Africa.

Zola. *Bhambatha*. Ghetto Ruff CDGRUF 040. *2004*: South Africa.

CHRISTOPHER BALLANTINE

Kwasa Kwasa

The term 'kwasa kwasa' (or 'kwassa kwassa') originated in the later twentieth century in the present-day Democratic Republic of Congo (known as Zaire from 1971 to 1997), where it denoted a music and dance that was part of the overall development of Congolese *rumba*. The invention of the dance itself is often attributed to Kinshasa motor mechanic and street dancer Jeannot Ra or Jeannorat (see https://vimeo.com/13206199), who adapted a traditional social dance of the Kongo people into a popular style that was later picked up by musicians Pepe Kalle, Kanda Bongo Man and others. Kanda Bongo Man was the musician who did most to bring the dance to wider attention. By 1979 he was based in Paris, from where he capitalized on the growing international popularity of *soukouss* (also *rumba*-related) by touring extensively in Africa and elsewhere. *Kwasa kwasa* developed as part of the 'fast-paced, stripped-down sound' (Stewart 2003, 325) of Kanda Bongo Man's band, centered around guitars (played by guitarists such as Dally Kimoko and Diblo Dibala) and rhythm section, and became very popular on dancefloors. In Kinshasha the music and dance were popularized among others by the band led by Pepe Kalle, Empire Babuka, who recorded an album for Leader Records in 1987 entitled *Kwasa Kwasa*.

In musical terms, *kwasa kwasa* is characterized by a basic rhythmic sequence punctuated by frenetic *ostinati* lead guitar breaks and a rhythm section that features light percussion and loud bass. Under the influence of Congolese musicians such as Kanda Bongo Man, Madilu System, Yondo Sister, Koffi Olomide and General Defao, Viva La Musica and others, seen in person on tours, heard on cassettes and on the radio and watched on videos, *kwasa kwasa* became popular in several African countries (e.g., in Swaziland and Namibia), where it developed in contact with other genres and performance practices. Though initially condemned as 'devilish', the *kwasa kwasa* beat and rhythm, and those of another *rumba*-based genre that followed it, *ndombolo*, also permeated many sub-Saharan gospel genres.

There follow two examples of this diffusion, in Botswana and in Malawi.

Bibliography

Salter, Tom. 2011. '"Being Modern Does Not Mean Being Western": Congolese Popular Music, 1945 to 2000.' *Critical African Studies* 3(5): 1–50.

Stewart, Gary, 2003. *Rumba on the River: A History of the Popular Music of the Two Congos*. London: Verso.

Discographical References

Empire Babuka. 'Kwassa kwassa': https://www.youtube.com/watch?v=RZCPYBdI-aY

'Jeannot Ra: Exhibition Kuasakuasa': https://vimeo.com/13206199

Kalle, Pepe, and Empire Babuka. *Kwasa kwasa*. Leader Records REPRO 01. *1987*: Nigeria. Online at: https://www.youtube.com/watch?v=g3uPqqo1HKo (accessed 8 June 2018). Video (accessed 8 June 2018_)

DAVID HORN AND JOHN LWANDA

Kwasa Kwasa (in Botswana)

The Botswana manifestation of the Congolese *kwasa kwasa* genre may be dated to the late 1990s, and the genre has continued to develop there over time.

The term *kwasa kwasa*, in Botswana, is understood metaphorically by Setswana-speaking people as 'dance-dance'. This translation often leads to the interchangeable use of other related terms during performance: *kwasa kwasa* is often replaced by 'bina bina' (*bina* is a Setswana word that means 'dance'). *Kwasa kwasa* in Botswana, essentially Congolese in stylistic origin, has become a hybrid of various other styles, such as *kwaito-kwasa* and gospel-*kwasa*. True to the assumed meaning of its name, the genre emphasizes dance extensively. In the dance, men and women are pitted against each other in competitive, but communicative, moves. The music aims for popular appeal through the dance moves and story line.

Musically, the manifestation of *kwasa kwasa* in Botswana is the same as *kwasa kwasa* elsewhere. The genre is distinguished mainly by a strong rhythm section, often including guitars and percussion at a moderately fast tempo. Although the name makes reference mainly to dance, the term is used in Botswana to identify a combination of the instrumentation, the singing and the dance. The guitar is the centerpiece instrument in *kwasa kwasa*. Not surprisingly, therefore, the pioneers of the genre in Botswana, both local and foreigners, are mainly guitarists.

When *kwasa kwasa* began in Botswana, artists adopted the personae of Congolese performers such as Kanda Bongo Man, Pepe Kalle and the Empire Bakuba band and Koffi Olomide. Radio airplay and videos of these artists were used extensively for this purpose. The airplay given to Congolese *kwasa kwasa*, together with video recordings of musicians, including those just mentioned, exposed audiences to the music and inspired prospective Botswana artists. The *kwasa kwasa* of Kanda Bongo Man, Pepe Kalle and Koffi Olomide was sung either in Lingala or French. However, in Botswana, the music was adapted to the local language of Setswana in its different dialects. Artists narrated stories and experiences, exploring many subjects in their song lyrics.

The initial catalysts for *kwasa kwasa*'s emergence in Botswana include the presence of foreign nationals, mainly from DRC and a few others from countries such as Tanzania. These artists include the late Biza Mupulu, Nathaniel Mwambona, Lawi Somana and Kapenda Katuta. Another contributing factor was the way the performance bands were formulated. For instance, some individual instrumentalists performed music freelancing work for different bands as dictated by the demand for their instrumental expertise. Others chose to permanently join working bands, while a few started their own bands. The effects of the collaborative works and breakaway bands helped to nurture the *kwasa kwasa* genre in Botswana. Most local artists who were younger at the time started as dancers, instrumentalists or lead or backing vocalists in the initial bands.

Alfredo Mos (Alfred Mosimanegape) and Les Africa Sounds may be viewed as the pioneer of *kwasa kwasa* in Botswana, judging by how many artists broke away from his band to form their own *kwasa kwasa* bands. For instance, Slizer, a renowned local female artist, was a backing vocalist and dancer for Alfredo Mos and Les Africa Sounds. Biza Mpulu, a Congolese guitarist and music producer, started with Super Powers Band in 1993, then joined Alfredo Mos and Africa Sounds, then formed The Dr. Biza Band in 1996. Frank Lesokwane (popularly known as Franco), with his Afro Musica band, broke away from Alfredo Mos and went solo in 2001. Frank Lesokwane immediately released the album *Ke Llela le Lona*, which has a dominant feel in the vocals and some rhythms reminiscent of the local *dikhwaere* music, a vocal traditional genre that is responsorial and often used as social commentary.

Alfredo Mos's first album in 1997 (*Botshelo*) and the following album in 1998 (*Motho*) may be considered the roots of *kwasa kwasa* in Botswana. The reciprocal encounters of its early performances in Botswana further defined *kwasa kwasa* and anchored it as a local genre. Nathaniel Mwambona, a Tanzanian guitarist from the group Nata Capricorn, released *Bula Matlho* in 1999, with vocals by Frank Lesokwane and with the long-selling hit song 'Maya'. In 2009 Frank Lesokwane and Jeff Matheatau collaborated on a *kwasa kwasa* album titled *Clash of the Giants*. This album was considered to have resulted in fresh creative energy that revitalized the genre and cultivated a newer and larger audience. Other significant local *kwasa kwasa* bands include Kups and Bwasa Stars, Bra Monty and Sakaye Kings, Taolo Moshaga, Jeff Matheatau, Chris Manto 7, Real Kwasa Melody, Tumza and Kennyboy Mckenzie.

Kwasa kwasa in the mid-2000s developed subgenres including *kwaito-kwasa*, house-*kwasa* and gospel-

kwasa. *Kwaito-kwasa* is a blend of *kwaito* music from neighboring South Africa with *kwasa kwasa*. *Kwaito-kwasa* albums include *Kasi Angels* by Vee, *Back to Kasi* by the Eskimos group and *Masupatsela* by Exodus. The origins of *kwaito-kwasa* are associated with Vee (Odirile Sento), who popularized the style by producing albums and grooming upcoming groups. In this development, the initial intent was to fuse two genres (*kwaito* and *kwasa kwasa*) that originated outside Botswana, but were popular locally, in a way that the youth of Botswana would understand. The melodic lines were simplified as the local language took precedence. Some local rhythmic patterns of indigenous dances were incorporated. The most obvious change was the up-tempo adjustment. The need for a faster tempo for dance gave rise to another subgenre: house-*kwasa*, a blend of house music and *kwasa kwasa*, as popularized by the duet formed by Vee and Slizer (Naledi Kaisara). Other artists of house-*kwasa* include Zolasco and K-Pist, Dr. Mickey (Michael Rankgomo), Mzulala, Cobra and Slizer Creations.

The localization of *kwasa kwasa* appears to be a defining moment for the development of music in Botswana. New styles have been influenced by *kwasa kwasa*, the younger generation looks up to artists of the genre as role models, and the media broadcasts of *kwasa kwasa* performances have sparked a general interest in performance. Traces of *kwasa kwasa* sounds are heard in gospel music, *kwaito* and other Botswana traditional popular genres. Thus, *kwasa kwasa* remains a point of reference for the majority of artists and it continues to develop as a genre.

Bibliography

Anusiem, Boniface Nkem. 2012. 'Globalizing an Authentic African Mediature.' Paper presented at the International Conference on Media and Culture, Pan African University, Lagos, Nigeria.

Mukuna, Kazadi wa. 1992. 'The Genesis of Urban Music in Zaïre.' *African Music* 7(2): 72–84.

Rapoo, Connie. 2013. 'Urbanised Soundtracks: Youth Popular Culture in the African City.' *Social Dynamics* 39(2): 368–83.

Steingo, Gavin. 2005. 'South African Music After Apartheid: Kwaito, the "Party Politic," and the Appropriation of Gold as a Sign of Success.' *Popular Music and Society* 28(3): 333–57.

Togarasei, Lovemore. 2012. 'Mediating the Gospel: Pentecostal Christianity and Media Technology in Botswana and Zimbabwe.' *Journal of Contemporary Religion* 27(2): 257–74.

Discographical References

Eskimos. *Back to Kasi*. Ramco loco and Black Moneymakers. *2004*: Botswana.

Exodus. *Masupatsela*. Black Moneymakers. *2006*: Botswana.

Lesokwane, 'Franco' Frank. *Ke Lela le Lona*. Franco Investments. *2001*: Botswana.

Matheatau, Jeff, and Franco. *Clash of the Giants*. Diamond Studios. *2009*: Botswana.

Mos, Alfredo and Les Africa Sounds. *Botshelo*. BOP recording studio. *1997*: South Africa.

Mos, Alfredo, and Les Africa Sounds. *Motho*. Label unknown. *1998*: South Africa.

Mwambona, Nathaniel and Nata Capricorn. *Bula Matlho*. BOP recording studio. *1999*: South Africa.

Sento, 'Vee' Odirile. *Kasi Angels*. Eric Ramco Records. *2004*: Botswana.

PINKIE GOMOLEMO MOJAKI

Kwasa Kwasa (in Malawi)

Kwasa kwasa arrived in Malawi at a time of transition. Toward the end of the 1980s Malawians yearned for less restrictive governance after nearly 25 years of strict one-party rule under Dr. Hastings Kamuzu Banda, who had been declared president for life in 1971. Dancing provided one such avenue and *kwasa kwasa* was a dance that, superficially or not, resembled genuine Malawi traditional dances. Malawians exploited this avenue, and authorities were unable to ban *kwasa kwasa* because of its resemblance to traditional dances that Dr. Banda favored, despite religious or other objections. Bands found *kwasa kwasa* easy to play; it only required the basic drums, bass, rhythm and lead configuration. In rural and peri-urban areas it was sometimes played with only drum or drum and bass accompaniment.

Kwasa kwasa was popularized in Malawi via Congolese cassettes and videos in the 1980s and consolidated by tours by Congolese stars such as Kanda Bongo Man. Kanda Bongo Man's 1989 CD entitled *Kwassa Kwassa*, featured several tracks that became extremely popular in Malawi, among them 'Sai' and 'Lela-lela.' And in 1991 singer Mbilia Bel toured Malawi and showed Malawi women at firsthand how to dance *kwasa kwasa* (Chimombo and Chimombo 1996, 128). *Kwasa kwasa*'s rhythmic dancing matched Malawi rhythmic and musical sensibilities. Indeed, there are similarities to some of Malawi's female dances, such as *chisamba*, associated with initiation ceremonies, although these were performed in private, and *mwinoghe*, a dance of entertainment.

Initially *kwasa kwasa* music was mostly played in bottle stores and bars in the urban areas and viewed as 'bar music.' One of the most popular venues was Lunzu Townhouse, owned by Leonard Banda. Banda and his disc jockey Captain Pazuzu initiated *kwasa kwasa* dancing competitions that attracted female dancers and hundreds of patrons. As Lunzu is a major stopover on the M1 motorway that runs between Malawi's two major cities, Blantyre and Lilongwe, it is no surprise then that, in the early 1990s, *kwasa kwasa* soon spread throughout Malawi via dancing competitions that saw many women take to the stage for the first time. These *kwasa kwasa* dancing competitions attracted male and female dancers from as far afield as Zambia, Tanzania and Zaire itself (Chimombo and Chimombo 1996). *Kwasa kwasa* dancing stars emerged, including Jean Nandau, Papaje Kayira and Nancy Moya, all of whom combined Congolese dance steps with local choreography (ibid.). Male *kwasa kwasa* dancers in the 1990s added breakdancing moves and local traditional dance moves, including *mazoma* and *gule wamkulu*, into the *kwasa kwasa* blend. Both male and female dancers chose costumes that exaggerated their body movements. Soon the competitions were being sponsored by commercial enterprises.

Although original Congolese music was used in *kwasa kwasa* competitions, the popularity of these competitions spurred the formation of local *kwasa kwasa* bands. Malawi electric musicians had played *rumba* for nearly two decades; groups including Super Kaso and Army Alpha Strings bands had experimented with Congolese *rumba* and *soukouss*, respectively, in the 1980s. However, it was not until the beginning of the 1990s that Malawi bands started experimenting with *kwasa kwasa*. One of the earliest bands was the short-lived Sapitwa, led by Patrick Tembo and Tepu Ndiche. Sapitwa featured a group of women dancers performing Malawi versions of *kwasa kwasa*. When Sapitwa disbanded, Collen Ali, a former Sapitwa member, Jack Kamwendo, Ben Michael and Peter Likhomo formed Mibawa, a group that opened Kanda Bongo Man shows in Malawi in 1994. Meanwhile, WEPAZ, a short-lived band led by Ethel Kamwendo, had also played *kwasa kwasa*.

Sapitwa's mantle was later briefly taken on by Mulangeni sounds and others. Since 1994 *kwasa kwasa* has been an integral part of the Malawi musical landscape, the template being used by gospel and secular musicians alike. Musicians such as Joseph Tembo routinely use *kwasa kwasa* elements in their productions.

Bibliography

Chimombo, Steve, and Chimombo, Moira. 1996. *The Culture of Democracy: Language, Literature, the Arts and Politics in Malawi, 1992–94*. Zomba: WASI.

Lwanda, John. 2006. 'Sounds Afroma.' In *The Rough Guide to World Music: Africa and the Middle East*, eds. Simon Broughton et al. London: Penguin, 210–18.

Discographical Reference

Kanda Bongo Man. *Kwassa Kwassa*. Hannibal HNBL 1343. *1989*: France/UK.

Discography

Mulangeni Sounds. *Tinadya chambo*. Mulangeni. *1994*: Malawi.

Sapitwa (featuring Patrick Tembo and Tepu Ndiche). *Malawi's Top Soukous, Manganje and Tchopa Band*. Studio K. *N.d.*: Malawi.

Sapitwa. *Pamudzi paMatola*. Sapitwa Band Productions. *1993*: Malawi.

JOHN LWANDA

Kwela

Kwela is a jazz-inspired form of black South African popular music that evolved in townships around Johannesburg during the 1950s, and is strongly associated with the penny whistle. Often described by musicians as 'our blues,' *kwela* is central to the *marabi*-influenced tradition of urban hybrid music. Chronologically the primary styles in this tradition are *marabi* (1920s and 1930s), *tsaba tsaba* (1930s), African jazz (1940s and 1950s), *kwela* (1950s) and *mbaqanga* (1960s), although in practice there is considerable fluidity between these styles. *Kwela* is not associated with a specific ethnic group, but does have a particular profile with regard to race, class, gender, age and the urban/rural divide; most *kwela* musicians were black working-class young men or boys who lived in city areas.

Throughout the twentieth and into the twenty-first century the fundamental driver in the evolution of urban black popular music in South Africa has been an ongoing dialogue between styles popular in the United States and various forms of indigenous South African music. The resulting 'circuits of recognition and desire' (Allen 2005) start with the exact imitation in South Africa of the American popular style of the era, which is then gradually indigenized through the introduction of elements from local music. It is usually the South Africanized variant of the American style that enjoys the greatest market success, as this best reflects the fluid identities of urbanized, or urbanizing, township residents. Fans are able to associate themselves with the latest trend from the United States, to which they aspire, while simultaneously remaining rooted in local musical traditions reflective of their past and present lived reality. The evolution of *kwela* succinctly illustrates the typical circuit of this musical dialogue with the United States: while firmly rooted in the *marabi* tradition, *kwela* musicians also produced their versions of blues, rhythm and blues, big-band swing and rock 'n' roll, and the mature version of *kwela* constituted an indigenized amalgam of elements derived from North American and South African musical sources.

Musical Structure

While, therefore, 'kwela' covers a relatively wide range of musical practices, both musicians and audiences understand what is meant by the term, and the definitive characteristics of the genre may be articulated in technical musical terminology (Allen 1999). Structurally, most *kwela* compositions are comprised either of motifs alternating with solo sections, or of an *ostinato* backing figure over which a soloist improvises. Harmonically, *kwela* compositions are generally based on a cyclically repeated four-chord harmonic progression. The chords are nearly always primary; sevenths and substitutions are rarely used. However, compositions based on longer chord progressions, for instance those in blues form, are also recognized as *kwela*, provided that other definitive aspects (particularly with regard to instrumentation) are present. The individuality of each *kwela* composition is ordinarily defined by its melodic motifs. These are often closely modeled on the chord tones of the harmonic progression, and arpeggiated and scale passages dominate the melodic contours.

Kwela rhythm is defined primarily by the guitar rather than the drum set and has been described as a 'lilting shuffle.' The most important rhythmic difference between *kwela* and *marabi*, *tsaba tsaba* and *mbaqanga*, is that *kwela* is swung whereas the styles by which it was preceded and followed are characterized by a driving straight beat. The swing beat is the most important characteristic that *kwela* shares with its contemporary township styles – African jazz, vocal jive and sax jive. It is also the element that enabled *kwela* to fulfill its primary social function: to provide dance music. *Kwela* fans can jive, jitterbug and rock 'n' roll to South African music.

The main characteristics that differentiate *kwela* from other global styles played on the penny whistle are timbre and amplitude. In order to produce the aesthetically desirable 'buzz,' and to make it possible to play loudly by blowing hard without cracking a note, *kwela* musicians physically altered the shape of the penny whistle's fipple opening and evolved an embouchure that slightly covered this opening. This alteration and the *kwela* embouchure is only possible on penny whistles with metal headpieces: the historically correct *kwela* timbre cannot be produced on plastic-headed instruments (Allen 1999).

Ultimately, however, instrumentation is the most important definitive aspect of *kwela* as a style. Even if a composition fulfills all the other stylistic criteria, if it does not contain a solo saxophone or a penny whistle, it is not likely to be recognized as *kwela*. The horn section in *kwela* compositions generally comprises a solo penny whistle or saxophone, often with a penny whistle or saxophone chorus. Sometimes the backing chorus is provided by vocals.

Like the vocal jive of the era, the lyrics usually entail an element of sociopolitical commentary on a topical subject (Allen 2003). Originally the *kwela* rhythm section consisted of one or two guitars, but with the advent of recording, guitar, string-bass and drum set became the norm. Later a banjo was added and, as the style developed toward 1960s *mbaqanga*, both rhythm and lead guitars were required. When other parameters remained constant and a penny whistle or a saxophone was included, the addition of vocals or other instruments (for instance, clarinet, piano or violin) did not prevent a composition from being recognized as *kwela*.

History

The history of *kwela* is largely synonymous with the rise and fall of the penny whistle as a core instrument in black South African popular music (Allen 2005). While penny whistles were played in South African townships as early as the 1900s, they were first used extensively in the 1930s and 1940s by marching bands known as 'the Scottishes.' Formed by black male youths in imitation of Scottish Pipe bands, these bands included 15 to 25 penny whistlers and two to five drummers. Band members wore costumes imitative of Scottish pipers, including tartan kilts, sporrans, spats and glengarries, and they marched in formation while playing.

During this period the penny whistle was also sometimes used in *marabi* and *tsaba tsaba*, styles whose primary function was to create a convivial atmosphere for dancing and drinking in township *shebeens* (informal, illegal drinking houses) and for *stokvel* (mutual savings society) parties. From the early 1940s local big-bands started playing covers of US big-band swing for dance concerts in township halls, and a swing-*marabi* style evolved called 'African jazz' (also sometimes referred to as *majuba* or *mbaqanga*). Young aspirant musicians unable to afford big-band instruments started to render African jazz on penny whistles. Groups of these youngsters moved this music style from the *shebeens* and township halls onto the streets, where they busked for coins from passers-by. The two groups best known for their pavement performances in the early 1950s were both from Alexandra Township near Johannesburg: the Lerole brothers (led by Elias and Jake), and Lemmy 'Special' Mabaso with the Alexandra Junior Bright Boys.

The instance that popularized the penny whistle nationally, however, was its appearance in *The Magic Garden*, the second South African film with an entirely black cast. Released in 1951, the film featured local residents from Alexandra Township including penny whistler Willard Cele, whose penny whistle blues and boogie-woogie provided apt background music for the film's many humorous chase scenes. The popularity of the penny whistle rose rapidly in the townships as many boys tried to emulate their 'homeboy' movie star and hero Willard Cele. However, although Cele did record his movie tracks, the music industry did not realize the penny whistle's commercial potential until 1954 when Spokes Mashiyane began his first recordings with guitarist France Pilane.

The reason for the instant success of Mashiyane's releases is that they shifted recorded penny whistle music into a new stage in its dialogue with contemporary US styles: Cele's recordings were US-style blues and boogie-woogie; Mashiyane's compositions completed the process of indigenization because they were constructed from local musical elements adapted to the swing beat. The music industry reacted quickly to Mashiyane's success and within a few months most of the best-known street buskers were signed on by different recording companies. Spokes Mashiyane became known as 'King Kwela,' but other well-known stars included Lemmy 'Special' Mabaso, Jake and Elias Lerole, and the Solven Whistlers, led by Ben Nkosi, whose style was closer to jazz than most other *kwela* artists.

Kwela's move into the recording studio resulted in several stylistic changes. First, asserting that the penny whistle and guitar sounded too thin on recordings, producers added a string-bass and drum set to the backing instrumental lineup. Then in 1958 Gallo Record Company producer Strike Vilakazi suggested that Spokes Mashiyane play *kwela* on a saxophone, and other *kwela* recording artists followed suit. With the introduction of electric guitars and bass guitar over the turn of the decade, the style came to be known 'sax jive,' which evolved into *mbaqanga* in the early 1960s.

The word *khwela* (meaning to climb, ascend, mount or mate in isiZulu) is audible in recordings of African jazz and related styles from the 1940s onwards, interjected as an imperative to 'get up,' either to dance or to take a solo. However, police vehicles were known colloquially as *khwela-khwela* vans (an iteration of the instruction shouted by police when making arrests), and a misunderstanding in relation to this use of the word led to *kwela*'s use as a stylistic label for South African penny whistle music. In 1958 the recording 'Tom Hark' by Elias and His Zig-Zag Jive Flutes was used as the signature tune for a British television series set in South Africa, and it subsequently did well on the British hit parade. Embedded in the spoken introduction to 'Tom Hark,' a cameo about pavement gambling, is the phrase *'Daar kom die Kwela-kwela.'* In the township lingua franca of the day this phrase means 'here comes the police van,' but it was mistranslated in Britain as, 'here comes the kwela music' (Rycroft 1958, 56). Entranced by the style's international success, the South African media started referring to it as *kwela*, retroactively entrenching the term as a stylistic label.

Kwela's cross-cultural appeal also manifested in South Africa, and the genre became the first black musical style to cross the color bar to a substantive degree. The two catalysts for this unprecedented success were: (1) white people identified with *kwela* because the musicians who busked on city streets and in the suburbs had made the penny whistle part of Johannesburg's every day soundscape, and (2) the style's swing beat made it possible for white youths to perform the dance styles of their era (rock 'n' roll, jive and jitterbug) to *kwela* music. *Kwela*'s interracial appeal enhanced both its reputation and its sociopolitical importance, but also contributed to its demise. Popular during the 1950s, the decade during which the ideology of apartheid (separate development along racial lines) was first legislated, *kwela* constituted a particular threat to apartheid authorities.

The primary way in which *kwela* was affected by apartheid laws and their enforcement was through an ongoing erosion of access to performance venues (Allen 1996). Laws that debarred black musicians from clubs and other formal venues included the Liquor Act, which prohibited black musicians from performing at venues where alcohol was sold, and the Separate Amenities Act, which prohibited racially mixed audiences and casts, and prevented black people from performing at venues reserved for whites. *Kwela* street buskers were particularly vulnerable to being arrested under the Pass Laws, and were also constantly harassed by the police under bylaws relating to alleged disruption of traffic or causing a public disturbance. In one series of incidents *kwela* musicians were arrested for possible contravention of the Immorality Act (legislation that outlawed sexual relations between races) because they were providing music that facilitated interracial dancing in a public park (Allen 2008). By the early 1960s both the streets and more formal venues had become unviable, and live performance of *kwela* largely died out. In the recording studios, the style evolved into sax jive and 1960s *mbaqanga*.

Penny whistle *kwela* did, however, enjoy a longer period of popularity in countries to the north of South Africa such as Zimbabwe and Zambia, and it was performed in Malawi until the 1980s (Kubik 1969, 1987).

Conclusion

In the late 1980s and 1990s *kwela* enjoyed something of a revival. In part this was supported by two niche global music industry trends: listening back in time (the revivals and archiving projects relating to the blues in the United States, for instance); and listening away in space from the northern metropole (captured commercially through the invention of the 'world music' marketing category). Largely, however, *kwela*'s reemergence in this period was due to the iconic status it had come to enjoy in relation to more local concerns: South African history and politics. As the anti-apartheid movement gathered momentum in the mid-1980s, it generated a surge of cultural production, part of which entailed a rediscovery and celebration of the 1950s as a time of hope and nonviolent resistance: a decade defined by the Defiance Campaign, which was underscored by Mahatma Gandhi's notions of passive resistance. Thanks to its bittersweet musical characteristics (it is simultaneously upbeat and plaintive, hopeful and haunting), and the iconic image of ragged black boys playing penny whistles for the enjoyment of all race groups despite ongoing police harassment, the penny whistle variant of *kwela* became a particularly potent visual and aural trope of this version of the 1950s and all that it stood for in anti-apartheid politics.

Bibliography

Allen, Lara. 1996. '"Drumbeats, Pennywhistles and All that Jazz': the Relationship between Urban South African Musical Styles and Musical Meaning.' *African Music* 7(3): 52–9.

Allen, Lara. 1999. 'Kwela: The Structure and Sound of South African Pennywhistle Music.' In *Composing the Music of Africa*, ed. Malcolm Floyd. Aldershot: Scolar, 225–62.

Allen, Lara. 2003. 'Commerce, Politics, and Musical Hybridity: Vocalising Urban Black South African Identity during the 1950s.' *Ethnomusicology* 47(2): 228–49.

Allen, Lara. 2005. 'Circuits of Recognition and Desire in the Evolution of Black South African Popular Music: The Career of the Penny Whistle.' *South African Journal of Musicology* 25: 31–51.

Allen, Lara. 2008. 'Kwela's White Audiences: The Politics of Pleasure and Identification in the Early Apartheid Period.' In *Composing Apartheid: Music For and Against Apartheid*, ed. Grant Olwage. Johannesburg: Wits University Press, 79–98.

Kubik, Gerhard. 1969. 'Afrikanische Elemente im Jazz: Jazzelemente in der popularen Musik Afrikas.' [African Elements in Jazz: Jazz Elements in Africa's Popular Music]. *Jazzforschung/Jazz Research* 1: 84–98.

Kubik, Gerhard. 1987. *Malawian Music: A Framework for Analysis*. Zomba: The Centre for Social Research and the Department of Fine and Performing Arts, University of Malawi.

Rycroft, David. 1958. 'The New Town Music of South Africa.' *Recorded Folk Music* 1 (September/October): 54–7.

Discographical References

Elias and His Zig-Zag Jive Flutes. 'Tom Hark.' Columbia YE 164. *1958*: South Africa.

Mashiyane, Spokes. *King Kwela*. Melody Music, CDZAC 50. *1958*: South Africa.

Discography

Soul Safari Presents Township Jive & Kwela Jazz (1940–1960). Ubuntu 2011.004. *2011*: Netherlands.

Soul Safari Presents Township Jive & Kwela Jazz. Volume 2. Ubuntu 2013.005. *2013*: Netherlands.

Soul Safari Presents Township Jive & Kwela Jazz. Volume 3 (1960–1965). Ubuntu 2014.006. *2014*: Netherlands.

Tin Whistle Jive and the Roots of Kwela. Volume 1 (1951–1956). Flat International / Electric Jive FXEJ 15. *2014*: South Africa.

Tin Whistle Jive and the Roots of Kwela. Volume 2. Spokes Mashiyane and Willard Cele. Flat International / Electric Jive FXEJ 16/TP4 Records. *2015*: South Africa.

Filmography

The Magic Garden, dir. Donald Swanson 1951. South Africa. 63 mins. Feature film.

LARA ALLEN

Litungu Music

The *litungu* is a seven-stringed lyre and is the main musical instrument of the Bukusu people of Kenya (Masasabi 2010), who also refer to it as 'lusia,' which literally means 'a string.' The words 'lusia lulayi' are used to describe good music and literally mean 'a good string' in reference to appealing music that is performed on the *litungu* (Masasabi 2002, 14). The *litungu* is associated with the *kamabeka* dance (Wanyama 2008). *Kamabeka* means 'shoulders' in Lubukusu, the language spoken by the Bukusu people. The dance, performed by Bukusu men and women to *litungu* music, is characterized by shaking both shoulders in response to the rhythm of the *litungu*. In the modern era, urban *litungu* ensembles often perform a mixture of traditional and modern styles, but such stylistic merges and compromises in both music and dance are viewed by upholders of Bukusu tradition as antagonistic to its survival.

The Instrument

The *litungu* is used among different Luiya (also spelled Luhya) subdivisions, but is mainly a Bukusu instrument (Senoga-Zake 2000). The traditional Bukusu lyre has seven strings, while the other Luiya *litungu* instruments sometimes have six strings.

The former measures about 75 centimeters long and approximately half of its length is taken up by its oval body. Over the open part of this sound-box a skin is stretched, usually that of a giant monitor lizard, but a cowhide is also commonly used. The skin is secured around the edges by wooden pegs or nails. Unlike the guitar, the sound hole of this instrument is near the edge of the sound-box. Two pieces of wood project from the sound-box upwards for about 45 centimeters, and the distance between them widens from 27.8 to 30 centimeters. At their widest part, these supports are joined by a crossbar around which the seven strings are wound. A wooden bridge lifts the strings clear of the skin belly. Where the strings are secured to the tail of the sound-box, an extra skin flap is glued, partly for additional strength against wear and partly to prevent the sound from escaping from the holes through which the strings are slotted. Around the crossbar, the surplus string forms a ball and each string may be tuned by twisting its corresponding ball in such a way that a part of the ball is trapped beneath the string and cannot, therefore, unwind when the hand is taken away.

The *litungu* uses a hexachord scale, tuned diatonically without the seventh or leading tone. Since the octave is found between the first and the seventh strings, the instrument has seven strings but six notes of the scale that have different names. As in other Luiya communities, it is not uncommon to find a *litungu* with an eighth or even ninth string. In such a case the leading note, *te*, and supertonic, *re*, are included.

Performance

In traditional *litungu* music, the main instrument is played by men and in most cases accompanies singing (Shitubi 2005). Women were not allowed to play or even to touch the *litungu* in the traditional setting (Masasabi 2010), but changes in the sociocultural context in the 1980s and 1990s led a few women to venture into *litungu* playing. For instance, as part of the requirements of the music education curricula at universities and other learning institutions in Kenya, the instrument is chosen and recommended as a course instrument for both male and female students.

To play the *litungu*, the player places the instrument either on his or her lap or in front. Although the players normally sit, when the excitement reaches a climax they stand up and join the dancers. Typically, a player or leader introduces himself or herself and the song before serious music commences, or accompanies himself or herself on the instrument while introducing the song to the listeners. Usually, the player returns to the address in the middle of the song, at times developing a dialogue with a person from the audience. Players may perform alone and sing in unison with the instrument, or they may play in groups of two or even three, plucking different strings as accompaniment rather than playing in unison with the vocal part.

Most *litungu* players have played the instrument since childhood, and they claim to have learned the art from their grandfathers, fathers or uncles within the clan (Wafula 2007). After acquiring the basic ability to handle the instrument, they build on and refine their skills by listening to other *litungu* players and through exposure to performances at occasions such as weddings, communal rituals, beer parties and other general entertainment occasions.

The performing styles of different *litungu* players are generally similar except for slight differences in tone, vitality in the plucking of the strings, timbre of voices and instruments, and ornamentation techniques and styles (Shitubi 2005). The player may maintain a steady rhythmic *ostinato* in compound quadruple meter while marking and keeping the tempo by stamping his or her foot on the ground. In most cases the steady tempo of the rattling jingle tied to the player's leg enhances the steadiness of the tempo.

Occasionally, the *litungu* player creates variation by singing in a different rhythm from that of the instrument (Wanyama 2008). He or she may also engage in a solo-response form with the instrument. Depending on the musician's experience and level of dexterity, he or she may also play a familiar folk song melody with the left hand while the right hand adds harmonic effects, a countermelody or other ornamental embellishments. The player may also sing in parallel thirds with the instrumental melodic line or an octave higher or lower than the instrument. Interest in the performance may be purposely initiated by varying singing with chants or normal conversation. As indicated earlier, while talking, the player may choose to introduce him or herself and may also mention and praise people in attendance at a political rally, a marriage ceremony or a fund-raising ceremony by calling out their names as well as their clan lineages. Most *litungu* players are fond of commenting metaphorically on sociocultural and political issues affecting the immediate and wider society, hence aesthetically and artistically giving their audience food for thought, and a *litungu* player's ability is generally judged in part on the ability to contextualize songs in this manner, in addition to improvisational skill (Shitubi 2005, 301).

The *litungu* is played to the accompaniment of the *luhengele*, also known as the *chimbengele* or *luengele*, a long, narrow, wooden board that is struck with two sticks in each hand. This rattling idiophone supplies the vibrant rhythmic accompaniment that plays a central role in the stimulation of the *kamabeka* (shoulder dance) peculiar to the Bukusu people.

The traditional *litungu* ensemble may include other instruments, such as *bichenje* (foot jingles played by stamping one foot in rhythm with the main beat of the music), *efumbo* (drum, plural *chifumbo*), *lulwika* (antelope horn) and *silili* (fiddle). According to Senoga-Zake (2000), the *efumbo* is found among the Bukusu, Samia and Marachi people. It is slightly longer than the *isukuti* and slightly shorter than the *embegete* of the Kuria, and it resembles the *musondo* of the Giriama. The *efumbo* is covered on one side with a skin and played on the covered side only. The tuning is done by warming the drum on a fire or leaving it in the hot sun.

As the performance goes on, people in attendance join in ad lib by dancing the *kamabeka* dance as they sing along in response to the soloist. Traditionally, the *kamabeka* dance is characterized by the freedom of individual dancers to display personal idiosyncratic flair without observing the strict patterns and formation that characterize school and college performances in the Kenya Music Festival. However, in most cases, dancers form circular patterns and/or dance in pairs.

Most of the songs performed are 'folk songs that refer to the history of the Bukusu community and its mythology' (Shitubi 2005, 301). Based on already existing tunes, composers, who are also performers, create new lyrics to address a current situation, or they may compose new tunes but maintain already existing words from other Bukusu folklore tunes or from Bukusu proverbs. In most cases, performers/composers belong to or are affiliated with a particular musical clan or relative(s) and therefore it is believed by the community that they inherit the skill from their parents or grandparents and perfect it through apprenticeship.

According to Wanyama (2008), the performance of *litungu* music by *litungu* players, along with the *kamabeka* dance, propagates and acknowledges the mythical-genealogical foundations and origins of the Bukusu community. Most players seldom complete a performance without mentioning Mwambu and his wife, Sela, who are believed to be the forefather and foremother of the Bukusu people. It is also worth noting that, apart from the prevalent use of symbolism, many other Bukusu myths and ogre stories form the basic fabric of quite a number of songs in the *litungu* musical repertoire. Another aspect unique to the performance of *litungu* music, and by extension the *kamabeka* dance, is that some songs allude to the historical continuum of events that the community has undergone. For instance, in some songs, the singers describe the wars fought between the Bukusu and their white colonial masters, the British.

Challenges to Tradition

Adherence to what is viewed as 'traditional authenticity' regarding cultural performances is difficult and elusive (Wanyama 2008). For instance, some materials that were used to manufacture traditional instruments, especially monitor lizard skin and antelope horns, have become rare as a result of most African countries' efforts to conserve wildlife. Violation or disobedience of rules in this regard often attracts severe penalties. The only option the artist is left with is to improvise by using available materials in the construction of instruments. For this reason, *litungu* ensembles in rural villages, urban centers and the Kenya Music

Festival improvise variations on the traditional drum, *efumbo*, using old tins of different sizes covered with cowhide, while aerophones, such as the traditional *lulwika*, are improvised by using plastic water pipes. Moreover, in the Kenya Music Festival it is not uncommon to come across *litungu* ensembles and *kamabeka* dance troupes in innovative and creative costumes in terms of color and structure. Often, deliberate efforts are made to capture the viewers' attention with visual aesthetic impact by amplifying the vibrant shoulder movements through the use of costumes that are gathered around the shoulder area.

In urban and rural areas most *litungu* ensembles mix traditional dance styles with popular styles from other cultures and countries (Wanyama 2008). An example is the Tindikti – Jua Kali band, which is featured mostly at political rallies. A common mixture combines traditional *litungu* dance styles and the Congolese-related *ndombolo* dance, including the use of the Lingala language (along with Lubukusu and Swahili), in an effort to appeal commercially to a wider audience outside the Bukusu community and also to compete for supremacy in the Kenyan and the wider East African popular music market. This trend occurs partly because most people in Kenya are fond of *lingala* music and dance ('lingala' was what Kenyans called Congolese music when it arrived in the 1960s and 1970s) and so it may be argued that this is an attempt by the local *litungu* ensembles to compete favorably with locally popular *lingala* music by fusing its rhythms and dance styles with the more familiar *litungu* music. However, the two dances are characterized by quite different dance styles. The *kamabeka* dance emphasizes vigorous shoulder movements, while the *ndombolo* dance, on the contrary, is mostly restricted to vigorous waist gyration movements, often with sexual connotations. While this fusion is 'creative' and expresses a dynamic culture process, it is perceived by some as posing a great threat to the traditional authenticity, identity and originality of *litungu* music and *kamabeka* dance. In this regard, critics argue that *litungu* music and *kamabeka* dance as agents of Bukusu traditional cultural-artistic identity are on the verge of collapse if cultural identity policy structures are not put in place to counter this negative and retrogressive 'creativity,' which may soon leave the community with nothing to claim as its own cultural expression.

Bibliography

Masasabi, Nancy A. 2002. 'Bukusu Litungu Music: An Analysis, Arrangement and Creative Composition.' Unpublished MA thesis, Kenyatta University, Nairobi. Online at: https://core.ac.uk/download/pdf/43167845.pdf (accessed 16 April 2018).

Masasabi, Nancy A. 2010. *Silao-Sikeleko as a Process of Performance Compositional Elaboration in Bukusu Litungu Music*. Unpublished Ph.D. dissertation, University of South Africa, Pretoria.

Senoga-Zake, George W. 2000. *Folk Music of Kenya for Teachers and Students of the Music-Loving Public*. Nairobi: Uzima Press.

Shitubi, Isaac W. 2005. 'External Influences on the Litungu Traditional Popular Music of the Luhya in Kenya.' In *Emerging Solutions for Musical Arts Education in Africa*, ed. Anri Herbst. Cape Town: African Minds.

Wafula, Mukasa S. 2007. Personal interview with the author.

Wanyama, Mellitus N. 2008. 'Dance as a Means of Cultural Identity: A Case of the *Bukusu Kamabeka* Dance.' *Journal of Music Research in Africa* 5(2): 213–22. Online at https://www.tandfonline.com/doi/abs/10.1080/18125980902797013 (accessed 24 August 2018).

Discography

Munialo, Godfrey. *Four Songs on Litungu*. Dagoretti Records. *2017*: Kenya. (Digital album.)

Original Musical Instruments of Kenya. Polydor POLP 315. *1972*: Kenya. (Includes three tracks featuring the *litungu*.)

YouTube

(accessed 16 April 2018).

https://www.youtube.com/watch?v=3bMkUiD4SGM

https://www.youtube.com/watch?v=3LmcCRLllws&list=RD3LmcCRLllws&t=3

MELLITUS NYONGESA WANYAMA

Luga Flow, *see* **Hip-Hop in Uganda**

Ma/Gaisa

The music genre *ma/gaisa* expresses united identity and cultural pride in the language and ethnicity of the Damara people of Namibia. 'Ma/gaisa' literally means 'true traditional music' and is based on Damara folklore modernized with contemporary instruments and influences. The genre's predecessor, traditional /gais (also known as !hu tsans or !hu dans) music, is a form of Damara play with storytelling, singing and chanting, based on highly complex clapping rhythms and dances in 6/8 and 4/4 meters. The term /gais refers to 'inheritance' and 'traditional music' in the Khoekhoegowab 'click sound' language of the Damara people of Namibia.

Namibia's independence in 1990 gave rise to expressions of the cultural pride that was undermined during apartheid (1948–90) in the era of South African rule. *Ma/gaisa* emerged as one of these expressions, and as a unique musical brand in Namibia. It was named by Brian Gonteb, cultural officer in the Ministry of Arts, Education, and Culture in the 1990s. According to Gonteb (interview, 2017), musicians had no name for their genre of music until the 1980s, when the *ma/gaisa* genre was formed by influences from *mbaqanga*, US funk music and South African styles such as *pantsula* and bubblegum disco, popularized by artists including Slush and Brenda Fassie. The genre is a mixture of different influences, and Gonteb further notes that musicians adopted the genre name Damara *pantsula*, later Damara *punchi* or Damara *punch*, because they wanted to be associated with whatever was well known or popular at the time. Some popular bands that played music in this genre were the Ras Cool Band, Tcoqma and Axue. The term 'Damara punchi' was coined by Mr. Peter Joseph !Auxab who, ironically, had the heaviest traditional /gais undertones in his music in comparison with fellow artists in the 1990s such as Mr. Nick Mokomelo and Mister Wille. Gonteb explains that the term 'punchi' was derived from the South African music/dance style of *pantsula* of the late 1980s and early 1990s. According to Mr. !Auxab (Gonteb 2017), the concept of 'Damara punch' is also connected to the English word 'punch' with its connotations of striking or hitting. The story goes that when United Nations Transition Assistance Group (UNTAG) was in Namibia in 1989 just before Independence, they saw people during a *besub* wedding festivity performing the !hu tsans /gais, a dance that involves hard stomping on the ground. UNTAG members asked what the commotion was about, to which, according to Mr. !Auxab, the people at the wedding party replied 'it is punching the ground,' hence 'Damara punch.'

However, in the late 1990s Gonteb and colleagues decided to change the genre name to *ma/gaisa*, stepping away from the South African terminology of *pantsula* and the tribal connotation of Damara, thus creating a new, unique Namibian genre that was not exclusive to one ethnic group. In the 1990s many Namibian musicians were frustrated with the inability to break through, either in the South African market or at home in Namibia, due to the lack of support from radio stations and promoters. Live music in Namibia was competing with electronic *kwaito*, which was taking Namibia by storm. Therefore, musicians decided to start their own *ma/gaisa* genre. In the late 2010s *ma/gaisa* is highly popular and prevalent on national radio stations.

Musically, the genre is characterized by pentatonic melodies, major triad chords, 4/4 and 6/8 meter, talking basslines of syncopated sixteenth notes and punchy up-tempo 'four-to-the-floor' beats with snares on the offbeats. *Ma/gaisa*'s sound is shaped by Auto-tune vocals, tone-bending synthesizers and melodies, rhythmic playing and various syncopated drum breaks. Generally, the diatonic major scale is used for melodies with occasional 'coloring' through a lowered fifth or seventh scale degree. Instruments such as synthesizers, horns, guitars or bass often repeat the song's main vocal melody. Typically, accompanying melodies include descending 'glides' from the octave (eighth) toward the major sixth, from the major fifth toward the fourth and between the major second and tonic. Harmonic progressions are based on various I-IV-V patterns hailing from Western European music. *Ma/gaisa* music is repetitive in structure, generally without different musical sections such as choruses and bridges, although producer Steven Alvin !Naruseb from Welwitchia Records creates songs that adopt these Western popular music forms.

Lyrics are sung, spoken and chanted in call-and-response forms, and they deal with personal stories of fun, love and the challenges of life. For example, Mr. Nick Mokomelo was known for songs such as 'Ta khom, aa sao khoen ga !Nari-o,' meaning 'Let's Not Go With People When They Travel,' referring to kids staying home to 'party' when parents travel or are out, and '/Gui #namisa /khubi tere mama,' which means 'Borrow Me One Hip, Mama.' Mr. PJ !Auxab had a popular song called '!Hao-khoese tanisen,' meaning 'Behave Like a Guest When You Visit Other People.' Brian Gonteb explains that since the 2000s most songs are about love, although traditional /gais music included more songs dealing with daily events and activities, such as herding, alongside love songs. Gonteb affirms that the rise of love songs reflects a change in society: taboos about love-related matters have diminished and women artists (who have been plentiful since the 2010s) such as T-Bozz and Staika tend to sing about matters concerning love and relationships including the high prevalence of gender-based violence.

Music During Apartheid

During apartheid, Namibia was divided into homelands ('bantustans') strictly segregating the population according to ethnicity. Damaraland was situated in northwest Namibia, which later became the Erongo and Kunene region. Due to labor migration, men were often forced to work outside their homelands. They gathered in new urban settings with people from different cultures, creating new subcultures. Namibia's capital, Windhoek, was a cultural hub, hosting a vibrant music scene during the days of the 'Old Location.' Old Location was an area in central Windhoek where black communities lived until they were violently removed by the apartheid regime in the late 1950s and sent to live in townships many kilometers outside of the city center. Between the 1920s and 1930s urban culture emerged in African-run dance halls and *shebeens*, where live bands played and people danced. Bands generally played covers of popular US and South African music using saxophones, double bass, drums and guitars. It was mostly instrumental music, but sometimes there were vocalists. This lively scene was disrupted by forced resettlement in the 1950s and 1960s, pushing people into the new ethnically segregated township Katutura. New nightclubs emerged in Katutura and Khomasdal, offering some live performance opportunities. Bands usually consisted of people from the same cultural background (Herero, Damara or Owambo, etc.), although there were also 'mixed' bands. Due to the censorship policies of the apartheid regime, music from the United States and South Africa dominated the radios. South African genres such as *mbaquanga* thus influenced many of Namibia's contemporary music genres.

In the 1970s various South African bands, such as the Crimsons and the Poppettes, were popular and frequently toured Namibia (former 'South West Africa'). However, local bands including the Ugly Creatures, Chicittos, Baronages, Children From Pluto, Bee Bop Brothers, the Black Five and the Chiclets offered ample competition. The Chiclets were mainly a Damara band that also sang in Damara/Nama. They played covers from South Africa and the United States but gradually started creating their own repertoire that incorporated their cultural heritage. The Black Five band, later renamed the 'Ama Africa Band,' was a revolutionary group that focused attention on the independence struggle with their song '#Anabeka #nu /goaro' or 'Black for Nothing Girl.'

As Gonteb explains, between the 1960s and 1980s local bands also covered traditional songs of /gais music that later evolved into the *ma/gaisa* genre. The /gais music was played mainly on guitars and accordion. A major stylistic change was the introduction of the electric keyboard in the 1980s. The development of *ma/gaisa* was heavily influenced by the possibilities and limitations this instrument brought with it; the keyboard had no 6/8 beats like those found in traditional /gais music, so the marching beat 1/2 was adopted instead, which was related to the bubble disco music popular at the time. The advent of the keyboard offered possibilities to play basslines together with the programmed drums and harmonic chords on one instrument. Gonteb describes how many people stopped playing guitar because they found that the keyboard produced sounds for drums, bass and melodies, making a one-man or two-man band possible. Economically this was also favorable since there was not much to earn. Thus, between the 1960s and the 1990s the development of *ma/gaisa* music went from instrumental-based bands of guitar, double bass, drums and sax to vocal-led groups on mainly keyboards and drums.

After Apartheid: The Emergence of *Ma/gaisa*

Ma/gaisa represents the cultural identity of Damara people in a postapartheid society where ethnicity was a tool for social segregation and indigenous cultural practices were undermined. After Namibia's independence from apartheid in the 1990s the various ethnolinguistic groups started 'defining, negotiating and legitimizing their identities in a new Namibian nation' (Markusic 2000, 1, cited in Mans 2003, 120). However, as Gonteb explains, they stepped away from Damara punch as a genre name because they found it too socially exclusive and wanted to 'open up' the genre.

Ma/gaisa originated in the western coastal towns of Namibia, in the Erongo region. In the 2000s the Welwitchia Music Production studio, led by producer and keyboardist Steven Alvin !Naruseb, developed the typical *ma/gaisa* sound. The first time the term appeared was on Phura's debut album *Tsuba Tes Go Ti /Namsa* (2006). Phura and other artists including Stanley (Ou Stakes) and Raphael & Pele popularized the term and genre. These artists represent various grooves and dance styles within the *ma/gaisa* style: Phura originated the style, while Stanley (Ou Stakes) and Dixon produced more jazzy and R&B-influenced *ma/gaisa* grooves. Raphael & Pele developed their own signature and performed a dance style called *marus gereseb*. In 2015 Simon Amunjera was one of a few artists who performed traditional *ma/gaisa* on keyboards. Musicians including Axue, Habasen, Stanley Hamaseb, Dennis Eiseb, Manneckey Khoe-Aob, Amakhoe Gawaseb and others specialized in incorporating traditional Damara music on modern instruments while mixing it with jazz. The 'M Connection Band' from Swakopmund was another major influence with their song '/Gamdisi /gui-/a' or 'Twenty One,' referring to the date of Namibia's independence.

Performance

Performances take place in concert halls, clubs and functions in various instrumental formations: either live (electric bass, keyboards, guitars and a drum set) or with keyboards that produce drumbeats. Beginning in the 2000s many vocalists performed only with a DJ for financial and practical reasons, although they were generally backed by dancers. Depending on the artist, fashion may range from traditional attire to the latest global trends and crossovers thereof.

Various artists represent this genre, including People's Choice, Backos and Stella. Leading names in the 2010s include Stanley, Dixon, Female Donkey, Lettie and Damara DikDing. These artists fuse musical elements from various genres (mainly *kwaito*, R&B and hip-hop) in their *ma/gaisa* music to reach audiences outside their language group. As noted earlier, contemporary *ma/gaisa* since the late 2000s has included more female artists; women performers were virtually nonexistent in the genre before the participation of Bulan, Titirtos, Letis and others.

In Namibia, most 'traditionally oriented music' is often confined to the specific ethnolinguistic groups; thus, special *ma/gaisa* festivals, tours and 'bashes' around the country present *ma/gaisa* artists. However, in the 2010s *ma/gaisa* became highly popular and has been much played on national radio since then. Crossover collaborations between artists of different ethnolinguistic groups take place, and thus the genre is becoming a valued contemporary aesthetic style, outside of purely ethnic-related significance. The genre will continue developing as artists go on innovating ways of combining music and performance styles from around the globe with their cultural Damara heritage.

Scholarship and Dissemination

Until 2015 practically no academic research existed on contemporary Namibian music styles. Other than YouTube videos, one could only find information and CDs through research in Namibia. This highlights the challenges in the distribution of Namibian music since independence. Also, until 2015 many field recordings of 'traditional music' as well as popular music from the 1950s to 1980s remained inaccessible due to the lack of functioning equipment (cassettes, LP players, reel-to-reel recordings). 'Stolen Moments – Namibian Music History Untold' is a collective of music researchers who started digitizing recordings from the National Archives in 2015, an initiative that will make it easier for people to access Namibian music through an online platform. Through an interactive Facebook page, the Ngoma Research Collective shares information on Namibian music practices – both old and new: https://www.facebook.com/pages/Ngoma-Research-Collective.

Bibliography

Gariseb, André J. 2006. 'Namibia: New Release from Phura.' *New Era*, 13 February. Online at: http://allafrica.com/stories/200602130630.html (accessed 10 January 2018).

Hartmann, Wolfram, Silver, Jeremy, and Hayes, Patricia, eds. 1997. *The Colonizing Camera: Photographs in the Making of Namibian History 1915–1950s*. Windhoek: Out of Africa.

Hayes, Patricia, Silvester, Jeremy, Wallace, Marion, and Hartmann, Wolfram, eds. 1984. *Namibia Under South African Rule: Mobility and Containment, 1915-46*. Oxford: James Currey.

Kambaekwa, Carlos. 2014. 'Down Musical Memory Lane – Baronages, One Time the Kasies Live Music Toast.' *New Era*, 9 May. Online at: https://www.newera.com.na/2014/05/09/musical-memory-lane-baronages-time-kasies-live-music-toast/ (accessed 10 January 2018).

Mans, Minette E. 2003. 'State, Politics and Culture: The Case of Music.' In *Re-Examining Liberation in Namibia: Political Culture Since Independence*, ed. Henning Melber. Uppsala: Nordiska Afrikainstitutet, 113–29.

Mans, Minette. 2015. 'Music in Africa: Traditional Music in Namibia.' Online at: http://musicinafrica.net/traditional-music-namibia (accessed 10 January 2018).

Matundu, Kae. 2013. 'Namibia: Is This Oviritje Moment of Truth?' *New Era*, 3 May. Online at: http://allafrica.com/stories/201305031299.html (accessed 10 January 2018).

Mupetami, Limba. 2013. 'Death by Damara Punch.' *The Namibian*, 13 December. Online at: http://www.namibian.com.na/indexx.php?archive_id=117688&page_type=archive_story_detail&page=1 (accessed 10 January 2018).

'Tate Boetie spits on Kwaito's popularity.' 2007. *Informanté*, 20 July. Online at: http://www.informante.web.na/node/861 (accessed 10 January 2018).

Interviews

Gariseb, André J. 2015. Interview with the author.
Gonteb, Brian. 2017. Interview with the author.
Kambaekwa, Carlos. 2015. Interview with the author.
Khoe-Aob, Mannecky. 2017. Interview with the author.
Naruseb, Steven Alvin. 2015. Interview with the author

Discographical References

Ama Africa Band. '#Anabeka #nu /goaro.' South West African Broadcasting Corporation (SWABC). *1984*: South West Africa.

Auxab, Pieter Jozef. '!Hao-khoese tanisen.' Gallo Records. *1990*: South Africa.

M Connection Band. '/Gamdisi /gui-/a.' Independent release. *1990*: Namibia.

Mokomelo, Nick. '/Gui #namisa /khubi tere mama.' SWABC radio. *1989*: Namibia.

Mokomelo, Nick. 'Ta khom, ta sao khoen ga !Nari-O.' SWABC radio. *1989*: Namibia.

Phura. *Tsuba tes go ti /namsa*. Welwitchia Music Productions. *2006*: Namibia.

Discography

Backos. *Jive*. Amaku Production. *2006*: Namibia.

Bulan. *//Naxu-te*. Desert Tunes Productions. *2013*: Namibia.

Damara Dikding. *Beats form the Heart*. Chossta Records. N.d.: Namibia.

Emy-Lee. *'/Gamiros' //Khoa i ge huka ra*. Welwitchia Music Productions. N.d.: Namibia.

Female Donkey. *Raak my aan*. Namibia Music Production. *2014*: Namibia.

King Phura. *Uts ha-i /kha #khi*. Welwitchia Music Productions. *2011*: Namibia.

Mannetjie Zulu. *!Narimari-e?* Khomas Music Productions. *2012*: Namibia.

Ou Stakes. *Tsarab a #an*. Ou Stakes Productions. *2014*: Namibia.

T-Bozz & Staika. */Asa //aeb ma/gaisa Vol. 1*. Coastal Beats Productions. *2011*: Namibia.

TukoroS. *Di-ünusen*. Desert Tunes Productions. N.d.: Namibia.

Facebook

Ngoma Research Collective (Namibia). Official Facebook page. https://www.facebook.com/Ngoma-Research-Collective-329144573899787/timeline/

Stolen Moments Namibia – Namibian History Untold. Official Facebook page. https://www.facebook.com/Stolen-Moments-Namibia-193689374012214/timeline/

SHISHANI VRANCKX

Makossa

Makossa is a dance music genre that emerged in the 1950s in the coastal regions of Cameroon, mainly in the country's largest city, Douala. It gained wide popularity in the country and was marketed as the only distinctive 'Cameroonian' popular music genre until the 1970s. *Makossa* is a guitar-based dance music in binary rhythm that developed in the wake of Cameroon's independence in 1960. Its musical foundation is the traditional music of the Sawa, the people living at the coast in and around Douala.

Noah (2010, 27–31) mentions in particular the *assiko*, *bolobo*, *essewe* and *ambass-bey* dances as main influences on *makossa*. In the same vein, *makossa* was also influenced by dance music current at the time such as highlife, Congolese *rumba/soukouss* and funk, as well as by the characteristics of church music. *Makossa* songs are commonly sung in Douala, the language of the Sawa people, which is a tonal language. As the twenty-first century progressed, *makossa* songs were sung increasingly in French and also, though much less often, in English.

There is some confusion over the term 'makossa' and its meaning. While there is a consensus that it is derived from the term 'kossa,' some claim that this term refers to a children's handclapping game; others state that 'kossa' is a Sawa dance. It is possible that both claims are accurate. Noah explains that the Douala word 'kossa' is itself a neologism and describes a joyful interjection, sometimes akin to a curse, used to stimulate and motivate dancers. As it concerns dance, 'di kossa' (singular) and 'm'a kossa' (plural) refer to contorted movements (Noah 2010, 23).

Instrumentation, Style and Lyrics

Makossa is music for both dancing and listening. While dancing occurs frequently, lyrics are also much in focus. The main musical instrument for *makossa* is the rhythm guitar on which are played arpeggiated chords in finger-picking style. Songs usually begin with a short introduction of solo arpeggiated guitar chords with percussion, bass guitar and keyboards joining in. Early *makossa* songs were commonly performed by two guitars and percussion with an upright bass sometimes included. In later years electric guitars were introduced as well as keyboards, the organ and brass sections. The electric bass guitar has held a special position in *makossa* since the 1970s when it became important to musical arrangements.

Makossa songs are played in a moderate tempo for ease of dancing, with a basic binary rhythm commonly in 4/4 time. The songs are generally in major keys and often use three chords or fewer. The principal, foundational feature of *makossa* consists of cyclic guitar patterns which fulfill both a melodic and a rhythmic function. While one guitar plays a melodic foundation in a steady pattern, the other either joins in with a complementary pattern or replays the song's main melody while the singers are quiet. In early *makossa*, *dongas* and rattles set the pulse and provide a characteristic rhythmic foundation which is later taken over by the drum set. Additional sounds are then provided by keyboards or an organ and a brass section. Over the course of several decades *makossa* songs have become quite open to outside influences, especially those from *soukouss*, *zouk* and other Latin American dance music. In early *makossa*, the songs have mostly been in strophic form, often sung in two vocal parts. As time went on, songs were also structured according to a verse and refrain model, with background singers also included. The lyrics, sung mainly in Douala and sometimes in French, cover topics such as love and relationships, daily life, social pressures and moral and political issues. Also, some *makossa* musicians have performed protest music.

The History of Makossa and Its Principal Performers

Makossa evolved in the 1950s around a group of musicians who performed in different lineups in the bars and cabarets of Douala. Elie Mbongue Diboue, Essombe Théodore, Lobè Lobè Rameau, Nginia Noe na Epe Valentin and Regine Mundo featured among the first generation of *makossa* musicians. Their music was released on shellac discs by European and Congolese labels, most notably Ngoma, Opika and Loningisa, and was widely available in Douala and its surroundings. The music of this time has not, however, lasted in collective memory and the recordings have become quite rare.

It is the second generation of *makossa* musicians, including some of the aforementioned musicians who were still performing and recording in the 1960s, who count as the genre's pioneers. These musicians contributed to *makossa*'s emergence and musical development in the first decade after Cameroon's independence from France in 1960 and the United Kingdom in 1961. These singers and guitarists included Nelle Eyoum, Mouelle Guillaume, Ebanda Manfred, Willy le Paape and Epée Mbende Richard. Most of them performed together in duos and groups at some point in their careers. Among these groups were Ambiance Jazz, with Paul Ebeny and Wille le Pape; Le Tout Puissant Negro Styl, with Nelle Eyoum and Eke Samuel; Uvucot Jazz with Epée Mbende Richard; Orfecam Jazz with Mouelle Guillaume and Nelle Eyoum; Toumba Africa with Ebanda Manfred and Villa Vienne; and Los Calvinos. Popular solo musicians included Eboa Lottin and Charles Lembe, who were both guitarists and singers.

Nelle Eyoum is commonly credited with having invented the name of the genre by exclaiming 'kossa, kossa' during performances to motivate dancers. He has consequently come to be known as the 'Father of Makossa.' The two-part singing at this time usually involved two male voices. However, in some cases the duos were sung by a man and a woman. This was the case, for example, with Ebanda Manfred and Villa Vienne, and Ekotto Robert and Ruth Soppo. The songs of these *makossa* bands were released by international labels such as Ngoma, Opika (Congo) and Decca (Europe), but also by newly established Cameroonian labels such as Africambiance in the 1960s and Disques Cousins in the 1970s. In comparison to the 1950s, the instrumentation of bands had been extended by the mid-1960s to sometimes include the upright bass, maracas and *congas*. However, *makossa* songs could also be performed solo with a guitar as, for example, was the case with Eboa Lottin. The influence of Congolese dance music in Cameroon – with heavy Cuban and Latin American characteristics – is immediately audible in early *makossa*. Musicians and bands at this time also included Latin American-derived and -influenced songs in the style of *merengue* or *soukouss* in their repertoire.

The guitarist and singer Francis Bebey, notable for his rather intellectual approach, represents a special case in the history of Cameroonian music. Active as a musician since the 1960s, Bebey included *makossa* songs in his repertoire. He studied at the Sorbonne in the 1950s and settled in Paris, writing some novels and working at UNESCO as an adviser on films and radio and television programs. In the 1960s he began releasing recordings of his solo guitar music, turning to make his living with guitar music in the 1970s. He released *makossa*-style songs with French lyrics in which he told humorous stories over his guitar playing, speaking rather than singing. Bebey later turned to instrumental music. His music was for listening rather than dancing.

The sound of *makossa* changed with the electrification of instruments. The third generation of *makossa* musicians evolved during the 1970s, the standard setup for a *makossa* band becoming two electric guitars (lead and rhythm), an electric bass, a drum set, percussion and – depending on availability – organ or keyboards and brass sections. *Makossa* became known as the only 'Cameroonian' popular dance music and was identified as being modern, urban and cosmopolitan. When school bands performed cover versions of Cameroonian artists alongside covers of international artists such as the Jackson Five and James Brown, the genre they covered was generally *makossa*. Les Black Styls Band, with popular musicians Nkotti François, Toto Guillaume, Nseke Robert and Emile Kangue, were particularly important at this time, being favored to accompany musicians such as Missè Ngoh François, Jean Paul Mondo, Koulle Paul and Axel Mouna.

In the 1970s *makossa* gained international popularity through the song 'Soul Makossa' by Manu Dibango. Dibango was a jazz rather than a *makossa* musician but, like many other musicians, included *makossa* pieces in his repertoire. The song was actually not in the *makossa* style, but rather a song in a jazzy disco style, and was on the B-side of a single for the Cameroonian market. The song's only links to Cameroonian *makossa* are thus the words in the song's title and refrain. This song nonetheless made Manu Dibango, Cameroon and *makossa* famous internationally and increased its popularity in Cameroon. Consequently, in many overviews of Cameroonian dance music, Manu Dibango and 'Soul Makossa' are given prominence, while others – popular and known locally – are not.

Meanwhile, there were considerable developments in *makossa*. The guitarist Toto Guillaume, already popular in Cameroon, left Douala and his band Les Black Styls in 1976 and moved to Paris, where he studied music. This move can be seen as the beginning of the Paris-based production of *makossa*, the start of a period of about ten years during which virtually all successful *makossa* songs were recorded, arranged and produced by a group of musicians based in Paris who were known in Cameroon as 'l'équipe nationale du makossa' (the National Makossa Team). The core of the group was Toto Guillaume and bassist Aladji Touré, and the recording studio where they primarily worked was the Johanna Studio in Paris. These two musicians, along with various other Cameroonian musicians who were based in Paris, were responsible for the main output of *makossa* music for the Cameroonian market. They arranged and produced records for – among others – Les Black Styl (as a group and in its role as an accompanying band), Penda Dalle, Axel Mouna, Ben Decca, Moni Bilé, Bella Njoh and Charlotte Mbango. During this time the bass lines in *makossa* became more prominent, while the foundational cyclic guitar pattern remained, as did the roles played by the drum set, the organ or keyboards and the brass section. The music also borrowed elements from contemporary global pop trends including reggae and funk, as well as incorporating elements from various African genres. Popular bass players at the time were Vicky Edimo and Jeannot Dikoto Mandengue. Many musicians of this generation started off in bands and then tried to pursue a solo career. In addition, because *makossa* was the most popular Cameroonian music genre of the time, musicians not from the Douala region such as Anne-Marie Nzié, Uta Bella, Rachel Tsoungui, Elvis Kemayou, Sam Fan Thomas and André-Marie Tala integrated *makossa* songs into their repertoires.

The split-up of the production team of Aladji Touré and Toto Guillaume in the mid-1980s ended a successful era for *makossa* and represented a breaking point in the genre's history. Until the mid-1980s *makossa* dominated the Cameroonian music market, although challenged from the beginning of the 1980s by the newly emerging dance music, *bikutsi*. As Mathias Eric Owona Nguini has shown, these two principal Cameroonian genres held a specific significance in terms of being for or against the government in the national political conflict that began in the early 1990s, with *makossa* becoming the music of opposition (Owona Nguini 1995).

While the breakup of the Paris-based 'National Makossa Team' was a rupture in the successful marketing and the immense output of records, *makossa* nevertheless continued to be composed and performed in Cameroon. Many musicians who had started their careers in Paris with Touré and Guillaume such as Ben Decca and Dina Bell continued to perform during the 1990s and 2000s. The 1990s also saw a rise in successful solo women *makossa* musicians such as the singers Sissi Dipoko, Charlotte Mbango, Nadia Ewande and Grace Decca. *Makossa* songs also made increasing use of synthesizers and digital audio workstations at this time. A musician particularly popular during the 1990s was Petit Pays, who combined a *zouk* rhythmic foundation with typical *makossa* guitar lines. The media referred to his music as 'makozouk,' and he became famous for provocative presentations, for example, posing naked on an LP cover, as well as for controversial lyrics, which were common in the Douala language.

In the politically tense and combative time of the early 1990s, during which protests were daily occurrences and Cameroon witnessed the introduction of a multiparty state system and the liberation of the press, *makossa* musician Lapiro de Mbanga became one of the most outspoken protest musicians, singing critically about socioeconomic and political issues and blaming the political elite for current conditions. Lapiro de Mbanga appeared on the musical scene in Cameroon in the mid-1980s. He sang in Pidgin English and regularly criticized the Cameroonian government, including the president, in his songs. He remained in opposition to the ruling party, with his political engagement resulting in his imprisonment in 2008, sentenced to a three-year term for his song 'Constitution constipée' (Constipated Constitution) about a change in the Cameroonian constitution that allowed the president to serve indefinitely. His imprisonment was heavily criticized by international NGOs, but Mbanga was only released in 2011. He and his family were granted asylum in the United States. Mbanga died in 2014 at the age of 56.

Since the turn of the millennium technological developments have influenced the production of *makossa* songs, with production mainly taking place in French or Cameroonian studios. Songs have increasingly been accompanied by video clips and have increasingly used the French language. The sounds of *zouk* and other Latin American-derived dance genres have persisted. Generally speaking, vocals and an electronically produced percussion foundation have come to the foreground, while guitar lines have taken more of a back seat. Since the 2000s Dora Decca, Sergeo Polo, Njorheur and Narcisse Pryze have emerged as popular *makossa* musicians of a younger generation. At the same time singers active for decades such as Salle John have continued to perform. Singer Claudia Dikosso launched a *makossa* festival in 2016 in Douala.

Makossa in Its Political and Social Context

Makossa developed at around the time that Cameroon became independent, evolving during a period in which there was a quest for genuine symbols of Cameroonian identity. It has been celebrated as the first popular style of 'Cameroonian' dance music. During the 1960s and 1970s *makossa* was widely disseminated through radio and records. In these decades of economic prosperity and the autocratic development of a national political identity, *makossa* was to become the musical companion of 'modernism,' of the desire to create a modern, up-to-date, but nonetheless genuinely Cameroonian society. In this sense, *makossa* was the first modern urban music in Cameroon. *Makossa* musicians were generally dressed in Western-style clothes – suits and ties – and performed in bars and discotheques in front of a middle- and upper-class public. With *makossa* musician and production moving to Paris and with the introduction of hi-fi systems, live performances of *makossa* in Cameroon became increasingly rare. While certain generations might have their *makossa* favorites, the music has continued to appeal to people of all ages and socioeconomic backgrounds. Contemporary musicians perform mainly in Douala cabarets at weekends, as well as at concerts and festivals, principally in Cameroon and France.

Bibliography

Dibango, Manu. 1994. *Three Kilos of Coffee: An Autobiography*. Chicago, IL: University of Chicago Press.

Nkolo, Jean-Victor. 1994. 'Makossa: 1. Bikutsi: 1. Cameroon: Music of a Small Continent.' In *World Music: The Rough Guide*, eds. Simon Broughton et al. London: Rough Guides, 324–33.

Nkolo, Jean-Victor, and Ewens, Graeme. 1999. 'Cameroon: Music of a Small Continent.' In *The Rough Guide to World Music Volume 1: Africa, Europe and the Middle East*. eds. Simon Broughton et al. London: Rough Guides, 440–7.

Noah, Jean Maurice. 2010. *Le Makossa. Une musique africaine moderne* [Makossa. A Modern African Music]. Paris: Harmattan.

Nyamnjoh, Francis B., and Fokwang, Jude. 2005. 'Entertaining Repression: Music and Politics in Postcolonial Cameroon.' *African Affairs* 104(415): 251–74.

Owona Nguini, Mathias Eric. 1995. 'La Controverse bikutsi-makossa: Musique, politique et affinités régionales au Cameroun (1990–1994)' [The Bikutsi-Makossa Controversy: Music, Politics and Regional Affinities in Cameroon (1990–1994)]. *L'Afrique politique*: 267–76. Online at: http://regards.in2p3.fr/fiche.php?id=7950 (accessed 20 June 2018).

Discographical References

de Mbanga, Lapiro. 'Constitution constipée.' JPS Production. *2008*: Cameroon.

Dibango, Manu. 'Soul Makossa/Lily.' Fiesta 51.199. *1971*: France.

Discography

Ashanty, Tokoto. *This and This*. Wea Filipacchi Music WE 3(4)1-50567. *1978*: France.

Bébé Manga. *Ami Oyomiya*. SIIS 0010. *1980*: Ivory Coast.

Bebey, Francis. *Bia So Nika*. Ozileka Records OZIL 3309. *1981*: France.

Bell, Dina. 'Yoma Yoma/Manaka.' (45 rpm 12-inch maxi single.) Azengue Productions AZEN 1080. *1979*: France.

Bilé, Moni. *Bijou*. Safari Ambiance SA 103. *1982*: France.

Bolanga, Ebongue. 'Ndolo Na Tondi No/Na Wasi Moni.' Fiesta 759. *ca. 1955*: France.

Dalle, Penda. *Ndut'a Diba*. Africa Oumba ADLP 004. *1981*: France.

de Mbanga, Lapiro. 'Pas Argent, No Love.' *Pas Argent, No Love*. Haissam Records MH 0101. *1985*: France.

Decca, Ben. 'Nyong'a Mulema/Wamsè Timbà.' (45 rpm 12-inch maxi single.) Tempo Records TP 111. *1981*: France.

Decca, Dora. *Aphrodite*. JPS Production CDJPS. *2002*: France.

Diboue, Elie Mbongue. 'Miango Ma Kwed'a Papa/Lidienne Ngon'a Misomba.' Philips P79.271 H. *ca. 1955*: France.

Dickson, Georges. 'Kiss me Doudou.' *Zambé*. BMCA 8701. *1987*: France.

Dikosso, Claudia. *Maturité*. Dri Production. *2008*: Cameroon.

Dikoume Lobbe Henri et son ensemble: 'Nabole Bolea Oa/Osi Wele Mba Bana.' Opika 1227. *ca. 1955*: Congo.

Djento Djene. *Debroussailler*. Safari Ambiance SA 103. *1985*: France.

Ebanda Manfred & l'Orchestre Toumba Africa. 'Elimbi/We Ntuba.' Africambiance AA 66. *ca. 1968*: Cameroon.

Ebeny, Paul, & l'Ambiance Jazz. 'A yo yo/Malea Ma Bobe.' Pathe Marconi G 20037. *1967*: France.

Ebongue, John Leng. 'Sangise Milema/Ndol'a Mpon.' Afro-Disc AD 034. *1976*: France.

Ekambi Brillant & Les Cracks. 'Djongele La N'dolo/Ngon A'boh.' African 90.507. *1971*: France.

Epée Mbende Richard & Uvocot-Jazz. 'Munyenge Mwa Dooh-Dooh/Je Nde Mbo A Mboa.' Africambiance AA 34. *ca. 1967*: Cameroon.

Eyoum, Nelle,& L'Orchestre Negro-Styl. 'Bosinga Be Nde Njon A Kwedi/Mambo Ma Timbi.' Jicco JC 48. *ca. 1970*: Nigeria.

Eyoum, Nelle, & Los Calvinos. 'Kembe/Mboa E Ma Pung Wea.' Africambiance AA87. *ca. 1968*: Cameroon.

Guillaume, Toto. 'Dibena.' *(Toguy)*. Disques Espérance ESP 165.551. *1981*: France.

Hen's, Jeannot, & Le Hen's Band. 'Longue.' Cheick Anta Diop Productions. *2001*: Cameroon.

Kingue, Jacky. Patou. Preya Music P.M.C. 0014. *2001*: Cameroon.

Kingué, Michel. 'Longe La Penya/Ndok'a Mun'asu.' Songhaï Son 875. *1975*: France.

Les Black Styl. *Les Black Styl à Paris*. Éditions Rétro 2000 EA 7811101. *1979*: France.

Manulo, Nguime. *Longe Le Nde Bila*. Africa Oumba AOLP 016 – AOK 16, *1984*: France.

Mbango, Charlotte. 'Maloko.' Vol. 3. Energy Production LP 54681. *1991*: Cameroon.

Mbondy Kollo Sadrack & l'Orchestre Super Estudiantine-Jazz. 'Bona Bito/Na Mawolo Makossa.' Jicco JC 13. *ca. 1970*: Nigeria.

Mboule, Joe. 'Ison/Julie.' Sonafric SAF 1808. *1976*: France.

Mouelle Guillaume et l'Orchestre Orfecam Jazz. 'Minya Ma Wenge/Mbanga Mo O Dimene.' Africambiance AA 64. *ca. 1968*: Cameroon.

Mouloby, Jean, et son Ensemble. 'Mawuse Ma Ndolo/Benyengue Ba Duala.' Opika 1357. *ca. 1955*: Congo.

Mouna, Axel. *Bobia*. Africa Oumba AOLP 005. *1981*: Cameroon.

Moussy, Pierre de. *Ndolo L'Amour*. Edition Decko MOU 060. *1984*: France.

N'johreur. *Harmattan*. JPS Production. *2003*: France.

Orchestre Festival Jazz – Gauthi – Ebenezer Ekwalla Bonny. 'L'amour n'est pas force/Na Dipi Babo.' Africambiance AA 83. *ca. 1968*: Cameroon.

Petit Pays et les Sans Visa. *Les morts ne sont pas morts*. Milan 813 043. *1992*: France.

Rameau et Jacquy Lobbe Lobbe. 'Myango Ma Duala/Mbongsan Ma Ngando.' Opika 1356. *ca. 1955*: Congo.

Samuel Same & les Black Styl. 'Bila/Etum na wa.' Sonafric SAF 1648. *1974*: Cameroon.

Valentin, Nginia Noe na Epe. 'Ngon'a Bo/Loa Nginia.' Ngoma 1019. *ca. 1955*: Congo.

ANJA BRUNNER AND JOACHIM OELSNER

Makwayela

Makwayela is a music and dance genre from the southern provinces of the Republic of Mozambique. Its presence has been documented from the early 1930s, when it was developed by the male population involved in the great Southern African labor migration to the rapidly growing mining industry of the South African Transvaal. This migration occurred during the nineteenth century and continued into the twenty-first century (Delius 2017). Ever since the discovery of gold in South Africa in 1886 and the subsequent bilateral agreement of labor migration between colonial Mozambique and South Africa in 1902, the male population of southern Mozambique has migrated in large numbers to the South African gold and coal mines. Within a framework negotiated between the Witwatersrand Native Labour Association and the Portuguese colonial authorities, over one-third of the active male population of southern Mozambique were working in the South African mines between the beginning of the twentieth century and Mozambican Independence in 1975 (Mercandalli et al. 2017, 18). Each year about 150,000 miners traveled from their homes in Mozambique for periods of 18 months to two years. The young miners worked long hours, mostly as unskilled laborers shoveling coal and pulling carts in dangerous working conditions where injury and death were not uncommon, conditions documented in the film, *Marrabentando: The Stories My Guitar Sings/Marrabentando: As histórias que a minha guitarra canta* (2005). They lived in squalid conditions in cramped male hostels divided according to ethnic origin. One of the ways these young men shared some of their troubles and found relief from hardship was through musical performance. This led to the increasing popularity of three southern Mozambican popular music genres: *marrabenta*, *timbila* and *makwayela*, each originating from different migrant mining communities in the region. The proximity to other miners from different regions of southern Africa facilitated the exchange of musical and dance practices among the hostel residents. Thus, *makwayela* displays musical and choreographic features similar to those found in Malawi, Lesotho, Swaziland and, perhaps most recognizable internationally, the South African male choral styles of *isicathamiya* and *mbube* made popular by the Grammy Award-winning male choir, Ladysmith Black Mambazo.

Makwayela performing groups consist of about 8 to 14 male dancers and singers, wearing Western suits, shoes and sometimes hats. They dance in a line known as 'kunfola,' and perform *canções* (songs) in local Bantu languages, in particular Ronga – the language spoken mostly in and around the Mozambican capital of Lourenço Marques (later known as Maputo) – and occasionally in the colonial language of Portuguese. The lyrics make reference to aspects of social life, life cycles, social criticism and public health among other relevant issues.

Makwayela groups carry distinctive names in both Portuguese and English. These names are designed to bring recognition to the groups in the *makwayela* competitions that occurred regularly, not only in the mines, but also in the Mozambican capital and in the villages and towns from which miners departed. The genre became a national symbol following the independence of Mozambique in 1975, with the formation of a new Mozambican government led largely by Mozambican ethnic groups from the south of the country where *makwayela* was popular. In a matter of years, *makwayela* was practiced throughout Mozambique and taught in schools and workplaces. *Makwayela* groups were created formally in the newly nationalized factories, hospitals, markets and urban neighborhood community centers as well as within public sector work forces and assemblages of public sector administrators. *Makwayela* was performed at public events across the country, including in the national parliament (Carvalho 2004).

A range of different *makwayela* styles was in evidence through groups performing in the capital city, Maputo, in the 1980s and early 1990s. A compact disc compilation, *Makwayela* (1998), documents these styles, and includes performances by noteworthy groups such as those of the public transport company TPM (Transportes Públicos de Maputo) and the national airline LAM (Linhas Aéreas de Moçambique).

The musical structure of *makwayela* is characterized by vocal polyphony (three to four voices) and repeated rhythmic patterns that include feet stamping. Most manifestations of *makwayela* display a common formal structure made up of four parts: *stokhozele*, *bomba*, *canção* and *istep*. The *stokhozele* (praise speech) is an introductory section in which the *maestro* announces to the public the first few words of the song in an *a cappella* solo, using a melodic formula that helps the performers identify their individual entry note for the second section, the *bomba* (bomb). This is the loudest section, in which a short verse is presented in homophonic harmony. The third section, the *canção* (song), exhibits more elaborate melodic and harmonic configurations and displays contrapuntal organizations of one or two soloists and the full four-voice choir. Finally, *istep* (stomp), the longest section, features a series of repetitions of the same lyrics: performers dance with lively movements, feet stamping and hand gesturing using carefully practiced routines.

With the installation of the Second Republic, after the death of President Samora Machel in a plane crash in 1986, authorities disinvested in *makwayela*. Within a few years only a few groups remained, singing at weddings and private parties. However, the tradition has remained strong in some parts of Southern Mozambique, in particular in the sugar cane-growing region of Manhiça, north of the city of Maputo, where local *makwayela* groups have continued to rehearse regularly and compete in local competitions.

The Makwayela dos TPM group, formed by members of the public transport trade union, became the best-promoted group performing *makwayela*. It performed in several European and African countries and became a representative of the state. In 1984 several of its members were killed in an attack by rebel army forces. In 2009 Makwayela dos TPM issued its only compact disc, *Xitimela Xa Kuya Manhiça*, under the leadership of Gil Mabjeca (d. 2014). The group commemorated its 40th anniversary in a public performance in 2016, once again bringing its surviving members to public attention.

Makwayela was both a factor in and a consequence of the colonial and postcolonial history of Mozambique. From ordeals in the Transvaal mines to the rural-to-urban migration in the southern provinces of Maputo, Gaza and Inhambane, to the genre's status during the 1980s as a state symbol and recognized musical emblem, *makwayela* gave life to social existence in southern Mozambique for over a century and, in some parts of the country, has continued to do so.

Bibliography

Carvalho, João Soeiro de. 1999. 'Makwayela: Choral Performance and Nation Building in Mozambique.' *Horizontes Antropológicos* 5(11): 145–82.

Carvalho, João Soeiro de. 2004. 'Makwayela: Um enunciado sonoro da experiência social no Sul de Moçambique' [Makwayela: A Sonic Statement of Social Experience in Southern Mozambique]. In *Sonoridades Luso-Afro-Brasileiras* [Luso-Afrobrazilian Sonorities], eds. José Machado Pais, Joaquim Pais de Brito and Mário Vieira de Carvalho. Lisbon: Instituto de Ciências Sociais, 143–54.

Delius, Peter. 2017. 'The History of Migrant Labor in South Africa (1800–2014).' In *The Oxford Research Encyclopedia of African History*, ed. Thomas Spear. Online at: http://africanhistory.oxfordre.com/view/10.1093/acrefore/9780190277734.001.0001/acrefore-9780190277734-e-93 (accessed 11 February 2018).

Mercandalli, Sara, Nshimbi, Christopher Changwe, and Moyo, Inocent. 2017. 'Mozambican Labour Migrations, Remittances and Development: Evidence, Practices and Implications for Policy.' In *Migration, Cross-Border Trade and Development in Africa*, eds. Christopher Changwe Nshimbi and Inocent Moyo. London and New York: Palgrave Macmillan, 15–42.

Discographical References

Makwayela: Moçambique. Tradisom VS 09. *1998*: Portugal.

Transportes Públicos de Maputo. *Xitimela Xa Kuya Manhiça*. Radio Moçambique. *2009*: Mozambique.

Discography

Ladysmith Black Mambazo. *Shaka Zulu*. Warner Brothers 9 25582-1, 1-25582. *1987*: USA.

Filmography

Marrabentando: The Stories My Guitar Sings/Marrabentando: As histórias que a minha guitarra canta, dir. Karen Boswall. 2005. Portugal. 52 mins. Documentary with stories and songs by Antonio Marcos and Dilon Djinji and English subtitles.

Online at: http://vimeo.com/43718451 (accessed 22 February 2018).

JOÃO SOEIRO DE CARVAHALLO AND KAREN BOSWALL

Malipenga

Malipenga is a syncretic music and dance art form that arose out of the colonial encounter between Western military traditions and African dance culture in Malawi. It is a costumed group dance for men, using mainly drums, gourd trumpets (kazoos) and whistles for accompaniment, and with elaborate, competitive, synchronized steps and call-and-response singing. The kazoos (trumpets or *malipenga* in the Chewa language) give the dance its name. Two main dance types are the *malipenga white* in which the uniforms are white and individual dance steps more fluid and individualistic and the *malipenga khaki* where khaki uniforms predominate. *Malipenga khaki* choreography is closer to the part-military origins of the dance. In *malipenga* dance, drama and marching mix to varying extents. *Malipenga* is typically performed as a competitive activity between two or more companies of dancers.

History and Related Genres

Malipenga originated when the imitations found in colonial military parades, such as the use of mimicry for entertainment and to resist colonialism in the late nineteenth and early twentieth centuries, were fused with local dances (Ranger 1975; Kamlongera 1986). This syncretization of traditional dances and military parade mimicry of colonial armies on the Swahili coast spread to Malawi, in the case of *malipenga* taking particular root in the Nkhata Bay district, which then included Likoma Island. The many Nyasa (Malawian) King's African Rifles soldiers involved in the East African campaigns of World Wars I and II consolidated these syncretic dances in the popular arena and spread them throughout Malawi and parts of Zambia, where the related *kalela* dance is found (Mitchell 1957).

Beni, *malipenga* and *mganda* have since been carried to Zimbabwe and South Africa by Malawi migrant workers. Like its close relation *mganda*, with which it shares many features, *malipenga* has the same historical roots as *beni*. *Beni*, another dance that resulted from a syncretism between local forms and military marches, is considered by most observers to be the first to result from the encounters between colonial and indigenous cultures. However, both *mganda* and *malipenga* differ from *beni* in some musical patterns, aesthetics and choreography. As a useful generalization, in Malawi *malipenga* is practiced by and shows features of Tonga aesthetics, *mganda* is popular with the Chewa and *beni* is associated largely with the Yao. Thus *mganda* is 'indigenous' to the central region districts of Kasungu, Lilongwe, Nkhota Kota, Ntchisi, Dowa and Salima, while *malipenga* has its spiritual and aesthetic home in the northern and lakeshore districts of Nkhata Bay, Karonga, Rumphi and Likoma Island district. In *beni* the uniforms more closely resemble khaki military ones, while in *mganda* and *malipenga* the uniforms are white, more closely resembling those of a colonial officer class. The starchy white uniforms resonate with the reputed 'fastidious smartness' of Tonga men. The version of *malipenga* called *malipenga khaki* shows the relationship between *beni* and *malipenga*: the uniforms (largely khaki) are similar and this form of *malipenga* has, like *beni*, a more militaristic choreography.

Function

Malipenga, like *mganda*, is performed for entertainment at rural and urban occasions throughout the year (Kamlongera 1986; Nthala 2009). It also carries social commentaries and has, since nationalist times, become a regular genre at political events and weddings. Chirwa (2001) observes that it was used during the fight for independence, a fact that later caused problems during Dr. Banda's era, between 1964 and 1992. After independence, President Banda preferred less critical social commentary. In an attempt at taming the *malipenga* societies, whose music was rich in social and personal commentary, and whose culture and very organization went against the ethos of the one-party state, Dr. Banda accused Nkhata Bay and Nkhota Kota men of being lazy 'bawo- [a chess board type game] playing and *malipenga*-dancing men' who shied away from farm work (Kamlongera 1986). The songs cover both historical and current events and, like the dance steps, evolve as new musical styles are incorporated. Songs may be purely for entertainment or for social praise or critique. Classic *malipenga* songs from the 1950s may be heard on ILAM recordings by Hugh Tracey, for example, 'Akapunda, Mungore' (ca. 1958).

Organization

Malipenga troupes are highly organized, usually at village or area level, showing their partly military origins. There is a quasi-military hierarchy of 'king,' 'adjutant,' 'doctor,' 'nurse' and a council. The 'king,' inevitably the local chief, is the fundraiser and the adjutant acts as the organizing secretary. A company, society or team of *malipenga* dancers is referred to as a *boma* or *bwalo*. Public performances are usually of *bomas* competing with each other in the presence of a hosting king. In the rural area, a chief's compound, a cleared *bwalo* (gathering place or ground, also referred to as *boma*) is used for performances, while in urban or peri-urban areas football grounds or stadia are used.

Instruments

Malipenga uses drums to mark out the dance rhythm and steps. Usually two drums are used: a two-sided bass (marching band type) drum and a cylindrical smaller tenor drum. In bigger *bomas*, other smaller drums and percussion may be used to accentuate the climactic dancing. Usually two people carry the bass drum slung on a pole, with the drummer in the rear beating the instrument. In addition to drumming, *malipenga* musicians use homemade kazoos constructed from gourds with resonators made of spiderwebs or, in modern times, plastic. These kazoos or 'trumpets' are what give the dance its name; *malipenga* means trumpets. *Malipenga* dancers use kazoos both as props and as instruments. The kazoos or 'trumpets' are flourished with pride and panache in 'military' unison. Kazoo playing may be solo, unison or in call-and-response form with a leader. Given the dance's origin, kazoos made from long gourds that resemble trumpets are preferred. Sometimes, however, *malipenga* is performed without kazoos and leaders' instructions are communicated with whistles. Songs of a political, social, entertaining or critical nature, sung in call-and-response, unison or polyphonic manner, set the tone for the kazoo players.

In each *boma* there are usually those who can play kazoos, those who can dance and those who do both. In multiline formations, for choreographic effect, good dancers are placed in the front row. Sometimes kazoo players and singers are grouped separately from the dancers. Dancers with no musical skills mime at playing their instruments as they execute their elaborate steps, while instrumentalists, who may dance less elaborately, provide rhythmic and melodic phrases on the kazoos.

In the classic form of *malipenga* practiced before independence, the tempo was slower, with the marching drum beating out the dance steps to be followed by the dancers. A second, smaller drum was also used to provide a counter beat. In contemporary *malipenga*, the tempo varies with the song-and-dance routine. A song may have several movements that include both a slower section and a frenetic, climactic dance phase.

Performance

Malipenga is to a large extent about the performance of a dance-drama (Kamlongera 1986). It features elaborate costuming and accoutrements; the smart, clean, white uniforms that never seem to get dirty despite the dust are often heavily starched and well ironed. Headgear of fez and feathers is common. With time, the uniforms have evolved to include newer fashions but, overall, white is the preferred garment color. As with most traditions, uniforms reflect prevailing socioeconomic circumstances and fashions. In the twenty-first century dancers are as likely as not to be wearing scarves of various colors. In terms of choreography, the dance movements and performances start with a slow build-up as the dancers move from their waiting places on to the main arena. The basic movements may be described as an elaborate mixture of a military march with dance moves in which the dancers, shoulders hunched and bent over, use their arms and legs to create elaborate, synchronized, gentle but manly dance patterns.

In the natural environment (also called *boma*), as opposed to the political arenas, where time may be a factor, *malipenga* performances start with an elaborate schedule of local and invited *boma* groups marching, similar to a New Orleans Mardi Gras, to collect the king and to introduce the king and his office bearers to the audience and guests (Anon 1980). This is followed by the 'march-dance,' with the king leading and the *malipenga* dancers in two lines, singing songs of praise to the king, being theatrically 'attended' to by the doctor and nurse. The king's role in *malipenga* is at once a symbol of authority to be praised and one to be blamed for any mishaps, which resonates with the evolving role of *malipenga* over the years from colonial to postcolonial times.

The procession circles the arena once or twice before the king addresses the gathering and sits down to watch the *bomas* compete. After some dancing the king is invited to inspect the dancers. The dancers respond with the most vigorous and inventive dancing, at once individual and in as much unison as possible, bowing low as the king inspects them.

Malipenga, like its sister dances *mganda* and *beni*, found a new lease of life in the twenty-first century. As one of Malawi's 'national' dances, it is performed at social and state occasions. At both regional and district levels, it is thriving in its social and its entertainment functions. In line with its syncretic origins, it has continued to adapt, bringing in influences, fashions and choreographies from the latest dance imports such as jazz and modern dance, *kwasa kwasa* and even hip-hop. In turn, local and international popular musicians have appropriated some aspects of *malipenga*. For example, Faith Mussa, a gospel singer, incorporates *malipenga* kazoo playing in his 'Timayenda ndi Mdidi,' while Patience Namadingo, one of Malawi's afro-jazz musicians, uses *malipenga* rhythms and choreography in 'Msati mseke' (see YouTube references).

Bibliography

Anonymous. 1980. 'Malipenga.' *This is Malawi*, October, 8.

Kamlongera, Christopher. 1986. 'An example of a Syncretic Drama from Malawi: *Malipenga*.' *Research in African Literatures* 17(2): 197–210.

Koma-koma, William P. 1965. *Mganda Kapena Malipenga*. Limbe: Malawi Publications Bureau.

McCracken, John. 2012. *History of Malawi 1859–1966*. London: Zed Books.

Mitchell, J. Clyde. 1957. *The Kalela Dance: Aspects of Social Relationships Among Urban Africans in Northern Rhodesia*. Manchester: Manchester University Press on behalf of the Rhodes-Livingstone Institute.

Mpata, Daniel. 2001. 'The Malipenga Dance in Nkhata Bay District.' *The Society of Malawi Journal* 54(1): 23–8.

Mphande, David. 2014. *Oral Literature and Moral Education Among the Lakeside Tonga of Northern Malawi*. Mzuzu: Mzuni Press.

Nthala, Grant Moloko. 2009. 'The Chewa Art of Drumming and Its Influence on Modern Malawian Music.' Unpublished MA thesis, University of Free State, Bloemfontein.

Ranger, Terence. 1975. *Dance and Society in East Africa*. London: Heinemann.

White, Landeg. 1982. 'Power and the Praise Poem.' *Journal of Southern African Studies* 9(1): 8–32.

Discographical Reference

'Muganda we chitonga banda' and 'Akapunda, Mungore' (sung by16 Tonga men and boys). *Music of Nyasaland*. Rhodes University Library of African Music ILAMTRO378. Grahamstown. *Ca. 1958*: South Africa.

YouTube

Bamudala6. 2008. 'Malipenga White': https://www.youtube.com/watch?v=gSpMOMONO64 (accessed 12 August 2015).

Bamudala6. 'Malipenga Khaki': https://www.youtube.com/watch?v=APGh7xJsBj4 (accessed 12 August 2015).

Colter Sol. 2015. 'Malipenga White': http://www.dailymotion.com/video/x2tto7p (accessed 20 August 2015).

'Malipenga Pictures': https://www.google.nl/?gfe_rd=cr&ei=1IhUVtXcK8GL-QbdlIH4Cw&gws_rd=ssl#q=malipenga+pictures (accessed 22 September 2015).

Mussa, Faith. 'Timayenda ndi Mdidi': https://www.youtube.com/watch?v=aUXHTNQa1zU (accessed 9 October 2017).

Namadingo, Patience. 'Msati mseke': https://www.youtube.com/watch?v=jMBc1FqmhTM&list=RDjMBc1FqmhTM#t=0 (accessed 9 October 2017).

Nkhani Digest. 'Beni – a Malawian Traditional Dance' (includes *malipenga* kazoo playing from 10 to 13.45 mins of the film): https://www.youtube.com/watch?v=b7wvrHgZTY0 (accessed 21 April 2016).

JOHN LWANDA

Maloya

In Réunion, a French overseas department in the Indian Ocean to the east of Madagascar, *maloya* refers to a diverse range of styles of singing and dancing which are generally recognized as having African origin. Traditionally, a *maloya* song is rather short and is repeated at length. It is performed by an alternating soloist and chorus and accompanied by an ensemble of percussion instruments and rattles. This musical form emerged during the nineteenth century in the colonial context of the sugar plantation society, which was responsible for the importation of slave labor and later contract workers from Africa, India and Asia. Until the mid-twentieth century this music, which was associated with the descendants of African slaves and hired workers, was instead referred to as *séga*. The term *maloya*, whose etymology (most likely Madagascan) remains unclear, later became widespread, with *séga* referring instead specifically to modernized Creole song (see separate entry).

As an element of social regulation within communities of sugar plantation workers, *maloya* was highly stigmatized by colonial and postcolonial ideologies. For example, during the slavery era, the recreational and musical gatherings of slaves were restricted by decree. However, these practices were common and were chronicled by colonial observers throughout the nineteenth century.

Most of the key instruments of *maloya* appeared during the nineteenth century, including the *rouleur* (a bass drum) and the *kayamb* (a rattle in the form of a raft). The use of the *piker* (an idiophone consisting of a bamboo cylinder struck with two sticks) and the *sati* (a metal drum struck with drumsticks) became more widespread in the 1970s and is linked to 1970s revivalism. Depending on the forms and contexts of performance, other instruments may be added, including the *bob* (a musical bow) and other percussion instruments introduced during the 1970s to 1980s, such as the *djembés* of West Africa or the *congas* of Latin America, along with modern instruments including guitars, synthesizers, bass, drums and so on.

Three main overlapping types of *maloya* may be distinguished. Firstly, *maloya* is practiced within the context of rituals called *servis malgas*, *servis kabaré* and *servis kaf*. These are annual ceremonies at which animals (cattle and poultry) are sacrificed as offerings to the Madagascan or continental African ancestors (and their Creole descendants) being honored. *Maloya* is then performed with its four main instruments (*rouleur*, *kayamb*, *piker* and/or *sati*). The songs are generally sung by those gathered together to initiate communication with the ancestors and maintain the trance of some participants. During the *servis*, the rhythm of the *maloya* varies between a binary form close to 2/4 (characteristic of the *maloya* heard during the *servis*) and a form close to 6/8 (which is much more common outside the ritual context). Historically practiced within the family and neighborhood circles, the *servis* has become increasingly public and some *maloya* groups even perform *servis* songs within the context of secular entertainment (Troupe Lélé, Lindigo, Destyn, Kozman Ti Dalon).

Until the 1960s the second type of *maloya* was also practiced in the context of festive events (*bals maloya*) with dancing and improvised songs of social commentary and critique (Autret 1993). *Maloya* garnered publicity in the media thanks to urban orchestras playing modernized or folkloric versions of *maloya* called *séga maloya*. From the late 1950s onwards *maloya* became an instrument of political struggle when the Communist Party of Réunion (PCR) prompted the creation of *maloya* 'troupes' to liven up their political meetings. During the years from 1960 to 1970 Réunion's political landscape was divided into two camps regarding the territorial status of the island: on the right, supporters of maintaining the island's department status and membership to France, and on the left, defenders of the autonomy or even independence of Réunion. These political positions entailed different approaches to the local culture, especially regarding Creole language and music. Seeking to highlight the non-Western and rural features of Creole culture, the PCR, which demanded the political autonomy of the island, produced the first *maloya* records in 1976. In this tense political context, *maloya* musicians who conveyed the ideas of the PCR, or ideas close to those defended by that party, could not sing freely in public areas without having to surmount restrictions that including power outages and the seizure of musical instruments. The widespread idea that *maloya* was banned originates from this period. However, when practiced in the context of folklore, *maloya* did not undergo political opposition.

A few leading figures, such as Firmin Viry and Simon Lagarrigue (nicknamed 'Gramoune Dada'), thus emerged. They quickly became iconic because they enabled the diffusion of this music outside of its traditional and restricted frameworks (*bals maloya*, *servis*) while simultaneously guiding the practice of young militant musicians. In conjunction with the renewal of insular literary forms (which were heavily influenced by both oral traditions and popular dialects), *maloya* participated in the establishment of a new field of artistic creation. This new field would go on to develop a discourse of resistance to the assimilation of Creole culture into dominant French culture.

In the 1980s, after the Left gained power in France with the election of François Mitterand as president, the proliferation of independent radio stations and the recognition of regional identities through cultural policy, headed in France by Jack Lang (Minister of Culture), together allowed for the official recognition of *maloya* as a fundamental part of island identity. Until then, *séga* and Creole 'folklore' of European origin dating from the late nineteenth century (such as *polka*, *mazurka* and *quadrille*) were the main musical symbols of the island. Danyèl Waro, Lo Rwa Kaf, Gramoune Lélé and Firmin Viry have been considered since then as exemplars of the genre, their music serving as a source of inspiration and as a traditional reference for a number of other groups (Melanz Nasyon, Kiltir, Ras Mélé, Salem Tradition). The aesthetics of this form of *maloya* could be described as neo-traditional. It incorporates the fundamentals of the genre (including its core instruments and alternating soloist – chorus form) while variably adding a plurality of new elements from other world music traditions (including *kora*, West African *djembés*, Moroccan *crotales* and diatonic accordion).

The official recognition of traditional *maloya* allowed for the creation of the third type: *maloya électrique*. Introduced in the late 1970s and early 1980s by five main groups (Les caméléons, Ziskakan, Baster, Ousa Nousava, Ti Fock), *maloya électrique* combines rhythmic and instrumental aspects of *maloya* with various stylistic influences from genres such as jazz (Sabouk), urban African music (Ti Fock), rock (Patrick Persée) and pop/folk music (Ziskakan, Tapok). In 1991 *malogué* was born from a fusion of *maloya* and reggae, modeled on the Mauritian *seggae* (*séga-*). This genre experienced great commercial success up until the mid-1990s, with lyrics mixing social protest and evasive references to Rastafarianism. The band Na essayé was the most famous *malogué* group. There have also been closer connections between ragga (dancehall reggae) artists (KM David, DJ Dan) and *maloya* musicians (Lindigo).

Bibliography

Autret, Frédérique. 1993. 'Introduction au maloya traditionnel de La Réunion, un genre musical en mutation' [Introduction to the Traditional Maloya of Réunion: A Changing Musical Genre]. Master's Thesis, University of Paris-Sorbonne, Paris.

Carpanin Marimoutou, Jean-Claude. 1989. 'Oralité et écriture: Les chansons créoles de Danyèl Waro et Ziskakan' [Orality and Writing: The Creole Songs of Danyèl Waro and Ziskakan]. In *Formes-Sens/Identités* [Forms-Meanings-Identities], eds. J.-C. Carpanin Marimoutou and Daniel Baggioni. Saint-Denis: University of Réunion Island, 151–208.

Chaudenson, Robert. 1992. *Des îles, des hommes, des langues: Essai sur les créolisations linguistiques et culturelles* [Islands, People and Languages: An Essay on Linguistic and Cultural Creolization]. Paris: L'Harmattan.

Desrosiers, Brigitte. 1996. 'Le discours sur la musique, le discours sur l'identité à La Réunion' [Discourse on Music, Discourse on Identity in Réunion]. In *Regards sur le champ musical* [Perspectives on the Musical Field], ed. B. Cherubini. Saint-Denis: University of Réunion Island, 29–47.

Desrosiers, Brigitte, and Desroches, Monique. 2000. 'Réunion Island'. In *The Garland Encyclopedia of World Music: South America, Mexico, Central America and the Caribbean*, Vol. 5, eds. Dale Olsen and Dan Sheehy. New York: Garland, 606–11.

Lagarde, Benjamin. 2007. 'Un monument à la mémoire des ancêtres malgaches: Le maloya (île de La Réunion) [A Monument to the Memory of Madagascan Ancestry: Maloya (Réunion Island)], *Conserveries mémorielles* 3: 27–46.

La Selve, Jean-Pierre. [1984] 1995. *Les musiques traditionnelles de La Réunion* [The Traditional Music of Réunion]. Rev. ed. Saint-Denis: Azalées Editions.

Samson, Guillaume. 2006. *Musique et identité à La Réunion: Généalogie des constructions d'une singularité musicale insulaire* [Music and Identity in Réunion: Genealogy of the Construction of an Insular Musical Singularity]. Unpublished Ph.D. Thesis, University of Montréal – Aix-Marseille III, Montréal/Aix-Marseille.

Samson, Guillaume, and Pitre, Shawn. 2007. 'Music, Poetry and the Politics of Identity in Réunion Island: A Historical Overview'. *Popular Music History* 2(1): 25–48.

Samson, Guillaume, Lagarde, Benjamin, and Marimoutou, Carpanin. 2008. *L'univers du maloya* [The Universe of Maloya]. Saint-Denis: Editions de la DREOI.

Yu Sion, Live, and Hamon, Jean-François, eds. 2004. *Diversité et spécificités des musiques traditionnelles de l'Océan Indien* [Diversity and Specificities of Traditional Music of the Indian Ocean]. *Kabaro* (2–3): 1–296.

Discography

Baster. *Lorizon kasé*. SEDM CD 33409. N.d.: France/Réunion.

DJ Dan. *Ker maron dann béton*. WR Prod 2007-05. *2007*: France/Réunion.

Kaf, Lo Rwa. *Somin galisé*. Discorama C.D. 9209, N.d.: France/Réunion.

Kiltir. *Pèp maloya*. Discorama 2007.02. *2007*: France/Réunion.

Lélé, Granmoun. *Soléyé*. Indigo/Label Bleu 25 28. *1995*: France.

Lindigo. *Misaotra mama*. Piros CDP5340. N.d.: France/Réunion.

Melanz Nasyon. *Dizan maloya*. MN0205. *2005*: France/Réunion.

Na Essayé. *Oté La Sère*. Discorama 9101. N.d.: France/Réunion.

Ousa Nousava. *Ousa Nousava*. S.E.D.M/Oasis 70 003. N.d.: France/Réunion.

Persée, Patrick. 'Ying yang.' TAMTAM Production. N.d.: France.

Progression. *Naviguer Mon Bato*. Discorama 97-02. N.d.: France/Réunion.

Ravan. *Ravan*. SEDM CD33406. N.d.: France/Réunion.

Sabouk. *Sézon*. Discorama 9707. *1998*: France/Réunion.

Salem Tradition. *Fanm*. Cobalt, CO 100. *2005*: France/Réunion.

Tapok. *Tapokopat*. JPR 20056. N.d.: France/Réunion.

Ti, Fock. *Aniel*. Celluloid/Mélodie, 64617-2 DK 016. N.d.: France.

Viry, Firmin. *Ile de La Réunion Maloya Firmin Viry*. Ocora C560138. *1999*: France.

Waro, Danyèl. *Bwarouz*. Cobalt. *2002*: France.

Ziskakan. *10 zan*. ZIS 016,PSB 747 K. N.d.: France.

GUILLAUME SAMSON (TRANSLATED BY ORLENE DENICE MCMAHON)

Mamaya

Mamaya is a music and dance genre that developed in the colonial-era metropolis of Kankan in northeastern

Guinea in the 1930s and 1940s. Originally based in Mande (specifically Maninka) xylophone traditions that flourished there, the genre came to symbolize modern, cosmopolitan, youth-oriented celebrations deeply rooted in local culture. It has enjoyed great longevity and is a staple in the repertory of Guinean and Malian popular music in the early twenty-first century. The term *mamaya*, which can refer either to a single recognizable song and its musical accompaniment or to a more general xylophone-based celebration, represents the first real flowering, still in living memory, of a widely influential Mande popular expressive culture (for a description of Mande music as a whole, see the entry on Mande Music in this volume).

Mamaya belongs to the generation born in Kankan in the late 1910s and early 1920s, which reached adulthood in the late 1930s. Part of a system of age groupings that define generations every three or four years, this cohort, named *san diya* ('year's happiness') partially embraced and reshaped European culture to fit their own lifestyles. The colonial economy helped produce a relatively affluent middle class, driven by long-distance traders and businessmen who acted as intermediaries between the large trading companies and local markets. Youth of this and subsequent generations tried to reconcile the rigid social and religious strictures of the important Islamic center of Kankan, which frowned on physical contact between male and female dancers, for example, with imported dances including the *tango*, waltz, *rumba* and *bolero*. *Mamaya* resulted as a new artistic public form that expressed a harmony between respect for tradition and youthful innovation.

The music was played by *jelis* (also known as *griots*), who were experts in Maninka xylophone (called *bala* or *balafon*) and praise-singing traditions, and it was danced by both young men and women of all social classes dressed up in their finest clothes. Kankan *bala* master Sidi Djéli Dioubaté and his three sons Sidi Karammò, Sidi Mamadi and Sidi Moussa are widely credited with pioneering the genre. The trio of sons was recorded in 1949 and 1952 by Arthur S. Alberts and Gilbert Rouget, respectively.

The piece of music called 'Mamaya,' as distinguished from the whole event of the same name, is an extended composition for *bala* and voice, comprising a long section of lyrics sung to an unusually long through-composed melody. *Mamaya* performances traditionally involved choral singing set to other melodies and punctuated by *bala* solos, praising the young Kankan notables of the day. Dancing was much more genteel compared to the high frenetic energy of *jembé* drumming and dancing that also flourished in the region. Part of the enduring charm of *mamaya* comes from the *bala* functioning as both a percussion instrument and a melody instrument in one; it is fully compatible with drums, and also with the quieter string instruments of the *jeli* (e.g., *kora* and *ngoni*). Modern, post-independence renditions of the piece 'Mamaya' often add other instruments, such as the *kora*, electric guitar and bass, keyboards and brass, while reducing the role of the *bala*. For Guineans and Malians born in the 1950s and later, *mamaya* symbolizes the music and culture of their parents' and grandparents' generations along with a Mande genius for innovation.

Bibliography

Charry, Eric. 2000. *Mande Music: Traditional and Modern Music of the Maninka and Mandinka of Western Africa*. Chicago: University of Chicago Press.

Charry, Eric, and Kaba, Lansine. 2000. 'Mamaya: Renewal and Tradition in the Manninka Music of Kankan, Guinea (1935-45).' In *The African Diaspora: A Musical Perspective*, ed. Ingrid Monson. New York: Garland, 187-206.

Discographical References

Alberts, Arthur S. *Field Recordings from Guinea and Mali*. Archives of Traditional Music, Indiana University. Accession no. 68-214-F, ATL 3564-3567, 3574-3577. *1949*: USA.

Alberts, Arthur S. *The Arthur S. Alberts Collection: More Tribal, Folk, and Café Music of West Africa*. Rykodisc RCD 10401. (Recorded 1952.) *1998*: USA.

Alberts, Arthur S. *The Field Recordings of African Coast Rhythms: Tribal and Folk Music of West Africa*. Riverside RLP 4001. *1953*: USA.

Rouget, Gilbert. *Guinée, music des Malinké/Guinea, Music of the Mandinka*. Le Chant du Monde/Harmonia Mundi CNR 2741112; 794881468829. (Recorded 1952.) *1999*: France.

Discography

Cissoko, Ba. *Sabolan*. Marabi 46808. *2004*: France.
Diabate, Nainy. *Nafa*. Stern's Africa STCD 1083. *1998*: UK.

Diawara, Djeli Moussa (aka Jawara, Jali Musa). *Soubindoor*. Mango CCD9832. *1988*: UK.

Dioubaté, Oumou. *Femmes d'Afrique*. Africando DK-041; Melodie 38147-2. *N.d.*: France.

Kaba, Baba Djan. *Kankan*. Sonodisc 5510. *1992*: France.

Keita, Mamady. *Mogobalu*. Fonti Musicali FMD 205. *1995*: Belgium.

Kouyaté, (El Hadj) Djeli Sory. *Guinée: Anthologie du balafon mandingue*, vols. 2 and 3. Buda 92534-2 & 92535-2. *1992*: France.

Koïta, Ami. *Songs of Praise*. Stern's STCD 1039. *1993*: UK. (Reissued, with some earlier material, as Ami Koïta, *Mamaya*. Melodie 38120-2. *1992*: France.)

ERIC CHARRY

Mande Music

The music of the Mande provides an important link between Africa's ancient empires and the modern era. The Mande hereditary musicians, the *jeliw*, are widely acknowledged as 'living libraries,' having preserved from generation to generation a rich oral tradition of stories and songs describing the major figures and events of their region's history (for a detailed description of the music of the *jeliw*, see the entry Jeliya in this volume). Mande music was also at the forefront of the politics of the postcolonial era, when African governments promoted revolutionary ideologies through popular music. In the 1960s and 1970s Mande musical groups toured the continent and had a profound influence on the development of popular music styles in Africa.

Mande peoples (Manden) inhabit large areas of West Africa and can be defined as a language group whose members trace their ancestry to the Empire of Mali (circa 1230 CE to circa 1550 CE). There are large populations of Manden in Mali, Guinea, Senegal and the Gambia, and significant populations in other West African nations. There are numerous subgroups of the Mande, including the Bamana (Bambara), Maninka (Malinké) and Mandinka. Mande music is closely associated with the traditions of its hereditary professional musicians, known as *jeli* (masculine) or *jelimousso* (feminine). Some other terms for these musicians are *jali* (male)/*jalimuso* (female) and the French term *griot* (male)/*griotte* (female). In this entry, the term *jeli* (Maninkakan language plural *jeliw*) is used in a non-gender-specific sense. Musical activity among the Mande is focused upon the *jeliw* but not limited to them. The music of hunters' societies (often featuring the *bolon*, a three-stringed arched harp) provides source materials, while regional specializations in particular instruments (such as the *dundun* and *jembé* drums) also produce distinctive musical styles that feed into *jeliya*, a term which describes the artistry of the *jeliw*.

Mande society is hierarchical and stratified into three social groups – the *horon*, who constitute the nobles, the *nyamakala*, who comprise the artisans, and the *jon*, who are the descendants of slaves. The *jeliw* are members of the *nyamakala*, and their role in Mande society incorporates several important functions. *Jeliw* serve as the oral historians of their societies, for example, for they transmit the histories, tales and stories of the Mande from one generation to the next. A *jeli*'s knowledge of oral histories also extends to the performance of epic narratives, which describe, either in song or in spoken narration, the life stories of important figures in Mande history. Mande epic narratives include those in honor of Soundiata Keita (circa 1218 to circa 1255), the founder of the Empire of Mali, and 'Da Monzon,' which honors Da Monzon Diarra, the seventeenth-century Bambara ruler. *Jeliw* also perform songs that celebrate the bravery of warriors, such as 'Duga' and 'Djandjon,' while other songs such as 'Malisajo' and 'Massané Cissé' present tales of morality and ethics. Praise singing to members of the *horon* also constitutes an important part of a *jeli*'s musical and social activity, for the *horon* are the *jeli*'s patrons. Other significant functions that a *jeli* fulfills in Mande society include maintaining a comprehensive knowledge of the genealogies of local families, which supports their role as the master of ceremonies at social occasions such as births, initiations, marriages and funerals. In the precolonial era *jeliw* were the court musicians for the Mande ruling families, and in the modern-era African presidents still employ *jeliw* for ceremonial functions.

Mande musical instruments include several from the chordophone, idiophone and membranophone families. Traditionally, many Mande musical instruments are played by men only, with women providing vocal and rhythmic accompaniment. The plucked chordophones played by Mande hunters include the *simbing* (*simbi*, *simbingo*), an arched harp of between five and nine strings, the *soron* (*seron*), a harp lute of between 15 and 19 strings, and the *bolon*, an arched harp of three strings which is usually associated with war and funeral music.

Chordophones associated with the *jeliw* include the *ngoni* (*koni*, *konting*), a plucked lute with four or five strings, and the *kora*, a plucked harp lute of 21 strings. Idiophones of the *jeli* include the *balo* (*balafon*), a hammered wooden xylophone of 19 keys, and the *né* (*négé*, *karinyan*), a tubular iron bell scraped with a rod, played only by women. A *nyenyemo*, an idiophone consisting of a flat piece of metal with wire loops along the edges, is often affixed to the end of the neck on instruments such as the *bolon* and the *kora*. A bracelet of iron bells on each wrist may also be worn by *balo* musicians when performing. Mande membranophones are not usually attributed to *jeliw*. They include single-face drums such as the *sabaro*, *kuturiba* and *kuturindingo*, which are often used together as an ensemble (Charry 2000, 201), as well as the *jembé* and the *dundun*. The *tama*, a goblet-shaped, single-faced drum with strips of leather affixed from the skin to the base, can attain variable pitch. The musician cradles the *tama* under his/her arm, and by applying pressure to the strips of leather the surface of the skin is stretched or slackened, thus producing variable tones.

The structure of the music of the *jeliw* is focused upon two stylistic elements. In instrumental music these are the *kumbengo* and the *birimintingo*. The *kumbengo* is a short *ostinato* pattern which persists throughout the performance. *Kumbengos* often employ the intervals of fifths and octaves, and can be played for long periods with only subtle variations to the melody occurring. In the music of the *jeliw* a specific *kumbengo* pattern is closely associated with a particular traditional narrative, thus each narrative is identifiable through its melody. *Birimintingo* refers to the ornamentation, variation and improvisation which a musician incorporates into a performance. Its purpose is to create interest through the exposition of musical passages that expand upon and augment the *kumbengo* (Counsel 2009, 47). In vocal music there are also two important stylistic considerations, the *donkilo* and the *sataro*. Like the *kumbengo*, the *donkilo* section of a vocal piece is a short melodic phrase. It may be employed by a singer to introduce a song, and it is also often performed by a chorus. The *sataro* is similar in function to the *birimintingo*, in that it refers to improvised passages within the vocal section. Melisma is a common device employed by vocalists in *sataro* sections, and as a general rule Mande melodies exhibit a downward terracing of pitch (Knight 1984, 110). A typical *jeli* song is strophic in form. The lyrical content will frequently have recourse to historical figures and events, and eloquent praise is used to honor the protagonists.

Mande Music in the Modern Era

Following independence (1958–74), many West African nations embarked on ambitious programs designed to reinvigorate the indigenous arts. The governments of Guinea and Mali, for example, enacted a series of policies whereby the state exercised a rigid control over musical activity. Some of the measures introduced in the early 1960s included barring foreign music from the national airwaves, forcing all private groups to disband, creating new state-funded musical groups in all major towns and regions, and instructing the musicians of the new groups in the modernization of their local traditional musical styles. In the independence era these new government policies encouraged artists to 'return to the source' for inspiration, a policy which was inspired by the *Authenticité* movement. *Authenticité* was a cultural philosophy that promoted a return to the values, ethics and customs found in traditional, 'authentic' African societies. First introduced by Guinea as the centerpiece for its cultural policy, other African nations (such as Mali, Burkina Faso, Chad and Zaire) incorporated its philosophies into their nation's cultural activities (see Counsel 2004a, b, 2009). Both Guinea (1968) and Mali (1967) announced Cultural Revolutions, though Mali's was short-lived following a coup d'état in 1968 which ousted the president.

The cultural policies adopted by these and other West African states resulted in Mande *jeliw* assuming important roles in many of the new orchestras. Their intimate knowledge of history and music was highly valued and gave them a distinct advantage over other musicians. The repertoires of many of the new orchestras were based upon *jeli* songs, positioning the Mande *jeliw* at the forefront of the modernization of African music. During the independence era (1958–74) many Mande epic narratives were presented by the state-funded orchestras in a new modern style, with the melodies of the *balo*, *kora* or *ngoni* transposed to Western instruments such as the electric guitar or saxophone. Some orchestras featured the traditional musical instruments of the *jeli* alongside Western instrumentation, thus representing a cultural revival and a union between the old Mande world and the new. Some notable modernized versions of Mande epic narratives include 'Soundiata' by Keletigui et ses Tambourinis, 'Alla l'aké' by Bembeya Jazz National and 'Massané Cissé' performed as an instrumental by the Quintette Guinéenne.

As the influence of Mande music grew, musical instruments such as the *kora* achieved iconic status and were used as a symbol for Mande music in particular and African music in general (Counsel 2009, 166–72). Guinean orchestras toured Cuba, the Eastern Bloc and the United States, releasing many recordings on the state-controlled Syliphone label – one of the first recording labels of West Africa's postcolonial era. Guinea's orchestras also toured widely in Africa, promoting their government's ideology and revolutionary cultural policy to new audiences throughout the continent. In 1969 Guinea sent a delegation to the First Pan-African Cultural Festival in Algiers, where its musicians were awarded a gold medal, five silver medals (including one in the *Orchestres Moderne* section) and the inaugural prize for culture.

Among the most popular of the Guinean groups of the independence era were Bembeya Jazz National, Keletigui et ses Tambourinis and Balla et ses Balladins. Recordings by these orchestras and many other regional and national groups were released solely by Syliphone, whose output spanned 750 songs released on 45 rpm and 33.3 rpm discs between circa 1967 and 1983. Bembeya Jazz National's 1969 Syliphone recording *Regard sur le passé* represented a landmark in African music. Here the group presented their version of the epic narrative of Samori Touré, and at nearly 38 minutes in length the song played on both sides of the LP disc – a first for an African orchestra. The song's narrative, spoken and sung in French and the Mande dialect of Maninkakan, explored the life of Samori Touré, whose long resistance to French rule ended with his capture in 1898. In the song favorable comparisons are made with the leadership of Guinea's President Sékou Touré, who was the grandson of Samori, and through music and verse the orchestra linked the values of the past with the objectives and goals of the present leadership. Thus, during Africa's independence era Mande music was not only modernized by government policy but also politicized. Many Guinean orchestras of the era performed material that was highly propagandist in theme, with numerous examples of praise songs to the Guinean leadership in evidence throughout the Syliphone catalogue. One example is 'Mandjou,' a song in praise of the Touré lineage, recorded by Keletigui et ses Tambourinis, which celebrated the Guinean presidency. This was in spite of the government's harsh repression of the Guinean people, a policy that resulted in thousands of deaths in custody, executions without trial and an exodus of close to 25 percent of the population. Such matters, however, were not addressed in the music of the era. Critics of the government risked severe reprisals, and as the state controlled all media (which was subjected to censorship) musicians had no public or commercial outlets to voice opposition (see Dave 2014).

Guinean solo artists, such as the *jeli* Kouyaté Sory Kandia, also recorded extensively for Syliphone. His recordings with the orchestra Keletigui et ses Tambourinis provide an excellent example of the *jeli* musical tradition transposed to an orchestra setting. Also of note are recordings by the singer Miriam Makeba, who was exiled from her native South Africa and lived in Guinea from 1968 to 1986. She recorded extensively with *jeliw* for Syliphone.

Guinea's revolutionary cultural policies were abandoned following the death of President Sékou Touré in 1984. Syliphone records ceased production and many of the orchestras disbanded, thus bringing their era to a close. A new generation of Mande performers arose, musicians who utilized electronic instrumentation and who recorded their materials in the studios of Côte d'Ivoire and France. Sékouba 'Bambino' Diabaté, a former lead vocalist with Bembeya Jazz National, forged a successful solo career and performed with the multinational group Africando. Mory Kanté produced Guinea's first international bestseller with his song 'Yéké yéké,' which topped the charts throughout Europe.

Malian orchestras of the independence era had fewer commercial opportunities and less exposure to the international market than their Guinean counterparts, though their influence was no less profound. Popular groups included the Super Rail Band, Les Ambassadeurs du Motel, the Super Djata Band and Kanaga de Mopti. The Malian approach to the modernization of Mande music is best encapsulated by songs such as 'Duga,' by the Regional Orchestre de Kayes, 'Djandjon' by Les Ambassadeurs du Motel, 'Soundiata' by the Orchestre Rail Band de Bamako and 'Mandjou' by Les Ambassadeurs Internationaux. The latter is of particular interest as it is performed as a praise song to President Sékou Touré in the manner of a *jeli*, yet is sung by a non-*jeli* singer – Salif Keita. Since the 1980s Keita has been the most commercially successful of all Mande musicians. He began his career with the Orchestre Rail Band of Bamako, before moving to Les Ambassadeurs du Motel and then to Les Ambassadeurs Internationaux. His solo career commenced in 1987 with the acclaimed 'Soro,' and his subsequent recordings have received numerous awards and nominations. Of the *jeli* musicians of the Malian independence era (1960–8), popular artists included Ba Zoumana Sissòko and Fanta Damba, both of whom were recorded in the early 1970s for the Bärenreiter-Musicaphon recording label as part of an extensive series on Malian music, and Kandia Kouyaté.

Though the governments of Senegal and The Gambia did not implement revolutionary cultural policies like *Authenticité*, both governments nevertheless encouraged the modernization of their indigenous musical traditions. In the Senegambia region the Wolof constitute the largest language group, and Wolof musicians were featured in many of the local orchestras. Wolof culture shares many similarities with the Mande. Both societies are comprised of three distinct social groups, with the Wolof *gewels* performing near-identical functions to that of their *jeli* counterparts in the Mande. Senegalese groups who popularized Mande music include Touré Kunda, who released several commercially successful recordings. Also of note are the songs of the Catholic monks of the Keur Moussa Monastery, who incorporated the *kora* and *balo* into their liturgical performances. The Gambia produced several popular Mande musicians, such as the *kora* players Jali Nyama Suso (who composed the national anthem in the mid-1960s), Jaliba Kuyateh and Dembo Konte.

In the 1990s the popularity of Mande music waned in West Africa, as the push for democratic reforms grew. Disenchanted with corrupt military regimes and the musicians who praised them, the public turned to new musical styles such as *wassoulou* and *mbalax*, whose singers were not bound by the hereditary social structures of the *jeli* but were instead free to criticize and provide social commentary (Durán 1995, 111). Some *jeliw*, too, have followed this path, and claim the right to sing about any topic (Eyre 1997, 45). Ami Koïta, one of Mali's most popular *jelimousso*, is a case in point, with her songs addressing issues such as women's rights, a theme taken up by other Mande singers such as Fantani Touré. The musical instruments of the Mande *jeliw* are also evolving, so that they are no longer the sole provenance of male musicians. Several women *kora* players have now established themselves as eminent musicians, and at l'Institut Nationale des Arts in Mali women are trained in the performance of the *kora* and the *balo*.

Mande music is thus adapting itself to the new settings and contexts of the modern age. Although the era when Mande orchestras dominated the West African music scene may have passed, interest in the music remains strong in the early twenty-first century, and an expanding collection of CD reissues are a testament to the musical style's lasting influence.

Bibliography

Charry, Eric. 2000. *Mande Music: Traditional and Modern Music of the Maninka and Mandinka of Western Africa*. Chicago: The University of Chicago Press.

Counsel, Graeme. 2004a. 'Popular Music and Politics in Sékou Touré's Guinea.' *Australasian Review of African Studies* 26(1): 26–42.

Counsel, Graeme. 2004b. 'Music in Guinea's First Republic.' In *Mande-Manding: Background Reading for Ethnographic Research in the Region South of Bamako*, ed. Jan Jansen. Leiden: Leiden University Department of Cultural Anthropology and Development Sociology, 284–301.

Counsel, Graeme. 2009. *Mande Popular Music and Cultural Policies in West Africa: Griots and Government Policy Since Independence*. Berlin: VDM.

Dave, Nomi. 2014. 'The Politics of Silence: Music, Violence and Protest in Guinea.' *Ethnomusicology* 58(1): 1–29.

Durán, Lucy. 1995. 'Birds of Wasulu: Freedom of Expression and Expressions of Freedom in the Popular Music of Southern Mali.' *British Journal of Ethnomusicology* 4: 101–34.

Eyre, Banning. 1997. 'A Griot Found.' *Folk Roots* 163–4: 43, 45, 101.

Knight, Roderic. 1984. 'The Style of Mandinka Music: A Study in Extracting Theory from Practice.' *Selected Reports in Ethnomusicology* 5: 3–66.

Discographical References

Bembeya Jazz National. 'Alla l'aké.' *Guinée an XI. Le Rendez-Vous Annuel des Grands*. Syliphone SLP 15. *1969*: Guinea.

Bembeya Jazz National. *Regard sur le passé*. Syliphone SLP 10. *1969*: Guinea. (Reissued as *Regard sur le passé*. Mélodie 38206-2. *1999*: France.)

Kanté, Mory. 'Yéké yéké.' *Akwaba Beach*. Barclay 833119. *1994*: France.

Keita, Salif. *Soro*. Island / Celluloid. CD 66883. *1997*: United Kingdom.

Keletigui et ses Tambourinis. 'Mandjou.' *Keletigui et ses Tambourinis*. Syliphone SLP 30. *1972*: Guinea.

Keletigui et ses Tambourinis. 'Soundiata.' *Guinée an X. Orchestres Nationaux. Grand Tierce Musical*. Syliphone SLP 10. *1968*: Guinea.

Les Ambassadeurs du Motel. 'Djandjon.' *Volume 1*. Sonafric SAF 50030. *1977*: France.

Les Ambassadeurs Internationaux. 'Mandjou.' *Mandjou*. Badmos BLP 5040. *1977*: Côte d'Ivoire. (Reissued as *Mandjou / Seydou bathily*. Universal Music 539529-2. *2010*: France.)

Orchestre Rail Band de Bamako. 'Soundiata.' *Orchestre Rail Band de Bamako*. Bärenreiter-Musicaphon BM 30 L 2606. *1970*: Germany.

Quintette Guinéenne. 'Massane Cissé.' *Musique sans paroles*. Syliphone SLP 54. *1976*: Guinea.

Regional Orchestre de Kayes. 'Duga.' *Les Meilleurs Souvenirs de la 1ère Biennale Artistique et Culturelle de la Jeunesse (1970)*. Bärenreiter-Musicaphon BM 30 L 2604. *1970*: Germany.

Discography

Africando. *Gombo Salsa*. Mélodie 38145-2. *1996*: France.

Authenticité. The Syliphone Years. Guinea's Orchestres Nationaux and Federaux 1965–1980. Sterns STCD 3025-26. *2007*: London.

Balla et ses Balladins. *The Syliphone Years*. Sterns STCD 3035-36. *2008*: London.

Bembeya Jazz National. *The Syliphone Years. Hits and Rare Recordings*. Sterns STCD 3029-30. *2007*: London.

Damba, Fanta. *Première anthologie de la musique malienne. Volume 6. La tradition épique*. Bärenreiter-Musicaphon BM 30 L 2506. *1971*: Germany.

Diabaté, Sékouba. 'Bambino.' *Le Destin*. Popular African Music PAM OA 22. *1992*: Germany.

Keletigui et ses Tambourinis. *The Syliphone Years*. Sterns STCD 3031-32. *2009*: London.

Keur Moussa. *Sacred Chants and African Rhythms from Senegal*. Sounds True 337. *1997*: USA.

Koïta, Ami. *Carthage*. Sonodisc 6840. *1995*: France.

Konte, Dembo, and Kausu Kuyateh. *Jaliology*. Xenophile XENO 4036. *1995*: USA.

Kouyaté, Kandia. *Kandja Kouyaté et l'Ensemble Instrumental du Mali*. Disco Stock DS 8003. *1983*: Côte d'Ivoire.

Kouyaté, Sory Kandia et son Trio de Musique Traditionnelle Africaine. *L'épopée du Mandingue. Volumes 1, 2, 3*. Syliphone SLP 36, 37, 38. *1973*: Guinea. Reissue: *L'épopée du Mandingue*. Mélodie 38205-2. *1999*: France.

Makeba, Miriam. *The Guinea Years*. Sterns STCD 3017. *2001*: London.

Sissòko, Ba Zoumana. *Musique du Mali. Volumes 1, 2. Banzoumana Sissòko. Le Vieux Lion. Volumes 1, 2*. Bärenreiter-Musicaphon BM 30 L 2552, 2553. *1971*: Germany.

The Soto Koto Band featuring Jaliba Kuyateh. *Kora Dance*. Soto Koto Music. *2010*: The Gambia.

Suso, Jali Nyama. *Gambie. Mandinka kora par Jali Nyama Suso*. Harmonia Mundi HM 558639. *1984*: France.

Touré Kunda. *É'mma. Africa*. Celluloid 67041-1. *1980*: France.

Touré, Fantani. *Awo*. France: Corner Shop. *2007*: France.

GRAEME COUNSEL

Marabi

Marabi was a pan-ethnic city music, developed in South Africa's urban slums (principally those of Johannesburg) during the second and third decades of the twentieth century. A rhythmically propulsive dance idiom that drew its melodic inspiration eclectically from a wide variety of 'traditional,' African-Christian and Western popular sources, *marabi* was forged mainly by unschooled slumyard musicians who were part of the notorious culture and economy of illegal backyard liquor dens known as shebeens. It was the music of a variety of secular social occasions – most famously the weekend-long slumyard parties – that usually involved dancing and the sale and consumption of alcohol. Normally associated with the keyboard (piano or pedal organ), *marabi* was sometimes played on other instruments, notably guitar and banjo.

For almost everyone not condemned to life in the ghetto, the music and culture of *marabi* were considered evil. Associated with illegality, police raids, sex and a desperately impoverished working class – large numbers of whom at any one time were unemployed – it was vilified as a corrupting menace, and it came in for especially vituperative treatment from ministers of the church, teachers, newspaper columnists, parents and other self-appointed guardians of the common weal. But such concerns masked and were prompted by a deeper worry. For the class of blacks who felt upward social and political mobility to be within their grasp if they played their hand correctly, the fear was that the culture of *marabi* would create the wrong impression, contaminate respectability and thus jeopardize class ambition. The word's associations seem to suggest as much, even if its origins remain obscure: the term *marabi* appears to be related to the Sotho phrase *ho raba raba* ('to fly around'), possibly a metaphor for the 'loose' behavior of its adherents. Certainly, in popular usage the term has come to refer to social behavior: at least one Sotho dictionary gives *marabi* as the plural form of *lerabi*, a slang word for a 'lawless person' or 'gangster' (Coplan 2007, 115).

History and Sociopolitical Context

Marabi in its 'classic' form had a short life. Made famous by legendary pianists and organists with names such as Ntebejana, Boet Gashe, Toto, Highbricks and Nine Fingers, the idiom and its associated culture flourished between about 1915 and 1935 – despite being subject to continuous police harassment, often of a particularly brutal kind. Since music – or 'noise,' to those antipathetic to the idiom – was involved, *marabi* events were easily discovered; and when nothing more incriminating could be found, the police used such 'noise' as a pretext for terminating them. But legislation soon gave local authorities more sweeping powers. The Urban Areas Act of 1923 enabled the local state to proclaim that inner city suburbs were 'white' living areas, and thus to start laying claim to them. Most visibly, in Johannesburg in 1924 and 1925, 6,000 black 'Africans' were ordered out of the city; by 1933 all but three areas of the city had been declared 'white.'

As the relocation of black residents began, so too did the definitive destruction of *marabi* culture. Essentially an intimate art, *marabi* had flourished in the small, informal, domestic spaces of the slumyards. But the new, sterile black dormitory suburbs to the southwest of Johannesburg in which blacks were resettled provided no opportunities for its nurturing. With 18,000 people living in nearly 3,000 houses in Orlando by 1935, the township could, in principle, perhaps have supported a *marabi* musical culture; but a number of municipal regulations made this impossible. Of these, perhaps the most repressive was a restriction issued by the Orlando Advisory Board, which in 1933 resolved that 'all night entertainments be not allowed in private houses – that is, entertainments that are conducted for money – by reason of disorder, rowdiness and being a nuisance to neighbours' (Koch 1983, 230). Nor were the new township 'community halls' an option, since their size and ambience made them quite unsuitable.

These circumstances provoked the development of a new genre, one that transformed *marabi* as much as it sought to conserve it. By the late 1920s and early 1930s black dance bands started to appear, modeling themselves directly on prototypes derived from the United States. Soon there was a profusion of such bands, and they played US (or US-inspired) swing numbers that were becoming familiar in South Africa through recordings and films. More significantly, these bands sought to fuse genres, by developing their own *marabi*-based pieces in big band, or swing style. It is this unique and prodigious genre that later came to be known as African jazz or *mbaqanga*. Symbols of what black people could achieve in a white-dominated world, swing-like bands flourished and began to play to capacity crowds in ramshackle township halls around the country. The best of them – such as the Jazz

Maniacs, the Merry Blackbirds, the Rhythm Kings, the Jazz Revellers, the Harlem Swingsters – achieved fame across the country, and sometimes beyond. Rooted in the heterogeneous, multi-class socioeconomic milieu of the new townships, the bands and their audiences were more diverse than had been the case with the *marabi* performance culture of the slumyards. Bands with frank working-class links (the Jazz Maniacs, for example) embraced the challenge of developing a swing-inspired *marabi* style, but even those bands that cultivated 'respectability' and courted a more elite following (the Merry Blackbirds, for example) found that the heterogeneity of township audiences exerted strong pressures toward the inclusion of at least some *marabi* tunes in their repertoire. All blacks suffered social and political repression, and this created certain commonalities, including a sense of shared destiny, whatever the manifest differences between black audience members. For this reason, the elite black vaudeville acts of the time (Griffiths Motsieloa's Pitch Black Follies, for example) sometimes incorporated in their programs clean, polished versions of some of the best-known *marabi* songs of the time.

So began a time of astonishing innovation of styles based on *marabi*. These included big band *marabi* and its successor, the *tsaba-tsaba*, during the 1930s; African jazz (*mbaqanga*) during the 1940s; *kwela*, the extraordinary *marabi*-derived pennywhistle music of the streets, developed during the 1950s by impoverished black children in creative imitation of their favorite jazzmen; the multitude of jazz-based, close harmony vocal groups, also during the 1950s; and the neo-traditional vocal and instrumental style introduced in the 1960s, again under the name of *mbaqanga*, though it had little in common with its eponymous style of two decades earlier.

The repression that was an intrinsic part of the 'grand apartheid' era stretched roughly from 1960 to the late 1980s, and it cut a swath through this pattern of rapid innovation. When, in the mid-1980s, a virile oppositional popular culture eventually began to reappear, it did so only because of the reemergence – on an irresistible scale – of black working-class and community politics, to sound the death knell of apartheid. Significantly, the recuperation of *marabi*-based jazz was central to this revival. After the country's first nonracial, democratic elections in 1994, the jazz scene was dominated by younger players, most of whom continued to seek an individual voice through a fusion of international styles with idioms that were locally rooted, such as *marabi*. An intriguing by-product was a growing number of popular music groups (Mafikizolo, for example) who made passing reference to the flavor of *marabi* or its progeny.

The Music

Arguably, *marabi* has been the most important single ingredient in the development of South African styles of jazz and popular music. Though the original idiom had a number of distinctive features (outlined below), it is the foundational harmonic structure that has lived on and given a strongly characteristic flavor to various manifestations of South African jazz and popular music. As such, the relationship between *marabi* and its progeny is similar to that between the blues and its offspring in the United States. Moreover, like the blues, *marabi* uses a simple, cyclical harmonic structure with origins in the repeated patterns (sometimes called 'root progressions' or 'harmonic segments') typical of many indigenous African musics. The basic *marabi* cycle characteristically extended over four bars, with one bar for each of the following chords: I-IV-I$^6_4$-V. The melodies superimposed on these endlessly repeating patterns sometimes became legendary – those known as 'Sponono' (a term of endearment) and 'uNtebejana ufana nemfene' (Ntebejana looks like a baboon), for example. On the very limited evidence available, it seems that songs were typically simple, unitary structures involving much repetition and some variation. Though *marabi* appears to have been a predominantly textless idiom, vernacular lyrics on topical subjects were sometimes invented – even on the spur of the moment – and in some instances these contained political commentary or protest. A significant proportion of the melodies appear to have been traceable to 'traditional' or 'indigenous' origins.

Other styles and repertoires also left their mark on the melodic and rhythmic structures of *marabi*. These included a familiar stock of 'black' Christian hymns and wedding songs, commercially popular tunes of the day, types of so-called 'colored' ('mixed-race') and 'white' Afrikaans dance music known as *tikkie-draai* and *vastrap*, and the *ghommaliedjies* of the Cape Malays. There appear also to have been varieties of *marabi* associated almost exclusively with certain groups of Xhosa and Zulu speakers. The Xhosa version – reputedly less polished than mainstream *marabi* – was named *tula n'divile*, after the words of a song first made popular by migrant workers in Durban in the late 1920s; the Zulu version – developed by Zulu migrant workers in Johannesburg – was termed *ndunduma*, after the Zulu word for the minedumps that seemed to them to symbolize that gold-rich city.

In *marabi* performance, cyclical repetitions of one melody or melodic fragment could yield eventually to a similar treatment of another melody or fragment, and perhaps then still others, each possibly from a different source. By loosely stringing melodies together in this manner, a performer – whether playing piano, pedal organ, guitar or banjo – could create extended medleys and play for long stretches without stopping. Throughout, a simple rhythmic accompaniment would be provided by a player shaking a tin filled with small stones, typically sounding the most basic and widespread drum patterns of 'traditional' Nguni music.

Descriptions suggest that *marabi* was danced in a highly sensuous manner, without fixed steps, and at a slowish pace. There were some typical styles of dress, if one is to believe the description of a newspaper commentator of the era. 'The ladies usually dress in red,' he wrote in *Bantu World* in 1932. 'These dresses are very short … They usually put on Japanese black shoes. Their hair [is] usually cut in what is known as the "French cut." The gentlemen dress in black shirts, black Japanese shoes and baggy trousers of various shades and colours.' He also noted the prevalence of scuffles and violence, in his estimation 'because the dancers were usually intoxicated' (ScipioAfricanus 1932).

Given the opprobrium attached to *marabi* culture by all who considered themselves above it, or who considered it a threat, it is not surprising that not a single one of the many early *marabi* musicians was ever recorded. What were recorded, however, were a number of performances that allude to, or 'refract,' the early music of the slumyards. In particular, these recordings include *marabi* imitations, recreations and arrangements, all of them typically 'cleaned up' and performed by elite groups (for the reasons discussed earlier). As such, these recordings are removed by one or two steps from slumyard *marabi*, but since they are our nearest approximations, many of them are of great historical importance. Often their titles contain orthographic errors – sure signs of either careless disregard or the white managers' lack of familiarity with the relevant vernacular or both (see Discography).

For a style that was cultivated by untutored musicians and that gave sustenance for just two decades to newly urbanized people living in the most desperate circumstances, *marabi* has had an impact on the formation and development of South African music that is in inverse proportion to its social genesis and standing. Marked from the start as proletarian and pan-ethnic, *marabi* evolved at a time not only of rapid socioeconomic expansion, change and dislocation, but also of the refining of the first legislative cornerstones of the 'race'-based capitalism that eventually came to be known as apartheid. At a crucial moment of South African history, this was a music of solidarity and survival. Despised, feared and disparaged like the slum dwellers who made it, *marabi* nonetheless fertilized a host of later stylistic developments in the flowering of South African music.

Bibliography

Allen, Lara. 1993. 'Pennywhistle Kwela: A Musical, Historical, and Socio-Political Analysis.' Unpublished M.Mus. thesis, University of Natal, Durban.

Allen, Lara. 2000. *Representation, Gender and Women in Black South African Popular Music, 1948–1960*. Unpublished Ph.D. thesis, University of Cambridge.

Allingham, Rob. 1994a. 'Hip Kings, Hip Queens: The Story of South African Jazz, at Home and Overseas.' In *World Music: The Rough Guide*, eds. Simon Broughton et al. London: Rough Guides, 391–6.

Allingham, Rob. 1994b. 'Township Jive: From Pennywhistle to Bubblegum – the Music of South Africa.' In *World Music: The Rough Guide*, eds. Simon Broughton et al. London: Rough Guides, 373–90.

Ballantine, Christopher. 1999. 'Looking to the USA: The Politics of American Male Close-Harmony Song Style in South Africa during the 1940s and 1950s.' *Popular Music* 18(1): 1–18.

Ballantine, Christopher. 2000. 'Gender, Migrancy, and South African Popular Music in the Late 1940s and the 1950s.' *Ethnomusicology* 44(3): 376–407.

Ballantine, Christopher. 2012. *Marabi Nights: Jazz, 'Race' and Society in Early Apartheid South Africa* (with accompanying CD). Pietermaritzburg: University of KwaZulu-Natal Press.

Coplan, David B. 1979. 'The African Performer and the Johannesburg Entertainment Industry: The Struggle for African Culture on the Witwatersrand.' In *Labour Townships and Protest: Studies in the Social History of the Witwatersrand*, ed. Belinda Bozzoli. Johannesburg: Ravan Press, 183–215.

Coplan, David B. 1981. '*Marabi*: The Emergence of African Working-Class Music in Johannesburg.' In *Discourse in Ethnomusicology II: A Tribute to Alan P. Merriam*, eds. Caroline Card et al. Bloomington: Ethnomusicology Publications Group, Indiana University, 43–65.

Coplan, David B. 2007. *In Township Tonight! Three Centuries of South African Black City Music and Theatre*. Johannesburg: Jacana Media.

Erlmann, Veit. 1991. 'Cultural Osmosis, Ethnicity, and Tradition in Black Popular Music in Durban, 1913–1939.' In *African Stars: Studies in Black South African Performance*. Chicago: University of Chicago Press, 54–94.

Hamm, Charles. 1988. *Afro-American Music, South Africa, and Apartheid*. I.S.A.M. Monographs, No. 28. Brooklyn: Conservatory of Music, Brooklyn College of the City University of New York.

Koch, Eddie. 1983. 'Doornfontein and Its African Working Class, 1914–1935: A Study of Popular Culture in Johannesburg.' Unpublished MA thesis, University of the Witwatersrand, Johannesburg.

ScipioAfricanus. 1932. 'A New Development of Dance Styles Takes Place Among the Reef Bantu.' *Bantu World*, 28 May.

Titlestad, Michael. 2004. *Making the Changes: Jazz in South African Literature and Reportage*. Pretoria: UNISA Press.

Discography

Amanzimtoti Players. 'Sbhinono' [sic] (Sponono). HMV GU 130 and JP 165. *1932*: South Africa.

Bantu Glee Singers. 'Ndunduma.' HMV GU 94. *1932*: South Africa.

Griffiths Motsieloa and Company. 'Sponono naMarabi.' Singer GE 67. *1931*: South Africa.

Hot Lips Dance Band. 'Marabi No. 2 Jive.' Rayma RB 5. *c. 1945*: South Africa.

Jazz Revellers Band. 'Seponono' [sic] (Sponono). Columbia AE 45. *1933*: South Africa.

Merry Blackbirds. 'E Chain Covers' [sic] (iChain Covers). Singer GE 94. *c. 1934*: South Africa.

Motsieloa's Pitch Black Follies. 'Tsaba Tsabake No.1' [sic] (Tsaba Tsaba ke No.1). Singer GE 853. *1939*: South Africa.

Nkandhla Guitar Players. 'Evelina.' Gallotone-Singer GE 975. *c. 1948*: South Africa.

Zikali, W. P. 'Ntebetshana' [sic] (Ntebejana). Columbia AE 45. *1933*: South Africa.

Zuluboy and his Jazz Maniacs. 'Izakalo Zika Z-Boy' [sic] (Izikhalo Zika Zuluboy). Better XU 9. *1939*: South Africa.

Zuluboy and his Jazz Maniacs. 'Tsaba Tsaba.' Better XU 9. *1939*: South Africa.

CHRISTOPHER BALLANTINE

Maringa

The term *maringa* is used in various African countries to designate a type of dance and/or a musical genre that became a key foundational element of what would later develop into modern African popular musics. It played a role also in the beginnings of urban identity in Africa and in the articulation of different social sectors. Existing documents suggest it emerged at the turn of the twentieth century, but it is possible that it predates that time. The roots of the genre lie in the historical process under which African traditions, having participated in a complex intermingling of influences in the Americas as a consequence of the slave trade, returned to Africa at the beginning of colonization. *Maringa* later spread to various African countries. In the 1950s what was known as *maringa* in Congo began to be called *rumba* (Aranzadi 2016).

Broadly, the word *maringa* represents a type of music linked to the *gumbe* drum (a square frame drum with legs) that Jamaican Maroons, rebel slaves, took with them to Sierra Leone when they were deported there at the turn of the nineteenth century. In Freetown, one may see *gumbe* still being performed today among Creoles or Krio, a group originally comprising Black Loyalists, Maroons and the slaves who were recaptured from slave trading vessels by the British Navy. (For further information on these groups, see the following entries and the entry on Gumbe/Goombay.) In Africa in the nineteenth century a diaspora of the Krio from Freetown formed elites in different countries, settling in Ghana, Nigeria, Equatorial Guinea (where they became great cocoa planters) and Congo (where thousands of migrant workers from Sierra Leone worked on the railroad from the coast to the capital Kinshasa); in all these countries, and also in Gabon, the *maringa* has been documented.

It is recognized that the genre exhibits Caribbean influences and that it shares characteristics with both *rumba* and calypso. Documentation of *maringa* via sound recordings did not begin until the third decade of the twentieth century. The most important recordings are those from Sierra Leone, especially those of Ebenezer Calender in the 1940s–60s. In Sierra Leone, *maringa* largely gave way to a more modern form, *Milo jazz*, while in Ghana and eastern Nigeria *maringa*, together with both *gumbe* and *asíkó*, was later partially absorbed into highlife.

There follow two entries that provide more detail on *maringa* and the relationships between *maringa* and other genres in two specific countries: Equatorial Guinea and Sierra Leone.

Bibliography

Aranzadi, Isabela de. 2016. 'La rumba congoleña en el diálogo afro-atlántico: Influencias caribeñas en África desde 1800' [The Congolese *Rumba* in the Afro-Atlantic Dialogue: Caribbean Influences in Africa Since 1800]. *Methaodos. Revista de Ciencias Sociales* 4(1): 100–18. Online at: http://dx.doi.org/10.17502/m.rcs.v4i1.108 (accessed 22 December 2016).

ISABELA DE ARANZADI (TRANSLATED BY PAMELA NARBONA JEREZ)

Maringa (in Equatorial Guinea)

In Equatorial Guinea, *maringa* may be performed either as a song with accompaniment or purely as an instrumental. There are two distinct styles, which share the same rhythm and timeline. The first style is sung at the end of a ritual dance, called *ñánkue* or *bonkó*, which is performed by Creoles (or Crió) in Malabo, the capital of the island of Bioko, and in which masked performers depict their ancestors in street processions. It is also performed by Annobonese on the smaller island of Annobon. The other style is a type of song accompanied by the Spanish guitar, using the two-finger guitar-picking technique and influenced by Iberian melodies (*bolero*, *fado*, *copla*, and so on) and African-Caribbean rhythms.

Equatorial Guinea, located on the west coast between Cameroon and Gabon, is the only Spanish-speaking country in Africa. *Maringa* is primarily associated with the country's island territories, Bioko Island, which lies across from Nigeria and Cameroon, and Annobon, which is located 600 kilometers south of Bioko and 300 kilometers from the Gabonese coast. Bioko was known as Fernando Po during the period of colonization, and for part of its history, from 1826 to 1843, was leased by the British. (The island's original and present-day name of Bioko will be used for the remainder of the entry.)

After independence from Spain in 1968, Equatorial Guinea remained isolated from other African countries and also from Spain during the dictatorship of the first president, Macias Nguema, until 1979. During this time the use of the Spanish language was forbidden, along with the performance of dances with Spanish names using the square drum. The *maringa* ritual dance was performed as an independence dance during the first decades of the twentieth century by Creoles and, because of its influence, was also performed by the Annobonese and by the Bubi people in Creole villages of Bioko (Malabo and Luba). Similarly, the guitar style of *maringa* is performed by both Annobonese and Bubi people and is considered an 'old style' that was very important during the twentieth century until independence in 1968.

Historical Overview

Tracing the history of *maringa* requires an exploration of the historical experience of a former colony that participated in multiple African and African-American trajectories. Social sectors are articulated around various powers – British, Creole and Spanish – with music constituting a means of connection between many Africans from the coast, Ghana, Nigeria, Sierra Leone and in a multiethnic society on the island of Bioko.

Among the significant movements involved in a 'back to Africa' process in music, such as that from coastal to rural areas, the earlier diasporic arrival of African-American and African-Caribbean music, which began in Sierra Leone at the turn of the nineteenth century and spread to other countries in the following years, reaching the island of Bioko from

1827 onwards, is of special importance to the origins of urban popular music.

As noted earlier, the British leased the island from the Spanish, mainly as a base for the navy to carry out antislavery patrols. The first group of Creoles came with the British from Sierra Leone in 1827 as workers. This group was to have a fundamental influence on the formation of Creole culture in the island. They were called 'fernandinos' (after the then name of the island) and they called themselves Crió (in Sierra Leone, usually Krio), meaning Creole. The Sierra Leonean diaspora brought with it African-Caribbean and African-American musical influences. The former included *gumbe*, a genre built around the square *gumbe* drum. Brought by Jamaican Maroons to Freetown in 1800, *gumbe* is considered the first 'back to Africa' style and formed the basis for other styles including palmwine, *maringa* and highlife, as documented by Kenneth Bilby (2011), John Collins (1992) and Fleming Harrev (1993; 2001). The second set of musical influences on Bioko from Sierra Leone had their origins with the Black Loyalists, liberated slaves who were evacuated by the British after the American War of Independence first to Nova Scotia then to Freetown, and who brought with them language, customs, music and a British cultural identity that persists among Creoles in Malabo (the capital of Bioko) and the Krio in Freetown. (For further information about this group in Sierra Leone, see the entry on Gumbe/Goombay.)

These diverse musical influences were spread through the movements of Sierra Leoneans along the coastal countries of Africa, including Bioko, where the square drum was played by Creoles up to 1976 (when local dance associations ceased operations in conjunction with a mass migration of Creoles from Bioko to Nigeria, fleeing the dictatorship of President Macias) and were conserved by the Annobonese people in Annobon. There have also been movements of workers from Bioko back to Sierra Leone, as well as influences or at least exchanges between Bioko and countries such as Gabon, Cameroon and Congo. This complex circulation makes it difficult to trace the lines of influence and development, but it is clear that *maringa* was a presence in all of these countries. It is not known whether the genre began in Bioko in the early nineteenth century (Cubans were deported from Cuba to Bioko during the nineteenth century and González Echegaray (1959) thinks that Cuban influence is evident in the genre) and was later diffused through the Sierra Leoneans and Liberian Kru people, or whether the new wave of *maringa* in Sierra Leone was the primary source influencing its emergence in Bioko.

Maringa, along with other genres such as *gumbe*, *aşíkò* and palmwine, was a highly important precursor of twentieth-century popular music in West Africa. In Equatorial Guinea the documentary sources for *maringa* go back to the first decade of the twentieth century, when it was reported in a newspaper on 2 August 1907 as being played in Bioko to celebrate the firstborn child of the King, Alfonso XIII. Performed by the Banda de la Marina (Navy Band), it featured dancing by *krumanes* (Kru) and *fernandinos* (Creoles) (Aranzadi 2016, 105). The known sources therefore predate those of Sierra Leone. In Bioko the so-called *sierraleonas* (Sierra Leoneans among the elite Creole community who maintained strong connections with their home country) kept up regular contact with Freetown during the nineteenth century up to 1893, the year in which passage through Freetown was limited to ships with commercial purposes. Through the influence of the Creoles on Bioko the heritage of Sierra Leone music reached the Bubi group who were native to the island, the Annobonese on Annobon and even the Fangs, who sang songs in Pidgin in some villages on the mainland and who were taken to Bioko by the Spaniards to work on cocoa plantations in the 1920s.

Black African Creoles from Bioko were a rare example of an African bourgeoisie. The island remained without effective colonial occupation during the mid-nineteenth century. The British left in 1835 and the Spanish did not effectively colonize it until 1900, even though it was under their domain. The commercial activity of the island's Creoles was very intense. The link between economic development and the birth of popular music, as well as the emergence of a new identity for the elite, was the basis for the exchange of musical culture in the island's urban area. For example, after World War I, Maximiliano Jones, a Creole descendant of Sierra Leone, brought machines from Germany to install electricity in the south of the island. As his son Daniel noted: 'This great event was celebrated with lots of fireworks and boat races. For three days, we danced *maringas* and *baleles*. ... His

Majesty Alfonso XIII sent his congratulations with a large reward' (Jones 1962, 265–6).

According to Fleming Harrev (pers. comm.), *maringa* may have spread from Bioko to other neighboring countries as a bridge between the Anglophone and Francophone countries in Africa. In the 1920s *maringa* was played in Nigeria, and the genre constitutes one of the roots of highlife (Waterman 1990, 45–6). It was played in cities including Lagos (Waterman 1988, 229), Accra and Douala, where in 1932 *maringa* and other music sung in African bars was under strict regulation by Europeans (Schler 2002, 325). In Gabon, *maringa* (or *malinga*) denotes a large square drum played with the heel of the foot; the song and the dance are accompanied by the drum and accordion (Pepper 1958, 49). In addition, there has been Cuban influence on Bioko Island since the nineteenth century, when hundreds of deported Afro-Cubans, among them a few musicians, joined the group of Creoles (Aranzadi 2012a, b). In the festivals of Santa Isabel in the late nineteenth century (Malabo), the *cha-cha-cha* (*chachachá*) was danced in *maringa* style (Sialo 1954).

Maringa (Ritual Version)

The ritual *bonkó* is sung and danced by the community of black African Creoles and, as a result of their influence, it is also danced by the indigenous Bubi people of Bioko Island and the Annobonese from Annobon Island. This ritual stems from the influence of the Ekpe secret society of Calabar in Nigeria, and also the related Cuban Abakuá, which was brought to Bioko by Cuban deportees. In the city of Malabo, in some villages in Bioko and in the only city on Annobon Island, a procession takes place every day during the Christmas season from 24 December until 7 January, with a ritual dance called *ñánkue* or *bonkó* (*mamahe* in Annobon) that features masked performers (called *ñánkue*) who represent the ancestors. The *bonkó* songs are in Pidgin or in Spanish. As the dance is about to come to an end, members of the secret Association of Bonkó or Ñánkue sing *maringa* and accompany the musicians and masked performers. The quadruple rhythm of *maringa* announces the finale of *bonkó* and contrasts with the triple 6/8 meter sung throughout the afternoon. It is possible that finishing *bonkó* with *maringa* is related to the fact that *maringa* was customarily the last piece performed by the colonial guard band at Sunday concerts during the era of Spanish colonization, and the only one in which Africans and Europeans danced together. This dance – a culmination of the meeting of numerous social and ethnic sectors – represented an expression of the celebration of urban African identity and of resistance in an oppressive colonial environment.

The group of singers, all dressed in the same clothing featuring West African textile weaving designs, follows the musicians and masked performers in the procession. The choir sings in a responsorial structure and answers the soloist in unison, sometimes singing in thirds. The lyrics describe the most important events and sentiments that took place during the year in the Creole community (ambition, sorrow, comic events, complaints, etc.) (Aranzadi 2009). The accompanying instruments are five single-headed skin drums of different sizes playing call-and-response polyrhythms in 6/8 time, along with idiophone instruments such as the *katá* (two sticks), the *kon-kon* (a metal bell on which Caribbean *clave* is played with a small stick) and the *sheek-sheek* (maracas).

Bonkó appeared at the beginning of the twentieth century in Annobon and has been performed in Malabo since the mid-nineteenth century (Aranzadi 2012a). There is evidence of the existence of *maringa* in the early twentieth century. In addition to the 1906 and 1907 occasions noted earlier, we also find it in 1907 on the small island of Corisco, on the mainland, where it was danced and treated by institutions 'as an immoral dance') (Aranzadi 2016; author's translation). The colonial guard played this dance in duple meter with a rhythm of alternating eighths and sixteenths, as documented in a score from 1910 (Saavedra Magdalena 1910, 121). Daniel Jones also mentions occurrences in the south of the island in 1913 (1962, 115, 146, 205, 246, 265). Another reference to *maringa* appears as a dance practiced in Guinea in 1919 (Mas 1931, 96).

Further, according to local Creole collective memory, during the nineteenth century and at the beginning of the twentieth century *maringa* was played as a dance independent of *bonkó*. In Guinea it was danced with the square drum *kunki* by the *sierraleonas*, who were accorded high status in Bioko. It is said that at the beginning it was accompanied by drums, then by the accordion and later by the Spanish guitar, but always accompanied by *kunki* (a large square drum with a double frame and legs),

Maringa (in Equatorial Guinea)

by *tambali* (small square tambourines) and by a saw (scraped with a stick) and bottle. It was associated with the square drum played with a Caribbean timeline and was thus part of the earliest roots of African popular music in countries such as Ghana, Nigeria and the Congo. The accordion was introduced to Africa in 1860 in Freetown (Harrev 1987, 6). Later, the instrument was associated with *maringa* and the *aṣíkò* style (with square tambourines) in Senegambia, where it was introduced by the Aku community (Yoruba) of the Krio group from Freetown. In the twentieth century the accordion was played along with square tambourines in Ghana, on the Ivory Coast and in other West African countries (Harrev 1993, 3) and Gabon (Pepper 1958, 49).

At the time of Spanish colonization of Guinea in the 1940s, the Sialo Claretian missionaries placed *maringa* among the 'immoral dances' nominally prohibited by the Ecclesiastical Authority of the Colony (Official Journal of the Vicariate, April 1943, No. 45 in Sialo 1954). In the 1950s in Guinea there were several dances in *maringa* style (*ekota, bolo* and *manchop*) (Sialo 1954); it was not danced by a single ethnic group but rather by all Guineans. It was a vehicle for expression in a multiethnic urban space that could be 'borrowed' by all ethnic groups in the city of Santa Isabel (later Malabo), precisely because of the trans-ethnic nature of the music itself, with its European, African-American and African roots.

In 2018 *bonkó* dance is a symbol of the city of Malabo and also participates in back and forth migration across the Atlantic. *Bonkó* is influenced by the Abakuá secret society, which deported Cubans brought to Bioko from 1862 until Cuba's independence in 1898. It is also directly influenced by the *Ekpe* ritual society from Calabar, which was transformed in Cuba into the *Abakuá* society, founded in 1836 in Havana by Carabalí slaves (from Calabar). In fact, it is one of the Afro-Cuban roots of Cuban identity (Aranzadi 2012a). Another factor is the intermingling of African-American styles, which go back to the Sierra Leonean diaspora and its heritage of Jamaican Maroons and Black Loyalists (who danced the *kunki* [*koonking* or *koonken*] in Freetown in 1830) with those of the recaptured slaves who also left a ritual heritage in Bioko (Aranzadi 2010, 2012b). (For further information on *maringa* in Sierra Leone, see the following entry.)

The *Maringa* Style with Guitar

This second style of *maringa*, which shares a common type of *clave* with the first style (one also found in highlife, *aṣíkò* and *cumbé*), is present in Bioko and Annobon, and elders remember that it was also practiced on the mainland, beginning in colonial times. It is associated with the Spanish guitar and with African-Caribbean influences in the rhythm, and it uses the two-finger-picking technique found in other African countries. The style combines European-influenced harmonies and melodies, interlaced with syncopated rhythms. The guitar melodies in one or two parts (usually in intervals of sixths) accompany the voice or are played as instrumental interludes between the verses. The scale used is diatonic and the harmony is European. This version of *maringa* (more diatonic) differs from the palmwine genre, in which the pentatonic scale is often used with a very strong I-IV-V harmony. While in Bioko this form of *maringa* is considered an 'old style' (common in the 1960s and earlier) and few musicians still play it, the Annobonese have conserved guitar-style *maringa* as popular music and play it frequently.

Maringa on Annobon Island is often sung in a minor mode with I-IV-V chord progressions and a repeated alternation of I and IV in the minor mode. The songs have different tempos, many having a slow tempo and very agile rhythmic accompaniment provided by the square little tambourine *tambali*, interlaced with the rhythm of all the instruments, in groups of eighth or sixteenth notes played with or without syncopation (see Example 1).

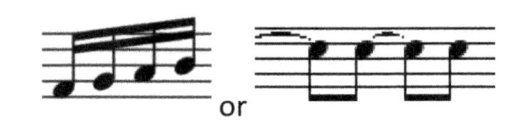

Example 1: *Maringa* rhythms

The songs use call-and-response structure. The vocalists sing in two parallel voices (with intervals of thirds and fourths). The percussion instruments used are the *tango*, the *dun*, the *tambali* and the bottle. The first two are conical membranophone drums, 50 centimeters high and about 15 or 20 centimeters in diameter. The *dun* provides the bass and the *tango* performs polyrhythms in dialogue with the *dun* in the unaccented beats, articulating rapid and flexible phrases that fill the spaces when the *dun* is silent. The *tambali* is constructed in the same way as the *cumbé* (the big square drum with legs). With the *tambali*, played with a thin stick, different shades of intensity are created. The *tango* and *dun* were incorporated from the 1960s into the folk songs of the Annobonese in *maringa* style with guitar, imitating Nigerian drums and other coastal African drums. The *tambali* and the *cumbé* were introduced in Annobon from the beginning of the twentieth century. Accompaniment with dialogue between the drums in Annobon Island songs also occurs in the songs without guitar.

An early style of *gumbe* with the square drum is one of the roots of other early styles that emerged later, including *maringa*, *aṣíkò* and *jùjú* music. In Equatorial Guinea, the Sierra Leoneans, who were the first settlers of the island, and their descendants played the *kunki* square drum brought from Freetown and *tambali* tambourines. They danced the *kunki* until 1976, the year when many Creoles left the island because of the political and social crisis after independence. There is no other reference to *kunki* in West Africa, except in 1830 in Freetown (mentioned above), where the settlers from Nova Scotia (Black Loyalists) danced the *koonken* or *koonking* (Rankin 1836).

Later, according to the older Creoles in Bioko, around the first half of the twentieth century, the guitar was introduced into the *kunki* dance, accompanied by the big square drum and the little square tambourine. The research of Fleming Harrev (1987) and Cynthia Schmidt (1998) has shown that the *maringa* guitar style spread to other countries in Africa where the Kru mariners went to work. The Kru arrived in Bioko from Liberia to work on cocoa plantations and learned *maringa* there, carrying it with them in subsequent travels to Gabon and both Congos.

The genre of *maringa* in other African countries is also linked to *cumbé* under other names. *Gumbe*, *Milo jazz* and *maringa*, according to Horton, were three instrumental music styles played by Creoles from Sierra Leone (1999, 231), and the term *maringa* designates the square drum in the Congo (Robinson 2003, 350). Another name for this drum in the Congo is *patenge* (Tchebwa 1996, 48). Thus, the square drum on a double frame together with the *maringa* constituted some of the roots in Zaire (later Democratic Republic of Congo), of what would explode as the Congolese *rumba* (Mukuna 2000, 112). According to Lema, a Congolese musician who played it in Kinshasa in the 1960s, the *patenge* or *maringa* drum in Congo was played astride (personal communication). It was played in the same way also in Sierra Leone, Gabon, Ghana and Equatorial Guinea. These drums are the same as the *kunki* of the Creoles in Bioko, the *cumbé* of Annobon Island and, among other similar names, the *goombay* or *gome* of Ghana. In Lagos, according to Harrev, the first band that played urban-style music in Yoruba in the 1930s imitated the *maringa* style on guitar (2001, 7).

In Moka, a village on Bioko Island, Gabriel Borikó plays *maringa* and has his own group with drums and *maracas*. As the present author can testify from personal experience, in 2007 he played the Spanish guitar, and when he was recorded in 2013 for the BBC Radio 3 *World Routes* program he used an electric guitar. In the village of Rebola near the capital Malabo, Luís Sorizo, a Bubi singer since colonial times, has a wide repertoire of songs in Spanish, Bubi and Pidgin, among which there are influential songs in the *maringa* style.

Popular Songs on Annobon Island: *Tômbô Plass'a* and *Tômbô Meté d'Ôluy'a*

In villages in the summer there is singing every day, and in the capital of Annobon Island, Palé, there is music on Saturdays and Sundays. A type of leisure dance is performed by the young Annobonese and, depending on where it is performed (in the square or in the middle of the street), it has different names: *tômbô plass'a* (songs sung in the only plaza of Palé, the only city on the island of Annobón) and *tômbô meté d'öluy'a* (the name for songs sung in the streets of Palé). The *tambali* is used in these dances, as well as the *tango*, the *dun* and the bottle. The topics are varied, and as for songs without guitar, the vocal style is closer to *cumbé*, without a diatonic scale and with similar vocal lamentations to flamenco. When songs have guitar accompaniment, it is the *maringa* style described above. When the guitar is introduced, although the accompanying instruments are the same, the rhythm becomes more regular and the melodies are diatonic.

In their *maringa* songs, the singer Desmali and his group D'Ambô de la Costa sing about various themes, such as love, grief, prison during the dictatorship and so on, with a melancholy that reflects the situation of the Annobonese for centuries, isolated on the small island of Annobon, where they still live today with a subsistence economy of fishing and harvesting. Their trip from Annobon to Malabo in search of new opportunities did not reap the hoped-for success and, although humor is present in several Annobon Island songs, in the case of Desmali, the melancholic character prevails and his themes are those of infidelity, love, sorrow, memories of his single mother and so on.

Conclusion

Maringa is a genre with a long history in Equatorial Guinea. It was present throughout the colonial period that began in the early twentieth century, as a precursor style of popular music. It was performed by the colonial bands and by small groups using both native and imported instruments (including the accordion) along with instruments that had made a double Atlantic crossing (such as the square drum). *Maringa* is recognized as having played an important part in the emergence of urban identity in Equatorial Guinea and in enabling social sectors and ethnic groups to express themselves. It is considered one of Equatorial Guinea's proprietary genres, especially among older generations.

Bibliography

Aranzadi, Isabela de. 2009. *Instrumentos musicales de las etnias de Guinea Ecuatorial* [Musical Instruments of Ethnic Groups in Equatorial Guinea]. Madrid: Apadena.

Aranzadi, Isabela de. 2010. 'A Drum's Trans-Atlantic Journey from Africa to the Americas and Back after the End of Slavery: Annobonese and Fernandino Musical Cultures.' *African Sociological Review* 14(1): 20–47. Online at: http://www.ajol.info/index.php/asr/article/viewFile/70227/58416 (accessed 22 December 2016).

Aranzadi, Isabela de. 2012a. 'El legado cubano en África. Ñáñigos deportados a Fernando Poo. Memoria viva y archivo escrito' [The Cuban Legacy in Africa. Ñáñigos deported to Fernando Poo. Living Memory and Written Record]. *Afro-Hispanic Review* 32(1) (Spring): 29–60.

Aranzadi, Isabela de. 2012b. 'Musical Objects and Identities in Transit within Groups in Equatorial Guinea: Musical Connections with Sierra Leone and Cuba following the Abolition of Slavery.' In *In and Out of Africa, Exploring Afro-Hispanic, Luso-Brazilian, and Latin-American Connections*, ed. Joanna Boampong. Newcastle upon Tyne: Cambridge Scholars Publishing, 190–215.

Aranzadi, Isabela de. 2013. *Memoria africana en el Atlántico y cultura (in)material de la música en un espacio de criollización: La isla de Bioko* [African Memory in the Atlantic and (Im)material Culture of Music in a Space of Creolization: The Island of Bioko]. Unpublished Ph.D. thesis, Autonomous University of Madrid.

Aranzadi, Isabela de. 2016. *La rumba congoleña en el diálogo afro-atlántico. Influencias caribeñas en África desde 1800* [The Congolese Rumba in the Afro-Atlantic Dialogue. Caribbean Influences in Africa Since 1800]. *Methaodos. Revista de Ciencias Sociales* 4(1): 100–18. Online at: http://dx.doi.org/10.17502/m.rcs.v4i1.108 (accessed 22 December 2016).

Bender, Wolfgang. 1989. 'Ebenezer Calendar – An Appraisal.' In *Perspectives of African Music*. Bayreuth: E. Breitinger, 43–69.

Bilby, M. Kenneth. 2011. 'Africa's Creole Drum. The Gumbe as Vector and Signifier of Trans-African Creolization.' In *Creolization as Cultural Creativity*, eds. Robert Baron and Ana C. Cara. Jackson: University Press of Mississippi, 137–77.

Collins, John. 1992. *West African Pop Roots*. Philadelphia: Temple University Press.

González, Echegaray, Carlos. 1959. *Estudios guineos* [Guinean Studies]. Madrid: Instituto de Estudios Africanos, Consejo Superior de Investigaciones Científicas.

Harrev, Flemming. 1987. 'Gumbe and the Development of *Krio* Popular Music in Freetown, Sierra Leone.' Paper presented at IASPM's 4th International Conference, Accra, Ghana, 12–19 August.

Harrev, Flemming. 1993. 'The Origin of Urban Music in West and Central Africa.' Paper presented at 23rd World Conference of the ICTM, Berlin, 16–22 June.

Harrev, Flemming. 2001. 'The Diffusion of Gumbe *Assiko* and *Maringa* in West and Central Africa.' Paper presented at 12th Triennial Symposium on

African Art by the Arts Council of the US African Studies Association, St Thomas, Virgin Islands, 22-9 April 2001.

Horton, Christian Dowu Jayeola. 1999. 'The Role of the *Gumbe* in Popular Music and Dance Styles in Sierra Leone.' In *Turn Up the Volume: A Celebration of African Music*, eds. Jacqueline Cogdell DjeDje and Ernest Brown. Los Angeles: UCLA Fowler Museum of Cultural History.

Jones Mathama, Daniel. 1962. *Una lanza por el Boabí* [A Lance by the Boabí]. Barcelona: Casals.

Más, José. 1919 [1931]. *En el país de los bubi. Escenas de la vida en Fernando Poo* [In the Land of the Bubi. Scenes of Life in Fernando Po]. Madrid: Pueyo, S.L.

Pepper, Herbert. 1958. *Anthólogie de la vie africaine. Congo-Gabon* [Anthology of African Life. Congo-Gabon]. Paris: Ducretet Thomson.

Rankin, F. Harrison. 1836. *The White Man's Grave: A Visit to Sierra Leone, in 1834*, 2 vols. London: R. Bentley.

Robinson, N. Scott. 2003. 'Frame Drums and Tambourines.' In *Continuum Encyclopedia of Popular Music of the World, Vol. 2: Performance and Production*, eds. John Shepherd et al. New York: Continuum, 362-72.

Saavedra y Magdalena, Diego. 1910. *España en el África Occidental (Río de Oro y Guinea)* [Spain in West Africa (Gold River and Guinea)]. Madrid: Imprenta Artística Española.

Schler, Lynn. 2002. 'Looking Through a Glass of Beer: Alcohol in the Cultural Spaces of Colonial Douala, 1910-1945.' *The International Journal of African Historical Studies*, 35(2/3): 315-34.

Schmidt, Cynthia. 1998. 'Kru Mariners and Migrants of the West African Coast.' In *Garland Encyclopedia of World Music. Vol. I. Africa*, ed. Ruth M. Stone. New York: Garland Publishing, 370-82.

Sialo, Joaquín Mª C.M.F. 1954. 'El archipiélago Mandji su capital Santa Mª de Corisco. Los bailes indígenas' [The Archipelago Mandji Its Capital Santa Mº of Corisco. Indigenous Dances]. *La Guinea Española* 1401, 25 January, Santa Isabel, 30-3.

Tchebwa, Manda. 1996. *Terre de la chanson: La musique zaïroise hier et aujourd'hui* [Land of Song: Zairean Music from Yesterday and Today]. Louvain la Neuve: Duculot.

Waterman, Christopher A. 1988. 'Àṣíkò, Sákárá and Palmwine: Popular Music and Social Identity in Inter-War Lagos.' *Urban Anthropology* 17: 229-58.

Waterman, Christopher A. 1990. *Jùjú: A Social History and Ethnography of an African Popular Music*. Chicago: University of Chicago Press.

Personal Communications

Cervera Liso, Desiderio (Desmali). 2007-15.
Flemming Harrev, 2007-9
Kinson, Daniel. 2007-13. Personal communications with the author.
Mukuna, Kazadi wa. 2000. 'Latin American Musical Influences in Zaïre.' In *The Garland Handbook of African Music*, Vol. 1, ed. Ruth M. Stone. New York: Taylor and Francis, 107, 112.
Lema, 2016.

Discography

Desmali and D'Ambò de la Costa. *Luga da Ambo*. ICEF. *2008*: Equatorial Guinea.
Música Tradicional de Guinea Ecuatorial. SGAE. España. CD accompanying Aranzadi. *2009*.
Various Artists. Recordings accompanying Aranzadi. *2013*.

ISABELA DE ARANZADI

Maringa (in Sierra Leone)

In Sierra Leone, *maringa* is a style of popular music primarily performed for wedding entertainment in Creole culture. It is used at the residences of the wedded couples and to accompany the revelers as they dance along the street toward the homes of the bride and bridegroom. In the hands of the musician credited with the creation of the Sierra Leonean version of the genre, Ebenezer Calender, it also became an important part of the country's commercial popular music. Although *maringa* in Sierra Leone is sometimes equated with palmwine music they are not equivalent, as the latter refers to a wide-ranging group of related idioms, of which, in Sierra Leone, *maringa* is one.

The Creole or Krio culture of Sierra Leone is an amalgam of cultural practices of the several groups: the Nova Scotian Settlers or Black Loyalists (former slaves and free African-Americans who were evacuated, mainly from Virginia, to Nova Scotia following promises from the British during the American War of Independence, and were sent to Sierra Leone in 1792, where they founded the settlement of Freetown); Jamaican Maroons (escaped slaves who fought the British and were deported first by the British to Nova Scotia in 1796, and then to Freetown in 1800); slaves who were recaptured from slave trading vessels by the British Navy on the open sea); and a mixture of ethnic groups from West Africa. (*See also* the entry on Gumbe/Goombay.)

In *maringa*, elements derived from the Aku (a Creole minority group in Sierra Leone originating primarily in Yoruba and also in Igbo and Hausa cultures) are most apparent, for example in the language used to denote the bridal party (namely, *iyawo* [bride] and *okor* [bridegroom], as well as the lyrics of some of the wedding songs, for example 'baio baio o mibeh' (which means 'please take good care of my daughter' in Yoruba).

Sierra Leonean *maringa* was originated by Ebenezer Calender (1912–85), a celebrated bandleader, who was the son of a Jamaican soldier and a Sierra Leonean mother (for an image of Ebenezer Calender's Maringa Band see Stewart 1993, 46). Calender's music formed part of the 'palmwine' tradition, introduced to Sierra Leone in the 1920s. In the early 1940s Calender also had a *gumbe* ensemble, a genre that by that time was popular enough in Sierra Leone to attract a musician of Calender's caliber. From that association he developed the style of popular music known in Sierra Leone as *maringa*. Since Decca began recording Calender's *maringa* band music in 1945, it is safe to assume that the *maringa* ensemble came into existence in Sierra Leone sometime between 1940 and 1945. The *maringa* band is said to have surpassed the *gumbe* ensemble in popularity in the 1940s (*Zensor Musikproduktion* 88, 1988), though the ongoing influence of *gumbe* was strong: as Rachel Jackson notes (citing John Collins), 'during the 1950s Calendar released almost 300 maringa songs which bore the influence of *gumbé*' (2012, 136).

The *maringa* of Sierra Leone is sometimes erroneously equated with the *merengue* of the Dominican Republic because the names sound similar, but their structure and instrumentation are different. The *maringa* of Sierra Leone is a lively, easy-going social dance music in calypso and *rumba* style. When *maringa* music emerged in the early 1940s, its instrumentation consisted of the following: the acoustic guitar (played by Calender, who had learned to play the guitar by 1935, and who was also the lead singer), the triangle, the *baba* (octagonal frame master drum used by the *asíkó* ensemble that accompanies a traditional masquerade known as *alikali*), the *bombadon* or bass tuba and the bass-box (similar to the one used in the *gumbe* ensemble).

In the late 1940s Calender's ensemble made several recordings for Decca and HMV, and reached the heyday of its achievement and popularity in the 1950s, by which time the instrumentation consisted of the *gumbe* drum, which was prominently used during this period; two frame drums, including the aforementioned *baba*, which has a bar handle in the frame to allow the player to keep time on the skin head with the other hand, and another drum resembling a cylindrical tambourine; the acoustic guitar, always the principal instrument of the ensemble; and a transverse flute made from cane wood. Calender came to love the acoustic properties of the flute during his association with a renowned flutist from the Sherbro–Mende ethnic group, who was so widely known by his nickname 'Never-Tire' (because he could play on his wooden flute for hours without stopping) that no one bothered to learn his real name. Calender also included another of his favorite instruments, the *bombadon*. By the 1980s the instrumentation was further transformed to include triangles, the *agogo* (metal gongs) and milk tins rubbed together as friction idiophones, in addition to the acoustic guitar. The type of songs used by Calender and his group ultimately became part of the prevailing *Milo jazz* of the 1970s and early 1980s.

The singing style is sometimes in call-and-response form in which the response is learned by rote; at other times, the leader sings a fragment of the song and the mixed-gender chorus completes it melodically or harmonically (see Example 1), either singing in unison or in parts (see Horton 1979, 95 and song number 6 on page 354).

Leader: 'Baio baio o mi beh' (Do-Do Do-Ti La-Sol)
Leader and Chorus (completes leaders' statement): 'Baio.baio o mibeh' (Do-Do-Mi-Mi-Do-Re-Do)
Example 1: Call-and-Response Song Text (*Maringa*) with Tonic Solfa syllables.

Calender learned his calypso-style *maringa* music in part from his mixed African-Caribbean parentage and partly from the influence of G. Brown, a Trinidadian who performed in Freetown in the 1950s (N.a., 1954).

Calender himself composed most *maringa* songs in a manner in keeping with the minstrel tradition of the folk entertainment groups of West Africa. For example, he narrated folk morality stories from which he selected themes for the songs that served as refrains. Most of those compositions were composed on the spur of the moment. Calender created the songs based on his experience of Krio culture, and his compositions were understood and appreciated by the elders, who also respected him as a purveyor of the culture.

Calender's compositions were classified as part of the palmwine guitar tradition that was introduced to Sierra Leone in the 1920s. The heyday of his dance band was also a period of continuing British colonial rule, during which the music of Sierra Leone reflected foreign influence in instrumentation (e.g., in the use of brass instruments). Wolfgang Bender (1989) reported that by 1984 Calender had composed some 270 songs, not including his *gumbe* and funeral wake-keeping songs. So the entire list of Calender's compositions must be even larger. Within this repertoire, some of his *gumbe* lyrics are identical to those of his *maringa* songs. For example, one such song, used in both *gumbe* and *maringa* music, goes, 'if na boy gi ahm ehn dadi name' (roughly, 'if it is a boy give him his father's name') and another includes the lyric 'konni rabbit kam luk we kondo de play wonder' (roughly, 'rabbit you say you are cunning, come and see how clever the lizard has become').

Song texts in Sierra Leonean *maringa* are usually short and repetitive. Calender's 'Double Decker Buses' is an exception in that it is a song of social history with several stanzas, composed in *maringa* style. Examples of short songs include the salacious 'Fire, Fire, Fire de Kam.' This song describes the bridegroom's anticipation of how pretty the bride will look and how excited he will be when he sees his bride for the first time. The bride and bridegroom are expected not to visit each other from the day before the wedding until the day of the wedding, when the bride is walked up the aisle by her father (see music examples in Horton 1979, 94–6). Another short song denounces idleness in women: 'Arrria bebi go buy yu ogboro' (roughly, the song exhorts the woman it addresses, instead of sitting idly, to purchase a large shopping basket, put her wares in it and sell them at the market, to make money to live independently of her lover). Finally, another salacious song goes 'Aunty Marie dance me saful ah a behg oh mi yai de turn' (roughly meaning 'Sister Marie, your dancing is too sexy and rough for me, I am feeling dizzy, I am begging you, let me go').

Calender defined *maringa* as deriving from the notion of a carousel, a dance to 'wake up the body' (interview with the author). This explanation is suggestive of a circular and repetitive dance; the music is repeated until the musicians tire themselves out as the variety of dance styles presented by the dancers encourage the musicians to continue playing. *Maringa* dance is related to *gumbe* in which four movements form the foundation of the dance: in the Creole language of Sierra Leone (Krio) the movements are named: (1) *Ole wase*; (2) *Shake wase*; (3) *Cut belleh*; (4) *Cut belle en shake wase*. Whereas in *gumbe* dance each movement must be emphasized by repeating it several times, in *maringa* a dancer does not have to go through all four movements. If a dancer joins in the dance when the tempo is already accelerated, he or she only has to keep the pace and make as much effort as possible to move the hips to the rhythm of the music. The dancing does not last as long as the *gumbe* dance.

Conclusion

While *maringa* is associated particularly with Creole wedding ceremonies, as Ebenezer Calender's career demonstrates, it is also an integral part of Sierra Leone's popular music. Thus, when the former Director of Broadcasting in Sierra Leone, John Akar, was asked in 1965 to assemble a National Dance Troupe for Sierra Leone, he selected Ebenezer Calender and his Maringa Band to represent music of Krio heritage. In fact, whenever a representative sample of popular music of Sierra Leone has been selected, Calender and his Maringa Band were always chosen to represent Krio culture (along with Isata Nyambe and Salia Koroma representing Mende traditional music and others representing various ethnic cultures).

Between 1965 and 1985, the year of his death, Calender was employed at the Sierra Leone Broadcasting Service to present his own style of popular music and folk yarns, in which he was well versed. In this capacity, he captured the interest and devoted following of most Sierra Leoneans. The late president of Sierra Leone, Siaka Probyn Stevens (1905–88), in his New Year's Day awards in 1984, presented Ebenezer Calender with a national certificate of honor for his contribution to the music of Sierra Leone.

Calender died on 5 April 1985. As a purveyor of Krio culture in Sierra Leone, his life and music have been attractive topics of research. Scholars who have studied and published on *maringa* music include Wolfgang Bender (1989), Gary Stewart (1993), Christian Horton (1979 and 1999) and Doreen Faux (1985). Alex Johnson transcribed and translated the lyrics of Calender's songs (1989). After Calender's death, Daddy Loco and his Calender Survivals came into being with the expressed desire to produce *maringa* music after the style of Ebenezer Calender. Unfortunately, the band folded, and no one else was subsequently able to perpetuate the style. Thus, the genre survives only in recordings of *gumbe, maringa* and *Milo jazz* played over the broadcasting system.

Bibliography

Anon. 1954. 'Entertainment.' *Daily Mail*, 2 July.
Anon. 1988. *Zensor Musik Produktion*: 88.
Bender, Wolfgang, ed. 1984. *Songs by Ebenezer Calender in Krio and English from Freetown, Sierra Leone*. Transcription and translation by Alex Johnson. Bayreuth: Iwalewa.
Bender, Wolfgang, 1989. 'Ebenezer Calender: An Appraisal.' In *Perspectives on African Music*, ed. Wolfgang Bender. Bayreuth: Bayreuth University, 43–68.
Bilby, Kenneth M. 1985, *The Caribbean as a Musical Region*. Washington DC: Woodrow Wilson International Center for Scholars.
Calender, Ebenezer. 1985. *Krio Songs*. Freetown: Peoples Educational Association of Sierra Leone.
Collins, John. 2001. 'Pan African Goombay Drum-Dance Music: Its Ramifications and Development in Ghana.' Paper Presented at Arts Council of the African Studies Association's 12th Triennial Symposium on African Art, US Virgin Islands.
Faux, Doreen Z. 1985. 'The Life and Work of Ebenezer Calender.' Unpublished BA thesis. Fourah Bay College, University of Sierra Leone.
Horton, Christian Dowu. 1979. *Indigenous Music of Sierra Leone: an Analysis of Resources and Educational Implications*. Unpublished Ph.D. dissertation, University of California, Los Angeles.
Horton, Christian Dowu Jayeola. 1999. 'The Role of the Gumbe in Popular Music and Dance Styles in Sierra Leone.' In *Turn up the Volume! A Celebration of African Music*, ed. Jacqueline Cogdell DjeDje. Los Angeles: UCLA Fowler Museum of Cultural History, 230–35.
Jackson, Rachel. 2012. 'The Trans-Atlantic Journey of Gumbé: Where and How Has It Survived?' *Journal of International Library of African Music* 9(2): 128–53. Online at http://www.jstor.org/stable/24877257 (accessed 12 May 2018).
Johnson, Alex. 1989. 'Transcriptions and Translations of Ebenezer Calender Repertoire.' In *Perspectives on African Music*, ed. Wolfgang Bender. Bayreuth: Institute for African Studies, 69–90.
Kabba, Muctaru R. A. 1980. '*Sierra Leone Heroes: Fifty Great Men and Women Who Helped to Build Our Nation.*' Freetown, Sierra Leone: Government Printing Press.
Stewart, Gary, 1993. 'The Music of Sierra Leone: Maringa, Roots, Roboto, Shoots.' *The Beat* 12(1): 45–7.
Ware, Naomi. 1978. 'Popular Music and African Identity in Freetown, Sierra Leone.' In *Eight Urban Musical Cultures: Tradition and Change*, ed. Bruno Nettl. Urbana, IL: University of Illinois Press, 296–320.

Discographical References

Calender, Ebenezer. 'Arria Bebi'/'Why yu nor go buy okroh.' Decca WA 2501. Late *1940s*: Sierra Leone.
Calender, Ebenezer. 'Double Decker Buses.' Decca WA 2641. Late *1940s*: Sierra Leone.
Calender, Ebenezer. 'Fire, Fire, Fire de Kam'/ 'Mi ko yu ti si.' Decca WA 2502. Late *1940s*: Sierra Leone.
Calender, Ebenezer. 'Gbe nyama'/'Koni rabbit ehn kondo.' HMV JZ 5241. Late *1940s*: Sierra Leone.
Calender, Ebenezer. 'If na boy gi am ehn dadi name, if na gial gi am ehn mami name.' HMV JZ 5237. Late *1940s*: Sierra Leone.
Calender, Ebenezer. 'Mu kpuelor'/ 'Aunti Marie dance mi saful.' Bassophone B3. *1964*: Sierra Leone.
Sierra Leone Music: West African Gramophone Records Recorded at Freetown in the 50s and Early 60s. Zensor ZS 41 *1988*: African Elegant (Original Music OMCD015).

Discography

African Elegant: Sierra Leone's Kru Krio Calypso Connection. Original Music: OMCD015. *1992*: USA. (Includes 13 tracks by Ebenezer Calender.)

Calender, Ebenezer. 'Don't lie mi lovin bebi' and 'Bebi lay yu poda now.' Decca WA 2519. Late *1940s*: Sierra Leone.

Calender, Ebenezer. 'Du yu yone lef mi yone' and 'Si mi no mohr.' HMV JZ: 5240. Late *1940s*: Sierra Leone.

Calender, Ebenezer. 'Kuma bebi.' Decca 1610. Late *1940s*: Sierra Leone.

Calender, Ebenezer. 'Mi na pooh ole man nor du mi so.' Decca WA 2520. Late *1940s*: Sierra Leone.

Calender, Ebenezer. 'Moni don don de' and 'Kost of livin in Freetown.' Decca WA 2630. Late *1940s*: Sierra Leone.

Calender, Ebenezer. 'Na marade ring yu want yu nohr go geht am' and 'Yuba noh geht paper.' HMV JZ 5256. Late *1940s*: Sierra Leone.

Calender, Ebenezer. 'Yu eat mi moni, yu say yu nohr want mi.' HMV JZ 5998. Late *1940s*: Sierra Leone.

Sierra Leone Music: West African Gramophone Records Recorded at Freetown in the 50s and Early 60s. Zensor ZS 41. *1988*: West Germany.

Various Artists. 'Tape 2: Maringa Music of Sierra Leone.' (Field Recording made by Christian Horton in Freetown, *1974*, to be deposited at UCLA music library.)

Sheet Music

Calender, Ebenezer. 1985. *Krio Songs*. Freetown: Peoples Educational Association of Sierra Leone.

CHRISTIAN 'DOWU JAYEOLA HORTON

Marrabenta

Ask Mozambicans from the South of Mozambique what is *marrabenta* and they might tell you that it is a dance, a rhythm and a musical genre from the 1960s and 1970s. They might also tell you that it is 'a state of being,' 'the essence of what is Mozambican' (out-take 1 from the film *Marrabentando: The Stories My Guitar Sings/Marrabentando: As histórias que a minha guitarra canta* – see Filmography and Visual Recordings). The verb 'to marrabenta' has in some ways become equated with an attitude unique to Mozambique, and 'marrabentando' (marrabenting) with a state of being that comes from living a life of challenges and hardships while still enjoying life to the best of one's ability. Despite a period of unpopularity, *marrabenta* has stood the test of time and taken its place as one of Mozambique's most popular urban music genres.

The rhythm and choreographic style of *marrabenta* were first developed in the 1930s in the southern provinces of the Republic of Mozambique. The music was originally sung and accompanied on handmade tin-can guitars popular among the migrant mining communities of the southern provinces of Maputo and Gaza (for an account of the importance of these migrant mining communities to the development of *marrabenta*, *makwayela* and *timbila*, see the entry on makwayela). The genre only later came to be known as *marrabenta*. It became popular among the white and ethnically mixed communities of the country's capital, Lourenço Marques (later known as Maputo), during the 1960s and 1970s. Electric guitars took the place of the tin cans, rhythm sections were introduced, records were produced and, by the early 1970s, *marrabenta* was a sound popular on the radio and in the nightclubs and discotheques across the country. Associated with a colonial bourgeois lifestyle, it was all but silenced in the communist era of President Samora Machel's post-independent Mozambique (1975–86), but regained popularity in the late 1980s and again through a third incarnation in the 2000s, with its offshoot genre *pandza* taking hold on the Mozambican airwaves and dance floors.

Origins and Early History

Discussions are common among musicians, journalists and researchers about what led to the emergence of *marrabenta*, as well as about the derivation of its name. The meaning of the term 'marrabenta' is thought to stem from the Portuguese word 'rebentar,' meaning to break, tear or blow up (Laranjeira 2014). The word is thus equivalent to sayings in the English language such as 'going through the roof' or 'taking the lid off,' used when referring to moments when the dizzying heights of musical and festive enjoyment are reached. In the 1950s and 1960s the imperative 'rebenta!' would have been called upon as a shout of encouragement as dancers reached breaking point or guitarists reached 'string-breaking' fever-pitch (out-take 2). Adding the prefix 'ma' to a Tsonga word indicates a noun, so a literal translation of this Tsonga/Portuguese hybrid term of 'marrabenta' could be 'the blow out' or 'the music that takes you through the roof.' One of the early *marrabenta* musicians, Dilon Djinji, has claimed a more sexual origin for the word, recalling times when he was apparently referred to as 'marrabenta': the one who 'tears or breaks'. In an unpublished interview conducted in 2004 and alluded to cursorily by his friends in the film *Marrabentando: As histórias que a minha guitarra canta*, Djinji claims the nickname 'marrabenta' was given to him in the 1950s because of the number of girls whose virginity he took during his vacations from the mines. Well dressed and playing his tin-can guitar, he apparently had the pick of the girls at the end of the night. Discussions about the origins of the genre and its name have nevertheless continued, and no agreement has been reached as to the origins of either the term or the genre.

It is thought that the *marrabenta* of the dusty black suburbs of Mozambique was brought into the capital city in the 1940s, when nightclubs and recreational associations such as the African Association of Lourenço Marques hosted live bands from the suburbs. The songs performed in these locations were accompanied by handmade instruments including the tin-can guitar, in which the strings were made from fishing line, the body from old oilcans and the neck from old wooden boards. The clubs in which this music was first played in an urban setting were frequented mainly by intellectuals and travelers looking for places to spend their leisure time (Filipe 2012; Laranjeira 2014). The clubs also had a reputation for attracting prostitutes, which may have been the root of the later criticisms laid against *marrabenta* by the first president of Mozambique, Samora Machel, whose post-independence 'socialist ethics' (Machel 1982, quoted in Arnfred 2011, 129) ultimately led to the closing of clubs and the decline of *marrabenta* after independence in 1975.

One of the first academic references to a musical genre called 'marrabenta' was made in 1957 in Norberto Santos Júnior's ethnomusicological study, *Algumas canções indígenas de Marracuene Moçambique* (Some Indigenous Songs of Marracuenne, Mozambique). In this study, Santos Júnior noted that *marrabenta* was played and danced by members of the Bantu ethnic group known as 'Tsonga,' with the genre's rhythm being one of its most characteristic elements, another being the musical interrelationship between the verse and the chorus (Santos Júnior 1957).

Ethnomusicological recordings of guitar music from Mozambique of the 1950s were released in the United States in 1997 as *Kerestina: Guitar Songs of Southern Mozambique 1955-1957* and in the Netherlands in 2003 as *Forgotten Guitars From Mozambique: Portuguese East Africa 1955 '56 '57*. These early recordings were of songs accompanied essentially by the guitar. The sleeve notes of both recordings designate the tracks on the albums as 'the antecedents of *marrabenta*,' despite their stylistic variety. This reinforces the idea put forward by Mozambican ethnomusicologist Rui Laranjeira that the term *marrabenta* refers to a musical style which combines various performative typologies (Laranjeira 2014, 31–44).

By the mid-1950s musical instruments were being imported from South Africa. New musical groups sought to emulate the sounds of South African artists, a trend that in the 1960s made possible the popular stylization of *marrabenta* by bands such as Conjunto Harmonia, Conjunto João Domingos and Orquestra Djambu (Laranjeira 2014).

The growing popularity of *marrabenta* during the 1960s also enabled its integration within the dance hall circuit. The dance movements of *marrabenta* evidence a clearly erotic character. This is specially the case among women, who engage in a circular motion of the hips that reflects the syncopation of the instrumental accompaniment. At the same time, the women's hands alternate between the waist and the head on opposite sides, while their feet twist and accentuate the light synchronized pulse.

In 1962 the statute known as 'indigenato' that legislated against certain rights of indigenous people was abolished and the Radio Club of Mozambique, the national radio station of colonial Mozambique, created programs aimed at promoting various Mozambican musical practices including *marrabenta* (Filipe 2012; Power 2000). Weekly programs such as *Voz de Moçambique* (Voice of Mozambique) and *África à Noite* (Africa at Night) finally brought the sounds of 'indigenous' Mozambicans to new audiences in the city. The Orquestra Djambu (originally Conjunto Yong Ussufo) became one of the most popular groups and some of their songs that were used as radio station jingles have remained popular. Popular with both black and white audiences, *marrabenta* was accepted by the Portuguese rulers who had their own particular colonial approach to cultural synthesis and inclusion, in particular through their policies of cultural assimilation (Freyre 1940).

Post-1960s Consolidation and Development

Over time, while instrumentation and vocal arrangements may have evolved, the *marrabenta* rhythm has remained essentially unchanged, with its distinctive common time shuffle at the start of the measure, its solid 4/4 meter and the distinctive offbeat emphasis just ahead of the fourth beat of the measure played on the guitar strings or snare (how far ahead is an important feature that, as it is felt more than measured, has yet to be studied). Such rhythmic features are found in the acoustic *marrabenta* of the 1960s and 1970s, recorded by musicians such as the late Fanny Pfumo (1928–87), Dilon Djinji and Xidimingwana. These rhythmic features are also to be found in the 12-piece Orchestra Marrabenta Star de Mocambique's big band arrangements of the 1980s and 1990s, the hip-hop derivatives of bands such as Mabulu in the early 2000s and the derivatives of *marrabenta* played in nightclubs during the 2010s. According to local accounts, the genre's sonic features derive from traditional rhythms and dances from southern Mozambique such as *zucuta* and *magika*. In both dances, which are generally performed in pairs, women and men twist their toes in the sand and gesture seductively to one another with their arms and faces (out-take 3). In both its acoustic and amplified forms, the instrumentation of *marrabenta* is generally characterized by the predominance of the guitar (Laranjeira 2014)).

The recording of the album *Marrabenta* by Orquestra Djambu in 1970 marks the consolidation of this band's repertoire as a musical genre. This recording is also an example of the 'Música de Moçambique' (Music of Mozambique) promoted by the colonial regime, and is in line with the various releases of the Alvorada label (produced by Radio Triunfo) which served as a vehicle for the dissemination of the 'folklore' of the overseas Portuguese provinces. The *Marrabenta* album, mostly instrumental, is commonly considered to be the stylistic model for the genre, due mainly to its popularization of the song 'Elisa Gomara Saia' (Swing Your Skirt Elisa). The song features a binary temporal organization with a sixteenth-note feel and a syncopated dynamic in the percussion and guitars. The guitars play regular beats on the lower strings and syncopated beats on the higher strings, a performance style known as the 'African finger style.' The short vocal lines use melodic intervals that emphasize the harmonic structure laid down by the guitar, alternating between syncopated and tuplet patterns (a 'tuplet' is any rhythm that involves dividing the beat into a different number of equal subdivisions from that usually permitted by the time signature, in this case 4/4).

During the early 1970s, in the later years of colonial power, several companies were created to promote live shows and take Mozambican artists into the recording studios. The two most influential of these companies were Produções 1001 and Produções Golo. Resistance to colonial power was growing at this time and the Mozambique Liberation Front (FRELIMO), formed in 1962, was running increasingly successful military insurgencies from their long-established 'liberated zones' in the north of Mozambique. There was strict censorship of all songs played on Mozambican radio, yet some *marrabenta* songs that incorporated protest lyrics sung in local languages, such as those by the *marrabenta* legend Fany Mpfumo, seemed to escape censorship (Matusse 2013, 34). This could have been due to the poor translations offered to the censors or to the use of allegory and metaphor often employed by *marrabenta* lyricists (out-take 4). The music of Fany Mpfumo was extremely popular in the period leading up to independence. His lyrics recounted different aspects of the lives of poor black Mozambicans as well as the living conditions of Mozambicans in general, and were critical of the Portuguese colonial empire. Fany Mpfumo, often referred to as one of the 'Kings of Marrabenta,' had a diverse stylistic repertoire, ranging from ballads to up-tempo dance tracks, only some of which could be identified as *marrabenta*.

After the proclamation of independence on 25 June 1975 the newly formed government of FRELIMO founded its cultural policy on their postcolonial version of concepts such as 'modernity' and 'culture,' which elevated the music defined during the Portuguese colonial period as 'tradition' and 'folklore' (Carvalho 2002). FRELIMO sought instead to project a cultural model that elevated rural music over popular urban music, and recognize it as a living, dynamic and contemporary cultural form. The original *marrabenta* of the black suburbs had been adapted to suit the urban tastes of the black and white Mozambican elite and was now associated with the decadence of the bourgeoisie and the moral and sexual corruption associated with colonialism. Dance halls were closed as uncertainty reigned as to whether or not dancing in public was, indeed, banned (out-take 5). As evidenced in the film *Marrabentando: As histórias que a minha guitarra canta*, Mozambican musicians who were used to having a relatively free hand in their compositions had to reconfigure their repertoire to be in line with the cultural policies promoted by the First Republic of President Samora Machel. From this time, the recordings by Ngoma, the record label of Radio Mozambique, reveal the influence of other musical cultures, particularly those from the Caribbean and Cuba, on the vocal style, rhythmic patterns and instrumental timbres of the music of this time. International pop music, including soul and R&B, also exercised a strong influence. However, despite the disapproval of FRELIMO, aspects of the repertoire continued to display characteristics similar to those previously associated with *marrabenta*, such as the recognizable syncopated emphasis at the end of each measure and the solo vocal and chorus dialogues. This continuity suggests that, regardless of the presumed public absence of *marrabenta*, its characteristics were still present in the musicians' performative styles.

After the death of Samora Machel in 1986 Joaquim Chissano took over as president of Mozambique. His policy was marked by structural changes aimed at progressive economic and social liberalization. At the same time, however, a civil war that had started in Mozambique soon after independence escalated, increasing levels of fear and hardship across the country. This increase led to the flight of many entertainment entrepreneurs, the closure of shops specializing in the sale of musical instruments and the increasing shortage of equipment essential for record production, including vinyl (Carvalho 2005). Recordings made at the national radio station Radio Mocambique were released on cassettes by the station's record label, Ngoma. A repertoire identified as *marrabenta* was featured among these recordings, including the posthumous editions of Fany Mpfumo and the series *Música de Moçambique* (1989) and *Ritmos de dança moçambicanos* (1989), which included songs by Dilon Djinji and Lisbon Mathavel. These two musicians from Maputo were identified by the producer of these recordings as leading performers of *marrabenta*. Djinji and Mathavel's recordings evidence a development of the sound established by Fany Mpfumo, with new approaches to musical texture and arrangement. The drum kit takes the place of Fany Mpfumo's disparate sets of percussion instruments and the bass guitar is more active with motifs that delineate the harmony and emphasize rhythmic polyphony, in these ways reflecting the influence of African-American pop music. The growing importance of the electric guitar and the characteristic percussive timbre of solid body models allowed for greater clarity of the guitar sound within the instrumental ensemble. These new musical elements from Djinji and Matavel became most pronounced in the repertoire of the Orchestra Marrabenta Star de Mocambique.

Established in 1987 with the political aim of promoting Mozambican popular music nationally and internationally, Orchestra Marrabenta Star de Mocambique represented a commercial initiative spearheaded by the businessman and cultural promoter Aurelio Le Bon. Orchestra Marrabenta Star de Mocambique was formed by inviting some of the most accomplished popular musicians of the capital to join the five-piece house band of Radio Mocambique to create a 12-piece big band, with the house band rhythm section boosted by two further percussionists, the horn section enlarged and women vocalists and dancers added. As had Orquestra Djambu before them, the group played the greatest hits of *marrabenta*, many from the colonial era, including the aforementioned 'Elisa Gomara Saia.' There was an apparent intention by the groups in their choice of repertoire to present a specific genre with its well-established features which might be identified by listeners and replicated in future compositions. In this way *marrabenta* was revived and transformed once again, and this time promoted around the world.

At the turn of the millennium, *marrabenta* flourished again at the hands of German businessman Roland Hoberg, producer of the hip-hop *marrabenta* fusion group Mabulu. The main aim of Mabulu was to modernize *marrabenta* for the twenty-first century through collaborations between younger and older musicians. Artists such as Lisbon Matavele, Dilon Djinji and Antonio Marcos were invited to re-record their 1970s repertoire, adding new sections performed by young rap singers. As documented in the film *Marrabentando: As histórias que a minha guitarra canta*, the old 'marrabentistas' were in many cases presented live with this new grouping, not only in Mozambique but also abroad.

Marrabenta and the Mozambican Identity

Following the popularity of Mabulu, *marrabenta* acquired an aspect distinctly reminiscent of earlier times. Mozambican musicians such as Stewart Sukuma or McRoger (MC Roger), whose music was popular on the dance floors in the 1990s and 2000s, reference *marrabenta* in a number of their songs, mimicking the rhythmic and melodic features of early *marrabenta* and combining these with other musical styles such as *passada* and rap.

In the lyrics of some of these songs, *marrabenta* is identified as a part of Mozambican identity, bridging social classes and age groups, occupying a role similar to *semba* in Angola, *sungura* in Zimbabwe or *kalindula* in Zambia. In 2003 the rap band Gpro Fam (G Pro Fam) used the expression 'País da *marrabenta*' (country of *marrabenta*) in a hip-hop track ('País da *marrabenta*') criticizing the elders of Mozambique for their failure to realize the dreams of the revolution:

O país da marrabenta vai de mal a pior
Mas paciência, moçambicanos têm de melhor
Foram 16 anos de uma guerra civil
Só de orelhas decepadas foram mais de mil
Ainda querem que o povo lhes de ouvidos
Dam! filhos da mãe desses politicos!!

The country of Marrabenta go from bad to worse
but, so be it, Mozambicans have the best
They were 16 years of civil war
Just those who were left with no ears were more than a thousand
They still want the people to give them their ears
Damn! The political sons of bitches!!

In this track, it is not the rhythmic or melodic character of *marrabenta* that is reflected in the title, but the *Mocambicanidade* or 'Mozambicanness' of *marrabenta*. The 'country of marrabenta' in the title of the Gpro Fam track is referring to the independent nation of Mozambique. The YouTube video of this track includes an archive recording of President Samora Machel's declaration of independence on 25 June 1975:

Mocambicanos e Mocambicanas
A nossa reppublica popular
Nasce do sange do povo

Men and Women of Mozambique
Our people's republic
Born from the blood of the people

Marrabenta has in this way come to represent an older generation who led their country into Independence and then to poverty and corruption.

This association between *marrabenta* and *Mocambicanidade* (Mozambicanness) was also reflected in 2010 by the founder of Mozambique's first contemporary dance company, Panaibra Gabriel Canda. In his choreographed presentation, *Time and Spaces: The Marrabenta Solos*, Canda looks at his own identity as a Mozambican born in the year of Mozambican independence. By entitling the piece 'The Marrabenta Solos,' the various facets of what is considered Mozambican are symbolized by the term 'marrabenta.'

A cultural festival created in 2008, Festival Marrabenta, has taken place 30 kilometers north of the capital, Maputo, in Marracuene, one of the places considered to be the true home of *marrabenta*. At this festival, the genre has again been promoted as the one that somehow defines Mozambique. The ninth Festival Marrabenta in 2016 brought together Mozambican artists from across the three *marrabenta* generations from Orquestra Djambu, Xidiminguana and Dilon Djindji to the early twenty-first-century promoters of *marrabenta*, Mabulu and Stewart Sukuma, as well as proponents of *marrabenta*'s musical successor, *pandza*, in the form of República do Pandza (the Pandza Republic). A variety of styles and genres of Mozambican popular music were also included in the festival program, reflecting the contemporary tendency to use the term 'marrabenta' to designate all Mozambican popular music.

Bibliography

Arnfred, Signe. 2011. *Sexuality and Gender Politics in Mozambique: Rethinking Gender in Africa*. New York: Boydell & Brewer.

Carvalho, João Soeiro de. 2002. 'Performance Culture in Maputo: Categories of Expressive Modes in the Changing of an African Urban Society.' *Revista Portuguesa de Musicologia* 12: 253–64.

Carvalho, João Soeiro de. 2005. 'Mozambique.' In *Continuum Encyclopedia of Popular Musics of the World, Vol. 6: Locations – Africa and the Middle East*, eds. John Shepherd, David Horn and Dave Laing. London and New York: Continuum, 94–7.

Erlmann, Veit. 1999. *Music, Modernity, and the Global Imagination: South Africa and the West*. Oxford: Oxford University Press.

Filipe, Eleusio. 2012. "*Where are the Mozambican Musicians?*" *Music, Marrabenta, and National Identity in Lourenço Marques, Mozambique, 1950s–1975*. Unpublished Ph.D. dissertation, University of Minnesota.

Freyre, Gilberto. 1940. *O mundo que o português criou* [The World the Portuguese Created]. Río de Janeiro: J. Olympio.

Laranjeira, Rui. 2014. *A Marrabenta: Sua evolução e estilização, 1950–2002* [Marrabenta: Its Evolution and Stylization, 1950–2002]. Maputo: Minerva.

Machel, Samora. 1982. 'Discurso na Província de Gaza, Marco 1982' [Speech Made in Gaza Province, March 1982]. Printed in *Revista Tempo* 600.

Matusse, Samuel. 2013. *Fany Mpfumo e outros ícones* [Fany Mpfumo and Other Icons]. Maputo, Mozambique: TDM (Telecomunicacoes de Mocambique) e FUNDAC Fundo Nacional da Cultura.

Power, Marcus. 2000. 'Aqui Lourenço Marques!! Radio Colonization and Cultural Identity in Colonial Mozambique, 1932–74.' *Journal of Historical Geography* 26(4): 605–28.

Santos Júnior, Norberto. 1957. 'Algumas canções indígenas de Marracuene (Moçambique)' [Some Indigenous Songs of Marracuenne, Mozambique]. *Revista de Gacia da Orta* 5(2): 327–43.

Discographical References

Forgotten Guitars From Mozambique: Portuguese East Africa 1955 '56 '57. Sharp Wood Productions SWP 025/HT 17. *2003*: Netherlands.

Gpro Fam. 'País da *marrabenta.*' *Um passo em frente*. Gpro Fam. *2003*: Mozambique.

Kerestina: Guitar Songs of Southern Mozambique 1955–1957. Original Music OMCD030 *1997*: USA.

Música de Moçambique, vol.4. Ngoma LPL 0151. *1990*: Mozambique.

Orquestra Djambu. 'Elisa Gomara Saia.' Marrabenta. (7-inch 45 rpm EP). Alvorada AEP 60 693. *1965*: Mozambique.

Orchestra Marrabenta Star de Mocambique. 'Elisa Gomara Saia.' *Independence*. Warner Bros Records SLH 6015 *1988*: Zimbabwe and Piranha pir 12 568.22012. *1988*: Germany.

Ritmos de dança moçambicanos nº2. Ngoma LPL 0149. *1989*: Mozambique.

Discography

Chiau, Gabriel. 'Xipalapala/Nkata.' Fonoplay. N.d.

Djinji, Dilon. *Dilon, by Dilon Djinji*. Riverboat Records ASIN B00006IIXX. *2002*: Mozambique.

Langa, Alexandre. *Amnistia*. Ngoma LPL 0147. *1988*: Mozambique.

Mabulu. *Soul Marrabenta*. Riverboat Records TUGCD1024. *2001*: UK.

McRoger. *McRoger & Mr. Arssen – Estamos Na Área*. Vidisco Moçambique 17.80 1400. *2002*: Mozambique.

Mpfumo, Fany. *Nyoxanini*. RM/Vidisco. *1999*: Mozambique.

Mpfumo, Fany. *O rei Fany Pfumo*. Ngoma LPL 0142. *1988*: Mozambique.

Orchestra Marrabenta Star de Mocambique. *Marrabenta Piquenique*. Piranha CD-PIR1043 *1996*: Germany.

Sukuma. Stewart. *Nkhuvu*. *2007*: Mozambique.

The Rough Guide to Marrabenta Mozambique. World Music Network RGNET 1063 CD. *2001*: UK.

Tsonga. 'Masesa.' *Southern Mozambique 1943 '49 '54 '55 '57 '63 Portugese East Africa*. SWP Records 021. *2003*: Netherlands.

Xidimingwana. *Xidimingwana*. Ngoma LPL 0148. *1989*: Mozambique.

Filmography

Marrabentando: The Stories My Guitar Sings/ Marrabentando: As histórias que a minha guitarra canta, dir. Karen Boswall. 2005. Portugal. 52 mins. Documentary with English subtitles, and stories and songs by Antonio Marcos and Dilon Djinji. Online at: http://vimeo.com/43718451 (accessed 22 February 2018).

Visual Recordings

Unreleased out-takes from the film *Marrabentando: As histórias que a minha guitarra canta*, from the personal video archives of Karen Boswall: all interviews conducted in Maputo, March 2004:

1. interviews with the general public.
2. interviews with marrabenta musicians from the radio house band Grupo RM (1975–2016).
3. interviews with artist and musician Malangata Valente Ngwenya (1936–2011).
4. interviews with marrabenta musician Xidiminguana (1936–).

5. interviews with marrabenta musicians from Orchestra Marrabenta Star de Mocambique: Wazimbo, Jose Guimaraes, Sox and Chico Antonio.

YouTube

Gpro Fam. 2015. 'País da marrabenta': https://www.youtube.com/watch?v=_qaKqSKWlYg (accessed 4 March 2018)

Panaibra Gabriel. 2010. *Time and Spaces – Panorama*: https://www.youtube.com/watch?v=m9JzdW7B61c (accessed 4 March 2018)

Website

http://www.kfda.be/en/program/time-and-spaces-the-marrabenta-solos (accessed 4 March 2018)

KAREN BOSWALL AND JOÃO SOEIRO DE CARVAHALLO

Maskanda

Maskanda is a South African popular neo-traditional performance genre, most commonly viewed simply as guitar music that is closely associated with the traditions of the Zulu people, the largest ethnic group of black South Africans. The musical resources of early *maskanda* lie in Zulu women's bow songs (characteristically songs of loss and longing), in regionally differentiated song and dance forms generically labeled as *ingoma*, in Afrikaans folksong and in popularly developing township styles such as *mbaqanga*.

The genre originated in the early decades of the twentieth century as a musical response to the radical shift in the lives and experiences of young Zulu men, which were brought about largely as a result of colonialism and the system of labor migrancy that accompanied it. This change involved much more than a shift in geographical location from a rural to an urban environment. For Zulu people, precolonial life was rooted in a patriarchal social structure with a rural homestead at its core, where cattle were the most valued economic asset, and where communities of homesteads had some security in the commonality of a religious ideology based on ancestor worship. By the early decades of the twentieth century, pushed by the hut and poll tax (a tax on people and homesteads introduced by the British colonial government in the 1850s that forced Zulu people into the labor market) and perhaps pulled by the idea of 'development,' many young men were confronted by a marked disjuncture between the ideologies of their heritage and those they encountered in the cities, most notably a cash-based capitalist economy and Christianity.

Maskanda is popularly affiliated with notions of Zuluness and many practitioners revere it as an expression of their Zulu identity and tradition. However, similar to other performance practices shaped under the directives of apartheid, *maskanda* did not escape the weight of that hegemony. *Maskanda*'s formulation around a call-and-response pattern between a lead singer and a chorus recalls community-based singing typical of precolonial Zulu music. The inclusion of *izibongo* (praise poetry) and the Zulu warrior images expressed in dance and dress all held Zulu identity captive in a historical moment as the place of authenticity, a place that separated it from the present and from other sectors of South African society. Hence, its form and aesthetic ideals often pay homage to a version of Zuluness that served the political aspirations not only of the apartheid regime but also of the Inkatha Freedom Party that controlled the Zulu 'homeland.' The Inkatha Freedom Party was formed in 1975 'as an exclusively Zulu organization . . . its leader could only be a chief and a Zulu' (Bonin et al. 1996, 164). This emphasis on ethnicity as a constitutive feature of the Inkatha Freedom Party rendered it complicit with the ideology of the apartheid regime (for further explication of this point see Maré 1995).

Maskanda began as a solo performance style, and although there is little documentation of early practice one may well assume that the idiosyncrasies of individual expression were part and parcel of the earliest versions of the genre. Competitions, as part of the leisure activities of migrant laborers and later the commercialization of *maskanda* in the 1950s and 1960s, contributed to the constitution of *maskanda* as a body of practice with prescribed elements of style, form and musical procedures.

Although applications of the label *maskanda* are quite varied, a number of features are regarded as typical of *maskanda* performance. These include a band lineup of amplified acoustic guitar, electric bass, drums, concertina and/or violin and a small group of backing singers who also are featured prominently as dancers; a non-improvisational, sectionalized structure; a picking style of guitar playing, often with a percussive texture; a section including *izibongo* (praise poetry); rhythms that recall various *ingoma* dance styles; and a mode of dress that references precolonial Zulu traditional practices. Different musicians favor some of these aspects over others, resulting in distinct musical trends within different contexts. For example, audiences with strong Zulu traditionalist affiliations expect *maskanda* performance to include *izibongo*, musicians dressed in traditional-type attire and a musical structure that is interspersed with vibrant displays of *ingoma* dance. Audiences with strong urban affiliations embrace a version of *maskanda* that includes synthesized sounds produced on keyboards, rhythms and melodic inflections of a variety of popular contemporary performance genres such as *kwaito* and gospel music, contemporary designer-styled versions of traditional dress and no *izibongo* section.

Maskanda's earliest association with the experience of change permeates the subsequent path of its development over more than a century. Indeed, landmarks in its development correlate with significant shifts in the political and social environment in South Africa. The history of *maskanda* can thus be divided broadly into three phases: the phase of inception in the early decades of the twentieth century, a period when, although no longer a colony, South Africa was dominated by a political economy that paid homage to British imperialism; the phase of formalization and stasis from the late 1950s to 1994, when *maskanda* was commercialized and became static in style, form and lyrics during the apartheid era; and the phase of expansion heralded by the 1994 democratic election and embedded in the era of liberal democracy.

Formative Phase: Early Decades of the Twentieth Century

There are many gaps in the documentation of early *maskanda*, a situation that is indeed a reflection of the political climate of the time. Apart from the music that developed under the influence of Christian missionaries, the creative expression of an urbanizing indigenous population was most often disregarded, or viewed with suspicion. Furthermore, ethnomusicologists and others interested in the documentation of South Africa's cultural heritage paid little attention to the syncretic styles that were developing in and around cities, since their main concern was the preservation of what was perceived as 'authentic' indigenous music.

The historiography of early *maskanda* has been shaped by two main factors: the stories that have been told about the responses of labor migrants to their lived experience, and the musical connections that can be made between different types of music that were documented at the time and the earliest recordings that are available of *maskanda*.

Maskanda began as a solo performance practice that brought together the musical sounds, styles and textures associated, on the one hand, with life 'at home' as a son, brother or lover in the setting of a rural Zulu homestead and, on the other, with life 'at work' as a unit of labor in an urban or unfamiliar Westernized setting. Solo performance was associated more commonly with women's music and hence women's bow music was an obvious resource; this music was characterized by many repeats of a descending vocal line, and bound by a texture that articulated a bi-tonal arrangement of the harmony. The lyrics of women's bow music characteristically mourned the loss of husband or lover to the cities (see Joseph 1983). Early solo versions of *maskanda* most often exhibit these same characteristics but they were recontextualized, most obviously through the lyrics, which spoke of a male experience of loss and disjuncture, the instrumental accompaniment (primarily on guitar) and the gradual inclusion of the sounds they encountered in the workplace (such as Afrikaans *liedjies*) and diatonic choral practices of music rooted in encounters with the missionaries.

Songs remembered as part of life in the rural homestead were thus reworked to incorporate new musical and material resources and to speak of new experiences. As they were readily available and relatively inexpensive, the guitar, and to a lesser extent the concertina, were obvious instruments of choice.

By the 1950s *maskanda* had been mobilized in cities and on the mines as a competitive medium through which young men could reinforce their sense of worth. The competitive spirit may certainly have been responsible for the development of a flamboyant introductory section that not only established the tonality and melodic outline of the piece to come, but also gave the musician an opportunity to show off his skill as a guitarist (at this point, musicians were always male, although women's bow songs were appropriated because they were songs of loss and a way of remembering the security of home). The rhythm of dance styles commonly practiced in the musicians' rural homes, together with the sections of *izibongo* that were inherently heavy with poetic allusions to local landscapes and personalities that would only have been understood by listeners from the same rural communities, were conducive to the development of a performance style that articulated feelings of pride and belonging that counteracted the hostile, dehumanizing world of labor migrancy.

Formalization Period: 1960–94

The popularization of *maskanda* by the record industry in the 1960s and early 1970s had a marked impact on both the constitution and the aesthetics of the music. What had begun essentially as a solo style was adapted to group performance and modified in keeping with commercial incentives. Musical characteristics, such as subtle implied downbeats, a nonhierarchical harmonic structure and a polyrhythmic layered melodic texture, gave way to a version with overtly articulated and regulated beats, a stronger reliance on a I-IV-V harmonic framework and a simplified melodic texture that relied heavily on call-and-response.

In 1971 John Bengu (1930–85), under the stage name Phuzeshukela (literally translated as 'Drinker of Sugar'), joined GRC studios at Gallo as a recording artist. Under the direction of successful *mbaqanga* producer Hamilton Nzimande, Phuzeshukela soon came to represent the sound and style that many *maskanda* musicians aspired to emulate. Rob Allingham (1990) describes Nzimande's impact on Phuzeshukela's style as follows: 'He took Bengu's [Phuzeshukela's] music and smoothed it out with modern production techniques, in many instances using an electrified backing band and vocals. He himself switched from acoustic to electric guitar. The result was a sound with vastly enhanced commercial appeal.' It had become common practice in the industry to single out and promote individual musicians as representatives of an entire body of practice in order to satisfy a particular market. Musical categories, particularly those used to describe the music of black South Africans, were constructed according to the ethnic divisions that were promoted in the political arena at the time. *Maskanda* was marketed, along with other genres including *isicathamiya*, as traditional Zulu music.

Ingoma dance was given a prominent role in *maskanda* performance of this era. This affirmed *maskanda*'s position as traditional Zulu music and to some extent compensated for the many aspects of *maskanda* performance that were being Westernized. *Maskanda*'s status as traditional music was also etched in the public imagination through the representation of artists on record covers in a rural setting, and at times even posing as Zulu warriors.

There is a considerable amount of uniformity in music recorded during this era. Most songs had the same formal structure: songs began with a short introduction on the guitar followed by alternating solo and chorus sections which were interrupted approximately two-thirds of the way through the song by an *izibongo* section of praise poetry and which ended with a final repeat of the chorus section. The lyrics were always in Zulu and the tonality was essentially diatonic. The songs were presented in a band lineup of amplified acoustic guitar, bass guitar, violin or concertina and a Western-style set of drums. The sacred status of tradition promoted in political rhetoric, particularly of the Inkatha Freedom Party, translated into prescriptive ideals of performance practice. There were nevertheless musicians who were not enthralled by popularly promoted versions of *maskanda*, and who followed individual instincts and aesthetic ideals. One such musician was Shiyani Ngcobo. He presented his music in solo performance, in duets of acoustic guitar and bass and in ensembles of guitar, bass, violin and/or concertina with a single female backing singer. He adamantly resisted the use of a drum kit and employed either the *ingoma* drum or the *djembe* for percussion. Ngcobo's music, which survives in recordings, is subtly layered, with many textures realized through his guitar wizardry and the variety in his vocal range and timbre.

Post-Apartheid: Since 1994

While the first nonracial democratic elections of 1994 heralded a new era in South Africa, it was some time before new experiences, attitudes and ideals started to be played out in and through *maskanda*. Musicians engage in *maskanda* for different reasons, not least of all because they see it as a possible source of income. Thus, there is tension between *maskanda*'s status as traditional music and its function in the contemporary music marketplace. While, as traditional music, it benefits from performance opportunities associated with major public events such as political rallies and international conferences, it is most often rejected in local performance venues and music festivals in favor of music associated with the cosmopolitan life style and tastes of a transforming middle class. There are varied responses to this tension. Some musicians are reticent in introducing new sounds and styles in their music for fear of alienating an established audience that celebrates *maskanda* as Zulu tradition. These musicians tend to follow the standards of practice formalized in the apartheid era. Others are comfortable infusing the genre with sounds associated with different 'soundscapes,' most notably those that capture the urban flavor of contemporary aspirations.

While the idea of *maskanda* as tradition is never completely abandoned by its practitioners, there is significant flexibility in the moments and versions of the past that are referenced, as may be seen, for example, in iHashi Elimhlophe's album *Muntuza* (2002). Bheki Ngcobo, better known by his stage name, iHashi Elimhlophe (The White Horse) stands out as one of the more adventurous contemporary *maskanda* musicians. His versions of *maskanda* range from examples that give precedence to the *izibongo* style of vocal delivery to songs that recall the iconic sounds and styles of Sophiatown or in which thumping rhythms are borrowed from *kwaito*. Thus, the hugely popular sounds of *kwaito* and gospel music have found their way into the *maskanda* domain.

The duet Shwi Nomtekhala, winners of the 2006 SAMA (South African Music Association) award for Best-Selling Album of the Year (*Wangisiza Baba*), also present *maskanda* in a different flavor. Their music, which is infused with the harmonies of *isicathamiya*, is often slower in tempo and seldom includes an *izibongo* section. Unlike many other *maskanda* musicians, they do not present themselves to the public in traditional Zulu style of dress.

A further recent trend is the significant increase in the number of women participating in *maskanda* in frontline roles rather than as backing singers. Female versions of *maskanda* tend to be more conservative than those of their male counterparts; there is a strong emphasis on vocals and dance rather than on the instrumental backing, which is almost exclusively performed by men. While there are some political songs such as Izingane Zoma's song 'Msholozi,' which is about recently appointed ANC president Jacob Zuma, for the most part songs are deeply personal, and they are often about betrayal in love, the burdens of poverty and the tragedy of AIDS.

Conclusion

Maskanda has always been a musical practice that is deeply embedded in everyday life. As with other popular music practices there are many informal practitioners who gather together in their spare time to practice and enjoy the performance experience. It is, however, primarily the successful recorded artists who give definition to the genre, and many amateur *maskanda* musicians aspire to standards of commercial success. Furthermore, while *maskanda* continues in an osmotic process of shaping and being shaped by social life in South Africa, its audience is not entirely local. A number of *maskanda* musicians have toured widely, not only to Europe and North America, but also as far afield as Japan and Cuba.

Bibliography

Allingham, Rob. 1990. Liner notes to *Singing in an Open Space: Zulu Rhythm and Harmony 1962-1982*. Licensed from Gallo Records, South Africa; Rounder Records Corporation. CD5027. USA.

Bonnin, Debby, Hamilton, Georgina, Morrell, Robert and Sitas, Ari. 1996. 'The Struggle for Natal and KwaZulu: Workers, Township Dwellers and Inkatha, 1972-1985.' In *Political Economy and Identities in KwaZulu-Natal: Historical and Social Perspectives*, ed. Robert Morrell. Durban: Indicator Press, 141-78.

Bourdieu, Pierre. 1993. *The Field of Cultural Production: Essays on Art and Literature*. Cambridge: Polity Press.

Clegg, Jonathon. 1981. 'The Music of Zulu Migrant Workers in Johannesburg – A Focus on Concertina and Guitar.' In *Papers Presented at the Symposium on Ethnomusicology*, ed. Andrew Tracey. Grahamstown: International Library of African Music.

Davies, Nollene. 1991. 'Aspects of Zulu Maskanda Guitar Music.' In *Papers Presented at the Tenth Symposium on Ethnomusicology*, ed. Andrew Tracey. Grahamstown: International Library of African Music.

Davies, Nollene. 1992. *A Study of Guitar Styles in Zulu Maskanda Music*. Unpublished M. Music thesis, Natal University.

Davies, Nollene. 1993. 'From Bows to Bands: On the Historical Development of the Maskanda Tradition.' In *Papers Presented at the Eleventh Symposium on Ethnomusicology*, ed. Andrew Tracey. Grahamstown: International Library of African Music.

Joseph, Rosemary 1983. 'Zulu Women's Music.' *African Music* 6(3): 53–89.

Maré, Gerhard. 1995. *Ethnicity as Identity and Ethnicity Politically Mobilised: Symbols of Mobilisation in Inkatha*. Unpublished Ph.D. thesis, University of Natal.

Morrell, Robert, ed. 1996. *Political Economy and Identities in KwaZulu-Natal: Historical and Social Perspectives*. Durban: Indicator Press.

Muller, Carol. 1995. '*Chakide* – The Teller of Secrets: Space, Song and Story in Zulu Maskanda Performance.' *Current Writin.* 7(2): 117–31.

Olsen, Kathryn. 2000. 'Politics, Production and Process: Discourses on Tradition in Contemporary Maskanda.' Unpublished MA thesis, University of Natal. Online at: https://researchspace.ukzn.ac.za/handle/10413/5156 (accessed 11 January 2018)

Olsen, Kathryn. 2002. 'Constructions of Zuluness in Contemporary Maskanda.' In *Papers Presented at the 2002 Symposium on Ethnomusicology*, ed. Andrew Tracey. Grahamstown: International Library of African Music.

Saul, John. 2001. 'Cry for the Beloved Country: The Post-Apartheid Denouement.' *Monthly Review* 52 (8): 1–51. Online at: https://www.researchgate.net/publication/297556352_Cry_for_the_beloved_country_The_post-apartheid_denouement (accessed 11 January 2018).

Schraeder, Peter J. 2004. *African Politics and Society: A Mosaic in Transformation*. 2nd ed. London: Thomson Wadsworth.

Discographical References

Ihash'Elimhlophe. *Muntuza*. DCC Records, Ihashi na Maponi Music CD DCC (WB) 004. *2002*: South Africa.

Izingane Zoma. 'Msholozi.' *Msholozi*. Izingane Zoma Music CDING 125 (FN). *2005*: South Africa.

Shwi Nomtekhala. *Wangisiza Baba*. Bula Music CDBULA 153. *2004*: South Africa.

Discography

Ihash'Elimhlophe. *Muntuza*. DCC Records, Ihashi na Maponi Music CD DCC (WB) 004. *2002*: South Africa.

Izingane Zoma. *Msholozi*. Izingane Zoma Music CDING 125 (FN). *2005*: South Africa.

Maskandi Gospel Hits. Gallo Record Company CDGSP 3077 (JN). *2006*: South Africa.

Ngcobo, Shiyai. *Introducing Shiyani Ngcobo. Zulu Guitars Dance: Maskanda from South Africa*. World Music Network SLCD 063. *2004*: South Africa.

Phuzekhemisi no Khethani. *Imbizo*. RPM Records Inc. CDTIG 456. *1994*: South Africa.

KATHRYN OLSEN

Masse Gohoun

Masse gohoun is a style of popular music that was created in the late 1960s by Yedenou Adjahoui (1930–95), a beloved Gun singer from the village of Avrankou, outside of Porto Novo, Benin. The style is characterized by an active lead drum (*kpezin*) part that interacts with the singer's vocal line and with two interlocking bell patterns. *Masse gohoun* has been developed, modernized and expanded in the decades since its creation.

Masse gohoun is rooted in *djegbe* and *djoglissohoun*, traditional rhythms used in the popular celebration of life ceremonies such as weddings and baptisms, as well as in drumming for the cult of the Vodun deity Sakpata, in which Adjahoui was initiated as a youth. Adjahoui took as his point of departure the basic bell pattern for *djegbe*, which is based around two simple, interlocking parts played on small, handheld curved iron bells with small metal sticks (in other parts of West Africa called *dawuro*, in Benin simply the generic *gan*) and the *assan* (shakers). He first introduced additional accompaniment parts on the *alekele*, a set of two high-pitched wooden drums with skin heads joined together. The iconic sound of *masse gohoun* developed when Adjahoui added the *kpezin*, a lead drum made of clay and wrapped in wicker that cuts through the ensemble to inspire dancing by the audience. The style is particularly characterized by exchanges between the *kpezin* and the singer's poetic, pentatonic improvisations in the language of Gun. Adjahoui's recordings, using only the percussion ensemble and his voice, recorded with long reverb and no modern instruments, became very popular in Porto Novo and other Gun-speaking regions.

Adjahoui was known for weaving spiritual themes, moral lessons and proverbs into his vocals, often with political lyrics that criticized the socialist government of Mathieu Kerekou, which was established in 1972. Adjahoui recorded for the Albarika Store label in Cotonou from 1969 to 1974, but in order to avoid any potential problems with Kerekou's administration, in the 1980s he recorded his albums in nearby Lagos, Nigeria. He established a large following in the Badagry region of far western Nigeria, where many Gun people still reside. While *masse gohoun* was certainly a creation of the twentieth century, it was more connected to traditional regional aesthetics than were some other genres that developed around the same time, suggesting that it might deserve the label 'neo-traditional.' Adjahoui called *masse gohoun* 'folklorique,' linking it closely to Porto Novo and the surrounding villages.

Adjahoui's student and later rival Dossou LeTriki (d. 2010) continued the development of *masse gohoun* in the 1980s. LeTriki introduced a practice of competitive verbal sparring in his vocal improvisations that called out other *masse gohoun* artists and reinforced his own claims to authenticity as the true master of *masse*. He also strengthened *masse gohoun*'s explicit associations with the *egungun*, also known as *les revenants*. The ancestral spirits of the masked *egungun* are Yorùbá in origin, but they appear widely in southern Benin, especially in Porto Novo and Ouidah. They are called *kuvito* in Fon. The link with the *egungun* reveals the closeness of Gun and Yorùbá culture in Porto Novo, where people from both ethnicities have lived side by side for several hundred years. The mask practice remains the same as in Yorùbáland, but in Benin the music is *masse gohoun* instead of *batá* drumming. Representing the spirits of venerated ancestors, the *egungun* wear brilliantly colored costumes of different pieces of cloth, and more pieces are added each year. Their faces, hands and feet are covered.

After Dossou LeTriki, the *masse gohoun* ensemble expanded even more. Performance has been professionalized since the 1990s, with groups, consisting of up to 10 members, covering multiple accompaniment parts on curved bells, *assan*, *alekele*, *kpezin* and also the *gidigbo*, a large lamellophone of Yorùbá origin with four or five metal keys, played seated. The leader of the group usually plays the long, standing drum *kpawle*, and sings the lead parts, while the other members, usually men, sing the chorus. These groups are hired to play for *egungun* ceremonies or occasionally concerts, but not normally for more everyday events such as weddings and funerals. Ensembles typically wear matching pants and shirts of all the same bright, traditional print, along with the Beninois-style fitted cloth cap, worn off to one side.

Most recently, musicians have started to modernize *masse gohun*, especially those in brass bands and in the jazz community. The jazz and rock drummer Jean Adagbenon, like Adjahoui a native of the village of Avrankou, also created a modernized version of *masse gohoun* called 'Mass-Go,' as in 'must go!' Adagbenon's new style also references 'GoGo,' a nickname for *djoglissohoun*, one of the older styles on which *masse gohoun* is based. Adagbenon began by adapting *djoglissohoun* to the drum set in the 1980s, and then, in 2015, released his first album in the new style 'Mass-Go.' In mixing *masse gohoun* with 'GoGo,' rock and even gospel, Adagbenon aims to convince the youth of Benin of the value of their own traditional music, and of studying it rigorously.

Bibliography

Médiohouan, Guy Ossito. 1993. 'Vodun et littérature au Bénin' [*Vodun* and Literature in Benin]. *Canadian Journal of African Studies* 27(2): 245–58.

Discographical Reference

Adagbenon, Jean. *Devo Premier*. Self-produced, vol. 6. *2015*: Benin.

Discography

Adjahoui, Yedenou. *Groupement Folklorique-Yedenou Adjahoui et Son Ensemble*. Albarika Store 001. *1969*: Benin.

Adjahoui, Yedenou. *Et Son Ensemble d'Avrankou – Dahomey*. Albarika Store ASEP 1050. *1972*: Benin.

Adjahoui, Yedenou. *Et Son Ensemble Folklorique d'Avrankou*. Albarika Store 032. *1975*: Benin.

Adjahoui, Yedenou. *Son Groupe Folklorique*. Vols. 1 & 4. Ola Oluwa Ni. *1983*: Nigeria.

Gangbé Brass Band. 'Tagbavo.' *Togbé*. Contrejour. *2001*: France.

Groupe Djomakon. *Les Revenants de Ouidah*. Discafric Carré DCF 005. *1976*: Benin.

LeTriki, Dossou. *Avec Son Groupe Masse Gohoun Super*. Albarika Store 139. *1984*: Benin.

SARAH POLITZ

Mbalax

Mbalax (pronounced 'mm-bah-lakh') is a distinctive 'Senegambian' (Senegalese and Gambian) genre of percussion-based dance music that arose shortly after Senegal gained independence from France in 1960. Named after a rhythm played on the *sabar* drum, which is prominently featured in this style of music, the term 'mbalax' has since been used as an umbrella term for this genre of Senegambian popular music as a whole. Made famous by Senegalese singer Youssou N'Dour, *mbalax* came to the fore fully in the 1970s and 1980s, and continues to be the dominant genre of modern Senegambian music in the twenty-first century. Although the Gambia has produced some *mbalax* artists, the Gambian music industry has been much less developed than that of its neighbor, Senegal. As a consequence, Senegalese *mbalax* artists have dominated the popular music scene in both Senegal and the Gambia.

Typical characteristics of an *mbalax* song include a strong rhythmic emphasis (provided by the *sabar* drums), repetitive chord progressions, fast, danceable tempos, syncopated guitar riffs and a highly syncopated keyboard part. The vocal style is drawn from Wolof *griot* vocal traditions, with lyrics covering a range of issues from praise songs for Muslim religious leaders to songs about everyday social pressures, relationships and moral issues. *Mbalax* music is first and foremost music to be danced to and is most frequently performed live in Dakar nightclubs, as well as being disseminated by way of radio, televised video clips, audio cassettes, CDs and via the Internet.

Mbalax is a genre that appeals to all ages and socioeconomic groups within Senegambia. It thus plays a very important role in Senegambian culture.

Rhythmic Roots

The rhythmic foundation and primary identifiable feature of modern *mbalax* is the *sabar*, a traditional drum played exclusively by Wolof *griots*. *Sabar* drumming has been an important part of everyday life in Senegambia for centuries, and is performed at traditional life cycle events, as well as for entertainment. Played with hand and stick, the *sabar* is a single-headed drum carved from the trunk of a *dimb* tree, with a goatskin head stretched across the top and held in place by seven pegs. The *sabar* is traditionally played in an ensemble ranging from four to a dozen or more percussionists. The ensemble consists of drums of different sizes, each of which have specific names (such as *nder*, the tallest drum and leader of the ensemble; *mbëng-mbëng*, a medium-sized drum which plays the accompaniment; *tungune*, the shortest drum; and *cól*, the egg-shaped bass drum). Despite these names, all can be referred to collectively or individually as 'sabar.'

In Wolof percussionist parlance, 'mbalax' literally means 'accompaniment.' Within a *sabar* ensemble, different drums play different roles, and 'mbalax' refers to the accompaniment parts played by the *mbëng-mbëng* drum. However, the *mbalax* part varies rhythmically from one dance to another. One of the most popular dance rhythms is *Kaolack* (named after the region), and it is the *Kaolack* accompaniment part (*mbalax*) that is most prominently featured in the *mbalax* that is known as the popular music genre – hence the name. This rhythm can be described in vocal mnemonics as 'te-tan pax, gin …,' and can be played in either a duple or triple meter. (In duple meter, this can be represented as 'te tan PAX - - gin - - …' or, in triple meter, as 'te tan PAX - gin - …,' with the 'PAX' serving as the downbeat. Because this particular rhythm is so widely used, it is commonly known as 'mbalax' rather than 'the mbalax part to *Kaolack*,' which results in some confusion.

Kaolack is the rhythmic backbone to the overwhelming majority of *mbalax* songs. Its simple contour, full range of sounds and flexibility in tempo have all contributed to its staying power. At the beginning of the twenty-first century, other dance rhythms found their way into the *mbalax* scene. The dance rhythm called 'lëmbël' has fast become a part of *mbalax* music and, subsequently, the *baar mbaye* dance rhythm has also been introduced. Nonetheless, *Kaolack*, or 'mbalax,' has remained the most prominent and widespread of rhythms used in its namesake genre.

Instrumentation and Style

A typical *mbalax* ensemble consists of *sabar*, electric guitars (rhythm and solo), bass guitar, kit drums, keyboards, optional horn section (trumpet and/or saxophone), backup vocals and/or *tama* (talking drum).

The roles of these instruments in an *mbalax* band is analogous to the roles of drums within a *sabar* ensemble, with the lead vocal as *nder* drum, the rhythm guitar as *mbëng-mbëng* drum, and the keyboard as *talmbat* (bass drum accompaniment). Thus an *mbalax* ensemble, although consisting primarily of modern electric instruments, can be seen as a transformation of the traditional *sabar* ensemble.

One of the main characteristics of *mbalax* style is the *sabar*. In addition to providing the rhythmic foundation for the music, *sabars* also serve as solo instruments, playing catch musical phrases (called '*bàkks*') that serve as 'breaks' at key points in the music. In this way the *sabars* function both as rhythmic accompaniment as well as solo instruments. There is also a close relationship between the *sabar* breaks and the dance, as dancers love to match the various *bàkks* with dance steps that perfectly accentuate the drumming.

A typical *mbalax* band has numerous (four to six) *sabars* played by one or two percussionists. Generally, one percussionist plays the *cól* (bass drum), which keeps a bass beat, solos frequently and plays *bàkks* (musical phrases); the other percussionist primarily plays mbalax (*Kaolack* or, occasionally, *lëmbël*) on the *mbëng-mbëng*, keeping the steady mbalax rhythm. This second percussionist also generally has two other *sabar* drums on either side of the *mbëng-mbëng*, which he can play simultaneously for a wider range of sounds.

Although one percussionist typically plays the *cól* and the other primarily *mbalax*, the two will join together to play *bàkks*, which are prominently featured in the introduction, at the end of a chorus section, in between verses or even as a special solo section.

Other salient musical features of the *mbalax* style include fast, danceable tempos, repetitive chord progressions, an emphasis on rhythm and syncopated guitar riffs. The keyboard also plays a highly syncopated, percussive part referred to as 'marimba' (imitating the marimba, a xylophone-like instrument). Played exclusively on the Yamaha DX7, the 'marimba' keyboard part is likened rhythmically to the *talmbat* (accompanimental bass drum part) in a traditional *sabar* ensemble, and is especially prominent in 'pure and hard' *mbalax* styles.

Harmonically, *mbalax* music follows a decidedly cyclic form, with simple patterns of chord progressions (often with just 2–4 different chords) repeating over and over again. This repetitive chord structure allows greater opportunities for improvisation, both on the part of the lead vocalist and the instrumentalists. The chord progressions emphasize both major and minor modes, with common progressions such as I–IV–ii–V, III–I–ii, or i–VI–i–VI.

The vocal style used in *mbalax* music has strong ties to traditional Wolof praise-singing and Islamic chant styles. Often in a high register, the vocal lines tend melodically to follow a Western diatonic scale, cascading in mostly conjunct motion, often with emphasis on repeated notes. In addition to singing, *mbalax* music sometimes contains *taasu* (rhythmically declaimed poetry, understood by the Senegalese to be a predecessor of rap). The *taasu* is usually performed by a member of the band other than the lead vocalist, such as the percussionist or dancer/animateur (like the beloved Alla Seck).

History of *Mbalax* Bands, Stars and Musicians

Many *mbalax* singers are *griots*, or hereditary musicians. The *griot* singers, as well as *griot* percussionists (masters of the *sabar*), are born into their profession, exposed to singing and drumming at an early age, and learn from elder members of their families. This is the way in which they receive their musical training.

The other instrumentalists in *mbalax* bands (keyboardists, guitarists, etc.) tend to be self-trained. Although some musicians attend the National Conservatory, few have formal training of any kind, and many simply learn by ear.

Historically, *mbalax* is very much a product of the post-independence era in Senegal and neighboring Gambia. By the end of World War II, Latin dance music dominated the airwaves, recording distribution and live performance venues. In celebration of independence in 1960, numerous new bands were formed in Senegal, including the Star Band and Orchestre Baobab. Although the music was still Latin in style, singers such as Laye Mboup began to sing Wolof lyrics (instead of Spanish), and eventually these bands began to incorporate traditional drums such as *sabar* and *tama* (talking drum) into the ensemble. This new style, coined 'mbalax' by Senegalese singer Youssou N'Dour, drew upon traditional *sabar* rhythms and Wolof lyrics to which the Senegalese people could relate.

The most important exponent of *mbalax* music has been Youssou N'Dour, the long-reigning 'King of Mbalax.' With his band, Super Étoile de Dakar, N'Dour has long been the most popular *mbalax* singer in the country. In addition to his larger-than-life status in his home country, and his success as a business mogul, Youssou N'Dour was the first artist to bring *mbalax* to the international scene. His golden voice, which holds enormous power in the upper register and has an extremely wide range, has made N'Dour one of the leading vocalists to come out of Africa onto the international scene.

Some other *mbalax* singers who have experienced considerable success include Fallou Dieng, Ndongo Lô, Omar Pène and Thione Seck. The new, younger generation is led by Pape Diouf, Alioune Mbaye Nder and Wally Seck. Female artists such as Ami Collé, Coumba Gawlo, Fatou Guewel, Kiné Lam and Viviane N'Dour have also reached the top of the charts. Since the 1990s, musicians have begun to experiment with more fusion styles, which have resulted in subgenres such as rock-*mbalax*, jazz-*mbalax*, folk-*mbalax* and salsa-*mbalax*. This 'mbalaxization' of other styles has provided an example of the growing global currency of many African music groups at the turn of the twenty-first century.

In the 1970s, the Gambian group the Super Eagles (who were later renamed Ifang Bondi) were extremely popular. However, due to an underdeveloped music industry, Gambia has played a relatively small role in the history of *mbalax*. Despite producing a few homegrown artists such as Moussa Ngom, Gambia's airwaves and concert venues have essentially been dominated by Senegalese *mbalax* bands, as well as by the more traditional music of Mande *griots*.

Music for Dancing

Although mbalax has been widely disseminated through cassette sales, radio, television and the Internet, the music is best experienced live in Dakar nightclubs. Throughout the city, live *mbalax* bands attract patrons from the upper middle class on a regular basis. Youssou N'Dour owns the famous Thiossane nightclub, where he plays regularly.

A soirée typically runs from after midnight to 4:00 a.m., with bands playing two one-and-a-half-hour sets. People come 'dressed to the nines,' as is typical of the Senegalese (they are known for their exceptional care and fine taste in dress). When the band begins playing, the dance floor fills up immediately and remains so until the end of the evening.

The basic style of *mbalax* dance involves carefully nuanced pelvic gyrations and knee movements. Occasionally, when a dancer responds to a *bàkk* or other *sabar* solo, they will break out into the more traditional *sabar* dance style, with elegant jumps and flailing limb movements.

In addition to these basic moves, new *mbalax* dance crazes are constantly emerging, often with the rise of a particular song. Examples of such dances are the *ventilateur* (electric fan, which describes the motion of buttocks swirling suggestively); *xaj bi* ('the dog,' when a dancer lifts their leg in imitation of a dog); *moulaye chigin* (which involves pelvic and knee movements that perfectly match the *sabar* breaks); *jelkati* (a dance in which the upper arms, bent at the elbows, move in parallel motion from left to right); and, more recently, *youza* (a dance in which the arms make a signature scooping motion). Interestingly, all of these dance crazes are tied closely to *sabar* breaks and some (such as *tawran tej*) are even named for the vocal mnemonics of the *sabar* rhythm they accompany.

Text and Lyrics

The lyrics of *mbalax* songs are of tremendous importance to the Senegalese public, with most covering social, religious, familial or moral issues. Common themes include the importance of respecting elders, women and children, taking care of one's family and having a strong work ethic. Some texts also address modern themes such as young lovers with disapproving parents, the complexities of polygamy and the pressures on Senegalese immigrants living abroad.

As in the tradition of griot praise singing, many *mbalax* songs praise important religious and/or historic figures such as Cheikh Amadou Bamba, the founder of the Mouride sect, the famous warrior, Lat Dior, and King Alboury Ndiaye. Occasionally, singers praise wealthy patron friends in song as well, continuing the griot tradition.

Mbalax as National Symbol

Mbalax is listened to and adored by most Senegambians, from young schoolchildren to the elderly. Unlike hip-hop, which appeals more to a youthful age group, *mbalax* is truly a genre that cuts across generations. *Mbalax* stars such as Youssou N'Dour have become important cultural icons and every time a new recording is released, it is heard on the airwaves throughout the country. Music videos appear frequently on all major Senegalese television stations and the careers and lives of *mbalax* stars are followed closely in the media.

In addition to being a national symbol, *mbalax* has been one of Senegal's most important commercial exports in the late twentieth century, competing with *soukous* as one of the best-known African music genres in the West. Ever since Youssou N'Dour broke onto the international scene through his participation in the Amnesty International tour in 1988 and collaborations with Peter Gabriel and Paul Simon, *mbalax* artists have begun to release recordings as well as tour internationally. Artists who have had considerable international success, aside from Youssou N'Dour, include Baaba Maal, Ismael Lö, Cheikh Lô and Orchestre Baobab.

As is the case for any artist trying to appeal to an international audience, *mbalax* musicians are faced with the problem of making their music more accessible to foreigners without compromising its integrity. Because the fast *mbalax* beat is said to be difficult to understand (and to dance to) for Westerners, *mbalax* bands often change their music rhythmically in order to emphasize beats 1 and 3 of 4, as well as simplify their texture (e.g., having less syncopated *marimba*). They also sing more songs in French or English, rather than in their native Wolof, which is understood only by people from Senegal and the Gambia. Some critics say that Youssou N'Dour oversimplifies his music for international release. Regardless, *mbalax* musicians have continued to make their mark on the international scene, with increasing numbers of young artists playing in important venues from Paris to New York.

Although *mbalax* has spread all over the world through recordings, the Internet and live tours, it remains a homegrown genre in that the vast majority of *mbalax* musicians are Senegalese. Some *mbalax* bands led by Senegalese immigrants exist in Europe and North America, but the most successful bands remain those from Senegal.

Conclusion

Mbalax is the popular music genre par excellence of the Senegambian people. From its birth in the 1970s, *mbalax* has infused Latin dance music with Senegambian elements, from Wolof lyrics to *sabar* percussion. It has not only become a musical form but also a national symbol for Senegal, and remains one of Senegal's most important exports. A dance music based rhythmically on the traditional *sabar* drum, *mbalax* is modern in its musical style, lyrical content and national status.

Bibliography

Castaldi, Francesca. 2006. *Choreographies of African Identities: Négritude, Dance, and the National Ballet of Senegal*. Champaign: University of Illinois Press.

Cathcart, Jenny. 2001. 'Mbalax.' *Songlines* (Winter 2001): 32–9.

Cathcart, Jenny. 1989. *Hey You! A Portrait of Youssou N'dour*. Oxford: Fine Line Books.

Celebrating Senegal's 50th Anniversary: Mbalax Fever – The Story of Popular Music in Senegal. Online at: http://afropop.org/hipdeep/HipDeep.html#progr amId=790&view=1.

Durán, Lucy. 1989. 'Key to N'Dour: Roots of the Senegalese Star.' *Popular Music* 8(3): 275–84.

Mangin, Timothy. 2013. *Mbalax: Cosmopolitanism in Senegalese Urban Popular Music*. Unpublished Ph.D., Columbia University, New York. Online at: https://academiccommons.columbia.edu/catalog/ ac:156952 (accessed 18 March 2018).

McLaughlin, Fiona. 1997. 'Islam and Popular Music in Senegal: The Emergence of a "New Tradition".' *Africa* 67(4): 560–81.

Panzacchi, Cornelia. 1996. *Mbalax Mi*. Wuppertal: Peter Hammer Verlag.

Shain, Richard M. 2009. 'The Re(public) of Salsa: Afro-Cuban Music in *Fin-De-Siècle* Dakar.' *Africa* 79(2): 186–206.

Tang, Patricia. 2005. 'Negotiating Performance in Senegalese Popular Music: Sound, Image and the Ethnomusicologist as Exoticized "Other".' *Journal of Popular Music Studies* 17(3): 275–300.

Tang, Patricia. 2007. *Masters of the Sabar: Wolof Griot Percussionists of Senegal*. Philadelphia: Temple University Press.

Discography

Collé, Ami. *Defar ba mou baax*. Prince Arts. *2013*: Senegal.

Diop, Mapathé. *Sabar Wolof: Dance Drumming of Senegal*. Village Pulse VPU-1003. *1992*: Senegal.

Diouf, Pape. *Partir*. Jololi. *2004*: Senegal.
Etoile de Dakar. *Xalis*. Popular African Music ADC 303. 1987; *1994*: Senegal.
Gawlo, Coumba. *Yo Male*. Rendez-Vous. *1998*: France.
Guewel, Fatou, and Groupe Sopey Noreyni. *Fatou*. Stern's Africa 1078. *1998*: Senegal.
Lam, Kiné. *Praise*. Shanachie 64062. *1996*: Senegal.
Lemzo Diamono. *Marimbalax*. Stern's Africa 1076. [1992–5] *1997*: Senegal.
Lô, Cheikh. *Né la thiass*. World Circuit/Nonesuch 79471-2. *1996*: Senegal.
Lô, Ismael. *Natt*. Syllart/Mélodie 38740-2. *N.d.*: France.
The Music in My Head. Stern's Africa 1081. *1998*: Senegal.
Nder, Alioune Mbaye, et le Setsima Group. *Nder et le Setsima Group*. Africa Fête Diffusion 002. *1999*: Senegal.
N'Dour, Youssou. *Nelson Mandela*. Polygram 831 294-2. *1986*: Federal Republic of Germany.
N'Dour, Youssou. *Set*. Virgin V2-86195. *1990*: Senegal.
N'Dour, Youssou. *The Guide (Wommat)*. Chaos/Columbia OK 53828. *1994*: Senegal.
N'Dour, Youssou. *Immigrés*. Earthworks. *2002*: Senegal.
N'Dour, Youssou. *Nothing's in Vain*. Nonesuch 79654-2. *2002*: USA.
N'Dour, Youssou. *I Bring What I Love*. Nonesuch. *2010*: USA.
N'Dour, Youssou. *Africa Rekk*. Jive/Epic. *2016*: Senegal.
Orchestre Baobab. *Bamba*. Stern's Africa 3003. [1981] *1993*: Senegal.
Orchestre Baobab. *Specialist in All Styles*. World Circuit/Nonesuch 79685-2. *2002*: Senegal.
Pène, Omar, and Super Diamono. *Fari*. Stern's Africa 1051. *1993*: Senegal.
Seck, Thione. *Daaly*. Stern's Africa 1070. *1997*: Senegal.
Seck, Wally B. *Ndeweneul*. Wally Family Production. *2014*: Senegal.
Streets of Dakar: Generation Boul Falé. Stern's STCD 1084. *1999*: Senegal.
Touré, Lamine, & Group Saloum. *Lamine Touré and Group Saloum*. Nomadic Wax. *2005*: USA.
Touré, Lamine, & Group Saloum. *Cosaan*. Nomadic Wax. *2010*: USA.
Viviane et Le Djoloff Band. *Tere Nelaw*. Mélodie. *2002*: Senegal.

PATRICIA TANG

Mbaqanga

Mbaqanga (isiZulu: 'cornmeal bread') refers to a range of musical styles that constitute urban black South African popular music since the 1940s, including African jazz, jive, *isimanje-manje*, *umgqashiyo*, soul *mbaqanga* and so-called township jive. Jazz pianist and composer Gideon Nxumalo is credited with disseminating the word *mbaqanga* to refer to African jazz in the 1950s via his weekly, one-hour jazz program, *This Is Bantu Jazz*. However, the term is said to have been first used in the 1940s to refer to African jazz by the Jazz Maniacs trumpeter Michael Xaba. In its application to jazz, *mbaqanga* described something homemade that was a quick way to earn money or daily bread. Throughout its fluid history and stylistic references, the music industry has used the term *mbaqanga* to refer to a consistently pan-ethnic urban style produced for ordinary township dwellers.

African Jazz

In the late 1940s and 1950s, black South African jazz musicians used the term *mbaqanga* to describe the African jazz that was the fusion by South African swing bands of US big band swing with local styles such as *marabi* and *tsaba tsaba*. *Marabi* was a pan-ethnic, urban, popular keyboard style from the 1920s whose harmonic and rhythmic features, especially its endlessly repeated harmonic cycle, I-IV-I6/4-V, served as a structuring principle for African jazz, paralleling the role of the blues for American jazz (Ballantine 1993). *Tsaba tsaba* music, a *marabi*-derived Rhodesian hybrid style, was a syncretism of African melody and rhythm, American swing, Latin American *conga* and *rumba*, but it was closer to *marabi* than to swing. It showed affinity with African migrants' dances, such as the BaSotho's *focho* dance, and Afrikaans folk dances such as the *vastrap*. Although it used chords similar to *marabi*, it was played in duple time with a fast quarter-note beat on the bass drum (without any swing feel), and a polyrhythmic sense of 'two-against-three.' *Tsaba-tsaba*'s influence was evident in the local musical features, mostly melodic and rhythmic, that were later incorporated into the style.

Typical characteristics of African jazz include cyclically repeated short progressions of primary chords on the bass, repeated or alternated melodies the length of the harmonic cycle and call-and-response and swung rhythm. Its ensembles included piano, double bass, drums, reeds and brass. Famous bands included the Jazz Maniacs and the Harlem Swingsters, who performed in township halls and venues such as the Bantu Men's Social Centre (in Johannesburg), for working- and middle-class audiences respectively. Such bands also performed in clubs patronized by white South Africans (for example, the Jazz Maniacs often performed in Johannesburg's Paradise Nightclub), at least until the ban instituted in 1942 was legally underwritten by the apartheid era's Reservation of Separate Amenities Act (1953). Both acts effectively expelled black show business from white city centers and performance venues.

African jazz musically expressed the move toward New Africanism (a model African national culture for all classes of African townsmen) characteristic of the 1940s. The ideology of the 'New African' was in many ways South Africa's later (1930s and 1940s) answer to black America's conception of a progressive or advancing community, the 'New Negro' (in the mid-1920s). Like its African-American predecessor, it was influential in the field of culture as espoused by both countries' black elites (Couzens 1982). In the spirit of New Africanism, local music and dance styles, compositions, orchestrations and arrangements were encouraged in jazz compositions by the black intelligentsia, while there was less acceptance of the increased use of *marabi*-based melodies and harmonies and *tsaba tsaba*, both conventionally viewed as belonging to the 'lower classes' (Ballantine 1993).

African jazz was popular with Westernizing Africans. It was a vehicle of class formation as well as a means of cultural communication and participation *across* classes – a cosmopolitan music that stressed equality, black unity and non-tribalism. This cosmopolitanism was achieved by jazz musicians' adoption of American and African-American popular culture – its dress, speech and mannerisms – to forge new urban cultural myths. This Americanization is evident in the prominence of US-style gangsters in African jazz's history, as well as in the conscious billing of certain musicians as 'local versions' of American stars. For example: the Manhattan Brothers' style, image and stage routines followed the Mills Brothers, Nathan Mdledle was described as 'the Bing Crosby of South Africa' and Dolly Rathebe was 'South Africa's Ella Fitzgerald.'

Alongside live concerts, the style was disseminated by the record industry, the radio, and print media (especially the jazz record review). Print publications such as *Zonk!* (1949), *Drum* and *Golden City Post* (1951) featured African jazz and record reviews. Todd Matshikiza's idiosyncratic style of reporting, called 'Matshikese,' retained the accents, style and rhythm of pre-1960s *mbaqanga*. The recording industry built its catalogues for black music on African jazz and later *kwela*. Gallo Africa and its subsidiary Gramophone Record Company, Trutone and Teal (both subsidiaries of EMI) and Troubadour Records hired African talent scouts and producers who shaped the sound of black South African popular music. Rupert Bopape established EMI as a giant of African jazz by employing jazz musicians on a permanent basis, including Isaac 'Zacks' Nkosi, Elijah Nkwanyane and Ellison Temba. In the 1950s the SABC presented radio programs featuring different African languages and musical styles on separate days. Once a week Gideon Nxumalo, a jazz pianist and composer known for disseminating the term *mbaqanga*, hosted an African jazz program entitled *This Is Bantu Jazz*.

By the mid-1950s African jazz was an established popular genre, evidenced by the formation of institutions dedicated to its performance: the Odin Cinema of Sophiatown; the Sophiatown Modern Jazz Club; the 'Jazz at the Odin' series; and Johannesburg's Dorkay House. Despite its popularity, by the mid-1950s African jazz big bands declined for economic reasons; their fate was also sealed by apartheid's racialized policing of leisure time and residential space. In the new townships, suitable performing venues were scarce and restrictions on performers were repressive. Many retreated to the recording studio.

Jive: Mid-1950s to 1960

In response to the economic, political and spatial obstacles of the mid-1950s, a new *mbaqanga* emerged in South Africa's townships. It was an amalgam of related popular music styles, performed and recorded in different languages and on various instruments and often marketed as jive. Jive refers to American-influenced urban African dancing, popular since the 1950s and accompanied by either American or African jazz. By the end of the 1960s 'jive' described 1950s and 1960s instrumental musics in South Africa. This section focuses on 'sax jive' and 'vocal jive' – two of the most distinctive and enduring forms of jive – and their contribution to *mbaqanga*.

After the *kwela* boom in this decade, particularly in the form of 'pennywhistle kwela' that was performed by young, male amateur and professional musicians (Allen 2005) subsided, sax jive and vocal jive dominated. Jive thrived in the slumyards and shebeens of black South Africa, particularly in the mining towns of Kimberley (diamonds) and Johannesburg (gold) and it remains, in its syncretism, a sonic palimpsest of those who were in closest physical proximity to the country's rapid industrialization. Vocal jive appropriated African jazz's characteristics. The musical characteristics evident in both sax jive and vocal jive were common in black popular music recorded during this time. Jive energized African jazz by infusing its tunes with *tsaba tsaba*, and it was less indebted to American swing than its predecessors melodically, rhythmically and harmonically; vocal jive emphasized the influence of local forms through its lyrics.

When the pennywhistle *kwela* musician Spokes Mashiyane recorded 'Ace Blues' in 1954, 'flute jive' was born and soon dominated the record industry. Persuaded by Trutone producer Strike Vilakazi, the same Spokes Mashiyane picked up the saxophone in 1958 and recorded 'Big Joe Special,' after which 'sax jives' dominated. Dorothy Masuka's 'Hamba Nontsokolo,' which was released in 1953 by Troubadour's producer Cuthbert Mathumba, exemplified 'vocal jive.' While definitive origins cannot be attributed to the genre, these events were important. Sax jives were built around simple, repeated melodic fragments grounded by *marabi*-derived harmonies. The melodies of sax and vocal jives showed *kwela's* influence (two or three short melodic motifs spanning the harmonic cycle interspersed with solo improvisations). Solo saxophonists, along with vocal soloists and groups, were backed by lead and rhythm guitars, acoustic string bass and drums. Prominent musicians of this style include sax jivers Zacks Nkosi, West Nkosi and Ntemi Piliso; vocal jivers Dorothy Masuka, Dolly Rathebe and Miriam Makeba; and groups such as The Skylarks and The Quad Sisters.

Record and media industries shaped the sound of the music and the image of the musicians. Primarily due to print media, vocal jive soloists and ensembles, especially women, had more exposure than their instrumental and male counterparts: they were 'stars' in the Hollywood mode. The pictorial press's commercial apparatus – pin-ups, cover girls, advertising – also presented jive musicians as gendered, sexualized bodies. Its audiences have reflected this consumerist mode; 1950s sartorial and linguistic 'hipness,' the latter expressed in the township *patois* known as 'tsotsi taal,' remain iconic in the twenty-first century, and the fashion, in particular, has often been revived as retro-chic. Due to their status as cultural icons, the dance styles developed by 1950s audiences are still recognizable to postapartheid South Africans.

Jive's importance for black cultural politics has often been underestimated, primarily because of its considerable commercial success; its branding as 'jive' led to its dismissal as inconsequential 'candy floss' (Allen 2003) by the leading black music intelligentsia of the time. For the record companies who knew that this music was popular, marketing the music as innocuous 'jive' evaded apartheid censorship and was thus a strategic trivializing of the style.

Vocal jive's lyrics referenced current events and social issues in local township lingo without analysis or commentary; they could only imply other meanings suggested by the stated theme. Cryptic lyrics were useful in South Africa's repressive climate as they implied significance while avoiding censorship, but even so, there was risk associated with promoting vocal jive. Vocal jive's prominence is partly due to its sponsorship by Troubadour Records, a company that was opportunistically daring about apartheid's censorship laws. For example, one of its star women singers, Mabel Mafuya, recalls that she made her money at Troubadour by singing the latest news, including songs about the controversial bus boycotts of 1956 and 1957. Yet another Mafuya song, 'Regina,' referred to the iniquities of the Immorality Act of 1950, which outlawed intimate relationships between blacks and whites (Regina was a white woman who had won a highly publicized case that allowed her to marry her Zulu partner). Another legendary Troubadour musician, Dorothy Masuka, recorded songs that specifically referenced apartheid laws and anti-apartheid resistance leaders. Such songs brought the security police to the company's offices, but Troubadour's owners, Israel Katz and Morris Fagan, defused the situation by claiming Masuka's songs were praise songs and, at worst, merely informative (Allen 2003). The Troubadour company also gave its producer and A&R man Cuthbert Mathumba relatively free rein over the music produced, and Mathumba built up Troubadour Records until it controlled about 75 percent of the black market. Mathumba successfully produced entertaining jive music with topical lyrics. Companies other than Troubadour, who were without Mathumba's singular talent, tended to favor instrumental sax jive rather than risk censorship, police raids or possible closure.

Mbaqanga: 1960s to Mid-1970s

Sax jive and vocal jive merged to form the bases of 1960s *mbaqanga*, backed by two electric guitars, an electric bass guitar and drums. Its rhythms were straight and driving; the lead guitar and bass guitar provided strong contrapuntal lines. With its broad-based popularity already eclipsed by *kwela* and vocal jive, African jazz and (instrumental) jive died out in the 1960s. Primary musicians of African jazz left with the musical *King Kong* or individually. Hugh Masekela, for example, was awarded a scholarship to study music at Julliard, while Miriam Makeba left to promote Lionel Rogosin's covertly made anti-apartheid film, *Come Back Africa* (1959). The multiracial musical theater project about the life and death of a legendary boxer, *King Kong: An African Jazz Opera*, had been a thorn in the apartheid government's side since its first rehearsal in 1958 and its premiere in February 1959, mainly because preparations for the show meant black musicians and actors had to break the apartheid curfew that curtailed their presence in 'white' areas of Johannesburg and because the organizers insisted on hosting the show's premiere in a racially integrated venue (the University of the Witwatersrand's Great Hall). Soon after the show was underway, the 'King Kongers' applied to travel outside the country. They eventually outsmarted apartheid bureaucracy and were reluctantly permitted to proceed to London, where they opened at the Princes Theatre in 1961. The *King Kong* exodus included foremost musicians of African jazz, such as members of the Jazz Maniacs, the pianist and *King Kong* composer Todd Matshikiza, the Woody Woodpeckers and the Manhattan Brothers. Once in London, *King Kong* musicians popularized styles including not only *kwela* and vocal jive, but also, most enduringly in their individual appearances, African jazz. Jive artists including Dorothy Masuka, after recording a song commemorating Patrice Lumumba's assassination, and Miriam Makeba, after making her anti-apartheid statement at the UN in 1963, were branded 'undesirable' and exiled, but black South Africa did not run out of talented musicians.

While still reliant on traded riffs and cyclical primary harmonies, in the early 1960s bands backing sax soloists became heavier and more elastic in rhythm. This was mainly due to Joseph Makwela's electric bass. Makwela, alongside electric guitarist Marks Mankwane, later formed the Makgona Tsohle Band, Gallo-Mavuthela's resident band, which would back Mahlathini and the Mahotella Queens. Makgona Tsohle's *mbaqanga* combined neo-traditional music with *marabi* rather than jazz. Its ensembles had two electric guitars, an electric bass guitar and drums (at times including accordion, concertina or violin). The vocal style of 1960s *mbaqanga* was a descendant of 1950s vocal jive, but had five instead of four vocal parts. *Mbaqanga* came closer to neo-traditional forms, set rural songs to *marabi*-based rhythms and was played at rapid tempo.

Soon such ensembles backed vocal groups, resulting in *isimanje-manje*, which drew on indigenous isiZulu female polyphonic singing and used five-part harmonies that included a male 'groaner,' who sang with a rough timbre in textural counterpoint to the female vocalists. The most prolific producer of this *mbaqanga* was EMI's Rupert Bopape, who combined neo-traditional musics with pre-1960s *mbaqanga*. *Isimanje-manje* was pioneered by Black Mambazo (not to be confused with Ladysmith Black Mambazo), featuring Zeph Nkabinde and the groaner Aaron 'Big Voice Jack' Lerole. Their female counterparts were the Dark City Sisters. Once Lerole left EMI in 1961, his role as groaner was taken over by Simon 'Mahlathini' Nkabinde.

With Mahlathini, the stage was set for *umgqashiyo*, consolidated after Bopape moved to Gallo-Mavuthela in 1964 with Mahlathini, the Makgona Tsohle Band and other EMI musicians. *Umgqashiyo* references a particular popular dance style and is not formally different from *isimanje-manje*. *Umgqashiyo* was popular during the 1960s to mid-1970s. Bands from other companies flourished, for example GRC's Amatshitshi, the groaners Saul and Bhekitshe Tshabalala, the backup band Abafana Bentuthuko and Izintombi Zesimanje-manje (immortalized in Meintjes 2003). The GRC lineup was produced by Hamilton Nzimande.

Umgqashiyo shows were presented in black townships and male-only hostels. Stage choreography, the correspondence between body movement, gesture, melody and rhythm were essential. Steps and movements were taken from traditional and urban dance styles. The shows were divided into several segments, from traditional to more urbanized music, dance and costumes. Songs in the opening segment began with a lead guitar introduction, followed by a bass melody pattern based on the F-C-G#-C *ostinato* formula, played over a bouncing 8/8 rhythm. Keyboard or accordion lines were laid on top in staggered fashion, each part cutting the phrase cycle at different points. Appreciation for repetition with slight variation, reminiscent of vocal jive, was basic to *umgqashiyo* shows. Most shows had a stand-up comedian as a master of ceremonies, who would perform comic sketches (reminiscent of the music and vaudeville format of earlier times). Unlike vocal jive's cryptic lyrics, this *mbaqanga*'s lyrical force lay in a mythical veneration of 'the old life' that possibly provided some degree of comfort for the landless, economically disempowered and politically disenfranchised migrant laborers who formed the bulk of its audience.

Late *Mbaqanga*: 'Soul *Mbaqanga*,' Mid-1970s to 1990s

After *umgqashiyo* waned in the mid-1970s, another style of *isimanje-manje* emerged. Distinguishable by its all-male, sweet-voiced frontline and the absence of a groaner, it was described as 'soul *mbaqanga*' and it endured in the South African soundscape for the next two decades. The style is characterized by florid song introductions on electric organ, a foregrounded horn lineup, distinctive two-part quavering vocal harmonies, synthesizers and an electric guitar rapidly picked, with high neck work.

US soul music from the 1960s and 1970s was popular in black urban South Africa and 'local soul' singles had been produced. Soul (and later disco) was preferred by black youth, indexing a generational gap that would widen in post-'Soweto Uprising' (1976–7) South Africa. The student-led revolt has been memorialized by the televised shootings of Soweto students by apartheid police on 16 June 1976, but in fact spread across the country and lasted far longer in the Eastern Cape, particularly in the coastal city Port Elizabeth. Its effects on black youth musical cultures, coupled with the violent murder of the Black Consciousness Movement leader, Bantu Steve Biko, at the hands of the police, were definitive. Henceforth, 'the youth' related to music as protest or rebellion (e.g., through reggae) and, equally tenaciously and rebelliously, as pleasure (through dance forms like disco). Older genres were now seen as government-tolerated, and their traditionalism was viewed as complicit with apartheid's tribalism and conservatism in general.

The most notable producer at this time was Hamilton Nzimande of the Gramophone Record Company, which he joined in 1966. It was Nzimande's suggestion that the Soul Brothers copy their vocal style from popular Zimbabwean township music (itself already influenced by *mbaqanga*'s style of bass playing). The Soul Brothers (David Masondo, Zakes Mchunu, Tuza Mthethwa, Moses Ngwenya and American Zulu) blended *mbaqanga* with local soul and disco to produce a style that emphasized a bouncing township beat, complex organ riffs and lead bass melody. They had male dancers who executed complex *mapantsula* dance routines in bright shirts, sneakers and creased trousers, singing in close harmony falsetto style. Their song lyrics, despite the music's association with a rebellious youth audience, were not often explicitly political. Rather, they addressed social issues familiar to their urban working-class audiences. They soon attracted imitators, and 'soul *mbaqanga*' has dominated South Africa from the mid-1970s to the postapartheid era through radio, albums and the television program *Ezodumo* (later called *Roots*), which regularly features groups of this kind.

Mbaqanga's Diaspora

Mbaqanga outside South Africa has a longer history than is often documented. This is in part due to the increasingly restricted way in which the genre has been defined (often equating *mbaqanga* solely with *isimanje-manje* or *umgqashiyo*). The 1960s saw most African jazz and jive artists leave South Africa because spaces for performing their music were closed down, including whole suburbs that kept these musical cultures alive, such as Sophiatown (in Johannesburg) and District Six (in Cape Town). They also left because the Government Proclamation R26 of 1965 formalized the (longer) prohibition of racially mixed bands, venues and audiences, which proved detrimental for African jazz. The cast of the *King Kong* show disseminated African jazz through the *King Kong* musical in London via stage, screen and record and found favor there with British traditional jazz musicians such as Chris Barber, the producer Denis Preston, and Britain's Afro-Cuban jazz exponent, Kenny Graham. *Mbaqanga* also found a home in the United States, through the musicians who chose the United States as their place of exile: Ndikho Xaba, Jonas Gwangwa, Hugh Masekela, Miriam Makeba, Caiphus Semenya and Letta Mbulu. Here, their type of jazz found some resonance with 1960s African-American cultural nationalism. The legendary Blue Notes – Chris McGregor, Dudu Pukwana, Johnny Dyani, Mongezi Feza, Louis Moholo – arrived in England in the mid-1960s as 'progressive' beboppers, but also introduced themselves to their new audiences (mostly through the BBC and the CIA-funded Congress of Cultural Freedom institution, the Transcription Centre's African Writers' Club) as interpreters of the African jazz/*mbaqanga* sound (along with Ronnie Beer and Gwigwi Mrwebi). Creating a 'free jazz' London scene with its nascent avant-gardists, the Blue Notes with South African (most importantly Harry Miller) and British jazz musicians, elaborated *mbaqanga* into improvised music in the form of the extremely influential big band, the Brotherhood of Breath. Later musicians who moved to the United Kingdom, such as Ernest Mothle, Pinise Saul, Lucky Ranku and Julian Bahula, disseminated *mbaqanga* to London's cosmopolitan audiences, forging a style now commonly known as 'London Township.' The most visible form of *mbaqanga* in 'world music' is *umgqashiyo*, whose reigning ambassadors are the Mahotella Queens (formerly Mahlathini and the Mahotella Queens). The revived careers of the Mahotella Queens, alongside the Soul Brothers' commercial success in the world music circuit, have raised *mbaqanga*'s international profile.

Historiography and the Problem of Definitions

The pervasiveness of the term *mbaqanga* as a descriptor of black urban popular music makes it difficult to describe as a genre; each new audience sought its own *mbaqanga*, and *mbaqanga* created specific audiences. The related term 'township jive,' for example, does not refer to anything specific and seems to belong more to 'world music' discourse than to the actual music and its sound, or to the way practitioners or consumers of the music in South Africa conceptualize it.

Historical writings have linked *mbaqanga* with its apartheid backdrop, and have drawn out how the tensions linking musical, political and commercial imperatives have influenced *mbaqanga*. Researchers agree that African jazz was a positive syncretism. It occupies an unchallenged space in black South Africa's cultural history (Ballantine 1993 and Coplan 2007). The music industry's position has been scrutinized (Coplan 1979), but recent scholarship shows that commercial and artistic ends do not inevitably clash (Allen 2003; Ballantine 1999; Meintjes 2003). This has benefited the study of vocal jive in particular (Allen 2003 and Ballantine 1999). The tense triumvirate of music, industry and politics is clearest in earlier writings on *umgqashiyo* or *isimanje-manje* styles (Ballantine 1993, 8). Here the argument (echoed by politicized black youth of the 1970s), is that its reference to older so-called 'tribal' forms of dance, music and dress complied with apartheid ideology. Similar arguments pertain with regard to the mislabeling of *isimanje-manje* and *umgqashiyo* as *mbaqanga* (Coplan 2007, 227–8). The dynamics of *isimanje-manje* production have been examined by Louise Meintjes (2003), and a richer picture has emerged. Finally, the addition of the Soul Brothers and similar bands (Coplan 2007) represents a new move in the genre's historiography. Previous articles on *mbaqanga* had not included the Brothers under this term (Allingham 1994b, 1999), even though they have been billed as foremost proponents of 'soul *mbaqanga*.'

Conclusion

Louise Meintjes (2003) concludes that *mbaqanga* is an institution as well as a set of musical and social practices. All of its manifestations must be viewed historically. A striking feature of *mbaqanga* is that it has consistently interpellated an urban (at times migrant working-class) audience. Their tastes at times leaned toward *marabi* and localized jazz (such as African jazz and sax jive). They sought music that vocalized their permanence in the city, with all its joys and woes (vocal jive). At other times, they demanded musical styles that recalled a space more secure than the 'unhomely' city (*umgqashiyo*, *isimanje-manje*). Finally, home groove persisted in soul- and disco-influenced *mbaqanga*. In postapartheid South Africa, this music has become truly popular music (perhaps more popular than genres such as *kwaito*). Its audiences transcend categories of class, generation, gender, language, rural/or urban and, increasingly, race. *Mbaqanga* has come full circle, then, since earlier African jazz, as a musical expression of New Africanism, sought to achieve just that.

Bibliography

Allen, Lara. 1993. 'Pennywhistle Kwela: A Musical, Historical and Socio-Political Analysis.' Unpublished M.Mus dissertation, University of Natal, Durban.

Allen, Lara. 2000. *Representation, Gender and Women in Black South African Popular Music, 1948-1960*. Unpublished Ph.D. thesis, Cambridge University.

Allen, Lara. 2003. 'Commerce, Politics, and Musical Hybridity: Vocalizing Urban Black South African Identity during the 1950s.' *Ethnomusicology* 47(2): 228-49.

Allen, Lara. 2004. 'Music, Film and Gangsters in the Sophiatown Imaginary: Featuring Dolly Rathebe.' *Scrutiny2* 9(1): 19-38.

Allen, Lara. 2005. 'Circuits of Recognition and Desire in the Evolution of Black South African Popular Music: The Career of the Pennywhistle.' *South African Journal of Musicology* 25: 31-51.

Allingham, Rob. 1994a. 'Hip Kings, Hip Queens: The Story of South African Jazz, at Home and Overseas.' In *World Music: The Rough Guide*, eds. S. Broughton, M. Ellingham and R. Trillo. London: The Rough Guides, 391-6.

Allingham, Rob. 1994b. 'Township Jive: From Pennywhistle to Bubblegum: The Music of South Africa.' In *World Music: The Rough Guide*, eds. S. Broughton, M. Ellingham and R. Trillo. London: The Rough Guides, 373-90.

Allingham, Rob. 1999. 'South Africa: Popular Music: The Nation of Voice.' In *World Music: The Rough Guide*, eds. S. Broughton, M. Ellingham and R. Trillo. London: The Rough Guides, 638-68.

Ansell, Gwen. 2004. *Soweto Blues: Jazz, Popular Music, and Politics in South Africa*. New York: Continuum.

Ballantine, Christopher. 1993. *Marabi Nights: Early South African Jazz and Vaudeville*. Johannesburg: Ravan Press.

Ballantine, Christopher. 1999. 'Looking to the USA: The Politics of American Close-Harmony Song Style in South Africa during the 1940s and 1950s.' *Popular Music* 18(1): 1-18.

Coplan, David B. 1979. 'The African Musician and the Development of the Johannesburg Entertainment Industry, 1900-1960.' *Journal of Southern African Studies* 5(2):135-64.

Coplan, David B. 2007. *In Township Tonight! South Africa's Black City Music and Theatre*. 2nd ed. Chicago: University of Chicago Press.

Couzens, Tim. 1982. '"Moralizing Leisure Time": The Transatlantic Connection and Black Johannesburg, 1918-1936.' In *Industrialisation and Social Change in South Africa: African Class Formation, Culture and Consciousness, 1870-1930*, eds. Shula Marks and Richard Rathbone. London and New York: Longman, 314-37.

Meintjes, Louise. 2003. *Sound of Africa! Making Music Zulu in a South African Studio*. Durham, NC: Duke University Press.

Discographical References

Mafuya, Mabel, and her Girl Friends. 'Regina/Baba.' Troubadour AFC 364. *1956*: South Africa.

Mashiyane, Spokes, and his Rhythm. 'Ace Blues.' Quality, TJ 24, matrix 4080/1. *1954*: South Africa.

Mashiyane, Spokes and his Magic Sax. 'Big Joe Special.' Quality, 45TJ 500, matrix 7607/8, *1958*: South Africa.

Masuka, Dorothy. 'Hamba Notsokolo.' Troubadour AFC 170. *1953*: South Africa.

Discography

African Jazz ñ Jive (50S & 60S): An Authentic Selection of South African Township Swing Classics from the 50s & 60s. Gallo/GSP, CDZAC75. *2000*: South Africa.

Dark City Sisters and the Flying Jazz Queens. *The Dark City Sisters and the Flying Jazz Queens*. Earthworks/Virgin CDEWV 31. *1993*: USA.

From Marabi to Disco: 42 Years of Township Music. Gallo Music, CDZAC61. *1994*: South Africa.

Mahlathini and the Mahotella Queens. *Paris-Soweto*. Polydor 839676. *1990*: UK.

Mahlathini and the Mahotella Queens. *Mbaqanga*. Polygram 314511 780-2. *1991*: UK.

Makeba, Miriam, and the Skylarks. *Miriam Makeba and the Skylarks, vol. 1*. Teal Records, African Heritage, TELCD 2303. *1991*: South Africa.

Makeba, Miriam, and the Skylarks. *Miriam Makeba and the Skylarks, vol. 2.*, Teal Records, African Heritage, TELCD 2315. *1991*: South Africa.

Mashiyane, Spokes. *King Kwela*. Gallo Music, CDZAC50. *1991*: South Africa.

Mrwebi, Gwigwi. *Kwela by Gwigwi's Band*. 77 Doug Dobell AFRO/101. *1967*: UK. (Reissue: Mrwebi, Gwigwi. *Mbaqanga Songs*. Honest Jons Records, HJRLP103. 2006: UK.)

Nkosi, West. *Sixteen Original Sax Jive Hits*. Gallo South Africa, CDZAC57. *1991*: South Africa.

Soul Brothers. *Ezinkulu: The Best of the Soul Brothers*. Gallo Music CDGMP 1040. *1996*: South Africa.

Township Swing Jazz! vol. 1. Gallo Music, CDZAC 53. *1991*: South Africa.

Township Swing Jazz! vol. 2. Gallo Music, CDZAC 54. *1991*: South Africa.

Filmography

Come Back Africa, dir. Lionel Rogosin. 1959. USA. 83 mins, Drama.

LINDELWA DALAMBA

Mbube, *see* Isicathamiya

Mbumba

Mbumba is the name given to songs and dances performed by women at political rallies in Malawi since the late 1950s. The genre uses music and dance that is appropriated and adapted from traditional music, dance and orature. *Mbumba* music is polyphonic, polyrhythmic and, by definition, sang and danced by women. The instrumental accompaniment is usually, but not exclusively, provided by men.

Historical Outline

In rural Malawi society, since colonial times, women have had distinct channels of musical expression, such as singing while working at the mortar (*pamtondo*) and lyrics sung in other traditional music and dance settings (Vaughan 1987, 147; Lwanda 1993, 119–42). Some *pamtondo* songs were later recreated as political songs, illustrating the appropriation process of the *mbumba* genre. For example, the pounding song 'Akweni ndatopa' (Aunt I Am Tired) was the template for the Malawi Congress Party's (MCP) rousing 1958 chant 'Tambala akamalira' (When the Cock Crows).

Malawi (formerly Nyasaland) became a British Protectorate in 1891. Lacking obvious natural resources, it effectively became a manpower reservoir for mineral-rich countries to the South and West, a factor that later contributed to a rise in female-headed single families. Various anti-colonial activities, responding to poor educational provision for Africans, racial inequality and poverty, led to the formation of the Nyasaland African Congress (NAC) in 1944. The establishment of the Federation of Central Africa, comprised of modern-day Malawi, Zambia and Zimbabwe, alarmed radical nationalists who saw the role of a Nyasaland/Malawi labor reservoir continuing. Younger nationalists thereafter sought a more radical anti-colonial struggle and looked to Dr. Hastings Banda for stronger leadership. After Dr. Banda returned from prolonged absence abroad, in the United States, Britain and Ghana, to lead the NAC in 1958, his lieutenants cultivated a personality cult around him to strengthen his negotiating power with the British colonial authorities. As part of this initiative, songs of praise, initially led by male politicians including nationalist leader Kanyama Chiume, were sung at political rallies with both men and women singing chorus. The politicians appropriated music from female traditional dances such as *chimtali, chinamwali, chiwoda* and *vimbuza* and used it as a crucial tool of nationalism. Female traditional dances and popular music were suitable because they had a preexisting protest/blues orientation, reflecting Malawi's largely patriarchal culture of the time.

A particular female figure was important in the process of setting a precedent. The Zimbabwe-born singer Dorothy Masuka was recruited by Yatuta Chisiza of the MCP to sing at political rallies in the 1961 election campaign (Mckay 2008, 133; Chechamba 1997, 32). Her pop hit 'Ei yow phata phata!' (Hail phata phata [a *kwela* dance]!) became 'Iyo Ngwazi Banda!' (Hail Ngwazi Banda!). After her tour, the MCP increasingly used women as political singers in general and praise singers for Dr. Banda in particular, and an *mbumba* national movement was soon established. In matrilineal Chewa culture the maternal uncle, or *nkhoswe*, has authority over and looks after the affairs of the nieces (*mbumba*), especially in regard to marriage. Dr. Banda regarded himself as *Nkhoswe* Number One (the paramount uncle or guardian) of the *mbumba* groups, using tradition as his legitimizing factor, a legitimation that he also used to justify his one-party regime (Lwanda 1993; Forster 1994, 491–20).

Between 1958 and 1964 a steady growth in the appropriation of mostly female traditional music for political reasons occurred, initially executed by both male and female politicians. Some male *makwaya* (*a cappella* choral) and foreign music, such as 'John Brown's Body,' which became 'Chitaganya ndiyo nyumba ya Welensky' (The Federation Is [Prime Minister] Welensky's House), were also used. After the Cabinet Crisis of 1964, in which Dr. Banda defeated his younger colleagues and consolidated his power, women became the main composers (Chirwa 2001, 5–8). The *mbumba* movement played an important role in establishing an MCP hegemony (Lwanda 1993; Chirambo 2009), culminating in Dr. Banda becoming president for life in 1971. The MCP's Women's League organized the various *mbumba* groups in the country, composing songs that preached 'unity, loyalty, obedience and discipline.' As an example, a wedding song 'Chikwati ichi! Chamatiki tiki!' (This Wedding Will Rain Tickeys! [money]) became '*Zonse zimene za Kamuzu Banda!*' (Everything Belongs to Kamuzu Banda!).

The *mbumba* movement unintentionally ensured the endurance of nonpolitical traditional music in localities as in colonial times. Gifted practitioners and singers were constantly drafted from these localities into the creative ranks of the *mbumba* music movement. Each region, district or grouping had its own distinctive *chitenje* (wrap-round skirt) cloth material, complete with a picture of Banda at the front and back. The best master drummers were co-opted by the government to back the women. Some of the *mbumba* music composed between 1964 and 1982 using appropriated traditional templates remains as popular and innovative as any compositions by the male popular professional musicians of the period with whom they competed for radio space (e.g., that by Dowa District MCP *mbumba*, or Dowa Mbumba, in its use of melody, counter melody, harmony and polyrhythm). The Dowa Mbumba's so-called Dowa Symphony (*Azimai aku Dowa*), is an example of traditional female music appropriated, extended and made politically potent. During Dr. Banda's era many males objected to the politically laden lyrics, which were often normative and directive, rather than the music and *mbumba* choreography.

Dr. Banda so valued *mbumba* music that he refused to allow it to be commercially recorded, regarding it as 'sacred' to the MCP and its ideals of nation-building. He enacted the Commercial Advertising (Traditional Music) Control Act of 1978 to protect *mbumba* music from commercial 'exploitation.' Only the Malawi Broadcasting Corporation (MBC) was allowed to record *mbumba* music (Chanunkha 2005, 2–28) (these recordings are available in the MBC archives).

Although opponents of the one-party state regarded *mbumba* as an abuse of women during Dr. Banda's one-party rule, after the transition to a multiparty dispensation in 1994 many of these same critics started their own *mbumba* movements. In some cases the same individuals who had praised Dr. Banda defected to the opposition, re-appropriated MCP *mbumba* songs and revised the lyrics in favor of the new leaders (Lwanda 1993; Chimombo and Chimombo 1996; Mkamanga 2000; Chirwa 2001). By the end of 1993 the male-dominated United Democratic Front (UDF), whose party color was yellow, had its own yellow *mbumba*. Verah Chirwa, who had spent 11 years as a prisoner of conscience after criticizing Dr. Banda, objected to what she saw as the resurgence of the exploitation of females as party cheerleaders. She was publicly vilified by President Bakili Muluzi (V. Chirwa, 2007, 158–65). Many senior UDF female politicians, like their male counterparts, had been in the MCP and preferred *mbumba* culture.

By May 1994 there were three varieties of *mbumba*, identified by political party color and associated with distinct political parties in the transition to a multiparty system: red *mbumba* (MCP), yellow *mbumba* (UDF) and the Alliance for Democracy's blue *mbumba* reflecting ideological, economic and ethnic and political differences which were not of obvious political advantage to female party members in terms of gender issues and advancement. In 2004 the blue color was appropriated by a newer and bigger party, the Democratic Progressive Party (DPP).

DPP *mbumba* was comprised of defectors from the UDF and the MCP. A number, including Mai Chiponda, were veterans of both the Dowa and UDF *mbumba* eras.

Music and Dance Characteristics

Mbumba utilizes a call-and-response format with one or more female lead singers. When there are two or more lead singers, parallel harmonies, often in thirds, are employed. Some of the younger *mbumba* leaders sing in unison. The rhythm of a particular song depends on the dance on which the song is based. Prior to 2004 the *mbumba* were usually accompanied by drummers, with the number, usually three to five, varying according to affordability. While the rest of the drummers kept time, one or more lead drummers played additive lead rhythms to accentuate and provide syncopated contrast with the dancers' steps. Again, the exact form depends on which traditional dance the particular *mbumba* song is based on, which may include *chiwoda*, *chimtali*, *visekese*, *mwinoghe*, *ingoma*, *vimbuza*, *mganda*, *chisamba* or other dances.

Mbumba melodies are comprised of praise narratives (for example, 'Apailoti'), storytelling ('Kwacha Kamuzu wabwera' [It's Dawn, Dr Banda Has Arrived]) and news-telling narratives which may praise the leadership ('Azimai akuDowa' [Dowa Women]) or attack opponents ('Muwalo ndiwoononga' [Muwalo Is a Confusionist]) (Dowa Mbumba 2004). *Mbumba* singers also suggest ('Amuna wanga ndigulileni nsalu ya chipani' [Husband, buy me a party cloth/dress]), criticize or complain whenever possible.

Mbumba music does not just appropriate and recycle traditional music, it also has syncretic aspects. Aspects of twist, *smanjemanje*, *rumba* and jive were incorporated into the choreography, especially by younger practitioners. Older singers and arrangers brought in more traditional elements such as parallel lead singing and lyrical and spontaneous melodic improvisation. Since 2004 electric bands have backed *mbumba* musicians. In 2009 Margaret Chiponda and pop musician Joseph Tembo introduced the *kwasa kwasa* beat into the *mbumba* tradition with a potent DPP political rally song 'Angwazi senderani' (Ngwazi Move!) that featured *kwasa kwasa* beats, steps and choreography.

Mbumba performances are highly choreographed and venues determine stylistic elements. Smaller venues favor circular dance patterns with women facing inwards toward the drummers in the center and away from the audience. Larger venue performances may involve hundreds of *mbumba* dancers in various patterns. *Kwasa kwasa*-derived choreographies feature performances by women dressed in party colors dancing *kwasa kwasa* steps in formation.

Reception

Mbumba is considered by some to have appropriated tradition and religion in order to praise and buttress Dr. Banda's rule between 1964 and 1993 (Lwanda 1993; Muyebe and Muyebe 1999; Chirambo 2009). Critics viewed it as political exploitation of females for little obvious gender gain (Semu 2002; Gilman 2001). But the *mbumba* phenomenon is also a top-down movement controlled by elite urban women. Moreover, in the constrained atmosphere of a one-party state, it provided rural women with entertainment and occasional release from drudgery. It also gave women some limited power over their husbands as they had 'to go *mbumba* dancing'. And in the democratic phase, unlike in the one-party era, some politicians do pay women dancers. The *mbumba* movement has also played a role in the modernization of various traditional musical styles which might have been publicly ignored had they not become reservoirs for appropriation. Certainly in 2014 the *mbumba* movement is at the forefront of creating new musical styles with, for example, the blue *mbumba* co-operating with music producer Joseph Tembo in their aforementioned *Angwazi sendera* creations.

Bibliography

Chanunkha, Robert. 2005. *Music Education in Malawi: The Crisis and the Way Forward*. Unpublished Ph.D. thesis, University of Pretoria.

Chechamba, Wyndham R. 1997. 'Chechamba's Music Story.' *WASI* 9(1): 32.

Chimombo, Steve, and Chimombo, Moira. 1996. *The Culture of Democracy: Language, Literature, the Arts and Politics in Malawi, 1992–94*. Zomba: WASI.

Chirambo, Reuben M. 2009. 'Democracy as a Limiting Factor for Politicized Cultural Populism in Malawi.' *Africa Spectrum* 44(2): 77–94.

Chirwa, Verah. 2007. *Verah Chirwa: Fearless Fighter*. London: Zed Books.

Chirwa, Wiseman J. 2001. 'Dancing Towards Dictatorship: Political Songs and Popular Culture in Malawi.' *Nordic Journal of African Studies* 10(1): 1–27.

Forster, Peter G. 1994. 'Culture, Nationalism, and the Invention of Tradition in Malawi.' *The Journal of Modern African Studies* 32(3): 477–97.

Gilman, Lisa. 2001. 'Purchasing Praise: Women, Dancing, and Patronage in Malawi Party Politicking.' *Africa Today* 48(4): 43–64.

Lwanda, John L. 1993. *Kamuzu Banda of Malawi.* Glasgow: Dudu Nsomba Publications.

Lwanda, John L. 2003. 'Mother's Songs: Male Appropriation of Women's Music in Malawi and Southern Africa.' *Journal of African Cultural Studies* 16(2): 119–42.

Mackay, Peter. 2008. *We Have Tomorrow: Stirrings in Africa, 1959–1967.* Norwich: Michael Russel.

Mkamanga, Emily. 2000. *Suffering in Silence.* Glasgow: Dudu Nsomba Publications.

Muyebe, Stanslaus P., and Muyebe, Alex. 1999. *The Religious Factor Within the Body of Political Symbolism in Malawi, 1964–1994.* Florida: Universal Publishers.

Semu, Linda. 2002. 'Kamuzu's Mbumba: Malawi Women's Embeddedness to Culture in the Face of International Political Pressure and Internal Legal Change.' *Africa Today* 49(2): 77–99.

Vaughan, Megan. 1987. *The Story of an African Famine: Gender and Famine in Twentieth Century Malawi.* Cambridge: Cambridge University Press.

Discographical References

Dowa Mbumba. 'Kokolilo ku Malawi,' 'Azimai akuDowa' and 'Muwalo ndri woononga.' MBC Archives. *c. 1979*: Malawi. (Reissued as Dowa Mbumba. 'Kokolilo ku Malawi,' 'Azimai akuDowa' and 'Muwalo ndri woononga.' *The Sizzling Seventies.* Pamtondo CD PAM070. *2004*: UK.)

Masuka, Dorothy. 'Ei Yow Phata Phata! (Pata Pata).' *1961*: South Africa. (Reissued as Dorothy Masuka, 'Pata Pata.' *The Definitive Collection: Dorothy Masuka, the Grande Dame of African Music.* Wrasse Records WRA SSO89. *2002*: South Africa.)

Rumphi Mbumba. 'Apailoti.' MBC Archives. *c. 1977*: Malawi. (Reissued as Rumphi Mbumba. 'Apailoti.' *The Sizzling Seventies.* Pamtondo CD PAM070. *2004*: UK.)

YouTube

DPP *Mbumba* and Joseph Tembo. DPP Moto moto eya/*Angwazi sendera.* 4 May 2009. Online at: https://www.youtube.com/watch?v=drt05jmyLL8 (accessed 27 January 2015).

Gloria Jane. 'John Brown's Body.' 29 September *2009.* Online at: https://www.youtube.com/watch?v=bSS n3NddwFQ (accessed 27 January 2015).

Kamuzu Banda's Women Dancers 2. Online at: https://www.youtube.com/watch?v=s4e4ZSGwHRc (accessed 27 January 2015).

JOHN LWANDA

See also Cultural Animation Groups

Mchiriku

Mchiriku is a Dar es Salaam street music, popular mainly with the poorer sections of society in Tanzania. The genre features a tiny Casio keyboard amplified to distortion via megaphones and a host of Zaramo drums. Despite a lack of promotion in terms of radio airplay and general media attention, *mchiriku* has become one of Tanzania's major youth musics, along with *bongo flava.* The output of *mchiriku* groups is prolific, with dozens of new releases on the market all the time. *Mchiriku* is performed exclusively for family celebrations, including weddings, male initiations and birthdays, to help the hosts to share the event with family, friends and the neighborhood.

Mchiriku emerged as one of the first new forms under the emerging laissez-faire Tanzanian political regime in the early 1990s. Its definitive sound emanates from a small Casio keyboard that became available in downtown electronics shops around 1991 to 1992. The keyboard also gives the music its alternative name *mnanda* (from *kinanda,* a 'small musical instrument/box'). As the name suggests, the small keyboard and its amplification through megaphones is the genre's distinguishing mark. The powerful sound and the typical aesthetics of distortion may well have been significant factors in *mchiriku*'s rise as an emerging youth music throughout the 1990s.

Mchiriku grew out of earlier types of *ngoma* (drum- and dance-based entertainments) prominent in the city area, namely *chakacha* and *vanga. Chakacha* originated as a female dance in Kenyan coastal towns such as Mombasa. The distinctive fast rhythm of *chakacha* and the character of its sexually charged lyrics were picked up and popularized beyond the

Kenya coast by Mombasa-based *taarab* groups including Zuhura Swaleh and Maulidi Juma. In Dar es Salaam the different strands morphed together and *chakacha* became a small-ensemble, low-cost version of *taarab* for performances at weddings in the city's suburbs.

Most early *mchiriku* groups grew out of *chakacha* groups by replacing the Indian harmonium with a Casio keyboard, which was lightweight, less prone to damage, and easy to amplify by simply plugging into an amplifier. The louder and more powerful sound of the amplified keyboard soon necessitated changes in the accompanying percussion instruments as well. The *tabla* was dispensed with and replaced by a pair of small local hand drums called *dumbaki* (roughly resembling the size of *bongos* and held the same way between the legs); initially the single *msondo* was replaced by a set of two, also positioned between the legs. In due course a third bass drum was added by the *msondo* player to give the music more bottom range and keep up with the volume of the amplified keyboard and voice. The percussion lineup of three *msondro (msondo)*, two *dumbaki*, *mkwasa* (timing sticks beaten on a stool) and *chekeche* became the standard used by all groups.

The earliest *mchiriku* recordings (e.g., Night Star Musical Club 's *Mabingwa wa mchiriku*, 1993) still exhibit the *chakacha* lineage, with the percussion played in an easily flowing manner, well tuned and interlocking, not yet displaying the dynamics and drive that was to characterize *mchiriku* in the early 2000s. The Casio players perform single-handed in the manner in which they learned on harmonium or accordion before moving to the keyboard. Soon, however, the best players developed a two-handed playing style, executing interlocking patterns and crossing arms to make use of the diminutive keyboard. The right hand plays a regular pattern, broken chords akin to the rhythm guitar playing in *muziki wa dansi*; the right hand then crosses over and adds an independent high-pitched solo pattern. These high-pitched sounds work especially well when the Casio is amplified with a megaphone and its cone, adding additional overtones that enable the music to be heard far and wide. From afar what is heard first when approaching a performance is usually a high-pitched din, and this has contributed to the music's most popular name, *mchiriku* (from Swahili *chiriku*, meaning 'finch').

The first groups to appear in the early 1990s were Night Star Musical Club and Jamhuri Musical Club, both based in Kariakoo (the central and oldest African living quarter). As the music became increasingly popular all over Dar es Salaam, groups popped up by the dozens in all local quarters. One of the longest-lived groups is Jagwa Music, whose origins lay in Mvita Orchestra, a *chakacha* group. In 1992 (immediately after the first Gulf War) some musicians left to form a new group called Scud; then, following a further rift, another new group was formed, named, Jaguar Musical Club (after the French fighter plane). That group has since recorded 15 albums, becoming the most popular *mchiriku* group around Dar es Salaam in the early 2000s. Jagwa Music became an internationally famous act, and since 2010 has toured many countries (including the United States in 2016) and performed at major festivals throughout the world.

Mchiriku street performances were prohibited by the local authorities in the second half of the 1990s and again in 2014, mostly for extramusical reasons such as robberies and killings taking place in the vicinity of performances. Yet despite these official bans, media neglect, and its reliance on channels outside the regular music industry for production, *mchiriku* is firmly established as the major alternative youth musical expression in the second decade of the twenty-first century. Jagwa Music's success on international stages may ultimately lead to wider acceptance within Tanzania, where most evaluations of the style are based on extramusical factors such as its association with the city's perceived low-life. An in-depth study of the style's history and social significance is urgently needed as hardly any documentation exists beyond the few surviving cassette recordings.

Bibliography

Graebner, Werner. 2006. 'Tanzania-Popular Music: The Land of Use-Your-Brain.' In *The Rough Guide to World Music: Africa and the Middle East*, eds. Simon Broughton et al. London: Rough Guides, 418–29.

Graebner, Werner. 2013. 'Respect, Man, Respect!' In *Herbst: Theorie zur Praxis* [Autumn: Theory for Praxis], ed. Steirischer Herbst. Graz: Steirischer Herbst Festival, 146–9.

Graebner, Werner. 2016. 'Other Flavas from Bongo: Mchiriku-Segere-Baikoko.' In *Mambo Moto*

Moto – Music in Tanzania Today, ed. Tiago de Oliveira Pinto and Bernhard Hanneken. Berlin: VWB – Verlag für Wissenschaft und Bildung, 73–94.

Discographical Reference
Night Star Musical Club. *Mabingwa wa mchiriku.* FKW. *Ca. 1993*: Tanzania.

Discography
Jagwa Music. *Bongo Hotheads.* Crammed Discs CRAW 80. *2012*: Belgium.

WERNER GRAEBNER

Mdundiko

Mdundiko is a *ngoma* (song/dance accompanied by drums) practiced in Dar es Salaam, Tanzania and surrounding areas. Its height of popularity was in the 1970s and 1980s when it became a popular evening pastime for young people around the city; by the 2000s it was a constitutive part of Tanzania's social imaginary.

Mdundiko's origins are with the Zaramo (the major ethnic group living in Dar es Salaam and the surrounding area), where it is one of the festive music and dance forms performed at life cycle events such as *jando* (boys' initiation), girls' coming of age or weddings. As a procession dance that moves from house to house or quarter to quarter to announce the festivity to relatives and friends, it is an especially visible part of musical life in Dar es Salaam. When it is stationary, the dancers form a circle, with individuals or pairs entering to show their skills. As the festivity continues into the night, *mdundiko* turns into *vanga*, its faster-paced twin. Percussion ranges from two to three smaller instruments for the procession to a full array of *chapuo, msondo, simba* (differently sized and tuned drums), *bati* (sheet iron or oil can) and *mkwasa* (short wooden sticks) for the stationary version. Also, for the procession, sometimes there is a crossover into *beni bati* (the modern-day coastal descendant of the old *beni* genre), with one trumpet and military bass drum added; the repertoire may also include rhythms and songs from both genres. *Mdundiko* songs are in Zaramo and Swahili languages; as suits the occasion of life cycle rituals, many songs touch on moral teaching and sexual matters. Typical Zaramo vocals are performed in hocket fashion, spreading individual notes and syllables among several singers.

With its high visibility and popularity in Tanzania's major city, *mdundiko* has come to be perceived as a synonym for 'traditional' dance, possibly also because in the national language of Swahili *mdundo* has a number of meanings associated with drums, rhythm and the sound of drumming. Thus the association is an immediate one for almost everyone. That *mdundiko* is an important part of the local imaginary is borne out by its frequent adoption and dispersal into other art forms. In the 1980s, for example, Remmy Ongala and Super Matimila paid tribute to the style in their song 'Mariamu wangu' with verbal and rhythmic/melodic references; and in the 2000s the band Young Stars Modern Taarab (now Segere Original) had a number of hit songs with a new style called *segere* that transferred rhythms and melodies of both *mdundiko* and *vanga* to modern instruments and production. On a more imaginary plane, in the 2010s a number of *bongo flava* hip-hop artists have referenced *mdundiko* either verbally or with imagery in songs and videoclips. A 2013 feature film carries *mdundiko* in its title, referencing 'traditional' *ngoma* practices rather than the original Zaramo *mdundiko*, and also carrying a rather moralistic undertone and critique of medical and mystical practices formerly attached to many *ngoma*.

Discographical Reference
Ongala, Remmy, and Super Matimila. 'Mariamu wangu.' *Songs for the Poor Man*. Real World RWLP 6. 1989: UK.

Discography
Ngoma za wazaramo. Radio Tanzania Dar es Salaam No. 57. N.d.: Tanzania.
Young Stars Modern Taarab. *Segere.* FKW. N.d. [*2002*]: Tanzania.

Filmography
Mdundiko, dir. Jackson Kabirigi. 2013. Tanzania. 129 mins. Feature film.

WERNER GRAEBNER

Medeh

Medeh (praise), or *medeh an-nabi* (praise of the Prophet), is the traditional religious music style of the Trab el-Bidhân region, particularly performed throughout Mauritania, Western Sahara and the Saharawi refugee camps in southwest Algeria. As in other North African countries such as Tunisia (Jankowsky 2010) or Morocco (Langlois 1998), this type of spiritual music is closely associated with the history of trade and slavery, particularly black slavery, in the West Saharan region.

The *medeh* praises are spiritual chants in Hassâniya – the local Bidhân dialect of Arabic – dedicated to the life and deeds of the prophet Mohamed and other similar subjects, usually accompanied by the *tbal* drum and characteristic clapping patterns. As a crossroads culture of Berber, Arab and sub-Saharan origins, the Bidhân have a mixture of social and cultural characteristics traditionally based on nomadism and oral transmission, and the great majority of the twenty-first-century population practices Islam. In particular, the performance of *medeh* is associated with Thursday evenings – the night before the Muslim day of rest – and religious festivities such as the holy month of Ramadan and the celebration of the Eid al-fitr (end of Ramadan) and the Eid al-adha (sacrifice of the lamb), among others.

The *medeh* is usually performed, although not exclusively, by black families associated with the *harâtîn* or descendants of former slaves (Norris 1968; Cleveland 2002). For centuries, the Western part of the Sahara accommodated a vital network of routes between strategic points and desert cities that were key to the development of important trans-Saharan trade camel caravans. These convoys transported all types of goods from north to south and vice versa: salt, gold, ivory, cloths, nutmeg, leather, and also slaves, mostly of sub-Saharan descent. Within the Bidhân culture, the black population was quickly assimilated into its own traditions, especially the speaking of Hassâniya, the practice of Islam, and their praises, although they have remained marginalized.

In the main cities in Mauritania (mostly) and Western Sahara, the *medeh* is usually performed in the evenings in private houses or spaces habilitated for special social gatherings, such as large marquees or tents on side streets. In the nomadic camps in the desert, it is also common to see *medeh* performed outside by the fire. Sometimes, but not always, these events have an open-door policy, and family and friends are invited to gather, share a meal, and get involved in the performance. Performers sit on the floor forming a semicircle around the drummer, who gives the cue for the polyrhythmic clapping to start. The lead singer – usually a man in Mauritania and Western Sahara, but almost always a woman in the Saharawi refugee camps – is the one in charge of performing the main vocal line, answered by the others in a call-and-response style. When the main singer is performing, it is common to hear the rest of the group encouraging him or her with *zgarit* (ululations) and typical vocal expressions such as 'aski,' 'hah' and 'shhh,' which show their appreciation. As a general norm, *medeh* performers are very specialized and committed to using their talent only to praise Allah and his Prophet Mohamed, thus securing their entrance into Paradise.

Bibliography

Cleveland, Timothy. 2002. *Becoming Walata: A History of Saharan Social Formation and Transformation*. Portsmouth: Heinemann.

Jankowsky, Richard C. 2010. *Stambeli: Music, Trance, and Alterity in Tunisia*. Chicago: University of Chicago Press.

Langlois, Tony. 1998. 'The Gnawa of Oujda: Music at the Margins in Morocco.' *The World of Music* 40(1): 135–56.

Norris, Harry Thirlwall. 1968. *Shinqiti Folk Literature and Song*. Oxford: Oxford University Press.

VIOLETA RUANO

Merengue in Angola

Angolan *merengue* is a localized interpretation of the Caribbean *merengue* that is popular in Haiti, Dominican Republic, Colombia and Venezuela. Angolan *merengue* developed in the 1960s and 1970s during the later years of Portuguese colonial rule as a local recorded music industry was emerging.

When record shops opened in Angola's capital, Luana, in the 1950s, singles of Caribbean genres, including *merengue* and *soca*, were among the most popular. As an influx of white Portuguese immigrants moved to Luanda, economic and political opportunities for the city's African residents diminished and many moved from the city center to the outlying neighborhoods, known as *musseques*. Angolans who had recently relocated from rural areas also moved into the *musseques*, and these areas became the cultural and political center of the country. Music clubs opened in the *musseques*, particularly Marçal and Sambizanga, and musicians performed original hybrid music, including *merengue*, *kazukuta* and *semba*, that drew on Caribbean music and local rhythms, lyrics and instrumentation.

Angolan *merengue* arrangements are up-tempo and based on four-beat rhythm patterns. The Angolan version differs from its Caribbean counterparts through the incorporation of local instrumentation and rhythms. Productions are also distinguished by their production values, as engineers favor saturated tones and bring mixed percussion and guitars to the fore, relatively de-emphasizing other melodic parts. Guitars feature as the main melodic instrument with a lightly distorted electric lead and a softer acoustic rhythm guitar, accompanied by bass guitar and occasionally horns. Percussion is performed predominantly by hand on *bongó*, *tumba* and *ngoma* drums. The *dikanza*, a long, hollow, ridged idiophone is scraped and tapped to create a cross rhythm throughout many *merengues* and is one of the characteristic sounds of the Angolan form. *Merengue* can be performed either instrumentally or with vocalists. Vocal arrangements such as 'Kiezo merengue' tend to feature a dominant lead singer with minimal harmonies.

By the late 1960s a local record industry had emerged that could record, manufacture, release and distribute local music. As Angolan-produced records started to emerge on labels such as Fadiang, Ngola, Valentim de Carvalho and Companhia de Discos de Angola (CDA), the musicians who developed skills and followings in the *musseques* were able to release their music. Some labels were independent and locally owned, while others had the backing of international labels such as EMI. CDA launched the subsidiary label Merengue in the mid-1970s and released work by singers Teto Lando, Carlos Lamartine and David Zé. The house band Conjunto Merengue was led by Carlos Vieira Dias and featured a large and revolving lineup that included Gregório Mulato, Zeca Tirilene, Vate Costa and Joãozinho Morgado.

A rapid decline in the recording industry followed independence in 1975. By 1978 the Angolan Civil War had affected cultural production and the recording industry had collapsed. The political and military conflict in Angola disrupted live performance and led to a scarcity of imported instruments. Many of the groups that performed *merengue* in the 1970s disbanded and the genre declined in prevalence. Although fewer groups performed *merengue* in the 1980s, elements of the music and dance influenced the *kizomba* genre. As *kizomba* dance clubs emerged internationally in the mid-2000s, interest in *merengue* returned and compilations of *merengue* singles were reissued internationally and became available in Angola. Alongside *semba*, *kazukuta* and *rebita*, *merengue* is recognized in Angolan national memory as synonymous with the cultural and political struggles and development of postcolonial Angolan identity, or *Angolanidade*.

Bibliography

Alves, Amanda. 2013. 'Angola: musicalidade, política e anticolonialismo (1950–1980)' [Angola: Musicality, Politics and Anti-colonialism (1950–1980)]. *Revista Tempo e Argumento* 5(10): 373–96.

Moorman, Marissa. 2008. *Intonations: A Social History of Music and Nation in Luanda, Angola, from 1945 to Recent Times*. Athens, OH: Ohio University Press.

Discographical Reference

Os Kiezos. 'Kiezo merengue.' *Memorias*. Luanda, Ngola Musica. (CD.) RNAPQ003. *2005*: Angola.

Discography

Angola Soundtrack: The Unique Sound of Luanda 1968–1976 (ed. Samy Ben Redjeb). Analog Africa AACD 069. *2010*: Germany.

Angola Soundtrack 2 – Hypnosis, Distortions & Other Sonic Innovations 1969–1978 (ed. Samy Ben Redjeb). Analog Africa AACD 075. *2005*: Germany.

Lamartine, Carlos, and Conjunto Merengue. *Angola Ano 1*. Companhia de Discos de Angola NALP-6001. *1975*: Angola.

Minguito. 'Merengue 16.' Rebita R.1016. *1973*: Angola.

GARTH SHERIDAN

Milo Jazz

Milo jazz is a popular street music genre in Sierra Leone. It involves vigorous dancing and loud percussion instruments that are played with great intensity. Its emergence in the early 1970s highlighted the beginning of a novel kind of street music that modernized the country's existing *gumbe* and *maringa* genres. Compared to the sound of the older genres, *Milo jazz* had a brighter, more modern sonority that seemed more in tune with the musical spirit of the age. *Milo jazz* remained a feature of street life in the capital, Freetown, until the Civil War of the 1990s devastated the city's cultural expressions.

Milo jazz was named after the signature percussion instrument created by filling Milo malted chocolate drink cans with stones, which produced what Sierra Leone-born poet Roland Eben Marke (2017[2007]) has described as a 'mesmerizing, soulful percussion music.' 'Milo' was also the nickname of a locally brewed alcoholic drink that was very popular among the working-class people of Sierra Leone. Such names were necessary as locally brewed spirits were illegal up to the end of the rebel war and anyone caught either distilling or drinking them was guilty of a crime punishable by fine or imprisonment. In the early twenty-first century the government of Sierra Leone seems to have relaxed the restrictions, but makers of the local spirit still continue to brew under cover.

Musical Characteristics

Milo jazz is strongly associated with the musician and bandleader Olohrunfeh Israel Johnson ('Dr. Oloh,' 1944–2007), who with his Milo Jazz Band gave this music its start (see Horton 1999, fig. 18.4). The compositions of Dr. Oloh's ensemble became the standard for other lesser-known *Milo jazz* ensembles.

When Milo jazz came into existence in the late 1970s, the number of skilled *gumbe* players had dwindled and the traditional instruments of the *gumbe* ensemble were gradually disappearing from use. At the same time, there was a growing emphasis on the uniqueness of African heritage. This was reflected in the quality and instrumentation of popular bands, which had in the past utilized a number of Western instruments at the expense of their traditional counterparts, and in the desire among those bands to focus on innovative use not only of the traditional instruments but also of attire and language.

This movement witnessed the formation of such bands as Masokoloko, which utilized the slit drums (*inkali*) of the Limba ethnic group and the traditional palm-frond attire used by Poro musicians of the Mende ethnic group (Limbas do not have Poro society but rather Matoma, which is their own secret society). The Group Afro Nationale featured vocalist Patricia Koroma, a Mende by ethnicity, who sang a number of popular songs in Mende. The group Sabanoh 75 formed in honor of I.T.A. Wallace-Johnson, a Creole politician, who used the slogan 'Sabanoh' (meaning 'victory') in reference to a high-profile court case he had won. Dr. Dynamite and his Afro-Rhythms, led by Johnson Johnson, was another representative band of this time.

Initially, the *Milo jazz* ensemble was formed by doubling the number of instruments characterizing the *gumbe* ensemble, adding instruments borrowed from other ethnic traditions as well as the signature instrument of *Milo jazz*, the Milo can rattle. Among the instruments added was the *kongoma*, a bass lamellophone from the Limba and Loko ethnic groups (see Horton 1999, fig. 18.5) made from a rectangular wooden sound box with a sound hole, over which three pieces of hack saw are usually fastened. When these metal pieces are plucked with the thumb and index fingers of both hands, they are amplified in the sound box. The *kongoma* plays the role of string bass, sounding a limited number of partials. According to Van Oven (1981), the three-pronged *kongoma* can play the tonic chord but with the harmonic background role limited to the sounding of only three pitches of that chord. The *kongoma* sometimes falls out of tune, resulting in frequent dissonant pitches, including the harsh-sounding augmented fourth interval. Another addition was a triangle, borrowed from the Limba and Loko and known by those groups as the 'koto' or 'kenken' (Horton 1979, 176). This unpitched idiophone is formed from a horseshoe-shaped piece of iron rod used in building construction. It is used to produce the metallic sound effect heard in *Milo jazz*. A bass-box, similar to that used in the *gumbe* ensemble, was also featured as an 'answer bass-box' or second bass-box, which alternated background rhythms with the first bass-box to give the players some respite (see Horton 1999, 232, fig. 18.3).

The master drum of the *Milo jazz* ensemble was the two-in-one drum (see Horton 1999, fig. 18.6), a borrowing from the Fula ethnic group, who call the drum 'jimberu' (see Horton 1979, 165). Made of a pair of conical *conga* drums, the *jimberu* lacks the traditional idiophonic attachment of metal strung with wire rings that rattle as the player drums on the skin. The two drums are fastened together to facilitate their playing.

Other instruments included various shakers and rattles that produced jingling effects. Originally, there was a mouth organ, but this was replaced by the bugle, which was used to add a brighter sound to a percussion-based ensemble. The bugle player was usually a novice who could play only two pitches, the tonic and dominant, which were alternated and repeated over and over in a rhythmic sequence, serving to coordinate the players in the absence of a conductor.

Gary Stewart (1987) suggests that Dr. Oloh considered (but decided against) the inclusion of some additional instruments in his ensemble in the late 1980s, including the electric guitar (as the acoustic guitar was felt to be growing out of style) and the *kondi*, another Limba lamellophone, which plays higher pitches than the *kongoma* but which also experiences the latter's tuning problems (Horton 1979, 337). Also under consideration was the *kilii* or *kalei* of the Mende ethnic group (see Horton 1979, fig. 1), a log drum with three slits that provide three different tone colors, capable of enhancing the overall sonority of the ensemble. Selecting traditional instruments was problematic, however, because of the difficulty of finding instruments that stay in tune. Dr. Oloh instead emphasized drums, bells, rattles and vocals.

In performance, Dr. Oloh's band used the gong drum and bass drum to lay the background foundation for the music and the tenor drum, with the Milo can rattles and friction bottles to color the sound. The *kongoma*, *koto*, *kenken* and *kondi* add dissonance and 'smear' the execution of the melody, creating a texture that is a mixture of monophony and heterophony. Dr. Oloh himself was the lead vocalist with a group of male voices as support. The rhythms of the songs were prominent and consistent to sustain the interest of the dancers. (Dr. Oloh and his band visited the United Kingdom several times during the 1990s and were recorded in London on 10 October 1991 and 3 September 1992 for a BBC radio program presented by the English DJ John Peel [see YouTube below]).

The lyrics of the songs were bold and daring and sometimes sensuous to the point of vulgarity. Lyrics for the most part addressed issues of street life, sexual attraction, marriage and political events that affected the everyday life of the people. Dr. Oloh was opposed to war and spoke out against violence, dictatorship and anarchy during the rebel wars of the 1990s. He advocated for peace, unity and happiness, and was beaten up during the rebel wars that ended in 2002. As if anticipating his demise in October 2007, he composed a song with the lyrics 'usai we get foh go when den rebel go kam foh kill wi' (roughly meaning 'where can we take shelter when the rebel come to kill us'). Another politically engaged song, 'Momoh noh worry,' celebrated the transfer of power from President Siaka Probyn Stevens, who governed from the late 1970s to the mid-1980s, to Brigadier J.S. Momoh, then the former head of the Sierra Leone military forces. Stevens resigned in hopes of forestalling a military coup d'état, but to no avail. Dr. Oloh used parabolic language to convey, roughly, 'what God has destined for anyone no man can stop from happening.'

Other songs were used for weddings, for example, 'Aleluyah Tumbay' ('admiring the rolling hips of women well dressed for the wedding') and 'Yawo Mami Ebi So' (roughly a reference to the well-dressed mother of the bride). Some of the content was explicitly sexual, for example, 'Ol Mi Bobbi Lef Mi Wase Foh Mi Man' (roughly meaning 'You can touch the boobs of the woman but not her buttocks because that part of a woman's body is privately reserved for her husband').

Performance Context and Dance Style

Milo jazz is street dancing music; at the sound of the drums, the arena would quickly fill with eager dancers. In the music's heyday, the band paraded through the streets amid great commotion. The musicians played vigorously and, with the bugle controlling the music, it was easy for the dancing to become rowdy, with participants bumping into each other. Everyone danced energetically within minutes of starting, as *Milo jazz* dancing usually lasted much longer than that in either *gumbe* or *maringa*. The dance was free but high-energy, continuing until the dancers were covered with perspiration. The participants called this type of dancing 'gee bodi wata' (roughly meaning 'dance until one is completely drenched with sweat'). Most dancers could last for only a single dance. Dancers performed a mixture of the same four steps found in the *gumbe* dance: (1) 'ole wase'; (2) 'shake wase'; (3) 'cut belleh'; (4) 'cut belleh en shake wase.' Whereas, in the *gumbe* dance, the dancer slowly developed the different steps, repeating each step as necessary to reach a climax, in *Milo jazz*, there was a total disregard for the sequence of the dance steps.

Milo jazz dancing had a large following since no one had to concentrate on the nuances as in the *gumbe* dance. However, because it ignored the classic *gumbe* style, many of the older generation of the 1970s and

1980s feared it was corrupting and could lead to a loss of tradition. In the twenty-first century young people still enjoy dancing to recordings of *Milo jazz* music because it is rhythmic and the most recent of all the local popular genres.

Bibliography

Deen, Akie. 2007. 'In Memoriam.' *Standard Times Press News*, 18 October.

Fadlu-Deen, Kitty. 2015. *Milo and All That Jazz*. N.p.: Createspace Independent Publishing.

Horton, Christian'Dowu. 1979. *Indigenous Music of Sierra Leone: An Analysis of Resources and Educational Implications*. Unpublished Ph.D. dissertation, University of California, Los Angeles.

Horton, Christian'Dowu Jayeola. 1999. 'The Role of the Gumbe in Popular Music and Dance Styles in Sierra Leone.' In *Turn Up the Volume! A Celebration of African Music*, ed. Jacqueline Cogdell DjeDje. Los Angeles: UCLA Fowler Museum of Cultural History, 230–5.

Marke, Roland Eben. 2017. 'Musician of the Week: Dr. Oloh.' *The Patriotic Vanguard* 22 February. Online at: http://www.thepatrioticvanguard.com/dr-Olohh-a-cornerstone-of-sierra-leonean-music (accessed 29 May 2018). (First published 2007.)

Stewart, Gary. 1987. 'Dr. Oloh's Milo Jazz.' *West Africa*, 22 June: 1202–3.

Discographical References

Dr. Oloh and Milo Jazz. 'Usai We Geht Foh Go Wen Denh Rebels Go Kam For Kill Wi,' 'Momoh Nor Worry,' 'Aleluyah Tumbay,' 'Yawo Mami Ebi So,' 'Ol Mi Bobbi Lef Mi Wase Foh Mi Man.' *Tape 3*. (Field recordings by Christian Horton, to be deposited at the UCLA music library.) *1999*: Sierra Leone.

Discography

Dr. Oloh. 'Du Yu Yone Lef Mi Yone.' HMV JZ 5240. *1980s*: Sierra Leone.

Dr. Oloh. 'Na Marade Ring Yu Want'; 'Yuba Noh Geht Paypa.' HMV JV 5256. *1980s*: Sierra Leone.

Dr. Oloh. 'Yu Eat Mi Moni, Yu Say Yu Nor Want Me.' HMV JZ 5998. *1980s*: Sierra Leone.

YouTube

(accessed 7 June 2018)

Dr Oloh & His Milo Jazz Band. 'Aleluyah Tumbay.' (Peel Session): https://www.youtube.com/watch?reload=9&v=hQY5j-NKU_k

Dr Oloh & His Milo Jazz Band. 'Yawohammi.' (Peel Session): https://www.youtube.com/watch?v=K_KNKLe9wEU

CHRISTIAN 'DOWU JAYEOLA HORTON

Moppie

The *moppie*, from the Dutch word *mopje* (little joke, pronounced mawpi), is a comic song, with a topical, coherent text, sung by the minstrel troupes and Malay Choirs in Cape Town, South Africa. It is used to ridicule often serious matters, which range in subject from politics to social issues around gender and sexual orientation. Satire and ridicule were ways in which subaltern peoples were able to voice their opinions on matters affecting them under the oppressive governments of the British administration and apartheid regime. It is believed that these songs emerged out of the period of slavery (1653–1838), initially under the Dutch, and that creating and singing songs were means of coping with the dire conditions of slaves (Martin 1999, 49).

Several *moppies* offer sociopolitical commentary or satire, often subversively; the words of one *moppie* in response to the 1952 tercentenary celebrations of Jan van Riebeeck's landing at the Cape, 'Hey, babariebab se ding is wim,' imply that van Riebeeck is impotent. Van Riebeeck was a key figure in colonial and apartheid symbology as the Dutch colonial administrator tasked with setting up a refreshment station at the Cape for the Dutch East India Company (VOC) along the trade route to Asia. During the height of apartheid this coded message clearly indicated the opinion of the subaltern peoples about the lavish celebrations held by white South Africans.

Another example of this kind of political critique is a *moppie* that emerged in the 1990s attacking the Value Added Tax first introduced in October 1991 that replaced general sales tax (see South African History Online and Martin 2005). Among the *moppies* most exuberantly appreciated by singers and audiences are those satirizing the *moffie* (a transvestite, pronounced mawfi), in which the soloist's actions often involve exaggerated, feminized hand and body movements. In 2018 people sang about the severe water crisis that affected Cape Town.

The *moppie* is a fast-paced responsorial action song with a soloist who mimes the lyrics energetically and comically, supported by a chorus that stands behind him, moving to the music and imitating some of the soloist's actions. Musical bricolage is apparent in the construction of these songs, with phrases from several well-known melodies, especially popular US hits and Christian songs such as 'Jerusalem' or 'O Tannenbaum,' strung together to create a new song. Musically, the excitement of the *moppie* results from the *ghoema* rhythm played on the *ghoema* drum and the accompanying rhythmic strumming of guitars and banjos. The banjo stridently drives this characteristic local rhythm, and is a salient marker of the timbral preferences of the music of Cape Town.

The *moppie* features primarily as a competitive genre sung at the Minstrel Carnival and Malay Choir competitions held during the summer months (January to March). It often uses *double entendre* alluding to sociopolitical situations or sexual matters. People enjoy this allusory kind of humor and the *moppie* remains very popular as many new songs in this genre are composed annually for the competitions ensuring its persistence as a local genre.

Bibliography

Martin, Denis-Constant. 1999. *Coon Carnival: New Year in Cape Town, Past and Present.* Cape Town: David Philip Publishers.

South African History Online: Towards a Peoples' History. Online at: http://www.sahistory.org.za/dated-event/value-added-tax-vat-replaces-general-sales-tax (12 September 2017).

Discography

The Tulips. *South Africa: The Cape Town Minstrels.* Musique du Monde. *1999*: France.

SYLVIA R. BRUINDERS

Morna

As one of the oldest genres of Cabo Verdean music, the *morna* has its roots in the nineteenth century. Like many Cabo Verdean traditions, it is thought to have absorbed a variety of influences, including the Portuguese *fado*, the Brazilian *modinha*, Angolan rhythms, Arabic music and even British sea shanties. In Cabo Verde, poverty, isolation and harsh climate have generated a society built around high rates of emigration, resulting in a ubiquitous theme of *sodadi* – an intense longing for something deeply missed. The *morna* embodies the essence of Cabo Verdean *sodadi* and beautifully conveys the pain of separation, the sadness of departure or lost love. It is considered by many to be the clearest manifestation of pan-Cabo Verdean identity, as well as its most sophisticated and erudite musical form.

Lyrics are always written in the vernacular language of Cabo Verde, Kriolu (Creole), which is a mix of archaic Portuguese and several African languages, and serves as an undeniable mark of Cabo Verdean identity. *Mornas* are written almost exclusively from a male perspective and most commonly have romantic themes and use images of nature associated with the islands to emphasize depth of sentiment. The narrative can relate to an individual idealized woman, a *cretcheu* (beloved), or it can be a larger metaphorical reference to Cabo Verde itself.

The music is in a slow 4/4 or 2/4 meter with wide-ranging melodies in which each strophe and refrain is repeated (AABB). Harmonically the *morna* vacillates between major and minor tonality, and is commonly set in the key of A minor. The melodies reflect this instability with pitch variation on the third and seventh notes of the scale, but also in microtonal upward *appoggiaturas* at the beginning of phrases, the frequency and depth of which vary by performer.

The genre's Iberian roots are clear from its primarily string accompaniment, which is traditionally composed of at least two guitars, a *cavaquiño* (a small four-string guitar similar to a ukelele), a violin and, if available, a piano or clarinet. Since the 1980s, however, it is not uncommon for *mornas* to incorporate Latin American, African or Middle Eastern musical instruments and elements. With the exception of some older Cabo Verdeans, few still dance the *morna*, an extremely slow couples' dance.

Because music, and the *morna* in particular, is seen as the crux of Cabo Verdean identity, pinpointing *morna*'s source, however elusive, is somewhat of an obsession for music scholars. It is generally believed that the *morna* originated on the island of Boa Vista. Due to its abundance of salt, this island was a frequent stop for ships of many nationalities between the seventeenth and nineteenth centuries, each leaving their own musical influences. There is, however, little agreement on the nature of that source. The possibilities include humorous songs of failed romances, women's call-and-response work songs, an Afro-Brazilian-influenced dance form known as the *lundum*, or the *landú*, a Boavistense version of the *lundum*, primarily sung at weddings. The oldest known *morna*, 'Brada Maria,' anonymously composed on Boa Vista around 1870, tells the story of an abandoned, heart-broken young woman, indicating a transition into more serious lyrics.

The first well-known composer of the *morna*, Eugénio Tavares, was born on the island of Brava in 1867. He is considered the 'father' of this form because of the beauty and clarity of his Kriolu lyrics. During his lifetime the populations of Brava and Fogo were decimated by large numbers of men joining American whaling ships which passed through their waters. One of his best-known compositions, 'Hora di bai' (Hour of Leaving), reflects the heartbreak of those leaving Cabo Verde, perhaps forever, and was traditionally sung at the docks in Brava as the men left. He died in 1930 as a national hero, leaving behind a large repertoire of *mornas*, many of which Cabo Verdeans learn by heart as children and carry through their lives.

If Tavares elevated the lyrics of the *morna*, the composer Francisco Xavier da Cruz, known as B. Léza (1905–58) from the city of Mindelo on the island of São Vicente, revolutionized the musical aspects of the form (Monteiro 1998, 22). Influenced by Brazilian music, he enriched and expanded the harmonic complexity by incorporating passing seventh chords and modulations. His many compositions, such as 'Miss Perfumado,' 'Tanha' and 'Terra longe' (Distant Land), are still an important part of the modern repertoire.

The earliest *morna* recordings were made in Lisbon in the 1950s, when a young Cabo Verdean singer, Fernando Quejas, recorded and promoted compositions of Eugénio Tavares, B. Léza and others (see Quejas 1994). The *morna* served as a strong symbol of resistance to Portuguese occupation, especially during the war of liberation in the late 1960s and early 1970s. At that time many singers, the most prolific of whom was Bana, recorded in Lisbon and Rotterdam. In 1965 Voz de Cabo Verde, headed by Luís Morais, transformed and modernized the *morna* with electronic instruments and added instrumentation.

At independence in 1975 Cabo Verdean youth ignored the *morna* in favor of more contemporary electrified music. The form languished until 1985 when Cesaria Évora, a well-known singer from Mindelo, was (re)discovered after a concert sponsored by the Cabo Verdean Women's Association (OMCV). Her subsequent international celebrity caused a renaissance in traditional acoustic (Bau 1996) and neo-traditional recordings (Fantcha 1997). Of particular note were the innovations of Paulino Vieira, Évora's producer and bandleader who, in the process of creating her sound, paved the way for new opportunities for many composers, including Antero Simas, Nhelas Spencer and Manuel D'Novas; and performers, such as Ildo Lobo, Maria Alice, Tito Paris and Bau. From the late 1980s, until her death in 2011, Cesaria was internationally admired. In 2004 she won a Grammy for Best Contemporary World Music Album for *Voz d'amor*.

Although not considered popular music by Cabo Verdean youths, the *morna* holds an important place in the world of Cabo Verdean music. At various times in its development the *morna* has been strongly associated with specific islands in the archipelago, but it should not be exclusively linked to any single island. Its lyrics, music and sentiment have made it larger than all of its influences, African and European, or separate stages of development, because it represents the shared experience of an entire archipelago.

Bibliography

Martins, Vasco. 1988. *A música tradicional cabo-verdiana – I (A morna)* [Traditional Cabo Verdean Music – Vol. I, Morna]. Praia, Cabo Verde: Instituto Cabo-Verdiano do Livro e do Disco.

Monteiro, Vladimir. 1998. *Les musiques du Cap-Vert* [The Musics of Cabo Verde]. Paris: Éditions Chandeigne.

Mortaigne, Véronique. 1997. *Cesaria Evora: La voix du Cap-Vert* [Cesaria Evora: The Voice of Cabo Verde]. Arles: Actes Sud.

Rodrigues, Moacyr, and Lobo, Isabel. 1996. *A morna na literatura tradicional: Fonte para o estudo histórico-literário e a sua repercussão no sociedade* [The Morna in Traditional Literature: Source for Historical-Literary Study and its Repercussions in Society]. Mindelo, São Vicente: Instituto Cabo-Verdiano do Livro e do Disco.

Tavares, Eugénio. 1932. *Mornas: Cantigas crioulas* [Mornas: Creole Songs]. Lisbon: J. Rodrigues.

Discographical References

Bau. *Tôp d'coroa*. Lusafrica 08649-2. *1996*: France.

Évora, Cesaria. *Voz d'amor*. Bluebird 54380. *2003*: France.

Fantcha. *Criolinha*. Lusafrica 262.34-2. *1997*: France.

Quejas, Fernando. 'Carta di nha cretcheu.' *Cabo Verde: Anthology 1959–1992*. Buda Records 92614-2. *1994*: Paris.

Discography

Bana. *A voz ouro: Mornas*. Zé Orlando: Sons D'Africa C 107. *1996*: Portugal.

Cabo Verde: Anthology 1959–1992. Buda Records 92614-2. *1994*: Paris.

Évora, Cesaria. *Miss Perfumado*. Melodie 79540-2. *1992*: France.

Évora, Cesaria. *Cesaria*. Nonesuch 79379-2. *1995*: France.

Évora, Cesaria. *Cabo Verde*. Nonesuch 79450-2. *1997*: France.

Évora, Cesaria. *São Vicente de Longe*. Windham Hill 01934115902. *2001*: France.

Évora, Cesaria. *Nha sentimento*. Lusafrica 562502. *2009*: France/Portugal.

Lobo, Ildo. *Nós morna*. Lusafrica 08834-2. *1996*: France.

Tito Paris ao Vivo no B.Leza. Lusafrica 262.72-2. *1998*: France.

JOANNE HOFFMAN

See also **Morna (in Europe) (Vol. XI, *Europe*)**

Mutia

Mutia (sometimes written as *moutya* or *moutia*) is a Creole musical form practiced in the Seychelles, an archipelago in the Indian Ocean to the east of Madagascar that was colonized by both the French and the British. Historically practiced in the colonial context by African workers and their descendants, the genre is characterized in its traditional form by songs performed in call-and-response (between soloist and chorus) and accompanied by two or three circular, single-headed drums. These formal characteristics demonstrate a clear relationship with the *séga typique* of Mauritius, the *séga tambour* of Rodrigues Island and, to a different extent, the *maloya* of Réunion. Lee explains the similarities between *mutia* and the *séga typique* of Mauritius by pointing to the movement of African slaves and, after Abolition, African contract laborers between the Seychelles and Mauritius during the nineteenth century (Lee 1990).

Until the 1960s *mutia* was practiced during events that were more or less condemned by both the Church and the French and English colonial powers, who viewed dancing as 'licentious.' These festive events gave rise to a significant distribution of musical and choreographic roles. As described by Henri Dauban (1984), two men improvised the lyrics and melody to be sung during the actual dance while drummers stretched the skin drumhead over a fire. Although all of the local young people attended the event, only married women were allowed to dance with men while the rest participated in the chorus, repeating or responding to the phrases sung by the soloists. Dauban notes that 'from time to time, the girls would let out shrill screams to express their pleasure' (1984, 173).

Texts, usually short but repeated over a long period of time, were improvised on themes of everyday life and the events that played out in small village communities. In this sense, *mutia* performed the role of a social regulator, with strong emphasis on interpersonal critique and community conflict management. Over the course of one evening, improvised songs could be integrated into jousts or sorts of duels between the people involved. Metaphors and figurative language also offered a context for creativity in which humor and mockery held an important place.

From the 1960s the traditional context of *mutia* became increasingly rare, almost disappearing completely in the following decades. In the 1970s the independence of the Seychelles led to a re-evaluation of musical traditions and to the development of tourism. *Mutia* was taken up again, played by folk groups, notably the National Cultural Troupe. It was also modernized through the integration of instrumental sounds coming from international trends (electric or acoustic guitar, bass, drum kit, keyboards), and by studio recording techniques (Naylor 1997). Lyrics, whose alternating soloist–chorus structure was sometimes replaced by the alternating verse–chorus structure (in which solo–chorus alternation might not always take place), expanded their aim by going beyond the framework of interpersonal and daily community relationships that had formed the basis of traditional *mutia*'s lyrics. In conjunction with the re-evaluation of African contributions to Creole culture in the Seychelles, *mutia* was recognized as a part of cultural and musical identity as well as an asset for tourism in the archipelago. Along these lines, artists such as Jean-Marc Volsy, John Vital and Patrick Victor composed songs in which *mutia* celebrates the African roots of national and Creole identity and preserves the memory of slavery.

In the 1990s a hybrid form of *mutia* called *mouggae* (*mutia*-reggae) appeared under the influence of reggae and, more specifically, Mauritian *seggae* (*séga*-reggae). El Manager's records had considerable impact in the Seychelles, resulting in the success of *mouggae* among the younger generations. The music is characterized by a ternary rhythm derived from *séga* (or from *mutia*), but in which the accents of the drums, keyboards and guitars have been modified to emphasize the second eighth-note in the triplets, thus drawing closer to the offbeat rhythm characteristic of reggae. Sometimes inspired by international reggae hits, song topics ranged from social protest to entertainment, as well as the advocacy of national pride. Recorded or partly mixed in Great Britain, *mouggae*, as a genre in itself, was no longer in style by the end of the 1990s. However, it helped diversify the practice of playing *mutia*. Artists from the Seychelles sometimes choose to include a *mouggae* in records that are primarily devoted to *séga* (John Vital), reggae (Sonny Morgan) or to a form of local pop music (Ralf).

Bibliography

Dauban, Henri. 1984. 'Propos en vrac d'agronomie sub-équatoriale et d'histoire des Seychelles par Henri Dauban' [Some Thoughts on Sub-Equatorial Agronomy and on the History of the Seychelles by Henri Dauban]. In *Les Seychelles et l'océan Indien* [The Seychelles and the Indian Ocean], ed. B. Koechlin. Paris: L'Harmattan, 151–74.

Koechlin, Bernard, ed. 1984. *Les Seychelles et l'océan Indien* [The Seychelles and the Indian Ocean]. Paris: L'Harmattan.

Lee, Jacques K. 1990. *Séga: The Mauritian Folk Dance*. London: Nautilus.

Mahoune, Jean-Claude. 2004. 'The Origin of the Traditional Music/Dances of the Republic of Seychelles.' *Kabaro* 2–3:285–93.

Naylor, Michael Lee. 1997. 'The Creativity in Culture: Creolization in the Musical Genres of the Seychelles Islands.' Unpublished Master's Thesis, University of Michigan.

Discographical References

Morgan, Sonny. *Island Massive: The Sonny Morgan Collection, Vol. 1*. Sonny Morgan SM 98 90127. *N.d.*: Seychelles.

Ralf. *Profil*, Seychelles Nut R.J.A. 02.98. *1999*: Seychelles.

Ralf. *Zoli zour. Muzik otantik Seychelles*. Seychelles Nut, 20.06. *2000*: Seychelles.

Vital, John. *Bonjour*. Bib's Agency 14 004. *N.d.*: Seychelles.

Discography

El Manager & The Mouggae Boys. *Nouvelle génération*. Disques Dom CM41513. *N.d.*: Seychelles.

Forgotten Music of the Islands. Ocora OCR 582055. *2002*: France.

Musiques populaires des îles Seychelles. Musique du monde/Music from the World, Buda Records, 1984862. *N.d.*: France.

Seychelles All Stars. NDC 02. *2000*: Seychelles.

Seychelles, nouvelles tendances. Night & Day NDCD062. *1999*: Seychelles.

Victor, Patrick. *Memory Lane*. Seychelles Artistic Production. *N.d.*: Seychelles.

Volcy, Jean-Marc. *Leko Bake*. Seychelles Artistic Production 009. *N.d.*: Seychelles.

GUILLAUME SAMSON (TRANSLATED BY ORLENE DENICE MCMAHON)

Muziki Wa Dansi

Muziki wa dansi is Tanzania's version of urban African dance band music. Typically performed in dance or social halls, it is a Swahili-language genre characterized by orchestras that feature electric guitars, a horn section and a host of vocalists. In the three decades following independence in 1961 *muziki wa dansi* established itself as the quasi-national style of Tanzania, dominating radio programming and the live music scene. Political and economic liberalization since the early 1990s also had its impact on the arts and the media landscape, leading to a proliferation of alternative musical entertainments. *Muziki wa dansi* has since lost some of its status, yet it is still acknowledged as the typical sound of Tanzania in the early twenty-first century.

Dansi: The Club Era ca. 1930–65

Popular music forms developed in the urban centers along the East African coast from the early decades of the twentieth century. A first impulse came from colonial marching bands; brass-band instrumentation was adopted into the games of local competitive *ngoma* (dance) societies, first in the Swahili coastal towns and then spreading all over East Africa in the years following World War I. Ranger

(1975) gives a vivid description of this *beni* (from the English 'band') phenomenon. From these groups emerged the earliest so-called *dansi* clubs with their associated bands, with the Dar es Salaam Jazz Band among the first in 1932. These bands were found in most towns of the mainland of what was then Tanganyika. They played foxtrots, waltzes and *son*, with instrumentation based on sets of local drums and stringed instruments including mandolin, ukulele or guitar. In due course, they adopted trumpets, flutes and clarinets. Like the *beni* clubs before them, these *dansi* clubs fostered friendly rivalry between clubs located in the major towns. Both the club structure and a lack of recording outlets for individual artists helped to foster the still-apparent strong group-based sound and identity in Tanzanian music.

The 1950s and early 1960s scene was dominated by the Dar, Kilwa and Western Jazz Bands (all based in Dar es Salaam), Cuban Marimba and Morogoro Jazz Band (Morogoro), Kiko Kids and Tabora Jazz (Tabora), Atomic and Jamhuri Jazz (Tanga). All these bands were very much collective efforts, with only one individual standing out: Salum Abdallah, founder and lead singer of Cuban Marimba, and the most famous Tanzanian musician throughout the 1950s and early 1960s. As the band's name indicates, it tried to strike a balance between the influence of Cuban *son* and the sound of the *marimba* (a local version of the handheld lamellophones called *mbira* or *sanza* elsewhere in Africa), and the band included melodies and rhythms from local *ngoma* dances in its repertoire. Salum Abdallah and Cuban Marimba was one of the few bands to be documented on recordings (the Mombasa-based Mzuri label released their songs in the 1950s and early 1960s). Some recordings by the Dar es Salaam Jazz Band and a few regional orchestras were made by Hugh Tracey/ILAM and released on Gallo Records in the early 1950s. Otherwise, the only recordings made in Tanganyika were those by the local radio station (Tanganyika Broadcasting Service, subsequently Radio Tanzania Dar es Salaam [RTD]), a situation that pertained in the post-independence era.

Ujamaa: The National Phase 1965–90

In the years following independence in 1961, the new government applied its Ujamaa policy of self-determination to the cultural sphere, trying to create a national culture by 'seek[ing] out the best of the traditions and customs of all our tribes' (Nyerere 1962/1966). Urban popular musics such as *muziki wa dansi* were suspect as colonial imports, yet the majority of the population did not accept as valid entertainment an artificial national *ngoma* style with its lyrics praising government and party. Official policy grudgingly accepted *muziki wa dansi* as the most popular style, but not without some attempts at engineering: with no independent music industry at hand, the state-controlled RTD and the Tanzania Film Company had a recording monopoly. Local bands continued to record for RTD on a regular basis (about once a year); however, bands were not permitted to record songs whose lyrics were deemed incompatible with government policies. It was RTD policy also only to broadcast songs with lyrics in Swahili.

The economic 'self-dependence' policy that restricted imports of nonessential items – for example, musical instruments and public address systems – in the long run dealt a death blow to almost all the music clubs. The late 1960s nonetheless saw the rise to fame of Mbaraka Mwinshehe, who had joined the Morogoro Jazz Band (one of the oldest bands in the country, founded in Morogoro in 1944) as a youth and worked his way to the top, becoming the bandleader in 1968. Like many other Tanzanian radio recordings, Mwinshehe's songs were released as singles by the Nairobi-based PolyGram (Kenya) label. In 1973 the label gave Mwinshehe a loan to buy a set of instruments and a public address system. He formed his own band, Super Volcano, which gave him some independence from the Tanzanian structures, but he was also bound to PolyGram as a recording artist and had to make frequent Kenyan tours to pay back the loan. Mwinshehe died in a car accident while on tour in Kenya in 1979.

With the restructuring of the economy, most Tanzanian bands began to operate under the patronage of state organizations, a system that continued until the end of the 1980s. The organization owned the instruments and employed the musicians, who drew regular salaries and received a percentage of the gate collection at performances. In 1964 the first group founded under this new regime was the Nuta Jazz Band (associated with the National Union of Tanzania, hence the acronym); there followed bands under the patronage of the police, army, national service, national insurance company, party youth wing, Dar es Salaam city council, Dar es

Salaam bus service and so on. By the 1970s *muziki wa dansi* was firmly entrenched as the national music style, with its songs dominating the programs of RTD from morning to night. The instrumentation also had become standardized with a basic lineup of three guitars (solo, second solo and rhythm guitar), bass guitar, drum set and *congas*, plus three trumpets and two or three saxophones sharing the front line with three to six singers.

This style achieved a most intricate and powerful realization in the early 1980s with the music of Mlimani Park Orchestra. Mlimani was formed in 1978, recruiting some of the best and longest-standing musicians on the Tanzanian scene. Under the guidance of Michael Enoch the group further developed the characteristic three-guitar interplay, with the second solo guitar filling out empty spaces between rhythm and solo guitar. Enoch himself organized the band's inimitable three-trumpet, three-saxophone horn arrangements. The band's music was firmly rooted in rhythms and melodies of *ngoma* of the Zaramo people inhabiting the Dar es Salaam area, giving it a strong local identity. The words of *muziki wa dansi* songs were invariably the most important part for the public. Mlimani's chief lyricists, Muhiddin Maalim, Hassani Bitchuka and Cosmas Tobias, together with Dar International's Marijani Rajab, took the art to new heights, on a par with the classical traditions of formal Swahili poetry. Other important bands of the period include Juwata Jazz (a new incarnation of Nuta, later to be renamed OTTU) and Vijana Jazz (the band of the party's youth wing) led by singer/composer Hemed Maneti.

The Dar music scene always had a strong contingent of musicians from the eastern regions of the Congo, most prominently the musicians of Orchestre Maquis, many of them resident in Tanzania since the early 1970s. Others were Mzee Makassy, Ndala Kasheba and Remmy Ongala. The latter entered Tanzania in 1978 to join his uncle Makassy's band and went on to lead Orchestra Matimila. Throughout the 1980s Ongala transgressed the ordinary fixed style of *muziki wa dansi* songs, creating a new style of verbal delivery that strung together long narratives with observations about everyday life, the plight of the poor, politics, AIDS and other social issues. Ongala was one of the few Tanzania-based musicians to make a name outside the country through international releases and touring.

New Diversity: The 1990s and Early 2000s

New musical trends began to evolve in the early 1990s, when the economic liberalization program, in effect since the mid-1980s, and the move away from a one-party system began to show results. The newly established media, private television stations and the spread of video as alternative forms of entertainment dealt a big blow to live music and especially to *muziki wa dansi*. Until the early 1990s 20 to 30 dance bands had played the Dar es Salaam circuit five or six nights a week; the number dwindled to a handful in the late 1990s, with fewer still in the 2000s. The remaining interest in live music and audiences shifted toward other genres (including modern *taarab* and *bongo flava*) during this time. Of the well-known *muziki wa dansi* orchestras, only Mlimani Park and Msondo Ngoma (formerly (Nuta/Juwata) survived. A number of smaller groups work as resident bands in clubs around the country, extending the legacy of the erstwhile national style by singing and playing the hits of a bygone era.

Bibliography

Askew, Kelly. 2002. *Performing the Nation: Swahili Music and Cultural Politics in Tanzania*. Chicago: Chicago University Press.

Graebner, Werner. 1989 [1997]. 'Whose Music? The Songs of Remmy Ongala and Orchestra Super Matimila.' *Popular Music* 8(3): 243–58. (Reprinted in *Readings in African Popular Culture*, ed. Karin Barber. Bloomington: Indiana University Press.)

Graebner, Werner. 2000. 'Ngoma ya ukae: Competitive Social Structure in Tanzanian Dance Music Songs.' In *Mashindano! Competitive Music Performance in East Africa*, eds. Frank Gunderson and Gregory Bartz. Dar es Salaam: Mkuki na Nyota Publishers, 295–318.

Graebner, Werner. 2007. 'The Ngoma Impulse: Club to Nightclub in Dar es Salaam.' In *Dar es Salaam: Histories from an Emerging African Metropolis*, eds. James R. Brennan, Andrew Burton and Yusuf Lawi Dar es Salaam: Mkuki na Nyota Publishers, 177–97.

Nyerere, Julius. 1962 [1966]. *Freedom and Unity: Uhuru Na Umoja: A Selection from Writings and Speeches 1952–65*. Dar es Salaam: Oxford University Press.

Perullo, Alex. 2011. *Live from Dar es Salaam: Popular Music and Tanzania's Music Economy*. Bloomington: Indiana University Press.

Ranger, Terence O. 1975. *Dance and Society in East Africa 1890-1970: The Beni Ngoma*. London: Heinemann.

Discographical References

Abdallah, Salum, and Cuban Marimba. 'Ngoma iko huku/Kacha cha.' Mzuri HL 7-28. *N.d.* [early 1960s]: Kenya.

Morogoro Jazz Band. 'Pole dada/Choyo uache.' Polygram (K) POL 7-051. *1970*: Kenya.

Morogoro Jazz Band. *Mfululizo wa muziki*. Polygram (K) POLP 502. *1972*: Kenya.

Morogoro Jazz Band. 'Sululu ya moro/Zima moto.' Polygram (K) POL 7-081. *1972*: Kenya.

Discography

Abdallah, Salum, and Cuban Marimba. *Ngoma iko huku: Vintage Tanzanian Dance Music 1955-1965*. Dizim 4701. *1999*: Germany.

Mwinshehe, Mbaraka, and Orchestra Super Volcano. *Masika: A Fresh Breeze from Tanzania*. Buda 860286. *2015*: France.

Ongala, Remmy, and Super Matimila. *Songs for the Poor Man*. Real World RWLP 6. *1989*: UK.

Zanzibara 3: Ujamaa – The 1960s Sound of Tanzania. Buda 860142. *2007*: France.

Zanzibara 5: Hot in Dar – The Sound of Tanzania 1978-1983. Buda 860184. *2007*: France.

Zanzibara 7: Sikinde vs Ndekule – A Battle of Bands in Dar es Salaam 1984-1987. Buda 860241. *2013*: France.

WERNER GRAEBNER

Muziki Wa Injili

Muziki wa injili (lit. gospel music) is a popular church music genre in Tanzania. It was an extension of the local church music traditions, which had begun to develop in the late nineteenth century among Lutheran and Anglican branches of the Protestant church, in which choirs sang Western church hymns that were translated into Kiswahili or other Tanzanian local languages (more than 120 languages or language dialects are spoken in Tanzania). Later, from the 1960s on, some choirs included in their repertoire songs with Christian religious lyrics set to traditional Tanzanian tunes. Most choirs sang without accompaniment. A few used the harmonium or traditional instruments such as *kayamba* (shakers) and drums (Weman 1960; Mbunga 1963; Barz 1997 and 2003; Sanga 2009).

Muziki wa injili began to be recognized as a distinctive genre in the late 1960s, 1970s and early 1980s especially in cities such as Dar es Salaam, Mwanza, Mbeya, Arusha and Tabora. It was distinguished by improvisation, the use of electric guitars and keyboards and the incorporation of a variety of popular music styles such as *rumba*, *soukouss*, reggae, *zouk*, R&B, rap and *salsa* (*charanga*-style). In some cases new styles are developed for specific songs while at other times rhythmic configurations (and even tunes) are adopted from selected Tanzanian traditional music and dance styles such as *sindimba* (of the Wamakonde), *mdundiko* (of the Wazaramo) and *ling'oma* (of the Wanyakyusa). Most of these features are uncommon in the mainstream, Western-oriented church choir music and hymns, which are normally written in either staff or solfa notation and performed either unaccompanied or accompanied by organ or electric keyboard. Likewise, unlike Western-oriented church choir music and hymns, *muziki wa injili* is largely composed, transmitted and preserved orally and aurally. The size of singing groups varies from smaller groups with two or three singers to large groups with up to 50 or 60 singers. The music is usually organized in four parts (soprano, alto, tenor, bass) for large groups and in three parts (soprano, alto and tenor) for smaller groups. These voices normally sing in parallel thirds, sixths and octaves. In other instances parallel fourths and fifths are also used. Sometimes the music is performed in homophonic manner while at other times the voices sing in call-and-response pattern with a lead singer or lead voice singing the call section and the rest of the group singing the response segment. Body movements are one of the distinguishing and important features of *muziki wa injili*. Two types of body movements are typical in the performance of this music: *stepu* (Kiswahili for steps) and *matendo* (Kiswahili for actions). *Stepu* include footwork in different directions such as right, left, forward or backward performed in relation to the rhythm and tempo of a given song. *Matendo* body actions use performers' hands and facial expressions as well as miming of other human activities and movements such as running, walking or kneeling. Normally these movements are created and performed as signs that help to convey various messages expressed in the lyrics of the songs.

The music is performed not only in churches during services but also in evangelical meetings (indoor or outdoors) and in concerts of *muziki wa injili* in cities such as Dar es Salaam, Arusha and Mwanza (Barz 2003; Sanga 2006 and 2008). Most of these concerts take place in church buildings and concert halls. The audiences for these concerts include Christians of all denominations as well as non-Christian music lovers. Apart from being performed by church choirs, *muziki wa injili* is also performed by individual musicians who record and sell their albums privately. With the increased broadcasting of the music by various television and radio stations, some of which are owned by church organizations, and the growing circulation of this music through CDs and DVDs as well as video, audio cassettes and Internet, *muziki wa injili* has grown rapidly in popularity and use.

In the late 1980s and 1990s *muziki wa injili* was popularized by recordings of Ulyankuru Choir (Tabora), Tumaini Choir (Arusha), Mabibo Youth Choir (Dar es Salaam) and Lulu Choir (Dar es Salaam). Later, many other choirs came onto the scene. The most famous of these choirs include Kwaya ya Uinjilisti Kijitonyama (Kijitonyama Evangelical Choir), Kwaya ya Uinjilisti Sayuni (Sayuni Evangelical Choir), Kinondoni Revival Choir, Bethel Gospel Singers and Kasulu Choir (Kigoma) to name only a few. There are also small groups such as Upendo Group (Dar es Salaam) and many individual musicians, including Rose Muhando, Upendo Nkone, Bahati Bukuku, Jennifer Mgendi, Sedekia Fanuel, David Robert, Cosmas Chidumule, Christina Shusho and Bon Mwaitege.

From its inception, *muziki wa injili* has interacted with other popular music genres in Tanzania and around the globe, leading to increased musical exchanges and hybridization. These interactions are likely to grow, thanks to increased use of computer and Internet technology. Apart from addressing issues related to Christian faith, practices and biblical texts, *muziki wa injili* lyrics have also increasingly engaged day-to-day economic, political and sociocultural matters such as gender, racial and class identities, relations and conditions. While research concerning *muziki wa injili* began in the disciplines of ethnomusicology, anthropology and religious studies, it is also being carried out in other fields such as literature and Kiswahili language.

Bibliography

Barz, Gregory F. 1997. *The Performance of Religious and Social Identity: An Ethnograhy of Post-mission Kwaya Music in Tanzania*. Unpublished Ph.D. dissertation, Brown University.

Barz, Gregory F. 2003. *Performing Religion: Negotiating Past and Present in Kwaya Music of Tanzania*. Amsterdam: Rodopi.

Barz, Gregory F. 2005. 'Soundscapes of Disaffection and Spirituality in Tanzanian Kwaya Music.' *The World of Music* 47(1): 5–32.

Bjerk, Paul. 2005. '"Building a New Eden": Lutheran Church Youth Choir Performances in Tanzania.' *Journal of Religion in Africa* 35(3): 324–61.

Kweka, Nsia. 2013. 'Uchambuzi wa Dhamira katika Nyimbo za *Muziki wa Injili* Dar es Salaam.' Unpublished MA thesis, University of Dar es Salaam.

Mbunga, Stephen B. G. 1963. *Church Law and Bantu Music: Ecclesiastical Documents and Law on Sacred Music as Applied to Bantu Music*. Schoneck-Beckenried: Nouvelle Revue de Science Missionnaire Suisse.

Sanga, Imani. 2006. 'Composition Processes in Popular Church Music in Dar es Salaam, Tanzania.' *Ethnomusicology Forum* 15(2): 247–71.

Sanga, Imani. 2007. 'Gender in Church Music: Dynamics of Gendered Space in *Muziki wa Injili* in Dar es Salaam, Tanzania.' *Journal of Popular Music Studies* 19(1): 59–91.

Sanga, Imani. 2008. 'Music and Nationalism in Tanzania: Dynamics of National Space in *Muziki wa Injili* in Dar es Salaam.' *Ethnomusicology* 52(1): 52–84.

Sanga, Imani. 2009. 'Teaching-Learning Processes in *Muziki wa Injili* in Dar es Salaam.' *African Music* 8(3): 132–43.

Weman, Henry. 1960. *African Music and the Church in Africa*. Uppsala: Lundequistska.

Discography

Bukuku, Bahati. *Yashinde Mapito (Vol. 1)*. GMC Wasanii Promoters. *2003*: Tanzania.

Chidumule, Cosmas. *Yesu ni Bwana*. F.M Music Bank. *1998*: Tanzania.

Mgendi, Jennifer. *Yesu Nakupenda* (Vol. 4). Global Sounds, Mamu Stores and Congo Corridor Stores (GMC). *2003*: Tanzania.

Muhando, Rose. *Uwe Macho*. Distributed by GMC Wasanii Promoters. *2004*: Tanzania.

IMANI SANGA

Mwomboko

The music and dance genre *mwomboko* emerged in Kenya with the arrival of Western musical instruments such as the accordion and guitar (Mahugu 1990). The name 'mwomboko' comes from the Agikũyũ (Gikuyu, Kikuyu) word 'kwomboko,' which means 'eruption' (King'ori 2008 in Wangechi 2013), and *mwomboko* was named in reference to the dancing style *kwomboka*, which involves rhythmic and patterned steps characterized by upward, downward and sideway body movements by male–female couples in response to accordion music (Nyambura 2008 in Wangechi 2013). The genre is called *mwomboko* to describe the atmosphere created by the vibrations of sounds played on the accordion. One of the distinguishing factors in *mwomboko* is the use of the instruments *kinanda kia mugeto* (accordion) and *karing'aring'a* (metal ring and gong). The *mwomboko* style of dancing was borrowed from European dance styles learned from former soldiers who fought in World Wars I and II. *Mwomboko* was first performed by young men and women but gradually the dance has been embraced by both young and old of both sexes. It is performed as an expression of local culture during public occasions and state functions (Mwangi 2004; Munene 1991).

History

According to Wangechi (2013, the most important scholarly source of information on the genre), *mwomboko* music emerged in the 1940s as a dance based on the traditional songs of the Agikũyũ (Kikuyu) people of Kenya. It was first brought to Murang'a from Kiambu by artists including Cinda wa Watiri, who was among the earliest *mwomboko* performers. John wa Nyambura, who started performing *mwomboko* in 1942 as a young woman, recalled (in Wangechi 2013) that all those who performed *mwomboko* were expected to keep high moral standards.

The emergence of *mwomboko* is highly associated with the arrival of the accordion in Kenya, brought by the African soldiers who participated in World Wars I and II, when they learned how to play and sing to the rhythms of the accordion by watching Europeans perform the waltz and schottische dances (Muchiri 2008 in Wangechi 2013). The Agikũyũ returnee soldiers then taught the Agikũyũ dancers how to perform these dances, which were later transformed into *mwomboko* around 1937 (Murefu 2008 in Wangechi 2013). John wa Nyambura (2008 in Wangechi 2013) indicated that the genre started after *murithigu* was banned by the colonialists between 1941 and 1942.

At first, the accordion players accompanied those who sang *muthirigu*, a protest dance performed to rebel against colonial rule and the foreign lifestyle that colonialists wanted to impose on the Agikũyũ (including the banning of female circumcision, which was viewed as an important rite of passage by the Agikuyu [Maina 2008 in Wangechi 2013]). After the colonialists banned *muthirigu*, accordion players developed the *mwomboko* genre, which they knew would not provoke the colonial government as much as *muthirigu*, arguably because of the latter's affiliation with European dance cultures and styles such as the waltz. *Mwomboko* was used to communicate various messages, especially of protest, affirming that the Agikũyũ would never accept a stranger to rule them. According to Mwangi (2008 in Wangechi 2013) *mwomboko* was banned around 1947 by the colonialists but was revived after a few years.

When *mwomboko* emerged, it was performed at night in the valley since the dancers feared being discovered by the colonial government, which opposed performance of the dance (Kihonge, Hunga et al. 2008 in Wangechi 2013). The dancers carried weapons so that, in case they were caught, they could fight back. They performed the dance from about midnight and then went home. After independence (1964) the genre was brought to public places. Thus, a dance that previously lasted for a whole night was reduced to just a few minutes, performed in stadia, churches and other public places, depending on the occasion and event.

Musical Characteristics

The musical instruments in *mwomboko* performance consist of the *kinanda kia mugeto* (accordion) and *karing'aringa* (metal ring and gong). *Mwatu* (an empty beehive) or *ithanduku* (a wooden box) is used to articulate the rhythm of the ring and also serves as a seat for the ring player (Maina 2008 in Wangechi 2013). The ring is played by striking its sides across the diameter with a *chuma* (a short metal rod). The ring and beehive provide the percussive accompaniment for the dance, whereas the accordion mostly complements the voice by filling in the gaps when the soloist is not singing.

The accordion is the lead instrument and therefore plays the most prominent role in *mwomboko*. Wangechi (2013) observes that the accordionist directs and coordinates both the player of the metal ring and the dancers; plays introductory sections; gives the preliminary statement of the next movement which determines the dance steps; plays interludes marking the end and the beginning of the next section; plays the concluding section (postlude); accompanies the solo voice; doubles the human voice; and pitches the vocal soloist.

The metal ring (*karing'aring'a*) is the highest-pitched instrument in the *mwomboko* ensemble and its rhythmic patterns are played in monotone. The instrument's pitch depends on the circumference of the ring; a *karing'aring'a* with a large circumference produces a low pitch while one with a small circumference produces a higher pitch (Mwangi 2008 in Wangechi 2013),

The *karing'aring'a* produces a percussive accompaniment to the dance. It is played by striking its sides across the diameter with a metal rod. An *ithanduku* (an empty wooden box) is sometimes used to mark the rhythm of the metal ring, to articulate a strong beat and to provide additional percussive effects for the dance. As observed earlier, the wooden box also serves as a seat for the metal ring player. The metal ring helps in directing the dance steps and formations and keeps a constant tempo for the performance. It is played with *ostinato* rhythms that vary slightly from one dance to another. The player of the instrument neither responds to the soloist vocally nor dances.

Since the early song texts of *mwomboko* were meant to convey messages of protest against colonial rule (John 2008 in Wangechi 2013), most were highly symbolic. To understand their meaning, one needed a good knowledge of the Agikūyū language. However, later song texts covered topics such as the social life of the Agikūyū or the accordionist, the political life of the community, historical events and other issues affecting the community. Wangechi (2013) points out that, since independence, song texts not only include topics dealing with Agikūyū cultural traditions, but also social and emerging issues, worship and many others, depending on the occasion for which the dance is being performed and the soloist's ability.

The player of the accordion (*kinanda kia mugeto*) in *mwomboko* song and dance doubles as the lead soloist/singer (*mukui*) and leader of the group. It is important to note that the role of soloist in *mwomboko* is exclusively male. The soloist takes charge of the whole performance and controls the dance troupe with his voice and his instrument. He is expected to have a strong voice that exhibits command and authority in singing; he decides when to change from one dance movement to another; he embellishes the dance with vocables that come at the end of a movement or mark the beginning of the next movement; he has the liberty to compose songs on the spot to suit the occasion, and his articulate choice of words and manner of playing the accordion render him popular. Wangechi (ibid.) maintains that there are usually no standard precomposed song texts since the soloist creates most of the texts as the dance goes on. He is, therefore, expected to have a good command of the Agikūyū language and culture in order to be able to use idiomatic expressions, metaphors, parables and symbolic language effectively, responsibly and creatively. The soloist combines the English, Kiswahili and Agikūyū languages to secure multicultural appeal and audience appreciation. Githee (in Wangechi 2013) adds that songs on current issues have gained popularity in the contemporary setting, while those whose themes are based on historical events are slowly disappearing. The soloist, therefore, tries to find a common ground acceptable to the audience's taste.

Dance Elements

As Wangechi (2013) has described it, the dance starts from outside the arena (in most cases a school playground) in a relatively slow tempo. The dancers enter the arena in male–female pairs, and the same couples dance with one another throughout the performance. Once inside the arena, the dancers create several formations depending on the dance movement being performed. The dance is graceful, unhurried and solemn and involves movement of various parts of the body. The predominant dance formation is *raini igiri* (two lines) where the dancers move in pairs.

In its initial stage, *mwomboko* was not noteworthy for its costumes (King'ori 2008 in Wangechi 2013) but, as the dance became more popular in the late 1960s and early 1970s, the young men started wearing baggy trousers and long-sleeved shirts with scarves around their necks, or sometimes ties. The ladies wore *ihuruto* (round skirts), which were allowed to flare out as they danced, exaggerating their dance movements. On the upper parts of the body, female dancers tied a *khanga* wrap that left one shoulder bare. Dancers wore shoes while performing (Wangechi 2013).

Mwomboko consists of several dance movements or sections, namely *machi ndogo, tindo, rumba, mbombo, matore, ndongomothi, njeki, machi korathi, machi ndaihu/machi imwe* and *kariara* (Wangechi 2013). Apart from *machi ndaihu* (long march), also called *machi namba imwe* (march number one), which is an entry-to-the stage dance and may also be performed while exiting the stage, the movements are not, necessarily, performed in any particular prescribed order.

Machi Namba Imwe/ Machi Ndaihu (long march): this movement's dance style is a military-type formation and march (Waititu 2008 in Wangechi 2013). Men and women form two lines and then march in pairs. The movement starts from outside the arena, and the performers enter the arena marching to the beat of the song and holding hands. The movement lasts longer than the others.

Ndongomothi (fool): in this movement, the dancers march and swing their feet while at the same time rotating and moving around in circular formation. The man's right hand is usually on the woman's left underarm area while the man's left hand holds the woman's right hand. The woman's left hand lies on the man's right shoulder. They also dance sideways in a leisurely manner.

Machi namba Igiri/Machi Ndogo/Nini (small march): this movement resembles *machi ndaihu* since it is also a military-style march. It is called 'small march' because it does not last as long as the other march and also because its formations are slightly different. In this particular movement, men dance in a linear formation, turning around rhythmically.

Njeki (jack): the name is derived from the mechanical tool used to raise a vehicle off the ground to change a flat tire. The pairs rotate in revolving forward and backward motions, pausing to lift one leg between directional changes. The *njeki* movement is performed at a much faster tempo than the others. The dancers make several formations within the arena.

Luba (*rumba*): this movement was adopted from the Cuban *rumba* style. The dancers copy the *rumba* dance style with formations of three steps performed to the *rumba* beat.

Machi Korathi (chorus): *Korathi* is the Agikũyũ word for 'chorus'. Formations are much simpler compared to the other movements. At times, this movement serves as an interlude allowing the singer and the dancers to reorganize themselves after performing other, more complex movements. *Korathi* lyrics are soothing and catchy in nature.

Mwomboko dance style: in the *mwomboko* dance style, the performers move in single file, count two steps, bend down and then move majestically back and forth in the dancing arena. This movement is the climax of the *mwomboko* performance.

Tindo (chisel): the dance formations of *tindo* are similar to those of the *mwomboko* movement. The main difference is that the dancers do not bend after counting two steps; instead they move their feet rhythmically, emulating the way a carpenter drives a chisel into a piece of wood while splitting it. The dancers move in single file, swinging their bodies in a zigzag posture, and then march majestically within the arena.

Kariara: in this movement, the dancers make formations whereby they turn around and then turn sideways while still holding hands as they file forward, back and forth inside the arena. *Kariara* originated from River *Kariara* in Kandara Division, Murang'a County.

Wangechi (2013) further observes that *mwomboko* dancers must master their minds, bodies and emotions. They must maintain a high level of coordination with the vocal soloist and they must show a high level of commitment in the performance. The members of the audience, who in most cases comprise both men and women of all ages, are an important part of the performance. They cheer and applaud a good performance and also give material appreciation, in the form of money, to an impressive dancer and soloist.

Survival and Change in *Mwomboko*

Wangechi's 2013 study concluded that several factors have contributed to the survival of *mwomboko*, including the following:

a. It is a genre that accommodates change. The soloists use *mwomboko* tunes to relay new themes which are relevant to contemporary society.
b. The song text of *mwomboko* music is specifically composed to cater to the interests of the target audience.
c. *Mwomboko* tunes appeals to people of all ages.
d. *Mwomboko* has been used as a means of conveying cultural values of the Agikũyũ, communicating important information and educating members of the community.

Regarding changes that have taken place in *mwomboko* dance song, Wangechi points out that:

a. *Mwomboko* was initially used as a protest dance against colonial rule but later symbolically expressed both Agikũyũ culture and emerging issues.
b. Themes, initially political and about protest in nature, later incorporated emerging issues, praise, religious and social concerns (such as encouraging virtues and condemning vices).
c. *Mwomboko* began as a protest dance against colonial rule but emerging new *mwomboko* dance spaces include political rallies and campaigns, public holiday celebrations, bars, nightclubs and restaurants.

Conclusion

Mwomboko serves the Agikũyũ at different levels (see Muchiri wa 2008 in Wangechi 2013). At the social level, it provides a platform for moral and social education on emerging issues such as HIV and AIDS, political issues and education for girls. At the recreational level, it offers a vehicle for enjoyment and personal satisfaction. At the functional level, it provides a spirit of togetherness and sharing which is important for the maintenance of ethnic identity and enhancement of social binding.

Bibliography

Mahugu, Peter. 1990. 'A Literary Investigation into the Agikũyũ Songs of Independence.' Unpublished MA thesis, University of Nairobi.

Munene, Ernest. 1991. *An Investigation into the Origin of Mwomboko Dance with Reference to Murang'a District*. Unpublished research project, Kenyatta University, Nairobi.

Mwangi, Peter M. 2004. 'Poetics of Gikũyũ Mwomboko Poetry: A Case Study of Selected Performing Artists.' Unpublished MA thesis, Kenyatta University, Nairobi.

Wangechi, Kinyua Hellen. 2013. 'Mwomboko and Music Traditions of the Agikũyũ of Murang'a County.' Unpublished MA thesis, Kenyatta University, Nairobi. Online at: http://ir-library.ku.ac.ke/handle/123456789/7484 (accessed 10 April 2018).

Informants Interviewed by Kinyua Hellen Wangechi (from Wangechi 2013)

Elijah – Dancer, Mũkangũ Dance Troupe (28 May 2008).
Hunja – Dancer, Kangema Dance Troupe (20 June 2008).
John wa Nyambura – Dancer, Kamune Dance Troupe (20 June 2008).
Kabura – Dancer, Kangema Dance Troupe (20 June 2008).
Kihonge – Leader, Kangema Dance Troupe (20 June 2008).
King'ori wa Mwangi – Leader of Kamune Dance Troupe (20 June 2008).
Mwangi Murefu – Dancer, Kangema Dance Troupe (20 June 2008).
Ndaiga Muchiri – Dancer, Kangema Dance Troupe (20 June 2008).
Ndaiga Muchiri wa Komu – Dancer, Kangema Dance Troupe (28 June 2008).
Nelius wa Mwangi – Elder (20 June 2008).
Waigwa – Leader, Mũkangũ Dance Troupe (16 November 2008).
Waititu – Dancer, Mũkangũ Dance Troupe (28 May 2008).
Wambui Maina – Dancer, Mũkangũ Dance Troupe (16 November 2008).
Wangeci – Dancer, Kangema Dance Troupe (20 June 2008).

YouTube

(accessed 23 April 2018).
https://www.youtube.com/watch?v=YteNFxPvEyo
https://www.youtube.com/watch?v=p23klL5tPBw

MELLITUS NYONGESA WANYAMA

Naija Pop

Naija pop is a general term that came into common usage around 2012 to describe the popular music of Nigeria. 'Naija' is Lagos slang for Nigeria. Naija pop music, purveyed by a new generation of artists including D'Banj, P-Square, Wizkid, Tiwa Savage, Yemi Alade, Flavour, Wande Coal and Davido, is light-hearted, danceable, celebratory, generally apolitical and, notably, not associated with any one ethnic group or language. Naija pop songs are often released accompanied by well-produced videos. These videos are typically created by professionals associated with Nollywood, Nigeria's powerful and influential popular film industry. For example, Clarence Peters, son of *jùjú* star Shina Peters, and founder and CEO of CAPital Dream Pictures, has directed many of the most popular Naija pop music videos. These videos tend to celebrate an upwardly mobile urban lifestyle, featuring fine houses, cars and clothing. Naija pop stars have become some of the most successful musicians in Africa – perhaps ever – touring widely around the continent and beyond, appearing frequently on satellite television broadcasts, acting as sponsors or spokespeople for commercial advertising campaigns and influencing a new generation of musicians around the continent.

While Naija pop has been widely used as a descriptor only since 2012, the music it describes originated in the late 1990s, following the death of Nigerian army general and *de facto* President Sani Abacha. Abacha's authoritarian regime (1993–8) capped decades of military rule in Nigeria, which had hampered the development of the country's creative industries. Producer and artist agent Rab Bakari, an acute observer of the Lagos scene, notes that, after Abacha's death, many young professionals returned from places including New York, London and Toronto and dedicated themselves to building a truly Nigerian entertainment industry in Nigeria.

Before the late 1990s Nigerian popular music had tended either to break down along familiar international genre categories – jazz, gospel, reggae, R&B, rap – or, in the case of more homegrown genres, to be linked to a particular ethnic group, such as Yorùbá *jùjú* and *fújì*, Igbo highlife, Hausa pop music in the north and many lesser-known popular music styles associated with Nigeria's 250 to 400 ethnic groups. Even Fela Kuti's internationally successful Afrobeat sound, a hybrid genre born in the 1970s, relied on identifiably Yorùbá elements in its language and rhythms. In contrast, Naija pop consciously aims at being pan-Nigerian. That does not mean local languages and rhythms do not appear in songs – they do. But there is no single Naija pop language or beat. The music's rhythms are created by producers using computers in recording studios. Auto-tuned vocals, with their characteristic electronic trilling effects, are prevalent. Producers may draw on any number of different sources, including ethnic rhythms from throughout the vast, culturally complex country of Nigeria. Naija pop hits have tended to work within a 4/4 time signature, although, ever since Davido's 2014 hit 'Aye,' which uses a distinctive 12/8 time signature, many other hit songs use variants of 6/8 rhythm.

In April 2014 Nigeria's National Bureau of Statistics proclaimed the country's GDP to be the largest in Africa, ahead even of some European countries. A former British colony cobbled together in the late nineteenth century from three dramatically different cultural and geographic regions, Nigeria has struggled to achieve unity and stability as an independent nation. With over 170 million people, it is Africa's most populous nation, and, despite its impressive GDP, one of the continent's nations with the highest level of poverty. This wealth paradox plays out in Naija pop songs. Wizkid's 2014 hit 'Ojuelegba' recounts his rise from a poor neighborhood in Lagos to stardom, and the song's video was filmed there. It is a success story, a song that seeks to tell any poor Nigerians that they, too, can overcome adversity with faith and hard work. The wealthy, luxurious lifestyle depicted in many Naija pop songs and videos has become a dominant imaginative space, one emulated all over Africa but perhaps especially resonant in Nigeria, where even the poorest know that they live in a rich country and deserve better.

Some critics complain that this emphasis on style and wealth is part of an unhealthy obsession with the United States, especially with African-American popular culture. US R&B and hip-hop are closely studied models for the architects of Naija pop; however, the genre cannot be reduced to imitation. While it has no specific ethnic identity, Naija pop embraces ethnic diversity, its lyrics – both sung and rapped – favoring the hybrid urban patois of major cities, especially Lagos. As such, Naija pop plays throughout the country. Rab Bakari notes that, at a wedding party in Jos in the predominantly Muslim north, one might hear songs sung in Yorùbá from Ogun State or Lagos, or by an artist such as Flavour, who works elements of Igbo highlife into his Naija pop sound. The music's modern aesthetic, clever use of pop hooks and seductive celebration of youth and opulence help it to transcend notoriously stubborn ethnic barriers.

Some consider Naija pop to be a subgenre of Afrobeat, the pan-African pop music of twenty-first-century African cities and diaspora communities in London, New York, Houston and elsewhere. The term 'Naija pop' was coined in Nigeria, whereas the term 'Afrobeat' came out of the DJ scene in London. Certainly, Naija pop stars contribute a great deal to the club mixes of music called 'Afrobeat' that is heard in DJ dance venues all over the world. But Naija pop is specific to Nigeria, a product of the country's unique history and its formidably ambitious, young creative community.

The vast majority of Naija pop stars are male. They may perform with a band, but more typically they are backed by a DJ and appear onstage and on video with dancers, typically women. There are some notable exceptions to Naija pop's male dominance, such as Yemi Alade, a singer of mixed Igbo and Yorùbá parentage, and Tiwa Savage, one of the top artists from Lagos's Mavin Records, one of many production houses dedicated to promoting Naija pop. Onstage, Tiwa Savage has a sassy, stylish demeanor, and a certain toughness, underscored by her powerful vocal delivery.

Physical music sales have never been a particularly reliable source of income for Nigerian musicians, especially after the decline of vinyl in the 1980s, when cassettes and CDs, both easily pirated, became the principle formats for music consumption. This history forced artists and producers to develop alternative funding strategies long before the arrival of MP3 and other digital formats did so worldwide. Naija pop artists make their money from large-scale performances, patronage and corporate sponsorship. The most lucrative funding source for popular musicians in Nigeria has been through alliances with titans of industry. This business model does not encourage artists to write politically outspoken or provocative songs. As Nigerian music promoter Cecil Hammond told CNN in 2015, 'The more neutral you are, the better – so just focusing your music, give us good music, let everybody dance and that's it.' However, obscenity has found its way into Naija pop lyrics. For example, releases by Wizkid and Davido are sold with the label 'Explicit.'

Because Naija pop is defined so loosely in musical terms, it can continue to morph and adapt with changing times and fashions. For this reason, and because Nigeria's media marketing juggernaut is squarely behind the term, it is likely to be with us for a long time to come.

Bibliography

Bakari, Rab. 2016. Interview with the author. New York.

Duthiers, Vladimir, and Kermeliotis, Teo. 2012. 'Afrobeats: The New Sound of West Africa That's Going Global.' *CNN* (19 December). Online at: http://edition.cnn.com/2012/12/19/world/africa/afrobeats-music (accessed 24 January 2018).

Veal, Michael E. 2000. *Fela: The Life and Times of an African Musical Icon*. Philadelphia: Temple University Press.

Discographical References

Davido. 'Aye.' HKN Music (digital download). *2014*: Nigeria.

Davido. *Son of Mercy EP [Explicit]*. Sony Music Entertainment International Limited. *2016*: New York.

Wizkid. 'Ojuelegba.' *Ayo [Explicit]*. Empire Mates Entertainment. *2014*: Nigeria.

Discography

Alade, Yemi. *King of Queens*. Effyzzie Music Group. *2014*: Nigeria.

Flavour. *Thankful*. 2Nite Entertainment. *2014*: Nigeria.

Savage, Tiwa. *R.E.D. (Deluxe Edition)*. Mavin Records/323 Entertainment. *2016*: Nigeria.

BANNING EYRE

Ndebele Pop

While Ndebele pop is not a musical genre as such, the contributions of Ndebele musicians to a number of South African and Zimbabwean genres popular within Zimbabwe are sometimes referred to as 'Ndebele pop.' Traditional music of the Ndebele ethnic group tends to feature choral arrangements, with rich, rhythmic vocal harmonies backed by spare percussion, including leg rattles (*amahlwayi*) and clappers (*izikeyi*). Ndebele artists have made an impact in Zimbabwean popular culture, especially in the 1940s to 1960s, when the jazz scene in Bulawayo produced some of the country's most popular acts. Since that time, the country's popular music has been dominated by the majority population, the Shona. While there have been Ndebele singers and groups of note, they have not coalesced into a distinct movement or musical style.

The Ndebele people established themselves in what is now Zimbabwe during the early nineteenth century. They were part of a large migration of people from the Nguni language group who surged north from present-day South Africa, fleeing the militant rampages of the king Shaka Zulu (1787–1828). This migration resulted in two new states, Gaza in the east (in present-day Mozambique) and Ndebele in the west. The Ndebele territory came to be known as Matabeleland, roughly the southwest third of present-day Zimbabwe, with its capital in Bulawayo. Two Ndebele kings, Mzilikazi and his son Lobengula, presided over tense relations, including warfare, with the majority Shona. After the establishment of Rhodesia in the 1890s, white leaders exacerbated these interethnic tensions as part of a divide and rule strategy.

This legacy of mistrust lingered after Zimbabwe's independence in 1980. The Shona-led government of Robert Mugabe pursued a violent campaign against 'dissidents' in Matabeleland in the early 1980s, killing thousands and deepening animosity among the Ndebele. Such violence has never recurred, but the Ndebele still occupy a secondary political position in Zimbabwe and this status is reflected in the cultural sphere, including music.

Because of their close ties to South Africa, Ndebele musicians in Bulawayo were more influenced by trends in Johannesburg than in Harare (formerly Salisbury). Starting in the 1930s Bulawayo bands began echoing the jazz-inspired *marabi* and *kwela* music of South Africa. Shona musicians also played so-called township jazz, but many of the key artists in this influential scene were Ndebele. Sometimes, popular jazz songs were simply translated into Ndebele. But as the movement grew, groups created their own compositions, which were played in elite venues, such as hotels, but also on national radio and later television. Groups such as De Black Evening Follies, the Cool Four and the City Quads became the most popular black Rhodesian acts of the day.

The charismatic singer Sonny Sondo left De Black Evening Follies to become the front man of the City Quads. Sondo was a sensational performer, considered by many one of the era's most talented entertainers. Another standout was Dorothy Masuka, who began with the Cool Four but went on to have a major international career as a jazz singer. This was an era in which foreign music, from the Mills Brothers to Jim Reeves, had a huge impact in Rhodesian cities. While there were many Ndebele artists in township jazz, the music was not ethnically identified. Soon, rock 'n' roll, and later more indigenous forms of pop music (such as *chimurenga* and *sungura*), came to dominate Zimbabwe's airwaves and concert venues. Though jazz would never regain its stature on the national scene, Bulawayo is still home to a vibrant jazz scene today, featuring many Ndebele artists.

After independence, Zimbabwe's popular music came into its own and a number of popular bands and singers emerged. Most of these were Shona, but not all. Lovemore Majaivana was the most popular of the Ndebele singer/bandleaders from Bulawayo. His actual last name was Tshuma, but he went by the name Majaivana, a reference to his great dancing. Majaivana moved through bands, the Real Sounds and the Zulus, before working as a solo artist and bandleader. He played the popular foreign styles of the day, but also released an album of Ndebele folk songs in 1984. Like the jazz musicians of the earlier era, Majaivana took his strongest cues from popular music in South Africa – township jive and soul and, as the 1990s began, the disco-influenced sound called 'bubblegum.' Despite his popularity, neither Majaivana nor his Ndebele peers succeeded in creating a distinctly Ndebele pop style.

Another noteworthy Ndebele singer of this era was Albert Nyathi, a poet/musician whose work often had a political element, whether lamenting the assassination of the African National Congress leader Chris Hani or singing the praises of the old Ndebele kings, Mzilikazi and Lobengula.

In the wake of Paul Simon's *Graceland* album (1986), the *mbube* (*isicathamiya*) choral vocal sound of Ladysmith Black Mambazo enjoyed worldwide popularity. This provided an opening for more folkloric Ndebele artists in Zimbabwe to venture into the popular sphere. By far the most prominent was the group Black Umfolosi, who toured internationally for many years. They incorporated the South African gumboots dance into their act, and sometimes donned fur pelts and wooden shields, like warriors. But the essence of their act was the strong choral arranging and delivery that has always been a hallmark of Ndebele music.

In the twenty-first century popular music in Southern Africa moved away from ethnic identification and became more and more subsumed into a global conversation dominated by hip-hop aesthetics and electronic production. It can be expected that some elements of language, choral arranging and also the ongoing political status of Ndebele people in Shona-dominated Zimbabwe will play a role in the work of future Ndebele musicians, however muted they may be by the globalizing trends transforming popular music in this region.

Bibliography

Beach, David. 1994. *The Shona and Their Neighbors*. Oxford: Blackwell.

Eyre, Banning. 2015. *Lion Songs: Thomas Mapfumo and the Music that Made Zimbabwe*. Durham, NC: Duke University Press.

Makwenda, Joyce Jenje. 2005. *Zimbabwe Township Music*. Harare: Storytime Promotions.

Turino, Thomas. 2000. *Nationalists, Cosmopolitans, and Popular Music in Zimbabwe*. Chicago: University of Chicago Press.

Zindi, Fred. 1985. *Roots Rocking in Zimbabwe*. Harare: Mambo Press.

Discography

Black Umfolosi. *Festival Umdlalo*. World Curcuit WCD 037. *1993*: UK.

Cool Crooners of Bulawayo, The. *Blue Sky*. Atelier Noaille EPC 502305 2. *2001*: France.

Cool Crooners, The. *Isatilo*. Atelier Noaille F001. *2004*: France.

Imbizo. *Amalombolomba/Endless Speech*. Womad Select WSCD 108. *2001*: UK.

Majaivana, Lovemore. *Isono Sami*. ZMC CD MUSI 873. *2000*: Zimbabwe.

Majaivana, Lovemore. *The Best of Lovemore Majaivana*. ZMC CD ZMUSI 845. *2012*: Zimbabwe.

Masuka, Dorothy. *Hamba Nontsolola, and Other Original Hits from the 50s*. Gallo Records cdzac 60. *1993*: South Africa.

Simon, Paul. *Graceland*. Warner Bros. 1-25447. *1986*: USA.

BANNING EYRE

Ndombolo

Ndombolo is widely used as a term for the generation of Congolese dance music that emerged in Kinshasa in the late 1990s and early 2000s. In fact, the word describes a dance, not a musical style, although non-Congolese music fans and writers have applied the name to the music accompanying the dance, much as they did with an earlier term for Congolese music, 'soukouss.' Congolese music aficionados are more likely to refer to the 'ndombolo era' as the 'fourth generation' of Congolese music – the first being the *rumba* of the 1940s and 1950s; the second being the big-band sound of artists such as Franco and TPOK Jazz or Tabu Ley Rochereau and Afrisa International in the 1960s; the third being the rock-influenced sound of Zaïko Langa Langa in the 1970s; and the fourth being 'ndombolo,' spearheaded by the band Wenge Musica.

The *ndombolo* dance was introduced by Wenge Musica in late 1997 or early 1998. Veteran Congolese music producer and presenter Lubangi Muniania notes that once Wenge Musica originated *ndombolo*, other groups started incorporating the dance (Muniania; interview with author, April 2018). People began to identify the dance move with the music, and the music with the dance. However, a 'purist Congolese music connoisseur' understands that *ndombolo* is actually a set of dance moves.

The word itself has unclear origins. One online dictionary, the Lingala/English Dictionary, claims it is a Kikongo word meaning 'to beg' or 'to ask.' Muniania (2018) believes it is a Bandundu term referring to the way a woman works her hindquarters while dancing to attract a man. (These definitions may not be mutually exclusive.) In any case, the term clearly has a sexual connotation as the *ndombolo* dance fits into a longer tradition of sexually suggestive dances accompanying Congolese popular music. Indeed, there have been attempts in Mali, Cameroon and Kenya to ban the dance as excessively vulgar. Congolese musicians have also faced resistance over obscenity at home. The late bandleader Franco was briefly imprisoned in the late 1970s because of obscene lyrics in two songs, 'Helene' and 'Jacky'. And *ndombolo*-era musicians, notably Koffi Olomide, have faced more recent censorship on similar grounds. Muniania (2018) also notes that, at one point, the word 'ndombolo' became Kinshasa street code referring to President Laurent Kabila (1997–2001).

Montreal-based Congolese singer Pierre Kwenders came of age during the *ndombolo* era, and sees it as an extension of innovations introduced by Zaïko Langa Langa decades earlier (Kwenders; interview with author, January 2018). Specifically, Zaïko continually introduced signature dances and showcased the role of the *atalaku*, or animator, who chants encouragement to listeners and often namechecks individuals who have supported the band financially or who may do so in the future – a practice known as *libanga* (to 'namecheck' is to mention the name of an individual in a public forum for promotional purposes). *Libanga* is a prominent feature in the popular music of the *ndombolo* era.

While it is not possible to pin down precise musical characteristics that identify a song as *ndombolo*, some general observations can be made. The music is generally a little slower than *soukouss*, which is seen as influenced by contact with Caribbean and mostly Antillean musicians in Paris. Also, the *ndombolo* era is seen in part as a reassertion of Congolese identity. Percussion plays a more prominent role in *ndombolo* songs, and specific rhythms often cue audiences to engage in particular *ndombolo* dance moves.

Ever since the early 2000s artists identified with earlier eras have chosen to include elements of *ndombolo* in their recordings and performances. Kwenders (2018) describes Papa Wemba's band Nouvelle Ecriture as a '*ndombolo*-friendly' version of his former band Viva la Musica. Muniania (2018) points out that old-school *rumba* artists know that they have to incorporate some *ndombolo* in their performances in order to remain relevant. Similarly, *ndombolo* artists need to ease into a classic Congolese *rumba* sound at certain points in order to satisfy that audience. Koffi Olomide – arguably the reigning elder of Congolese music – also moved away from his ballad-oriented *tha tcho* sound of the 1990s to incorporate *ndombolo* music and dance. Given his stature, he surpassed the popularity of *ndombolo* pioneers, the former leaders of Wenge Musica, Werrason and J.B. Mpiana. Muniania (2018) asserts that by the early 2000s Olomide had become the chief representative of *ndombolo*, edging out all competitors.

Such observations underscore the fluid nature of the term 'ndombolo'. In a sense, all these varieties of Congolese music – *soukouss*, *kwasa kwasa*, *ndombolo* – are really extensions of the original *rumba* sound. One important characteristic of the *ndombolo* era is near fanatical fan loyalty to specific artists. Once collaborators, Werrason and J.B. Mpiana became fierce competitors in the eyes of their respective fans in the early 2000s. Similar divisions have since emerged between the fans of younger artists Fally Ipupa and Ferre Gola. Muniania (2018) links this devotion to particular artists in part to public disillusionment with political leaders, specifically Joseph Kabila, son of Laurent Kabila and president of the Democratic Republic of Congo (DRC) from 2001. When people feel abandoned by their leaders they look elsewhere for role models, and musical artists have chiefly been the ones to fill this void.

Given war and scarcity in the DRC, many Congolese have moved to European cities, particularly Paris and Brussels. Some, such as Maitre Gims, the son of one of Papa Wemba's former vocalists, have become major crossover pop stars. Through these developments, *ndombolo* moves have made their way into French and other varieties of hip-hop, a source of pride for Congolese musicians and fans. *Ndombolo* has continued to remain in the mix as a new, sixth generation of Congolese artists emerges, often in diasporas, with a stress on unity rather than division. Congolese music is a phenomenon that subsumes and incorporates all its previous incarnations, growing and changing but leaving nothing behind.

Bibliography

Ewens, Graeme. 1994. *Congo Colossus: The Life and Legacy of Franco & OK Jazz*. Norfolk, UK: Buku Press.

Stewart, Gary. 2000. *Rumba on the River*. London and New York: Verso.

White, Bob W. 2008. *Rumba Rules: The Politics of Dance Music in Mobutu's Zaire*. Durham, NC: Duke University Press.

Discographical References

Franco. 'Helene.' *1978*: DRC. Online at: https://www.youtube.com/watch?v=pwBzMiyXnRg (accessed 13 June 2018).

Franco. 'Jacky.' *1978*: DRC.

Discography

Fally Ipupa. *Droit chemin*. Obouo Music. *2006*: DRC.

Gola, Ferre. *Qui est derrière toi?* Kiki Productions. *2009*: DRC.

Mpiana, J. B. *Feux de l'amour*. Le Monde des Artistes. *1997*: France.

Werrason. *Kibuisa Mpimpa*. JPS Production CDJPS 132. *2001*: France.

Websites

'Afropop Worldwide': http://afropop.org/, in particular 'Congolese Music: The Fifth Generation.' 2018, http://afropop.org/audio-programs/congolese-music-the-fifth-generation (accessed 15 May 2018).

Lingala/English Dictionary: https://dic.lingala.be/en/ndombolo (accessed 15 May 2018).

'Ndombolo.' Wikipedia: https://en.wikipedia.org/wiki/Ndombolo (accessed 15 May 2018).

Interviews

Lubangi Muniania, April 2018, Brooklyn, NY.

Pierre Kwenders, January 2018, New York City.

BANNING EYRE

Nederlandslied

The *Nederlandslied* (Dutch song, pronounced near-der-lunds-lead, often referred to as just the *Nederlands*) is a prestigious and competitive genre of the Malay Choirs, which are all-male choral groups that host annual choral competitions during the summer months (January to March) in Cape Town, South Africa. Musically, the genre is a responsorial song of moderate tempo between a soloist and chorus, in which the soloist often joins the chorus for part of the response. The *Nederlands* is a Creole song in which there is a fusion of a number of musical traits that arrived in the Cape under conditions of slavery during the Dutch colonial period. These traits were mainly from Indian Ocean locations such as Indonesia, India, Mozambique and Madagascar, whence slaves were taken by the Dutch East India Company (VOC). European musical characteristics are also prevalent, as are Arabic influences, which came through the Islamic religion of the slaves (see Davids 1985; Desai 1985; and Martin 1999).

Nederlandsliedere (pl.) ostensibly began as old Dutch songs (reflected in the High Dutch and older forms of Creole Dutch) brought to the Cape by settlers, sailors and soldiers (Martin 1999, 26–7). Slaves emulated this singing, localizing the songs and thereby forming a new musical genre. The most distinctive feature of the *Nederlandslied* is the nasal vocal quality of the soloist and the rather high-pitched vocal melismatic ornamentation called *karienkels* (pronounce kah-ring'-kils). The practitioners and the culture-bearers hold these qualities to be innate or a gift, which cannot be taught. The *karienkels*, consisting of *glissandi*, turns and *acciaccaturas* around certain melodic pitches of longer duration, along with the minor tonality of the piece, lend a rather Eastern feel to the soloist's singing. The soloist's voice floats above the rest of the music as he produces these melismatic ornaments with intonational fluctuations and a rather constricted throat; he is also rhythmically freer than the chorus and accompaniment. His singing provides a contrast to the choir, which sings in Western block harmonies with a steady slow tempo and a rather even and controlled sound production compared to the more emotional quality of the soloist. The accompaniment, consisting of string instruments, has an Iberian feel to it, reflecting the earlier Portuguese influence in some of the locations from which the slaves originated (Martin 1999, 172–3). Earlier, the instrumentation comprised only mandolins, guitars and banjos, but these days it also includes violins and cellos.

The most widely known *Nederlandslied* is 'Rosa,' a love song popularly sung at Cape Muslim weddings, extolling the moral virtues of fidelity. In the past, weddings were prolonged affairs of several days' duration with the families of the bride and bridegroom taking turns to sing various types of songs as entertainment (Martin 1999, 72–3).

According to Martin (1999, 26–7), some 20 *Nederlandslied* songs were known to have existed around the end of the 1800s. A concerted effort was made by Malay choral music enthusiast Rasdien Cornelius and retired Dutch sailor Frans de Jongh to collect and record these songs from the elderly and from the Netherlands, so there are about 200 to

300 songs in existence. The repertoire is considered closed and no one composes these songs any longer.

Bibliography

Davids, Achmat. 1985. 'Music and Islam.' In *Papers Presented at the Fifth Symposium on Ethnomusicology, Faculty of Music, University of Cape Town, August 30th–September 1st 1984*, ed. A. Tracey. Grahamstown: International Library of African Music, 36–8.

Desai, Desmond. 1985. 'Cape Malay Music.' In *Papers Presented at the Fifth Symposium on Ethnomusicology, Faculty of Music, University of Cape Town, August 30th–September 1st 1984*, ed. A. Tracey. Grahamstown: International Library of African Music, 39–44.

Martin, Denis-Constant. 1999. *Coon Carnival: New Year in Cape Town, Past and Present*. Cape Town: David Philip Publishers.

Discography

Central Malay Choir. *Central Malay Choir*. Gallo. *1973*: South Africa.

The Tulips. *South Africa: The Cape Town Minstrels*. Musique du Monde. *1999*: France.

YouTube

Marines Malay Choir 1st Prize Nederlandslied: https://www.youtube.com/watch?v=mC9kKEg4BOk (accessed 23 April 2018)

SYLVIA R. BRUINDERS

Ngoma

In Bantu languages (spoken over a vast area covering Central, Eastern and Southern Africa), including the widely spoken Swahili, *ngoma* is the common word denoting any kind of 'drum' or 'drums.' *Ngoma* also refers to all genres of music–song–dance that are (primarily) accompanied by drums or drumming, to the whole context of such events or performances (which may include any kind of festive arrangements) and also to a particular *ngoma*'s healing or mystical aspects. In many Bantu languages, including Swahili, *ngoma* has also been employed since the mid-twentieth century to refer to 'traditional music' in general and to create a distinction between it and contemporary or urban genres – though making and maintaining such distinctions and divisions is increasingly futile.

The spelling of *ngoma* can vary according to language or language subgroup: *ngoma* (also sometimes *ng'oma*) is current in parts of Central and many parts of Eastern Africa, while in Uganda it is *engoma* (Kiganda), and in many Southern African languages *ingoma*. Variants and modifications of the root ('goma') according to the Bantu language noun class system are possible. For example, in Swahili an amplicative *goma* (sg.)/*magoma* (pl.) is used for a bigger drum or drums but also for a specific genre of drum–song–dance–performance linked (formerly) to state functions or the annual Nairuz festival, while *kigoma* (sg.)/*vigoma* (pl.) denotes a smaller drum. Abstract derivations are also possible, for example *mgoma* signifying a specific drum pattern for dancing as distinguished from the lyrical or song section of a performance.

Ngoma may denote any kind of drum (of differing designs or sizes), or an ensemble of drums. It may also denote a particular drum design (which may be different according to ethnic group), or (again different from one ethnic group to another) a particular genre of drum–song–dance. While any percussion instrument may be subsumed under the term *ngoma*, more particularly the term refers to membranophones.

Many *ngoma* genres are named after the leading drum or a drum characterizing the genre. *Msondo*, for example, is the lead instrument in the *msondo* genre (in many ethnic groups in Eastern Africa part of initiation/*rites de passage*); while *kidumbak* (a more recent genre from Zanzibar) is named after a set of small clay drums that characterize and differentiate the genre from others in Zanzibar.

The meaning of *ngoma* evolves also as part of everyday language use. In post-independence Tanzania, for example, *ngoma* – seen as 'traditional' and the true expression of the emerging new nation – was placed in opposition to genres seen as foreign imports (such as dance band music or *taarab*). In recent decades these imaginary boundaries have become more blurred. For example, the contemporary Tanzanian *muziki wa dansi* orchestra Mlimani Park reference their style with the Zaramo language *Sikinde, ngoma ya ukae*, 'Sikinde, the *ngoma* from home/from the tradition,' alluding to the musical traditions of the Dar es Salaam area and the rootedness of their decidedly contemporary style in the musical traditions of Tanzania. Another long-established dance band, Nuta Jazz Band, now call themselves and their style *Msondo Ngoma*.

There follows an example of *ngoma* in one particular country, Malawi.

Bibliography

Janzen, John M. 1992. *Ngoma: Discourses of Healing in Central and Southern Africa*. Berkeley: University of California Press.

WERNER GRAEBNER

Ngoma/Ingoma (in Malawi)

Ngoma and *ingoma* are very similar and related dances associated with two branches of the Ngoni people of Malawi who are the descendants of the Zulu of South Africa. The genre was originally a war dance.

The Ngoni arrived in Malawi as a result of the *mfecane* period of scattering among the Zulu (cf. Eldredge 1992, 1–35). Inkosi ya Makosi Zwangendaba Jere's followers are descended by the Ngoni Jere of the northern region of Malawi, while Inkosi ya Makosi Ngwana Maseko's followers' descendants constitute the Maseko Ngoni. The northern Ngoni (Jere Ngoni) call the dance *ingoma* while the Maseko call it *ngoma*. In the past the dance was performed to prepare for war as well as to celebrate victory. Since 1891, when Malawi became a British protectorate, the dance has been performed at traditional events including weddings, the installation of chiefs, funerals and political rallies.

In performance, both men and women wear traditional decorations that include headgear made of feathers or animal skins for males and beads for women, animal skin or other beadwork for the neck and shakers and rattles or iron bells on the legs. The men wear animal skin kilts (*zibiya*) and are bare-chested. Because of the political context in Malawi between 1964 and 1994, which forbade the use of any militaristic tools, carrying spears was problematic; and clubs (*zibonga*) tend to be used in Malawi instead. Shields are part and parcel of the choreography; and since 1994 some spears have made a comeback. In public performances since independence in 1964, many women, apart from Ngoni beadwork and token traditional decorative items, wear modern clothes, wraparound cloths (*zirundu*) and either head beadwork or *duku* (*doeks* head covering).

Song texts address social, political or cultural issues in Tumbuka and Chichewa, performed in polyphonic and call-and-response form, accompanied by a foot-stamping dance that provides the rhythm. Animal horns are used to provide a drone background. *Ngoma* has characteristic staccato handclaps that also provide rhythm; a basic triple meter tends to be the most frequently used. Characteristically no drums are employed.

Ngoma provides an example of an old war dance that has been transformed in the modern era to provide both entertainment and continuity with the past. The legacy of the old war tradition is evident in the 'war' choreography involved in the performances. In the dance, women sing as they proudly circle the men who dance in the middle; this is a carry-over from the days when the women needed to ritually protect the men before they went to war. The women are also responsible for wiping the men's brows and for picking up any items that fall from their costumes. The men, positioned in straight lines, dance rhythmically while stamping the ground and waving and shaking their shields and clubs. The women, apart from providing the music, which is sung in unison, ululate and provide the rhythmic handclap background.

Bibliography

Eldredge, Elizabeth. 1992. 'Sources of Conflict in Southern Africa, c. 1800–30: The "Mfecane" Reconsidered.' *The Journal of African History* 33(01): 1–35.

Maluwaya, McDonald (Kwacha National Dance Troupe choreographer). 2001. Personal written communication with the author.

Phiri, Dudwa Desmond. 2004. *History of Malawi: From Earliest Times to the Year 1915*. Blantyre: CLAIM.

Discography

UNESCO. 'Boya boya.' *Music Tradition of Malawi*. UNESCO Collection CD AUVIDIS D 8265. *1996*: France.

Filmography

Ngoni Traditional Dance and Music (Mchinji Ingoma Troupe), dir. John Lwanda. 2004. Malawi. 90 mins. Documentary.

JOHN LWANDA

Nidal

Nidal – literally meaning 'struggle' in Hassâniya, the characteristic Arabic dialect of the northwest African Bidhân region – is the most representative Saharawi music style. It was developed in the Saharawi refugee camps in southwest Algeria during the 16-year-long war that followed the Moroccan invasion of their country, Western Sahara, and the subsequent exodus in 1975. This music is also simply known as the 'Saharawi revolutionary song.'

El-nidal has its origins in the anti-colonial poetry that was developed in Western Sahara during the final years of Spanish colonial rule, in the late 1960s and early 1970s (Mahmud Awah 2015). In particular, the development of the early *nidal* is closely associated with the foundation of the Polisario Front – the Saharawi liberation movement – in 1973. Around this time, the Polisario leaders encouraged the composition of revolutionary songs inspired by the music and resistance poetry of neighboring countries such as Mauritania and Algeria. These songs were performed in secret political gatherings, recorded in cassettes and transported clandestinely across the country (Ruano Posada and Solana Moreno 2015).

When, in 1975, Spain transferred the administration of Western Sahara to Morocco (and for a few years, also to Mauritania), instead of starting the decolonization process demanded by the United Nations since the 1960s, the Moroccan army disregarded the pro-independence claims of the Polisario Front and took the country by force. Half of the Saharawi population went into exile and became refugees in southwest Algeria. They declared Western Sahara an independent nation in exile – the Saharawi Arab Democratic Republic (SADR) – on 27 February 1976, and started a desert war against Morocco. Once in the camps, the Saharawi refugees developed all the basic infrastructure of a nation, such as administration, hospitals, schools and a Direction of Culture that was in charge of the development and promotion of the 'revolutionary song' and its maximum representative, the national band El Uali.

The previously clandestine resistance songs were turned into symbolic anthems of the revolution, accommodating a myriad of musical influences along the way. *Nidal* music in the late 1970s and 1980s was mainly played on guitar, first the acoustic guitar that had been incorporated into traditional Saharawi music during the Spanish presence in the territory, and later on the electric guitar, which had already become a symbol of modernity throughout Africa (Kaye 2008). Musically speaking, the songs were a mixture of traditional *azawaan* modes, *tbal* drum playing and call-and-response singing, Arabic lute playing and singing, desert blues, rock and even hints of Spanish flamenco. The lyrics were praises in honor of the Saharawi liberation army, the newly formed nation, and the courage and pride of the Saharawi people.

Throughout the late 1980s *nidal* music was developed again with the introduction of new instruments such as the keyboard, saxophone and drum kit, as well as quicker, more danceable beats in some songs, in imitation of the national dance bands that had spread out throughout West Africa in the previous decades (e.g., Mali, Guinea and Senegal; Charry 2000). All these changes, together with intense international touring of the band El Uali, were attempts to promote the Saharawi self-determination struggle abroad.

After the ceasefire between Morocco and the Polisario in 1991, the production of Saharawi revolutionary music went into a holding period. However, it was revived years later through the international careers of Saharawi singer Mariem Hassan and, later on, Saharawi singer and percussionist Aziza Brahim. Aziza uses her music to advocate for a just and peaceful solution in Western Sahara, as well as to denounce Morocco's marginalization and mistreatment of those Saharawis who remained under occupation. Today, the Saharawis, both in the refugee camps and in occupied Western Sahara, still wait to be granted their right to vote in a self-determination referendum; and their music is the perfect embodiment of this hope.

Bibliography

Charry, Eric. 2000. *Mande Music: Traditional and Modern Music of the Maninka and Mandinka of Western Africa*. Chicago and London: University of Chicago Press.

Kaye, Andrew L. 2008. 'The Guitar in Africa.' In *The Garland Handbook of African Music*, ed. Ruth M. Stone. New York: Routledge, 88–109.

Mahmud Awah, Bahia. 2015. 'Generaciones literarias: Intelectualidad y política en el Sahara Occidental,

1850–1975' [Literary Generations: Intellectuals and Politics in Western Sahara, 1850–1975]. *Les Cahiers d'EMAM*: 24–5. Online at: https://emam.revues.org/774#article-774 (accessed 28 March 2018).

Ruano Posada, Violeta, and Solana Moreno, Vivian. 2015. 'The Strategy of Style: Music, Struggle, and the Aesthetics of Saharawi Nationalism in Exile.' *Transmodernity: Journal of Peripheral Cultural Production of the Luso-Hispanic World* 5(3). Onlineat:https://escholarship.org/uc/item0/4hm2f4pf (accessed 28 March 2018).

VIOLETA RUANO

Odonson

The Ghanaian *odonson* style of highlife evolved from coastal maritime-influenced forms of local guitar and accordion palmwine music (*osibisaaba, aṣíkò* [*ashiko, assiko*] and 'blues') that spread, beginning in the 1930s, into the Akan Ashanti, Brong-Ahafo and Nzima hinterlands, as well as the Kwahu mountains (see Asante-Darkwa 1974). As this music was taken inland, it became progressively indigenized and became known as 'odonson' (from the Akan word for love, 'odo'), 'Ashanti blues' or (according to the folk guitarist Koo Nimo) 'atini.'

Early History and Musical Characteristics

The indigenization or regionalization of coastal music took place because in the small inland towns and villages the guitar gradually replaced an old Akan six-stringed (occasionally seven- or eight-stringed) harp-lute or bridge-harp instrument. The Akan call this instrument the *seprewa* (or *seperewa*), which, according to *seprewa* player Osie Korankye, means an instrument that 'speaks when touched.' The *seprewa* is a squarish resonance box made of wood and animal skin and two lines of gut and fiber strings that pass over a high bridge and are attached to a wooden neck. Each string attachment is covered by a leather bracelet around the neck that can be adjusted to fine-tune each string (see Korletey 1989).

The *seprewa* itself was acquired by the Ashanti in the 1740s when their army defeated the neighboring Akan kingdom of Gyman in present-day Bondoukou in central Côte D'Ivoire. The Ashanti captured both the Bondoukou royal court *seprewa* and its one-legged player. Both were taken to the Ashanti capital of Kumasi where, as the gilded '*sika sankua,*' it became a favorite court instrument of the Ashanti king or Asantehene. This early use of the word 'sankuo' (or 'sanko' or 'sanku') for the *seprewa* is, according to Osei Korankye, derived from a Mande word. This would certainly make sense since Bondoukou is an old Sahelian trading town at the southernmost tip of the medieval trans-Saharan trade route operated by Mande-speaking peoples. So the *seprewa* can be treated as a small version of the harp-lute found throughout the Sahelian subregion, such as the 21-stringed Malian *kora*.

Beginning as the sole instrument of the Asantehene (king), the Akan *seprewa* was gradually democratized as it was taken up by Akan sub-chiefs. By 1815, when the British African Company agent Thomas Bowdich visited the Asante capital of Kumasi, the inland capital of the Asante forest kingdom, the *seprewa* or 'sanku' was in wide general use (Bowdich 1819). By then it was employed not only for the appellation and praising of chiefs, but also to accompany philosophical and topical songs played at funerals and places where the local alcoholic palmwine beverage was served.

As a result of cross-fertilization, some of the songs, techniques and modalities of the *seprewa* were transmitted in the 1930s to the *odonson* style of guitar playing. *Odonson* was played in slow 4/4 or 6/8 time, and it was sung exclusively in Akan (cf. the earlier coastal use of some Pidgin English) and in recitative (rather than verse) form. *Odonson* music also utilized the traditional Akan scale and modal practice of the melody, moving between two tonal centers a full tone apart, rather than the Western I/IV/V chord progression of coastal music.

The *seprewa*'s tuning is a relative one (related to the singer's pitch center) based on the traditional Akan heptatonic scale, which for the purpose of this discussion may be treated as a hexatonic scale with the addition of a flattened seventh. The melodies and harmonies (in parallel thirds) based on these scales, however, are not like the closed Western diatonic ones that go through various sequences and progressions that finally resolve on the single fixed tonic or 'do.' As mentioned earlier, Akan melodies alternate around two tone centers, a full tone apart. This is typical of Akan traditional music genres such as 'nnwonkoro' (Nketia 1973) and 'adenkum' (Aning 1968, 68), that are sung in the Akan modality starting on either the 'do' or 're' note of the scale. When the first six (hexatonic) notes of the Akan scale are divided into ascending thirds, the 'do' mode of *nnwonkoro* and *adenkum* is made up of the notes doh-me-so, and the 're' mode consists of the notes re-fa-la (respectively equivalent to a major triad and a superdominant minor triad). An identical modal arrangement is found in the music of the six-stringed Akan *seprewa*. Indeed, its very construction and tuning is modal, with the three left-hand strings tuned to do-mi-so, and the right-hand ones to re-fa-la. With this hexatonic tuning, the *seprewa* is played by continually swinging to and fro from one mode or tonal center to the other. In the key of G this would be equivalent to moving between the notes of a G major triad (G, B, D) and the superdominant one of A minor (A, C, E). These exact hexatonic modal sequences of GBD/ACE are used in some forms of *odonson* or 'Ashanti blues' guitar highlife, although on this Western instrument the three modal notes may also be simultaneously played as a triadic chord.

It should be noted, as mentioned earlier, that a flattened seventh can be added to these hexatonic scales, making them heptatonic, either for the singing or as an extra note for melodic instruments, such as a seventh string for the *seprewa*. In this case the extra flattened seventh note or 'te' (i.e., the flattened 'ti' note) then acts as the fourth ascending note in the 'do' mode (i.e., doh-me-so-te). Moreover, an eighth string can even be added to the *seprewa*'s 're' mode, thus resulting in the ascending sequence of re-fa-la-do, and so completing the octave.

For the sake of simplicity the remainder of this discussion will be limited to the simpler hexatonic arrangement. Another hexatonic modal sequence used by Akan guitarists consists of the notes of the superdominant triad with those of the relative minor, rather than the major of the 'do' triad. In the key of G, for instance, the modal sequence would alternate between A minor and E minor. There are also varieties of modal playing on the guitar that the six-stringed *seprewa* players cannot perform, as they involve the addition of the flattened seventh note that, although part of the Akan heptatonic scale, is usually missing from the traditional *seprewa* harp-lute. This means that in the key of G, for example, the guitarist need not only play a modal arrangement between G and the next tone up (i.e., the previously mentioned G/A minor sequence), but can also play such arrangements as between G (or triad G, B, D) and the next full tone below (i.e., the flattened seventh or F or triad F, A, C, based on F). Furthermore, the G triad can be substituted for its relative E minor so that the modal alternation can also be between the E minor triad and the F major (or major seventh) triad. An example is the 'Kwaa' form of Akan blues (after its composer the late Fanti guitarist Kwaa Mensah) that spans two cycles of a polyrhythmic 6/8 *adowa*-type bell pattern.

In Ghana a huge internal record market developed for palmwine highlife music. This began with the mid-1920s coastal *osibisaaba* style (of Kwame Asare, William Aingo, etc.), followed by the more indigenized or 'Akanized' *odonson* style of the 1930s. This was part and parcel of the 'native records' released by the European companies Zonophone, HMV, Parlophone and, according to Waterman (1990, 27, 47) the Lagos-based German Odeon company. Distributers were the United Africa Company and the Basel Mission's United Trading Company. By the 1930s tens of thousands of *odonson* records were being released annually by Ghanaian guitarists and occasionally by accordion/concertina players), including Kwese Manu, Osei Bonsu, Kwerki Bibi, Kwese Pepera, Kamkan, Piasah, Appiah Anning and Mireku. This lucrative pre–World War II industry was a result of lucrative cash crops (such as cocoa and oil palm) that enabled many Ghanaians (and Nigerians), including cash crop farmers, to buy wind-up gramophones. In fact, in Ghana this rustic style of palmwine music also became known as 'coco-ase' (under the cocoa tree) music.

From the 1950s to Date

During the late 1950s and 1960s the guitar bands became amplified; nevertheless the *odonson* style was maintained within the repertoire, although played on electric guitars. An example is Dr Gyasi's enormous 1972 record hit 'Sikyi Highlife' which was based on an *odonson* song played in 4/4 time and in which the melody moves between two minor chords a tone apart.

Since the 1970s a number of Ghanaian guitarists have returned to the older acoustic palmwine and *odonson* tradition. These include Koo Nimo, Kwabenah Nyama, the late T.O. Jazz and the younger

Kyekyeku (Eugene Oppong). Furthermore, since the 1980s the *seprewa* itself has made a comeback, beginning with Little Noah of Koo Nimo's band combining the *odonson seprewa* and guitar styles. Koo Nimo himself was based at the KNUST University in Kumasi, where he taught both guitar and *seprewa*, and he has continued teaching both instruments in his Adadan Cultural Resource Centre. Since the mid-1990s the *seprewa*, including its associated *odonson* style, has been played and taught by other younger university-based artists including Osei Korankye, Aaron Bebe Sukura and Balfour Kyeremanten. They have added an extra four to eight strings to the instrument's original six and they utilize Western tuning 'machine head' pegs instead of leather bands.

Following in Koo Nimo's footsteps, since the late 1990s Aaron Bebe Sukura and highlife guitarist John Collins have likewise combined the *seprewa* and guitar on stage and in recordings to play *odonson*-style highlife compositions as well more contemporary African music styles such as Afrobeat and *soukouss* (e.g., *N'yong* 2003). Recordings of the *seprewa* combined with modern band instrumentation have also been released by Osei Korankye with the former Osibisa Afro-rock band guitarist Kari Bannerman (*Seperewa Kasa* 2008), and Aaron Bebe Sukrua with the Ghanaian rap (hiplife) artist Wanluv the Kubolor (*Greencard* 2007), while the Australian-based 'world music' artist Afro Moses (Ernest Safo) occasionally uses the *seprewa* on stage.

Conclusion

A number of important points arise from this discussion of Akan *odonson* highlife. First, the eighteenth-century Akan acquisition of a Sahelian West African harp-lute demonstrates that there were musical exchanges between the forest and the Sudanic West African kingdoms long before European colonization. A second point is that Akan *seprewa* music played by guitars is another example of what Kauffman (1975, 132), in the context of Zimbabwean Shona guitar playing, has called the successful transfer of non-Western 'processal' practices onto new musical instruments. In the case of *odonson* highlife the traditional Akan 'processal' modes, scales and rhythms were not only transferred to acoustic guitars but, from the 1960s on, also were employed by electric highlife guitar bands. Third, in recent years the *seprewa* has been revived in Ghanaian universities where improvements have been made in terms of tuning, range of notes and even the addition of microphone pickups for stage performances. As a result, since the 1990s the instrument has been used on stage and in recording studios by highlife bands that combine guitars and *seprewas* and/or play various types of modern contemporary African music that range from Afro-rock and Afrobeat to local rap and 'world music.'

Bibliography

Aning Ben, A. 1968. 'Melodic Analysis of Adenkum.' *Papers in African Studies* (Legon: Institute of African Studies) 3: 64–80.

Asante-Darkwa, Kwadwo. 1974. *New Musical Traditions in Ghana*. Unpublished Ph.D. dissertation, Wesleyan University.

Bowdich, Thomas Edward. 1819. *Mission from Cape Coast Castle to Ashantee*. London: John Murray.

Catalogue of Zonophone West Africa Records by Native Artists. 1929. Hayes: British Zonophone Company.

Collins, E. John. 1985. *Music Makers of West Africa*. Washington DC: Three Continents Press.

Collins, E. John. 1994. *The Ghanaian Concert Party: African Popular Entertainment at the Crossroads*. Unpublished Ph.D. dissertation, SUNY Buffalo.

Collins, E. John. 1996. *Highlife Time*. Accra: Anansesem Press.

Collins, E. John. 2006. 'African Guitarism: 100 Years of West African Highlife.' *Legon Journal of the Humanities* 27: 173–96.

Kauffman, Robert. 1975. 'Shona Urban Music: A Process Which Maintains Traditional Values.' In *Urban Man in Southern Africa*, eds. C. Kileff and W. C. Pendelton. Zimbabwe: Mambo Press, 127–44.

Korletey, S. C. 1989. 'The Seprewa Harplute of the Akan People of Ghana.' Legon: Diploma in African Music for the Music Department of the University of Ghana.

Nketia, J. H. Kwabena. 1973. *Folksongs of Ghana*, Accra: Ghana University Press.

Waterman, Christopher A. 1990. *Jùjú: A Social History and Ethnography of an African Popular Music*. Chicago: University of Chicago Press.

Discographical References

Gyasi, Dr. K. and His Noble Kings. *Sikyi Highlife*. Essiebons EBL 6117. *1972*: Ghana.

Korankye, Osie, and Bannerman, Kari. *Seperewa Kasa*. Riverboat Records. *2008*: UK.
Local Dimension. *N'yong*. Arion S.A. Records. *2003*: France.
Wanluv the Kubolor and Aaron Bebe Sukura. *Greencard*. Pidgin Music. *2007*: Ghana.

Discography

Music in Ghana: A Selection of Popular African Music from the Archives of the Institute of African Studies, University of Ghana, Legon. PAMAP 601. *1997*: Germany.
Nimo, Koo. *Koo Nimo – Osabarima*. Shanachie. *1990*: USA.
Nimo, Koo. *Koo Nimo: Highlife Roots Revival*. Riverboat Records and World Music Network. *2012*: USA.
Nyama, Kwabena. *Sunday Monday*. Arion Disques. *2000*: France.
Rhythm of Life, Songs of Wisdom: Akan Music from Ghana, West Africa. Smithsonian/Folkways SF CD 40463. *1996*: USA.
Vintage Palmwine: Kwaa Mensah, Koo Nimo and T. O. Jazz. Otrabanda Records OTB02. *2003*: Netherlands.

Filmography

Crossing Over: Trinidad to Ghana /Ghana to Trinidad, dirs. Christopher Laird and Wallace Bampoe Addo. 1988. Ghana, Trinidad and Barbados. 60 mins. Documentary. (Features Koo Nimo.)
Rhythms of the World: Highlife in Ghana, dir. Wolfgang Huschert. 1993. Germany. 28 mins. Documentary. (Includes *odonson* guitar.)
Sounds from Ghana, dirs, Jochen Schell and Lucia Arias Ballesteros. 2012. Germany. 26 mins. Documentary. (Includes *seprewa* playing by Osei Koranky.)

E. JOHN COLLINS

Omutibo

Omutibo is a popular music genre performed among the Luhya of western Kenya for entertainment purposes in celebrations, parties, restaurants and cultural festivals. It is lively and danceable and is laced with lyrics describing love affairs and gender relations. It is regularly aired on regional vernacular radio stations such as Mulembe FM, to which the majority of people in Western Kenya listen frequently for general entertainment

According to the research carried out by Fred Wekesa Kusienya (hereafter Wekesa 2012), the pre- and post–World War II eras marked the beginning of guitar music in the nation of Kenya. The guitar was accepted by various ethnic communities in Kenya, among them the Abaluhya community, which adapted, traditionalized and appropriated the instrument to make it part and parcel of Luhya cultural music expression. In *omutibo* music, the technique of playing the guitar was borrowed from that of playing a Luhya lyre known as *litungu*. *Omutibo* music originated from Khayega village in Kakamega District in 1960, and spread to other parts of the Western Province (ibid.). While some of the instruments have been replaced or enhanced using new technology, the capoed rhythm guitar and its mode of playing have remained constant.

Origin

It is believed that, until the early 1950s, the main percussion instruments among the Abaluhya of Kakamega District of Kenya were the sticks or concussions. Shem Tupe, whose guitar playing and singing made him a legendary figure in western Kenya, explains (in Wekesa 2012) that when *isukuti* drums were invented, the rhythm of the small drum replaced the rhythm of the sticks. (For further information on *isukuti* drums see the entry on Isukuti.) The smallest *isukuti* drum produces a thinner and somewhat sharper sound that almost resembles the human voice or surrogate sounds. Wekesa observes that Nzewi (2005) describes the sounds (*tibo, tibo, tibo, tibo*, etc., as illustrated in Example 1, below) as mnemonic, because they reference the last two syllables of the name of the genre *omutibo*.

Example 1: The mnemonic sounds of *Isukuti mwana* (lead drum)

This sound later formed the basis of a new name 'omutibo' for the lead drum (Wekesa 2012).

Omutibo emerged as a style of music expression in Kenya in the early 1960s when the dry or box guitars were brought to the Western Province by returning war veterans. According to Tupe (2011 in Wekesa 2012), when the guitars arrived in Luhya land, it was a very exciting phenomenon. Guitarist Roland Isese (2011 in Wekesa 2012) observes that the first person to play the guitar in the *omutibo* style was known as Mr. Shisundi from Khayega village in Kakamega District; hence Isese attributes the origin of *omutibo* as a style of music expression to that village. George Mukabi, regarded as one of the main pioneers of *omutibo* music, evidently learned the *omutibo* style from Mr. Shisundi, later developing great versatility as a guitarist and surpassing his tutor in his performance skill level. Mukabi went on to become the popular agent of publicity of *omutibo* music through his recordings (ibid.).

Another guitarist, John Nzenze, (in Wekesa 2012) remembers that, when the guitar reached the Luhya community, the precursors of Luhya guitar music adopted the instrument and began learning how to play traditional melodies in the idiom of the *omutibo* drum. The guitar player was accompanied by percussion instruments including a Fanta soda bottle, a metal ring and a wooden board. This gave rise to another level of the definition of *omutibo*. It was later believed among the locals of Kakamega District that any instrumental ensemble consisting of one capoed guitar, a Fanta bottle, a metal ring and a wooden box was an *omutibo* jazz band, even before the band performed anything. Wekesa notes that, even if the instrumental ensemble described above played a different popular music genre, it was still believed to be *omutibo* music.

Musical Characteristics of Early *Omutibo* Music

Omutibo music, as the name suggests, employs the rhythmic idiom associated with the drum that was originally called the *omutibo* – played on *isukuti* drums. This music idiom is defined by a rhythmic pattern in simple time (Example 2) and a similar rhythm in compound time (Example 3).

Example 2: The *isukuti* rhythm in simple time (source: Wekesa 2012, reprinted with permission of the author)

Example 3: The *isukuti* rhythm in compound time (source: Wekesa 2012, reprinted with permission of the author)

According to Wekesa, *omutibo* music was generally performed in both simple and compound time meters in the following categories: compound duple, compound triple, compound quadruple, simple duple, simple triple and simple quadruple. The many types of meters contribute to the complexity, identity and beauty of *omutibo* music. The basic beat in compound time is a dotted note. In practice, the dotted note has three equal divisions: the first division is independent while the second and third divisions are tied together. This creates a syncopated effect that is characteristic of this music and that is sometimes referred to as the Luhya or *isukuti* beat. The *isukuti* beat conspicuous in the recordings of the 1960s is in both simple and compound time signature.

George Mukabi, one of the pioneer *omutibo* musicians, never recorded any of his songs in any language other than Swahili. This is because in the early 1960s the Kenyan government encouraged artists to record in the Swahili national language to foster national unity, identity and patriotism (Isese 2011 in Wekesa 2012). Wekesa argues that, with regard to recorded songs in the 1960s, though the name of the genre is derived from the traditional *omutibo* drum beat or rhythm, the *omutibo* drums were still not incorporated in the performances as part of the instrumental ensemble.

Generally, in the *omutibo* songs of the 1960s, the melody of the voice and the rhythm of the wooden board were in simple meter with the exception of the rhythm of the Fanta bottle, which was in groups of three pulses per every one rhythmic throb of the wooden board (Example 4).

Example 4: The Fanta soda bottle rhythm

Wekesa's analysis of selected early *omutibo* music revealed relatively short and repetitive melodies.

The songs were in simple strophic form without a refrain or chorus. The lyrics were mostly about love relationships and general social commentary on peaceful co-existence. The lyrics were simple and relatively few, hence easy to comprehend and memorize. The language generally used was plain and not figurative or symbolic.

Changes in *Omutibo* Music from the 1960s to 2008

Research by Wekesa established that the elements characterizing *omutibo* music, described above, remained unchanged between 1960 and 1970. He observes that 1970 to 1980 was a transition period for *omutibo* in a number of areas. During the 1960s, for instance, instrumentation of the *omutibo* ensemble included a Fanta bottle, a metal ring, a wooden board and one, or sometimes two, capoed acoustic guitars. From 1971 onwards some instruments were replaced immediately while others gradually faded from the ensemble. The capoed acoustic guitar was replaced immediately by electric guitars (lead, rhythm and bass). The metal ring, Fanta bottle and wooden board did not disappear until toward the end of the 1970s. The ensemble in this period comprised the original and 'new' instruments playing together, creating a hybrid effect. Recorded *omutibo* songs of the 1960s reveal a supportive style of accompaniment by the capoed acoustic guitar. However, this style changed, with the electric lead, rhythm and bass guitars all playing independent accompaniment for the vocal melody. The resulting sound is a blend of the many instruments and the vocal melody.

In addition, Wekesa notes that during the 1960s all *omutibo* musicians were men, though women became part of the *omutibo* ensembles from the 1970s onwards. The main role of the female musicians was to provide backup or response in a call-and-response song pattern. Wekesa observes that *omutibo* songs of the 1960s did not employ call-and-response form, though interview sources indicated that the solo-and-response technique was practiced in informal contexts. In a recording scenario, the call-and-response technique was first evident in the recorded *omutibo* songs of early 1971.

Omutibo songs of the 1960s contained only two male vocal parts, and harmony was borrowed from the Western style of two-part singing in intervals of thirds and sixths. However, from the 1970s to 2008, the voice parts increased from two male voices to three, and in some cases four, mixed voices. The harmony borrows from the Western style of soprano, alto and tenor, though not quite strictly. There is a tendency for voices to find themselves in unison at some points and to split into parts at others (Wekesa 2012).

Finally, Wekesa's analysis of the selected *omutibo* music reveals a notable change in duration. In the 1960s songs lasted between two and two-and-a-half minutes. From 1971 to 2008 songs began lasting between five and eight or sometimes ten minutes, especially in the latter portion of that period. From 2008 to 2017 there has been no significant change in song duration.

Omutibo in World Music

Some familiarity with the sounds of *omutibo* among the worldwide audience for world music became possible in the late 1980s thanks to the release by UK label Globestyle of a selection of records by the group Abana Ba Nasery, led by Shem Tupe, entitled *Classic Recordings of West Kenya*. Encouraged by the response to this recording, Globestyle also made a new recording by the group, *Nursery Boys Go Ahead*, in 1992. In 2017 US label Olvido released three recordings of historical *omutibo* recordings, using the recordings owned by Shem Tupe, including one devoted to the music of George Mukabi.

Bibliography

Nzewi, Meki E. 2005. 'Instrumental Music Ensemble as a General Musicianship Training Strategy.' In *Emerging Solutions for Musical Arts Education in Africa*, ed. Anri Herbst. Cape Town: African Minds, 203–10.

Wekesa Kusienya, Fred. 2012. 'The Evolution of Omutibo Guitar Music of the Abaluhya of Kakamega District of Kenya, from 1960 to 2008.' Unpublished MA thesis, Maseno University, Kisumu.

Informants Interviewed by Fred Wekesa Kusienya (from Wekesa Kusienya 2012).

John Nzenze, Kakamega Town (12 August 2011).
Roland Isese, Kakamega Town (2 February 2011).
Shem Tupe, Luanda Town (10 March 2011).

Discographical References

Abana Ba Nasery. *Classic Acoustic Recordings From West Kenya*. Globestyle CDORBD 052. *1989*: UK.

Abana Ba Nasery. *Nursery Boys Go Ahead!* Globestyle CDORBD 076. *1992*: UK.

Country Music of Western Kenya: 45s From the Archive of Shem Tupe. Limited edition. Olvido Records. No number. *2017*: USA.

Mukabi, George. *Furaha wenye gita*. Olvido Records OLV004. *2017*: USA

Usiende Ukalale, Don't Sleep: Omutibo From Rural Kenya. Olvido Records OLV005, *2017*: USA.

MELLITUS NYONGESA WANYAMA

Oromo Popular Music

Oromo is the name for a number of interrelated ethnic groups found largely in southern Ethiopia and northern Kenya. Ethno-linguistically defined, it is the third largest group on the entire African continent. Traditional Oromo music is pentatonic, heavily vocal and uses instruments that are common to other ethnic groups in Ethiopia, including the *krar* (a five- or six-stringed harp), the *masenko* (a single-stringed fiddle) and the *washint* (a bamboo flute). Unlike much traditional music in western sub-Saharan Africa, Oromo music is usually monorhythmic, featuring little in the way of cross-rhythms or complex syncopation. Triplet rhythmic feel is by far the most common (especially compound meters such as 6/8). Much Oromo popular music traces its origin to distinct traditional styles that have been repurposed to fit an increasingly modernized and urbanized existence. One such song style is *girarsa*.

Girarsa is traditionally sung by hunters or warriors, either to rile themselves up before action or to recount their exploits upon returning home. It is, therefore, typically sung extemporaneously by a solo male performer, and the rhythms are either free or dictated heavily by the poetic rhythm of the text. The text details images of rural life and themes of bravery, and it often contains double meanings used to disguise or complicate larger conceptual points. The warrior/hunter protagonist is the main reason why *girarsa* has become popular as a song style expressing political dissent, especially against successive Ethiopian governments, with which there has been tension since the overthrow of Emperor Haile Selassie in 1974. Many Oromo were imprisoned or forced into exile because of lyrics with thinly veiled references to perceived colonial outsiders (typically the Amhara and Tigray ethnic political groups from the north) as alien beasts or crops (especially as metaphorical 'weeds' damaging indigenous flora). These lyrics are a prominent example of an ethnic group using traditional elements from their past to deal with issues in the present.

Much Oromo popular music is composed and performed primarily on a Western keyboard (especially Casio, Roland or Triton). Most recording studios are found in homes and are minimally equipped with only one or two keyboards and a small mixer. Nearly all the music makes use of a particular horn timbre for the melody, which is considered the most important aspect of Oromo music because it is the vehicle through which the words are declared. Oromo musicians in the capital city Addis Ababa make use of the percussion sounds of the Western drum kit on the keyboards to arrange a rhythmic loop that is characteristic of the region from which it came (e.g., Wellega, Illubabur, Jimma, Shewa, Arsi, Harer, Bale and Borena).

Oromo popular music within Ethiopia has been heavily scrutinized by various governments over the last century and, as a consequence, musicians must be careful about choosing their topics. Accordingly, most pop songs are about love. In the diaspora, however, musicians may be openly political, hence the ubiquity of political songs in Oromo music coming out of Minneapolis, Norway and Australia. Well-known Oromo popular music performers include Ali Birra, Kamal Ibrahim, Mohammed Sheika, Dagim Makonnen, Jambo Jolte and Zerehun Wedejo.

Bibliography

Jalata, Asafa. 2005. *Oromia and Ethiopia: State Formation and Ethnonational Conflict 1868–1992*. Trenton, NJ and Asmara, Eritrea: The Red Sea Press.

Jalata, Kulani. 2009. 'The Role of Revolutionary Oromo Artists in Building Oromummaa: The Case of Usmayyoo Musa and Ebissa Addunya.' Paper presented at the July 2009 Oromo Studies Association conference at Georgia State University in Atlanta, Georgia. Online at: http://gadaa.com/oduu/?p=1782 (accessed 27 September 2017).

Mollenhauer, Shawn. 2011. *Millions on the Margins: Music, Ethnicity, and Censorship among the Oromo of Ethiopia*. Ph.D. dissertation, University of California Riverside. Online at: http://escholarship.org/uc/item/4v51v3wbP (accessed 27 September 2017).

Tolesa, Addisu. 1999. *Geerarsa Folksong as the Oromo National Literature: A Study of Ethnography, Folklore, and Folklife in the Context of the Ethiopian Colonization of the Oromo*. Lewiston, NY: The Edwin Mellen Press.

YouTube

Birra, Ali and Shabbo, Ali. *Ali Birra & Ali Shabbo Collections of Guitar Songs (Old Oromo Music)* (1974). https://www.youtube.com/watch?v=m39ovmrITe4

'Geerarsa.' Performed by Luuccee. 3.22 mins. https://www.youtube.com/watch?v=m5e0Jv3hqbM

SHAWN MOLLENHAUER

Oviritje

Oviritje is a genre of music sung in Otjiherero, the language of the Herero people in Namibia. It is performed and danced to at social gatherings and concerts, and represents the cultural practices and pride of the Herero people in Namibia's postcolonial society.

Oviritje is characterized by 4/4 meter and punchy up-tempo 'four-to-the-floor' beats with offbeat snares. Its sound typically features syncopated drum breaks, tone-bending synth effects, and rhythmic keyboards with distinctive dissonant harmonic variations. Deep and heavy vocal timbres and an open-throat style of singing and chanting are common to both male and female vocals, and most songs recorded between 2000 and 2015 used Auto-tune. Generally, the diatonic major scale is used for melodies, with a lowered seventh, creating a distinct musical color. The song's main vocal melody is often repeated by keyboards emulating organ or accordion sounds. Harmonic progressions are based on various I-IV-V patterns hailing from Western music. Lyrics dealing with personal stories of love, life and its challenges are sung, spoken and chanted in call-and-response form.

History

Namibia was a German colony from 1890 until 1915. During this period, Herero and Nama populations revolted against German rule, which led to a genocidal killing of 80 percent of the Herero, numerous San people and 35 percent of the Nama populations between 1904 and 1908. Many of the traditional songs in Herero culture commemorate the suffering of this period. Traditional music is performed *a cappella*, accompanied by handclapping and foot-stomping dances, with different repertoires for women and men.

During South Africa's occupation of Namibia (1915–90), apartheid divided the country into homelands, segregating the various ethnolinguistic groups. The territory of former Hereroland (northeast Namibia) now falls within the regions Omaheke and Otjozondjupa. The names of the former homelands (Hereroland, Owamboland, etc.) are no longer official terms, yet they are commonly used in everyday speech. Most Herero people have family houses and farms based in 'Hereroland,' yet people live in different areas of the country depending on their profession.

Before independence, men often were forced to work outside their homelands, which led to the creation of new cities where people of all backgrounds would mingle socially and musically. Black urban culture developed in the Namibian capital Windhoek between the 1920s and 1930s with various bands performing mainly covers of popular music from South Africa and the USA. The Bee Bob Brothers was a popular live band among the Otjiherero-/Ovambanderu-speaking community in the 1960s to 1970s, playing *mbaquanga* and pop music. Only from 1969 did the South African Broadcasting Corporation (SABC) start broadcasting Namibian music in vernacular languages through the launch of Radio Bantu. Various Namibian artists were recorded by SABC but Namibian music was not published or distributed until the country's independence in 1990. Still, in 2015, distribution is a challenge for the majority of Namibian artists. Most *oviritje* music is solely available in Namibia.

Between the 1960s and 1970s artists started repackaging their cultural heritage in modernized forms. Apartheid and the influence of Christianity oppressed local cultures and many cultural expressions were suppressed and lost. However, people found ways to make their music adapt and survive in modern society. Artists including Kareke

Henguva, Kakazona Kavari, Meisie Henguva, Oomzulu Pietersen, Matuarari Kaakunga and Bella Kazongominja started combining traditional *a cappella* Herero music – generally referred to as *konsert* – with modern instruments. Keyboards were introduced in Namibia from the 1980s and played a particularly important role in the development of this style. Between the early 2000s and the late 2010s the keyboard has been the main instrument from which the harmonies and drumbeats are played.

According to artist Big Ben, *oviritje* music was once performed *a cappella*. Melodies were vocal interpretations of the instrumentation of popular styles from South Africa such as *mbaqanga*, *kwela* and *maskandi*. These 'konsert' groups mainly existed in schools. Their performances were mostly in school halls and occasionally in tents in villages during school holidays. When modern instruments became more available to the black communities, most churches in Namibia started adding organs and keyboards to their sets, and these became part of *oviritje* music too, as most organists and keyboardists at that time started playing in churches. Big Ben also notes that *oviritje* music was originally mid-tempo but became a fast-paced style of dance music to compete with other locally popular genres such as *kwaito* and house.

Performance

Performances usually take place in concert halls and at festivals as well as at social functions and parties. Dance is an integral part of *oviritje* performances, with various dancers performing specific choreographies to show off their skills. Audiences are encouraged to dance along and sometimes called on stage during shows. Some shows host a full-band instrumentation including keyboards, live drums, electric bass and guitars.

Most artists follow the latest global fashion trends. However, the group Bullet ya Kaoko performs in traditional Himba attire (animal skins, red skin ointment and traditional hairstyles), captivating audiences with their original looks and performance style and combining *oviritje* with some *kwaito* elements. Most music videos feature both rural and urban locations and stylistic features (props, symbols, fashion), depending on the artists and where they are based. Most artists travel for music and other types of jobs between Namibia's capital Windhoek and north-east Namibia, where many Herero people still live and important sociocultural practices take place. Leading *oviritje* artists since 2000 have included Big Ben, Kappa Kamaheke, Tura Horns, Ondarata, Eto,' Ovikango, Otjiteke Tjowawa, Ozoseua, Oviku Viomuriro, Zulla boy, Fora Diego, Condest, Lovers and Doll, the Wild Dogs, Tuponda, Katja, Millenium, Kareke and Kakazona ua Kavari.

Conclusion

Almost no academic research was conducted on modern-day Namibian music styles until 2015, when the music history research group 'Stolen Moments – Namibian Music History Untold' started digitizing recordings from the National Archives. Up until then, no digitalized material was available apart from videos on YouTube, and access to field recordings of 'traditional music' as well as to popular Namibian music from between the 1950s and 1980s was hampered by the absence of working equipment. The digitization process will make Namibian music more accessible to the general public. Also, the Ngoma Research Collective studies contemporary and more traditional cultural practices in Namibia and shares its findings on its Facebook book page: https://www.facebook.com/pages/Ngoma-Research-Collective.

After Namibia's independence from apartheid in the 1990s, the various ethnolinguistic groups started 'defining, negotiating and legitimizing their identities in a new Namibian nation' (Markusic 2000, 1 in Mans 2003, 120). *Oviritje* represents the cultural identity of Herero people after the apartheid era, in which ethnicity was a tool for social segregation and indigenous cultural practices were undermined. The genre will continue developing as artists keep innovating ways of combining music and performance style from around the globe with their cultural Herero heritage.

Bibliography

Mans, Minette E. 2003. 'State, Politics and Culture: The Case of Music.' In *Re-Examining Liberation in Namibia: Political Culture Since Independence*, ed. Henning Melber. Uppsala: Nordiska Afrikainstitute, 113–29.

Mans, Minette. 2015. 'Traditional Music in Namibia.' *Music in Africa*, 2 October. Online at: http://musicinafrica.net/traditional-music-namibia (accessed 4 January 2017).

Matundu, Kae. 2013. 'Namibia: Is This Oviritje Moment of Truth?' *New Era*, 3 May. Online at: http://allafrica.com/stories/201305031299.html (accessed 4 January 2017).

Neshiko, Selma. 2015. 'The Live Music Scene in Namibia.' *Music in Africa*, 8 February. Online at: http://musicinafrica.net/live-music-scene-namibia (accessed 4 January 2017).

Powel, Azizi. 2013. 'Namibian Band Ovikango – "Omundu" (with partial English translation).' *Pancocojams*, 17 April. Online at: http://pancocojams.blogspot.be/2013/04/ovikango-omundu-with-partial-english.html (accessed 4 January 2017).

Steinmetz, George. 2005. 'The First Genocide of the 20th Century and Its Postcolonial Afterlives: Germany and the Namibian Ovaherero.' *Journal of the International Institute* 12(2). Online at: http://quod.lib.umich.edu/j/jii/4750978.0012.201/--first-genocide-of-the-20th-century-and-its-postcolonial?rgn=main;view=fulltext (accessed 4 January 2017).

Interviews

Big Ben. 2015. Interview with the author.
Gariseb, Andre J. 2015. Interview with the author.
Hoffmeyer, Retha-Louise. 2015. Interview with the author.
Kambaekwa, Carlos. 2015. Interview with the author.
Reid, Burton. 2015. Interview with the author.
Tjituka, Chris. 2015. Interview with the author.

Websites

African Promo Zone. Official Facebook page: https://www.facebook.com/permalink.php?id=550211878453743&story_fbid=585178834957047.

Artist directory: Bullet Ya Kaoko. 2015. Music in Africa: http://musicinafrica.net/directory/bullet-ya-kaoko.

Ngoma Research Collective. Official Facebook page: https://www.facebook.com/Ngoma-Research-Collective-329144573899787/timeline/

Official Myspace Page of Oviritje Contemporary: https://myspace.com/oviritje1/music/songs.

Stolen Moments Namibia – Namibian History Untold. Official Facebook page: https://www.facebook.com/Stolen-Moments-Namibia-193689374012214/timeline/

Discography

Bullet. *Maturi Pambara*. Label unknown. *2013*: Namibia.
Dr. Kareke. *Pone Peja*. Label unknown. *2012*: Namibia.
Kakoro & Waelly. *Muzepaui*. Label unknown. *2013*: Namibia.
Kazoozu Kaarondo. *Ombuharua ja Kaoko*. Label unknown. *2014*: Namibia.
MBM Music Production. *Old but not Cold*. Label unknown. *2014*: Namibia.
Ngoro no Mundu. *Mission Accomplished*. Label unknown. *2013*: Namibia.
Okazera. *Jeheja*. Label unknown. *2013*: Namibia.
Onyoka. *Ezorongondo*. Label unknown. *2008*: Namibia.
Otja Kariazu. *Mbinapuje*. Label unknown. *2013*: Namibia
Ozosondora zOndarata. *White Shoes*. Label unknown. *2013*: Namibia.
Rax. *Unreachable*. Label unknown. *2014*: Namibia.
Wild Dogs Dancing Club. *Yakindja*. Label unknown. *2014*: Namibia.

SHISHANI VRANCKX

Palmwine Music

'Palmwine' music is a term used retrospectively to describe collectively various early twentieth-century West and Central African music styles that originated from a combination of local instruments with the portable ones of visiting seamen, such as the concertina and guitar (and also banjo, harmonica, mandolin and pennywhistle) played at low-class dockside bars and rustic palmwine bars. These included subgenres and regional variants such as Ghanaian *osibisaaba* and *odonson*, Sierra Leonian *aṣíkò* (*ashiko, assiko*) music, Nigerian native blues and Central African *maringa*. All these in turn had a profound impact on the popular dance music of the guitar and dance bands of these countries beginning in the 1930s and 1940s, such as Ghanaian highlife, Nigerian *jùjú* music, Sierra Leonian *maringa*, Cameroonian *makossa* and Central African Congo jazz or *soukouss*.

The maritime origins of palmwine music go back to the Liberian Kru (or Kroo) people, who were traditionally long-distance canoe-men and were therefore employed by the Europeans as navigators and, beginning in the late eighteenth century, as seamen, first on sailing boats and then, in the mid-nineteenth century, in British and American steamships (Brooks 1972 and Schmidt 1998). Beginning in the late nineteenth century, these cosmopolitan Kru mariners Africanized the guitar on the high seas by developing the distinct West African two-finger plucking guitar technique and by creating distinct music styles such as *dagomba* (the name of a ship), fireman (ship's coal-stoker) mainline and *krusbass (*Kru guitar bass line). These they spread along the West/Central African coast through offshore visits, or via the Kru-town settlements established in major ports. The following will examine palmwine music and its regional variants and offshoots in more detail in the Central and West African countries of Sierra Leone, Nigeria, Ghana, Democratic Republic of Congo and Cameroon.

Sierra Leone

There was a Kru-town in Freetown from the nineteenth century, and by the 1920s it had grown to around 5,000 people. The sort of music the Kru musicians there played can be gleaned from some of the later 1930s to 1950s recordings (by Decca) of the Kroo Young Stars Rhythm Group. Kru music influenced both the local palmwine and *maringa* music of the Krio (Creole) people of Sierra Leone's capital. According to the Freetown percussionist Samuel Oju King (Collins 1985, 39), palmwine music was played in Freetown's low-class bars by guitarists such as 'Useless Man' Foster and the seaman Eku, who were accompanied by percussionists on cigarette tins and bottles. Other instruments included concertinas, musical saws, the giant *congama* lamellophone and *aṣíkò* frame drums. *Maringa* appeared later and was sung in Krio or an indigenous ethnic language and was popularized in recordings beginning in the 1940s by Ebenezer Calender and later Sooliman Ernest Rogie. Some titles of early palmwine/*maringa* songs are 'King Jimmy,' 'Lazy Woman,' 'Trungayaise' (Ruffian), 'Sweetie Palmwine,' 'Fire Fire' and 'River Rokel' (ibid., 39–41). According to Nicodemus Fru Awasom, a historian at Gambia University (personal communication), Sierra Leone's nearby English-speaking neighbor, Gambia, also developed a guitar palmwine style called 'Mbuh' during the colonial period in working-class areas such as Abakpa-Bamenda.

Nigeria

Both Waterman (1990, 47 and 1988, 130/137) and Alaja-Browne (1985) refer to the 'Krusbass' two-finger technique of Lagotian palmwine music in the 1920s and 1930s. In fact, Lagos's largest interwar palmwine group, the Jolly Orchestra, was based at the harbor-front marina and its leader was the Kru ex-seamen 'Sunday Harbour Giant.' Its songs were often sung in Kru or Pidgin English, the *lingua franca* of the coast. Later palmwine exponents were Ambrose Campbell and Julius Araba. As noted by Christopher Waterman, palmwine music underwent regionalization before World War II as it dispersed from the port city of Lagos into the hinterland, where, combined with influences from *aṣíkò* (*ashiko*) and *agidigbo* lamellophone music, it evolved into 'native' blues and later *jùjú* music (Waterman 1988, 247 and 1990, 39, 45). Early native blues exponents were the Yorùbá guitarists Irewolede Denge and S.S. Peters (from eastern Ijaw, Nigeria), both based in Lagos in the 1930s. Native blues was also popularized in eastern Nigeria during the 1940s and 1950s by Okonkwo Adigwe's Three Night Wizards, Stephen and Aderi Olariechi, and Stephen Amechi. Their acoustic music fed into the 1960s eastern and midwestern Nigerian highlife music of Victor Uwaifo, Stephen Osita Osadebe (Soundmakers), Paulson Kalu, Raphael Amanabae (Peacocks), Michael Eleagha (Music Royals) and the Oriental Brothers. Jùjú on the other hand was created in western Nigeria in the early 1930s by Tunde King, Ojoge Daniel and Ayinde Bakare from a combination of various elements, one being the small rectangular samba frame drum introduced by the thousands of freed Brazilian slaves who settled in Lagos in the late nineteenth century. From the African side came palmwine music and *aṣíkò* (*ashiko*) that was combined with Yorùbá *agidigbo* music and traditional Yorùbá praise music.

Ghana

There was also a Liberian Kru musical influence through their Kru-towns in the coastal Fanti towns of Ghana, while Fanti fisherman themselves had communities on Liberian offshore islands. Around 1900 in the Fanti port towns of Cape Coast and El Mina the Kru concertina/accordion and guitar music, as well as imported Sierra Leone *aṣíkò* (*asíikò*) music, was combined with local Fanti recreational styles.

This led to early coastal palmwine music styles such as *annkadaamu* (Mensah 1971 and 1972), the slow tempo Akan 'blues,' *opim* or *eho/oho* (Collins 1996, 3) and the *osibisaaba* style and its accompanying ring dance. In fact, the Fanti fishermen had a traditional recreational music known as *osibi* which is probably the origin of the name *osibisaaba*. However, beginning in the mid-1920s the word *osibisaaba* gradually became replaced by the generic Ghanaian term for its popular music 'highlife,' coined when local street music began to be played by local high-class dance orchestras.

The Fanti Kwame Asare (a.k.a. Jacob Sam) is considered to be the godfather of Ghanaian *osibisaaba* style of palmwine music and according to his nephew, the guitarist Kwaa Mensah (Collins 1985, 13), Asare learned guitar from a Kru man. Asare's Fanti group was formed around 1918 and consisted of two guitars and a member playing either the *adaka* (wooden box) or castanets (wooden *claves*). In the 1920s Asare's group became known as the Kumasi Trio when it relocated to the inland Ashanti capital of Kumasi where its three members worked for the Tarkwa Trading Company. This company arranged their first recording in London for Zonophone (EZ label), which in 1928 released the first recorded versions of the well-known Ghanaian highlife 'Yaa Amponsah' (a woman's name). Like the Kru styles, 'Yaa Amponsah' is played in a major scale and uses Western chord progressions. However, instead of the calypso-type *clave* rhythm of Kru music it utilizes a traditional Akan triple offbeat bell rhythm, found for example in Akan *sikyi* music.

During the 1930s *osibisaaba*, along with other coastal accordion/guitar styles, percolated into the rural hinterlands of southern Ghana, where it gradually replaced the traditional Akan *seperewa/seprewa* harp lute associated with praising chiefs, funerals and palmwine drinking. This resulted in the development of guitar styles based on this local instrument's modes that became known as *odonson*, *atini* or Ashanti 'blues,' a slow form of highlife played in either 2/4 time or an alternation of duple and triple time related to the traditional polyrythmic 6/8 bell rhythms of traditional Ashanti *kete* and *adowa* drum-dances (Nketia 1957, 15; Sprigge 1961, 78, 80). Records of both the coastal *osibisaaba* and later rural *odonson* forms of palmwine music were part of the large prewar 'native artists' record industry of companies like Zonophone (1929), HMV, Odeon and Parlophone. Both forms also helped lay the foundation for the guitar bands of the 1950s, when the smaller palmwine trio format was expanded in the 1940s by Appiah Adjekum (who added three *konkoma* frame drums), followed in around 1950 by E.K. Nyame (an ex-Adjekum member), whose guitar band utilized highlife dance-band instruments such as the double bass, trap-drums and Afro-Cuban bongos. However, the two-finger guitar-picking palmwine style was retained, even when E.K.'s, and the other numerous guitar bands modeled on it, became amplified or went electric beginning in the 1960s.

In the music of one of Ghana's outstanding guitarists of the later twentieth century, Koo Nimo, older traditions of palmwine music are rediscovered with pride, together with other aspects of Ashanti heritage such as poetry and proverbs, and melded with modern ideas and sensibilities (see Kaye 1992 and 1999; Obeng-Amoako Edmonds 2016). In the early 2000s Koo Nimo was central to the process by which Ghanaian palmwine music became part of the world music scene.

Central African Congolese Music

The Liberian Kru people were a component of the 5,000 English-speaking West African 'coastmen' recruited between 1885 and 1908 by King Leopold of the Congo Free State (now Democratic Republic of Congo) to perform contract work as clerks, artisans, sailors and railroadmen at the port of Matadi at the mouth of the Congo River (Cornet 1958) It was these 'coastmen' who both set up the country's first dance orchestra (the Excelsior Orchestra) and influenced the earliest recognized Congolese style of popular dance music, *maringa*, played on frame drums, the *likembe* lamellophone, accordions and guitars. This informal barroom music, sung in the evolving trans-ethnic Lingala trade-language of Central Africa, surfaced around 1914 in the coastal Matadi–Kinshasa area and, during the 1920s, spread as far as Shaba in eastern Congo, via the navigable Congo River, railways and migrant mine workers (Kazadi 1973). It was also the West African 'coastmen' who introduced the two-finger palmwine guitar technique that was used by the local Congolese sailor-musicians Dondo Daniels and Antoine Kolosoy Wendo (Ewens 1994).

These techniques were subsequently used in the 1950s by both the early Kinshasa and Brazzaville-based Congo jazz (*soukouss*) dance bands of Kalle, Franco and Les Bantous, as well as the guitarists from Swahili-speaking eastern Congo such as Jean Bosco (Rycroft 1961 and 1962) and Losta Abelo, who played acoustic or 'dry' (i.e., non-amplified electric) guitar accompanied by rhythms tapped out on a bottle.

Cameroon

Makossa is a southern Cameroonian popular dance music that emerged in the 1940s as a blend of local recreational music styles with the *maringa* of the neighboring Congos and the *aṣíkò* (*ashiko*, *assiko*) form of guitar/accordion palmwine music introduced by English-speaking West African seamen. The most popular *aṣíkò* groups in the Cameroons in those days were those of Jean Aladin Bikoko and Uncle Jospeh Medjo. *Aṣíkò* was followed by the *makossa* of the 1950s and 1960s, pioneered by bands (acoustic and later amplified/electric) run by Eboa Lotin, Misse Ngoh, Mama Obandja and Ebanda Manfred.

Conclusion

In short, beginning in the late nineteenth century, along the West/Central African coast from Freetown to Matadi, the music and instruments of cosmopolitan African sailors resulted in early coastal forms of transcultural palmwine music such as *aṣíkò*, *osibisaba* and 'native blues'. These in turn helped lay the foundation for twentieth-century popular music styles such as West African *maringa*, highlife, *jùjú* music and *makossa* – and Central African *soukouss*.

Bibliography

Alaja-Browne, Afolabi. 1985. *Juju Music: A Study of Its Social History and Style*. Unpublished Ph.D. dissertation, University of Pittsburgh.

Bender, Wolfgang. 1989. 'Ebenezer Calender – An Appraisal.' In *Perspectives on African Music*, ed. Wolfgang Bender. Bayreuth African Studies Series 9. Bayreuth: Bayreuth University/German Research Council, 43–68.

Brooks Jr., George E. 1972. *The Kru Mariner in the 19th Century: An Illustrated Historical Compendium*. Newark, DE: Liberian Studies Association in America.

Catalogue of West African Native Artists. 1929. Hayes, Middlesex: British Zonophone Company.

Collins, E. John. 1985. *Music Makers of West Africa*. Washington DC: Three Continents Press.

Collins, E. John. 1996. *Highlife Time*. Accra: Anansesem Press.

Cornet, René J. 1958. *La Bataille de Rail: la construction du chemin de fer de Matadi au Stanleypool* [The Rail Battle: The Construction of the Railway from Matadi to Stanleypool]. Brussels. Edition Cuypers.

Ewens, Graeme. 1994. *Congo Colossos: Franco and OK Jazz*. N.p. (UK): Buku Press.

Kaye, Andrew Laurence. 1992. *Koo Nimo and His Circle: A Ghanaian Musician in Ethnomusicological Perspective*. Unpublished Ph.D. dissertation, Columbia University.

Kaye, Andrew L. 1999. 'Koo Nimo: A Contemporary Ghanaian Musician.' *Journal of the International Library of African Music* 7(4): 147–65.

Kazadi, Pierre. 1973. 'Trends in 19th and 20th Century Music in Zaire Congo.' In *Musikulturen Asiens Afrikas und Oceaniens* No. 9, ed. Robert von Gunther. Regensburg: Gustav Bosse Verlag, 267–88.

Mensah, Atta Annan. 1971/2. 'Jazz - the Round Trip.' *Jazz Forschung/Jazz Research* 3/4: 124–37.

Nketia, J. H. Kwabena. 1957. 'Modern Trends in Ghana Music.' *African Music Society Journal* 4: 13–17.

Obeng-Amoako Edmonds, E. 2016. *Six Strings and a Note: Legendary Agya Koo Nimo in His Own Words*. Accra: Ink City Press.

Rycroft, David. 1961. 'The Guitar Improvisations of Mwenda Jean Bosco,' Part One. *African Music Society Journal* 2(4): 81–98.

Rycroft, David. 1962. 'The Guitar Improvisations of Mwenda Jean Bosco,' Part Two. *African Music Society Journal* 3(1): 86–102.

Schmidt, Cynthia. 1998. 'Kru Mariners and Migrants of the West African Coast.' In *Garland Encyclopaedia of World Music, Volume I: Africa*, ed. Ruth M. Stone. New York and London: Routledge, 370–81.

Sprigge, Robert. 1961. 'The Ghanaian Highlife: Notation and Sources.' *Music in Ghana* 2: 70–94.

Stewart, Gary. 2000. *Rumba on the River: A History of the Popular Music of the Two Congos*. London and New York: Verso.

Waterman, Christopher A. 1988. 'Aṣíkò, Sákárà and Palmwine: Popular Music and Social Identity in

Inter-War Lagos, Nigeria.' *Urban Anthropology* 17(2/3): 229–58.

Waterman, Christopher A. 1990. *Jùjú: A Social History and Ethnography of an African Popular Music*. Chicago: University of Chicago Press.

Discographical References

Bokoor Band. 'Trungayaise.' *Electric Highlife*. Naxos. *2002*: USA/Hong Kong.

Calender, Ebenezer. 'Fire Fire.' Decca West Africa WA 2502. *1950–1*: West Africa.

Kumasi Trio. 'Yaa Amponsah. Parts 1 and 2.' Zonophone EZ 1001. *1928*: UK.

Discography

Calender, Ebenezer. 'Double Decker Bus.' Decca West Africa 26411. *1952*: West Africa.

Dairo, I. K. *Definitive Dairo*. Xenophile. *Late 1990s*: USA.

Early Guitar Music from West Africa 1927–9. Heritage Records HT CD 33. *2003*: UK.

Fatai Rolling Dollar Returns. Jazzhole Records. *2010*: Nigeria.

Ghana Muntie: Recordings from the GBC Ghana Radio Gramophone Library 1947–62. Centre for World Music. *2012*: Germany.

Golden Afriques Volume 2 (Congolese music 1956–82). Network Medien. *2005*: Germany.

Juju Roots 1930–50s. Rounder Records 5017. *1999*: USA.

Kroo Young Stars Rhythm Group . 'A Se To Kpa.' Decca WA 2523. *Early 1950s*: West Africa.

Marvellous Boy: Calypso from West Africa. Honest Johns HTRCD 38. *2009*: UK.

Ngoma Fleurs musicales du Cameroun. FMC/Afrovision. *Early 1980s*: Cameroon.

Ngoma: Souvenir ya l'indépendance. PAMAP. *1997*: Germany.

Nimo, Koo. *Highlife Roots Revival*. Riverboat Records/World Music Network TUG1064. *2012*: USA.

Nimo, Koo. *Osabarima*. Adasa ADCD 102. *1990*: UK.

Nyama, Kwabena. 'Sunday Monday.' *Ghana musique de vin de palme*. Buda Musique 1979352. *2000*: France.

Popular Music Ghana 1931–57. Disques Arion. *2002*: France.

Rogie, Sooliman Ernest. *Dead Men Don't Smoke Marijuana*. Realworld/CEMA. *1997*: UK.

Roots of Highlife. Heritage Records. *1992*: UK.

Sam, Jacob, and the Kumasi Trio. *Jacob Sam and the Kumasi Trio*. Heritage HTCD 28. *1995*: UK.

Sierra Leone: West African Gramophone Records. Zenzor Germany ZS 41. *1988*: Germany.

The Arthur S. Albert Collection: More Tribal, Folk and Cafe Music of West Africa. Ryko 10401 *1998*: USA. (Library of Congress Endangered Music Project.)

The Palmwine Sounds of S.E. Rogie. Workers Playtime LP9. *1989*: UK.

The Roots of Juju Music 1928: Domingo Justus. Heritage Records. *1993*: UK.

The Rough Guide to African Guitar Legends. Rough Guide RGNET 1259CD. *2011*: UK.

The Rough Guide to Congo Gold. World Music Network 1200. *2008*: UK.

The Rough Guide to Congolese Soukous. World Music Network RGNET 1050. *2002*: UK.

Vintage Palmwine. Otrabanda Records. *2003*: Holland.

Filmography

Highlife: From Yaa Amponsah to Telephone Lobi, dir. Theo Uittenbogaard. 1999. Holland. 30 mins. Dutch NPS TV documentary.

Konkombe: The Nigerian Pop Music Scene, dir. Jeremy Marre. 1989. UK. 60 mins. Documentary.

On the Rhumba River, dir. Jack Sarasin. 2007. France. 80 mins. Documentary.

Rhythms of the World: Highlife in Ghana, dir. Wolfgang Huschert. 1993. Germany. 30 mins. Documentary.

E. JOHN COLLINS

Pandza

Pandza is one of Mozambique's youngest popular music genres. It was born in the club scene of the early 2000s when DJs in the capital, Maputo, were looking for a Mozambican sound that would encourage people to dance. At a time when the clubs were dominated by imported dance music, predominantly from South Africa, Angola and the Democratic Republic of Congo, there was clearly a need for something more homegrown. The unmistakably Mozambican *marrabenta*, although popular at parties and listened to by every generation, was lacking contemporary subject matter and the prerequisite electronic club sound. However, played alongside dancehall *ragga*, the *marrabenta* mash-up never failed to fill the dance floors. It had the same tempo or bpm (beats per minute) essential for effective live mixing, and the emphasis on the downbeat of the *ragga* drum patterns fused well with the instantly recognizable guitar shuffle of *marrabenta* from the 1970s. The contemporary beats and sounds brought the iconic voices of Xidiminguane, Dilon Djinji and Antonio Marcos into the twenty-first century. Coming at a time when recording technology was becoming more accessible, DJs soon became producers and recording artists in their own right. They took their experience from the clubs into the small studios proliferating around the city and built on the winning *ragga-marrabenta* groove to sing of the day-to-day realities of the young audience in a light and irreverent manner that suited the party scene. It took some time to settle on a name for this new sound but, in 2005, the first recognized *pandza* track, 'Foto,' was released by DJ Ardiles and became an overnight success. A vibrant cassette distribution network quickly took the sound to all parts of the country and *pandza* soon took over from Congolese *kwasa kwasa*, Angolan *kizomba* and South African *kwaito*, becoming the genre of choice in the parties, clubs and streets of Mozambique. Despite some challenges, *pandza* has grown into an internationally recognized African dance genre that has continued to reflect the challenges, aspirations and perhaps necessarily irreverent spirit of young Mozambicans.

Mention *pandza* in Mozambique and two names will soon come up: Ziqo and DJ Ardiles. These names will often be followed by a declaration of affinity with one or the other as to who actually invented *pandza*. DJ Ardiles cites others such as hip-hop artist N'Star as being part of this early group of key players in the history of *pandza*, while recognizing that the early partnership between himself and Ziqo was fundamental:

> I never want to talk about who was the first, who wasn't, but I know me and Ziqo were very important – and it wasn't just the two of us, there were 15 or 20 of us – and in addition to them there were those who developed the dance, and those who listened; proud of what was happening and helped take it to the next level. Many people made us grow into what we are now.
> (DJ Ardiles: interview with author, January 2014)

Unlike its forerunner *marrabenta*, *pandza* is a product of a young generation growing up in the postcolonial, post-communist and commercialized Mozambique of the twenty-first century (Mozambique gained independence from Portugal in 1975; from 1977 to 1992 the country was governed by the Marxist regime of President Samora Michel, a period plagued by civil war). This 'modernity' is reflected in the branding, the iconography and the lyrics, as well as in the dance that accompanies the music. Equally homegrown, *pandza* dance steps reflected the increasingly individualized world of Mozambique's post-communist generation, where individual expression was celebrated and 'anything goes.' Unlike *marrabenta*, in which a specific dance step was identified as the genre began to flourish in the 1960s and has continued to be performed in a relatively unembellished form, a *pandza* dancer makes their mark by infusing the dance steps with individual creativity. *Pandza* has remained a very male genre, and the dancing is generally performed either solo, where individual self-expression is paramount, or in tightly choreographed routines by male duos or troops who set the bar for the public and other dancers participating in the genre for the first time. Although constantly evolving, deft footwork reminiscent of South African *mapantsula* is generally present, imaginatively combined with the sensual hip movements of *zouk*, the acrobatics of break dance and the swagger of hip-hop. *Pandza* producer Mr. Dino, who worked with DJ Ardiles and Ziqo from the outset, puts the need to satisfy the Mozambican's love of dance at the center of the creation of *pandza* in the film, *Pandza Land (Pais do Pandza)*: '*Pandza* is African music and African people love to dance and move, so it needs to have a good drums and percussion, mastering that gets you dancing and a message that you enjoy, because it's not a music to concentrate to, it's dance music, there for joy, happiness and to party.'

As for the music, DJ Ardiles brought his knowledge of branding and marketing from his undergraduate studies of business administration to the conscious creation of this new genre: 'I began as a DJ, then in 2005 became a professional musician, producer, composer. The artists I produced didn't have a clear "line," and I became interested in creating one. I wanted to enter into the market with an Ardiles different to the artists I produced' (DJ Ardiles: interview with author, January 2014).

The use of the term 'pandza' was another considered element in the creation of the genre. Key players at the time were all asked to propose names for the genre; other terms such as 'dzukuta' and 'moza' were also in use before 'pandza' was settled upon. Perhaps this term prevailed because, in the local languages of Changana and Ronga, 'pandza' describes beating or ripping something up, much as when certain grooves take over the body and get people dancing despite themselves. The word 'pandza' also conjures up the kind of confusion typically found in Mozambican daily life, a confusion which can be viewed with exasperation or laughter. When something is 'pandza,' it is so full of contradictions or light and shade that it is difficult to know whether to laugh or cry.

Although designed as dance music and not for serious contemplation, the themes of *pandza* tracks generally make a point of reflecting on daily life in the Mozambican cities and surrounding suburbs. Some *pandza* tracks have addressed issues related to the day-to-day challenges of life in Mozambique, much as the older, socially critical genre of *marrabenta* had previously done. However, until about 2010, much *pandza* tended to reflect what the South African DJ Le Blanc has described as 'the same things that bug young people today all over the world: partying, money, fancy cars, brand clothes, love, and girls' (DJ Le Blanc, quoted in Jentzsch 2013). These realities were new to the *pandza* generation in Mozambique, and the light-hearted lyrics reflected the rosy economic climate of the late 2000s when, for the first time in Mozambican history, young urban Mozambicans were discovering what it was like to have money. The songs celebrated branded clothes, smartphones, chic clubs and beach bars. This was a life these young people had only previously seen in movies. Nevertheless, there was generally a simple message to mull over, hidden in the laughter and fun. For example, in the track 'Foto' the theme is the use of the cameras in smart phones, which had become an important element of a cool young upwardly mobile urban Mozambican wardrobe. With his simple repeated hooks and call-and-response riffs, DJ Ardiles sings of a world of which the parents of this *pandza* generation had never dreamed. The young were embracing the modern world of the Brazilian soaps and Hollywood movies that Mozambique seemed to have finally adopted.

DJ Ardiles also reminded listeners, albeit in a light-hearted way, to reflect on the potential misuse of this new technology:

VERSE:	Todo lado onde eu vou	Everywhere I go
	Tem alguem que me tira uma foto	Someone's taking my picture
CALL:	Na barraca	In the street bars (barraca),
RESPONSE:	Foto!	Photo!
CALL:	Discoteca	Discoteque
RESPONSE:	Foto!	Photo!
CALL:	Minha mulher	My woman
RESPONSE:	Foto!	Photo!
CALL:	Em casa,	At home
RESPONSE:	Foto!	Photo!
CHORUS	Deixa minha vida	Leave me be
	Deixa minha vida	Leave me be
	Deixa minha vida	Leave me be

Another successful early DJ Ardiles track reflecting this new wealth and social transformation was 'Meninas bonitas' (Pretty Girls) (2009). In the video, girls dance in their designer shorts and bikinis on a yacht. The lyrics of the song reflect the thoughts of a man wanting to pick up a girl, one of these girls perhaps: he wants a pretty one, but now also one with high social status, one with a car, one who studies:

Nesta vida ja nao quero stress, pa! / In this life I don't want stress, pa!

Uma dama que nao de-me cash pa! / A woman who doesn't give me cash, pa!

This song could be taken to reflect an intermediary stage in women's shifting place in Mozambican society. With girls' attendance at the growing number of state and independent universities reaching an all-time high, and while women remained objectified, a woman's education and financial autonomy was now also celebrated. It is possible that this song represents the *pandza* way of celebrating a new place for educated, independently thinking women in Mozambican society.

Despite what refined international producers and DJs saw as the 'lo-fi production' of these early *pandza* tracks, with its 'cheap-sounding midi synths, digital drum kits, funky basses and live guitar licks, glued together by sweet auto-tuned voices' (DJ Le Blanc quoted in Jentzsch 2013), the mastering process worked well for the 'lo-tech' sound systems and home speakers for which the tracks were produced. *Pandza* was effectively home-produced and this represented a significant advance in the Mozambican popular music industry where previous generations of popular musicians had had to hand production over to strangers.

In 2010 economic growth began to come to a standstill. The development of *pandza* suffered a setback when the closing of two Mozambican record labels pushed production and distribution back into the hands of international labels in South Africa, Portugal, Angola and Brazil. In response to the image of *pandza* among the international community as 'rough around the edges,' as well as to the challenges of depending on a local market, Ziqo and DJ Ardiles decided to 'upgrade.' They teamed up with three other *pandza* artists, Mr. Kuka, DH and DJ Junior, to form an umbrella organization, the *Republica de Pandza* (Pandza Republic), which could support and promote *pandza* artists and promote them further in the global arena:

> By 2010 fewer people were making *pandza* tracks. That's when I decided to start a group, something which we had never had in Mozambique before, which was where *pandza* would be created. If a new artist appears on the market playing *pandza*, they will come out of the *Republica de Pandza*. If they want to sell a record, make a music video, the *Republica de Pandza* will help them. If there's a talented musician becoming successful, they can remain independent, but we can advise and support. The *Republica de Pandza* would have a '*pensamento da pandza*' (*pandza* thinking) at its center. We started with talent and passion, nothing else. Three years later in 2013 we managed to reach our objective. People had been saying '*pandza* is dead' and we said no rhythm dies! [People] … stop doing what they were doing and [we] stop talking about the genre. But if we give it a new 'tonic' it can come back to life.
>
> So, we made an 'upgrade' and in 2013 we could see it paid off.
>
> (DJ Ardiles: interview with author, January 2014)

One aspect of this '*pandza* upgrade,' in addition to the quality of the recordings and videos, was a shifting direction in the themes of the songs. In 2013 the economic boom seemed a thing of the past, and the country was heading toward a prolonged financial crisis. The songs reflected the impact of this economic downturn on the average Mozambican *pandza* fan. For example, one major hit in 2013 was Ziqo's 'Barrakeni,' in which a wife is portrayed as being angry with her husband for drinking all the wages and leaving the family with nothing. The husband, unrepentant, declares that when he dies from drink, he would like to be buried in the street bar or 'barraka' he frequents. This classic combination of satiric humor, reflecting real-life challenges while raising real contemporary Mozambican issues, became an identifying characteristic of *pandza*. As the economic crisis has continued to put an increasing strain on the Mozambican pocket, this theme of managing finances during hard times has remained a common feature of many *pandza* hits. The 2015 DJ Ardiles & Mr. Kuka hit 'Meio rico, meio pobre' (Half Rich, Half Poor) and DJ Ardiles's 'Uma cerveja, um bloco' (One Beer, One Brick) (2016) are two additional hits in which this theme is developed in typical tongue-in-cheek *pandza* style, as illustrated first in the chorus of 'Meio rico, meio pobre':

Recebo dia 30	I receive on the 30th,
gasto no dia 30	spending begins on the 30th,
e acaba dia 30	and ends on the 30th,
Chila no dia 30	Chilling begins on the 30th,
Compra no dia 30	shopping begins on the 30th.
Comeca e acaba no da 30	It begins and ends on the 30th,
Sou meio bobre, meio rico	I'm half poor, half rich,

In contrast, 'Uma cerveja, um bloco' promoted a tongue-in-cheek 'campaign' that would *resolver muitos problemas aqui em Mocambique* (resolve many problems here in Mozambique). The suggestion was that if the listener bought a brick every time they had a beer, they would eventually build themselves a home. In classic *pandza* style, however, DJ Ardiles is keen to clarify that this is not a suggestion not to drink; the suggestion is to have a good time while also ensuring there is a roof over one's head:

Meus estimagens jovens ...	My esteemed youth
cada vez que voces bebem três, cem,	Every time you buy three for a hundred
podia comprar 5 blocos (Bai) ...	You could buy 5 bricks
uma casa não e muitos blocos ...	A house doesn't take many bricks
Uma cervez, um bloco (x 8)	One beer, one brick (x8)
Adir a nossa campanha	Follow our campaign
Uma cervez, um bloco ..	One beer, one brick
Não e para parar de beber	It's not to stop drinking
E para garantir habitação	It's to guarantee somewhere to live
Não e para parara de curtir	It's not to stop having fun
E para garantir habitação	It's to guarantee somewhere to live

Sung in the official language of Portuguese and the languages of southern Mozambique, Shangana and Ronga, the upgraded *pandza* sound has attracted a global audience in Brazil, Angola and Portugal as well as across southern borders into South Africa and Zimbabwe. Many stars of Mozambican popular music such as Lisa James, Mr. Bow, MC Roger and Rosalia Mboa include *pandza* tracks in their repertoire. Mr. Bow, one of the most popular Mozambican artists of the 2000s, combines *pandza*, *marrabenta* and Mozambican hip-hop. Singing in Shangana, he celebrates living the life of a US superstar while never forgetting his roots in the suburbs.

For the post-*marrabenta*, postwar, post-communist generation of young Mozambicans, artists such as Mr. Bow, DJ Ardiles and Ziqo instil a pride that comes from self-recognition:

> We are Mozambicans and we sing of the Mozambique in our blood and the public feel this. Our music reaches the whole of Mozambique because we sing what the people are and people feel themselves and see themselves in the music. *Pandza* also makes others talk of Mozambique, and that gives strength to the Mozambican people. Many already speak of our paradise beaches, we want the same with the music ... so we can be recognized internationally, and this brings us pride. (DJ Ardiles: interview with author, January 2014)

After the challenges that began in 2010, *pandza* made its way back into the limelight and, in 2013, its role in instilling national pride and provoking discussions around the everyday issues facing young Mozambicans began to be recognized in the local and the international press: *pandza* was celebrated as being 'characteristic of living and being in art' (Laranjeira 2015). In a society in which space for freedom of expression has been shrinking and the division between rich and poor growing, it has been playing its part in finding ways for struggling Mozambicans to overcome hardship through laughter. Such a capacity has become as important as it was in the times of *marrabenta*, revealing, as Laranjeira (2015) puts it, that the 'vitality and transformative power of the creative imagination of the young generation ... [is] not just for Mozambique but for humanity.' In the words of one of *pandza*'s founders, 'It's more than a style of music, the themes we sing about are themes that identify the way we live in this society. I think it existed for a lot longer than this but we hadn't "materialized" it. That's *pandza*!' (DJ Ardiles; interview with author, January 2014).

Bibliography

Jentzsch, Corinna. 2013. 'Mozambique's Pandza Music.' *Africa Is a Country*. Online at: https://africasacountry.com/2013/10/mozambiques-pandza-music (accessed 17 June 2018).

Laranjeira, Rui Guerra. 2015. 'O Dzukuta-Pandza está a bater em Moçambique' [Dzukuta-Pandza Is Becoming a Hit in Mozambique]. *Buala*. Online at: http://www.buala.org/pt/palcos/o-dzukuta-pand

za-esta-a-bater-em-mocambique (accessed 17 June 2018).

Nhalivilo, Reinaldo Luís. 2015. 'DJ Ardiles e Mr. Kuka educam a sociedade com "Meio Rico Meio Pobre"' [DJ Ardiles and Mr. Kuka Educate Society with 'Half Rich, Half Poor']. *A verdade.* Online at: http://www.verdade.co.mz/cultura/52219-dj-ardiles-e-mr-kuka-educam-a-sociedade-com-meio-rico-meio-pobre (accessed 17 June 2018).

Discographical References

DJ Ardiles. 'Foto' [Photo]. Musica Antiga. *2005*: Mozambique. Online at: https://www.youtube.com/watch?v=8wD83tjGpuE (accessed 17 June 2018).

DJ Ardiles. 'Meninas bonitas' [Pretty Girls]. Musica Antiga. *2009*: Mozambique. Online at: https://www.youtube.com/watch?v=KVAQeWwqiFU (accessed 17 June 2018).

DJ Ardiles. 'Uma cerveja, um bloco' [One Beer, One Brick]. Musica Fresca. *2016*: Mozambique. Online at: https://www.youtube.com/watch?v=HpG_z4Ig5P0 (accessed 17 June 2018).

DJ Ardiles and Mr Kuka. 'Meio rico, meio pobre' [Half Rich, Half Poor]. *2015*: Mozambique. Online at: https://www.dailymotion.com/video/x2iu5aa (accessed 17 June 2018).

Ziqo. 'Barrakeni' [Street Bar]. Musica Fresca. *2013*: South Africa. Online at: https://www.youtube.com/watch?v=-NA3ggVT3Pc (accessed 17 June 2018).

Filmography

Pandza, dir. Heike Roch. 2018. Germany/Mozambique. 9 mins. Documentary. Online at: https://www.youtube.com/watch?v=_-Di0TyS658 (accessed 25 June 2018).

Pandza Land [*Pais do Pandza*], dir. Heike Roch. 2017. Mozambique. 67 mins. Documentary. Trailer. Online at: https://www.youtube.com/watch?v=t-8_DMYJqh8 (accessed 25 June 2018).

Interview

DJ Ardiles, January 2014.

KAREN BOSWALL

(all translations by the author)
All lyrics reproduced with the permission of DJ Ardiles

Rap Galsen, *see* **Hip-Hop in Senegal**

Rebita

Rebita is a music and dance genre formed in the region of Luanda, Angola. Scholars (dos Santos 1999; Moorman 2008) date the origins of its choreographic style to the mid-eighteenth century within a process of local interpretation of European music and dance genres such as *quadrille* and *contradance* (which were danced among the Portuguese white colonial elite and the *mestizo* social group in Angola's capital) by Kimbundu populations (the predominant ethnic and cultural group in the Luanda region). The genre's origins and development are usually credited to the fishermen communities living on the Cape Island off the city's coast.

Sources provide a more detailed characterization of the performance contexts and the instrumentation of the *rebita* as a music and dance genre during the first decades of the twentieth century. During this period the term *rebita* denoted a music and dance practice with highly formalized bodily and visual codes, performed in the so-called rebita clubs (Kubik 1997) in the Luanda region. The instrumental accompaniment consisted of the harmonium or the button diatonic accordion (called *ngaieta* in the Kimbundu language), a scrapper (*dikanza*), a small gourd with seeds inside (*saxi*) and, sometimes, a bottle (used as a wind instrument). Women and men performed a collective partners' dance, developed in a closed form (involving physical contact between pairs) and in a circular mode. The dancers formed a circle, which the men abandoned to address their female partners individually, taking a bow and then bending their body backward. The women responded with the same movement. During the dance, men and women approached each other and, at a moment signaled by the music, stamped 'their feet touching each other lightly with the abdomen, thus giving acoustically the impression of a violent shock' (Kubik 1997, 409). This configuration of movements, known as *massemba* (a Kimbundu term frequently used as a synonym of *rebita*), is considered to be the origin of the *umbigada*, a similar Brazilian choreographic form. The hybrid contours of *rebita*'s sound practices are also observed through its dress codes, with the female dancers dressed as urban elite women (known as *bessanganas*), wearing layers of cloths under a long sleeve blouse and a smaller cloth wrapped around the head, and the men wearing European suits and ties (Moorman 2008, 61).

Musically, the *rebita* is a strophic song without refrain, with a tonal harmonic and melodic structure, organized in quadruple meter and performed in a moderate tempo. At the beginning of each song and under the overlapped rhythmic patterns of *saxi* and *dikanza*, the master of ceremonies addresses the dancers in French and Portuguese, transmitting general directions regarding the dance formation. The song develops then in a call-and-response structure. Sung in Kimbundu, *rebita*'s lyrics comment on daily episodes and social experiences. *Rebita* is characterized by a polyphonic texture with autonomous and overlapping rhythmic and melodic layers. The intertwined patterns of percussion instruments, played in *ostinato* (with ornamental variations) throughout a song, provide the rhythmic support to the autonomous and dialogic melodies of voice and accordion. The specific choreographic moment of *umbigada* or *massemba* is configured with a brief change in rhythmic accentuation (a small, offbeat, rhythmic motive).

From the late 1940s a cultural movement with a nationalist and anti-colonial sensibility, led by musician Carlos 'Liceu' Vieira Dias and his group N'Gola Ritmos, sparked an interest in Kimbundu cultural practices. Together with *kazuguta* and *kaduke* rhythms, as well as Luanda's Carnival rhythms, *rebita*'s rhythms were reconfigured within new popular music styles also influenced by genres from Latin and South America (*rumba*, *merengue* and *samba*), and from the 1960s onwards by rock 'n' roll, rhythm and blues and soul music. Resulting from the creative processes developed by young musicians issuing from the city's peripheral neighborhoods (known as *musseques*), these new styles were subsumed under the general category of *semba* – an encompassing term denoting new rhythmic styles as well as appropriations of Kimbundu sound practices and international popular music genres and styles, all performed on acoustic guitars, Kimbundu percussion instruments and voices.

In the late 1960s Portuguese recording companies such as Fadiang (Fábrica de Discos de Angola) and Valentim de Carvalho built recording studios and factories that produced vinyl discs in the territory, as part of a larger colonial investment of Portuguese and non-Portuguese capital in different sectors of the Angolan economy (particularly in extractive industries such as oil production, mining and cash crop agriculture) (Moorman 2008, 162). The articulation of recording infrastructures, radio broadcasting and record shops throughout the Angolan territory in the late colonial period (1968–74) gave rise to a local recording industry which favored the commodification and circulation of Angolan music. During this period the accordionist and singer Minguito stood out among Luanda's *rebita* musicians, having recorded several singles (Minguito n.d.; 1975) launched through the popular labels Rebita/Fadiang and Merengue/Companhia de Discos de Angola, backed up by guitar-based groups such as Os Kiezos and Os Merengues. Minguito, as the singer Paulino Pinheiro, presented a hybrid style of *merengue rebita*, which the latter brought to the title of two of his recorded songs (Pinheiro 1973; 1974). While *rebita* as an expression of a silenced social experience under colonial rule was becoming culturally and politically meaningful among the *musseques*' populations, it was also being mobilized within colonial policy and presented through festivals of folklore in Portugal. This political context motivated the presentation of the *rebita* group led by Mestre Geraldo (also known as Santa Bárbara) at the Festival Folclórico das Províncias Portuguesas, in Santarém, Portugal (1969).

After Angolan National Independence (1975) four *rebita* groups remained active in the Luanda region (Muxima Angola, Agostinho Neto, Santa Bárbara and Novatos da Ilha), performing in clubs throughout the city's neighborhoods, at political ceremonies and occasionally as representatives of Angolan culture outside the country, as in the cultural delegation Canto Livre de Angola, which toured Brazilian cities (1983). Since the 1990s groups such as the Luanda-based Banda Maravilha (1997; 2006) and the migrant group in Portugal Jovens do Hungu (1995), as well as the singer and percussionist Bonga (2004; 2005), who developed his musical career in Europe from the 1970s, have drawn strongly on *rebita* as a source of inspiration. In Bonga's musical style, crafted with the group Semba Masters, the *rebita*'s allusive accordion sound was transferred to synthesized keyboard instruments. The use of the *dikanza* and of *rebita* rhythms in recordings and live performances became hallmarks of his identity as a musician and performer.

Bibliography

Cidra, Rui. 2010a. 'Bonga.' In *Enciclopédia da música em Portugal no século XX, A–C*, ed. Salwa Castelo-Branco. Lisbon: Círculo de Leitores/Temas e Debates, 149–51.

Cidra, Rui. 2010b. 'Jovens do Hungu.' In *Enciclopédia da música em Portugal no século XX, C–L*, ed. Salwa Castelo-Branco. Lisbon: Círculo de Leitores/Temas e Debates, 664.

Cidra, Rui. 2010c. 'Migração, música e' [Music and Migration]. *Enciclopédia da música em Portugal no século XX, L–P*, ed. Salwa Castelo-Branco. Lisbon: Círculo de Leitores/Temas e Debates, 773–93.

Cidra, Rui. 2010d. 'Rebita.' In *Enciclopédia da música em Portugal no século XX, P–Z*, ed. Salwa Castelo-Branco. Lisbon: Círculo de Leitores/Temas e Debates, 1103.

Cidra, Rui. 2010e. 'Semba.' In *Enciclopédia da música em Portugal no século XX, P–Z*, ed. Salwa Castelo-Branco. Lisbon: Círculo de Leitores/Temas e Debates, 1195–6.

dos Santos, Jacques Arlindo. 1999. *ABC do Bê Ó*. Luanda: Edições Chá de Caxinde.

Kubik, Gerhard. 1997. 'Cultural Interchange between Angola and Portugal in the Domain of Music since the Sixteenth Century.' In *Portugal e o mundo. O encontro de culturas na música*, ed. Salwa Castelo-Branco. Lisbon: Publicações Dom Quixote, 407–30.

Moorman, Marissa. 2008. *Intonations. A Social History of Music and Nation in Luanda, Angola, from 1945 to Recent Times*. Athens: Ohio University Press.

Discographical References

Banda Maravilha. *Angola Maravilha*. RMS. *1997*: Luanda.

Banda Maravilha. *Zungueira*. Ruben Produções. *2006*: Luanda.

Bonga. *Kaxexe*. Lusafrica. *2004*: France.

Bonga. *Maiorais*. Lusafrica. *2005*: France.

Jovens do Hungu. *Sembele*. Strauss. *1995*: Portugal.

Minguito. *Bangú Muna Ditari/Emengué Koufelé*. Rebita/Fadiang R 1021. *N.d.*: Angola.

Minguito. *Mamã Muxima/Minguito na Armónica*. Rebita/Fadiang R 1036. *N.d.*: Angola.

Minguito. *Merengue 16/Cisma da Minha Vida*. Rebita/Fadiang R 1016. *N.d.*: Angola.

Minguito. *N'Gandala ku N'Ganhala Oh Fuma/O Ritmo do Meu Bossa*. Rebita/Fadiang R 1010. *N.d.*: Angola.

Minguito. *N'Gi KalaKala Mivu Ioso/Pensando Conforme o Tempo*. Merengue/Companhia de Discos de Angola MPA 4056. *1975*: Angola.

Pinheiro, Paulino. *Desforra do Merengue Rebita/Saudades do Huambo*. Rebita/Fadiang R 1215. *1974*: Angola.

Pinheiro, Paulino. *Merengue Rebita/Rumba Rubrica*. Rebita/Fadiang R 1105. *1973*: Angola.

Discography

Angola 90's. Buda Musique CD 82962-2. *1997*: France.

Duo Ouro Negro. *Por um Chamiço/ Rebita/ Alucinado/ Ana Ngola Dilenue*. Columbia ESRF 1736. *1966*: Portugal.

Os Jovens do Prenda, Os Kiezos and Urbano de Castro. *Rebita: Apresentando Jovens do Prenda, Os Kiezos, Urbano de Castro* (LP.) Fadiang: Angola (reissued on Analog Africa AADE-04. *2013*: Germany.)

RUI CIDRA

Reggae in sub-Saharan Africa

Jamaicans are predominantly of African descent, and most enslaved Africans who were transported to Jamaica between the sixteenth and nineteenth centuries originated from regions of Central Africa (present-day Congo-Brazzaville, the Democratic Republic of Congo, Gabon, Sao Tome and Angola) and West Africa (present-day Ghana, Nigeria, Guinea-Bissau, Côte d'Ivoire, Togo and Benin). Reggae, like most genres of Jamaican popular music, is rooted partly in African musical forms, and Jamaican reggae artists frequently sing about Africa, which Rastafarians view as their spiritual homeland. It is no wonder, then, that reggae music has spread to the African continent.

Reggae first emerged in the late 1960s in the slums of West Kingston, Jamaica. Musically, reggae incorporates elements of its Jamaican predecessor genres – mento, ska and rocksteady – which, in turn, were inspired by genres including African-American rhythm and blues. One of the most easily recognizable elements is the rhythmic accents on the offbeat – usually played by guitar and/ or piano – known as the 'skank.' Other dominant features are the drum and bass. The bass guitar sound is the driving force, thick and heavy, and, along with the backbone provided by the drums, holds a steady groove throughout reggae songs. The roots reggae subgenre is noted for its spiritual lyrics praising Jah (the Rastafarian black God) and Africa, as well as for its tradition of social criticism. Jamaican reggae has historically carried strong political messages, and many singers attempt to raise the sociopolitical consciousness of the audience by denouncing materialism, racism, colonialism, capitalism and many other types of social evil. Thus, Jamaican reggae music and Africa seem interconnected at many points; and indeed, beginning in the 1970s, Africa not only offered a welcome for the arrival of roots reggae on its soil, but offered it an excellent breeding ground.

Reggae superstar Bob Marley's music first arrived on the continent around the end of the 1970s with hymns to a free and united Africa such as 'Africa Unite' (1979) and 'Zimbabwe' (1979). Reggae in Africa was then boosted by Marley's visits to Gabon on 4 and 5 January 1980 and to Zimbabwe on Independence Day, 18 April 1980. During the postcolonial period, Marley rapidly became a symbol for African youth revolting against racial and social injustices, the foreign policy of former colonial powers and African dictatorships, among other things. Africans also listened to cassette tapes and LPs of reggae artists including Burning Spear, Peter Tosh and Jimmy Cliff. Many started identifying themselves with Jamaicans, reggae music and Rasta culture. Indeed, it was easy for young Africans to recognize themselves in the daily lives of their Jamaican counterparts because both groups were black, lived in harsh ghetto conditions and, above all, were politically, economically and socially oppressed. The early reggae audience in Africa was composed primarily of the lower classes, but as time elapsed middle- and upper-class audiences were also attracted to its strong sociopolitical message.

As African reggae developed in the late 1970s to early 1980s, it merged elements of Jamaican roots reggae with indigenous characteristics such as local languages (Côte d'Ivoire's Alpha Blondy often sings in his native Dioula, for example) and traditional musical instruments (Tiken Jah Fakoly of Côte d'Ivoire, for instance, employs traditional African instruments such as the *kora* and the *balafon* in his arrangements). Many African countries have witnessed the rise of numerous local reggae voices, including Majek Fashek in Nigeria, the Black Missionaries in Malawi, Shasha Marley in Ghana, Takana Zion in Guinea, Jah Verity in Burkina Faso, Black African Positive in Senegal, Papa Cidy in Uganda, Zeleke Gessesse in Ethiopia, Koko Dembele in Mali, Lucky Dube in South Africa, and Alpha Blondy and Tiken Jah Fakoly in Côte d'Ivoire, to name just a few. Numerous artists use this subversive style of music to point an accusing finger at the ills gnawing away at the continent, including neocolonialism, the plundering of African natural resources, African dictatorships, bribery, ethnic conflicts and AIDS. In the eyes of many reggae practitioners and consumers, the advent of African reggae corresponds to the most important stage of the long and tumultuous history of Jamaican popular music: reggae, born in Jamaica, has returned to its motherland, Africa.

There follows a set of entries devoted to reggae in four specific, representative sub-Saharan African countries: Côte d'Ivoire, Ghana, Malawi and South Africa. They are intended to offer a cross-section of the diverse (and sometimes similar) ways that reggae has developed in different regions of the African continent, and the extent to which it has prospered and declined in importance. For further information on reggae and related genres in Jamaica and the Caribbean, including the influential visit of Ethiopian emperor Haile Selassie to Jamaica in 1966, see the entries in Vol. IX, *Genres: Caribbean and Latin America*.

Bibliography

Bebey, Francis. 1975 [1969]. *African Music: A People's Art*. London: Harrap.

Briard, Frédérique. 2008. *Tiken Jah Fakoly: L'Afrique ne pleure plus, elle parle* [Tiken Jah Fakoly: Africa No Longer Cries but Speaks]. Paris: Editions Les Arènes.

Chevannes, Barry, ed. 1997. *Rastafari and Other African-Caribbean Worldviews*. New Brunswick, NJ: Rutgers University Press.

Cheyney, Tom. 1991. 'The African Reggae Phenomenon.' *The Beat* 10(1): 24. Online at: http://www.afropop.org/wp-content/uploads/2015/12/Beat101africanreggae.pdf (accessed 13 February 2017).

Davis, Stephen, and Simon, Peter. 1982. *Reggae International*. New York: R&B Publishing.

King, Stephen A. 1998. 'International Reggae, Democratic Socialism, and the Secularization of the Rastafarian Movement, 1972–1980.' *Popular Music & Society* 22(3): 39–60.

Konaté, Yacouba. 1987. *Alpha Blondy*. Paris: Karthala.

Kroubo Dagnini, Jérémie. 2009. 'Rastafari: Alternative Religion and Resistance against "White" Christianity.' *Études caribéennes N°12/April 2009*. Online at: https://etudescaribeennes.revues.org/3665?lang=fr (accessed 13 February 2017).

Kroubo Dagnini, Jérémie. 2010. 'The Importance of Reggae Music in the Worldwide Cultural Universe.' *Études caribéennes N°16/August 2010*. Online at: https://etudescaribeennes.revues.org/4740?lang=fr (accessed 13 February 2017).

Kroubo Dagnini, Jérémie. 2011. *Vibrations jamaïcaines: L'Histoire des musiques populaires jamaïcaines au XXe siècle* [Jamaican Vibrations: The History of Jamaican Popular Music in the Twentieth Century]. Rosières-en-Haye: Camion Blanc.

Kroubo Dagnini, Jérémie. 2013 [2008]. *Les origines du reggae: retour aux sources* [The Origins of Reggae: Back to the Roots]. Rosières-en-Haye: Camion Blanc.

Roberts, G. Woodrow. 1957. *The Population of Jamaica*. Cambridge: Cambridge University Press.

Savashinsky, Neil. 1994. 'Rastafari in the Promised Land: The Spread of a Jamaican Socioreligious Movement Among the Youth of West Africa.' *African Studies Review* 37(3): 19–50.

Waters, Alan. 1994. 'Reggae Music in Africa.' *Passages. A Chronicle of the African Humanities*. Online at: https://quod.lib.umich.edu/p/passages/4761530.0008.004/--reggae-music-in-africa?rgn=main;view=fulltext (accessed 5 April 2018).

Discographical References

Bob Marley & the Wailers. 'Africa Unite.' *Survival*. Island Records ILPS 9542. *1979*: UK.

Bob Marley & the Wailers. 1979. 'Zimbabwe.' *Survival*. Island Records, ILPS 9542 *1979*: UK.

Filmography

Alpha Blondy: Un combat pour la liberté [Alpha Blondy: A Struggle for Liberty], dirs. Antoinette Delafin and Dramane Cisse. 2010. France. 90 mins. Music documentary.

Le souffle du reggae [Reggae Blowing through the Air], dir. Jérémie Cuvillier. 2015. France. 52 mins. Music documentary.

JÉRÉMIE KROUBO DAGNINI

Reggae in Côte d'Ivoire

In no African country is reggae more prominent than in Côte d'Ivoire, where it is one of the most prevalent forms of popular music. Arguably the most significant reason that Ivorian musicians and fans have embraced reggae is its transnational reputation as a medium associated with liberatory politics and resistance to oppression against peoples of African descent (Schumann 2009, 118; Salm 2010, 1336; Reed 2012, 95–6). Much of Ivorian reggae features texts about social issues and politics, and since the early 1980s the genre and its star performers have played important roles at key moments in Ivorian political life.

Reggae first arrived in Abidjan in the late 1970s in the form of LP records by Jamaican artists such as U Roy, I Roy, Peter Tosh, Bunny Livingston Wailer and, of course, Bob Marley, whose name is almost synonymous with the genre. Soon afterwards, Ivorian national radio began broadcasting reggae records, and the genre quickly spread to dance clubs in the popular Abidjan neighborhood of Treichville. Though Treichville was primarily a poorer, working-class neighborhood, its dance clubs were patronized by people of various socioeconomic levels, including many residents of wealthier neighborhoods such as Cocody and Résidential. Early Ivorian reggae audiences thus included rich, poor and middle-class fans (Aster 2004). Once this broad listenership for Jamaican reggae was established, the scene was set for the emergence of the first homegrown superstar in this increasingly popular style.

In 1980 a relatively unknown reggae singer named Alpha Blondy (Seydou Koné) gave his first live concert in the streets of Treichville (Aster 2004). Blondy would go on to become the first major reggae star not only in Côte d'Ivoire, but across the African continent. His first album, *Jah Glory* (1982), achieved immediate success, launching a career of renown in French-speaking countries that, by the late 2010s, had considerably exceeded 30 years (Salm 2010, 1336). *Jah Glory* featured a number of characteristics that would become general standards for Ivorian reggae:

singing in the Ivorian trade language Jula, French and occasionally English; a 'roots reggae' sound; and lyrical themes concerning social issues, politics and spirituality.

Like Blondy, nearly all other major Ivorian reggae artists are from the northern savanna region of Côte d'Ivoire where northern Mande languages such as Maninka and Jula predominate. It is not unusual for Ivorian reggae songs to be sung entirely in Jula; equally common are songs in French, the national language, or Ivorian street French ('Nouchi'), while still others mix Jula and French. In 1990s Côte d'Ivoire, differences between the north and south became politicized, resulting in a civil war that divided the country from 2002 until 2011. In that context, reggae became increasingly associated with the north and the fight by northerners to counteract prejudice and political disenfranchisement. Many Ivorian reggae albums also include a song or two in English, a pattern established by Blondy, who had spent time studying in the United States. Singing in English enables Ivorian artists to try to transcend the linguistic barrier that prevents them from achieving popularity in the English-dominated, global reggae market. Regardless, the popularity of Ivorian reggae has largely remained restricted to the Francophone world, including other former French colonies and especially France itself, home to some 4.5 million African immigrants (INSEE).

The 'roots reggae' sound preferred by most Ivorian reggae artists was popularized in the 1970s by Bob Marley, Peter Tosh and other Jamaican artists. Instrumentation generally consists of bass and electric guitar, organ and/or keyboard, drum kit, a male lead singer backed by a female chorus, and sometimes a horn section and additional percussion. The foundation of roots reggae, the rhythm section, operates thus: the bass guitar, relatively loud and melodic, plays a prominent role (as it does in many other African popular music styles); the rhythm guitar plays staccato chords on beats two and four of the measure; and the drummer plays the kick or bass-drum on beats one and three along with complex eighth and 16th note patterns on the high-hat cymbals. Some popular Ivoirian reggae artists, including Alpha Blondy and Tiken Jah Fakoly (Doumbia Moussa Fakoly), occasionally stretch beyond roots reggae instrumentation by adding African instruments such as the *kora* or the *ngoni*, or electronic drums and synthesizers.

The term 'roots reggae' refers not just to the music sound but also to the Rastafarian religion, the lifestyle associated with it and the concern for social issues that Bob Marley's music and legend embody. These extramusical associations also appealed to Ivorian musicians. For many Ivorian listeners, the very sound of reggae is imbued with a sense of pan-African identity and resistance to injustice, rendering it an effective medium for spreading such messages. Tiken Jah Fakoly, a successor to Alpha Blondy, whose fame rivals that of his predecessor, recognized the genre's inherent associations when at the beginning of his career he was looking for a vehicle for his politically charged messages. Discussing this choice, Fakoly noted, 'Reggae is a militant music. It's the music of those without means. It's the music of opinions … it is a music that is the soul of the poor' (quoted in Reed 2012, 96).

By the 1990s reggae had become the primary music of rebellion and political protest in Côte d'Ivoire. Ivorian President Henri Konan Bédié's policy of 'Ivoirité' (Ivorian-ness) promoted a radically conservative view of Ivorian citizenship that disenfranchised northerners as well as the immigrants from Burkina Faso, Mali and other northern West African countries who made up 25 percent of the population of Côte d'Ivoire. Blondy's lyrics became increasingly confrontational (Schumann 2009, 120–1), and younger artists such as Fakoly and Fadal Dey had smash hits protesting against the government and 'Ivoirité' (Akindes 2002, 96). Songs by Dey and Blondy were banned by the Bédié government until the regime fell in a bloodless coup in 1999, at which point mutinying soldiers 'seized the state radio station and put back on the air the recording of Ivorian [reggae] musicians whose banned music had inspired them' (Vick 2000; cf. Akindes 2002, 96; Reed 2012, 96–7). The following year Fakoly's 'Promesses de caméléon' (Promises of the Chameleon) so harshly criticized Bédié's successor Robert Gueï that Fakoly and members of his family began receiving death threats. Recognizing that in the government's eyes he had crossed a line, Fakoly chose to go into exile, first to Burkina Faso and then Mali, where he was still living in the late 2010s.

Ivorians tend to associate reggae with northerners, both culturally and politically (Akindes 2002, 97). During the civil war, however, southern reggae artist Serges Kassy aligned himself with the 'Alliance of Young Patriots,' a militant group whose passionate support for the south was equaled by its xenophobic rhetoric toward northerners (Schumann 2009, 131). Reggae is more than a musical genre in Côte d'Ivoire; it is a social field within which fundamental political and cultural conflicts are debated and fought. Ivorian reggae artists are far more than mere protest singers; indeed, they are 'political actors' (Schumann 2015) who are deeply and directly engaged in the power struggles that have plagued the country since the late twentieth century.

No artist has been more actively engaged in social and political action than Tiken Jah Fakoly. Fakoly comes from a family of *griots* ('jeli') – traditional bards and oral historians whose societal role includes criticizing injustice and unethical behavior. Fakoly has embraced this role but uses reggae as his medium of expression (Eyre 2009; Dieng 2012). Arguably, all Ivorian reggae artists do the same: adopt the role of the *griot* and also adapt it by utilizing a musical genre whose very sound evokes a sense of the pan-African struggle for justice. Using reggae, Ivorians wrap powerful social messages in an appealing aesthetic package that stimulates both light-hearted pleasure and serious contemplation.

Bibliography

Akindes, Simon. 2002. 'Playing It 'Loud and Straight': Reggae, Zouglou, Mapouka and Youth Insubordination in Côte d'Ivoire.' In *Playing with Identities in Contemporary Music in Africa*, eds. Mai Palmberg and Annemette Kirkegaard. Uppsala: Nordiska Afrikainstitutet, 86–103.

Aster, Bente E. 2004. *The 'Terrible' Child from Treichville*. Hovedoppgave: University of Oslo.

Dieng, Cheikh Ahmadou. 2012. 'Reggae Griots in Francophone Africa.' In *Global Reggae*, ed. Carolyn Cooper. Kingston, Jamaica: Canoe Press, 213–20.

Eyre, Banning. 2009. 'African Reggae: Obscure Roots, Modern Twist.' Online at: http://www.npr.org/templates/story/story.php?storyId=100810488 (accessed 29 March 2018).

INSEE (Institut National de la Statistique et des Etudes Economiques). 'Répartition des immigrés par pays de naissance.' Online at: http://www.insee.fr/fr/themes/tableau.asp?reg_id=0&ref_id=immigrespaysnais (accessed 29 March 2018).

Konaté, Yacouba. 1987. *Alpha Blondy: Reggae et société en Afrique noire*. Abidjan: Ceda.

Reed, Daniel B. 2012. 'Promises of the Chameleon: Reggae Artist Tiken Jah Fakoly's Intertextual Contestation of Power in Côte d'Ivoire.' In *Hip Hop Africa and Other Stories of New African Music in a Globalized World*, ed. Eric Charry. Bloomington: Indiana University Press, 92–108.

Salm, Steven J. 2010. 'Globalization and West African Music.' *History Compass* 8(12): 1328–39.

Schumann, Anne. 2009. 'Popular Music and Political Change in Côte d'Ivoire: The Divergent Dynamics of Zouglou and Reggae.' *Journal of African Media Studies* 1(1): 113–32.

Schumann, Anne. 2015. 'Music at War: Reggae Musicians as Political Actors in the Ivoirian Crisis.' *Journal of African Cultural Studies* 27(3): 342–55. Online at: https://www.tandfonline.com/doi/abs/10.1080/13696815.2015.1028027?journalCode=cjac20 (accessed 29 March 2018).

Toynbee, Jason. 2007. *Bob Marley: Herald of a Postcolonial World?* Cambridge: Polity Press.

Vick, Karl. 2000. 'Reggae Artists Voiced Nation's Discontent.' *Washington Post*, January 30.

Discographical References

Alpha Blondy and the Natty Rebels. *Jah Glory*. Moya Production MOY 33001. *1982*: Côte d'Ivoire.

Fakoly, Tiken Jah. 'Promesses decaméléon.' *Le caméléon*. JAT Music. *2000*: Côte d'Ivoire (reissued on Barclay 531059-5. *2008*: France.)

Discography

Alpha Blondy. *Apartheid Is Nazism*. Pathé 2404491. *1985*: France.

Alpha Blondy and the Solar System. *SOS guerre tribale*. Jimmy's International Production JIP031. *1991*: France.

Dey, Fadal. *Méditations: Le Dey de Dieu*. Koné Dodo. *2000*: Côte d'Ivoire.

Fakoly, Tiken Jah. *Mangercratie*. JAT Music. *1996*: Côte d'Ivoire; Louma BS 50754. *1999*: France.

Fakoly, Tiken Jah. *L'Africain*. Barclay 530 130-6. *2007*: France.

Kassy, Serges. *Tous ensemble positifs*. Serges Kassy Productions. *2013*: Côte d'Ivoire.

DANIEL B. REED

Reggae in Ghana

Reggae is one of three Jamaican styles of music that became popular in Ghana from the nineteenth century. First there was the Jamaican *goombay* frame drum music introduced to West Africa by Jamaican Maroons in 1800, beginning in Freetown, Sierra Leone and then spreading to Ghana and elsewhere. Second, syncopated African-Caribbean music was introduced by black colonial soldiers from the English-speaking West Indies stationed in Ghana during the late nineteenth century. Then, from the late 1960 and 1970s reggae became popular with Ghanaian youth when it was introduced through records, films and visits by Jamaican artists.

This Jamaican influence resulted not only in local bands copying reggae sung in Jamaican Patois but also in local versions of reggae that were sung in Ghanaian languages and which integrated some of its offbeat and syncopated rhythmic features, such as the 'skanking' guitar, the backbeat and the 'one-drop' drum beat. This is not surprising, as the offbeat musical features of reggae are also found in Ghanaian traditional music and highlife music.

Before reggae, a predecessor of this Jamaican music known as ska was popularized in West Africa by Jamaican-born singer Millicent 'Millie' Small, who visited Ghana and other parts of West Africa in the late 1960s. Her music was followed by records of the pioneering reggae singers Toots and the Maytals, the Heptones, Desmond Dekker and also Jimmy Cliff, who starred in the 1972 reggae film *The Harder They Come* and who toured Nigeria in 1974. Almost immediately, Ghanaian and Nigerian highlife artists began blending the offbeat guitar and percussion of reggae into some of their highlife songs. This began with Ghanaian guitar bands in the early 1970s, including the African Brothers (Nana Ampadu and Eddie Donkor), the City Boys and Teacher Boateng and his Africana, and later the Kumapim Royals, Amakye Dede and K.K. Kabobo. Likewise, in Nigeria, Victor Uwaifo and Sonny Okosun began combining reggae and highlife in the late 1970s.

Reggae became even more popular after 1977 when the Rastafarian musician Bob Marley released his *Exodus* album. That was also the year that the first reggae sound system was brought to Ghana by the Jamaican Raas Wolde Mikael who set up base in Tema and Accra. Then came visits to Ghana by Jamaican artists during the 1980s such as Misty in Roots, Musical Youth and Yellow Man. Moreover, in 1984 another reggae sound system called Hi Power was brought to Ghana by the British West Indian Jah Power with the Ghanaian MCs Preacher Levi, General Marcus and Wahesh Simeon. Some of these Jamaican visitors were followers of the Jamaican Rastafarian movement inspired by Marcus Garvey, with its distinctive dreadlock hairstyle and gold, green and red colors.

As a result of this reggae–rasta influence, from the early 1980s Ghanaian reggae bands appeared that consisted of dread-locked young musicians performing imitative cover versions of Bob Marley's music. One was the Classic Handels, later called the Classic Vibes (with Kwadwo Antwi, Osibio and Ayi Soloman), which left Ghana for Europe in 1983. Another was Roots Anabo, formed in Germany by the Ghanaians Ekow Savage Alabi and Sammy Nukpere. These bands tended to remain faithful to the Jamaican format and they sang exclusively in Patois – as did other reggae bands and artists in Ghana at the time such as Felix Bell, the SO2 Squad, Kojo Ashakanor, Kindred, Grassroots and the later Black Empire, Nazarite Vow (with Ras Korby and General Stano) and Ras Kente's Root of David.

As mentioned, highlife bands in Ghana (and Nigeria) began to indigenize reggae in the 1970s. However, it was the Afrocentric 'roots' message of Bob Marley's music that helped trigger a creative move by Ghanaian reggae bands to indigenize their music in terms of language, instrumentation and lyrical themes. This use of local languages was also encouraged in the mid-1980s by the success of the Mande and Baoule reggae records of Côte d'Ivoire's Alpha Blondy, whose Solar System band toured neighboring Ghana. As a result, Kwadwo Antwi (formerly of the Classic Vibes) began to sing in Akan, while Ellis Salaam's Cultural Imani Band performed folkish reggae songs using traditional percussion and sung in the Ga language. In the 1990s came a host of other reggae bands and artists that performed in English or local languages and expressed the militant and Afrocentric-type message of Bob Marley's 'roots-reggae': Fred Dred's Kente band, Shasha Marley (who usually wears a monk's cloak onstage), Sly Dennis's Exodus group from the University at Kumasi, Alaine Courage Man, Ras Tonto, Ekow Micah's Sunlife Band,

Carlous Man, the Rasta musician Black Prophet and United Spirit (which included the German musician Chris Luhn).

Particularly important is Kwadwo Antwi who, from his first 1986/1987 albums *All I Need Is You* and *Saman*, released a string of romantic songs in the Akan language that blended the 'lovers rock' reggae style of Gregory Isaacs with highlife. As a result of Antwi's success, he received the USA Black Entertainment Television (BET) Award in 2010 for best international act in an event hosted by Queen Latifah.

Another important Ghanaian figure is Rocky Dawuni, whose reggae career began in 1991 when he set up his Local Crisis band at the university in Accra where he was studying. His lyrics are of a much more political nature than those of Kwadwo Antwi, as can be gathered from some of the titles of the albums Dawuni released from 1996, such as *Movement, Awakening, Book of Changes* and *Hymn for a Rebel Soul*. Although he sings in English, Dawuni has added some traditional instruments to his band and is fusing reggae with Afrobeat in a style he calls 'Afro Roots.' Based in the USA for many years, he also makes regular trips to Ghana. He has collaborated and performed with Stevie Wonder, Peter Gabriel, Bono and John Legend and was named one of Africa's Top 10 global stars by CNN.

Rocky Dawuni was born in Accra, but his family is from Yendi in Ghana's Northern Region. Also from this region comes Sheriff Ghale, who sings reggae songs in Dagbani. He is based in Tamale, the local capital of the Northern Region, and since the 1990s has released nine albums that focus on themes concerning interethnic peace and nation building. For instance, his 2005 *Sochira* ('Crossroads') album is about the Dagbon chieftaincy conflict. More recent artists from Ghana's Upper and Northern Regions who play local versions of reggae are Blakk Rasta, Sirina Issah, Zinjina and Ras Queysen.

Since the 1990s, there have been numerous visits to Ghana by foreign reggae artists. Some examples are the Nigerian reggae bands of Ras Kimono and Evi Edna Ogholi-Ogosi, South Africa's Lucky Dube and the Jamaican artists Gregg Isaacs, Jimmy Cliff, Mutabaruka and Ziggy Marley. Some Jamaican musicians settled in Ghana, such as some of the members of Zion's Children. Rita Marley built a house and recording studio on the Aburi Hills just north of Accra, and ran her Rita Marley Foundation in Ghana till her death in Miami in 2017.

As mentioned earlier, several sound systems were brought to Ghana by West Indians from the late 1970s, and the electronic Jamaican reggae style associated with them became popular in Ghana in the late 1980s. This Jamaican music, known as ragga or dancehall, includes DJs who toast (a form of Jamaican rap) over the music. From the 1990s Jamaican ragga and dancehall began to influence some of the Ghanaian artists who play local hip-hop and rap known as 'hiplife,' such as Mad Fish, the late Terry Bonchaka, Bandana, Slim Busterr, Aberewa Nana and Samini (Batman). Dancehall was given a boost in the early 2000s through visits to Ghana by the USA-based Jamaican Shabba Ranks and the US/Panamanian reggaeton artist General Phullos. Reggae beats have also found their way into the local gospel dance music that developed in Ghana from the 1980s and represents the country's single biggest commercial music genre in the early twenty-first century. An exponent of this reggae gospel is K.K. Kabobo. (For more on gospel music in Ghana, see the entry on Highlife.)

What is so interesting about the impact of Jamaican music on Ghana is that many black Jamaicans are the descendants of slaves from Ghana who in Jamaica became known as 'Kromantis' or 'Coromantins.' It was they who led the various eighteenth-century Maroon slave revolts that the British could never control and which resulted in some Maroons being first deported to Nova Scotia then transported (repatriated) to West Africa. Several militant back-to-Africa Jamaicans, including Marcus Garvey and Bob Marley, were of Maroon extraction.

Not only are the ancestors of some Jamaicans Ghanaian, but even as early as the nineteenth century the music of Jamaican former slaves and soldiers found its way to Ghana. With these long-term and continuous transatlantic criss-crossing connections it is of no surprise that reggae resonates so strongly in Ghana.

Bibliography

Collins, E. John. 1996. *Highlife Time*. Accra: Anansesem Press.

Collins, E. John. 2012. 'Contemporary Ghanaian Popular Music since the 1980s.' In *Hip Hop Africa:*

New African Music in a Globalising World, ed. Eric Charry. Bloomington: Indiana University Press, 211–33.

Discographical References

Antwi, Kwadwo. *All I Need Is You*. Label unknown. *1986*.

Antwi, Kwadwo, and Classic Vibes of Ghana. *Saman*. Kame Records 66-24023-01 *1985*: Germany.

Dawuni, Rocky. *Awakening*. Aquarian Records AQRN3102-2. *2001*: Ghana/USA.

Dawuni, Rocky. *Book of Changes*. Aquarian Records. *2005*: Ghana/USA.

Dawuni, Rocky. *Hymn for a Rebel Soul*. Aquarian Records. *2010:* Ghana/USA.

Dawuni, Rocky. *Movement*. Aquarian Records. *1996*: Ghana/USA.

Marley, Bob. *Exodus*. Island Records ILPS 9498. *1977*: UK.

Oksoun, Sonny. *Fire in Soweto*. EMI NEMI (LP) 0330. *1978*: Nigeria.

Oksoun, Sonny. *Papa's Land*. EMI NEMI 0232. *1977*: Nigeria.

Sheriff Ghale. *Sochira (Cross Roads)*. With D.J. Nash. *2005*: Ghana. Title song online at www.youtube.com/watch?v=MvTyyqauTBE (accessed 4 April 2018).

Uwaifo, Victor. 'Five Days a Week Love' and 'When the Sun Shines.' *Five Days a Week Love*. Phonogram Ltd. Nigeria POLP 012. *1977*: Nigeria.

Discography

Antwi, Kojo/Kwadwo, *Don't Stop The Music.* 2000. Online at: www.myghanaradio.com/kojo-antwi-don-t-stop-the-msic (accessed 4 April 2018).

Antwi, Kojo/Kwadwo. *Densu*. CD Baby 5637653806. *2002*: Ghana.

City Boys.'Nya Asem Hwe.' Scottie Records Onitsha LDR 2001. *1977*: Nigeria.

Dede, Amakye. *Greatest Hits*. Online at: https://www.youtube.com/watch?v=6ry1B62cC0o (accessed 4 April 2018).

Marley, Shasha, *Lost and Found*. Holy Trinity Records. *2007*: Ghana.

Roots Anabo. *Civilization*. Sinus Musik. *1987*: West Berlin.

Salaam Cultural Imani Group. 'Mama Shille Oga' and 'Moko Baba.' *The Guitar and Gun: Highlife Music from Ghana*. Stern's Music STEW50CD. *2003*: UK.

Filmography

The Harder They Come, dir. Perry Henzell. 1972. USA. 120 mins. Original music by Jimmy Cliff, Desmond Dekker, The Slickers and The Maytalls. Feature film.

E. JOHN COLLINS

Reggae in Malawi

In Malawi, reggae has been played since the 1960s and comes second only to gospel in popularity. There is, however, a large overlap because some Malawi gospel music uses reggae backing. Thus, reggae is a prevalent genre in both the secular and religious arenas. Malawi reggae musicians use the same chord patterns as their West Indian comrades for 'pure' reggae but they also incorporate reggae into the *afroma*-based style of diverse musicians including Alleluya Band and the Malawi Police Orchestra. Generally, Malawians tend to prefer a lighter ska-tinged reggae, although in concert most bands play with the bass turned high.

History

Reggae took root in Malawi, via ska and 'lovers' reggae,' much earlier than in many other African countries. There were a number of entry points. The original entry occurred in the 1960s with hits including Millicent Small's 'My Boy Lollipop' (1964), Desmond Dekker's 'The Israelites' (1968), the Beatles version of reggae, 'Ob-la-di Ob-la-da' (1969), Jimmy Cliff's 'Wonderful World' (1969) and early 1970s lovers' reggae radio hits such as Eric Donaldson's 'Cherry Oh Baby.' This type of early reggae and ska found resonance with Malawians because of the similarities of some local dance rhythms, such as *beni*, to the jerky ska/reggae. Indeed, the Malawi Broadcasting Band (MBC Band) recorded a reggae version of 'Zivute zitani tili pa mbuyo pa Kamuzu' ('Come Hell or High Water We Are Behind Dr Banda') in 1974, the same year as Bob Marley's 'No Woman No Cry' was released in the UK, and nearly a decade before South African reggae artist Lucky Dube's breakthrough. Thus, the later influence of bands, including the Wailers, Culture and Aswad and musicians such as Bob Marley and Peter Tosh, consolidated roots reggae rather than introduced reggae to Malawi. Further, the Malawi Young Pioneers, a paramilitary organization, popularized reggae in the rural areas with its Spearhead Band.

The secondary route for reggae came, much later, via the work of African musicians including Ivorian Alpha Blondy and South African Lucky Dube. However, it must be noted that by the time of Lucky Dube's LP *Rastas Never Die* (1984) reggae had been well established in Malawi, and the Malawi Police Orchestra ('Ulanda' [Poverty]), the MBC Band ('Anthu ndiobvuta' [People Are Troublesome]) and the Army's Alpha Strings all played reggae at functions. Kalimba had a BBC top 20 hit in 1982 with their poppy rock reggae, 'Sometimes I Wonder,' even before Dube recorded *Rasta*.

It has been speculated that musicians may have taken to reggae in such high numbers because of the paucity of musical instruments in the late 1960s and 1970s; a single lead guitar and bass guitar could provide a good backing. The introduction of keyboards and personal computers in the 1980s revolutionized the making and performance of music; at the switch of a knob one could have a 'decent' reggae backing. Unfortunately, this coincided with shortages of foreign exchange, which inhibited the purchase of drum kits and guitars and leveraged the increased use of keyboards. Bands including the MBC and Alleluya featured keyboards prominently, often as the backbone of the reggae rhythm section.

Alleluya Band, a gospel group that became a training ground for many future reggae musicians and bandleaders, was formed in 1978. Initially, this group's sound featured a gentle, lilting reggae beat underpinning various Malawi beats and melodies. At the time of the Pope's visit to Malawi in 1989 the band had reached the peak of its musical experimentation, producing a gentle synthesis of gospel and *afroma* with a reggae tinge. From Alleluya Band arose prominent reggae artists including Mlaka Maliro, Billy Kaunda, Coss Chiwalo, Charles Sinetre and Paul Chaphuka. The success of Alleluya Band and its role in the success of Pope Paul's visit encouraged other religious organizations to fund gospel musical activities, and reggae-backed music benefited. The role of Alleluya Band as a youth band that mixes the secular and the religious cannot be overemphasized.

Another reggae school grew up around the band from Chileka called the Black Missionaries, led by the late prominent reggae artist Evison Matafale. There is a small Rastafarian community in Malawi to which Matafale belonged. After Matafale's death, the sons of the 1980s bandleader Robert Fumulani, who were part of Matafale's backing band the Black Missionaries, continued with his work.

The most popular reggae musician in Malawi from 1994 to 2014 was Lucius Banda. Beginning in the Alleluya Band, he carved out a career as a 'soldier of the people.' As a 'multiparty dispensation' supporter, Lucius Banda sang about President Banda's autocracy during the transition to multiparty democracy. Then, fed up with the corruption of the multiparty politicians (most of them holdovers from the one-party era), he observed about all politicians that 'Ali ndi njira zawo' ('They have their sly ways') and rapped in 'Cease Fire,' a no-holds-barred reggae rap track in English, about political corruption and exploitation of the poor (Chirambo 2002, 103–22). However, by 2004 Lucius, formerly known as the 'people's champion,' had succumbed to political patronage and was an opposition United Democratic Party Member of Parliament (MP), and one of the *mabwana* (big men) he had formerly criticized. Despite being an MP he continued singing and upset President Bingu wa Mutharika, earning himself a prison sentence in 2006 after being found guilty of forging a secondary school leaving certificate to qualify as an MP. He was found not guilty on appeal.

Conclusion

Though popular, reggae in Malawi has its critics, some of whom are musicians. Because it can be produced by computers or keyboards, it is sometimes viewed as lazy music that kills Malawi musical innovation. But it is very popular with both rural and urban youth, both for its carrying messages and as a sociocultural phenomenon associated with modes of dress and secular behavior. It is equally popular among born-again Christian groups who use it to back their gospel tunes.

Bibliography

Chirambo, Reuben Mayamiko. 2002. '*Mzimu wa soldier*: Contemporary Popular Music and Politics in Malawi.' In *A Democracy of Chameleons: Politics and Culture in the New Malawi*, ed. Harri Englund. Uppsala: Nordic Africa Institute, 103–22.

Lwanda, John. 2008. 'Music Advocacy, the Media and the Malawi Political Public Sphere, 1958-2007.' *JAMS (Journal of African Media Studies)* 1(2): 135-54.

Seebode, Jochen. 2012. 'Popular Music and Young Male Audiences in Contemporary Malawi.' In *Hip hop Africa: New African Music in a Globalising World*, ed. Eric Charry. Bloomington: Indiana University Press, 234-60.

Discographical References

Banda, Lucius. 'Ali ndi njira zawo.' *Cease Fire*. Balaka: IY Productions. *1996*: Malawi.

Banda, Lucius. 'Cease Fire.' *Cease Fire*. Balaka IY Productions. *1996*: Malawi.

Banda, Lucius. *Survivor*. Balaka: IY Productions. *2006*: Malawi.

Beatles, The. 'Ob-la-di Ob-la-da.' Parlophone GMSP 137. *1969*: UK.

Cliff, Jimmy. 'Wonderful World.' Trojan Records TR 690. *1969*: UK.

Donaldson, Eric. *Cherry Oh Baby*. Dynamic Sounds DYN-420. *1971*: UK.

Dekker, Desmond, and the Aces. *Israelites*. Pyramid PYR 6058. *1968*: UK.

Dube, Lucky. *Rastas Never Die*. Gallo CD GSP3000. *1984*: South Africa.

Kalimba. 'Sometimes I Wonder.' Dephon Promotions SCL 5302. *1982*: South Africa.

Malawi Police Orchestra. '*Ulanda*.' MBC Archives. *c. 1982*: Malawi.

Marley, Bob, and the Wailers. 'No Woman No Cry.' *Natty Dread*. Island Records ILPS 9281. *1974*: UK.

MBC Band. *Anthu ndiobvuta*. MBC Archives. *c. 1985*: Malawi.

MBC Band. '*Zivute zitani tili pa mbuyo pa Kamuzu*'On *Kokoliko ku Malawi*.' MBC Ngoma Records MW LP001. *1974*: Malawi.

MBC Band and the Chichiri Queens. *Kokoliko ku Malawi*. MBC Ngoma Records MW LP001. *1974*: Malawi.

Small, Millicent. *My Boy Lollipop*. Fontana TF449. *1964*: UK.

Discography

Alleluya Band. *The Best of Alleluya Band*. MC. IY Productions. *1994*: Malawi.

Matafale, Evison, and the Wailing Brothers. *Kuimba*. MC Studios. *2000*: Malawi.

Matafale, Evison, and the Black Missionaries. *Kuyimba 2*. M'mbomba Promotions KYCD002. N.d.: Malawi.

JOHN LWANDA

Reggae in South Africa

South Africa enjoys a unique and relatively prominent role in the world of reggae music. Reggae from Jamaica and the United Kingdom first found an audience in South Africa during the 1970s, with several local record labels licensing albums by major reggae acts and others imported into the country. In the early 1980s three of the genre's biggest stars performed live in southern Africa: Bob Marley in Harare, Zimbabwe, in April 1980, Jimmy Cliff in Soweto a month later and Peter Tosh in Swaziland in December 1983. Even though its origins were foreign, reggae was soon adopted by South African artists and audiences.

Initially, popular artists who normally specialized in other genres recorded reggae songs or made reference to the genre in their lyrics, which helped pave the way for dedicated reggae artists. Two of the earliest examples of this were the Movers' 1975 album *Black Reggae* and Kori Moraba's album *Sotho Reggae* in 1977. This trend continued in the early 1980s, with popular disco acts such as Blondie & Pappa and Neville Nash including reggae tracks on their albums between 1980 and 1983. Singer Steve Kekana recorded the reggae song 'Sounds of Africa' in 1981 and wrote 'Reggae Music' for another early South African reggae album, the Dread Warriors' self-titled album on Gallo in 1983. Kariba released several reggae albums in the early 1980s, predominantly made up of cover versions of international reggae hits. Benjamin Ball meanwhile successfully fused reggae and disco on songs including 'Flash a Flashlight' (1984). Over time, these and other artists were able to craft a distinctively South African brand of reggae music, still reminiscent of its Jamaican originators but typically characterized by the abundant use of synthesizers (often instead of guitars) and the incorporation of indigenous South African languages and musical influences.

Of the dedicated reggae artists that emerged in the 1980s three stand out as pioneers of the South African scene: Colbert Mukwevho, Carlos Djedje and Lucky Dube. Colbert Mukwevho started his career performing with his father and uncles in the Thrilling Artists. Their 1983 album *Ha Nga Dzule* (She Did Not Stay) featured the reggae track

'Luimbo Lwa Reggae' (The Reggae Song), arguably the earliest attempt at reggae sung in Tshivenda, one of South Africa's indigenous languages. During the mid-1980s Mukwevho fronted the Comforters, a band that fused reggae (with English lyrics) and the popular 'bubblegum' disco sound of the day. In 1990 Mukwevho recorded a reggae duet, 'Hero's Party,' with Brenda Fassie, the country's biggest pop star at the time, produced by Sello 'Chicco' Twala, who also produced Mukwevho's 1991 album *Lion in a Sheep Skin,* using the name Harley & The Rasta Family.

Though influenced by Jamaican roots reggae in terms of vocal delivery, Carlos Djedje's lyrics addressed local issues and audiences (Martin 1992, 202). Djedje, whose albums include *Remember Them* in 1989, considered his role as a reggae musician to be closely linked to the popular struggle against apartheid, and his lyrics therefore frequently referred to oppression and injustice in South Africa (Djedje 2012).

Lucky Dube was the artist who brought reggae into the South African mainstream, appealing to a broad audience that extended beyond ethnic and racial categories, rivaling the country's biggest pop stars in terms of sales and popularity and even finding success throughout Africa and the rest of the world. His global success, particularly when considered in relation to other South African reggae artists, may have been due to a number of factors, including an ambitious management team that facilitated Dube's regular tours all over the world as well as his ability to write catchy songs with simple yet deeply profound and reconciliatory lyrics that resonated with both South African and global audiences.

Dube's reggae career began after his cousin, producer Richard Siluma, saw Jimmy Cliff's performance in Soweto in 1980. Siluma eventually persuaded his younger cousin Dube, then specializing in traditional Zulu *mbaqanga* music, to record some reggae tracks. Dube's first reggae releases were *Rastas Never Dies* (1984) and *Think About the Children* (1985). His subsequent reggae albums, such as *Slave* (1987), *Together as One* (1988) and *Prisoner* (1989), sold in large quantities, cementing reggae's popularity in South Africa and launching Dube's international career (Dagnini 2011; Goldstuck 2007; Siluma 2010).

Djedje, Mukwevho and Dube, as well as Jambo and the band O'Yaba, were some of the genre's biggest local stars. Indeed, by the late 1980s South Africa had become one of the countries outside Jamaica where reggae enjoyed its most dedicated following (Martin 1992, 202). Reggae was consumed by South Africans of all races, who bought albums in large numbers and frequently attended live (albeit typically racially segregated) concerts.

Reggae During Apartheid

Central to reggae's lyrical message are themes of empowerment and liberation from social and political oppression. This was part of the reason for its widespread appeal, both locally in South Africa and globally. Reggae also provided South Africans with a powerful link to the rest of the African continent and its diaspora, particularly significant at the time given the country's growing isolation from the rest of the world (Tenaille 2002, 152–3).

From the late 1970s South African politics – specifically its system of minority rule and racial segregation known as apartheid – was a regular theme for many prominent reggae artists from Jamaica and the UK, including Bob Marley ('War') and Jacob Miller ('Forward Jah Jah Children') in 1976, and Peter Tosh ('Apartheid') in 1977. Throughout the 1980s apartheid remained a common subject for reggae artists, including many of the genre's most popular figures.

With listeners who cut across racial, ethnic and linguistic divisions and with its revolutionary message, reggae in South Africa had the power to mobilize people against apartheid oppression and was therefore seen as a threat by authorities (Chawane 2012, 173–4; Martin 1992, 202; McNeill 2012, 84, 93). Many of Bob Marley's songs, for example, were banned from the airwaves by the South African Broadcasting Corporation (SABC) (McNeill 2012, 84). Other reggae songs were frequently banned for their use of the word 'Jah,' the Rastafarian term for God (Jansen van Rensburg 2013, 99–100).

Despite attempts at censorship, reggae developed a loyal following in South Africa during the 1980s, not only among the general public but also among the country's political leaders imprisoned on Robben Island near Cape Town. James Mange, sentenced to 20 years, turned to Rastafarianism while in prison and formed a reggae band that performed for political prisoners on special occasions (Dreisinger 2013;

missLee 2013; Reggae Moonshine Festival 2013). Mange later released several albums with his band The Whiplashes.

Outside the country, one of South Africa's many political exiles, Aura Msimang, studied at the Jamaican School of Arts (JSA) in Kingston during the 1970s. In 1977 she recorded an album (as Aura Lewis) with her band Full Experience and influential producer Lee 'Scratch' Perry at his Black Ark Studios in Jamaica. Msimang later moved to the United States, where she worked on two musical tours with Jimmy Cliff, the first in 1980.

In the early 1990s, as the end of apartheid approached, South African reggae artists continued to use their music for political ends. For example, Jambo released the song 'No Man Kill Another Man' in 1990, a call to end the violence erupting between the rival Inkatha Freedom Party (IFP) and African National Congress (ANC). The following year, in May 1991, the Reggae Strong for Peace concert in Johannesburg featured many of South Africa's top reggae artists, including Dube, Djedje, Mukwevho and O'Yaba. Money raised by the event and its subsequent live album and video were donated toward charitable causes in Soweto.

Reggae in Democratic South Africa

The dismantling of apartheid legislation in the early 1990s, leading to South Africa's first democratic elections in 1994, brought rapid change to South African society. The popularity of reggae in South Africa has largely been synonymous with the career of one artist, Lucky Dube, and his global appeal continued to grow during the postapartheid era until his tragic murder in Johannesburg in 2007. Undoubtedly the most successful, prolific and popular of South Africa's reggae musicians, Dube during his career worked with several artists who continue to fly the flag for reggae in South Africa.

For example, Dube's cousin, Richard Siluma, performs under the reggae moniker Saggy Saggila and released *Endless Love Racing* in 2013. Dube's former backing singer Phumi Maduna refashioned herself as Sister Phumi, one of the genre's few female stars. Keyboardist Thuthukani Cele parted ways with Dube to form The Slaves, who released several albums in the early 1990s before changing their name to the One People Band, releasing *The Spirit of Reggae* in 2014. Maduna and Cele attract a loyal international following, touring Papua New Guinea in 2015 and Malawi in 2017, among other places. Cele in 2016 released a new album, *Eyes for My Babe*. Also keeping Dube's legacy alive is the Lucky Dube Band, made up of Dube's former backing musicians, which released *Celebrate His Life* in 2015. Dube's children Nkulee and Thokozani Dube have embarked on their own musical careers.

Among the pioneers of the genre in South Africa, Carlos Djedje has continued to remain active after many decades in the industry. In 2014 he was invited to perform in Germany and Malaysia, and in 2015 he released a new album, entitled *Conscious Reggae*. In 2017 he was recognized by the government of Jamaica for his contribution to the genre. Djedje's contemporary Colbert Mukwevho also remains a respected figure in South African reggae. He continues to record new material and to perform regularly, often alongside his son Percy, known by the stage name P. Postman.

One of the most popular names in South African reggae in the postapartheid period has been Dr. Victor and his band the Rasta Rebels. After a successful career as both a session musician and a frontman for various disco acts in the 1980s, Victor Khojane began releasing reggae albums as Rasta Rebels in the early 1990s. These included *Pump up the Reggae* in 1990, a medley of popular reggae songs, and *Restless World* in 1991, an album of cover versions of songs by British reggae artist Eddie Grant, whose 1988 anti-apartheid anthem 'Gimme Hope Jo'Anna' was a global hit but banned in South Africa. The Rasta Rebels' version of the song was a hit in South Africa and led to Dr. Victor's prolonged career in pop-reggae.

Of the younger generation of reggae talent to emerge in South Africa since 2000, Tidal Waves have established a loyal following, performing regularly at music festivals and events around the country, often as the sole proponents of reggae music on diverse lineups of artists. In 2016 they released their sixth album, *Tomorrow Starts Today*.

In other parts of the country, Rastaman Nkushu from Limpopo province is another popular reggae artist who has long been active on the local scene. In Cape Town, groups including the Azania Band and The Rudimentals are keeping reggae alive, while in Durban, Kwazulu-Natal, reggae is still performed regularly by groups such as The Meditators and family band Undivided Roots. A band made up of Mozambican musicians based in South Africa, 340ml developed a loyal following in South Africa with their dub- and ska-inspired sound, releasing the albums *Moving* (2003) and *Sorry for the Delay* (2008).

As in other parts of the world, the related genre of dancehall is growing in popularity in South Africa. One of its leading figures is Black Dillinger, born Nkululeko Madolo in Gugulethu, Cape Town. After being featured in German magazine *Riddim* in 2004, he relocated to Berlin and signed to German reggae label MKZWO. He has since released albums such as *Live And Learn* (2007), *Love Life* (2009) and *Better Tomorrow* (2011), dividing his time between Germany and South Africa. In 2015 he performed in Jamaica.

In South Africa in the late 2010s reggae no longer enjoys the commercial and popular success it once experienced in the 1980s and 1990s. Although the genre still has a loyal following, particularly among the country's large Rastafarian community (Chawane 2012), it sits firmly outside the mainstream, with limited airplay or media exposure. The South African Music Awards (SAMAs) do not offer a dedicated reggae category, and have only attempted to acknowledge the genre since 2013 with the introduction of the category 'Best R&B/Soul/Reggae.' This may well be due to a decline in the number of reggae albums being released in South Africa every year. It also suggests a gradual decline in the genre's popularity, despite its significant historical role in the country's political and cultural landscape.

Bibliography

Chawane, Midas. 2012. 'The Rastafari Movement in South Africa: Before and After Apartheid.' *New Contree* 65: 163–88.

Dagnini, Jérémie Kroubo. 2011. 'The Importance of Reggae Music in the Worldwide Cultural Universe.' *Études caribéennes* 16. Online at https://journals.openedition.org/etudescaribeennes/4740?lang=en (accessed 4 September 2018).

Djedje, Carlos. 2012. Telephone interview with the author. 18 September.

Dreisinger, Baz. 2013. 'In South Africa, A Reggae Legacy Lives On.' National Public Radio. Online at: http://www.npr.org/2013/03/30/175583890/in-south-africa-a-reggae-legacy-lives-on (accessed 4 September 2018).

Goldstuck, Arthur. 2007. 'Lucky Dube: A Complete Human Being.' *Mail & Guardian Thought Leader*. Online at: www.thoughtleader.co.za/amablogoblogo/2007/10/19/lucky-dube-a-complete-human-being (accessed 5 April 2018).

Jansen van Rensburg, Claudia Elizabeth. 2013. 'Institutional Manifestations of Music Censorship and Surveillance in Apartheid South Africa with Specific Reference to the SABC from 1974 to 1996.' Unpublished MA thesis, University of Stellenbosch.

Järvenpää, Tuomas. 2017. 'From the Margins, Reggae in South Africa Continues to Struggle for Human Dignity.' *The Conversation*, 4 July. Online at: http://theconversation.com/from-the-margins-reggae-in-south-africa-continues-to-struggle-for-human-dignity-80419 (accessed 5 April 2018).

Martin, Denis-Constant. 1992. 'Music Beyond Apartheid?' In *Rockin the Boat: Mass Music and Mass Movements*, ed. Reebee Garofalo. Cambridge, MA: South End Press, 195–207.

McNeill, Fraser G. 2012. 'Rural Reggae: The Politics of Performance in the Former "Homeland" of Venda.' *South African Historical Journal* 64(1): 81–95.

missLee. 2013. 'A Night of Political History with James Mange.' *Mzansi Reggae*. Online at: www.mzansireggae.co.za/a-night-of-political-history-with-james-mange-2 (accessed 5 April 2018).

Mochoele, Lenah. 2015. *Walking a Mile In Your Shoes: My Spiritual Journey With Lucky Dube*. Johannesburg: Walking a Mile.

Mojapelo, Max. 2008. *Beyond Memory: Recording the History, Moments and Memories of South African Music*. Cape Town: African Minds.

Reggae Moonshine Festival 2013. 'Press Release.' Online at: www.reggaemoonshinefestival.blogspot.com/p/in.html (accessed 5 April 2018).

Siluma, Richard. 2010. Interview with the author. 12 January. Johannesburg, South Africa.

Tenaille, Frank. 2002. *Music Is the Weapon of the Future*. Chicago: Lawrence Hill.

Discographical References

340ml. *Moving*. Sheer Sound SLCD 3401. *2003*: South Africa.

340ml. *Sorry for the Delay*. Arame Farpado AFCD 3402. *2008*: Mozambique.

489

Ball, Benjamin. 'Flash a Flashlight.' *Paulina.* Third World Music TWL510. *1984*: South Africa.
Blondie & Pappa. *24 Hour Service.* CCP Record Company CCP1011. *1980*: South Africa.
Blondie & Pappa. *Together.* Family FLY(V)2. *1982*: South Africa.
Black Dillinger. *Better Tomorrow.* Richvibes Records. *2011*: Austria.
Black Dillinger. *Live and Learn.* MKZWO Records. *2007*: Germany.
Black Dillinger. *Love Life.* IMmusic. *2009*: Germany.
Cele, Thuthukani. *Eyes for My Babe.* Ingomuso Music Publishing. *2016*: South Africa.
Djedje, Carlos. *Conscious Reggae.* Self-released. *2015*: South Africa.
Djedje, Carlos. *Remember Them.* Umkhonto Records. *1989*: South Africa.
Dread Warriors. 'Reggae Music.' *Dread Warriors.* Gallo BL455. *1983*: South Africa.
Dube, Lucky. *Prisoner.* Gallo LUCKY5. *1989*: South Africa.
Dube, Lucky. *Rastas Never Dies.* Plum HUL519. *1984*: South Africa.
Dube, Lucky. *Slave.* Gallo HUL40141. *1987*: South Africa.
Dube, Lucky. *Think About the Children.* Gallo HUL40110. *1985*: South Africa.
Dube, Lucky. *Together as One.* Gallo HUL40171. *1988*: South Africa.
Fassie, Brenda. 'Hero's Party.' *Black President.* CCP Record Company BREN(V)4064851. *1990*: South Africa.
Full Experience. *Aura Meets Lee 'Scratch' Perry at Black Ark Studio.* Blue Moon. Productions BM116. *1990*: France.
Grant, Eddie. 'Gimme Me Hope Jo'Anna.' Ice Records, ICE128701. *1988*: UK.
Harley & The Rasta Family. *Lion in a Sheep Skin.* CCP GAE(V)4065141. *1991*: South Africa.
Jambo. 'No Man Kill Another Man.' *Bad Friend.* Cool Spot SPOT (V) 007. *1990*: South Africa.
Kekana, Steve. 'Sounds of Africa.' *Raising My Family.* EMI 7C 062-83242. *1981*: Sweden.
Lucky Dube Band. *Celebrate His Life.* Different Colours Productions. *2015*: South Africa.
Marley, Bob. 'War.' *Rastaman Vibration.* Island Records GSC340. *1976*: South Africa.
Miller, Jacob. 'Forward Jah Jah Children.' *Tenement Yard.* Jam Sounds. *1976*: Jamaica.
Moraba, Kori. *Sotho Reggae.* RPM RPM7032. *1977*: South Africa.
Movers, The. *Black Reggae.* City Special CYL 1034. *1975*: South Africa.
Nash, Neville. 'Friday Morning.' *Diamonds & Pearls and Solid Gold.* Nash NALP(L)3317. *1982*: South Africa.
One People Band. *The Spirit of Reggae.* OPB/Mbix Music. *2014*: South Africa.
Rasta Rebels. *Pump up the Reggae.* CSR Records/One Way OWL2000. *1990*: South Africa.
Rasta Rebels. *Restless World.* CSR Records CSRL117. *1991*: South Africa.
Reggae Strong For Peace. Gallo. *1991*: South Africa.
Saggy Saggila & The Ras Band. *Endless Love Racing.* RSR Records CDRSR368JN. *2013*: South Africa.
Thrilling Artists, The. 'Luimbo Lwa Reggae.' *Ha Nga Dzule.* *1983*: South Africa.
Tidal Waves. *Tomorrow Starts Today.* Simply Audio Records. *2016*: South Africa.
Tosh, Peter. 'Apartheid.' *Equal Rights.* Columbia PC34670. *1977*: USA.

DAVID DURBACH

Rumba

Before its association with a succession of commercial pop music styles, the term *rumba* referred to a neo-African traditional dance/music form in Cuba that has remained popular into the twenty-first century. Some of the musical roots of traditional *rumba* can be traced to the slave barracks of rural Cuba, which housed slaves from West and Central Africa, most notably the Congo area of Central Africa. *Rumba* then coalesced as a style among free black and mulatto dockworkers in Havana and Matanzas during the late nineteenth century after slavery in Cuba was abolished. It is a festive, secular practice involving call-and-response singing, percussion emphasizing the *clave* rhythm – which links the music back to much older Congolese traditions – and sexually suggestive dancing. With variants including *guaguancó*, *yambú* and *columbia*, traditional *rumba* remains a vibrant and ever-evolving music and dance form, performed by both professional Afro-Cuban folkloric groups and amateur musicians in Cuba and abroad.

However, in the second quarter of the twentieth century the term *rumba* began to be applied – some would say misapplied – to a quite different music, *son*, an ensemble music style that featured the paired-stringed *tres* and swept to huge popularity in Havana in the 1920s. *Son* developed when the more rudimentary *son montuno* from the eastern province of Oriente, which featured call-and-response singing over simple chords, absorbed some musical elements from *rumba* and *trova* in Havana, such as the use of the *clave* and the addition of a sung verse section. In the 1930s the term 'rumba' (often spelled 'rhumba') began to be used as a label for marketing Cuban *son* to foreign audiences, since the word 'son' does not carry over into English well. This commercial *rumba*, however, was far removed from traditional *rumba*. The former was usually a watered-down version of Cuban *son* performed by white Cuban jazz bands for elite Cubans and foreign audiences (Moore 1995, 1997).

The international (commercial) *rumba* craze of the 1930s was driven largely by the dissemination of 78 rpm records. Aside from the success of the genre in the United States, Europe and Latin America, it also gained widespread popularity in Africa with the proliferation of the GV record series. Records including Don Azpiazú's 'El Manicero' ('The Peanut Vendor'), first released in 1930, arrived all at once in colonial African cities, forever changing their popular music. While Cuban music influenced directly a number of African nations – for example, Senegal and Tanzania – the most striking impact was in Kinshasa and Brazzaville, two cities facing one another across the Congo River. In the early 1950s in the Congo the dance known as *maringa* began to be called *rumba*. At first, this was essentially African folk music with simple backing and the *clave* rhythm. But everything changed with the introduction of the electric guitar in the late 1950s. This new *rumba* was urban dance music, suitable for nightclubs and radio play.

Rumba, in the modern African sense, then, refers to the danceable, guitar-driven, choreographed music genre that emanated out of the Congolese cities of Brazzaville and what was then Léopoldville beginning in the 1950s. Essentially an Africanized adaptation of the era's internationally popular Cuban dance music, Congolese *rumba* was the first in a succession of related genres, variously known as *zairois*, *soukouss*, *kwasa kwasa* and *ndombolo*, among other names. Often, the names initially referred to dances but became popularized as names for the music itself. As the Congolese sound spread throughout much of Africa in the 1960s, 1970s and 1980s, it influenced the dance music of many countries, such as Kenya and Tanzania, as well as Zambia and Zimbabwe, to varying degrees. Following the section on Congolese *rumba*, this entry concludes with brief sections on *rumba* in Kenya and *rumba* in Zimbabwe.

Congolese *Rumba*

Congolese *rumba* is most commonly sung in Lingala, a regional African language, but this has not prevented it from being well known and immensely popular across the African continent. Musically, it is most easily recognized by its distinctive high-pitched, repetitive, rhythmically complex electric guitar patterns and the presence of the *atalaku*, specialized singers with a characteristic vocal style that includes long, quasi-improvisational melodies and triadic harmonies, sung mostly in high registers with a 'strained' timbre. While Congolese *rumba* is based on Cuban music, it has also drawn liberally on African as well as non-African sources throughout its evolution. The lyrics spare almost no topic, but the most common themes are romantic love and married life in the modern urban capitals of the two Congos. Also called 'la musique moderne,' it is considered a national music, and it has contributed a great deal to a sense of national identity in the Democratic Republic of Congo (formerly Zaïre) in particular. Detailed accounts of Congolese *rumba* are provided by Manda Tchebwa (1996) and Gary Stewart (2000).

While the style has evolved significantly since its beginnings, certain characteristics have remained consistent. From very early on, songs most commonly have a two-part form, with the beginning section(s) (*chant*, *couplet* or *couplet-refrain*) dominated by sung lyrics and a final section characterized by choreographed dance and repetitive electric guitar sequences. Since the 1980s this is most often the *sebene*, sometimes spelled *seben*, a stylistic element which crystallized in the 1960s and 1970s, made up of repeated syncopated phrases (usually one or two measures in length) played on effects-heavy electric guitars, accompanied by dance shouts instead of vocal melodies.

Genres: Sub-Saharan Africa

Terminology and Basic Principles

In Congolese musical culture, the word 'rumba' refers to a specific rhythm and its variations, closely related to the *clave* beat that is the rhythmic foundation for Afro-Cuban *rumba*, *son* and other genres (see Example 1). The *rumba* rhythm in Congolese music is characterized by a light high-hat, which sketches something resembling a *clave* beat with a smooth, easy feel.

The same term 'rumba' is also used as a more general term for Congolese popular music, despite the fact that many Congolese songs do not, strictly speaking, use the *rumba* rhythm. Other terms such as 'soukouss,' 'kwasa kwasa' or 'ndombolo' are used to refer to Congolese music in general, especially in parts of Africa outside the Congo. These other terms, like the term *rumba*, can each designate a particular rhythm and the dance that accompanies it. At times when a particular rhythm/dance combination was extremely popular, people began using that term to refer to the broader musical practice. In the Congo, the most common terms used for the genre as a whole are 'la musique moderne' or 'la musique typique,' both of which distinguish *rumba* from traditional music (usually called 'folklore' or *la musique folk* in the Congo) and from religious music (much religious music is very similar to *rumba*, and also has a large following).

Example 1: *Clave* rhythm

A modern *rumba* band, designated by the French word *orchestre*, is typically made up of the following: a rhythm section with a drum set, *conga* player and one or more other percussionists (shakers, bongos, etc.); at least three electric guitars (a bass guitar, lead guitar and *accompagnement* guitar [rhythm guitar]) and often a fourth, middle or *mi-solo* guitarist; a horn section and/or one or more keyboard synthesizers (synthesizers began replacing horn sections in the 1970s and 1980s); usually a dance troupe, often divided into male and female dancing corps; and generally at least five, and sometimes up to ten, singers. The band leader is usually a singer, although the lead vocal part of each song is not necessarily sung by him or her, and another set of singers have a specialized role as 'animators' (referred to most commonly as 'atalaku,' but also by using the French word 'animateur'), whose role is to make dancers and listeners excited during the dance sections of songs. This general configuration has been constant for most of the history of the genre, although the role of the *atalaku* was neither formalized nor the term coined until the third generation of music (see history section below).

Not all musicians and singers are on stage at the same time or on every recorded track: most bands have more guitarists, drummers and singers than are ever necessary at one time, and each song has a set of instrumentalists and singers 'assigned' to it. The vocal labor is even divided within songs, where the first part of the songs is typically sung by one or two lead singers and an optional background chorus, with the *atalakus* taking over in the second dance section to sing or shout out dance moves, *libanga* and other supplementary vocal parts.

Many Congolese describe their music history in terms of four generations: the first generation roughly covers the 1940s to mid-1950s, the second from the 1950s to mid-1970s, the third from the 1970s to around 1990, and the fourth lasts from the 1990s to the early twenty-first century. Musicians are sorted along these generational lines and associated with a particular time period and thereby a particular age demographic where audiences are concerned. In practice, there is much stylistic overlap, many artists produce music across multiple generations, and it is rare that an individual listener's taste remains squarely within these boundaries, but the terms are useful and meaningful, especially to the Congolese listening public.

History: First Generation, 1940s to 1950s

The earliest recordings of *rumba* in the Congo were modeled after the Cuban music that, marketed as *rumba*, become a global sensation, and was introduced to the Congo through phonograph records brought by Belgian colonists. Some early Congolese songs were even sung in Spanish. Musicians soon created their own lyrics in African languages, however, and commercial recordings of Congolese artists in the *rumba* style were produced beginning in the 1940s in both Brazzaville and Léopoldville (the colonial name for the city that today is called Kinshasa). Lingala, a regional *lingua franca* in Kinshasa and Brazzaville, eventually became the musical language of choice, and in some parts of Africa (Kenya and Tanzania, for example), *rumba* is called 'Lingala music.' Lingala's dominance was driven by its regional status in the urban centers of the recording industry, the use of Lingala as a *de facto* language of the military (giving it a trans-ethnic and trans-regional 'national' status), and its public use by early national leaders, such as Mobutu in the Democratic Republic of Congo (called Zaïre from 1971 until the end of Mobutu's reign in 1997). Despite Lingala's dominance, many songs include lyrics in other languages, usually either local languages from other parts of the Congo (Kikongo, Tshiluba, Swahili, etc.) or French or English, reflecting the trans-ethnic and multilingual nature of the musical culture.

These early days of Congolese music were accompanied by a fashion culture and street slang for Congolese men who called themselves 'les Bills' after Buffalo Bill. This culture, dominant during the 1950s, came from the dual influence of Indian cinema and Western films from the United States, and the dialect spoken was called Hindoubill (a term made up of 'hindou' from the French term for Hindu and 'bill' derived from Buffalo Bill). Singers adopted nicknames and fashion styles from cinematic culture.

The first generation is often referred to as 'ntango ya ba Wendo' ('the time of Wendo and the like'), referring to 'Papa' Wendo Kolosoy. Wendo's most famous song was 'Marie Louise,' which features a single voice over acoustic guitars and a sparse rhythmic background, a sound characteristic of the recordings from this time. These early recordings often employed acoustic instruments, including various types of accordion, piano and acoustic bass, instruments that are much rarer in later generations of Congolese *rumba*. The music of the first generation is quite similar in structure and feel to the internationally disseminated versions of Cuban music styles of the time (*chachachá*, *rumba*, *son*, etc.).

History: Second Generation, 1950s to Mid-1970s

The second generation of music had two main musical 'schools': the O.K. Jazz school, begun in 1956 with Luambo Makiadi 'Franco' as its figurehead, and the African Jazz school, founded by Joseph 'Grand Kalle' Kabasele in 1951 and continued most prominently in the stardom of Tabu Ley Rochereau. Advances in recording and amplification technology made larger bands possible, and the popularity of the music and musicians created a large and competitive professional music scene. Each band had 'defectors' throughout its history who left to start their own groups, a practice that continued into later generations. African Jazz split into several camps, with the splinter group African Fiesta (led by Rochereau and guitarist Dr. Nico) having the most success before eventually splitting again.

Both schools presented mannered, sophisticated images: three-piece suits, tightly arranged horn sections and smooth musical styles dominated by *rumba* rhythms. African Jazz is considered more refined in terms of its music and lyrics, with a focus on idealistic love narratives and rich poetic language, as opposed to the O.K. Jazz school's engagement with social issues and rhythms more suited to dancing. In practice, both groups produced repertoires of dazzlingly wide range, and this generation represents something of a 'classical' period of the music: the style crystallized into a genre, distinguishable from other regional, African or international genres, and the 'modern' *orchestre*, with its distribution of personnel and roles, was established. This ensemble included extended vocal sections alternating between solo or duo singers and a chorus of male voices; extended instrumental solos (usually horn or guitar), which would eventually evolve into the *sebene* style; and choreographed dance, which was still fairly subtle in the second generation but would grow to be more central to the musical practice. At this point, Congolese *rumba* had an established canon of stars and hit songs, with intertextual references to songs or lyrics from the past playing an important role in giving the music a sense of itself as a genre and a continuing relationship to its own history.

Among the best-known hits of this second generation are 'Mario' by O.K. Jazz (sung by Franco) and 'Mokolo nakokufa' by African Fiesta National, a splinter group with its main members from African Jazz (sung by Tabu Ley Rochereau). 'Mario' recounts the woes of a woman whose younger lover spends her money and will not make his own, typical of the kind of 'morality' piece O.K. Jazz is known for, as well as Franco's continued pushing of the limits of what was considered 'decent' for public speech. 'Mokolo nakokufa,' which translates as 'The Day I Will Die,' reflects upon the fact that the time and manner of one's death are unknown, and speculates about what may flash through the minds of different people at the moment of their departure: the working woman thinks of her children and the boat she used to cross the river to the market; the rich man thinks of his automobile and his children in Europe; the drunk thinks about drinking beer with his friends on payday. Both songs offer visions of the social and economic realities of life in the Congolese city from the perspectives of fictional narrators. Franco's 'Mario' is devilishly playful in the overtness of its language and its critique of the characters involved, whereas Rochereau's 'Mokolo nakokufa' presents a more philosophical and gentle perspective. These songs typify the character of this generation and its most influential actors.

Both Franco and Rochereau continued to be active into the 1980s, and both made attempts to establish themselves abroad. Rochereau had some success on the world music circuit during its initial market boom in the 1980s. Franco apparently began to establish a studio presence in Brussels, and according to lore, the success of the song 'Maya,' released by O.K. Jazz in 1984 during this long absence, threatened the musical authority he had established in Kinshasa and compelled him to return.

History: Third Generation, 1970s to 1990

The third generation, whose flagship band was Zaïko Langa Langa, marks a significant stylistic break from the earlier generations, one characterized by a general acceleration of the music, an increasing importance of choreographed dance and music videos that accompany albums, and a thinner musical texture. The bands were often 'slimmed down' (the economic downturn that began in the region around 1980 certainly contributed to this process), with keyboard synthesizers taking the place of horn sections, two guitars instead of three, and a guitar style that was generally cleaner, higher-pitched and faster. Many songs of the third generation have two-part 'verse-*sebene*' or 'refrain-*sebene*' structures, while others have more complex structures. Still, the vast majority of third-generation songs end with a *sebene*, and the tight, sparse sound, both of the vocal sections, and of the high-pitched guitar and snare drum in the *sebene*, makes the style of this period the most easily recognized as distinctively Congolese. Some slower subgenres emerged in reaction to the trend of tempo acceleration (such as *tcha-tcho*, created by Koffi Olomide and influenced by Caribbean *zouk*).

This is also the generation associated with the fashion phenomenon called *la sape* in which designer clothing and accessories (mostly European) became a *sine qua non* of musical culture, along with an intensification of European migration from the two Congos (also related to political and economic instability). The Zaïre 74 music festival that accompanied the boxing match in Kinshasa between US boxers Muhammed Ali and George Foreman, known as 'The Rumble in the Jungle,' brought Congolese musicians and audiences into direct contact with African-American music acts, most notably B.B. King and James Brown, and historians suggest some kind of resulting influence, perhaps in both directions. This era also saw the production and dissemination of made-for-television concerts related to Mobutu's *animation culturelle*.

Zaïko Langa Langa, who continue to operate in the twenty-first century, were the trailblazing group of the third generation, powered by the leadership and guitar wizardry of Manuaku Waku and the vocal talents of stars such as Nyoka Longo, Bozi Boziana, Papa Wemba and Dindo Yogo. It was also Zaïko Langa Langa that pioneered the role of the *atalaku*, or *animateur*, formalizing and specializing the role of a singer who shouts dance moves, calls out to supporters and friends, and otherwise fills in the dance *sebene* section. Papa Wemba, the artist most commonly associated with *la sape*, left Zaïko Langa Langa to form Viva la Musica, and has become one of the Congolese artists best known to non-African audiences in the world music crossover tradition of Tabu Ley Rochereau. 'King' Kester Emeneya and Koffi Olomide both began their careers working with Papa Wemba, but have had such subsequent success that they have become rivals to Wemba, and all three of these artists have careers that have endured well into the time of the fourth generation. One of Zaïko Langa Langa's chief competitors was Orchestre Bella Bella, founded by brothers Maxim and Emile Soki (Les Frères Soki), which enabled such enduring stars as Pepe Kalle and Diblo Dibala to begin their careers. Dibala has also had some success outside Africa, and was one of the motors that pushed Congolese bands (such as Loketo and Kanda Bongo Man's band, both of which Diblo played in) to some degree of success in Europe and the United States in the late 1980s and 1990s under the generic term *soukouss* (see separate entry).

History: Fourth Generation and Beyond, 1990s to the Early Twenty-First Century

The band Wenge Musica ushered in the fourth generation, known as the 'Wenge' generation ('Ba Wenge'). First formed in 1981, Wenge Musica became a sensation in the 1990s, in particular with hit songs such as 'Kin é bougé' (1991). With the Wenge clan, the quick, clean guitar sound of the third generation gave way to a more relaxed, almost 'retro' tempo, and many artists of this generation draw explicitly on contemporary Latin music (such as *salsa*) and US pop styles (such as R&B, one example being Fally Ipupa's 2006 album *Droit chemin*).

As in earlier generations, their success led to a splintering of the group, and today Wenge Musica is roughly divided into two main camps: Wenge Musica BCBG, led by J.B. Mpiana, and Werra Son's Wenge Musica Maison Mère. The Werra school (Maison Mère) is associated with high-energy dance and rough edges, and appeals to a more popular mass audience, whereas the BCBG groups are seen as smoother and more sophisticated, playing to a more refined audience with middle-class aspirations, mirroring the second-generation split between O.K Jazz and African Jazz (respectively). Other artists exist somewhat independently of this dual structure, such as Felix Wazekwa, and many others from earlier generations have remained active, like Papa Wemba (1949–2016) and Koffi Olomide (b. 1956). Stars of the early twenty-first century include Bill Clinton Kalonji and Ferre Gola (both from the Maison Mère school), as well as Fally Ipupa (who originally sang with Koffi Olomide).

The fourth generation saw in particular the rise of the subgenre of *générique*, or theme song, and an even louder, denser sound than prior styles (musically, *générique* may be compared to a long series of *sebene* sections with no lyrical vocal section). It is also associated with the increasing prominence of *libanga*, the names of friends, sponsors and other associates that are inserted in the songs. This is related to gradual shifts in the economics of the music business in the Congo region. Artists have reacted to the economic decline of Mobutu's Zaïre that began in the late 1970s, as well as intermittent political unrest and increasing piracy. Instead of being sponsored by a charismatic government or record sales, much of their support comes from the informal relationships created through *libanga*. These artists do give small concerts, for which they charge large fees, and large concerts which are free and usually sponsored by beer companies, but even these are more for promotion than for profit. The *libanga* 'phenomenon' has led many critics, especially older fans of earlier generations of music, to denigrate the more recent music for its lack of substance, as well as for a lack of refinement and even 'brutality' in the musical practice.

The success of young, innovative stars in the early twenty-first century such as Fally Ipupa and Ferre Gola suggested the possibility of a fifth generation of musicians influenced by US R&B and other African styles such as *coupé-décalé*.

Thematic Trends and Musical Characteristics

The vast majority of *rumba* songs focus on the subject of romantic love and on the problems of marriage in particular. Although some songs take the form of professions of dedication and undying love, conflict and infidelity are more common themes, most often in the form of fear of betrayal or a demand for justice for wrongdoing. Conflict between spouses often involves neighbors, in-laws and family friends, with the singer complaining about the behaviors of these members of the community, and often pronouncing judgments about them. Because lyrics address relationships and responsibilities, political and social questions may be addressed indirectly through the theme of love, marriage and family affairs.

The marriages and communities described are almost exclusively in modern urban settings. Most historians of Congolese music mention the importance of the city, and *rumba* songs are often explicitly set in Kinshasa or Brazzaville (or recount the experience of life between the two cities). In the music, Kinshasa is referred to by many nicknames, such as 'Kin,' 'Léo' (in pre-independence times), or 'Lipopo,' and Brazzaville is often called 'CFA.' Specific areas of the cities are also named in songs, especially sections of the city with certain reputations, such as Matonge, Kimbanseke or Poto Poto. Papa Wemba has referred in his music to a section of his neighborhood (in Matonge, Kinshasa) as the 'Village Molokai,' a composite of street names.

Congolese *rumba* is also, to some extent, a music of the river: the Congo (also called the Zaïre during Mobutu's regime), which separates the two capitals. This explains, in part, the recurrence of yet another theme: travel. Many songs recount either the experiences of the musicians on their concert tours, or travel as a source of conflict for an amorous couple, separated because one partner leaves to work or study. In the early days, these travels were related to the river, as in the classic 'Ebale ya Zaïre' ('The Zaïre River') by O.K. Jazz. In the 1990s and early 2000s, songs increasingly described travel to Europe and the United States, but in similar terms.

Early songs exhibited repetitive song forms (with verses and a refrain), but since the third generation (1970s), it has become increasingly typical for a song to be through-composed, with little or no exact repetition of either lyrics or melodic material. Songs tend to have tightly choreographed introductions and transitions between the various sections of the song, and instrumental solo sections are called 'solfège' sections. A typical form is intro-verse-solfège-transition-refrain-transition-*sebene*-fadeout (recordings typically end with a fadeout, whereas concert performances usually end after a much-extended *sebene*).

The lyrics to the verse and refrain sections usually describe a poetic 'moment,' as opposed to a linear narrative through time, and these sometimes take the form of a litany, punctuated by refrains sung by a chorus. One example is the song 'Nakoma mbanda na mama ya mobali' ('My Mother-in-Law Has Become My Rival for the Attentions of My Husband') by O.K. Jazz, which begins with an introduction that transitions into a verse, sung chorally, describing problems with a mother-in-law (from a female perspective). There is a break and short transition into a refrain section, where the same chorus sings different lyrics summarizing the problem. Between refrains Franco sings alone, developing the details of the problems. Finally, another transition leads into a *sebene*, and the song fades out. The musical material and *tempi* are quite different from section to section, although the musical material from the introduction returns in the transition to the *sebene* section. More recent music (that of the third and fourth generations) tends to have more sections and more variation in the musical material within a song, although the basic structure is generally the same. While this is the most common song form, many songs throughout the repertoire have only a single section, and still more have multiple sections, but without the final *sebene*.

The guitar style has evolved over the years, but has almost always featured a picked, melodic approach exhibiting great polyphony (within each guitar part as well as between instruments) and rhythmic sophistication (through syncopation, hemiola and rhythmic displacement). Lead guitars at times play improvised melodies like guitars in Western jazz and pop genres, but more often play repetitive patterns with continuing variation. Strumming is uncommon in Congolese guitar style, and is found mostly in the music of the first generation or as a special effect in later practice. Open strings are exploited in guitar practice, as well as in the bass parts, which are similarly polyphonic and rhythmically sophisticated compared to guitar parts. The 'Hawaiian' guitar style (steel or slide guitar) was very popular during the early generations (1940s to 1960s), and guitar effects such as delay pedals and distortion have become the norm, although at times more or less in fashion (especially during the third and fourth generations).

Congolese *rumba*'s harmonic practice is restrained, and most songs follow one of several progression patterns of major chords, such as I-IV-V-IV or I-IV-I-V. Minor harmonies are rare, as are non-triadic harmonies, although dominant seventh and sixth chords are used, usually according to the rules of functional tonal harmony (e.g., V_7-I or V_7/IV-IV). Vocal harmonies follow a rule of parallel motion at consonant intervals (according to Western definitions, that is, thirds, sixths, fourths and fifths), and the 'chord' instruments (guitars, bass and keyboard) follow similar rules.

The Congolese Legacy

In the twenty-first century the success of the Ivoirian-Parisian *coupé-décalé* style has influenced and even threatened the dominance of the Congolese style on the African continent. This style, while associated with Côte d'Ivoire and the Ivoirian diaspora in Paris, is heavily influenced and inspired by Congolese music, and one of its biggest early stars, Jesse Matador, is of Congolese origin. But in general, Congolese *rumba* has remained remarkably independent of large-scale global music trends, despite its historical relationship to the global recording industry through commercial Cuban music and the success of certain musicians in the world music market. Even when it borrows from R&B, reggae, *salsa* and the like, these other styles are integrated into a musical grammar that is distinctively Congolese in that artists rarely stray from the melismatic vocal style, subject matter of life in Kinshasa, syncopated guitar patterns, or the song structure appropriate to their musical generation. The genre has endured, despite an industry based on a listening public that in general possesses only a microscopic purchasing power, and a history of states that have been either repressive (in the case of both pre- and post-independence times) or have had little or no ability to enforce intellectual property rights (in times of economic hardship and civil unrest since the 1990s). One could understand this persistence as a Congolese musical miracle, but the case of Congolese *rumba* may also be instructive as the global music industry moves forward into new economies and new technologies of reproduction.

In the face of the region's political and economic troubles, Congolese *rumba* has remained vibrant, with lasting popularity among diverse audiences across Africa, most of whom do not speak the language in which the music is sung. While its continental dominance seems to have waned since the late 1990s, its musicians have left a vast and rich repertoire of recordings which are likely to inspire, entertain, educate and make audiences dance for many years to come.

Rumba *in Kenya*

Congolese *rumba* has thus had a long-lasting impact on the history of African popular music. As Ewens observes, 'No other music in the history of African pop has had such a widespread and lasting impact as the guitar-based music of Zaire and Congo' (Ewens 1991, 126). Kenya was no exception in this regard. *Rumba* was popularized in Kenya by itinerant Congolese musicians during the 1960s and 1970s (Atsiaya 2014a), where it became known as 'lingala,' the language in which it was performed. This movement of musicians increased in the 1970s as deteriorating political conditions in the Democratic Republic of the Congo resulted in many Congolese musicians migrating to Kenya and Tanzania.

Atsiaya (2014a) accounts for one of the very few sources available on *rumba* in Kenya. In this publication, he expands on these reasons for the influence of Congolese *rumba*. He contends that the spread of *rumba* to Kenya may be linked to two factors in particular. The first was an active recording environment in the Congo with rival bands seeking to outdo each other. According to Atsiaya, this motivated the Americans to set up a radio station in Congo (Radio Congolia, later Radio Congo Belge) which broadcast with such a wide radius that its music reached many parts of East, Central and West Africa. In addition, the Congo, with its vibrant musical life, became a focal point for musicians in East Africa; as Atsiaya observes, 'These musicians would observe what was happening in the Congo and strive to reproduce it' (Atsiaya 2014a).

Secondly, because of the vibrant recording and production environment in the Congo, Congolese recordings began finding markets beyond the country's borders. Kenya was one such market. According to Atsiaya, Congolese *rumba* acquired quick and widespread local acceptance in Kenya, even though the language in which it was sung, Lingala, was unknown to most Kenyans. However, the preponderance of Lingala did not mean that Swahili and other local languages were not used in Kenya to perform *rumba*. For example, Samba Mapangala – a Congolese musician who settled for a short time with his band, Orchestra Virunga, in Kenya and East Africa – mixed Swahili and Lingala in his music, especially in songs such as 'Vunja mifupa.'

In addition, some Kenyan bands chose to adopt *rumba* to local Kenyan dialects. That is how Kabasselleh Ochieng of the Luna Kidi band and Musa Juma of the Limpopo International band established themselves as successful *rumba* artists. They played music comparable in quality to Congolese *rumba*, but sang in Dholuo (a dialect spoken by the Luo people of Kenya and Tanzania) interspersed with Swahili. In the same vein, the late Habel Kifoto, who worked with the Kenya Army, led an army dance band – the Maroon Commandos Band – that sang songs such as 'Charonyi ni wasi' and 'Kristina dada' in Swahili and his native Taita (the language of the Taita people, a Bantu ethnic group of Kenya). Other key Kenyan musicians who embraced *rumba* but sang in Swahili were Fundi Konde, Daudi Kabaka and Fadhil William. Yet other musicians chose to remain heavily influenced by Congolese *rumba* to the extent that their local identities became almost imperceptible – except to listeners with a keen ear. One such musician is Kombo Kombozee from Taita ('Taita' also refers to a mountainous region near the coast of Kenya), whose musical identity remained heavily influenced by Congolese *rumba*, with lyrics sung in Lingala (Atsiaya 2014a).

Atsiaya points out that *rumba* has become an indelible part of the Kenyan musical landscape. It has become the preferred music of sophisticated urban music-lovers. Despite the fact that most *rumba* popular in Kenya has been sung in Lingala, it has not prevented the music from touching the hearts of such audiences. According to Atsiaya, one of the reasons for this loyal following is the character of *rumba* songs. Most *rumba* songs, as those of Musa Juma, Mzee Makassy, Les Wanyika and Simba Wanyika reveal, recount a story about love, broken hearts, sad encounters, aspirations for a better future or a celebration of good times. The lyrics are woven together in a poetic manner and delivered with engaging melodies and accompaniments. *Rumba*'s appeal has increased with time. In most entertainment spots in Kenya, especially those patronized by people middle-aged and older, resident bands always reserve a place for *rumba*, even if the rest of the repertoire is made up of contemporary, fast-paced music. *Rumba* often serves as the basis for the rest of the performance. Even when the performance moves into related genres such as *soukouss* and *techno*, the basis of the music always remains *rumba*. To many people in East and Central Africa, *rumba* is a mark of identity, the music of the people (Atsiaya 2014a).

Rumba *in Zimbabwe*

From the 1950s on Congolese *rumba* spread nearly everywhere in Africa, projected in the main by vinyl records. Right away, the music was heard and played in Zimbabwe (then Rhodesia). In fact, *rumba* became so popular so quickly that local groups simply *had* to play it. A band from Kinshasa, Lipopo Jazz Band, moved to Harare (Salisbury) in 1964, becoming the first fully Congolese band to reside in Zimbabwe. Jackson Phiri, a Malawian, joined to sing *rumba* songs in local languages, and Lipopo enjoyed a good run at the upmarket Federal Hotel. When the Congolese members were deported in 1969, Phiri took over. From there, Lipopo Jazz Band became a training ground for some of the most important guitarists in Zimbabwe.

When it comes to Zimbabwean *rumba*, it is important to note as well a few non-Congolese influences. First, there was *benga* and related, *rumba*-derived styles from Kenya and Tanzania. During Zimbabwe's independence struggle (1966–79), resisters and fighters moved back and forth to these countries, and brought music and dances with them. There were in addition styles from South Africa, especially the guitar-driven *mbaqanga* sound emanating from the townships around Johannesburg. Musically speaking, the East African *rumba* variants featured more transparent guitar interplay than did the Congo sound. In other words, the distinction between accompaniment and lead guitar was less pronounced. Similarly, the *clave* feel was more understated. This de-emphasizing of *clave* was further reinforced in Zimbabwe by the solidly 4/4 *mbaqanga* influence – South Africa was one of the few places in Africa where this era's Cuban music had exerted only a muted impact.

Local Zimbabwean traditions had relatively little influence on *rumba* because they tended to work with 12/8 rhythm structures, fundamentally different from the succession of *rumba* variants. But Zimbabwe's *rumba* bands sang in local languages, especially Shona, and gradually developed a distinct local identity. In the 1970s and 1980s groups including the Real Sounds, O.K. Success, the Harare Mambo Band and the Marxist Brothers enjoyed widespread popularity playing *rumba*. Musicians from the Congo, such as the original members of the Lubumbashi Stars, hewed closer to the Kinshasa sound, while others, such as Devera Ngwena Jazz Band, had a more Zimbabwean character, tending toward the music that soon became widely known as *sungura*.

As time went on, these distinctions became harder to make. In the 1990s and early 2000s popular singers such as Simon Chimbetu and Leonard Zvakata led *rumba* bands, but their melodies, themes and stylized dances were not all that different from what *sungura* artists John Chibadura, Leonard Dembo and other artists were doing. Harare's live music scene was extremely active during these years, with many bands playing affordable gigs in beer halls and outdoor gardens with dance floors, all around the city, all night long, every weekend. The competition to come up with new songs, new dances, new outfits – anything to enlarge a band's share of a dance-hungry local audience – was intense.

Despite their popularity, *rumba* and *sungura* have been subject to criticism as 'foreign' sounds, in some way a betrayal of the nationalist, revivalist sentiments that drove Zimbabwe's defining liberation struggle. At the same time, *rumba* has remained at the heart of the most popular dance genres of modern Africa. Dancing enthusiasts throughout the continent love it, and it sells recordings and concert tickets. So it seems clear that Zimbabwean variants of *rumba* will persist despite economic and political hardships and the ongoing encroachment and evolution of more contemporary popular music styles.

Bibliography

Atsiaya, Amadi Kwaa. 2014a. 'Effects of Rumba on Kenyan Pop Scene.' *Music in Africa*. Online at: https://www.musicinafrica.net/magazine/effect-rumba-kenyan-pop-scene (accessed 27 December 2017).

Atsiaya, Amadi Kwaa. 2014b. 'The Recording Industry in the DRC and Its Impact on Kenyan Popular Music.' *Music in Africa*. Online at: https://www.musicinafrica.net/magazine/recording-industry-drc-and-its-impact-kenyan-popular-music (accessed 27 December 2017).

Bemba, Sylvain. 1984. *Cinquante ans de musique du Congo-Zaïre* [Fifty Years of Music in Congo-Zaire]. Paris: Présence Africaine.

Drake-Boyt, Elizabeth. 2011. *Latin Dance*. Santa Barbara, CA: Greenwood.

Ewens, Graeme. 1991. *Africa O-Ye! A Celebration of African Music*. New York: Da Capo Press.

Ewens, Graeme. 1994. *Congo Colossus: The Life and Legacy of Franco & OK Jazz*. Norfolk, VA: Buku Press.

Eyre, Banning. 2015. *Lion Songs: Thomas Mapfumo and the Music that Made Zimbabwe*. Durham, NC: Duke University Press.

Khazadi, P. 1971. 'Congo Music: Africa's Favourite Beat.' *Africa Report* 16(4): 25–9.

Moore, Robin. 1995. 'The Commercial Rumba: Afrocuban Arts as International Popular Culture.' *American Music Review/Revista de Música Latinoamericana* 16(2): 165–98.

Moore, Robin. 1997. *Nationalizing Blackness: Afrocubanismo and Artistic Revolution in Havana, 1920–1940*. Pittsburgh, PA: University of Pittsburgh Press.

Moore, Robin. 2006. *Music and Revolution: Cultural Change in Socialist Cuba*. Berkeley, CA: University of California Press.

Moore, Robin. 2009. *Music in the Hispanic Caribbean: Experiencing Music, Expressing Culture*. Oxford: Oxford University Press.

Palmberg, Mai, and Kirkegaad, Annemetter. 2002. *Playing with Identities in Contemporary Music in Africa*. Uppsala: Nordic African Institute.

Perez, Louis A., Jr. 2012. *On Becoming Cuban: Identity, Nationality and Culture*. Chapel Hill, NC: University of Carolina Press.

Roberts, John Storm. 1972. *Black Music of Two Worlds*. Tivoli, NY: Original Music.

Roberts, John Storm. 1979. *The Latin Tinge*. Oxford: Oxford University Press.

Steward, Sue. 1999. *Musica! The Rhythm of Latin America: Salsa, Rumba, Merengue & More*. San Francisco, CA: Chronicle Books.

Stewart, Gary. 2000. *Rumba on the River: A History of the Popular Music of the Two Congos*. London: Verso.

Sublette, Ned. 2004. *Cuba and Its Music: From the First Drums to the Mambo*. Chicago: Chicago Review Press.

Tchebwa, Manda. 1996. *Terre de la chanson: La musique zaïroise hier et aukourd'hui* [The Land of Song: Zairian Music Yesterday and Today]. Louvain-la-Neuve: Duculot.

Turino, Thomas. 2000. *Nationalists, Cosmopolitans, and Popular Music in Zimbabwe*. Chicago: University of Chicago Press.

White, Bob W. 2002. 'La rumba congolaise et autres cosmopolitismes' [Congolese Rumba and Other Cosmopolitanisms]. *Cahiers d'études africaines* 42(168): 663–86.

White, Bob W. 2008. *Rumba Rules: The Politics of Dance Music in Mobutu's Zaire*. Durham, NC: Duke University Press.

White, Bob W., ed. 2012. *Music and Globalization: Critical Encounters*. Bloomington: Indiana University Press.

White, Bob W. and Yoka, Lye Andre. 2010. *Musique populaire et société à Kinshasa: Une ethnographie de l'écoute* [Popular Music and Society in Kinshasa: An Ethnography of Listening]. Paris: L'Harmattan.

Yvonne, Daniel. 1995. *Rumba: Dance and Social Change in Cuba*. Bloomington: Indiana University Press.

Zindi, Fred. 1985. *Roots Rocking in Zimbabwe*. Gweru: Mambo Press.

Zindi, Fred. 2013. *Music Rocking from Zimbabwe*. Harare: Zindisc Publishing.

Discographical References

African Fiesta National. 'Mokolo nakokufa.' *Le Seigneur Rochereau*. Sonodisc CD36515. *1992*: France.

Don Azpiazú. 'El Manicero' [The Peanut Vendor]. Victor Records 22483. *1930*: USA.

Fally Ipupa. *Droit chemin*. Baierle Records. *2007*: Germany.

Maroon Commandos Band. 'Charonyi ni wasi.' *Hit Parade Number 1*. Polydor POLP 516. *1979*: Kenya.

Maroon Commandos Band. 'Kristina dada.' *Riziki Haivatu*. Polydor POLP 518. *1981*: Kenya.

O.K. Jazz. 'Ebale ya Zaïre.' *Franco, Simaro et le TP OK Jazz*. Sonodisc CD36520. *197?*: France.

O.K. Jazz. 'Mario.' *Franco et le Tout Puissant O.K. Jazz*. Sonodisc CD8461. *1989*: France.

O.K. Jazz. 'Maya.' *1984*: Zaïre.

O.K. Jazz. 'Nakoma mbanda na mama ya mobali.' *Franco: Nakoma Mbanda na Ngai*. Sonodisc CD36571. *1997*: France.

Samba Mapangala and Orchestra Virunga. 'Vunja mifuba.' *Vunja Mifuba*. CBS Kenya IVA 40 071. *1989*: Kenya.

Wendo Kolosoy. 'Marie Louise.' *Nani akolela Wendo*. Franc'Amour FC 075. *1993*: Belgium.

Wenge Musica. 'Kin é bougé.' *Kin e bouger*. Next Music. *1991*: Belgium.

Discography

African Jazz. *Grand Kalle & African Jazz: Succès des années 50/60*. Sonodisc CD36579. *1997*: France.

Chibadura, John. *The Essential John Chibadura*. CSA CD5002. *2001*: Zimbabwe.

Chimbetu, Simon. *African Panorama, Chapter 1*. Gramma CD KSA 184. *1999*: Zimbabwe.

Chimbetu, Simon. *Takabatana*. Sheer Sound SLCD 041. *2003*: South Africa.

Mpiana, J. B. and Wenge Musica BCBG. *T.H. (Toujours Humble)*. Simon Production-SIPE. *2000*: France.

O. K. Jazz. *20ème Anniversaire*. Sonodisc 360 082/83. *1976*: France.

Olomide, Koffi. *Force de Frappe*. Sonodisc. *2001*: France.

Papa Wemba & Viva la Musica. *Foridoles*. Suave. *1994*: USA.

Roots Rock Guitar Party: Zimbabwe Frontline, Volume 3. Stern's Africa STEW40CD. *1999*: UK.

Werra Son and Wenge Musica Maison Mère. *Solola bien*. JPS Production CDJPS 047. *1999*: USA.

Zaïko Langa Langa. 'Pa Oki.' Veve TS-44. *1979*: Zaïre.

Zvakata, Leonard Karikoga. *Greatest Hits*. ZMC CDKLZ5. *1996*: Zimbabwe.

BANNING EYRE AND JOHNNY FRIAS (INTRODUCTION), JOHN NIMIS (CONGO), MELLITUS NYONGESA WANYAMA (KENYA) AND BANNING EYRE (ZIMBABWE)

See also **Rumba (Vol. IX, Caribbean and Latin America)**

Sákárà

Sákárà is a contemplative Islamic-influenced Yorùbá popular musical genre. The dominant stylistic characteristics of *sákárà* music include recitative/declamation, the drone-like melody of the *gòjé* (fiddle), instrumental preludes and interludes by *gòjé*, playing in octaves, repetition of successive stanzas that may contain variations of the same music, quotations from the Holy Qur'an, philosophical texts and call-and-response. The genre is plaintive, melancholic and sober in nature.

Scholars including Eúbà (1971) and Waterman (1999) date the genre's origin to the 1940s. It came to Yorùbáland from the northern region of Nigeria through Ilorin and other towns that had early contact with Islam and the Hausa people. The Islamic and Arabic musical attributes found in *sákárà* are quite visible in its instrumentation, which comprises *gòjé* (fiddle), *sákárà* drums, *igbá* (calabash), *kannango* drums and *sèkèrè* (rattle). Some of these instruments, especially the *gòjé* and the *sákárà* drums, are borrowed from the Hausa-Arabic culture (Daramola 2005, 144); many Hausa musical typologies employ *gòjé* or other traditional fiddles as a leading instrument in their ensembles. In discussing the Arabic prototype of the gòjé, Omíbíyí (1979) noted that it is called the *emzhad* and is used purely for recreational and entertainment occasions, while the Hausa employ it to accompany male singers, acting as a cue for their music and dance steps.

Sákárà evolved in the early 1940s and was used for various occasions such as weddings, naming and burial ceremonies and other social functions of the Yorùbá Muslim. It was popularized by artists such as Sànúsí Àká and Yùsúfù Olátúnjí (fondly called Bàbá Légbá). Olátúnjí was the undisputed icon of *sákárà* music. He hailed from Ìséyìn in Òyó state, Nigeria, and was based in Abéòkúta, a town regarded as the home of *sákárà* music in Yorubaland. Another pioneer of *sákárà* music was Sànúsí Àká, popularly called 'Chief Composer.' Àká was a contemporary of Yùsúfù Olátúnjí. His philosophical songs are full of thought-provoking lyrics laden with native wisdom and sung in Ègbá dialect addressing topics such as social order and current events, cultural values, folk idioms, myths and the oral history of the Yorùbá, among others.

Sákárà musicians of the 1990s and beyond include Jámíù Lefty Balógun, Ola Baba Ibeji, Latifu Adisa, Ahbedeen Olátúnjí, Jnr, Lukman Babatunde Ajao and Abimbola Omojesu (the latter performing gospel *sákárà*, a variant that incorporates Christian religious texts). Jámíù Lefty Balógun, the scion of late Pa Sàlámì Lefty Balógun (a contemporary of late Yùsúfù Olátúnjí), was born in Lagos. He reached the peak of his musical career in 1983 when he released an album titled *Mo wa ri Faye* which is rooted in and built on the fusion of *fààjì èkó* (Lagos traditional music) as its thematic basis. This distinct style separated Jámíù's *sákárà* music from that of others. He used the idiom to prove that *sákárà* is a 'Lagos home grown music' especially in Ìsàlè Èkó, Ìta Fájì and other downtown Lagos areas. Aside from this fusion, he also experimented by applying modern technology and incorporated Western instruments in his music.

While *sákárà* still maintains its musical status as music for 'the elderly' because of its slow tempo, in the early twenty-first century it has been modernized by young musicians who used themes from the genre in their music, particularly those performing 'naija hip-hop music' – a blend of a fast indigenous music with hip-hop.

Bibliography

Dáramólá, Abayomi. M. 2005. *The Musical Concept of the Alásàlátù in Yorùbá Islamic Music*. Unpublished Ph.D. thesis, Department of Music, Obáfémi Awólówò University, Ilé-Ifè.

Eúbà, Akin. 1971. 'Islamic Musical Culture Among the Yorùbá: A Preliminary Survey.' In *Essays on Music and History In Africa*, ed. Klaus P. Wachsmann. Evanston, IL: Northwestern University Press, 171–81.

Mustapha, Oyebamiji. 1975. 'A Literary Appraisal of Sákárà: A Yorùbá Traditional Form of Music.' In *Yorùbá Oral Tradition*, ed. Wándé Abimbola. Ilé-Ifè: University of Ifè, 517–49.

Olusoji, Stephen O. 2009. *Comparative Analysis of the Islam-Influenced* Ápálá, Wákà, Sákárà *Popular Music of the Yoruba*. Unpublished Ph.D. thesis, Institute of Africa Studies, University of Ibadan, Ibadan.

Omíbíyí, Mosunmola A. 1979. 'Islam Influence on Yorùbá Music.' *African Notes* III(2): 37–54.

Waterman, Christopher Alan. 1999. *Jùjú: A Social History and Ethnography of an African Popular Music*. Chicago: Chicago University Press.

Sheet Music

Olusoji, Stephen O. 2010. *Nigerian Dances for Piano, Vol. 1*. Lagos: Right-Time Services.

Discographical Reference

Balógun, Jámíù Lefty. *Mo wa ri Faye*. Label unknown. *1983*: Nigeria.

STEPHEN OLUSOJI

Salegy

Salegy is an electric dance music style born in the nightclubs and urban bars of Madagascar. It differs from traditional dances in that it is danced freestyle, usually in male–female couples, but sometimes individually. It is generally associated with the island's northern and northwestern coastal towns including Majunga, Nosy Be and Diego Suarez (Antsiranana). Despite its regional focus, *salegy* is heard and performed in various parts of this vast and culturally diverse country. Musically, it is driving, fast, 6/8 party music with roots in Malagasy folklore, but also with clear affinities with mainland Afropop dance music styles in places including Zimbabwe and Mozambique. *Salegy* is characterized by gently rippling guitar work, organ or keyboards and sometimes accordion, simple harmonic progressions and powerful vocal harmonies.

Salegy developed from the bar and nightclub scene in coastal cities during the period of French colonial rule that preceded Madagascar's independence in 1960. Even after independence, these port towns were centers for French military personnel who had money to spend and an appetite for dancing and nightlife. *Salegy* began alongside other local popular music genres using Malagasy rhythms, including *watcha watcha*, but *salegy* surpassed all competitors to become the most widely disseminated local pop music of Madagascar during the 1970s and 1980s. *Salegy* remains vibrant in the early twenty-first century, although, with the exception of national stars such as Jaojoby and Lego, neither practitioners nor recordings of the music have seen sustained success on the international market.

Origins

Madagascar is the third largest island in the world, and its physical isolation has made it home to unique flora, fauna and culture. The island has a complex history characterized by successive waves of immigration from Southeast Asia, Africa, the Middle East and Europe. Its 18 distinct ethnic groups perform a broad range of traditional music types, using varieties of harps, zithers, lutes, wind and percussion instruments found nowhere else in the world. Close vocal harmonies emphasizing thirds and sixths characterize many Malagasy music styles, and are thought to reflect the island's Polynesian cultural roots. Pervasive triplet rhythms, often played at breathtaking speed – upward of 225 BPM – reflect continental African influences. Harps, including the tubular *valiha*, typical of the central highlands, are used to play music with melodious elegance evocative of European Renaissance music.

Although *salegy* is a modern contemporary genre, it carries echoes of these older traditions. As one *salegy* guitarist, Lucien Jaojoby, described it, 'The first Malagasy musicians to make salegy with a guitar tried to imitate the sound of the *valiha* or the sound of the *marovany* [box zither]' (personal communication with the author). These guitarists developed open tunings for the guitar. Despite this link to tradition, *salegy* did not develop from any single ethnic genre or style, and this hybrid character helps to explain its popularity in social settings in various parts of the country. *Salegy* asserts a general Malagasy identity rather than a particular ethnic one. The music is heard in relatively upscale restaurants and nightclubs in Antananarivo, the capital, though it is more often heard in much more humble, rural settings such as private parties and public dances, especially in the north.

From the Nightclub to the Recording Studio

Eusèbe Jaojoby – known simply as Jaojoby – is a world-famous *salegy* singer and bandleader, and his story and music are representative of the music overall. He has described the genre as 'Malagasy folk songs played with modern Western instruments like accordion, organ, piano, synthesizer, electric guitar, and drums' (interview with author, 2001).

Indigenous folk music is a crucial ingredient in the development of *salegy*, but as with so many African pop music styles, pioneering musicians also have some knowledge of foreign music. When Jaojoby started out in music in the 1960s, bands covering the international hit parade began experimenting with the fast-triplet *salegy* rhythm but, he says, 'mainly as instrumentals.' Jaojoby was 15 in 1970 when he moved to the port city of Diego Suarez to pursue his studies. By night, he sang in clubs, mimicking mostly American popular music artists of the day – Percy Sledge, Otis Redding, James Brown and others. 'As customers,' recalled Jaojoby, 'we had French soldiers and Malagasy people also. We played rhythms from all over the world – slow, cha-cha-cha, jerk, *valse passo*, tango, bolero – and we began to introduce the *salegy*.'

A good singer, Jaojoby began writing *salegy* songs, mostly about love and romantic situations, the main concern of *salegy* songs. 'We went anywhere people called us,' Jaojoby recalled, 'in town, in village, in the field, in markets, in open air. We used an energy generator. We played more African and Malagasy rhythms: *kwassa-kwassa*, *sigoma*, and also rhythms from the Indian Ocean, like *séga*. We played most of the African rhythms, but we made them Malagasy.' A slower 'lover's' variety of *salegy* was called *malesa*, but the core *salegy* repertoire was always fast and furious.

During the 1970s the island's Disco-Mad label produced hot-selling *salegy* singles by artists including Jean Feddy, Abdallah, Jaojoby and one of the style's first originators, Tianjama, with his group Orchestre Liberty. As the economy and recording industry declined in the 1980s – the product of general economic decline and increased media interest in foreign music – there was a dry spell in *salegy* recordings, but the groups kept playing. Early 1990s *salegy* recordings tended to feature drum machine production, as was the trend in much African popular music of this era.

With the 1990s rise of Mars as Madagascar's record company goliath, well-produced, full-band *salegy* recordings entered the market. Younger *salegy* singers including the charismatic Lego – half-brother of Malagasy pop star Rossy – and Dr. JB with his highly professional band the Jaguars came to dominate the *salegy* scene, and subsequently, a new generation of acts emerged.

Lyric Content in *Salegy*

Whereas Jaojoby's songs derive from Antankarana folk songs, performed informally in the island's extreme north, Lego's sound owes more to the Sakalava people who live to the south and west, around the city of Majunga. The subject of folk songs in both cases is generally love and romance; however, Lego said that his personal road to *salegy* stardom began with spirituality, specifically trance music. 'I grew up in Ananalalava,' he said. 'It's a sacred island.' Lego recalls being cured of an early illness by a *tromba*, a traditional healer who 'treats you with music' (interview with author, 2001). Once cured, Lego began playing his accordion at *tromba* ceremonies, and this eventually led to his career as a *salegy* musician.

Lego's song 'Capote,' an ode to condoms, became a sensation in 2001 due to its unusually forthright popular music message about avoiding sexually transmitted diseases such as HIV/AIDS. Women waved condoms in the air each time he performed it. 'Imagine in Majunga,' he said, 'almost 7000 people holding up condoms. They demanded the song by blowing up the condoms like balloons. It was bizarre. Incredible. But it sends a message.' This anecdote illustrates that songs with social messages do exist in *salegy*; however, the genre remains principally associated with dancing, celebration and love songs.

Media Challenges for Local Popular Music

One of Madagascar's paradoxes is the national media's indifference to the island nation's rich traditional and roots pop music. *Salegy* bands have packed local clubs in northern towns including Majunga, Antsiranana (Diego Suarez) and Nosy Be for decades, but their music is rarely heard on national radio and even less on television. More rhythmically bland forms of music highly imitative of Western pop receive far more media attention and commercial promotion, likely reflecting the aspirations of an elite market more attuned to foreign than local music culture. While *salegy* recordings and artist tours have had some limited success internationally, the trend has not been sufficiently robust to inspire a serious re-evaluation of the genre in national media and industry. In Antananarivo, the curious visitor is more likely to locate a live *salegy* concert with the assistance of a well-informed local than by relying on radio, television or print media.

Bibliography

Anderson, Ian. 1996. Liner notes for the CD *Salegy!* by Jaojoby. Green Linnet Records, Xenophile 4040.

Anderson, Ian. 2006. 'Madagascar, a Parallel Universe.' In *Rough Guide to World Music, Volume 1: Africa, and Middle East*, eds. Simon Broughton et al. London: The Rough Guides, 197–210.

Rakotomalala, Mireille. 1998. 'Performance in Madagascar.' In *The Garland Encyclopedia of World Music, Volume 1: Africa*, ed. Ruth M. Stone. New York and London: Garland Publishing, Inc., 781–91.

Discography

Dr JB et les Jaguar. *Aza M'Derange*. Mars MA1043. *2000*: Madagascar.

Jaojoby. *Salegy!* Green Linnet Records, Xenophile 4040. *1996*: USA.

Jaojoby. *Aza Arianao*. Indigo LBLC 2573. *2001*: France.

N'Dour, Youssou. *Set*. Virgin V2-86195. *1990*: Senegal.

BANNING EYRE

Séga

Séga is a modern form of Creole song common to the Creole islands of the Indian Ocean: Réunion, Mauritius, Rodrigues and the Seychelles. In Réunion, 'Creole' refers to people born in Réunion, whatever their origin or characteristic cultural practices. In Mauritius and Rodrigues, the term is used more specifically for the descendants of Africans and Madagascans as opposed to descendants of Europeans,

Indians and Asians. However, these meanings are not exclusive and the use of the term may vary in different contexts. Since the 1950s *séga* also has been practiced in Madagascar, where it is, however, less culturally rooted. *Séga* is one of the fundamental genres of regional recording production. It is almost exclusively produced locally and is widely broadcast on radio. Deeply rooted in Creole choreographic habits, it is danced both in nightclubs and at family celebrations.

The Historical Development of *Séga*

During the eighteenth and nineteenth centuries in the Mascarene and Seychelles islands the word *séga* referred to the practices of slaves and hired workers of African and/or Madagascan origin. According to Robert Chaudenson, the term '*séga*' seems also to have etymological origins in Swahili, in which language it means 'to roll up, to pick up one's clothes' (Chaudenson 1992, 192). This gesture can still be seen in traditional forms of *séga*. In Mauritius and Rodrigues, these old *séga* forms (practiced since the nineteenth century) are accompanied by two or three circular, single-headed drums, which are equipped with bells. These drums are called *ravann* in Mauritius and *tanbour* in Rodrigues. More often than not, they provide a basic rhythm in duple meter with ternary subdivisions and frequent *hemiola* (Desrosiers 2005). The song is structured around alternating form between a soloist and a chorus (responsorial or antiphonal). Until the 1960s the lyrics of *séga* were often improvised in Creole, treating themes of everyday life. It thus served as a social regulator in village and neighborhood communities, enabling more or less autonomous management of interpersonal conflicts. The genre accompanied dances performed by one or more male–female pairs in the center of a circle of participants. The dancers performed small steps opposite one another, rotating around themselves and their partners.

In Réunion, *séga* was known by the name *maloya* during the first half of the twentieth century (La Selve 1995). In the Seychelles, it corresponded instead to *mutia* (see also separate entries on Maloya and Mutia). Since the end of the twentieth century the practice of improvised singing is no longer in existence or is at least very rare. This type of music is practiced either as part of tourist entertainment or within the framework of cultural revivalism and identity claims.

The term *séga* also refers to a modernized form of Creole song built on the alternating verse–chorus form. The origin of this form of *séga* is dated to the beginning of the twentieth century, with the writing of the first Creole *quadrille* by the colonial bourgeoisie in Réunion and Mauritius. Creole composers sought to integrate the rhythmic features of *séga* derived from the descendants of slaves by adapting them to the form of the Western *quadrille*. During the twentieth century *séga* thus encompassed, for the peoples of both the Mascarene and the Seychelles islands, all forms of Creole song performed in local rhythms with Western instruments.

Performed by musicians at dances, *séga* has integrated the influence of international dance repertories throughout the twentieth century. In Réunion, it was practiced mostly by bands, self-taught accordion and violin players (called '*jouars*' in Réunion), and by orchestras made up of stringed instruments (mandolin, banjo, guitar). Odéon recordings from Réunion by Georges Fourcade gave the genre its first publicized existence in the media during the Colonial Exhibition of 1931. These recordings allow us to understand the importance of humor and satire in the genre, with the sung forms of *séga* touching upon all areas of social life, including race relations and marriage.

In the years from 1950 to 1960 the development of the media (radio, TV) and of a small regional record industry gave *séga* a commercial dimension by fostering the emergence of a star system. Maxime Laope and Benoîte Boulard in Réunion, Serge Lebrasse and Jean-Claude Gaspard in Mauritius, Stanley Beaufond in the Seychelles and Henri Ratsimbazafy in Madagascar were among the artists who gained their reputations thanks to *séga* records. During this period *séga* was influenced by African-Caribbean and Latin American repertories (with the integration of the *maracas*, *bongos* and *conga*), and by accordion music, particularly in Réunion, with the integration of the chromatic button accordion. Borrowings from African-Caribbean music (most notably in Réunion by the group Club Rythmique) occurred essentially at the levels of instrumentation and melody, with certain *séga* occasionally being constructed around adaptations of international tunes. Since the 1960s *séga* has continued to integrate external stylistic elements, resulting in a myriad of substyles that are often ephemeral: *séga conga* (Narmine Ducap), *séga mambo* (Michel Admette), *séga pop* (Luc Donat), *disco séga*, *Bollywood séga* (in Mauritius) and so on.

Contemporary Forms of *Séga*

Since the 1980s three new forms of *séga* have particularly marked regional record production. In the mid-1980s the invention of *seggae* (*séga*-reggae) by the Mauritian group Racinetatane had a major regional impact. It gave rise to the creation of *malogué* (*maloya*-reggae) in Réunion by Na Essayé and *mouggae* (*mutia*-reggae) in the Seychelles by El Manager. Accompanying antiestablishment texts sometimes referring to Rastafarianism, *seggae* went out of fashion in the mid-1990s. The violent death in prison of Kaya, the leader of Racinetatane, as well as the imprisonment of Ras Natty Baby for drug trafficking, brought an end to *seggae* as a style in itself. However, many *séga* and reggae groups still integrate *seggae* into their repertoire. In the early 2000s, faced with the enthusiasm of the people of Réunion for Caribbean *zouk love*, a group from Réunion called Analyse popularized *séga love*, which aimed to provide a romantic and sentimental dimension to *séga* (Hidalgo 2000). Analyse's success, in terms of both record sales and nightclub appearances, was quickly followed by that of Dominique Barret with his 2001 hit 'Po ou mam'zel'. In Mauritius, Alain Ramanissum also carved out a name for himself in this genre of *séga*, most notably by adapting the song 'Je t'aime' by French singer Lara Fabian. Finally, the more recent trend of Indian Bollywood films has led to the popularization of Bollywood *séga* in Mauritius, notably by Claudio Veeraragoo. Based on the use of texts in Bhojpuri or Hindi as well as in Creole, Bollywood *séga* is in particular derived from the translation (from Creole to Bhojpuri or Hindi) of preexisting *séga* songs and by adding sonorities reminiscent of Bollywood movie soundtracks (Servan-Schreiber 2010, 316). For the latter, this mainly consists of adding Indian drum sounds performed on a synthesizer and Indian singing style.

Amid this stylistic diversity, *séga* has maintained some common denominators, which, in a certain way, constitute its dominant form. In terms of instrumentation, the electric guitar and bass along with the synthesizers and drums all remain indispensable to the genre. Moreover, *ségas* are usually structured around two alternating sections, which correspond to the verse and the chorus. And finally, it is the rhythm that constitutes the key element of *séga*. It consists of the vertical juxtaposition of duple meter in ternary subdivision with triple meter in binary subdivision. This hemiola, characteristic of traditional *ségas* (Desrosiers 2005), is particularly audible in the bass-drums intersection. In Mauritius, the group Cassiya distinguishes itself by its brass arrangements (usually performed on a synthesizer) and by the insertion of saturated guitar solos. The impact of Cassiya and of Mauritian *séga* in general on Réunion's 'ségatiers' (*séga* players) was still very strong from the late 1990s to the early 2000s.

Séga **and Regional Identity**

The existence of record production and regional stardom has heavily favored the dynamics of exchange between islands. Collaborations between artists from Mauritius and Réunion are regular, such as that of Gérard Louis (Cassiya's guitarist) and Bruno Escyle (leader of the band Apolonia) in 2005. Similarly, *ségas* that are successful on one island are often picked up and translated by artists from neighboring islands. Across the Mascarene and Seychelles islands, intense circulation takes place, which adds to the stylistic malleability of *séga*. This exchange contributes to the cementing of a regional identity and to the assertion of a kind of Creole community that transcends the respective boundaries of each island. But it also promotes strong competition, in which Mauritian artists seem to be faring best. In Réunion, the 'Mauritian Fiesta' brings on stage the most famous Mauritian artists (Cassiya, Claudio Veeraragoo, Tian Corentin, etc.). The show attracts thousands of spectators each year in a theater that, under normal circumstances, rarely hosts artists from Mauritius.

Conclusion

Séga remains the most popular musical genre of the Mascarene and Seychelles islands. Beyond island particularities and community differences, it constitutes a strong symbol of Creole identity in the Indian Ocean. Rarely exported outside of this region, it is nonetheless very popular with the Creole public. In Mauritius, it can even be considered as a veritable national symbol.

Bibliography

Boonzajer Flaes, Rob. 2000. *Brass Unbound: Secret Children of the Colonial Brass Band.* Amsterdam: Royal Tropical Institute.

Chaudenson, Robert. 1992. *Des îles, des hommes, des langues: Essai sur les créolisations linguistiques et culturelles* [Islands, People and Languages: An Essay on Linguistic and Cultural Creolization]. Paris: L'Harmattan.

Chaudenson, Robert. 1995. *Les créoles* [The Creoles]. Paris: PUF.

Desrosiers, Brigitte. 1996. 'Le discours sur la musique, le discours sur l'identité à La Réunion' [Discourse on Music, Discourse on Identity in Réunion]. In *Regards sur le champ musical* [Perspectives on the Musical Field], ed. B. Cherubini. Saint-Denis: University of Réunion Island, 29–47.

Desrosiers, Brigitte. 2005. *Les chants de l'oubli. La pratique du chant traditionnel à l'île Rodrigues (île Maurice). Exemple d'autonomie sociale et culturelle d'une musique créole* [The Songs of Oblivion: The Practice of Traditional Singing on the Island of Rodrigues (Mauritius Island). An Example of the Social and Cultural Autonomy of a Creole Music]. Unpublished Ph.D. thesis, University of Montréal, Montréal.

Desrosiers, Brigitte, and Desroches, Monique. 2000. 'Réunion Island.' In *The Garland Encyclopedia of World Music: South Asia: The Indian Subcontinent*, eds. Bruno Nettl and Alison Arnold. New York: Garland, 606–11.

Hidalgo, Fred. 2000. 'Séga-Maloya: La grande réconciliation' [Séga-Maloya: The Great Reconciliation]. *Chorus* 34: 108–16.

La Selve, Jean-Pierre. [1984] 1995. *Les musiques traditionnelles de La Réunion* [The Traditional Music of Réunion]. Rev. ed. Saint-Denis: Azalées Editions.

Samson, Guillaume. 2006. *Musique et identité à La Réunion. Généalogie des constructions d'une singularité musicale insulaire* [Music and Identity in Réunion: Genealogy of the Construction of an Insular Musical Singularity]. Unpublished Ph.D. thesis, University of Montréal – Aix-Marseille III, Montréal/Aix-Marseille.

Samson, Guillaume, and Pitre, Shawn. 2007. 'Music, Poetry and the Politics of Identity in Réunion Island: A Historical Overview.' *Popular Music History* 2(1): 25–48.

Servan-Schreiber, Catherine. 2010. *Histoire d'une musique métisse à l'île Maurice – Chutney indien et séga Bollywood* [The Story of a Hybrid Music of Mauritius: Indian Chutney and Bollywood *Séga*]. Paris: Riveneuve Editions.

Soupe, Paul. 1990. 'L'ethnicité: discours officiels, discours populaires et ségas' [Ethnicity: Official Discourse, Popular Discourse and Ségas]. In *Vivre au pluriel. Production sociale des identités à l'île Maurice et à l'île de La Réunion* [Pluralist Living: Social Production of Identities in the Islands of Mauritius and Réunion], ed. J-L. Alber. Saint-Denis: University of Réunion Island, 63–81.

Yu Sion, Live, and Hamon, Jean-François, eds. 2004. *Diversité et spécificités des musiques traditionnelles de l'Océan Indien* [Diversity and Specificities of Traditional Music of the Indian Ocean]. Kabaro series, vol. 2, nos 2–3. Paris: L'Harmattan.

Discographical References

Barret, Dominique. 'Po ou mam'zel.' *Po ou mam'zel.* Discorama. *2001*: France/Réunion.

Ramanissum, Alain. 'Je t'aime.' *Suprem séga 2*. KDM. *2004*: France/Réunion.

Discography

Arlanda, Jules. *Jules Arlanda et ses interprètes*. Takamba, Taka 0306. *2003*: France/Réunion.

Cassiya. *Ici Cote Nou Eté*. Production Cassiya. N.d.: Mauritius.

Cassiya. *Séparation*. Cassiya Productions. *1993*: Mauritius.

Donat, Luc. *Le Roi du séga*, Takamba, Taka 0408. *2004*: France/Réunion.

Escyle, Bruno, and Louis, Gérard. *Séga maloya*. CD JBE 010. *2005*: France/Réunion.

Fourcade, Georges. *Le barde créole*. Takamba, Taka 015. *2001*: France/Réunion.

Île Maurice: Séga Ravanne mauricien, Séga Tambour de l'Île Rodrigues. Ocora Rado France France/Harmonia Mundi C 580060. *1994*: France.

Jean-Claude. *Pile Pile*. Piros P5088. *1987*: France/Réunion.

Jean-Claude. *Ségas de l'Île Maurice*. Piros 5125. *1988*: France/Réunion.

Kaya. *Ersatz of Bob Marley*, Méli Mélo, BEE 960303. *1996*: Mauritius.

La compile Bollywood Séga. Majik Records, MJP 2019. N.d.: Réunion/France.

Laope, Maxime. 'Hommages'. Piros 5209. *N.d.*: France/Réunion.
Le Club Rythmique avec Michel Adélaïde. *Mémoires du Séga*. Playa Sound/Auvidis 65139. *N.d.*: France.
Lebrasse, Serge. *Le Prince Du Séga*. Tambour Music TAMB 4. *1995*: UK.
Les ségatiers de l'Île Maurice. Audivis S65126. *1994*: France.
Les ségatiers de l'Île Maurice. Playa Sound, PS 65126. *1994*: France.
Les Windblows. *Fiesta Kréol*. S.E.D.M. / Oasis 33500. *N.d.*: France/Réunion.
Madoré, Henri. *Le dernier chanteur de rue*. Takamba, TAK 9701. *N.d.*: France/Réunion.
Mauritius Island – Séga Dance. Playa Sound/Auvidis Distribution 65126. *1994*: France.
Musiques en cuivre. Fanfares de La Réunion. Frémeaux & Associés FA 5098. *2004*: France.
Musiques populaires des îles Seychelles. Musique du monde/Music from the World, Buda Records 1984862. *N.d.*: France.
Na Essayé. *Oté La Sère*. Discorama 9101. *N.d.*: France/Réunion.
Racinetatane. *Seggae Nu Lamizik*. Power Music Shop/Cyper Production. *1989*: Mauritius.
Ras Natty Baby. *Vibration Rasta Zom*. Déclic Communication 50574-2. *1996*: France.
Ras Natty Baby. *Seggae Time*. Déclic Communication. *1998*. France.
Ravannes sans Frontières. *Noire, La Rivière Noire*. Sonolynn/Tambour Music. CD TAMB 7. *1996*: UK.
Seychelles, nouvelles tendances. NDCD 062. *1999*: Seychelles.
Ti Frère. *Ile Maurice—Hommage à Ti Frère*. Ocora C560019. *1991*: France.
Vital, John. *Bonjour*. Bib's Agency 14 004. *N.d.*: Seychelles.
Volcy, Jean-Marc. *Leko Bake*. Seychelles Artistic Production 009. *N.d.*: Seychelles.

GUILLAUME SAMSON (TRANSLATED BY ORLENE DENICE MCMAHON)

Semba

Semba is an Angolan song and dance genre of the Luanda region. The word *semba* means 'touch of bellies' in the Kimbundu language, referring from at least the beginning of the twentieth century to a choreographic element of the Angolan music and dance genre *rebita* (Kubik 1997). During a particular moment, the male and female dancers approached each other and touched abdomens lightly while stamping their feet. Acoustically signaled by the musicians, this motion was performed by the dancers to give the impression of a 'violent shock' (Kubik 1997, 409). The term reemerged in the 1950s to denote songs performed with guitars and native percussion instruments that adapt and transform rhythms and melodies of rural and urban expressive practices, especially of Ambundu cultural origin. The Ambundu are a Kimbundu-speaking Bantu people of the northeastern region of Luanda and historically were the main ethnic group of the city's surrounding areas. After the arrival of Portuguese merchant explorers and the foundation of Luanda (1576), they were brought to the orbits of Angola's colonial society and deported as slaves to the New World, especially to Brazil. Historically, Luanda's colonial encounter involving Ambundu and other ethnic groups also gave rise to new urban *mestizo* social groups and to syncretic cultural configurations centrally involving expressive culture.

Since the 1950s the word *semba* has denoted a new genre of music and dance that resonates with Ambundu expressive practices, particularly with dance, a central element of *semba*'s social experience and aesthetics. In its post-1950s form, *semba*'s foundations as a music and dance genre are closely related to the creative work of Ngola Ritmos, a music group formed in Luanda's Bairro Operário neighborhood in 1947 by musicians who took part in the activities of an emerging nationalist class. These musicians included Carlos Aniceto Vieira Dias (known as Liceu Vieira Dias, guitar, voice and composition), the main artistic and political figure of the group, Manuel António Rodrigues Júnior (known as Nino Ndongo, guitar and voice) and José Maria dos Santos (guitar and voice). Ngola Ritmos is consensually considered the precursor of *semba* and Angolan contemporary popular music. In addition to composing an extended body of *semba* songs, the group established the aesthetic principles and creative processes upon which the development of the genre was based. In the 1960s and 1970s the group's cultural and political legacy propelled musicians and groups mostly based in Luanda to develop new *semba* styles that were commodified through a rising local recording industry.

Mostly coming from the educated native middle strata of Luanda's colonial society (from the 'assimilados' social group, whose members were considered to be complying with the social rules of the official Portuguese colonial society), the musicians of Ngola Ritmos conceived of the valorization of Angolan culture, especially music, poetry and dance, as the primary means to spark anti-colonial political consciousness and elicit nationalist sentiments. At that time, cultural practices and social behaviors understood as African were disparaged in Angolan colonial society, especially under the politics of 'assimilation' (*assimilação*) that posited the adoption of Portuguese and European cultural values and practices as the sole condition for Angolans to reach a desired level of social, legal and political status.

In this sociopolitical context, the group Ngola Ritmos began adapting rhythms, melodies, oral materials and dialogic textures from Ambundu-Kimbundu expressive practices to popular music song forms performed through acoustic guitars and percussion instruments such as the *dikanza* (a wood scraper) and drums. According to one of the group's leaders Amadeu Amorim (drums and voice), the Luandan Carnival rhythms of *cidrália, lisanda, caixa corneta, kabetula* and *cabocomeu* (Milonga and Vaz 2009) were particularly employed and fused in the creation of *semba* songs and their different rhythms. These materials were reframed according to the musicians' cosmopolitan sensibilities, including cultural influences from Cuban, Congolese, Brazilian and Portuguese popular musics. Under a dense percussive layer foregrounding the steady beats of the drums and the *dikanza* rhythmic variations, the songs were structured around a characteristic guitar style combining arpeggios, plucked chords and fingerpicked melodies. This instrumental accompaniment provided the rhythmic and harmonic structure for the exposition of short voice melodies sung in a dialogic structure by a female or male solo voice and a chorus. Besides composing *semba* songs the group recreated traditional 'lamentos' (an emotionally charged vocal genre usually sung by women at a slow tempo), and interpreted both Brazilian *samba* songs and Portuguese *fado* with a 'tropical flavor' (Milonga and Vaz 2009). The use of the Kimbundu language was a crucial element of Ngola Ritmos' aesthetics of processing folklore materials.

Their *lamentos* and *semba* songs spoke of Angolan cultural symbols and of the realities of everyday life under colonial rule, conveying encoded messages of suffering, resistance and future sociopolitical change.

The group began playing for friends at weekend lunches and backyard parties (*festas de quintal*) in the Bairro Operário, a transitional area between the colonial center of the city (*baixa*) and the urban shantytowns (*musseques*) where most of the black Angolan population lived. There followed performances in other neighborhoods, at the Liga Nacional Africana (National African League) and at the Rádio Nacional de Angola (Angola's National Radio). In conjunction with the musical and artistic activity, the members of the group developed covert political action, stimulating the circulation of anti-colonial and nationalist sentiments through clandestine debate and the distribution of political pamphlets. In 1959 a Portuguese police operation known as 'trial of the 50' (processo dos 50) aimed at silencing the opposition to Portuguese colonialism in Angola, leading to the arrest of Liceu Vieira Dias, Amadeu Amorim and José Maria dos Santos and to their deportation to the political prison camp of Tarrafal, in the Island of Santiago, Cape Verde. Euclides Fontes Pereira, the *dikanza* player of the group and a civil servant also suspected of involvement with nationalist activities, was professionally transferred to the isolated town of Luso (today Luena) in the eastern central Angolan territory. Despite its loss of members, the remaining group integrated new elements and achieved some popularity in Angola among the *assimilados* and in Portugal among Portuguese metropolitan publics. In 1964 the group traveled to Lisbon, performing on a Portuguese national television show and recording three EPs (Ngola Ritmos 1964).

In her thorough research on Angolan music and nation building, historian Marissa Moorman (2008) showed how, after the popular rebellions (1961) that marked the beginning of the armed struggle fought by Angolan liberation movements against colonial rule (1961–74), the colonial government enacted a set of economic and social policies aimed at pacifying the Angolan population and bringing it closer to the Portuguese state. During this period, the investment of Portuguese and non-Portuguese capital in different sectors of the Angolan economy (particularly in extractive industries such as oil production, mining and cash crop agriculture) (Moorman 2008, 162) increased significantly. Development projects and social reforms propelled Angola's rapid economic growth and social change. Angolans' legal status as Portuguese citizens (1961), along with access to new jobs and improved wages in the civil service, industry and commerce sectors, had a significant impact on the population's cultural experience and musical life, especially in urban *milieus*. In the mid-1960s the changing conditions of urban life in Luanda stimulated new production and consumption practices related to music and dance. Recently opened nightclubs, recreational clubs and associations based in the city's *musseques* began featuring music groups and singers performing *semba*, *plena*, *merengue*, *rumba*, *bolero* and *samba* to dancing audiences (Moorman 2008). The growth of urban popular music gave rise to a local recording industry based in Luanda but connecting different regions of the country through a network of record stores and radio stations (ibid.). Among the five record companies operating in the country between 1968 and 1974, two of them, Fadiang–Fábrica de Discos de Angola (Factory of Angolan Records, also known as Rádio Reparadora do Bié) and Valentim de Carvalho, built recording studios and vinyl pressing plants in the country.

Extensive recording configured *semba* as a music category comprising multiple rhythmic styles inspired by different regional Angolan expressive practices and international genres and performed with electric musical instruments, especially guitars, and Angolan percussion instruments. Despite its plurality of styles, the genre is structured around a set of core traits as a duple meter dance song set in strophic form. Songs contain one or two short and simple melodies, repeated with small rhythmic and melodic variations and interspersed with short motivic choral responses. The instrumental accompaniment is comprised of elaborate heterophonic instrumental sections that highlight the melodic and soloistic role of the electric guitar, as well as rhythmic variations on the percussion instruments, especially the *dikanza*. Given the wide spread of the recording industry, musicians from different urban centers and regions also produced *semba* sung in Bantu languages other than Kimbundu, such as Umbundu (in the central highlands) and Kikongo (in the northernmost region

of the territory), integrating regional stylistic traits and cultural influences as well. Accompanied by groups such as Os Jovens do Prenda, Os Kiezos, Bongos and Águias Reais, women singers such as Sara Chaves, Lourdes Van-Dunem, Belita Palma, Lilly Tchiumba, Alba Clington and Mila Melo, and men such as Artur Nunes, David Zé, Urbano de Castro, Artur Adriano, Dionísio Rocha and Elias Dia Kimuezu (nicknamed 'the king of Angolan music') became local popular music stars in the second half of the 1960s and early 1970s.

Semba after Independence

After the military coup of 25 April 1974 in Portugal, which overthrew the Estado Novo dictatorship and brought the end of Portuguese colonial rule, *semba* musicians became important actors in the Angolan nation-building process, whether participating in the efforts of the Movimento Popular de Libertação de Angola (MPLA) to establish itself as the state representative or engaging in the activities of civil society groups based in Luanda's *musseques* (Moorman 2008). Following national independence on 11 November 1975, the Civil War (1975–2002) between three opposing political organizations (the MPLA controlling state power, the União Nacional para a Independência Total de Angola [UNITA] and the Frente Nacional de Libertação de Angola [FNLA] rebel forces) caused the decline of the recording industry and diminished *semba* production. Cultural production was entirely supervised by the state and positioned at the service of nation building and party propaganda. On 27 May 1977 three of the main figures of *semba* and Angolan popular music – Urbano de Castro, David Zé and Artur Nunes – were murdered in the repression following an alleged attempted coup led by MPLA's dissenting voice Nito Alves. Their bodies were never found. After the events of 1977, *semba* became part of a politically silenced past, demonstrated by the prohibition of the screening of António Ole's documentary film on Ngola Ritmos in Luanda in 1978 (*O Ritmo do Ngola Ritmos*; Ole 1978). The cultural politics of the MPLA privileged the production of a new music with a revolutionary tone (especially the genre known as *trova*) with no audible connection with the recent past.

The few groups performing *semba* in the late 1970s and early 1980s such as Agrupamento

Kissanguela (with Elias Diakimuezu, Manuel Faria, Santos Junior, Carlos Lamartine), Semba Tropical (with Carlos Burity, Carlitos Vieira Dias, Joy Artur), Os Merengues (with Teta Lando, Carlos Lamartine, Carlitos Vieira Dias) – all in the orbit of MPLA's cultural institutions – and Os Jovens do Prenda began to include wind instrument sections (usually alto and tenor saxophone, trumpet and trombone, a probable outcome of the influence of Cuban popular music (increased by the presence of Cuban troops in Angola and the training of Angolan musicians in Cuba). Examples include Agrupamento Kissanguela's eponymous album (1979), Os Jovens do Prenda's *Música de Angola* (1983) and Semba Tropical's *Angola* (1985). Along with the electric guitar, wind instruments assumed an increasingly prominent role in *semba* song structure and arrangements that remains in the twenty-first century.

During the years of state monopoly of cultural production (1978–92), also coinciding with the most intense years of the Civil War between the MPLA and UNITA, the commercial recording of new *semba* repertoires came mainly from musicians living in Europe, especially in Portugal, such as Bonga (also known as Bonga Kwenda) and then political exile Waldemar Bastos. In contrast to the musicians living in Angola, expatriate musicians enjoyed the freedom of expression to voice, through song, their discontent with the political predicament of the country, especially the war and the social suffering it triggered.

Bonga, for example, a former athlete and musician (*dikanza* and voice) in Luanda and in the Metropole during the late colonial period (1966–72), went into exile in the Netherlands in 1972 after his engagement with the anti-colonial struggle. There, he started a career as a singer, making three records (Bonga 1972, 1974, 1976) with the musical accompaniment of Angolan, Cape Verdean and Brazilian musicians, and presenting a creative synthesis of *rebita*, *lamento*, *semba* and Luanda's Carnival rhythms. Over the rich melodic and rhythmic support provided by acoustic guitars and percussion instruments, he sang about the conflicts of Angola's social reality under late colonial rule and post-independence political transformation, with an emotion-loaded vocal style that became one of his hallmarks. After Angola's national independence he developed a successful career in France and, from 1985, in Portugal. Surrounded by Angolan and other Lusophone African musicians living in the country in the period (from Mozambican António Costa Neto, to Angolans Nanuto, Betinho Feijó, Dom Lanterna, Carlitos Semba and the group Semba Masters), he commented critically upon Angola's social and political reality and expressed new desires for the country's future. In *semba* hits such as 'Olhos Molhados' (Bonga 1988), 'Frutas de Vontade' and 'Mariquinha' (Bonga 1989), among many others, he addressed themes, including the political management of intimacy, and the loss of creativity, community values and destruction inflicted by the war.

Another critical voice of Angola's political context in the 1980s and 1990s was singer and composer Waldemar Bastos. Bound to the cultural politics and events of the Angolan state after national independence (1976–82), he detached himself from the state's tutelage on the occasion of a theater festival in Portugal (1982). He headed to Germany and, later, Brazil, where he recorded his first album, *Estamos juntos* (1983), with the collaboration of renowned Brazilian musicians he had met years before in Luanda under a project of cultural exchange between Angola and Brazil (Projecto Kalunga) including Chico Buarque, Martinho da Vila and João do Vale. Having settled in Europe in 1984, he continued his musical career with the Portuguese label Valentim de Carvalho (Bastos 1990, 1992) and later, after the interest in his work shown by the American musician and producer David Byrne, with the world music label Luaka Bop (*Pretaluz*, 1998). Composed at the confluence of multiple musical styles, ranging from Angolan and Congolese popular musics to the Brazilian Tropicália movement, some of his emblematic songs, such as the *lamento* 'Sofrimento' and the *semba* 'Querida Angola' (Bastos 1998) were conceived as calls to the values of humanity, fraternity and justice as solutions to Angola's political conflict (Cidra 2010).

After the implementation of a free market economy by José Eduardo dos Santos's political regime in 1992 and the end of state-supported cultural production, new networks of music production and commodification gradually took place in the country. By the end of the decade, recording studios were built and *semba* recordings of the 1960s and

1970s, including those of David Zé, Artur Nunes and Urbano de Castro, were reissued on CD (Moorman 2008, 188). Since the end of the war in 2002, *semba* has been increasingly acknowledged as a meaningful expression of Angolan culture and history.

Stylistic Links and Innovations

Since the mid-1980s Angolan popular music, including *semba*, has been strongly influenced by Caribbean *zouk*. The genre's popularity was at the origin of a new Angolan music and dance genre (*kizomba*) and of significant stylistic intersections with locally performed genres. While in the 1960s and 1970s *semba* was performed according to multiple rhythmic configurations inspired by different Angolan expressive practices and international genres, since the 1980s its rhythmic foundation seems to have unified around a groove and a set of rhythmic patterns akin to *zouk* and *kizomba*. Given the close rhythmic proximity of *semba* to *kizomba*, listeners and dancers distinguish them according to felt parameters such as timbre (*kizomba* is based on synthesized sounds while *semba* is based on acoustic ones), tempo (slower in *kizomba*, moderate and fast in *semba*), melodic and vocal styles as well as lyrical content. One important stylistic change in *semba* in this period was the prominence of the bass guitar in the definition of the genre's aesthetics and rhythmic foundation. *Semba*'s *ostinato* and melodic basslines, featuring a slower movement than the guitar's dense textures and thus conveying the feeling of two contrasting internal tempos within songs, became one of the genre's signature elements. Creative processes of intertextuality between *semba* and *kizomba*, expressed by the central role of the bass in the definition of the dance groove, the overlapping of contrasting rhythmic layers and, above all, the similar rhythmic configuration, have been particularly explored by Paulo Flores, a musician who started as a *kizomba* composer and singer in the late 1980s and became the main innovator of *semba* in the first two decades of the twenty-first century. A gifted songwriter, merging in his songs autobiography, the observation of Angolan daily life and cosmopolitan cultural references through a poetically sophisticated language, Paulo Flores is very much responsible for a new creative breadth of *semba* and for its popularity among newer generations.

Bibliography

Cidra, Rui. 2010. 'Bastos, Waldemar.' In *Enciclopédia da música em Portugal no século XX, A–C*, ed. Salwa Castelo-Branco. Lisbon: Círculo de Leitores/ Temas e Debates, 132–3.

Cidra, Rui. 2010. 'Bonga.' In *Enciclopédia da música em Portugal no século XX, A–C*, ed. Salwa Castelo-Branco. Lisbon: Círculo de Leitores/ Temas e Debates, 149–51.

Cidra, Rui. 2010. 'Semba.' In *Enciclopédia da música em Portugal no século XX, P–Z*, ed. Salwa Castelo-Branco. Lisbon: Círculo de Leitores/ Temas e Debates, 1195–6.

Kubik, Gerhard. 1997. 'Cultural Interchange between Angola and Portugal in the Domain of Music since the Sixteenth Century.' In *Portugal e o mundo: O encontro de culturas na música*, ed. Salwa Castelo-Branco. Lisbon: Publicações Dom Quixote, 407–30.

Milonga, Sílvia, and Vaz, Pedro. 2009. 'Amadeu Amorim.' *Semanário Angolense*, 29 September. Online at: http://angola-luanda-pitigrili.com/who%E2%80%99s-who/a/amadeu-amorim.

Moorman, Marissa. 2008. *Intonations: A Social History of Music and Nation in Luanda, Angola, from 1945 to Recent Times*. Athens, OH: Ohio University Press.

Discographical References

Agrupamento Kissanguela. *Agrupamento Kissanguela*. Companhia de Discos de Angola NALP-6005. *1979*: Luanda.

Bastos, Waldemar. *Angola minha namorada*. EMI Valentim de Carvalho 077779392520. *1990*: Portugal.

Bastos, Waldemar. *Estamos juntos*. EMI Odéon Brasil 31C 062 421258. *1983*: Brazil.

Bastos, Waldemar. *Pitanga madura*. EMI Valentim de Carvalho 0 777 7 99430 2 9. *1992*: Portugal.

Bastos, Waldemar. 'Sofrimento' and 'Querida Angola.' *Pretaluz*. Luaka Bop 9 46481-2/ Warner Brothers 9 46481-2. *1998*: USA.

Bonga. *Angola 72*. Morabeza Records 6802 932 Y. *1972*: Netherlands.

Bonga. *Angola 74*. Morabeza Records 6810442. *1974*: Netherlands.

Bonga. *Angola 76*. Morabeza Records 6810 865. *1976*: France.

Bonga. 'Olhos Molhados.' *Reflexão*. Discossete LP 605. *1988*: Portugal.

Bonga. 'Frutas de vontade' and 'Mariquinha.' *Malembe Malembe (Devagar e Bem)*. Discossete LP 678. *1989*: Portugal.

Os Jovens do Prenda. *Música de Angola*. IEFE Discos IEFE 042. *1983*: Portugal.

Semba Tropical. *Angola*. Dacapo APO 30005. *1985*: UK.

Discography

Angola 60's 1956–1970. Buda Musique 829912. *1999*: France.

Angola 70's 1972–1973. Buda Musique 82992-2. *1999*: France.

Angola 70's 1974–1978. Buda Musique 82993-2. *1999*: France.

Angola 80's 1978–1990. Buda Musique 829942. *1999*: France.

Angola 90's. Buda Musique 82962-2. *1999*: France.

Bonga. *Raízes*. Morabeza Records 6810 619. *1978*: Netherlands.

De Castro, Urbano. *Reviver Volume 5*. Teta Lando Produções TPL03/98. *1998*: Angola.

Flores, Paulo. *Canta meu semba*. R.M.S. CD 011 2, *1996*: Angola.

Flores, Paulo. *Recompasso*. Vidisco 11.80.7997. *2001*: Angola.

Flores, Paulo. *Excombatentes*. Terra Eventos. *2009*: Angola.

Flores, Paulo. *Excombatentes Redux*. Rue Stendhal 3700409810480. *2012*: France.

Flores, Paulo. *O país que nasceu meu pai*. Kubiku 0040232749308. *2013*: Portugal.

Kimuezu, Elias Diá. *Elias*. Ngola NGLP 9001. *N.d.*: Angola.

Kimuezu, Elias Diá. *Elias Diá Kimuezu*. Ngola NGLP 9009. *N.d.*: Angola.

Kimuezu, Elias Diá. *Xamavo*. Nováfrica CD015. *1999*: Portugal.

Ngola Ritmos. *Conjunto N'Gola Ritmos. N'Ga Sakidila/ Chico/ Xikéla/ N'zage*. Decca Records PEP 1113. *1964*: Portugal.

Ngola Ritmos. *N'Gola Ritmos 1: N'Biri Birin/ João Domingos/ Chapéu Preto/ Timpanas*. Alvorada 60 637. *1964*: Portugal.

Ngola Ritmos. *N'Gola Ritmos 2: Mona Ami/ Kuaba Kuaie Kalumba/ Maria da Luz/ Margarida Vai à Fonte*. Alvorada AEP 60 638. *1964*: Portugal.

Nunes, Artur. *Memórias*. 2 CDs. Ngola Música RNAPQ20. *N.d.*: Angola.

Os Kiezos with Jivago and Artur Adriano. *Kenieke Tuene/ Nós Somos Assim*. Endipu LP-126. *1992*: Angola.

Zé, David. *Memórias*. 2 CDs. Ngola Música RNAPQ19. *N.d.*: Angola.

Zé, David. *Mutudi Ua Ufolo/ Viúva da Liberdade*. Ngola NALP-6002. *1975*: Angola.

Zé, David. *Reviver*. Teta Lando Produções TLP02/98. *1998*: Angola.

Filmography

O Ritmo do Ngola Ritmos, dir. Antonio Ole. 1978. Angola. 60 mins. Documentary. Original music by Ngola Ritmos.

RUI CIDRA

Shambo

Shambo is a contemporary music based on the traditional culture, melodies and rhythms of the Aawambo people of north-central Namibia. Beginning in the 1960s–70s, Aawambo musicians started to introduce innovations into their traditional songs by including acoustic instruments such as guitar and saxophone. Use of the term 'shambo' itself to denote the music became current in the early 2000s when musicians such as Ngatu, Setson Wahengo and Tunakie further revamped the traditional Aawambo *a cappella* music by incorporating electronic beats and keyboard instruments.

The sources of *shambo* therefore lie in Owamboland, the home of the Aawambo people. In modern-day Namibia, the Aawambo are often referred to as 'Wambos' by other communities, a term dating from the colonial period. The term 'shambo' derives from 'Oshambo Shakambode,' which refers to Aawambo people.

Musically, *shambo* is characterized by medium-tempo rhythmic patterns in 6/8 meter, although some songs are played in 4/4. Harmonic progressions are based on various I-IV-V patterns. Melodies are often sung in a typical Aawambo high-pitched vocal style. These melodies may be traditional songs but can also be singers' personal compositions and improvisations. Lyrics often comment on social realities and ululations create links to traditional Aawambo cultural practices.

History

Oshiwambo, the language in which *shambo* is sung, is the umbrella term for the seven mutually understandable languages spoken by the Aawambo. Singing in Oshiwambo was restricted during the period when Namibia (known as South West Africa until 1968) was controlled by South Africa, whose government began to impose apartheid there during the 1940s. Only from 1969, with the launch of Radio Bantu by the South African Broadcasting Corporation (SABC), was singing in vernacular languages allowed on the radio. The first steps in the modern history of *shambo* music occurred as a result of migration of labor, in which vast numbers of Aawambo men were recruited to work outside Owamboland through the exploitative contract labor system.

Traditionally, Aawambo music is *a cappella*, based on vocals, handclapping and the foot-stomping that is part of dance. When performed in groups, there are vocal call-and-response structures accompanied by specific handclapping patterns, often syncopated, and the *ngoma* (*ngoma* means 'drum' in various Bantu languages including Oshiwambo; see separate entry). Traditional music is organized along divisions of age and gender and all people who are part of the community take part in performances. Foreigners and outsiders may also be encouraged to take part in the celebrations. These performances happen mainly in Owamboland during social occasions such as weddings, births and harvest celebrations. People (women, men or children) stand in a circle and sing and clap, while everyone takes a turn dancing in the circle to showcase their creativity with ingenious footwork and other dance moves.

In the 1970s artists began to reinterpret traditional music using 'modern' instruments such as guitars, saxophones and accordions, inspired by new influences experienced through migrant labor. South Africa was an important meeting point for various cultures, as the mining industry brought in labor forces from all over southern Africa. The musical influence of the United States was huge at the time, with jazz and jive having already played a significant role in the creation of new genres, including *mbaquanga* and *kwela*, inspired by the new harsh urban realities. In all probability Tate Kwela ('Mister Kwela'), one of *shambo*'s leading musicians, acquired his name during his time in South Africa. The music he and other labor migrants brought back to Namibia is a mix of traditional local elements and South African influences.

Solo artists including Kwela were generally both singers and instrumentalists and were crucial in developing *shambo* into a genre with instruments. Other *shambo* artists of this era include Naimbudu ya Shilengifa, Kanghondi kaTimo Haimbodi ya Shomwele Johannes 'Warmgat' ('Hot ass') Mureko, Iita ya Kadha, Lexington, Boetie Simoni and Kangwe Keenyala.

Kwela, Lexington, Boetie Simoni and Nanghili Nashima were among the first Namibian artists to record in the studios of the former South West African Broadcasting Corporation in the 1970s, and they all released hits on the local-language radio stations (Kambaekwa 2014). However, Namibian music was never distributed in Namibia, as only 'approved' music from the United States and South Africa was sanctioned during apartheid's censorship. Only after independence in 1990 did the promotion and distribution of Namibian music begin, which explains the shortage of internationally known Namibian music.

Since the 1990s *shambo* has developed into music played with a full-band setup including drums, electric bass, synthesizer and electric guitars. This modern version of *shambo* was developed and promoted by artists such as Ngatu and Setson & the Mighty Dreads. These reggae-influenced artists were especially influential in promoting the sound of *shambo*. In her first album *Omwila* in 2005, singer/dancer Tunakie fused traditional melodies with synthesizers and electronic beats, marking a new sound for this genre. Tunakie subsequently became known as the 'Queen of Shambo,' after many successful years.

Many artists who perform *shambo* spent time in exile during the war against South Africa's apartheid regime. During that exile reggae music and its ideologies played an important role and influenced many artists to assert a sense of cultural pride. Ras Sheehama – and particularly his song 'Cassinga,' which commemorates the massacre of Namibians by South Africans in a SWAPO camp in Cassinga, Angola, in 1978 (Mans 2017, 21) – played an important role in this movement. Since independence in 1990 reggae bands have reinvigorated the live music scene in Namibia with original music. Reggae has its own place in the industry, although *kwaito*, house and Afropop have proved to be far more popular.

Performance of *Shambo*

Most *shambo* performances take place in concert halls, in both urban and rural areas, due to the need for musical equipment and amplification. Artists (both men and women) often wear traditional attire or incorporate it in modern creations. Rastafarians played an important role in *shambo*'s development and thus many *shambo* artists have a Rastafarian image (clothing and dreadlocks). Both *shambo* and Rastafarianism are in stark contrast with other local genres of music, which promote the latest Western trends in music and fashion.

Artists including Tunakie, Jackson Wahengo, Hishishi Papa, Castro ('Etondo'), Naxa & Joseph Nakale, Nakale-ya-Nakale, D-Naff, Samuele, Kamati, Ndawana, Young-T, Blossom and Sally all use traditional Aawambo elements in original ways, creating new crossover forms of art. Nashilongweshipwe Mushaandja, for example, experiments with unique performance styles combining theater, poetry and chant. Sally incorporates old folktales in a new approach to storytelling through her lyrics in the Afropop genre. Hishishi Papa uses traditional melodies and rhythms with pan-African musical influences. Jackson Wahengo reinterprets 'classics' by contemporary Aawambo legends Nanghili Nashima and Tate Kwela, as well as fusing West African sounds, blues and jazz in his own compositions. He and Ngatu perform *okwiitanga* in their music, a traditional form of praise and storytelling. In 2014 Wahengo released a cover of a song by Nanghili Nashima, 'Eeloli,' incorporating the traditional *okwiitanga* vocal style into a modern-day version of *shambo* (see https://www.youtube.com/watch?v=5zIDbFLLVYI). As explained by Wahengo (personal communication), 'Eeloli' is a word borrowed from Afrikaans or English probably referring to lorries or trucks. Nashima's song refers to the trucks that were used to transport contract laborers from northern Namibia to the south to work in mines, farms and so on. It was a big occasion when boys were accepted as contract laborers, so Nashima sings 'Eeloli odeuya da Shiwanela (Swanla),' meaning 'the trucks of SWANLA (South West Africa Native Labour Association) have arrived to pick up our boys for work.' An important traditional singer, Nashima was known for her unapologetic honesty when she sang about critical social issues and sex, which was culturally unheard of for women in the late 1960s. (She may be seen on the film *The Power Stone* [1999].)

In 2005 *shambo* was recognized by the Namibia Society of Composers and Authors of Music (NASCAM) as one of Namibia's folk music genres, but in 2018 the Namibian Annual Music Awards (NAMAs) removed it as a category from its annual showcase event, citing a lack of interest on the part of artists and audience, and causing some anguish among its continuing performers (Mouton 2018). In this contrasting situation *shambo*'s ongoing development will depend on artists continuing to find innovative ways of combining music and performance styles from around the globe with their cultural Aawambo heritage.

Bibliography

Fenner, Louise. 2007. 'Namibian Musicians Bring Traditional Music to Washington.' Online at: http://iipdigital.usembassy.gov/st/english/article/2007/10/20071009154243xlrennef0.551037.html#axzz3nQ33PUvx (accessed 4 January 2017).

Kambaekwa, Carlos. 2014. 'Boetie Simoni, Pioneer of Shambo Genre.' *New Era*, 2 May. Online at: https://www.newera.com.na/2014/05/02/musical-memory-lane-boetie-simoni-pioneer-shambo-genre/ (accessed 4 January 2017).

Kambaekwa, Carlos. 2014. 'Down Musical Memory Lane – Pioneer of Traditional Music, Lexington, to Date Has to Earn a Cent From His Works.' *New Era*, 16 May. Online at: https://www.newera.com.na/2014/05/16/musical-memory-lane-pioneer-traditional-music-lexington-date-earn-cent-works/ (accessed 4 January 2017).

Mans, Minette, with Ngoma Research Collective. 2017. *The Changing Faces of Aawambo Musical Arts*. Basel: Namibia Resource Centre & Southern Africa Library.

Mouton, Rineda. 2018. 'The Death of Shambo Music.' *Windhoek Observer*, 16 March. Online at: http://www.observer.com.na/index.php/entertainment/item/9489-the-death-of-shambo-music (accessed 11 June 2018).

Musariri, Confidence. 2006. 'Tunakie Is Not Done Yet.' *New Era*, 16 January. Online at: https://www.newera.com.na/2006/01/16/tunakie-is-not-done-yet/ (accessed 4 January 2017).

Nkomo, Philani. 2014. 'Nakale's Eluwa Talitende Rides High.' *Confidente*, 13 February. Online at: http://www.confidente.com.na/2014/02/nakales-eluwa-talitende-rides-high/ (accessed 4 January 2017).

Sister Namibia. 2006. 'Tunakie Uushona – The Queen of Otyaka.' Online at: http://www.thefreelibrary.com/Tunakie+Uushona--Queen+of+Otyaka%3A+as+a+child+she+sang+and+danced+to..-a0151652750 (accessed 4 January 2017).

'Tate Kwela's Legacy to be Honoured at the NAMA Awards.' 2015. *The Namibian*, 19 March. Online at: http://www.namibian.com.na/indexx.php?archive_id=134861&page_type=archive_story_detail&page=1 (accessed 4 January 2017).

Vranckx, Shishani. Forthcoming. 'Journeys of Transformation: Identity formations Among Urban Oshiwambo-Speaking Artists in Post-Apartheid Namibia.' MA thesis, University of Amsterdam.

Personal Communication

Jackson Wahengo, 2013–18. Various in-person interviews and email communications.

Discographical References

Ras Sheehama 'Cassinga.' *King's Music*. Paul Joubert's Music. *1991*: Namibia. (Reissued on *Ras Sheehama's Early Years*. RasShee Records. *2013*: Namibia. Online at: https://www.youtube.com/watch?v=nmQs0cNyivk (accessed 13 June 2018.)

Tunakie. *Ombwila*. Arise Africa. *2005*: Namibia.

Discography

(1) Shambo

Etondo *Etondo*. Shiiva Entertainment. *2012*: Namibia.

Formula Band. *Shaamboka*. Irie Music Production. *2006*: Namibia.

A Handful of Namibian & Papa Wemba. Hothouse Productions. *2003: Namibia*.

Hishishi Papa. *Aantu Aantu*. Omalaeti Productions OMHP001. *2010*: Namibia.

Hishishi Papa. *Shili Mekunde*. Omalaeti Productions OMHP003. *2011*: Namibia.

Hishishi Papa. *Toshendjelekendje*. Independent release. *2015*: Namibia.

Kamati. *Ekanda*. Omalaeti Productions. *2012*: Namibia.

Kamati. *Elenga*. Omalaeti Productions. *2013*: Namibia.

Mushaandja, Nashilongweshipwe. *Black Bantu Child*. (EP.) Desert Digital Distribution, *2014*: Namibia. Online at: https://itunes.apple.com/us/album/black-bantu-child-ep/id940020743.

Nakale, Naxa. *Haishuna kEkoka*. Independent release. *2012*: Namibia.

Ndawana. *Eengano*. Independent release. *2014*: Namibia.

Ngatu. *Extra Mile*. Independent release, available in Namibia. *2013*: Namibia.

Set-son & the Mighty Dreads. *Kula Umone*. Independent release. *2004*: Namibia.

Set-son & the Mighty Dreads. *Wisdom Fundamental*. Independent release. *2005*: Namibia.

Set-son & the Mighty Dreads. *The Drama of Cain and Abel*. Independent release. *2007*: Namibia.

Tunakie. *Going Back to the Roots*. Arise Africa. *2008*: Namibia.

Tunakie. *Eendunge*. House of Legends. *2009*: Namibia.

Tunakie. *Ondjila*. House of Legends. *2013*: Namibia.

Wahengo, Jackson, *Akutu Hewa*. Independent release. *2012*: Namibia. Online at: https://itunes.apple.com/us/album/akutu-hewa/id572827796.

(2) Other Oshiwambo-Speaking Music: Afropop, Reggae and Hip-Hop

Blossom. *Komuthima Gwomeya*. GMP. *2012*: Namibia.

Blossom. *Indikupapatele*. Independent release. *2013*: Namibia.

D-Naff *Greatest Hits*. D-Naff Entertainment. *2012*: Namibia.

Ras Sheehama. *Pure Love*. Africa Cream Music. *2002*: Namibia.

Sally. *Courage*. Boss Madam Records. *2012*: Namibia.

Sally. *I Am Mukwanekamba*. Omake. *2015*: Namibia.

Tate Boetie. *Oshitenda*. Omalaeti Music Productions. *2005*: Namibia.

Young T. *Philosophical Pages*. Independent release. *2014*: Namibia.

Filmography

The Power Stone: A History of the Kwanyama People, dirs. Andrew Botelle and Kelly Kowalski, 1999. Namibia. 53 mins. Documentary. Online at: https://www.youtube.com/watch?v=y5bmViJJvCc. Extract featuring Nashima Nanghili online at https://www.youtube.com/watch?v=BjNextQYpOM (accessed 11 June 2018).

Websites

Hishishi Papa discography: http://www.discogs.com/artist/2716488-Hishishi-Papa

Jackson Wahengo website: http://jacksonwahengo.com

Ngoma Research Collective Official Facebook page: https://www.facebook.com/Ngoma-Research-Collective-329144573899787/timeline/

Set-son and the Mighty Dreads: Namibian Shambo and Reggae: http://setsonandthemightydreads.blogspot.be/p/shambo-reggae.html

Stolen Moments – Namibian Music History Untold Official Facebook page: https://www.facebook.com/Stolen-Moments-Namibia-193689374012214/timeline/

YouTube

Wahengo, Jackson, 'Eeloli': https://www.youtube.com/watch?v=5zIDbFLLVYI

SHISHANI VRANCKX

Simpa

Simpa music evolved in the Dagbon traditional area of northern Ghana in the 1930s out of a combination of indigenous Dagomba and Hausa music with southern Ghanaian *goombay* (*gombe* or *gome*) frame drum music and highlife, introduced from southern Ghana through records, brass bands and itinerant *concert party* bands. Simpa's local features include the use of the Dagbani language, dance rhythms and the hourglass-shaped pressure drum. *Simpa's* southern roots are implied by the name 'simpa' itself, for this is the local name for Winneba, one of the coastal Fanti port towns in which highlife was born.

Simpa was and still is a recreational music of the young but is also played at weddings and funerals as well as at 'out-doorings' (christenings) of newborn infants. In April 1974 there were 12 *simpa* groups in the royal capital of the Dagomba state; the two most popular at the time were the Wait and See and the Real Unity Stars formed by Halaru Sayiba in 1967. These bands consisted of six or seven young male musicians and a chorus of girls between the ages of 10 and 16. The instruments they employed were two or three frame drums, a set of locally Tamale-made trap drums (snare and two side drums), twin *congas* (a copy of the Afro-Cuban drum but with a metal body), a bell, metal rattles and sometimes a trumpet and local pressure hourglass-shaped drum. Their songs consisted of traditional Dagomba dances, highlife songs (e.g., 'Nimpa Rebree' by C.K. Mann) sung in Akan, and Ga *kpanlogo* songs such as Otoo Lincoln's 'ABCD.' Foreign numbers included soul and twist songs by James Brown and Chubby Checker with new lyrics in Dagbani, and 'Congo jazz' songs by O.K. Jazz and others, sung in Lingala and Hausa.

Simpa was in fact the third of three genres of transcultural recreational dance music that appeared in the Dagbon traditional area during the 1930s. The first was *gombe* or *gome*, a popular recreational dance of the Ga in Accra. Shani Abraham, who was one of the six Dagombas who introduced this music to Yendi, stated in 1974 that he learned it from Hausa and Kotokolis in Prang in the Brong-Ahafo Region (120 miles south of Yendi) (personal communication with the author). A second style that appeared about the same time was *amidziro* music ('amidziro' means 'stranger' in the Ewe language), which was played on large kerosene cans and local *congas* and was introduced to Yendi by Hausas from Salaga, 70 miles south of Yendi. *Simpa* music, which first appeared in Yendi and then spread to Tamale and throughout Dagbon, drew on both of these earlier imported southern styles. Shani Abraham recalls that the name 'gombe' was changed by the young people of the time to 'simpa' in the 12th year of Na Abdallah's reign (1932), whereas Issaca-Bukari, who helped organize the first *simpa* group, dated the change to the early reign of Na Muhammad (1938–48). This phenomenon, whereby the name of a recreational drum-dance music style is changed by Ghanaian youth or age-sets of a particular era, who modify or modernize the music of an earlier generation, also occurred with other forms of neo-traditional music, such as the Ewe *borborbor* of the 1950s and Ga *kpanlogo* of the 1960s, which drew respectively from the *kolomashie* and *konkoma* of the older generation.

As an informal recreational music, *simpa* has always been associated with gatherings of young people and so was generally frowned upon by the older generation. Furthermore, *simpa* music became embroiled in the traditional political divisions within Dagomba society that have emerged since Ghanaian independence in 1957. Customarily, Dagbon was ruled through the rotation of the two royal Andani and Abdullah/Abudu families, but British colonialists, who favored the single dynasty of the Abdullah/Abudu family, altered this tradition in the early 1900s. Not surprisingly, the Andanis supported the anti-British Convention People's Party of Kwame Nkrumah (CPP) and this division continued after independence, with the Abdullah/Abudu House becoming linked to the anti-Nkrumah 'Busia-Danquah' political axis. A serious dispute consequently erupted in the Dagbon traditional area three years after Nkrumah's overthrow in 1969, when the new Busia government expelled the Andani king. The various *simpa* groups took sides in this dispute, and their songs were considered so inflammatory that a six-month police ban was placed on their performances.

In 1994 the Ghana Folkloric Board of Trustees discovered that there were 16 operating *simpa* groups still active in the Dagbon town of Tamale. A decade later, serious violence again erupted between the two royal families of Dagbon. Further research is needed to determine the extent to which the *simpa* groups may have been involved in this dispute.

Bibliography

Chernoff, John. 1979. *African Rhythms and African Sensibility*. Chicago: University of Chicago Press, 129–30.

Collins, E. John. 1985. *Music Makers of West Africa*. Washington DC: Three Continents Press, 33–8.

Collins, E. John. 1996. *Highlife Time*. Accra: Anansesem Press, 105–8.

Discographical Reference

Mann, C. K. and the Carousel Seven. 'Nimpa Rebree.' *Party Time with Ceekay*. Essiebons Label EBL 6114. 1973: Ghana.

E. JOHN COLLINS

Sokwe

Sokwe (sometimes written *soukwé*) is a form of music, dance and theater. In the Seychelles, it is part of a group of musical traditions of African origin along with *tsinge* songs and *mutia*. Some Africans arrived in the Seychelles as slaves between 1770 and 1812, when the archipelago belonged to France, and others came after the slavery period in the second half of the nineteenth century, working mainly as agricultural laborers. According to Jean-Claude Mahoune, *sokwe* may have been practiced within the context of rituals but, due to the impact of Christianity, 'was later deprived of its ritualistics elements' (Mahoune 2004, 288). Whatever its origins, it provides a rare example of mask tradition in the Indian Ocean's Creole islands.

Structured in call-and-response form when performed collectively, the melodic part of *sokwe* can also be sung solo. In this case, it is accompanied by a musical bow (*bombe*) or by a monochord zither (*zèz*) (Naylor 1997, 49), which both produce a kind of drone accompaniment played by two or three notes. The song thus consists of a modal melody which is interspersed with spoken interjections, chattering teeth and a vocal effect produced by rapidly exhaling while vibrating the vocal chords as if coughing. It is also punctuated by words spoken in the bass register. The lyrics of *sokwe* mix Creole and Afro-Madagascan linguistic traits.

In terms of its theatrical and choreographic dimension, *sokwe* seems to have given rise to several types of staging. In general, it is described as a dance in which the dancers, wearing masks and costumes made from foliage, mimic birds (Bollée 1993, 451). However, Bernard Koechlin compares *sokwe* to a kind of *commedia dell'arte* where 'the troupe is comprised of a king ... with his court ..., a wizard ..., a doctor with his stethoscope (*kuta-kuta*), which gives life, a man armed with a gun and an appointed *tramontagne*' (Koechlin 1984, 8). In this form, the *sokwe* performance thus alternates between comic dialogues, songs and dances.

Since the end of the twentieth century to hear or see *sokwe* in one of these two older versions is very rare, as rare as it is to meet *bombe* or *zèz* players (Naylor 1997). Some of the most iconic traditional musicians from 1970 to 1980 (such as Ton Pa), who preserved the memory of *sokwe*, are now deceased. However, since the 1980s and 1990s *sokwe* has been a source of inspiration for popular music composers in the Seychelles who seek to revitalize the musical heritage of the archipelago, while at the same time modernizing it with the influence of other music from Africa and the Indian Ocean. For example, in a song called 'Otto ek Kamil' (Otto and Kamil), Jenny Letourdie proposes a modernized form of *sokwe* based on recordings of Ton Pa made by Bernard Koechlin for the Ocora label (*Forgotten Music of the Islands*, 2002). This has resulted in the adaptation of certain characteristic traits such as the melodic outlines, the drone accompaniment (the *zèz* being replaced by the guitar and electric bass), the chattering teeth (reproduced on the synthesizer), alternating the treble and bass vocal registers, as well as the vocal effects. Added to these adaptations are drum sections, brass section breaks performed on the synthesizer, as well as various sound effects.

According to Précourt (2009, 38), *sokwe* is no longer practiced much in the Seychelles. Its importance remains primarily symbolic insofar as it inspires contemporary art. However, *sokwe* is still performed as part of shows in the Festival Kréol, which is the most important cultural event in the Seychelles, and at tourist events.

Bibliography

Bollée, Annegret. 1993. *Dictionnaire étymologique des créoles français de l'océan Indien. Deuxième partie. Mots d'origine non-française ou inconnue* [Etymological Dictionary of French Creoles of the Indian Ocean. Part Two. Words of neither French nor Known Origins]. Hamburg: Helmut Buske Verlag.

Koechlin, Bernard, ed. 1984. *Les Seychelles et l'océan Indien* [The Seychelles and the Indian Ocean]. Paris: L'Harmattan.

Mahoune, Jean-Claude. 2004. 'The Origin of the Traditional Music/Dances of the Republic of Seychelles.' *Kabaro* 2–3:285–93.

Naylor, Michael Lee. 1997. 'The Creativity in Culture: Creolization in the Musical Genres of the Seychelles Islands.' Unpublished Master's thesis, University of Michigan, Ann Arbor.

Précourt, Fanie. 2009. CD Liner notes. *Ton Pat'. Memwar lamizik seselwa*. Takamba TAKA 1017. 2009: France.

Discographical References

Létourdie, Jenny. 'Otto ek Kamila.' *Seychelles, nouvelles tendances* [The Seychelles: New Trends]. NDCD 062. *1999*: Seychelles.

Ton Pa. 'Sokwe.' *Forgotten Music of the Islands*. Ocora OCR 582055. *2002*: France.

Ton Pat'. *Memwar lamizik seselwa*. Takamba TAKA 1017. *2009*: France.

GUILLAUME SAMSON (TRANSLATED BY ORLENE DENICE MCMAHON)

Soukouss

Congolese popular dance music has a long history within Africa and on both sides of the Atlantic. Generally referred to as 'Congolese rumba,' this quintessentially modern tradition is a source of national pride for the nearly 80 million people who call the Democratic Republic of the Congo home. Within the Congo, especially in the capital city of Kinshasa where Congolese *rumba* was born, people often refer to the musical genre as 'musique moderne' in order to distinguish it from the other primary genres of popular music in the region: *musique religieuse* and *musique traditionnelle*.

Outside the Congo, however, the terms used to refer to Congolese popular music are somewhat less clear. During most of the 1990s and 2000s Congolese popular dance music outside the Congo came to be known by the term 'ndombolo,' a particular dance style that became associated with Wenge Musica, the flagship group of the fourth generation of musicians hailing from Kinshasa (see the entry on Ndombolo). During the previous generation (especially during the 1980s) people outside the Congo referred to Congolese popular music as 'soukouss.' Much like the term 'ndombolo,' the term 'soukouss' would seem to be the name of a dance style, though the particular trajectory of Congolese popular music during this period sheds some doubt on this theory.

Following the global oil crisis in the mid-1970s and a series of nationalization measures put into place by the increasingly authoritarian and corrupt Mobutu regime, many Congolese set out to make lives for themselves and their families abroad, some for political reasons and others with economic motivations. This wave of Congolese emigration in the late 1970s and early 1980s corresponded with the early stages of 'world music,' a cultural phenomenon driven primarily by Western consumer desire for exotic music from the global South. Central African musicians living abroad, including a small number of musicians from the Congo, attempted to ride the wave of world music, especially following the huge success of *zouk* music popularized by the Caribbean supergroup Kassav.

Soukouss, while generally considered to be a genre of Congolese *rumba*, displays certain characteristics which make it distinct from *rumba*, most notably in that it targets non-Congolese audiences. Indeed, the vast majority of people living in the Congo are not familiar with the term 'soukouss' or with the musical genre to which the term refers. But there are also important stylistic elements that make *soukouss* an outlier. For many years Congolese popular music followed the song structure of most of Western popular music, alternating between verses and choruses with songs lasting somewhere between three and five minutes. Changes in the aesthetics and the performance of popular music in the Congo in the 1970s led to a song structure involving longer songs with a series of verses followed by a series of choruses. The choruses functioned as a bridge into the extended dance sections that would quickly become the trademark of Congolese popular music.

The extended song structure, which placed greater emphasis on dancing (both in the audience and on stage), was very popular among audiences. During this period musicians began to rely on the potential of the extended dance segment (often referred to as 'seben') as a means of distinguishing themselves from the competition. Seeing the effect of these changes on audiences, Congolese musicians living abroad in Africa and in Europe decided to capitalize on this popularity. They did this not only to attract the increasingly eager audiences for world music to attend concerts, but also because they claimed that non-Congolese audiences preferred the dance sections since they were unable to understand the lyrics of the verses and choruses (sung almost exclusively in Lingala). For what would seem like very pragmatic reasons, artists in the Congolese diaspora began composing and performing songs which reduced verses and choruses into the space of a short introduction in order to focus primarily on the *seben*, which in some live settings can last as long as 35 to 40 minutes. *Soukouss* was often associated with a particular type of rhythm on the snare drum and a somewhat more rapid tempo in order to contribute to a sense of excitement during live performances.

The origin of the term 'soukouss' is the subject of some discussion (White 2000). Popular *soukouss* artists in the 1980s claimed that the term comes from a dance step of the same name. However, this dance step, while relatively popular for a short period of time, was popular also in the 1960s, and it is unlikely that musicians in the Congolese diaspora of the 1980s are referring to the same phenomenon. Another explanation, probably more likely, proposes that during the dance segments of *soukouss* performances musicians would encourage audience members to dance by shouting 'secoues-ça' (French for 'shake it'). This recurring motif came to be transformed into 'soukouss' and (much like the expression 'kwassa kwassa') became a generic term for the musical style more generally.

The popular artists most often associated with *soukouss*, notably groups such as the legendary supergroup Soukouss Stars, guitarist Diblo Dibala and singers such as Kanda Bongo Man and Aurlus Mabele, were actively touring in Africa, Europe and even in the Americas (the United States, Canada and parts of the Caribbean) for much of the 1980s and 1990s. In some cases these artists were able to participate in the rapidly growing circuit of world music concerts and festivals and were able to gain a certain degree of notoriety. However, they experienced difficulties in renewing or rejuvenating the genre and *soukouss* music, despite numerous expectations, never seemed capable of 'breaking through' to larger mainstream audiences, at least not to the same degree as other tropical genres such as reggae, *zouk* or, subsequently, *reggaetón*. One exception to this rule, and one that had yet to be fully documented in the late 2010s, is the influence of *soukouss* (especially the particular style of electric solo guitar) in the evolution of *champeta* music in certain Caribbean nations in the northern part of South America.

Bibliography

Stewart, Gary. 2000. *Rumba on the River*. London and New York: Verso.

Taylor, Tim. 1997. *Global Pop: World Music, World Markets*. New York: Routledge.

Tchebwa, Manda. 1996. *Terre de la chanson: La musique zaïroise hier et aujourd'hui* [The Land of Song: Zairean Music Yesterday and Today]. Brussels: Éditions Duculot.

White, Bob W. 2000. '*Soukouss* or Sell-Out? Congolese Popular Dance Music as Cultural Commodity.' In *Commodities and Globalization: Anthropological Perspectives*, eds. Angelique Haugerud, M. Priscilla Stone and Peter D. Little. Lanham, MD: Rowman & Littlefield, 33–58.

White, Bob W. 2008. *Rumba Rules: The Politics of Dance Music in Mobutu's Zaire*. Durham, NC: Duke University Press.

Discography

Aurlus Mabele with Loketo. *King of Soukous*. Sound Wave Records 89005-2. *1991*: USA.

Dibala, Diblo. *Ami Eh! Bougez!* Kadance K4244. *1985*: France.

Kanda Bongo Man. *Kanda Bongo Man.* Kanda Bongo Man BM 0057. *1987*: France.

Kanda Bongo Man. *Soukous in Central Park.* Hannibal Records HNCD 1374. *1993*: UK/USA.

Soukouss Stars. *Rumba Soukous – The Heartbeat of Africa.* Cassava Records CASV -04327. *2001*: USA.

BOB W. WHITE

Sungura

Sungura is a genre of guitar-driven popular music in Zimbabwe that draws on a wide range of regional styles, especially Congolese *rumba*, Kenyan *benga*, South African township music and Zimbabwean *jit* (*jiti*). Characterized by multiple, layered guitar lines, driving 4/4 rhythms, syncopated hi-hat patterns and long performances, *sungura* accommodates dancing both on stage and in the audience. *Sungura* is also called *museve* or *rumba museve*. The Kalanga people's version of *sungura* is called *tshova-tshova*.

The genre emerged as Zimbabwe won its independence from white minority rule in 1980 and it became the most successful genre of popular music in the country. It has historically been performed primarily for male working-class audiences in the bars, clubs and municipal venues of Zimbabwe's urban and peri-urban communities. A typical concert starts shortly after dusk and lasts all night long, with performances sometimes lasting more than eight hours. Unlike other styles of Zimbabwean popular music, such as *chimurenga* and *jiti*, the performance of *sungura* is not dominated by Zimbabwe's Shona majority. Zimbabwe's growing post-independence recording industry quickly capitalized on *sungura*'s broad appeal by recording singles and cassettes that dominated the local industry during the latter decades of the twentieth century. In the twenty-first century music piracy and a fading recording industry are, for the first time, threatening *sungura*'s hold on the local population. Despite *sungura*'s massive appeal to a broad spectrum of Zimbabwean society, in the early twenty-first century it had yet to receive much notoriety abroad.

Sungura has its roots in the 1970s, a vibrant musical time in Zimbabwe as locals waged a successful military campaign in their struggle for independence from white minority rule. The first important influence on *sungura* was Congolese *rumba*, a guitar band music style based on recordings of Cuban *son* that swept the former Zaire (now the Democratic Republic of Congo) and the continent as a whole during the middle of the twentieth century. *Rumba* musicians employed the Cuban *clave* timeline pattern, vocal melodies and two-part *montuno* form from *son*. After independence from Belgium, Zaire fell apart economically and *rumba* musicians spread throughout eastern and southern Africa. Several Congolese bands ended up in colonial Zimbabwe (then Southern Rhodesia), where jobs were more plentiful than in Zaire. Among them were the Real Sounds, O.K. Success and Lipopo Jazz. Lipopo's repertoire reflects the musical diversity of Zimbabwe in the 1960s, playing South African, Congolese and Zimbabwean styles, as well as genres from the United States.

Benga is the second important influence on *sungura*. A form of Luo guitar-band music from Kenya based on *rumba*, *benga* is faster and higher-pitched than *rumba*, relying primarily on two guitars and two vocalists in parallel thirds. There are two paths along which *benga* arrived in Zimbabwe: (1) via Zimbabwean guerrilla soldiers who trained in Tanzania during Zimbabwe's war of independence, often forming bands that played *benga* and *rumba*, and through recordings on Kenyan labels such as Kanindo and Sungura that arrived with these traveling soldiers (as music consumers), and (2) through the close political and commercial ties between Zimbabwe, Tanzania and Kenya during this period of colonial transition. Since it was largely these 45 rpm records that Zimbabwean audiences listened to, they referred to *benga* music as *kanindo*. *Sungura* is not a Shona word but a Swahili one (meaning 'rabbit'), further evidence of Kenya and Tanzania's role in the history of Zimbabwean popular music.

Another key influence on the genre comes from South African musicians who have performed their driving duple rhythms, acoustic guitars and heavy bass lines in Zimbabwe since the nineteenth century. By the time Congolese *rumba* and East African *benga* made their mark in the 1960s and 1970s, many local guitar bands were combining indigenous Shona musical characteristics and South African style.

Several bands in the late 1970s collectively shaped *sungura*. The Kassongo Band, formed by soldiers training in Tanzania, was heavily influenced by both *benga* and Swahili *rumba*. The Sungura Boys used instruments from returning soldiers, named themselves after a Kenyan record label and were one of the first bands to combine influences of *benga* and South African township music. The Marxist Brothers relied on the Sungura Boys as backing musicians and played music heavily influenced by Congolese *rumba*. Devera Ngwena called their music *tsava tsava*, based on their South African style, and catered to the multinational population at Zimbabwe's mines. Finally, the Mother Band and the Vhuka Boys, while musically overshadowed, serve as an important link to older musicians including Tineyi Chikupo (from Lipopo Jazz) and Shepherd Chinyani, who helped train the next generation of *sungura* stars, including John Chibadura, Nicholas Zakaria and Alick Macheso.

By the time of independence in 1980 bands had combined the Cuban heritage and guitar work from Congolese *rumba* with the speed and repetitive texture of *benga*. They also added a stronger South African bass and an emphasis on I-IV-I-V chord progressions, employed interlocking guitar lines and highlighted the high-hat in the drums to recall the melodic lines and rattle patterns of much local music, thus creating *sungura*. Lyrics have typically addressed issues of morality or love. Over time, dancing became more important to the popularity and success of *sungura* bands. The audiences were and are predominantly men who dance in a manner similar to Congolese styles. Bands began emphasizing dance steps marked by intricate footwork and flexibility in their stage shows. Alick Macheso, for instance, became hugely popular after developing his signature 'Borrowdale' dance that includes fast footwork reminiscent of the horses racing in Harare's Borrowdale horse track. His more recent variants include 'Razor Wire' and 'Zora Butter.'

Zimbabwe's mining and industrial sectors have long been the destination for migrant labor from throughout the region and *sungura*'s musicians reflect this diversity. Nicholas Zakaria and Alick Macheso are both Chewa speakers of Malawian heritage, Simon and Naison Chimbetu from the Marxist Brothers have Swahili heritage from Tanzania and John Chibadura of the Sungura Boys is of Mozambican descent. In the Kassongo Band alone, Ketai Muchawaya and Knowledge Kunenyati are Ndau from southeastern Zimbabwe, Marko Sibanda is Ndebele, and Lee Roy Lunga is a Sena speaker from Mozambique. The mines catered to their diverse labor force by hiring bands to perform for their workers, even sponsoring their own 'house bands.' Devera Ngwena, for instance, formed while playing for miners at the Mashaba Asbestos Mine (Zindi 1985, 55–6). Because of its regional foundation, *sungura* has emerged in other parts of southern Africa, with Comando & Chova Chova in Mozambique and both Eugene Kubwima and Simon Chidhuza in Namibia.

Despite misplaced labels of early *sungura* as 'rumbira,' none of this music has much to do with the *mbira* (a well-known local lamellaphone or 'thumb piano' played during religious ceremonies in some Shona communities) or other Shona indigenous music. Attempts to associate *sungura* with the *mbira* are often efforts to capitalize on the *mbira*'s popularity abroad and its explicit associations with Shona-based Zimbabwean nationalism. In the early days, many performers also played *jit*, partially inspired by rural Shona drumming styles, but *sungura* quickly developed its own musical trajectory defined largely by Zimbabwe's multinational working population.

There are several reasons why *sungura* became the dominant popular music in Zimbabwe. First, as mentioned above, it placed little reliance on indigenous Shona musical material, but still used musical material drawn from various regional sources, thus appealing to a broader spectrum of Zimbabwe's immigrant communities as well as the Shona majority, who heard the sounds of a potential African modernity in *rumba*, *benga* and their offshoots. Second, because of that migrant base and the efforts of mines and commercial farms to provide entertainment to their workers, *sungura* was performed live more widely than many other more Shona-centric genres. The long, energetic live shows characteristic of *sungura* could be heard everywhere from urban clubs in Harare to the mines, commercial farms and peri-urban communities (growth points) in Zimbabwe's rural areas. Finally, as record companies including Gramma, ZMC and RTP moved to capitalize on this new, post-independence style of music, they pressured performers to emphasize *sungura* because of its reliable popularity. This became even more important during Zimbabwe's twenty-first-century economic collapse, as record companies grew more stylistically conservative in their production of cassettes and CDs.

Sungura solidified its position as Zimbabwe's dominant popular music in the 1980s and 1990s. The leading performers in the 1980s included Leonard Dembo, John Chibadura, Simon Chimbetu and the Khiama Boys led by Nicholas Zakaria. Dembo's album *Chitekete* in 1992 was the first local album to sell 100,000 copies. Former Khiama Boys members System Tazvida, Cephas Karushanga and especially Alick Macheso learned from Zakaria's guidance and went on to form their own successful bands. During the 1990s Leonard Zhakata became one of the most popular *sungura* artists with his poetic interpretation of *rumba*. However, Alick Macheso and Orchestra Mberikwazvo soon replaced Leonard Dembo as the best-selling musicians in Zimbabwean history, largely due to Macheso's combination of guitar virtuosity and signature dance moves. Sadly, many of *sungura*'s biggest stars have died prematurely, devastated by the AIDS epidemic and other causes. John Chibadura, Leonard Dembo, Simon Chimbetu, System Tazvida, Ketai Muchawaya and Tongai Moyo all passed away at the pinnacle of their respective careers. In many cases, as with Chimbetu's son Sulumani and Moyo's son Peter, their children carry on their father's legacy.

Surprisingly, as Zimbabwe descended into economic and political turmoil in the twenty-first century, *sungura*'s popularity only grew. Record companies emphasized the reliability of *sungura* to the detriment of other genres, audiences attended shows despite economic hardships, and musicians such as Macheso, Tongai Moyo, Somandla Ndebele, Pengaudzoke, Sulumani Chimbetu, Sugar-Sugar and the Njerama Boys offered joy and hope to a troubled population. In the second decade of the twenty-first century, members of Alick Macheso's Orchestra Mberikwazvo branched off on their own to form Extra Kwazvose, one of the first successful *sungura* bands to include the electric keyboard prominently in their music. But with the passing of several important *sungura* artists and shifts in the music industry favoring young, urban performers in genres such as dancehall and hip-hop, in the late 2010s *sungura*'s importance locally is lower than it has been in decades. Macheso is still performing, and younger artists suh as Simon Mutambi keep emerging, but their public presence is fading. Still, unlike the 'traditional' popular genres of *chimurenga* and *jit* or the foreign foundations of urban grooves, *sungura* offers working-class Zimbabweans the sound of an indigenous modernity that speaks to their own daily realities as they struggle with the turmoil of postcolonial Zimbabwe.

Bibliography

Eyre, Banning. 2001. *Playing With Fire: Fear and Self-Censorship in Zimbabwean Music*. Copenhagen: Freemuse.

Eyre, Banning. 2006. *Africa: Your Passport to a New World of Music*. Van Nuys, CA: Alfred Publishing.

Muranda, Richard, and Maguraushe, Wonder. 2013. 'Sungura Music's Development in Zimbabwe: The Emergence of Trendsetters, Emulators and Copycats.' *Journal of Music and Meaning* 12: 1244–62.

Perman, Tony. 2012. 'Sungura in Zimbabwe and the Limits of Cosmopolitanism.' *Ethnomusicology Forum* 21(3): 374–401.

Pfukwa, Charles. 2010. 'When Cultures Speak Back to Each Other: The Legacy of Benga in Zimbabwe.' *Muziki: Journal of Music Research in Africa* 7(1): 169–78.

Turino, Thomas. 2000. *Nationalists, Cosmopolitans, and Popular Music in Zimbabwe*. Chicago: University of Chicago Press.

Zindi, Fred. 1985. *Roots Rocking in Zimbabwe*. Gweru: Mambo Press.

Discographical Reference

Dembo, Leonard, and the Barura Express. *Chitekete*. Gramma L4 KSALP 132. *1991*.

Discography

Chibadura, John. *The Essential John Chibadura*. CSA CD5002. *2001*: Zimbabwe.

Chimbetu, Simon, and Orchestra Dendera Kings. *Lullaby*. Gramma L4 KSALP 117. *1997*: Zimbabwe.

Chimbetu, Sulumani, and Orchestra Dendera Kings. *Syllabus*. Sulu Music SC12. *2012*: Zimbabwe.

Dembo, Leonard, and the Barura Express. *Mazano*. Gallo MCGMP 40404. *1992*: Zimbabwe.

Devera Ngwena. *Devera Ngwena 1*. Gramma L4 ZML 1001. *1980*: Zimbabwe.

Extra Kwazvose. *Ndizvo Zviripo*. CD Gramma 760. *2013*: Zimbabwe.

Kassongo Band. *The Evergreen Ketai (Featuring Kassongo)*. ZMC ZMUSI 824. N.d.: Zimbabwe.

Khiama Boys. *Singles Collection Volume 1 (Mabhauwa)*. Gramma ZCD 177. *2001*: Zimbabwe.

Macheso, Alick, and Orchestra Mberikwazvo. *Zvido Zvenyu Kunyanya*. Gramma CDJLP1084. *2003*: Zimbabwe.

Macheso, Alick, and Orchestra Mberikwazvo. *Zvinoda Kutendwa*. Last Power Media LPM 030. *2010*: Zimbabwe.

Macheso, Alick, and Orchestra Mberikwazvo. *Tsooka Dzerwendo*. Alema Music ALEMA 001 CD. *2016*: Zimbabwe.

Marxist Brothers. *Mwana We Dangwe*. Gramma ZMUSI 300. *1983*: Zimbabwe.

Moyo, Tongai, and Utakataka Express. *Samanyemba*. Gramma 210. *2002*: Zimbabwe.

Mesi, Paradzai, and Njerama Boys. *Chitaurirwa*. CD Gramma 595. *2010*: Zimbabwe.

Mutambi, Simon, and The Cobra Kings. *Zvese Ndezvako*. Gramma. *2014*: Zimbabwe.

Pengaudzoke. *Tokudai Mese*. RTP PENLP105. *2002*: Zimbabwe.

Sugar Sugar. *Chimwe nechimwe*. ZMC MNCD 35. *2010*: Zimbabwe.

Tazvida, System, and Chazezesa Challengers. *Wadenha Mago*. Gramma L4 KSALP 166. *1996*: Zimbabwe.

Zakaria, Nicholas, and Khiama Boys. *Munongedzo*. Gramma CD JLP 1088. *2006*: Zimbabwe.

Zakaria, Nicholas, and Khiama Boys. *Ruvheneko*. Gramma CDJLP 2002. *2010*: Zimbabwe.

Zhakata, Leonard K. *Maruva Enyika*. ZMC KLZ 1. *1994*: Zimbabwe.

Zimbabwe Hits Volume Two: Goodbye Sandra. Discafrique. *1989*: Zimbabwe.

TONY PERMAN

Taarab

Taarab is the popular music of the Islamic Swahili people of the East African coast – encompassing the coasts of Tanzania and Kenya and the islands of Zanzibar. Originally a wedding music, it spread widely by way of records, cassettes and radio, and later via television and video, to become a general feature of the aural landscape along the coast.

At first hearing, *taarab* may sound like other forms of Arab music, especially the Zanzibar variety with its Egyptian film orchestra-style lineup. In Mombasa one may be struck by its links with Indian film music. Yet, *taarab* lyrics are invariably in Swahili, and in its voice quality, melodies and local *ngoma* (drum-based dance music) rhythms it is equally reminiscent of typical African musical aesthetics. Indeed, the combination of Africa, Arabia and India in this Indian Ocean musical culture expresses the complex identity of the Swahili people well.

Taarab is sung poetry, so the lyrics and vocals are especially important. Vocals that cut through the instrumentation are popular among the Swahili and there is a distinct preference for high, clear female voices. Rhythm is crucial, too, and no band features fewer than three percussion players, most often on *dumbak* and *bongos* (small drums) and *rika* (tambourine). *Taarab* is generally based on the rhythms of local *ngoma*, the *kumbwaya* and *chakacha* being the most prominent on the coast. Latin American rhythms are part of the mix, too, through the influence of Cuban records in the 1940s, as are rhythms from the Arabian Peninsula.

While some instruments utilized in *taarab* are Near Eastern in origin, including the Arab *oud* (lute), *qanun* (zither), *nai* (flute) and *tashkota* (originally derived from the Japanese *taishokoto*, also called *benju* along the coasts of India and Pakistan), most instruments used in ensembles since the mid-twentieth century are of Western provenance. The first to enter were single violins; from the 1950s, the *firqah*-type orchestras included larger string sections with the occasional cello, and many ensembles also featured the double bass. Accordions followed, before organs and electric keyboards started to be substituted for many of the instruments mentioned so far. A heavier sound first developed in the late 1960s and 1970s, with the inclusion of electric guitars and bass guitar and occasionally a drum set by *taarab* groups in Tanga and Mombasa. A more expansive trend has taken place in *taarab* since the 1990s: so-called modern *taarab*, with a basic lineup of two synthesizers, solo guitar, bass guitar and a drum machine supporting the vocals.

Taarab Roots and Early *Taarab*

The word *taarab* derives from the Arabic *tariba* – 'to be moved or agitated by playing or listening to the sound of music' – yet it gained currency only in the 1950s in the wake of the popularity of Egyptian films screened in cinemas along the coast. The word has since been adopted into Swahili to cover the whole musical style and its context. Zanzibaris generally cite the establishment of the Ikhwani Safaa Musical Club and its orchestra in 1905 as the source of all *taarab* music. The then-ruling sultan, so the story goes, ordered instruments such as the *qanun*, *oud* and violin from Egypt. He also sent a Zanzibari to Cairo to learn to play these instruments and to instruct his fellow club members. This puts the music squarely in the realm of an imported entertainment, played in upper-class circles around the sultan's palace. Yet this version of *taarab* history ignores the older traditions of classical Swahili poetry, which also determine the formal canons of *taarab* lyrics, and the presence of older Swahili musical styles played on instruments including the *gambus* or *kibangala* (*qanbus*; seven-string lute), widely in use along the coast until the early decades of the twentieth century. An original document outlining the foundation of Ikhwani Safaa even mentions the popularity and practice by the club itself of playing Swahili songs from Lamu to the accompaniment of the *gambus* (Graebner 2004a and 2015).

While the later official history of Ikhwani Safaa mentions that the club's orchestra performed songs in Arabic exclusively until the 1950s, the 1920s saw the rise to fame of a group of musicians around the female singing star Siti bint Saad. The members of this group, led by Maalim Shaban, were among the first East African artists to make commercial recordings, traveling to Bombay three times between 1928 and 1931 and recording hundreds of Swahili songs and instrumentals for HMV. The same musicians also recorded for the Odeon and Columbia labels in 1930 (as well as on the French Pathé label), as did a number of musicians from the Kenya coast.

The *taarab* recording industry is an interesting story in itself. From 1928 to 1931, all the major record companies active in Africa, including HMV and Columbia, recorded *taarab*. Brisk business was carried out for a short while until the world recession. In the postwar years, activity was left to local, mostly Asian-owned music stores. The most prominent of these was the Mombasa-based Assanand & Sons, which under the Mzuri label recorded and released hundreds of *taarab* records from Kenya and Tanzania from the 1950s to the mid-1970s. Releases then shifted to the cassette format and local cassette copying shops. Since the early 2000s the most popular groups and singers have been released on CD-Rs (Graebner 2004b).

The Kenya Coast: Lamu and Mombasa

Mbaruk Talsam was a prominent member of the aforementioned Zanzibar-based Siti bint Saad/Maalim Shaban group. A blind singer and lute player, Mbaruk was born in Mombasa in the 1880s. It is reported that as a young man he went to Lamu to learn from the 'true masters of Swahili poetry and song' of the time, Mohamed Kijumwa and Bwana Zena. A few songs recorded by Mbaruk are the only aural link that we have with pre-*taarab* style Swahili sung poetry that was previously accompanied by the *kibangala* (an instrument linked to the Yemeni *qanbus*; cf. D'Hérouville, Graebner, et al. 2013; Graebner 2014). Oral sources suggest musical links to the *sawt* genre of the Persian Gulf, notably from Kuwait, music coming in via musicians on board *dhow* sailing ships visiting with the north-east monsoon (Graebner 1991).

The Zein Musical Party, led by Zein l'Abdin until his death in 2016, is the heir of Lamu's old *taarab* tradition. Together with the Swahili poet Sheikh Nabhany, Zein unearthed a number of old poems and songs, dating back to the nineteenth century, which he included in his repertoire. Zein was not just an accomplished singer and composer but also ranked as the finest *oud* player in East Africa and his name is well known throughout the Islamic world. Like many Lamu musicians, Zein was based in Mombasa for decades as it is in this large port town that performance opportunities and a small recording industry exist.

With the migration of most major singers to Mombasa, since the 1970s the Lamu Archipelago wedding *taarab* has been served by a few amateur groups. One of these is a small group led by Famau Mohamed, who accompanies himself on the Indian harmonium. As most areas in the Lamu archipelago are still without electricity, acoustic instruments have to be used and the harmonium is loud enough to cut through the din of percussion and wedding ambience. For the weddings of more well-to-do townspeople, professional groups from Mombasa or Malindi are bussed in. One of the best-loved and most prolific singers from the early 1960s was Juma Bhalo, who represents the mainstream of Kenya coast *taarab* with its strong leanings toward Bollywood songs. A well-versed poet as well as singer, he ingeniously translated the ambience of these movies into Swahili poetry and song. For a long time Bhalo's main rival on the scene was singer Maulidi Juma, leader of Maulidi Musical Party, who play both traditional Swahili wedding songs and the Hindi-style songs. The group is a typical Mombasa ensemble, with a sound based on keyboards (with a strong harmonium flavor), with accordion, guitar, bass guitar and percussion fills.

Preceding the wave of Bollywood-styled *taarab* that became a dominant trend in the 1960s was the culture of music clubs, springing up in the wake of *ngoma* societies and gaining currency in the 1930s with the popularity of Egyptian sound films starring Um Kulthum and Mohamed Abdel Wahhab. Two prominent orchestras founded in the 1930s include Jauhar Orchestra and Morning Star, both active until the 1980s. From the 1960s Morning Star was led by Matano Juma, one of the most distinctive voices in *taarab* and also a musical innovator who included heavily amplified organ and violin and a Western drum set in the music and came up with a kind of *taarab* that sounded like psychedelic rock by the late 1960s.

Zuhura Swaleh became the leading female *taarab* singer in the 1970s. Her first impact on the Mombasa scene was with the Zein Musical Party, after which she formed her own group. Zuhura was responsible for the popularization of the *chakacha*-style *taarab*, very much loved by the female audiences and a precursor to today's *mipasho* (back-biting) lyrics. Performed for women exclusively as a part of wedding celebrations, *chakacha* is a fast dance rhythm and it usually features very ribald lyrics. Zuhura introduced both the rhythm and the cutting-edge lyrics into *taarab*, with great success. An interesting musical feature of her group was the *tashkota*, a very distinctive sound in Mombasa *taarab* since the 1950s. A second female singer, and for a while the undisputed queen among *taarab* singers, was Malika (Asha Abdo Suleiman). In the 1970s she occasionally sang with Zein, but then was married in Somalia, where she performed as part of the country's national ensemble. In the 1980s she occasionally performed and recorded in Mombasa, backed by Maulidi Musical Party. When civil war erupted in Somalia she resettled in Mombasa and started her own group. In the early 1990s Malika had one of the biggest hits in *taarab* history, 'Vidonge,' a song that was widely covered, even by dance bands from Nairobi, including Samba Mapangala (Orchestre Virunga).

With the aging of former stars and the focus of the industry moving to Dar es Salaam since the 1990s, Mombasa *taarab* has lost much of its former might and focus. Most of the current groups indulge in copies of the latest hits from the leading Dar es Salaam ensembles.

Tanzania

Organization in social clubs was one of the main features of *taarab* from the 1930s to the 1960s. Political changes, economic pressures and evolving lifestyles ultimately resulted in the demise of this organizational form. While, on the Kenya coast, the club orchestras gave way to individualistic expression and bands typically headed by the lead singer, on the Tanzanian side of the border it was political and economic constraints – Ujamaa austerity politics – that led to the formation of new groups under the umbrella of state or para-statal organizations. Thus Dar es Salaam's Egyptian and Al-Watan Musical Clubs that had been the city's pride up to independence were fading away for lack of instruments, with the leading singers and musicians being lured by steady income as members of the entertainment sections of state organizations including JKT Taarab (National Service), Magereza Taarab (prisons administration) or DDC Kibisa (the City Council's Dar es Salaam Development Corporation). Paradoxically, it was the state's austerity politics and the closing off of Zanzibar after the revolution in 1964 that kept *taarab* music clubs and their orchestras up and running into the late 1990s and early 2000s.

Zanzibar's oldest music club, Ikhwani Safaa, was founded in 1905 as a men's social and recreational club. Members met at the club's premises after the final Muslim prayer of the day to rehearse and play for their own amusement, yet they would not perform in public. A rival club, Nadi Shuub, was also formed at the time. The initial phase of Ikhwani Safaa's history ended around World War I but the club surfaced again with the general popularity of clubs and orchestras in the 1930s and 1940s. The band that initially featured only *'ud*, violin, *nai* and percussion soon swelled to an orchestra adding *qanun*, accordions, *tashkota*, cello, double bass, a violin section, and later also organ and electric guitar. With the popularity of Egyptian cinema, this *firqah*-type lineup was the standard fare of all the name clubs from Mombasa to Dar es Salaam and was emulated in Zanzibar to some degree also by a number of less well-known ensembles like Miembeni and Michenzani Social Clubs.

Shime Kuokoana (originally a small *kidumbak* group), formed around 1958 by some musicians close to the Afro-Shirazi party's youth wing then fighting for independence, in time included more *taarab* instruments and after the 1964 revolution grew into a quasi-national *taarab* orchestra, uniting the island's leading musicians also from the other clubs present in Zanzibar town. As it was originally under the Ministry of Information and Culture, the new club was ultimately called Culture Musical Club (Mila na Utamaduni in Swahili) in the 1970s, gaining complete independence in 1980. Ikhwani Safaa and Culture Musical Club came to represent the sound of Zanzibar with frequent recordings for radio and television and a plethora of cassettes – usually live recordings for new songs premiered at the important annual shows on Idd-el-Fitr and Idd-el-Haj holidays. Both clubs and their respective orchestral style were in decline after the 1990s, with the leading singers and musicians being lured to join the fashionable modern *taarab* circuit and audience allegiance completely shifting to the new style.

In the 1960s the Black Star Musical Club of Tanga, a small town on the northern Tanzanian coast, turned around the whole *taarab* scene. Up until then, *taarab* had been the near-exclusive province of Islamic Swahili – people who claimed long Swahili ancestry and often overseas origins. Then Black Star introduced a new modern style, with guitar and bass and a more danceable rhythmic base. *Taarab* was revolutionized and began crossing national boundaries to audiences as far away as Burundi and Congo/Zaire. Since the 1970s most *taarab* groups active in Tanzania, Burundi and Kenya have been modeled on the style and instrumentation of the Black Star Musical Club, its offspring Lucky Star, and their star female singers Shakila, Sharmila and Asmahan.

The political and economic liberalization of the early 1990s led to new developments on Dar Es Salaam's *taarab* scene. Two large (and rival) orchestras were at the forefront of this evolution: Muungano Taarab, owned by a businessman, and TOT (Tanzania One Theatre), which was closely related to the ruling CCM party. Both groups offered a variety of styles – a kind of integrated family entertainment including stage versions of ethnic *ngoma*, *kwaya*, theatrical plays and *taarab*. Shows were performed on Saturday and Sunday afternoons at social halls all over the city. Yet, the climax of their performances was the *taarab*: TOT and Muungano presented the flashiest *taarab* ever heard in East Africa, adding synthesizer and a dance band-style rhythm section to regular *taarab* instruments including violin, accordion and local percussion. With the advent of the group East African Melody in 1995 a musical standardization process occurred in which the typical lineup was reduced to two keyboard players, solo and bass guitar, plus drum machine. This process was driven mainly by a kind of cut-throat competition between the bands that focused on obtaining the most famous female star singers and having the sharpest hottest *mipasho* lyrics attacking the other band's singer(s), rather than musical innovation. In the 2010s the premier bands in this style are Jahazi Modern Taarab led by Mzee Yusuf and Zanzibar Stars Modern Taarab.

Another development of the 2000s on the Dar es Salaam scene was a crossover between *taarab* and Zaramo *ngoma*, called 'Segere' after the genre's initial big hit song. The first proponents of this style were Young Stars Modern Taarab. *Segere* is an electrified mix of Zaramo *mchiriku*, Swahili *chakacha* and *taarab*. The songs are extended medleys stringing together various lyrics, choruses and melodic lines from various sources. Young Stars has since split; members of the original band now continue as Segere Original. Tandale Modern Theatre is another group representing this style.

While modern *taarab* has branched out to engage new audiences beyond the confines of Islamic coastal society – and in the 2000s has forfeited much of its original flavor by including elements of dance band music and *bongo flava* pop – the sound and repertoire of mid-twentieth-century acoustic *taarab* has been embraced as part of coastal Swahili society's cultural heritage and identity formation. In the late 2010s it is on the verge of becoming a kind of classical sound emulated by younger musicians either with modern electronic instruments or by picking up defining acoustic instruments including the *'ud* or *qanun*. This revival is again led by Zanzibari musicians. A major example of innovation within this context is provided by Rajab Suleiman and his group Kithara.

Bibliography

Askew, Kelly. 2002. *Performing the Nation: Swahili Music and Cultural Politics in Tanzania*. Chicago: Chicago University Press.

D'Hérouville, Pierre, Graebner, Werner, et al. 2013. 'Les migrations du luth yéménite dans l'Océan Indien' [The Migrations of the Yemeni Lute Around the Indian Ocean]. In *Qanbus, Tarab: Le luth monoxyle et la musique du Yemen* [*Qanbus, Tarab:* The Single-Piece Lute and the Music of Yemen], eds. Jean Lambert and Samir Mokrami. Paris: CEFAS, Geuthner, 109–36.

Fair, Laura. 2001. *Pastimes and Politics: Culture, Community and Identity in Post-Abolition Urban Zanzibar*. London: James Currey.

Fargion, Janet Topp. 2014. *Taarab Music in Zanzibar in the Twentieth Century: A Story of 'Old is Gold' and Flying Spirits*. New York: Routledge.

Graebner, Werner. 1991: 'Tarabu – populäre Musik am indischen Ozean' [*Tarabu* – Popular Music on the Indian Ocean Coast]. In *Populäre Musik in Afrika*, ed. Veit Erlmann. Berlin: Museum für Völkerkunde, 181–200.

Graebner, Werner. 2004a. 'Between Mainland and Sea: The Taarab Music of Zanzibar.' In *Island Musics*, ed. Kevin Dawe. Oxford: Berg, 171–97.

Graebner, Werner. 2004b. 'The Interaction of Swahili Taarab Music and the Record Industry. A Historical Perspective.' In *African Media Cultures – Cultures de médias en Afrique*, eds. Rose Marie Beck and Frank Wittmann. Cologne: Rüdiger Köppe, 171–92.

Graebner, Werner. 2014. 'The *Qanbus* Connection: Pre-*Taarab* Roots on the Northern Kenya Coast.' In *From the Tana River to Lake Chad: Research in African Oratures and Literatures*, eds. Hannelore Vögele et al. Cologne: Rüdiger Köppe, 311–23.

Discographical References

Malika [Asha Abdo Suleiman]. 'Vidonge.' *Cassette No. 8*. Mbwana Radio Service Mombasa. *1990*: Kenya.

Samba Mapangala and Orchestre Virunga. 'Vidonge.' *Feet on Fire*. Stern's Africa 1036. *1991*: UK.

Discography

Black Star and Lucky Star Musical Clubs. *Nyota*. GlobeStyle CDORB 044. *1989*: UK.

Ikhwani Safaa Musical Club. *Music of Zanzibar: Taarab 2*. GlobeStyle CDORBD 040. *1988*: UK.

Mila na Utamaduni/Culture Musical Club. *Spices of Zanzibar*. Network Medien 24210. *1996*: Germany.

Poetry and Languid Charm: Swahili Music from Tanzania and Kenya: From the 1920s to the 1950s. Topic Records TSCD936. *2007*: UK.

Rajab Suleiman and Kithara. *Chungu*. Buda Musique 860248. *2013*: France.

Samba Mapangala and Orchestre Virunga. *Feet on Fire*. Stern's Africa 1036. *1991*: UK.

Swaleh, Zuhura and Maulidi Musical Party. *Jino la Pembe*. GlobeStyle CDORBD 075. *1992*: UK.

Young Stars Modern Taarab. *Segere*. FKW no cat. number. *N.d.* [*2002*]: Tanzania.

Zanzibara 2: The Golden Age of Mombasa Taarab (1965–1975). Buda Musique 860119. *2005*: France.

Zein Musical Party. *The Style of Mombasa*. GlobeStyle CDORBD 066. *1990*: UK.

Filmography

Poetry in Motion: A Hundred Years of Zanzibar's Ikhwani Safaa Musical Club, dir. Ron Mulvihill. 2016: France. 71 mins. Documentary.

Zanzibar Musical Club, dir. Philippe Gasnier and Patrice Nezan. 2009. France. 85 mins. Documentary.

WERNER GRAEBNER

Tabanka

In Cabo Verde, the word *tabanka* (sometimes spelled *tabanca*) is generally understood to refer to an annual Afro-Christian religious re-enactment, but it is also used to designate the mutual aid organization which sponsors that event and may also be a reference to the music which accompanies one part of the larger event. It is associated with a group known as the Badiu from the island of Santiago, who were the ancestors of slaves who escaped to the center of the island in times past. *Tabanka* has existed in Cabo Verde since the eighteenth century, but the word itself comes from Guinea-Bissau and means fence or village.

The annual *tabanka* ritual officially begins on 3 May, the Feast of the Cross (Santa Cruz), which was historically designated by masters as a symbolic holiday in honor of humanity's liberation. The irony of this was not lost on slaves who took advantage of this day to celebrate themselves, and over time a complex series of events developed in which traditional societal roles were reversed and participants, satirizing those who oppressed them in daily life, adopted roles similar to those of a colonial court. The events extend to include several important feast days in June, including St John the Baptist's day on 24 June, but primarily revolve around the theft and recovery of an object that is a symbolic representation of a saint.

Opening festivities are heralded by the playing of drums and the distinctive call of horns made of conch shells, known as *búzios*. In the days immediately preceding the main events women gather to grind corn and take part in lively sessions of dancing and singing known as *batuque*, which involve a single performer in the center of a circle of women singing in chorus while striking a folded cloth held between their legs. Festivities accelerate on the saint's day with a Catholic mass, after which the 'thief,' who is traditionally male, steals the 'saint' from the church designated as the *tabanka* chapel. After the theft, a complex ritual takes place in the chapel where members pay their respects to the stolen 'saint,' accompanied by two drummers who beat patterns specific to *tabanka* music known as *salvas* at certain points in the ceremony, and by members who may also perform *ladainha*, a unique form of sung group prayer based on the Catholic liturgy. *Ladainhas*, sung in a mixture of Portuguese, Latin and Krioulu, are sung by a leader and small group and accompany many religious rituals. The passing harmonies produced by the vocal polyphony and strident vocal technique can be quite dissonant and haunting.

The high point of the festivities occurs seven days later when the 'thief' and his fellow conspirators lead a large procession through the streets, comprised of the organization's members in costumes designating their role in the proceedings, to recover the 'saint' from its hidden location. This is when the music most associated with *tabanka* is performed. The group is accompanied by drummers playing military-style metal drums with skin heads carried over the shoulder and played with two wooden sticks on one side, along with several *búzio* players and marchers carrying whistles. The rhythm is strongly in 2/4 time (see Example 1), with *búzios* alternating between two pitches a minor third apart; one generally playing on the beat and one with repeated notes in a syncopated rhythm, often using the sixteenth note as a pickup. Women sing traditional songs and perform a dance similar to the one that accompanies *batuque*. The songs are short, perhaps one phrase, with a narrow range and are sung open-voiced, similar to the singing for *batuque* or *funana*. Lyrics, describing the hardships of daily life, were interpreted as rebellious by the Church and state.

Example 1: Drum rhythm

In a ritualized process, the king and the benefactor negotiate the return of the 'saint.' When the process is complete, the festivities continue with a large feast followed by celebrations, including long sessions of animated *batuques*, throughout the night. In the morning the group returns to the *tabanca* chapel and restores the 'saint' to its rightful place.

Under the Portuguese colonial administration, *tabanca* was seen as seditious in nature and, starting as early as 1723, it was often severely restricted or prohibited, particular in the capital city of Praia. After independence it received government support and the *tabanka* rhythms were heard in street processions and at presentations during official state functions. Since the 1990s *tabanca* has declined in popularity and membership and like many genres seen as resistance, it is still finding its way in an independent Cabo Verde; in the future it may only survive in a touristic version of its original self.

The distinctive rhythm and sound of the *búzio*, however, can be heard in Cabo Verdean popular music, including *cabo-zouk* and *funana*, where even a small amount immediately transports the listener to the island of Santiago. Throughout the 1990s a popular and well-known performer from Santiago known as Orlando Pantera championed the use of *batuque* and *tabanka* rhythms in his compositions, which included *Vasulina* (Vaseline) and *Lapidu na bô* (Stuck on You). After Pantera died tragically in 2001 at the age of 33 without producing his first CD, a group of young artists, including Tcheka, Lura and Mayra Andrade, sometimes called the *Geracão*

Pantera (Pantera Generation), have carried on what he started and expanded on his innovative use of the sound and rhythm of the *buzio* in their performances and compositions.

Bibliography

Gonçalves, Carlos Filipe. 1998. 'Kap Verd Band.' In *Descoberta das Ilhas de Cabo Verde* [Discovery of the Cabo Verde Islands], coordinated by José Maria Almedia. Praia, Cabo Verde: Archivo Histórico Nacional (Cabo Verde), 177–, 208.

Hurley Glowa, Susan. 1995. 'Tabanka.' In *Historical Dictionary of the Republic of Cabo Verde*. 3rd edn., eds. Richard Lobban and Marlene Lopes. Metuchen, NJ: The Scarecrow Press, 195–8.

Monteiro, Félix. 1948–9. 'Tabanca: Evolução semantica' [Tabanca: Semantic Evolution]. *Claridade* 6 (July 1948): 14–18 and 7 (December 1949): 19–26.

Monteiro, Vladimir. 1998. *Les musiques du Cap-Vert* [The Musics of Cabo Verde]. Paris: Éditions Chandeigne.

Semedo, José Maria, and Turano, Maria R. 1997. *Cabo Verde: O ciclo ritual das festividades da tabanca* [Cabo Verde: The Cycle of Tabanca's Ritual Festivities]. Praia: Spleen-Edições.

Discography

Andrade, Mayra. *Navega* [Sail]. BMG/Sony BMG/Sony Music Distribution 0564. *2006*: France.

Capo Verde: An Archipelago of Music. Ocora Radio France C-560146/57. *1999*. France.

Dez Granzin di Tera [Ten Grains of Sand]. *A viagem dos sons / The Journey of Sounds: Cabo Verde*. Tradisom, Lda VS11. *1998*. Portugal.

Ferro Gaita. *Rei di Tabanka*. Ferro Gaita Productions (no number). *1999*: Cabo Verde.

Lura. *Di korpu cu alma* [Of Body and Soul]. Lusafrica, distributed by Escondida Music ESC6511-2. *2005*: Portugal/Cabo Verde/France.

Lura. *Best of Lura*. Lusafrica. Amazon Digital Services. *2010*: Portugal.

Tcheka. *Boka Kafé*. Amazon Digital Services. *2017*: Portugal.

JOANNE HOFFMAN

Takamba

Takamba is a dance and music style of the Songhai people, centered in Gao, Mali. As practiced since the early twentieth century, the dance is slow and sensuous with a graceful intensity that reflects the pace and character of life in the Sahara Desert. It is enjoyed by men and women, young and old, in social and concert settings. *Takamba* is also a genre of accompanied songs and instrumental pieces. As both a musical style and a dance, *takamba* has deep roots, going back at least as far as the Songhai Empire in West Africa in the fifteenth and sixteenth centuries, and probably much further. Modern *takamba*, accompanied by calabash gourd percussion and a spike lute called *kurbu*, emerged in the mid-twentieth century. While other forms of Songhai music conjure spirits or bring about possession, *takamba* is intended to entertain. Its popularity in recent decades reflects the way it has been embraced by young artists and used to express the concerns of youth (such as finding potential spouses and ways to make a living) and, to a degree, urban culture in the Sahara.

Takamba's Evolution

Knowledge of the origins and evolution of this region's music only extends to the period when recordings began to be made in the early twentieth century. The oldest remembered forms of *takamba* were slow songs, accompanied only by the *kurbu*. Songhai musician Abdoulaye Alhassane Touré (founding member of the Niger band Mamar Kassey), recalls hearing *takamba* songs as a boy in the 1960s, both in Niamey, Niger and Gao, Mali. Performed by Touré's elders, these songs were serene and reserved, often without rhythm, and accompanied only by single-line *kurbu* melody. Sometimes the *kurbu* player would tap out a gentle rhythm using the extra fingertips on his picking hand to strike the hard, stretched skin of the instrument's drum-like body. Listeners might participate with sporadic handclapping. The rhythm, when it emerged, was in 6/8, but rhythm was not emphasized.

By the early 1970s the more rhythmic *takamba*, accompanied by calabash percussion, had emerged, to better support a distinctive dance (described below) that was gaining in popularity. The calabash is a large, dried and halved gourd played with fist and fingers; younger players emphasize the finger rhythms by wearing metal rings. The *kurbu* lute, typically with three strings, is also ubiquitous, its sound often enhanced with an electronic pickup so it can be played through a guitar amplifier or public address system. The music of *takamba*, like most music in the southern Sahara, uses pentatonic scales, including the minor pentatonic scale, which has caused much speculation about historic connections between this region's music and American blues. This association is not lost on musicians, who are known to amplify their ancient lutes using distortion effects pedals that lend their fleet, dark melodies a Jimi Hendrix-like air.

The music of contemporary *takamba* is typically organized around a two-part rhythm with an underlying 12-beat cycle, as follows:

Example 1: *Takamba* rhythm

The strong triple feel of the second measure gives *takamba* its elegant, stately character. However, in performances, especially by modern electric bands, the rhythm can shift to 4/4, with the pulses organized into four groups of three beats (instead of three groups of four). This gives the music a rolling momentum that overrides the basic rhythm, but does not completely obscure it.

Precolonial *takamba* songs were used to praise heroes and chiefs, although in independent Mali, they are as likely to praise the beauties and pleasures of youth. This is largely because, since the 1970s, this region has seen the rise of popular, recorded music, singers and songwriters – male and female, solo and in groups – who compose contemporary songs using the *takamba* rhythm. The rhythm is distinctive and easily recognized, and to a degree influences the format of lyrics. However, singers and composers are free to accommodate the *takamba* rhythm within their songs in any way they like. *Takamba* is a tradition that has been thoroughly adapted within the evolving language of the region's popular song.

The Dance

The *takamba* dance is focused on the upper body, with slow undulating movement of the torso, shoulders, arms and hands. The arms are held extended, wavering and flicking in continuous fluid motion. *Takamba* is danced by both men and women, separately or together.

The *takamba* dance was a great passion of the late Malian guitarist and singer Ali Farka Touré, who performed it brilliantly. In his later life, Touré was never without his cassettes of *takamba* groups from northern Mali. Since 1999 an annual festival in northern Mali, *Le Festival au Desert*, has brought international attention to *takamba*. At this festival, popular artists including Touré (prior to his death in 2006) and the popular singer Khaira Arby of Timbuktu share the stage with more traditional *takamba* groups such as Super 11, sometimes fielding multiple calabash and *kurbu* players, who give the music robust power. During nearly every performance at this festival, people can be seen on the stage dancing *takamba*, even when the music is only distantly related to the fundamental *takamba* rhythm. Partly as a result of the global attention this festival has received, *takamba* is now accessible to the world through commercial recordings, touring ensembles, documentary films and YouTube videos.

Takamba among the Tuareg

The modern *takamba* became popular among the nomadic Tuareg during the late twentieth century. The Tuareg lute called *tehardent* – essentially identical to the *kurbu* – is the featured accompaniment instrument in the Tuareg version. For this reason, some musicians refer to the genre and dance as 'tehardent.' This creates confusion as there are many other styles of music played on *tehardent* – *takamba* being but one. Fatimata Oletouma of the Tuareg traditional group Tartit described the Tuareg dance, which she calls *tehardent*, as related to, but distinct from, Songhai *takamba*. '*Takamba* and *tehardent* are almost the same thing,' she noted in a 2003 interview with the author, 'But generally the *takamba* is danced standing, and the *tehardent* is danced seated, with the movement confined to arms, shoulder, and neck. These are populations that live together, and when two cultures live together, it is certain that each will give something to the other.'

Takamba music and dance disseminated from Mali during the 1960s and reached for example Tamanrasset, a major city of the Algerian Tuareg, by 1974. For the Tuareg, as for the Songhai, *takamba* is an expression of urban life and contemporary values, and is generally disparaged by conservatives and Islamic religious authorities.

Bibliography

Durán, Lucy. 2006. 'Mali, Gold Dust by the River,' *World Music, Volume 1: Africa, and Middle East*, eds. Simon Broughton, Mark Ellingham and John Lusk. London: The Rough Guides, 219–38.

Morgan, Andy. 2013. *Music, Culture and Conflict in Mali*. Copenhagen: Freemuse.

Wendt, Caroline Card. 1998. 'Tuareg Music.' In *The Garland Encyclopedia of World Music, Volume 1: Africa*, ed. Ruth M. Stone. New York and London: Garland Publishing, 574–95.

Personal Communication

Fatimata Oletouma. Interview with author, 2003.

Discography

Arby, Khaira. *Timbuktu Tarab*. Clermont Music 7 11574 67652 1. *2010*: USA.

Festival in the Desert. World Village 468020. *2003*: USA.

Super 11. *Super Onze*. Two Speakers Rec, Rec Two: 003. *2010*: Netherlands.

Tartit with Imharhan. *Live from the Sahara*. Clermont Music 7 11574 76172 2. *2013*: USA.

Filmography

Ali Ag Amoumine – Takamba. Online at: https://www.youtube.com/watch?v=4uyjMmXVAws.

Haidara Aïchata Cissé dit CHATO danse le Takamba de Super11. Online at https://www.youtube.com/watch?v=FM2CdpoT2h4.

BANNING EYRE

Takiboronsé

Takiboronsé (*takboronsé*) came into being in Burkina Faso in 2005 at a time when the country's music scene was dominated by music from elsewhere in Africa and beyond. It has been estimated that approximately 80 percent of the music broadcast on the radio and played in discos at this time originated from outside the country (Smockey; interview with first author, February 2018). This situation had led many music lovers, cultural actors, media personalities and commentators such as Jean Philippe Tougouma (2007) to complain about the invasion of the country by sounds from the Côte d'Ivoire such as *zoblazo*, *zouglou* and *coupé-décalé* and, to a lesser extent, the Democratic Republic of the Congo. The popularity of *zouglou* and *coupé-décalé* was such that many young Burkinabè musicians adopted these musical styles. The emergence of *takiboronsé* marked a departure from this trend and signaled a new beginning in the development of urban music in Burkina Faso.

The roots of this change can be traced back to the 1990s. Before this time, a number of factors militated against the development of a national urban popular music. One, as Batamaka Somé puts it, is 'the diverse tastes of the five dozens of national ethnicities' (2012, 62). Another was the undeveloped state of Burkina Faso's music industry. A final one was an unstable and inhospitable political climate that predominated during the 1980s. The result was that the urban popular music of the Côte d'Ivoire and the Democratic Republic of the Congo, countries whose music industries had 'developed very fast and efficiently in terms of infrastructure, production and invention of cadenced danceable rhythms' (Somé 2012, 63), became the staple musical fare for Burkinabè young people, for whom jobs were precarious and unemployment high. Many Ivorian and Congolese musicians performed in Burkina Faso. Conversely, these industries provided an opportunity for Burkinabè musicians to 'find a place for themselves in the world of music' (Somé 2012, 63). However, the financial challenges for Burkinabè musicians wanting to record in the Côte d'Ivoire or the Democratic Republic of the Congo were daunting.

A number of important changes occurred during and after the 1990s that set the scene for the development of *takiboronsé* as a national urban popular music. The political climate opened up and permitted a greater degree of democracy, fueling increased creativity among musicians. Technological developments from the 1970s through the 1990s, including the spread of the phonograph, the cassette, VHS and the CD-ROM, the expansion of news through radio and television, the birth of the compact disc, the accessibility of cable television and the Internet, and the advent of websites such as YouTube all provided the infrastructure for a much more vibrant popular music scene. As was the case in other African countries, the development and growth of national television became a major force in the dissemination of popular music. Added to this was the establishment of a few production and recording studios. All these innovations resulted in a growing infrastructure capable of underwriting the advent of a national music such as *takiboronsé* (Somé 2012, 66).

The Birth and Development of *Takiboronsé*

Takiboronsé was launched by Ahmed Smani (also known as Hamed Smani), who is recognized as the founding father of the genre through the release of his first album *Zalissa* in 2005. *Takiboronsé* was not thought of as a musical genre in 2005. At the time of its release *Zalissa* was simply a hit. However, after the success of *Zalissa* artists such as Yeleen, Faso Kombat and Smockey were inspired to think of ways of creating a popular music typical of Burkina Faso in a manner similar to the way in which *coupé-décalé* has symbolized the Côte d'Ivoire. Following the Ivorian model, the practice for Burkinabè bands and artists became that of including *takiboronsé* in every album they released. According to Smockey, *takiboronsé* was inspired musically by Congolese *rumba*, particularly that of Pamelo M'munka, as well as by rhythms performed on traditional Burkinabè instruments, most notably the tri-string Kundé employed in the Mossi kingdoms of the upper Volta river in central Burkina Faso (Smockey; interview with first author, February 2018). Musically, therefore, *takiboronsé* became a fusion of traditional rhythms, to a significant extent those of the traditional *warba* and *wiire* dances of the Moosi people (also known as the Mossé), and modern sounds drawn principally from the popular musics of the Côte d'Ivoire and the Democratic Republic of the Congo.

As is the case with popular music genres in many other parts of West Africa, *takiboronsé* is a form of both music *and* dance, something, as Somé observes, that is reflected in the genre's name. The name derives from Mooré, the language of the Moosi people (the largest ethnic group of Burkina Faso, making up more than 50 percent of the population). According to Somé, '*takiboronsé* is a compound word that derives from [the] local Mooré word *tak/taki* that means "to pull"; and *borenga* that denotes the upper part of the human body … literally, then, Takiboronse or Takboronse … means to "pull the upper parts of the bodies"' (2012, 71). The dance embodies this description: 'The dance consists in moving gracefully and rhythmically the upper part of the body back and forth … one must bend from the waist and swing the body back and forth, while keeping the arms moving harmoniously with the rest of the body' (Somé 2012, 72). The music encapsulates this movement: a syncopated polyrhythm slower than that of Congolese dances that oscillates gently through melodies that are sweet and engaging. (All these characteristics can be seen and heard in the YouTube video of Ahmed Smani performing the title song from his *Zalissa* album [see YouTube videos listed below]).

Takiboronsé went from being just one hit to a genuinely popular genre with the appearance of the band Le Gouvernement (the Government). Its members were Smockey, Yeleen, Faso Kombat, Floby and Madson Junior. The release in 2005 of Le Gouvernement's maxi-single 'Bouge' marks a high point in the emergence of *takiboronsé*. According to Smockey, the thinking behind *takiboronsé* was to produce a music that could make people dance and think at the same time: 'We wanted to prove that we could make a music that moves, but also a music that has substance and depth. And since we were all politically engaged artists, we asked ourselves, why not call our band "Le Gouvernement"? It allowed us to be ironic' (Smockey; interview with first author, February 2018). Smockey adds that combining movement and irony was a way for the band to inject some humor into their music, to expose the absurdity of the state apparatus and the banana democracy of Burkina Faso. In order to create a buzz around the new genre, promoters contrived 'clashes,' false competitions between bands. These 'clashes' were conducted through the lyrics and performances of the bands' songs. A women's band called Les Premières Dames (The First Ladies) clashed with other bands, for example, by criticizing them for 'being all male and ignoring women's concerns' (Somé 2012, 74). These 'clashes' helped maintain the genre's popularity while this popularity lasted.

Ahmed Smani's hit, *Zalissa*, was followed not only by groups such as Le Gouvernement and Les Premières Dames but also by other groups such as Le Pouvoir (The Regime/The Power) and La Cour Suprême (The Supreme Court). If *takiboronsé* was inspired partially by traditional rhythms, the groups that promoted it did not use the traditional languages of Burkina Faso. Rather, the chosen language of these musical groups was French. French allowed artists to transcend ethnic and regional differences and produce an urban music in which all Burkinabès could recognize themselves. The central theme of *takiboronsé* was a gentle, humorous, social and political satire – as evidenced by the names of the musical groups – often aimed indirectly at the government and some of its members.

In these ways, *Zalissa* and the music that followed represented an outburst of pride on the part of Burkinabè artists, making people dance to Burkinabè sounds produced by local artists and rooted in the values and realities of the country. Those who promoted this new style were young, elegant, full of charm and sartorially dressed. Their first objective was to convince Burkinabè youth that they were witty and had musical talent, so much so that some analysts have said that the purpose of *takiboronsé* was as much to showcase the musicians as to support traditional local music. If so, they were certainly successful.

Influence and Reputation

The phenomenon of *takiboronsé* lasted only two years. However, its influence has persisted beyond its brief existence. It had a multidimensional influence on the evolution of Burkina Faso's popular urban music, as it triggered a cultural nationalist surge that has continued to impact the urban music of the country, even beyond its borders. According to Somé, the effects of *takiboronsé* on the popular culture of Burkina Faso have been multiple and contradictory. As Somé explains: '[*Takiboronsé*] provides an avenue for some artists to voice a humorous and indirect criticism of the government and some social behaviors in highly self-aware commitment, but it also promotes less political agendas' (Somé 2012, 73).

Takiboronsé provided a pretext for artists to criticize public figures and denounce certain social behaviors and practices. It has also stimulated the advent of several musical groups which furthered the development of Burkinabè music. For example, the song 'Faire le Malin' was created by the group Le Pouvoir in response to Le Gouvernement's 'Bouge,' and the all-women's group Les Premières Dames was established in response to the music of Le Gouvernement, Le Pouvoir and La Cour Suprême. The 'clash' or musical jousting that was thereby instigated between artists and musical groups created a space for creative expression and generated genuine artistic and cultural innovations. In the same vein, *takiboronsé* helped to breathe new life into Burkina Faso's music, which in turn helped to create a feeling of cultural nationalism.

Takiboronsé also breathed new life into the Burkinabè music industry. It allowed the people of Burkina Faso to consume their own music and generated money for everyone involved in the production of the music. According to the members of Le Gouvernement, *takiboronsé* made it possible for them to tour the country and to be well remunerated for their performances. *Takiboronsé* also favored the creation and strengthening of lobbies for the distribution and dissemination of Burkinabè music. The period during which *takiboronsé* was popular also coincided with the predominance of the Seydonie Production cassette tape. Seydonie's mass duplication of cassette tapes allowed distributors to organize themselves into a lobby to buy new releases and resell them. The monopoly of the distribution lobby reduced profits for artists but guaranteed them a regular income. This situation compelled artists to sell their products to distributors rather than selling them directly to the public. Smockey explains further:

> The distributors worked as a cooperative to bring down the price of cassette tapes to the point at which it became embarrassing not only for Seydonie, which duplicated the tapes, but also for us, the artists, because the distributors managed to reduce prices by establishing a sort of blackmail system. They put all their money together and used this huge amount of cash to buy cassettes. After that, you ran the risk of having no distribution at all if you did not sell them your own tapes. When the system worked well, the distributors would immediately come to you and buy several boxes of cassettes. Today this distribution circuit has completely disappeared. (Smockey; interview with first author, February 2018)

Even if inspired by tradition, *takiboronsé* was the first modern popular music genre to symbolize Burkina Faso. As such, it was an influential innovation. It was the first to inspire Burkinabè artists to create other musical artifacts. One such artist was Basebill, who created a dance, the 'Glissement-Glisser,' that enjoyed a modest success in Burkina Faso. Another was Prince Zoetaba, who created another dance, the Jetgo, that enjoyed relative success in the capital, Ouagadougou. In terms of rhythm, the contribution of *takiboronsé* has persisted. *Takboronsé*'s distinctive rhythm, as demonstrated in the YouTube video of 'Zalissa,' has continued to be used by many Burkinabè guitarists.

However, not all cultural commentators have had such a positive view of *takiboronsé*. It has been criticized by such commentators as being a mere flash in the pan with no lasting value. Jean-Philippe Tougouma, for example, has argued that 'Burkina, a country of culture with great cultural events, is unfortunately the only country in our subregion that cannot make its "children" dance to the sound of a national rhythm. We are confined to talking only about Coupé-Décalé, Zouk this or Zouk that, as most merely echo those sounds' (Tougouma 2007). While it is true that there were fewer studios during *takiboronsé*'s popularity than subsequently, when Tougouma was commenting, there was a greater level of production because artists recorded albums rather than singles, which has since become the practice. More than being a passing fad, therefore, *takiboronsé* has helped to position Burkinabè music among the most important urban musical styles of the West African subregion. *Takiboronsé* represented a moment of awakening for both artists and music lovers.

Takiboronsé's ephemeral existence was due in part to the end of the 'clashes.' The original promoters of *takiboronsé* were groups of musicians who had previous careers as individual artists. After the success of *Zalissa*, for example, Ahmed Smani decided to join Le Pouvoir. The disappearance of *takiboronsé* resulted in part, therefore, from the frustrations of individuals who felt that the unique character of their bands was being absorbed by a mass phenomenon. As a consequence, many groups stopped touring and the basis for the 'clashes' vanished. However, the principal reason for the genre's demise was the breakup of the real creators of *takiboronsé*: Le Gouvernement. The breakup resulted in *takiboronsé* losing its soul. Smockey explains the disappearance of the 'clashes' in terms of the eventual isolation of Le Pouvoir:

> As soon as the initiators withdrew, the driving force of the movement vanished. I think that contributed to bringing the movement to an end. There could no longer be clashes. Le Pouvoir used Le Gouvernement and Les Premières Dames to make a name for itself by slapping us in the face all the time. From the moment that Le Pouvoir was all alone, who could they clash with? The band became just a gimmick and people became disinterested (Smockey; interview with first author, February 2018)

Despite its brief existence, the greatest contribution of *takiboronsé* was without a doubt the development of pride in a national culture. Indeed, since the appearance of *takiboronsé*, Burkinabè music has opened up to the world and has come to be consumed both nationally and internationally, as the subsequent production of YouTube videos in France and elsewhere evidences (see YouTube videos listed below). The spread of this music has served to further develop the Burkina Faso music industry. One of the foremost symbols of this Burkinabè cultural industry has been the creation of an Internet portal for the promotion of Burkina Faso's culture. Wherever they might be located, those active in the world of culture have been able and proud to promote and market Burkinabè music. *Takiboronsé* has proven the ability of Burkinabè artists and helped divest themselves of an inferiority complex in relation to other music and artists. The web portal, Tackborsé TV, is an emanation of this newfound pride (https://www.tackborse.tv). Tackborsé TV is a web media created in 2007 by a young Burkinabè living in the United States which, according to its sponsors, is dedicated to the promotion of the culture of Burkina Faso. Indeed, whether it is music, dance, cinema or Burkinabè fashion, Tackborsé TV makes a point of honoring all these cultural forms through its self-promotion as 'the official cultural portal from Burkina Faso.' The term 'Tackborsé' or 'Takborsé' has become a brand for this sense of national pride.

Bibliography

Kaboré, Auguste Ferdinand, and Kaboré, Oger. 2004. *Histoire de la musique moderne du Burkina Faso: Genèse, évolution et perspectives* [A History of Modern Music in Burkina Faso: Genesis, Evolution and Perspectives]. Ouagadougou: EDIPAP International.

Smockey. 2018. Interview with first author, February.

Somé, Batamaka. 2012. 'An Emulating Beat: The Takiboronse Effect in Burkina Faso Popular Culture.' In *Music, Performance and African Identities*, eds. Toyin Falola and Tyler Fleming. London: Routledge, 62–77.

Tougouma, Jean Philippe. 2007. 'Production artistique: Exit le "Takiborsé "?' [Artistic Production: Exit 'Takiboronsé'?]. Online at: http://lefaso.net/spip.php?page=impression&id_article=18349 (accessed November 2017).

Discographical References

Le Gouvernement. 'Bouge.' Abazon. *2005*: Burkina Faso.
Le Pouvoir. 'Faire le Malin.' Adonis Production. *2005*: France.
Smani, Hamed. 'Zalissa.' *Zalissa*. *2005*: Burkina Faso.

Discography

La Cour Suprême. *To Djakala*. ETK Production. *2005*: Burkina Faso.
Le Pouvoir. *Le Retour*. Senghor Distribution. *2007*: Burkina Faso.
Les Premières Dames. *Les Premières dames*. Jovial Productions. *N.d.*: Burkina Faso.
Smockey. 'Tout le monde sur la Steupi !' Odéon 7243 8 87162 2. *1999*: France.

YouTube

Hamed Smani. 'Zalissa.' France. 2015: https://www.youtube.com/watch?v=92K2OWqx3uM (accessed 9 November 2017).
La Cour Suprême. 'Le Verdict.' 2012: https://www.youtube.com/watch?v=B9MrMyC8tOg&list=RDB9MrMyC8tOg&t=275 (accessed 15 May 2018).
Le Gouvernement. 'Bouge.' Burkina Faso. 2012. Tackborsé TV: https://www.youtube.com/watch?v=TTrm5xESGeM (acccessed 7 March 2018).
Le Pouvoir. 'Le Malin.' France. 2008: https://www.youtube.com/watch?v=UBrSoB1mlRk (accessed 9 November 2017).

Website

Tackborsé TV: https://www.tackborse.tv (accessed 9 November 2017)

Interview (with first author)

Smockey, February 2018.

CHRISTOPHE HIEN WITH JOHN SHEPHERD
(translated by André Loiselle with John Shepherd)

Tchinkoume

Tchinkoume is a genre of traditional drumming, singing and dancing that originated in Mahi country, north of Abomey in the south central area of the Republic of Benin. The city of Savalou is the center of *tchinkoume* practice, but the style has been popularized in Abomey and Cotonou as well. *Tchinkoume* was originally a ceremonial genre for funerals in the Mahi court, but, according to oral tradition, the Mahi noble Alokpon was taken captive in a war with Abomey during the reign of King Kpengla (1775–89). Alokpon is said to have established the practice of *tchinkoume* in Abomey, alongside other royal ceremonial genres such as *zenli*. *Tchinkoume* remains a style with symbolic weight that is summoned in local contexts, mostly for funeral celebrations. It has been modernized and recorded with electronic instruments by later twentieth-century artists such as Stan Tohon, who created Tchink System, and le Roi Alokpon (Anatole Houndeffo), a singer from Savalou who took his stage name from the eighteenth-century Mahi noble.

Like early versions of *zenli*, the *tchinkoume* ensemble is composed of the *sinhun* ('water drum'), which consists of two calabashes of different sizes turned over in pails of water and struck with sticks; *assan* (shakers); three or four double *gan* (iron bells), assembled and played as a set (*batterie*); the large gourd *gota*, similar to the gourd played for *zenli*; and the *kpete*, or traditional flute. The *kpete* sets *tchinkoume* apart from other genres in Abomey and southern Benin, and it summons associations of the Mahi country just to the north. The flute plays a high, repeating set of five or six tones. *Tchinkoume* ensembles also include a lead vocalist, choir, dancers and wooden clappers, which double the bell pattern. The similarities with *zenli* instrumentation reveal a common ancestral root in Allada and Adja-Tado, the kingdoms of the south that preceded the establishment of Abomey and Savalou prior to 1600. The *gota* was the Mahi version of the *kpezin* drum, which was difficult to construct in the hills of Savalou because of the scarcity of clay.

The general division of labor assigns men as instrumentalists and women to the choir. Both men and women dance *tchinkoume,* linking their quick pelvic and shoulder snaps with the ensemble's fastest underlying rhythms. Men's *tchinkoume* dance styles are especially dynamic, and may involve gymnastic poses and jumps, often by two or three people together. Dress for *tchinkoume* performances is typically traditional, with men and women wearing matching, brightly patterned outfits in local prints. The lead singer usually wears kingly apparel, such as a royal hat, robes and a curved staff over his shoulder. The most well-known *tchinkoume* artists are able to make a living through their performances, but the majority of singers performing at funerals around Savalou and Abomey also have other professions.

Tchinkoume singers perform mostly in the Mahi language, which practitioners see as necessary for achieving the appropriate vocal style and intonation. Topics center around the intersection of traditional proverbs and local politics. Very good *tchinkoume* singers are often hired to sing at funerals for the purpose of poetically praising the dignified departed and his or her family members. Vocal melodies are improvised and pentatonically based. They typically fit closely with the tonal structure of the lyrics.

Le Roi Alokpon (Houndefo Anatole) from Savalou began recording *tchinkoume* in the late 1960s and became the most widely recognized singer within the local market in Benin, earning him the title of the 'king of Tchinkoume.' He focused on recording the most acoustic sound possible from the *tchinkoume* ensemble, especially the deep sound of the *gota*, which functions as the group's bass-drum. He died in 2013.

In 1978 the recording artist Stan Tohon, from Abomey, created his project Tchink System, a group that developed a modern, funky, electric version of *tchinkoume*. Tohon focused the sound especially on the *sinhun* and all of its possible permutations in recording effects and loops. He also added electric guitar and keyboard to his recordings, and dressed in stylish Western clothes when he performed and sang in Fon, not Mahi, the language of the style's origin, addressing his 'Tchink System' to a more southern and urban Beninois audience. Tohon, among other Beninois musicians, appreciated the connections between *tchinkoume* and the African-American funk they heard from James Brown, and channeled it into Benin's own version of Afrobeat. Tohon began working in hip-hop and reggae production in Europe in the 1980s and 1990s, applying his *sinhun* sounds to other diasporic genres.

Tchinkoume is best known among audiences in twenty-first-century Benin through the work of the late Roi Alokpon and the singer Gbezawe in Abomey, and other similar artists who perform at the funerals of notable figures. It carries associations of royalty, along with the dignified joy expressed in funeral contexts. Compared to *tchinkoume* performed in local contexts with traditional instruments and singers, the modernized Tchink System has had less staying power with local Beninois audiences. With the death of Alokpon in 2013, speculation began about who might become his successor. His son Yalekpon responded with the release of his first album, *Azagoun Loko Vi*. *Tchinkoume* is a living tradition with a vibrant future ahead.

Bibliography

Médiohouan, Guy Ossito. 1993. 'Vodun et littérature au Bénin' [*Vodun* and Literature in Benin]. *Canadian Journal of African Studies* 27(2): 245–58.

Discographical Reference

Yalekpon. *Azagoun Loko Vi*. Gangan Productions. *2016*: Benin.

Discography

Alokpon. *Ali Ma Yi Se Gon*. Les Echos Sonores du Dahomey. *1970*: Benin.
Alokpon. *Roi du Gotta*. Akiyo & Fils. *1980*: Nigeria.
Tohon, Stanislas. *Yallow*. SATEL 100. *1977*: Benin.
Tohon, Stanislas. *Stanislas Tohon dans le Tchink System*. Editions Les Vedettes ⊢ EV 001. *1979*: Benin.
Tohon, Stanislas, and The Tchink System. *Tchink Attack*. CRC Éditions (Blue Silver). *1994*: France.

SARAH POLITZ

Tigrinya Music

Tigrinya music (*tigrigna*) is the popular music of the Tigrinya-speaking people of Eritrea and of Ethiopia's northern region of Tigray. Although the term 'Tigrinya music' may also be used to refer to the traditional music of the Tigrinya people, since the 1960s it has increasingly been used to designate modern popular music, while folkloric music and music that emphasizes traditional elements is referred to as *bahlawi* ('cultural') Tigrinya. Modern Tigrinya music emerged in the late-1950s and 1960s and, having undergone significant changes during the following decades, is still very popular in the 2010s. Because the Tigrinya constitute about half of Eritrea's population and play a dominant role in the political and cultural life of the country, Tigrinya music occupies a prominent position in the popular music landscape of Eritrea. The same may be said for Ethiopia's Tigray region, where the Tigrinya constitute over 95 percent of the population. As such, Tigrinya music is both the main popular music genre of Eritrea and a regional subgenre of Ethiopian popular music. During Eritrea's 30-year-long struggle for independence from Ethiopian rule (1961–91), Tigrinya popular music was also an important vehicle for asserting Eritrean nationalism against foreign occupation, and the first decades of the genre's history were significantly affected by the unfolding of the armed struggle.

History

Tigrinya popular music emerged as the result of the encounter, in urban contexts, between traditional Tigrinya secular music and the modernizing forces affecting Eritrea and the Tigray region in the postwar era. Eritrea was an Italian colony from 1889 to 1941, and during this period the Italians introduced Western music and instruments into the country, mainly through their military bands. However, Tigrinya popular music started to emerge only in the 1950s when, after a decade of British administration, Eritrea became an autonomous province of the Ethiopian federation. In a similar way to what was happening in Ethiopia's capital Addis Ababa, foreign genres such as jazz and rock 'n' roll gained popularity among the urban youth. The first modern bands and dance ensembles were started in the cities of Asmara and Massawa by local garrisons of the Ethiopian Police and Imperial Body Guard, as well as by groups of Italian expatriates. It was, however, within a number of artists' associations promoting national theater and music that a truly Tigrinya modern music started to emerge. The most important of these groups was the Mahber Theatre Asmara (Asmara Theatre Association), mostly known by its acronym: MaTA.

MaTA was founded in 1961 as an association of independent performing artists, and although it also organized small theatrical productions, its name became mostly associated with the modern music ensemble it hosted. The MaTA ensemble included Western instruments such as accordion, guitar, drum kit, and brass and woodwind instruments, and it was the first independent band to employ said instrumentation to perform Tigrinya music, as part of a repertoire which also included Amharic, European and Sudanese songs as well as music from other Eritrean nationalities. Many well-known exponents of the first period of Tigrinya modern music started their careers at MaTA. Tewelde Redda, a founding member of the association, acted as guitar player, composer and music entrepreneur, and is credited by many as the first Eritrean electric guitarist. Other musicians of MaTA's early years were *krar* player Ateweberhan Segid, accordion and keyboard player Asres Tessemma, and singers Osman Abdulrahim and Alamin Abdeletif. One of Eritrea's most beloved female singers, Tiberih Tesfahuney, also began her career at MaTA.

In 1962 Haile Selassie I revoked Eritrea's autonomous status and unilaterally annexed it to Ethiopia. This new situation made MaTA's role in promoting Tigrinya identity through music all the more important, even though the patriotic character of some songs had to remain covert because all public activities were under close scrutiny for anti-Ethiopian propaganda. Despite these constraints, MaTA's success with local audiences led in the mid-1960s to the opening of the eponymous club in Asmara. As in many other cities around the world, this was a period of exciting modernization, particularly for the younger generations, and music was no exception. In the 1960s and early 1970s several music clubs opened in the cities of Asmara and Massawa, where dance bands performed a mixed repertoire of Eritrean, Ethiopian and Western popular music. The influence on local popular music of US genres such as jazz, rock 'n' roll and rhythm and blues was also facilitated by the radio broadcasts of the US military base of Kagnew, located just outside Asmara. The music broadcast by Radio Kagnew became so popular among the local youth that those new foreign genres were often simply defined as 'Kagnew music.' The early 1970s saw the emergence of several new bands, such as the Rockets, the Flames, the Jaguars and the Zeray Deres Band, all clearly influenced by 'Kagnew music.' Other Tigrinya musicians decided to pursue their career in Addis Ababa rather than Asmara. Possibly because of their proximity to Kagnew, Tigrinya musicians were considered particularly modern and innovative in Addis's thriving music scene, and many of them played a crucial role in the musical revolution that was sweeping the Ethiopian capital in the late 1960s and early 1970s.

In 1974, with the overthrow of Haile Selassie I and the rise of the Derg military junta in Ethiopia, the struggle for Eritrean independence increased in intensity, as did the military repression from Addis Ababa. Throughout the 1970s many popular Tigrinya performers joined the armed resistance led by the ELF (Eritrean Liberation Front), the EPLF (Eritrean People's Liberation Front) and the TPLF (Tigrayan People's Liberation Front). Among their ranks were Tigrinya musical icons from the 1960s such as singer and *krar* player Tsehaytu Beraki, singers Tiberih Tesfahuney and Bereket Mengisteab and guitarist Tewelde Redda. Younger performers who gained prominence in the 1970s also joined the struggle, most notably singer Yemane Barya. Throughout the 1970s and 1980s, song lyrics became increasingly nationalistic, as the various liberation groups used music as an instrument of active propaganda. Eventually, several musicians involved in the struggle left the country and settled abroad.

In 1991 the Eritrean pro-independence guerrillas defeated the Ethiopian army and entered Addis Ababa. In 1993 Eritrea became formally independent, and several artists who had left the country during the 1970s and 1980s returned home. After the mid-1990s, however, a new generation of Tigrinya singers and musicians came to the fore, expanding the ranks of Tigrinya national musical icons. Among the most popular are singers Helen Meles and Elsa Kidane, as well as Abraham Afewerki, a beloved musical innovator, singer and instrumentalist who passed away prematurely in 2006.

Musical Description

Tigrinya music almost always includes vocals, which are sung in the Tigrinya language. Song lyrics encompass the usual subject matter of popular music, such as romantic love, autobiography and social commentary. However, because the history of Tigrinya music is inextricably linked to Eritrea's struggle for independence from Ethiopia, patriotic and pro-independence lyrics have been common in the country's popular music, at least until Eritrea's liberation in 1991. Due to close scrutiny by the Ethiopian censors, nationalist and political messages were usually disguised through metaphor and allusion, but this did not prevent several songs from being censored by the Ethiopian authorities. Some commentators (Mesfin 2006) argue that – even after independence – Eritrean music is still very much centered around nationalist sentiments, to the detriment of other subject matter.

Singers are the central and most recognized performers in Tigrinya music. Singing is generally led by a solo voice, although antiphonal call-and-response vocals are not uncommon, especially in the climactic finale of a song. The style of solo singing is often melismatic, and since the 2000s the use of Auto-tune software to process a singer's voice has become very popular.

One of the main features distinguishing modern Tigrinya music from its traditional version is the use of Western instruments. Starting from the 1950s and more commonly in the 1960s music ensembles began incorporating brass and woodwind instruments, a drum kit, electric guitar and bass guitar, and in some instances an accordion or electric organ. Since the 1980s keyboards and drum machines have come to replace some if not all of these instruments. Whereas the drum machine usually replaces live drum playing, keyboards and synthesizers are used both to produce new sounds and to replicate the sound of 'real' instruments, for example that of a brass section. In addition to Western instruments, Tigrinya music may also employs traditional instruments, most notably the *krar*, a six-stringed lyre with metal strings that is usually strummed (as opposed to the Ethiopian *krar*, which normally has five nylon/gut strings and is plucked). Also, the *kabaro* drum may be found in popular music ensembles, in addition to or instead of a modern drum kit or drum machine. Handclapping is another common feature of Tigrinya music, and usually handclaps stress the main accents of a song's rhythm. With the diffusion of electronic instruments, handclaps are also increasingly reproduced with drum machines.

Although Western functional harmony is used more and more in Tigrinya modern music, the main elements of the genre remain lyrical content, melody and rhythm, as is the case with most Tigrinya traditional music. Most songs are modal – in the sense that they are based on a single central pitch and do not modulate – and the melodic material is mostly pentatonic.

Tigrinya songs employ several different rhythms. The most common by far, and considered the 'trademark' Tigrinya beat, derives from Tigrinya folk music and is based on a repeated rhythmic cell in 6/8 in which the main accent – usually provided by a drum in conjunction with handclapping – falls at the beginning of the cycle:

Example 1: *Tigrinya rhythm*

This rhythm is usually altered for the final section of the song, in what is normally called 'doubling' ('*dereb*'). One more accent/handclap is added to the rhythmic pattern, thus increasing the cross-rhythmic tension of the song's finale:

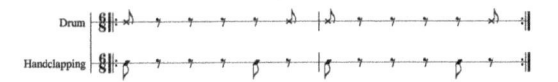

Example 2: *Tigrinya rhythm (final song section)*

Slower songs, usually played by a solo singer with instrumental accompaniment but no percussion, are characterized by looser rhythms with different cycle lengths. Finally, Tigrinya popular music may also employ rhythms that are borrowed either from neighboring styles (e.g., Tigre music), or from Western popular music (the latter practice being increasingly common since the 1990s).

Guayla

Tigrinya *guayla* (which translates as 'dance' or 'party') is a subgenre of Tigrinya music whose main function is to accompany dancers. It is a traditional style of Tigrinya music and dance that has successfully crossed over to the modern/popular music landscape. Tigrinya music and *guayla* are thus overlapping categories, with *guayla* indicating the faster, dance-oriented Tigrinya music played at parties and celebrations such as weddings. *Guayla* music normally employs the characteristic Tigrinya beat with its 'doubled' finale and, during the first part of a song, a group of dancers form a circle and slowly move along its circumference following the main accents provided by the drums and handclapping. During this stage the dancers do not interact much with each other. When, toward the end of the song, the rhythmic 'doubling' starts, the dance becomes faster. The dancers stop moving in a circle and face each other, dancing more vigorously and shaking and twisting their shoulders. In this stage, the women dancers may also punctuate the music with high-pitched ululations. In modern performance settings, *guayla* can be either *bahlawi* ('cultural') or *zemenawi* ('modern'), mostly depending on whether a real *kabaro* drum or a drum machine are used.

Conclusion

Tigrinya music is Eritrea's most widespread popular music genre, and as such it is a useful lens through which to look at the history of the region. Born when Eritrea was still a province under Ethiopian sovereignty, it has been an essential tool in defining Tigrinya – and by extension Eritrean – identity during the struggle against the powerful Ethiopian neighbor. Twenty years after the end of the armed struggle, in the 2010s, Tigrinya popular music is still an important arena in which the younger generations that have come of age after independence negotiate their values and identities between past, present and future.

Bibliography

Falceto, Francis. 1999. Liner notes to *Éthiopiques 5: Tigrigna Music 1970–1975*. Buda Musique 82965-2. 1999: France.

Kimberlin, Cynthia Tse. 2006. '"Who Dared?": Twenty-two Təgrəñña Songs From Mändäfära, Eritrea.' In *Proceedings of the XVth International Conference of Ethiopian Studies, Hamburg 2003*, ed. Siegbert Uhlig. Wiesbaden: Harrassowitz Verlag, 446–68.

Mesfin, Dawit. 2006. 'Eritrea: Songs of the Patriots.' In *The Rough Guide to World Music: Africa & Middle East*, ed. Simon Broughton et al. London: Rough Guides, 103–7.

Teffera, Timkehet. 2005. 'Music, Making Music and Dancing: Ethnomusicological Observations in Mekele/Tigray.' *Guandu Music Journal* 3: 126–47.

Discography

Beraki, Tsehaytu. *Selam.* Terp Records AS-072004. *2004*: Netherlands.

Éthiopiques 5: Tigrigna Music 1970–1975 (ed. Francis Falceto). Buda Musique 82965-2. *1999*: France.

MICHELE BANAL

Township Pop, see Bubblegum

Tsaba Tsaba

Tsaba tsaba is an urban dance music of black South Africans that emerged in the 1930s and came to the attention of the wider world in 1954 following US radio broadcasts of 'Skokiaan,' and the tune's immediate release under a new title as 'Happy Africa.' With its infectious bouncy rhythm and catchy saxophone-led melodic phrases, 'Skokiaan' had been composed by saxophonist August Musarurwa from neighboring Southern Rhodesia and recorded with his African Band of the Cold Storage Commission of Southern Rhodesia for the Gallo label in 1947. In a routine international marketing exercise the single had been sent over by an unimpressed Gallo manager in Johannesburg to his American counterparts, with a disparaging note on which he had written: 'See if anything can be done with this. I think it's awful' (quoted in Ballantine 2012, 139). Surprisingly, however, 'Skokiaan,' now renamed 'Happy Africa,' became an instant hit, with US sales of the single quickly topping the 250,000 mark and subsequent publication as sheet music in more than 17 countries worldwide. The tune's other remarkable achievements included 'coverage' by many international groups and musicians, among them Louis Armstrong, and topping the US Hit Parade in 1954. A few years later in 1960 'Satchmo' traveled to Rhodesia (today's Zimbabwe) to meet the originator of the song that had captivated his, and the world's, imagination. Over the decades rearrangements of the original song were recorded by countless musicians, including South Africans Hugh Masekela, Nico Carstens, Sam Sklair, Spokes Mashiyane, Ntemi Piliso's African Jazz Pioneers and the Soweto String Quartet – who all rerecorded the song under its original title 'Skokiaan.'

An alumni of the Rhodesian British South African Police Band (formed in 1939), August Musarurwa was a musically literate saxophonist who had gone on to become one of Zimbabwe's most highly respected composers and jazz saxophonists. On leaving the Police Band in 1947 he formed a Bulawayo-based band and in the same year recorded 'Skokiaan' for Johannesburg-based Gallo Records (GB.1152.T). Initially issued in Gallotone label's broad 'Jive' category, 'Skokiaan' appeared on Side B of the 78-rpm disc with the subtitle 'Tsaba Tsaba Dance' (http://www.45worlds.com/78rpm/record/gb1152t&c=66764#66764). On the label of the 1947 recording, August Musarurwa (wrongly spelled as Msarurgwa) is listed as leader of the African Dance Band of the Cold Storage Commission of Southern Rhodesia. Later reissues of the tune (e.g., on Decca [UK] F10350) credited the recording ensemble as Bulawayo Sweet Rhythms Band, a name by which Musarurwa's band was also known. The changed details significantly erase the original band's migrant status in Johannesburg. The origins of 'Skokiaan' were regionally attributed to 'Bulawayo,' while the music production industry category was changed from that of [South African] 'jive' to 'Shona Dance' – Shona being the inclusive identity of several Zimbabwean ethnic groups. Besides the structural similarity of 'Skokiaan' to early *marabi*-swing dance music, its unchanged official subcategorization points to the tune's links to *tsaba tsaba*, a fashionable dance that was popular among black South Africans in the late 1930s.

The South African Roots of *Tsaba Tsaba* Dance

'Tsaba tsaba' is a derivative of the verb 'tsaba,' the essential meaning of which is shared among several southern Bantu dialects (in Sesotho, *tshaba*; in sePedi, *tsāba*; and in isiNguni, *saba*), meaning to be 'scared,' 'afraid' or 'fearful.' Grammatically, the verbal repetition denotes a diminutive form of the verb root '-tsaba,' indicating in this case 'half-afraid,' 'half-scared' or 'half-frightened.' In the prevailing cultural adaptive contexts *tsaba tsaba* is understood as a response to behavioral censorship and gendered paternal dominance in practices of both Christian and traditional African morality. Eyewitness accounts of *tsaba tsaba* as a black South African social dance all concur with the following description:

> A male and a female danced towards each other, shaking the knees in what is sometimes described as a 'rubber-legged' style; pelvic movement was also

emphasised in addition to footwork. Just before the couple made contact, a shout of the word 'Tsaba!' was given and they danced backwards to their starting points. (Mensa 1971, 128)

As both a dance- and swing jazz-influenced popular music *tsaba tsaba* is a ramification of similar historical processes of modernity which articulate to Southern Africa's shared ethnic origins, colonialism, industrialization, economic labor migrancy and the region's social cultures of urbanization. Prior to its appropriation as a global sound of post–World War II popular music and jazz, *tsaba tsaba* emerged in the 1930s as a dance craze of black South Africans. An urban social dance, *tsaba tsaba* symbolically enacted the identification by middle-class African youth with the subversive resistance of *marabi* proletarian culture and its music. Initially, *tsaba tsaba* was the subject of an uncharacteristic consensus between elite, Christian and indigenous cultural values, and was broadly vilified as contributing to the moral breakdown of African society. However, by the beginning of the 1940s the dance had gained acceptance by the most vociferous critics of black urban social culture. Leading African cultural commentators in local print media – among whom were literate musicians, composers and civic entertainment innovators – came to regard *tsaba tsaba* as a cultural achievement of New Africanism and an indigenous response comparable to influential Harlem social dance fashions such as La Conga, the Big Apple, the Shag and others.

The Dance Music Origins of *Tsaba Tsaba*

Tsaba tsaba is rooted in the cultural condition of the African urban working class and its social performance innovations. In the early decades of the twentieth century it was an informal musical entertainment for adolescents, who performed to the accompaniment of singing and handclapping provided by onlookers. The origins of *tsaba tsaba* are historically attributed to Sophiatown (the suburb of Johannesburg demolished during apartheid, under the Natives Resettlement of 1954), which is still celebrated for its uniquely diverse musical performance practices and vibrant social entertainment culture. In this context, the adult *marabi* social occasions and youthful *tsaba tsaba* dances were closely related and significantly coeval as adaptive cultural practices of working-class urbanizing Africans.

By the late 1930s *tsaba tsaba* had inspired compositions of dance music by swing-influenced vaudeville and early South African jazz orchestras. Among the first such dance bands to popularize *tsaba tsaba* in recordings were Motsieloa's Pitch Black Follies, Zuluboy and his Jazz Maniacs, and Wilfred Sentso. Wilfred Sentso was a jazz musician, composer, vaudeville troupe leader, educationist and black music rights activist who initiated the earliest formations of music unionism in South Africa. Among his many achievements was the founding of several vaudeville troupes, including the Synco Down Beats Orchestra and Synco Fans. In the mid-1930s Sentso established the Wilfred Sentso School of Modern Piano Syncopation, a performing arts academy in Johannesburg's Orlando township. Within five years of its establishment the school was claiming among its alumni talented musicians who were members of prominent music formations or had become celebrated performing artists in their own right. The performing arts school's programs also included the publishing of sheet music. Although composed by Wilfred Sentso, the celebrated 'Tsaba-Tsaba Baby' was, like the majority of *marabi* melodies, orally transmitted and thereby found its way into popular repertoires of *marabi*-style swing-influenced dance bands. Besides Wilfred Sentso's well-trained groups, the best-known were Solomon 'Zuluboy' Cele's Jazz Maniacs, Griffiths Motsieloa's Pitch Black Follies, Peter Rezant's Merry Blackbirds, Nimrod Makhanya's Bantu Glee Singers, Snowy Hadebe and Company, Sonny Groenewald's Jazz Revellers Band, William Mseleku's Amanzimtoti Players and John Mavimbela and Company.

Tsaba Tsaba Dance Music and *Marabi*-Swing Influence in 'Skokiaan'

Two tracks, recorded in 1939 by two different bands, bear direct references to *tsaba tsaba* in their titles. 'Tsaba Tsaba ke No.1' (Tsaba Tsaba is No. 1) was recorded by (Griffiths) Motsieloa's Pitch Black Follies for Gallo Pty Ltd and issued under its Singer (GE) catalogue, and in the same year 'Tsaba Tsaba' was recorded by Zuluboy and his Jazz Maniacs and issued by Gallo Music Publishers under its Better catalogue's XU series. Considered to be fine examples of the fusion of US big-band swing with *marabi*, both recordings are remarkable in their inclusion of choral voices in their arrangements. 'Tsaba Tsaba ke No.1' celebrated the *tsaba tsaba* dance and also included exclamations of the name 'Highbricks!' – a popular pianist in Johannesburg of the *marabi* era. The lyrics of 'Tsaba Tsaba,' in which a male singer laments his condition of migrant itinerancy, the loneliness of which only a lover would relieve, are comparable to those of a blues. Both tunes are built on a repeating *marabi* harmonic pattern, which typically employs roots I IV (I or I6/4) V of the western European diatonic scale. Regarded as the prototype *tsaba tsaba* dance tune, August Musarurwa's 'Skokiaan' has a duple-time meter and a four-bar form based on a cyclic harmonic progression indistinguishable from that of *marabi*. In his later compositions Musarurwa went on to consolidate the South African influence of 'jive' and 'tsaba tsaba' in a style that closely resembled 'Skokiaan' in form and harmonic structure.

The close resemblances between South African *marabi*-influenced jazz and 'Skokiaan' went far beyond metrical, harmonic and orchestrational musical elements, with both idioms mirroring similar sociopolitical, economic and contested power subjectivism of their African innovators. The kind of African jazz referred to as 'jive' in Gallo's South African recordings was popularly referred to as *tsava tsava* in Zimbabwe. Just as *marabi* was an outlawed proletarian socioeconomic entertainment institution of urban black South Africa, so was *tsava tsava* associated with the working class in Zimbabwe, where equivalent social dance occasions were known as 'tea parties.' In both *marabi* and 'tea-parties' were sold illicit home-brewed alcohol, which patrons imbibed as they danced to harmonically cyclic *marabi* and *tsava tsava* music, respectively.

Popular music narratives and historical music studies acknowledge the importation of *tsaba tsaba* into Zimbabwe by migrants returning home from the more industrialized metropolises of the Reef mining towns and elsewhere in South Africa. In the late 2010s the legacies of such influential exchanges are largely deposited with the polyglot popular dance music of contemporary Zimbabwe, contestably and collectively referred to as *jit* or *jiti*, originally spearheaded by both liberation struggle and post-liberation struggle era musicians, among them Thomas Mapfumo. Oliver Mutukudzi, Bhundu Boys and many others.

Bibliography

Abrahams, Randall. 2003. *Spinning Around: The South African Music Industry in Transition*. Cape Town: HSRC Publishers.

Allen, Lara. 2005. 'Circuits of Recognition and Desire in the Evolution of Black South African Popular Music: The Career of the Penny Whistle.' *SAMUS: South African Journal of Musicology* 25(1): 31–51.

Ansell, Gwen. 2005. *Soweto Blues: Jazz, Popular Music, and Politics in South Africa*. New York: Continuum.

Ballantine, Christopher John. 2012 [1993]. *Marabi Nights: Jazz, 'Race' and Society in Early Apartheid South Africa*. 2nd ed., Pietermaritzburg: University of KwaZulu-Natal Press. (1st ed. published as *Marabi Nights: Early South African Jazz and Vaudeville*. Johannesburg: Ravan Press, 1993).

Chikowero, Mhoze. 2015. *African Music, Power, and Being in Colonial Zimbabwe*. Bloomington: Indiana University Press.

Coplan, David B. 2008. *In Township Tonight! South Africa's Black City Music and Theatre*. 2nd ed. Chicago: University of Chicago Press.

Mensa, Atta Annan. 1971/2. 'Jazz – the Round Trip.' *Jazz Forschung /Jazz Research* 3(4): 124–37.

Turino, Thomas. 2000. *Nationalists, Cosmopolitans, and Popular Music in Zimbabwe*. Chicago: University of Chicago Press.

Zindi, Fred. 1985. *Roots Rocking in Zimbabwe*. Gweru, Zimbabwe: Mambo Press.

Discographical References

African Dance Band of the Cold Storage Commission of Southern Rhodesia (leader August Musarurwa). 'Karekwangu'/'Skokiaan.' Gallotone GB.1152. *1947*: South Africa.

Armstrong, Louis. 'Skokiaan,' Parts 1 and 2. Decca 9-29256. *1954*: USA.

Bulawayo Sweet Rhythms Band. 'Skokiaan'/'In the Mood.' Decca F10350. *1954*: UK.

Motsieloa's Pitch Black Follies. 'Tsaba Tsaba ke No.1.' Gallo. *1939*: South Africa. (Reissued in accompanying CD to Ballantine 2012.)

Zuluboy and His Jazz Maniacs. 'Tsaba Tsaba.' Gallo. *1939*: South Africa. (Reissued in accompanying CD to Ballantine 2012.)

Discography

Alpert, Herb, and Masekela, Hugh. 'Skokiaan.' *Herb Alpert/Hugh Masekela*. A&M SP-728. *1978*: USA.

Cogan, Alma. *Skokiaan*. (E.P.) La Voz de Su Amo 7EML28.093. *1955*: Spain.

Four Lads, The. 'Skokiaan'/'Why Should I Love You?' (45 rpm single.) Columbia 4-40306. *1954*: USA.

Graves, Josh. 'Skokiaan.' *Alone at Last*. Epic KE 33168 *1974*: USA.

Marterie, Ralph, and His Orchestra. 'Skokiaan'/'Crazy 'Bout Lollipop.' (45 rpm single.) Mercury 70432X45. *1954*: USA.

Prado, Perez, and His Orchestra. 'Skokiaan'/'The High and the Mighty.' (45 rpm single.) RCA Victor 47-5839. *1954*: USA.

Websites

45worlds: http://www.45worlds.com/

South African Music Archive Project: http://samap.ukzn.ac.za

SAZI DLAMINI

Tsapiky

Tsapiky (sometimes *tsapika* and generally pronounced tsa-PEEK) is a genre of electric guitar-driven popular music that developed in southwest Madagascar beginning in the late 1970s and early 1980s. This is communal, celebratory music, not explicitly tied to any local ethnic group. Just the same, in the late twentieth and early twenty-first centuries *tsapiky* has become a cultural music of deep significance, particularly in the region's rural villages. This amplified, modern music has largely supplanted older traditional genres as the soundtrack for funeral ceremonies and gatherings. Rituals surrounding death and veneration of ancestors are central to traditional Malagasy social life – somewhat like weddings in many other parts of the world. In southwest Madagascar, a funeral is the principle time when neighbors gather and distant relatives travel to be together. A funeral ceremony typically lasts three days and nights, with food, drink, exchanges of gifts and non-stop music and dancing. As the dominant music style for these occasions, *tsapiky* has become an emblematic cultural feature of this large, arid, mineral-rich region of Madagascar.

Tsapiky coalesced from at least three preexisting musical influences. First, there were traditional village folk songs composed and sung among the Bara, Tsimihety, Vezo, Makoa and other local ethnic groups. Malagasy people all speak essentially one language, and their division into distinct ethnic groups is somewhat arbitrary, in part a convenient construction of French colonists. However, groups do adhere to characteristic customs, lifestyles, taboos and professions, such as cattle herding among the Bara, and fishing among the Vezo. These village songs are typically accompanied by handmade box-lutes known as *kabosy* or mandolins. They may also be played on accordion, a common instrument in many forms in Madagascar. Before the rise of *tsapiky*, these songs often unfolded in the fast 12/8, 6/8 or ternary rhythm that typifies most traditional music around the island.

A second influence on early *tsapiky* is the music of the large box-zither known as the *marovany*. This instrument is often used in *tromba*, spirit possession ceremonies. The instrument is strung on opposite faces of a rectangular box, and the player uses two hands to pick on both sides simultaneously. The music's complex rhythmic cycles and distinctive phrasing have strongly influenced local guitar players, and so found their way into the textures of *tsapiky*.

The third crucial element in prefiguring *tsapiky* is popular music from South Africa. Tulear, the capital city in this region, and much of the south-west Malagasy coast, is within reception range of South African radio stations. In the 1960s and 1970s South African *mbaqanga*, *maskanda*, sax jive and other styles became popular and influential in this region. Some of this music also made it onto Madagascar's own national airwaves, but its impact in the Tulear region was significantly greater – to the point where local artists and groups began performing songs in South Africa's strongly pronounced 4/4 (binary) time signature, often using simple I-IV-V chord progressions. One South African artist, Lulu Masilela, became so popular in Madagascar that people in the Tulear region came to refer to South African popular music generally as 'Lulu music.'

These elements first coalesced in a local style known as *pecto*, named for a strong-flavored candy. Important guitar-playing musicians, notably Bloko and Kaboto, achieved regional fame in the 1970s, a time when Tulear was on the rise economically.

Madagascar has known a long-standing tension between the more politically powerful ethnic groups of the central highlands and the marginalized ones of the coastal regions. So there was a distinct element of local pride in the new sound.

It is unclear exactly when *pecto* became *tsapiky*. Even the word *tsapiky* has no exact translation. Some musicians relate it to the movement of a local bird, imitated by dancers to *tsapiky* music. Others link the word to the French phrase 'ça pique,' meaning 'it stings' like a wasp or a mosquito. There is no consensus on the word's meaning or origin. However, it is clear that the music's lack of ethnic identity allowed it to appeal across sometimes fraught identity lines, and this helps explain its rapid rise in regional popularity.

Though some recordings of *pecto* music were made, it was mostly as *tsapiky* that this music began to be documented and widely disseminated on cassettes and later videos sold on VHS tape and shown on local television. A system emerged in which producers in Tulear recorded and filmed *tsapiky* bands and contracted them out to the countryside to play at ceremonies. Most of the musicians came from rural villages, so these producers in Tulear became middlemen in a growing grassroots music economy. Musicians worked hard and were paid poorly, but at least they were working. Competition among the groups drove professionalism, as groups quickly became stronger, tighter and more inventive in order to get more and better contracts.

Tsapiky songs revolve around short, cycling fingerpicked guitar riffs. There is a distinctive stop-and-dash quality to the phrasing, and phrases repeat with successive variations, some arranged, some improvised. The classic *tsapiky* band is led by and named after a single electric guitarist whose riffing signals the arrangement of a song. The group also includes a bass player whose pumping lines, often reminiscent of those heard in South African *mbaqanga*, interact with the guitar lines, a drummer and two or more singers and dancers. Currently, groups may also use keyboards, though in addition to, not in place of, the guitar. At a ceremony, songs run long. At intervals, the drummer will signal a stop, after which the band revs into a higher gear, jumping in at a faster tempo and with more intensity. This faster section is called the *kilatsaky*, meaning literally 'to fall.' This is similar to the *seben* section of a Congolese pop song – a concluding segment in which freewheeling guitar playing and cries and chants from a singer or MC (*animateur*) encourage the dancers and celebrants. As for the dancing, it is stylized, though not strictly prescribed. Common moves include a fluttering of extended arms – like a bird – and, importantly, carefully isolated rotation of the buttocks, a move known as *kinikike*.

Tsapiky lyrics are neither narrative- nor message-oriented. They tend to unfold, like the guitar playing, in short bursts. Sometimes the words simply egg on the crowd, but they can make references to the concerns of daily life, including serious issues: famine, drought, prostitution and the current scourge of this region, organized cattle rustling, which has created security risks in the countryside, and greatly complicated the logistics of organizing ceremonies.

Tsapiky has produced a succession of popular bands, generally named for their guitarist/leader: Jean Noel, Alexis, Damily, Teta. One singer, the late Rasoa Kininike, achieved national fame when her recordings were released around Madagascar. But she is the exception. More typically, the most successful *tsapiky* guitarists seek fortunes outside the constrained dynamic of the Tulear-based scene. Teta moved to the capital Antananrivo and collaborated with jazz and other musicians, though he has now returned to Tulear to record his own hybrid of *tsapiky*, aimed at an international audience. Damily married a French wife and moved to France. He performs classic *tsapiky*, playing both electric and acoustic guitar. As of 2015 Damily was the only bona fide *tsapiky* musician/bandleader to bring this music to the international stage. Meanwhile, in south-west Madagascar, more and more *tsapiky* groups were operating out of remote villages, reducing the importance of Tulear in the regional *tsapiky* scene.

Bibliography

Damily. 2014. Interview with the author in Madagascar.

Mallet, Julien. 2009. *Le tsapiky, une jeune musique de Madagascar* [Tsapiky: A Young Music of Madagascar]. Paris: Karthala.

Mallet, Julien. 2014. Interview with the author in Madagascar.

Teta. 2014. Interview with the author in Madagascar.

Discography

Damily. *Ravinahitsy*. Helico, HWB 58004. *2007*: France.

Damily. *Ela Lia*. Helico, HWB 58120. *2009*: France.

Teta. *Fototse/Racines/Roots*. Buda Musique. 860214. *2012*: France.

Tsapiky: A Panorama from Tulear. Arion. RRN64661. *2004*: France.

Tulear Never Sleeps. Sterns Africa. STEW49CD. *2003*: UK.

BANNING EYRE

Tuareg Guitar Music

Tuareg (or Kel Tamasheq, 'Speakers of Tamasheq') are traditionally seminomadic people who inhabit the Sahara and Sahel desert regions of Niger, Mali, Algeria, Libya and Burkina Faso. A diasporic community of Tuareg exiles from Mali and Niger migrated to Algeria and Libya beginning in the 1960s, where they developed a new style of guitar music as a means for community building and political protest. Their songs became popular among the wider Tuareg community in the 1990s through the clandestine circulation of cassette recordings promoting armed resistance in Mali and Niger. By the late 1990s peace accords allowed for public performances, shifting the genre's main messages away from resistance to other topics of interest to Tuareg. Since the early 2000s Tuareg guitar music has gained recognition worldwide through touring bands and tourism in the Sahara. On account of the diverse linguistic and political contexts in which Tuareg guitar music has circulated, it is known by several names, including *ishumar*, *tishumaren*, Tuareg blues and simply 'guitar.'

Emergence and Early Circulation in the Sahara

Drought, conflict with government military forces, state policies antagonistic to marginalized nomadic populations, and increasing reliance on a wage-labor economy led many Tuareg in Mali and Niger, mostly young men, to migrate to cities in southern Algeria and Libya beginning in the late 1960s. Their mobility usually involved crossing borders illegally and without official identity papers. In new urban contexts, these *ishumar* (a term likely adapted from the French *chômeur*, 'unemployed person') established diasporic enclaves and broke with the traditionally hierarchical structure of Tuareg society, developing new forms of social solidarity in support of each other's pursuits of housing, employment and financial aid.

In Tamanrasset, Algeria, the *ishumar* community organized around festive occasions known as *zahuten*, which were often held in private residences or outside of town to avoid confrontation with local authorities. These gatherings featured *tende*, a Tuareg drumming and singing tradition performed primarily by women; poetry and songs accompanied by *anzad*, the Tuareg monochord fiddle played exclusively by women; and they were accompanied by informal choruses of men and women. Often, the plastic jerrycans that serve as water vessels in the region replaced the traditional *tende* drum, which is constructed from a mortar; among children these containers were also converted into *guitares-bidons* (can guitars). The new performance settings reformulated aspects of rural traditions but also introduced novel poetic forms and themes relating to the emerging *ishumar* lifestyle. One of the important early singers and hosts of *zahuten* was Lalla Badi, a Tuareg woman whose songs were recorded on cassette and shared with those who could not attend.

By the late 1970s these practices, as well as men's poetic composition (*assak*), were synthesized in a new guitar form that was primarily performed by *ishumar* men. The earliest figureheads of the emerging guitar music in Tamanrasset were Ibrahim ag Alhabib and Inteyeden ag Ablil, both originally from Mali. Together with several other *ishumar* in the area, these musicians formed the group Taghreft Tinariwen ('Reconstruct the Deserts,' later shortened to Tinariwen), which became the most important force for popularizing *ishumar* guitar music in the Sahara and, later, worldwide. Accompanied by a jerrycan drum and women who would sing call-and-response phrases, the early guitarists drew inspiration from an eclectic array of regional and international musical styles, including the *takamba* dance popularized by *agiwwin* (griots) from Timbuktu, star Malian guitarists (e.g., Ali Farka Touré, Kar Kar [Boubacar Traoré]), Sahrawi guitar songs of the Polisario Front in Western Sahara, *raï* and *chaabi* music from the Maghreb and artists with global popularity such as Jimi Hendrix, Dire Straits and Bob Marley.

The early *ishumar* songs were ruminations on the experiences of *ishumar*, frequently referencing hunger, thirst and the soul; foremost among their

545

themes was *essuf*, the nostalgia and isolation one encounters in the uninhabited desert. Cultural autonomy, language preservation and protest became similarly important topics due to the marginalization of Tuareg in Saharan nations. As increasing numbers of *ishumar* men sought military training during the 1980s, particularly in Libya, their songs took on an increasingly militant nature; in fact, most *ishumar* guitarists at this time were not regarded as professional musicians but as militants. They began promoting values of endurance, bravery and sacrifice, and advocated revolutionary projects based on the concept *toumast* ('Tuareg people' or 'nation'), aspiring to unite Tuareg in ways circumventing their traditional social structure.

The messages of these songs became of primary importance; on cassette recordings circulated and duplicated among *ishumar* throughout the Sahara, song texts were frequently recited before being performed so that their meaning was clear. Because of the subversive nature of these songs, public performances and cassette recordings of *ishumar* guitar music were outlawed in Algeria, Mali and Niger. Yet, *ishumar* ideologies and guitar music continued to circulate clandestinely, particularly through the work of Tinariwen and, in Niger, the group Takrist-n-Akal led by Abdallah ag Oumbadougou. In the early 1990s the simmering tension among *ishumar* led them to undertake major armed rebellions against the governments of Mali and Niger as they sought to improve Tuareg political self-determination.

Post-Rebellion Developments and Global Recognition

Peace accords in Niger (1995) and Mali (1996) brought some resolution to the rebellions. As one condition of post-rebellion reconciliation, which saw a new emphasis on regional semi-autonomy and privatized development in Niger and Mali, public performance of Tuareg guitar music was not only permitted by these states but integrated into political life. Where guitarists sang of resistance before, since the peace accords they increasingly valorize reconciliation, democracy and dialogue among Tuareg and multiethnic national communities, while retaining an interest in revitalizing Tuareg culture and language. They are often hired to perform for political rallies and nongovernmental organizations, or are sent by Saharan governments on tours promoting peace. Guitar groups also regularly participate in youth festivities that in preceding decades had featured only *anzad* and *tende*. In all of these cases, professional ensembles have emerged among Tuareg where professional music-making was traditionally regarded with ambivalence. Guitarists are not just former *ishumar* but may be from any number of social backgrounds, although many hail from the elite stratum of traditional Tuareg society known as *imajeghen*. The popularity of the style is not limited to Tuareg alone, and it has been adapted by members of other ethnic groups and in multiethnic bands (e.g., Etran Finatawa).

The release of one of the earliest albums of this music available outside Africa, Tinariwen's *The Radio Tisdas Sessions* (2001), introduced European, North American and other global listeners to the blues- and rock-inflected sounds of Tuareg guitar, to the mythic narratives of *ishumar* engaged in rebellion and to contemporary Tuareg concerns. Several groups have formed among the Tuareg diaspora in Europe, particularly in France, while others have formed in refugee camps where many Tuareg fled during conflict and drought since the 1990s (e.g., Tartit). International tours by Tuareg bands and the production of albums by both major and independent record labels, which tap into world music as well as indie rock listener bases, attract large audiences worldwide today. For example, the cult following for Tuareg guitar supported a US-based crowdfunding campaign to produce *Akounak Tedalat Taha Tazoughai* ('Rain the Color of Blue with a Little Red in It,' 2015), an adaptation of the film *Purple Rain* (1984, starring the US artist Prince) set in Agadez, Niger; mainstream support was evidenced when Tinariwen won the 2012 Grammy Award for Best World Music Album with *Tassili*.

This large international audience provides Tuareg with a venue for garnering support for their political aspirations and to attract travelers to the Sahara, where festivals (e.g., the Festival in the Desert), desert treks and other opportunities support cultural tourism, one of the major avenues for economic development among Tuareg. However, both tourism and the mobility of Tuareg musicians are restricted by recurring concerns about terrorism in the Sahara, and visa fees occasionally prove prohibitive for some performers. Nonetheless, contrary to being a passing fad (see Borel 2006), Tuareg guitar music continues to draw sustained interest from both Saharan and global audiences.

Musical Characteristics

At their most fundamental level, Tuareg guitar music performances feature a solo voice and an acoustic or electric guitar. More frequently, the music is performed in groups of three or more musicians and includes one or more rhythm guitars (and occasionally a bass guitar), which draw on *tende* rhythms and play drones and simple chords, sometimes in a style reminiscent of reggae. The lead guitarist often plays the lowest string with the thumb as a drone as well, likely an adaptation from the performance techniques of West African lutes. Frequently, the guitarists are accompanied by percussion. This usually takes the form of handclapping, tapping on an acoustic guitar or drumming on a *tende*, but it is not unusual to have accompaniment on drum kits (more common in Niger), calabash gourds or *djembes*.

Song melodies are usually strophic in form, pentatonic, and sung with minimal ornamentation, which differs from highly ornamented poetic traditions. These characteristics in particular lend much Tuareg guitar a 'bluesy' appeal for international listeners. A chorus, sometimes made up of spectators during community performances, will often sing responses to the solo singer. Song lyrics are almost always in Tamasheq, the Tuareg language, although French, Arabic and local indigenous languages may be mixed into the texts; occasionally songs will include rapping. The guitar is performed almost exclusively by men, which is remarkable given that women traditionally are held in great prestige in Tuareg musical practice. Although a few women guitarists do exist, when women participate in Tuareg guitar music it is generally by singing and clapping.

Bibliography

Amico, Marta. 2013. *La fabrique d'une 'musique touarègue': Un 'son du désert' au prisme de la* World Music [The Making of a 'Tuareg Music': A 'Desert Sound' in the Prism of World Music]. Unpublished Ph.D. thesis, L'Ecole des Hautes Etudes en Sciences Sociales (EHESS).

Belalimat, Nadia. 2003. 'Qui sait danser sur cette chanson, nous lui donnerons la cadence: Musique, poésie et politique chez les Touaregs' ['Whoever Can Dance to this Song, We Will Give Him the Rhythm': Music, Poetry and Politics among the Tuareg]. *Terrain* 41: 103–20.

Belalimat, Nadia. 2010. 'The *Ishumar* Guitar: Emergence, Circulation, and Evolution from Diasporic Performances to the World Scene,' trans. Anne Saint-Girons. In *Tuareg Society Within a Globalized World: Saharan Life in Transition*, eds. Anja Fischer and Ines Kohl. New York: I.B.Tauris, 155–70.

Borel, François. 2006. 'Tuareg Music: From Acoustic to Electric.' In *Art of Being Tuareg: Sahara Nomads in a Modern World*, eds. Thomas K. Seligman and Kristyne Loughran. Los Angeles: Iris and B. Gerald-Cantor Center for Visual Arts at Stanford University and UCLA Fowler Museum of Cultural History, 117–33.

Genthon, Anouck. 2012. *Musique touaregue: Du symbolisme politique à une singularisation esthétique* [Tuareg Music: From Political Symbolism to Aesthetic Distinction]. Paris: L'Harmattan.

Lecocq, Baz. 2010. *Disputed Desert: Decolonisation, Competing Nationalisms and Tuareg Rebellions in Northern Mali*. Boston, MA: Brill.

Rasmussen, Susan. 2000. 'Between Several Worlds: Images of Youth and Age in Tuareg Popular Performances.' *Anthropological Quarterly* 73(3): 133–44.

Rasmussen, Susan. 2005. 'A Temporary Diaspora: Contested Cultural Representations in Tuareg International Musical Performance.' *Anthropological Quarterly* 78(4): 793–826.

Rasmussen, Susan. 2006. 'Moving Beyond Protest in Tuareg *Ichumar* Musical Performance.' *Ethnohistory* 53(4): 633–55.

Discographical References

Tinariwen. *Tassili*. Anti- 87148. *2011*: USA.
Tinariwen. *The Radio Tisdas Sessions*. World Village 468010. *2001*: USA.

Discography

Desert Rebel, Vol. 1. Original Dub Master ODM07820. *2006*: France.

Etran Finatawa. *Introducing*. World Music Network LC11067. *2006*: UK.

Group Bombino. *Guitars from Agadez, Vol. 2*. Sublime Frequencies SF046. *2009*: USA.

Ishumar: Music of Tuareg Resistance. Reaktion TAP012. *2008*: France.

Ishumar 2: New Tuareg Guitars. Reaktion RE20. *2011*: France.

Tartit. *Ichichila*. Network 36.584. *2000*: Germany.

Tinariwen. *Amassakoul*. World Village 468026. *2004*: USA.

Filmography

Akounak Tedalat Taha Tazoughai, dir. Christopher Kirkley. 2015. 75 mins. USA. Drama/ Feature film. Original music by Mdou Moctar.

Festival in the Desert, dir. Lionel Brouet. 2004. 64 mins. USA. Documentary.

Purple Rain, dir. Albert Magnoli. 1984. 111 mins. USA. Feature film. Original music by Prince.

The Last Song Before the War, dir. Kiley Kraskouskas. 2014. 74 mins. USA. Documentary.

ERIC J. SCHMIDT

Tufo

Tufo is one of the most popular musical song and dance styles of coastal communities in northern Mozambique. It is a soft, lyrical vocal music sung by groups of women and accompanied by four tuned frame drums. The interweaving rhythms of the *tufo* drums and the accompanying rising and falling movement of the dancers are said by many Mozambican *tufo* singers and dancers to reflect the undulating waves and ripples of the Indian Ocean, which is at the heart of their music and their culture. An original version of *tufo* is thought to have been brought to the northern coast of Mozambique by Arab traders as early as 900 AD, while its present form dates back to the 1930s. The vocal lines, lyrics and rhythm draw on the diverse cultural influences of the region, fusing the Bantu and Sufi traditions of the Swahili Coast. Loved and respected throughout Mozambique for its delicate sensuality, *tufo* song and dance combines the nation's relationship with the sea, its pride in its rich cultural history and the legendary beauty and strength of its women.

It is said that when the Portuguese explorer Vasco da Gama first landed on Mozambique Island (*Ilha de Moçambique*) in 1498 he was greeted by four boats 'under sail and oar, with people *tangendo e cantando* [loosely, swaying and singing]' (Joao de Barros, *Primeira écada da Ásia*, Book IV, cited in Lutero and Pereira 1980, 20). More than 400 years have passed between this recorded event and the formation of contemporary *tufo* groups during the re-Islamization of the region in the early 1930s. Oral history tells of a trader called Iussufe who came from Quíloa (var. Kilwa), an area of Tanzania founded in the tenth century AD whose power, at its height in the eleventh century, stretched along the Swahili coast. Iussufe is said to have spent long periods of time on Mozambique Island in the 1920s and 1930s, continuing to visit until the 1970s (Lutero and Pereira 1980, 20). It is thought that Iussufe was behind the formation of some of the older *tufo* groups on Mozambique Island such as Estrela Vermelha, the oldest *tufo* group still active there, having been formed in 1931 (Arnfred 2011, 281). Estrela Vermelha was previously named Mahafil Islam; the group changed its name following Mozambican Independence in 1976 and the new secular communist rule of the liberation front FRELIMO (Frente de Libertação de Moçambique).

Originally *tufo* was performed by men, in particular at Maulid to celebrate the birthday of Prophet Mohammed. The name *tufo* originates from the Arabic name for the frame drum known as the *daf* or *duff*. The Portuguese colonizers of Mozambique pronounced this 'adufe' or 'adufo,' which the Emakhua speakers of northern Mozambique then transformed to 'tufo' (Lutero and Pereira 1980, 19). Women's dances and songs similar to *tufo* may be found across the Arab world. They are often associated with the Prophet Mohammed's arrival in Medina, where he was greeted in the streets by girls singing and playing the *duff* (Doubleday 1999). Such performances may be found throughout coastal East Africa, and *tufo* singing and dancing still forms an essential part of Maulid celebrations among the Islamic coastal communities of Mozambique. However, the male *tufo* groups were eclipsed by the women's ensembles, whose songs and dances are popular both at Islamic celebrations and festivities and during secular occasions.

Although *tufo* has become increasingly secularized, the clothes worn by the women still reflect the Islamic values of women's piety and the modesty of the genre's early beginnings. The women dress in matching brightly colored *capulanas* (printed cloth worn by women across Mozambique) covering their heads and stretching down to their ankles. The men dress in a matching color scheme, their heads also covered with woven or embroidered *kofios* (Islamic skull caps). *Tufo* women nevertheless take pride in the subtle sensual movements of the dance and in their physical beauty, famously treating their skin with a ground tree bark called *msiro*, which is a traditional beauty mask worn during performances. The women kneel or stand in rows, swaying, rocking and gesturing to the lyrics with graceful arm movements. Over time, more energetic and playful Bantu dance styles such as *nzope* have been fused with the synchronized dance movements of traditional *tufo*, and room has been made for individual flair and fun. *Tufo* groups often also include *nzope* song and dance in their repertoire, singing and dancing like children with skipping ropes and cane sticks.

New women's *tufo* groups continue to form across the country. The practices of mutual support and community benefit of the Islamic *tariqas* (known in Mozambique as *confrarias*) upon which they were founded stretch beyond the more visible practices of the songs, dances and colored cloths that identify them with all aspects of the women's lives. They are, in fact, just one aspect of complex familial and neighborhood networks, connected like children and grandchildren to the founding 'mother' groups in Mozambique Island and Angoche (two of the earliest Arab trading centers on the East Coast of Africa), and they contribute to maintaining and strengthening the position of women in northern Mozambique. Through them, women learn skills, not only in singing, drumming, dancing and songwriting, but also in social organization. Large social events known as *carramas* are planned and managed by the members, some of whom are illiterate and many of whom are single mothers in varying degrees of financial difficulty. At the *carramas*, sister groups come together and sing and dance through the night, often competing with one another for the best dances, costumes, vocals and compositions. This competitive element of *tufo* performances is also reminiscent of Swahili traditions of the Beni and Lelemama singing and dancing societies found across East Africa. Signe Arnfred argues that this is as much a sign of secularization of *tufo* as it is a sign of the increasing importance of women in the genre and a reflection of how the traditional matrilineal social structure of northern Mozambique has been absorbed into the Islamic hierarchies of the region (Arnfred 2011, 277–90). The African Muslims in northern Mozambique stem largely from two Sufi Tariqas, Qadiriya and Shadhilya, who were flexible in their incorporation of Bantu traditions into their practices. Men still play an important part in *tufo* organization and performance, however, and while in the 1950s the women drummers of the female *tufo* groups were reported to play 'to perfection' (Borba and Lopes Graça 1962, 33–4) it is common in the early twenty-first century to find men making up the rhythm section of many *tufo* groups and still holding important roles both within the administrative structures and as composers.

Musical and Lyrical Characteristics

The Arabic origins of *tufo* songs may be heard in the melismatic melodies, which float on the lilting rhythm of the four frame drums, like the *dhows* (square-sailed sailing boats typical of the Swahili coast) that first carried this music to Africa on the waves of the Indian Ocean. The melodic lines are normally introduced by two vocalists in canon form. The vocal leader introduces the melody, followed by the second vocalist, who takes the phrase and often adds a small variation before she settles on a harmony to complete the phrase. These melodies are taken up by a chorus of between 10 and 20 women, who, guided by the drums, build the intensity and pace of the song to an often fast and ecstatic conclusion. The women's powerful vocal style enables their voices to carry not only over the increasing volume of the drums, but also across distances, reminding many listeners of the nautical origins of the music, sung on boats in the open water. The rhythm is provided by four tuned frame drums, with goat, sheep or cow hide stretched over matching round, hexagonal or square wooden frames of different sizes. The larger of the four, known as the *bazuca*, works in partnership with the second largest, the *ngajiza*, to set the rhythmic foundation of the songs and determine the speed. The two smaller drums, the *apústua* and *duassi*, provide a polyrhythmic counterpoint with sharp slaps and light patters that increase in speed, volume and intensity, becoming more prominent as the song builds. The relationship between the two pairs of drums reflects the fusion between *tufo*'s Arabic and African origins.

The core patterns played by the larger two drums resonate with the genre's Arabic roots, while the syncopation and improvised dialogue of the *apústua* and *duassi* have their origins in the Bantu culture of the Mozambican host (Lutero and Pereira 1980, 20).

Over the decades of social transformation in Mozambique, *tufo* groups have, rather pragmatically, accepted the role of transmitting the various messages of government and nongovernmental institutions in their songs, while also maintaining their connection to the past with the older Islamic repertoire. The religious songs are normally sung in seated rows with restrained upper body movements, and they are still generally sung in Arabic. Satirical and humorous secular songs reflecting daily life are generally sung in the local Bantu languages, of which Emakhua is the most widely spoken in the region. These are more likely to be sung standing with more physical movement, as are the songs for official dignitaries or foreigners, which are more often sung in the country's official language of Portuguese. In a single public performance such as those during national and regional holiday celebrations, rather militaristic songs reminiscent of the revolutionary hymns of the 1970s may still be heard alongside songs promoting condom use for the prevention of HIV and mosquito nets for the prevention of malaria. These may be mixed with songs that are sung in the local languages of the region (Emakhuwa-Emoniga, Ekoti or KiSwahili) and intended for more local audiences. Among *tufo* groups, there has been a tradition of including political comment and protest in the lyrics of the songs; sometimes the message is still hidden from Portuguese-speaking outsiders by singing in the local language.

Conclusion

The varied social functions of the *tufo* groups and their music reflect the breadth and importance of the role of *tufo* groups for many men and women in the towns and villages of coastal Mozambique and across the country. One of Mozambique's most valued music genres, *tufo* is not only considered beautiful to hear and watch but it also plays a social role in the lives of women in the groups, helping them find their voice, learn skills, socialize with one another and provide each another with emotional and material support wherever in the country they may have settled.

Bibliography

Arnfred, Signe. 2011. *Sexuality and Gender Politics in Mozambique: Rethinking Gender in Africa*. Oxford: James Currey.

Borba, Tomas, and Lopes Graça, Fernando. 1962. *Dicionário da música* [Dictionary of Music]. Lisbon: Edições Cosmos.

Doubleday, Veronica. 1999. 'The Frame Drum in the Middle East: Women, Musical Instruments and Power.' *Ethnomusicology* 43(1): 101–34.

Durán, Lucy. 2005. 'Tufo Song and Ghorwane.' BBC radio broadcast. Online at: http://www.bbc.co.uk/programmes/p005xkvq (accessed 6 February 2018).

Lutero, Martinho, and Martins, Pereira. 1980. 'A influência Àrabe na música tradiçional' [The Arab Influence on Traditional Music]. In *Música tradiçional em Moçambique* [Traditional Music in Mozambique], ed. Paolo R. Soares. Maputo: Gabinet de Organização do festival da canção e música tradicional, Ministério da Educação e Cultura, 18–31.

Discography

Associacao a Luta Continua. 'Onhipiti Ossanta Toniyo.' *Mozambique* (Vol. 2). Globestyle CDORBD 087 DVORBD 086. *1994*: UK.

Grupo Beira Mar. 'Unabadera Uhema.' *Mozambique* (Vol. 1). Globestyle CDORBD 087 DVORBD 086. *1994*: UK.

Grupo Estrela Vermelha De Bairro Carrupeia, Nampula. 'Mocambicano.' *Mozambique* (Vol. 2). Globestyle CDORBD 087 DVORBD 086. *1994*: UK.

Grupo Estrela Vermelha De Bairro Carrupeia, Nampula. 'Unabadera Uhema' *Mozambique* (Vol. 1). Globestyle CDORBD 087 DVORBD 086. *1994*: UK.

Grupo Estrela Vermelha Do Ilha De Moçambique. 'Enhipiti Equissirua.' *Mozambique* (Vol. 1). Globestyle CDORBD 087 DVORBD 086. *1994*: UK.

Grupo Estrela Vermelha Do Ilha De Moçambique. 'Enhipiti Kahi Yankhani.' *Mozambique* (Vol. 2). Globestyle CDORBD 087 DVORBD 086. *1994*: UK.

Mozambique (Vols 1 and 2). Globestyle CDORBD 087 DVORBD 086. *1994*: UK.

KAREN BOSWALL

Umbholoho

Umbholoho is a lively, secular genre of unaccompanied vocal music with step dance movements performed by male ensembles in Swaziland. Closely related to the South African Zulu genre *isicathamiya*, *umbholoho* is also referred to by the English word 'bombing' or '*ingom' ebusuku*' ('song of the night'). It is performed by a handful of contemporary adult ensembles countrywide, as well as by a growing number of youth groups attached to schools.

Swaziland is a small, landlocked country bordering South Africa and Mozambique. With a population of approximately 1.2 million people, many citizens live in and around the two largest urban hubs, Mbabane (the national capital) and Manzini. Beyond the central urban areas, numerous smaller towns have grown up around key industries including the sugar plantations of Simunya and the logging and paper mills of Mhlabanyatsi and Bhunya. It is in these towns, where large numbers of men congregate for industrial labor, that *umbholoho* ensembles have historically existed.

From the early twentieth century Swaziland acted as a labor reservoir for South African industry and, through this relationship, many cultural practices were shared and exchanged across the porous national borders. It is believed that *umbholoho* as a musical practice came to Swaziland from South Africa in the early 1930s (Malinga 2014).

Veit Erlmann traces the term 'boloha' or 'umbholoho' to Xhosa or Afrikaans terms for 'polka.' Within Zulu *isicathamiya*, 'umbholoho,' 'amaleki' and 'boloha' were terms that historically referred to a style of wedding song performed in a straight line from the 1930s onward (Erlmann 1996, 53–4). Vusabantu Ngema's writing on Zulu dance forms cites *umbholoho* as a type of communal wedding dance, along with *ukgqumushela* and *isigekle* (Ngema 2007, 40, 46). Influenced by these musical practices in the hostels of the mining areas surrounding Johannesburg, groups of *umbholoho* singers started up in Swazi towns such as Siteki, Lavumisa and Bhunya, often in areas where large industries existed.

Since 2009 this musical style has been best known in its interpretations by contemporary ensembles such as the Bhunya Bombers (who performed at Swaziland's major annual musical festival 'Bushfire' in this same year), Sibane Semaswati (also based in Bhunya), and two performing ensembles based at the Manzini City Council and the University of Swaziland Kwaluseni campus respectively (Malinga 2014). *Umbholoho* music is sung in the national Swazi language, Siswati, and performed in groups of 15 to 20 performers. *Umbholoho* singers dress in formal uniforms and are led by a conductor or lead singer (sometimes known as *maskanda*) (Nkabinde 1997, 75). Competitions are a common occurrence within this tradition, where groups perform and are judged by musical and choreographic criteria (how uniformly and how well movements and gestures are performed in the group), as well as visual appeal, costumes and neatness. Competitions are coordinated by local judges who have been trained by South African specialists, and competing ensembles must adhere to strict regulations to be considered.

Besides competitions, 'bombing' groups or *umbholoho* ensembles often perform alongside *sibhaca* dance troupes at community events and conventions and before national sports games. Active ensembles are organized through the Swaziland National Umbholoho Association (SNUA), headed in 2014 by Innocent Malinga. The Association has been in existence since 1999 and exists to bring a higher profile and further opportunities to *umbholoho* performers.

In terms of structure, *umbholoho* songs are created from four-part harmony (leader, alto, tenor, bass), with a distinctive leader or *maskanda* initiating call-and-response textures. This close harmony singing is accompanied by carefully choreographed hand gestures and stepping dance movements (known as *istep*) (Dlamini 1998). These gestures are initiated and sometimes improvised by the leader. In *umbholoho*, the preferred harmonies are triadic (often revolving around I, IV and V chords). A soft vibrato (especially in the leader's calls) is distinctive of the genre. The leader will often call out a short phrase which is answered by a substantially longer choral response, above which the leader can improvise. The ensemble can also set up repeated sung structures on vocables that form a rhythmic basis upon which the leader can improvise lyrics above in a higher register. Song lyrics tell stories local to the area, recount tales of love with underlying moral messages or deal with community matters. Like other Siswati language songs, the lyrics are often poetic, with numerous meanings operating simultaneously.

Umbholoho music is very similar to the *isicathamiya* choral music of well-known South African ensembles such as Ladysmith Black Mambazo, the King Star Brothers and the African Music Bombers of northern KwaZulu-Natal. Differences between the genres can be seen, however, in lyrical content and local references. *Umbholoho* songs often have an underlying moral commentary but they recount Swazi stories and local events in the Siswati language. The Swaziland National Umbholoho Association claims this musical tradition requires more national support, but with choirs starting in schools and tertiary educational facilities, the audience for *umbholoho* continues to grow slowly. That said, there are no commercially available recordings of *umbholoho* ensembles and so this tradition lives on solely in live performance. In terms of research into both musical and social aspects of the genre, *umbholoho* remains undeveloped in the late 2010s.

Bibliography

Dlamini, Sazi. 1998. 'Township Music: The Performance and Compositional Approaches of Three Neotraditional Musicians in Durban.' Unpublished Masters thesis, University of KwaZulu-Natal, Durban, South Africa.

Erlmann, Veit. 1996. *Nightsong: Performance, Power, and Practice in South Africa*. Chicago: University of Chicago Press.

Malinga, Innocent. Interview with the author, 19 September 2014.

Ngema, Vusabantu. 2007. 'Symbolism and Implications in the Zulu Dance Forms: Notions of Composition, Performance and Appreciation of Dance among the Zulu.' Unpublished Masters thesis, University of Zululand, Richards Bay, South Africa.

Nkabinde, Thulasizwe. 1997. 'Indigenous Features Inherent in African Popular Music of South Africa.' Unpublished Masters thesis, University of Zululand, Richards Bay, South Africa.

CARA L. STACEY

Uukorasa

The term *uukorasa* (Oshindonga) or *oukorasa* (Oshikwanyama) originated in northern Namibia among Aawambo and Kavango people. *Uukorasa* (sing. *okakorasa*; the term was adapted from the English 'choruses') are multipart group songs performed with rhythmic movements (*okwiinyenga*) in a call-and-response form. As a popular youth genre innately tied to the Christian religion, these songs function as a medium through which questions about identity, society and politics may be articulated. Even though indigenous musical expressions differ widely across the region, these choruses are remarkably similar throughout Namibia, whatever the language be. Hence, such songs are variously called *!khoǂuisa !obodas* in Khoekhoe, *konsertliedjies* or *aksieliedjies* in Afrikaans lingua franca and they also lie at the root of *oviritje*. They are also referred to as 'hitsongs' by practitioners, providing an indication of their popularity.

Historical Outline

The history of *uukorasa* traces the bilateral musical influences of European missionaries and indigenous Namibian musical traditions. When choral music in the form of hymns was introduced by missionaries in the mid-nineteenth century, it spread throughout the region and was widely adopted by church congregations. Precolonial vocal music in north-central Namibia had been sung by men and women separately, mostly in harmonies of parallel thirds. Following the missionary influence, however, men and women began to sing together in the new hymnal genre. Hymns were even sung at home or while performing daily chores. Aawambo men, for instance, began to sing hymns while traveling, thus partly replacing the traditional *uupongo* or loneliness songs of previous times (Löytty 2012). The typical hymnal homophony and homorhythm slowly became embedded in the aural imagination of the people. But although men and women began to perform these hymns together, the singing retained its African roots – mainly in descending bends of long notes and anticipation of beats. During the 1960s, as the struggle for independence began to take hold, the texts of *uukorasa* were influenced by anti-apartheid sentiments, leading to the inclusion of praises and hopes for the better future of all.

Through initiatives of a new Student Christian Movement founded in 1967, increased contact between Namibian, South African, Botswanan, Zimbabwean and Angolan chapters occurred, contributing to the exchange and sharing of song styles. The nature of the SCM meetings and the shared political values provided a framework for freedom songs during the anti-apartheid struggle in the 1970s, with political contents continuing into the present. Young people took their inspiration from popular culture, blending indigenous traditions with Western genres. Thus, the chorus style of the *makwaya* (originating in South Africa with elements of American spirituals, ragtime and gospel, blended with the rhythms of *vastrap* and the *riel* dances of Griqwa, Boer and Malay people) took root readily and flourished in Namibian churches, schools and community organizations. According to Veikko Munyika (in an interview with Sakari Löytty [Löytty 2012]), *uukorasa* were initially sung in IsiZulu or IsiXhosa, but soon Namibians started composing songs in their own vernaculars. This also applies to *!khoǂuisa !obodas* in the central region, where performers often did not know what the borrowed texts meant, but had learned the songs by ear at interparish song competitions or when meeting with other congregations.

Many of the songs reflect the birth of spiritual revival among young people who wanted to express their cultural as well as spiritual feelings through song and dance. Their popular nature, joyously expressed in the rhythmic dance movements, combined with a new need to rehearse, led to the songs being performed at schools, homes and other meeting places. Since performances even took place at shebeen bars in northern Namibia, and at social gatherings in central regions, the apparent dissociation between church and secular spaces, as well as the happy and light melodies, initially drew the criticism of missionaries. They expressed fear that serious hymnal melodies might be used in the 'moondances' of local people. A concerned missionary, Saari, claimed that the lighter 'English and Salvation Army kind of religious songs' were used in such contexts (Löytty 2012, 61). Yet it was exactly the easy acceptance of these songs, this embedded dialogue between indigenous traditions and modernity, that contributed to the genre moving comfortably between religious and secular spaces.

Namibia gained its independence in 1990, and since that time these choruses have become very popular with formal choirs, as they easily cross racial and ethnic boundaries. Thus, *uukorasa* are now performed at many international venues and competitions by choirs such as the National Youth Choir, the College of the Arts Youth Choir, University of Namibia Choir, Mascato Youth Choir, Gabriel Taapopi Secondary School Choir and others. These formal choirs therefore provide the only recordings of the genre, although many less formal video clips may be found on YouTube. This does not negate the fact that *uukorasa* are performed mainly by self-initiated groups on entry to church meetings and school halls – in public and personal spaces – across the country.

Musical Characteristics

Uukorasa are sung in multipart arrangements by groups of young women and men to lively tempos. They begin with a compelling rhythmic foot or arm movement without voices, or with a short solo vocal introduction or call. The response may be a repetition of the call pattern or a shorter repetitive phrase. Songs may also be introduced with a slow, hymn-like passage without accompanying physical movements. Then the more up-tempo arm and foot movements begin. The music is largely homophonic and homorhythmic, based on the primary chords I, IV and V. Melodies typically consist of short phrases with repeating lyrics, set to a catchy rhythm. Often one of the voice groups (soprano, alto, tenor or bass) initiates the call, which is then taken up by another voice part, until all the parts have sung it. When this happens, call parts may be matched by a solo or group dance, taken up in turn as the song progresses. In other words, while tenors, for example, sing the solo part, they are also responsible for a solo or group movement sequence. New songs are generally composed by one (or more) of the performers, who selects a spiritually uplifting phrase and creates the melody around that.

Performance Modes and Spaces

For performance, chorus groups perform dressed in some kind of matching outfit or color, so as to be distinguishable. They set themselves up in lines, women normally in front and men at the rear. Performed as a kind of dancing procession, led by either women or men, the songs are sung to lead a group into the church (after which singing stops) or onto a stage. Similar processions are also popular at weddings. Movements are well synchronized and typically consist of foot brushes along the floor to create a swishing sound, sideway steps and small stamps, forward and backward steps, hand claps, arm swings from side to side, half-turns and so on. Articulation between upper and lower body is enhanced by shoulder- and hip-swinging actions. Movements tend to be symmetrically repeated on both sides and in sets of two or four times the sequence. During performance the short songs are repeated as many times as desired, but may also be cut short by a speaker or on reaching the procession destination, where it simply peters out.

Song Texts

Words and messages are significant in these songs (Löytty 2012; Haugh 2014). The texts often make use of verses from the Bible, but typically contain words of general encouragement, praise and strength (this was especially true during the armed struggle in the 1960s to 1980s). For example, a Khoekhoe-language song in the central part of the country praises a local spiritual leader, Hosea/Narib. The lyrics begin with a call of 'O Nanajo' (meaningless syllables) and each call is repeated by the four-part chorus, as follows: 'O Nanajo, O /Nariroba, O Priester /Nariroba, O Silwerstroom [the farm where they work] O Nanajo.' Sometimes songs are even used to support the topics of discussion in meetings, where they serve as interludes between speeches, so that people may stretch and refresh themselves (Löytty 2012, 87). As popular avenues of expression, songs travel significant distances in terms of language and space. For example, an *okakorasa* text in RuKwangali (a Kavango language) documented by the author at a secondary school in 1993 simply goes: 'Sikama medina lya Jesus' (Stand up in the Name of Jesus). The exact same song in the Khoekhoe language was documented by the author in the same year in the central region, 1,000 kilometers south.

Cultural Significance

According to Avorgbedor (2004, 270), church music and popular music exist in a dialectical relationship, 'a creative space for the common interchange and negotiation of musical ideas.' *Uukorasa* represent this discourse on culture, nation, identity and religion, and, according to Haugh (2014), the construction of a Christian and Namibian identity by praising the nation, yet discussing problematic issues. Haugh's description of the genre in the context of the Roman Catholic Church in Namibia reveals the performative nature of nationalism, wherein singing and song both reflect and shape the new nationalism.

Further, in the competitions that are undertaken between different parishes, young people have found a way through this genre of music to embrace popular culture as well as the traditional culture of play. Performance at church or competitions is generally preceded by rehearsals. Singers gather in schools, university lecture rooms or somebody's home. Movement sequences are carefully planned and choreographed, then memorized. New songs are created or passed on from a previous experience. Because of the collective form of creation and practice, *uukorasa* present a constantly evolving style and performance, mixing aspects of hymnody with popular dance moves.

An *okakorasa* is distinct from a 'song' (*eimbilo*) or hymn in the sense that *uukorasa* display a directed energy aimed at worthy, uplifting goals. Hence, !khoǂuisa !obodas are described as a welcome to the church, even though they are performed outside. The song 'Ada dti netse khat !gaia ha saob ikha,' for example, is a text prepared by a chorus group 'to approach the altar singing' (Namises 1999). The intention as well as style of *uukorasa* and !khoǂuisa !obodas are the same, despite being expressed in different languages and different regions.

Conclusion

As a widespread southern African complex of song, dance and worship, *uukorasa* (and other vernaculars of similar songs) play an important role in creating a Christian and national identity, and in preparing spiritually for worship in an enjoyable and rhythmic manner. They express relations to fundamental matters (social, religious and political) while creating an atmosphere of joy and participation.

Bibliography

Avorgbedor, Daniel Kodozo. 2004. 'Music: Musical Innovation in African Independent Churches.' In *African Folklore: An Encyclopedia*, eds. P.M. Peek and K. Yankah. New York: Routledge, 268–72.

Haugh, Wendy A. 2014. *Lyrical Nationalism in Post-Apartheid Namibia: Kings, Christians, and Cosmopolitans in Catholic Youth Songs*. Lanham: Lexington Books. Online at: https://books.google.co.za/books (accessed 23 November 2015).

Jordaan, Gerrit. 2013. 'Hymn Singing in Sesotho/Setswana/Sepedi Speaking Churches: A Process of

Claiming and Reclaiming.' *Muziki: Journal of Music Research in Africa* 10(2): 39–55.

Löytty, Sakari. 2012. *People's Church, People's Music: Contextualization of Liturgical Music in an African Church*. Helsinki: Sibelius Academy. Online at: https://helda.helsinki.fi/bitstream/handle/10138/235058/nbnfife201204183233.pdf?sequence=1 (accessed 17 September 2018).

Mans, Minette Elaine. 2000. 'Using Namibian Music/Dance Traditions as a Basis for Reforming Arts Education.' *International Journal of Education and the Arts* 1(3). Online at: http://ijea.asu.edu (accessed 23 November 2015).

Namises, Milka. 1999. Interview with the author. Khomas Region.

Discography

Damara Kau Odia. MP3 Download. Online at: onlymuzic.com/site_damara-kau-odia-album-songs.xhtml (accessed 3 October 2017).

YouTube

(all accessed 3 October 2017)

COTA Youth Choir at RIGA World Choir Games. 2014. Online at: https://www.youtube.com/watch?v=7DMipdBu06A.

Gabriel Taapopi Secondary School Choir, Oshana Region. Online at: https://www.youtube.com/watch?v=wkW-TGNYLJQ.

'Jesus om 'na Gwa Kalunga.' Track 4 on 'Namibian Images and Sound by National Youth.' Choir. Online at: http://www.awesometapes.com/national-youth-choir-of-namibia-namibian-images-sound/.

Western Youth Choir. 2012. Online at: https://www.youtube.com/watch?v=UHzVRs3w4Cs

MINETTE MANS

Wákà

Wákà is a neo-traditional Islamic-inspired Yorùbá genre popularized by women performers from Ijebu areas in the Ogun and Lagos States in southwestern Nigeria. Originally for use in Muslim ceremonies, it developed during the twentieth century into a genre with a broader audience performed by professionals and from the 1980s was incorporated into Nigerian society as a musical genre used for all occasions, including life rites, social functions and national functions. At the same time, it was internationalized through concert tours by some of its leading exponents.

Research suggests that the genre's origin and development were influenced by both the Hausa music of northern Nigeria and the Islamic *àsàlátù* genre. First, the word *wákà* can be traced to the word *wakar*, meaning song in the Hausa language, which, through the acceptance of Islam by Hausa-Fulani people, has its root in the Arabic language. Waterman (1999, 2000) and Jimba (1997) affirm that *wákà* originally evolved from Hausa music of northern Nigeria.

It has been argued by exponents of *wákà* that it evolved from Islamic socio-religious services and that, although *wákà* is practiced and popularized by musicians from the Ijebu area, it developed from the *àsàlátù* music practiced by Islamic women before it finally carved out its own identity. These women, it has been said, usually gather outside the mosque to rehearse songs laden with verses from the Qur'an, extolling the greatness of Allah, Mohammed his prophet and other notable religious personalities. Later, these songs incorporated themes built around social events and topical issues, giving them a wider appeal and attracting more patronage from various societies (*egbe*) in Ijebu-Igbo and its environs.

Wákà began life in the early nineteenth century as a vocal music style performed *a cappella* and continued in that way until *séélí* (small pairs of cymbals with jingles) were added in the 1920s (Waterman 2000, 172), By the 1940s drums and percussion had been added, and the vocal ensemble numbered five or six (ibid.). In its modern form it combines membranophones and idiophones. The major instruments include *séélí* (used until 1970), *agidigbo* (box piano), *bembe* (membrane drum), *gangan* (hourglass drum), *akuba* (membrane drum), *kannango* (membrane drums) and *sèkèrè* (rattles), which accompany the vocal part in call-and-response form. Modern acculturated instruments include guitar, keyboard, synthesizer, saxophones and trap drum. In Waterman's view, the presence of some new instruments, such as *agidigbo*, and the rhythmic patterns evident on recordings of the 1940s 'suggest the influence of *àpàlà*' (another Yorùbá genre linked to the same Ijebu group) (ibid.).

The dominant vocal performance styles include recitative, solo/responsorial, chain-song technique, vocal unison sometimes ending with cadential homophony and an elongation of theme through repetition of sections. Lyrics use quotations from the Qur'an and are performed using the Ijebu dialect and the central Yorùbá language.

The first commercial recordings of *wákà* were made in Lagos for the Odeon label by Majaro Acagba in the 1920s (e.g., 'Waka Orin Imale'/'Waka Kanpa' [Odeon A 248014]). The evolution of *wákà* in the modern era may be attributed specifically to the pioneering efforts of Batile Àlàké, who was the first to incorporate *séélí*, when she started her group in the 1950s. Àlàké (who died in 2013) was also the first to make a commercial *wákà* album. The major exponent since then has undoubtedly been Sàláwà Àbèní, who further popularized the genre by modernizing it and taking it around the world through musical tours, including (for example) London in 2001 and again in 2013. Since her debut recording, *Late General Murtala Ramat Mohammed* (dedicated to the then recently assassinated head of state), released on Leader Records in 1976, Àbèní has made over 80 albums. She was crowned the Queen of Wákà Music by the Aláàfin of Òyó, Ọba Làmídì Adéyemí III in 1992 at Adámásíngbà Stadium, Ìbàdàn, in recognition of her contribution to fostering traditional music through the *wákà* genre in Yorùbáland.

Others who have performed *wákà* music since the 1940s include Kuburatu Alaragbo, Mesitura Akanke, Folake Awoleye, Kokumo Serah (who performs *wákà* gospel, a type of *wákà* with religious texts played at Christian social gatherings), Muyidatu, Ogunfolu Amudatu, Apeke Abike Ola, Fatimuta Akingbade, Adetoun Abeke and others in Ijebu waterside areas of Ogun State, Epe and Ikorodu in Lagos State.

Bibliography

Àjàní, S. A. 1975. 'Wákà Songs in Yorùbáland.' Unpublished BA essay, Department of Linguistics and Nigerian Languages, University of Ìbàdàn.

Denselow, Robin. 2001. 'Queen Salawa Abeni.' *The Guardian*, 20 July. Online at: https://www.theguardian.com/culture/2001/jul/20/artsfeatures10 (accessed 30 May 2018).

Jimba, Moshood. 1997. *Ilorin Waka, a Literary, Islamic and Popular Art*. Ilorin: Taofiqullah.

Olusoji, Stephen O. 2005. 'Apala, Sakara and Waka as Entertainment Music.' *African Notes: Journal of the Institute of African Studies, University of Ibadan* 29(1/2): 98–112.

Olusoji, Stephen O. 2009. *Comparative Analysis of the Islam-Influenced Apala, Waka and Sakara Popular Music of the Yoruba*. Unpublished Ph.D. thesis, Institute of African Studies, University of Ibadan, Ibadan.

Waterman, Christopher A. 1999. *Jùjú: A Social History and Ethnography of an African Popular Music*. Chicago: University of Chicago Press.

Waterman, Christopher A. 2000. 'Yoruba Popular Music.' In *The Garland Handbook of African Music*, ed. Ruth M. Stone, 169–86.

Discographical References

Àbèní, Sàláwà. *Late General Murtala Ramat Mohammed*. Leader. Number unknown. *1976*: Nigeria.

Acagba, Majaro. 'Waka Orin Imale'/'Waka Kanpa.' Odeon A 248014, N.d. *(192–?)*: Nigeria.

Àlàké, Batile. *Batile Alake and Her Waka Group*. Star SREP 49. N.d. *(196–?)*: Nigeria.

Discography

Àbèní, Sàláwà. *Omi Yale*. Leader LRCLS 29. *1980*: Nigeria.

Àlàké, Batile. *The Waka Queen*. Subsaharan Trading SUB-7350-2. *1996*: USA.

Sheet Music

Olusoji, Stephen O., comp. 2010. *Nigerian Dances for Piano, Vol. 1*. Lagos, Nigeria: Right-Time Services Ltd.

YouTube

(accessed 30 May 2018).

Bàtílè Àlàké, 'Aje Onire': https://www.youtube.com/watch?v=ZedutGxrkAw

Bàtílè Àlàké and Her Waka Group: https://www.youtube.com/watch?v=mSmc9ZyqroA

Queen Sàláwà Àbèní & Her African Waka Modernisers, 'Jomi Jomi': https://www.youtube.com/watch?v=TDAf5LUyQEw

Sàláwà Àbèní, 'This Is Waka Music': https://www.youtube.com/watch?v=siDUkVLRk4M

STEPHEN OLUSOJI

Wassoulou

Wassoulou is a popular Malian music genre named after the forest region of Wassoulou, located in southwestern Mali and southeastern Guinea. It is characterized by a robust repertoire of rhythms, dances and instruments, and a distinct vocal style unique to the region. It is also distinguished by its open, democratic nature, as young people and women participate fully in performance and creation regardless of caste. Most notably, the pentatonic, calabash harp-lutes known as the *kamalen n'goni* and *donson n'goni* and virtuosic female singers are icons of the *wassoulou* sound. *Wassoulou* is considered by many to be 'the true reservoir of Malian music' (Diarra 1998).

The people dwelling in the Wassoulou region (Wassoulounkaw) are united in language and culture, despite their separate nationalities. In Mali, they are held in high esteem for their musical prowess, especially in the areas of popular song and dance music (Maxwell 2008). The densely forested region provides abundant resources for unique musical instruments: strings, vines, gourds and rattles of all sorts of shapes and sizes, skins and, of course, the human body and voice. Centuries-old metalsmithing in Wassoulou has also provided a musical treasure of unique, deeply traditional metallaphones, but non-indigenous metals and plastics have also made their way into the local pallet of instrument building and design since the mid-twentieth century.

Wassoulou emerged as the leading new genre of Malian popular music around 1989 when singer Oumou Sangaré made a splash on the popular music scene with her hit recording of 'Diarabi Nene' (Love's Chill). Oumou's interpretation of this well-known traditional love song enchanted the nation almost instantaneously. Her voice was considered lovely and a classic expression of traditional Wassoulou song, yet her lyrics were shockingly sensual for that era in popular Malian music. Other hit songs on Sangaré's cassette, however, such as 'Moussolou' (Women), carried messages of women's empowerment that pleased national audiences. The blend of old and new ideas from a deeply traditional, regional voice defined a large part of the *wassoulou* sound.

Equally shocking to Malian listeners was the irreverent, electric *kamalen n'goni*: a neo-traditional 'youth harp' made of a gourd, six strings and a pick-up. The instrument was invented in the late 1960s by Alata Brulaye, a young man from the village of Yanfolila, in response to severe music and dance restrictions placed on the youth by their elders' society of hunters. Also known as the 'prostitute's harp' and the 'devil's harp,' Alata's *kamalen n'goni* revolutionized youth music culture in the Wassoulou, branding it as irreverent and marking it forbidden in families of good moral standing. Its infectious, syncopated rhythms and sharp, twangy timbre were so irresistible, as local legend has it, that even decent, married women were known to sneak out of their windows at night just to follow its music.

The *kamalen n'goni* was featured predominantly in Oumou Sangaré's music, but it was also partnered with more symbolically benign, traditional musical instruments from Wassoulou such as the *jembe*, the Fula flute, hand clapping and calabashes to create a rich, organic, forest sound. What distinguished *wassoulou* as a commercial pop music genre, however, was the incorporation of electronic instruments into this traditional layer of forest sound. Electric bass, keyboard and later drum set added the element of modernity to the sound that defined and continues to define *wassoulou*.

Other vocalists have also contributed tremendously to the development of *wassoulou* as a popular commercial genre, among them first-generation stars Nahawa Doumbia and Coumba Sidibé and second-generation singers including the late Ramata Diakité and Tata Diakité, and Oumou Sangaré. Nahawa Doumbia from Bougouni, also known as the 'breaker of taboos' and a powerful clairvoyant, introduced the pentatonic *balafon* and the Didadi rhythm into the *wassoulou* sound in the mid-1980s. The late Coumba Sidibé recorded traditional music of the region for decades, beginning as far back as the late 1960s during live broadcasts of radio sessions at the singular national radio and television stations ORTM. This early style featured her solo voice accompanied by acoustic *jembe* and *kamalen n'goni*, the latter played by its inventor, Alata Brulaye. In the decades that followed Coumba made numerous studio recordings in Bamako and later in New York of heavily synthesized sounds that came to be known as the Wassoulou Explosion in the 1980s. Ramata introduced an electronic, techno sound into the style with her cassette *Na* in 1998.

Second-generation singer Oumou Sangaré put commercial *wassoulou* music on the map in the African and international world music market in 1993 with her release of *Ko Sira*. This pivotal recording launched Sangaré's status as a successful international artist. Sangaré's lyrics addressed African women's rights in ways that resonated worldwide and that had never been voiced to such a mass audience. Since *wassoulou*'s debut on the world music scene, next-generation female vocalists such as Kon Kan Kon Siata Sidibé and current international sensation Fatoumata Diawara have continued to develop its sound. While lyric messages and instrumentation change, *wassoulou* remains, at its core, a 'youth' music for dance and entertainment, characterized by freedom of expression, dynamic rhythms, and creative blends of electronic and indigenous *wassoulou* sounds.

Bibliography

Diarra, Boubacar S. 1998. 'Review of Djeneba Djakité: Nouvelle Cassette *Foruou*.' *Le Mag* (February).

Durán, Lucy. 1995. 'Birds of Wassulu: Freedom of Expression and Expressions of Freedom in the Popular Music of Southern Mali.' *British Journal of Ethnomusicology* 4: 101–34.

Durán, Lucy. 2000. 'Women, Music, and the "Mystique" of Hunters in Mali.' In *The African Diaspora: A Musical Perspective*, ed. Ingrid Monson. New York: Routledge, 137–85.

Maxwell, Heather A. 2002. *Destiny's Divas: Wassolu Singing, Music Ideologies, and the Politics of Performance in Bamako, Mali.* Unpublished Ph.D. thesis, Indiana University, Bloomington.

Maxwell, Heather A. 2003. 'Divas of the Wassoulou Sound: Transformations in the Matrix of Cultural Production, Globalization, and Identity.' *Consumption, Markets, and Culture* 6(1): 43–63.

Maxwell, Heather A. 2008. 'Of Youth Harps and Songbirds: The Sweet Music of Wasulu.' *African Music* 8(2): 26–55.

Discographical References

Diakité, Ramata. *Na*. Mali K7. *1998*: Mali.
Sangaré, Oumou. 'Diarabi Nene.' *Moussolou*. Samassa/World Circuit 021. *1989*: Mali/UK.
Sangaré, Oumou. *Ko Sira*. World Circuit 036. *1992*: UK.

Discography

Diawara, Fatoumata. *Fatou*. World Circuit: *2011*: UK.
Doumbia, Nahawa. *Yankaw*. Mali K7. *1996*: Mali.
Sangaré, Oumou. *Moussolou*. Mali K7. *1991*: Mali.
Sidibé, Coumba. 'Wary.' *Divas of Mali*. Shanachie. *1996*: USA.

HEATHER MAXWELL

Yéla

Yéla forms an important aspect of the artistic heritage associated with the Haal Pulaar (also known as the Fulbe, Fulani or Tukulor), an ethnic group of Senegal and Mauritania with related groups in neighboring countries. Through poetry and music, *yéla* evokes the history and identity of these communities and is a source of pride for their members. The Haal Pulaar who identify with their culture recognize the knowledge and values to which *yéla* songs refer and feel challenged by these songs to act according to these values, known as *pulaaku* (Schareika 2010). Audiences who are less familiar with the Pulaar language and culture may still appreciate the melodies, the catchy rhythms and the fine choreography that characterize this genre. These elements and the genre's adaptability to styles of modern music are the reasons for *yéla*'s longevity, as it has continued to play an indispensable role in enlivening family ceremonies and other community events.

The performance of *yéla* has primarily been the preserve of *griots* and *griottes* (West African historians, storytellers, poets and praise singers; *gawlo* [sing.], *awlube* [pl.] in Pulaar). These *griots* and *griottes* are the custodians and masters of traditional oral knowledge and are also virtuoso musicians. *Yéla* made up the principal repertoire of the royal *griots*, that is, those *griot* families that were directly linked to successive governing dynasties. An artistic form that combines poetry, song, music and dance, the mastery of which requires careful learning, *yéla* is transmitted within families. As in neighboring groups such as the Wolof and Mandinka, the status and function of the *griot* are hereditary (Wane 1966; Dorsch 2006). Initiation occurs at an early age. Mothers teach their daughters vocal techniques and how to play musical instruments, while fathers teach their sons the epic stories and genealogies of the historical personae that are celebrated in songs. Students perfect their abilities by accompanying their parents or elders at ceremonies and by performing with them, as evidenced in the documentary film *Yéla, les mélodies de la mémoire* (Yéla: Melodies of Memory) (2008).

Yéla has in these ways been transmitted through the ages, carried on in each era by a generation of interpreters who have been rigorously trained. The griots of the Haal Pulaar have preserved their legacy despite many economic, political and social changes. The disappearance of the traditional means of performing *yéla* has not prevented its survival. *Yéla* accompanies all the festive events that punctuate the social life of the Haal Pulaar; these include marriages, baptisms, circumcisions, the hosting of a distinguished guest and welcoming a returning emigrant. While it has remained primarily the domain of *griots* and *griottes*, *yéla* has also been a folk art accessible to all and adaptable to various circumstances.

Classic *yéla* is performed by a group of richly dressed women sitting on mats on the floor. They tap on calabashes or hit the ground with dried hollowed-out squashes. Once the rhythm is well established, the lead singer launches the song, the verses of which are punctuated by a chorus that serves as a refrain. As the mood of the song becomes established, women and girls take turns dancing and waving a scarf in the middle of the circle. Men, especially the elderly, intervene from time to time to recite the genealogy of heroes and sing about their deeds, as shown in the film, *Yéla, les mélodies de la mémoire*.

Yéla was originally a court music made up of war songs sung by *griottes* during vigils to rally warriors or to celebrate their warlike exploits and immortalize heroes on their return from the battlefield (ASAK 1967; Sow 2009). It originated during the reign of the Déniyanké, a Fulani dynasty that governed Foûta Tôro, a kingdom covering northern Senegal and southern Mauritania, from the early sixteenth century to the end of the eighteenth century (Kane 2004). Individuals representative of this dynasty such as Koli Tenguella (sixteenth century), Samba Guéladiégui and Soulé Ndiaye (eighteenth century) provided the dominant themes of the songs of this period. Another regional center of *yéla* is Boundou in eastern Senegal, a kingdom founded at the end of the seventeenth century by the *almamy* Malick Sy, who came originally from Foûta Tôro (Gomez 1992) ('almamy' is a title used to refer to West African Muslim rulers). Originating in a historical context marked by violent military confrontations involving wars of succession and resistance against the colonial conquest, *yéla* is essentially a hymn praising courage, honor and generosity. It evokes the glorious rides of heroes and extols the values embodied by warriors. The rhythm of the *griottes*' instruments imitates the sound of galloping warhorses.

Yéla has continued to evolve and grow as a dynamic genre over the centuries. This evolution has made it a vehicle for remembering and reflecting on current issues. Its lyrics serve to glorify illustrious ancestors and to address contemporary everyday social situations. Musically, too, innovations have been made continuously. The rhythms of calabashes played by *griottes* are often accompanied by the melodies of the *hoddu*, a lute with four strings played by a *bambado*, a Haal Pulaar musician. Since the 1970s the Western guitar has been added to or has even replaced the *hoddu*. The role of men has thus changed. Traditionally they devoted themselves to epic narration and the declamation of genealogies, while women sang and played. Subsequently, however, more and more men began to sing and, as *hoddu* and guitar players, they became increasingly important for the performance of *yéla*.

Modernization

As a performance tradition *yéla* is located at the confluence of ethics and aesthetics and functions as a kind of bridge between the Haal Pulaar of different regional and social origins. As such it has served as an interesting source of inspiration for an increasing number of performers in modern West African music scenes. The genre has been modernized by many groups that have seen it as their mission to promote the Haal Pulaar cultural heritage. They have adapted the music by performing *yéla* on instruments such as drums, keyboards and guitars.

The first and most prominent representative of this modernization movement has been the Senegalese singer Baaba Maal, referred to since the 1980s as the 'King of Yela' by the media. Singer, guitarist and dancer Baaba Maal has from the beginning of his career turned for inspiration to the classics of Pulaar music, aided in this search by his friend the griot Mansour Seck. Through his recordings and performances Maal popularized the songs and hymns of *yéla* well beyond Senegal and Mauritania (Ly 2000). After a few years of training at the National Conservatory of Music of Senegal, he devoted himself entirely to the exploration of Pulaar and West African artistic traditions. He traveled with his group Yellitaare Fuuta (which means 'Renaissance of Foûta' in Pulaar) and later with Daandé Leñol ('Voice of the People') through the towns and villages of northern and eastern Senegal before visiting neighboring countries such as Mauritania, Mali, Burkina Faso and the Ivory Coast. These trips allowed him to meet the people of the countryside as well as the custodians of different traditions and discover treasures of West African cultures that would serve as a resource throughout the rest of his career (Ba 2016).

Baaba Maal introduced international audiences to *yéla* through albums such as *Lam Toro*, which was released in 1992 by Island Records and produced by Chris Blackwell. Island Records also released 'Yelé (Hamady Bogle),' a remix of the song 'Hamady Boiro,' which was recorded with Jamaican toaster Macka B and based on the Jamaican dance, the bogle. The resonance of this song in the Caribbean and the United States at the time was due, among other things, to rhythmic affinities between *yéla* and reggae. Baaba Maal's next album, *Firin' in Fouta*, was nominated for a Grammy Award in the Best World Music Album category in 1996.

Within Senegal, Baaba Maal established *yéla* in the context of the dominance of *mbalax*, a genre strongly associated with the Wolof and seen as an expression of the 'Wolofization' of Senegal. Inviting Mandinka musicians and playing Mandinka songs such as the Mandinka griot piece 'Ceddo' ('Thiédo' on the album *Firin' in Fouta*), Maal's music did not just represent an expression of historical Pulaar–Mandinka encounters and the strong, local musical influences emanating from the former Mandinka empires. It could also be interpreted as a way to counter Wolof dominance by means of a trans-ethnic form of music that is both traditional and popular. In fact, Maal's approach to modernizing *yéla* partly influenced the modernization of Mandinka *kora* by exponents of the *yenyengo* style (McLaughlin 1995; Dorsch 2006, 2017). The modernization of *yéla* went hand in hand with Youssou N'Dour's success in modernizing Wolof rhythms and Ismael Lô's approach to popularizing Mandinka music. Recognized as one of the most charismatic and influential artists on the Senegalese scene, Baaba Maal received the Grand Prix of the President of the Republic of Senegal for the Arts in 2017 in recognition of his exemplary career. Young Pulaar or Pulaar-influenced musicians from Senegal and all over West Africa followed in his footsteps. Among the Senegalese numbered artists such as Les Frères Guissé, Thiedel Mbaye, Coumba Gawlo and Aliou Guissé, as well as the hip-hop bands Bideew Bou Bess and the short-lived Tim Timol. All these musicians drew inspiration from Baaba Maal and the traditions he revived.

Yéla has continued to play an important role in the social life of the Haal Pulaar as a hallmark of their identity and motivation. It has immortalized the illustrious men and great deeds that have marked the history of the Pulaar and neighboring communities, and has extolled the values (courage honor, dignity, generosity and faith) that are considered to be the foundation of these communities and the pillars of social cohesion. From an aesthetic point of view *yéla* has enlivened West African popular music by ennobling ceremonies and other festivities.

Bibliography

ASAK. 1967. 'Petite introduction à la musique sénégalaise' [A Short Introduction to Senegalese Music]. *Sénégal Carrefour* 2: 39–49.

Ba, Oumar Demba. 2016. *Baaba Maal: Le message en chantant* [Baaba Maal: The Message in Song]. Paris: L'Harmattan.

Bâ, Oumar Moussa. 1977. *Le Foûta Tôro au carrefour des cultures* [Foûta Tôro at the Crossroad of Cultures]. Paris: L'Harmattan.

Dorsch, Hauke. 2006. *Globale Griots: Performanz in der afrikanischen Diaspora* [Global Griots: Performance in the African Diaspora]. Münster: Lit.

Dorsch, Hauke. 2017. 'Making Manding in the Concert Hall – Jali Pop in Paris.' *Journal of African Cultural Studies* 29(2): 177–93.

Gomez, Michael. 1992. *Pragmatism in the Age of Jihad: The Precolonial State of Bundu*. Cambridge: Cambridge University Press.

Guèye, Tène Youssouf. 1980. *Aspects de la littérature pulaar en Afrique occidentale* [Aspects of Pulaar Literature in Africa]. Nouakchott: Les Presses de l'imprimerie nouvelle.

Kane, Oumar. 2004. *La première hégémonie peule* [The Initial Hegemony of the Peul People]. Paris and Dakar: Karthala/Presses universitaires de Dakar.

Ly, Amadou. 2000. 'L'identité culturelle pulaar, son importance, et le rôle de l'artiste dans sa défense et son expansion,' [The Pulaar Cutural Identity, Its Importance, and the Role of the Artist in Its Defense and Expansion]. In *Parole essentielle ... mélanges offerts à Ferdinand Diara* [The Essential Word ... Miscellaneous Essays Presented to Ferdinand Diara], ed. Papa Guèye. Département de Lettres modernes: Université Cheikh Anta Diop de Dakar, 295–310.

McLaughlin, Fiona. 1995. 'Haalpulaar Identity as a Response to Wolofization.' *African Languages and Cultures* 8(2): 153–68.

Sadji, Abdoulaye. 1985. *Ce que dit la musique africain* [What African Music Says]. Paris and Dakar: Présence Africaine.

Schareika, Nikolaus. 2010. 'Pulaaku in Action: Words at Work in Wodaabe Clan Politics.' *Ethnology* 49(3): 207–27.

Sow, Abdoul Aziz. 2009. *La poésie orale peule (Sénégal–Mauritanie)* [Peul Oral Poetry (Senegal–Mauritania)]. Paris: L'Harmattan.

Sy, Harouna 2016. *L'esthétique sociale des Pulaar. Socioanalyse d'un groupe ethnolinguistique* [The Social Aesthetic of the Pulaar: A Social Analysis of an Ethnolinguistic Group]. Paris: L'Harmattan.

Wane, Ibrahima. 2018. 'Le yelaa, hymne au martyre et mémorial des martyrs.' [Yéla: A Hymn to the Martyr and a Memorial for Martyrs]. In *Le héros et la mort dans les traditions épiques* [Heroes and Death in Epic Traditions], eds. Muriel Ott and Romuald Fonkoua. Paris: Karthala, 121–7.

Wane, Yaya. 1966. *Les toucouleurs du Fouta Toro: Stratification sociale et structure familiale* [The Tukulor of Foûta Tôro: Social Stratification and Family Structure]. Dakar and Paris: IFAN/CNRS.

Discographical References

Maal, Baaba. 'Hamady Boiro.' (CD single.) Island Records 864 061-2. *1992*: UK.

Maal, Baaba. *Lam Toro*. Island Records CIDM 512 519-2. *1992*: UK.

Maal, Baaba. 'Thiédo' ('Ceddo'). *Firin' in Fouta*. (CD.) Mango CIDM 1109, 524 024-2. *1994*: UK.

Maal, Baaba. 'Yelé (Hamady Bogle).' (12-inch single.) Island Records 2295. *1993*: France.

Filmography

Yéla, les mélodies de la mémoire [Yéla: Melodies of Memory], dir. Ibrahima Wane and Fatimata Ly-Fall. 2008. Senegal. 52 mins. Documentary.

IBRAHIMA WANE AND HAUKE DORSCH

Yenyengo

Yenyengo is a West African popular musical genre centered on the *kora*, a bridge harp or harp-lute played by Mande *griots*. With a repertoire of songs based on traditional tunes used by *griots* for the accompaniment of epics and praise songs, the performers of *yenyengo* incorporate rhythms of successful West African popular genres such as highlife, Afrobeat or *mbalax* to reach a wider and mostly younger audience in the West African countries Senegal, Gambia and Guinea-Bissau. The lyrics of *yenyengo* songs frequently address local, national as well as global social and political issues, but also personal and emotional subjects. In keeping with the *griots*' tradition of praising wealthy and powerful persons, performances and also recorded songs often include praises for businessmen, politicians and other patrons.

Griots are hereditary musicians and specialists in different fields of communication, including musicianship, praise singing, genealogy, historical narrations, epics, storytelling, counseling and diplomacy. *Griots* are often seen as constituting a caste, because of their endogamy. The institution of the *griot* was established in the West African Sahelian empires in the ninth century AD. In the twenty-first century *griots* are a common institution among those groups in West Africa that claim historical connections to one or more of these empires. Thus, there are different terms for *griots* in local languages: in most Mande languages, they are called *jeli*, while in Mandinka, one of many Mande languages, they are called *jali*.

Yenyengo is mainly played in the Mandinka-speaking regions of Gambia, southern Senegal and Guinea-Bissau. It was established in the mid-1950s in the southern Senegalese region called Casamance. So far, few scholars have described *yenyengo*, Sidia Jatta being an exception. Oral history sources provide conflicting versions of the style's early days. Different sources credit either the *kora* player Salif Jobarteh (different spellings of this name include Jebate, Diabaté or Dioubaté), Menseng Sissoko (also spelled Cissokho) or Menseng Kuyateh (also spelled Kouyaté) with having invented this genre by playing a tune of this title. Sources agree that *yenyengo* was inspired by a tune called *jimbasengo* played by the Gambian-born *kora* player Jali Mama Jobarteh. This was the first *kora* tune created to accompany dancing audiences. The etymology of *yenyengo* is also disputed, but several sources claim that this word, uncommon in Mandinka language, is associated with notions of noise and shouting, reflecting the criticism of the elder generation of the 1950s who disliked the quick danceable rhythms. Others imply that *yenyengo* is an onomatopoetic imitation of the sound of laughter, referring to the style's entertaining character.

Yenyengo is best understood as a popular style of music that was based on traditional court music played by *griots*. It thus mirrors the developments of popular genres in neighboring countries, such as *mamaya* in Guinea-Conakry and *jarabi* in Mali. The latter style's name translates as 'love' or 'passion' and refers to the fact that from the 1960s onward some young *griots* and *griottes* started to sing about these personal feelings and desires rather than refer to old epics and more generally give counsel on how to live a decent life. *Yenyengo* may have influenced the later developments of *mbalax* and *yela* in northern Senegal, both of which were traditional Wolof and Tukulor rhythms transformed to popular music genres and made famous by musicians such as Youssou N'Dour and Baaba Maal.

Yenyengo is characteristic of the Mandinka-speaking region of Senegambia since the *kora*, its main instrument, serves as a symbol representing the Senegambian empire of Gabu (also Kaabu, N'Gabou) that covered the region of what became Gambia, Casamance and Guinea-Bissau. The *kora* is a double-bridge harp-lute with usually 21 strings, a calabash body, a cow skin as resonator, a wooden neck and two hand-posts. According to oral tradition the *kora* was established in the eighteenth century by *griots* serving as entertainers and counselors to the royal families of the empire of Gabu. In the twentieth century the *kora* was brought to other Mande-speaking groups in Mali and Guinea. Thus, the repertory of the *kora* is mainly based on Mandinka songs and melodies but has been extended to include transcriptions of tunes originally composed for other traditional instruments, such as the lute *ngoni* or the xylophone *balo*. One can easily distinguish between the slower, solemn tunes from Mali and Guinea and the quick *tempi* of the Senegambian region, which may help explain why it was in this latter region that the meditative music of traditional Mande string instruments was transformed into a dance style. Both in traditional music and in *yenyengo* most *kora* players are still men, which is because *griots'* traditional gender roles allowed only men to play most musical instruments (including the *kora*) while female *griottes* sang and played only certain percussion instruments.

Historical Outline

Yenyengo's history may be divided into two phases, the first starting in the 1950s when *kora* players used their instrument to entertain audiences at dance events instead of playing pieces linked to Gabu history and Mande epic. Although the song *yenyengo* and most other songs that belong to this style are in the traditional *tomora ba* tuning, the text as well as the rhythms differ from the traditional repertoire. The texts focused on new subjects and included love songs and songs about war, social problems, or contemporary events such as the Apollo missions to the moon. The rhythms of *yenyengo* songs differ widely and are often compared to Afrobeat or highlife, probably more because of their role as a popular style than their rhythmic semblance. However, *mbalax* rhythms are easily discernible in *yenyengo* tunes.

Often, *kora* players replaced the drum ensembles that were the only common form of dance entertainment before the use of Western musical instruments. The late *kora* player and *griot* Malamini Jobarteh explained this transfer economically: audiences had to pay less for one *kora* player than for a drum ensemble. *Kora* players played either solo or accompanied by one or two musicians, using the body of the *kora* as a percussion instrument by tapping on the calabash. The new role of *kora* players as entertainers for the younger generation and the new fast-paced tunes were strongly criticized by some musicians and audiences of the elder generation for being a break with the tradition and a profanation of the art of the *griot*. The very name of the style *yenyengo* could be understood as a mockery of elders' lack of understanding for this style. Once they grew older, the *kora* players of this first phase ceased playing *yenyengo* and afterward performed only those tunes that are regarded as traditional, such as 'Kelefa Sanneh,' 'Masaane Ceesay' and so on. Thus, a musician's spectrum may include pop as well as traditional tunes, making it problematic to classify local music according to Western terminology (court music, folk, traditional, popular, etc.).

From the 1970s the *kora* became known internationally; Alex Haley's novel *Roots* (1967) and the related subsequent television series introduced the instrument to Western audiences, and Gambian *kora* players Jali Nyama Suso, Amadou Bansang Jobarteh and Alhaji Bai Konte toured Europe and the United States. Later, Konte took his son Dembo Konte and his adoptive son Malamini Jobarteh on tour. However, although Jobarteh had played *yenyengo* in Gambia, Senegal and Guinea-Bissau, he would play only traditional tunes when touring abroad, because *yenyengo*, he said, required dancers, and Europeans and Americans did not know how to dance to it.

Modern *kora* music became known in the West through the Gambian *kora* player Foday Musa Suso, who in 1977 emigrated to the United States where he founded the group Mandingo Griot Society and played with musicians of different genres, most prominently with US jazz pianist/composer Herbie Hancock. In 1987 Guinean *kora* player Mory Kante had a huge international success with his hit 'Yékéyéké,' which reached the Top 20 in numerous European countries, topping the charts in some of them. Its mixture of traditional Maninka tunes with disco rhythms, synthesizer and brass sounds served as an inspiration for the second wave of *yenyengo* musicians.

Since the mid-1980s, Western pop and rock instruments such as electric guitar, electric bass, saxophone, trumpet, drum set and synthesizer have been common in *yenyengo* bands, but the bands themselves are always led by a *kora* player, who usually also sings. Traditionally, *koras* have 21 strings, whereas most *yenyengo kora* players use 22, 23 or even more strings on their instruments and amplify them with microphones or pickups. Usually, bass strings are added to produce a deeper, stronger and more danceable sound. However, the higher number of strings may also be reminiscent of the style's origin in the Casamance region, where a 22nd string has been kept as a reminder of the first *kora* player, Jalimadi Wuleng. Since the 1980s, the combination of the *kora* with Western instruments – and sometimes also local traditional instruments, such as the *tama*, *djembe*, *sabar* or *dundunba* drums, or the *balo* – has been seen as the typical *yenyengo* group. Groups in the Casamance, such as the Ucas Jazz Band of Sédhiou, established this combination in the 1970s; however, due to his outstanding success since the late 1980s, the Gambian *kora* player Jaliba Kuyateh is regarded by his fans as the inventor of *yenyengo* – very much to the dismay of musicians and fans of the older generations.

Although *yenyengo* could rightly be credited with having allowed Mandinka music to cross linguistic and ethnic boundaries – because as a dance music it was also enjoyable to people who did not understand Mandinka – it remains a local Senegambian phenomenon. Jaliba Kuyateh tours internationally but performs mainly to Senegambian diasporic audiences. His most famous student, Tata Dindin Jobarteh, who is dubbed 'King of Yenyengo' in The Gambia, reaches his Western audiences mainly by playing traditional Mandinka tunes.

The international success of the *kora* calls into question gender, regional and caste restrictions concerning this instrument formerly exclusively played by male Mandinka *griots*. When Sidia Jatta, Gambian politician and scholar, played the *kora* in the 1990s, despite his noble family background this was still a scandal and he never recorded or performed professionally. This changed in the early twenty-first century. In the booklet to his album *22 Strings / 22 Cordes*, published in 2015, the Senegalese *kora* player Sekou Keita openly addresses his mixed noble and *griot* background. UK-based female *kora* player Sona Jobarteh may not be the first woman to play the *kora* publicly, but she has achieved unprecedented success and an enduring career. The most internationally successful *kora* players in the early twenty-first century are not from the Senegambian region but rather Malians such as Toumani Diabaté and Ballaké Sissoko and the Guinean Mory Kanté. Locally, however, *yenyengo* continues to be successful in The Gambia and Casamance with a new generation of *kora* players, educated in the late 1990s, who are often younger relatives of Jalibah Kuyateh and Tata Dindin Jobarteh such as Jobarteh's younger brothers Pa Bobo Jobarteh and cousin Dawda Jobarteh.

Sources

The author is indebted to the late Gambian *griots* Malamini Jobarteh and Dembo Konte and also to Aziz Kuyareh, Bakary Sidibe, Malaine Diabaté, Jalibah Kuyateh and Tata Dindin Jobarteh who shared their knowledge on *yenyengo*.

Bibliography

Barry, Boubacar. 1988. *La Sénégambie du XVe au XIXe siècle: Traite négrière, islam et conquête coloniale* [Senegambia from the Fifteenth to the Nineteenth Centuries: Slave Trade, Islam and Colonial Conquest]. Paris: L'Harmattan.

Charry, Eric. 2000. *Mande Music: Traditional and Modern Music of the Maninka and Mandinka of Western Africa*. Chicago: University of Chicago Press.

Charters, Samuel B. 1981. *The Roots of the Blues: An African Search*. London: Boyars.

Diawara, Mamadou. 1996. 'Le griot mande à l'heure de la globalisation' [The Mande Griot in Times of Globalization]. In *Cahiers d'Études Africaines* 36(144): 591–612.

Diawara, Mamadou. 1997. 'Mande Oral Popular Culture Revisited by the Electronic Media.' In *Readings in African Popular Culture*, ed. Karin Barber. Bloomington, IN: Indiana University Press, 40–53.

Dorsch, Hauke. 2005. 'Cosmopolitans, Diasporists, and Griots: The Role of Diasporic Elites.' In *Religion in the Context of African Migration*, eds. Cordula Weisskőppel and Afe Adogamé. Bayreuth: Eckhard Breitinger, 56–77.

Dorsch, Hauke. 2006. *Globale Griots: Performanz in der afrikanischen Diaspora* [Global Griots: Performance in the African Diaspora]. Münster: Lit Verlag.

Dorsch, Hauke. 2010. '"Indépendance Cha Cha": African Pop Music since the Independence Era.' *Africa Spectrum* 45(3): 131–46.

Dorsch, Hauke. 2013. 'Griots Navigating the Black Atlantic and Scholars Constructing the African Diaspora.' In *Diaspora as a Resource: Comparative Studies in Strategies, Networks and Urban Space*, eds. Waltraud Kokot, Christian Giordano and Mijal Gandelsmann-Trier. Zürich and Münster: Lit Verlag, 171–97.

Durán, Lucy. 1995. 'Jelimuso: The Superwomen of Malian Music.' In *Power, Marginality, and African Oral Literature*, eds. Graham Furniss and Liz Gunner. Cambridge: Cambridge University Press, 197–207.

Ebron, Paulla A. 1999. 'Tourists as Pilgrims: Commercial Fashioning of Transatlantic Politics.' *American Ethnologist* 26(4): 910–32.

Ebron, Paulla A. 2002. *Performing Africa*. Princeton, NJ: Princeton University Press.

Hale, Thomas. 1998. *Griots and Griottes – Masters of Words and Music*. Bloomington & Indianapolis: Indiana University Press.

Haley, Alex. 1976. *Roots: The Saga of an American Family*. New York: Doubleday.

Haley, Alex. 1987. 'Black History, Oral History, and Genealogy.' In *Oral History: An Interdisciplinary Anthology*, eds. David K. Dunaway, Willa K. Baum. Nashville, TN: American Association for State and Local History, 264–87.

Jansons, Marloes. 2003. *The Best Hand Is the Hand that Always Gives: Griottes and Their Profession in Eastern Gambia*. Leiden: CNWS.

Jatta, Sidia. 1985. 'Born Musicians: Traditional Music from The Gambia.' In *Repercussions: A Celebration of African-American Music*, eds. Geoffrey Haydon and Dennis Marks. London: Century, 14–29.

Knight, Roderic C. 1991. 'Music out of Africa: Mande Jaliya in Paris.' *The World of Music* 3 (1): 52–69.

Niane, Djibril Tamsir. 1989. *Histoire des Mandingues de l'Ouest – Le royaume du Gabou* [History of the Manding of the West – the Kingdom of Gabou]. Paris: Karthala.

Panzacchi, Cornelia. 1994. 'The Livelihoods of Traditional Griots in Modern Senegal.' *Africa* 64(2): 190–210.

Panzacchi, Cornelia. 1996. 'Dañuy Gewel – Nous sommes des griots – Les griots sénégalais, vus par eux-mêmes' [We are the Griots – Senegalese Griots as Seen by Themselves]. In *Genres autobiographiques en Afrique*, eds. Janos Riesz and Ulla Schild. Berlin: Reimer, 101–12.

Pfeiffer, Katrin, ed. 1997. *Mandinka Spoken Art: Folk-Tales, Griot Accounts and Songs*. Cologne: Köppe.

Schulz, Dorothea. 2001. *Perpetuating the Politics of Praise: Jeli Singers, Radios, and Political Mediation in Mali*. Cologne: Köppe.

Sidibe, Bakary K., ed. 1980. *Sunjata: The Story of Sunjata Keita, Founder of the Mali Empire*. Banjul: Oral History and Antiquities Division.

Zemp, Hugo. 1966, 'La légende des griots malinké' [The Legend of the Malinke Griots]. *Cahiers d'Études Africaines* 6(24): 611–24.

Interviews and Personal Communications

Jobarteh, Ebrima. 'Tata Dindin.' 2001. Personal communications with the author, 13 January, 17 August.

Jobarteh, Ebrima. 'Tata Dindin.' 2015. Online communication with the author, 13–16 November.

Jobarteh, Malamini. 1999. Personal communications with the author, 22 October and 6 November.

Konte, Dembo. 1999. Interview with the author, 1 December.

Kuyateh, Aziz. 2015. Interview with the author, 11 October.

Kuyateh, Aziz. 2015. Personal communication with the author, 10 November.

Kuyateh, Jaliba. 1999. Interview with the author, 30 October.

Sidibe, Bakary K. 1999. Interview with the author, 26 October.

Discographical References

Kante, Mory. 'Yékéyéké'/'Akwaba Beach.' Barclay 887 048-7. *1987*: France.

Keita, Sekou. *22 Strings / Cordes.* ARC Music EUCD2585. *2015*: UK.

Discography

Diabaté, Toumani. *Djelika.* Hannibal HNCD1380. *1995*: USA.

Diabaté, Toumani. *Jarabi – The Best of … Palm Pictures.* Hannibal HNCD1462. *2001*: USA.

Diabaté, Toumani, and Sissoko, Ballake. *New Ancient Strings-Nouvelles Cordes Anciennes.* Hannibal HNCD1428. *1999*: USA.

Diabaté, Toumani, and Diabaté, Sidiké. *Toumani & Sidiki.* World Circuit WCD087. *2014*: UK.

Dindin, Tata. *Salam – New Kora Music.* World Network 56.981. *1994*: Germany.

Dindin, Tata, and Lüdemann, Hans. *Piano Meets Kora – African Dialogues.* RISMEdition RISM. *2001*: Germany.

Dindin Jobarteh, Tata. *Kanake.* Sam Productions 9016. *2008*: Italy.

Hancock, Herbie, and Suso, Foday Musa. *Village Life.* CBS FC 39870. *1985*: USA.

Jalikunda – Die Grios Westafrikas und der übrigen Welt (Buch & CD). Ellipsis Arts ELLI 50452. *1996*: Germany.

Jobarteh, Amadu Bansang. *Tabara – Gambian Kora Music.* Music of the World MOW 129. *1993*: USA.

Jobarteh, Dawda. *Northern Light, Gambian Night.* Stern's Africa STCD 1112. *2012*: UK.

Jobarteh, Malamini, and Konte, Dembo. *Jaliya.* Stern's Africa 1010. *1985*: UK.

Jobarteh, Pa Bobo, and Trio, Kaira. *Kaira Naata.* Real World WSCD103. *1997*: UK.

Kairo – Songs of The Gambia. GRTS / Africa Productions. *1999*: The Gambia.

Kante, Mory. *Akwaba Beach.* Barclay 833 119-1. *1987*: France.

Konte, Alhaji Bai. *Kora Melodies from the Republic of The Gambia, West Africa.* Rounder – 5001. *1973*: USA.

Konte, Alhaji Bai, Konte, Dembo, and Jobate, Ma Lamini. *Gambian Griot Kora Duets.* Folkways FW 8514. *1979*: USA.

Konte, Dembo, Kuyateh, Kausu, and The Jali Roll Orchestra. *Jali Roll.* Rogue Records FSML 2020. *1990*: UK.

Konte, Dembo, and Kuyateh, Kausu, with Mawdo Suso. *Jaliology.* Xenophile – XENO 4036. *1995*: USA.

Konté, Lamine. *Chant du Nègre … Chant du Monde.* Arion – 33 395. *1977*: Italy.

Maal, Baaba. *Firin' in Fouta.* Mango CIDM 1109. *1994*: UK.

Mali – Cordes Anciennes. Syllart/Buda Records. 1977822 Ca. *2000*: France. (First released by Bärenreiter-Musicaphon BM 30 L 2505. *1970*: Germany.)

Mandinka and Fulani Music of The Gambia – Ancient Heart. Axiom 314-510 148-2. *1990*: UK.

Mandekalou: The Art and Soul of the Mande Griots. Syllart Records – 79663-2. *2004*: France.

N'Dour, Youssou. *Immigrés.* Virgin 7 91020-1. *1988*. UK.

Oppermann, Rüdiger. *KlangWelten* (featuring Tata Dindin and others). KlangWelten Records, SMD KW 20011. *2000*: Germany.

Oppermann, Rüdiger, with Malamini Jobarteh et al. *Same Sun – Same Moon.* Shamrock 1017-1. *1992*: Austria.

HAUKE DORSCH

Zamrock

Zamrock emerged in Zambia in the jubilant atmosphere that followed independence (1964) in the late 1960s and early 1970s. The influences of Zamrock artists can be traced to the Merseybeat sound from Britain; rock 'n' roll, funk and psychedelica from the United States; *soukouss* from Congo as well as traditional Zambian folk music. As there was little emigration from or immigration to Zambia at the time, Zambian musicians found almost all of their inspiration on the radio. While, for example, the Nigerian jazz-funk scene was inspired by the at-the-time Nigerian-based English musician Ginger Baker, and the Ghanaian rock scene was indebted to Ghanaian artists based outside of Ghana through bands such as Osibisa, Zamrock consisted of almost solely homegrown musicians (Yoruba 2013).

Zamrock emerged as the music of optimism and good times. After independence, an attitude of self-celebration set in among Zambian musicians and their audience. The period in Zambia was marked by rapid urbanization, social upheavals, flares, fluorescent colors, flamboyant hairstyles, generational differences and powerful music. Mass migration into Zambia's rich mining districts meant musicians were suddenly exposed to different musical styles. Traditional instruments – from drums (such as the high-pitched 'talking' *vimbuzza*) to stringed instruments (such as the *babatoni*) to the *kalimba* (handheld lamellophone) – joined with instruments brought into the country by the British ruling classes, such as the accordion and guitar.

Soon after independence, the Zambia Broadcasting Service (ZBS), Zambia's first national radio station, was formed. ZBS led a drive to focus on domestic musical talent and made a concerted effort to collect Zambia's ceremonial, festival and work songs nationwide. President Kenneth Kaunda, an amateur musician himself, passed a law that at least 95 percent of music on the radio had to be of Zambian origin (Hament 2013). His intention was to help create a uniquely Zambian musical presence. Ironically, however, this policy turned out to be instrumental in creating one of the most interesting Western-fusion music styles of all time.

The Zamrock sound was epitomized by the electric guitar that, in post-independence Zambia, became a symbol of the idealized 'West': of freedom, economic prosperity and the future. The guitar solos of Western artists that filtered through to the streets of Lusaka by means of radio waves and bootleg records acted as a template for a uniquely hybrid sound mixing Zambian traditional music, optimism and pride with the fuzzed-out, psychedelic sounds of Jimi Hendrix's bluesy acid guitar, James Brown's funk, and the rock rhythms of the Rolling Stones; songs such as the Zamrock band Five Revolution's 'Respect Yourself' would not have sounded out of place on the Rolling Stones' album *Exile On Main Street*.

The iconography of the Zamrock era was very much that of the Western rock bands, including stage antics with joyous exuberance and a flamboyant sartorial style. One legendary gig by the band Amanaz in 1974 reportedly saw the singer jumping out of a coffin wearing a skeleton suit with flared trousers. Considered hippies and eccentrics in their home country, Zamrockers were part of a closely knit community that often traded members between bands (Alapatt 2010). However, the scene was not without its rivalries; a vicious war of words between Keith Mlevhu, unusually most famous as a solo artist in a scene consisting almost entirely of groups, and Rikki Ilionga, frontman of Musi-O-Tunya, broke out with each one bragging in the media, and on stage, that he was the country's only superstar. But Zamrock was a musical genre with many superstars, such as Paul Dobson Nyirongo, frontman of the Ngozi Family and one of the founding members of Musi-O-Tunya – believed by many to be the first ever Zamrock group. He went by the stage name Ngozi, meaning 'danger.' Paul Ngozi is credited with creating the Zambian version of *kalindula*. *Kalindula* was a homegrown music style of southern Africa which in part inspired Zamrock, and which typically features a lead electric guitar and a rock-*rumba* beat mixing English and local languages (Lumbwe 2013). However, it was as a Zamrock artist, mixing the *kalindula* sound with the funky and fuzzy sounds of Western psychedelic music and rock 'n' roll, that Ngozi became famous. He was also known for his spectacular stage antics, which included playing the guitar with his teeth. Zambian music lovers adored him. With poignant, relevant lyrics, he won many awards and represented Zambian music in both Europe and the United States, and he even went on a controversial tour of South Africa at the height of apartheid.

One of the most loved bands of the era was called the W.I.T.C.H. or Witch. While originally just a shortening of the previous name of the band, the Footswitch, the band's name became an acronym for 'We Intend

To Cause Havoc.' The W.I.T.C.H.'s charismatic lead singer, Emmanuel Chanda, was known as 'Jagari,' an Africanization of Mick Jagger's name. The W.I.T.C.H. toured all over southern and eastern Africa, from Botswana to Kenya, playing to thousands at stadium shows (Göransson Sandberg 2013).

The years following the oil crisis of the 1970s which coincided with a slump in the price of Zambia's main export commodity, copper, caused unemployment and inflation rates to skyrocket and made the music scene in Zambia a more challenging work environment. This period saw many Zamrock groups disband. The decline of Zamrock was also facilitated by changing tastes brought about by new radio stations, television and video flooding the country with outside musical influences, such as reggae, ragga, rhythm & blues, hip-hop and gospel. Musical piracy hit Zamrock artists hard, and with no safeguards in place, bootleggers in neighboring countries were able to make money by copying and selling the music of Zambian artists. Many musicians of the era therefore left the profession to find other work to sustain themselves and their families. Jagari, for example, became a teacher, and then a miner (RBMA Radio 2013). Many others fell victim to the new disease that wreaked havoc among Zambian musicians at this time, AIDS. However, the style is remembered for its pure and simple entertainment value – the way in which it was experienced as dangerously dance-inducing, funky and cool. Songs that exemplify this sound include 'Chifundo' by the W.I.T.C.H., an effortlessly groovy song with tight rhythm guitar; and 'Size Nine' by Paul Ngozi and the Ngozi Family, with a catchy wah-wah guitar and jerking rhythms under the smooth voice of Paul Ngozi, who wails at a mother-in-law to stop interfering in her daughter's affairs.

There is a shortage of scholarly articles on Zamrock; however, in the early 2010s there was a revival in attention to the genre. While the original Zamrock records can be very difficult to find, some of the Zamrock classics have been reissued by Now-Again records (Okay Africa 2013), providing another chance to experience the music of this era.

Bibliography

Alapatt, Eothen. 2010. CD liner notes, 'Rikki Ililonga and Musi-o-Tunya – Dark Sunrise.' *Dark Sunrise* (reissue). Now-Again Records B0045CD6HI.

Göransnon Sandberg, Henning. 2013. 'Why Zamrock Is Back in Play.' Online at: http://www.theguardian.com/world/2013/jul/22/zamrock-zambia-music-rerelease (accessed 5 October 2017).

Hament, Ellyn. 2013. 'Zambia: A Melting Pot of Musical Styles.' Exploratorium. Online at: https://www.exploratorium.edu/eclipse-archive/zambia/music.html (accessed 5 October 2017).

Lumbwe, Kapambwe. 2013. 'Indigenous Mfunkutu and Contemporary Ubwinga (Wedding) Music of the Bemba-Speaking People of Zambia.' *Journal of the Musical Arts in Africa* 10: 71–101.

Okay Africa. 2013. 'Zamrock: The Best 1970s Zambian Psychedelic Rock Tracks.' Online at: http://www.okayafrica.com/audio/zambia-music-zamrock-top-songs/ (accessed 5 October 2017).

RBMA Radio. 2013. Zamrock Special. Online at: http://www.rbmaradio.com/#shows/emmanuel-jagari-chanda-zamrock-special (accessed 2 December 2014).

Yoruba, Cosmic. 2013. 'The Barely-Documented History of Zamrock.' Online at: http://archived.thisisafrica.me/music/detail/19916/the-barely-documented-history-of-zamrock (accessed 22 February 2015).

Discographical References

Five Revolution. 'Respect Yourself.' *I Am a Free Man*. ZMPL 18. *1976*: Zambia.

Ngozi, Paul, and the Ngozi Family. 'Size Nine.' Paul Ngozi Greatest Hits. Yamene Records. *2003*: Zambia.

Rolling Stones. *Exile on Main Street*. Virgin Records. *1994*: USA.

The W.I.T.C.H. 'Chifundo.' *W.I.T.C.H.: We Intend To Cause Havoc!* Now Again Records B00AFIPGFQ. *2011*: USA.

Discography

Amanaz. *Africa*. Label unknown. *1975*: Zambia. (Reissued as Amanaz. *Africa*. Now-Again Records 4047179438728. *2010*: USA.)

Five Revolutions. *I Am a Free Man*. ZMPL 18. *1976*: Zambia.

Ililonga, Rikki, and Musi-o-Tunya. *Dark Sunrise*. MOT Records LMOT 1017. *1975*: Zambia. (Reissued as Ililonga, Rikki, and Musi-o-Tunya. *Dark Sunrise*. Now-Again Records 0659457506728. *2010*: USA.)

Ngozi, Paul, and the Ngozi Family. *Zambia. 1977*: Zambia.

The W.I.T.C.H. *Lazy Bones!!*. Zambezi ZTZ 1. *1975*: Zambia. (Reissued as The W.I.T.C.H. *Lazy Bones!!*. Now Again Records NA5105. *2013*: USA.)

The W.I.T.C.H. 'Chifundo'. *W.I.T.C.H.: We Intend To Cause Havoc!*. Now Again Records B00AFIPGFQ. *2011*: USA.

HENNING GÖRANSSON SANDBERG

Zenji Flava

Zenji flava, also referred to as *zenji fleva*, from the English word 'flavor,' is a musical genre that emerged in the 1980s on the Isles of Zanzibar (United Republic of Tanzania). Within the upsurge of *bongo flava* as popular Tanzanian music performed and produced mainly by very young musicians – and therefore considered *muziki wa kizazi kipya* (music of a new generation) – *zenji flava* has developed as a distinctive genre, articulating the disrupted and intense cultural, social and geopolitical identities of Zanzibari youth. Their choice to shape a clear Zanzibari identity rather than a comprehensive Tanzanian one mirrors and enacts the geopolitical discourses ascribed to the critical relationship between mainland Tanzania and the archipelago of Zanzibar, dating back to the union between Tanganyika and Zanzibar officialized in 1964. The musical heritage of the Islands, comprising long-standing *ngoma* performances (including *ndege, kibati, msewe, gonga, uringe*) as well as initiation rituals (*unyago*), *kidumbak* music and *taarab* music, resonates in *zenji flava*, responding to the historical and sociocultural context of the islands (Brunotti 2005a, b). Further, the *zenji flava* scene differs from that of other Tanzanian musical performances in its language, topics and musical patterns.

While the term *bongo flava* links the genre's emergence to the urban context of Dar es Salaam, Tanzania's largest city (*bongo* translates from Swahili as 'big brains' and emphasizes the shrewdness and craftiness needed to survive in the metropolis) (Englert 2008; Reuster-Jahn and Hacke 2011; Suriano 2007), Zanzibari young people increasingly refer to their music as *zenji flava*. The term *zenji*, derived from the Arabic word *zanjibār*, which in turn comes from the Farsi term *zang-bār* (*zang* means 'black' and *bār* means 'coast'), is employed as a conscious act of self-identification (Omari 2013) that emphasizes the unicity of performance aesthetics, musical motives and particular playing styles, vocal techniques and timbral features, due to the historical and musical context.

In the early twenty-first century, prominent *zenji flava* performers include Alhaji Goya, AT, Baby J, Berry Black, Berry White, Chidi Yobo, Cool Muza, Didah, Dorica, Offside Trick, Rama B, Rico Single, Short Gun, Sultan King and Warda Baby. Through forms of dissemination including television, radio and the Internet, *zenji flava* articulates lived experiences in contemporary Zanzibar to a local and a global audience, affirming itself as an ever-growing phenomenon.

Emergence

Zenji flava emerged in Zanzibar in the 1980s, albeit maturing as a relevant cultural and musical genre only in the 1990s. To trace the history of *zenji flava* is partly to trace that of *bongo flava*, since the distinction between the two genres surfaced later for geopolitical reasons. Nevertheless, Zanzibar has been a cosmopolitan context for a longer period of time. Situated at the intersection of the maritime routes across the Indian Ocean, along which peoples from the surrounding littoral societies have been traveling for centuries (Sheriff 2010), Zanzibar is a threshold to the African mainland and a harbor, providing access to a continuous flow of commodities and peoples. Musical genres have traveled with their performers and molded the original soundscape of the islands.

In the 1980s a few privileged young Zanzibari musicians who came into contact with US rap and hip-hop because of studying abroad or having relatives overseas (Englert 2008) began imitating these genres, singing in English. A decade later musicians started rapping in Swahili, first translating lyrics by US rappers and then composing and rapping their own lyrics, appropriating foreign patterns and innovating on sounds, beats, language and creeds (Perullo 2012), in a continuous negotiation between local and global flavors. Thus, while *bongo flava* was considered a mere imitation of North American hip-hop and rap styles when it emerged, it developed as an innovative and creative genre, appropriating and reinventing several further genres, such as R&B, reggae, ragga, *zouk, bongo banghra* and *takau* (Perullo 2012; Suriano 2007). As for two other prominent Swahili musical genres, *muziki wa dansi* and *taarab*, the emergence of *zenji flava*, as well as of *bongo flava*, confirms how the appropriation and accommodation, also referred to as Swahilization, of foreign performing elements are fundamental characteristics of Swahili culture (Askew 2002).

The founders of *zenji flava* include, among others, DJ Saleh, DJ Kim, Dula Ukasha, Abdullah and Cool Para, later joined by Cool Muza, SJ in the crew 'the Struggling Islanders' (Omari 2013). At the time, there were only the state-owned radio station Sauti ya Tanzania Zanzibar and Television Zanzibar, both of which aired only music that was considered representative of an exclusively Tanzanian identity, acquiescing in the cultural project of nation building (Askew 2002; Fair 2001). Yet, it was Television Zanzibar, established in 1974 and owning the proper equipment and technology, which in the mid-1990s produced the first *bongo flava* music videos, among them the first videos from Zanzibari musicians, featuring songs by Cool Para and 'the Struggling Islanders' (Juma4 2011). The liberalization of the media and the establishment of private radio stations and recording studios, as well as the digitalization of the media, facilitated the diffusion and growing popularity of *zenji flava*, although the local context reveals important disparities in the access to the production and the consumption of the genre.

Since the early 2000s several radio stations have been established on Unguja Island, the biggest and most famous within the archipelago: Coconut FM, Bomba FM, Zenji FM, Spice FM and others; on Pemba Island, on the contrary, there are only Radio Micheweni and the religious stations of Radio Istiqama and Radio Maria (Omari 2013). This partly reflects the controversial history of the archipelago, which plays a relevant role in molding the unicity of *zenji flava*. Alhaji Goya, a musician from Pemba, addresses the issue in his famous song 'Hali ya Pemba,' portraying precisely the challenges faced in everyday life on the island, never directly criticizing the Zanzibar government, but using rhetorical figures proper to the long-standing Swahili poetic tradition. In fact, until the 2010 Tanzanian general elections, when a Government of National Unity was established after a popular referendum that enabled the setting-up of a power-sharing government (31 July 2010), the political context was characterized by the denial of political and civil rights. In that framework the use of cultural performances as a counter-narrative to the mainstream culture was not allowed (Brunotti 2005a; Omari 2013). The new political scenario enabled young people to address diverse feelings of belonging and identification, letting an overall Zanzibari identity arise as a conscious act in the reinvention of a powerful unifying identity to oppose the disputed national Tanzanian one.

Unguja Island, a major tourist destination, provides opportunities for *zenji flava* artists to gain the attention of a wider and more varied audience. Nevertheless, this audience never compares to the massive attraction *bongo flava* counts on in Dar es Salaam and elsewhere on the mainland. Although many *zenji flava* artists regard Dar es Salaam as the center of growth for musicians, especially because of promotion and distribution and improved quality of life, *zenji flava* is not confined to a geographical context. Production and consumption of *zenji flava* music have been changed and facilitated by digital social networks, which allow easy downloads of songs and videos and constitute commentary platforms and provide updated information on venues, concerts and new releases, eventually contributing to the popularity and success of the artists. Since music video production seems to be taking the place of earlier means of diffusion, communication and reception, in the early twenty-first century the role played by the Internet is becoming impressively significant to the musicians' visual self-expression (Hacke 2014).

Performance and Identity

At the intersection of global and local youth culture (Perullo 2012; Perullo and Fenn 2003), *zenji flava* claims a space within the past and present African diaspora (Hacke 2014), while voicing contextual cultural and sociopolitical challenges. Like the music style identified as *taarap*, a fusion between *taarab* and rap, experimented by one of the most prominent Zanzibari musicians, Cool Para (Khamis 2001), the repositioning of *bongo flava* into strong recognition as *zenji flava* is grounded in the musical and poetic heritage of the islands. In Zanzibar, producers craft lyrics employing verbal interplay, prosodic rhythm and proper intonation of *taarab* tradition. They produce tracks that replicate the instruments used in traditional live performances, such as *kinanda* (harmonium), *udi* (lute), *ganuni* (Arab zither with 78 strings), violins, accordion, cello, but also Western drum kits, electric guitar, double bass and other percussion instruments. Instrumentals also reproduce *ngoma* performances distinctive of the islands. In 'Dege,' a song performed by the Offside Trick crew (2012), the lyrics, dancing and musical instruments are related to the *ndege, ngoma* genre from Pemba: this was traditionally performed at weddings and used to display a unique mimicry, representing and enacting the social identities involved in the ritual, and in society at large. Yet, 'Dege Hilo' introduces musical forms, beats and sounds that figure in different musical and cultural discourses too, eventually embarking on a project of hybridization of the soundscape, suggesting patterns of both inclusion and exclusion, of self-identification as well as detachment (Vierke 2015).

The poetic adaptation of the language reveals features proper to the *zenji flava* genre. For instance, in the song 'Ahmada,' by Offside Trick (2010) featuring the late Bi Kidude, renowned as the 'queen of Zanzibar,' *zenji flava* encounters *unyago* traditional initiation rituals. Swahili language alternates with 'lugha ya ndani' (the term used by Swahili people to describe the specific 'hidden' language used in the rituals and understood only by participating women), revealing the creativity of the poetic project that makes the genre unique. The music, enriched by *msondo*, the big drum played by Bi Kidude, mixes genres and cultural significance, eventually creating a profound piece of *zenji flava*'s history. The dancing is molded according to the initiation ritual's gestures, coupled with the *flava* tempo and dancing styles. Vocalization, motifs, imageries and themes derive inspiration from a vast repertoire resounding with local and global tunes.

Lyrics address local audiences, sometimes criticizing accepted social values, not completely denying them but rather reaffirming them, enriched with aspects pertaining to Zanzibari youth. Themes can vary from daily life issues to political concerns, disclosing beliefs, customs and creeds pertaining to the islands. Poetic stanzas may make reference to the existence of spirits, whose realm is commonly accepted as interfering with the human one, or a variety of other topics. Zanzibari cuisine, specific ways to differentiate social categories and to define private and public relationships, debated social issues such as bride-wealth payment, economic constraints and generational clashes are all communicated through *zenji flava* music. Sometimes ascribed as a strategic choice to gain easy reception and reach fast economic success (Englert 2008; Omari 2013), the topic of love, which is profoundly embedded in Swahili poetic tradition (Khamis 2004), is also a prominent theme. Various images of love permeate *zenji flava* songs, some locally derived, others rising from cultural exchange, repositioning the genre within local/global narratives.

Locality is not only portrayed in song lyrics and musical patterns; it is elaborated and creatively evoked in *zenji flava* music videos. *Zenji* 'flavors' are constantly perceptible in the choice of stage costumes, makeup, settings and common use objects. Further, minimal gestures and dramatic mimicry promote an aesthetic that is distinctively Zanzibari.

Conclusion

Through *zenji flava*, Zanzibari young people address local contexts, singing them and, therefore, claiming a space in the restrictive gerontocratic sociopolitical Zanzibar (Burgess 2005). At the same time, they find a position in global youth culture, defying geopolitical borders in an era of rapid globalization. Self-expression has become global; as soon as songs and music videos are released, they are played on the Internet, allowing Zanzibari young people to conceptualize globalization and modernity through their performance (Suriano 2007), in local and trans-local contexts.

Driven by the need for societal acceptance, *zenji flava* artists struggle to introduce themselves to their own society as young people, and not as a marginalized and problematic subculture. Often regarded by Zanzibari society as *wahuni* (hooligans), not exclusively because of the specificity of the genre, but for the simple reason that they are stigmatized as musicians (Brunotti 2005b), Zanzibari young people build, through the *zenji flava* genre, their own creed and interpretation of authenticity and 'Zanzibariness.'

Bibliography

Askew, Kelly. 2002. *Performing the Nation: Swahili Music and Cultural Politics in Tanzania*. Chicago: University of Chicago Press.

Brunotti, Irene. 2005a. *Chake/Wete in Ng'ambo: Ngoma e costruzioni identitarie a Zanzibar in età contemporanea* [Chake/Wete in Ng'ambo: Ngoma and Identity Constructions in Contemporary Zanzibar]. Unpublished Ph.D. thesis, Università degli Studi di Napoli 'L'Orientale.'

Brunotti, Irene. 2005b. 'Ngoma ni uhuni? Ngoma za kisasa mjini Zanzibar.' [Are Ngoma Hooliganism? Contemporary Ngoma Performances in the Urban Zanzibar] *Swahili Forum* 12: 161–71.

Burgess, Thomas. 2005. 'Youth and Citizenship in East Africa.' *Africa Today* 51(3): vii–xxiv.

Englert, Birgit. 2008. 'Kuchanganyachanganya: Topic and Language Choices in Tanzanian Youth Culture.' *Journal of African Cultural Studies* 20(1): 45–55.

Fair, Laura. 2001. *Pastimes and Politics: Culture, Community, and Identity in Post Abolition in Post-Abolition Urban Zanzibar, 1890-1945*. Athens, OH: Ohio University Press.

Hacke, Gabriel. 2014. 'Tanzanian Music Videos in the Black Atlantic: The Production, Distribution and Visual References of Bongo Flava Video Clips.' In *Bongo Media Worlds. Producing and Consuming Popular Culture in Dar es Salaam*, eds. Matthias Krings and Uta Reuster-Jahn. Cologne: Rüdiger Köppe Verlag, 79–107.

Juma4. 2011. 'Zanzibar Nineties Rap: the VHS Vault.' Online at: http://www.africanhiphop.com/zanzibar-nineties-rap-the-vhs-vault/ (accessed 27 February 2016).

Khamis, Said Ahmed Mohamed. 2001. 'Redefining Taarab in Relation to Local and Global Influences.' *Swahili Forum* 8: 145–56.

Khamis, Said Ahmed Mohamed. 2002. 'Wondering about Change: The Taarab Lyric and Global Openness.' *Nordic Journal of African Studies* 11(2): 198–205.

Khamis, Said Ahmed Mohamed. 2004. 'Images of Love in the Swahili Taarab Lyric: Local Aspects and Global Influence.' *Nordic Journal of African Studies* 13(1): 30–64.

Omari, Shani. 2013. 'Hip Hop Music as a Youth Medium for Cultural Struggle in Zanzibar.' *The Journal of Pan African Studies* 6(3) (September): 133–55.

Perullo, Alex. 2012. 'Imitation and Innovation in the Music, Dress, and Camps of Tanzanian Youth.' *English and Cultural Studies Book Publications* 11: 187–207.

Perullo, Alex, and Fenn, John. 2003. 'Language Ideology, Choices, and Practices in Eastern African Hip Hop.' In *Global Pop, Local Language*, eds. Harris M. Berger and Michael Thomas Carroll. Jackson: University Press of Mississippi, 19–51.

Reuster-Jahn, Uta, and Hacke, Gabriel. 2014. 'The Bongo Flava Industry in Tanzania and Artists' Strategies for Success.' In *Bongo Media Worlds. Producing and Consuming Popular Culture in Dar es Salaam*, eds. Matthias Krings and Uta Reuster-Jahn. Köln: Rüdiger Köppe Verlag, 24–42. (Reissue of Uta Reuster-Jahn and Gabriel Hacke, 'The Bongo Flava Industry in Tanzania and Artists' Strategies for Success.' *Arbeitpapiere / Working Papers* 127 (2011): 1–21.)

Suriano, Maria. 2007. '"Mimi ni Msanii, Kioo cha Jamii." Urban Youth Culture in Tanzania as Seen Through Bongo Fleva and Hip-Hop.' *Swahili Forum* 14: 207–23.

Vierke, Clarissa. 2015. 'Comparing the Incomparable? On the Poetic Use of Language in Swahili Hip Hop and "Classical" Swahili Poetry.' In *Habari ya English? What about Kiswahili? East Africa as a Literary and Contact Zone*, eds. Lutz Diegner and Frank Schulze-Engler. Leiden and Boston: Brill Rodopi, 81–112.

Discographical References

Goya, Alhaji. 'Hali ya Pemba.' MJ Records. *2000*: Tanzania.

Offside Trick ft. Bi Kidude. 'Ahmada.' Akhenaton Records. *2010*: Tanzania.

Offside Trick ft. Hammer Q. 'Dege.' Golden Heart Studio (GHS). *2012*: Tanzania.

Discography

Baby J. 'Nimempenda Mwenyewe.' Akhenaton Records. *2014*: Tanzania.

Berry Black. 'Nafsi Yako.' Teddy Records. *2009*: Tanzania.

Berry Black, Berry White ft. Shiriko. 'Na Wewe 2.' Teddy Records. *2007*: Tanzania.

Cool Muza and Montago. 'Wanangu wa Mtaani.' Jupiter Records. *2010*: Tanzania.

Offside Trick. *The Best of Offside Trick*. Akhenaton Records. *2012*: Tanzania.

Rico Single. 'Wafanyakazi.' Jupiter Records. *2012*: Tanzania.

Sultan King. 'Mahari.' Jupiter Records. *2011*: Tanzania.

Filmography

Zenji Flava, dirs. Bram Vergeer and Raymond Verhoef. 2006. The Netherlands. 54 mins. Documentary.

Visual Recordings

AT. 2011. 'Bao la Kete.' Kwetu Studio/Kiri Rec (video).
Cool Para. 1990s. 'Kwenye Matata.' TVZ (video).
Dorica. 2012. 'Bado Nampenda.' Mac Media (video).
SJ. 1990s. 'Baby Lone.' TVZ (video).

IRENE BRUNOTTI

Zenli

Zenli (also known as *zinli*) is a funereal style of drumming, singing and dancing practiced in Republic of Benin. *Zenli* is characterized by the prominent use of the lead *kpezin* clay drum, which responds to the vocalist's poetic and melodic improvisations and inspires participants to dance, using a rippling arm and torso motion, which is another important part of *zenli* practice. Over time, *zenli* has undergone a series of transformations, mostly through changing instrumentation, performance context and lyrical content.

Recent music scholarship in Benin has shown that there are, in fact, many different varieties of *zenli* throughout the southern part of the country. The Conservatoire des Danses Cérémonielles d'Abomey (2013) identifies five different forms of *zenli* present in Benin: Adja, Kotafon, Fon, Ouémé and Sahoue. The Fon variety originating in Abomey (*zenli d'Abomey*) is described here. The Sahoue variety, from southwest Benin, was developed and given increased visibility in the 2010s by the female percussionist and vocalist Norberka, who calls her version *zenli gbete*. The Kotafon variety, from western Benin into Togo, has been popularized by the artist known as Gbefa, and *zenli* from the eastern Ouémé region (Avivozenli) is practiced by Anice Pepe. The Adja variety, sometimes called *avizenli*, is lesser known, originating from the ethnically Mina section of western Benin and Togo.

Historical Development

Zenli has been practiced since the time of the precolonial Danxomean Empire, possibly as early as the reign of King Agadja in the Fon capital of Agbome (called Abomey by the French) in the first part of the eighteenth century. At first during the reign of King Agadja (1708–28), *zenli* was performed only on the *sinhun* (literally, 'water drum'), two calabashes of different sizes and tones overturned in pails of water and struck with sticks, producing a high pitch and a low pitch; and on the *zenli* itself, a large gourd which both kept time and played lead parts, producing a deep vibration that could be felt as well as heard. The bell (*gan*), shakers (*assan*) and clay *kpezin* drums were introduced later, during the reign of King Guezo (1818–58).

Zenli was originally only played for the funerals of the royal family in Abomey. 'Zen' in the Fon language refers to the ritual fan used to close the tomb of the departed and 'li' to the tomb itself. Local historians suggest that *zenli* may have originally been borrowed from the drumming repertoire for Fa divination, which was brought to Abomey by Yorùbá traders during the time of King Agadja. King Agonglo, who ruled from 1789 to 1797, was said to have called on *zenli*'s ritual power to resolve his difficulty producing an heir.

During the reign of King Guezo (1818–58), *zenli* underwent a dramatic transformation in instrumentation with the addition of the *kpezin* drums. According to both *zenli* singer Alekpehanhou and oral historian Gabin Djimasse, Guezo requested that his son, the future King Glele, organize a *zenli* orchestra for the funeral of Guezo's close friend Tometin. Glele decided to introduce some innovations into the *zenli* formula to surprise his father. A few days in advance of the funeral, he brought in a couple of *kpezin*, drums made of pottery and wrapped in wicker with skin heads that are capable of producing a great variety of timbres at great volumes, from deep resonances to sharp cracks. He taught the orchestra a new rhythm to go along with the old rhythm played on the *zenli* drum, and he added the *kpezin* along with *assan* and *gan* while phasing out the *sinhun*. Glele's father was very pleased with the rhythm when he heard it on the day of his friend's funeral and called it *zenli blibli*, a new form of *zenli* that was much more majestic and moving than it had been before. Guezo then requested that this style be played at his own funeral. This new style of *zenli* became popular throughout the region of Abomey for funerals around the late nineteenth century. Glele appointed a different *zenli* group to play for the princes and chiefs in each neighborhood in Abomey, which meant that some drummers made a living exclusively by playing *zenli* for the royal families. This practice has continued into the twenty-first century, but due to increased cost of living, nearly all *zenli* musicians engage in other work to earn the majority of their income.

After independence in 1960, a new generation of musicians introduced further innovations into the *zenli* genre, each claiming a personal style and documenting their work through newly available recording technology. They also began performing *zenli* outside of funeral contexts, at weddings, birthdays and other celebrations. For the funeral contexts, only men could perform in the group, but at other celebrations, women could play and dance as well. The artist Akpinkpa was among the first to specialize in love songs in *zenli* style in the 1960s. Although he did not produce many recordings, Akpinkpa became the mentor of Le Roi Alekpehanhou, who began his prolific recording career in the 1980s. Alekpehanhou introduced several innovations into what he called his *zenli rénové* or 'renewed *zenli*'. He continued his mentor's interest in expanding *zenli*'s lyrical topics, including love, politics, philosophy and personal relationships. Alekpehanhou insists that only one song per album be on a funereal topic, in order to bring a more joyful spirit to his audience. He has also introduced different bell sounds into his music, including the twin bell (*ganvinon*) borrowed from sacred Vodun repertoires, giving it a distinctive stamp. Alekpehannhou produced over 40 albums from the 1960s to the early twenty-first century, and he is known as a skilled improviser when he sings in Fon. He is also well known for his music videos, which make use of traditional imagery to bring his language to life, and which are ubiquitous on local television in Benin. Alekpahanhou's ensemble grew increasingly larger, including between 6 and 10 musicians and as many as 20 backup singers.

Zenli dancing also changed in the second half of the twentieth century as it migrated into other performance contexts. In a royal funeral context, *zenli* dancers isolated their torsos, smoothly rippling their back muscles from top to bottom with their elbows out. This dance was perceived in traditional communities as cool and dignified. At weddings and other celebrations since the 1960s, *zenli* dancing has become increasingly acrobatic and more and more physically demanding, as dancers have added pelvic and shoulder pops and larger arm gestures to the dance. Outside of Abomey in Cotonou and in the Beninois diaspora in the United States, *zenli* rhythms and dancing have become emblematic of a playful attitude toward traditional heritage. Customarily, the men who perform *zenli* wear a *pagne* (wrapped skirt) around their waists and a loose-fitting white tunic called a *boba*.

Musical Description

Zenli focuses on the voice of the singer, whose improvisations on mostly pentatonic melodies are prized for their lyrical and poetic innovations. These vocals may reference traditional proverbs, praise powerful personalities or signify on political events. The *gan* and the *assan* provide the timeline (see *gan* timeline patterns in Example 1), while the *zenli*

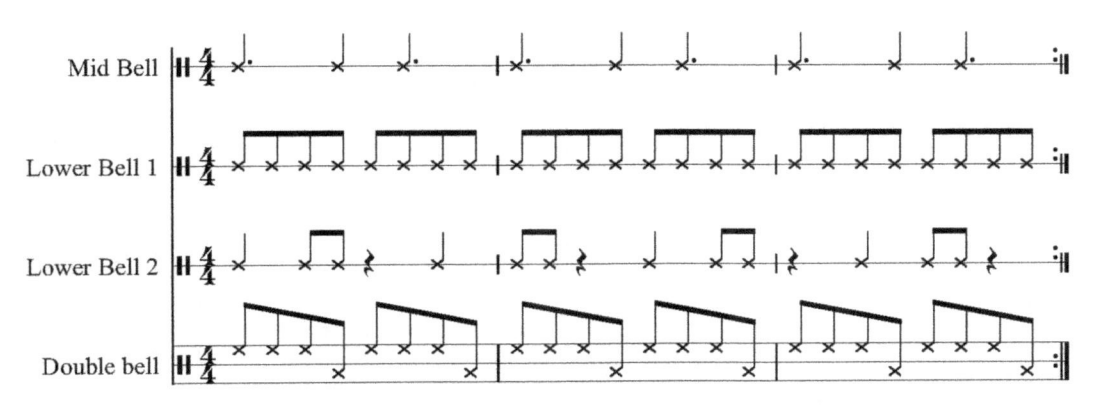

Example 1: *Zenli* bells (*gan*) timeline

and *kpezin* trade off accompaniment and lead roles, always interacting closely with the singer. The choir's interactions with the singer are also important, as they echo the major themes of the song, singing in unison.

The presentation of *zenli* extends from live performance at funerals and celebrations to CD and cassette recordings, and to music videos for television and YouTube. The lead vocalist and the choir may be amplified, while the instruments are not. The lead vocalist will often dress in the style of an Abomean king, with a traditional hat appliqued with the symbols of his lineage, a curved royal staff engraved with similar symbols and a long, flowing, white *boba* tunic over a long *pagne* skirt. Imagery in music videos has become particularly important, since singers make reference to everyday activities through proverbs and parables, and the videos bring these references to life.

Zenli has also achieved some international circulation in specific examples. It has been adapted in brass band and jazz arrangements by the Gangbé Brass Band on their track 'Ajaka' (2001 and 2015) and by the jazz guitarist Lionel Loueke in his duet with vocalist Angélique Kidjo on 'Vi Ma Yon' on his album *Mwaliko* (2010). One of the difficulties in performing *zenli* outside of Benin is that the *kpezin* drums are very fragile and break easily when transported. The Gangbé Brass Band has introduced an innovative solution by covering a set of three *kpezin* together with welded iron to protect them. This also gives the drums a deep metallic resonance.

Conclusion

The transition of *zenli* from sacred funereal genre to ubiquitous popular style is an important one, and mirrors similar transitions in other traditional styles. This was the case with *tchinkoume,* which was originally a Mahi funeral genre, and *kaka* and *masse gohoun,* which have roots in the music of secret societies and Vodun practice near Porto-Novo. Because of its wide dispersion and many different local variants, *zenli* is the most commonly practiced of these genres, both in traditional and popular contexts. While Benin has not developed a leading single national style out of its many rhythmic traditions, *zenli*'s popularity and widespread adaptations give it unifying resonance as a musical marker for southern Benin.

Bibliography

Alekpehanhou. 2014. Interview with the author, 7 December. Abomey, Benin.

da Cruz, Clement. 1954. *Les instruments de musique dans le Bas-Dahomey (Populations Fon, Adja, Kotafon, Péda, Aïzo)* [Musical Instruments in Lower Dahomey. (Fon, Adja, Kotafon, Peda and Aïzo Populations)]. *Études dahoméennes* [Dahomey Studies], XII. Porto-Novo, Benin: Institut Français d'Afrique Noire.

Djimasse, Gabin. Interview with the author, 6 December. Abomey, Benin.

Discographical References

Gangbé Brass Band. 2015. 'Ajaka.' *Go Slow to Lagos.* Buda Musique. *2015*: France.

Gangbé Brass Band. 2001. 'Ajaka.' *Togbé*. Contre-jour. *2001*: Belgium.

Loueke, Lionel, and Kidjo, Angélique. 'Vi Ma Yon.' *Mwaliko*. Blue Note. *2010*: New York.

Discography

Le Roi Alekpehanhou. *Roi du Zenli Rénové*. SATEL ACM 17. *2008*: Benin.

Le Roi Alekpehanhou. *Sato Na Hanga*. SATEL ACM 19. *2010*: Benin.

Les visages du Zenli (Sonorités Endogènes d'Afrique) [The Faces of Zenli (Indigenous Sounds of Africa)]. Conservatoire des Danses Cérémonielles et Rituels d'Abomey. *2013*: Benin.

SARAH POLITZ

Zikiri

The term *zikiri* is a phonetic alteration in the Bambara language of the Arabic word *dhikr* (invocation of the name of Allah), which refers to Islamic praise songs. The music genre *zikiri* was created in Mali in the early twenty-first century and has spread into many West African countries. It constitutes a major phenomenon of popular religious music produced *by* and *for* the young people. This Islamic pop music is articulated in several musical styles, from *griot* songs to international pop music including rap and reggae, and it is characterized by the use of amplified instruments and by its extensive media coverage. *Zikiri* combines the practice of a panegyric to the glory of a religious guide with traditional music drawing on oral culture and blended with a globalized cultural modernity, and it promotes Afro-Islamic values in response to the cultural hegemony of the West. Its development is one of the consequences of the emergence of new popular Islamic organizations that appeared in the wake of the 1991 Malian democratization process and that are characterized by an opening to civil society, a religious transnationalism, and the reaffirmation of a popular religiosity under the influence of Sufism (Holder 2009, 2013). Thus, in an unprecedented manner, *zikiri* articulates the processes of re-Islamization and national identity reaffirmation as well as entertainment (Olivier and Djebbari 2015).

From *Madh* to *Zikiri*

At the beginning of the 1970s, when Racine Sall, the son of a *cadi* (Muslim judge) established in the region of Kayes near the border with Senegal, created a new genre of Islamic praise songs, they were circumscribed to the holy cities of Timbuktu, Jenne, Dilly and Nioro in Sahel (Holder 2012b; Hunwick 2003; Olivier 2004, 2012, 2016). These panegyrics, called *madh* in Arabic, were addressed to the Prophet Muhammad, to his mediators (saints, sheikhs and *ulemas*), but also to powerful living people. Furthermore, they belonged to a larger repertoire that had spread in the Sufi Muslim world for over a millennium, in particular in Africa. The *madh* panegyrics constituted very effective forms of proselytizing with the purpose of educating and feeding the imagination about the lives of the holy people. The *Ta'rîkh as-Sûdân*, famous chronicles of Timbuktu and Jenne written by Al-Sa'di (1594–1655 or 1656), testify that *madh* have been performed at least since the beginning of the seventeenth century (Hunwick 1999), seeming to confirm that these praise songs have survived across history, or at least have been a recurring feature and have shaped a strong identity. *Madh* is a poetic and musical genre that embodies the style of a learned music and even of classical music, since the poetic lyrics and melody are based on the rules of Arabic classical poetry (metrics, rhythm and structure), codified and theorized in numerous treaties, even though some melodies in Mali stem from popular music (Olivier 2012, 2016). *Madh* is a monody performed *a cappella* by a single individual or a choir according to social circumstances. When the performance is collective, in particular during the annual religious ceremonies (Ramadan, Mawlid), *madh* adopts an antiphonal or responsorial form by being sung by two male choirs in a relationship of ritualized rivalry (Holder and Olivier 2015).

For a long time, *madh* remained the major artistic sound expression of Islam in Mali, very closely associated with the urban and learned culture of the cities situated on the border of the Sahara. When Racine Sall began to compose religious praise songs at the very beginning of the 1970s, this regional and cultural specificity spread to the rest of Mali. He did not compose the lyrics in Arabic, however, but in vernacular languages, and particularly in Bambara, the most widespread language in Mali. Sall launched the process of popularization of Islamic music by making a religious body of knowledge accessible to an audience that was Muslim but not familiar with the Arabic language. He modernized his music, drawing on griotic and international pop music alike to attract his Malian audience. While *madh* was sung *a cappella*, Sall's *zikiri* was performed with upside-down calabash, underarm drum, *balafon*, *kora*, electric guitar, drums or synthesizer. This instrumental ensemble accompanied solo sung verses to which the chorus responded. *Zikiri* adhered to the standards of the popular music broadcast on Radio Mali in the 1970s, which allowed its introduction into the popular culture and entertainment market. Racine Sall was indeed one of the very first Malian artists to record an album in a studio in 1973, later appearing on national television (ORTM) from its outset in 1983. Nevertheless, in spite of Sall having recorded a dozen albums, there was no emulation of his achievement. For about 20 years, he was the only one to promote this new popular religious genre in Mali, where griotic music (Charry 2000) and the orchestras playing modern popular music, stemming from the Artistic and Cultural Biennale – the Rail Band, Les Ambassadeurs du Motel or the Super Biton de Segou (Mazzoleni 2011) – were prominent.

Nevertheless, at the beginning of the 1980s the popularization of the analog cassette allowed some preachers of Segou and Bamako to begin recording religious praise songs in studios. At the same time, Chérif Ousmane Madani Haïdara released his first preaching cassettes, inspired by the famous Egyptian Sheikh 'Abd al-Hamîd Kishk, whose productions had been circulating in the Muslim world, western Africa included, since the 1970s (Holder 2012a). The religious cassette thus became a new product in the Malian media economy. And the same trend was observed in nearby countries, especially in Senegal and in Ivory Coast, where musical production was more developed at the time.

However, religious praise songs remained marginal in the Malian musical scene of the 1980s. *Zikiri* emerged as popular music only at the end of the 1990s, in the wake of the Sufi reformist movements led by charismatic figures such as Chérif Ousmane Madani Haïdara, the spiritual guide of the Ançar Dine association, or Sheikh Sufi Bilal Diallo, leader of the Muslim Community of Sufis.

Zikiri as Islamic Pop Music

Over the course of a few years in the early twenty-first century *zikiri* became increasingly popular, illustrated by its spectacularization and media coverage. In reality, this phenomenon went hand in hand with the expansion of Mawlid ceremonies (commemorations of the birthday of the prophet Mohammad) throughout Mali, which reached their peak in 2005 when Mawlid was established as a national religious holiday. These commemorations were transformed into proper music festivals hosted in stadia, with hundreds of thousands of people gathering for the entire week between the anniversary of the date of birth and that of the 'baptism' of the prophet (Olivier 2014b). From then on, *zikiri* evolved into the real hymns of Muslim organizations, such as Ançar Dine or the Muslim Community of the Sufis, and, at the same time, *zikiri* singers (*zikiridala*, lit. 'the one who lays *zikiri*') increased in number dramatically and gave birth to a new form of religious profession (Prud'homme 2010). Some decided to be in the service of a specific preacher; for example, Souleymane Diarra, whose stage name is Zikiri Solo, along with Nouhoum Dembélé, has become affiliated with Chérif Haïdara, and Ba Ka Bouraïma Samaké and the Anwar Orchestra both work for Sheikh Sufi Bilal. However, others are polyvalent and praise several preachers, or are even independent, as is the case with Mohamed Diaby, whose talent for *zikiri* was showcased by the reality show *Case Sanga* broadcast on the Africable television channel in 2007. Finally, some Malian musicians who are not labeled as such have also begun composing *zikiri* on specific occasions. This is the case for *griot* Almami Bah, reggae singer General Balodi and guitarist Baba Salah. Although most *zikiri* singers are young men, some young women also have achieved success in the media, such as Alima and Sana Koné, both established in Ivory Coast, but natives of Mali.

Zikiri is in vogue in the early twenty-first century, and is growing in popularity along with the phenomenon of re-Islamization of Malian society (Holder 2009). Some *zikiri* singers have even become stars in competition with the *griots* and *griottes* when it comes to performing at wedding and 'baptism' celebrations (Schulz 2001), a development which sometimes prompts the *griots*' anger and sometimes their conversion to the field of religious music. These *zikiri* star singers circulate between Mali, Ivory Coast and Burkina Faso, in the so-called Manding cultural area, to perform during private parties, public concerts or television programs, living as idolized artists.

This festive use of *zikiri* blurs the line between the sacred and the profane: it is not rare for audiences, carried away by the singer's performance, to burst into applause, or for the singers to sketch dance steps, both acts considered highly inappropriate in a strictly religious context. Besides, these festive performances inevitably provoke criticism and condemnation, relayed by the media, from the religious authorities. Articles appear in Malian newspapers regularly, often inspired or drafted by Muslims who advocate orthopraxy, denouncing the mingling of men and women which the performances of *zikiri* favors, as well as the practice of 'impertinent' dancing (*coupé-décalé*, *balani* show and so on), and sometimes even the 'blasphemous' character of these songs.

In spite of these criticisms, the *zikiri* phenomenon is becoming more and more prominent in Malian popular music in the early twenty-first century, as *zikiri* singers organize themselves and professionalize. With regard to the popular craze and the economic perspectives it generates, the Malian authorities cannot but interfere with *zikiri* as it fits in the public cultural policies that aim, in particular, to professionalize the music industry.

Media coverage is largely accountable for the popularization of *zikiri* (Schulz 2012). But the situation has changed immensely since the 1980s when the first analog cassettes of religious praise songs were released in the music market. The turning point toward digital dissemination occurred in the early 2000s and accelerated after 2005. However, the analog medium was not replaced immediately; a hybrid technology arose and until 2011 both media coexisted, in response to various uses, audiences and modes of consumption of music. The extensive production and distribution of analog cassettes and video-CDs (a less complex and less expensive technology than DVD) generates a small informal economy (shops, market stalls and street vendors). But just like the rest of Malian musical production, *zikiri* is the victim of massive pirating and most of the singers prefer to offer their cassettes and video-CDs as professional 'business cards' rather than to sell them. This allows them to earn notoriety, and thus to be invited to entertain at lucrative private parties or participate in concerts, and possibly be spotted by pop or world music producers. In general, the service economy, based on remuneration from live performances, seems better adapted than the copyright system to the widely informal economy of *zikiri* (Olivier 2014a).

Since 2011 *zikiri* has been played on and exchanged via smartphones; it is watched on television (in religious and variety programs or reality shows alike) and on the Internet; it is played on FM and Internet radio channels (religious radio stations included); it can be downloaded from streaming websites and via smartphone applications thanks to the 3G mobile telephony network; it is promoted via the personal Facebook pages of *zikiri* singers and the pages of religious organizations; related mobile ring tones and ring-back tones can be downloaded; and, finally, it is stored on USB drives and MP3 memory cards. *Zikiri* takes advantage of all the media available in Mali and thus is no different from the rest of the Malian popular music industry.

The Making of a 'Bambara Sound'

The popularization and media coverage of the *zikiri* genre in Mali, and more generally in western Africa, accounts for increasing competition among singers in the regional music market. This has driven some market stakeholders (producers, radio and television hosts) to label *zikiri* performed in Mali as Malian, and in so doing to impart a national identity to it *de facto*, thus offering it better visibility and a qualitative identity marker or 'logo' in the field of new religious music (Prud'homme 2015). But this assignment of a Malian identity, which is primarily part of an economic strategy, is not entirely unfounded from a musical perspective. Indeed, many Malian singers of *zikiri* seek to produce what they themselves call the 'Bambara sound.'

The main features of the 'Bambara sound' are as follows:

a. lyrics written in Bamanakan, the *lingua franca* in Mali that is also understood in many of its neighboring countries;
b. the use of instruments: calabashes or turned-over cans struck by two wooden sticks, an instrumental configuration which is the basis of most Malian music;
c. the pentatonic scale that is the basis of the melody, and that is common to most Malian music, be it profane or religious. However, the melodies sung by *zikiri* singers often rely on a harmonic base performed by a synthesizer on a heptatonic scale that some musicians call 'the French scale.' This harmonic density is supposed 'to modernize' *zikiri* and obviously belongs to the Western musical language, widely spread in Western Africa via globalized music, but also by Christian songs;
d. the responsorial form, consisting of a chorus responding to a soloist, which is the most widespread musical pattern in Mali, but also found in the globalized music industry;
e. specific rhythmic patterns, in particular: *cumba*, *jazz-wassoulou*, *takamba* and *bamana foli*. Allegedly, *cumba* rhythm is from Segou, the capital of one of the most important states in precolonial Mali and a symbolic emblem of the country's culture. Yet, this rhythm is much more likely to have been imported from Cuba, a country with which Mali has developed important cultural exchanges since its independence. Cuban music had a major influence on Malian, and more generally West African, musical production (Shain 2002). But if *cumba* rhythm illustrates this musical circulation between the two sides of the Atlantic Ocean, this legacy was largely forgotten in favor of the perception – which eventually prevailed – of a uniquely Malian origin. Similarly, *bamana foli* refers to Bambara cultural identity – it means 'Bambara's greeting' – but this group of several

rhythms played by *jembe* and *dunun* drums was popularized at first by the various national groups (The Instrumental Ensemble and the National Ballet) before Malian world music percussionists, such as Abdoul Doumbia or the Drum Brothers, appropriated them; they have even become the primary rhythms taught during the training courses organized for Westerners. Traditionally played by the musicians of the *ngoni* lute in the region of Gao, the *takamba* rhythm was revived in the 1980s and 1990s, when it was transferred to amplified instruments by such bands as Gao's Super Onze, before Andy Morgan, one of the organizers of the Festival au Désert, discovered it in the early 2000s. Since then, *takamba* has been considered 'world music,' and it represents one of the typical musical expressions of Northern Mali, even though it has remained popular in Bamako, thanks to musicians such as Baba Salah or Habib Koité who have kept it up-to-date. As for the *jazz-wassoulou* rhythm, the renowned 'cantatrice' Oumou Sangaré popularized it in the 1990s, coining the 'Wassoulou style' that blends various types of local music with jazz, salsa, funk, rock or technodance. Oumou Sangaré owes her success to the 'Wassoulou style' to such an extent that it has become one of the emblems of Malian music on the international stage. By appropriating the *jazz-wassoulou* rhythm, *zikiri* singers stand in the field of the new Malian music, being part of both a local identity and a global economy.

The making of the identity of the 'Bambara sound' may be viewed as a process of the folklorization of *zikiri*, or better still, as a 'folklorization 2.0' which places this genre between Islamic religious music, griotic music and globalized popular music.

Conclusion

Through the recent phenomenon of *zikiri,* Islam appears as a new cultural and artistic offering in Mali. But far from being restricted to Mali, this phenomenon may be observed in other West African countries and beyond, across the Sufi Muslim world. Whether they are named *zikiri* (in Ivory Coast, Burkina Faso and Ghana), *bandiri* (in Nigeria), *inshad* (in Egypt), *nasheed* (in Algeria), *taarab* (in Tanzania and in Kenya), or *qasidah* modern (in Indonesia), these new types of Sufi Music have in common the production of a national and popular cultural imagination that is connected to the global.

Bibliography

Charry, Eric. 2000. *Mande Music: Traditional and Modern Music of the Maninka and Mandinka of Western Africa*. Chicago: Chicago University Press.

Holder, Gilles, ed. 2009. *L'islam, nouvel espace public en Afrique* [Islam, New Public Space in Africa]. Paris: Karthala.

Holder, Gilles. 2012a. 'Chérif Ousmane Madani Haïdara et l'association islamique Ançar Dine' [Charif Ousmane Madani Haïdara and the Ançar Dine Islamic Association]. *Cahiers d'Études africaines* 206–7:389–425.

Holder, Gilles. 2012b. 'Djenné, "la ville aux 313 saints." Convocation des savoirs, "lutte des classements" et production d'une ville sainte au Mali' [Jenne, 'The City of 313 Saints.' Convocation of Knowledge, 'War of Classification' and Production of a Holy City in Mali]. *Cahiers d'Études africaines* 208: 741–65.

Holder, Gilles. 2013. 'Un pays musulman en quête d'État-nation' [A Muslim Country in Search of Nation-State]. In *La tragédie malienne*, eds. Patrick Gonin, Nathalie Kotlok and Marc-Antoine Pérouse de Montclos. Paris: Vendémiaire, 135–60.

Holder, Gilles, and Olivier, Emmanuelle. 2015. 'Le Maouloud de Djenné: Stratégies patrimoniales de l'islam, mémoire urbaine et identité nationale' [The Maouloud of Djenné: Heritage Strategies of Islam, Urban Memory and National Identity]. In *Le Mali contemporain*, eds. Joseph Brunet-Jailly, Jacques Charmes and Doulaye Konaté. Paris: Éditions Tombouctou/IRD Éditions, 252–83.

Hunwick, John O. 1999. *Timbuktu and the Songhay Empire: Al-Sa'di's Ta'rikh al-sudan Down to 1613 and Other Contemporary Documents*. Leiden, Boston and Cologne: Brill.

Hunwick, John O. 2003. *Arabic Literature of Africa: The Writings of Western Sudanic Africa*, Vol. 4. Leyden: Brill.

Mazzoleni, Florent. 2011. *Afro Pop: L'âge d'or des grands orchestres africains* [Afro Pop: The Golden Age of African Orchestras]. Paris: Le Castor Astral.

Olivier, Emmanuelle. 2004. 'La petite musique de la ville: Musique et construction de la citadinité à Djenné (Mali).' [The Little Music of the City. Music and Construction of Urbanity in Jenne (Mali)]. *Journal des Africanistes* 74(1–2): 97–123.

Olivier, Emmanuelle. 2012. 'Les louanges islamiques au Mali: Un art de la filiation' [Islamic Praise Songs in Mali: An Art of Filiation]. In *Musiques au monde: La tradition au prisme de la création* [Music in the World : Tradition Through the Prism of Creation], ed. Emmanuelle Olivier. Sampzon: Éditions Delatour, 93–116.

Olivier, Emmanuelle. 2014a. 'Droits d'auteur *vs* usages locaux de l'autorité: Réflexion à partir d'une K7 de louanges islamiques au Mali' [Copyright vs Local Uses of Authority: Reflection from a Cassette of Islamic Praise Songs in Mali]. *Volume. La revue des musiques populaires* 10/2: 151–71.

Olivier, Emmanuelle. 2014b. 'Musiques et globalisation: "Techno-logiques" de la création musicale' [Music and Globalization: 'Techno-logics' of Musical Creation]. *Le temps des médias* 22: 134–48.

Olivier, Emmanuelle. 2016. *Islam et art poétique au Mali: Les madih de Aboubakar b. Al-Hadi Ko Yaro (1940–1999)* [Islam and Art of Poetry in Mali: The madih of Aboubakar b. Al-Hadi Ko Yaro (1940–99)]. Bamako: Éditions Tombouctou.

Olivier, Emmanuelle, and Djebbari, Élina. 2015. 'Des "religions du terroir" à l'islam et *vice versa*: Politiques culturelles et pratiques artistiques croisées' [From the Local Religions to Islam and Vice Versa: Cross-Cultural Politics and Artistic Practices]. In *Le Mali contemporain: Regards de scientifiques*, eds. Joseph Brunet-Jailly, Jacques Charmes and Doulaye Konaté. Paris and Bamako: IRD Éditions/Tombouctou Editions, 333–63.

Prud'homme, Pierre. 2010. *Louangeurs islamiques et économie politique du panégyrique à Bamako, Mali: Ethnographie d'une nouvelle profession religieuse* [Islamic Praise Singers and Political Economy of the Panegyric in Bamako : Ethnography of a New Religious Profession] Unpublished Master's thesis, Université de Provence Aix-Marseille 1.

Prud'homme, Pierre. 2015. '"Les griots d'Allah," ou l'émergence d'une musique religieuse populaire' ['Allah's Griots': The Emergence of a Popular Religious Music]. In *Le Mali contemporain: Regards de scientifiques*, eds. Joseph Brunet-Jailly, Jacques Charmes and Doulaye Konaté. Paris and Bamako: IRD Éditions/Tombouctou Editions, 317–32.

Shain, Richard. 2002. 'Roots in Reverse: Cubanismo in Twentieth-Century Senegalese Music.' *The International Journal of African Historical Studies* 35(1): 83–101.

Schulz, Dorothea E. 2001. *Perpetuating the Politics of Praise: Jeli Singers, Radios, and Political Mediation in Mali*. Cologne: Köppe.

Schulz, Dorothea E. 2012. *Muslims and New Media in West Africa. Pathways to God*. Bloomington: Indiana University Press.

Discographical References

Alima. *Louange à Allah*. Akwaba production. *2016*: Ivory Coast.

Alima. *Sebe Allah Ye*. (Cassette.) N.d.: Ivory Coast.

Dembele, Nouhoum. *Droit des femmes*. (Cassette.) *N.d.*: Mali.

Dembele, Nouhoum. *Folikan. Vol. 3*. (Cassette.) N.d.: Mali.

Dembele, Nouhoum. *Kira Mahamadou kanou bè anw na*. (Cassette.) N.d.: Mali.

Diaby, Mohamed. *Djangou Gallo*. 3GMuzik production, CD B00I46TZ8K. *2014*: Ivory Coast.

Diarra, Souleymane. *12 mai. Champion*. (Cassette.) *2011*: Mali.

Diarra, Souleymane. *Allah Ka Bamourou*. (Cassette.) *2010*: Mali.

Diarra, Souleymane. *Chérif Valeur*. (Cassette.) N.d.: Mali.

Diarra, Souleymane. *Kira Ka San Nayèlè*, Yeleen Production. (Cassette.) N.d.: Mali.

Diarra, Souleymane. *L'union fait la force*. (Cassette.) N.d.: Mali.

Diarra, Souleymane. *Souleymane Zon*. (Cassette.) *2016*: Mali.

Koné, Sana. *Nourou Mohammed*. DisqueKoné production. *2012*: Ivory Coast.

Koné, Sana. *Salam*. Disquekoné production. *2014*: Ivory Coast.

Sall, Racine. *Wale Niouma Do*. (Cassette.) N.d.: Mali.

YouTube

Alima, Nouhoum Dembélé, Mohamed Diaby, Souleymane Diarra (Zikiri Solo), Sana Koné, Racine Sall and Ba Ka Bouraïma Samaké's *zikiri*, as well as Chérif Ousmane Madani Haïdara's preachings, are broadcast on the following YouTube channels:

Cherifla TV: https://www.youtube.com/user/MrSere Brahima

Djinè Prod.: https://www.youtube.com/channel/UC_RzkXPkNQpiLNo0AiYcDKQ

Haraniani Dembele: https://www.youtube.com/channel/UCJubvgjYecmMERmCmq-uoFA

Maitre Gaba: https://www.youtube.com/user/maitreGABA/videos

Oumar Pichichi: https://www.youtube.com/channel/UCTqgN5NzhkVp2tejmGNWv1w/videos

Sere Brahima: https://www.youtube.com/channel/UCTVJvdMBdtQKo_EMs5BOZbA

Soufi Bilal Diallo: https://www.youtube.com/channel/UCc7HoNnjHeAiY8ZNlR2KyRg

EMMANUELLE OLIVIER

Zilizopendwa

Zilizopendwa is a Swahili term commonly used interchangeably with 'golden oldies' to describe songs recorded in Kenya since the 1980s based on idioms of early Kenyan popular music genres. The term literally means 'those that were liked'. Initially the term referred to Kenyan popular music of the 1940s to 1970s, a period that marked the recording of classic popular hits in several distinct genres such as *benga*, *omutibo*, *bango*, *rhumba* and twist (Ondieki 2010b, 24). From the late 1980s into the 1990s surviving seminal musicians and a few other contemporaries rerecorded these 'golden oldies' and repackaged them as *zilizopendwa*. These musicians, who recorded when the oldies originally emerged, were regarded as the pioneers of Kenyan popular music. Among them were Kenyan household names Daudi Kabaka, Fundi Konde, Fadhili William, Joseph Ngala a.k.a. Mzee Ngala, Paul Mwachupa, Gabriel Omolo and John Ogara. Their music in these various genres appropriated and incorporated indigenous local musical idioms (Roberts 1972, 255; Kubik 1981, 93; Low 1982, 17; Ondieki 2010c, 7). Originally recorded on a single box guitar accompanied by either a Fanta bottle or wooden blocks with two male singers, this music has over the years been reproduced with a full-band setup of several guitars, keyboards, drum set (in some cases electric drum set), *congas* and many other arrangements.

Most of the music ultimately considered part of the *zilizopendwa* category was first recorded between the 1940s and the late 1970s. Though some of the veteran artists are still alive in the early twenty-first century and continue to perform this music in club settings, new bands performing cover versions of the genre have been in existence since the 1980s. *Zilizopendwa* cover versions are the mainstay of many resident club bands in Kenya (Akuno, Ogama and Ondieki 2014).

When *zilizopendwa* emerged in the 1980s, the Nairobi music scene was declining due to a number of factors: the proliferation of cassettes and consequent piracy problems; the introduction of discotheques and preference for jukeboxes which led to reduced performance by live bands; the flooding of the market with foreign music through the multinational record companies; and a lack of policies to protect the music industry. The once-vibrant recording industry in Nairobi that attracted musicians from East, Central and southern Africa began to close shop with the departure of multinational record companies such as EMI, CBS and Polygram. This trend, coupled with poor media policies, resulted in a reduction of new recordings of local popular music. The decline was further exacerbated by the preference of young bands to perform and record imported genres such as funk, soul and rock. However, toward the end of the 1980s and into the early 1990s, most of the local Kenyan citizenry, especially those in rural areas who did not appreciate foreign genres, began to seek the older music styles that were dubbed *zilizopendwa*. Seminal bands such as Them Mushrooms released albums of medleys of *zilizopendwa* songs that sparked a new wave of re-recording the old songs, sometimes with the original musicians, but with better instruments and a bigger band and thus a fuller sound (Nyairo 2005, 33).

Them Mushrooms released their first album, *Zilizopendwa*, in 1991. Mainly comprising remixes of songs from early Kenyan popular genres, the album was so successful that the following year the band reworked more *zilizopendwa* songs in their second album, *Zilizopendwa 1992*. The two collections were ultimately made available in 2001 as *Zilizopendwa – Wazee Wa Kazi* (The Veterans) (Nyairo, 2004). These works established Them Mushrooms as one of Kenya's favorite bands. Their venture sparked other remixes of *zilizopendwa* by groups such as those by another very popular band, Kayamba Afrika. Kayamba Afrika gave the *zilizopendwa* remixes a new sound by combining the *zilizopendwa* grooves with *a cappella* harmonies. By the late 1990s hip-hop artists joined the craze of remixing and sampling *zilizopendwa*, providing the music with yet another point of entry into the top charts. One such example is the duo Jawabu (Kallaway and Shaky) that honored their father, Peter Akwabi, by remaking his 'Dada Njoo,' a very popular tune of the 1970s (Nyairo 2005, 35).

The late 1990s also marked the appropriation and adaptation of the genre into choral arrangements. In the early twenty-first century *zilizopendwa* remains the most popular choral style for Kenyan composers and arrangers in both secular and religious music (Akuno, Ogama and Ondieki 2014). Thus, *zilizopendwa* has been further repackaged through various Kenya music festivals to appear at other cultural festivals, in televised choral competition programs and in entertainment programs for national holiday celebrations.

Zilizopendwa continues to play a major role as one of the definitive expressions of national popular culture. The fact that the genre represents a mixture of styles that dominated the music industry from the 1940s to the 1970s means that the music resounds in the hearts of many Kenyans as popular memory. The repositioning of the genre is propelled by evolving live performances, remixes and choral adaptations. These newly emerging renditions brighten the future of the genre as more and more composers arrange and adopt hits, giving *zilizopendwa* new life in a distinct package. The genre also forms an immense part of the repertoire of live band music in Kenya, more often than not dominating the opening set of almost all Kenyan bands. This has continued to enhance the reputation of the genre.

Zilizopendwa has promoted interest in the styles it repackages, and many young musicians, in the 2010s, are composing in these styles, such as *benga*, *omutibo* and *rhumba*, among others. These and other scenarios have stimulated academic discourse in relation to the genre in popular music studies, music and culture, popular culture, representation and identity (Akuno, Ogama and Ondieki 2014; Nyairo and Ogude 2003; Nyairo 2004, 2005; Ogama 2009b; Okumu 1998; Ondieki 2010a, b). Some styles of *zilizopendwa*, such as *bango*, *benga* and *omutibo* have continued to enjoy new recordings each year, as commercially viable products in the Kenyan market. In addition, other styles such as twist continue to be heard in remixes and choral arrangements that endear them to Kenyan audiences, thus sustaining the genre.

Bibliography

Akuno, Emily Achieng,' Ogama, Sylvester Otieno, and Ondieki, Donald Otoyo. 2014. '*Zilizopendwa*: The Ramifications for Development and Revival.' In *Zili(zo)pendwa: Dance Music and Nostalgia in East Africa*, eds. Birgit Abels, Barbara Titus and Frank Gunderson. Berlin: VWB, 47–62.

Anyumba, Henry Owunor. 1970. 'Historical Influences on African Music: A Survey.' *Hadith* 3: 192–204.

Graebner, Werner. 1987. 'Popular Music in Kenya – a Historical Overview.' In *The Rough Guide to Kenya*, ed. Richard Trillo. London: Routledge, 359–60.

Graham, Ronnie. 1989. *Stern's Guide to Contemporary African Music*. London: Pluto Press.

Harrev, Flemming. 1989. 'Jambo Records and the Promotion of Popular Music in East Africa.' *Perspectives on African Music* 9: 103–23.

Kavyu, Paul Ndilya. 1978. 'The Development of Guitar Music in Kenya.' *Jazz Research* 10: 111–19.

Kazadi, Pierre. 1971. 'Congo Music: Africa's Favourite Beat.' *Africa Report* 16(4): 25–9.

Kidula, Jean. 1996. 'Cultural Dynamism in Process: The Kenya Music Festival.' *Ufahamu: A Journal of African Studies* 24(2–3): 63–81.

Kubik, Gerhard. 1981. 'Neo-Traditional Popular Music in East Africa since 1945: Folk or Popular? Distinctions, Influences, Continuities.' *Popular Music* 1: 83–104.

Low, John. 1982. 'A History of Kenyan Guitar Music 1945–1980.' *Journal of International Library of African Music* 6: 17–36.

Lukalo, Fibian Kavulani. 2008. 'Outliving Generations: Youth Traversing Borders Through Popular Music in Everyday Urban Life in East Africa 1.' *Cultural Studies* 22(2): 254–72.

Manuel, Peter. 1988. *Popular Music of the Non-Western World*. London: Oxford University Press.

Martin, Stephen H. 1991. 'Popular Music in Urban East Africa: From Historical Perspective to a Contemporary Hero.' *Black Music Research Journal* 11: 39–53.

Nyairo, Joyce. 2004. *"Reading the Referents": (Inter) Textuality in Contemporary Kenyan Popular Music*. Unpublished Ph.D. thesis, University of Wiwatersrand, Johannesburg.

Nyairo, Joyce. 2005. '"*Zilizopendwa*" 1: Kayamba Afrika's Use of Cover Versions, Remix and

Sampling in the (Re)Membering of Kenya.' *African Studies* 64(1): 29–54.

Nyairo, Joyce, and Ogude, James. 2003. 'Popular Music and Negotiation of Contemporary Kenyan Identity.' *Social Identities* 9(3): 383–400.

Nyairo, Joyce, and Ogude, James. 2005. 'Popular Music, Popular Politics: *Unbwogable* and the Idioms of Freedom in Kenyan Popular Music.' *African Affairs* 104(415): 225–49.

Ogama, Sylvester Otieno. 2009a. 'Selection, Arrangement and Choral Performance of African Contemporary Popular Tunes (*Zilizopendwa*).' Unpublished paper presented during National Adjudicators/Trainers Workshop organized by the Kenya Music Festival.

Ogama, Sylvester Otieno. 2009b. 'Choral Music: Impact of Analytical Hearing on the Adaptation and Arrangement of Kenyan *Zilizopendwa*.' Unpublished paper presented during the National Music Symposium organized by the Permanent Presidential Music Commission, Eldoret.

Ogude, James. 2012. 'The Invention of Traditional Music in the City: Exploring History and Meaning in Urban Music in Contemporary Kenya.' *Research in African Literatures* 43(4): 147–65.

Okumu, Caleb Chrispo. 1998. 'The Development of Kenyan Popular Guitar Music: A Study of Kiswahili Songs in Nairobi.' Unpublished MA thesis, Kenyatta University, Nairobi.

Ondieki, Donald Otoyo. 2010a. 'The Development of the Popular Music and the Recording Industry in Kenya.' A commissioned paper presented on 13 April 2010 during the Sixth National Symposium on Kenyan Music organized by the Permanent Presidential Music Commission held at Government Training Institute, Mombasa.

Ondieki, Donald Otoyo. 2010b. *The Analysis of Zilizopendwa for the Development of Instructional Materials for Music Education*. Unpublished Ph.D. thesis, Kenyatta University, Nairobi.

Ondieki, Donald Otoyo. 2010c. *Zilizopendwa Fake Book, A Teaching Resource*. Kisumu: Emak Music Services.

Opondo, Patricia A. 2000. 'Cultural Policies in Kenya.' *Arts Education Policy Review* 101(5): 18–24.

Paterson, Doug. 1987. 'The Live Music Scene.' In *The Rough Guide to Kenya*, ed. Richard Trillo. London: Routledge, 361–2.

Paterson, Doug. 1999. 'Life and Times of Kenyan Pop.' In *World Music: The Rough Guide, Vol.1*, eds. Simon Broughton, Mark Ellingham and Richard Trillo. London: Penguin, 509–22.

Pfukwa, Charles. 2010. 'When Cultures Speak Back to Each Other: The Legacy of *Benga* in Zimbabwe.' *Muziki* 7(1): 169–78.

Ranger, Terence Osborn. 1975. *Dance and Society in East Africa 1890–1970: The Beni Ngoma*. Berkeley: University of California Press.

Roberts, John Storm. 1968. 'Popular Music in Kenya.' *African Music Society Journal* 4(2): 53–5.

Roberts, John Storm. 1972. *Black Music of Two Worlds*. New York: Praeger.

Salim, Ahmed Idha. 1973. *Swahili Speaking Peoples of Kenya's Coast 1895–1965*. Nairobi: East African Publishing House.

Senoga-Zake, George. 1988. *Folk Music in Kenya*. Nairobi: Uzima Press.

Stapleton, Chris, and May, Chris. 1987. *African All Stars: The Pop Music of a Continent*. London: Quartet Books.

Discographical References

Kayamba Afrika. *Kayamba Afrika*. Samawati Productions. *2001*: Kenya.

Kayamba Afrika. *Sherehe*. Samawati Productions. *2004*: Kenya.

Them Mushrooms. *Zilizopendwa*. Mushroom Records. *1991*: Kenya.

Them Mushrooms. *Zilizopendwa 1992*. Mushroom Records. *1992*: Kenya.

Them Mushrooms. *Zilizopendwa – Wazee wa Kazi Collection*. Mushroom Records. *2000*: Kenya.

Discography

Abbasi, Thomas, Nandwa, Edward, and The Bottletops. 'Mulimi Kwanje' and 'Bibi Maringo.' Equator Records 7 EU 329. *1969*: Kenya.

Agade, George, and Equator Sound Band. 'Mchumba wa Chati' and 'Mijini Kuna Hatari.' Equator Records 7 EU 385. *1970*: Kenya.

Kabaka, Daudi, and Agade, George. 'Western Shilo' and 'Helule Helule.' Equator Records EU 195. *1966*: Kenya.

Kabaselleh, Ochieng', Ochome and Equator Sound Band. 'Wach Awacha Japuonj' and 'Nyiwa Makawuono.' Equator Records 7 EU 321. *1969*: Kenya.

Kilimambogo Brothers Band. 'Katulu na Bell-Bottom' and 'Eka Kuia Beatrice.' Kilimambogo Brothers. KLB 7-001. *1976*: Kenya.

Konde, Fundi. *Fundi Konde Retrospective Vol.1 (1947–1956)*. RetroAfric RETRO 8CD 4910610. *1997*: Kenya.

Misiani, D. O., and the Shirati Jazz Band. *Benga Beat*. World Circuit WCB 003. *1987*: UK.

Mwale, John, and Navongo Succes. 'Hakuna cha Bure' and 'Ludya Wazia.' Equator Records 7 EU 387. *1970*: Kenya.

Ogara Boys Band. 'Selestina Juma.' AGS Records. *1963*: Kenya.

Omolo, Gabriel, and the Apollo Komesha Band '71. 'Lunchtime' and 'Tutakula Vya Ajabu.' Apollo. APL 618. *1971*: Kenya.

Rhino Boys. *Rumba yetu*. HMV *Rhumba* N 17102. N.d.: Kenya.

William, Fadhili, and the Black Shadows. 'Malaika' and 'Hakuna Mwingine.' Equator Records, EU 130. *1963*: Kenya.

William, Fadhili, and the Equator Sound. 'Jitu la Madaraka' and 'Wacha Nikae Chonjo.' Equator Records 7 EU 384. *1970*: Kenya.

CALEB CHRISPO OKUMU AND
DONALD OTOYO ONDIEKI

Zoblazo

The popular music and dance genre *zoblazo* (zoe-blah-zoe) utilizes musical elements from ethnic groups rooted in the southern and eastern regions of Côte d'Ivoire (especially the Apollo [Appolo] or Nzema). The genre's creator, Frederic Desire Ehui, popularly known as Meiway, was born and raised among the Nzema in Grand Bassam, in the southeast of the country. Meiway developed the premise of his new style after moving to Paris in 1985. Through fusing the traditional rhythms and dance of his ethnic group with modern instrumentation, *zoblazo* was born. Meiway draws primarily from the music of his Nzema (also known as Apollo) ethnic group, a subgroup of the Akan (Kwa) linguistic cluster. But, to relate to a younger audience, he also infuses his style with a popular dance rhythm (see Example 1) that is heard throughout West Africa, displaying creativity and versatility as a music artist.

Meiway's musical life is rooted in his many years of singing for his church choir and participating in vocal groups in both Abidjan and Paris. His first album, *Ayibebou* (1989) set the precedent for the style *zoblazo*. This style draws aurally and chorographically from the Nzema to create a neo-traditional musical style and dance. As heard on the tracks 'Ayibebou,' 'Aya,' 'M'mapa' and 'Simali' from the album *Ayibebou*, Meiway commonly uses Nzema rhythms on various instruments, such as the guitar, bell, keyboard and scraper, creating a polyrhythmic effect. In addition to his creative use of layered rhythmic patterns, the aforementioned tracks exemplify the artist's use of the Apollo language within his songs, further distinguishing *zoblazo* from other popular genres. Occasionally, Meiway demonstrates his versatility and knowledge of the music scene by creating songs which follow the style of other genres, such as *zouglou* and *coupé-décalé*, as is audible in his song '200% Zoblazo,' which aurally resembles early *zouglou* in its vocal style and predominant use of the popular dance rhythm:

Example 1: Popular dance rhythm

Although established in Paris, the genre *zoblazo* is most popularly known within Francophone Africa, where Meiway became one of the best-known artists, releasing new hits and albums nearly every two years beginning with his premiere album *Ayibebou* in 1989. Although Meiway's *zoblazo* style is unique, he is an artist who adjusts with the times. Thus, while *zoblazo* is known for its unique neo-traditional sound, Meiway's many albums (14 as of 2016) incorporate various sounds from other genres, both popular and traditional. For instance, the simple song 'Essika' (1991) is reminiscent of choral music, 'Mbalax Groove' (1997) merges the Senegalese Wolof *mbalax* with bagpipes and the Anglophone song 'Africa Unite' (1997) merges the organ and northern African flute with reggae rhythms. Meiway's *zoblazo* also borrows elements from the popular Ivoirian genres *zouglou* and *coupé-décalé*. For instance, the song 'Miss Lolo' (2001) is similar to *zouglou* in its vocal performance and style, while 'Voila String' (2004) and 'Oh Lele' (2004) are constructed in the *coupé-décalé* style, with dance breaks and onomatopoeias (*blockage*).

Lyrically, Meiway speaks of a variety of topics: love, war, ethnic pride, national unity and women to name just a few. Some of Meiway's most popular and legendary singles have been songs that express his admiration for the physical assets of the female body, for example, 'Rouler Moutou' (Roll the Bottom, 2012) and 'Miss Lolo,' while 'Voila String' comically tells of the search for the fabric when women wear thongs.

The above-mentioned songs musically reflect the influence of contemporary Ivoirian popular music styles, such as *coupé-décalé*, with its dance breaks, rhythms and guitar riffs, as well as *zouglou* with its vocal harmonies and narrative-style lyrics. However, whereas the lyrics of *coupé-décalé* are primarily composed in an argot language called Nouchi, primarily spoken among urban youth in Abidjan (a compilation of French, Dioula, Baoulé and Bété), Meiway typically uses French and Apollo (his indigenous language) and he employs instrumental accompaniments instead of remixed and digitized beats heard in *coupé-décalé*.

Meiway's creative blend of traditional and contemporary dance and music is most evident in his video 'Soukou aka Nanan,' from his 1995 album release *Meiway: Appolo 95 (400% Zobalzo)*. Visually, this neo-traditional performance displays Meiway's Akan roots, demonstrating a traditional Akan female dance. The women use white handkerchiefs as a sign of joy and purity and Meiway himself is adorned in *kente* cloth and gold, also signifiers of his Akan heritage. In addition to the intricate and brightly woven *kente* cloth and gold adornments that visually demonstrate the artist's ethnic roots, musically Meiway uses the vocal harmony of parallel thirds commonly heard among the Akan and a neighboring ethnic group, the Bété, and the arrangement includes accordion, drum set and castanet, blending modern instrumentation with traditional sights and sounds.

The artist's 2012 album *Professeur*, inspired by the 2010–11 political crisis over presidential elections in Côte d'Ivoire, includes tracks that promote peace. For example, the song 'Attié Oyé' advocates peace and nonviolence by stating in a whimsical manner that it is better to shoot a snail to eat than to kill a man and bury him. The comical video clip, demonstrating a clumsy hunter tripping through the 'jungle' with a large, dated rifle in search of snails, tones down the very direct anti-war message of the song.

Similar to previous Ivorian popular genres (*ziglibithy* and *dopé*), *zoblazo* is unique to its creator Meiway's ethnic roots as the musical and chorographical foundation. Therefore, as the sole creator and performer, Meiway can shift and alter the genre as he pleases, reinventing himself every few years. In 2014 Meiway, nearly 50 years old, was continuing to release top music hits seen, heard and danced to by African youth. Meiway's songs and videos continued to be streamed on music channels such as Trace Africa and to place in the top ten countdown for African hits. Although Meiway is the creator and, for many, the sole performer of *zoblazo*, other artists have performed in this style (including Zo Gang [a group started and led by Meiway], Deza XXL and Oren'Tchy). However, nearly 30 years after its creation these artists have come and gone, and Meiway remains the only star of *zoblazo*. Consequently, if *zoblazo* follows the path taken by other solo creator/performers (such as *ziglibithy*, founded by Ernesto DjeDje, and *dopé*, founded by Amédée Pierre), the genre will likely fade after Meiway retires.

Bibliography

'Les leçons de vie du Professeur Meiway: nouvel album du Maître du Zoblazo.' 2012. RFI Music (10 October). Online at: www.rfimusic.comhttp://musique.rfi.fr/actu-musique/musique-africaine/album/20121019-lecons-vie-professeur-meiway (accessed 12 October 2017).

'Meiway.' 2007. RFI Music (1 November). Online at: www.rfimusic.com/artist/world-music/meiway/biography.html (accessed 12 October 2017).

Moussa, Sidibi. 2014. Interview with the author, 30 June.

Valsecchi, Pierluigi. 2001. 'The "True Nzema": A Layered Identity.' *Africa: Journal of the International African Institute* 71(3): 391–425.

Discographical References

DjeDje, Ernesto. *Le Roi du Ziglibithy*. Badmos BLP 5021. *1977*: Côte d'Ivoire.

Meiway. 'Africa Unite,' 'Mbalax Groove.' *Les génies vous parlent (500% Zoblazo)*. Lusafrica 262.30-2. *1997*: France.

Meiway. *Appolo 95 (400% Zoblazo).* Meiway Organisation 4/Sonodisc. *1995*: France.

Meiway. 'Attié Oyé.' *Professeur (M23).* Meiway Organisation 11/Lusafrica. *2012*: France.

Meiway. 'Aya.' *Ayibebou.* Meiway Organisation 1/Sonodisc. *1989*: France.

Meiway. *Ayibebou.* Meiway Organisation 1/Sonodisc CD67373. *1989*: France.

Meiway. '"Essika."' *200% Zoblazo.* Sonodisc LPS 5501. *1991*: France.

Meiway. 'Mbalax Groove.' *Les génies vous parlent (500% Zoblazo).* Lusafrica 262.30-2. *1997*: France.

Meiway. 'M'mapa.' *Ayibebou.* Meiway Organisation 1/Sonodisc. *1989*: France.

Meiway. 'Miss Lolo.' *Eternel.* JPS CDJPS158. *2001*: France.

Meiway. 'Oh Lele.' *Golgotha 800% Zoblazo.* Lusafrica 46218-2. *2004*: France.

Meiway. 'Rouler Moutou.' *Professeur (M23).* Meiway Organisation 11. *2012*: Côte d'Ivoire.

Meiway. 'Simali.' *Ayibebou.* Meiway Organisation/Sonodisc. *1989*: France.

Meiway. '"Voila String."' *Golgotha 800% Zoblazo.* Lusafrica 46218-2. *2004*: France.

Discography

Meiway. *200% Zoblazo.* Sonodisc. CDS5501 *1991*: France.

Meiway. *Jamais 203 (300% Zoblazo).* Sonodisc. *1993*: France.

Meiway. *Best of Meiway.* Afriba 88808 *1997*: France.

Meiway. *Les génies vous parlent (500% Zoblazo).* Lusafrica 262.30-2. *1997*: France.

Meiway. *Extraterrestre.* Lusafrica 362142/ Meiway Organisation 6. *1999*: France.

Meiway. *Eternel.* JPS CDJPS158/Meiway Organisation 7. *2001*: France.

Meiway. *Golgotha.* Lusafrica 46218-2/ Meiway Organisation 8. *2004*: France.

Meiway. *9ème commandement.* Meiway Organisation 9. *2009*: Côte d'Ivoire.

Meiway. *M20.* Lusafrica LS235/Meiway Organisation 10. *2009*: France.

Meiway. *Professeur (M23).* Meiway Organisation 11. *2012*: Côte d'Ivoire.

Meiway. *Illimtic.* Musicast 3700187664587/Meiway Organisation 12. *2016*: France.

Pierre, Amédée. *Live (Live Concert, Vol. 1).* Musiki. *2012*: France.

Zo Gang featuring Meiway. *Hold Up.* Lusafrica 56725262742. *1998: France.*

YouTube

Meiway. 'Meiway-Soukou.' Available at: http://www.youtube.com/watch?v=bcBpRtyD11A (accessed 30 October 2013; uploaded 14 September 2008).

TY-JUANA TAYLOR

Zouglou

Zouglou (zoo-gloo), a popular urban music and dance genre blending highly syncopated traditional dance rhythms and vocals with modern electronic instrumentation, is considered by some scholars to be the premier music genre of Côte d'Ivoire, due to its national popularity and its pan-ethnic appeal. In contrast to previous Ivorian popular genres that were commonly comprised of very specific musical elements signifying and appealing to ethnic-identified Ivoirian traditions, such as *dopé, ziglibithy* and *zoblazo, zouglou* has no specific ethnic or religious affiliation. To further its pan-ethnic appeal, the lyrics of *zouglou* are primarily sung in French and some artists also utilize a popular urban argot spoken primarily among impoverished Ivorian youth – Nouchi – in their lyrics. Nouchi blends French and a variety of local languages (including, but not limited to, Bété, Dioula, Baoulé and Ebrie), enabling *zouglou* to reach a broader multiethnic audience while masking the satirical critique of national politics that commonly is heard in *zouglou* lyrics. This creative linguistic blend gives the genre the ability to articulate the sentiment of the everyday Ivoirian, while incorporating diverse musical influences from Côte d'Ivoire.

History

The term *zouglou* has many contested definitions. For instance, it is popularly translated from the Baoulé language to mean 'pile of rubbish' (perhaps reflecting the feelings of many students of Abidjan about how their government was treating them), though it has linguistic roots and other definitions in Bété and Wè (other languages and ethnic groups present in Côte d'Ivoire). Others have suggested that *zouglou* was taken from the dance *zougloubehi*, created by two Ivoirian brothers and university students, Christian Gogoua and Bruno Porquet. It has also been suggested that *zouglou* came from the Baoulé phrase 'Otile Zouglou' meaning *rassembles comme des imbéciles idiots* ('gathering like idiot imbeciles') which refers to the way in which students at the university were forced to pile into their dormitories.

Determinations of the genre's date of establishment are as inexact as the etymology of its name. During the late 1980s and early 1990s (the exact date is debatable) the youth of Abidjan, Côte d'Ivoire created *zouglou*. The genre can be divided into two musical forms: a traditional form drawing from the musical elements of the indigenous groups Wè and Bété (both part of the larger ethnolinguistic cluster Krou [Kru]) in rural western and central Côte d'Ivoire, and a modern-traditional form composed of a mix of non-traditional and traditional instrumentation. The Wè lends performative aspects to *zouglou* performance from its mask dance genre *touhourou*.

The traditional form, originally known as *wôyô*, uses strictly percussion instruments (*djembe*, bell, scraped bottle) and voice. *Wôyô*, before being transformed into the popular genre *zouglou*, was used initially as a form of entertainment at school games and musical accompaniment at funerals (the term itself denotes a percussion ensemble that accompanies school sports and funerals). *L'ambiance facile* is a generic term used to describe *wôyô*.

The traditional-modern form of *zouglou* has its roots in *wôyô* as well, but is most noted for its use of nontraditional instrumentation such as guitar, drum set and synthesizer. This form of *zouglou* is what is most popularly known and heard today throughout Côte d'Ivoire and the African diaspora.

The genre, in both forms, uses its lyrical content as a platform to critique historical events and express discontent with the living conditions of students and citizens of Côte d'Ivoire. Through time the thematic content evolved, addressing various topics beyond dissatisfaction with the economy and government. Other lyrical themes include, but are not limited to, knowledge (imparting wisdom), humor (e.g., Magic System's 'Premier Gaou'), homages, mood setting, love, revindication, derision, social criticism, social justice, national history, mourning, France (life abroad) and gender relations.

While the lyrical content and themes differ between artists, there are musical components of the genre that remain constant. Many authors have claimed that Bété patterns are the rhythmic foundation of *zouglou*. Some percussionists, however, maintain that this notion is too general. *Zouglou* does have Bété roots in its rhythmic construction, along with influences from music of other Ivoirian ethnic groups. The *cloche* (bell) pattern (Example 1) is the most distinguishable pattern in *zouglou* and another more recent Ivoirian popular genre, *coupé-décalé*. This bell pattern is popular in Afropop music throughout many regions of West and Central Africa, but has its roots among the Krou who have origins in Liberia, have migrated and are of the same linguistic cluster as the Bété in southern Côte d'Ivoire. In addition, this rhythm can be heard in early Ghanaian highlife (palmwine) (e.g., 'Please Go Easy With Me' by S.E. Rogie), and it is closely related to what has been described as the first popular music of Africa, *gumbe/goombay* (*gombey, gomé*), which laid the foundation for palmwine highlife music in Ghana, Congolese *soukouss* and various other popular music genres of Africa.

Example 1: *Zouglou*'s popular bell rhythm

After nearly a century of migration, this dance rhythm has been appropriated by the youth in Abidjan and used to cheer their teams (akin to pep bands) during sports events, political events and funerals. This recreational use of the music (then called, as noted, *ambiance facile [wôyô]*), set the stage for the emergence of a new genre. Eventually during the 1980s the urban college youth attending the University of Abidjan (later called University of Félix Houphouët-Boigny) appropriated the recreational musical form to forge a genre – *zouglou* – that would enable them to vocalize their problems.

To accompany lyrics describing both their own unhappiness and the political injustice rife in the nation, and to further demonstrate their conditions and pleas, the students created the *zouglou* dance. With hands lifted in the air, the dance first demonstrated the students' public plea to God for help, and then depicted their cry for freedom and liberation, as they posed their arms horizontally like a bird taking flight.

In response to the sudden global fall of cocoa and coffee prices (Côte d'Ivoire's primary export crops) in the 1980s and the devaluation of the country's CFA

(*Communauté Financière African* [African Financial Community]) currency by half in 1994, which led to dismal living and studying conditions, college youth transformed *wôyô* from a recreational form of music into a national platform to express frustration. Previously performed, as noted, to accompany school sports and activities, *wôyô*, henceforth called *zouglou*, now served as a national platform to vent youth contestations against the government one-party system (PDCI), run for over 30 years by reigning president Félix Houphouët-Boigny, and the declining economic climate for many within Côte d'Ivoire. The genre articulated the cruel effects of economic issues and a number of national calamities: (1) the overnight devaluation of the CFA currency; (2) the transformation of Côte d'Ivoire from one of the leading countries in Africa in education, national growth and wealth to a debt-ridden country lacking the funds to offer the promises of education and prosperity given to previous generations; and (3) the lack of true democracy due to the one-party system overseen and dictated by the reigning president for over 30 years.

It was in this political context that the music used for recreation to support sport teams and amuse the audience was transformed into a musical style that articulated the needs of university students and Ivoirian youth. Didier Bilé and Les Parents du Campus was one of the first *zouglou* groups. Bilé adapted *wôyô* songs to articulate the socioeconomic climate and to declaim for better living conditions. Bilé's group, while not the first *zouglou* group, had a powerful and impacting presence in mediating *zouglou* with the release of the hit 'Gboglo Koffi.' They took a musical style most familiar to them and altered it to serve as a platform for their musical and political purpose. Other early *zouglou* groups include Les Poussins Chocs and Les Salopards.

Zouglou remained a relatively local Ivoirian genre until the release of the single 'Premier Gaou (1er Gaou)' (1999; rereleased 2002) by Magic System. Many believe this track to be the catalyst for popularizing the genre nationally and internationally. 'Premier Gaou' creatively weaves a variety of popular music components from genres throughout the world to manifest a sound strangely familiar, yet simultaneously unique. In the 2002 re-release of 'Premier Gaou' one can hear how the performance includes a plucked guitar popular in much Congolese *soukouss* music. The song utilizes vocal parallel thirds and fuses traditional instrumentation, including the *djembe* and both shaken and scraped idiophones, with studio-produced beats. All of these musical elements are layered with the popular dance rhythm.

As other dance-based genres, such as *coupé-décalé*, grew into popularity, the *zouglou* dance faded into obscurity, except among the generation who grew up during the 1990s. However, in the early twenty-first century children still perform the dance when a classic *zouglou* song is played. With the growth and development of other dance-based genres, *zouglou* became most known for its lyrical content. While the content is usually serious, the performers often use humor through irony and satire to discuss politically driven topics and to create narratives related to the aforementioned themes. Through the narration of real events *zouglou* acts as a mediator, expressing public sentiment regarding the socioeconomic, historical and political status of the nation. These sentiments are commonly masked by satire and humor, an element of *zouglou* performance that is further enhanced through the occasional use of Nouchi.

Zouglou Today

In early twenty-first-century Abidjan, *zouglou*'s popularity has waned with the growth of *coupé-décalé*, hip-hop, *zouk* and other globally popular genes. *Zouglou* artists such as Les Patrons and Magic System remain well-known, high-selling exponents of the genre, and live *zouglou* performances are still held weekly in certain regions of the city, such as Koumassi, Blockhauss, Yopougon, and in select clubs. These performances take place for audiences of hundreds of people seated at the *maquis* (open-air restaurant), where they are served grilled meats, other dishes and drinks while listening to countless *zouglou* groups singing to prerecorded music. While the quality of singers varies, the *maquis* is most commonly a place to unwind and relax with friends on the weekend.

In addition to these weekly performances, one can experience the genre in its more traditional live form with *djembe*, bottles and vocal performance on Grand Bassam beach, where drastically inflated drink and food prices are also found. The performers circulate the beach looking for those willing and able to pay for their talents. For the right price, the performers serenade listeners at their table, but for those unwilling to pay, the performers only pause briefly and continue their circulation in search of paying customers.

Conclusion

The songs of *zouglou*, which began as accompaniment music to athletic events in the 1980s, evolved into anthems among disenchanted college youth and spread quickly to embrace the sentiments of much of the Ivoirian youth population. After two civil wars and the increasing decline of the Ivoirian economy and political system, the revolutionary voice of *zouglou* was muted. Consumers and artists began to look abroad, appropriating themes popular in much US hip-hop, such as materialism and hedonism. Only a few *zouglou* artists continued to address political matters, and the continued growth of genres such as *coupé-décalé*, *zouk* and hip-hop has diminished the popularity of the genre among Ivoirian youth in the twenty-first century.

Bibliography

Akindes, Simon. 2002. 'Playing It "Loud and Straight": Reggae, Zouglou, Mapouka and Youth Insubordination in Côte d'Ivoire.' In *Playing with Identities in Contemporary Music in Africa*, eds. Mai Palmberg and Annemette Kirkegaard. Uppsala: Nordiska Afrikainstituet, 86–103.

Collins, John. 1992. *West African Pop Roots*. Philadelphia: Temple University Press.

Collins, John. 1996. *Highlife Time*. Accra: Anansesem Publications.

Impey, Angela. 2008. 'Popular Music in Africa.' In *The Garland Handbook of African Music*, ed. Ruth M. Stone, 2nd ed. New York: Garland, 124–47.

Kadi, Germain-Arsene. 2013. '"*Gbê est mieux que drap*" : La musique urbaine, le Nouchi et la révolte des jeunes en Côte d'Ivoire depuis les années 1990' ['It's best to be honest than allow someone to follow the wrong path and be mocked publicly': Urban Music, Nouchi, and the Revolt of Youth in Ivory Coast Since the 1990s]. *The Postcolonialist* 1(1): 1–13.

Mitter, Siddhartha. 2011. 'The Hip Hop Generations: Ghana's Hip Life and Ivory Coast's Coupé Décalé.' Online at: http://www.afropop.org/tag/west-africa/page/3/ (accessed 12 October 2017).

N'Guessan, Lou Gonezie Sylvie Isabelle. 2010. 'Le zouglou comme identité musicale de la Côte d'Ivoire: cas du groupe Magic System' [Zouglou, a Part of the Musical Identity of Ivory Coast: A Case Study of Magic System']. Thesis, Institut National Supérieur des Arts et l'Action Culturelle [The National Institute of High Arts and Cultural Activities] (INSAAC), Côte d'Ivoire.

Ogola, George, Schumann, Anne, and Oluttayo Olatunji, Michael. 2009. 'Popular Music, New Media, and the Digital Publishing Sphere in Kenya, Côte d'Ivoire, and Nigeria.' In *African Media and the Digital Public Sphere*, eds. Okoth Fred Mudhai, Wisdom J. Tettery and Fackson Banda. Palgrave: Macmillan, 203–23.

Schumann, Anne. 2009. 'Popular Music and Political Change in Côte d'Ivoire: The Divergent Dynamics of "Zouglou" and Reggae.' *Journal of African Media Studies* 1(1): 117–33.

Schumann, Anne. 2010. *Danse Philosophique!: The Social and Political Dynamics of Zouglou Music in Abidjan, Côte d'Ivoire, 1990–2008*. Unpublished Ph.D. dissertation, University of London, School of Oriental and African Studies.

Schumann, Anne. 2012. 'A Generation of Orphans: The Socio-Economic Crisis in Côte d'Ivoire as Seen Through Popular Music.' *Africa* 8(4): 535–55.

Discographical References

Les Parents du Campus Ambiance. 'Gboglo Koffi.' *Les Parents du Campus Ambiance: Zouglou Dance*. Fan Club. *1991*: Côte d'Ivoire (Reissued on *20 Years History: The Very Best Of Syllart Productions*. Next Music CDS 8984. *2002*: France).

Magic System. 'Premier Gaou.' *Premier Gaou*. Abidjan: Showbox International. *1999*: Côte d'Ivoire. (Reissued on Next Music CDS 8933, *2002*: France)

Rogie, S. E. 'Please Go Easy With Me.' *Palm Wine Guitar Music: The 60s Sound*. Cooking Vinyl COOK 010. *1988*: UK.

Discography

Espoir 2000. *Espoir 2000*. Kiki Productions. *2001*: France.

Espoir 2000. *Gloire à Dieu*. Bana Music BA010. *2006*: France.

Espoir 2000. *4éme Mandat*. Jober Entertainment. *2007*: USA.

Les Patrons. *Haut Niveau (14 Zouglou Hits)*. Afrik'arts-prod. *2012*: Côte d'Ivoire.

TY-JUANA TAYLOR

Index

Page numbers in bold indicate major headwords and in italics indicate maps.

!hu dans/!hu tsans 366
'/Gui #namisa /khubi tere mama' (song) 366-7
'200% Zoblazo' (song) 583
+268 (group) 292
12 Gauge (group) 229
1Xtra (radio program) 20
23.3 Wisdom Connection (group) 261
241 (duo) 239, 240
2Face Idibia (Afropop artist) 176, 224, 256
2Pac (rapper) 256, 259
2Shotz (rapper) 255
340ml (group) 489
3D Crew 245
50 Cent (rapper) 259
5FM (radio station) 287, 349
5kiem Underground (group) 261, 263
5th Generation (group) 230
II Proud (hip-hop artist) 85

!Auxab, Pieter Jozef 366, 367
A Long Way to the Beginning (album) 17
Aawambo people. *See* Owambo/Aawambo people
AB Sounds (band) 25
Ababio, Desmond 211
Ababio, Emmaneul (Promzy) 276
Abacha, Sani 448
Abafana Bentuthuko (group) 422
Abaga, Jude (M.I./Mr. Incredible) 256
Abagusii people 68, 71
Abakuá Society 394, 395
Abaluhya/Abaluyia people 68, 460
Abana Ba Nasery (group) 462
Abayomi, James 13
Abba (band) 137
Abdallah (*salegy* artist) 502
Abdallah, Salum 440
Abdeletif, Alamin 537
Abdi, Said 166
Abdillahi dj 167
Abdulkareem, Eedris 256, 259
Abdullah (*zenji flava* artist) 569
Abdullahi Mighty (technopop artist) 177
Abdulrahim, Osman 537
Abeid, Bakari 337

Abeke, Adetoun 556
Abelo, Losta 469
'Aben Wo Ha' (song) 209
Abènì, Sàláwà 556
Abiodun, Dele 16, 324
Abiodunn, Shina 13
Ableton Live (software) 66
ag Ablil, Inteyeden 545
Aboagye Da Costa, Nana 209
Abodam (hiplife artist) 276
'Aboodatoi' (song) 51
Abraham, Kofi 210
Abraham, Shani 516
'Abrentsie' (song) 275-6
Abrewa Nana (singer-songwriter) 277
Abu-Andani, Wilhemina (Mimi) 277
Abubakar, Aminudeen Ladan 173
AC/DC (band) 180
Acagba, Majaro 556
accordion 35, 54, 75, 80, 81, 106, 132, 135, 140, 155, 160, 167, 204, 205, 217, 300, 323, 394, 395, 397, 421, 422, 429, 457, 458, 464, 467, 468, 469, 476, 501, 502, 503, 504, 513, 523, 525, 526, 537, 538, 566, 569-70, 584. *See also* chromatic button accordion; diatonic button accordion; *kinanda kia mugeto*; piano accordion
Accra Excelsior Orchestra 205
Accra Rhythmic Orchestra 205
'Ace Blues' (song) 420
Ace of Base (band) 349
Ace/Afro-Jùjú Series 1 (album) 325
Acheampong, Nana 209
Acid Band 102
acoustic guitar 70, 217, 235, 310, 312, 319, 326, 327, 338, 399, 408, 410, 434, 438, 456, 462, 469, 493, 512, 520, 544, 547. *See also* guitar
acoustic slide guitar 24. *See also* guitar
Acquah's brass band 10
'Ada Ada' (song) 224
Adabraka Drama Troupe 115
Adadan Cultural Resource Centre (Kumasi, Ghana) 459
Adagbenon, Jean 413

adaha 9-11, 34, 35, 36, 89, 204, 341-2
adaka (musical instrument) 468
adakim/adakam 34, 35
Adawa Super Ten: Elemu Nget On (album) 324
adawa system 324
Addis Ababa Municipality Orchestra 141
Addo, Javes 210
Addo, Nicholas 13
Addy, Mustapha Tettey 346
Addy, Obo 346
Ade, King Sunny (Sunday Adeniyi) 16, 146, 212, 321, 322, 324
Adegbolu, Olumide Edwards (Olu Maintain) 256-7
Adegetor, Ayinla 44
Adejobi, Emmanuel Adeleke 46
Adeniyi, Sunday. *See* Ade, King Sunny
adenkum gourd calabash 35. *See also* calabash
adenkum orchestras 35
adesim 341
Adewale, Segun 16, 324, 325
Adewale, Sir Shina and His Super Stars International 325
Adidas (company) 265
Adigwe, Okonkwo 217, 467
Adinkra Clan (group) 275
Adio, Kasumu 44
Adisa, Latifu 501
Adja 572
Adjahoui, Yedenou 412-13
Adjekum, Appiah 205, 342
Adjepong, Akosua 212
Admette, Michel 505
adowa 35, 275, 458, 468
Adriano, Artur 509
Adu, Allan Cosmos 209
Adzei, Senyoh 343
adzewa/denzim 35
aerosol art 228, 231-2. *See also* graffiti art
Afar music 165. *See also* Djibouti (Volume VI, *Locations: Africa and the Middle East*)
Afewerki, Abraham 538
AFJ Productions 240

589

Index

afkloplied. See ghoemaliedjie/ghommaliedjie
Afra Sound Stars (group)   337, 340
Africa '70 (band)   13, 16, 17. *See also* Egypt '80 (band); Koola Lobitos (band); Nigeria '70 (band)
África à Noite (radio program)   403
Africa Express (band)   25
Africa n°1 (radio station)   237
Africa O-Ye!: A Celebration of African Music (Ewens)   29
Africable (TV network)   576
African All-Stars: The Pop Music of a Continent (Stapleton and May)   29
African Association of Lourenço Marques   403
African Beats (group)   16, 324
African Brothers Band (aka African Brothers Band International of Ghana)   138, 207, 208, 483
African Dance Band of the Cold Storage Commission of Southern Rhodesia   540
'African dancehall'   276. *See also* dancehall
'African Dances' (song)   66
African Fiesta National (group)   493
'African Girls' (song)   51
African Gramophone Stores (Nairobi, Kenya)   69
African Heritage Library (Medie, Ghana)   211
African jazz   285, 358, 359, 360, 361, 388, 389, 418-19, 420, 421, 423, 424, 540, 542. *See also* mbaqanga
African Jazz (band)   493
'African kick'   327
'African metal'   182, 184
African Music Bombers, The (group)   552
African National Congress (ANC)   39, 302, 350, 411, 488
African National Congress (ANC) Youth League   289
African Pride Singers   302
'African Queen' (song)   256
African Rhythms Band   99
African Show Boys (group)   212
African Songs (record label)   323, 324
African Virtuoses (group)   312
African Writers' Club   423
African Zulu Male Voice Choir   301
African-American music   16, 109, 161, 165, 166-7, 170-1, 202, 205, 208, 236, 254-5, 285, 287, 392, 494. *See also* blues; funk; hip-hop; house music; jazz; reggae; rhythm and blues; soul
African-Caribbean/Afro-Caribbean music   10, 124, 137, 138, 204, 236, 392-3, 395, 482, 504
Africando (group)   23, 313, 385
africano   17. *See also* Afrobeat
Africulturbain (hip-hop cultural center: Pikine, Senegal)   262
Afrigo Band, The   57-8
Afrika Shrine (club: Lagos, Nigeria)   15
Afrikaans metal   194, 195
Afrikaners   78-82, 195, 266, 418, 553
Afrisa International (group)   451
Afro Celt Sound System   313
Afro jazz   25-6
Afro Messengers (band)   17
Afro metal   186
Afro Moses (musician)   212, 459

Afro National (band)   138, 433
'Afro roots'   483
Afro, Teddy   144
Afrobeat   11-19, 29, 31, 32-3, 59, 91, 145, 148, 202, 208, 211, 227, 254, 257, 324, 330, 448, 459, 483, 536, 561, 562
'afrobeat'   335
Afrobeats/Afro Beats   19-22, 84, 87
Afrobeats (radio program)   20
Afro-Cuban music   27, 206, 490, 492
  in Senegal   22-4
Afro-Cubists (band)   206
Afrodelic funk   32
Afrodelics, The (band)   32
Afro-Disco (record label)   138
Afrodisia (record label)   32
Afro-fusion   211, 212
'afrohili' style   208
Afroma   24-7, 484, 485
Afro-Music (periodical)   29
Afro-National (group)   46
Afropop (radio program)   29
'AfroPop Around the Bay' (article)   28
Afropop Worldwide (radio program)   21, 29
Afropop! An Illustrated Guide to Contemporary African Music (Barlow and Eyre)   29-30
Afropop/Afro pop/Afro-pop   27-30, 176, 275, 277, 513, 514, 586
Afro-rock   30-4, 208, 459
Afro-Succès (group)   124
Afrozla, Djeff (DJ)   334
Afutuo Nsakra Nnipa (play)   118
agahu. See gahu/agahu
Agbajda music   182
agbehun   92
agbotchebou   92
agídìgbo/agidigbo   223, 342, 467
agídìgbo/agidigbo (musical instrument)   43, 44, 413, 555. *See also* lamellophone
Agìkūyū people. *See* Kikuyu people
agiwwin   545. *See also* griots
agogo (musical instrument)   43, 147, 223, 399. *See also* gong
Agorosso (musician)   26
Agostinho Neto (group)   476
Agro (band)   195, 196
Agrupamento Kissanguela (group)   509-10
Aguda slaves   222
Águias Reais (group)   334, 509
Agyeman, Eric   212
Agyempong, Akosua   210
Agyepong, May   277
Ahababu Rasulillah (group)   175
Ahawul Nabiyyi (group)   175
'Ahmada' (song)   570
Ahmed, Mahmoud   94, 142, 143
Ahmed, Musbahu   173
ahweya/ahwiya/aways   35-6, 342
Aidarus, Houssein   167
Aingo, William   458
Airport Hotel (Maseru, Lesotho)   344
AIT (record label)   69
'Aja t'o foju d' Ejo' (song)   44-5
Ajadi, Y.K.   44
'Ajaka' (song)   574
Ajao, Lukman Babatunde   501
Ajilo, Chris   224
ajísari. See were/wéré

AK (Henry Tsehpo Segopa)   230
AKA (hip-hop artist)   123, 231
Àká, Sànúsí   501
akalela   332, 333
Akamba people   68, 71
Akan blues. *See odonson* highlife
Akan people   205, 276, 341, 457-9, 468, 583, 584
Akan recreational music   34-7, 342
Akan Trio   112, 113, 207
Akanite, Oliver Sunday (Oilver De Coque)   216, 217, 218, 219
Akanke, Mesitura   556
akapoma   35
Akar, John   400
Akatakye (hiplife artist)   211
Akébé II (group)   125
Akendengué, Pierre Claver   238
Akingbade, Fatimuta   556
Akins, Laolu   32
Akijnsanya, Adeolu   223, 224, 342
Akiwumi, Diana   210
Akon (singer)   256, 277
'Akoo Te Brofo' (song)   209
Akosua Tuntum   34, 36
Akounak Tedalat Taha Tazoughai (film)   546
akpese recreational music   90
akrodo   34-5
aksieliedjies   552
Aku people   135, 395, 399
àkúbà/akuba (musical instrument)   43, 223, 323, 555. *See also* drums
Akwabi, Peter   581
Akwaboa Band   113
'Akweni ndatopa' (song)   425
Akweza (group)   125
Akyeame (duo)   211, 274-5, 276
akyewa. See ahweya/ahwiya/aways
Alabi, Ekow Savage   209, 482
Alade, Yemi   123, 448, 449
Aladura Mission   46
'Alagbon Close' (song)   15
Alaine Courage Man (highlife artist)   482
Àlàké, Batile   556
Alaragbo, Kuburatu   556
Alayameta, Adisa   43
Albarika Store (record label)   413
Albarn, Damon   32, 313
Alberts, Arthur S.   382
Al-Burda (Al-Busiri)   174
Al-Busiri (poet)   174
al-Tijani, Sidi Ahmad   175
alcohol and alcoholism   10, 25, 55, 80, 114, 120, 198, 205, 207, 222, 279, 281, 286, 331, 334, 344, 360, 361, 388, 453, 473, 474, 494, 542, 543, 587
alekele (musical instrument)   412, 413. *See also* drums
Alekpehanhou (singer)   572, 573
'Aleluyah Tumbay' (song)   434
Alesh (hip-hop artist)   269
Alexandra Junior Bright Boys (group)   360
Alexis (*tsapiky* musician)   544
Al-Fazazi, Abu Zayd Abd al-Rahman ibn Yakhlaftan ibn Ahmad   174
algaita (musical instrument)   170
Algeria   8, 168, 545, 546, 578
  Saharwai refugee camps   430, 431, 456
  Tamanrasset   530, 545
ag Alhabib, Ibrahim   545
Ali, Collen   358

590

Index

Alif (group)   262
alikali   399
Alikali society   46, 47
Alima (singer)   576
'Alingo' (song)   256
'Allah Ya Isa' (song)   260
Alleluya Band   484, 485
'Allen Avenue' (song)   255
Allen, Tony   11, 13–14, 15, 16–17, 223, 287
Allenby College (Johannesburg, South Africa)   288
Alliance for Democracy (Malawi)   426
Alliance of Young Patriots (militant group)   481
Allkiniah (band)   191
Alokpon (Anatole Houndeffo)   535, 536
Alokpon (Mahi noble)   535
Alpha Blondy (Seydou Koné)   121, 478, 479, 485, 512
Alpha Blondy and the Solar System (band)   482
Alpha Waves (group)   211
Alpha-Omega (band)   32
alto saxophone   510. *See also* saxophone
'Alu Jon Jonki Jon' (song)   12
Alves, Kim   340
Alves, Nito   509
Alvorado (record label)   404
Al-Watan Musical Club (Dar es Salaam, Tanzania)   525
Ama Africa Band   367
Amachie Dede (group)   217
amacoons   299
Amaculo ase Lovedale (album)   39
Amado, Tony   347
amahlwayi (musical instrument)   450. *See also* rattle
amahubo   38
amakwaya/makwaya   **37–42**, 298, 553
amaleki   551
Amanabae, Raphael   467
Amanaz (band)   180, 566
Amandine (singer)   129
Amandzeba (Nat Brew)   212
Amanzimtoti Male Voice Choir   302
Amanzimtoti Players (group)   541
'Ama-Oxford Bags' (song)   300
Amarteifio, G.W.   346
Amartio, Sol   31
amaskwaito   352
Amatshitshi (group)   422
Amayenge (band)   332–3
Amazon (ecommerce company)   260
Ambassador Records   208
ambass-bey   370
Ambolley, Gyedu-Blay   208, 212, 275–6
Ambolley, Gyedu-Blay and Steneboofs (group)   32
Ambondrona (band)   192
Ambundu people   507, 508
Amechi, Stephen   216, 217, 467
American Zulu (guitarist)   422
Amha Records   143
Amhara people   139, 140, 141, 463
amidziro   516
Amimo, Fanuel   71
Amin, Idi   58
Amini (singer)   87
Ammunition (Amukelani Tshawani)   288
Amoah, Charles   209
Amoah, Nana Akua (Mzbel)   277
Amoaku, Komla   211

Amoateng, Daniel Kofi (Okyeame Quophi)   274–5
Amorim, Amadeu   508
Amougou, Richard   77
Ampadu, Nana   208, 210, 482
amplification equipment   43, 322, 323, 428, 429, 469, 493, 574
Ampofo, J.A. 'Black Chinese'   212
amponga drum   280. *See also* bass drum; drums
Amponsah, Ofori   211
Amudatu, Ogunfolu   556
Amunga, David   68, 71
Amunjera, Simon   368
A Nous Les Petits (group)   122–3
Analyse (group)   505
Ananse the trickster   109, 206
Anansesem   109, 115
ANC. *See* African National Congress
Ançar Dine (organization)   576
Ancien Koutchoua Mbada (album)   65
Anderson, Kimba   26
Andersson, Reverend and the Joyful Way Singers (band)   210
Anditi, Olima   69
Andrade, Mayra   528–9
Andrianampoinimerina, King of Imerina   278–9, 281
Andrianjaka, Ludger   53
Angola   4, 7, 20, 96, 98, 131, 181, 183, 226, 248, 252, 333–4, 337–40, 406, 431–5, 436, 470, 471, 473, 474, 477, 507–11, 552
   Cape Island   475
   Luanda   7, 333, 338, 347–8, 431, 475–6, 507–8, 509, 510
   Luanda, Bairro Operário   333, 507, 508
   Luanda, Marçal   431–2
   Luanda, Sambizanga   333, 431–2
Angola Itokiana (ensemble)   54
Angra (band)   190
angul (musical instrument)   133, 135
'Angwazi senderani' (song)   427
'Ani Yali Amanyi' (song)   272
Anikulapo-Kuti, Fela   11–13, 14–16, 17–18, 21, 32, 208, 212, 223, 254, 255, 256, 257, 287, 288, 335, 448
Anikulapo-Kuti, Femi   17, 32
Anikulapo-Kuti, Seun   17, 21, 32
animal horns (as musical instrument)   455. *See also* horn; *lulwika*; *olwika*
Animasaun, Lekan   13
Aniocha/Anioma people   218
Aniyameta, Adisa   44
Anjonu Elere (album)   44–5
ankle/foot bells and rattles   65, 455. *See amahlwayi; bichenje; inzogera; kwa'*
Ankobra (group)   211
Anning, Appiah   458, 468
annkadaamu   468
Annobonese people   131, 133, 135–6, 392, 393, 394, 396, 397
Anoff, Panji   275
Ansah, Bob   109–10, 111, 207
Ansah, Reverend Owusu   210
Anta (rapper)   262
Antananarivo Teatra (troupe)   53
Antankarana folk songs   503
antelope horn. *See lulwika*
anti songs   201
Antibalas (band)   16, 17
Antivirus movement (Tanzania)   87

Antoine, Bamou   66
Antwi, Kojo/Kwadwo   208, 482, 483
Anwar Orchestra   576
Anyo (highlife artist)   219
anzad (musical instrument)   545, 546. *See also* fiddle
apaa   50–1
Apagya Show Band (band)   32
apala/àpàlà   **43–6**, 221, 555
apartheid/anti-apartheid   15, 39, 78–9, 94, 154, 155, 183, 194, 195, 227, 265, 266, 267, 288, 302, 349, 350, 361, 367, 389, 408, 419, 421, 422, 423, 435, 487–8, 513, 553, 566
Apollo Diablo (MC)   230
Apollo people. *See* Nzema/Apollo people
Apolonia (group)   505
Apost (band)   190, 191, 192
Appau, Kwame Nsiah (Okyeame Kwame)   211, 274–5, 276
Appianing (palmwine artist)   205
apústua (musical instrument)   549–50. *See also* drums; frame drums
Aquai, Khodjo   209
Arab/Arabic music   165, 166, 179, 198, 202, 323, 436, 453, 500, 523, 548, 549
Araba, Julius O.   323–4, 467
Arba Lijotch (band)   93, 141
Arby, Khaira   530
ARC (Associated Recording Co.) Studio   31
Arch Enemy (band)   190
ardin (musical instrument)   179. *See also* harp
Arewa24 (TV show)   259
Aribido, Folorunsho   44
Arinoti *beni*   75
Arinze, E.C.   216, 217, 219, 224
Arka'n (band)   182
Arkhurst Hall (Sekondi, Ghana)   108
ARM (hip-hop artist)   270
Armstrong, Louis   206, 540
'Army Arrangement' (song)   15, 16
Army Band (Ethiopia)   93, 141, 142
aro (musical instrument)   147. *See also* idiophone
Aro Kanton'ny Fahiny (ensemble)   54
'Arrey' (song)   167
'Arrria bebi go buy yu ogboro' (song)   400
Art Ensemble of Chicago, The (band)   12
Art on the FrontLine (online series)   270
Artur, Joy   510
Arungu, Aliyu Dandawo   169, 173
Arungu, Buda Dantanoma   169
Aryittey, Nii Edmund   209
asaadua   34, 36
Asaba people   218
àsàlàtù   555
Asante, Okyerema   32, 212
Asare, Kwame (Jacob Sam)   35, 112, 113, 205, 458, 468
Asare, Kwame and His Fanti Group   205, 468
Asase-Ase (band)   32
Ashakanor, Kojo   482
Ashanti 'blues. *See odonson* highlife
Ashanti Nkramo Band   205
Ashanti (Asante) people   9, 35, 342, 457, 468
Ashiratu Nabiyyi (group)   175
Ashong, Mildred (Eazzy)   277
Asia   184

591

Index

aṣíkò/ashiko/assiko **46–8**, 133, 135, 160, 205, 217, 234–5, 321–2, 323, 370, 392, 393, 395, 396, 399, 457, 466, 467, 469. *See also gumbe/goombay*
  in Nigeria 47–8, 91
  in Sierra Leone 46–7, 162
assiko/sikko (musical instrument) 135. *See also* square tambourine; tambourine
asivui (musical instrument) 89. *See also* drums; peg drum
Asmahan (singer) 526
Assagai (band) 32
assan (musical instrument) 92, 330, 412, 413, 535, 572, 573–4. *See also* shakers
Assanand & Sons (music store: Mombasa, Kenya) 524
Astatke, Mulatu 94, 139, 143–4
Aswad (group) 484
AT (*zenji flava* artist) 568
atalaku 491, 492, 494
'Atannawa Musolo' (song) 329
ATI (hip-hop artist) 232
atika-tika 35
atini. See odonson highlife
Atkins, Chet 301
Atlantis (club: Paris) 120
'Atoba' (song) 272
Atologbe, Rotimi 44
Atomic Jazz Band 440
Atsiaya, Amadi Kwaa 497, 498
Attuquayefio, Jones 346
Aushi people 331, 332
Australia 315, 340
Authenticité movement 268, 332, 384, 386
Auto-Tune (software) 20, 140, 172, 235, 448, 464
'Aux choses du pays' (song) 238
Avengers (band) 31
avizenli 572
awaasa (musical instrument) 341. *See also* rattle
Awadi, Didier 240, 314
aways. See ahweya/ahwiya/aways
Awe ke, Aster 143
'Awisia Ye Mobo' (song) 113
Awoleye, Folake 556
Awotoye, Anthony Olanrewaju (Tony Tetuila) 256
Awudome, Tsito 343
awukye 51
axatse (musical instrument) 89, 153. *See also* rattle
Axim Trio 111–12, 206, 207
Axue (band) 366
Axue (Semlou Gomachab) 368
AY Fashion (singer) 177
Ayagi, Sani Yusuf 173
Àyàn lineage 146
Ayefele, Yinka 325
Ayers, Roy 16
Ayi, Majoie 77
Ayibebou (album) 583
Àyìndé, King Wasiu Marshal (K1 De Ultimate) 145
Àyìnlá, President Kollington 146, 147
Àyìnlá, President Kollington, and His New Fuji System 146
Ayitey, Mr. (schoolmaster) 108, 109
Ayivor, Kofi 33
Azagaia (Edson da Luz) 250–2
Azangeo, Amoah 32

Azania Band 488
azawaan 179, 456
Azike, Okecukwu. *See* Junior and Pretty (duo)
azikir 148
azmari music **48–50**, 141, 142
azmaribets (performance venue) 49
azonto 19, 21, 36, **50–2**, 123, 347. *See also* Afrobeats/Afro Beats
'Azonto' (song) 51
Azuma, Christie 32
Azziz (hip-hop artist) 230

ba gasy **52–4**
Ba, Amadou Fall 262
baakisimba 327
baar mbaye 414
baba (musical instrument) 46, 47. *See also* drums
Baba Ngani Agba (Haruna Ishola) 43, 44, 323
Baba, Rabi'u Usman 175
Baba, Yakasai, Alee 173
Babaluku (rapper) 273
babaton/babatoni (musical instrument) 309, 331, 566. *See also* banjo
Baby J (*zenji flava* artist) 568
Bachelors (band) 31
Backos (*ma/gaisa* artist) 368
'Bad Girl' (song) 252
Badakala (film) 173
Badejo Sound Studio 323
Badejo, Peter 323
Badi, Lalla 545
Badinaz Band 58
Badiu people 62–3, 151, 152, 527
badjo di gaita 151–2
Badu, Ewurama 211
Baganda people 326, 327, 328, 335
bagpipes 74, 75, 151, 583
Bah, Almami 576
Bahamas 132
Bahula, Julian 423
Baidoo, Reverend Yaw Agyeman 210
baikoko **54–6**
Baird, Michael 332
Bajarou: Big String Theory (album) 56
bajourou **56–7**
Bakare, Ayinde 322–3, 467
Bakari, Rab (DJ/Producer) 20, 21, 275, 448, 449
Baker, Ginger 16, 31, 32, 566
bakisimba 57
Bakwena people 186
bala/balafon/balo (musical instrument) 56, 310, 311, 312, 316, 382, 384–5, 386, 563. *See also* xylophone
Ball, Benjamin 486
Balla et ses Balladins (group) 385
ballet 317, 318
Ballets Africains de la République de Guinée, The 318
ballroom music 112, 205, 222, 223
balo. See bala/balafon/balo (musical instrument)
Balogun, Ayodeji Ibrahim. *See* Wizkid (musician)
Balogun, C.A. 323
Balógun, Jámíù Lefty 501
Balogun, Queen Ayo 325
Balógun, Sàlámì Lefty 501

Baloji (MC and hip-hop artist) 270
bals maloya 380
Balsher, David 'Draztik' 229, 230–1
Bamako Beat (documentary) 312
bamana foli 577–8
Bamana/Bamara people 383
'Bambanani' (song) 352
Bambara people 179, 577–8
Bamboo (hip-hop artist) 245
bamboo stamping tubes (musical instrument) 35
Bamou, Antoine 64
Bana (*morna* artist) 437
band (Uganda) **57–60**
Banda de la Marina 393
Banda Likute 252
Banda Maravilha 476
Banda, Hastings Kamuzu 126, 357, 377, 425–6, 427
Banda, Leonard 358
Banda, Lucius 485
Banda, Robson and The New Black Eagles (band) 103
Bandana (hiplife artist) 483
bandiri 578
bandiri (musical instrument) 168, 175. *See also* drums; frame drum
banga (musical instrument) 170. *See also* drums
bango **60–2**, 580
Bango Sounds Band 61, 62
Bango Teusi Five (album) 61
bangwe (musical instrument) 309. *See also* zither
banjo 22, 24, 75, 78, 80, 112, 155, 205, 300, 309, 321, 323, 331, 360, 388, 436, 453, 466, 504
Bankole, Rafiu 323
Bannerman, Kari 33, 138, 459
Banpoe, Y.B. 115
Bantou Pô-si (group) 234, 235
Bantsi, Game 'Zeus' 231, 232
Bantu Glee Singers 541
Bantu Men's Social Centre (Johannesburg, South Africa) 419
Bantu people 158, 331, 403, 454, 498
Banyore, Adolf 69
BAPMAF. *See* Bokoor African Popular Music Archives Foundation
baptisms/christenings 43, 53, 63, 90, 91, 412, 516, 559, 576
Bara people 543
Barbados 9
Barber, Chris 423
bard music/bards. *See* griots
Bärenreiter-Musicaphon (record label) 386
Barijaona (composer) 53
baritone horn 75, 91. *See also* horn
baritone saxophone 13, 223. *See also* saxophone
Barlow, Sean 29
barmât 179
Barnaba (singer) 87
Baronages (band) 367
Barons (band) 32
'Barrakeni' (song) 473
Barre, Ibrahim 167
Barre, Maxamed Siyaad 199, 200
barrel drum. *See ghoema* drum
Barret, Dominique 505
Barrister, Síkírù Àyìndé 145, 146, 148

592

Index

Barrister, Síkírù Àyìndé, and His Supreme Fuji Commanders (group) 146
Barristers, The (band) 31
bars and taverns 113, 192, 205, 222, 238, 239, 326, 343, 344, 358, 370, 373, 394, 466, 467, 501. *See also* nightclubs; restaurants and cafes; *shebeens*; *tej bets*; *tombo* bars
Barya, Yemane 538
Basa Basa (band) 32
Basebill (musician) 533
Basitsile, Sidney (DJ Sid) 229, 230, 231, 290
Basotho people 343–5, 418
bass drum 14, 61, 75, 91, 92, 102, 124, 134, 154, 182, 320, 341, 377, 418, 429, 430, 480, 505. *See also amponga* drum; *ćol* drum; drums; *dun*; gong drum; *rouleur*; *talmbat*
bass, electric 152, 181, 320, 368, 408, 421, 465, 513, 517, 557, 563
bass guitar 13, 14, 61, 68, 77, 140, 167, 199, 218, 235, 324, 331, 360, 370, 410, 414–15, 421, 432, 441, 462, 477–8, 485, 492, 511, 523, 547. *See also* guitar
Bass, Kotto 65
Baster (group) 380
Bastos, Waldemar 510
Bat'haillons Blin-D (group) 261
bàtá fújì 147
bàtá/bata drum 12, 17, 48, 146–7, 162, 413. *See also* drums
Bataka Underground (Bataka Squad) (group) 272, 273
bati (musical instrument) 430
Batida (group) 348
Batman Samini (Emmaneul Samini) 211, 276, 483
batuque/batuko 62–3, 151, 528
Bau (composer) 437
Bavabuka Foundation, The (Uganda) 273
Bawasaba (band) 33, 212
Bawuta-Kin (group) 269
bax ragga 59
Bazoka (group) 55
bazuca (musical instrument) 549–50. *See also* drums; frame drums
BBC 423, 434, 485
BBC Radio 20
BBC Radio 3 396
BBC Radio 3 Awards for World Music 251
beaches 272, 287, 587–8
'Beasts of No Nation' (song) 15
beat music 208
Beat Premiers (DJ duo) 229
Beat Street (film) 226
beatboxing 243
Beaters, The (band) 31
Beatles, The (band) 31, 208, 484
Beatsters, The (group) 102
Beaufond, Stanley 504
Bebe Cool (reggae artist) 335
Bebey, Francis 371
bebop 11, 206
Bediako Band 32
Bee Bop Brothers (band) 367, 464
Beecham, Joe 210
beer halls 298, 499
Beer, Ronnie 423
Beeskraal (group) 82
beguine 236

Behind the Mask (band) 191
Behrenroth, Lars 290
Behringer mixing console 259
Bekele, Bizunesh 142
Bekele, Hirut 142
bel (musical instrument) 46, 47. *See also* drums
Belgium 160, 318
  Brussels 452, 494
bell (musical instrument) 34–5, 36, 205, 221, 331, 346, 412, 413, 434, 458, 516, 573, 583, 586. *See also* ankle/foot bells and rattles; cowbell; *dawuro*; finger bell; *gan*; *gangbo*; *gankogui*; *ganvinon*; *né/négé*
  bracelet of bells 384
Bell, Dina 373
Bell, Felix 482
Bella, Uta 372
Bello, Shittu 44
Bellow, Bella 31
belwo 165, 197–8, 201
bembe (musical instrument) 555. *See also* drums
Bembeya Jazz National (group) 312, 385
Benaadiri songs 200
bend skin 63–8, 234
'Bend Skin' (song) 64, 65
benga 68–73, 308, 498, 520, 521, 580, 581
Bengu, John (Phuzeshukela) 410
beni 73–6, 308, 376, 377, 378, 430, 440, 484
beni bati 76, 430
beni ngoma. *See beni*
Benin 8, 32, 44, 64, 90–3, 153, 161, 221, 330, 412–13, 477, 535–6, 572–4
  Abomey 92, 535, 536, 572, 573
  Avrankou 412
  Cotonou 91, 92, 153, 535
  Ouémé region 572
  Ouidah 91, 92, 413
  Porto Novo 8, 91, 92, 330–1, 412, 574
  Savalou 92, 535, 536
Benny B (hip-hop artist) 268
Benson, Bobby 11, 14, 31, 206, 223, 224
Benson, Bobby and His Combo (band) 224
Benson, Leke 13
Beraki, Tsehaytu 538
Berber people 179
Berry Black (*zenji flava* artist) 568
Berry White (*zenji flava* artist) 568
Berry, Chuck 142
bessanganas 475
BET Awards 256, 257, 483
Bété people 584, 586
Bethel Gospel Singers 443
Beti people 76, 77
Beynaud, Serge 121, 122
Bhalo, Juma 524–5
BHIPMA. *See* Botswana Hip-Hop Music Awards
Bholoja (guitarist) 291
bhor 179
Bhosle, Asha 172
Bhundu Boys, The (group) 320, 542
Bhunya Brothers (group) 551
Bi Kidude (singer) 570
Bibi (percussionist) 338
Bibi, Kwerki 458
bichenje (musical instrument) 364. *See also* ankle/foot bells and rattles

Bichi, Auwalu Habib 175
Bideew Bou Bess (group) 227, 262, 560
Bidhân people 179, 431
Big Beats (band) 32, 208
Big Ben (*ovirtije* artist) 465
'Big Blind Country' (song) 12
Big Dawg Productions 290
Big Dudes (band) 94
Big Five Band 58
Big Gold Six, The (group) 332
'Big Joe Special' (song) 420
Biggy, Okatch 71
Bikoko, Jean Aladin 469
bikutsi/bikudsi 66, 67, 76–8, 234–5, 372
Bilé, Didier 587
Bilé, Moni 372
Billboard Magazine 28
Billy-O (Bello Ibrahim) 177
Bin G (hip-hop artist) 270
bina bina 356
Biney's brass band 10
Bini people 343
birimintingo 384
Birra, Ali 463
birthday parties and celebrations. *See* parties: birthday parties and celebrations
Birungi, Sarah 58
Bis bi Clan (group) 261
Bisa Goma (band) 32
Bishop's School (Accra) 107, 108
Bitchuka, Hassani 441
BK Studios 58
Black African Positive (group) 478
Black and White Spots (group) 206
Black Ark Studios 488
Black Beats (group) 206
Black Box (group) 349
Black Caesar (hip-hop artist) 230
Black Chinese (J.A. Ampofo) 212
Black Coffee (DJ) 287, 288, 291
Black Dillinger (reggae artist) 489
Black Eagles (club: Accra, Ghana) 346
Black Empire (group) 482
Black Entertainment Television (BET) Awards. *See* BET Awards
Black Five, The (band) 367
Black Ghosts (band) 32
Black Intellect (MC) 230
Black Loyalists 132, 159, 391, 392, 393, 395, 396, 398
Black Mambazo (group) 421
black metal 185, 186, 190, 191
Black Missionaries (band) 478, 485
Black Music of Two Worlds (Roberts) 28
Black Noise (group) 265
Black President (album) 94
Black Prophet (reggae artist) 483
Black Reggae (album) 486
Black Sabbath (band) 180, 181
Black Santiago (group) 206, 330
Black Star Musical Club (Tanga, Tanzania) 526
Black Star Square (Accra, Ghana) 346
Black Stars (soccer team) 51
Black Tigers, The (group) 65
Black Umfolosi (group) 451
blackface minstrelsy. *See* minstrelsy
blacksmiths 160, 311, 316
Blackwell, Chris 560
Blakey, Art 13
Blakk Rasta (reggae artist) 483

593

Index

Blekete (band)   33
Blekete music   182
'Blessed Assurance' (hymn)   325
B. Léza (Francisco Xavier da Cruz)   437
Blitz the Ambassador   17
BLO (band)   32
Bloko (guitarist)   543
Blom, Paul   195
Blondie & Papa (duo)   486
Blossom (*shambo* artist)   514
Blue Cheer (band)   181
Blue Knights (band)   31
Blue Magic (band)   31
blue *mbumba*   426, 427
Blue Notes (group)   423
blues   64, 142, 161, 308, 359, 360, 456, 514, 530, 542. *See also* rhythm and blues
Blues Syndicate (band)   31
Bluetooth technology   177, 259, 266
BMG Records   289
BMG. *See* Boeremusiekgilde (South Africa)
Boargazm (band)   188
Boateng, Vanessa   51
boba (musical instrument)   153. *See also* drums
Bobbito (DJ)   231
Bobo, Abdi   167
Bodenstein, Manie   80, 82
boeremusiek   **78–83**
Boeremusiekgilde (Boeremusiek Guild) (BMG) (South Africa)   79, 80–1
bogle   560
boites   152. *See also* discotheques; nightclubs
Bokoor African Popular Music Archives Foundation (BAPMAF) (Accra, Ghana)   211
Bokwe, John Knox   39
'Bolanle' (song)   255
bolel   49
bolero   382, 392, 509
Bollywood films/filmi music   172, 505, 523. *See also* Hindi films/filmi music
Bollywood séga   505
bôlo/bolo   239, 395
bolobo   370
boloha   551
bolon (musical instrument)   383, 384. *See also* harp
Bomba FM (radio station)   569
bombadon (musical instrument)   399
Bombardier, Zélé le   77
bombe (musical instrument)   517. *See also* musical bow
Bon, Aurelio Le   405
Bonchaka, Terry   211, 483
Bond of 1844 (play)   112
Bone Thugs-n-Harmony (group)   229
Bones Nkasei (hiplife artist)   211
Bonet, Pep   186
Boney M (band)   137, 209
Bonga (singer-songwriter)   476, 510
bongo banghra   568
bongo flava/bongo fleva   **84–9**, 226, 246, 272, 428, 430, 441, 526, 568–9. *See also* hip-hop: in Sub-Saharan Africa
Bongo Maffin (group)   349, 350, 351, 352
Bongo Records   85, 86
Bongo, Ali   129, 239, 241
Bongo, Josephine (Patience Dabany)   125
Bongo, Omar   124, 125, 126, 127, 128, 129, 236, 241

bongo/bongó (musical instrument)   22, 206, 207, 269, 334, 429, 432, 468, 492, 504, 523. *See also* drums
Bongos (group)   509
Bongos Ikwue (band)   32
bonkó. *See ñánkue/bonkó*
Bono (singer-songwriter)   32, 483
Bonsu, Osei   205, 458
Bonsu, Reverend Michael Osei   210
boogie-woogie   360
Boom Shaka (group)   289, 349, 352
Boombaya (group)   32, 208
Boomerang (album)   262
BOP (Brothers of Peace) (group)   289, 349, 352
Bopape, Rupert   419, 421
'Borankana Metal' (song)   186
Borankana music   186
borborbor   35, **89–90**, 516
Borikó, Gabriel   396
Born Free Crew   103
borrowdale dance   521
Bosch, Fanie   80
bosoe   36
Boss, Lytto   59
Botchwey, Emmanuel Abrompah (Kwaw Kese)   276
Botha, P.W.   15
Boti, Marc   332
Botshelo (album)   356
Botswana   7, 181, 185–7, 188, 226, 228–32, 289–91, 552
  Gaborone   7, 186, 229
  Kweneng District   186
  Maun   186
Botswana Hip-Hop Music Awards (BHIPMA)   230, 213
bottle (as musical instrument)   121, 131, 134, 135, 395, 396, 467, 469, 475
  Fanta bottle   70, 461, 462, 580
  scraped bottle   586
'Bouge'   532
Boulard, Benoîte   504
Boulaye, Patti   138
bow songs (Zulu)   39, 408, 409
Bowen, Judith   64, 66
Bowie, Lester   16
box guitar   460–1, 580. *See also* guitar
box zither. *See marovany*
box-bass (musical instrument)   162, 433
box-drum   35. *See also* drums
Boziana, Bozi   494
Bra Monty and Sakaye Kings (group)   356
Bracket (duo)   219, 224
'Brada Maria' (song)   437
braggadocio (rap)   255
Brahim, Aziza   456
Brahms, Johannes   40
Brako, Ben   209
brass band music   13, 36, 47, 61, 73, 89, 112, 115, 204, 209, 222, 223, 341, 413, 439, 574. *See also adaha; beni*
  in Benin   **90–3**
  in Ethiopia   **93–4**, 141
  in Gabon   124–5
brass bands jazz/brasso   75
brass section/instruments   23, 56, 93, 94, 127, 140, 205, 217, 370, 372, 382, 400, 518, 537, 538, 563
Brazil   46, 47, 48, 91, 190, 222, 315, 333–4, 340, 436, 437, 467, 473, 474, 475, 507, 508, 510

breakdance   225, 228, 229–30, 234, 237, 243, 252, 262, 265, 347, 471
Breakin' (film)   229
BreBre Ohaa Hemma (album)   275
Brew, Nat 'Amandzeba'   212
Britain. *See* United Kingdom
Broadway (band)   36, 206
'Broken Heart' (song)   51
Brotherhood of Breath (group)   423
Brothers of Peace (BOP) (group)   289, 349, 352
Brown, Andy   103
Brown, Chris   257
Brown, G.   399
Brown, James   12, 13, 31, 125, 208, 254, 494, 516, 536, 566
Brulaye, Alata   557
Buabeng, Adelaide   114, 116
Buarque, Chico   510
bubblegum   **94–5**, 289, 336, 366, 450, 487
Bubi people   132, 392, 393, 394
Bucknor, Segun   32, 342
Bucknor, Segun and the Assembly (band)   31
Buena Vista Social Club (ensemble)   313
bugle   9, 74, 89, 163, 334, 433–4
Bugolobi Youth (group)   272
Buk Bak (group)   210, 211
Bukoto Youth (group)   272
Bukuku, Bahati   443
Bukusu people   362, 364, 365
Bukutu (band)   32
Bula Matlho (album)   356
Bulan (*ma/gaisa* artist)   368
Bulawayo Sweet Rhythms Band   540
Bulimundo (group)   97, 152
Bullet ya Kaoko (group)   465
'Bum Bum' (song)   87
bumps-a-daisy   342
Bunzus, The (band)   32
Buraka Som Sistema (group)   348
burger highlife   138, 205, 209, 219
Burity, Carlos   510
Burkina Faso   8, 315, 317, 384, 478, 480, 531–4, 545, 560, 576, 578
  Ouagadougou   8, 533
Burma Jokers (troupe)   112, 207
Burna Boy (singer-songwriter)   257
Burning Spear (reggae artist)   478
Burning Tone Records   195
Burundi   4, 7, 526
Bus Stop (group)   209
Bushfire Festival (music festival: Swaziland)   551
busipa   226, 270
busking   360, 361
Buung Pinz (rapper)   241
'Buy Africa' (song)   14
'Buya Afrika' (song)   302
búzio (musical instrument)   528, 529. *See also* horn
bwalo/boma   158, 377, 378
bwiti   240
Byrne, David   16, 510

Caban Bamboo (nightclub: Lagos, Nigeria)   224
Cabaret des Artistes (concert hall: Libreville, Gabon)   237
cabarets   370, 373. *See also* nightclubs
Cabdiraxmaan, Hodan   200

594

Index

Cabo Verde 62–3, 96–7, 105–6, 337, 338, 339, 340, 527–9
   Mindelo 105, 106
   Praia 528
   Santiago 62, 63, 106, 151–2, 528
Cabo Verde Show (group) 96, 340
Cabo Verdean *zouk*. *See cabo-zouk/cola-zouk*
cabocomeu 508
cabo-love 339
cabo-zouk/cola-zouk 96–8, 106, 339, 528
Cabral, Kino 34
cacha, Ruperto 131
caixa (musical instrument) 46. *See also* drums; snare drum
caixa corneta 508
Cakewalk Pro (software) 259
calaacal 202
calabash (musical instrument) 35, 170, 529, 530, 547, 557, 559, 562, 575. *See also adenkum* gourd calabash; *igbá*
Calender, Ebenezer 132, 160, 163, 164, 392, 398, 399–401, 467
Calender, Ebenezer and His Maringa Band 400
Calloway, Cab 109
Caluza, Reuben Tholakele 38, 39, 298, 300
Caluza's Double Quartet 300
calypso 9, 11, 13, 23, 57, 137, 161, 204, 206, 216, 392, 399
Camara, Ladji 318
Cameroon 4, 8, 32, 47, 63–7, 76–7, 162, 168, 172, 181, 183, 234–5, 239, 369–73, 393, 451–2, 466, 469
   Bamiléké plateau 64, 65
   Douala 64, 66, 369, 370, 372, 373, 394
   Douala, Bangangté district 64–5
   Ndé 63, 65
   Noun 64
   Yaoundé 4, 76, 77, 234
Cameroon Radio and Television (CRTV) 65
Campbell, Ambrose 11, 224, 467
Canabasse (rapper) 262
Canada 92, 519
   Toronto 200
Canda, Panaibra Gabriel 406
Cannibal Corpse (band) 181, 190
cans and tins (as musical instrument). *See also* Milo jazz; tin-can guitar
   cigarette tins 467
   jerrycans 545
   kerosene cans 516
   milk tins 399
   petrol cans 197
cantata 107, 108, 109
Canto Livre de Angola (cultural embassy) 476
Cape Coast Akrampa Number Six Asafo (Warrior) Company 9
Cape Coast Sugar Babies (group) 205
Cape Verde. *See* Cabo Verde
CAPital Dream Pictures 448
Capital FM (radio station) 246
Capital XTRA (radio station) 20
'Capote' (song) 503
Captain Moro 209
Captain Pazuzu (DJ) 358
Cardoso, André 249
Caribbean 11, 22, 46, 47, 57, 131, 135, 137–8, 159–60, 162, 323–4, 352, 392, 395, 405, 431, 432, 452, 478, 519, 560

Carlous Man (reggae artist) 483
carnivals 75, 154–5, 156, 157, 160, 299, 333, 334, 338, 347, 436, 476, 508, 510
Carnivore (restaurant: Nairobi, Kenya) 188, 244, 245, 246
carpenter's saw (musical instrument). *See* musical saw
carpenters 160, 342
carpentry tools 135
carramas 549
'Carry Am Go' (song) 255
Carstens, Nico 80–1, 82, 540
Carstens, Nico and Boereqanga 82
Case Sanga (TV series) 576
Cashless Society (hip-hop collective) 230–1
Casio keyboard 428, 429, 463. *See also* keyboard
   Casiotone MT-140 173, 176
Casio synthesizer 172. *See also* synthesizer
cassette recordings 28, 59, 61, 66, 77, 84, 86, 116, 143, 199, 200, 208, 210, 226, 229, 234, 236, 237, 261, 268, 285, 312, 317, 332, 339, 348, 355, 357, 368, 405, 414, 416, 443, 456, 471, 478, 520, 522, 523, 524, 526, 531, 533, 544, 545, 546, 557, 574, 575–6, 577, 580
'Cassinga' (song) 513
Cassiya (group) 505
Cast (singer) 177
castanet (musical instrument) 35, 36, 584. *See also clave/*clips
Castro (hiplife artist) 51
Castro (*shambo* artist) 514
Castro, Okonfo Kwade 211
Cato, Aurora 108
Cats Paw (band) 30. *See also* Osibisa (band)
Cavaquim, Frank 105
cavaquiño (musical instrument) 105, 436. *See also* guitar
CBS (record label) 580
CCP Records 284
CD. *See* compact disc
CDA (record label). *See* Companhia de Discos de Angola (record label)
CDJs 291
CD-R. *See* compact disc-recordable
Cele, Thuthukani 488
Cele, Willard 360
Celestial Christian Church 91
Celi, Gadji 122–3
cell phones/mobile phones/ smartphones 28, 55, 174, 177, 472, 577
cello 155, 205, 453, 523, 525, 569–70
censorship 49, 91, 105, 106, 143, 177, 183, 199, 201, 227, 260, 367, 385, 404, 452, 487, 513
Central Africa 4, 120, 159, 161, 162, 181, 216, 225, 338, 454, 466–9, 477, 497, 518, 586. *See also specific nations*
Central African Republic 4, 6, 8, 181
Central Intelligence Agency (CIA) (US) 423
Central Johannesburg College 288
Central Volcano Band 58
Centre-ville (group) 125
CFAO (trading company) 113
chaabi 545
chachachá 57, 394, 493

Chad 4, 6, 8, 168, 181, 384
Chaguo la Teenies Awards 246
Chaka Chaka, Yvonne 94, 95
chakacha 98–100, 428–9, 523, 525, 526
Chali, Kris 332
Chamber Squad (group) 85
Chameleone, Jose 335
Chanda, Emmanuel 'Jagari' 567
Channel Four (TV network) 346
Channel O Music Video Awards 87, 231
Chantre, Téofilo 106
chants and chanting 12, 16, 147, 179, 210, 221, 234, 243, 275, 280, 349, 351, 364, 366, 415, 431, 514
chapa 308
Chaphuka, Paul 485
Chaplin, Charlie 108, 109
chapuo (musical instrument) 430. *See also* drums
charanga 23, 442
Charles, Leon 138
Charles, Ray 166
Charleston (dance and rhythm) 66
Charter House Production and Events Management company, The (Accra, Ghana) 276
'Chave Chimurenga' (jingle) 103
Chaves, Sara 509
Chebaibai (*benga* artist) 71
Chechamba, Wyndham 25
Checker, Chubby 24, 31, 208, 346, 516
chekeche (musical instrument) 429
chela 61
chemanjemanje 320
'Chemsha bongo' (song) 85
'Chemutengure' (song) 102
Chepkoech, Angelica 71
Chepkorir, Elizabeth 71
chera 54
cherewa (musical instrument) 336. *See also maracas*; rattle
Cherubim Church 47–8, 91, 323
Chewa people 158, 377, 426, 521
Chibadura, John 499, 521, 522
Chicago (hiplife artist) 210
Chicago, Roy 223, 224
Chicco (Sello Twala) 94–5, 289
Chicittos (band) 367
Chicken Run Band 31
Chiclets, The (group) 367
Chico, Igo 13
Chidhuza, Simon 521
Chidinma (singer-songwriter) 257
Chidumule, Cosmas 443
Chief Abioro (entrepreneur) 320, 324
Chief Commander Ebenezer Obey and his Miliki Sound (album) 324
Chief of the Ghosts (album) 186
Chief Olayegbe (entrepreneur) 323
chifumbo/efumbo drum. *See efumbo/chifumbo* drum
'Chifundo' (song) 567
Chikinchi (highlife artist) 209
Chikowa Jazz Band 308, 309
Chikuni, Lewis 26
Chikupo, Tineyi 521
Chilala, Brian 'Rebel' 333
Children From Pluto (group) 367
Children of Bodom (band) 190
chimbengele (musical instrument). *See luhengele/luengele*
Chimbetu, Naison 521

595

Index

Chimbetu, Simon 103, 498–9, 521, 522
Chimbetu, Sulumani 522
Chimezie, Bright 217
Chimombe, James 320
Chimombo, Overton 25
Chimora (band) 94
chimtali 425, 427
chimurenga **100–5**, 227, 320, 331, 333, 450, 520
chin (musical instrument) 131, 135
chinamwali 425
Chingaira, Dick 'Comrade Chinx' 101, 103
chinungu 320
Chinyani, Shepherd 521
Chipembere, Masauko 26
Chiponda, Mai Margaret 427
Chiquito (rapper) 251
Chirwa, Verah 426
Chisala, P.K. 332
chisamba 358, 427
chisekele (musical instrument) 331. *See also* shakers
Chisiza, Yatuta 425
chitelele 332, 333
Chitipi Capital Sounds (group) 25
Chiume, Kanyama 425
Chiwalo, Coss 485
Chiweshe, Ashton 'Sugar' 102
Chiweshe, Stella 103
chiwoda 308, 425, 427
Chiyangwa, Leonard 'Pickett' 102
Chizi, Dan 72
Choge, Sa'adatu Barmani 170
Choice Breakfast (radio program) 51
Choices Pub and Restaurant (Nairobi, Kenya) 188
'Chop Money' (song) 256
choral music/singing 382, 409. *See also amakwaya*; *muziki wa injili*; *nederlandslied*; *uukorasa/oukorasa*
Chris Manto 7 (*kwasa kwasa* artist) 356
Christ Apostolic Church 47–8
Christian metal 194
Christian missions and missionaries 37–8, 74, 204, 221–2, 298–9, 300, 395, 409, 552, 553
Christianity 15, 47–8, 158, 321, 436, 501, 517, 552–3, 554. *See also* church; church music
Christmas 9, 153–4, 155, 299
Christmas bands 154, 155, 156, 157
chromatic button accordion 504. *See also* accordion
Chura (group) 74
church 10, 47–8, 51, 62, 90, 91, 107, 108, 151, 251–2, 297–8, 299, 388, 438, 444, 465, 552, 553, 554
church music 64, 91, 101, 209–10, 212, 213, 219–20, 221–2, 252, 323, 370, 442–3, 465
CIA (US). *See* Central Intelligence Agency (US)
Cicada (band) 32
cidrália 508
Cigaal, Axmed Cali 199
Circuit Five (band) 31
City Arts Monthly (San Francisco) 28
City Boys (group) 207, 208, 482
City Quads, The (group) 450
Cklub 103 (radio program) 290
C.K. Jazz (Continental Kilo Jazz Band) 69

clarinet 80, 105, 280, 436, 440
clash cymbals 76. *See also* cymbals
Clash of the Giants (album) 356
Clash Raaboon/Movaizhaleine 238, 240
Class Suicide (band) 188
Classic Handels (group) 482
Classic Recordings of West Kenya (album) 462
Classic Vibes (group) 482
clave 10, 13, 14, 20, 22, 23, 35, 131, 204, 346, 395, 468, 490, 491, 492, 498, 520
claves/clips (musical instrument) 13, 34–5, 36, 205, 323, 336, 394, 468
clay drum. *See kidumbak/vidumbak* drum; *kpezin* drum
Clegg, Johnny 32
Cliff, Jimmy 208, 478, 482, 483, 484, 486, 487, 488
Climi Boodhari (poet) 198
Clington, Alba 509
Clouds FM (radio station) 85, 87
Clouds Media Group 87
Club Afrique (London) 224
Club Ellesse (Pretoria, South Africa) 284, 286
clubs 22, 23, 85, 97, 120, 123, 142, 176, 177, 188, 195, 244, 294, 334, 338, 346, 361, 368, 403, 431–2, 470–1, 475, 476, 479, 503, 521, 537, 587. *See also* nightclubs; social clubs
CNN (TV network) 186, 252, 483
Coal, Wande 448
coast-nite concerts 75
Cobra 357
coco-ase music 458
Coconut FM (radio station) 569
'Coffin for Head of State' (song) 15
Coker, Fred 33
Coker's brass band 10
cól drum 414, 415. *See also* bass drum; drums
cola SanJon 105
coladeira 9, **105–6**, 338, 340. *See also coladeira* [in Europe] (Volume XI, *Genres: Europe*)
cola-zouk. *See cabo-zouk/cola-zouk*
Cole, Bob 207
Cole, Rabiu Ishola 43–4
Coleman, Ornette 12
Collé, Ami 416
College of the Arts (COTA) Youth Choir Namibia 553
Collinet, Georges 29
Collins, John (musician and author) 28–9, 30, 459
Collins, William 'Bootsy' 16
Colombia 28, 431
colonialism 14, 37, 73, 74, 100–1, 107–9, 110–12, 120, 141, 152, 158, 165–7, 181, 183–4, 198, 202, 217, 277, 298, 317, 342, 345, 374, 375, 376–7, 379, 382, 408, 439–40, 444, 475, 476, 482, 508, 528
Coltrane, John 12
columbia 490
Columbia Records 53, 300, 524
Comando & Chova Chova (group) 521
Come Back Africa (film) 421
Comets (group) 206
Comforters, The (group) 487
coming-of-age ceremonies 54–5, 430
Common (rapper) 17

Communauté Black (group) 240
communism and communist regimes 101, 207, 248, 380, 402, 471, 548
Communist Party of Réunion (PCR) 380
compact disc (CD) 28, 29, 62, 77, 86, 129, 143–4, 148, 173, 174, 175, 177, 188, 210, 220, 236, 237, 259, 260, 282, 285, 312, 313, 331, 333, 339, 349, 357, 368, 375, 386, 414, 443, 449, 522, 528, 531, 574. *See also* digital versatile disc (DVD); video-CD
compact disc-recordable (CD-R) 337, 524
Companhia de Discos de Angola (CDA) (record label) 334, 432, 476
competitions
 amakwaya 40
 breakdance 229
 Clash Raaboon/Movaizhaleine 238
 concertina 79
 heesaha hirgalay 199
 hip-hop 237, 246
 isicathamiya 297–8
 isukuti 306
 jembel/djembe music
 jùjú 323
 klopse 154–5
 kwasa kwasa 358
 Malay Choirs 155, 436, 453
 malipenga 376
 MCing 230
 rap 244
 takiboronsé 532, 533, 534
 umbholoho 551
 uukorasa 554
 were/wéré 146, 147
computers 86, 140, 191, 193, 235, 243, 244, 291, 443, 448, 485
Comrade Chinx (Dick Chingaira) 101, 103
concert halls 192, 222, 237, 368, 443, 465, 514, 443, 450, 465, 514
concert party **106–20**, 205, 206, 207–8, 217, 516
Concert Party Show (fortnightly event) 116–19
concertina (musical instrument) 78, 79, 80, 81, 82, 112, 160, 205, 300, 321, 408, 410, 421, 458, 466, 467
Concertina Club of South Africa, The 81–2
concerts and live perfomances 21, 31, 33, 37, 54, 57, 58, 75, 77, 85, 86–7, 91, 97, 101, 121, 135, 148, 175, 177, 181, 186–7, 188, 191, 192, 202, 210–11, 212, 234, 262, 263, 269, 297–8, 300, 302, 309, 317, 318, 338, 344, 351, 360, 361, 367, 373, 394, 419, 432, 439, 440, 441, 449, 464, 479, 484, 486, 487, 488, 494, 495, 496, 520, 555, 567, 576, 577, 587. *See also* open air/open space performances; school concerts
conch (musical instrument). *See búzio*
Condest (group) 465
conductor (musical instrument) 70
confrarias. *See tariqas/confrarias*
'Confusion Break Bone' (song) 12
conga 418
conga drum 13, 70, 99, 206, 217, 379, 433, 441, 492, 504, 516, 580. *See also* drums; *tumba* drum
congama (musical instrument) 467. *See also* lamellophone

596

Index

Congo, Democratic Republic of the (DRC)   4, 5, 7, 25, 27, 47, 68, 69, 125, 126, 128, 132, 160, 162, 181, 226, 227, 239, 267–70, 320, 331, 355, 356, 357–8, 365, 384, 392, 393, 395, 396, 441, 451–2, 468, 470, 477, 491, 493, 497, 518–19, 526, 531, 532, 566
  Goma   269, 270
  Kinshasa/Léopoldville   4, 181, 269, 270, 355, 396, 451, 468, 469, 491, 492–3, 495–6, 497, 518
  Kinshasa/Léopoldville, Kimbanseke   496
  Kinshasa/Léopoldville, Matonge   496
  Kisangani   269, 270
  Lubumbashi   269, 270, 331
  Matadi   468, 469
Congo, Republic of   4, 7, 236
  Brazzaville   4, 120, 181, 469, 477, 491, 492–3, 495, 496
  Brazzaville, Poto Poto   496
Congo *jazz*   466, 469, 516
Congo, River   496
Congolese music   19–20
Congolese *rumba*   70, 72, 84, 86, 102, 235, 308, 331, 358, 370, 391, 396, 451, 452, 491–7, 498, 520, 521, 532. *See also* rumba; *soukouss*
Congress of Cultural Freedom (advocacy group)   423
Congress of South African Trade Unions (COSATU)   302
Conjunto Harmonia (group)   403
Conjunto Merengue (group)   432
Conjunto Yong Ussufo (group)   403
'Conscience' (song)   270
'Constitution constipée' (song)   372
Continental Kilo Jazz Band (C.K. Jazz)   69
contradance   475
Convention Peoples Party (CPP) (Ghana)   90, 206, 207
Cook, Michael   275
Cool Four, The (group)   450
Cool Muza (rapper)   568, 569
Cool Para (rapper)   569
Coolio (rapper)   269
Coon Carnival (Cape Town, South Africa)   299
copla   392
Copland, Stewart   32, 212
copyright   62, 97, 208, 263, 301, 577
Corentin, Tian   505
Cornelius, Rasdien   453
cornet   280
Coromantins/Kromantis   483
Coronation of King George VI, The (play)   111–12
COSATU. *See* Congress of South African Trade Unions
Cosmic Four Dots (group)   102
Costa, Nina da   138
Costa, Vate   432
COTA Youth Choir Namibia   553
Côte d'Ivoire   8, 20, 47, 66, 112, 115–16, 120–3, 132, 135, 160, 162, 168, 239, 315, 317, 385, 436–7, 477, 478, 479–80, 497, 531, 532, 560, 576, 578, 583–4, 585–8
  Abidjan   8, 120, 121, 122, 318, 479, 586, 587
  Abidjan, Blockhauss   587
  Abidjan, Cocody   479
  Abidjan, Koumassi   587

Abidjan, Résidential   479
Abidjan, Treichville   479
Abidjan, Yopougon   587
Boa Vista   436, 437
Bondoukou   457
Bouake   8, 122
Brava   437
Fogo   437
Cothoza Mfana! (radio program)   301
Coulibaly, Soungalo   318
coupé-décalé   20, 66, **120–4**, 239, 495, 496–7, 532, 576, 583, 584, 586, 587, 588
Couto, Zeca   106
cow horn. *See olwika*
cowbell (musical instrument)   70, 341. *See also* bell; *gankogui*
CPP (Ghana). *See* Convention Peoples Party (Ghana)
Crab, Clifford   195
Crabs in a Bucket (album)   212
Crackdust (band)   186
Cradle of Filth (band)   190
Crammed Discs (record label)   331
Crane Band, The   57–8
Crazy Gang (band)   57
Cream (group)   31, 208, 332
Créas, J.J.   66
Crentsil, A.B.   210, 211
Creole people
  Fernandino   132–3, 134, 135, 392, 393–4
  Indian Ocean islands   503–5, 517
  Mauritius   182
  Seychelles   438–9
  Sierra Leone   159, 160, 162, 391–2, 395, 398, 400, 401, 467
  Western Cape   154, 157
Crimsons, The (group)   367
Crió people. *See* Creole people
Crocodile Male Voice Choir   301
Crossbones, The (group)   332
crotales (musical instrument)   380. *See also* cymbals
Crouch, Andrae   352
'Crowd Mentality' (song)   256
CRTV. *See* Cameroon Radio and Television
Cruz, Francisco Xavier da (B. Léza)   437
Cthonic (band)   182
Cuba   23, 46, 135, 137, 222, 385, 393, 394, 395, 405, 411, 490–1, 497, 508, 521, 523, 577
  Havana   490, 491
  Matanzas   490
  Oriente   491
Cubaliwa (album)   251
Cuban Marimba (group)   337, 440
Cubase (software)   86, 259
cultural animation groups
  in Congo, Democratic Republic of the   125, 126, 128
  in Gabon   **124–31**
Cultural Imani Band   482
Culture (group)   484
cumba   577
cumbé   **131–7**, 160, 395. *See also gome/gombe/le gombe*; *gumbe/goombay*
cumbé drum   131, 132, 133, 134, 396. *See also* drums; frame drum; square drum
cumbia   28, 105
Cunha, Yuri da   334

cut belle en shake wase   400, 434
cut belleh   400, 434
cuud (musical instrument)   198, 199, 201. *See also* lute
Cyclops (band)   31
cymbals   91, 283, 326. *See also* clash cymbals; *crotales*; *séélí*
Czechoslovakia   44

D.O. 7 Shirati Jazz Band   69
D'Banj (musician)   176, 257, 448
D 'N' D Slam (hip-hop artist)   272
D'Novas, Manuel/Manel   105, 437
Da (band)   440
Da Brains (group)   262
Da Capo Guide to Contemporary African Music, The (Graham)   29
Da Nu Eagles (band)   59
Da Rappatainer (Weird MC/Adesola Adesimbo Idowu)   255
Da Silva, Luís   96
Da Trybe (trio)   255
Da'ar, Jama Nur   166
Daahir, Khadra   199
Daara J/Daara J Family (group)   227, 240, 262
Dabany, Patience (Josephine Bongo)   125
Dabatram (band)   33, 212
Dadapaoly (composer)   53
Daddy Bibson (MC)   261
Daddy Fresh (singer)   259
Daddy Loco and His Calender Survivals (group)   401
Daddy Lumba (Charles Kojo Fusu)   138, 209
Daddy Saj (hip-hop artist)   138
dadj'i   135
Dadson, E.K.   111–12
daf/duff (musical instrument)   548. *See also* drums; frame drum
Dagbon people   161, 516–17
dagomba   205, 447
Dagomba people   35, 342
Dairo, I.K.   47, 323
Dairo, I.K. and His Blue Spots (group)   223, 323
Dairo, I.K. and the Morning Star Orchestra   223, 323, 525
Dairo, Paul Play   224
Dako, Seth   209
'Dalibom ka Ntsikana' (hymn)   38
Dalom Kids (band)   95
Dama Do Bling (Ivânnea da Silva Mudanisse)   273
DAMAC PAC (hip-hop artist)   272
Damara DikDing (musician)   368
Damara *pantsula*   366
Damara people   366, 367–8
Damara *punch*   366, 368
Damba, Fanta   56, 386
dambwe (initiation places)   158
Damelin College (Pinetown, South Africa)   288
Damily (musician)   544
Dan Anace, Muhammadu Bawa   169
Dançando com Voz de Cabo Verde (album)   106
dance-band highlife   204, 205, 206–7, 208, 209, 216–17, 222, 343, 466, 468
dance bands   388–9, 441, 454, 455, 469, 526
'dance-hall' (sample)   176, 177

597

Index

dance halls   105, 124, 367, 404–5, 439. *See also* discotheques; nightclubs
dancehall   57, 78, 84, 176, 177, 257, 334–5, 470, 483, 489, 522. *See also* ragga
'Dancing Shoes' (song)   231
Dandogarai, Kabiru   175
Danfo O Si'Ere/Ema Tori Owo Pa'nia (album)   44–5
Danger, Francis   71
Danialou Sagbohan & Les Astronautes (album)   330
Danialou, Sagbohan   330
Daniel, Ojoge   467
Daniel, Ojoge and His Juju Band   323
Daniels, Dondo   468
Dankwairo, Musa   169
Danmaraya Jos   169, 170
dansa   317
dansi. *See muziki wa dansi*
dansi clubs   439–40
Danso, Robert   217
Dany, Edson   340
danzón   22, 23
Dar Akhbar (building: Djibouti City)   166
Dar International Orchestre   441
Dark City Sisters   421
Darko, George   138, 209
Darko, Kwabena Okyere (Obrafour)   210, 276, 277
Darling, Tommy   32
'Dats Wassup' (song)   231
Daughters of Glorious Jesus (group)   210
Davido (singer)   87, 123, 176, 448, 449
Davies, Teddy   138
Davis, Spencer   31
Dawuni, Rocky   483
dawuro (musical instrument)   412. *See also* bell
dB Studios   332
DDC Kibisa   525
De Black Evening Follies (group)   450
De Castro, Urbano   509, 511
De Coque, Oliver (Oliver Sunday Akanite)   216, 217, 218, 219
De Kock, Bosman   81
De Lange, David   80, 82
de Mbanga, Lapiro   372
De Souza, Ignace   330
Deaf Ears (band)   6
death metal   185, 186, 190, 191, 194
decalé chinois   122
Decca Records   53, 113, 300, 323, 324, 467
Decca West Africa (record label)   44, 218, 399
Decca, Ben   372
Decca, Dora   372
Decca, Grace   372
Dede, Amakye   208, 212, 482
Deen, Akie   137–8
Deep Horizon (band)   103
deep house   284
Deep Purple (band)   180
Def Dara Studio   261
Def Leppard (band)   181
Definitive Jux (record label)   231
'Dege' (song)   570
Dekker, Desmond   482, 484
Delgado, Justino   340
Delta Igbo people   218
Dembele, Koko   478
Dembéle, Nouhoum   576
Dembo, Leonard   499, 522

Democratic Progressive Party (DPP) (Malawi)   426–7
Democratic Republic of Congo (DRC). *See* Congo, Democratic Republic of the
Demogoroth Satanum (band)   196
denbafòli   316, 317
Denero, Kao   138
Denge, Irewolede   467
densewu   35
Denti d'Oro, Antoni (António Vaz Cabral)   62
denzim/adzewa   35
desert blues   456
Desmali (singer)   136
Desmali e Dambo de las Costa (group)   132, 135, 397
Desparate Chicks (group)   219
Destyn (group)   380
Devera Ngwena (group)   498, 521
Dey, Fadal   480
Dey, Kofi   153
Deza XXL (group)   584
d'gong   349
DH (*pandza* artist)   473
Dharaar, Khadiija Ciye (Khadiija 'Belwo')   197
'Dhulkayaga' (song)   198
Dhuule, Cumar   198, 199
Diabaté. *See also* headings beginning Dioubaté; Jobarteh
Diabaté, Aboubacar 'Badian'   56
Diabaté, Foussenou   56
Diabate, Kasse Mady   311, 313
Diabaté, Lanfia   56
Diabate, Papa   312
Diabaté, Sékouba 'Bambino'   311, 312, 385
Diabaté, Sira Mory   56
Diabaté, Toumani   312, 313, 563
Diaby, Mohamed   576
Diakité, Ramata   557
Diakité, Tata   557
Diallo, Sheikh Sufi Bilal   576
Diamond Platnumz (recording artist and dancer)   87
Diamond Players (band)   10
Diamond Production (band)   58–9
Diamonds in the Rough: A Ugandan Hip-Hop Revolution (documentary)   273
'Diarabi Nene' (song)   557
Diarin'ny Kintana (ensemble)   54
Diarra, Souleymane (Zikiri Solo)   576
Dias, Beto   340
Dias, Carlitos Vieira   510
Dias, Carlos Aniceto Vieira. *See* Dias, Liceu Vieira
Dias, Liceu Vieira   334, 432, 476, 507, 508
diaspora   11, 19, 21, 27, 28, 30, 275, 278, 569
 Angolan   510
 Beninois   573
 Batswana   229
 Cabo Verdean   96–7, 339, 340
 Congolese (DRC)   270, 452, 518, 519
 Ethiopian   143, 463
 Gabonese   241
 Ghanaian   51–2, 209
 Ivorian   120–3, 497
 Lusophone African   337, 338, 339
 Malian   313

 Nigerian   449
 Sierra Leonean   132–3, 134, 135, 392, 393–4, 396
 Somalian   200
 South African   422–3
 Tuareg people   545–6
 West African   19
diatonic button accordion   380. *See also* accordion; *gaita*; *ngaieta*
Diawara, Djeli Moussa (Jali Musa Jawara)   312
Diawara, Fatoumata   558
Dibala, Diblo   355, 494–5, 519
Dibango, Manu   32
Diboue, Elie Mbongue   370
Didah (*zenji flava* artist)   568
Die Antwoord (group)   227, 266
Die Kaapse Affodille Dames Boereorkes (group)   82
Diego, Fora   465
Dieng, Fallou   416
'Diepkloof' (song)   352
digital audio workstation   372
digital technology   192–3, 335, 349
digital versatile disc (DVD)   148, 282, 331, 339, 443, 577. *See also* compact disc (CD); video-CD (VCD)
Digo people   54, 75
dihy   280
dikanza (musical instrument)   334, 432, 475, 476, 508, 509. *See also* scraper
dikhwaere   356
Dikosso, Claudia   372
Dimossi (group)   125, 127
Dioubate, Oumou   312
Dioubaté, Sidi Djéli   382
Dioubaté, Sidi Karammò   382
Dioubaté, Sidi Mamadi   382
Dioubaté, Sidi Moussa   382
Diouf, Pape   416
Dioum, Mbacke   261
Dire Straits (band)   545
Director, Nya   64
disc jockeys. *See* DJ(s)
disco   44, 137, 170, 254, 422, 486, 531, 563. *See also* burger highlife
disco séga   505
discolypso   **137–9**
Disco-Mad (record label)   502
discotecas africanas ('African discos')   338
discotheques   84, 96, 137, 152, 188, 209, 244, 312, 373, 402, 580; *See also* nightclubs
Dix-Covian Jokers (troupe)   112
Dixon (*ma/gaisa* artist)   368
Dixon, Marshal   269
DJ(s)   121, 225, 228, 229, 234, 237, 243, 262, 283, 284–6, 287, 288–9, 290–2, 348, 349, 368, 449, 470, 471, 472, 483
DJ Abrantee   20
DJ Arafat (Yoro Gang)   121, 122
DJ Ardiles   471, 472, 473, 474
DJ Awadi   261
DJ Bass   229
DJ Berry   272
DJ Boogie Sid   291
DJ Caloudje   121
DJ Chrispin   291
DJ Christos   284, 286, 288, 289, 349, 350
DJ Cleo (Cleopas Monyeapo)   288, 291
DJ Cosmo   290

598

Index

DJ Couleur 270
DJ Dan 380
DJ Dext 229
DJ Dolphus 290
DJ Eddie Ed 229
DJ Edu 20
DJ Fondo Fire 291
DJ Fresh 285, 287, 288, 290
DJ Ganyani 284, 285
DJ Gérard Ben 66
DJ Glen Lewis 285
DJ Guto 251
Dj Iggy Smallz 284
DJ Jacob 121
DJ Jazzy Jeff and the Fresh Prince (duo) 255
DJ Jonathan 121
DJ Junior 473
DJ Khabzela 287
DJ Khenzo 229
DJ Kicking Clectic 229
DJ Kim 569
DJ Le Blanc 472, 473
DJ Lewis 121
DJ Mass 229
DJ Mosse the Darkchild 246
DJ Sabside 292
DJ Saleh 569
DJ Sbu 289
DJ Sebem 348
DJ Sid (Sidney Basitsile) 229, 230, 231, 290
DJ Sid Presents P-Side (album) 230
DJ Simza 291, 292
DJ Skizo/Ski (David Molosi) 290–1
DJ Tira 289
DJ Tony 290
DJ Tunez 21
DJ Vetkoek (Mahoota/Zynne Sibika) 289
DJ Vinny Da Vinci 284
DJ Young Mullar 291
DJ Ziyawa (Mduduzi Matsenjwa) 291
dja' (musical instrument) 65. See also xylophone
Djan, Abraham Ohene 275
Djan, Ohene 275
Djedje, Carlos 486, 487, 488
DjeDje, Ernesto 584
Djedje, Percy (P. Postman) 488
djegbe 412
djelingoni (musical instrument) 56. See also lute
djembe (musical instrument). See *jembe/djembe/dyembe* drum
Djeyim, Jack 66
Djibouti 6, 164, 165, 166–7, 200
Djibouti City 6, 165, 197, 198
Djily Bagdad (hip-hop artist) 263
Djinji, Dilon 251, 402–3, 404, 405, 406, 471
djoglissohoun 412, 413
DJs@Work (group) 284
djun-djun (musical instrument). See *dùndún/dundun* drum
DK (Daniel Kamau Mwai) 71
'DKW' (song) 82
Dladla, Nomalungelo 292
Dlamini, Nomzamo 292
Dludlu, Jimmy 288
DMX (rapper) 259
D-Naff (rapper) 514
Dobeez (hip-hop artist) 245

doblá (musical instrument) 134. See also square tambourine; tambourine
Doc Shebeleza (*kwaito* artist) 289
dockworkers 490
dodo dance 69, 70
Dog Murras (singer-songwriter) 334
Dogo Dogo Stars Baikoko (group) 55
dogole (musical instrument) 54. See also drums
Dolphus (DJ) 229
Dom Lanterna (musician) 510
Domingos, Camilo 340
Dominican Republic 399, 431
Domino, Antoine "Fats" 208
Dompo, Confort 114
Don Azpiazú 22, 491
Don Bosco (recording studio) 85
Don Juan (hip-hop artist) 232
Donaldson, Eric 484
Donat, Luc 505
dondo drum. See *odonno/dondo* drum
donga (musical instrument) 370
donkielong (musical instrument). See concertina
Donkor, Eddie 482
donson n'goni (musical instrument) 557. See also harp lute
Dookom (group) 266
doom metal 194
dopé 584, 585
Dorica (*zenji flava* artist) 568
Dorkay House (music venue: Johannesburg, South Africa) 419
Dorsey, Jimmy 301
dos Santos, José Maria 348, 507, 508
double bass 80, 140, 206, 207, 367, 468, 523, 525–6, 569–70
Double D (singer) 177
'Double Decker Buses' (song) 400
Doukouré, Stephane Hamidou (Douk Saga) 120–1
Doumbia, Abdoul 578
Doumbia, Nahawa 557
doundoun (musical instrument). See *dùndún/dundun* drum
Dowa Mbumba (group) 426
Dowa Symphony (*Azimai aku Dowa*) 426, 427
'Down on One' (song) 51
Dowuona, B.B. 209
DPP (Malawi). See Democratic Progressive Party (Malawi)
Dr Pure (hip-hop artist) 259
Dr. Biza Band, The 356
Dr. Deep (hip-hop artist) 269
Dr. Dynamite and His Afro-Rhythms (group) 433
Dr. Footswitch (rock musician) 183
Dr. JB et les Jaguars (group) 503
Dr. Kareke (Henguva Kareke) 464–5
Dr. Mickey (Michael Rankgomo) 357
Dr. Nico (guitarist) 493
Dr. Oloh and His Milo Jazz Band 433, 434
Dr. Victor (reggae artist) 488
Dr. Victor and The Rasta Rebels (group) 488
Drake (rapper) 257
Dramé, Adama 318
Draztik (MC/record producer) (David Balsher) 229, 230–1
DRC. See Congo, Democratic Republic of the

Dread Warriors (group) 486
Droit chemin (album) 495
drugs and addiction 95, 505
Drum (periodical) 419
Drum Brothers (group) 578
drum machine 56, 94, 96, 137, 138, 140, 143, 144, 209, 251, 283, 284, 295, 523, 538
drum machine, electronic 312
drum set/drum kit 13, 14, 68, 76, 81, 99, 140, 145, 149, 152, 167, 199, 205, 217, 228, 309, 324, 326, 330, 331, 332, 359, 360, 368, 372, 410, 413, 414–15, 438, 441, 456, 463, 473, 480, 485, 492, 523, 525, 537, 538, 547, 557, 563, 569–70, 580, 584, 586
drum set/drum kit, electric 580
drum, electronic 480
drums 35, 38, 55, 56, 61, 65, 66, 70, 105, 108, 127, 158–9, 163, 166, 167, 173, 181, 201, 205, 221, 229, 231, 307, 326, 332, 333, 337, 340, 345, 367, 376, 377, 378, 382, 394, 408, 420, 421, 427, 428, 438, 440, 442, 465, 477, 478, 502, 505, 508, 513, 518, 528, 544, 545, 575. See also *àkúbà/akuba*; *alekele*; *baba*; *banga*; bass drum; *bàtá/bata* drum; *bel*; *bembe*; *boba*; bongo/bongó; boxdrum; *chapuo*; conga drum; *dogole* drum; *duman girke*; *efumbo/chifumbo* drum; *embegete*; *embuutu* drum; *empuunyi* drum; *engoma* drum; frame drum; *ganga*; *ghoema* drum; *gumbe/goombay* drum; hand drum; hourglass drum; *isukuti* drum; *jembe/djembe/dyembe* drum; *jimberu*; *kabaro*; *kagan* drum; *kalangu* drum; *kamkumbe* drum; *kannango* drum; *kebero*; *kidi* drum; *kotso*; *kpawle/kpahwle* drum; *kunda* drum; *kunké*; *kuru*; *kurya*; *kuturiba*; *kuturindingo*; *kwadum* drum; *kwaira*; marine; *mbalule* drum; *mbandambanda* drum; *mbëngmbëng* drum; *moropa*; *mosomba* drum; *mpanje* drum; *msondo* drum; *musondo*; *nankasa* drum; *nder* drum; *ndu'*; *ngoma/ingoma* drum; *ngoma ya kuchanganya*; *ngoma ya kudunda*; *nkali*; *oge* drum; *omele ako* drum; *omele méta* drum; peg drum; *ragga* drum; *ravann*; *rollin*; *sabar* drum; *sákárá/sakara* drum; *samba* drum; *sati*; *simba*; *sinhun*; slit drum; snare drum; *sogo*; square drum; *tabla*; talking drum; tambourine; *tango* drum; *tauje*; *taushi*; *tbal* drum; *tende* drum; tin drum; tomtom; trap drum; *turu*; *zenli* drum
Drygun (rapper) 263
DSTV (TV network) 87
duassi (musical instrument) 549–50. See also drums; frame drums
dub 489
Dubazane, Jubele 'Lumbu' 299
Dube (group) 103
Dube, John Langalibalele 39, 300
Dube, Joseph Hlomayi 102
Dube, Joshua 102, 103
Dube, Lucky 289, 478, 483, 484, 485, 486, 487, 488

599

Index

Dube, Nkulee 488
Dube, Thokozani 488
dubstep 235
Ducap, Narmine 505
duff (musical instrument). *See daf/duff*
Dugan, Stella 210
duman girke (musical instrument) 170. *See also* drums
dumbaki/dumbak (musical instrument) 429. *See also* drums; hand drum
dun (musical instrument) 395–6. *See also* bass drum; drums
Dundee Wandering Singers 301, 302
dùndún/dundun drum 12, 17, 43, 146, 147, 223, 383, 384, 563, 578. *See also* drums; *dundunba* drum; hourglass drum; talking drum
dundunba drum 563. *See also* drums; *dùndún/dundun* drum
dunun (musical instrument). *See dùndún/dundun* drum
Duo Ouro Negro (group) 334
Duodu, Lee 209
Duol (record label) 69
Durán, Lucy 313
Durban Humming Bees (choir) 301
Durban Youth Radio 285
Durdur (group) 199
Dutiro, Chartwell 103
DVD. *See* digital versatile disc
dwae 34
Dyani, Johnny 423
Dynamics (band) 31
Dzidudu (band) 33, 212
Dzimba, Jimmy 61
dzukuta. *See pandza*

E.L. (musician) 51
Eagles Production (band) 58–9, 335
East Africa 5, 6, 73–6, 86, 100, 157, 216, 225, 308, 365, 376, 439–40, 454, 497, 498, 523, 548, 549. *See also* Horn of Africa; *specific nations*
East African Melody (group) 526
East Coast Team 86, 87
Easter 9
'Easy Dancing' (song) 138
Easy FM (radio station) 246
Easy Kabaka (band) 32
Eazzy (Mildred Ashong) 277
Ebaahi Sounds (group) 346
Ebanda Manfred & l'Orchestre Toumba Africa (group) 370
Ebanda Manfred (singer) 370, 469
EBEN Entertainment (record label) 240
Ebeny, Paul & l'Ambiance Jazz (group) 370
Ebogo, Tonton 77
Ebonies (band) 58
Echoes (band) 31
Eder, Alan 153
Edikanfo (band) 32
Edimo, Vicky 372
Edu Magicians (band) 10
Edwards, Dennis 352
'Eeloli' (song) 514
Efik people 218
efumbo/chifumbo drum 364, 365. *See also* drums
Efya (singer) 21
'Egbe Mi O' (song) 14

Ege, Akanbi 322
eggono 327
Egun people 153, 161
egungun 413
egwe 217
egwu ekpiri 217
egwu ogene 217
Egypt 524, 578
Egypt '80 (band) 15, 17. *See also* Africa '70 (band); Koola Lobitos (band); Nigeria '70 (band)
Egyptian films 523, 525, 526
Egyptian Musical Club (Dar es Salaam, Tanzania) 525
eho/oho 468
Ehui, Frederic Desire (Meiway) 583–4
Eid al-adha 431, 526
Eid al-Fitr 75, 431, 526
Eiseb, Dennis 368
Ekemode, O.J. (Orlando Julius) 28, 32
ekengele (musical instrument) 306
Ekiti people 323
ekota 395
Ekpe Society (Calabar, Nigeria) 394, 395
Eku (guitarist) 467
El Manager (musician) 439, 505
'El Manisero' ('The Peanut Vendor') (song) 22, 491
El Pollos (band) 31
El Uali (group) 456
Elanga Maurice et Les Grands Esprits (band) 77
eLDee (rapper) 255
Eleagha, Michael 467
election campaigns and rallies 85, 86, 227, 241, 245–6, 261, 281, 425. *See also* political events and rallies; politics and political songs
electronic dance music 28, 291. *See also* azonto; cabo-zouk/cola-zouk; house music; kuduro/kuduru; salegy; techno
Elegancia (group) 132
Elias and His Zig-Zag Jive Flutes (group) 361
Elias Dia Kimuezu (group) 334
'Elinqukuva lika Ntsikana' (hymn) 38
'Elisa Gomara Saia' (song) 404
elombo 127–8
Ema Fowo S'oya Si Wamo (album) 44–5
Emancipation Day (Ghana) 211
embegete (musical instrument) 364. *See also* drums
embuutu drum 327. *See also* drums
Emeneya, King Kester 494
Emerent, Ange Ebogo 77
'Emi Ni Baller' (song) 257
EMI Records 32, 205, 323, 344, 419, 421, 432, 580
Eminem (rapper) 277
emotional rap 277
empancipados 321
Empire (sociocultural group) 129
Empire Babuka (group) 355, 356
Empire Day concerts (Gold Coast) 107, 108, 109
empuunyi drum 327. *See also* drums
emzhad 501
endingidi (musical instrument) 326, 327. *See also* fiddle; tube fiddle
engoma drum 327. *See also* drums; *ngoma/ingoma* drum

Eno, Brian 16, 32
Enoch, Michael 441
Enow, Stanley 235
enseege (musical instrument) 326. *See also* gourd rattle; rattle
'Enyeε nyame a' (song) 276
Epiphany feast day 133
EQ (hip-hop artist) 230
Equator Sound Band 57
Equatorial Guinea 8, 131–6, 392, 392–7. *See also* Guinea; Guinea-Bissau
  Annobon Island 8, 131, 132, 133–4, 135, 392, 394, 395, 396, 397
  Basakato village 132
  Bioko/Fernando Po 8, 47, 132–3, 136, 160, 162, 392–3, 394, 395, 396
  Bioko/Fernando Po, Moka village 132, 396
  Bioko/Fernando Po, Rebola village 396
  Corisco 394
  Luba 132
  Malabo/Santa Isabel 8, 131, 132, 133, 135, 392, 393, 394, 395, 396, 397
  Palé 131, 133, 396
Erasmus, Rassie 81
Eritrea 6, 536–9
  Asmara 6, 537
  Massawa 537
Es'khaleni (album) 288
Escyle, Bruno 505
Eshete, Alemayehu 142, 143
Eskimos (group) 357
Essah, Kojo 212
essewe 370
'Essola' (song) 65
Estamos juntos (album) 510
Estonia 340
Estrela Vermelha (group) 548
esukuti. *See isukuti/isikuti/esukuti*
Ethio-groove 139
Ethio-jazz 93–4, 139, 143–4
Ethiopia 6, 48–9, 93–4, 139–44, 182, 463, 478
  Addis Ababa 49, 141, 142, 142, 143, 463, 537–8
  Arsi 463
  Bale 463
  Borena 463
  Harer 463
  Illubabur 463
  Jimma 463
  Kagnew 142
  Shewa 463
  Tigray Region 536, 537–8, 539
  Wellega 463
Ethiopian modern music (*zemenawi muzika*) **139–45**
Éthiopiques CD series 143–4
Ethio-rock 182
ethnicity and race 64, 68, 78–9, 80, 84, 92, 97, 110, 124, 126–7, 132, 133, 144, 153, 154, 159, 182, 189, 196, 218, 225, 226, 227, 234, 238, 239, 255, 256, 266, 287, 295, 296, 302, 311, 316, 317–18, 327, 328, 329, 331, 333, 350–1, 359, 361–2, 367–8, 374, 375, 389–90, 395, 397, 400, 402, 408, 410–11, 418, 419, 421, 423, 424, 443, 448–9, 454, 463, 465, 487, 502, 504, 543, 553, 585
Eto' (Eto O Rorooso) (*oviritje* artist) 465
Étoile de Dakar (group) 23, 416

600

Index

Etondo (group)   514
Etran Finatawa (band)   546
Europe   86, 92, 94, 96, 180, 182, 184, 186, 187, 189, 208, 222, 226, 235, 262, 270, 296, 313, 315, 318, 320, 338, 348, 349, 411, 417, 491, 495, 496, 510, 519, 546, 563. *See also specific nations*
Eva (rapper)   257
Evans, Chris   59
Eve (rapper)   257
'Everybody Likes Saturday Night' (song)   9
Évora, Cesaria   105, 106, 437
Évora, Grace   340
Ewa Brothers (troupe)   115
Ewande, Nadia   372
Ewe people   35, 89–90, 153, 161, 341, 342, 516
Ewi songs   147
Ex Doe (hiplife artist)   210, 211
Excelsior Orchestra   468
Execution Diary (album)   276
Exodus (group)   357, 482
Expression (album)   269
Extra Kwazvose (group)   522
Eyadema, Gnassingbé   126
Eye of Liberty (band)   183
Eyo'nlé Brass Band   91, 92
Eyoum, Nelle   370, 371
Eyoum, Nelle et le Tout Puissant Negro Styl (group)   370
EZ (record label)   468
Ezodumo (TV show)   422

fààjì èkó   501
Faarax, Xuseen Aw   198
Fa-Baako (rapper)   259
Fabian, Lara   505
Fábrica de Discos de Angola (record label). *See* Fadiang
Facebook   20, 174, 190, 200, 249, 465, 577
Fada Freddy (musican)   262
Fadaka, Wura   224
Fadar Bege (Umar Abdul'aziz Wudil)   175
Fadiang (record label)   432, 476, 509
fado   392, 436
FAG. *See* Forces armées gabonaises
Fagan, Morris   421
fâghu   179
Fahnbulleh, Miatta   138
Fair Play Anti-Corruption Youth Voices Award   270
'Faire le Malin' (song)   533
Faki, Makame   337
Fakoly, Doumbia Moussa (Tiken Jah Fakoly)   478, 480, 481
Fakoly, Tiken Jah   478, 480, 481
Fal G (hip-hop artist)   270
Falceto, Francis   144
Fall, Pape   23
Fally Ipupa   452, 495
famadihana (reburials)   53
family and kinship   129, 146, 182, 209, 240, 261, 262, 268, 272, 279, 295, 304, 306–7, 317, 320, 336, 338, 379, 383, 415, 416, 425, 428, 431, 453, 495, 536, 549, 558
famo   344, 352
fanfares   91, 92–3
F.A.N.G. (rapper)   239
Fang people   239–40, 393
Fantasma (band)   291

Fanti people   9, 34–5, 89, 205, 342, 467–8
Fantimoti, Maryam   173
Fanuel, Sedekia   443
Faransiskiyo Somaliland (album)   200
Faria, Manuel   510
Faroe Islands   187
Faru, Sa'idu   169
Fashek, Majek   478
fashion   120, 186, 263, 346, 351, 465, 494
Faso Kombat (group)   532
Fassie, Brenda   94, 95, 366, 487
Fat Free (MC)   230–1
Fatai Rolling Dollar (highlife artist)   324
Fatim (rapper)   262
Fatima CIA (hip-hop artist)   269
feast days   63, 105, 527–8
  Feast of the Cross (Santa Cruz)   527–8
  Festival of SanJon (Cape Verde)   105
  Saint Anthony's Day   133
Feddy, Jean   502
Federal Hotel (Harare, Zimbabwe)   498
Feedback (band)   182
Feijó, Betinho   510
Fela! (musical show)   16, 17
Female Donkey (*ma/gaisa* artist)   368
ferro (musical instrument)   151, 152
Ferro Gaita (group)   152
festas de quintal (backyard parties)   338, 508
Festival au Desert (music festival: Mali)   530, 546, 578
Festival Folclórico das Províncias Portuguesas (Santarém, Portugal, 1969)   476
Festival Kréol (cultural festival: Seychelles)   518
Festival Marrabenta (cultural festival: Marracuene, Mozambique)   406
festivals   49, 75, 90, 105, 125, 160, 317, 321, 368, 372, 380, 385, 394, 406, 460, 465, 494, 518, 581. *See also* social events and celebrations; *specific festivals*
Feuyang, Irene   65
Feza, Mongezi   32, 423
fiddle   69. *See also anzad; endingidi; gòjé/goge; iningiri; kuntigi; masenko/masinqo; silili;* tube fiddle; violin
FIFA World Cup (2010: South Africa)   51
fife (musical instrument)   9, 107, 112, 204
Fight to Win (album)   17
fikhuli (musical instrument)   306. *See also* rattle
films and film music   31, 32, 33, 84, 86, 108, 109, 110, 114, 115, 148, 186, 205, 226, 229, 249, 261, 265, 273, 320, 340, 346, 347, 360, 374, 388, 402, 403, 405, 421, 430, 448, 471, 482, 509, 514, 530, 546, 559. *See also* Bollywood films/filmi music; Egyptian films; Hausa *nanaye* filmi music; Hausa video films; Hindi films/filmi music; silent films; Western films
finaçon   63
'Financial Women' (song)   219
Fineran, Gene   108
finger bell (musical instrument)   341. *See also* bell; *firikyiwa*
Finland   182, 190

'Fire, Fire, Fire de Kam' (song)   400
firikyiwa (musical instrument)   35. *See also* bell; finger bell
Firin' in Fouta (album)   560
Fischian, Bob   209
fishermen   35, 133, 153, 160, 204, 205, 222, 343, 345–6, 467–8, 475
Fitiyanul Ahbabu (group)   175
Five Revolutions (band)   333, 566
fiyano (musical instrument)   173, 259. *See also* piano
F. Kenya's Riches Big Sound (group)   207, 208
FL Studio (software). *See* Fruity Loops/FL Studio (software)
Flack, Roberta   208
flamenco   396, 456
Flames, The (group)   537
Flavour (singer-songwriter)   219, 224, 448, 449
Fleck, Bela   313
Fleetwood, Mick   32, 33
Floby (musician)   532
Flores, Paulo   338, 340, 511
Florida 2000 Discotheque (F2) (Nairobi, Kenya)   244
flute   74, 167, 198, 235, 291, 309, 440, 583. *See also* Fula flute; *kpete; nai;* penny whistle/pennywhistle; tranverse flute; *washint*
flute jive   420
focho   418
Foes, Okule   345
fòli   317
folk jazz gospel   308
folk-*mbalax*   416
Fon people   92, 161, 572
'Fonksionera sy Sofera' (song)   280
foot jingles (musical instrument). *See bichenje*
For Your Dancing Feet (TV show)   211
Forces armées gabonaises (FAG)   125
Ford Choirs in Contest   40
Forgotten Guitars From Mozambique: Portuguese East Africa 1955 '56 '57 (album)   403
Fote Mogoban (album)   312
'Foto' (song)   471, 472
fouka-fouka   122
Foumalade (rapper)   261, 262
'Founding Fathers' (song)   260
Four Brothers, The (band)   320
Fourcade, Georges   504
Fourie, Jacques   195, 196
Fourie, Jo   81
foxtrot   108–9, 205, 206, 223, 342, 440
frafra (musical instrument)   32. *See also* rattle
frame drum   35, 36, 46, 48, 90, 153, 160, 161, 321–2, 399, 467, 516. *See also apústua; bandiri; bazuca; cumbé* drum; *daf/duff;* drums; *duassi; goombay* drum; *konkoma/konkomba* drum; *ngajiza; sákárà/sakara* drum; *tufo* drum
France   44, 53, 92, 127, 138, 234, 236, 237, 261, 262, 312, 337, 339, 340, 385, 480, 510, 546
  Paris   96, 97, 120, 121, 313, 372, 373, 452, 497, 583
Réunion   3, 181, 182, 379–80, 438, 503, 505

601

Index

Franco (Franco Luambo)   212, 451, 452, 469, 493, 494, 496
Franco (Frank Lesokwane) and Afro Musica (group)   356
Fred Dred (singer)   482
Freestyle (rapper)   255
FRELIMO. *See* Frente de Libertação de Moçambique (Mozambique Liberation Front)
French Cultural Center (Dakar)   261
Frente de Libertação de Moçambique (Mozambique Liberation Front) (FRELIMO)   249–50, 404–5
freestyling   263
Friday, Billy   224
Fruity Loops/FL Studio (software)   86, 244, 259, 348
fújì   43, 44, 45, **145–51**, 254, 256, 257, 325, 448
Fújì Musicians Association of Nigeria, The (FUMAN)   148
Fuji, Dekunle   325
Fuk n Kuk (group)   262
Fula flute   557. *See also* flute
Fulani people   46, 555
Full Experience (group)   488
FUMAN. *See* Fújì Musicians Association of Nigeria, The
Fumulani, Robert   485
Fumulani, Robert and Likhubula River Dance Band   25
Funa, Senhor (musician)   152
funaná   97, 106, **151–2**, 528. *See also* Volume XI, *Genres. Europe*; *funaná* [in Portugal]
fund-raising   297, 364
funerals/funeral wakes   35, 43, 47, 65, 90, 91, 147–8, 158, 294, 304, 384, 400, 413, 455, 468, 501, 516, 535, 536, 543, 572–3, 574, 586. *See also shimambo*
funk   11, 28, 31, 143, 208, 254, 324, 366, 370, 372, 536, 566, 578, 580
Funkees, The (band)   32
Funkiest Mallam (singer)   177
funky highlife   208
'Funky Horn' (song)   13
Fu-Schnickens (trio)   85
Fuse ODG (hip-hop artist)   51
Fuster, Francis   31–2
Fusu, Charles Kojo (Daddy Lumba)   138, 209
Fusu, K.K.   211
fwanda fwanda-ing'oma yabalala   332
Fynn, Nana (highlife artist)   211

Ga people   35, 50–1, 133, 160, 205, 341, 345–7, 516
Gabao Hip-Hop Festival (Gabon)   235
gabay   165
Gabhy (*ba gasy* artist)   53
gaboma rap   236, 239
Gabon   4, 7, 8, 47, 124–30, 132, 135, 162, 226, 227, 235–41, 392, 393, 394, 396, 477, 478
    Estuaire province   127–8
    Libreville   124, 125, 236–7, 238, 239, 241
    Ogooué Maritime province   127–8
    Owendo   236
Gaborone Club (Gaborone, Botswana)   290

Gaborone Secondary School (Gaborone, Botswana)   229
Gabriel Taapopi Secondary School Choir, Oshana Region   553
Gabriel, Aderan   44
Gabriel, Peter   32, 212, 417, 483
Gabrielle (singer)   349
gada   172. *See also* handclapping
Gadiaga, James   23
gahu/agahu   47, **153**, 161
gaisa. *See ma/gaisa*
gaita (musical instrument)   151. *See also* accordion; diatonic button accordion
Gallo Africa (record label)   419, 421
Gallo Record Company   289, 290, 296, 300, 301, 302, 360, 440, 486, 540, 541, 542
Gallo, Eric   300
Gallotone (record label)   300, 301, 540
Gambia   8, 31, 383, 386, 414, 415, 416, 417, 467, 561, 563
    Abakpa-Bamenda   467
gambus/qanbus (musical instrument)   524. *See also* lute
gan (musical instrument)   92, 535, 572, 573–4. *See also* bell
ganga (musical instrument)   170. *See also* drums
gángán/gangan drum   43, 44, 146, 322, 323, 555. *See also* drums; hourglass drum; talking drum
Gangbé Brass Band   91, 92, 574
gangbo (musical instrument)   330, 331. *See also* bell
Gangsters with Matatizo (GWM) (band)   85
gankogui/gonkogui (musical instrument)   89, 153. *See also* bell
ganuni (musical instrument)   569–70. *See also* zither
ganvinon (musical instrument)   330, 331, 573. *See also* bell
Garang, Muki   24
garaya (musical instrument)   170. *See also* lute
Garcia, Robert 'Bobbito'   231
Garvey, Marcus   482, 483
Gashe, Boet   388
Gaskia, Kaidan   259
Gasmilla (hiplife artist)   50, 51
Gaspard, Jean-Claude   504
Gaston (hip-hop artist)   261
Gathu, Jimmy   244–5
Gawaseb, Amakhoe   368
gawlo   311. *See also* griots
Gawlo, Coumba   416, 560
Gaye, Marvin   245
Gazo music   182
'Gbagada Gbogodo' (song)   12
Gbefa (*zenli* artist)   572
gbeohe   51
Gbezawe (singer)   536
G.B. Olivant (trading company)   108, 113
GCPU. *See* Ghana Concert Party Union
Gee Bayss (DJ)   261
gee bodi wata   434
Geelqaad, Hawa   166
Geenyo, Yurub   200
geerar   165
Gena (Gendarmerie nationale) (group)   124–5

gender
    Akan recreational music   34, 35
    ba gasy   53–5
    band (Uganda)   59
    batuque   62–3
    bend skin   64, 65–6
    benga   69, 71
    bikutsi   77
    boeremusiek   82
    bongo flava   87
    bubblegum   94
    cabo-zouk/cola-zouk   97
    chakacha   98–9
    coladeira   105
    concert party   114, 115, 116, 117
    coupé-decalé   122
    cultural animation groups   124, 125, 126, 127, 128, 129, 130
    cumbé   133
    Ethiopian modern music   142
    famo   344
    fújì   148
    Gabonese rap   237–8
    gospel highlife   210
    Hausa *nanaye filmi* music   171, 172, 173, 174
    Hausa rap   259
    Hausa technopop   176
    Hausa traditional music   169, 170
    heavy metal   194
    hees   197, 201
    highlife   207, 213
    hip-hop   227, 262
    hiplife   277
    hira gasy   279, 280
    imbyino   294, 295
    isukuti   307
    jazz band (Malawi)   308–9
    jelis   311–12, 313
    jembe/djembe   316, 317
    jive   420
    koriana le moropa   344
    kunke/kunki   133
    kwasa kwasa   358
    litungu   363
    ma/gaisa   367, 368
    makossa   372
    marabi   386
    maskanda   408, 409, 411
    mbumba   425–7
    MCs   230
    medeh   431
    ngoma/ingoma (in Malwai)   455
    pandza   472
    rebita   475
    reggae   488
    taarab   525
    takiboronsè   532, 533
    tchinkoume   535–6
    Tuareg guitar music   545, 547
    tufo   548–9
    wáká   555
    yéla   559
General Balodi (singer)   576
General Defao (singer)   355
General Marcus (MC)   482
General Phullos (reggae artist)   483
General Stano (reggae artist)   482
générique (rumba theme song)   495
Genesis Gospel Singers   210
genge   246
Genja (hip-hop artist)   270

602

Index

'Gentleman' (song)   14
Geracão Pantera   528–9
Germany   209, 262, 290, 318, 340, 482, 488, 489
   Hamburg   209
Gessesse, Tilahun   142
Gessesse, Zeleke   478
Getz, Stan   60
gewel   311. See also *griots*
G-Fresh (rapper)   259, 260
GH rap   275, 277
Ghana   8, 9, 11, 12, 28, 31, 32, 33, 34–6, 44, 47, 50–2, 107–19, 121, 132, 133, 134, 135, 138, 153, 161, 162, 168, 170, 172, 181, 183, 204–12, 217, 219, 221, 226, 273–8, 300, 316, 323, 333, 341–3, 345–7, 355, 392, 395, 396, 457–9, 466, 467–8, 477, 478, 482–3, 494, 516–17, 566, 578, 586
   Accra   8, 32, 50, 90, 108, 116–17, 132, 204, 273, 345, 394, 482, 483, 516
   Accra, Bukom   50, 345–6, 347
   Agona Swedru   10, 204
   Ashanti region   457
   Brong-Ahafo Region   457
   Cape Coast   8, 9, 10, 35, 107, 108, 204, 210, 211, 467
   Chorkor   50
   El Mina Castle   9, 10, 204, 467
   Jamestown   50
   Kpandu   90
   Kumasi   35, 457, 468, 482
   Mumford/Dwanba   341
   Prang   516
   Salaga   516
   Sekondi   108, 109
   Tamale   8, 516, 517
   Tema   50, 482
   Volta Region   10, 89, 90, 153, 343
   Winneba   10, 204, 516
   Yendi   516
Ghana Arts Council   346
Ghana Broadcasting Band   211
Ghana Broadcasting Corporation   115
Ghana Concert Party Union (GCPU)   116–18
Ghana Dance Ensemble   90
'Ghana le a azoli dzi' (song)   90
Ghana Music Awards (GMA)   276
Ghana National Theatre   116–18
Ghana Trio   112, 207
Ghanaba, Kofi (Guy Warren)   206, 211
Ghansah, Mary   210
'Ghetto Fabulous' (song)   350
Ghetto Luv (group)   350
Ghetto Radio   246
Ghetto Ruff (record label)   349
ghoema drum   155, 157, 436. See also drums
ghoema musical complex   153–7
ghoemaliedjie/ghommaliedjie   157–8, 389
Gidi Gidi Maji Maji (duo)   245, 246
gidigbo (musical instrument). See *agídigbo/agidigbo*
Gigi (singer)   143–4
'Gijima' (song)   231
Gil and Perfects (band)   97
'Gimme Hope Jo'anna' (song)   488
girarsa   463
'Girgiza Kai' (song)   260
Giriama people   364

Girlfriend: filamu ya muziki na maisha (film)   86
gita   54
Gitara, Rasamy   53
Gitta, Ssekyanzi Jessy   58
Glasper, Robert   17
Glass and Grant (duo)   108
Glastonbury Festival (music festival: Somerset, UK)   251
Glele, King of Dahomey   572
glissement-glisser dance   533
Globestyle (record label)   462
GMA. See Ghana Music Awards
gnawa   168
GNL Zamba (hip-hop artist)   272, 273
Gobir, Wari Mai Zarin   169
Godefroy, Keng   65
Godzilla   286. See also Oskido (DJ/producer)
goge (musical instrument). See *gòjé/goge*
Gogoua, Christian   585
gòjé/goge (musical instrument)   170, 500–1. See also fiddle
Gokh bi System (group)   262
Gola, Ferre   452, 495
Gold Coast (British colony). See Ghana
Gold Coasters (band)   211
Golden City Post (periodical)   419
Golden Nuggets (group)   211
Golden Production (band)   59, 335
Golden Strings (band)   31
Golgotha (band)   191
goma/magoma drum   454. See also *ngoma/ingoma* drum
gombay. See *gumbe/goombay*
gombe. See *gome/gombe/le gombe*
gombey. See *gumbe/goombay*
gome/gombe/le gombe   47, 50–1, 132, 133, 134, 160, 345, 396, 516, 586. See also *cumbé*; *gumbe/goombay*
Gomi/Gomes, Nácia   63
Gonçalves, António Manuel   334
Gonçalves, Gregório (Ti Goy)   105
Gondoliers, The (band)   32
gong (musical instrument)   35, 218, 306. See also *agogo*; *karing'aring'a*; *krəəh*
gong drum   434. See also bass drum; drums
gonga   568
gonkogui (musical instrument). See *gankogui/gonkogui*
Gonteb, Brian   366, 367, 368
Goode, Roger (DJ)   287
Goof (hip-hop artist)   230
goombah. See *gumbe/goombay*
goombay. See *gumbe/goombay*
gospel folk   325
gospel *fuji*   325
gospel highlife   209–10, 213, 219, 221
gospel highlife, Igbo   219–20, 224
gospel *kwaito*   352
gospel *kwasa*   356–7
gospel music   325, 351, 355, 409, 411, 413, 448, 483, 484, 485, 553, 567. See also gospel music (Volume XIII, International); *muziki wa injili*
gospel rap   276
gospel *sákárá*   501
gota (musical instrument)   535
Gotale (hip-hop collective)   262
goumbé. See *cumbé*; *gumbe/goombay*

gourd rattle (musical instrument)   322. See *enseege*; rattle; *sèkèrè/sekere/ṣè.kè.rè*
gourd trumpet. See kazoos
Goya, Alhaji   568, 569
G Pange Hip-hop Challenge (Kenya)   246
Gpro Fam (group)   250, 406
Graceland (album and tour)   32, 212, 296, 450
graffiti art   225, 228, 237, 243, 252. See also aerosol art
Graham, Kenny   206, 423
Gramma Records   521
Grammy Awards   437, 546, 560
Gramophone Museum (Cape Coast, Ghana)   211
Gramophone Record Company (GRC)   419, 422
gramophone recordings   25, 66, 114, 143, 218, 234, 324, 368, 370, 385, 449, 478, 479, 491, 492, 508, 520, 524, 531. See also sound recording and recordings
Gramoune Dada   380
Granadians, The (band)   32
Grand Bassam beach (Abidjan, Côte d'Ivoire)   587–8
Grant, Eddie   488
Grassroots (group)   482
Gravity Omutujju (rapper)   273
GRC. See Gramophone Record Company
GRC Studio   410
'Great Pretender, The' (song)   24
Great Trek Centenary (South Africa)   79–80
Green (band)   190, 191, 192
Green Arrows (group)   102, 320
Green Spots (group)   324
grindcore   194
griots   49, 316, 326, 414, 415, 416, 481, 561, 574, 575. See also *agiwwin*; *azmari* music; *iggǎwen*; *jeliyal/jaliya*; minstrels/minstrel music; *yéla*
Griqwa people   553
Groenewald, Sonny   541
Groove Cartell (DJ)   291
Groove FM (radio station)   211
Groove Meditation Sessions   291–2
groupes d'animation culturelle. See cultural animation groups
groupes de choc (shock groups)   126
Grupo dos Sambas   333
Grupo Estrela Vermelha   548
GSelector (software)   66
guaguancó   490
guajira music   23
guantanomo   122
guayla   539
gube   47, 132, 160. See also *cumbé*; *gumbe/goombay*
Guewel, Fatou   416
Guezo, King of Dahomey   572
Guilbault, Jocelyne   339
Guillaume, Mouelle   370
Guillaume, Toto   372
Guinea   8, 29, 44, 179, 310, 311, 312, 315, 317, 340, 383, 384, 394, 456, 478, 557. See also Equatorial Guinea
   Conakry   8, 318, 562
   Kankan   381–2
Guinea-Bissau   8, 337, 339, 477, 527, 561
guiro (musical instrument)   70. See also scraper

603

Index

Guissé, Aliou 560
Guissé, Fères 560
guitar 13, 23, 24, 35, 51, 54, 56, 68, 69, 71–2, 75, 80, 101, 102, 103, 105, 109, 112, 113, 116, 124, 127, 133, 152, 155, 160, 161, 198, 204, 205, 209, 216, 223, 231, 255, 295, 309, 320, 321, 334, 342, 345 356, 359, 360, 367, 368, 369, 372, 379, 388, 403, 404, 408, 436, 439, 440, 441, 453, 457, 458, 459, 460, 465, 466, 467, 468, 469, 471, 473, 477, 482, 486, 494, 495, 496, 501, 504, 507, 513, 517, 521, 526, 537, 545–7, 555, 559, 566, 580, 583, 586. *See also* acoustic guitar; acoustic slide guitar; *balafon*; bass guitar; box guitar; *cavaquiño*; *guitares-bidons*; lap steel guitar; lead guitar; pedal steel guitar; rhythm guitar; Spanish guitar; tenor guitar; tin-can guitar
guitar, electric 22, 24, 70, 76, 81, 138, 140, 145, 167, 179, 181, 217, 229, 235, 284, 310, 312, 323, 327, 331, 332, 333, 340, 360, 370, 382, 385, 396, 402, 405, 410, 414–15, 421, 422, 432, 434, 438, 442, 456, 462, 480, 491, 492, 502, 505, 509, 510, 513, 523, 525–6, 536, 538, 543, 544, 547, 563, 566, 569–70, 575. *See also* wah-wah pedal
guitar-band highlife 204, 207, 208, 209, 210, 216–17, 222, 223, 342, 343, 458, 466, 482
guitares-bidons (musical instrument) 545. *See also* guitar; tin-can guitar
gule wa mkulu 158–9, 308, 358
gumbay. *See* gumbe/goombay
gumbe/goombay 46, 47, 132, 133, 135, 153, **159–61**, 345, 392, 393, 396, 399, 400, 401, 432, 433, 434, 516, 586. *See also asíkò/ashiko/assiko*; *cumbé*; *gome/gombe/le gombe*; goombay (Volume IX, *Genres: Caribbean and Latin America*)
 in Sierra Leone **162–4**
gumbe/goombay drum 132, 159–60, 161, 162, 391, 393, 482. *See also* drums
gumbeh. *See* gumbe/goombay
gumbia. *See* gumbe/goombay
Gumede, Willie 301
Gun people 92, 412, 413
Gurage people 139
Guru (rapper) 51
guux **164–7**. *See also hees*; Djibouti (Volume VI, *Locations: Africa and the Middle East*)
Guux Brothers Band 167
guz 349
GV record series 491
Gwaladi, Joe 309
Gwale, Nasir 176
GWM (Gangsters with Matatizo) Band 85
Gyamena, Daasebre 210, 211
Gyamfi, Rex 209
Gyamfi, Sloopy Mike 209
Gyan, Asamoah 51
Gyan, Kiki 33
Gyasi, Dr. K. and His Noble Kings (group) 35, 207, 458
G'z Mobb (band) 85

Ha Nga Dzule (album) 486–7
Haal Pulaar people 558–9, 560
Haastrup, Joni 32
Habasen (*ma/gaisa* artist) 368
Habyarimana, Juvénal 296
Haïdara, Chérif Ousmane Madani 575, 576
Haile Selassie I, Emperor of Ethiopia 93, 141, 142, 143, 478, 537, 538
hainteny 181, 280
Haiti 159, 431
Halgan, Sahra 200
'Hali ya Pemba' (song) 569
Hallelujah Chicken Run Band 102
Hamargod, Abdo 167
Hamargod, Said 166–7
Hamaseb, Stanley 368
'Hamba Nontsokolo' (song) 420
Hammond, Cecil 21, 449
Hamziyya (Al-Busiri) 174
Hancock, Herbie 313, 563
hand drum 89, 319, 346. *See also* drums; *dumbaki/dumbak*; *ngoma/ingoma* drum
handclapping 35, 47, 158, 172, 186, 294, 370, 455, 464, 513, 529, 538, 539, 547, 553, 557
Handel, George Frederic 40
Hango, Tiwonge 26
Hannibal Records 312
Hansen, Jerry & the Ramblers Dance Band 206, 211–12
Happy Stars (band) 208, 210
Happy Trio 112
Harare (band) 32
Harare Mambo Band 498
Harare Mambos (group) 102
harâtîn 431
Harbours Band 224
Harcourt-White, Ikoli 219
Hard Blasterz (group) 85
hard bop 13
Harder They Came, The (film) 482
hardrockmg.com (website) 190
Hardstone (Ngunjiri Harrison) 245
Hargeysa Cultural Centre 200
Harlem Swingsters (band) 389, 419
Harley & The Rasta Family (group) 487
harmonica 112, 205, 217, 466
harmonium 205, 429, 442, 475, 524. *See also kinanda*
harp 238, 240, 383, 502. *See also ardin*; *bolon*; lyre; *ngombi*; *simbing/simbi*; *tashkota*
harp lute 459. *See also* donson n'goni; *kamalen n'goni*; kora; *mvet/mvett*; *seprewa/seprerewa*; *soron/seron*
Harris, Clifford 'T.I.' 231
Harris, Faan 81
Harrysong (singer) 219
Hart, Kevin 51
Hassan, Mariem 456
Hassâniya poetry 179
Hausa *nanaye filmi* music 168, 170, 171–4, 176, 177
Hausa people 46, 168, 227, 259, 342, 399, 500, 516, 555
Hausa popular music **168–78**, 448
Hausa rap 170, 258–60
Hausa technopop 170, 176–7
Hausa traditional music 168–71, 173

Hausa video films 171–4, 176
Hausahiphop (blog) 259
hawl/el-hawl **178–80**
Hay'oe (group) 237, 241
Haya, Mntwan' Omkhulu! 39
Heartbeats (band) 31
heavy metal. *See also* black metal; Christian metal; death metal; doom metal; melodic death metal; symphonic metal; thrash metal; Viking metal
 in Africa **180–5**
 in Botswana **185–8**
 in Kenya **188–90**
 in Madagascar **190–4**
 in South Africa **194–7**
Hedzoleh Soundz (band) 28, 32, 208
Hedzoleh, Amartey 33
heello 198
heello yar-yar 165, 166
hees **197–204**
hees jacayl 199, 201
hees siyaasadeed 197, 199
hees waddani 201
'Hellbangers: Botswana's Underground Metal Culture' (Bonet) 186
Helwani, Faisal 32
Henderson, Dick 109
Hendrix, Jimi 31, 180, 199, 208, 332, 530, 545, 566
Henguva, Kareke (Dr. Kareke) 464–5
Henguva, Meisie 465
Herero people 367, 464–5
Henshaw, Inyang 224
Heptones, The (group) 482
Heron, Gil-Scott 275
Hewale Sounds (group) 212, 346
HHP (Hip-Hop Pantsula) (rapper) 231
Hi Power sound system 482
'Hiddiiyooy Hiddi' (song) 167
Hiddo Dhawr (restaurant: Hargeysa, Somali) 200–1
high hat (hi-hat) (musical instrument) 99, 102, 231, 283, 284, 320, 492
Highbricks (pianist) 388, 542
highlife 10, 11, 13, 20, 27, 29, 31, 32, 34, 35, 36, 47, 89, 112–13, 114, 118, 119, 133, 137, 148, 161, **204–16**, 222, 226, 275, 324, 370, 392, 393, 394, 395, 448, 449, 466, 468, 469, 482, 483, 516, 561, 562. *See also adaha*; hiplife; *odonson* highlife; palmwine music
 in Nigeria 235, 342–3. *See also* highlife, Igbo; highlife, Yorùbá
highlife, Igbo **216–21**, 254
highlife, Yorùbá **221–5**, 254
highlife-jazz 12–13
Hindi films/filmi music 168, 170–2, 173, 174–5, 198, 323, 493, 523. *See also* Bollywood films/filmi music
hip-hop 20, 44, 45, 95, 103, 138, 144, 149, 161, 219, 261, 273, 274, 275, 335, 347, 349, 368, 378, 404, 416–17, 448, 451, 471, 474, 522, 567, 587, 588. *See also* Hausa hip-hop; hiplife; Swahili hip-hop; *zenji flava*
 in Botswana **228–34**
 in Cameroon **234–5**
 in Gabon **235–43**
 in Kenya **243–8**
 in Mozambique **248–54**. *See also marrabenta*; *pandza*
 in Nigeria **254–8**

604

Index

in Nigeria (Hausa rap) **258–60**
in Senegal **260–5**
in South Africa **265–7**
in Sub-Saharan Africa **225–8**. *See also* bongo flava/bongo fleva; hiplife
in the Democratic Republic of Congo **267-71**
in Uganda 59, 226, 246, **271–3**
Hip-hop Halisi Freestyle Challenge (Kenya) 246
hip-hop highlife. *See* hiplife
Hip-Hop Pantsula (HHP) (rapper) 231
hiplife 20, 51, 138, 204, 205, 209, 210–11, 213, 219, 226, **273–8**, 346–7, 483
hira gasy **278–83**
hira taloha 54
hira teatraly 53
hira tranainy 54
hirwo 165
Hishishi Papa (musician) 514
historiography/scholarship
  Afropop 28–30
  azonto 50–1
  benga 68–9
  beni 74–5
  Ethiopian modern music 144
  mal gaisa 368
  maringa in Equatorial Guinea 393
  maringa in Sierra Leone 401
  marrabenta 403
  maskanda 409
  mbaqanga 423
  oviritje 465
  umbholoho 551
  yenyengo 561–2
'Hit the Road Jack' (song) 166
HIV/AIDS 84, 85, 117, 127, 262, 289, 309, 328, 332, 351, 411, 441, 447, 478, 503, 550, 567
HMV (His Master's Voice) (record label) 113, 205, 300, 323, 399, 458, 468, 524
Hoberg, Roland 405
hoddu (musical instrument) 22, 559. *See also* lute
Hofmeyr, Steve 82
Holbrook-Smith, Paa K. 211
'Holla At Yo Boy' (song) 257
Holland. *See* Netherlands
Holy Trinity Church (Accra, Ghana). Mass (Anglican) Sunday School Choir 107
Homme d'Orchestre 330
Honey I'm Home (abum) 232
'Hora di bai' (song) 437
horn 13, 14, 55, 56, 112, 116, 147, 149, 206, 209, 223, 284, 330, 359, 414–15, 480, 492, 494. *See also* animal horns; baritone horn; *búzio*; *ihembe*; *shellela*
Horn Cable TV 200
Horn of Africa 164, 165, 166
Horns, Tura 465
Horseed (band) 199
Hosanna Gospel Band 333
hosho shakers (musical instrument) 102. *See also* shakers
hostels (male-only) 422, 551
Hot Boys (group) 269
Hot Mix 5 (radio program) 286
Hot Springs Band, The 58
Hot96 FM (radio station) 246

hotels 22, 26, 57, 61, 62, 85, 90, 220, 222, 272, 344, 450, 498. *See also* hostels; restaurants and cafes
hotnotsmusiek 79
Houndeffo, Anatole (Le Roi Alokpon) 535, 536
Houon, Ange Didier (DJ Arafat/Yoro Gang) 121, 122
hourglass drum 516. *See also* drums; *dùndún/dundun* drum; *gángán/gangan* drum; *jauje*; *odonno/dondo* drum
House Afrika Records 284, 286
House Afrika Records. CDGUMBA series 285
house music 95, 229, 257, 265, 347, 348, 349, 513
  in Botswana 289–91
  in South Africa 284–9
  in Southern Africa **283–93**
  in Swaziland 291–2
house-*kwasa* 356-7
house warmings 43
'How Long' (song) 270
Hoyte, Mr. (variety artist) 108
H.T. (MC) 230
Huambo Metal Festival (music festival: Angola) 183
Hughes, Brewster 11
Humming Bees Quartet, The 300
Hungary 44
hunters 383–4, 463, 557
Hurley, Steve 'Silk' 286
Hush Hush Studio 211
Hussein, Juma (Maya) 55
Hutton, Charles 109–10, 111
Hykkers (band) 31
hymns 37, 38, 48, 90, 91, 101, 112, 148, 155, 219, 221–2, 267, 298, 321–2, 323, 325, 389, 442, 552, 554

!kho╪uisa 552
!obodas 552
Iary (rock musician) 192
Iba (hip-hop artist) 261
Ibe, Muddy (highlife artist) 216
Ibeji, Ola Baba 501
Iberian peninsula 392, 436, 453
Ibeto, Uche 218
Ibex Band 143
Ibibio people 218
'Ibofolo' (song) 288
Ibrahim, Abdul Hamidu (MC Lazzy) 276
Ibrahim, Bello (Billy-O) 177
Ibrahim, Kamal 463
Ibrahim, Njike 65
Ice Cube (rapper) 176
'Ice Ice Baby' (song) 84
Ice Prince (hip-hop artist) 257
Ice Queen (MC) 230
ICMAD. *See* International Centre for African Music and Dance
'I Colour Ba' (song) 302
ICU Hall (Durban) 297
Idakho people 304
idiophone. *See* *aro*; *ndu*'; *nyenyemo*; *piker*; *sanza*; *upatsu*
Idlios Studio 61
Idowu, Adesola Adesimbo (Weird MC/Da Rappatainer) 255
Ifang Bondi (group) 31, 416
Ifediorama, Larry 32

Iftiin (band) 199
igbá (musical instrument) 500. *See also* calabash
Igbo highlife **216–21**, 254
Igbo people 216–20, 254, 324, 399, 448
iggâwen 179. *See also* griots
I Got Skills (competition) 230
ihembe (musical instrument) 295. *See also* horn
Ihhashi/iHashi/Ihash' Elimhlophe (guitarist) 352, 411
Iita ya Kadha (grouo) 513
Ijaw people 218
Ijebu people 555–6
Ika people 218
ikembe (musical instrument) 295. *See also* lamellophone
Ikenga Super Stars of Africa (group) 216, 217
Ikhwani Safaa Musical Club 524, 525–6
'Ikoyi Mentality versus Mushin Mentality' (song) 14
'Il y a pas de match' (song) 66
ILAM. *See* International Library of African Music
Ilanga (group) 103
Ilionga, Rikki 566
Ill Bliss (rapper) 257
Illegal Act (album) 230
Illustrate (hip-hop artist) 230
imashi 298
imbyino **294–6**
Imfiraji (Namangi) 168–9
imfunkutu 332, 333
imharamba 294
'I'm in Love with a DJ' (song) 95
Immortal (band) 190
Imperial Bodyguard Band (Ethiopia) 93, 141
'I'm So Hood Our Way (Ghana)' (song) 277
In Da So Da Kauna (film) 172–3
In Oath (band) 188
'Ina Ran' (song) 44
inanga (musical instrument) 294–5. *See also* zither
independence 10, 12, 15, 24, 28, 31, 57, 63, 75, 90, 91, 96, 97, 101, 102–3, 105, 112, 114, 120, 124, 127, 151, 152, 153, 164–6, 167, 171, 183, 190, 198, 202, 206–7, 236, 240, 244, 249–50, 251, 252, 268, 279, 296, 308, 312, 317, 320, 324–5, 336, 366, 367–8, 369–70, 372–3, 375, 377, 378, 380, 384–6, 392, 395, 396, 402, 403, 404, 405, 406, 414, 415, 432, 437, 438, 439, 440, 444, 445, 450, 454, 455, 456, 464, 465, 471, 476, 502, 509–11, 513, 516–17, 520, 521–2, 525, 526, 528, 530, 537, 538, 539, 548, 552, 553, 565–6, 573, 577. *See also* nationalism
India 154, 157, 453
Indian music 86, 166, 197, 202
Indian films/filmi music. *See* Bollywood films/filmi music; Hindi films/filmi music
indlamu 298
Indonesia 154, 157, 453, 578
Infanteria (band) 196
'Ingoduso' (song) 300
ingoma. *See* *ngoma/ingoma*

605

Index

ingomabusuku (night music) 297
ingom' ebusuku. *See umbholoho*
iningiri (musical instrument) 295. *See also* fiddle
initiation rituals and ceremonies. *See* rites of passage
inkali (musical instrument) 433. *See also* drums; slit drum
Inkatha Freedom Party (South Africa) 408, 488
Innocent Malinga 551
inshad 578
Inside Africa (TV series) 186
Instagram 174
Instrumental Ensemble, The (L'Ensemble Instrumental National) (Mali) 578
intambo 294
Intellectual Metamorphosis (album) 182
Inter Jazz Band 102
International Brothers (group) 324
International Centre for African Music and Dance (ICAMD) (Accra, Ghana) 211
International Library of African Music (ILAM) 377, 440
Internet 19, 28, 30, 51–2, 77, 174, 180, 183, 188, 190, 192, 224, 232, 258, 282, 339, 414, 416, 443, 531, 534, 568, 577
'Intsimbi ka Ntsikana' (hymn) 38
Invader (musician) 137
inzogera (musical instrument) 295. *See also* ankle/foot bells and rattles; rattle
Ionic Revolt (band) 32
iPods 177
IQ (rapper) 259, 260
Iroku Club (London) 32
Iron Maiden (band) 181, 190
I Roy (DJ) 479
Isa, Ibrahim Narambada 169
Isaacs, Gregory 483
Isese, Roland 461
isgubhu 349
Ishola, Haruna (Baba Ngani Agba) 43, 44, 323
Ishola, Haruna and His Apala Group 44
Ishola, Musiliu 44, 45
Ishriniyyat (Al-Fazazi) 174
ishumar. *See* Tuareg guitar music
isicathamiya 227, 291, **296–303**, 375, 410, 411, 450–1, 551, 552
isikhunzi 299–300
isikhwela Joe 296, 297
isimanje-manje 418, 421–2, 423, 424
isishameni 299
iskista 141
Islam 15, 43, 147, 158, 168, 321, 323, 415, 548–9, 550
Islamic praise music 171, 175–6. *See madheel/madhu/madh*; *medeh*; *sákárà/sakara*; *zikiri*
Islamiyya schools 174
Island Records 261, 324, 560
Israel 182, 340
  Jerusalem 93, 141
Issaca-Bukari 516
Issah, Sirina 483
istep 141
Isukha people 304–7
isukuti drum 304–7, 364, 460. *See also* drums

isukuti mama/ikhasi/mukhasi drum 304. *See also* drums
isukuti mwana/ngapa/omutiti/mutiti drum 304, 307. *See also* drums
isukuti papa/isatsa/musatsa drum 304. *See also* drums
isukuti/isikuti/esukuti **304–8**, 461
Iszadore, Sandra 12
Italy 44, 236
ithanduku (musical instrument) 444, 445
I Told You So (film) 114
'I.T.T. (International Thief Thief)' (song) 12, 15
iTunes (media player) 232
Itz Tiffany (Afro-pop artist) 51
Iussufe (trader) 548
Ivory Coast. *See* Côte d'Ivoire
Iwegbue, Charles 219
Iyan-Tama, Hamisu Lamido 173
Iyan-Tama Multimedia Studio 173
Iyanya (singer) 87, 257
izibongo 408–9, 410, 411. *See also* praise music and songs
Izibongo ZikaShaka (Khumalo) 39
izikeyi (musical instrument) 450
Izingane Zoma (trio) 411
Izingoma zomshado 298–9
Izintombi Zesimanje-manje (group) 422
Izon T (singer-songwriter) 59

Jabuya, Samuel Aketch (Aketch Oyosi) 69
Jackson, Michael 125, 137, 236, 349
Jacob Sam. *See* Asaare, Kwame
Jaga-Jaga (album) 259
'Jaga Jaga' (song) 256, 259
Jagari (Emmanuel Chanda) 567
Jaguar Jokers (troupe) 115, 207, 208
Jaguar Musical Club (group) 429
Jaguars, The (group) 537
Jagwa Music (group) 429
Jah Glory (album) 479–80
Jah Power 482
Jah Verity (reggae artist) 478
Jahazi Modern Taarab (group) 526
jaliya. *See jeliya/jaliya*
Jaluka (band) 32
jama/djama hiplife 211, 212, 347
Jamaica 9, 46, 132, 133, 135, 159, 161, 334–5, 477–8, 482, 483, 486, 487, 488
  Kingston, West Kingston 477
Jambo (reggae artist) 487, 488
James, Lisa 474
Jamhuri Jazz Band 440
Jamhuri Musical Club (group) 429
Jamnazi Band 71
jando 430
Jano Band 182
Jaojoby (Eusèbe Jaojoby) 502, 503
Jaojoby, Lucien 502
Japan 315, 411
jarabi 562
'Jarabi' (song) 56
Jatta, Sidia 563
Jauhar Orchestra 525
jauje (musical instrument) 169. *See also* drums; hourglass drum
Jaune Toujours (group) 92
Jawabu (duo) 581
Jawara, Jali Musa (Djeli Moussa Diawara) 312

jazz 11, 28, 38, 57, 60, 61, 64, 75, 79, 80, 81, 91, 92, 93, 106, 141–2, 161, 206, 216, 254, 267, 288, 308, 324, 330, 351, 358, 368, 378, 380, 389, 413, 418, 448, 450, 496, 513, 514, 537, 541, 542. *See also* African jazz; Afro jazz; Ethio-jazz; highlife-jazz; jazz (Volume XIII, *International*)
jazz band (Malawi) **308–10**
jazz blues 308
Jazz Giants (band) 24–5
jazz jazz 308
Jazz Kings (band) 205
Jazz Revellers Band 301, 389, 541
Jazz, T.O. 210, 212, 217, 458
jazz-mbalax 416
jazz-wassoulou 577, 578
'Je t'aime' (song) 505
Jean-Claude (singer) 504
Jean-de-Boulon, Nami 64, 66
Jeannette, Marie Jeanne 53
Jeannot Ra (dancer) 355
Jeannot, Tala 65, 66
Jebiyay (Saxardiid Maxamed) 198
Jeeta (album) 177
'J'Ehin J'Ehin' (song) 14
jelis/jeliw. *See jeliya/jaliya*
jeliya/jaliya 49, 56, **310–15**, 382, 383, 384–5, 386. *See also azmari* music; griots
jelkati 416
jembe/djembe/dyembe drum 121, 315, 317, 380, 383, 384, 410, 547, 557, 563, 578, 586, 587. *See also* drums
jembe/djembe/dyembe music **315–19**
jenbefòli 317
Jeneraal Daa'uud (band) 199
jetgo dance 533
Jewel Ackah 210, 212
Jezzabelle (MC) 230
jiibka iyo jaanta 165, 166
jiifto 165, 201
'Jiim' Sheekh Muumin (musician) 199
Jilani, Sheikh Abdul Qadir 175
jimbasengo 562
jimberu (musical instrument) 433. *See also* drums
Jit (film) 320
jit/jiti 103, 308, **319–21**, 520, 522, 542
Jitsvinger (hip-hop artist) 266
jitterbug 359, 361
jive 319, 359, 361, 418, 419–21, 423, 427, 513, 542. *See also mbaqanga*
JKT Taarab 525
J-Man (rapper) 259
João Domingos, Conjunto 403
Jobarteh. *See also* headings beginning Diabaté; Dioubaté
Jobarteh, Amadou/Amadu Bansang 563
Jobarteh, Dawda 563
Jobarteh, Jali Mama 562
Jobarteh, Malamini 562, 563
Jobarteh, Pa Bobo 563
Jobarteh, Salif 562
Jobarteh, Sona 563
Jobarteh, Tata Dindin 563
Jobe, Badou 31
Joe Da Crazy Boy (producer) 241
Jofabro Records 323
John (hip-hop artist) 245
'John Brown's Body' (song) 426
John Canoe/Jonkonnu festival 160

Index

John Mavimbela and Company (group) 541
John, Salle 372
Johnson, Aaron 17
Johnson, Ani 210
Johnson, Bob 112, 206, 207
Johnson, Bola 224
Johnson, Dexter 23
Johnson, Ishmael 109–10, 111–12, 114
Johnson, Johnson 433
Johnson, Olohrunfeh Israel (Dr. Oloh) 433, 434
Johnson, Peter (Peter na Lepet) 163
Joint, The (radio program) 246
Jolly Orchestra 11, 467
Jolof4Life (record label) 261
Jolson, Al 108, 109, 110
Jolte, Jambo 463
Jones, Addy Foster 138
Jones, Berkley 32
Jones, Bill T. 16
Jones, Quincy 352
Jongh, Frans de 453
Journey, The (album) 200, 288
Jovens do Hungu (group) 476
Jovi (rapper) 235
Joy Sr, Aloysius Matovu 58
JPS Productions (record label) 65, 67
Jua Cali (Paul Julius Nunda) 246
Juba, Crosdale 224
Judas Priest (band) 180
jùjú 16, 43, 47, 145, 146, 148, 161, 221, 223, 254, 257, **321–6**, 342–3, 396, 448, 466, 467, 469
Jùjú Music (album) 324
jukebox 580
Juliani (hip-hop artist) 246
Juliano, Fosta (Mista Doe) 230
Juma Nature (hip-hop artist) 85, 86
Juma, Adam 87
Juma, Matano 525
Juma, Maulidi 429, 525
Juma, Musa 497, 498
Jungle Brothers (group) 249
jungle rock 32. *See also* Afro-rock
Junior and Pretty (duo) 254–5, 256
'Just Like That' (song) 16
Juwata Jazz (band) 441
Jy sal dit nie glo nie (album) 82

K1 De Ultimate (King Wasiu Marshal Àyìndé) 145
Kaakunga, Matuarari 465
Kabaka, Daudi 498, 580
Kabanda, Bernard 328
Kabara, Sheikh Nasiru 168
kabaro (musical instrument) 538. *See also* drums
kabary 278, 280, 281
Kabasele, Joseph 'Grand Kalle' 469, 493, 495
Kabasele, Jsoeph 308
Kabaselleh, Ochieng' (Hajullas Nyapanji) 69, 497
Kabelo (*kwaito* musician) 352
kabetula 337, 508
Kabila, Joseph 452
Kabobo, K.K. 208, 482, 483
Kaboom (rapper) 255
kabosy (musical instrument) 543. *See also* lute
Kaboto (guitarist) 543

Kabral, Bibina 63
Kachaba Brothers (band) 25
Kachamba, Daniel 25
Kachamba, Donald 25
Kacki Disco (rapper) 129
Kadongo Kamu Super Singers 328
kadongo-kamu 57, 272, **326–30**
KADS Band 58
Kaf, Lo Rwa 380
Kafeero, Paulo (Prince Paul Job Kafeero) 326, 328–9
Kafinga, Sani Hasasan 168
kagan drum 153. *See also* drums
Kagnew music 537
Kai-Lewis, Jerry 'Black Intellect' 230
kainka 341
Kaisara, Naledi (Slizer) 356, 357
kaka 92, **330–1**, 574
kaka (musical instrument) 330, 331
'Ka Kacaay' (song) 198
Kakadu Night Club (Lagos, Nigeria) 223
kakagbo 330
Kakaiku's Band 113, 207
kakaki (musical instrument) 170. *See also* trumpet
Kalabari people 218
Kalakuta Show (album) 15
Kalamashaka (trio) 245, 246
Kalambe Jazz Band 308, 309
kalanga people 520
kalangu drum 168, 169, 170. *See also* drums
Kalawa Jazmee (record label) 289, 290, 349
Kalawa Records 289
kalei/kilii (musical instrument) 434. *See also* drums; log drum
kalela
Kalenjin people 68
Kalenjin Sisters (duo) 71
Kaliati, E. (Elias) 25
Kalimba (band) 25, 485
kalimba (musical instrument) 269, 566. *See also* lamellophone
kalindula 308, **331–3**, 406, 566
Kalindula Kings (Serenje Kalindula Band) 332, 333
Kallaway, Joseph 581
Kalle, Pepe 355, 356, 494–5
kalon'ny fahiny 54
Kalonji, Bill Clinton 495
Kalu, Paulson 216, 220, 467
Kalule, Angela 58, 335
Kama (hip-hop artist) 245
kamabeka 362, 364, 365
Kamaheke, Kappa 465
kamalen n'goni (musical instrument) 557. *See also* harp lute
Kamande wa Kioi (*kikuyu* artist) 71
Kamati (*shambo* artist) 514
Kamba *benga* 68, 71
Kamenyo, Victor 273
Kamikaze (hip-hop artist) 270
Kamkan (highlife artist) 458
kamkumbe drum 158–9. *See also* drums
Kampala City 6 (band) 57
Kampala Sound – 1960s Ugandan Dance Music, The (album) 57
Kamtchoum, Jean-Berlin 65
Kamwendo Brothers Band 308, 309
Kamwendo, Jack 358
Kanaga De Mopti (group) 386

Kanda Bongo Man (*kwasa kwasa* artist) 355, 356, 357, 495, 519
Kanda Kid (dancer) 99
Kaney, Lakal 259
Kanindo (record label) 70–1, 520, 521
kanindo benga 70–1, 308
Kanindo, Phares Oluoch 68, 69
kannango drum 500, 555. *See also* drums
Kano Music Express (radio program) 259
Kano Riders (group) 259
Kano State Censorship Board 177
Kantah, Kwah 35
Kante, Manfila 312
Kante, Mory (Djessou Mory) 29, 312, 314, 385, 563
Kanyomozi, Juliana 335
kaolack 414
Kapingdbi (band) 32
Kaponda, Ally Bhutto 269
kapuka 246
kar 179
KAR. *See* Kings African Rifles
Kar Kar (Boubacar Traoré) 545
Kareem, Aderan 44
kariara 446
Kariba (group) 486
karienkels 453
Karimaura, Ephraim 102
Karimbo (album) 251
Karimu, Bisiriyu 44
Karindula Sessions, The (album) 331
karing'aring'a (musical instrument) 444–5. *See also* gong
karinyan (musical instrument). *See né/négé*
Kario, Karitas 59
K-Arrowz (hip-hop artist) 259
Karushanga, Cephas 522
Kasambwe Brothers (band) 308
Kasheba, Ndala 441
Kasiwukira (studio) 59
Kassav (group) 337, 518
Kassongo Band 520–1
Kassy, Serges 481
Kast (hip-hop artist) 230
Kasulu Choir 443
katá (musical instrument) 131, 134, 135, 394
Katchás (musician) 152
Katenga Humming Bees (group) 25
Kathi, Mthokozisi 289
Katino (K-Tino) (singer) 77
Katja (*oviritje* artist) 465
Katsaitis, Christos. *See* DJ Christos
Katsina, Muhammadu Sarkin Taushin Sarkin 169
Katumba, Jimmy 58
Katuta, Kapenda 356
Katya, Emma 270
Katz, Israel 421
Kauma, Sam 58
Kaunda, Billy 485
Kaunda, Kenneth 332, 566
Kavari, Kakazona 465
Kawalya, Joanita 58
Kay, John 209
Kaya (*seggae* artist) 505
kayamb (musical instrument) 379, 442. *See also* shakers
Kayamba Afrika (group) 580
Kayira, Papaje 358
Kazar (band) 190, 191, 192
Kazibwe, Travis 59

607

Index

Kazongominja, Bella 465
kazoos (musical instrument) 376, 377. *See also* trumpet
kazukuta **333–4**, 337, 432
KBC. *See* Kenya Broadcasting Corporatoin
K-Bos (hip-hop artist) 230
K-Boys (group) 259
K-Cee (singer-songwriter) 123
Ke Llela le Lona (album) 356
KEB (hip-hop artist) 232
kebero (musical instrument) 49. *See also* drums
Kedjevara, Kiva 121
'Kedu America' (song) 218
Keenyala, Kangwe 513
Keita, Fodeba 317
Keïta, Mamady 318
Keita, Salif 212, 311, 312
Keita, Sekou 563
Kekana, Steve 486
kekere (masqueraders) 47
Kele, Chris 26
Kelele Studios 62
Keletigui et ses Tambourinis (group) 285
Keleza, Consciencia 252
Kelimann (MC) 230
Kemayou, Elvis 372
Ken wa Maria (*benga* artist) 71
Kenis, Vincent 331
kenken (musical instrument) 433, 434. *See also* triangle
kente 35
Kente (group) 482
Kenya 5, 6, 7, 20, 21, 32, 60–2, 68–72, 74, 98–100, 181, 182, 188–9, 226, 243–7, 304–7, 362–5, 444–7, 451–2, 460–2, 463, 491, 493, 497–8, 520, 523, 524–5, 526, 578, 580–1
  Eldoret 5, 71, 226
  Giriama 61
  Kakamega County, Itumba village 304–5
  Kakamega County, Khayega village 460, 461
  Kamba 75
  Kiambu 444
  Kisii 71
  Kisumu 71
  Lake Victoria 68
  Lamu 74, 98, 524
  Malindi 5, 61, 74, 98, 524
  Mazeras 75
  Mombasa 5, 55, 61, 74, 75, 98, 428–9, 523, 524–5
  Murang'a 444
  Nairobi 5, 57, 62, 70, 75, 99, 100, 188, 243, 244–5, 246, 525, 580
  Nairobi 'Mombasa Village' 75
  Nairobi 'Pangani Village' 75
  Nairobi, Dandora 245
  Nairobi, Kariobangi South 245
  Nairobi, Kibera 245
  Nyanza region 68, 69
  Rabai 61
  Rift Valley region 68, 71
  Tanga 523
Kenya Broadcasting Corporation (KBC) 71
Kenya Music Festival 306, 307, 364–5
Kenya Television Network (KTN) 245
Kenya, F. 210

Kerestina: Guitar Songs of Southern Mozambique 1955–1957 (album) 403
Keta Trio 112
Ketama (flamenco group) 312–13
kete 35, 468
Kete Warriors (band) 212
Keur Gui (duo) 261, 262
Keur Moussa (monastery: Dakar, Senegal) 386
Keurtyce E. (rapper) 241
Key Soap Concert Party Show 117, 118–19
Keya (group) 74
keyboard 51, 65, 81, 94, 116, 138, 144, 146, 152, 179, 181, 217, 228, 284, 309, 326, 368, 370, 372, 382, 409, 414–15, 418, 422, 438, 439, 442, 456, 463, 464, 465, 476, 480, 485, 492, 494, 496, 501, 536, 538, 544, 555, 557, 580, 583. *See also* Casio keyboard
keyboard, electric 327, 367, 442, 522, 523
keyboard, electronic 25, 140, 143
Keyti (hip-hop artist) 261
Khaba, Isaac Fana (DJ Khabzela) 287
Khadiija 'Belwo' (Khadiija Ciye Dharaar) 197
Khalifa, Wiz 257
khaliji 28
Khiama Boys (group) 522
Khoe-Aob, Mannecky 368
Khoi people 79
Khoza, Solly 344
Khumalo, Bakithi 296
Khumalo, Mzilikazi 39
Kiaka (band) 190, 192
kianja (theaters) 280
kibangala (musical instrument) 523, 524. *See also* lute
kibati 568
Kibuuka, Andrew Benon 58
kick drum. *See* bass drum
Kickboxer (film) 347
kidandali **334–6**
Kidane, Elsa 538
kidi drum 153. *See also* drums
Kidjo, Angélique 32, 212, 574
kidumbak **336–7**, 454, 568
kidumbak/vidumbak drum 336, 454. *See also* clay drum; drums
Kifoto, Habel 497–8
kignit/qenet system 139–40
kigoma/vigoma drum 454. *See also* drums; *ngoma/ingoma* drum
Kigozi, Fred 57, 58
Kijitonyama Evangelical Choir 443
Kijumwa, Mohamed 524
Kiko Kids (band) 440
Kikuyu *benga* 68, 71
Kikuyu people 68, 245, 444, 445, 447
kilatsaky 544
Kilifeu (rapper) 261
kilii (musical instrument). *See kalei/kilii*
Kilimambogo Brothers Band 71
Kilonga, Sidney 61
Kilonzo, Kakai 71
Kiltir (group) 380
Kilwa (band) 440
Kimani, Tim (Bamboo) 245
Kimbandas do Ritmo (group) 334

Kimbundu people 475, 476
Kimoko, Dally 355
Kimuezu, Elias Dia 509, 510
kinanda (musical instrument) 569–70. *See also* harmonium
kinanda kia mugeto (musical instrument) 444. *See also* accordion
Kindred (group) 482
Kinetic P (DJ) 290
King Ayisoba (*kologo* player and singer) 212
King Karo, The (troupe) 118
King Kong: An African Jazz Opera (musical film) 421, 423
King Ming (hip-hop artist) 230
King Star Brothers, The (group) 552
King, B.B. 494
King, Kenny Tone 224
King, Samuel Oju 467
King, Tunde 321, 323, 324, 467
Kingi (*beni* association) 74
Kingi Beni (group) 74
Kingi Jazz Band 75
Kings African Rifles (KAR) 24, 74, 376
Kingston Trio 301
kinikike 544
Kininike, Rasoa 544
Kino Clan (band) 85
Kinondoni Revival Choir 443
Kintana Telonohorefy (theatre company) 53
Kipchamba arap Butuk (*benga* artist) 71
Kipchamba arap Tapotuk (*benga* artist) 71
'Kirari' (song) 259
Kishk, Sheikh 'Abd al-Hamid 575
Kisii *benga* 71
ki-taarab 337
kitchen knife (as musical instrument) 151, 162
Kitchener (singer) 11, 137, 138
Kizito, Tim 'Dr. T' 59, 335
kizomba 96, 98, 248, 249, **337–41**, 347, 348, 432, 471, 511
Klasick (hip-hop artist) 232
Klear Kut (group) 272
klopse 79, 154–5, 156, 157
KM David (ragga artist) 380
Knuckles, Frankie (DJ/producer) 286, 349
Ko Sira (album) 558
Kobus! (band) 195
Koch FM (radio station) 246
Kode di Dona (*gaita* player) 152
ko'dja' music 65
Koechlin, Bernard 517
Kofi Sammy (highlife artist) 207, 210
Kofi, Prince Osei 212
Koilonget Band 71
Koita, Ami 56, 311–12, 313
Koite, Habib 314, 578
Kokoliko ku Malawi (album) 25
kokoma/kokomba 217, 222
kolamashie/kolomashie 35, 160, 341, 345, 516
Kologbo, Oghene 13
Kom, Esi 114
Kombozee, Kombo 498
Konadus International Band 217
Konaté, Famoudou 318
Konde, Fundi 498, 580
kondi (musical instrument) 434. *See also* lamellophone
Kondo, Joseph 61

608

Index

Koné, Sana 576
Koné, Seydou. *See* Alpha Blondy
kongoma (musical instrument) 433, 434. *See also* lamellophone
koni/kontig (musical instrument). *See ngoni*
konkoma/konkomba 10, 89–90, 161, 206, **341–3**, 516. *See also adaha*; highlife
konkoma/konkomba drum 341, 342, 468. *See also* drums; frame drum
kon-kon (musical instrument) 394
Konkrete (rapper) 230
Konte, Alhaji Bai 563
Konte, Dembo 386, 563
Kontihene (hiplife artist) 211
Konvict Musik Africa (record label) 277
Konvict Records 277
Kool Koc VI (MC) 261
Koola Lobitos (band) 11–13. *See also* Africa '70 (band); Egypt '80 (band); Nigeria '70 (band)
koonken/koonking. *See kunke/kunki*
Koppo (hip-hop artist) 235
kora (musical instrument) 49, 56, 179, 263, 310, 311, 312, 313, 316, 380, 384–5, 386, 457, 478, 480, 560, 561, 562–3, 575. *See also* harp lute
Kora All African Music Awards 97, 251, 340
Korankye, Osie 457, 459
Korby, Ras 482
korgon 51
koriana le moropa **343–5**
Koroma, Patricia 433
Koroma, Salia 400
Korpiklaani (band) 182
Kotafon 572
koto (musical instrument) 162, 163, 433. *See also* triangle
kotokoli people 516
kotso (musical instrument) 169. *See also* drums
Kouchouam Mbada (group) 64, 65, 67
Kounabeli et Orchestre Banowita 123, 125, 127
Kouyaté. *See also* headings beginning Kuyateh
Kouyaté, Bala Faseke 311
Kouyaté, Bassekou and Ngoni Ba (group) 313
Kouyaté, Kandia 56, 311–12, 386
Kouyaté, Modibo 56, 312
Kouyate, N'faly 313
Kouyaté, Sory Kandia 385
Kouyaté, Tata Bambo 56, 311–12
Kowa, Dan 259
Kozman Ti Dalon (group) 380
kpahwle drum. *See kpawle/kpahwle* drum
kpanlogo 35, 50–1, 160, **345–7**, 516
Kpanlogo Party (album) 346
kpawle/kpahwle drum 92, 330. *See also* drums
kpe 51
Kpehe Gome Group 133
kpete (musical instrument) 535. *See also* flute
kpezin drum 92, 330, 412, 413, 535, 572, 573–4. *See also* clay drum; drums
K-Pist (*kwasa kwasa* artist) 357
Kraftwerk (band) 137, 209
krar (musical instrument) 48, 49, 140, 463, 538. *See also* lyre

Kream Production (band) 59
krəəh' (musical instrument) 65. *See also* gong
Krio people. *See* Creole people
Kroo Young Stars Rhythm Group 467
Krotal (hip-hop artist) 235
KRS One (rapper) 272
Kru people 205, 222, 345, 393, 396, 466–7, 586
krusbass 222, 467
K-South (duo) 245, 246
K.T. (MC) 230
K-Tino (Katino) (singer) 77
KTN. *See* Kenya Television Network
'Ku Hemba' (song) 352
Ku weet xam sa bop (album) 261
Kuaté, Emmanuel 66
Kubik, Gerhard 25
Kuboye, Tunde 32
kubumburuwa (musical instrument) 170
Kubwima, Eugene 521
kuduro/kuduru 98, 226, 248, 252, 334, **347–8**
Kuffour, Bice Osei (Obour) 211, 274
Kuffour, John 212–13
kukuma (musical instrument) 170. *See also* lute
Kukurudu (band) 32
Kumalo, Alfred Assegaai 39
Kumapim Royals (band) 207, 482
Kumasi Trio 35, 205, 468
kumbeh/goumbe 160. *See also cumbé*; *gumbe/goombay*
kumbengo 384
kumbwaya 523
'Kumutongo' (song) 102
kunda drum 99. *See also* drums
Kunene, Madala 288
Kunenyati, Knowledge 521
Kungiyoyin Yabon Annabi 175
kunke/kunki 132, 135
kunke/kunki drum 132, 133, 394–5, 396. *See also* drums; square drum
kuntigi (musical instrument) 170. *See also* fiddle
kununku/kurunku 34–5
Kups and Bwasa Stars (group) 356
kurbu (musical instrument) 529–30. *See also* lute
Kuria people 364
kuru (musical instrument) 169. *See also* drums
kurya (musical instrument) 169. *See also* drums
Kurya, Ata Mai 169
Kusasira, Catherine 59
Kusasira, Cathy 335
Kuti, Fela. *See* Anikulapo-Kuti, Fela
kuturiba drum 384. *See also* drums
kuturindingo drum 384. *See also* drums
Kuwa, Kara Buzu Mai Kan 169
Kuwait 524
Kuyateh. *See also* headings beginning Kouyaté
Kuyateh, Jaliba 386, 563
Kuyateh, Menseng 562
'Kuzanga' (song) 102
kwa' (ankle rattle) 65. *See also* ankle/foot bells and rattles; rattle
Kwabena Kwabena (highlife artist) 211
kwadum drum 35. *See also* drums

kwaira (musical instrument) 170. *See also* drums
kwaito 87, 95, 226, 229, 230, 248, 265, 284, 286, 288, 289, 291, **348–55**, 366, 368, 409, 411, 424, 465, 471, 513
kwaito-jazz 352
kwaito-kwasa 356–7
kwaito-kwela 352
kwaito-maskanda 352
Kwaku-T (hip-hop artist) 275
kwamsa (musical instrument) 170. *See also* lute
Kwanza Unit (band) 84–5
kwasa kwasa/kwassa kwassa 25, 230, **355**, 378, 427, 452, 471, 491, 492, 502
in Botswana **355–7**
in Malawi **357–8**
Kwassa Kwassa (album) 357
Kwaw Kese (Emmanuel Abrompah Botchwey) 276
Kwaya ya Uinjilisti Kijitonyama (Kijitonyama Evangelical Choir) 443
Kwaya ya Uinjilisti Sayuni (Sayuni Evangelical Choir) 443
kwela 25, 298, 308, 352, **358–62**, 389, 419, 420, 421, 450, 465, 513
Kwela, Tate 513, 514
Kwenders, Pierre 452
Kwesi, Dzikum 343
kwomboka 444
Kyekyeku (highlife artist) 458–9
Kyeremanten, Balfour 459

La Cour Suprême (group) 532, 533
la musique moderne 491, 492
la musique typique 491, 492
'La parole aux jeunes' (song) 241
la sape 494
Labaran, Binta 'Fati Nijar' 173
ladainha 528
Ladies Club of Cape Coast 108
Ladies Musical League (Accra, Ghana) 108
'Lady' (song) 14
Lady B (Lady Bantu) (hip-hop artist) 235
Lady Jaydee (singer) 87
Lady Ponce (singer) 77
Lady Wanja (*kikuyu* artist) 71
Ladysmith Black Mambazo (choir) 296, 375, 450–1, 552
Ladzekpo, Kobla 153
Lafayette (record label) 300
Lagarrigue, Simon (Gramoune Dada) 380
Lagbaja (Bisade Ologunde) 17, 32, 224
Lagos No Shaking (album) 17
Laka, Don 289, 349, 352
Lala people 332
Lalao, Noelson 53
Lam Toro (album) 560
Lam, Kiné 416
LAM. *See* Linhas Aéreas de Moçambique
Lamartine, Carlos 432, 510
Lamasy (band) 191
l'ambiance facile 586
lamellophone 342. *See also agidigbo/agidigbo*; *ikembe*; *kalimba*; *kondi*; *kongoma*; *likembe*; *mbira*; *premprensua*; *sana kissinge*; *ubo aka*
lamento 508, 510
Lamu people 74
Lando, Teto 432, 510

609

Index

landú 436
Lane, Frankie 345
langarm 79
Laope, Maxime 504
lap steel guitar 324. *See also* guitar
'Lapaz Toyota' (song) 51
Last Poets (group) 275
Last Year's Tragedy (band) 188
'Late Orimolusi Adeboye' (song) 44
Latin America 57, 105, 225, 338, 352, 370, 372, 418, 436, 476, 491, 504, 523
Latvia 182
Laubscher, Japie 79
Lauemi, Lasisi 44
Lawi (Francis Phiri) 26
Lawson, Rex Jim 206, 219, 224
laxamiste 201, 202
laxan 197
Layemi, Lasisi 43
Laylizzie (Edson Abel Jeremias Tchamo) 252
Lazzy (MC) (Abdul Hamidu Ibrahim) 276
Le Club Rythmique (group) 504
Le Gouvernement (group) 532, 533, 534
Le Grande Kalle (Joseph Kabaselé) 469, 493, 495
Le Pouvoir (group) 532, 533, 534
Le Roi Alekpehanhou 572, 573
Le Roi Alokpon 535, 536
Le Roux, Gabi 349, 350
Le Wise (slammer) 239
lead guitar 25, 68, 70, 72, 77, 217, 309, 331, 355, 361, 420, 421, 422, 432, 462, 485, 492, 496, 498. *See also* guitar
Leader Records 355, 556
Lebrasse, Serge 504
lebteit 179
Lee, George 138
Legend, John 483
Lego (*salegy* artist) 502, 503
Lélé, Gramoune 380
lëmbël 414, 415
Leñol, Daandé 560
Lerole, Aaron 'Big Voice Jack' 421
Lerole, Elias 360
Lerole, Jake 360
Les Ambassadeurs du Motel (group) 386, 575
Les Ambassadeurs Internationaux (group) 312, 386
Les Bantous (group) 469
les Bills de Buffalo 493
Les Black Styl (group) 371-2
Les caméléons (group) 380
les Diablotins (group) 125
Les Escrocs (group) 314
Les Ogres de Barback (group) 92
Les Parents du Campus Ambiance (group) 587
Les Patrons (band) 121, 587
Les Poussins Chocs (group) 587
Les Premières Dames (group) 532, 533, 534
Les rappeurs de la Côte ouest africaine (radio program) 237
Les Salopards (group) 587
Les Têtes Brulées (group) 77
Les Titans (group) 77
Les Vétérans (group) 77
Les Volcans de la Capitale (band) 91
Lesokwane, 'Franco' Frank 356

Lesotho 7, 343-5, 375
Letis (*ma/gaisa* artist) 368
Letourdie, Jenny 517
LeTriki, Dossou 413
Letsale, Thabo 'Grandpa' 230
Letsatle, Mmphala 230
Lettie (*ma/gaisa* artist) 368
Lewis, Aura 488
Lexington (*shambo* artist) 513
Lexxus Legal (rapper) 269
libanga 452
Liberia 8, 31, 32, 44, 112, 205, 222, 345, 393, 396, 466-7, 586
Libya 4, 8, 168, 545, 546
Lido Beach (Entebbe, Uganda) 272
Lifeline Family (group) 210
Liga Nacional Africana (Luanda, Angola) 508
light Afrikaans music 80-1
Lijadu Sisters (group) 32
likembe (musical instrument) 468. *See also* lamellophone
Likhomo, Peter 358
Lima, Manu 96
Limba people 433, 434
L'Imby (band) 191
Limpopo International Band 497
Linah (singer) 87
Lincoln, Otoo 345-6, 516
Linda, Solomon 301, 302
Linda, Solomon and His Evening Birds (choir) 296, 301
Lindigo (group) 380
Linengwe River Jazz Band 308, 309
ling'oma 442
lingala 365, 493, 497
Linhas Aéreas de Moçambique (LAM) 375
l'Institut Nationale des Arts (Mali) 386
Lion King, The (musical film) 301
'Lion Sleeps Tonight, The' (song) 301
Lion's Hearts, The (band) 10
Lipopo Jazz (band) 102, 498, 520, 521
lisanda 508
'Little Louie' Vega (DJ/producer) 286, 287
Little Noah (*seprewa* artist) 459
litungu (musical instrument) 362-3, 364, 460. *See also* lyre
litungu music **362-5**
Liundi, Taji 85
Livity (group) 97, 340
Lô, Cheikh 417
Lô, Ismael 417, 560
Lô, Ndongo 416
Lobo, Ildo 106, 437
Local Crisis (band) 483
Local Dimension (group) 212
locomotive style 208
log drum. *See kalei/kilii; nkali*
Loggerenburg, Glenn Van 284
Loketo (band) 495
Lokömotiva (band) 190
Lolwe (record label) 69
London Township (musical style) 423
Long, J.P. 109
Longo, Nyoka 494
Loningisa (record label) 370
'Look, Think, Stay Alive' (song) 244-5
Lopes, Dabs 340
L'Orchestre Kanaga De Mopti (group) 386
Lord Alajiiman (hip-hop artist) 262

Lord Kenya (musician) 210, 211
Los Calvinos (group) 370
Lotin, Eboa 469
'Lotto' (song) 287
Loueke, Lionel 574
Louis, Gérard 505
'Love Adure' (song) 219
Love Aquarius (band) 25
'Love Me Love You Forever' (song) 138
Love Nortey (highlife artist) 210
Lovers and Doll (group) 465
lovers' reggae 484
Luaka Bop (record label) 510
Luanda Carnival 333, 338, 476, 508, 510
luba 446
Lubrano, Suzanna 97, 340
Lubumbashi Stars (group) 498
Lubum-Connection (hip-hop artist) 270
Lubwama, Kato 58, 59
Lucky Dube Band 488
Lucky Star Musical Club (Tanga, Tanzania) 526
luga flow. *See* hip-hop: in Uganda
luga ragga 59
luhengele/luengele (musical instrument) 364. *See also* rattle
Luhn, Chris 483
Luhya *benga* 71
Luhya people 460, 461
'Luimbo Lwa Reggae' (song) 486-7
Lulu Choir 443
Lulu music 543
lulwika (musical instrument) 364, 365. *See also* animal horns; horn
Lumba Brothers (group) 209
Lumumba, Patrice 421
Luna Kidi Band 497
'Lunchtime' (song) 69
lundum 436
Lunga, Lee Roy 521
Lunzu Townhouse (peformance venue: Malawi) 358
Luo *benga* 69-70
Luo people 68, 69, 71
Luo Sweet Band 69
Lura (singer) 63, 528-9
Lusaka Radio 24
lusia. See litungu
Lust of a Dying Breed (band) 188
Lutaaya, Geoffrey 58, 59, 335
Lutaaya, Philly 58
lute 502, 547. *See also cuud; djelingoni; gambus/qanbus; garaya; harp lute; hoddu; kabosy; kibangala; kukuma; kurbu; kwamsa; molo; ngoni; oud/'ud; tehardent; tidinit; udi; ukulele; xalam*
Luz, Edson da (Azagaia) 250-2
lyre 69. *See also* harp; *krar; litungu*
lyrics
 aṣíkò/ashiko/assiko 46, 48
 band (Uganda) 59
 bango 62
 benga 70
 bongo flava 84, 85
 bubblegum 94
 burger highlife 209
 chakacha 99
 coladeira 105
 cultural animation groups 126, 127
 cumbé 133

610

Index

gumbe 163–4
Gabonese rap 237–8
heavy metal 181, 182–3, 188
Hausa rap 260
kizomba 339
kwaito 351
hees 198–9, 201
highlife 207
hip-hop 248–9, 250–2, 255–6, 266
hira gasy 281
imbyino 295
kadongo-kamu 328–9
jazz band (Malawi) 308–9
isicathamiya 301–2
ma/*gaisa* 366–7
makossa 372
maringa 397, 400
marrabenta 404, 406
maskanda 409
masse gohoun 413
mbalax 416
Milo jazz 434
moppie 435
mwomboko 445
Naija pop 449
Oromo popular music 463
pandza 472, 473–4
reggae 478
rumba 493–4, 495–6
salegy 503
Tigrinya music 538
tsapiky 544
Tuareg guitar music 545–6
tufo 550
umbholoho 552
uukorasa 554
vocal jive 420–1
zenji flava 570
zoblazo 584
zouglou 586, 587

M-1 (rapper) 17
'MaAfrika' (song) 231
Maaka Maka (album) 276
Maal, Baaba 212, 417, 559–60, 562
Maalim, Muhiddin 441
maandagraundi 86
Mabaso, Lemmy 'Special' 360
Mabele, Aurlus 519
Mabiaku, Dede 32
Mabibo Youth Choir 443
'Mabingwa wa mchiriku' (song) 429
Mabjeca, Gil 375
Mabulu (group) 251, 404, 405, 406
mabumbumbu 61
Mabuse, Sipho 'Hotstix' 94
mabuyu/*maboya* (musical instrument) 54, 55. *See also* trumpet
Mac Mooger (hip-hop artist) 85
McAdoo, Orpheus M. 299
Mcanyana, Gershon 301
McCartney, Paul 16, 31
McCormack, Cecil Bunting (Bunny Mack) 138
McGod (highlife artist) 209
McGregor, Chris 423
Machel, Samora 403, 405, 406
Macheso, Alick and Orchestra Mberikwazvo 521, 522
machi korathi 446
machi namba igiri/*machi ndogo*/*nini* 446
machi namba imwe/*machi ndaihu* 446

machi ndaihu. *See machi namba imwe*/ *machi ndaihu*
machi ndogo/*nini*. *See machi namba igiri*/ *machi ndogo*/*nini*
Mack, Bunny (Cecil Bunting McCormack) 138
Macka B (reggae artist) 560
McKah (hip-hop artist) 246
MacLean, Jordan 17
'Maçonaria' (song) 251–2
Mad Fish (hiplife artist) 483
Madagascar 3, 7, 27, 52–4, 154, 157, 190–3, 181, 278–82, 453, 501–3, 504, 543–4
  Antananarivo 3, 52, 53, 190, 280, 281, 502, 503
  Antsiranana/Diego Suarez 501, 503
  Majunga 501, 503
  Manjakandriana 280
  Nosy Be 501, 503
  Tulear 543, 544
Made in South Africa (album) 82
madhee/*madhu*/*madh* 168, 171, 173–6, 575–6. *See also* praise music and songs
Madibo (hip-hop artist) 270
Madilu System (singer) 355
Madinka people 383
Madonna (singer-songwriter) 352
Madson Junior (musician) 532
Maduna, Phumi (Sister Phumi) 488
Mafara, Ibrahim Gurso 169
Mafikeng Sixties Festival (South Afica) 287
Mafikizolo (duo) 287, 291, 349, 352
Mafokate, Arthur 349
Mafuya, Mabel 420
Magagula, Bhemani 291
ma/*gaisa* 366–9
Maganga, Luka 23
Mage4 (band) 191
Magereza Taarab 525
Magic Aliens (Psychedelic Aliens) (band) 31, 32, 208
Magic Garden, The (film) 360
Magic System (group) 587
magika 404
Magogo KaDinzulu, Princess 39
magoma drum 454. *See also ngoma*/*ingoma* drum
Magool, Xaliimo Khaliif 199
Magoola, Rachel 58
Magosi (hip-hop artist) 230
Mahabbatu Rasul (group) 175
Mahafil Islam (band) 548
Mahber Theatre Asmara (MaTA) (group) 537
Mahi people 92, 535, 574
Mahlasi, Thakane 344
Mahlathini and the Mahotella Queens (group) 352, 421, 423
Mahoota (DJ Vetkoek/Zynne Sibika) 289
Mahotella Queens, The (group) 423
Maiga, Boncana 313
Main Mall (Gaborone, Botswana) 229
Maina, Kefa 71
Maintain, Olu (Olumide Edwards Adegbolu) 256–7
Maiso, Fred 58, 59
Maître Gims (rapper) 270, 452
Maiyafe, Sheikh Bala 168
Majaivana, Lovemore 450

Majalisa, Patricia 95
majalisi 175
Majoos (hip-hop artist) 270
Majoro, Dede 58
majuba 359
makada 169
makadan jama'a 169–70
makadan sana'a/*maza* 169, 170
makadan sarakuna 169, 170
makadan yaki 169
Makassi Plus Studio 65
Makassy, Mzee 441, 498
Makasu (band) 25
Makeba, Miriam 25, 28, 301, 352, 385, 420, 421, 423
Makgona Tshole Band 421
Makhanya, Nimrod 541
makhoyane (musical instrument) 291. *See also* musical bow
Makiadi, Franco Luambo. *See* Franco (Franco Luambo)
Makindye Youth (group) 272
Makini, Jackson Ngechu (Prezzo) 246
Makoa people 543
Makonde (band) 32
Makonnen, Dagim 463
makossa 27, 29, 32, 64, 234–5, 325, 288, **369–74**, 466, 469
'makozouk' 372
makwaya. *See amakwaya*/*makwaya*
makwayela **374–6**
Makwayela dos TPM (group) 375
Makwela, Joseph 421
Malagasy operetta. *See ba gasy*
Malan, Rian 82
Malawi 7, 24–7, 68, 74, 95, 126, 158, 308–9, 331, 357–8, 375, 376–8, 425–7, 455, 478, 488
  Dowa 377
  Karonga 377
  Kasungu 377
  Likoma Island 376
  Lilongwe 7, 377
  Nkhata Bay district 376, 377
  Nkhota Kota 377
  Ntchisi 377
  Rumphi 377
  Salima 377
Malawi Army Strings Band 25, 358, 485
Malawi Broadcasting Band (MBC Band) 25, 484, 485
Malawi Broadcasting Corporation (MBC) 308, 426
Malawi Congress Party (MCP) 126, 425–7
Malawi Congress Party. Women's League 426
Malawi Police Orchestra 25, 484, 485
Malawi Young Pioneers (paramilitary organization) 485
Malay choirs 154, 155, 156, 157, 435, 436, 453–4
Malaysia 488
Malewezi, Qabaniso 26
Mali 8, 47, 56, 132, 160, 162, 179, 310, 313, 315, 317, 382, 383, 384, 385–6, 456, 478, 480, 484–5, 529–30, 545, 546, 557–8, 560, 562, 563, 574–8
  Bamako 8, 313, 315, 317, 318, 451–2, 557, 575, 578
  Gao 529, 578
  Segou 575, 577
Malika (Asha Abdo Suleiman) 525

611

Index

Malikula, William   25
Malinké people   315, 317
malipenga   **376-9**
malipenga khaki   376, 377
malipenga white   376
Maliro, Mlaka   485
'Malitaba (singer)   344
Mallett, Emmanuel (Zapp Mallett)   275
malogué   380, 505
maloya   182, **379-81**, 438, 504, 505
maloya électrique   380
Mama Ohandja (singer)   77
Maman Dédé (singer)   129
Mamar Kassey (group)   529
mamaya   **381-3**, 562
'Mamaya' (song)   382
mambo   105, 161, 322
Mame Xa (hip-hop artist)   262
MaMohato of Lesotho, Queen   344
Mamu Stores (distribution company)   85
Man Nito (trumpeter)   334
Manatsa, Zexi   32
manchop   395
Mande music   **383-7**, 416. See also *jeliya/jaliya*
Mande people   263, 310-11, 315, 316, 382, 383, 386, 416, 561, 562
Mandela, Nelson   94, 95, 349
Mandengue, Jeannot Dikoto   372
Mandingo Griot Society (musical group)   563
Mandinka people   558, 560, 562, 563
'Mandjou' (song)   385
mandolin (musical instrument)   205, 440, 453, 466, 504
Mandoza (musician)   350-1
Man-E (MC)   230
Maneti, Hemed   441
mangabeu   234-5
mangambeu   64, 66
Mange, James   487-8
Mangeshkar, Lata   172
Mango (record label)   261
Mango Groove (group)   288
'Manhanga Kutapira' (song)   102
Manhattan Brothers (group)   288, 419, 421
Maninka/Malinké people   382, 383, 563
Mankwane, Marks   421
Mann, C.K.   35, 208, 210, 212
mantyantya   332, 333
Manu, Kwese   458
manyenenyene   344
Manzekele, Jerry (Dobeez)   245
mapanes (slums)   236, 238-9. See also slumyards
mapantsula   351, 422, 471
Mapfumo, Thomas   29, 31, 101, 102-3, 212, 320, 542
Mapfumo, Thomas and the Blacks Unlimited (band)   102
Mapfumo, Thomas and the Springfields (band)   102
Maphumulo, Nkosinathi (DJ Black Coffee)   287, 288, 291
Mapine, Tebogo 'Nomadic'   230, 231
maqām   202
maquis (open-air restaurants)   121, 587. See also bars and taverns; restaurants and cafes
marabi   298, 319, 358, 359, 386, **387-91**, 418, 424, 450, 504, 541-2
marabi-jazz   352

maracas (musical instrument)   322, 323, 504. See also *cherewa*; rattle; *sheek-sheek*
Marachi people   364
maraka-dòn   317
Marathons (group)   25
Marbel, Joseph   108, 109
Marcos, António   251, 405, 471
Maria Alice (singer)   437
'Marie Louise' (song)   493
Marijata (band)   32
marimba (musical instrument)   56, 269, 334, 440. See also xylophone
marine (musical instrument)   46, 47. See also drums
maringa/malinga   47, 132, 135, 137, 160, 162, 163, **391-2**, 432, 434, 466, 467, 468, 491. See also *gumbe/goombay*
   in Equatorial Guinea   **392-8**
   in Sierra Leone   **398-402**
'Mario' (song)   493-4
Marlene, Ivete Rosária Mafundza (Yveth)   248-9, 250, 252
Marley, Bob   208, 324, 478, 479, 480, 482, 483, 484, 486, 487, 545
Marley, Bob and the Wailers (band)   484, 485
Marley, Rita   483
Marley, Shasha   478, 482
Marley, Ziggy   483
maroka   168, 170
Maroon Commandos Band   498
Maroon   46, 132, 153, 160, 162, 391, 393, 395, 398-9, 482
marovany (musical instrument)   502, 543. See also zither
marrabenta   248, 252, 374, **402-8**, 470-1, 472, 474. See also *pandza*
Marrabenta (album)   404
Marrabentando: As Histórias que a minha guitarra canta (film)   403, 405
Marriots (band)   211
Mars (record label)   503
Marsalis, Branford   16
Marshall, Hugh   186
Martin, Messi   76, 77
Maru-a-Pula School (Gaborone, Botswana)   229
Maru, Abu Dankurma   169
marus gereseb   368
Marxist Brothers (group)   498, 521
Masagazi, Fred   57, 326, 328, 329
Masaka Band   25, 332, 333
Mascarene Islands   504, 505
Mascato Youth Choir   553
Mascots, The (band)   57
Masekela, Hugh   16, 28, 32, 287, 288, 421, 540
masenko/masinqo (musical instrument)   48, 49, 140, 463. See also fiddle
Mashifta (duo)   246
Mashifta (group)   246
Mashiyane, Spokes   360, 420, 540
Masilele, Lulu   543
Masinga, King Edward   299-300
masinqo. See also *masenko/masinqo* (musical instrument)
maskanda/maskandi   267, 287, 288, 352, **408-12**, 465, 543
Masokoloko (band)   46, 433

Masondo, David   422
masquerade   46, 47, 221, 321
Massassi (rapper)   241
masse gohoun   **412-13**, 574
massemba   334, 475, 476
'Mass-Go'   413
Masuka, Dorothy   420, 421, 425, 450
MaTA (Mahber Theatre Asmara) (group)   537
Matador (rapper)   262
Matador, Jesse   497
Matafale, Evison   485
Matan, Abdi   166
Matassa, Lafiya   259
Matata (band)   32
Matavel, Lisboa   251
Mathambo, Spoek   291
Mathavel/Matavele, Lisbon   405
Matheatau, Jeff   356
Mathew Chapter Five and the Saints (band)   31
Mathew, John De   71
Mathosa, Lebo   350
Mathumba, Cuthbert   420, 421
Matlabaphiri, Thato 'Scar'   230
matore   446
Matovu, Moses   58
Matsane, Emmanuel 'Mjokes'   289
Matsenjwa, Mduduzi (DJ Ziyawa)   293
'Matshikese'   419
Matshikiza, Todd   419, 421
Matshikos (band)   95
Matthews, Thabo 'Shakes the Mix'   229
Matthysse, Paul   86
Maulana, Kabiru   175
Maulidi Musical Party (group)   525
Maulidi, Maurice and Songani Swing Stars (group)   25
Mauritania   8, 178-9, 430-1, 558, 559, 560
   Trab el-Bidhân   178-9, 430, 456
Mauritian Fiesta (musical festival: Réunion)   505
Mauritius   3, 181, 182, 380, 438, 439, 503, 504, 505
   Rodrigues Island   438, 503, 504
Mavin Records   449
Mavuthela Music Company   421
mawaki (singers)   169
Mawanga, Peter   26
M'awensem (album)   276
Mawingu Studio   85
Mawlid/Maulid   548, 576
mawwâl   179
Maxamed BK (singer)   200
Maxamed, Saxardiid 'Jebiyay'   198
Maya (Juma Hussein)   55
Mayanja, Stacia   59
Mayena Production   240
Mayinja, Ronald   58, 59, 335
Mazee, Collela (Richard Owino)   69
Mazeras Brasso Band   75
mazoma   358
mazurka   79, 380
mbabadoni   331
'Mbagala' (song)   87
mbalax   23, 27, 29, 226, 262, 386, **414-18**, 560, 561, 562, 583
Mbalire, Frank   58
mbalule drum   158-9. See also drums
mbandambanda drum   158-9. See also drums

612

Index

Mbango, Charlotte   372
mbaqanga/mbaquanga   27, 82, 296, 298, 352, 358–9, 360, 361, 367, 388, 389, 408, **418–25**, 464, 465, 487, 498, 513, 543, 544
Mbare Chimurenga Choir   103
Mbarga Soukouss (*bikutsi* artist)   77
Mbarga, Prince Nico   216, 218, 219, 224
Mbarga, Prince Nico and Rocafil Jazz (group)   138
Mbaruk Talsam   524
Mbaye, Thiedel   560
MBC Band (Malawi Broadcasting Band)   25, 484, 485
MBC. *See* Malawi Broadcasting Corporation
mbëng-mbëng drum   414, 415. *See also* drums
mbeni bands   10
Mbenjere, Lawrence   309
Mbiľasuku (group)   123
Mbilia Bel (singer)   357–8
Mbilinyi, Joseph (Mr. II/Sugu)   85, 86, 87
mbira (musical instrument)   101, 102, 103, 320, 440, 521. *See also* lamellophone
M'biro, Guy   66
Mboa, Rosalia   474
mbombing   296–7
mbombo   446
mbome mvet   240
Mboup, Laye   415
Mbowa, Bill   57
mbube. *See* isicathamiya
'Mbube' (song)   296, 301
mbuh   467
Mbuli, Mzwake   95
Mbulu, Letta   288, 423
mbumba   126, **425–8**. *See also* cultural animation groups
Mbundu people   334
mbwa kachoka   75
MC(s)   228, 229–31, 243, 248–9, 251, 276, 277, 348
MC Afrik   272
MC Hammer   349
MC Kallé   269, 270
MC Lida   261
MC Lph   219
MC Mickey   245
'MC Moçambique' (song)   248–9, 250
MC Roger (McRoger/Stewart Sukuma)   251, 406, 474
MC Solaar   261, 268
MCA/Universal   16
mchiriku   **428–30**, 526
Mchunu, Sipho   32
Mchunu, Zakes   422
M Connection Band   368
MCP. *See* Malawi Congress Party
McRoger (MC Roger/Stewart Sukuma)   251, 406, 474
mdindiko   54
Mdledle, Nathan   419
Mdlongwa, Oscar Bonginkosi. *See* Oskido (DJ/producer)
M.D. Rhythm Success (band)   102, 320
M'du (M'du Masilela)   289, 349, 351
M'du Music (record label)   349
mdundiko   76, **430**, 442
mdurenge   98
medeh   179, **430–1**. *See also* praise music and songs
medeh an-nabi   **430–1**

media   19, 67, 77, 80, 84, 87, 124, 186–7, 196, 208, 226, 252, 261, 262, 265, 276, 284, 380, 385, 419, 420, 428, 429, 489, 503, 569, 576. *See also* radio; television
Meditators, The (band)   488–9
Medjo, Uncle Joseph   469
Meek Shall Inherit the Earth, The (album)   195
Megalodon (band)   196
megaphone   428, 429
Megastar Band   211
Meintjes, Louise   423
'Meio rico, meio pobre' (song)   473
Meiway (Frederic Desire Ehui)   583–4
Mekuria, Getatchew   94
Melanz Nasyon (group)   380
Meles, Helen   538
Mellesse, Netsanet   143
Melo, Mila   509
melodic death metal   192
Mende people   433, 434
Mendelssohn, Felix   40
Mendes, Gerard   106
Mendes, Gida   63
mendzan xylophone   76–7, 235. *See also* xylophone
Mengisteab, Bereket   538
'Meninas bonitas' (song)   472
Mensah, E.T. (Emmanuel Tettey)   206, 207, 217, 222–4, 275, 342
Mensah, E.T. and His Tempos (group)   206, 207, 342
Mensah, Joe   36, 224
Mensah, Kwaa   207, 458, 468
mento   11, 477
Menu, Kwesi   205
merengue   105, 137, 337, 338, 399, 476, 509
   in Angola   **431–2**
Merengue (record label)   432, 476
merengue rebita   476
Merry Blackbirds (troupe)   301, 389, 541
Merseybeat   566
Messengers (band)   206
Messiah (Handel)   40
Mestre Geraldo (*rebita* artist)   476
Metal Orizon (band)   186
metal ring (musical instrument)   461. *See also* ekengele
Metal4Africa (website)   195
Metallica (band)   181, 190, 194
metaly gasy. *See* heavy metal: in Madagascar
Metro FM (radio station)   285, 286
Metro FM Music Awards   287, 292
'metro songs'   14
Metshe, Azizz   229
meuteu music   65
mganda   376–7, 378, 427
Mgendi, Jennifer   443
Mhango, Griffen   25
M.I. (Mr. Incredible/Jude Abaga)   256
Mi Casa (group)   288
Mibawa (group)   358
Mic Flammer (rapper)   259
Micah, Ekow   482
Michael, Ben   358
Michelle (MC)   230
Michenzani Social Club   526
Mick Fleetwood: The Visitor (film and album)   32, 33
Middle East   184

midi synthesizer   473. *See also* synthesizer
Miembeni Club   525
Mighty Sparrow (musician)   137
'Mignoncité' (song)   67
migrant labour   343–5, 352, 374–5, 376, 390, 402, 408, 409–10, 418, 422, 424, 468, 513, 521, 542
migration and migrant communities. *See* diaspora
Mijikenda people   54, 60, 61, 75, 98
Mikael, Raas Wolde   482
Mike's Car Wash (performance venue: Kafue Road, Lusaka)   332
Mikoko Jazz (band)   308, 309
Mikouagna de Mounana (group)   125
Mila na Utamaduni (Culture Musical Club) (Zanzibar)   337, 526
miliki system   324
military bands   9, 24, 36, 73, 74, 75, 141, 204, 222, 537
Millenium (group)   465
Miller, Baller   224
Miller, Harry   423
Miller, Jacob   487
Mills Brothers (group)   419, 450
Milo jazz   47, 135, 162–3, 392, 396, 399, 401, **432–5**
Mimi (Wilhemina Abu-Andani)   277
Mind Assault (band)   195, 196
Mindoti, Kaskon W.   304–5, 306, 307
'Mine Bengidzakiwe' (song)   292
miners/mining communities   343–5, 374–5, 376, 390, 402, 409, 420, 521, 542, 551
Minguito (concertina player)   476
Minha Banda e Eu, A (documentary)   340
Minor Mistake (rapper)   259
minstrelsy   78, 79, 108, 109, 110, 115, 154, 205–6, 227, 299, 400, 435–6
mipasho   525
Mireku (highlife artist)   205
Misiani, D.O. (Daniel Owino)   69
Missema (group)   125, 129
Mista Doe (Fosta Juliano)   230
Misty in Roots (band)   482
'Mitala' (song)   309
Mitchell, Joni   352
Mitoche Brothers Band   308, 309
Mixter Bash (rapper)   259
Miya, Florence N.   306–7
Mjimba, Jimmy   61
M Joe (hip-hop artist)   270
MK Ondergrond (radio station)   195
Mkandawire, Mjura   25
Mkandawire, Wambali   25–6
Mkatshwa' Choir   301
Mkhize, Themba   288
Mkukupha, Isaac   25
Mkukupha, Nassau   25
mkwasa (musical instrument)   429, 430
MKZWO (record label)   489
Mlevhu, Keith   566
Mlimani Park Orchestra   441, 454
M'munka, Pamelo   532
mnanda. *See* mchiriku
Mngoma, Khabi   39–40
Mnisi, Paul (Rudeboy Paul)   286, 287
Mo wa ri Faye (album)   501
Mobambo, Yvonne   138
Mobb Deep (duo)   85

613

Index

Mobutu Sese Seko   126, 268, 269, 332, 493, 494, 495, 518
modinha   436
Moeletsi, Mokhabi 'Bumpy'   229
Moemba, Patrick   61
moffie   435
Mofokate, Arthur   289
Mofokeng, Mandla 'Spikiri'   289
Mohamed, Famau   524
Mohapeloa, Polumo Joshua   39
Moholo, Louis   32, 423
'Mokolo nakokufa' (song)   493, 494
Mokomelo, Nick   366-7
Molare (singer)   120, 121
Molelekwa, Moses   352
Moletsane, Modise 'Dee'   229
molo (musical instrument)   169, 170. *See also* lute
Molosi, David (DJ Skizo/Ski)   290-1
Mombasa Roots Band   99
'Momoh noh worry' (song)   434
Monare, Ignatius   300
Mondo Music Corporation (record label)   333
'Money' (song)   219
Mono-Mono (band)   32
Monroe farm (Mahikeng, South Africa)   287
Monsoh, David   120
Monsters of the East (band)   85
Mont Arrey (band)   167
Montreux Jazz Festival   251
montuno   23
Monyeapo, Cleopas (DJ Cleo)   288, 291
Monyoncho, Christopher   71
Moosi/Mossé people   532
'Mooyi' (song)   166
moppie   155, 157, **435-6**
Moraba, Kori   486
Morais, Luis   105, 106, 437
Morales, David   349
Morgado, Joãozinho   432
Morgan, Andy   578
Morgan, Sonny   439
morna   96, 97, 105, 151, **436-8**. *See also morna* (in Europe) (Volume XI, Europe)
Morocco   8, 20, 168, 431, 456
Morocco, Emeka   216
Morogoro Jazz Band   337, 440
moropa (musical instrument)   343, 344. *See also* drums
Mortal Soul (band)   188
Mos Def (rapper)   17
Mos, Alfredo and Les Africa Sounds (group)   356
Mosako (hip-hop artist)   230
Mosco, Harry   32
'Moses' (song)   352
Moshaga, Taolo   356
Mosidinyane, Salim 'Fat Free'   230-1
Mosimanegape, Alfred (Alfredo Mos)   356
mosomba drum   127. *See also* drums
Mo-T (trumpeter)   288
Mother Band, The   521
Mothiba, George   288
Mothiba, Joseph   288
Mothle, Ernest   423
Motho (album)   356
Mothus, Jerah (One Eyed Monkey)   288, 289
Motloheloa, Forere   344

Motshegoa, Vincent (DJ Vinny Da Vinci)   284
Motsieloa, Emily   301
Motsieloa, Griffiths   300, 301, 389, 541
Motsieloa's Pitch Black Follies (troupe)   300, 301, 389, 541-2
motswako flow   226, 228, 229, 231
Mouelle Guillaume et l'Orchestre Orfecam Jazz   370
mouggae   439, 505
moulaye chigin   416
Mouna, Axel   372
Moussa, Zara (ZM)   259
'Moussolou' (song)   557
mouth organ   433
moutia/moutya. *See mutia/moutia/moutya*
Movaizhaleine (group)   237, 238, 239, 240, 241
Movers, The (group)   486
Movimento Popular de Libertação de Angola (MPLA)   509-10
Moya, Nancy   358
Moyo, Jonathan   103
Moyo, Peter   522
Moyo, Tongai   522
moza. *See pandza*
Mozambique   3, 5, 7, 74, 154, 157, 158, 181, 183, 248-52, 337, 338, 374-6, 402-6, 453, 470-4, 521, 548-50
 Gaza   375, 402, 450
 Inhambane   375
 Likoma Island   376
 Manhiça   375
 Maputo/Lourenço Marques   7, 375, 402, 403, 470
 Marracuene   403, 406
Mozambique Liberation Front. *See* Frente de Libertação de Moçambique (FRELIMO)
Mozika Mavesatra Malagasy (web page)   190
MP3 technology and portals   28, 174, 177, 259, 449
mpanje drum   158-9. *See also* drums
Mpfumo, Fany   404, 405
Mphatlalatsane, Khwezi   231-2
Mphila, Khokhiwe   291
Mpiana, B.   452, 495
mpihira gasy/mpihiran'ny andrianana/mpilalao   53, 278, 279, 281
mpilalao. *See mpihira gasy/mpihiran'ny andrianana/mpilalao*
MPLA. *See* Movimento Popular de Libertação de Angola (MPLA)
mpre music   35
Mpulu, Biza   356
Mr. Arssen (rapper)   251
Mr. Bow (singer)   474
Mr. Dino (*pandza* artist)   471
Mr. II (Sugu/Joseph Mbilinyi)   85, 86, 87
Mr. Incredible (M.I./Jude Abaga)   256
Mr. Kuka (*pandza* artist)   473
Mr. Shisundi (guitarist)   461
Mr. T (MC) (Nomadic)   230, 231
Mrubata, McCoy   288
Mrwebi, Gwigwi   423
Mseleku, William   541
msewe   568
Msimang, Aura   488
msondo dance   98, 454

msondo drum   54, 99, 429, 430, 454, 570. *See also* drums
msondo ngoma   455
Msondo Ngoma (band)   441, 455
Mthethwa, Eugene 'Donald Duck'   289
Mthethwa, Tuza   422
'Mtsinje' (song)   25
Mtukudzi, Oliver   102, 320
MTV (TV network)   87, 257, 272
MTV Africa Music Awards   87, 256
MTV Europe Music Awards   87
Muambi, Peter   71
Mubiru, Haruna   58, 59
Muchawaya, Ketai   521, 522
Mucheca, Alberto   251
Mudanisse, Ivânnea da Silva   252
'Mudde Eri Mukama' (song)   328
Mugabe, Robert   101, 103, 183
mugambo   86
Mugula, Dan   328
Muhammad, Yakubu   173
Muhammad/Mohamed, Prophet   171, 173, 174, 175, 430-1, 548, 555, 575, 576
Muhando, Rose   443
Mujuru, Ephat   103
Mukabi, George   461, 462
Mukaiba, Ligali   44
Mukalazi, David   335
'Mukamfwila' (song)   332, 333
Mukasa, Hope   58
mukhasi drum. *See isukuti mama/ikhasi/mukhasi* drum
Mukiibi, Abbey   58
Mukwevho, Colbert   486-7, 488
Mulangeni Sounds (group)   25, 358
Mulanje Mountain Jazz (band)   308
Mulato, Gregório   432
Mulembe FM (radio station)   460
Mulwa, Bosco   71
Mun G (hip-hop artist)   273
Mundo, Regine   370
Muniania, Lubangi   451, 452
Muntuza (album)   411
Mupulu, Biza   356
Murcia, Juan   135
Mureko, Kanghondi kaTimo Haimbodi ya Shomwele Johannes 'Warmgat'   513
Murimi, Mike   71
Mursal, Maryam   200
Musa, Simon Kichera   71
Musaimo (*kikuyu* artist)   71
Musarurwa, August   540, 542
musatsa drum. *See papa/isatsa/musatsa* drum
museve. *See sungura*
Mushaandja, Nashilongweshipwe   514
Mushrooms (recording studio)   62
Music for Your Movement (album)   230
music hall   106, 109, 110, 205
Music Royals (group)   467
music videos/video clips   20, 51, 55, 59, 65, 77, 87, 89, 128, 129-30, 138, 144, 148, 192, 209, 210, 211, 218, 224, 226, 231, 234, 239, 240, 244-5, 252, 256, 257, 272, 276, 339, 355, 356, 357, 372, 414, 417, 430, 441, 448, 449, 465, 472, 473, 523, 567, 569, 570, 573, 574, 584. *See also* YouTube
Música de Moçambique (album)   405
musical bow. *See bombe; makhoyane; umuduri*

614

Index

musical saw 48, 109, 131, 135, 162, 321, 395, 467
musical theater 53, 113, 115, 118, 421
Musical Youth (band) 482
Musicians Union of Ghana (MUSIGA) 116, 207, 208, 274
MUSIGA. *See* Musicians Union of Ghana
Musik Maker (software) 66
Musi-O-Tunya (group) 180, 566
Musique de Mali (album) 56
Muslim Community of the Sufis (organization) 576
musondo (musical instrument) 364. *See also* drums
Mussa, Faith 378
musseques (informal settlements) 333, 334, 348, 431–2, 508, 509
Mustafa, Khamis 74
Mustapha, Rabi 173
Musungilo, Peter 332
Mutabaruka (poet and musician) 483
Mutambi, Simon 522
muthirigu 444
mutia/moutia/moutya 438–9, 504, 517
mutuashi 333
Mutukundzi, Oliver 542
Muungano Taarab (group) 526
Muxima Angola (group) 476
Muyenga Youth (group) 272
Muyidatu (*wákà* peformer) 556
muziki wa dansi 75, 84, 429, **439–42**, 454, 569
muziki wa injili **442–4**
Muzipasi (goup) 25
mvet/mvett 239–40
mvet/mvett (musical instrument) 235, 239–40. *See also* harp lute
Mvita Orchestra 429
Mwachupa, Paul 580
Mwafrika (rapper) 246
Mwai, Daniel Kamau (DK) 71
Mwaitege, Bon 443
Mwakasungura, Kapote 25
Mwalale, Ndiche (guitarist) 24
Mwambona, Nathaniel 356
Mwamwaya, Esau 26
Mwanafalsafa (hip-hop artist) 85
Mwansa, John 332, 333
Mwasiti (singer) 87
mwatu (musical instrument) 444, 445
Mwenda, Jean Bosco 60, 69, 469
mwinoghe 358, 427
Mwinshehe, Mbaraka, and Orchestra Super Volcano 440
mwomboko **444–7**
'My Car' (song) 256
'My Lady Frustration' (song) 13
'My Life' (song) 277
'My Life Time' (song) 325
Myeni, Mazwi 22
MySpace (social media) 174, 259
Mzbel (Nana Akua Amoah) 277
Mzee Ngala/*Mzee Bango* (Joseph Ngala) 60–2, 580
Mzekezeke (*kwaito* artist) 289, 351
Mzobe, Isaac 301
Mzulala (house-*kwasa* artist) 357
Mzuri Records 440, 524

!Naruseb, Steven Alvin 368
Nabhany, Sheikh 524
Nabiryo, Immaculate 58

Nadi Shuub (music club: Zanzibar) 525
Na Essayé (group) 380, 505
Naeto C (rapper) 257
nagtroepe (night troupes). *See* Malay choirs
Nagudu, Mahmud 173
Nahari, Taha 166
nai (musical instrument) 523, 525. *See also* flute
naija jams 219
Naija pop 21, 27, **448–9**. *See also* Afrobeats/Afro Beats; Afropop/Afro pop/Afro-pop
naija rap 138
Naijabeats 87
nails (as musical instrument) 131, 135, 306, 316
Nairobi Cinema (Nairobi) 244
Nairobi Metal Festival (Kenya) 188
Nairobi Rock Fest (Kenya) 188
Nairuz festival 454
'Naitaka Bango' (song) 61
Nakakaawa (radio drama) 328
Nakale, Joseph 514
Nakale, Naxa 514
Nakale-ya-Nakale (*shambo* artist) 514
Nakitare, Hubert (Nonini) 246
'Nakoma mbanda na mama ya mobali' (song) 496
NAKOREX (group) 212
Nalbandian, Kevork 93, 141
Naly, Jeanne 53
NAMA. *See* Namibian Annual Music Awards
Namadingo, Patience 378
Namakwa Brothers Band 308
Namangi, Aliyu 168–9
Namatovu, Irene 59, 335
Namibia 7, 181, 183, 355, 366–8, 464–5, 512–14, 521, 552–4
  Erongo region 368
  Hereroland 464
  Owamboland 464, 512, 513
  Windhoek 7, 464, 465
  Windhoek, Katutura 367
  Windhoek, Khomasdal 367
  Windhoek, Old Location 367
Namibian Annual Music Awards (NAMA) 514
naming ceremonies 147–8, 153, 170, 342, 501
  gorilla-naming ceremonies 294
Namoko, Alan and Chimvu Jazz Band 308
Namukasa, Bettina 59
Nana King (hiplife artist) 210
Nana, Aberewa 483
Naná, Senhore (musician) 152
nanaye filmi music. *See* Hausa *nanaye filmi* music
Nandau, Jean 358
Naneth (hip-hop artist) 237
nankasa drum 327. *See also* drums
ñánkue/bonkó 392, 394
'Nantabuulirirwa' (song) 329
Nantongo, Sofia 59
Nantume, Maureen 59
Nanuto (saxophonist) 510
Napoleon Club (Accra) 32
NARC. *See* National Rainbow Coalition
Nash, Neville 486
nasheed 578
Nashima, Nanghili 513, 514
Nata Capricorn (group) 356

Nation FM (radio station) 246
national anthems 39, 141, 246, 386
National Ballet of Mali 578
National Choir Festival (South Africa) 40
National Cultrual Troupe (Seychelles) 438
National Dance Company (Ghana) 90
National Festival of Concert Parties (1973: Ghana) 114
National Isicathamiya Festival (South Africa) 302
'National Makossa Team' 371-2
National Music Eisteddfod (South Africa) 40
National Party (South Africa) 195
National Rainbow Coalition (NARC) 245–6
National Resistance Movement (NRM) (Uganda) 273
National Star Search Competition (Kenya) 244, 245
National Theatre (Hargeysa, Somali) 199
National Youth Choir of Namibia 553
nationalism 39, 40, 79–80, 100–1, 102, 112, 198, 206–7, 334, 425, 498, 537, 538. *See also* independence
nationalization 125, 126, 199, 268, 332, 440–1, 566
native blues 466, 467. *See also* odonson highlife
Native Funk Lords (band) 210
Natongo, Carol 59
Naughty by Nature (trio) 84, 85, 272
Navio (hip-hop artist) 272
'Nawuliranga' (song) 272
Nazari (rapper) 259
Nazarite Vow (band) 482
Nazizi (hip-hop artist) 246
Ndagire, Mariam 58, 59
Ndani ya Bongo (album) 85
Ndau people 521
Ndawana (*shambo* artist) 514
Ndebele people 100, 101, 449–51, 521
Ndebele pop **449–51**
Ndebele, Somandla 522
ndege 568, 570
ndem 239
nder drum 414, 415. *See also* drums
Nder, Alioune Mbaye 416
Ndiche, Tepu 358
Ndichu, John 71
Ndingo Brothers Band 308, 309
ndombolo 121, 128, 226, 267, 268, 269, 355, 365, **451-3**, 491, 492, 518
Ndonfeng, Samuel (Sam Fan Thomas) 65, 372
Ndong Ndoutoume, Tsira 240
Ndongo D (rapper) 262
Ndongo, Nino (guitarist) 507
ndongomothi 446
N'Dour, Viviane 416
N'Dour, Youssou 212, 262, 311, 414, 415–16, 417, 560, 562
'Ndozvireva' (song) 102
ndu' (musical instrument) 65. *See also* idiophone
Ndugwa, Omugave 58
ndunduma 390
Ndzengue, Fam 77
nél/négé (musical instrument) 384. *See also* bell
Nederlandslied 155, **453–4**
Negra Soul (group) 269

615

Index

Negrissim (group)   234, 235
Négro Tropical (group)   124
Neji, Sunny   219
neo-traditional music   35–6, 38, 218, 351, 352, 408, 413, 421, 555–6
NEPA (Never Expect Power Always) (album)   17
Nest (*ba gasy* artist)   53
Netherlands   97, 337, 339, 340, 510
  Rotterdam   96, 97, 106
Neto, António Costa   510
Neto, Jorge   340
Never-Tire (flautist)   399
New Africanism   419, 541
'new age' *kwaito*   289
New Crossbones, The (band)   332
New Florida Nightclub (F1) (Nairobi)   244
New Scene (Jazz Giants) (band)   24–5
New School (group)   237
New Wave of British Heavy Metal (NWOBHM)   182, 186
New Year   153–4, 155, 279, 299
Newman, Amy   210
NFL (group)   275
NG Bling (rapper)   239
ngaieta (musical instrument)   475. *See also* accordion; diatonic button accordion
ngajiza (musical instrument)   549–50. *See also* drums; frame drums
Ngala, Joseph (Mzee Ngala/*Mzee Bango*)   60–2, 580
Ngatu (*shambo* artist)   512, 513
Ngcobo, Bheki (IHhashi Elimhlophe)   411
Ngcobo, Shiyani   410
'Ngisebenzel' u My Love' (song)   300
Ngogo Highlife Orchestra   212
Ngoh, Misse   469
Ngola (record label)   432
Ngola Ritmos (group)   334, 476, 507, 508, 509
Ngom, Moussa   416
Ngoma (record label)   370, 405
Ngoma Research Collective (Namibia)   368, 465
ngoma ya kuchanganya (musical instrument)   336. *See also* drums
ngoma ya kudunda (musical instrument)   336. *See also* drums
ngoma ya ndani   54–5
'Ngoma Yarira' (song)   102
ngoma/ingoma   54, 73, 75, 98, 157, 226, 408, 409, 410, 427, 428, 430, 439, 440, 441, 454–5, 523, 525, 526, 568, 570
  in Malawi   455
ngoma/ingoma drum   294, 295, 299, 320, 331, 432, 454, 513. *See also* drums; hand drum
ngombi (musical instrument)   240. *See also* harp
ngom (musical instrument)   127
ngoni (musical instrument)   179, 310, 311, 312, 316, 382, 384–5, 480, 578. *See also* lute
Ngoni people   455
Ngozi, Paul   180, 566
Ngozi, Paul and the Ngozi Family (band)   180, 566, 567
Ngqawana, Zim   288
ngueuguia music   65

ngumbé   340
nguni music   390
Nguni people   38, 299, 450
Ngunjiri, Harrison (Hardstone)   245
Ngwenya, Moses   422
Niamu Mbaam (group)   262
Nicholas II, Tsar of Russia   141
nidal   179, 456–7
Niger   4, 8, 168, 170, 172, 259, 545, 546, 547
  Niamey   8, 529
Nigeria   4, 8, 9, 11–12, 13, 15, 16, 20, 21, 28, 29, 31, 32, 43–5, 46, 47–8, 64, 84, 91, 95, 111, 112, 115–16, 121, 132, 133, 138, 145–8, 160, 162, 180, 181, 183, 204, 208, 216–20, 221–4, 241, 254–7, 258–60, 342–3, 392, 393, 394, 395, 448–9, 466, 467, 477, 478, 482, 483, 500-1, 555–6, 566, 578
  Abeokuta/Abéòkúta   47, 501
  Argungu   169
  Badagry   153, 221, 413
  Calabar   222, 395
  Edo State   343
  Epe   556
  Gobir   169
  Ibadan   47, 323, 343
  Ijebu Igbo   44
  Ikorodu   556
  Ilọrin   148, 500
  Isale Eko/Lagos Island   43, 222
  Jos   256, 449
  Kano   8, 171–2, 175–6, 177, 259, 260
  Kebbi   169
  Lagos   8, 14, 15, 16, 21, 91, 221, 222, 223, 254, 255, 321–5, 342, 394, 413, 448, 467, 501, 556
  Lagos State   555
  Lagos, Agege   255
  Lagos, Ajegunle   257
  Lagos, Apapa   255
  Lagos, Festac   255
  Lagos, Ikeja   255
  Lagos, Isolo   255
  Lagos, Ojuelegba   257
  northern Nigeria   168–77
  Ọ̀yọ́   146
  Ogun State   555, 556
  Onitsha   222
  Sokoto State   169
Nigeria '70 (band)   13. *See also* Africa '70 (band); Egypt '80 (band); Koola Lobitos (band)
Nigga Raw (rapper)   219
Niggaz 2 Public (band)   85
Night Star Musical Club (group)   429
nightclubs   15, 20, 23, 57, 76, 90, 93, 97, 98, 120, 177, 208, 222, 223, 224, 236, 239, 244, 249, 284–5, 286, 287, 290, 291, 348, 367, 402, 403, 414, 416, 419, 491, 501, 502, 505. *See also* bars; clubs; dance halls; discotheques
Nightwish (band)   186, 190
Nii Funny (hiplife artist)   51
nikabheni performers   299
Nimo, Koo   212, 457, 458, 459, 468
Nine Fingers (pianist)   388
Ning'anga, Kenneth   25
Nini (heavy metal musician)   192
Nix (hip-hop artist)   261
njeki   446
Njerama Boys (group)   522

Njiké, Daniel   64
Njoh, Bella   372
Nkabinde, Simon 'Mahlathini'   421
Nkabinde, Zeph   421
'Nkalakatha' (song)   350–1
nkali (musical instrument)   46. *See also* drums; log drum
Nketia, Joseph Hanson Kwabena   211
Nkhata, Brite   25
Nkhoma, Maria Chidzanja   25
Nkhuhku, Monametsi 'Apollo Diablo'   230
Nkol Engong (group)   125, 127, 129
Nkone, Upendo   443
'Nkosi siklel' iAfrika' (song)   39
Nkosi, Ben   360
Nkosi, Isaac 'Zacks'   419, 420
Nkosi, West   420
Nkrumah, Kwame   112, 206, 207–8, 346
nkul (musical instrument)   127
Nkushu, Rastaman   488
nkwa   217
Nkwanyane, Elijah   419
Nkwe, Jairus 'Jakarumba'   289
Nneka (singer)   17
No Discrimination (album)   17
'No Man Kill Another Man' (song)   488
Noel, Jean   544
Noella (hip-hop artist)   232
Nomadic (MC) (Tebogo Mapine)   230, 231
Nomiis Gee (hip-hop artist)   259
Nonini (Hubert Nakitare)   246
Norberka (*zenli* artist)   572
North Africa   181, 225, 430–1
North America   86, 180, 187, 226, 267, 296, 308, 313, 315, 359, 411, 417. *See also* Canada; United States
Northern Solidierz (group)   259
Nosey Road (band)   186
Nouvelle Ecriture (group)   452
Novatos da Ilha (group)   476
Now Again (record label)   180, 567
NRM (Uganda). *See* National Resistance Movement (Uganda)
Ntabanyane, Apollo   344
ntcham   239
Ntebejana (organ player)   388
Ntiskana Gaba   38
Ntoni, Victor   288
Nuatro, Francis Cudjoe   90
Nuatro's Osagyefo's Own Borborbor Group   90
Nukpere, Sammy   482
Number 1 (band)   23
'Number One' (song)   87
Nunda, Paul Julius (Jua Cali)   246
Nunes, Artur   509
Nursery Boys Go Ahead (album)   462
Nuta Jazz Band   440, 441, 455
Nuting But De Stone (album)   245
Nuura, Hibo   199
Nwaba, Israel   217
Nwanne, King Oge   224
NWOBHM. *See* New Wave of British Heavy Metal
Nxumalo, Gideon   418, 419
Ny Sakelidalana (ensemble)   54
Ny Tropy Analamanga (theatre company)   53
Nyali Beach Hotel (Mombasa, Kenya)   61
Nyama, Kwabena   212, 458
Nyambe, Isata   400
Nyambura, John wa   444

Index

Nyame Bekyere Band 210
Nyame, E.K. 112–13, 119, 207, 217, 468
Nyapanji, Hajullas (Ochieng' Kabaselleh) 69, 497
Nyasaland. *See* Malawi
Nyathi, Albert 450
Nyathi, Flavian 103
nyatiti 69, 70
nyau. See *gule wa mkulu*
nyenyemo (musical instrument) 384. *See also* idiophone
Nyenzi (group) 125
Nyirongo, Paul Dobson (Paul Ngozi) 180, 566
Nyolo, Sally 77
Nyovest, Cassper 123
Nytro (Batswana hip-hop artist) 230
Nzeka, Ephraim 16
Nzema/Apollo people 583
Nzenze, John 461
Nzeru Records 25
Nzié, Anne-Marie 372
Nzima people 457
Nzimande, Hamilton 41, 422
nzope 549
nzumari (musical instrument) 99

obaka (musical instrument) 127
Obandja, Mama 469
Obey Reocrds 323
Obey, Chief Commander Ebenezer 146, 323, 324
OBOUO Music 120
Obour (Bice Osei Kuffour) 211, 274
Obrafour (Kwabena Okyere Darko) 210, 276, 277
Obrah (TV series) 208
Obuade (group) 346
Ocansey, Albert 108
Ochieng, Henry (Octopizzo) 245, 246
Ochieng', Nelson (Nelson Ochieng' Orwa) 69
Ochoa, Eliades 313
Ocora (record label) 517
Octopizzo (Henry Ochieng) 245, 246
Odeon Records 53, 458, 468, 504, 524, 556
Odide music 343
Odin Cinema (Sophiatown, Johannesburg) 419
Odondi, John Ogara (Ogara Taifa) 69
odonno/dondo drum 36. *See also* drums; hourglass drum
odonson highlife 204, 205, 456, **457–60**, 466, 468
'Odoya' (song) 64
Odumosu, Mike 33
Ofege (band) 32
Office Malagasy du Droit d'Auteur (OMDA) 191
official events and ceremonies 80, 93, 124, 125, 126, 127, 128, 129, 130, 281, 317, 528, 550
Offside Trick (group) 568, 570
Ofo and the Black Company (band) 32
Ofori, Joseph Nana (Prodical) 276
Ogara Boys Band 69, 70
Ogara, John 580
oge drum 345. *See also* drums
Ogholi-Ogosi, Evi Edna 483
ògìdo (musical instrument) 323
Ogunkoya, Kola 224
ohangla 69, 70

Ohlange Institute Choir 38, 298, 300
Oja (band) 32
ojazibantshi 297
Ojeah, Okalue 13
'Ojo Davies/Elekole of Ikole' (song) 323
Ojo, Dele 323, 324
'Ojuelegba' (song) 257, 448
Okafor, Pretty. *See* Junior and Pretty (duo)
Okalla, Bob 118
Okeke, Prince Gozie 220
O.K. Jazz (band) 493–4, 495, 496, 516. *See also* TPOK Jazz (band)
O.K. Success (group) 498, 520
Okonta, Eddy 224
Okoss (rapper) 240
Okosun, Sonny 16, 32, 138, 482
Okotie, Chris 138
Okoye, Paul. *See* P-Square (duo)
Okoye, Peter. *See* P-Square (duo)
Okukuseku (band) 207, 208
okwiitanga 514
Okwoha, Amaka 220
Okyeame Kwame (Kwame Nsiah Appau) 211, 274–5, 276
'Ol Mi Bobbi Lef Mi Wase Foh Mi Man' (song) 434
Ola, Apeke Abike 556
Olaiya, Moses 324
Olaiya, Victor 11, 206, 223–4, 342
Olaleye, Isaac 13
olalomi music 44
Olang, Prechard Pouka (Poxi Presha) 245, 246
Olaribigbe, Aminu 44
Olariechi, Aderi 467
Olariechi, Stephen 467
Olátúnjí Junior, Ahbedeen 501
Olátúnjí, Yùsùfù 146, 501
Olayigbade, Saka 44
ole wase 400, 434
Ole, António 509
Oletouma, Fatimata 530
Ologunde, Bisade (Lagbaja) 17, 32
Olomide, Koffi 35, 356, 452, 494, 495
Olvido Records 462
olwika (musical instrument) 306. *See also* animal horns; horn
OM Studios 275
Omaboe, Grace 208
Omar, Rex 212
OMDA. *See* Office Malagasy du Droit d'Auteur
omele akọ drum 146–7. *See also* drums
omele mé.ta drum 147. *See also* drums
Omengo (group) 129
Omo Oba Eledua (Opeoluwa Orobiyi) 325
Omojesu, Abimbola 501
Omolo, Gabriel 69, 580
Omo-Rali, Ayinla 44
Omowura, Akeem 45
Omowura, Ayinla ('Alhaji costly') 43, 44–5
Omowura, Dauda 45
ompe 34
omutibo 307, **460–3**, 580, 581
Omwila (album) 513
Ondarata (*oviritje* artist) 465
One (album) 125
One Africa Music Festival (Brooklyn, USA, 2016) 21
One Eyed Monkey (DJ) (Jerah Mothus) 288, 289
One People Band 488

OneBeat (music program) 262, 269
ONFG. *See* Organisation nationale des femmes gabonaises
Ongala, Remmy and Super Matimila (group) 430, 441
Ongaro, Sukuma Bin (Wilson Omutere) 71
Onieede, Lasisi 44
Ontos (rapper) 259
Onwenu, Onyeka 218
Onwuka, G.T. 217
Onyia, Zeal 206, 217, 224
Onyina's Royal Trio 207
Opambo (band) 217
open air/open space performances 10, 165, 192, 196, 198, 279–80, 287, 336, 502, 587; *See also bwalo/boma*; concerts and live performances
bwalo 158, 377
'spinner' events 209
opera 39
Opera Africa (band) 39
Opika (record label) 370, 371
opim 468
Opoku, A.M. 153
Oppikoppi (music festival: Limpopo Province, South Africa) 350
Oppong, Eugene (Kyekyeku) 458–9
Optimism Club (Sekondi, Ghana) 108, 109
Optimism Club Dance Orchestra (Sekondi, Ghana) 112
Orakle (hip-hop artist) 230
Orchestra Marrabenta Star de Mocambique 404, 405
Orchestra of the National Police Forces, The (Gabon) 125
orchestras 124–5, 126, 204, 205, 206, 236, 310, 468, 504
Orchestre Baobab 23, 415, 417
Orchestre Bella Bella 494–5
Orchestre Black Santiago 206, 330
Orchestre Liberty 502
Orchestre Los Camaroes 77
Orchestre Maquis 441
Orchestre National de la Gendarmerie (Benin)
Orchestre National du Jazz (Benin) 91
Orchestre Rail Band de Bamako 386
Oren'Tchy (group) 584
organ (musical instrument) 113, 199, 219, 222, 370, 371, 372, 442, 464, 465, 480, 501, 502, 523, 525–6, 583
organ, electric 422, 538
Organisation nationale des femmes gabonaises (ONFG) 125
oriengo 129
Oriental Brothers (group) 216, 217, 224, 467
'Original Sufferhead' (song) 12
Origo, Owiti 69
oríkì 145–6, 147. *See also* praise music and songs
O Ritmo do Ngola Ritmos (documentary) 509
Orlando Julius (O.J. Ekemode) 28, 32
Orlando, Zé 339
Orobiyi, Opeoluwa (Omo Oba Eledua) 325
Oroki Social Club (album) 44
Orombo people 49, 139
Oromo popular music **463–4**
Orphaned Land (band) 182

617

Index

Orpheus M. McAdoo's Minstrel, Vaudeville and Concert Company 299
Orquesta Aragon 23
Orquesta Broadway 23
Orquestra Djambu 403, 404, 406
ORTM (TV network) 557, 575
Oru, Ajao 44
orutu 69, 70
Orwa, Nelson Ochieng' (Nelly Ochieng') 69
Os 5 elementos (documentary) 252
Os Jovens do Prenda (group) 509, 510
Os Kiezos (group) 476, 509
Os Merengues (group) 476, 510
Os Tubarões (group) 106
Osadebe, Osita 216, 217, 218, 219, 220, 467
Osadebe, Stephen 224
Osei, Teddy 31
Oshimili people 218
osibi 35, 468
Osibio, Nana 482
Osibisa (band) 30-1, 32, 33, 208, 566
Osibisa Kete Warriors (band) 33
osibisaaba 31, 34, 35, 205, 457, 458, 466, 468, 469
Oskido (DJ/producer) 286, 289, 290, 349
Oskido's Church Grooves (album) 286
Osofo Dadzie (TV series) 115, 208
'Osondi Onwendi' (song) 219
osoode/osode 34, 35
Ossei, Reginald Yaw Asante (Reggie Rockstone) 210, 273, 275, 276
Ossy (*ba gasy* artist) 53
Osumare, Halifu 274, 275
Osunlade (musician) 287
oswenka 297
Oti, Sunny 224
'Otto ek Kamil' (song) 517
OTTU (band) 441
Ou Stakes (Stanley) 368
Ouassoulounké/Wasulunka people 315
oud/ʻud (musical instrument) 166, 167, 198, 313, 337, 523, 524, 525, 527. *See also* lute
Ouémé 572
oukorasa. See uukorasa/oukorasa
ag Oumbadougou, Abdallah 546
Ousa Nousava (group) 380
Out Here Records 86
'Overtake Don Overtake Overtake' (song) 112
Overthrust (band) 186-7
Ovikango (group) 465
oviritje 464-6, 552
Owambo/Aawambo people 367, 512-13, 514
Owino, Richard (Collela Mazee) 69
Owiyo, Suzanna 72
Owonikoko, Raji 44
Owusu, Felix 212
Oxygen (band) 32
O'Yaba (band) 487, 488
Oyesiko, J.O. 323-4
Oyosi, Aketch (Samuel Aketch Jabuya) 69
Oyundi (record label) 69
Ozimzim (band) 211
Ozoseua (*oviritje* artist) 465
Ozzidi (band) 32

Pa Araico (drummer) 163
Paa Bobo (hiplife artist) 211
Paapa Mensah (musician) 138
Paape, Willy le 370
Pacheco, Johnny 23
Pagadeja (band) 32
Paim, Eduardo 337, 338, 340
Paliani, Eric 26
Palladium Theatre (Accra, Ghana) 108
Palma, Belita 509
palmwine music 113, 204-5, 207, 212, 213, 217, 222, 226, 321, 322, 393, 398, 399, 400, 457, 458-9, **466-70**, 586
pamtondo 308, 425
Pan African Historical Theatre Festval. *See* PANAFEST
PANAFEST (Pan African Historical Theatre Festval) 211
Pan-African Cultural Festival (1st: Algiers) 385
pandza 249, 402, 406, **470-5**. *See also marrabenta*
Pantera, Orlando 63, 528, 529
pantsula 252, 366
Papa Cidy (singer-songwriter) 478
'Papa Pavil' 131
Papa Shee (highlife artist) 211
'Papa Stop the War' (song) 95
Papa Wemba (singer and musician) 115, 212, 452, 494, 495, 496
Papua New Guinea 488
Paradise Nightclub (Johannesburg, South Africa) 419
Paranoid (band) 182
Paris Colonial Exposition (1931) 504
Paris, Tito 437
Parking Lot Grass (band) 188, 189
parks 97
Parlophone (record label) 113, 205, 322, 323, 458, 468
Parow, Jack 266
Parti démocratique gabonais (Gabonese Democratic Party) (PDG) 124, 125, 127, 128, 129, 236
parties 23, 49, 125, 145, 151, 152, 223, 238, 272, 284, 290, 334, 360, 363, 375, 460, 465, 470, 471, 502, 539, 576. *See also* nightclubs; social events and celebrations
    backyard/slumyard parties 338, 387-8, 390, 420, 508
    birthday parties and celebrations 43, 107, 148, 428, 548, 573, 576
    coronation parties 43
    inkera 294
    'kitchen party' 55
    'tea parties' 542
Paseli Brothers (band) 24
Passy La Noblesse 66
patenge 132, 396
patenge drum 396. *See also* drums; square drum
Pathé Records 524
pati drum 36, 89, 90, 341. *See also* drums; snare drum
patriotism/patriotic songs 71, 90, 201, 202
PaxAfro (band) 103
PCR. *See* Communist Party of Réunion
PDG. *See* Parti démocratique gabonais (Gabonese Democratic Party)
Peace, The (band) 180
Peacocks, The (group) 224, 467
'Peanut Butter' (song) 25
pecto 543-4
pedal organ 109, 344, 388
pedal steel guitar 145, 146, 147, 149. *See also* guitar
Pee Froiss (group) 261
Peel, John (DJ) 434
peg drum 153, 159, 161. *See also asivui*; drums
'Peka' (song) 344
pekee (musical instrument) 70. *See also* shakers
Pekiwe, Taurai and the Legal Lions (band) 103
Pène, Omar 416
Pengaudzoke (group) 522
penny whistle/pennywhistle 205, 358-61, 389, 420, 466. *See also* flute
People's Choice (group) 368
'People's Club' (song) 218
Pepe, Anice 572
Pepera, Kwesi 205, 458
Pereira, Euclides Fontes 508
Perna, Martín 17
Pernambuco, Joana 338
Perry, Lee 'Scratch' 488
Persée, Patrick 380
Persian Gulf 28, 524
'Personally' (song) 26
Peter na Lepet (Peter Johnson) 163
Peters, Clarence 448
Peters, S.S. 467
Peters, Sir Shina 325, 448
Peterson Mutebi and the Tames (band) 57
Petit Pays (singer) 372
Pfumo, Fany 404, 405
'Phambili siyaya' (song) 352
Philips Records 218, 323
Phiri, Francis (Lawi) 26
Phiri, Jackson 498
Phiri, Ray 296
Phiri, Saleta 25
Phiri, Stain 25
Phonodisc Records 44
Phuka, Morson 24-5
Phura (*ma/gaisa* artist) 368
Phuzeshukela (John Bengu) 410
Phyno (rapper and singer) 219
piano 54, 78, 80, 108, 112, 124, 140, 167, 205, 300, 301, 388, 436, 477, 502. *See also fiyano*
piano accordion 343, 344. *See also* accordion
piano, electric 12, 13
Piasah (highlife artist) 458
Pickett, Wilson 31, 115, 208
pickup (music technology) 322
Pierre, Amédée 584
Pierrot troupes 106
Pietersen, Ozzmzulu 465
piker (musical instrument) 379. *See also* idiophone
Pilane, France 360
Piliso, Ntemi 420, 540
Pinheiro, Paulino 476
Pino, Geraldo 12, 31
Pinodo, Bob 209, 212
Pinodo, Bob & His Sound Casters 32
Pio Macheka and The Black-Ites (band) 103
Pitch Black Follies (troupe) 300, 301, 389, 541-2
Pitcho (rapper) 270

Index

Placid Muhinder (hip-hop artist) 270
Plange, Stan 211
Plantashun Boyz (group) 256
pipes (as musical instrument)
 plastic drainage pipes 55
 plastic pipe with a funnel 306
 plastic water pipes 365
plantation workers 22, 379, 393, 396, 551
Platters, The (group) 24
Play for Me (album) 324
Player for Life (album) 229
Playhouse Company 302
Playhouse Opera (theatre: Durban, South Africa) 39
plena 509
PNDC. *See* Provisional National Defence Council
POC (Prophets of the City) (group) 265
'Pog Official' (song) 239
POK (record label) 69
Police Band (group) 540
Police Orchestra (Ethiopia) 93, 141, 142
Polisario Front 456, 545
political Afrobeat 14–15, 17–18
political events and rallies 207, 244, 246, 294, 302, 349, 364, 365, 411, 425–7, 447, 455, 546, 586. *See also* election campaigns and rallies; official events and ceremonies
politics and political songs 173, 227, 241, 245–6, 249–51, 261–2, 268, 269–70, 273, 281, 346, 372, 377, 380, 385, 406, 434, 463, 480, 485, 508, 509, 510, 517. *See also* apartheid/anti-apartheid; election campaigns and rallies; nationalism; nationalization; protest songs
polka 79, 380
'Poll Tax' (song) 302
Polo, Segeo 372
Polydor Records 53, 223
Polygram (record label) 208, 218, 440, 580
Pongo Rista (MC) 230
pop jazz 308
pop music 20, 31, 87, 95, 125, 219, 313–14, 405, 464, 495, 497, 503. *See also* Afropop/Afro pop/Afro-pop; *kidandali*; Naija pop; Ndebele pop; *zikiri*
Poppettes, The (band) 367
Pops Mohammed (multi-instrumentalist) 288
Poro people 433
Porquet, Bruno 585
Portugal 248, 337, 339, 436, 453, 473, 474, 508, 510
 Greater Lisbon area 338, 339, 340
 Lisbon 97, 338, 348, 437, 508
Positive Black Soul (group) 227, 261
Positive Force (band) 17
Positive Power (group) 272
Potgieter, Nic 81
Pothole (band) 194
Poun (rock musician) 192
power ballads 191–2
Poxi Presha (Prechard Pouka Olang) 245, 246
Pozo, Omanhene 211
P. Postman (Percy Djedje) 488
PPS the Writah (rapper) 262
praise music and songs 12, 43, 122, 124, 126, 127, 168, 171, 175–6, 218, 244, 262, 295, 311, 321, 324, 382, 385, 414, 415, 416, 421, 425, 426, 427, 467, 514, 554, 559, 561, 574, 575–6. *See also izibongo*; *madhee/madhu/madh*; *medeh*; *oríki*; *sákárá/sakara*; *zikiri*
Praye (band) 211
Preacher Levi (MC) 482
'Premier Gaou' (song) 587
premprensua (musical instrument) 36. *See also* lamellophone
Presley, Elvis 142, 208, 346
Presley, Kagiso 229
Preston, Denis 423
Prezzo (Jackson Ngechu Makini) 246
Prim and Propa (duo) 272
Prince Adekunle & His Western Brothers (band) 325
Prince Patrice 66
Prince Zoetaba (musician) 533
Princess Farida (dancer) 99–100
Princess Magogo kaDinizulu (opera) 39
Princes Theatre (London) 421
Proclamation R26 of 1965 (South Africa) 423
Prodical (MC) (Joseph Nana Ofori) 276
Produções 1001 (record label) 404
Produções Golo (record label) 404
Professeur (album) 584
Professional Seagulls (band) 224
Professor Jay (hip-hop artist) 85
progressive rock 208
Promedia 240
'Promesses de caméléon' (song) 480
Promzy (MC) (Emmanuel Ababio) 276
propaganda songs 103
Prophets of the City (POC) (group) 265
protest songs 100–1, 250–1, 320, 338, 405, 422, 444. *See also* nationalism; *nidal*; politics and political songs; Tuareg guitar music
ProVerb (hip-hop artist) 288
proverbs 43, 44, 45, 48, 53, 113, 276, 281, 324, 330, 468
Provisional National Defence Council (PNDC) (Ghana) 208
prudenica 122
Pryze, Narcisse 372
Pryze, Njorheur 372
P-Side (group) 229, 230
P-Square (duo) 123, 176, 256, 448
Psychedelic Aliens (Magic Aliens) (band) 31, 32, 208
psychedelic rock 31, 143, 180, 525, 566
Psychedelic Six (band) 31
Public Enemy (group) 84, 249, 261
Puerto Rico 137
Pukwana, Dudu 32, 423
Pullo, Buzu Dan 259
Punu people 240

qanbus (musical instrument). *See gambus/qanbus*
qanun (musical instrument) 523, 524, 525, 527. *See also* zither
qaraami 198, 201, 202
Qarshe, Cabdullahi 197, 198
qasidah 578
Qbio (MC) (Tumelo Segopa) 230
qhum music 291
Q-Masters (band) 32
Quad Sisters, The (group) 420
quadrille 380, 475, 504
Quainoo, Margaret 114
Quame, Nana (highlife artist) 211
Quaye, Asabre 33
Quaye, Jeff 211
Queen Jane (*kikuyu* artist) 71
Queen Latifah (rapper) 272, 483
Quejas, Fernando 437
quicksteps 108, 109, 205, 206
Quintette Guinéenne 385
Quophi, Okyeame (Daniel Kofi Amoateng) 274–5
Qur'an 500, 555, 556

R&B. *See* rhythm and blues
Raaboon (group) 237, 238
Rabadaba (*luga flow* artist) 273
Rabemanantsoa, Naka 53
Rachabane, Barney 296
Rachel (singer) 87
Racinetatane (group) 505
Radebe, Mark 40
Radebe's Trio 300
Radek Supreme (hip-hop artist) 269
radio 20, 317, 328, 355, 491, 504, 523, 577
 Angola 334, 338, 476, 508
 Botswana 229, 231, 232, 290, 356
 Burkina Faso 531
 Cabo Verde 106
 Cameroon 66, 77, 234, 373
 Congo, Democratic Republic of the 269, 497
 Côte d'Ivoire 123, 479, 480
 Djibouti 166
 Gabon 237, 241
 Ghana 114, 207–8, 209, 210, 211, 212, 276
 Kenya 71, 244, 246, 247, 460
 Madagascar 191, 282, 543
 Malawi 308, 426, 484
 Mali 557, 575
 Mozambique 249, 402, 403, 404
 Namibia 366, 368, 513
 Netherlands 97
 Nigeria 171, 174, 176, 177, 254, 259, 323
 Rwanda 296
 Senegal 22, 23–4, 261, 263, 414, 416
 Sierra Leone 400
 Somalia 197, 198, 199, 200
 South Africa 80, 81, 194, 196, 285, 286, 287, 301, 344, 349, 350, 418, 419, 422, 487, 489, 543
 Tanzania 85, 86, 428, 439, 440, 441, 443, 526
 UK 396
 US 29, 540
 Zambia 332, 566, 567
 Zanzibar 568, 569
 Zimbabwe 103, 450
Radio 5 287
Radio Bantu 301, 302, 464, 513
Radio Bop 285
Radio Botswana 2 (RB2) 229, 231, 290
Radio Club of Mozambique 403
Radio Congo Belge 497
Radio Congolia 497
Radio Djibouti 166
Radio Freedom 177, 259
Radio Hargeysa 197
Radio Istiqama 569
Radio Kagnew 537
Radio Kalahari Orkes (group) 82

619

Index

Radio Laurenco Marques 24
Radio Malawi 24
Radio Mali 575
Radio Maria 569
Radio Micheweni 569
Radio Mozambique/Mocambique 405
Radio Muqdisho 197, 200
Rádio Nacional de Angola 338, 508
Radio One 85
Rádio Reparadora do Bié (record label). *See* Fadiang (record label)
Radio Sesotho 344
'radio songs' 328
Radio Tanzania Dar es Salaam (RTD) 440, 441
Radio Tisdas Sessions, The (album) 546
Radio Triunfo 404
Radio Xhosa 287
Radio Zulu 287
Raeburn, Michael 32
raga 276
Rag-a-Jazzbo (band) 205
ragamuffin *apala* 45
ragga 95, 229, 235, 245, 286, 470, 483, 567, 568
ragga drum 471. *See also* drums
raggamuffin music. *See* ragga
ragtime 38, 205, 206, 298, 299, 553
raï 27, 545
Rail Band 56, 312, 575
Rainbow (band) 190
'Rainy Season' (song) 177
Rajab Suleiman and Kithara (group) 527
Rajab, Marijani 441
Rajoro, Justin 53
Rakers (band) 206
Rakotofiringa, Naly 53
Ralf (musician) 439
Rama B (group) 568
Ramadan/Ramadhan 43, 75, 145, 431
Ramanisum, Alain 505
Ramarokoto (*ba gasy* artist) 53
Ramco Records 230
Rameau et Jacquy Lobbe Lobbe (duo) 370
RAMfest (musical festival: South Africa) 195
Ramilison (*hira gasy* artist) 281
ramogi 69
Ramogi, George and C.K. Dumbe Dumbe Jazz Band 69
Ranarivelo, Ranaivo 53
Rancho Boys (band) 342
Ranger, Terence Osborn 74
Rankgomo, Michael (Dr. Mickey) 357
Ranks, Shabba 352, 483
Ranku, Lucas 'Lucky' 423
Ransome-Kuti, Fela. *See* Anikulapo-Kuti, Fela
Ransome-Kuti, Funmilayo 15
Raolifahanana, Fredy 53
rap 28, 57, 84, 85–6, 98, 123, 138, 149, 170, 176, 225, 226, 228, 234–5, 237–8, 243, 258, 265, 267, 274, 275, 348, 349, 442, 448, 459, 568, 574. *See also* GH rap; Hausa rap; hip-hop; *taarap*; zef-rap
Rap 'Em (TV show) 245
Rap Activity Jam (radio program) 230, 286
Rap Blast (radio pogram) 229
rap *bwiti* 240
Rap Face (André Cardoso) 249
Rap Galsen (movement) 85

rap galsen. *See* hip-hop: in Senegal
rap ikoku 240
rap jazz 308
Rap Kamer. *See* hip-hop: in Cameroon
Rap Mboa. *See* hip-hop: in Cameroon
Rap Priest (Obrafour) 210, 276, 277
Rap Sofo (Obrafour) 210, 276, 277
Rap'Adio (group) 261
Raphael & Pele (duo) 368
rapid intervention music 251–2
Ras Cool Band 366
Ras Kimono(reggae artist) 483
Ras Mélé (group) 380
Ras Natty Baby (reggae artist) 505
Ras Kente (reggae artist) 482
Ras Queysen (reggae artist) 483
Ras Sheehama (singer) 513
Ras Tonto (reggae artist) 482
Rash (band) 188
Rashid, Madier 252
rasp (musical instrument). *See ferro*
Rastafarianism 477, 478, 482, 485, 487, 489, 505, 514
Rathebe, Dolly 419, 420
Ratianarivo, Andrianary 53
Ratianarivo, Paul 53
Ratsimbazafy, Henri 504
rattle (musical instrument) 34–5, 36, 55, 65, 291, 322, 370, 433, 434, 455, 516. *See also* ankle/foot bells and rattles; *awaasa*; *axatse*; *fikhuli*; *frafra*; *luhengele/luengele*; *maracas*; *saxi*; *segure*; *sèkèrè/sekere/sè.kè.rè*; *shû' shû'*
ravann (musical instrument) 504. *See also* drums
Raven in Flesh (band) 186
Rawlings, J.J. 208, 210
'Rayuwa Cikin Kunci' (song) 259
razor wire dance 521
Razzmatazz Night Club (Johannesburg, South Africa) 286
RB2 (radio station). *See* Radio Botswana 2
RBC. *See* Rhodesian Broadcasting Corporation
RCA Records 301
Reagan, Ronald 15
Real Elements, The (band) 26
Real Kwasa Melody (group) 356
Real Sounds, The (group) 450, 498, 520
Real Unity Stars (group) 516
Rebirth Brass Band of New Orleans 92
rebita 432, 475–7, 507, 510
Rebita (record label) 334, 476
record clubs (in Dakar) 23
Red Bull (company) 265
red *mbumba* 426, 427
Red Spot (band) 206
Red Stars (band) 31
Redda, Tewelde 537, 538
Redding, Otis 208
reel (dance) 107
Reeves, Jim 450
Regard sur le passé (album) 385
reggae 28, 64, 84, 86, 95, 102, 121, 144, 161, 208, 235, 257, 276, 337, 372, 380, 422, 439, 442, 448, 497, 505, 513, 547, 567, 568, 574, 583
in Côte d'Ivoire 479–81
in Ghana 482–4
in Malawi 484–6
in South Africa 486–90

in Sub-Saharan Africa 477–9
Reggae Strong For Peace (concert: Johannesburg, 1991) 488
reggae-highlife 208
'Regina' (song) 420–1
Regional Orchestre de Kayes 386
Reinalda, Zeca di Nha 152
reinihira 280
Relate Soul (group) 269
Remedies, The (group) 256
Renegades (photographic exhibition: Marshall) 186
Rentoz, Emmanuel 33, 138
Repercussions (TV series) 346
República do Pandza (group) 406, 473
Reskape (rapper) 262, 263
restaurants and cafes 60, 121, 286, 502. *See also* bars and taverns; hotels; *maquis*
Resurrection (band) 191
Retribution Denied (band) 195
Réunion. *See* France: Réunion
Reverbnation (website) 232
Revolution (duo) 288
Rezant, Peter 301, 541
Rhodes Music Radio 285
Rhodes University (Grahamstown, South Africa) 285
Rhodesia. *See* Zambia; Zimbabwe
Rhodesian Broadcasting Corporation (RBC) 320
rhumba. *See* rumba
rhythm and blues (R&B) 57, 84, 87, 91, 161, 170, 229, 241, 245, 254, 257, 267, 268, 359, 368, 442, 448, 477, 495, 497, 567, 568
Rhythm Aces (band) 206
rhythm guitar 13, 25, 68, 70, 78, 217, 285, 324, 361, 370, 414–15, 420, 429, 432, 441, 462, 480, 492, 547, 567. *See also* guitar
Rhythm Kings (troupe) 301, 389
Rhythm of the Saints (album) 212
Ribeiro, Abeeku (The Witch Doctor) 275
Richard, Epée Mbende & Uvocot-Jazz (group) 370
Richie (hiplife artist) 276
Rico Single (*zenji flava* artist) 568
riel 553
Rihanna (singer) 257
rika (musical instrument) 523. *See also* tambourine
R'Imbosa (ensemble) 54
Ritchie, Lionel 352
rites of passage 151, 157, 158, 240, 308, 358, 383, 428, 430, 454, 568, 570. *See also* rituals, ceremonies and practices
Ritmos de Dança Moçambicanos (album) 405
rituals, ceremonies and practices 12, 16, 92, 128, 162, 279, 294, 295, 316, 326, 330–1, 358, 379, 517, 528, 543, 555. *See also* rites of passage
RJ Kanyera 270
Road Runners, The (band) 31
Roba (hip-hop artist) 245
Robert, David 443
Roberts, John Storm 28, 30
Rocha, Dionísio 509
Rochereau, Tabu Ley (singer-songwriter) 451, 493, 494

620

Index

rock 28, 64, 82, 183, 324, 380, 456, 566, 578, 580. *See also* zamrock
student rock bands 31–2
rock 'n' roll 31, 102, 140, 142, 208, 346, 450, 537, 566
Rock No Rio Festival (Catumbela, Angola) 183
Rockets, The (group) 537
rock-*mbalax* 416
rocksteady 477
Rockstone, Reggie (Reginald Yaw Asante Ossei) 210, 273, 275, 276
Rodgers All Stars Recording Studio (Awka) 218
Rodrigues Junior, Manuel António (Nino Ndongo) 507
Roger M (hip-hop artist) 272
Rogers Club (Ghana) 107–8
Rogie, S.E. (Sooliman Ernest) 467, 586
Rogosin, Lionel 421
Roha Band 143
Roland keyboard 463
rollin (musical instrument) 46, 47. *See also* drums
Rolling Stones, The (band) 31, 566
Rollins, Sonny 13
Romule (*ba gasy* artist) 53
Root of David (band) 482
Roots (Haley) 563
Roots (TV series) 422, 563
Roots Anabo (band) 482
roots reggae 478, 480, 482, 484, 487
Roots, The (band) 25
'Rosa' (song) 453
Rossy (pop singer) 503
Rouget, Gilbert 330, 382
Rough Guide CD series 29
rouleur (musical instrument) 379. *See also* bass drum; drums
Royal African Corps 9
RT Production House 67
RTD. *See* Radio Tanzania Dar es Salaam
RTP Records 521
Rudeboy Paul (DJ) (Paul Mnisi) 286, 287
Rudimentals, The (band) 488
rumba 57, 61, 69, 75, 127, 137, 161, 226, 267, 268, 320, 332, 333, 342, 358, 382, 392, 399, 418, 427, 442, 446, 452, 476, **490–500**, 509, 522, 580, 581. *See also* Congolese *rumba*; *muziki wa dansi*; *rumba* (Volume IX, *Caribbean and Latin America*); *soukouss*
in Kenya 497–8
in Zimbabwe 498–9
rumba museve. *See sungura*
Rumba, Jack 338
rumbira 521
Run DMC (group) 259
Ruyonga (hip-hop artist) 273
Rwanda 5, 294–6
Rwenzori Ballroom (Sheraton Kampala Hotel, Uganda) 272
Rwenzori Band 57

S3 (rapper) 270
Saad, Siti bint (singer) 524
Sabanoh 75 (band) 138, 433
sabar 143
sabar drum 22, 414–15, 416, 563. *See also* drums
sabaro drum 384. *See also* drums

SABC. *See* South African Broadcasting Corporation
sabon alkawari 173
Sabouk (group) 380
Sacko, Bouba 56, 312
Sacko, Fanta 56
Sacraphyx (band) 194
Sadla Jazz Band 75
Safari Sound Band 99
Saga, Douk (Stephane Hamidou Doukouré) 120–1, 122
'Sagacité' (song) 120, 122
Saggy Saggila (Richard Siluma) 488
Sahara Desert 529, 545–6
Saharawi revolutionary song. *See nidal*
Saharwai people 430, 431, 456
Sahel region 545, 575
Sahondrafinina (*hira gasy* artist) 281
Sahoue 572
Sahra Halgan Trio, The 200
Saïk1ri (rapper) 241
sailor's hornpipe 365
sailors/seamen 22, 35, 109 204, 205, 217, 222, 321, 345, 393, 396, 453, 466–7, 468, 469
St. Augustine (highlife artist) 219
St. Mary's Church (Accra, Ghana), Mass (Anglican) Sunday School Choir 107
St. Peter's Hostel Choir 300
Saint Paul's Band 102
Saka-Saka (band) 33
Sakalava people 503
sákárà/sakara 43, 47–8, 221, **500–1**. *See also* praise music and songs
sákárà/sakara drum 146, 147. *See also* drums
Sakkwato, Salihu Jankidi 169
Salaam (album) 261
Salaam, Ellis 482
Salaam's Cultural Imani Group 212
Salah, Baba (guitarist) 576, 578
salegy **501–3**
Saleh J (hip-hop artist) 84
Salem Tradition (group) 380
Sall, Racine 575
Sally (*shambo* artist) 514
Salomon (*ba gasy* artist) 53
salsa 22, 91, 137, 236, 330, 442, 495, 497, 578. *See also* Afro-Cuban music: in Senegal
salsa mbalax 23, 416
Salt (band) 32
Saltpond Trio 112
salvas 528
SAMA. *See* South African Music Awards
Samaké, Ba Ka Bouraïma 576
Samar (band) 191
Samatar, Xasan Aadan 199
samba 137, 161, 216, 342, 476, 508, 509
samba drum 46, 321–2, 467. *See also* drums
Samba Mapangala and Orchestra Virunga 497, 525
sambuna. *See batuque/batuko*
Samia people 364
Samini, Emmanuel (Batman Samini) 211, 276, 483
samples 228, 238, 251, 267, 272
Samuel, Eke 370
Samuele (*shambo* artist) 514

sana kissanje (musical instrument) 334. *See also* lamellophone
Sandji, Boro 121
sanduku (musical instrument) 336. *See also* box-bass
Sanekoye (band) 33
Sangalukani Jazz Band 308, 309
Sangaré, Oumou 212, 313, 557, 558, 578
'Sangaya' (song) 173
Sango, Bobo 120
Santa Bárbara (group) 476
Santana (band) 31, 208
Santana (Ugandan hip-hop artist) 273
Santos Junior 510
Santos Júnior, Norberto 403
'Sanya Zobe' (song) 177
sanza (musical instrument) 66, 440. *See also* idiophone
São Tomé and Príncipe 8, 131, 337, 338, 339, 477
S.A.P.E. *See* Société des Ambianceurs et des Personnes Elégantes
sapeurs 120
Sapitwa (group) 358
Sar, Jean Pierre 65, 67
Sarakasi Trust 246
'Sarie Marais' (song) 82
Sarkodie (hip-hop artist) 20, 50, 51, 209, 277
Sasamaso (band) 191
sati (musical instrumnet) 379. *See also* drums
SATMA. *See* South African Traditional Music Association
Saudi Arabia 44
Saul, Pinise 423
sauté-mouton 122
Sauti ya Tanzania Zanzibar (radio station) 569
Savage, Tiwa 448, 449
Savannah Band 58
Savuka (band) 32
Sawa people 369, 370
Sawaaba Soundz (band) 32, 208
'Sawale' (song) 219
sawt 524
sax jive 359, 360, 361, 420, 421, 424, 543
saxi (musical instrument) 475. *See also* rattle
saxophone 66, 94, 124, 145, 146, 147, 199, 359, 360, 367, 385, 414–15, 420, 441, 456, 512, 513, 555, 563. *See also* alto saxophone; baritone saxophone; tenor saxophone
Sayiba, Haralu 516
Sayuni Evangelical Choir 443
Scar (band) 182
Scar (MC) 230, 231
school concerts 107, 108, 110, 343
school halls 82, 465, 553
school sports 586
schottische. *See* settees/schottische
SCIM. *See* Soul Candi Institute of Music
SCOA (trading company) 113
Scorpion Records 138
Scorpions (choir) 301
Scorpions (rock band) 190
Scotchi Beni (band) 74, 75
Scottishes marching band 360
scraper (musical instrument) 583, 586, 587. *See also dikanza*; *guiro*
Scud (group) 429

621

Index

sebene/seben 491, 495, 496, 519
Sebitlo, Bruce 'Dope' 289
Sebunya, Eria 59
Seck, Mansour 559
Seck, Thione 416
Seck, Wally B. 416
séélí (musical instrument) 555, 556. *See also* cymbals
Seema, Puseletso 344
séga 182, 379, 502, **503–7**
séga conga 505
séga love 505
séga maloya 380
séga mambo 505
séga pop 505
séga reggae 439
séga tambour 438
séga typique 438
'Segarin Kano' (song) 259
segere 526
Segere Original (group) 526
seggae 380, 505
Segid, Ateweberhan 537
Segopa, Henry Tshepo (AK) 230
Segopa, Tumelo (Qbio) 230
segure (musical instrument) 46. *See also* rattle; *sèkèrè/sekere/sè.kè.rè*
Sehatra Ba Gasy (association) 54
Seismic (band) 188
Sekamatte, Grace 58, 59
Seke, Naison 24
sèkèrè/sekere/sè.kè.rè (musical instrument) 13, 43, 147, 223, 322, 323, 500, 555. *See also* rattle; *segure*
Sekondi Nanshamak (band) 205
Sekyedumasi Gospel Singers 210
'Selestina Juma' (song) 69
Selolwane, John Longwe 24
Semakula, Mesach 58, 59, 335
semba 334, 338, 340, 347, 348, 406, 432, **507–12**
Semba Masters (group) 476, 510
Semba Tropical (group) 510
Semba, Carlitos 510
Semedo, Gil 97, 340
Semenya, Caiphus 28, 423
Semi Lopi (*gaita* artist) 152
Sempre a Subir (TV show) 348
Sen Kumpë (group) 261
Senegal 8, 22–4, 64, 179, 226–7, 239, 260–3, 311, 315, 317, 383, 386, 414, 415, 416, 417, 456, 478, 491, 558, 559, 560, 561
  Casamance 561, 562, 563
  Dakar 8, 19, 22, 23, 96, 261, 318, 414, 416
  Dakar, Medina 261
Senegambia 310, 311, 386, 395, 414–17, 562. *See also* Gambia; Senegal
Sengo, Tony 58
senima 179
Senkebejje, Tony 58
Senkubuge, Charles James 58
Sensational Wulomei (group) 212, 346
Sento, 'Vee' Odirile 357
Sentso, Wilfred 541
Senyah, Jimmy 138
Senyaka (rapper) 352
seprewa/seprerewa (musical instrument) 205, 457, 458, 459, 468. *See also* harp lute
'Septembre noir' (song) 269

Serah, Kokumo 556
Seraphim Church 47–8, 91, 323
serenda 320
Serenje Kalindula Band (Kalindula Kings) 332, 333
seron (musical instrument). *See soron/seron*
servis kabaré 379–80
servis kaf 379–80
servis malgas 379–80
Set-son & The Mighty Dreads (group) 513
Set-son, Wahengo 512
Setswana people 356
Setswana traditional music 182
settees/schottische 79, 444
'Sevena Nhamo Ichanya' (song) 320
Sewanyana, Herman 58
Sewava, Jeff 58
Sewer, Kitu 246
'Sexual Healing' (song) 245
Seychelles 3, 438–9, 503, 504, 505, 517–18
Seydonie Production 533
Shaba (Kabiru Shariff) 177
Shabalala, Joseph 296
Shaban, Maalim 524
Shabani Records 269
Shades (band) 31
Shago, Muhammadu 169
'Shake Bodi' (song) 255
shake wase 400, 434
shakers (musical instrument) 54, 99, 121, 158, 291, 309, 319, 433, 455, 492, 587. *See also* assan; chisekele; hosho shakers; *kayamb*; *pekee*
Shakila (singer) 526
Shakur, Tupac 84
Shaky (Pius Aloyo) 581
Shalawambe (band) 332
Shallah, Feeno 230
shambo **512–16**
shangara 103
Shangara Jive (band) 103
Shango Babies (band) 32
Shareero (band) 199
Sharifai, Sadi Sidi 173
Shariff, Kabiru (Shaba) 177
Sharing Youth (group) 272
Sharks (band) 191
Sharmila (singer) 526
Shata, Mamman 171
shebeens 284, 287, 360, 367, 420, 553. *See also* bars and taverns; *tej bets*; *tombo* bars
sheek-sheek (musical instrument) 394. *See also* maracas; rattle
Sheika, Mohammed 463
shellela (musical instrument) 94. *See also* horn
Sherbro-Mende people 399
Sheriff Ghale (reggae artist) 483
Sheriff, Hassan M. 259
Shikow FemiOne (rapper) 246
shimambo 306
Shime Kuokoana (group) 337, 526
Shinamania/Afro-Jùjú Series 2 (album) 325
shiremba 306
Shoki Shoki (album) 17
Shona people 100–1, 102, 103, 450, 459, 520, 521, 540
'Shoot Them Before They Grow' (song) 94
Shoprite Zambia Hit Parade (album) 333
Short Dog (MC) 230

Short Gun (*zenji flava* artist) 568
Shorty (singer) 137
Showcase (TV series) 115
shũ' shũ' (musical instrument) 65. *See also* rattle
Shuffering and Shmiling (album) 15
shuffle 167
Shusho, Christina 443
Shwi Nomtekhala (duo) 411
Si'ya Po'ossi XI (group) 236–7, 238
Sialo Claretian missionaries 395
Sibanda, Marko 521
Sibane Semaswati (group) 551
sibhaca 551
Sibika, Zynne (DJ Vetkoek/Mahoota) 289
side drum. *See* snare drum
Sidi, Ibrahim Autan 175
Sidibé, Coumba 557
Sidibé, Kon Kan Kon Siata 558
Sidonie, Toubet 65
Sierra Leone 8, 9, 31–2, 46–7, 48, 112, 132, 135, 138, 159, 162–4, 205, 221, 222, 321, 345, 391, 392–3, 396, 398–401, 432–5, 466, 467
  Freetown 8, 31, 132, 133, 135, 153, 160, 161, 391–2, 393, 395, 396, 398, 399, 432–3, 467, 469, 482
sigoma 502
Sikinde, ngoma ya ukae 454–5
sikko (musical instrument). *See assiko/sikko*
sikuti. *See isukuti/isikuti/esukuti*
Sikwane, Thalo (DJ Fresh) 285, 287, 288, 290
sikyi 35, 468
'Sikyi Highlife' (song) 35, 458
silent films 108, 205
sililí (musical instrument) 364. *See also* fiddle
Siluma, Richard 487, 488
Silver, Horace 13
Silvera, Edmund 60–1
Simas, Antero 437
simba (musical instrument) 430. *See also* drums
Simbangoma Band 58
simbing/simbi (musical instrument) 383–4. *See also* harp
Simelane, Senzo 292
Simeon, Wahesh 482
Simon Bisbi Clan (hip-hop artist) 261
Simon, Paul 32, 212, 296, 417, 450
Simonelli, Victor 290
Simoni, Boetie 513
simpa 35, 47, 161, **516–17**
Sina Chuki (group) 337
sindimba 442
Sinetre, Charles 485
Sinewave Productions 230
Singer (record label) 300, 301
sinhun (musical instrument) 535, 536, 572. *See also* drums
Sinimo, Abdi (Cabdi Deeqsi) 165, 197, 198
sinjonjo 308
Sir Warrior (highlife artist) 216, 219
Sisqo (singer) 256
Sissi Dipoko (singer) 372
Sissòko, Ba Zoumana 386
Sissoko, Ballake 313, 563
Sissoko, Menseng 562
Sista Coumbis (rapper) 262
Sista Dia (rapper) 262

622

Index

Sista Joyce (hip-hop artist)   261
Sister Fa (rapper)   262
Sister P (hip-hop artist)   85, 87
Sister Phumi (reggae artist)   488
Sithole, Jonah   102, 103
siyomboka   332, 333
'Size Nine' (song)   567
SJ (*zenji flava* artist)   569
ska   477, 484, 489
skank   477, 482
Skepta (rapper)   257
Skinflint (band)   182, 186, 187, 188
Sklair, Sam   540
'Skokiaan/Happy Africa' (song)   540, 542
Skotchi Jazz Band   75
Skyforger (band)   182
Skylarks, The (South African vocal group)   420
Skype   180
slam   239
Slam Cup (Libreville, Gabon)   239
slave beat   182
slaves   46, 74, 79, 132, 133, 151, 154, 157, 161, 162, 182, 222, 391, 393, 395, 398–9, 431, 435, 438, 453, 467, 482, 483, 490, 504, 507, 517, 527, 528
Slaves, The (band)   488
Slim Busterr (hiplife artist)   211, 483
slit drum   235. *See also* drums; *inkali*; *ndu'*; woodblock/wood block
Slizer (singer)   356, 357
Slizer Creations (group)   357
slumyards   387–8, 389, 390, 420. *See also mapanes* (slums)
Slush (singer)   366
Sly and the Family Stone (band)   31, 208
Sly Dennis   482
Small, Millicent 'Millie'   482, 484
Smani, Ahmed/Hamed   532, 534
smanjemanje   308, 427
Smart Abbey   110
Smart Nkansah (highlife artist)   208
smartphones. *See* cell phones/mobile phones/smartphones
Smilin' Osei (highlife artist)   212
Smirnoff Party Mix, The (radio program)   290
Smockey (hip-hop artist)   532, 533, 534
snare drum   9, 14, 75–6, 91, 92, 516. *See also caixa*; drums; *pati* drum
SNM. *See* Somali National Movement
Snoop Dogg (rapper)   176, 259, 272
Snowy Hadebe and Company (group)   541
SNUA. *See* Swaziland National Umbholoho Association
SO2 Squad, The (band)   482
sobom   34
soca   28, 137, 348, 431
Sochira (album)   483
social clubs   43, 81, 90, 107–8, 110–11, 153, 313, 525–6, 537. *See also* clubs
social events and celebrations   38, 43, 48, 53, 76, 107, 125, 131, 147–8, 153, 160, 179, 223, 294, 297–8, 316, 318, 338, 344, 378, 460, 464, 465, 501, 539, 543, 549, 553, 573, 574. *See also* festivals; parties; rites of passage; rituals, ceremonies and practices; weddings
social halls   439, 526. *See also* township halls

social media   19, 21, 30, 173, 174, 180, 249. *See also* Facebook; Internet; YouTube
Société des Ambianceurs et des Personnes Elégantes (Society of Tastemakers and Elegant People) (S.A.P.E.)   120
Soga, Tiyo   39
sogo (musical instrument)   153. *See also* drums
Soki, Emile   494
Soki, Maxim   494
sokwe/soukwé   **517–18**
soldiers   9–10, 22, 46, 101, 103, 204, 206, 342, 376, 444, 453, 480, 482, 520–1. *See also* war
Solika (ensemble)   54
Sollo, Jake   32
Solo Beton (singer)   120, 121
Solo Thang (hip-hop artist)   85
Solo, Jake   138
Soloman, Ayi   482
Solven Whistlers (group)   360
Somali blues   165
Somali National Movement (SNM)   200
Somali people   49
Somalia   5, 6, 74, 164–6, 197–202, 525
    Boorame   197
    Hargeysa   198, 199
    Kismayu   74
    Muqdisho/Mogadishu   6, 198, 199
Somana, Lawi   356
'Sometimes I Wonder' (song)   25
son   22, 23, 226, 440, 491, 492, 493, 520
Sondo, Sonny   450
Songhai people   529
Sonko, Charles   57, 272
Sonko, Freda   272
sonobete   32. *See also* Afro-rock
Sontonga, Enoch Mankayi   39
Sony Music (record label)   289
Sophiatown Modern Jazz Club   419
Sorciers Noirs (group)   124
Sorizo, Luís   396
soron/seron (musical instrument)   384. *See also* harp lute
Sororenzou, Murenga   100
SOS (group)   337, 338, 340
Sosseh, Laba   23
Sotho Reggae (album)   486
'Soukou aka Nanan' (video)   584
Soukouss Stars (group)   519
soukouss   27, 55, 57, 91, 121, 227, 268, 269, 330, 338, 355, 358, 370, 442, 451, 452, 459, 466, 469, 491, 492, 495, 498, **518–20**, 566, 586, 587. *See also* Congolese *rumba*
soukwé. See sokwe/soukwé
soul   13, 31, 32, 57, 61, 161, 208, 254, 267, 285, 324, 422, 450, 516, 580
Soul Brothers (group)   422, 423
Soul Candi Institute of Music (SCIM)   288
Soul Candi Records   285
Soul Marrabenta (album)   251
soul *mbaqanga*   418, 422, 423
Soul to Soul (concert: Accra, 1971)   31, 208
Sound Forge (software)   259
sound recording and recordings   392. *See also* cassette recordings; compact disc (CD); compact disc-recordable (CD-R); digital versatile disc (DVD);

gramophone recordings; tape recordings
sound systems   482, 483
Soundcloud (website)   232
Soundcrafters (recording studio)   85
Soundmakers (group)   467
Sounds from the Other Side (album)   257
Sounds of Zambia (album)   333
South Africa   7, 20, 31, 32, 37–41, 69, 78–82, 94–5, 180, 181, 183, 186, 188, 194–6, 226, 227, 228–9, 232, 241, 248, 252, 265–7, 269, 284–9, 296–302, 308, 315, 319, 320, 336, 343–5, 348–53, 357, 358–61, 366, 367, 375, 376, 387–90, 403, 408–11, 418–24, 449, 450, 451, 453–4, 455, 464, 465, 470, 471, 473, 474, 478, 483, 486–9, 498, 513, 520, 521, 540–2, 543, 551, 552, 553, 566
    Bloemfontein   194
    Cape of Good Hope/Cape Colony   7, 155, 157
    Cape Town   7, 79, 153–6, 194, 228, 265, 266, 267, 287, 299, 435–6, 453, 488
    Cape Town, District Six   423
    Cape Town, Rose Street   155
    Dundee   197
    Durban   7, 194, 266, 267, 286, 287, 291, 297, 302, 390, 488–9
    Durban, Cato Manor   299
    Eastern Cape   302
    Empangeni   297
    Estcourt   297
    Gauteng   302
    Harrismith   297
    Johannesburg   7, 19, 194, 265, 266, 284, 285, 287, 291, 297, 299, 344, 349, 358, 360, 361, 387–8, 390, 420, 421, 450, 498
    Johannesburg, Alexandra Township   360
    Johannesburg, Orlando   388, 541
    Johannesburg, Sophiatown   419, 423, 541
    Johannesburg, Soweto   284, 287, 422, 486, 488
    Karoo   266
    Kimberley   420
    KwaZulu-Natal   286, 297, 298–9, 302, 488–9
    Ladysmith   297
    Mpumalanga province   297
    Newcastle   297
    Port Elizabeth   7, 266
    Port Shepstone   297
    Pretoria   7, 194
    Transvaal   374–5
    Western Cape   154, 157, 266
South African Broadcasting Corporation (SABC)   80, 81, 285, 287, 301–2, 419, 464, 487, 513
South African Music Awards (SAMA)   287, 411, 489
South African Traditional Music Association (SATMA)   297
South African Traditional Music Awards   265
South Cross (group)   269
South West African Broadcasting Corporation   513
Southeast Asia   184
Southern Africa   7, 181, 183, 225, 283–91, 374–5, 454, 521, 566. *See also specific nations*

623

Index

Soweto String Quartet 540
Soweto Uprising 422
Spain 340, 392
  Ibiza 287
Spanish guitar 392, 394, 395-6. *See also* guitar
speakeasies 343
Spearhead Band 485
Spencer, Nhelas 437
Spice FM (radio station) 569
spike lute. *See kurbu*
Splash (South African group) 95
Splash! (Cabo-Verdean group) 97, 340
spoon (as musical instrument) 135
Sprite Rap Activity Jam. *See Rap Activity Jam* (radio program)
square drum 132, 133, 135, 392, 394, 397. *See also cumbé* drum; drums; *kunké/kunki* drum; *patenge* drum
square tambourine 133, 135. *See also assiko/sikko; doblá; tamalin; tambali;* tambourine; *tan tuk*
Squire Addo (musician) 160
Ssebaduka, Christopher 328
Ssenkebejje, Tony 58
Ssesanga, Juliet 58
stadiums 97, 155, 158, 567, 576
Stagga (Ralph Williams III) 230
Stanley (Ou Stakes) 368
Stansfield, Lisa 352
Star 2000 (company) 67
Star Band 23, 415
Star Records 323
Stargazers (band) 206
S-Team (group) 235
'S'telel Ama Kanda' (song) 302
Stella (*ma/gaisa* artist) 368
Stephanie, Noumi 65
Steyn, Neels 80, 81
Sting (singer-songwriter) 32
stokvel (mutual savings society) 360
Storm, The (band) 103
Stormex (singer) 219
Strangers (band) 31
Stratovarius (band) 190
street festivals/parades 9, 10, 75, 76, 154, 155, 204, 299, 392, 528
street jibes 43, 45
street music 10, 299, 346, 468. *See mchiriku; Milo jazz*
Strength (band) 182
Strictly Hip-hop Live (radio program) 231
Struggling Islanders, The (group) 569
Student Christian Movement 552-3
Studio Mix (TV show) 287
Studios Kabako 269
Sub Pop Records 313
Sub-Saharan Africa 225-7, 328, 335-6, 431, 463, 477-8. *See also specific nations*
Sudan 4, 6, 166, 168, 174, 202
Sufi music. *See zikiri*
Sugar Babies Band 111, 222
Sugar Sugar (*sungura* musician) 522
Sugar, Ayitey (drummer) 345
Sugu (Mr. II/Joseph Mbilinyi) 85, 86, 87
sugudi/sukuti. *See isukuti/isikuti/esukuti*
'Suikerbossie' (song) 80
suku 317
Sukuma, Stewart (MC Roger/McRoger) 251, 406, 474

Sukura, Aaron Bebe 212, 459
Suleiman, Asha Abdo (Malika) 525
Sultan King (*zenji flava* artist) 568
Sultani (*beni* association) 74
Sumac, Yma 301
Summers, Donna 137, 209
Sun Ra (musician) 12
sungura 71, 103, 320, 406, 450, 498, 499, **520-3**
Sungura (record label) 69
Sungura Boys (group) 521
Sunjata Keita, Emperor of imperial Mali 310-11, 312, 313
Sunlife Band 482
Supa, Nasir Garba 169, 173
Super 11 (group) 530
Super Biton de Segou (group) 575
Super Combo (band) 32, 138
Super Djata Band 386
Super Eagles (group) 31, 416
Super Étoile de Dakar (group) 23, 416
Super Kaso (group) 25, 358
Super Onze (band) 578
Super Powers Band 356
Super Rail Band 386
Super Volcana (band) 440
Susan, Henrik 80, 81
Suso, Foday Musa 563
Suso, Jali Nyama 386, 563
Suzzy and Matt (band) 210
Swahili hip-hop 84-5
Swahili people 73, 74-5, 98, 521, 523, 524, 526, 570
Swahili Rap (album) 84
Swahili *rumba* 60, 521
swaito 349
Swaleh, Zuhura 429, 525
Swart, Valiant 82
Swazi Pride (group) 291
Swazi tribal (subgenre) 291
Swaziland 7, 291-2, 355, 375, 486, 551-2
  Bhunya 551
  Lavumisa 551
  Manzini 7, 291-2
  Mbabane 7, 291-2
  Mhlabanyatsi 551
  Simunya 551
  Siteki 551
Swaziland National Umbholoho Association (SNUA) 551, 552
Sweden 44, 58, 265
Swedru Twelve Apostles (group) 107
swing 58, 206, 359, 360, 361, 388, 389, 418, 420, 540, 541-2
Sydney (hiplife artist) 211
Syliphone (record label) 312, 385
Symmetric Orchestra 313
symphonic metal 190, 192
Synco Down Beats Orchestra 541
Synco Fans (troupe) 301, 541
syncro system 324
Syncro System Movement (album) 16, 324
synthesizer 50, 66, 94, 96, 138, 145, 147, 149, 170, 171, 172, 173, 202, 209, 228, 284, 295, 324, 338, 340, 372, 379, 422, 480, 486, 492, 494, 502, 505, 513, 517, 518, 523, 526, 555, 563, 575, 586. *See also* Casio synthesizer; midi synthesizer; Yamaha synthesizer
Szaabu Sounds (band) 32

'Ta khom, aa sao khoen ga !Nari-o' (song) 366
taarab 55, 76, 84, 336, 337, 429, 441, 454, **523-7**, 568, 569, 578. *See also zikiri*
taarap 569
taasu 415
Tabane, Philip 288
tabanka/tabanca **527-9**
Tabansi (record label) 138
tabla (musical instrument) 429. *See also* drums
Tabora Jazz (band) 440
Tabula, Joe 58, 335
'Tafsiri hii' (song) 245
Taghreft Tinariwen (band) 545, 546
Tagoe Sisters 210
Taifa, Ogara (John Ogara Odondi) 69
Taiwan 182
Taj Mahal (musician) 313
Taka (album) 177
takamba **529-31**, 545, 577, 578
Takashi (band) 212
takau 568
Takborsé TV (web portal) 534
takiboronsé/takboronsé **531-5**
Takrist-n-Akal (band) 546
Tala, André-Marie 64, 65, 372
talantalli 202
talking drum 9, 159, 235, 322. *See also* drums; *dùndún/dundun* drum; *gángán/gangan* drum; *tama* drum; *vimbuzza*
Talking Drums (group) 275
talmbat (musical instrument) 415. *See also* bass drum; drums
tama drum 22, 384, 414-15, 563. *See also* drums; talking drum
tamalin (musical instrument) 135. *See also* square tambourine; tambourine
'Tambala akamalira' (song) 425
tambali (musical instrument) 131, 134-5, 394-5, 396. *See also* square tambourine; tambourine
Tambaoga (musician) 103
tambourine 166, 198, 322, 337, 385. *See also* drums; *rika*; square tambourine
tan tuk (musical instrument) 134. *See also* square tambourine; tambourine
Tana in Rock (music festival: Madagascar) 192
tanbour (musical instrument) 504
Tandale Modern Theatre (group) 526
Tanganyika. *See* Tanzania
Tanganyika Broadcasting Service 40
Tanganyika, Lake 74
Tangent Records 346
tango 60, 108, 216
tango drum 395, 396. *See also* drums
Tanzania 4, 5, 7, 20, 21, 54-5, 68, 74, 75, 84-7, 95, 226, 269, 272, 331, 332, 337, 356, 358, 439-41, 442-3, 454-5, 491, 493, 497, 498, 520-1, 523, 524, 525-7, 578
  Arusha 442, 443
  Dar es Salaam 5, 19, 54, 55, 76, 84-5, 86, 428-9, 430, 440-1, 442, 443, 454, 525, 568, 569
  Dar es Salaam, Kinondoni 85
  Dar es Salaam, Masaki 85
  Dar es Salaam, Oysterbay 85
  Dar es Salaam, Temeke 85, 86
  Dar es Salaam, Upanga 85

624

Index

Dodoma 5, 85
Kariakoo 429
Kigoma 443
Kisosora 55
Lindi 71
Mbeya 442, 443
Mwanza 5, 442, 443
Tabora 442, 443
Tanga 54, 55, 75, 526
Zanzibar 5, 54–5, 74, 75, 76, 157, 226, 336–7, 454, 523, 524, 525–6, 527, 568–70
Zanzibar, Pemba Island 569, 570
Zanzibar, Unguja Island 569
Tanzania Film Company 440
Tanzania House of Talent (THT) 87
Tanzania One Theatre (TOT) (group) 526
tap-dance 205
tape recordings 85, 171, 180, 193, 231, 234, 269, 478, 533. *See also* video home system (VHS)
Tapok (group) 380
tarika (troupe/company) 279–80
Tarika Ramilison Fenoarivo (troupe) 279, 281
tariqas/confrarias 549
Tarkwa Trading Company 468
Tartit (band) 530
tarumbeta (musical instrument) 99. *See also* trumpet
tashkota (musical instrument) 523, 525. *See also* harp
Tassili (album) 546
Tau Ea Matskeha (ensemble) 344
tauje (musical instrument) 170. *See also* drums
taushi (musical instrument) 169. *See also* drums
Tausi Band 69
Tavares, Eugénio 437
tawran tej 416
Taylor, Cecil 12
Taylor, Ebo 208, 212
Tazvida, System (*sungura* musician) 522
tbal drum 179, 431, 456. *See also* drums
TBK. *See* Traditional Boer Music Club of South Africa
T-Bozz & Staika 367
Tchakounté, Pierre Didy 64, 66
tchamassi 234–5
Tchamba, Marole 66
Tchamo, Edson Abel Jeremias (Laylizzie) 252
tcha-tcho 494
Tchatchoua, Justin 66
Tcheka (singer) 63, 528–9
Tchengang, Raymond 67
Tchetche, Prince 66
Tchink System (group) 535, 536
tchinkoume 535–6, 574
Tchiumba, Lilly 509
Tchokui (Kouchouam Mbada group member) 65
Tchounou, Justin Bowen 64, 66
Tcoqma (band) 366
Teacher & His Afrikana (band) 208, 482
Teacher Boateng (highlife artist) 482
Teal (record label) 419
TEAxY (rapper) 259, 260
Technics Heart of the Beat (TV show) 285
techno 95, 348, 498

technopop 138, 168, 347. *See also* Hausa technopop
Technotronix (band) 349
Teddy, Ozi F. 232
Tee Mac & Afro-Collection (band) 32
Tee, Doug E. 261
Teek (rapper) 234, 235
Tefari Makonen, Prince Regent of Ethiopia. *See* Haile Selassie I, Emperor of Ethiopia
tehardent (musical instrument) 530. *See also* lute
tej bets (drinking houses) 49, 142. *See also* bars and taverns; *shebeens*; *tombo* bars
television (TV) 20, 23–4, 87, 317, 328, 504, 523, 577
Angola 348
Benin 573, 574
Burkina Faso 531
Cameroon 65, 234
Congo, Democratic Republic of the 494
Côte d'Ivoire 121, 123
Gabon 129
Ghana 114–15, 116, 117, 207–8, 211, 276, 346
Kenya 244, 245
Madagascar 191, 192, 282, 503, 544
Mali 557, 575
Mauritius 182
Netherlands 97
Nigeria 171, 254, 323, 448
Senegal 261, 263, 414, 416, 417
Somalia 200
South Africa 196, 285, 287, 349, 422
Tanzania 87, 441, 443, 526
UK 361
Zambia 332, 567
Zanzibar 568, 569
Zimbabwe 450
Television Zanzibar 569
Telfer, Ricky 31
Temba, Ellison 419
Tembo, Joseph 358, 427
Tembo, Patrick 358
tende 545, 546, 547
tende drum 545, 547. *See also* drums
tenor guitar 13, 324. *See also* guitar
tenor saxophone 510. *See also* saxophone
Tersch (group) 269
Teruel, Hipólito 135
Tesfahuney, Tiberih 537, 538
Tessemma, Asres 537
Teta (guitarist) 544
Tetteh, Charles 209
Tetuila, Tony (Anthony Olanrewaju Awotoye) 256
Teusi Five Band 61
tezeta 141
Tha Suspect (rapper/record producer) 257
Thailo and Kapiye (duo) 24
Thandiswa (singer) 350
Thatcher, Margaret 15
ThatodaPoet (hip-hop artist) 232
'The Twist' (song) 24
theater 53, 58, 59, 112–13, 115, 118, 141, 207, 278, 279–81, 328, 421, 514, 517, 526. *See also* concert party; musical theater
Thekisho, Thabio (ProVerb) 288
Them Mushrooms (band) 99, 100, 580

Théodore, Essombe 370
Therack (*ba gasy* artist) 53
Thiat (rapper) 261
Thiossane (club: Dakar, Senegal) 416
Third Mind (group) 229
This Is Bantu Jazz (radio program) 418, 419
This Is Me (album) 260
'This is Sad' (song) 13
Thomas, Pat 209, 212
Thomas, Sam Fan (Samuel Ndonfeng) 65, 66, 372
Thompson, Cindy 210
thrash metal 191, 194
Three Night Wizards (group) 467
Thrilling Artists, The (group) 486–7
THT. *See* Tanzania House of Talent
thumb piano. *See agidigbo*; *mbira*
T.I. (MC) 231
T.I.D. (hip-hop artist) 85
Ti Fock (group) 380
Ti Goy (Gregório Gonçalves) 105
Tianjama (*salegy* artist) 502
Tic Tac (hiplife artist) 210, 211
Tidal Waves (group) 488
tidinit (musical instrument) 179. *See also* lute
Tigray people 463
tigrigna. *See* Tigrinya music
Tigrim Bi (group) 261
Tigrinya *guayla* 539
Tigrinya music **536–40**
Tigrinya people 139
Tijaniyya Sufi order 175–6
tikkie-draai 389
Tim Timol (group) 560
Timaya (singer) 123, 219
timbila 374
Time and Spaces: The Marrabenta Solos (dance show) 406
Time for Music (TV show) 332
timitins (tea-meetings) 297–8
tin drum 198. *See also* drums
Tina (hip-hop artist) 237, 241
Tinariwen (band) 545, 546
tin-can guitar 402, 403. *See also* guitar; *guitares-bidons*
Tindikti-Jua Kali (group) 365
tindo 446
Tinyade Sounds (band) 308
Tirilene, Zeca 432
tishumaren. *See* Tuareg guitar music
Titirtos (*ma/gaisa* artist) 368
Tiyamiu, Abass 44
Tjovawa, Otjiteke 465
TKZee (group) 349, 352
Tlakula, Pansy 40
Tobias, Cosmos 441
Todd, Stanley 31
Toffin people 92
Togo 8, 31, 64, 126, 128, 153, 168, 181, 182, 342, 477, 572
Kpalime 90
Tohon, Stanislas 535, 536
Tokens, The (group) 301
Tokyo Joes 346
Toli Bangando 238–9
'Tolotolo' (song) 219
'Tom Hark' (song) 361
tombo bars 217. *See also* bars; *shebeens*; taverns
tômbô meté d'ôluy'a 396

625

Index

tômbô plass'a   396
tomtom   43. *See also* drums
Ton Pa (musician)   517
Toncha (*bend skin* artist)   65
Tonga   377
Tontoh, Mac   31
Tony Nobody (rapper)   234
Tony's Crazy Disco (party)   290
Too $hort (rapper)   255
Toots & the Maytals (group)   482
Top Ten Band   57
'Tora Gidi Uzvitonge' (song)   101
Torto, Frank   160
Tosh, Peter   478, 479, 480, 484, 486, 487
TOT (Tanzania One Theatre) group   526
Toto (pianist)   388
Tougouma, Jean-Philippe   534
touhourou   56
Tounkara, Djelimady   56, 312
Tounkara, Mamadou   56
Touré Kunda (band)   386
Touré, Abdoulaye Alhassane   529
Touré, Aladji   372
Touré, Ali Farka   212, 313, 530, 545
Touré, Fantani   386
Touré, Samori   385
Touré, Sékou   312, 385
Toussa (rapper)   262
township halls   360, 388, 419. *See also* social halls
township jazz   450
township jive   418, 423, 450
township music   422, 520, 521
township pop. *See* bubblegum
toyi-toyi   349
T-Pain (rapper/record producer)   256
TPM. *See* Transportes Públicos de Maputo
TPOK Jazz (band)   451. *See also* O.K. Jazz (band)
Trace Africa (music channel)   584
Trace Africa (TV network)   123
Tracey, Hugh   377, 440
tradi-rap   239–40
Traditional Boer Music Club of South Africa (TBK)   81–2
Transcription Centre (recoding studio: London)   423
Transportes Públicos de Maputo (TPM) (company)   375
Transvaal National Eisteddfod   38, 40
tranverse flute   399. *See also* flute
Traoré, Boubacar (Kar Kar)   545
Traore, Rokia   313
trap drum   109, 113, 116, 468, 516, 555. *See also* drums
Traxsource Charts (website)   291
Trey Songz (rapper)   257
triangle (musical instrument). *See* koto; kenken
tribal house   291
tribal metal   186
Triffis (band)   32
Trigmatic (hiplife artist)   277
Trinidad   9, 28, 132
Triple 9 (record label)   349
Triton keyboard   463
Triumph Club Dance Orchestra   222
tromba (spiritual possession ceremonies)   543
trombone   66, 75, 91, 223
Trompies (group)   289, 351
Troubadour Records   419, 420–1

Troupe Jeannette   53, 54
Troupe Léle   380
Troupe Théâtrale Malgache   53
trova   337, 338, 491, 509
truck drivers   321. *See also* Sinimo, Abdi
True Jit (album)   320
True Tones (band)   25
trumpet   13, 66, 75, 89, 91, 99, 124, 223, 280, 334, 414–15, 430, 440, 441, 510, 516, 563. *See also* kakaki; kazoos; *mabuyu/maboya; tarumbeta*
Trutone Reocrds   300, 419, 420
Trybesmen (trio)   255
tsaba tsaba   319, 320, 358, 359, 360, 389, 418, 419, 420, **540-3**
'Tsaba Tsaba ke No.1' (song)   541–2
'Tsaba Tsaba' (song)   541–2
tsapiky/tsapika   **543-5**
tsava tsava   521, 542
Tseheno (*ba gasy* artist)   53
Tselatra (band)   190, 192
Tshabalala, Ganyani (DJ Ganyani)   284, 285
Tshabalala, Saul   422
Tshabalala, Bhekitshe   422
Tshanda, Dan   94, 95
Tshawani, Amukelani 'Ammunition'   288
Tshiamo, Peter   290
Tshinaba, Mpotseng (DJ Glen Lewis)   285
tshova-tshova   520
Tsiboe, Nana (highlife artist)   212
Tsimihety people   543
tsinge songs   517
Tsonga people   403
'Tsoo boi' (song)   275
tsotsi taal   420
Tsoungui, Rachel   372
Tsuba Tes Go Ti/Namsa (album)   368
Tsui Shito (troupe)   115
Tu te croix likolo (album)   269
Tuareg blues. *See* Tuareg guitar music
Tuareg guitar music   **545-8**
Tuareg people   530, 545
tuba   75
tube fiddle   295. *See also* endingidi; fiddle
Tudo pa bo (album)   97
Tuffour, Nana   212
tufo   **548-50**
tufo drum   548. *See also* drums; frame drum
tuidzi   35, 90
Tukul Band   143
tula n'divile   390
Tumaini Choir   443
tumba drum   334, 432. *See also* conga drum; drums
Tumi (rapper)   231
Tumza and Kennyboy McKenzie (group)   356
Tunakie (*shambo* artist)   512, 513, 514
Tunde the Western Nightingale   323
tungba gospel   325
Tunisia   168, 431
Tupac (rapper)   269
Tupe, Shem   460, 461
Tuponda (group)   465
Turino, Thomas   320
turmas (youth groups)   333
Turner, Tina   31, 208
Turpin, Charles   111–12
turu (musical instrument)   169. *See also* drums

Turunen, Tarja   186
TV. *See* television
Twala, Sello 'Chicco'   94–5, 289
Twelfth Night (festival)   155
Twin Seven Seven (painter and musician)   32
Twi-pop   275
twist   31, 142, 208, 346, 427, 516, 580
Two Bobs and Their Carolina Girl (troupe)   109–10, 111, 114
Tyamzashe, Benjamin   39
Tyr (band)   187

'U Go Kill Me' (song)   51
U Roy (singer)   479
Ubaxa Kaccanka (group)   199
ubo aka (musical instrument)   217. *See also* lamellophone
ubugxagxa   298
Ubuntu Kraal (music venues)   287
Ucas Jazz Band   563
Uchendu, Nelly   224
'ud (musical instrument). *See* oud/*'ud*
UDF. *See* United Democratic Front
udi (musical instrument)   569–70. *See also* lute
UDM. *See* underground dance music
UFPDG. *See* Union des femmes du Parti démocratique gabonais
Uganda   4, 5, 6, 57–9, 68, 69, 95, 181, 183, 226, 271–3, 326–9, 334–6, 454, 478
  Buganda Kingdom   326, 327, 328, 335
Uganda Kezaala Band, The   57
Ugly Creatures (band)   367
ugubhu bow (musical instrument)   39
'Uhiki' (song)   245
Uhuru Dance Band   36, 206
'Uhuru Special/Bosoe' (song)   36
Uit die jaar vroeg (radio program)   81
Ujamaa policy   440–1, 525
UK. *See* United Kingdom
Ukasha, Dula   569
Ukhozi FM (radio station)   287
Ukoo Flani (group)   246
Ukoo Flani Mau Mau (hip-hop collective)   246
ukulele (musical instrument)   155, 323, 440. *See also* lute
ukureka   298, 299
ukusina   299
Ukwu, Celestine   216, 217, 219
Ukwuani people   218
Ulaeto, Martha   138
'Ulo Tixo 'Mkulu' (hymn)   38
Ulyankuru Choir   443
'Uma cerveja, um bloco' (song)   473–4
umbholoho   291, **551-2**
umbigada   475, 476
umdudo   38
umgqashiyo   418, 421–2, 423, 424
umhlanga   291
Umhlobo Wenene (radio station)   287
'Umoja wa Tanzania' (song)   86
'Umqombothi' (song)   95
umqongqo   299
umudiho   294
umuduri (musical instrument)   295. *See also* musical bow
umuganara   294
umuhamirizo   294
umushagiriro   294
'Un homme qui m'aime' (song)   66

626

Index

Unbwogable (album) 245
'Unbwogable' (song) 245, 246
Uncanny Sessman (hip-hop collective) 230
underground dance music (UDM) 290
underground hip-hop 246
Undivided Roots (band) 488–9
União Operário Kabocomeu (Group) 334
Unilever Ghana 117, 118
Union des femmes du Parti démocratique gabonais (UFPDG) 124, 125, 129
Union Trading Company 113
United Africa Company 113, 458
United Democratic Front (UDF) 426–7
United Kingdom (UK) 29, 33, 44, 87, 106, 171, 205, 230, 281, 284, 331, 361, 423, 434, 486, 487, 566
   London 11, 19, 28–9, 32, 51, 122, 138, 200, 205, 275, 283, 421, 449, 468, 556
United Spirit (band) 483
United States (US) 28–9, 31, 32, 44, 84, 85, 92, 94, 97, 98, 125, 138, 142, 171, 176, 189, 205, 206, 208, 222, 227, 228, 229, 234, 235, 236, 239, 241, 245, 248, 249, 255, 256, 257, 259, 260, 261, 262, 263, 267, 272, 273, 274, 275, 277, 284, 290, 299, 320, 323, 331, 347, 348, 349, 359, 360, 366, 367, 385, 388, 403, 418, 419, 422, 423, 434, 436, 448, 464, 491, 493, 495, 496, 513, 519, 520, 537, 540, 560, 563, 566, 568, 573
   Chicago 283, 286
   Detroit 283
   Houston 449
   Louisiana 27
   Minneapolis 200
   New York 122, 229, 249, 283, 290, 313, 449, 557
   San Francisco Bay Area 28
   South Bronx 225
   Washington, D.C. 290
United States. Department of State 262
United Trading Company 458
University of Abidjan 586, 587
University of Ghana, Department of Music 212, 343
University of Ghana, School of Performing Arts 153, 211
University of Namibia Choir 553
University of the Witwatersrand (Johannesburg, South Africa) 285
University of the Witwatersrand, Great Hall 421
'Unknown Soldier' (song) 15
Unreleased Records 231
upatsu (musical instrument) 99. *See also* idiophone
Upendo Group 443
Uplifted (album) 219
Uppers International (band) 32
Uproxx (website) 196
urban music 28, 64, 66, 84, 105, 161, 170, 173, 176, 246, 331, 373, 402, 404, 498, 531, 532, 533, 534, 585. *See also* Afrobeats/Afro Beats; Afropop/Afro pop/Afro-pop; *bend skin*; *bongo flava/bongo fleva*; bubblegum; *gumbe/goombay*; Hausa *nanaye filmi* music; *kwela*; *marrabenta*; *mbaqanga*; *tsaba tsaba*; *zouglou*

uringe 568
Urukererea (troupe) 296
US. *See* United States
Usanii Kona Hip-hop Challenge (Kenya) 246
'Useless Man' Foster (guitarist) 467
Usshaqul Nabiyyi (group) 175
uukorasa/oukorasa 552–5
uupongo 522
Uwaifo, Victor 206, 223, 224, 467, 482
Uwaliya Mai Amada 170

V2A4 (group) 237
Vadú (*batuque* performer) 63
Vadzimba (band) 103
Valdo, Gabby Nick 31
Vale, João do 510
Valentim de Carvalho (record label) 334, 432, 476, 509, 510
Valentin, Nginia Noe na Epe 370
valiha (musical instrument) 502. *See also* zither
Valinotti, Antonio (DJ Tony) 290
Valsero (rapper) 234
VaMugabe Chete Crew 103
Van Damme, Jean-Claude 347
Van Halen (band) 180, 190
Van Riebeeck, Jan 435
Van-Dunem, Lourdes 509
Van-Dunem, Ruca 340
vanga 428, 430
Vanilla Ice (rapper) 84
Vans, Andy 209
Vans, Bob 112
vastrap 79, 389, 418, 553
vaudeville 108–9, 110, 205, 297, 300, 301, 389, 422, 541. *See also* concert party
VCD. *See* video-CD
Vee (*kwasa kwasa* artist) 357
Veeraragoo, Claudio 505
Venezuela 431
ventilateur 416
Verdades, Irmãos 340
Versace, Lino 120, 121, 122
Versatile Eight (troupe) 109, 206
Vezo people 543
VHS. *See* video home system
Vhuka Boys (group) 521
Victor, Patrick 438
Victoria Jazz Band 69
Victoria, Queen of Great Britain 280
video clips/videos. *See* music video/video clips
video-CD (VCD) 577. *See also* compact disc (CD)
video home system (VHS) 171, 268, 531, 544. *See also* tape recordings
Vidisco (record label) 339
'Vidonge' (song) 525
vidumbak drum. *See kidumbak/vidumbak* drum
'Vie de haine' (song) 238
Vieira, Paulino 106, 437
Vier Transvalers (group) 80
vigoma drum. *See kigoma/vigoma* drum
Vijana Jazz (band) 441
vijiti (musical instrument) 336
Viking metal 187
Vila, Martino da 510
Vilakazi, Strike 360, 420
Viljoen, Ollie 82
Villa Vienne (singer) 370, 371

vimbuza 425, 427
vimbuza (musical instrument) 566. *See also* drums; talking drum
violin 198, 205, 280, 301, 336, 337, 408, 410, 421, 436, 453, 504, 523, 524, 525–6, 569–70. *See also* fiddle
Viomuriro, Oviku 465
VIP. *See* Vision in Progress (trio)
viras 151
Viry, Firmin 380
visekese 427
Vision in Progress (VIP) (trio) 210, 211, 276
Visions (band) 211
Visual Lab (recording studio) 87
Vital, John 438, 439
Viva La Musica (band) 355, 452, 494
'Viva la vida' (song) 291
Vivid Vision (firm) 230
vocal jive 359, 360, 420–1, 422, 423, 424
Vodún/voodoo 91, 92, 159, 330, 412, 573, 574, 573, 574
Voice of Destruction (band) 195
Voice of Rock (radio station) 195
Voice of the Cross (album) 219
Voice of the Cross (duo) 219–20
Voice of Wits (radio station) 285
Volsy, Jean-Marc 438
voodoo. *See* Vodún/voodoo
Voz de Cabo Verde (band) 97, 106, 437
Voz de Moçambique (radio program) 403
vugo 98
Vusi (hip-hop artist) 232
Vusi Dube (DJ/producer) 292
Vuur en Vlam (album) 82
VVIP (group) 276
Vyf Takhare (band) 80
Vyf Vastrappers (band) 80

Wa BMG 44 (group) 261, 262
Waaberi (collective) 199
Wacken Open Air Festival (Germany) 187, 196
Wade, Adboulaye 261
Wagadugu (band) 138
Wagëblë (group) 262
Wagosi wa Kaya (band) 85
Wahengo, Jackson 514
wah-wah pedal 31, 567. *See also* guitar; guitar, electric
Wailer, Bunny Livingston 479
Wainaina, Eric 72
Wait and See (group) 516
wàká 148, 555–6
wàká gospel 556
Waka Waka Band, The 58
Wakar Tsuntsaye (Danmatawalle) 169
Wakilisha (radio program) 246
wakokin gargajiya. *See* Hausa traditional music
Waku, Manuaku 494
Walaalaha Hargeysa (group) 166, 198, 200
Walaalaha Sweden (band) 200
Walias Band 143
Wallace-Johnson, I.T.A. 433
Walt Disney Company 301
Walton, William 108
waltz 28, 60, 79, 108–9, 151, 223, 382, 440, 444
'Walumbe Zaaya' (song) 328
Wamakonde people 442

627

Index

Wamala, Elly   57, 272, 326, 328
Wambua, Sammy   71
Wan Pop Sojas (hip-hop artist)   138
Wanaume TMK (band)   86
Wank's Nya (*bend skin* artist)   66
Wanluv the Kubolor (hiplife artist)   459
Wantu Wazuri (band)   32
Wanyakyusa people   442
Wanyika, Les   498
Wanyika, Simba   498
WAPI (hip-hop competition: Kenya)   246
war and armed conflict   169, 384, 455, 463, 559. *See also* soldiers
warba   532
Warda Baby (*zenji flava* artist)   568
Waro, Danyèl   380
Warona, Oscar   286. *See also* Oskido (DJ/producer)
Warren, Guy (Kofi Ghanaba)   206, 211
washint (musical instrument)   463. *See also* flute
wassoulou   313, 386, **557–8**
Wassoulou Explosion   557
Wassy, Brice   66
water drum (musical instrument). *See sinhun*
Waters, Ethel   108
Watiri, Cinda wa   444
Watson, Ed   137
Watson, Guy   66
Wayam, Hassan   169, 173
'Wayo (1st version)' (song)   13
Wazaramo people. *See* Zaramo/Wazaramo people
Wazekwa, Felix   495
WBMX (radio station)   286
'We Miss You Manelo' (song)   94–5
Wè people   586
'Weakness for Your Sweetness' (song)   138
Weavers, The (group)   301
wedding *beni*   75–6
wedding music/weddings   37, 38, 40, 43, 47, 59, 60, 61, 62, 63, 75, 90, 98–9, 147–8, 162, 163, 170, 179, 294, 295, 298–9, 304, 336–7, 366, 375, 377, 389, 398, 399, 400, 412, 413, 426, 428, 429, 430, 434, 436, 453, 455, 501, 516, 523, 524, 525, 539, 543, 551, 553, 559, 570, 573, 576
Wedejo, Zerehun   463
'Weekend Special' (song)   94
Weird MC (Da Rappatainer/Adesola Adesimbo Idowu)   255
Wekesa Kusienya, Fred   460, 461–2
Wellington's Band   211–12
Wells Fargo (band)   183
Welwitchia Music Production (record label)   368
Wendo, Antoine Kolosoy   468, 493
Wenge Musica (group)   451, 452, 495, 518
Wenge Musica BCBG (group)   495
Wenyeji (rapper)   246
WEPAZ (group)   358
were/wéré   43, 44, 145–6, 147, 221
Werra Son and Wenge Musica Maison Mère (group)   495
Werrason (musician)   452
Wesley (Methodist) Church (Ghana, Accra). Choir   107
Wesley, Fred   125

West Africa   8, 9, 11, 19, 21, 22, 31–2, 46, 47, 92, 132, 137–8, 153, 159, 160, 161, 162, 181, 204, 205, 206, 216, 222, 225, 227, 275, 277, 310–14, 315–18, 321, 383–6, 396, 399, 456, 466–7, 469, 477, 482, 497, 514, 560, 561–3, 574, 583, 586. *See also specific nations*
West African Theatre   206, 207
West Indies   9–10, 96, 204, 222, 225, 321, 482, 483, 484. *See also* Caribbean
West, Kayne   277
Western Diamonds (band)   211
Western films   493
Western Jazz Band   440
Western Nigeria Broadcasting Service   323
Western Sahara   8, 178–9, 430–1, 456, 545
Weston, Randy   16
Wham! (band)   352
Whiplashes, The (band)   488
whistle   65, 376, 377, 528
White, Tim   284
'Who Can Bwogo Me?' (song)   245
'Who're You' (song)   12
Why Self Government by Ultimatum (variety show)   112
Wicked Sounds (record label)   349
wiglo   165
wiire   532
Wilberforce Institute Singers   300
Wild Dogs, The (group)   465
Wild Style (film)   229, 261, 265
Wilfred Sentso School of Modern Piano Syncopation (Johannesburg, South Africa)   541
William, Fadhil   498, 580
William, Prince, Duke of Cambridge   51
Williams III, Ralph (Stagga)   230
Williams, Augustus   108, 109, 110
Williams, Ola   210
Williams, Tunde   13
'Wimoweh' (song)   301
Windhoek Metal Fest (Namibia)   183
Wings (band)   31
Winneba Orchestra   205
W.I.T.C.H/Witch, The (band)   180, 566–7
Witch Doctor, The (Abeeku Ribeiro)   275
Witchdoctor Records   195
Witchfest (music festival: South Africa)   195
Wizboy (musician)   219
Wizkid (singer-songwriter)   21, 123, 176, 257, 448, 449
WJLB (radio station)   286
Wolof people   179, 386, 414, 415, 558, 560, 583
Womad (World of Music, Arts and Dance) (music festival)   251
'Won Da Mo' (song)   257
Wonder, Stevie   16, 483
Wonderful Three, The (choir)   300
woodblock/wood block (musical instrument)   223, 580. *See also* drums; slit drum
Woody Woodpeckers, The (group)   421
Workers Brigade Concert Party   14
working class   14, 15, 40, 78, 79, 80, 116, 120, 133, 153–4, 160, 266, 279, 300, 301–2, 335, 344, 359, 374, 388, 389, 419, 422, 423–4, 433, 467, 479, 520, 522, 541, 542

world music   16, 23, 27, 28–9, 32, 33, 77, 92, 96, 121, 138, 143, 212, 227, 251, 262, 310, 312–13, 335, 361, 380, 423, 459, 468, 494, 518, 560
World Music Network (record label)   251
World of African Music, The (Graham)   29
World Routes (radio program)   396
worldbeat   28, 29
'Wosum Brodie A.' (song)   113
wôyô   586–7
Wozo Vacances (TV show)   123
wrestling matches   35
Wright, Jaguar   17
Wrust (band)   182, 186
Wudil, Umar Abdul'aziz (Fadar Bege)   175
Wuleng, Jalimadi   563
Wulomei (Sensational Wulomei) (group)   212, 346
Wunluv (hiplife artist)   211
Wuta (hiplife artist)   211
Wu-Tang Clan (group)   249

Xaba, Michael   418
Xaba, Ndikho   423
xaj bi   416
xalam (musical instrument)   22, 179. *See also* lute
X-Dough (singer)   177
Xhosa people   38, 390
Xidigaha Geeska (band)   200
Xidimingwana (musician)   404, 406, 471
Xido, Jeremy   183
Xitimela Xa Kuya Manhiça (album)   375
X-Man Sarari (rapper)   259
Xolo Home Boys (choir)   302
X-Plastaz (group)   86
Xudeydi (musician)   199
Xuman (rapper)   261
xylophone   76, 382. *See also bala/balafon/balafon; dja'; marimba; mendzan* xylophone

Y culture   285
Y Mag (magazine)   285, 349
ya Shilengifa, Naimbudu   513
'Yaa Amponsah' (song)   468
Yabon Annabi poets   175
'Yahooze' (song)   256–7
Yalekpon Alokpon (musician)   536
YALI. *See* Young African Leaders Initiative
Yalley, Mr. (teacher)   108–9, 112
Yamaha synthesizer   168, 172. *See also* synthesizer
  DX7   415
  PSR series   175, 176, 258, 259
  PSR-220   173
  PSR-730   173
yambú   490
Yamoah's Guitar Band   10, 207
yan amshi   169
Yankson, Paapa   210, 212
'Yantandu, Mallam Magaji   168
Yao people   377
Yarona FM (radio station)   232
Yasimika (album)   312
Yassi, Bob   29
Yatfu (group)   261, 262, 263
Yauri, Sani Aliyu Dandawo   169
'Yawo Mami Ebi So' (song)   434
Yebuah, A.K.   210
yefun pee   115

628

Index

'Yéké yéké' (song)   385, 563
yéla   **558–61**, 562
Yéla, les mélodies de la mémoire (documentary)   559
Yeleen (group)   532
Yellitaare Fuuta (group)   560
yellow *mbumba*   426, 427
Yellowman (DJ)   482
Y'en a Marre ('We've had enough') movement   261-2
yenyengo   **561–5**
'Yetul' isigqoko' (song)   302
YFM (radio station)   246, 285, 286, 287, 288, 289, 349, 350
Yobo, Chidi   568
yodeling   102
Yogo, Dindo   494
Yole!Africa (cultural center: Goma, DRC)   270
Yondo Sister (musician)   355
Yonkeu, Charly   66
yo-pop music   324
Yoro Gang (DJ Arafat)   121, 122
Yorùbá people   11, 12, 17, 43, 47–8, 145–6, 147, 148, 221–4, 254, 321, 323, 324, 342–3, 399, 413, 448, 467, 501, 555
'You Knows Me' (song)   231
Young African Leaders Initiative (YALI)   269
Young Stars Modern Taarab (group)   430, 526
Young T (musician)   514
Young Vibrations (group)   272
Youssoupha (rapper)   270
youth   227, 478
  Angola   333, 338, 347
  Botswana   228, 229
  Cabo Verdean   96
  Congo, Democratic Republic of the   268
  Ethiopia   142
  Ghana   34, 50, 51, 113, 342, 345–6, 482, 516
  Guinea   382
  Hausa   170–4, 176–7
  Ivorian   121, 585–8
  Kenya   188
  Madagascar   190
  Malawi   308, 485
  Mozambique   471, 472
  Namibia   552
  Nigeria   254, 259
  Senegal   260–1, 263
  South Africa   94, 95, 265, 284, 349, 359, 360, 422, 423
  Tanzania   54, 84–6, 428, 429
  Uganda   272
  Wassoulou region   557, 558
  West Africa   31–2, 137
  Zanzibar   568, 570
YouTube   20, 51, 55, 129–30, 174, 177, 180, 192, 200, 201, 232, 368, 406, 465, 530, 531, 534, 553, 574
youza   416

Yugoslavia   44
Yusuf, Mzee   526
Yveth (Ivete Rosária Mafundza Marlene)   248–9, 250, 252

zahuten   545
Zaïko Langa Langa (band)   451, 452, 494
Zair ak Batine (group)   261
Zaire. *See* Congo, Democratic Republic of the
Zaïre 74 (music festival: Kinshasa, 1974)   494
zairois   491
Zakaria, Nicholas   521
'Zakeline Mama' (song)   281
Zalissa (album)   532, 533
'Zalissa' (song)   532, 534
Zambia   5, 7, 20, 25, 74, 158, 180, 308, 331–3, 358, 361, 376, 406, 491, 568–7
  Luapula Province   331, 332
  Lusaka   566
Zambia Broadcasting Service (ZBS)   566
Zamrock   180, 332, 333, **565–8**
zanakira (children's songs)   280
Zangado, Mateus Pelé do   338
Zangbeto secret society   330–1
'Zangbeto' (song)   330
Zango, Adam A.   173, 177
ZANU-PF. *See* Zimbabwe African National Union-Patriotic Front
Zanzibar. *See* Tanzania: Zanzibar
Zanzibar Stars Modern Taarab (group)   526
Zapp Mallet (Emmanuel Mallett)   275
Zaramo/Wazaromo people   428, 430, 441, 442, 526
Zay B (hip-hop artist)   87
ZBS. *See* Zambia Broadcasting Service
Zé Orlando/Sons d'África (record label)   339
Zé, David   432, 509, 511
Zebrons, The (band)   102
zef-rap   266
Zein l'Abdin   524
Zein Musical Party (group)   524, 525
zemenawi muzika. *See* Ethiopian modern music
Zena, Bwana   524
zeni d'Abomey   572
zenji flava   226, **568–72**
Zenji FM (radio station)   569
zenli bibli   572
zenli drum   572. *See also* drums
zenli rénové   573
zenli/zinli   535, **572–4**
zenti gbete   572
Zeray Deres Band   537
Zeus (MC)   231, 232
Zeyna (DJ)   262
zèz (musical instrument)   517. *See also* zither
Zhakata, Leonard K.   522
ziglibithy   584, 585
Zikhali, W.P.   300

zikiri   **574–80**. *See also* praise music and songs; *taarab*
Zikiri Solo (Souleymane Diarra)   576
zilizopendwa   **580–3**
Zilizopendwa – Wazee Wa Kazi (album)   580
Zilizopendwa (album)   580
Zilizopendwa 1992 (album)   580
Zimba, Atongo   212
Zimbabwe   7, 25, 29, 31, 66, 68, 69, 70–1, 100–3, 180, 181, 183, 227, 308, 319–20, 331, 361, 406, 422, 459, 451, 459, 474, 478, 491, 498–9, 520–2, 542, 552
  Bulawayo   7, 450
  Harare   7, 102–3, 450, 486, 499, 521
  Matabeleland   450
  Murehwa   320
Zimbabwe African National Union-Patriotic Front (ZANU-PF)   101, 103
Zimbabwe Music Awards   103
Zimbabwe Music Corporation (ZMC)   521
Zinjina (reggae artist)   483
zinli. *See zenli/zinli*
Zion's Children (group)   483
Zion, Takana   478
Ziqo (*pandza* artist)   471, 473, 474
Ziriums (rapper)   260
zirombo   158
Ziskakan (group)   380
zither   502. *See also bangwe; ganuni; inanga; marovany; qanun; valiha; zèz*
ZM (Zara Moussa)   259
ZMC (record label). *See* Zimbabwe Music Corporation
Zo Gang (group)   584
zoblazo   531, **583–5**
Zola (*kwaito* artist)   350, 351, 352
Zolasco (*kwasa kwasa* artist)   357
Zombie (album)   15
Zombies Ate My Girlfriend (band)   196
Zonglo Biiz, The (band)   32, 208
Zonk! (periodical)   419
Zonophone (record label)   35, 205, 458, 468
zora butter dance   521
zouglou   121, 122, 531, 583–4, **585–8**
zougloubehi   585
zouk   57, 84, 86, 87, 340, 348, 370, 372, 442, 471, 518, 568, 587, 588. *See also cabo-zouk/cola-zouk*
  Antillean *zouk*   96, 97, 137
  Caribbean *zouk*   337, 338, 339, 494, 505, 511
zouk-love   96, 505
zucuta   404
Zulla Boy (*oviritje* artist)   465
Zulu people   40, 301, 352, 390, 408, 409–10, 455, 551
Zulu Squad (group)   272
Zuluboy (hip-hop artist)   266
Zuluboy and his Jazz Maniacs (band)   388–9, 418, 419, 421, 541–2
Zulus, The (band)   450
Zumratul Madahun Nabiyyi (group)   175
Zvakata, Leonard Karikoga   498–9

629